Contemporary
Literary Criticism

Guide to Gale Literary Criticism Series

For criticism on	Consult these Gale series
Authors now living or who died after December 31, 1999	**CONTEMPORARY LITERARY CRITICISM (CLC)**
Authors who died between 1900 and 1999	**TWENTIETH-CENTURY LITERARY CRITICISM (TCLC)**
Authors who died between 1800 and 1899	**NINETEENTH-CENTURY LITERATURE CRITICISM (NCLC)**
Authors who died between 1400 and 1799	**LITERATURE CRITICISM FROM 1400 TO 1800 (LC)** **SHAKESPEAREAN CRITICISM (SC)**
Authors who died before 1400	**CLASSICAL AND MEDIEVAL LITERATURE CRITICISM (CMLC)**
Authors of books for children and young adults	**CHILDREN'S LITERATURE REVIEW (CLR)**
Dramatists	**DRAMA CRITICISM (DC)**
Poets	**POETRY CRITICISM (PC)**
Short story writers	**SHORT STORY CRITICISM (SSC)**
Literary topics and movements	**HARLEM RENAISSANCE: A GALE CRITICAL COMPANION (HR)** **THE BEAT GENERATION: A GALE CRITICAL COMPANION (BG)**
Asian American writers of the last two hundred years	**ASIAN AMERICAN LITERATURE (AAL)**
Black writers of the past two hundred years	**BLACK LITERATURE CRITICISM (BLC)** **BLACK LITERATURE CRITICISM SUPPLEMENT (BLCS)**
Hispanic writers of the late nineteenth and twentieth centuries	**HISPANIC LITERATURE CRITICISM (HLC)** **HISPANIC LITERATURE CRITICISM SUPPLEMENT (HLCS)**
Native North American writers and orators of the eighteenth, nineteenth, and twentieth centuries	**NATIVE NORTH AMERICAN LITERATURE (NNAL)**
Major authors from the Renaissance to the present	**WORLD LITERATURE CRITICISM, 1500 TO THE PRESENT (WLC)** **WORLD LITERATURE CRITICISM SUPPLEMENT (WLCS)**

ISSN 0091-3421

Volume 173

Contemporary Literary Criticism

Criticism of the Works
of Today's Novelists, Poets, Playwrights,
Short Story Writers, Scriptwriters, and
Other Creative Writers

Janet Witalec
PROJECT EDITOR

Detroit • New York • San Diego • San Francisco • Cleveland • New Haven, Conn. • Waterville, Maine • London • Munich

Contemporary Literary Criticism, Vol. 173

Project Editor
Janet Witalec

Editorial
Tom Burns, Jenny Cromie, Kathy D. Darrow, Jeffrey W. Hunter, Justin Karr, Lemma Shomali

Research
Michelle Campbell, Tracie A. Richardson

Permissions
Shalice Shah-Caldwell

Imaging and Multimedia
Lezlie Light, Dave G. Oblender, Kelly A. Quin, Luke Rademacher

Composition and Electronic Capture
Kathy Sauer

Manufacturing
Stacy L. Melson

© 2003 by Gale. Gale is an imprint of The Gale Group, Inc., a division of Thomson Learning, Inc.

Gale and Design™ and Thomson Learning™ are trademarks used herein under license.

For more information, contact
The Gale Group, Inc.
27500 Drake Rd.
Farmington Hills, MI 48331-3535
Or you can visit our internet site at
http://www.gale.com

ALL RIGHTS RESERVED
No part of this work covered by the copyright herein may be reproduced or used in any form or by any means—graphic, electronic, or mechanical, including photocopying, recording, taping, Web distribution, or information storage retrieval systems—without the written permission of the publisher.

This publication is a creative work fully protected by all applicable copyright laws, as well as by misappropriation, trade secret, unfair competition, and other applicable laws. The authors and editors of this work have added value to the underlying factual material herein through one or more of the following: unique and original selection, coordination, expression, arrangement, and classification of the information.

For permission to use material from this product, submit your request via the Web at http://www.gale-edit.com/permissions, or you may download our Permissions Request form and submit your request by fax or mail to:

Permisssions Department
The Gale Group, Inc.
27500 Drake Rd.
Farmington Hills, MI 48331-3535
Permissions Hotline:
248-699-8006 or 800-877-4253, ext. 8006
Fax 248-699-8074 or 800-762-4058

Since this page cannot legibly accommodate all copyright notices, the acknowledgments constitute an extension of the copyright notice.

While every effort has been made to secure permission to reprint material and to ensure the reliability of the information presented in this publication, the Gale Group neither guarantees the accuracy of the data contained herein nor assumes any responsibility for errors, omissions or discrepancies. Gale accepts no payment for listing; and inclusion in the publication of any organization, agency, institution, publication, service, or individual does not imply endorsement of the editors or publisher. Errors brought to the attention of the publisher and verified to the satisfaction of the publisher will be corrected in future editions.

LIBRARY OF CONGRESS CATALOG CARD NUMBER 76-46132

ISBN 0-7876-6746-3
ISSN 0091-3421

Printed in the United States of America
10 9 8 7 6 5 4 3 2 1

Contents

Preface vii

Acknowledgments xi

Literary Criticism Series Advisory Board xv

Tariq Ali 1943- 1
Pakistani nonfiction writer, novelist, editor, playwright, historian, and journalist

Mary Daly 1928- 53
American critic, nonfiction writer, and autobiographer

Slavenka Drakulic 1949- 167
Croatian novelist and essayist

Carolyn Heilbrun 1926- 222
American novelist, critic, essayist, nonfiction writer, short story writer, and biographer

Toni Morrison 1931- 271
American novelist, nonfiction writer, essayist, playwright, and children's writer; entry devoted to the novel The Bluest Eye *(1970)*

Literary Criticism Series Cumulative Author Index 373

Literary Criticism Series Cumulative Topic Index 469

CLC Cumulative Nationality Index 479

CLC-173 Title Index 493

Preface

Named "one of the twenty-five most distinguished reference titles published during the past twenty-five years" by *Reference Quarterly*, the *Contemporary Literary Criticism* (*CLC*) series provides readers with critical commentary and general information on more than 2,000 authors now living or who died after December 31, 1999. Volumes published from 1973 through 1999 include authors who died after December 31, 1959. Previous to the publication of the first volume of *CLC* in 1973, there was no ongoing digest monitoring scholarly and popular sources of critical opinion and explication of modern literature. *CLC*, therefore, has fulfilled an essential need, particularly since the complexity and variety of contemporary literature makes the function of criticism especially important to today's reader.

Scope of the Series

CLC provides significant passages from published criticism of works by creative writers. Since many of the authors covered in *CLC* inspire continual critical commentary, writers are often represented in more than one volume. There is, of course, no duplication of reprinted criticism.

Authors are selected for inclusion for a variety of reasons, among them the publication or dramatic production of a critically acclaimed new work, the reception of a major literary award, revival of interest in past writings, or the adaptation of a literary work to film or television.

Attention is also given to several other groups of writers—authors of considerable public interest—about whose work criticism is often difficult to locate. These include mystery and science fiction writers, literary and social critics, foreign authors, and authors who represent particular ethnic groups.

Each *CLC* volume contains individual essays and reviews taken from hundreds of book review periodicals, general magazines, scholarly journals, monographs, and books. Entries include critical evaluations spanning from the beginning of an author's career to the most current commentary. Interviews, feature articles, and other published writings that offer insight into the author's works are also presented. Students, teachers, librarians, and researchers will find that the general critical and biographical material in *CLC* provides them with vital information required to write a term paper, analyze a poem, or lead a book discussion group. In addition, complete biographical citations note the original source and all of the information necessary for a term paper footnote or bibliography.

Organization of the Book

A *CLC* entry consists of the following elements:

- The **Author Heading** cites the name under which the author most commonly wrote, followed by birth and death dates. Also located here are any name variations under which an author wrote, including transliterated forms for authors whose native languages use nonroman alphabets. If the author wrote consistently under a pseudonym, the pseudonym will be listed in the author heading and the author's actual name given in parenthesis on the first line of the biographical and critical information. Uncertain birth or death dates are indicated by question marks. Single-work entries are preceded by a heading that consists of the most common form of the title in English translation (if applicable) and the original date of composition.

- A **Portrait of the Author** is included when available.

- The **Introduction** contains background information that introduces the reader to the author, work, or topic that is the subject of the entry.

- The list of **Principal Works** is ordered chronologically by date of first publication and lists the most important works by the author. The genre and publication date of each work is given. In the case of foreign authors whose works have been translated into English, the English-language version of the title follows in brackets. Unless otherwise indicated, dramas are dated by first performance, not first publication.

- Reprinted **Criticism** is arranged chronologically in each entry to provide a useful perspective on changes in critical evaluation over time. The critic's name and the date of composition or publication of the critical work are given at the beginning of each piece of criticism. Unsigned criticism is preceded by the title of the source in which it appeared. All titles by the author featured in the text are printed in boldface type. Footnotes are reprinted at the end of each essay or excerpt. In the case of excerpted criticism, only those footnotes that pertain to the excerpted texts are included.

- A complete **Bibliographical Citation** of the original essay or book precedes each piece of criticism. Source citations in the Literary Criticism Series follow University of Chicago Press style, as outlined in *The Chicago Manual of Style,* 14th ed. (Chicago: The University of Chicago Press, 1993).

- Critical essays are prefaced by brief **Annotations** explicating each piece.

- Whenever possible, a recent **Author Interview** accompanies each entry.

- An annotated bibliography of **Further Reading** appears at the end of each entry and suggests resources for additional study. In some cases, significant essays for which the editors could not obtain reprint rights are included here. Boxed material following the further reading list provides references to other biographical and critical sources on the author in series published by Gale.

Indexes

A **Cumulative Author Index** lists all of the authors that appear in a wide variety of reference sources published by the Gale Group, including *CLC*. A complete list of these sources is found facing the first page of the Author Index. The index also includes birth and death dates and cross references between pseudonyms and actual names.

A **Cumulative Nationality Index** lists all authors featured in *CLC* by nationality, followed by the number of the *CLC* volume in which their entry appears.

A **Cumulative Topic Index** lists the literary themes and topics treated in the series as well as in *Literature Criticism from 1400 to 1800, Nineteenth-Century Literature Criticism, Twentieth-Century Literary Criticism,* and the *Contemporary Literary Criticism* Yearbook, which was discontinued in 1998.

An alphabetical **Title Index** accompanies each volume of *CLC*. Listings of titles by authors covered in the given volume are followed by the author's name and the corresponding page numbers where the titles are discussed. English translations of foreign titles and variations of titles are cross-referenced to the title under which a work was originally published. Titles of novels, dramas, nonfiction books, and poetry, short story, or essay collections are printed in italics, while individual poems, short stories, and essays are printed in roman type within quotation marks.

In response to numerous suggestions from librarians, Gale also produces an annual cumulative title index that alphabetically lists all titles reviewed in *CLC* and is available to all customers. Additional copies of this index are available upon request. Librarians and patrons will welcome this separate index; it saves shelf space, is easy to use, and is recyclable upon receipt of the next edition.

Citing *Contemporary Literary Criticism*

When citing criticism reprinted in the Literary Criticism Series, students should provide complete bibliographic information so that the cited essay can be located in the original print or electronic source. Students who quote directly from reprinted criticism may use any accepted bibliographic format, such as University of Chicago Press style or Modern Language Association (MLA) style. Both the MLA and the University of Chicago formats are acceptable and recognized as being the current standards for citations. It is important, however, to choose one format for all citations; do not mix the two formats within a list of citations.

The examples below follow recommendations for preparing a bibliography set forth in *The Chicago Manual of Style,* 14th ed. (Chicago: The University of Chicago Press, 1993); the first example pertains to material drawn from periodicals, the second to material reprinted from books:

Morrison, Jago. "Narration and Unease in Ian McEwan's Later Fiction." *Critique* 42, no. 3 (spring 2001): 253-68. Reprinted in *Contemporary Literary Criticism.* Vol. 169, edited by Janet Witalec, 212-20. Detroit: Gale, 2003.

Brossard, Nicole. "Poetic Politics." In *The Politics of Poetic Form: Poetry and Public Policy,* edited by Charles Bernstein, 73-82. New York: Roof Books, 1990. Reprinted in *Contemporary Literary Criticism.* Vol. 169, edited by Janet Witalec, 3-8. Detroit: Gale, 2003.

The examples below follow recommendations for preparing a works cited list set forth in the *MLA Handbook for Writers of Research Papers,* 5th ed. (New York: The Modern Language Association of America, 1999); the first example pertains to material drawn from periodicals, the second to material reprinted from books:

Morrison, Jago. "Narration and Unease in Ian McEwan's Later Fiction." *Critique* 42.3 (spring 2001): 253-68. Reprinted in *Contemporary Literary Criticism.* Ed. Janet Witalec. Vol. 169. Detroit: Gale, 2003. 212-20.

Brossard, Nicole. "Poetic Politics." *The Politics of Poetic Form: Poetry and Public Policy.* Ed. Charles Bernstein. New York: Roof Books, 1990. 73-82. Reprinted in *Contemporary Literary Criticism.* Ed. Janet Witalec. Vol. 169. Detroit: Gale, 2003. 3-8.

Suggestions are Welcome

Readers who wish to suggest new features, topics, or authors to appear in future volumes, or who have other suggestions or comments are cordially invited to call, write, or fax the Project Editor:

Project Editor, Literary Criticism Series
The Gale Group
27500 Drake Road
Farmington Hills, MI 48331-3535
1-800-347-4253 (GALE)
Fax: 248-699-8054

Acknowledgments

The editors wish to thank the copyright holders of the criticism included in this volume and the permissions managers of many book and magazine publishing companies for assisting us in securing reproduction rights. We are also grateful to the staffs of the Detroit Public Library, the Library of Congress, the University of Detroit Mercy Library, Wayne State University Purdy/Kresge Library Complex, and the University of Michigan Libraries for making their resources available to us. Following is a list of the copyright holders who have granted us permission to reproduce material in this volume of *CLC*. Every effort has been made to trace copyright, but if omissions have been made, please let us know.

COPYRIGHTED MATERIAL IN *CLC*, VOLUME 173, WAS REPRODUCED FROM THE FOLLOWING PERIODICALS:

African American Review, v. 27, Summer 1990 for "*The Bluest Eye*: Notes on History, Community, and Black Female Subjectivity," by Jane Kuenz; v. 32, Summer 1998 for "The Fourth Face: The Image of God in Toni Morrison's *The Bluest Eye*," by Allen Alexander. Copyright © 1990, 1998 by the authors. Both reproduced by permission of the publisher and the authors.—*America*, v. 130, January 19, 1974. © 1974. All rights reserved. Reproduced with permission of America Press, Inc., 106 West 56th Street, New York, NY, 10019.—*Antioch Review*, v. 52, Spring 1994. Copyright © 1994 by the Antioch Review Inc. Reproduced by permission of the Editors.—*Asian Affairs*, v. 15, February 1984. Copyright © by American-Asian Educational Exchange, Inc. Reprinted by permission of the publisher.—*Belles Lettres*, v. 9, Fall 1993. Reproduced by permission.—*British Journal of Sociology*, v. 52, June 2001. Reproduced by permission.—*Callaloo*, v. 13, Summer 1990. © The Johns Hopkins University Press. Reproduced by permission.—*Chicago Tribune Books*, May 2, 1993. © 1993 Tribune Media Services, Inc. All rights reserved. Reproduced by permission.—*Christian Century*, v 91, January 16, 1974; v. 96, April 11, 1979. Both reproduced by permission.—*Christian Science Monitor*, v. 81, February 10, 1989. © 1989 The Christian Science Publishing Society. All rights reserved. Reproduced by permission from *The Christian Science Monitor*.—*CLA Journal*, v. 25, June 1982. Copyright, 1982 by The College Language Association. Used by permission of The College Language Association.—*Commonweal*, v. 99, February 1, 1974; v. 18, December 2, 1988. Copyright © 1974, 1988 Commonweal Publishing Co., Inc. Both reproduced by permission of Commonweal Foundation.—*Communication Monographs*, v. 60, June 1993 for "Women as Communicators: Mary Daly's Hagography as Rhetoric," by Cindy L. Griffin. Reproduced by permission of the Speech Communication Association and the author.—*Contemporary Sociology*, v. 5, July 1976 for "Review of *Beyond God the Father: Toward a Philosophy of Women's Liberation*," by Marie Augusta Neal. Copyright © 1976 American Sociological Association. Reproduced by permission of the publisher and the author.—*Critique: Studies in Contemporary Fiction*, v. 41, Spring 2000. Copyright © 2000 Helen Dwight Reid Educational Foundation. Reproduced with permission of the Helen Dwight Reid Educational Foundation, published by Heldref Publications, 1319 18th Street, NW, Washington, DC, 20036-1802.—*Cross Currents*, v. 49, Winter 1999-2000; v. 50, Fall 2000. Copyright 1999-2000 by Cross Currents Inc. Both reproduced by permission.—*Dalhousie Review*, v. 79, Autumn 1999 for "Review of *Women's Lives: The View from the Threshold*," by Sarah Emsley. Reproduced by permission of the author.—*East European Politics and Societies*, v. 15, Fall, 2001. Reproduced by permission.—*English Language Notes*, v. 30, September 1992. © copyrighted 1992, Regents of the University of Colorado. Reproduced by permission.—*The Explicator*, v. 51, Summer 1993; v. 53, Fall 1994. Copyright © 1993, 1994 Helen Dwight Reid Educational Foundation. Both reproduced with permission of the Helen Dwight Reid Educational Foundation, published by Heldref Publications, 1319 18th Street, NW, Washington, DC, 20036-1802.—*Hypatia*, v. 7, Spring 1992. Reproduced by permission.—*Indian Journal of American Studies*, v. 23, Fall 1993. Reproduced by permission.—*Journal of Asian Studies*, v. 44, November 1984. Reproduced by permission.—*Journal of Popular Culture*, v. 25, Summer 1992. Copyright © 1992 The Board of Regents of the University of Wisconsin System. All rights reserved. Reproduced by permission.—*Journal of the Midwest Modern Language Association*, v. 22, Spring 1989 for "Toni Morrison's 'Allegory of the Cave': Movies, Consumption, and Platonic Realism in *The Bluest Eye*," by Thomas H. Fick. Copyright 1989 by The Midwest Modern Language Association. Reproduced by permission of the publisher and the author.—*London Review of Books*, v. 14, April 23, 1992 for "Self-Disclosing Days," by Jenny Turner; v. 14, July 9, 1992 for "Here Is a Little Family," by Amit Chaudhuri; v. 20, June 4, 1998 for "Acts of Violence in Grosvenor Square," by Christopher Hitchens; November 30, 2000 for "I Prefer to Be an Ottoman," by Justin Huggler. All appears here by permission of the *London Review of Books* and the author.—*Los Angeles Times Book Review*, May 20, 1984; May 19, 1985; October 3, 1995; February 16, 1997. Copyright, 1984, 1985, 1995, 1997, Los Angeles Times. Reproduced by permission.—*MELUS: The Journal of the Society for the Study of The Multi-Ethnic Literature of the United States*, v. 21, Winter 1987. Copyright, MELUS: The Society for the Study of Multi-Ethnic Literature of the United States, 1987. Reproduced by permission.—*Michigan Quarterly Review*, v. 29, Winter 1990 for

"The Shape of Women's Lives," by Linda Simon. Copyright © The University of Michigan, 1990. All rights reserved. Reproduced by permission of the author.—**Midwestern Miscellany,** v. 24, 1996. Reproduced by permission.—**Modern Drama,** v. 36, December 1993. Copyright © 1993 University of Toronto, Graduate Centre for Study of Drama. Reproduced by permission.—**Monthly Review,** v. 41, October 1989. Copyright © 1989 by MR Press. Reprinted by permission of Monthly Review Foundation.—**The Nation** (New York), v. 248, June 5, 1989; v. 256, May 17, 1993; v. 261, November 6, 1995; v. 275, July 8, 2002. © 1989, 1993, 1995, 2002 The Nation Magazine/ The Nation Company, Inc. All reproduced by permission.—**National Catholic Reporter,** v. 35, March 5, 1999. Reproduced by permission of National Catholic Reporter, www.natcath.org.—**National Review,** v. 48, January 29, 1996. Copyright © 1996 by National Review, Inc, 215 Lexington Avenue. New York, NY, 10016. Reproduced by permission.—**The New Criterion,** v. 20, January 2002 for "A Lost Lady," by Jeffrey Hart. Copyright © 2002 by The Foundation for Cultural Review. Reproduced by permission of the author.—**New Directions for Women,** v. 18, January 1989 for "Outlaw Stories Empower & Inspire," by Marian Sandmaier. © Copyright 1989, New Directions for Women, Inc., 25 West Fairview Ave., Dover, NJ, 07801-3417. Reproduced by permission of the author.—**The New Leader,** v. 76, June 14, 1993; v. 84, November-December 2001. © 1993, 2001 by The American Labor Conference on International Affairs, Inc. Both reproduced by permission.—**The New Republic,** v. 169, November 10, 1973; v. 192, May 27, 1985. © 1973, 1985 The New Republic, Inc. Both reproduced by permission of *The New Republic*.—**New Statesman,** v. 106, July 22, 1983; v. 108, October 5, 1984; v. 109, March 1, 1985; v. 114, November 6, 1987; v. 126, April 11, 1997; v. 27, November 13, 1998; v. 128, January 8, 1999; v. 129, April 24, 2000; v. 13, September 11, 2000; v. 131, May 13, 2002. © 1983, 1984, 1985, 1987, 1997, 1998, 1999, 2000, 2002 Statesman & Nation Publishing Company Limited. All reproduced by permission.—**New Statesman and Society,** v. 3, October 12, 1990; v. 5, January 24, 1992; v. 5, May 22, 1992; v. 6, January 29, 1993. © 1990, 1992, 1993 Statesman & Nation Publishing Company Limited. All reproduced by permission.—**New York Review of Books,** v. 90, May 1993. Copyright © 1993 Nyrev, Inc. Reproduced with permission from *The New York Review of Books*.—**Off Our Backs,** v. 23, January 1993; v. 28, December 1998. Both reproduced by permission.—**Partisan Review,** v. 61, Winter 1994 for "Bosnia: Guilt By Dissociation? A Discussion with Slavenka Drakulic," by William Phillips and others. Copyright © 1994 by *Partisan Review*. Reproduced by permission of the publisher and author.—**Perspectives in Psychiatric Care,** v. 35, April-June 1999. Reproduced by permission.—**Problems of Communication,** v. 40, January-April 1991. Reproduced by permission.—**The Progressive,** v. 66, January 2002. Copyright © 2002 by The Progressive, Inc. Reproduced by permission of *The Progressive,* 409 East Main Street, Madison, WI, 53703, www.progressive.org.—**Publisher's Weekly,** v. 242, September 11, 1995; v. 247, November 6, 2000. Copyright 1995, 2000 by Reed Publishing USA. Both reproduced from *Publishers Weekly,* published by the Bowker Magazine Group of Cahners Publishing Co., a division of Reed Publishing USA., by permission.—**Slavic and East European Journal,** v. 42, Summer 1998; v. 42, Fall 1998. © 1998 by AATSEEL of the U.S., Inc. Reproduced by permission.—**Slavic Review,** v. 53, Fall 1994. Copyright © 1994 by the American Association for the Advancement of Slavic Studies, Inc. Reproduced by permission.—**Southern Humanities Review,** v. 18, Spring 1984; v. 29, Fall 1992. Copyright 1984, 1992 by Auburn University. Both reproduced by permission.—**Spectator,** v. 277, October 19, 1996. © 1996 by *The Spectator.* Reproduced by permission of *The Spectator.*—**Studies in the Novel,** v. 32, Summer 2000. Copyright 2000 by North Texas State University. Reproduced by permission.—**Times Literary Supplement,** no. 4491, April 28, 1989; no. 4566, October 5, 1990; no. 4571, November 9, 1990; no. 4635, January 31, 1992; no. 4648, May 1, 1992; no. 4713, July 30, 1993; no. 4861, May 31, 1996; no. 4970, July 3, 1998; no. 4992, December 4, 1998; no. 5083, September 1, 2000; no. 5175, June 7, 2002. © The Times Supplements Limited 1989, 1990, 1992, 1993, 1996, 1998, 2000, 2002. All reproduced from *The Times Literary Supplement* by permission.—**Washington Post Book World,** August 10, 1997. © 1997, Washington Post Book World Service/Washington Post Writers Group. Both reproduced by permission.—**The Washington Report on Middle East Affairs,** v. 21, November 2002. Reproduced by permission—**Women's Review of Books,** v. 1, August 1984 for "Famous Lust Words," by Marilyn Frye; v. 4, December 1986 for "She Done It," by Maureen T. Reddy; v. 5, December 1987 for "Erratic, Ecstatic, Eccentric," by Julia Penelope; v. 6, February 1989 for "Questioning the Quest," by Emily Toth; v. 10, March 1993 for "Mary, Mary, Quite Contrary," by Carol J. Adams; v. 12, July 1995 for "Postmurderism," by Lillian S. Robinson; v. 13, December 1995 for "Career Feminist," by Wini Breines; v. 15, January 1998 for "Free at Last," by Annette Zilversmit; v. 17, March 2000 for "No Place Like Home," by Valerie Jablow. Copyright © 1986, 1987, 1989, 1993, 1995, 1998, 2000. All reproduced by permission of the authors.—**Women's Studies International Forum,** v. 22, September-October 1999. Copyright © 1999 Pergamon Press Ltd. Reproduced by permission of the publisher.—**World Literature Today,** v. 66, Winter 1992; v. 73, Winter 1999; v. 74, Summer 2000; v. 74, Winter 2000; v. 75, Winter 2001. Copyright 1992, 1999, 2000, 2001 by the University of Oklahoma Press. All reproduced by permission of the publisher.

COPYRIGHTED MATERIAL IN *CLC*, VOLUME 173, WAS REPRODUCED FROM THE FOLLOWING BOOKS:

Awkward, Michael. "Roadblocks and Relatives: Critical Revision in Toni Morrison's *The Bluest Eye*." From **Critical Essays on Toni Morrison.** Edited by Nellie Y. McKay. G. K. Hall & Co., 1988. Copyright © 1988 by Nellie Y. McKay. All rights reserved. Reproduced by permission.—Dickerson, Vanessa. "The Naked Father in Toni Morrison's *The Bluest Eye*." From **Refiguring the Father: New Feminist Reading of Patriarchy.** Edited by Patricia Yaeger and Beth Kowaleski-

Wallace. Southern Illinois University Press, 1989. Copyright © 1989 by the Board of Trustees, Southern Illinois University. All rights reserved. Reproduced by permission.—Gray, Frances. "Elemental Philosophy: Language and Ontology in Mary Daly's Texts." From *Feminist Interpretations of Mary Daly*. Edited by Sarah Lucia Hoagland and Marilyn Frye. The Pennsylvania State University Press, 2000. Copyright © 2000 by Pennsylvania State University. All rights reserved. Reproduced by permission.—Korte, Anne-Marie. "Deliver Us from Evil: Bad versus Better Faith in Mary Daly's Feminist Writings" and "Just/ice In Time: On Temporality in Mary Daly's Quintessence." From *Feminist Interpretations of Mary Daly*. Edited by Sarah Lucia Hoagland and Marilyn Frye. The Pennsylvania State University Press, 2000. Copyright © 2000 by Pennsylvania State University. All rights reserved. Reproduced by permission.—Ledbetter, Mark. "Through the Eyes of a Child: Looking for Victims in Toni Morrison's *The Bluest Eye*." From *Literature and Theology at Century's End*. Edited by Gregory Salyer and Robert Detweiler. Scholars Press, 1995. Copyright © 1995 by The American Academy of Religion. All rights reserved. Reproduced by permission of the publisher and the author.—Harris, Trudier. "Reconnecting Fragments: Afro-American Folk Tradition in *The Bluest Eye*." From *Critical Essays on Toni Morrison*. Edited by Nellie Y. McKay. G. K. Hall & Co., 1988. Copyright © 1988 by Nellie Y. McKay. All rights reserved. Reproduced by permission.—Mbalia, Doreatha Drummond. "*The Bluest Eye*: The Need for Racial Approbation." From *Toni Morrison's Developing Class Consciousness*. Susquehanna University Press, 1991. Copyright © 1991 by Associated University Presses. All rights reserved. Reproduced by permission.—Miner, Madonne M. "Lady No Longer Sings the Blues: Rape, Madness, and Silence in *The Bluest Eye*." From *Conjuring: Black Women, Fiction, and Literary Tradition*. Indiana University Press, 1985. Copyright © 1985 by Indiana University Press. All rights reserved. Reproduced by permission.—Ratcliffe, Krista. "De/Mystifying Herself and Her Wor(l)ds: Mary Daly." From *Anglo-American Feminist Challenges to the Rhetorical Traditions: Virginia Woolfe, Mary Daly, Adrienne Rich*. Edited by John K. Wilson. Southern Illinois University Press, 1996. Copyright © 1996 by the Board of Trustees, Southern Illinois University. All rights reserved. Reproduced by permission.

PHOTOGRAPHS AND ILLUSTRATIONS APPEARING IN *CLC*, VOLUME 173, WERE RECEIVED FROM THE FOLLOWING SOURCES:

Ali, Tariq, photograph by Bernd Kammerer. AP/Wide World Photos. Reproduced by permission —Daly, Mary, Cambridge, Massachusetts, 1999, photograph by Christopher Pfuhl. AP/Wide World Photos. Reproduced by permission.—Drakulic, Slavenka, photograph by Filip Horvat. Corbis Saba. Reproduced by permission.—Heilbrun, Carolyn, photograph by Katy Raddatz. Corbis. Reproduced by permission.—Morrison, Toni, photograph. AP/Wide World Photos. Reproduced by permission.

Literary Criticism Series Advisory Board

The members of the Gale Group Literary Criticism Series Advisory Board—reference librarians and subject specialists from public, academic, and school library systems—represent a cross-section of our customer base and offer a variety of informed perspectives on both the presentation and content of our literature criticism products. Advisory board members assess and define such quality issues as the relevance, currency, and usefulness of the author coverage, critical content, and literary topics included in our series; evaluate the layout, presentation, and general quality of our printed volumes; provide feedback on the criteria used for selecting authors and topics covered in our series; provide suggestions for potential enhancements to our series; identify any gaps in our coverage of authors or literary topics, recommending authors or topics for inclusion; analyze the appropriateness of our content and presentation for various user audiences, such as high school students, undergraduates, graduate students, librarians, and educators; and offer feedback on any proposed changes/enhancements to our series. We wish to thank the following advisors for their advice throughout the year.

Dr. Toby Burrows
Principal Librarian
The Scholars' Centre
University of Western Australia Library

David M. Durant
Reference Librarian, Joyner Library
East Carolina University

Steven R. Harris
English Literature Librarian
University of Tennessee

Mary Jane Marden
Literature and General Reference Librarian
St. Petersburg Jr. College

Mark Schumacher
Jackson Library
University of North Carolina at Greensboro

Gwen Scott-Miller
Fiction Department Manager
Seattle Public Library

Tariq Ali
1943-

Pakistani nonfiction writer, novelist, editor, playwright, historian, and journalist.

The following entry presents an overview of Ali's career through 2002.

INTRODUCTION

Ali has been recognized as an important political and social commentator, establishing a reputation as a left-wing activist and journalist during the 1960s and 1970s. His work as an activist, journalist, editor, historian, playwright, and novelist has made him a familiar figure in British political and literary circles. In recent years, his writings have focused on the turbulent relationship between the countries of India and Pakistan and on British policies in the Middle East.

BIOGRAPHICAL INFORMATION

Ali was born on October 21, 1943, in Lahore, India, a region that is now part of Pakistan. In 1963 he received his B.A. from Punjab University, and then attended Oxford University in England. During his college years in England, Ali developed his talents as a writer and served as the president of the Oxford Union. He gained attention for his activities as a left-wing political activist, protesting British involvement in the Vietnam War as well as its policies toward the Soviet Union. After graduating from Oxford, Ali began working as a journalist, writing about a variety of political, social, and cultural issues while also serving as a member of the editorial board of the *New Left Review*. During the 1980s, he owned his own independent television production company, Bandung, which produced programs for the British Broadcasting Company (BBC). He has been a regular broadcaster on BBC Radio and has also contributed articles and journalism to magazines and newspapers including *The Guardian* and the *London Review of Books*. Ali resides in England and continues to expound on current political conditions, such as the cultural conflicts in the Middle East and Persian Gulf regions.

MAJOR WORKS

Ali has written a broad range of nonfiction, publishing first-hand accounts of life in the Soviet Union and in post-Soviet Russia, memoirs and studies of the student

movement in the 1960s, explanatory texts on Stalinism and Trotskyism, and modern political histories of India and the Balkan crisis. *1968 and After: Inside the Revolution* (1978) and *Street Fighting Years: An Autobiography of the Sixties* (1987) both delineate events of the 1960s and comment on the turbulent political and social climate of the era. In *Revolution from Above: Where Is the Soviet Union Going?* (1988), Ali displays his investigative talents in an exploration of the sociopolitical conditions in the Soviet Union before and during the fall of communism. Turning his focus toward his homeland, Ali presented his personal analysis of the political relations between India and Pakistan in *Can Pakistan Survive?* (1983). Ali continued his examination of Indian culture with *An Indian Dynasty: The Story of the Nehru-Gandhi Family* (1985) which traces the history and influence of the Nehru-Gandhi family in Indian politics. As a response to the September 11, 2001, terrorist attacks on the United States, Ali published *The Clash of Fundamentalisms: Crusades, Jihads, and Modernity* (2002). The work explores the history of spiritual fundamentalism, arguing that the September 11 attacks were caused by a conflict between religious dogma and modern imperialism.

During the 1990s, Ali began to write and publish fiction that explores his interest in Muslim history and culture. *Shadows of the Pomegranate Tree* (1993) is his first novel in a planned quartet detailing confrontations between Islamic and Christian civilizations. The book chronicles events surrounding the Banu Hudayl—an aristocratic Muslim family—in late fourteenth-century Spain. The novel opens with the burning of all Muslim books by Ximenes de Cisneros, Queen Isabella's confessor, and relates the misfortunes of the Hudayl family, including the struggles of patriarch Umar Hudayl, his son Yazid, and the fall of Islam in Spain. Ali's 1999 novel, *The Book of Saladin,* the second novel in the quartet, is a fictitious memoir of the ruler Salah-al-Din, who wrested Jerusalem from Christian control in the twelfth century. The work seeks to dismiss the stereotype of Saladin as a ruthless and godless conqueror, employing a modern sensibility in its depiction of European Crusaders in a distinctly negative light. The third installment in the series, *The Stone Woman* (2000), focuses on the decline of the Ottoman Empire in the nineteenth century as viewed through the eyes of one family, and in particular, through the eyes of its patriarch, Iskander Pasha. Iskander suffers a stroke, which leaves him partially paralyzed. As his lengthy rehabilitation progresses, many of his friends and family members come to visit. Over the course of the novel, Iskander seeks answers to the reasons behind the decline of his empire and attempts to reconcile his past behavior with his present emotions. Much of the narrative also focuses on his daughter, Nilofer, her relationship with Iskander, and the feelings and opinions of their other relatives. Ali's novel *Fear of Mirrors* (1998) is written in an epistolary style, taking the form of a letter from Professor Vladimir Meyer to his estranged son, Karl, in an attempt to explain the family history. The novel moves back and forth in place and time, covering several generations of Vladimir's family as well as the development of the early communist movement. Ali intersperses fictional characters with well-known historical figures, creating a narrative that recounts the rise and fall of communism and the reunification of Germany.

All of Ali's dramatic works have been written in collaboration with Howard Brenton, focusing strongly on the genre of "Instant History" plays—plays which are composed quickly to address timely social and political issues. Written in just over five days, Ali's play *Iranian Nights* (1989) was intended to act as a metaphorical response to the Islamic furor surrounding the release of Salman Rushdie's *Satanic Verses.* The plot utilizes several characters from Arabic folklore, including The Caliph and Scheherezade, in a tale about religious blasphemy and the nature of storytelling. *Moscow Gold* (1990) deals with the history of communism in the Soviet Union, following three women—Zoya, Katya, and Lena—as they experience and are affected by some of the major events in Soviet history, including the Russian invasion of Afghanistan, the election of Russian president Mikhail Gorbachev, and the dismantling of the Berlin Wall. *Ugly Rumours* (1998) satirizes the British New Labour movement, taking its title from the band that British Prime Minister Tony Blair formed while attending Fettes College. The play centers around Blair as he struggles to deal with national politics while being haunted by the ghost of Margaret Thatcher who lives in the attic of No. 10 Downing Street. Ali and Brenton have also joined with Andy de la Tour to produce *Collateral Damage* (1999), which concerns the Serbian-Croatian conflict, and *Snogging Ken* (2000), a satire about a London mayoral election.

CRITICAL RECEPTION

Ali's fiction and drama have met with mixed reviews, with critics generally favoring his plays over his novels. The plays *Iranian Nights* and *Moscow Gold* have been particularly singled out for their provocative political themes and nontraditional structures. His novels, in contrast, have received harsher criticism with some reviewers deeming them unimaginative and stylistically inferior. Several critics have faulted Ali for inadequate characterizations in his novels, while others have criticized his fiction citing such faults as overabundant metaphors, overuse of political jargon, and heavy-handed exposition. However, many commentators have applauded the pacing of Ali's storytelling as well as his humor and concern for authenticity in his historical novels, arguing that his later work appears more confident and mature. Critical consensus regarding Ali's political and historical studies has generally been favorable, with scholars noting his knowledgeable and intelligent treatment of Soviet and Middle Eastern politics. Nevertheless, some critics have found Ali's nonfiction to be needlessly polemic and marred by exaggeration, superficiality, and a lack of original information. In addition, several commentators have made similar observations regarding Ali's fiction, claiming his prose is predictable and overly driven by his own political beliefs. Julian Ferraro, for example, has stated that despite Ali's gripping subject matter, his writing often displays a "leaden touch." In general, reviewers have praised the epic historical detail in many of Ali's novels, but have conversely panned the author's abilities with narrative and prose. In his review of *Fear of Mirrors,* Ferraro continued, "The dialogue is either turgid with political analysis or wooden to the point of bathos. . . . and the trite conclusion provided by the final scenes seriously undermines the bleak complexities of the rest of the book." Overall, many commentators have agreed that Ali's unique background provides him with a valuable and intriguing perspective regarding world affairs.

PRINCIPAL WORKS

The New Revolutionaries: A Handbook of the International Radical Left [editor] (nonfiction) 1969
Pakistan: Military Rule or People's Power? (nonfiction) 1970
The Coming British Revolution (nonfiction) 1972
1968 and After: Inside the Revolution (history) 1978
Trotsky for Beginners (nonfiction) 1980
Can Pakistan Survive? (nonfiction) 1983
The Stalinist Legacy: Its Impact on Twentieth-Century World Politics [editor] (nonfiction) 1984
What Is Stalinism? [editor] (nonfiction) 1984
An Indian Dynasty: The Story of the Nehru-Gandhi Family (history) 1985
Street Fighting Years: An Autobiography of the Sixties (history) 1987
Revolution from Above: Where Is the Soviet Union Going? (nonfiction) 1988
Iranian Nights [with Howard Brenton] (play) 1989
Moscow Gold [with Howard Brenton] (play) 1990
Redemption (novel) 1990
*Shadows of the Pomegranate Tree (novel) 1993
Fear of Mirrors (novel) 1993
1968: Marching in the Streets [with Susan Watkins] (nonfiction) 1998
Ugly Rumours [with Howard Brenton] (play) 1998
*The Book of Saladin (novel) 1999
Collateral Damage [with Howard Brenton and Andy de la Tour] (play) 1999
Masters of the Universe?: NATO's Balkan Crusade [editor] (nonfiction) 2000
Snogging Ken [with Howard Brenton and Andy de la Tour] (play) 2000
*The Stone Woman (novel) 2000
The Clash of Fundamentalisms: Crusades, Jihads, and Modernity (nonfiction) 2002

*Shadows of the Pomegranate Tree, The Book of Saladin, and *The Stone Woman* are the first three novels in a planned four-part series focusing on the confrontation between Islamic and Christian civilizations.

CRITICISM

Premen Addy (review date 22 July 1983)

SOURCE: Addy, Premen. "State of Faith." *New Statesman* 106, no. 2731 (22 July 1983): 24.

[*In the following review, Addy credits Ali for his overview of the geopolitics of India in* Can Pakistan Survive?, *but faults him for not going beyond the "commonly held perceptions of the Left" in the book.*]

The creation of Pakistan was for its founder, Mohammed Ali Jinnah, a triumph of will and tactical acumen. For the Muslims of the subcontinent, whose cherished homeland this was to be, its consequences were fraught with tragedy. Jinnah had fondly hoped to build the new state in his own image: liberal, cosmopolitan, secular. But, as Tariq Ali observes [in *Can Pakistan Survive?*], it was a house built on sand. With Islam as its raison d'être, the country's ruling class consisted mainly of an unholy crew of Punjabi landlords and bureaucrats, a Punjabi-dominated military and a middle-class refugee element from Uttar Pradesh in India who had first voiced the idea of a promised land, only to lose out to the military-bureaucratic rump for whom any prospect of sharing office was an anathema.

The subject masses, Punjabi, Sindhi, Pathan, Baluchi, and the majority Bengalis separated from the rest by 1,000 miles of Indian territory, resisted all attempts, to chasten them into a common Islamic shape. Conflicting national, social, political and economic currents joined to fuel an explosive Bengali uprising in 1971, leading to the emergence of an independent Bangladesh.

In perhaps the strongest part of this book, Tariq Ali discusses the civilian interlude of Zulfiquar Ali Bhutto which followed this débâcle. The new Prime Minister's quicksilver intelligence was anchored to few moral constraints. He could be in turn coarse and charming, a man of the crowd and an aristocrat; but, like most demagogues, was prone to trim his sails to the prevailing wind. He appeased the Shah abroad and the mullahs at home in a desperate bid to retain power. However, every concession to his Islamic clerics emboldened them to ask for more. In the end they got in General Zia the obscurantist of their dreams and Bhutto paid for his weakness with his life.

As with Bhutto, so also with Jinnah. Recalling Lenin's observation that Shaw was a good man fallen among Fabians, Tariq Ali gives the impression that the Quaid-i-Azam was similarly placed in the Muslim League. Whatever Jinnah's early or inner distastes for mass politics he became a past master at manipulating these for his own ends. The ruthless methods by which he destroyed the Unionist inter-communal party of Muslims, Hindus and Sikhs in the Punjab would have done credit to a Tammany Hall mobster. Pirs and mullahs were pressed into service in the 1946 provincial elections. Their price inevitably was to be confessional politics in a confessional state. For Jinnah to have expected otherwise was a delusion.

Tariq Ali stresses correctly the contributions of the other players in the tragedy of India's partition: British deviousness, Congress obduracy, Hindu fanaticism and communist stupidity. In conclusion, a lot is said about the geopolitics of the region and the pressures facing

Pakistan from Iran and Afghanistan without adding significantly to the commonly held perceptions of the Left. A deeper exploration of India's position and confidence would surely have been more fruitful.

The ties between India and the Soviet Union constitute one expression of this confidence. They are a fact of life and a stable one at that in a highly unstable world. However severe the buffetings from China and America, Indian foreign policy has proved exceptionally durable. Wisely, Tariq Ali refrains from prophesying a quick end to Zia's regime. Short of a military adventure it could be with us for some years yet. But go it will, eventually.

William Crawley (review date February 1984)

SOURCE: Crawley, William. Review of *Can Pakistan Survive?*, by Tariq Ali. *Asian Affairs* 15, no. 1 (February 1984): 87-8.

[*In the following review, Crawley outlines Ali's major thematic concerns in* Can Pakistan Survive?]

Theorists of the left have been few in number in Pakistan and very limited in their influence. [In *Can Pakistan Survive?*] Tariq Ali writes from the position of one who though well known internationally is an outsider in his country's politics. He is equivocal about the validity and viability of Pakistan as a state. He dissects the political solutions and experiments which have been tried over the past thirty-five years, from the "military-bureaucratic" partnership culminating in President Ayub Khan's regime, through the "populism" of Zulfiqar Ali Bhutto to the "martial law with an Islamic face" practised by President Zia ul Haq. He pays particular attention to the Pakistani left, whose weakness and ineffectiveness he traces back to the errors of the Indian Communist Party both before and after independence in following the Moscow line too closely. By 1954 the communist party in both West and East Pakistan had been banned and its former members submerged in other parties. With the break-up of the two wings in 1971 the party reemerged in Bangladesh but not in the western half. Tariq Ali answers his own question "Can Pakistan Survive?" with a tentative and heavily qualified yes, the condition being that it must undergo a social transformation. Somewhat curiously for a Marxist, he believes that the mass mobilisation which he regards as the essential catalyst for such a transformation, can best be achieved in alliance with the regional sub-nationalities which are so evident in the politics of both Pakistan and India today. Tariq Ali's ideal is a federation of South Asian States, but he recognises that it seems far-fetched. He does not underestimate the power of a modern state to defend itself in the face of internal dissent, and he rejects terrorism (as practised in Pakistan by the so called "Al-Zulfiqar" organisation), as a viable policy. He sees Pakistan's future as a prey to superpower influences and the undertow of events in neighbouring Iran and Afghanistan. As a view from the left this tract poses some pertinent questions, and despite the polemics it illuminates the dilemmas which successive Pakistan governments have faced.

Nicholas Murray (review date 5 October 1984)

SOURCE: Murray, Nicholas. Review of *Who's Afraid of Margaret Thatcher?*, by Tariq Ali. *New Statesman* 108, no. 2794 (5 October 1984): 33.

[*In the following review, Murray provides a favorable assessment of Ali's introduction to* Who's Afraid of Margaret Thatcher?]

This short book [*Who's Afraid of Margaret Thatcher?*] consists of two long conversations which took place at County Hall in June 1983 and April 1984 between the two red horned and tailed demons whom Steve Bell delineates on the cover. It is an essential sequel to the unpolitical *Citizen Ken* and a must for all Livingstone-fanciers.

Tariq Ali's trenchant introduction aims its fairground rifle at a row of targets including the 'pink professors' (Crick and Hobsbawm), the 'fashion conscious editors of *Marxism Today*' who have done for radical *chic* what the Princess of Wales has done for parturition, the 'charade' of the block vote and (for the provenance of these talks is the Olympian *New Left Review*) the massed vices of Labourism.

The interview format is peculiarly well suited to the episodic and anecdotal temper of Ken Livingstone's political intelligence. He is explicit about his lack of any theoretical apparatus and at the end of his introduction Uncle Tariq leans over and administers a gentle slap on the wrist to young Ken for this ('Yet, I'm afraid, he will have to plough through some of the socialist classics sooner or later.')

What Livingstone does possess, of course, is an abundant political chutzpah. He has made socialism popular, deflected the arrows of media malignity and charmed the pants off us. What comes across most forcefully in these conversations is his optimism that we will see another Labour Government in 1987 or 1988, that it will be qualitatively different from its predecessors and that people can be won back in large numbers to the socialist cause. Given the self-flagellating gloom that prevails in many parts of the Labour movement this buoyancy is refreshing.

Livingstone, who joined the Labour Party in 1968, when other socialists were leaving it in droves—a fact that bemuses Tariq Ali—is decidedly a child of the *mille neuf soixante huit*, both in his laid-back manner and in his receptivity to the new politics of feminism and antiracism. He is not in the old corporatist mould of hidebound Labour politicians—what Tariq Ali, in a witty coinage, calls the 'Stabians' (product of a collision between 'Stalinist' and 'Fabian', describing those right-wing authoritarians in the upper reaches of the Labour Party who go about in horror of the grassroots).

Above all, he believes in the need for rebirth in the Party, 'basically refounding the Labour Party', which will come about as much from recognising what people outside it are demanding as from internal debate: 'This means *us* changing.' It is a tonic to hear a prominent Labour politician talking in this way. If this book does not go straight to the top of the alternative best seller lists in *City Limits* then I'm a member of Labour Solidarity.

Akbar S. Ahmed (review date November 1984)

SOURCE: Ahmed, Akbar S. Review of *Can Pakistan Survive?*, by Tariq Ali. *Journal of Asian Studies* 44, no. 1 (November 1984): 239-41.

[*In the following review, Ahmed criticizes* Can Pakistan Survive?, *calling the work simplistic, polemical, and "marred in general by non sequiturs and by exaggeration."*]

Tariq Ali, the professional polemical student leader long resident in England, has written a polemical book [*Can Pakistan Survive?*]. The title, subtitle, and photograph on the jacket (Pakistan in flames) may be termed "sensational." The question in the title has been asked since 1947; the subtitle is premature.

Tariq's view of South Asian political history is simplistic. Pakistan was a mistake: "Pakistan was an irrationality, a product of imperialist penetration of the subcontinent—its interior was diseased from birth—an experiment doomed to failure" (p. 145). It is a position held by most Indian leaders. Tariq's villains are black and his heroes are white. In the former category he includes the judiciary, the army, the civil service, and the journalists of Pakistan. In the latter category are the small group of Pakistani leftists. No one can deny that Pakistan has numerous problems. It has hostile neighbors; it has had serious ethnic divisions (in Bengal in 1971 and in Sind in 1984); there is tension between fundamentalists and other Muslims; the problem of martial law is chronic. But this book offers neither perceptive analysis nor solution.

In places the text reads like an official Party tract. The Pakistan army leaders come from the "kulak gentry of the Punjab and Frontier" (p. 65) and the "semi-fascist" clergy is "lumpen" (p. 187). What relieves the monotony of the Party prose are the flashes of temper and contempt for Pakistan (the "Islamic banana republic" [p. 161]) and Pakistanis (Jinnah was "elitist" [p. 27], inconsistent [p. 33], and did not understand communalist politics [p. 39]). Ayub Khan and his generals, like Azam Khan, were "bland and insipid"—their intellectual pastime was the *Reader's Digest* (p. 66); Yahya Khan was "a dim and slothful alcoholic" (p. 96). Zia is "Machiavellean" (p. 136). Tariq's contempt for the army generals almost reaches hysteria; "The fools!" he exclaims of them (p. 192).

But Tariq's special wrath is reserved for the Jamaat-i-Islami, "closely linked to Saudi Arabia and the United States, the closest thing in Pakistan to a fascist party" (p. 139). Tariq argues that "Islam is regarded by its fanatics as a complete and total code of life" (p. 184). It may surprise Tariq to learn that not only "fanatics" believe in Islam. Islam as a sociological and cultural force enjoys deep support in Pakistan society at every level. Islam may be interpreted in a thousand different ways, but its importance is an undisputed fact of life in Pakistan.

Islam is not Tariq's only villain. He singles out China and the United States as well. In a flight of emotion he argues that acquiring F-16s "might encourage Islamabad to embark on an adventure vis-à-vis its powerful Eastern neighbour" (p. 190). A statement that even Indira Gandhi may not be able to pull off with conviction.

The argument of the book is marred in general by non sequiturs and by exaggeration. Tariq writes that *Dawn* published Ayub Khan's photograph sixty-nine times in one issue in order to humor him; in his next sentence, he argues that this action illustrates how the bureaucracy was isolated from the people (p. 76). He charges with no evidence that ten thousand Pakistani prostitutes were dispatched to the Gulf States by the United Bank to earn foreign currency (p. 125). Baluch women, according to Tariq, were raped systematically by members of the Pakistan army (p. 121). He notes, again with exaggeration, that "for all Pakistan's women, life itself is a prison" (p. 161), "the Islamic code having reduced them to ciphers and objects" (ibid.).

Tariq's most basic conclusion, that because Pakistanis may be fed up with General Zia-ul-Haq they have rejected Pakistan, is seriously awry. On the contrary, the sense of insecurity felt by Pakistanis has induced them to rally around unpopular leaders. And what is the alternative? Since 1947, an entire generation to whom India is another country has grown up in Pakistan.

Tariq argues that the rulers of Pakistan—like Ayub Khan—were sustained from abroad: one may well apply the same arguments to Tariq. He is a creature of the British press. He obviously fills a need to have an ageless student leader providing sensationalism and journalistic coups. Although advertised as A Pelican Original, there is little that is original in this book.

Zareer Masani (review date 1 March 1985)

SOURCE: Masani, Zareer. "Tensions." *New Statesman* 109, no. 2815 (1 March 1985): 29-30.

[*In the following excerpt, Masani notes the lack of new research and serious analysis in* An Indian Dynasty.]

The lives of India's modern Caesars have already been the subject of copious biography; and Tariq Ali relies almost wholly on the work of his predecessors. But was there any point in a tedious repetition of the story if there was nothing new to add? There was certainly room for a study of the making of the dynasty and of the political culture that legitimised it. But that would have required new research and some serious analysis, neither of which appear in this hastily improvised dog's breakfast [*An Indian Dynasty: The Story of the Nehru-Gandhi Family*].

Tariq Ali implies that the dynasty owes its fortunes to founding-father Jawaharlal, whose achievements take up more than half the book. But his long-winded and discursive account of the nationalist movement misses out the most interesting part of the story—how the Congress Trinity of Father, Son and Holy Ghost (as Motilal and Jawaharlal Nehru and Mahatma Gandhi were sometimes affectionately known) assured the younger Nehru's political succession. Tariq Ali does not seem to know that when Jawaharlal took over as Congress President in 1929, his father, the outgoing president, had been pulling strings for him behind the scenes. He also misses the importance of Nehru's alliance with Gandhi in scuttling Subhas Bose, his main challenger for the nationalist succession.

Tariq Ali rightly suggests that the dynasty proper came into being in recent years, with Mrs Gandhi's blatant promotion of her sons. Yet his final section on the Brothers Gandhi, which should by this logic have been the core of the book, is astonishingly thin. There is no attempt to analyse the ingredients of populist leadership in India or to explain why a politically mature electorate, which so decisively rejected Mrs Gandhi's dynasticism in 1977, succumbed to it in 1980 and 1984.

Instead of including digressions on the dacoit queen, Phoolan Devi, surely he would have done better to examine the non-dynastic charisma of Opposition leaders like Jayaprakash Narayan or 'J. P.', heir to the mantle of Mahatma Gandhi, whose popular crusade brought down Mrs Gandhi's emergency regime. In a book which has several factual errors, the most serious is the misinformation about J. P.'s career, which leads to the suggestion that he was a pro-Hindu leader who adopted 'Bonapartist airs'.

Tariq Ali's neglect of alternative leadership creates the misleading impression that the Nehru-Gandhi dynasty is India's natural form of government. Indeed, his account of recent events, such as the storming of the Sikh Golden Temple and the massacre of Sikhs after Mrs Gandhi's assassination, reads alarmingly like an apologia for the dynasts.

What this book ignores is the complex political and social context of Indian dynasticism—the importance of caste and kinship networks, the strength of communal Hindu sentiment, the decline of parliamentary government, the centralising technocracy of business élites and the alienation of a cynical electorate. Apart from a throw-away reference to 'lumpen-feudalism', Tariq Ali does not address these issues. Instead, relying on the most banal Western stereotype of Third World politics, he blames the 'low level of culture' in the Indian countryside, and a 'belief in all sorts of religious individuals'.

Pratapaditya Pal (review date 19 May 1985)

SOURCE: Pal, Pratapaditya. "An Indian Dynasty." *Los Angeles Times Book Review* (19 May 1985): 7.

[*In the following review, Pal contends that although* An Indian Dynasty: The Story of the Nehru-Gandhi Family *"was written and produced in less than six months, it is well documented, generally accurate and very readable."*]

Thirty years ago, the non-aligned movement was born in an obscure town called Bandung in Indonesia. The chief architects of that conference were four remarkable men of this century: Tito of Yugoslavia, Chou en Lai of China, Nasser of Egypt and Nehru of India. Tito and Chou were rulers of communist governments; Nasser had come to power through military rather than democratic means; only Nehru was the freely elected leader of what was then—and still is—the largest democracy in the world. All four men died some time ago, and neither in the communist countries nor in partially democratic Egypt has any of the descendants of Tito, Chou or Nasser staked a claim to their country's political leadership as their birth-right. Ironically, only in the world's largest "democracy" has there been a perpetuation of dynastic rule for 34 years of its 37-year existence.

Tariq Ali's book [*An Indian Dynasty: The Story of the Nehru-Gandhi Family*] narrates the strange saga of perhaps the most extraordinary dynasty of modern times. Jawaharlal Nehru (1889-1964) was the first prime minister of independent India from 1947 until 1964. Except for a brief interregnum of a few months, he was succeeded by his only daughter Indira (1917-1984), who ruled longer than her father and, like him, died with her boots on, though not of natural cause but by bullets. Within a few hours after her assassination on Oct. 31, 1984, she was succeeded by her only surviving son, Rajiv Gandhi (1944-), whose claim to the throne at the time was based solely on heredity rather than merit or political experience. It must be pointed out that Indira and Rajiv Gandhi have only a surname in common with Mahatma Gandhi, who led India into freedom and was assassinated in 1948. Indira Nehru's husband Feroze Gandhi, who predeceased her by many years, was a Parsi (a non-Hindu minority who are descendants of Persian Zoroastrians who emigrated to India many centuries ago), while the Mahatma was a Gujarati Hindu. The two were not even remotely related, contrary to what most Americans think.

The book is undoubtedly timely, for India has been much on the American mind, thanks to unfortunate events that the mass media have reveled in reporting (the Sikh problem, the storming of their Golden Temple in Amritsar and consequent assassination of Indira Gandhi, and the even more tragic man-made catastrophe at Bhopal) and thanks as well to such cultural events in this country as David Lean's (rather than E. M. Forster's!) *A Passage to India* and the much touted PBS soap opera about the Indian jewel in the British crown. Indeed, as the book's American publisher's news release admits, it was commissioned by Ali's British publisher immediately after Mrs. Gandhi's death no doubt to cash in on the current India craze.

Considering that the book was written and produced in less than six months, it is well documented, generally accurate and very readable. A few minor errors are surprising though not crucial. Prayag is certainly much older than AD 600, and Alexander was *not* "stopped by the Indian ruler Chandra Gupta (sic), not far from Allahabad." Much less excusable is the statement that "Nepal, Sikkim and Bhutan are monarchies of a sort." Surely, Ali knows that the ruler of Sikkim was shamelessly dethroned three years ago by the very Mrs. Gandhi who has been characterized as the "Empress of India" in the heading of the book's fourth chapter. As a matter of fact, it is somewhat surprising that Ali ignores this ignominious episode in Mrs. Gandhi's political career.

Nevertheless, the author has deftly sketched the political portraits of four generations of Nehrus against the background of India's turbulent history of almost the entire 20th Century and has tried, on the whole, to be objective and impartial in his assessments and comments, by no means an easy task when reviewing one's own time. One must also admire Ali's restraint, for as Salman Rushdie, the author of *Midnight's Children*, writes in an incisive introductory essay to the book, "It has often seemed that the story of the Nehrus and the Gandhis has provided more engrossing material than anything in the cinemas or television, a real dynasty better than 'Dynasty,' a Delhi to rival 'Dallas.'"

Ali could easily have given us more titillating accounts of Nehru's apparent loveless marriage to a bride chosen by his patrician father, or of his later "affair" with Lady Edwina Mountbatten, the wife of Lord Mountbatten, the last viceroy of India. He could have written at greater length about Kamala Nehru's attachment to a much younger, witty and entertaining Feroze Gandhi who later married her daughter He could have probed further into the reasons why Indira Gandhi "did not like but loved Feroze" and yet abandoned him to devote herself entirely to her father. Hardly the appropriate behavior of an Indian wife, and yet she was exalted by the populace as a goddess! Her strange and obsessive devotion to her sons, her paranoid fear of losing power, her dependence on astrology, her paradoxical insecurity despite enormous popular support, her arrogance and her ruthlessness—all these make her one of the most intriguing and fascinating personalities in history. One can also ask why in a country of 700 million people (roughly 200 million of whom are literate) no other family in two generations has produced a single political personality to challenge the Nehrus.

Ali's emphasis has been more on the political rather than on the personal lives of his heroes and villains; actions and decisions are explained in political terms rather than with psychological insight. The personalities, therefore, seem somewhat dehumanized. Nevertheless, the book is well worth reading, for it clearly demonstrates the insidiously corruptive game of power, in which ultimately there are no winners.

Shiva Naipaul (review date 27 May 1985)

SOURCE: Naipaul, Shiva. "Family Affair." *New Republic* 192, no. 21 (27 May 1985): 26-30.

[*In the following review, Naipaul discusses Ali's perception of and attitude toward twentieth-century Indian politics in* An Indian Dynasty.]

No one interested in the 20th-century history of the Indian subcontinent can contemplate its dramas without the accompanying sensations of disquiet and distaste—even, on occasion, of outright revulsion. The plot, beginning with the struggles of the nationalist movement, is a complex and devious one, a spider's web of often incompatible ideals (Gandhi and Nehru may have been guru and disciple, but they also represented quite different images of Indian destiny), of hostile interests and confusions of motive. Toward the end, which we might say for the sake of convenience comes with the coronation of Rajiv Gandhi, the ideals have disappeared altogether. All that survives are the interests, which have become more naked, and the emotions to which they give rise, which have become more crude. How did it happen that the Gandhi-Nehru legacy decayed into the shabbiest idolatry of family? How was it that India—a country, despite all its poverty and squalor, with a substantial industrial base, powerful armed forces, a sophisticated civil service, a well-educated middle class—how was it that India maneuvered itself into the voodoo politics of Mama and Baby Docs?

I shall take a scene or two from what now passes for political life in India. Toward the end of 1983, Tariq Ali (in England those who still remember the intoxicating days of student revolt will also remember Tariq Ali, who achieved prominence as a radical president of the Oxford Union) was present at a session of the All India Congress Committee, one of the manifestations of the ruling party. It should have been a glittering occasion. Present were emissaries from East Germany, Tanzania, France, the Soviet Union. Indira Gandhi and her heir apparent, Rajiv, presided. Rajiv, so far as our information goes, had been perfectly content piloting the aircraft of Indian Airlines, the internal carrier. There is no reason to doubt that he would have gone on doing so but for the sudden death, in 1980, of his younger brother Sanjay. Cruelly robbed of one heir apparent, Indira Gandhi reached out for the only other available. It takes years of training, I am told, to qualify as an airline pilot. But it seems that nothing of the sort is required to become the leader of 800 million Indians.

"The Congress session," Tariq Ali tells us [in ***The Indian Dynasty***], "was a one-family show . . . Sitting on the floor of the wooden platform were Indira Gandhi and Rajiv, surrounded by provincial leaders. In the audience were 'delegates' from Congress branches in the country as a whole. 'Delegate' is perhaps a euphemism. They seemed like people picked up on the street and promised a good time. . . . Some of them were constantly being rescued from police, cells and brothels." They chanted slogans ("'Who is the leader of our nation?'" "'Rajiv Gandhi!'") when called on to do so by their cheerleaders. Only Indira and Rajiv could command their attention and deference. When other speakers tried to address them, the rabble grew noisily restive and drifted away from the hall in droves. Mindful of the presence of her distinguished overseas guests, the prime minister was vexed, becoming especially so when it was the turn of her most prominent guest (a member of the Central Committee of the Communist Party of the Soviet Union) to speak. In desperation, she rose to her feet. "'Look here,'" she appealed, resorting to the privacy of Hindi, "'. . . it looks very bad for foreigners when you all leave after I've spoken. Sit down! You near the door, sit down! . . . '"

It is possible that Tariq Ali has embellished the scene, that he has exaggerated the infantilism. Nevertheless, his description rings true. It is of a piece with the essentially personal and devotional nature of political allegiance in India. Indira Gandhi ought not to have been so discountenanced by the behavior of her admirers. She had raised no objections when it was proclaimed that "India is Indira and Indira is India." If that were indeed so, why should time be wasted listening to anyone else? Congress, as a party, was pure facade; no more than a front organization for Indira Gandhi and her family. Everybody knew that.

Politics as such—the battle of parties, the conflict of ideologies—had virtually ceased to exist. In that debased atmosphere a quarrel between mother-in-law and daughter-in-law automatically acquired vibrant public significance. After the death of Sanjay, it came to light that his widow, Maneka—never too enamored of her brother-in-law Rajiv and his Italian wife—was reacting badly to her sudden eclipse and the rapid elevation of her rivals. Whether the disaffected Maneka was expelled, or expelled herself, from the house of the Gandhis remains obscure. However it was, she lost her resident status. Not everybody who falls out with her mother-in-law responds to the challenge by forming a political party. Maneka did. One morning 800 million Indians woke up to discover that their political choice had been enriched by the birth of the *Rashtriya Sanjay Manch*—the National Sanjay Organization.

Her party, Maneka declared; would fight for socialism, democracy, and secularism; a trinity of aspiration, as Tariq Ali remarks, not usually associated with Sanjay Gandhi. Maneka fought an election against Rajiv. Socialism, democracy, and secularism featured little in her campaign. Tariq Ali sums it up well. "Maneka's main angle at the political rallies was to present herself to the poor peasants as a wronged widow, cast out on to the streets by a tyrannical mother-in-law and under the cold eyes of her late husband's cruel elder brother and his foreign wife."

Politically, India seems to have gone full circle, to have regressed to the shallow but deadly intricacies of the Moghul court on the eve of the British conquest. Is it too fanciful to suggest that one can already discern the dim outlines of future civil wars? The dramatis personae exist—one doesn't have to invent them. Maneka has her little princeling, Feroze; and Rajiv has his Rahul. The dynasticism that, to some, has seemed a blessing, offering India stability and continuity, could become a rather messy business if the claimants to the inheritance continue to multiply. Whatever its successes under the benign guidance of "Captain Rajiv," the intrinsically capricious character of the dynastic principle will ultimately subvert the too cheaply acquired illusions of stability and continuity. It is a papering over of the cracks that have developed in the foundations of Nehru's "secular" state. Today India may embrace the civilized Rajiv; but only yesterday it was recoiling in terror from Sanjay and the demons he had threatened to unleash.

Yet, when we turn our attention away from the Congress Party, when we survey the Indian landscape in search of an alternative, what do we see? We see factionalized Marxist sects not obviously anointed with any conviction of their revolutionary destiny; narrowly based "chauvinist" movements like the Sikh Akali Dal (Party of Immortals) in the Punjab; in the "anti-Aryan" south, regional alliances with a purely regional appeal. And we see too, through a polluted mist, those discredited, disgruntled gerontocrats, the Congress "Old Guard," maneuvered into the borderlands by the palace coup Indira Gandhi had engineered in 1969 to secure her ascendancy after the death of the ephemeral Lal Bahadur Shastri.

These, roughly speaking, were the men who, in 1977, were to be given a second chance by the Indian people, emerging triumphant from the post-emergency general election, which had swept away Indira and Sanjay. The failure of their jerry-built Janata (People) coalition went deeper than mere popular disenchantment with the disconcerting eccentricities of a urine-drinking prime minister; went deeper than the gross corruption that accompanied the urine-drinking—Indians, after all, were inured to corruption; went deeper, even, than the absurdities: the minister of health, for example, didn't believe in modern medical practices. Mutilated by the cutthroat ambitions of the leading protagonists who shamelessly warred with each other, the coalition vandalized the fragile fabric of Indian democracy. Its sordid, self-inflicted suttee prepared the way not only for the return of Indira Gandhi and the feared Sanjay, but signaled a surrender to the dynastic principle. If Nehruian democracy was to be raped, who better to do the ravishing than the descendants of Nehru? They might even do it with some style. And maybe some sort of rape had always been inevitable. How do you govern and hold together a country that defies the very idea of nationality? Nearly 40 years after the coming of independence and the secular state, the most fundamental questions persist.

"What is Mother India?" Jawaharlal Nehru had asked one of his audiences some years before the attainment of independence. His listeners, until that moment ebullient, fell uneasily silent. In India nearly everything conspires toward fragmentation. The challenge to the unity of India comes not from without but from within. The specific evolutions of history, religion, language, castes, subcastes, sub-subcastes—nearly everything tends to divisiveness. In the poorest and most squalid of villages, communities will isolate themselves from one another. Some years ago, while traveling in Maharashtra, I visited such a village. It was a stricken place, barely able to coax one crop of rice a year from the stony soil, inhabited by low-caste Hindus and Untouchables. Not many years before, the Untouchables had converted en masse to Buddhism; others seek salvation by embracing Christianity or Islam.

Conversion had made little difference to their condition. Relations between the two groups in the village were no less strained than they had been formerly. The "Buddhists"—to take just a couple of examples—could not draw water from the same well as the Hindus and had to locate their huts at a discreet distance. They were all, Hindu and Buddhist alike, hopelessly destitute, hopelessly separate—and all citizens of the Indian republic. In any of the neighboring villages, these same low-caste Hindus might find themselves similarly discommoded and reviled by those adjudged their superiors. In India, degradation and sublimity are subject to the most delicate shadings. Caste maintains and defines a sense of self that might otherwise disintegrate into nothingness. It is contagious, infiltrating its sensibilities even where it is formally denied. Neither Indian Christianity nor Islam—nor Buddhism—has been immune to the infection. Add to caste the other major lines of fracture randomly listed, and the question "What does Mother India mean to *you*?" assumes alarmingly chaotic implications. When meditated upon, the "India" invoked by nationalist favor begins to lose its solidity, melting away into spectral abstraction. Hence, perhaps, the silence that fell when Nehru asked his question.

There is another equally pertinent version of the question. What did Mother India mean to Jawaharlal Nehru? One way of trying to answer this is to consider the background of the man. The Nehrus, interestingly enough, had their ancestral roots in Kashmir, a region peripheral to the main currents of Indian life and, with its Moslem majority, still squabbled over by India and Pakistan. It is possible that this inherited marginality allowed Nehru to distance himself from the constrictions of the subcontinent's cellular mosaic and to see a "whole" where a whole may never have existed; or, at nay rate, not existed in the sense premised by nationalist fervor.

Although he never actually lived there—the Nehrus migrated to Delhi in the early 18th century—the picture-book romance of Kashmir, its snows, its lakes, its flowered meadows, did always remain with him, coloring his dreams. How subliminally un-Indian the images bequeathed by Kashmir! It smuggled into his perceptions the poetic license to which the privileged quasi-outsider is always vulnerable. Jawaharlal himself was born in Allahabad, a city on the confluence of the sacred rivers, Ganges and Yamuna. The Nehrus, Brahmans of impeccable quality, were aristocrats. British India, one imagines, could have furnished few better examples of adaptation and assimilation.

Motilal Nehru (Jawaharlal's father), a prosperous lawyer, an ostentatious Anglophile, lived in the grand Victorian manner. One of his son's earliest memories is of his father, warmed by claret, laughing resonantly at the dinner table. Motilal's house, with its terraces, columns, and cupolas, its rose garden, swimming pool, and croquet lawn—splendors picked out at night by flood-lighting—reflected its owner's worldly ease. India in its living reality Jawaharlal would discover only in his maturity. His childhood was sheltered, Motilal hiring an English tutor (albeit a somewhat unconventional one—he was a theosophist) for his son. For his daughters he acquired English governesses. Later, Jawaharlal was sent to Harrow, thus sharing an alma mater with Winston Churchill, the great enemy of Indian independence. But Anglophilia couldn't provide perfect protection. At Harrow Nehru experienced the first twinges of colonial unease and anxiety. "I was never an exact fit," he wrote in his autobiography. "Always I had a feeling that I was not one of them." In due course he went on to Cambridge, where he read geology, chemistry, and botany.

Imperial life continued on its measured way. Motilal was delighted when he was summoned to attend the durbar of the visiting king-emperor, George V. This event took place in Delhi in 1911. He ordered his clothes for the occasion from London. The future prime minister of India rose with a matter-of-fact aplomb to the demands made on him. "I suppose," he wrote to his father from Cambridge, "you want the ordinary levee dress with sword and everything complete. . . . The shoes for the court dress will be made at Knighton's and the gloves at Travelette's. . . . Heath's man has managed to fish out your old measures and cast, and he will shape your hats accordingly."

Motilal remained sufficiently Indian, nevertheless, to want to seek out a suitable bride for his son. Jawaharlal, in response to the threat, fished out his own up-to-date notions on love and marriage. "There is not an atom of romance," he countered, "in the way you are searching out girls for me . . . the very idea is extremely unromantic." Motilal, though, had his way in the end. On his return to India, Jawaharlal married the Kashmiri Brahman girl who had been found for him. He was 26; she was 16. Somehow his romantic modernity survived this setback. Its ardors and commitments were transferred to the nationalist battlefield, to his vision of India reborn.

The Nehrus, through all the later generations—Motilal's, Jawaharlal's, Indira's—have been Janus-headed: simultaneously martyrs to the nationalist crusade (the youthful Indira was detained by the British during World War II) and fairly typical embodiments of the colonial yearning for "cosmopolitan" sophistications, the victims and the beneficiaries of what nowadays is called cultural imperialism. I do not mean to suggest that these tendencies are necessarily discordant. On the contrary. It is no accident that Toussaint L'Ouverture was a pampered house slave. Revolutions are more often than not the stepchildren of underprivileged cognoscenti. They are the ones who most keenly feel the slings and arrows of outrageous fortune. It is always terrible to realize you are not "one of them." Cultural imperialism is no bad thing. Many of us could do with more rather than less of it. The Nehrus have had few inhibitions about it. The sicklier members of the family were in and out of Swiss and American sanatoriums. Indira—Tariq Ali tells us that her favorite city was Florence—was patchily educated in Swiss and English boarding schools, and spent a couple of inconclusive years at one of Oxford's women's colleges. At a time when it was difficult for Indian students to travel abroad, Indira insisted that her sons should be exceptions. "I couldn't care less what people say," she remarked, "I thought it was necessary for my boys to go to England."

Westernism—"phoreigness," as the Indian satirists put it—can assume many disguises. In Indira Gandhi, Nehruian modernity betrays degenerative symptoms. That an English education—and this, note, nearly a generation after the coming of independence—should still be a "necessity" for her boys is disturbing: Westernism is slipping into a crude devotion to the phoreign. With Sanjay it slipped further down the scale of values, expressing itself in an obsession with motorcars, tall buildings with lots of glass, wild ecological fantasies of a verdant India, and a savage contempt for his poverty-stunned countrymen. Rajiv (his wife, incidentally, is Italian) has softened the Sanjayite crassness and talks, instead, of the computer revolution. "Oh," said one of his close advisers, a fellow Cambridge graduate, to an interviewer, "we were the Beatles generation." A century ago his equivalents in Calcutta would have been discussing Jeremy Bentham and John Stuart Mill. Only in Jawaharlal Nehru, conspicuously the most erudite, cultured, and gifted of the clan, did the emphatic Westernizing strain in the Nehrus escape caricature and bear its noblest fruit.

The fruit was a noble one. Yet it has soured and grown bitter. Nehru's romanticism coexisted with a no less powerful rationalism. In fact, the two were linked: dependent on each other, present in each other. His rational romanticism—or, one could say, romantic rationalism—imposed on India the ideal of the secular, non-communal state. This might indeed, in some distant future, be a desirable consummation. But given the circumstances, few documents are further removed from the human realities they are supposed to regulate than the constitution of the Republic of India. "Communalism" has become a byword for all that is bad in India, associated with religious obscurantism, caste degradation, and warfare, and the riots and massacres that arise as a consequence. It resurrects, in particular, all the horrors of Partition, of mobs of Moslems, Sikhs, and Hindus gathering at railway stations with sword and knife and gun to let loose their blood-lust on the refugee trains transporting the displaced populations.

I do not for a moment gloss over these darknesses. But what is called communalism is not merely the sum of its assorted delinquencies—as Tariq Ali's flawless, textbook socialism would make it out to be. Nehru, unlike Tariq Ali, sensed the arduous and improbable nature of the task he had set himself and imposed on the country. When André Malraux asked this "un-English English gentlemen" (the characterization is Malraux's) what had been his greatest difficulty since independence, Nehru mentioned, first of all, "the creation of a just state by just means." He paused, then added more concretely: "Perhaps too creating a secular state in a religious country."

Communalism, for better or worse, articulates the Indian diversity. Looking down on it from Olympian heights we might wish that it had been otherwise. But it is a brute fact and, however hard we try, there is no running away from it. The Marxists might murmur about false consciousness; but consciousness, false or otherwise, remains consciousness. The divisions and distinctions and traditions bred by centuries of evolution cannot be wished away. The paradox, such as it is, is this. Communalism, while articulating Indian diversity, also expresses the unity of India. Not, obviously, the kind of unity presupposed or required by the "secular" state, but those broader unities characteristic of an old and intricate civilization. The old argument about the unity of India comes down to that. India *does* exist; India *is* a unity. Its existence and its unity, however, belong to a more ancient order of things. Rome began as a state and, as its power increased, became a civilization. India, more slowly, more undirectedly, accumulated a civilization and never quite managed to create the patterns of a consistent, self-conscious statehood. Those, like Tariq Ali, who would abolish "communalism" by waving the magic wand of class war and revolution, are, in effect, asking India to abolish itself. That is rather a lot to expect.

For Tariq Ali, despite his irreproachable radicalism, is also one of the victims and beneficiaries of cultural imperialism. How effortlessly he writes about "peasant spontaneity," "class demands" and all the rest. When Indira Gandhi's Parsi husband is said to come from a "petit bourgeois" background, one is overwhelmed by genuine distraction. Marx's man doesn't hesitate to fish out alien measures and casts. Motilal had at least taken the trouble of having his unique dimensions ascertained.

Is there a more fashionable cause around today than the pursuit of "identity"? All along the way, the secular ideal has had to make concessions to the Indian reality in its various guises. The carving out of states on the basis of language is a major example. So is the "positive discrimination" practiced on behalf of the Untouchables. By what sleight of hand does it become "chauvinist"—not to say fascist!—for the Hindus of Hindustan to proclaim themselves as such? The secular Indian state, so wary of its minorities, so wracked by the defection of Pakistan, has sacrificed Hindustan as a notion, has refused to accord it legitimacy. Only in the machinations of back-room political calculation and intrigue is it accorded weight. Forced into the shadows, is it any wonder that so many of its manifestations surface out of its murkier depths? Tariq Ali, as the following outburst will reveal, is not in a position to offer remedies. "The continued strength of religion in the modern world," he informs us with schoolboy intensity, "is the most telling indictment of this century. . . . The members of the Ku Klux Klan in the United States are all firm believers in Christianity."

Nehru, that un-English English gentleman, was more subtle. In his will he requested that a portion of his ashes be consigned to the Ganges—although, ever mindful of his famous agnosticism, he was careful to disown any apostasy on his part. "The Ganga," he wrote,

> . . . is the river of India, beloved of her people, round which are intertwined her racial memories. . . . She has been a symbol of India's age-long culture and civilization. . . . I am conscious that I too, like all of us, am a link in that unbroken chain which goes back to the dawn of history. . . . That chain I would not break, for I treasure it and seek inspiration from it.

The reinstatement of Hindustan—and I am not advocating the rebirth of some archaic, unhistorical dreamworld composed of Gandhian self-regulating village republics: no one, including the Hindu, is exempt from the necessities and tribulations of change—might conceivably restore to stationary Hinduism the burden of movement, the burden of moral and intellectual responsibility, which, in part because of secularism, it has relinquished. In that restoration might lie the resolutions that secularism—now ever more weakened by the dynastic cult based on the Nehrus—has so far failed to provide.

Nigel Fountain (review date 6 November 1987)

SOURCE: Fountain, Nigel. "Summer's Here and the Time Is Right." *New Statesman* 114, no. 2954 (6 November 1987): 28-9.

[*In the following review, Fountain describes Ali as an "informative, funny, and illuminating writer," lauding his prose in* Street Fighting Years.]

Is it the right title? Mick Jagger joined the Vietnam Solidarity Campaign marchers as they moved on Grosvenor Square in March 1968 and, hey presto, two months later, out popped 'Street Fighting Man' and thus, I suppose, the cue for the title of Tariq Ali's autobiography [*Street Fighting Years*]. Yet brooding on his entertaining reminiscences of those times my mind slipped to a 1964 waxing by the West Coast's Beach Boys, who reported that they were getting tired of going down the same old strip and were going to find a new place where the kids were hip. There isn't really very much *fighting* in *Street Fighting Years,* but boy, Ali can—and does—say he Got Around.

Indeed, the only restriction on his movement seems to have been the attention of the then Home Secretary, James Callaghan. The risk of losing his residency in Britain deterred the author from joining the action on the Paris barricades in May 1968. 'To have missed Paris that spring,' he writes, 'was unforgiveable.'

Well, up to a point; Lenin missed February 1917 so had the whole show rerun with a new script in October, and Mao had the good fortune to miss the Shanghai massacre in 1927. History, when it gets round to checking its files, will probably absolve Ali for his absence.

He can be an informative, funny, and illuminating writer. His description of childhood and adolescence in the hybrid state of Pakistan in the 1950s and early '60s is fascinating. The state floated between the Empire's legacy and the arrival of American imperialism, and was rooted in uncertain military rule. His upper-class family floated between memories of partition, faith in Stalin and uncertainty about the new world, and new colonial uprisings.

That experience, I guess, provides him with a breadth of vision and a sympathy with struggle across the globe singularly lacking from most other British socialists. But what it doesn't free him from is an often exasperating inability to take the piss out of himself. When not ruminating on the Beach Boys, my reference point turned to those military memoirs so beloved of the *Sunday Times* during Ali's—and my—childhood. Had it been the memoirs of Major-General Sir Tariq Ali MC, DSO I would not have been greatly surprised.

Having arrived in England, and Oxford University in the early '60s, we find him rapidly assuming command of the Oxford Union before a posting under Julian Critchley at Michael Heseltine's *Town* magazine. By then the Bertrand Russell Peace Foundation and its ubiquitous organiser Ralph Schoenman was on hand to provide him with field service in Prague, Hanoi and Bolivia. Much of this, too, is fascinating, including the information that his access to an imprisoned Régis Debray in Bolivia was obtained via a deftly forged credential from *Town* complete with a bogus signature from Heseltine. Should the Tory in better times rub shoulders with the now born-again rightist Debray in some vulgar act of diplomacy they might pause to think of the man who first brought them into peripheral contact in Che Guevara's mountain graveyard all those years ago.

Pausing is not really Ali's style. News from Vietnam demanded 'immediate responses'; arrival in Berlin meant immediate briefings from German SDS leaders; he would go 'straight from the LSE' to top level discussions on distribution of the *Black Dwarf.* Throughout, 'politics had to remain in command'.

But what politics? Talking on the 1960s underground recently Germaine Greer noted that everybody thought that the revolution—whatever that might be—was going to be easy. On the one hand Ali's travels wised him up to the violence, the horror, the tenacity that parts of those radical movements of the times were confronting and displaying. Yet his travels were those of a member of the upper classes won to radicalism, and despite the Trotskyism he had espoused by 1968—or possibly because of it—the workers remain largely offstage in a world of Tynans, Sartres and Schoenmans, with the odd eccentric aristocrat thrown in. It had practical implications: while the media ritualistically identified Ali as the 'leader' of the VSC, the International Socialists beavered away within its structures and picked up for their cause what recruits there were to be found.

Which, as the tide of revolution ebbed, left Tariq Ali—together, it should be said, with plenty of others—marooned on a sectarian sandbank shouting vainly for a pick-up from the Labour boat he had correctly rejected back in the days of Che. There are still heroic guerrillas, but no Debrays bother to write about them, and the radicalism has gone out of chic.

It hasn't, however, gone out of Ali, as in the closing pages of the book he details some of the legion lost to the right, and those like Clive Goodwin—the inspiration behind the *Black Dwarf* and much that was good in '60s London left politics—who just died. Gone are the theses from the Fourth International that concluded his 1970s *1968 and After,* and gone too is the author from the now dormant—or extinct?—International Marxist

Group, its always feeble British arm. But he fortunately has forgotten nothing, and learned some things along the way.

I was never much of a reader of *Town*. '*Marxism Today,*' Ali suggests, '. . . celebrates bourgeois existence far more forcefully than *Town* ever did.' Which would, he concludes, disqualify Critchley as a potential *MT* apparatchik. An interesting thesis. One way and another a job on *Town* seems to have been a guarantee of a one-way ticket to political oblivion. But that is a conclusion that its one-time proprietor, and Ali its erstwhile drama critic, would doubtless and perhaps accurately contest. 'History has not yet given us her final verdict on the century that is approaching its end,' says the author. No, but the bloody jury's been out long enough.

Robert Irwin (review date 28 April 1989)

SOURCE: Irwin, Robert. "The Poet and the Infidel." *Times Literary Supplement,* no. 4491 (28 April 1989): 456.

[*In the following review, Irwin compliments* Iranian Nights, *calling the play humorous and thought-provoking.*]

"'Why it's Ali Baba!' Scrooge exclaimed in ecstasy. 'It's dear old Ali Baba . . . And the Sultan's Groom turned upside-down by the Genii; there he is upon his head! Serve him right. I'm glad of it. What business had *he* to be married to the Princess!'" [In *Iranian Nights*] Tariq Ali and Howard Brenton, depressed and challenged by book-burnings, clenched-fisted mobs, death threats, fire-bombings and holy gangsterism, have found both solace and inspiration in the same source which the repenting Scrooge turned to, *The Arabian Nights*. The curtain opens on a stage set drawn from Dulac. The Caliph, a gaudily got-up Rumpelstiltskin played by Nabil Shaban, is waiting for the next story from Scheherezade (Fiona Victory), but her story-telling role is often usurped by Omar Khayyam (Paul Bhattacharjee). Together, Omar and the Caliph act out the story of a poet from an infidel isle who, sentenced to death for blasphemy, travels east to meet his judge, the Imam, in an attempt to save his life by talking (the Scheherezade tactic). He talks a lot, but the tactic does not work for him. Then Scheherezade relates an authentic story from the *Nights,* that of "The Qadi Yusuf with Harun al-Rashid and Queen Zubeidah".

Finally, the scene switches to Bradford and the Caliph and the poet are reincarnated as father and son, first and second generation immigrants. The father argues for assimilation against his son who, as "just a soldier of Islam", believes that the propagation of fear can be a way of propagating the Faith.

Iranian Nights is very loosely structured. It is really a rigged debate in which the Imam has few of the good lines (though Shaban delivers them with impeccable timing when he gets them). Some may feel that the Imam does not deserve good lines, and the authors are inclined to see the sentencing of Salman Rushdie as a corrupt political tactic, an aspect of the *Realpolitik* of the mullahs. Similarly, they interpret the Bradford Muslims' response to *Satanic Verses* as a social phenomenon, Islamic pride as an assertion of immigrant identity. There may be some truth in all this, but it may be that, in taking these lines, the authors are failing to engage fully with the otherworldly intransigence and intelligence of fundamentalist rigour. Moreover, the subtlety of censorship's fellow travellers in this country deserves fiercer scrutiny.

It was a good idea to draw on older and pleasanter representatives of Islamic culture, the medieval poets, al-Ma'ari and Umar Khayyam, as well as the anonymous contributors to *The Arabian Nights,* in order to demonstrate that bigotry has always had its critics within Islam itself. Very short, running for under an hour, *Iranian Nights* is still a comic night out, provoking and enjoyable. Its run at the Royal Court is not 1001 nights, but only nine. However, those interested (and that ought to be everyone), will be able to see it on Channel Four shortly.

Boris Kagarlitsky (review date 5 June 1989)

SOURCE: Kagarlitsky, Boris. "The Truth about *Perestroika.*" *Nation* 248, no. 22 (5 June 1989): 765-67.

[*In the following review, Kagarlitsky compares Ali's* Revolution from Above *to Anthony Barnett's* Soviet Freedom.]

The Soviet Union is too important to be left to Sovietologists. This precept is central to *Revolution from Above,* by Tariq Ali, but it could just as easily be applied to *Soviet Freedom,* by Anthony Barnett, which was published in London six months earlier. The two books almost beg for comparison. Both authors are radicals; neither had studied Soviet society before. Tariq Ali had edited a very interesting collection of materials on Stalinism, but as a British socialist he was interested in the overall theoretical and international aspects of the problem. Meanwhile, in these books both Ali and Barnett are mainly concerned with nothing less than the everyday political life of my country.

Who in the West could have imagined something like this five or six years ago? When many authors of books about the Soviet Union touched on politics, they set about describing the functioning of various official agencies or providing biographies of Politburo members. The study of politics came down to Kremlinology. Few people would have applied the phrase "political struggle" to the Soviet Union. The Western reader had an image of a hopelessly conservative and drearily bureaucratic society in which nothing happened for decades. All the greater, then, was the perplexity and ecstasy when new events started to occur and the process of reform charged ahead with dizzying speed.

Paradoxically, the more convinced the public in the West was that our society was hopelessly conservative, the more inclined it was to euphoria and wholly unrestrained exaggeration of the radicalism of any proclaimed Soviet reforms once it became clear that those were not fictions. People called it not liberalization but liberation. Every official decree was inevitably declared revolutionary, bold and progressive. Today even the censored official Soviet press sometimes offers more sober and critical analyses of current policy than the majority of serious Western publications. Misconceptions beget misconceptions. The Western public may have traded dark glasses for rose-tinted ones, but neither the right nor the left has come close to an understanding of the complex and possibly tragic processes under way in the Soviet Union.

Yet, good always comes out of bad. If not for the current universal fascination with the Soviet Union, probably neither Barnett nor Ali would have undertaken to travel around this "enigmatic country." Another thing in common is that both authors' interest in the country was piqued by *perestroika*. Further, as socialists, they inevitably connect the prospects for reform in the Soviet Union with the political struggle in the West. Ten or twenty years ago reference to the "Soviet experiment" only strengthened the arguments of the right by showing the uselessness of "socialist experiments." But now socialists can take pleasure in the news from Moscow. However it is happening, in the homeland of Stalinism they've begun to talk about socialism with a human face.

In this case Sovietology holds the losing hand. Didn't people representing this science present a generalized and schematic view of the Soviet Union in the West for many long years? Of course, Western authors have written many substantial books, especially on Soviet history (the works of Stephen F. Cohen, Moishe Levin and Alec Nove have had a great influence on Western historians). But the mass-produced works of dozens of rank-and-file Sovietologists of the 1970s and the "expert" newspaper commentaries are not likely to be of much interest now. It's not surprising that people like Barnett and Ali wanted to spend time in the Soviet Union themselves, to see everything with their own eyes and then share what they saw.

Of course, they don't rely solely on their own impressions. From the very first pages of their books it is clear that these authors—careful readers of *Moscow News* and *The Guardian*—examine news reports that may go unnoticed by other authors. Unfortunately, the limited circulation of *Moscow News* makes it nearly as inaccessible to the average Soviet reader as *The Guardian* or *The Nation,* and many events that I witnessed were strikingly different from the way they were depicted in even the most liberal issues of *Moscow News* or *Ogonyok*. But in the end these are the journals that are used to judge the development of *glasnost* in the Soviet Union, since in a society traditionally based on monopoly and centralism the monopoly on liberalism is guarded with particular zeal. Although Barnett and Ali are dependent on official sources of information, they aren't any more so than the average Soviet citizen. This makes their view of Soviet society sufficiently objective, albeit not always sufficiently analytical.

Barnett's *Soviet Freedom* is written impressionistically. Short chapters are devoted to a single event, personal observation or serious political issue. The descriptions of hotels or street scenes are given almost as much space as discussions of strikes and nascent worker activism. Ali tries to be more systematic in **Revolution from Above,** tracking the sources of events, citing social interests and the ideological orientation of the opposing sides. But he cannot resist sharing his personal impressions either. Both authors characteristically find a similarity between what they saw in the West in the 1960s and what is going on in Soviet society today. Such comparisons appear more and more often in Western literature. (I can't help but gloat that when I first noted this in the pages of the *New Left Review* in 1987, I was assailed for confusing desire with reality.)

Barnett's view of events is the view of an intellectual who made contacts with Moscow intellectuals. Ali's view is primarily that of an activist who likewise found people similar to himself in Moscow—and in unexpectedly great numbers. There were rallies on Pushkin Square in the summer of 1988, run-ins with the militia, heated discussions about the salvation of humanity and the fate of socialism. A clear tendency toward anarchy and a keen need for discipline, the Leninist phraseology of liberals and the authoritarian leanings of the champions of universal liberation—this is hardly new for someone who lived through 1968. But it in no way repeats what has already occurred. Events are moving at a different pace and the stakes are far higher. In April 1989 the young men and women at Tbilisi University personally experienced the difference between the Latin Quarter and Prospekt Rustavelli. The rapidly growing bitterness, the increasingly difficult situation in the economy, the skeptical and self-critical analysis of left ideologists—all have little in common with the lovely European dream of 1968. There is no time at Moscow

University to write beautiful slogans about love and revolution on the walls. The blood spilled in Sumgait and Tbilisi is clearly not the last. People speak of revenge more often at rallies, and movement activists know that no one guarantees their safety. Discussions of "revolution from above" and "Soviet freedom" are likely to be regarded as bitter irony. Both revolution and freedom still lie ahead—in the best of circumstances.

That Ali's book was published six months after Barnett's is its main advantage. Both authors are most concerned with the formulation of a civil society and the growth of political identity, but Ali clearly had more material. The Nineteenth Communist Party Conference took place in the interim between the publication of these two books in Britain. The election of delegates, which was conducted by purely bureaucratic methods, set off a powerful movement of protest in various parts of the country. Huge crowds of demonstrators appeared on the streets of Kuibyshev and Yaroslavl. Mass meetings were held in Omsk and Yuzhno-Sakhalinsk. In the non-Russian republics a situation that had already been quite tense quickly grew worse.

The public upsurge of the summer of 1988 gave rise to the People's Front movement. In the Baltic republics the movement has been primarily national in character, while in Moscow, Leningrad and the Russian provinces the People's Front has appeared as a coalition of the democratic left.

All of these events are reflected in Ali's account. As a Marxist, however, he doesn't limit himself to listing facts but rather tries to give a historical explanation for them. The heroes of the book are not simply people demonstrating in the streets of Moscow (heroes such as movement activists Mikhail Maliutin or Andrei Babushkin, who are still not very well known in the West). The author of **Revolution from Above** cites representatives of various ideological trends: left radicals, liberals, technocrats, conservatives and neo-Stalinists. He tries to give the reader a sense of the body of these people's ideas and how they took shape. In this sense Ali's book is a valuable traveler's guide to the ideological labyrinth of *perestroika*.

Barnett's work is to some extent already out-of-date. This isn't his fault—events have progressed too rapidly. Barnett gives the Western reader a sense of the Moscow political and cultural atmosphere in 1987, Tariq Ali writes about 1988—and here we are in 1989.

Unfortunately, only some of the two British travelers' predictions and conclusions have been borne out by the unfolding events. Although they are trying to get away from the clichés of Sovietology, they don't always succeed, often becoming captives of the very myths they wish to refute. Neither author believes in the myth of the totally controlled and completely centralized Soviet society, for instance. But their sense of the transformations conducted from above is to a large degree a continuation of this myth of Sovietology, which has merely been modified to suit the new circumstances. Instead of seeing an elemental, spontaneous process completely out of control, the vortex of a crisis, they still believe in the wisdom of reform. They are ready to blame conservative forces when transformations are not successful, without considering that the changes were, from the outset, a profoundly conservative attempt to re-establish control over an economy and society that was slipping out of control. They mistakenly identify the core of the unfolding changes as radical reform, though these changes had been predetermined by the urgency and tragic crisis gripping the country.

In reality, there has been no comprehensive reform in the economy or even in the political system. Everyone who has studied the legislation passed and political decisions made from 1986 to 1989 is amazed above all by how little has been accomplished. Many new documents are far from liberal. The law on elections and the decrees on special military units, on rallies and on demonstrations have made Soviet legislation much worse than it was even during the Brezhnev years. Stories on the failures of economic reform have become commonplace in the official press. The most astounding thing about *perestroika* is how much is changing in society despite the total failure of initiatives of reform from above. The greatest sensation of the spring 1989 elections was not the successes of the left in Moscow—where one of the coordinators of the People's Front, Sergei Stankevich, was unexpectedly turned into a key figure in the progressive deputy bloc—but the landslide defeat of official candidates in Leningrad, candidates who had no competition in elections conducted by the old rules!

As Western observers continue to extol wise reforms, we see that the complete failure of moderate reform attempts has opened the way to uncontrolled elemental processes. What do we have, a prerevolutionary situation or a prereactionary period? It may very well be both.

The course of events makes us delay our optimistic predictions. The Western public, which has begun to believe in these new myths of Sovietology, has another disappointment in store. But pessimistic prophesies would probably not be trusted, and in any case the country will never be the same again. The British travelers Barnett and Ali sensed this on the streets of Moscow. I can confirm that the same has been felt in Irkutsk, Sverdlovsk, Kiev and many other cities, at every end of this enormous land. The question of whether the reforms are irreversible is a question of whether people are willing to fight for their freedom. We saw that they were when 35,000 Muscovites responded to the appeal of the People's Front in March by attending a rally for the radical political leader Boris Yeltsin and the candidates of the "progressive bloc."

Perhaps my most vivid impression of those days was the work of the group organizing the rally. The young people wearing the Front's blue armbands were able to maintain order in the crowd, pass out fliers and listen to the speakers. These people don't believe a single word without thinking it over, but they are willing to fight for what they believe in. They already know what freedom is and they won't give up their rights. Because they can no longer live any other way.

You ask where the guarantees of irreversible democratization are? One is in these people.

Daniel Singer (review date October 1989)

SOURCE: Singer, Daniel. "The Intelligentsia and Soviet Change." *Monthly Review* 41, no. 5 (October 1989): 61-4.

[*In the following excerpt, Singer applauds the thought-provoking nature of Ali's* Revolution from Above.]

Tariq Ali is no Sovietologist. Born in Pakistan, educated at Oxford, he was one of the leaders of the protest movement in Britain in the 1960s and has been a prominent figure of the New Left ever since. Because he is essentially an activist and not a Kremlinologist, the author conveys the feeling that history is here in the making, that the Soviet Union is at the very beginning of a period of monumental change. A stranger, a visitor, he manages to pass on to the reader the excitement of a country where serious periodicals sell like hot cakes, where books, films, plays are political events, where people simultaneously discover their past and the art of political debate.

The purpose of the book [**Revolution from Above**] is polemical, and it is aimed at the western left. The author proclaims himself the champion of this "revolution from above." Naturally he too would have preferred to see a mass movement from below. "That would have been very nice, but it didn't happen that way," he remarks rather rhetorically, attacking left-wing skeptics for their over-critical attitude toward the Gorbachev experiment. While agreeing that one should never quarrel with history or sulk because the red mole is not digging in the expected fashion, I am not quite convinced that to welcome *perestroika* one must somehow identify with the Soviet leadership.

Indeed, in this lively book its Marxist author does not really deal much with social forces. Admittedly, the social analysis of the Soviet Union is not very easy, but its absence leads to ambiguous conclusions. Tariq Ali, whose heart is on the left, instinctively rejects, say, the proposition of a Nikolai Shmelev that "everything that is effective is moral," or Tatyana Zaslavskaya's tendency to confuse payment according to productivity with social justice. Yet to what extent do they represent the views of a professional intelligentsia defending its own interests against those of the *nomenklatura*? And what is the position of Gorbachev, or of Yeltsin for that matter, in the unfolding struggle between the managers and the *apparatchiks*? Ali aptly points out that Gorbachev "has to effectively dismantle a gigantic bureaucratic apparatus, and he wants to do this with the agreement of those whose privileges will be swept overboard." But whose interests does he represent? To say "the reformist wing of the Soviet elite" does not quite answer the question.

To dig deeper one would have to take a position on Gorbachev's own stand on equality, his distorted emphasis on the slogan "to each according to his labor" as *the* Marxist gospel. One would have to analyze further what the author calls "socially-controlled marketization." Granted that Soviet citizens have every reason to be mad as consumers or that a "mixed economy" is inevitable during a long period of transition, the real problems are the direction in which the economy is moving, the inner logic of the system, and its proposed property relations. It is in this context that one should also examine the reentry into a world capitalist market of an economy which still has a much lower level of productivity.

Ultimately it all comes down to Rosa Luxemburg's famous argument about the superiority of an erring mass movement over an infallible central committee. To seek signs of a movement from below should not be interpreted as teaching Russians lessons. It is a natural consequence of a certain conception of socialism based on the growing political consciousness of the masses. This attitude in no way neglects the importance of changes from above. Yet, in the last analysis, Tariq Ali himself welcomes Gorbachev and his *perestroika* because they are likely to, indeed because they have already, set the masses in motion. But does it necessarily mean that one should "establish direct contacts with official bodies in the Soviet Union and Eastern Europe"? (To say that the overwhelming majority of Soviet socialists are in the CPSU does not mean that they are a majority in the party.)

What I have said above attests to the author's achievement. His purpose is to provoke, and in this he clearly succeeds. His book deserves to be read by all Western leftists interested in the fate of the Soviet Union, which should be a pleonasm. Whether one agrees with him or not, his chapters raise all the issues the left must tackle: the resistance of bureaucracy, market and planning in a single state, the relevance of memory, the power to be granted to the soviets, and, finally, Russia's relations with the outside world. Besides, the book is topical despite the furious pace of events. It ends with a plea for Lenin's mummified body to be removed from the mausoleum. As I write these lines, in June 1989, the same proposal made by writer Yuri Karyakin at the Moscow Congress of People's Deputies has provoked passion throughout the Soviet Union.

Carol Rumens (review date 5 October 1990)

SOURCE: Rumens, Carol. "The *Perestroika* Pageant." *Times Literary Supplement*, no. 4566 (5 October 1990): 1069.

[*In the following review, Rumens calls* Moscow Gold *"gripping," and lauds the play for its bold, contrasting scenes and innovative stage construction.*]

Three hours' worth of *perestroika* for beginners ought to be boring. While alive to the broader issues at stake in Moscow, Tariq Ali and Howard Brenton add little to the arguments already sketched for us elsewhere in the media and, some neat one-liners notwithstanding, their language is often as clichéd. Yet **Moscow Gold** is gripping. Dramatically as well as visually it evokes the bold, *ad hoc* style of Constructivism, its sharply contrasted scenes as immediate as a series of revolutionary posters brought to life. Borrowing from many genres, Ali and Brenton vindicate the risk-taking that is their avowed dramatic policy—and also part of the real-life drama of *perestroika*. Unlike Gorbachev's reconstruction, though, this one is a triumph of collaboration.

Stefanos Lazaridis's set is dominated by the Politburo's enormous, circular, scarlet table-cum-dais, which springs trap-doors to allow the oppressed to burst forth at suitable moments—an effective use of symbolism, enhanced by the large downward-pointing finger of Stalin's semi-visible statue. Meyerhold is the presiding genius, and the earthy spirit of the circus is conjured by the revolving stage, bespattered with Cyrillic letters suggesting an astrological chart of the heavens, and the trapeze-like seats hanging above, variously occupied by TASS reporters, Lenin's ghost and Reagan's stargazer. Bill Connor's score matches the pastiche, now suggesting a Shostakovich symphony, now a Kurt Weill cabaret, and effectively using snatches of the Song of the Volga Boatmen to create a new litany of accusing serfdom. The director Barry Kyle keeps all this diversity moving along fast.

The play shifts into naturalistic gear for a subplot which, filled out, would have made a fine drama in itself. Zoya (Paola Dionisotti), one of a salty trio of Kremlin women-cleaners, learns that her youngest son has been killed in Afghanistan, and forces Grisha, her husband, to confess to Boris, the remaining son, the real nature of his activities in Dzerzhinsky Square. Grisha (Joseph O'Connor) is an old Bolshevik and an "honest" secret policeman, responsible for making the copy of the anti-Stalin poem which sent Mandelstam to his death. When he recites this poem, the moment carries unexpected dramatic conviction. Boris's later metamorphoses, first into a radical anti-*perestroishchik* (this hints at Lenin's own political conversion following the execution of his brother), then into a would-be émigré, needs, however, more space to make its impact. Later, the writers miss another opportunity in their suggestion that Lithuanian nationalists are simply folk-singing racist idiots.

They seize on that gift of history to the dramatist, the antagonism between Gorbachev the puritan, and Yeltsin, the natural cavalier. It seems almost as much a matter of chemistry as ideology that the two men cannot fail to oppose one another: their single handshake, initiated by the tenderer-hearted Yeltsin, swiftly deteriorates into a bout of arm-wrestling. The ideological opposition, of course, provides some fiery confrontation, and Gorbachev's commitment to the "third way" of humane socialism against Yeltsin's demand for the full bourgeois-capitalist works are given a force and clarity which often seem absent from the leader's attitudes in reality.

Both David Calder (Gorbachev) and Russell Dixon (Yeltsin) are convincing to the last gesture. Clive Merrison's sardonic Lenin is an equally fine performance, though perhaps a less credibly written character, surely presented as a better democrat than he in fact was.

Of the relatively small cast of villains, the ghastly puppet that Richard Earthy creates from Ceausescu's ghost has a whiff of evil. The heroine is clearly Raisa (Sarah Kestelman) with her worldly good sense and humour ("I'm just a simple Soviet girl who does for Misha"). Misha himself, though often the tormented hero, is not excessively idealized. The play's collective hero is the people. The Perestroika Pageant, a revolving parade of opinionated Muslims, Jews, gangsters, punks, loony nationalists, is the set-piece that stays longest in the memory. The picture of teeming, many coloured life is undercut by a sense of desperation. The ravenous hunger for both the bread and the circuses of the West is strongly captured. The East Berliners' cry of "we want" reminds us of what *perestroika* at heart is about.

David Widgery (review date 12 October 1990)

SOURCE: Widgery, David. "Berty Khan's Revenge." *New Statesman and Society* 3, no. 122 (12 October 1990): 42-3.

[*In the following review, Widgery offers a mixed assessment of* Redemption, *contending that too much of the novel "smacks of an adolescent desire to violate the orthodoxies the author once staunchly propounded."*]

Comic novels about the left, like Ethyl Mannin's *Comrade, O Comrade,* about the 1945 split in the Anarchist Federation of Britain, have a habit of not being very funny. The wittiest accounts are, like Claude Cockburn's true. Tariq Ali's qualifications as the Evelyn Waugh of Trotskyism are debatable, though his publisher, whose idiosyncratic list's only theme is desperation for a bestseller, feels that some sort of intellectual bodice-ripper might prove profitable consolation for us distressed '68ers to curl up with.

Ali used to issue severe tomes with relentlessly red and black typography and titles like **The Stalinist Legacy. Redemption** is served up with plenty of serifs, an Orozco detail and the inscription "a novel", just in case you thought it was a watering can. And T Ali's vanguard role in the leadership of the Fourth International is suppressed in the blurb, where he is described as "a writer and film-maker". But the only people this romp will please are the readers of the *Daily Mail* (glad that another escapee from bourgeois norms is safely redomesticated) and the juvenile left, whose knowledge of Trotskyism has been gleaned from Julie, rather than Ian, Burchill. The uninitiated wouldn't see the point and those who do know their AFL from their FLN will want something a bit more sophisticated than this mildly amusing Marxisant campus novel whose Rushdiesque *Ambition* doesn't quite come off.

The Trot-plot is simple and the characters, despite the publisher's disclaimer, bear a great deal of resemblance to actual persons. Ezra Einstein (Ernest Mandel), the polymathic genius of world Trotskyism, aware that the century is ending on "an ironic crescendo", calls a conference on the future of the revolutionary left with the aid of his ex-comrades, Kominsky (Alaine Krivine) and Diabolo (Michael Pablo). It is attended by his arch rivals: Jim Rock (Tony Cliff); Jed Burroughs (Ted Grant); Francois Pelletier (Pierre Frank); the editor of the *NLJ,* Jemima Wilcox (*NLR,* Robin Blackburn); Laura Shaw (Vanessa Redgrave), bearing the embalmed corpse of Frank Hood (Gerry Healey); and Uncle Terry Contraband and all (Gery Lawless).

Einstein, mystically affected by breastfeeding the baby newly delivered by his child-bride encountered during the Brazilian election campaign for Lula (Lula), devastates the conference by proposing mass entryism into the great world religions. The only person missing is, let's say, Berty Khan, the moustachioed ex-Trot *bon viveur,* who makes a living by feeding his notes from a radical youth through a series of word-processors and is filming the conference for the Channel 4 series, *Expletive Deleted* (ex-Trots love a laugh . . . as long as it's not at their own expense).

There are many in-jokes, some delightfully and *fatwa-*earningly tasteless, concerning Hood-Healey's dildo, Burroughs-Grant's repressed homosexual crush on Norman Tebbit and the movement's early fund-raising activities in a politically OK bordello. Some of the intellectual parodies are brilliant: the faxed critique of Einstein's theses on the East German working class sent by Ricky Lysagh (Perry Anderson) from Papua New Guinea (Los Angeles) is exquisite because it is political rather than just fun-poking. The more fabulous and audacious the book becomes (with Trotsky himself scandalously reincarnated up to tricks with Frida Kahlo), the more interesting it gets. When Ali's imagination really goes wild he is superb, with sex changes, Mother Courage on acid and a KGB encyclopaedia of Trotskyana, whose compilers plead for transfer to Novosibirsk.

But too much of **Redemption** smacks of an adolescent desire to violate the orthodoxies the author once staunchly propounded. This becomes a repudiation not just of the dishonesties of doctrinaire Trotskyism's various love affairs with leaders great and small (long overdue), but also of the left itself. Commitment to Marxism is portrayed as ridiculous (which small groups with big ideas can always be), ineffectual (which it is not), and inherently destructive intellectually.

Beneath the knockabout, Ali clearly feels that Einstein-Mandel could have been an influential figure if only he had not squandered his talent on political organisation. And Alex Mango (Paul Foot) is attacked as an inevitable and cynical corruptor of youthful idealism because he remains a member of an organised group. Given this defeatism, it is not so implausible that socialists who managed to persuade themselves that the east European states were somehow, underneath it all, based on socialist economic relations (which includes most of the traditional Labour left, the CPGB and most ortho-Trots) now enter a bona-fide church.

Thank God things are not turning out quite like this. Indeed, it is a tribute to the turbulent times we live in that Ali's jocular pessimism already seems dated. Just as **Moscow Gold** mirrors the Gorbachev obsession prevalent among western socialists when the Soviet Premier appeared to be singlehandedly transcending Russia's impasse, **Redemption** reflects late eighties capitalist triumphalism, when it seemed possible that western capitalism would effortlessly swallow eastern Europe in its inexorable expansion. Those of us who droned on about imperialist wars and economic recession then certainly looked fair game for parody. But in the nineties, it looks more and more as if Alex Mango, Sugar Brink and Nutty Shardman will have the last laugh.

Paul Kincaid (review date 9 November 1990)

SOURCE: Kincaid, Paul "Iron Curtain Call." *Times Literary Supplement*, no 4571 (9 November 1990): 1214.

[*In the following review, Kincaid derides Ali's prose in* Redemption, *noting several weaknesses in the plot and stating that the book "is a comedy, but humour is less in evidence than silly portentousness."*]

Far from the promised redemption, this crude first novel [***Redemption***] smacks of revenge. The various factions of Trotskyism, for which Tariq Ali was such a vocal and visible spokesman during the 1960s, are here mercilessly ridiculed as invariably brutish, ignorant and sexually perverse. Most of the factions appear to consist of no more than a handful of louts whose sole purpose in life is to do down rival factions and produce a newspaper detailing the tedious utterances of their leader. Those utterances, furthermore, are couched only in empty jargon; so that a sexual rejection is the cue for "vigorous polemic", and one character is described thus: "the rapist side of the Cuckoo was amply fulfilled in the politico-organizational sphere". Some of this, undoubtedly, is intended as satire; unfortunately the idiom is used so unvaryingly throughout the narrative that it seems Ali is unable to distance himself from the vocabulary, beliefs and attitudes he is supposedly parodying.

Redemption is a comedy, but humour is less in evidence than silly portentousness. The story concerns a Congress of Trotskyists staged in the first months of 1990 to consider a response to the events in Eastern Europe. There is never any sense that the rhetoricians respond to world events in any way that relates to their words; and since the book relies so heavily on gimmicks (a prosthetic metal penis which speaks, a seventy-five-year-old man who breast-feeds his own baby), neither is there any sense that any of it matters. It is a timely book, certainly, but everything seems to have been jettisoned in the cause of speed. We might charitably suppose that it is a shared ideology which makes every character indistinguishable from the rest, but it is inexcusable that Paris, London, New York and Mexico City should be presented as if they were identical. The sentence structure is irredeemable.

Alfred Evans, Jr. (review date January-April 1991)

SOURCE: Evans, Jr., Alfred. "Gorbachev's Unfinished Revolution." *Problems of Communication* 40, nos. 1-2 (January-April 1991): 133-43.

[*In the following excerpt, Evans praises certain portions of* Revolution from Above, *but faults others, asserting that the book ignores many complexities of the Soviet political arena.*]

[***Revolution from Above***,] by Tariq Ali is similar to the on-the-scene reporting of well-informed political journalists in Western and Asian democracies. A series of topical essays on Soviet politics in 1987 and 1988, the book is based largely on extensive interviews with well-placed Soviet sources. Ali expresses the enthusiasm of one who is caught up in the excitement of increasing political openness and intellectual honesty in the USSR under Gorbachev, and sees in *perestroyka* and *glasnost* the prospect for the revitalization of the socialist idea.

Ali describes political processes in the USSR as characterized by increasingly open debates among those defending contending positions, and by ever more open appeals by political leaders for support from a wide range of groups in the population. Also, although he is aware of each leader's desire to maximize his power, he attributes leaders' policy positions primarily to their objectives for Soviet society and their affinity for the interests both of groups of citizens and of officials in authoritative institutions.

Ali sees the reforms since 1985 as creating a basic conflict between reformers, led by Gorbachev and supported most ardently by intellectuals, on the one hand, and conservative mid- and lower-level party and state *apparatchiki*, whose apprehensions were expressed by Yegor Ligachev, on the other. However, this dichotomous view overlooks much of the complexity of the contemporary Soviet political spectrum. For example, Ali does not attempt to assimilate his description of Boris Yel'tsin's divergence from Gorbachev after October 1987 to his classification of supporters and opponents of reform.

Ali correctly observes that the 19th Conference of the CPSU in the summer of 1988 "represented a political stalemate and a compromise" (p. 56), and it may be added today that the stalemate that became evident on that occasion has persisted to the present, posing ever greater problems for the functioning of the Soviet system. He is also on target in reporting that the process of change opened up under Gorbachev is so deeply rooted "that halting the process now and standing still would create an enormous backlash," and that what has already taken place in the USSR "is merely the beginning of a process," or "the opening shots of what might be a long battle" (pp. 205, 218). Although Ali's analysis is optimistic, he reaches no definite conclusion about the prospects for the success of reform in the Soviet Union.

Alamgir Hashmi (review date winter 1992)

SOURCE: Hashmi, Alamgir. Review of *Redemption*, by Tariq Ali. *World Literature Today* 66, no. 1 (winter 1992): 210-11.

[*In the following review, Hashmi outlines the major themes of* Redemption.]

Tariq Ali comes to fiction from a respectable writing career in politics, history, biography, and, most recently, stage drama with a sharp focus on the contemporary world. On Christmas Eve 1989, in Paris, [in *Redemption*,] as the seventy-year-old Trotskyist patriarch Ezra Einstein watches on TV a Ceauşescu executioner make the sign of the cross, he seems even to forget the bliss of his late married life, he whose "fingers had rested more often on the keys and body of his antique writing aid [his fifty-five-year-old typewriter] than on the more intimate sections of the female anatomy." He issues a letter forthwith to convene a congress to discuss the world situation following the collapse of the East European regimes and the changes in the Soviet Union. As the oppressed classes have generally failed to be responsive to their program, the brigade considers changing its methods. Ezra himself proposes "that we go into these religions and fight to establish a connection between Heaven and Earth," because "one of the weaknesses of Marxism and all other isms descended from it has been a lack of understanding of ethics, morality, and, dare I say it, spirituality."

The possibility of redemption, however, is always considered tongue-in-cheek, and the gloom caused by the collapse of the Alternative System is beaten out with wit and banter. Although the new challenges include the formation of a new goulash religion called Christ-lamasonism and moving into the Catholic Church itself, the world congress falls short of evolving any workable theme or strategy; but there is a plenitude of jokes born of an earthy realism, as most matters are thought worthy of being "sorted out through friendly negotiations under the quilt."

While the larger issues of ideas and society are far from being resolved, solace and even blessedness (with a real halo over Ezra's infant daughter's head) are found in the formation of positive personal relations and private worlds. Ali's novel itself [*Redemption*] is a detached commentary on the enterprise. Dissentient comrade Cathy Fox refuses to attend the congress or join the excavation of Trotsky's grave in Mexico in search of some documents, but she views the dying ideological world with hope: "Something will be reborn . . . but how and when and in what shape it is impossible to predict. The whole world has to be remade." The *New Life Journal* is cited as derriding Kundera's sexist and nihilistic attitudes, and Maya, Ezra's wife, notes (in "The Chapter of Learning and Forgetting"—an obvious parody) her own reservations about the new cult novelist. The entries cited from the *Encyclopedia Trotskyana* and the narrator's comments together make up a hilarious text which is mock-learning and police work at the same time. This clever device also provides for a latter-day dramatic aside and a metafictional source of both fact and its factitious extensions. The lie about the existence of the Trotsky letters turns out to be a truth, even if their contents are different from those presumed and announced. Although the Movement and its saints must all be seen without their robes, as well as frequently without their undergarments, all the gains are in achieving true humanity of character, with Ezra preaching plain morals and finding his peace amid his family, earnestly if comically lactating and feeding Ho, his baby. The ending, with Maya reading Ezra's journal written for Ho's tenth birthday, contains a poem, an exhortation ascribed to Goethe in which Ali, with all his riotous energy and wit, has found the right note with which to *cure* a cynical world: "Build it again, / Great Child of the Earth, / Build it again / With a finer worth / In thine own bosom build it on high! / Take up thy life once more: / Run the race again! / High and clear / Let a lovelier strain / Ring out than ever before!"

Beneath the poetic fancy, the narrative suggests screen adaptations and a simpler field-sequential of events. Surely, if Goethe and Trotsky gang up together in the "Bandung File" (BBC's Channel 4 program which Tariq Ali produced for several years), a redemption will become inevitable.

Robert Irwin (review date 1 May 1992)

SOURCE: Irwin, Robert. Review of *Shadows of the Pomegranate Tree*, by Tariq Ali. *Times Literary Supplement,* no. 4648 (1 May 1992): 20.

[*In the following review, Irwin discusses Ali's utilization of exposition and metaphors, faulting what he deems to be Ali's lack of imagination in* Shadows of the Pomegranate Tree.]

> "We are living in the most difficult period of our history. We have not had such serious problems since Tarik and Musa first occupied these lands. And you know how long ago that was, do you not?"
>
> Yazid nodded. "In our first century and their eighth."

Tariq Ali's second novel [*Shadows of the Pomegranate Tree*], a work of historical fiction, is about the misfortunes of a family of Moors living in the province of Granada in 1500, eight years after the region had been conquered by the Spanish Catholic armies of Ferdinand and Isabella. It is the sort of historical novel in which people like to talk history ("We destroyed two great empires. Everything fell into our lap. We kept the Arab lands and Persia and parts of Byzantium. Elsewhere it was difficult, wasn't it? Look at us. We have been in al-Andalus for seven hundred years . . .") and debate such matters as women's rights, the problems of minority communities, the evils of book burning, and the origins of Western imperialism.

Tariq Ali prefers telling to showing and much of his narrative in *Shadows of the Pomegranate Tree* is conveyed through flashback and reminiscence. A man may enter "the deepest recesses of his memory", while a woman may be "assailed by memories of her own youth". Elsewhere, another character contemplates "the layers of guilt which still lay congealed somewhere in his mind", and another finds that the "cellars of his memory were overflowing". The author is fond of metaphors, particularly confused ones. "Bishop and sceptic, for a moment they remained motionless, facing each other. They had once belonged to the same sunken civilisation, but the universe which each inhabited had been separated by an invisible sea." The dialogue is decorated with duff proverbs, like "The broken glass has no saviours" and "Only a blind man dares to shit on the roof and thinks he cannot be seen!".

This is the sort of book where the good are very good indeed. Not only is Zuhayr, the hero, a brave fighter and very handsome, he is also a good committee man and a fine speech-maker: he will mature into a well-respected guerrilla leader, an early Islamic precursor of Zapata and Che Guevara The Grand Inquisitor, by contrast, is hook-nosed, cold-hearted, greedy, fanatical, and very cynical. His eyes burn and he sneers and snarls a lot. He seems to have stepped out of the pages of a much earlier novel by, Ouida, say, or Talbot Mundy.

There are a number of minor anachronisms. But the chief anachronism stems from a failure of imagination on the part of the author. Having failed to imagine that religious belief can ever be a serious option, Tariq Ali has reclassified all its manifestations. Religion, here, is either the marker of a politically disadvantaged minority community, or it serves as a convenient ideological cover for exploitation and imperialism. So, oddly for a novel which is set in one of the great ages of faith and which deals with the clash between Christianity and Islam, profound spiritual experience plays little or no part in the lives of the protagonists.

As I struggled towards the end of the book, it began to cross my mind that perhaps I was missing the joke and that *Shadows of the Pomegranate Tree* was intended to be a parody, a sort of *Cold Comfort Farm* in fancy dress. However, I regretfully conclude that this is not the case, and despite the unconscious comedy, the novel is hard going. As one of the characters in this desperately earnest work remarks, "All that is left . . . is for us to be inquisitioned. Yes! And to the very marrow of our sorry bones!"

Akbar Ahmed (review date 22 May 1992)

SOURCE: Ahmed, Akbar. "The Moors Murdered." *New Statesman and Society* 5, no. 203 (22 May 1992): 39-40.

[*In the following review, Ahmed provides an overview of Ali's life and career, tracing his development as an author through* Shadows of the Pomegranate Tree.]

A review of Tariq Ali's new novel [*Shadows of the Pomegranate Tree*] requires a review of the author. In the 1960s, when he emerged as a student star in Oxford, I admired him, in common with most Pakistani undergraduates in England then, for his rebellious energy and boldness. He appeared to capture the mood of his generation.

When he became President of the Oxford Union, the press was predicting that he would become prime minister of Pakistan. Although another Union president, Benazir Bhutto, did assume that office, Tariq never really had a chance. In Pakistani politics it matters who you are, and Benazir's father had been prime minister.

In one important sense, Tariq's career has been downhill ever since. Too much was expected of him, and because of that his life remains a disappointment. He compensated by remaining in the public eye through his writing and media appearances. The range of his interests was boundless: from the Nehru dynasty to Genghis Khan to a bawdy satirical novel, *Redemption.* But his ideas tended to be inflexible. Even the name he chose for his television company, Bandung, reflected an idea of third-world unity which, attractive in its time, was nonetheless rooted in his youth.

Not accepted by the academics for his serious writing, Tariq turned to television journalism. Here his energy and flair made an impact. Over this trajectory we see him moving from his earlier Marxist student position to the more complex stance of a media figure in Mrs Thatcher's Britain. In his success he appeared to parody the very culture he denounced.

Tariq's novel about Muslims in Spain is commercially correct, because 1992 is the 500th anniversary of the fall of Granada. And Muslim Spain is important because it challenges many assumptions Europeans have of themselves. On the one hand, it is an example of a harmonious, plural society with public libraries, baths and parks, ordered by Muslims who are today powerless and unwelcome. On the other, it is a society abruptly terminated by Christians. The stanchions were set in place for the European religious and racial persecution that followed. Notions of a "final solution" thus find a resonance in history.

While tapping the market, Tariq could also be discovering his cultural roots. Muslim Spain—and especially Andalusia—is irresistible as a source of fascination to Muslims. I felt its melancholic and romantic attraction when I visited Andalusia as an undergraduate, and later called it the "Andalus syndrome" in my book *Discovering Islam.*

Perhaps Tariq is now responding to the Andalus syndrome. This is mnemonically appropriate. The first victorious Muslim general in Spain was also called

Tariq, and Gibraltar commemorates his name: a derivation of Jabal-al-Tariq, or the Rock of Tariq. Clearly, there is much in the learning and culture of the Muslims of Spain that he admires. Those who expect a Marxist diatribe about decadent sultans and harems will be disappointed. Even the title is suggestive of romantic novelists such as M M Kaye, author of *Shadow of the Moon*.

For a writer, Andalusia is a rich treasure chest and anyone may dip in to pick up a bauble or two. Tariq tells us the story of a Muslim family after the fall of Granada to Ferdinand and Isabella. Young Yazid, the favourite, is at its centre. His father, Umar, is pressed by his uncle Miguel, a Christian convert and now Bishop of Cordoba, to convert and thus save the family's property and also to give his 17-year-old daughter, Hind, in marriage to Miguel's son. Hind, however, is determined to marry the man of her choice. Yazid's brother prefers death to becoming a Catholic.

These were dangerous times for Muslims. Juan, the village carpenter, has carved a chess set for the tenth birthday of Yazid. The black queen is a savage caricature of Isabella while the white sultan resembles Yazid's great-grandfather, a Moorish knight.

The novel begins with a book-burning. The Christians have gathered all the books in the private libraries of the town and are preparing to burn them. Here is a nod to our own age, with the roles reversed. Its end is a tear-jerker. Yazid is killed by Cortes, who goes on to plunder America. In the epilogue, 20 years after the story ends, Cortes arrives in the city of Tenochtitlan where Montezuma is king. The death of Muslim Spain is thus linked to the birth of America.

The story moves well and quickly and the prose is restrained. Tariq's quest for authenticity is admirable, but few people will recognise Qurtuba (Cordoba), Gharnata (Granada) or Dimashk (Damascus). What is the reader to make of Gharnatinos, who sound like a new pop group? Although he uses the word "Moors" in the author's notes, scholars now prefer Arab or Muslim. Indeed, the word Moriscos, little Moors—describing Muslims who remained after the fall of Granada—is considered derogatory.

The novel reflects the Andalus syndrome and will strike a chord in Tariq's own community in Britain, from which he has remained generally isolated. Others were also isolated, such as his friend Salman Rushdie (he, too, is writing a novel set in Muslim Spain). Representing élite Asian families and education (mainly at Oxbridge), this group formed an almost self-consciously "superior" class, distinct from their compatriots in Bradford and Birmingham. In their work—cynical, ironic, irreverent—they reflected British literary taste. The anger against *Satanic Verses* also reflected anger against them. ***Iranian Nights,*** which Tariq co-authored with Howard Brenton, depicted Muslims as cardboard characters, fanatic, corrupt and hypocritical. It did not help.

In the past, Tariq's work lacked the qualities of introspection, self-criticism and compassion. The bluster and theorising prevented him from hearing "the still, sad music of humanity". This novel suggests he may be moving towards a new maturity. If that is so, it is to be welcomed.

Amit Chaudhuri (review date 9 July 1992)

SOURCE: Chaudhuri, Amit. "Here Is a Little Family." *London Review of Books* 14, no. 13 (9 July 1992): 18-19.

[*In the following excerpt, Chaudhuri maintains that* Shadows of the Pomegranate Tree *is "a strangely refreshing work in that it gives us a warm and indulgent picture of a certain section of Islamic life."*]

Tariq Ali's novel [***Shadows of the Pomegranate Tree***] is about a noble family of great renown in Moorish Spain. The lives and culture of this family and its retainers are on the edge of extinction: either they must convert from Islam to Christianity, or die at the hands of the armies of Ferdinand and Isabella. The emotions, conflicts and shifts in this novel are no more complex and layered than those to be found in the exhilarating lyrics of an Arab song about love or heroism, but it is a strangely refreshing work in that it gives us a warm and indulgent picture of a certain section of Islamic life. Though it is set in Medieval times, it serves as a corrective to some of our images of the contemporary Muslim world, and reminds us, for instance, that its culture is made up not only of men with machine-guns in their hands and chequered handkerchiefs on their heads, but of sprawling, extended families, meeting-places, kitchens with their own aroma and cuisine, weddings, and a large number of personable and clear-headed women. On the brink of imminent destruction, courtships continue in the novel, pledges are made, long-winded arguments about politics and tiresomely inexhaustible family anecdotes fill the hours, as they no doubt do even now in Lebanon. It is all a little like peacetime, till one sees these figures from a distance and realises that they have gathered, in that innocent and communal fashion, upon a precipice. Some of the characters are extremely talkative, even boring, but one forgives them because one knows they are to be silenced for ever. Their verbosity has to be seen in the context of the silence out of which it has arisen and to which it will soon return, and of a culture which feels passionately wronged, but often lacks the right words to say the right things. There is a cook in this story, a dwarf, who makes 'heavenly delights' for the noble family from 'secret recipes' that only he knows. History has completely wiped out that family and their village by the end of the novel: only the dwarf survives, with the secret recipe, which is part of the unwritten history of a people, still in his head.

Douglas Allen (review date fall 1992)

SOURCE: Allen, Douglas. Review of *Revolution from Above*, by Tariq Ali. *Southern Humanities Review* 29 (fall 1992): 361-63.

[*In the following review, Allen examines the central issues discussed in* Revolution from Above.]

Since he came to Oxford University from Pakistan and became one of the radical leaders of the 1960s, Tariq Ali has been a prominent figure on the British Left. His books include **Can Pakistan Survive?, An Indian Dynasty: The Story of the Nehru-Gandhi Family,** and **Street Fighting Years: An Autobiography of the Sixties.** His orientation can best be described as that of an independent, democratic, anti-Stalinist Marxist/socialist: very familiar with the classical socialist writings of Marx, Engels, Lenin, Luxemburg, and others and strongly influenced by the writings of Deutscher, Trotsky, and Mandel (i.e., a strong, but not uncritical, Trotskyist influence).

The subtitle of the book [***Revolution from Above***] aptly describes its central question: Where is the Soviet Union going? During the post-Stalinist period of the mid-fifties, Khrushchev opened many gates for political and cultural revelations and changes, but he had to retreat under pressure from the bureaucracy and was finally deposed. The conservative Brezhnev period was marked by bureaucratic retrenchment, "mafiocracy" and corruption, and finally stagnation. Mikhail Gorbachev became General Secretary of the Communist Party of the Soviet Union in 1985, and we entered the turbulent period of *perestroika* and *glasnost.*

Tariq Ali visited the Soviet Union in 1985 and twice during 1988. Much of this book tries to make sense of where the Soviet Union is going by analyzing the Gorbachev period, from changes inaugurated at the Twenty-Seventh Party Congress in February 1986 through the remarkable Nineteenth Party Conference of June 1988, at which there was a public show of dissent and issues were openly debated for perhaps the first time since the 1920s.

The title, ***Revolution from Above,*** gets at the extraordinary potential but also the dangers that can undermine the struggle for radical change. This revolution, marking the beginnings of a long and unpredictable process, started from above: from Gorbachev, Alexander Yakovlev, Boris Yeltsin, and other party reformers and politicians. It includes Yuri Afanasiev, Rector of the Moscow State Institute of Historical Archives, and other reformist scholars; the playwright Mikhail Shatrov and other writers and filmmakers; Boris Kagarlitsky and other socialist dissidents struggling for perestroika.

Such a movement for radical change faces a powerful, entrenched, conservative bureaucracy, with many braking mechanisms in place and determined to defend its power and privileges. Gorbachev is the leader of those in favor of democratization, but he also wants to avoid a head-on clash with the party hierarchy, the bureaucratic apparatus, and the military

Time and again Tariq Ali maintains that the leaders of the "revolution from above" will not succeed unless there develops a *"revolution from below"*: working class soviets (councils) and other democratic mass forces, ensuring that reformers not become bogged down or deposed by the bureaucracy, and backing them and joining them in struggles against the entrenched forces resisting systematic change.

Revolution from Above presents a wide range of topics, starting with the cultural, economic, and political situation in the late 1980s. It also provides valuable background information and penetrating insights into the key issues and struggles defining Soviet history for seven decades after the October 1917 revolution. It is commonplace to read publications in the United States and the West attacking the Stalinist and Brezhnevite Soviet system. What is unusual is that Tariq Ali's attacks on the Soviet system come from *the Left*. For him, Soviet history, at least since the late 1920s, does not prove the failure of socialism; Stalinism is in fact a *crime against socialism,* a betrayal and liquidation of a progressive, democratic socialist potential.

As a critic from the Left, Tariq Ali offers startling observations and analyses rarely appearing in Western publications. For example, in describing and analyzing "the new renaissance" in politics and culture since April 1985, he contends that discussion and debate in influential Soviet newspapers and magazines is "far higher and [more] intense that anything in the West." In exploring whether democracy is possible in the USSR, Tariq Ali argues that perestroika could lead to a new soviet democracy, recapturing some of the original impulse of the Revolution, a "higher model of democracy which combines substantial equality and participatory rights with the procedures of democratic choice."

Tariq Ali is not uncritically romantic or utopian about Soviet history and future prospects. He follows his study of "the new renaissance" with a counterbalancing chapter on "Who's Afraid of Boris Yeltsin? The Resistance of the Bureaucracy." When this book was completed, Yeltsin, greatly admired by Tariq Ali, had been removed as Moscow Party leader and had not made his remarkable comeback, resulting in his 1991 election as President of the Russian Republic.

Chapter three provides extensive historical background and contemporary analysis of the Soviet economy, including the crisis of past centralized autarchic planning and why democratization and a socialist emancipatory program are essential social mechanisms for any successful socialist planning and development. The next chapter focuses on key individuals and struggles in Soviet history and argues that many of Trotsky's main ideas converge with the new reformism in the Soviet Union today. This is followed by a study of the earlier destruction and present potential for the revival of democratic soviet power. A chapter beginning "The Soviet Union is far too important to be left to the Sovietologists" surveys the leading American Kremlinologists during the Cold War and how their ideologically-based "totalitarian theories" were used to shape public opinion and policy-making. This is followed by a chapter on foreign policy which explores the place of the Soviet Union in the world and a concluding chapter which analyzes disturbing national and ethnic questions and conflicts within the country.

Revolution from Above is a provocative and challenging book. It is full of important but little-known information and surprising insights. It combines historical perspective with contemporary material, including documents and interviews with political and cultural figures and scholars at the heart of contemporary debates in the Soviet Union. Tariq Ali's attitude can be described as hopeful, apprehensive, and cautiously optimistic in the long run.

One wonders how developments since 1988 might have altered some of Tariq Ali's formulations. For example, he certainly acknowledges and analyzes the fundamental crises of the economy of the Soviet Union, but the more recent lack of successful reforms, widespread corruption, sense of anarchy, and extreme rapid economic deterioration have been staggering. Or, to provide a second significant example, Tariq Ali certainly differentiates between Gorbachev, who wants to avoid open conflict, and Yeltsin, who wants to confront pressing problems directly, often going outside the normal structures of power. But he considers both Gorbachev and Yeltsin as leaders in the same struggle for a progressive, democratic, socialist, pluralistic society. More recent tensions, splits, and even open hostility between the two leaders might have affected Tariq Ali's analysis of the Soviet reform process. Probably Tariq Ali's basic historical, political, economic, and cultural analysis remains unchanged, but he might be more apprehensive, more cautious, and less optimistic about Soviet revolutionary prospects at least in the short run.

Reviewer's Note: This review was completed in May 1991. Although Tariq Ali points to the tendencies that led to the attempted conservative coup against Gorbachev and deteriorating conditions in the Soviet Union, he obviously did not anticipate the consequences of the rapid economic and political collapse of late 1991: the complete dismemberment of the Soviet Union, the overthrow of Gorbachev, the dominance of Yeltsin, the strength of ethnic and regional separatist movements, and a very uncertain and dangerous future. In this regard, the struggles for a progressive, democratic, socialist, pluralistic society, with which Tariq Ali identifies, came too little and too late to overcome the deep-rooted historical and structural weaknesses of the Soviet Union, but they may have considerable significance for future struggles throughout the world.

Carl Caulfield (essay date December 1993)

SOURCE: Caulfield, Carl. "Moscow Gold and Reassessing History." *Modern Drama* 36, no. 4 (December 1993): 490-98.

[*In the following essay, Caulfied analyzes the role of history in* Moscow Gold.]

> The Revolution has shifted the theatre of our critical operations. We must review our tactics.[1]

Moscow Gold is Howard Brenton and Tariq Ali's second theatrical collaboration, after their satirical, metaphorical response in 1989 to the Rushdie affair in **Iranian Nights**. **Moscow Gold** dramatizes what its authors see as a need for a reassessment of Soviet history and Communist ideologies, but the play can also be seen as revealing a state of crisis in Howard Brenton's overview of world history and his earlier views on historical progression. Prior to the collapse of the Communist regimes in Eastern Europe, Brenton believed that Western Europe was on the verge of a political renaissance, an inevitable historical movement towards a more "communistic" society. As he stated in 1986: "It began with the Paris Commune in 1871. The Russian Revolution, whether you regard it with hope, hope betrayed, or with horror, has changed world history forever."[2] The "second Renaissance" Brenton describes is a transmutation from mercantile capitalism to a "communistic world view."[3] This "huge conviction" of Brenton's has been the source of his "utopian" plays, particularly *Greenland* (1989), and informs much of his work. In many ways, Brenton's development as a dramatist has been towards forging a drama that shows characters involved in a dialectical struggle with history, to show characters "trying to deal with history."

His characters, he has said, "suddenly find themselves with a torch in their hands which they realize is world history."[4] He often shows his characters (unaware that history is moving) struggling from the "micro" level of everyday living towards what he has described as a "macro-overview of history" or the "grand historical vision." To Brenton, this "historical vision" is the consciousness of a faith in a rational, communistic future. In many ways Brenton's work attempted to promote an historical enlightenment, in which individuals connect with "history" and gain a vision of the future. As he has described his characters: "But millions do not have that vision, confidence and heroism, and some are traumatised by defeat. It is they whom I write about. [. . .] I try to dramatise them coming to life, gaining visions, confidence and courage in their own way. If the Left convinces and wins people like them, the British revolution will be unstoppable."[5]

Throughout his career, Brenton has worked collaboratively with writers such as David Hare, Tunde Ikoli, and Tony Howard. Tariq Ali's role in *Moscow Gold* was to provide historical knowledge with Brenton as dramatist. In the play, there are traces of ideas from Ali's book on the USSR and the view that reform began as "a movement from above," a "revolution" within the Soviet elite.[6]

Moscow Gold took a year to research, including a visit to Moscow for Brenton. The play was performed by the Royal Shakespeare Company at the Barbican Theatre on 20 September 1990, directed by Barry Kyle. It was an opportunity for Brenton to make use of a large space and to return to an epic form of drama, which he'd developed at the National Theatre with plays such as *Weapons of Happiness* (1972), *The Romans in Britain* (1980), and *Pravda* (1985), the last co-written with David Hare. To deal with the massive scope of their subject—the changes in the former Soviet Union since *glasnost* and *perestroika*—Brenton and Ali decided that they must extend the non-naturalistic, panoramic approach used in *Iranian Nights*: "The only model we had was the work of the great Soviet theatrical genius Vsevelod Meyerhold. He attempted a theatre of great breadth, trenchant but nimble-footed, which was not documentary, but 'living history,' played out upon the stage at many levels of meaning with many techniques."[7] The visual design of the play, according to Barry Kyle, was intended to emphasize that it was not "photographic realism," as reflected in the circus-like sets of Stefanos Lazaridis.[8] Inevitably, through evoking the memory of Meyerhold productions such as *Mystery-Bouffe* and *The Magnanimous Cuckold*, the authors foregrounded as many difficulties as similarities. Like *Mystery-Bouffe*, performed a year after the October Revolution, *Moscow Gold*, performed a year after *glasnost*, tried to show not only life that's real, but "life transformed by the theatre into a spectacle."[9] The difference between the two lies in the dynamic of Meyerhold creating a form appropriate for Mayakovsky's play, while Brenton and Ali are imposing their conception of the same form seventy years later. "Quoting" Meyerholdian techniques in a play about *glasnost* may merely be a means of problematizing a contemporary audience's awareness of the historical situation depicted. It does, however, indicate a shift in Brenton's approach to dramatizing history; whereas previously he appeared more clearly aligned to a Marxist epic theatre, as defined by Brecht, the conventions adopted for *Moscow Gold* imply that these are no longer adequate. Meyerhold's notion of the theatre of the grotesque is not too far removed from Brecht's *Verfremdungseffekt*: "Is it not the task of the grotesque in the theatre to preserve this ambivalent attitude in the spectator by switching the course of the action with strokes of contrast? The basis of the grotesque is the artist's constant desire to switch the spectator from the plane he has just reached to another which is totally unseen."[10] Meyerhold's theories do allow greater dramaturgical latitude than Brecht's and seem particularly suited to a writer of Brenton's temperament, with his predilection for exaggeration, caricature, and disrupting the spectacle. In *Moscow Gold*, however, the authors run the risk of trivializing aspects of Soviet history, such as Stalinism, and turning the play into an empty spectacle.[11]

Moscow Gold is, according to the authors, a "song of history as it *is,* not as it should be and, apart from one utopian lapse, not as we would like it to be."[12] In a poem, Brenton describes Moscow as "this continent of old dreads," and the first Act of *Moscow Gold* certainly creates this sense of a place haunted by the past.[13]

Act One (subtitled "Before the Wall") attempts to give a historical backdrop to events which led up to the dismantling of the Berlin Wall. It begins with the image of the huge oval table of the Politburo, behind which sits Lenin with fist raised. Then the audience witnesses a pageant of the Revolution of 1917. The spectacle reflects the violent movement of the revolution, while the choreographed sequences show the sense of fluidity and purpose behind the tides of history. "TROTSKY *consigns the enemies of the Revolution to the dustbin of history*" and "LENIN *establishes some order in the chaotic dance.*"[14] This sequence flows into a funeral dirge and Sailors carry Lenin off, as if he were in a coffin. The image of the dead Lenin is ambiguous for a 1990s audience, which has witnessed his denigration as an icon of the revolution. Moreover, historically, the death of Lenin ushered in the reign of Stalin, but the spectacle simplifies much recent historical reassessment of the revolution, which questions the notion of a spontaneous explosion in 1917.[15]

As the pageant ends, three women, Zoya, Katya, and Lena, move forward. The three cleaning women are reminiscent of the three women in Brenton's *Thirteenth*

Night in that they represent the people, struggling towards enlightenment after the dark years underground. As Brenton said of *Thirteenth Night*: "The three 'free spirits' in the play, the three 'witches', were unidentifiable to the author when he was writing the play. Now, suddenly, there seem to be millions of them in the Soviet Union, climbing up to the clean air from the underground bunker where the tyrant's body rots, to quote the final image of Jack Beaty's dream . . .'[16] Zoya, who ages before the audience as the play jumps forward to 1982, gives voice to the feeling that she is beginning to wake from the nightmare of Soviet history. "What did I come from? The years of hopes and fears. Civil war. Famine. The Terror. Hitler. [. . .] And now all that's left . . . is the mess, and we clean it up every day" (2). In this sense, the three women are cleaning up the rubble of history in the Politburo, where so much history has been made. The presence of the oval table suggests that this is the only constant in Russian history; the leaders come and go, but the table remains, symbol of indomitable power.

The 1982 Politburo assemble, *"most of them looking old and sick"* (2). The spectacle of these old, powerful men shambling towards the oval table suggests that the Soviet leaders are decaying under the weight of an oppressive history and an old, dead ideology. The Stalinist inheritance, says Gorbachev (who is apart from the main group) is: "Dust, dust, poverty and dust" (4).

The notion that history lurks in every corner of Moscow is dramatized through Zoya and her family. Zoya has received news that her son Andrushka has been killed during the Afghanistan war, another victim of decisions made behind the oval table. In her grief, Zoya attacks the capitulation of her husband, Grisha, who has been a secret policeman for fifty years (23). Her other son Boris knows nothing about this and realizes that the family has been living a lie. The suggestion here is that the real history has been buried and stored secretly, guarded by policemen like Grisha. Boris thought that his father worked at the Mayakovsky museum, whereas, in actuality, Grisha's job has been to torture dissidents and "enemies of the state." Grisha has witnessed the deaths of Meyerhold and Osip Mandelstaum, who symbolize those who speak out against oppression as well as being "historians" who record the suffering and tyranny of the age. Grisha is able to recall Osip Mandelstaum's Stalin poem, which Stalin attempted to obliterate, revealing Brenton's belief that history suppressed will rise up and haunt the future (an idea explored in 1990 in his play about Nazi war criminal Rudolph Hess, *H.I.D (Hess Is Dead)*). Certainly, in the era of *perestroika* (as Ali and Brenton found), much of the hidden history of what happened to dissenters and so-called "dissidents" is becoming known. Grisha evokes some of the tragedies of Soviet history in the hope that his son Boris will understand his predicament. He tells Boris that individual morality seemed irrelevant: "But morality never entered into it. We had lost a few million during the First World War. Then came the civil war. Millions more died. People were tired. They wanted stability." (24). The speech gives a sense of how the tragic history of the Soviet Union itself tended to dwarf the individual and engender fatalism. Yet, ***Moscow Gold*** never really uses history in an enlightening way, other than in this scene. Although the scene is somewhat contrived, with its self-conscious references to artists and the Mayakovsky museum (which Brenton visited), the situation illustrates the peculiar dilemma that many Soviet families would find themselves in. It is interesting to compare this to Caryl Churchill's *Mad Forest* (1989), which follows the everyday lives of two families before and after the revolution in Romania. Because totalitarianism seeps into the heart of people's private lives, it is much more illuminating to witness the details of how those lives are conducted, as they often reflect more forcefully the effects of the State. In the original production of *Mad Forest*, for example, at the Central School of Speech and Drama in London, many family scenes were like silent tableaux, suggesting the fear of freedom of expression. Unfortunately, in ***Moscow Gold***, the writers never really explore the impact of historical events on individual and family lives.

In Ali and Brenton's perception, Gorbachev is shown as following on from Lenin and the aims of the 1917 revolution.[17] This is dramatically portrayed with Gorbachev in communion with the ghost of Lenin, who is seen as a detached joker, suspended in mid-air, as though enjoying his Godlike perspective on Gorbachev's dilemma. (In the Barry Kyle production, both Gorbachev and Lenin were suspended in mid-air.) It is Lenin who pushes Gorbachev to complete his revolution, which he interprets as rebuilding Socialism. But Brenton and Ali do not address or challenge the revisionist interpretations of Lenin and his legacy to present-day Russia.[18] History is often evoked in ***Moscow Gold***, but never analysed. Lenin suggests that everything was poisoned in 1917 by the First World War. "Then the well of Soviet socialism itself was contaminated," he says (62). Yet these comments are never explored or any reasons given why this vast country slid into Stalinism. There is an ellipsis of controversial issues—such as, say, Lenin's creation of the Cheka or War Communism—under Bolshevik rule. As far back as the 1920s, Bertrand Russell criticized the Bolsheviks for their "harsh and dictatorial spirit" and predicted Stalinism.[19] The play does not rise to the challenge of *glasnost* or fulfil its own claims: to reassess history.

After his conversation with Lenin, Gorbachev is shown more readily accepting the changes and the new currents of historical change. Yet Gorbachev is in conflict with both those who hold historical flow in check and those who want to break away from Socialist tradition (such as Boris Yeltsin) and move radically towards a capitalist economy. Gorbachev argues with Marxist hardliners within his own Politburo, but also in Germany he faces the intransigence of Egon Krenz and Erich Honecker. "You froze history in your country," Gorbachev tells them (45). The squabbles between Honecker, Krenz, and Gorbachev are shown to be irrelevant to the flow of history in any case as these scenes are juxtaposed with the destruction of the Berlin Wall. (The dramatic spectacle, actors tearing holes in the wall, made of paper, and jumping through, inevitably pales in comparison with the tremendous excitement of the real event.)

The "perestroika" pageant, beginning Act Two, is a complete contrast to the "Revolution pageant." It is *"chaotic, unfocused, bad tempered"* (47), suggesting that the myriad problems—economic, social, racial—that had been hidden for so many years under Stalinism suddenly erupt. Ali and Brenton give voices to disparate groups, which include Azerbaijan Muslims, Baltic folklorists, miners, and Russian fascists. Yet this speedy evocation betrays some of the flaws in *Moscow Gold* in their attempt at evoking the breadth of Russia.[20] According to Barry Kyle, *Moscow Gold* attempted to go beyond mere "descriptive journalism" and thus make it possible for "these events to be understood."[21] After the spectacle of the first act, the audience need analysis of the issues raised. And while the play certainly suggests the overwhelming sense of the myriad problems assailing Gorbachev, the playwrights do not follow through these issues, and it is perhaps this fragmentary evocation of complex problems that left Nick Curtis with "the feeling that perhaps the problems of the USSR aren't such a big deal after all."[22]

The exorcism of the Stalinist inheritance is given much more symbolic meaning through the representation of the Ceauşescus. The play shows some of the darker undercurrents working against "perestroika" (before the failed military coup), particularly through the hardliners within the Politburo. The old guard is presented with "*the corpse of* NIKOLAI CEAUŞESCU *dangling between them*" (71). They appear as puppets of history, as though manipulated by the dead ghost of Stalin and speaking in a dead language.

Gorbachev is shown still attempting to make sense of history and apply the notion that history is scientific. "Why is our destiny so impenetrable? The *point* of government is to know what you are doing. To do that, you need to know what will happen. That is why history must be a science" (58).

From this point of view, the Marxist historical materialist view of history is shown to be in a state of crisis. The notion of a "scientific" Socialism (the term used by Engels), which could predict historical development, is in doubt.

Gorbachev is seen as advancing the goals of Alexander Dubcek, which would be to bring about the potential of the Prague Spring before it was crushed by Soviet tanks. Gorbachev recognizes that the present is too riddled with ghosts and problems, but looks forward to "twenty years" in the future. "It's a sad business, making history under circumstances out of your control," he says (69).

Ali and Brenton voice alternative views about Gorbachev's creation of a "third way" in the Soviet Union in the future. Boris, who decides to leave Russia to teach Russian literature in Florence, considers a Russia in ten years' time which has degenerated into a "second Brazil" with shanty towns and "Gimcrack economics" (77). Boris Yeltsin voices his idea of a Russian Utopia where the country becomes "The California of Europe" (82). Of course, this is not the Utopia imagined by Gorbachev, or indeed by the authors of *Moscow Gold.* The play ends by putting forward three alternatives for the future of Gorbachev's "perestroika." The first ending is pessimistic in that Gorbachev is assassinated by three gangsters, with the logical consequence a return of power for the old guard. The second is optimistic, with the authors allowing themselves a "Utopian lapse." It is set in a future (unspecified) Russia where Gorbachev has rebuilt his Socialist state and decides to send aid to Washington, a complete turn-around of the present situation. The third "utopian" ending sees history as a logical progression from the 1917 revolution. Writing in 1936, Karl Mannheim associated "man's will to shape history" and understand it with the utopian mentality. Inevitably, the utopian mentality is connected to a sense of history as progress; progress not only in history, but concurrently in human potential.[23] The endings reveal the authors' ambiguity about history and progress, but show them still clinging desperately to ideology. The ambiguity is a recognition (however partial) by the authors that history cannot easily be viewed as part of a progression when it is so obviously in a state of flux. As Brenton and Ali point out: "The changes in the East have transformed world politics. Uncertainty has replaced the tried and tested formulas of both Right and Left. The nettle we had to grasp, as socialist writers, was that there are no longer easy ideological solutions."[24] This recognition has yet to lead to a reassessment by Brenton of his often simplistic and overoptimistic historical schema and his belief that society is moving towards a "second renaissance."

In many ways, *Moscow Gold* reveals similar problems to those of *Iranian Nights* in that the authors have failed to digest contemporary history and analyse its complexities in a convincing way. As Michael Billington concluded: "Theatre cannot compete with history."[25] If drama is to compete with "living history," it needs to go much further in deepening understanding of its issues than what can already be gleaned from the media.

Events in Russia since the production—including the failed coup, the resignation of Gorbachev as party leader, the banning of the Communist Party, the dissolution of the Soviet Union—again further underline the unpredictability of history and the difficulty of prophesying any "utopias." Boris Yeltsin's ascendancy over a year ago has brought about a government struggling to create a free market in a country riddled with massive inflation, corruption, unemployment, and ethnic conflict after seven decades of authoritarian rule. In its historical and dramatic inadequacies, **Moscow Gold** reflects a continuing need for the British Left to rise to the challenge of *glasnost* and move beyond naïve and schematic Marxist analytical frameworks.

Notes

1. V. Mayakovsky, "Who Has Lef Got His Teeth Into?" (1923), in *Plays/Articles/Essays,* vol. 3, (Moscow, 1987), 172.

2. Howard Brenton, Preface to *Brenton Plays: One,* (London, 1986), xiv.

3. Ibid.

4. Howard Brenton, "Address given at the University of New South Wales," Sydney, Australia, 23 May 1984.

5. Howard Brenton, Preface, (London, 1986), xv.

6. Tariq Ali, *Revolution from Above: Where is the Soviet Union Going?* (London, 1988), xii.

7. Howard Brenton and Tariq Ali, "Explanatory Note," in *Moscow Gold* (London, 1990). All page references will be to this edition.

8. Martin Esslin, "Barry Kyle Talks about *Moscow Gold*: Contemporary History Stages," *Plays International* (October 1990), 10-11.

9. See prologue to 2nd ed. of *Mystery-Bouffe,* contained in James M. Symons's *Meyerhold's Theatre of the Grotesque: The Post-Revolutionary Productions, 1920-1932* (Coral Gables, 1971), 52.

10. Edward Braun, ed., *Meyerhold on Theatre* (London, 1969), 139.

11. This is especially disappointing given that Tariq Ali edited *The Stalinist Legacy: Its Impact on Twentieth-Century World Politics* (Harmondsworth, Middlesex, 1984).

12. Howard Brenton and Tariq Ali, "Explanatory Note," vi.

13. Howard Brenton, *Sore Throats and Sonnets of Love and Opposition* (London, 1979), 45.

14. Howard Brenton and Tariq Ali, *Moscow Gold,* 1.

15. See, for example, Richard Pipes's *The Russian Revolution 1899-1919,* (New York, 1990), which argues that there is no "clear beginning or neat end" (xxi) to the revolutionary movement. Also see Edward Acton's *Rethinking the Russian Revolution* (London, 1990).

16. Howard Brenton, Preface to *Brenton Plays: Two* (London, 1989), xi.

17. Ali's book sees Gorbachev as revitalizing the Socialist project along Leninist lines. See *Revolution from Above,* 100. Ali never raises the suggestion that Gorbachev's invocation of Lenin may well have been a political tactic to signal to the old guard that reform was merely a return to the original aims of the Party.

18. Richard Pipes's chapter on "The Red Terror," for example, in *The Russian Revolution* (789-840), examines Lenin's responsibility for the terror and the regime that Stalin inherited.

19. Bertrand Russell, *The Practice and Theory of Bolshevism* (London, 1920), 170. In the book, Russell professes a belief in Communism, but "not Bolshevism" and his critique in the early 1920s might suggest a way for Ali and Brenton to argue from their ideological position while confronting the issues of the late 1980s/early 1990s.

20. The Chernobyl Man, for example, seems an unfortunate creation for dealing with the tragedy of Chernobyl. He is *"heavily sun-tanned"* and dressed in shabby country clothes. Yet, the presentation seems somewhat fey, as Chernobyl Man sings: "Ring a ring o' roses, pocket full o' posies, it's blown up, it's blown up, we all fall down" (56). The character is on stage briefly and states what is already known about the effects of radiation. There is a sense that the authors are not following through the implications of the issue.

21. Esslin, "Barry Kyle Talks about *Moscow Gold*," 10-11.

22. Nick Curtis, *Plays and Players* (November 1990), 27.

23. Karl Mannheim, *Ideology and Utopia: An Introduction to the Sociology of Knowledge* (London, 1936; reprinted 1966). See chapter on "The Utopian Mentality."

24. Tariq Ali and Howard Brenton, "Explanatory Note," viii.

25. Michael Billington, "All That Glitters Hides Gold," *Guardian* (28 September 1990), 44.

Christopher Hitchens (review date 4 June 1998)

SOURCE: Hitchens, Christopher. "Acts of Violence in Grosvenor Square." *London Review of Books* 20, no. 11 (4 June 1998): 14-15.

[*In the following excerpt, Hitchens contends that Ali provides a vivid portrayal of the 1960s world climate in* 1968: Marching in the Streets.]

I was just beginning to write about 1968 when I learned of the death in New Orleans of Ron Ridenhour, the GI who exposed the massacre at My Lai. He was only 52, which means that he was in his early twenties when, as a helicopter gunner in the area, he learned of the murder of nearly 660 Vietnamese civilians. This was not some panicky 'collateral damage' firefight: the men of Charlie Company took a long time to dishonour and dismember the women, round up and despatch the children and make the rest of the villagers lie down in ditches while they walked up and down shooting them. Not one of the allegedly 'searing' films about the war—not *Apocalypse Now*, not *Full Metal Jacket* or *Platoon*—has dared to show anything remotely like the truth of this and many other similar episodes, more evocative of Poland or the Ukraine in 1941. And the thing of it was, as Ron pointed out, that it was 'an act of policy, not an individual aberration. Above My Lai that day were helicopters filled with the entire command staff of the brigade, division and task force.'

A few weeks ago, at the Vietnam Veterans Memorial in Washington DC, the state finally got round to recognising the only physical hero of the story, a decent guy named Hugh Thompson who saw what was going on, landed his helicopter between Lieutenant Calley's killing-squads and the remnant of the inhabitants, called for back-up and drew his sidearm. His citation had taken thirty years to come through. It was intended as part of the famous 'healing process' which never seems quite to achieve 'closure'.

Ron wasn't interested in any stupid healing process. He wanted justice to be done, and it never was. A single especially befouled culprit, the above-mentioned Calley, was eventually court-martialled and served a brief period of house-arrest before being exonerated by Nixon. The superiors, both immediate and remote, got clean away. A canny young military lawyer near the scene, Colin Powell by name, founded a lifelong reputation for promise and initiative by arranging to have the papers mixed up at the office of the Judge-Advocate General.

I once asked Ron Ridenhour what had led him to risk everything by compiling his own report on the extermination at My Lai and sending it to Congress. He told me that, poor white boy as he was (he left school at 14 and was drafted without protest), he had been in basic training when, in the hut one night, a group of good ol' boys had decided to have some fun with the only black soldier in the detail. The scheme was to castrate him. Nobody was more astonished than Ron to hear his own voice coming across the darkened bunks. '"If you want to get to him, you've got to come through me." I'd've been dead if I hadn't been white and poor like them, but they gave up.' Later, when his troopship called in at Hawaii en route for Saigon, he went ashore and bought a book about Vietnam by the late Bernard Fall. 'Shit, this is what I'm getting into.'

A revolutionary moment requires both extraordinary times and extraordinary people, and Ron Ridenhour, despite his laconic attitude, was one of the latter. He wouldn't have denied, however, that there was 'something in the air' in those days. It was getting to the point where you couldn't shove black people around so easily, or invade any country that took your fancy. There were people who wouldn't take it, and even people in the press and in the academy who were prepared to make an issue of that. (Though this can be underestimated: it took more than a year for the My Lai story to get into print—in the *Cleveland Plain Dealer*.) Nonetheless, the climacteric that was 1968 had been building for some time. What fused it into critical mass, and provided its most indelible slogans and imagery, was undoubtedly the correspondence between the Civil Rights and anti-war movements, both of them American and both of them therefore, in a time when 'global village' was a new cliché, universal in scope and appeal and reach.

Something has to be done to rescue that time from the obfuscations that have descended over it and to fend off the sneers and jeers that now attach so easily. Some people, of course, take a kind of pleasure in repudiating their own past. Some, whether they wish to or not, live long enough to become negations or caricatures. Or indeed partial confirmations: I am thinking of Lionel Jospin, now chief minister of France and in those days a member of an unusually dogmatic *trotskisant* group; a *groupuscule*, indeed, and perhaps an excellent school for the inflexible later canons of neo-liberalism. Robert Lowell once said that he was glad not to have been a revolutionary when young, because it prevented him from becoming a reactionary bore in his old age. I see the point: the fact remains that in mid-life and in 1968 he acted eloquently and well, as a citizen of the republic of Emerson and Whitman should when the state is intoxicated with injustice and war. 'Retrospectives' which emphasise flowers, beads, dope and simplistic anarchism tend to leave him out, as they also omit the Ron Ridenhours.

I didn't really lift a finger to stop the colonial bloodbath in Vietnam which was, let it never be forgotten, prosecuted by liberal Democrats and robotically supported by an Old Labour Government. I did *give* some blood for the Vietcong, at a Blackfriars monastery which had been swept into enthusiasm by the mood of the time. ('Brother, your blood group is a rare AB. Do you think you might possibly make it two pints?' 'No.') I invited Eduardo Mondlane, the soon-to-be assassinated leader of the rebels in Mozambique, to my rooms, and helped organise a public meeting where he hailed the Vietnamese revolution for presaging the defeat of Salazarism in both Africa and Portugal, which indeed it did. I undertook a little work in helping American draft resisters in Oxford, thereby earning my first but not last file held by creepy people nobody had voted for. I went out with the brush and the poster-paint. And I took part in a good-sized punch-up outside the American Embassy in London, thus disproving (as a pamphlet of the time pointed out) Lady Bracknell's piercing words in *The Importance of Being Earnest*: 'Fortunately, in England at any rate, education produces no effect whatsoever. If it did, it would prove a serious danger to the upper classes, and probably lead to acts of violence in Grosvenor Square.'

The My Lai massacre had taken place the day before: we weren't to know that but it did seem very important to us that, half a world away, the Vietnamese might get to hear about this riot and somehow, I don't know, take heart. Mike Rosen, who was arrested and roughed up along with one or two other people who might be embarrassed if I printed their names today, wrote a rather fine agitprop poem making this simple point. It was a beautiful spring day and as one looked up from the big heaving, horse-battered, clod-throwing tussle around the Roosevelt memorial one could see the reflection of binoculars and spy-glasses as various members of the ruling class, foregathered on the roofs of North Audley Street, strove to catch the mood of the nation's supposedly insurgent youth. The editor of the *Daily Telegraph* the next morning published some sort of 'I was there' piece in which he got all the slogans wrong, perhaps from listening through an ear-trumpet. One of the fun things that year was to monitor the hopeless efforts of a rattled establishment to 'keep up'. At Oxford the authorities had a solemn discussion about covering the medieval cobbles with tarmac, lest there be a *nuit des barricades,* and in the PPE examination papers an anxious and 'with-it' question asked for elucidation of the sage 'Herbert Maracuse'. That was good for a chuckle. But it wasn't all doddering and quavering: Home Secretary Callaghan, that red-faced beadle, knew his stern duty. All the Fleet Street rags, the day after Grosvenor Square, printed a leering pic of a girl demonstrator in the grip of several stout bobbies, her skirt round her waist while one especially beefy constable administered a spanking. (For all I know, this is one of the many triggers that may have set Paul Johnson off.)

Tariq Ali was the moving spirit of that rally and this book [*1968: Marching in the Streets*]—which includes the spanking picture—brings it all back with exquisite vividness. It's hard to recall what a hate-figure he was in those days. I had a friend, a moustachioed Parsee Marxist named Jairus Banaji, who was forever getting picked up and smacked around by the forces of law and order just for the sake of appearances, as you might say. But then, 1968 was also the year when, also to the gloat and awe and wonder of the Tory press, London dockers marched to Westminster in support of Enoch Powell. Seeing the Kenyan High Commissioner entering the precincts of Parliament, they bellowed 'Go back to Jamaica' and were much admired in the suburbs for their John Bull spirit. The Communist Party, which was strong on the docks in those times and had the famous Jack Dash as *its* hate-figure, took the day off and later tried to organise a conciliatory East End meeting addressed by the concerned priesthood. But this is to get ahead of the story somewhat.

Like most such 'years', 1968 began a few months early. Premonitory rumbles, in my memory, include the American-inspired military coup in Greece on 21 April 1967, which seemed to challenge the endlessly reiterated notion of reliable ideological 'convergence' between Western European political forces (and also allowed us a second look at the 'defensive posture' of Nato). One would have to add the hunting down, by CIA men and the agents of a brutal dictatorship, of Che Guevara in Bolivia in October 1967, in which the local Communist Party also played a complaisant part. And, in quite another key, I recall the death at about that time of Isaac Deutscher, who had done so much in the early years of the teach-in movement to remind the young that 'the end of ideology' was itself an ideological construct, and that there still existed factors such as class and power. (When he spoke at the main event in Berkeley, the Communists tried to keep his appearance until last and then cut off the microphone.)

There's a kaleidoscopic feel to the pages of the Ali-Watkins volume. Turn the pages in a hurry and you go from the Tet offensive in Vietnam to the strikes in Poland to the murder of Dr King and the ghetto insurrection, getting no time to take breath for les évènements in France and the shooting of Robert Kennedy. Then comes the invasion of Czechoslovakia, the drama in the streets at the Chicago Democratic Convention, the butchery at the Mexico Olympics and the brave (now seemingly almost quixotic) We Shall Overcome moments of the first citizens' movement in Ulster. Some of these produced imperishable vignettes: microcosmic glimpses that were better recollected in tranquillity. I remember Terry Barrett, a Tilbury docker, giving a brilliant rasping reply to the racists from a May Day platform, and the workers at the Berliet plant outside Paris rearranging the letters of their company logo to read Liberté, and Mayor Daley being lip-read by the cameras as he shouted across the Convention floor at the composed, dignified figure of Senator Abraham Ribicoff: 'Fuck you, you Jew son of a bitch. Fuck you. Go home.' I also remember Dr Frantisek Kriegel, the only member of the Czechoslovak leadership who refused to sign the humiliating post-invasion document. He was a veteran of the International Brigades, the Chinese revolution and the wartime resistance, and is often left out of the record (including, though not for this reason, of the Ali-Watkins book) because he put the signers to shame and also because he was attempting to save the honour of socialism.

Not entirely with hindsight, one can now identify the significance of 1968 as being perhaps the critical year in that Death of Communism that is now such a commonplace. Some of my best friends in those days, as well as some of my worst enemies, were members of the Communist Party. It was very striking to be able to observe, in both cases, to what a huge extent a year of crisis and opportunity exposed them to awkwardness, put them on the defensive, found them stammering and unprepared. Their international fraternity of parties had become so contorted and congested by past lies and compromises and reversals that they yearned mainly for a quiet life. Thus: the spring developments in Prague could not be accepted in their entirety even by the reform supporters, because they contained a frontal challenge to 'the leading role of the Party'. But the prospect of a Warsaw Pact fraternal intervention would compromise at one stroke the careful edifice of peace campaigns and 'broad fronts' through which the Party had ingratiatingly tried, with some success, to keep in with the Labour Left and the trade-union apparat, I used to read the *Morning Star* (which had changed its name from the *Daily Worker* to become, as one comrade put it, a version of the *Daily Employee*) attentively. The Vietnam Solidarity Campaign was denounced, because the Soviet Union ostensibly put its faith in the good offices of U Thant. Enoch Powell was to be challenged by a bureaucratic fiat: prosecution under the incitement clause of the Race Relations Act. The Jew-baiting of the Polish authorities in the 'anti-Zionist' purge in Warsaw in March 1968 was to be discussed only in a whisper. Most revealing of all, the stony and mediocre nomenklatura of the French Communist Party (those 'crapules Staliniennes', as Daniel Cohn-Bendit invigoratingly termed them) exerted their entire negative weight in order to abort the anti-Gaullist upheaval in France. We know now what we knew then: the Soviet Union had given the PCF a direct instruction to become 'the party of order'. In a recent edition of the Paris magazine *L'Evènement du Jeudi*, one can read the testimony of Yuri Dobrynin, former fixer at the Soviet Embassy in Paris, who recalls in round terms: 'La ligne dictée par Moscou était précise: pas toucher à de Gaulle.' Thus, when the General returned in mid-rebellion from a fraternal visit to Ceausescu's Romania, and disappeared to Germany to consult with his military caste and agreed to release the Algerian war-criminals Raoul Salan and Jacques Soustelle as part of the deal, he had a porte-parole from the Kremlin in his pocket. The Fifth Republic with its cynical and fluctuating anti-Americanism didn't have long to run in fact, but George Marchais and Jacques Duclos and the others weren't to know that, any more than they did when they became the 'party of order' once more and supported the 'normalisation' of Czechoslovakia a few months later. Somewhere between those two moments, the remaining breath fled the body of monolithic Communism, which continued to decompose steadily in ways that some soixante-huitards found relatively easy to follow. (I was to have arguments with truly believing Communists only once more, among certain American pro-Sandinistas in the late Eighties, but by then it was like dealing with the squeaks emitted long ago from a dead planet. The real laugh came when dealing with the neo-conservatives who needed the illusion of an unsleeping and keenly ideological foe.)

Julian Ferraro (review date 3 July 1998)

SOURCE: Ferraro, Julian. Review of *Fear of Mirrors*, by Tariq Ali. *Times Literary Supplement*, no. 4970 (3 July 1998): 20.

[*In the following review, Ferraro praises* Fear of Mirrors *for its examination of characters who serve political ideals, but faults the novel for its trite conclusion and "wooden" dialogue.*]

Fear of Mirrors, Tariq Ali's third work of fiction, is a political novel. The book's narrative spans the twentieth century, from the last years of the Austrian Empire to the collapse of Communism in Eastern Europe and the reunification of Germany. Its central character, Professor Vladimir Meyer, is an East German Communist, a former dissident, who has been dismissed from his university post by the "Westies". Politically and emotionally estranged from his son, Karl, and abandoned by his wife, Helge, he tries to make sense of his own history and that of his country. The novel unfolds in a series of accounts, from various perspectives, of the present and the past, which are framed by the device of Vlady's attempt at a family history for his son. Moving fluidly between significant historical moments, this tells the interconnected stories of Vlady, of his mother, Gertrude, and his supposed father, Ludwik, a Soviet master-spy and the recruiter of Kim Philby. Vlady's account has a clear (and worthwhile) political agenda: "What I want . . . is to rescue the people in this story from the grip of those whose only interest in the past is to justify their version of the present."

Towards the beginning of the novel, Vlady recommends Alfred Döblin's Marxist epics of the 1940s to Karl, who is rapidly rising in the Social Democratic Party of the new Germany. The terms in which he does so might serve as an artistic manifesto for *Fear of Mirrors* itself:

> The subject of a novel is reality unchained, reality that confronts the reader completely independently of some firmly fixed course of events. It is the reader's task to judge not the author's! To speak of a novel is to speak of layering, of piling in heaps, of wallowing, of pushing and shoving.

At one point in Döblin's *A People Betrayed: November 1918: A German Revolution,* one of the characters is described in the following terms: "It seems to me that a man like you, who has long seen things so clearly, who stands in the midst of life, that such a man can explain to us what the world looks like now." Dispensing with all Döblin's ironies, Tariq Ali makes use of his own characters, such as Ludwik, who "moved in the thought-channels of his century", as a means of launching the sophisticated political discourse that distinguishes his book.

Fear of Mirrors is at its best in its examination of the painful and morally doubtful consequences of the compromises forced on those who live their lives in the service of political ideals, charting as it does the movement from utopian world revolution to Stalinist terror to the unsatisfactory realities of post-Communist Europe. Ali tells an intellectually and emotionally engaging story—even a reasonably gripping one, though the final twists in the tale are predictable. Other aspects of the writing betray a leaden touch. The dialogue is either turgid with political analysis or wooden to the point of bathos ("'It's all over, Vlady! Unlike the phoenix, your DDR will never rise again. And I'm glad.' Vlady smiled. 'So am I, but what has any of that to do with Marxism?'"), and the trite conclusion provided by the final scenes seriously undermines the bleak complexities of the rest of the book.

Kate Kellaway (review date 13 November 1998)

SOURCE: Kellaway, Kate. "Playing at Politics." *New Statesman* 27, no. 4411 (13 November 1998): 36.

[*In the following review, Kellaway discusses the tone and pacing of* Ugly Rumours.]

There is a madwoman in the cellar of No 10 Downing Street. Her name is Margaret Thatcher. Her triple-stringed pearls are intact but her twin-set suit, though tightly buttoned, is adrift with cobwebs. She needs dusting but does not know it. She is, in Sylvia Syms' entertaining portrayal of her, a merry but slightly sinister ghost. She still sees herself as the most influential person in the country. She carries about her person a "Thatcher extractor", a sort of portable Hoover designed to suck socialism out of the body. It seems to work on Tony Blair—and she is pleased with him.

Howard Brenton and Tariq Ali have done wisely to include Thatcher in their satire of new Labour, *Ugly Rumours.* For Blair does not lend himself to biting comedy quite as naturally as Thatcher has always done. The problem is that in life Blair resembles a moderately talented actor who has been badly directed (think of his awful over-emphatic rendition of Corinthians 14 at Diana's funeral; he made it sound as though he were trying to sell love as party policy).

In this production, Blair is played by a moderately talented actor (Neil Mullarkey) but at least he has been well directed by Christopher Morahan and Stephen Rayne. Tony-Boy, as he is known, has a habitual look of aggrieved naivety. He is someone who wants others to agree with him at any cost. ("Let's just agree to agree. I love agreements.") He shows a child's bafflement when crossed. He slaps the word "new" on everything, even referring to the "new future". I laughed aloud at Blair's re-write of Churchill's "fight them on the beaches" speech which includes the revision: "We must go down to the beaches with some fluffy towels." But Tony-Boy is, elsewhere, more depressing than amusing. He is nothing like so much fun as Mrs Thatcher.

More sport is to be had with Cherie Blair (brilliantly played by Carla Mendonca), otherwise known as Cherry-Pop. She dangles in the play like her sparkling but pointless New Age pendant, practising her painful smile and making brittle remarks about life as an "ordinary" QC. She has enough intelligence to suspect that Tony is being spoilt by power.

Much more powerful than Blair or his wife, though, and competing even with Thatcher are two PR girls: Polly Mendacity (Jaye Griffiths) and Charlie Ferrago (Carla Mendonca again). Charlie looks after Gordon Brown (known here as Gordon Macduff); Polly minds Blair. The women, dressed in black, behave with the mindless energy of a pair of over-keen aerobics instructors. I tired of them quickly. They are sadly necessary to the story but are wrapping without substance. Bunny Christie's design is a more interesting, slick package: the screen at the back of his set an inescapable reminder of television's role in politics.

Gordon Brown/Macduff (Gordon Kennedy) is steeped in quasi-Shakespearean quotes so far that should he wade no more returning were as tedious as to go o'er.

He is mainly in the grip of a Hamlet fantasy: his "father" is the late John Smith (Tony Selby), who keeps appearing to tell him that he finds new Labour's policies (and Brown's last Budget) "horrible, horrible, most horrible".

Rupert Murdoch (Tony Selby again) is nastily and amusingly rendered as the reluctant, foul-mouthed God with a toy koala bear on his knee and a map of the world in front of him. He is boorish, domineering and, it is dismally clear, made of much stronger stuff than any of the politicians with whom he plays. Richard Branson is also wonderfully rendered as "Biggles", borne aloft by red balloons and boasting fatuously that his company is "always moving".

The production is always moving, too, the structure of the play sees to that: it is organised into sound—or sight—bites. The structure is appropriate to the play's bleak vision of a world where politics is debilitated by technology (we are definitely in the digital age here). The writing is properly aggressive and, as the PR girls would say, "on-message". But there is an obvious difficulty about satirising blandness that Ali and Brenton never quite overcome. In a programme note we are told that "the play takes place in a very real world". Not so. This is a very unreal world that weirdly excludes ordinary people and their problems. But that, presumably, is the point.

Ranti Williams (review date 4 December 1998)

SOURCE: Williams, Ranti. "The Heart of a Warrior." *Times Literary Supplement*, no. 4992 (4 December 1998): 23.

[*In the following review, Williams asserts that* The Book of Saladin *vividly depicts the sweep of history, but fails to develop its characters adequately.*]

Saladin is one of the few figures to have emerged from the bloody, brutal history of the Crusades with any measure of dignity. Legend and history concur in presenting the Kurdish warrior who led the Muslim reconquest of Jerusalem in 1198 as a man whose integrity and compassion more than matched his sense of religious destiny and military skills. [In ***The Book of Saladin***,] Tariq Ali's fictional account of Saladin does not attempt to sully history's portrait of this liberal Muslim hero. Instead, it attempts to add to the conventional view of this humane, generous leader a sense of indecision and loneliness by presenting the contradictions at the heart of the great man.

The historical Saladin was the first Muslim leader to see the recapture of Jerusalem as part of a greater jihad. Ali's Saladin, despite an eventual sense of religious destiny, has a history of youthful scepticism—much is made of his failure to visit Mecca, which is seen as a conscious youthful decision, then a constant adult regret. Similarly, despite the historical Saladin's reputation for clever military strategy, Ali's version is strangely indecisive, poignantly susceptible to the opinions of those around him. Finally, Ali transforms the historical Saladin, the habitual frequenter of his large harem, into a man who, even in middle age, nurses the broken heart inflicted on him by an adolescent rejection. For all these attempts to make Saladin a more complex human being, Ali's Saladin does not live on the page and simply serves to prove that a mass of contradictions does not a character make.

The novel is in the form of a fictional memoir dictated by Saladin to Ibn Yakub, a Jewish scribe who talks to family and friends to gain a fuller picture of his subject. Of the fictional characters Ali creates to support his stellar historical cast, Ibn Yakub is, perhaps unsurprisingly, the best realized. Even as he is chronicling the lives and histories of the great and good, the humble scribe is fighting his own battles of wounded pride and bitterness occasioned by his wife's adultery. After a time, however, Ali seems to lose interest in his fictional alter ego, and so do we.

The other imagined characters in the novel do not fare anywhere near as well as the narrator. Ali points out in his introduction that "Women are a subject on which medieval history is usually silent". To remedy the historical balance, he creates two particularly spirited member of Saladin's harem—Jamila and Halima. Jamila, the more attractive of the two, is as radical in her religious philosophy (she is a sceptic) as she is in her sexual orientation (she is a lesbian). But the problem with Ali's portrayal of life beyond battles and councils of war is that his women and eunuchs, rather like his constant references to homosexual practice, all seem part of a worthy educational exercise. His efforts to portray those marginalized by history are commendable, but this should not have kept him from making them something more than ciphers or symbols. Considering the vibrancy of the period and culture chosen, ***The Book of Saladin*** is surprisingly flat. Ibn Yakub's uninspired style and a dialogue laden with platitudes do not help; neither does a strange lack of any sense of the passage of time.

Unlike Mary Renault's Alexander trilogy, which conveys Alexander's military genius and personal vulnerability, ***The Book of Saladin*** manages the grand historical sweep with a fair amount of colour and incident, but the core of the novel, where character should be, is empty.

Bruce King (review date winter 1999)

SOURCE: King, Bruce. Review of *Fear of Mirrors*, by Tariq Ali. *World Literature Today* 73, no. 1 (winter 1999): 219.

[*In the following review, King offers a negative assessment of* Fear of Mirrors, *calling the work confusing, poorly written, and clichéd.*]

Fear of Mirrors belongs to a literary subgenre that has not been fashionable during recent decades. Like many political novels, it attempts a grand story and has an epic feel resulting from the characters' involvement in major historical events. Tariq Ali tells of the rise and fall of communism as experienced by some Central European Jews who, rebelling against their enclosed society and against violent persecutions, were early communists. The novel moves back and forth between characters and places and times as several generations of family, friends, and lovers devote themselves to the revolution, become disillusioned, are betrayed and exterminated, or want to learn about, explain, or justify the past.

The story takes place against such events as Lenin's distrust of Stalin, Stalin's gaining control of the Communist Party, the failure of the revolution in Germany, the shift in the party line from global revolution to defense of the Soviet Union, the Spanish Civil War, the many purges, the way those who knew of Stalin's crimes hid them either from fear or because of the need first to defeat fascism, the fate of reform movements, the fall of the Berlin Wall, and the reunification of Germany. Fictional characters are mixed with well-known public figures, including known spies. As in many political novels the movement is from hopes to disillusionments; a constant theme is betrayal, either from fear of others and the truth, personal weakness, lies, or for political reasons. Husbands are betrayed by their wives, children by their mothers, and all are betrayed by their dream of a future of social justice.

Most of the novel takes the form of a long letter concerning family history from a father to his son in which he tries to explain the generations who gave their lives and killed others for a now lost cause. The novel curiously ends happily with several reunions, forgiveness, and even the suggestion that some form of Marxism is likely to be a major force once more as global capitalism is unable to be a solve the world's economic and social problems. Ali implies that communism was a noble experiment which went off the track because of Stalin. While he sees his characters as deluded, they have no other alternatives. Although ambiguity is rather mechanically worked into the comments characters make about Marxism, there is not a good word in the book for anything noncommunist. There is none of the considered criticism of communism often found in Europe, where, after examining what Marxism had produced around the world, many intellectuals feel that the faults were inherent in the theory and utopianism.

Ali is a well-known editor and author of New Left political publications, but ***Fear of Mirrors*** is a badly written novel. There is hardly a paragraph without clichés, political jargon, textbook political summaries, unbelievable dialogue, inappropriate diction, heavy-handed explanations. The characters seldom are credible as presented. The structure of the novel is over-elaborate, confusing, and requires rereading. The characters blur into one another. Drama is faked by ellipses and revelations. While there is the power that comes from a crude version of a thriller, Ali has shown that the distinction between creative and other forms of writing still holds true.

Jane Jakeman (review date 8 January 1999)

SOURCE: Jakeman, Jane. "Novel of the Week." *New Statesman* 128, no. 4418 (8 January 1999): 55.

[*In the following review, Jakeman maintains that* The Book of Saladin *is a fulfilling read, utilizing "sparse prose" filled with exotic settings in order to create a realistic portrait of the sultan.*]

[***The Book of Saladin***] is a work of fiction based on a historical character who has attained quasi-mythical status in both east and west. To the Muslim world, he is a rallying cry, an almost superhuman conqueror, an utterly virtuous religious figure as the commander of a holy war, leading the charge onward at sword point as the famous equestrian statue at Damascus. To the Christian world, he has long been the redeeming light in a world perceived generally as obscure and cruel: the rare courtly opponent surrounded by oriental darkness and wiles.

It was this western version of the Saladin legend that enabled the 19th century to create the concept of a superior warrior breed, wielders of damascened weapons as described in Lane-Poole's *Art of the Saracens*. Saracens, not Muslims or Arabs or Kurds. By splitting off certain aspects of Islamic history, it was possible for the west to appreciate a refined aristocratic culture unconnected with the inconvenient real peoples in the Muslim world. The Saladin myth was a powerful one that still informed Eden's aristocratic viewpoint in the Suez crisis, when he clearly could not believe that an ordinary little city clerk like Nasser, holding a pen instead of a sword and dressed in trousers instead of chain mail, could be an acceptable Arab leader.

We are used to the Saladin legend told from the Christian point of view, a set iconography of encounters between east and west glamourised by writers from Sir

Walter Scott to Graham Shelby, a version that has sided with the Crusaders except for the occasional excursion to concede Saladin's chivalry. This version has been ultimately derived from the western chronicles. Historians who would have been shamed not to read Greek and Latin sources in the original had no compunctions over ignoring the Arab accounts. Sir Steven Runciman, the definitive modern western historian of the Crusades and a master of Byzantine Greek, did not think it necessary to learn Arabic.

It is illuminating, then, to have the Saladin story told by a writer who has immersed himself in the other side. Tariq Ali's novel creates an authentic-seeming court, full of intrigue, dominated by a man who is charismatic yet not a hero of romance, a rather hesitant limping figure, a sultan whose preferred diet is soup and beans.

The life of Saladin is recounted by a Jewish chronicler, Ibn Yakub, an attractive figure whose own story is told in the intervals. The narrative is partly dictated by the sultan himself, partly by others such as the elderly scholar Imad al-Din, and the fascinating figure of Maimonides hovers in the background. The innocent Ibn Yakub is thrown into a dangerous world of shifting alliances, deceptive appearances and military calculation.

As well as the great scenes—the defeat of the Crusaders at Hattin, the encounter with Reynald of Chatillon, the taking of Jerusalem—this is the private life of the sultan, with lively characters who will not be treated as ciphers and a good deal of humour and directness of speech. In Saladin's entourage are strong and intelligent women, the Sultana Jamila and her female lover, and their story is interwoven with that of the sultan's public life. It may be controversial to assign such dominance to the women in a harem, but these are characters in a convincing story with a reality beyond that of historical cliché.

This is a satisfying novel, told, despite its exotic settings, in sparse prose carrying a ring of authenticity reminiscent at times of Naguib Mahfouz. The book deals in complex and subtle people who question the nature of the relationship between body and soul and ponder the purposes of war, not in easy stereotypes or generalisations, even in an area which has traditionally been replete with them. It gives a feeling of how it must have been to be in the company of a great but harried genius and also paints a pluralistic and tolerant Islam, a world of philosophical inquiry as well as military prowess. Saladin's despair of perpetuating such a world and his anguish over lack of Muslim unity, as his life moves towards its conclusion, are moving. "The sultan often asks himself if this bad dream will ever end or is it our fate as the inhabitants of an area which gave birth to Moses, Jesus and Mohammed to be always at war."

It is here, perhaps, that one senses in the author the sadness of a radical who has seen the failure of ideals in his own lifetime. If this novel offers little comfort for the Crusader side of the story, its dense and multifaceted explorations are also a plea against all religious bigotry.

Nina Raine (review date 24 April 2000)

SOURCE: Raine, Nina. "Three Men and a Manifesto." *New Statesman* 129, no. 4483 (24 April 2000): 43-4.

[*In the following review, Raine discusses the collaboration between Ali, Howard Brenton, and Andy de la Tour and the resulting play* Snogging Ken.]

Somewhere in Highgate, north London, three men are sitting round a kitchen table writing a play about the London mayoral election. One of them frets. One of them soothes. And one of them complains about ugly sentences. They are Andy de la Tour, Tariq Ali and Howard Brenton respectively.

I sit on the sofa, next to a pink book entitled *Socialism and Democracy,* an Arsenal scarf and a cap which claims that "Skateboarding is not a Crime". We are in Ali's freezing cold kitchen. He doesn't switch on the central heating. There is silence, broken only by the soft plink of the laptop in front of de la Tour. Ali watches him. Suddenly he speaks.

"Andy—you're not happy."

"No—it's just that, well, I've lost the mouse again."

Brenton gets up to investigate. He looks like a great dour farmer, but when his mouth opens, a surprising finicky chirrup comes out.

"If you had a nipple, this wouldn't happen, you know. I have a nipple. I love them."

They have almost finished *Snogging Ken.* It has taken them one week. By the time this piece is printed, the play, a late-night show using the restaurant set of Pinter's *Celebration,* will already have opened at the Almeida Theatre in London.

Ali and Brenton have collaborated before, with *Moscow Gold* (about Mikhail Gorbachev's struggle for power), *Iranian Nights* (the fatwah), and *Ugly Rumours* (the friction between Tony Blair and Gordon Brown). Last May, Andy de la Tour joined them to write *Collateral Damage* (the bombing of the Balkans). The last three are "Instant History Plays". Brenton is eager to maintain a distinction between "proper" plays, which he still writes, and the "disposable theatre" of their alliance, Stigma, which trades in "annoyers"—"specifically political knockabout".

But don't these annoyers relate to the agitprop of the Seventies, and the angry political plays that Brenton, David Hare, Trevor Griffiths, and David Edgar were writing? I quote Hare: "Our aggression stems . . . from a basic contempt for people who go to the theatre." Brenton bursts out laughing.

"When did David say that?"

"1972."

"That was 28 years ago!" He chuckles wistfully. "Oh, in those days, we were terribly . . . well, we were . . . John Osborne said we were very hairy-armpitted."

This trio don't take *themselves* so seriously nowadays. But they still share the same left-wing politics. They all went on the same marches. And they still feel, Brenton says, that theatre "should be bright and outrageous and hot". But they are older, more relaxed, more jovial. This new play displays their fundamental benevolence. Ali says: "It's a sort of joy, really. It's a celebration of Ken—we're delighted that he's decided to stand as mayor."

However, there is definitely a sense of duty as well as pleasure. These are men of conscience who are politically passionate enough to write the plays that everyone else lazily leaves to them. While others kept mum, they wrote **Iranian Nights**. Ali says: "People were just genuinely scared to speak up about it at that moment." Brenton chimes in: "We were trying to do a job—disperse the fear." **Snogging Ken** is another job they feel ought to be done—a satire on the absurdities of the mayoral election. "Unfortunately, nobody else is going to write it and put it on," says de la Tour, "so I suppose we've got to do it."

Collaboration helps. To write the play on your own, de la Tour reflects, "would be a totally miserable experience". They can enjoy improvising it as a triumvirate. "The process is speeded up. The fundamental principle of democracy is that you need an odd number," says de la Tour. In other words, two people continually gang up against a third.

A morning with them, and it's comically clear how each personality contributes. Take a scene in which two Blair babes—one naive, the other knowing—plot Ken's downfall. Brenton, the natural playwright, is the only one who worries about character, continually glossing lines. "Pandora's tetchy here, isn't she? She's saying . . ." And he is leery of speeches. "Thing is, she's running on a bit, couldn't we break it with a Lola line?"

He also objects to de la Tour's liberal use of exclamation and question marks. "I mean, Andy, you've got double question marks in here. What is all this? And then all these exclamation marks. Take them out."

"I thought some of them read quite well. In fact, one of them was yours."

"Take them all out."

They are ruthless with each other. Brenton's own weakness is for the poetic turn of phrase. As the computer crashes once more, he murmurs, "the Alzheimer's of technology". The others are aware of his foible. When he reaches the line "Flash bulbs in front of flash restaurants", Ali asks suspiciously: "What's all this? A bit of Brenton poetry?"

"Any fucking poetry—out of the door, mate," says de la Tour.

The contemporary nature of their subject is both a pleasure and a problem. The *Guardian* criticised **Collateral Damage.** Do we really want the theatre to rehearse the same argument we've been having all day? Don't we go to the theatre to escape current affairs? Not necessarily. When Harold Pinter's *The Dumb Waiter* was performed in Iran, under the Shah, the Iranian audiences immediately identified with a situation where enigmatic orders arrived from a mysterious power above. They allegorised the play to fit their own political situation. But Pinter is a special case. His plays, such as *Mountain Language* or *One for the Road,* though undeniably political, are deliberately set in a non-specific no-man's-land, and therefore they are endlessly relevant. The very specificity that guarantees the relevance of Stigma plays makes them perishable.

However, the authors aren't worried about the afterlife of the play. Let it die. Their real worry is that their parodic predictions could be fulfilled before the curtain even goes up. But topicality, as Ali admits, is "what gives the whole thing a buzz, if you can comment on something that's going on, that isn't even finished—and put it on stage to intervene in that process."

They turn their attention back to a particularly stubborn gag—a homophobe's vision of Ken orchestrating gay marriages.

BRENTON:

    Standing there, chain of office round his neck . . .

ALI:

    . . . Oscar Wilde in his hand—instead of the Bible.

DE LA TOUR:

    Too wordy and not funny.

BRENTON:

In some robe? We need visual comedy.

DE LA TOUR:

A priest's robe?

BRENTON:

No—a made-up robe. Like a druid.

ALI:

Dirty raincoat.

BRENTON:

(*Worried*) Why is a dirty raincoat particularly gay?

ALI:

Who was the gay saint?

BRENTON:

Some kind of pink robe, perhaps.

ALI:

(*De Profundis*) . . . no, they won't get it.

BRENTON:

(*Brightly*) A pink dressing-gown!

ANDY:

Problem is—what's the joke? There is no joke.

ALI:

(*Lets his glasses drop from his forehead onto his nose*) I think we've wasted too much time on gay marriage. (*He sighs*) Let's move on.

Disposable theatre. By the yard. I loved it. Maybe someone should write a play about it.

Royce Mahawatte (review date 1 September 2000)

SOURCE: Mahawatte, Royce. "At the Summer Palace." *Times Literary Supplement*, no. 5083 (1 September 2000): 11.

[*In the following review Mahawatte contends that although* The Stone Woman *is "rich, erudite and admirable," it tries to achieve too much and fails on a number of levels.*]

The Stone Woman, the third instalment in Tariq Ali's Islamic Quartet, owes a great deal to the nineteenth-century tradition of humanistic drama within historical debate. Although the novel is rich, erudite and admirable, it is overambitious in its aims and uneven in its achievements. Set near Istanbul at the end of the nineteenth century, the novel centres on the conflicts experienced by a noble Ottoman family, and in particular the stroke-afflicted patriarch, Iskander Pasha. Family members, young and old, arrive at the seaside palace to see the paralysed pasha, and they reflect on the past and prepare to face a new future. The slowly recuperating pasha seeks reasons for the demise of his empire and his heritage, and finds himself engaged in conversations with his family and with a visiting German baron. The pasha is unable to reconcile his feelings and past behaviour towards his modern children, especially his strong-willed daughter, Nilofer. The younger generation are caught between the dark world of decaying aristocrats and the dawning future ahead, yet they lament the loss of a time when their lives were less complicated. Not far from the palace is an arrangement of stones which resembles a female form, and the narrative is interleaved with the confessions of different family members who tell what has happened to them to this silent witness. We find that personal history differs markedly from common knowledge.

This Chekhov-like scenario of intense emotion within a creaking social structure constructs a rich picture of history and the way we think about history. We are presented with different explanations and interpretations of cultural decline, from the theoretical and the dynastic down to the plainly wrong and prejudiced. Uncle Memed, Halil and the Baron come to blows over the links between the Ottomans and the Florentines, and although the Baron wins the match thanks to his dreadful pedantry, Memed's abject boredom and Halil's pursuit of exact context, however, win the higher ground.

The voices of the young spice up the world of ideas. The intimate first-person confessions of Nilofer, the Circassian maid, Selim, and the Paris journals of the young pasha are difficult to place. On one level, they are a homage to the different literary perspectives and textures found in the nineteenth-century novel. They also show that the way we interpret both the past and present is subjective and prone to change. Unfortunately, these parts, with their lyrical love-scenes, render the whole uneven. The fact that we are furnished with chapter summaries only encourages the reader to ignore the intellectual discussion in favour of chapters entitled "Nilofer tells the Stone Woman that Selim has stroked her breasts in the moonlight and that she is falling in love with him". It is difficult to tell whether the youthful chapters are a metaphor for the freedom found in a time of cultural change or a need to feed the current delight in lavish settings and racy moments. Ali's female characters take full advantage of cultural instability, and their rebellion is a sexual one, not only in what they do, but most strikingly in what they feel. At times, it seems that Nilofer's sexual psychology has been teleported into her straight from the pages of Marilyn French. That is not to say that going against your parent's wishes, running away with a visiting school inspector and enjoying moonlit sex are recent inventions, but Nilofer's confessions seem a little wishful and oddly dated.

Such historical transparency is not necessarily a criticism, but it seems at odds with the impressive precision found elsewhere in the work. For this reason, although well constructed, **The Stone Woman** reads like a model answer in post-colonial novel writing, complete with liberal readings of history, feminist characterization and nineteenth-century pastiche. It is poetic and subtle in style and yet fragmented and difficult to engage with. However beautiful and evocative, the historical and the human do not couple in this novel, and we are left with a union that is a little forced.

James Hopkin (review date 11 September 2000)

SOURCE: Hopkin, James. "Turkish Delight." *New Statesman* 13, no. 662 (11 September 2000): 56.

[*In the following review, Hopkin argues that* The Stone Woman *is a captivating and complex novel.*]

The third novel in a planned quartet charting the tensions between Islam and Christianity, Tariq Ali's **The Stone Woman** sets up the Pasha family from Istanbul as a microcosm of the Ottoman empire at the end of the 19th century. Drawing on a rich tradition of mythmaking and storytelling, Ali creates an enchanting, sometimes harrowing, fable of a family whose stability and harmony, like the empire to which they belong, is largely predicated on undisclosed information and recycled myths.

Ali teases out these secrets with the grace and guile of a natural storyteller. A weathered sculpture of a pagan goddess—"the repository of all our hidden pain"—becomes the focal point for those concealing difficult truths. Each character approaches her and confesses a story (of forbidden love, real fathers, desires beyond the codes of Islam). Each riveting disclosure has its own voice, but they are all a little wise, sad and humane.

When not in confessional mode, the novel is narrated by Nilofer, returning from an exile imposed on her when she married a Greek. Determined to prevent the household from dictating the course of her life, Nilofer meets Selim, a young barber, and they begin a romance that Ali invigorates with many touches of tenderness. Eventually, Nilofer marries the barber—which would once have been scandalous—and, by having his child, she signals her will to disregard anachronistic codes and expectations.

Yet the novel does not operate solely on an allegorical level. As you might expect from a writer who is also a historian, there are many discussions of politics, philosophy and the past; and for a family whose status quo has been maintained by endless stories from the glory days of the Ottoman empire, there is also plenty of mischief-making. It is here that Ali's gently tweaking revisionism comes in. Nilofer's brother, the cynical Salman, challenges tales of Memed the Great's heroism by pointing out that Memed acted brutally towards his own family. Impatient with the rituals of Istanbul life, Salman also bemoans how "the empire has been irreparably decadent for three hundred years".

Most of the political discourse is saved for family friends, Memed and the Baron. They talk of the empire's decline in relation to the Russians, the Austrians and Bismarck's Germany. They call for a rational approach and for modernisation during a time of radical change that has turned "many ordinary people into madmen and assassins". In effect, the Baron is a mouthpiece for the author's not always subtle historicising; there are details of defeats suffered, territory lost and speculation on what might have been.

The Baron's numerous debates allow Ali to offer conflicting opinions on the demise of the Ottoman empire, and to convey the uncertainty of the times through the clamour of competing voices. As Memed and the Baron argue the veracities of Islamic history, there is talk of the army deposing the sultan and establishing a republic. Salman, however, like his sister, is in favour not of wars, but of planning against "tradition and obscurantism at home".

It is this intertwining of political, religious and national posturing with simple tales of family life and love (suicide, madness, defiance) that makes **The Stone Woman** so captivating.

Justin Huggler (review date 30 November 2000)

SOURCE: Huggler, Justin. "I Prefer to Be an Ottoman." *London Review of Books* 22, no. 23 (30 November 2000): 35.

[*In the following review, Huggler explores the major thematic concerns of* The Stone Woman.]

No country in the Islamic world has embraced the West as eagerly as Turkey has, which makes it an intriguing setting for the third novel in Tariq Ali's Islamic Quartet: a series of snapshots of the great historic collisions between the two cultures, taken from the Eastern point of view, **The Stone Woman** is set as the 19th century draws to a close. With the Ottoman Empire in terminal decline, Ali sends the members of a wealthy and aristocratic Turkish family hurrying to the bedside of the patriarch, Iskander Pasha, who has had a stroke. As he slowly recovers, the family, their friends and servants debate whether their country, 'the sick man of Europe', can get better too.

At first sight it seems that Ali has set out to write an Eastern *Magic Mountain,* if only in the sense that his characters, withdrawn from the world, discuss the historic events taking place around them. As the narrator, Nilofer, Iskander Pasha's daughter, puts it: 'Outside in the world a great deal was going on Rebellions were being plotted. Resistance was being prepared. Sultans and Emperors were becoming uneasy. History was being made. Here, in the beautiful fragrant gardens . . . all that seemed very remote.' But this is a little disingenuous: Ali's characters are not detached from the outside world. Iskander Pasha's country retreat teems with intrigue. There is a political murder. The Young Turks, plotting a nationalist revolution against the Ottoman Sultan, hold one of their secret meetings in the house. Even Ataturk makes a brief appearance. He is not named, but simply referred to as a 'young officer from Salonika'. The previous novel in the Quartet, **The Book of Saladin,** was a panegyric to the formidable Kurdish general who turned the Crusaders out of Jerusalem. **The Stone Woman,** by contrast, is the story of forgotten people who lived through great changes, and shaped them unwittingly.

It is to the **The Stone Woman**'s advantage that it is not primarily concerned with the great men of history. One of **The Book of Saladin**'s weaknesses was its stock characters: the heroic, self-denying general; the irreverent but faithful old retainer; the comically self-important academic. The characterisation in **The Stone Woman** is subtler: Mariam, for example, the cruel wife of Nilofer's brother Salman, has a fear of emotional commitment which is traced back to her abandonment by her mother, while Iskander Pasha himself, strict and puritanical in the eyes of his family, but a drinker and womaniser during his time as Ambassador to Paris, has the classic split personality of the Islamic patriarch (one brilliantly explored in Naguib Mahfouz's Cairo Trilogy). Ali's explanation for this lies in Iskander Pasha's past, however. We learn that he was once a dervish, a Sufi mystic who believed that God could be found through sensual ecstasy, and that it was the death of his first, Sufi wife which turned him into such a solemn figure.

Not all the characters in the novel are so well developed—in fact, some are hardly developed at all. Ali has 'stuffed **The Stone Woman** with more characters than he can handle. Nilofer's half-sister Zeynep, for instance, has so little to do that Ali has to pack her off to Istanbul to get rid of her. And, even with his stronger characters, his control slips from time to time. Some of the dialogue is unconvincing: what is said is interesting enough, but people just don't talk this way. 'I am starved of information concerning your life' seems an extraordinary turn of phrase for a mother comforting her weeping daughter. More alarming, the characters do not react realistically to dramatic events. Nilofer may no longer be in love with her first husband, Dmitri, but when he is murdered, you would expect her to feel horror or pity—or at least guilt at her own lack of feeling—but she has recovered her poise within a few paragraphs. When a spy is discovered at a Young Turks' meeting and dragged off to be murdered, the characters are unmoved. 'Poor man,' the old German tutor comments—which seems something of an understatement.

As the title implies, **The Stone Woman** is a novel about women, history's (and Islam's) most forgotten figures. This is a world of arranged marriages, where it is taken for granted that although a man can have several wives, a woman can have only one husband. On the other hand, Ali knows that women weren't, as the myth has it, entirely powerless. The aristocratic Nilofer is at a considerable advantage in her relationship with her first husband, the Greek school-teacher Dmitri, who is decidedly middle-class, and a member of a subject people, while the Young Turk Selim, Nilofer's second husband, is a strong supporter of women's rights. Interestingly, abolishing the veil is the only one of his stated aims that still troubles modern Turkey. The irony is that Ali has set out to explore difficult historical and cultural issues through the accessible medium of fiction, but his writing is at its best when he is dealing with these complex factual matters.

The Stone Woman herself, the statue of an ancient goddess, is a narrative device intended to compensate for the limitations of a first-person narrator. For centuries, the women on Iskander Pasha's country estate have told their secrets to the statue in the dead of night—which allows Ali to break away from Nilofer's narrative and reveal the thoughts of other characters. But it is an unnecessary device. The characters' secrets are more interesting when they're modulated via an unreliable narrator. Nilofer herself is convinced that the reason her Greek husband is willing to die at the hands of Turkish nationalists is that she no longer loves him, despite the fact that he has written to her that it is a 'political act'.

In a sense, the two reasons are inextricable: Ali's characters represent the dilemma facing the dying Ottoman Empire. The family's old tutor is German (Germany was the major European influence on the Ottoman Empire in its last years) and is having an affair with the intellectual of the family, Uncle Memed, which is used to symbolise the meeting of East and West. Iskander Pasha's split personality serves much the same function. He was Ambassador in Paris during the Prussian siege of 1870, when Napoleon III was overthrown;

and as Nilofer reads his diaries from that time it is made clear that drastic change is now underway in Ottoman Turkey. 'Only the French could topple their king in these circumstances,' Iskander writes. 'How I envy them this capacity.' Turkey soon enough would do the same. As the Western powers set about carving up the Ottoman Empire, confining the Turks to a small area of barren steppe, Ataturk, the 'young officer from Salonika', forced the Sultan from power and set up the Turkish Republic.

A seemingly inconsequential exchange between Nilofer and her second husband shows how infatuated the Ottoman Turks of the novel are with the West—and how much the Islamic world has changed since the 12th century, in which Ali's last novel was set. Selim tells Nilofer that he dreams of becoming a photographer: she is astonished. 'Is it that you could not imagine a future for me other than that dictated by my past and my origins?' Selim asks. 'Do you think only Italians can be photographers? This new art is beyond the reach of a poor boy from Anatolia?' This is a far cry from the world of *The Book of Saladin,* where the Westerners are 'barbarians', to be converted or despised, not the masters of new technologies to be emulated. Both the first and second novels in the Quartet dealt with high points of Islamic civilisation (the first was set in the Arab Caliphate of Cordoba). In *The Stone Woman* the last of the great Muslim empires has been reduced to 'a poor boy from Anatolia', peering in at the window of the West's camera shop.

The novel may look forward to the rise of the Turkish Republic from the ashes of the Ottoman Empire, but the Empire in its time had represented much more than Turkey, and its collapse meant the end of a united Islam's challenge to Western hegemony: there would no longer be a caliph, a successor to the Prophet Mohammed. *The Stone Woman* shows the last Islamic empire in its death throes, its rulers desperate to forge a new state in emulation of the West. This is often seen today as a triumph of the allegedly Western values of democracy and human rights, but Ali does not see it that way. When Nilofer and Selim debate the form of a new Turkish state, she tells her husband: 'I have no desire to be described as Turkish. I prefer to be an Ottoman.' It is not just that Turkishness is 'soulless', as Nilofer petulantly puts it. Her mother's family is Jewish, and whereas the Ottoman Empire was a political concept that embraced many ethnicities and all three religions 'of the Book', the Turkish national movement aimed to build a Western state around a single ethnic nation: Muslim Turks. Ali's portrayal of the Ottoman Empire is a little rosy, but it is essentially accurate.

'What of the Greeks who do not wish to leave Istanbul or Izmir?' Nilofer asks. 'You will either force them to be Turks or drive them into the sea?' When her son asks if his father Dmitri's killers will be punished when the Sultan is overthrown, one of Nilofer's brothers tells him the truth. The men who murdered his father because he was Greek are the very ones who are planning the brave new Turkish world. Even more chilling is the case of Petrossian, the family servant, an Armenian. Petrossian tells the Stone Woman that his sister's house has been set on fire in an attempt to drive the Armenians out of her village. He says that Nilofer's brother Halil, an Ottoman general, used to prevent this sort of thing, but can no longer do so. The old multiethnic state is crumbling—and more than a million Armenians will be systematically massacred by the Turks during the First World War.

There is one last twist in the novel's great debate—and an unexpected one. At the end of this serious novel of assassinations and ethnic cleansing, Ali introduces a genuinely comic character: Iskander Pasha's brother Kemal, a shipping magnate. Kemal claims that he 'could fly the Japanese flag' on his ships, 'if I wished'—national identity is not of much importance to an international businessman.

Bruce King (review date winter 2000)

SOURCE: King, Bruce. Review of *The Book of Saladin,* by Tariq Ali. *World Literature Today* 74, no. 1 (winter 2000): 245.

[*In the following review, King surveys the strengths and weaknesses of* The Book of Saladin.]

Tariq Ali is not only a journalist and filmmaker; he is also an old-fashioned novelist who likes to write large books on important issues and big themes. *The Book of Saladin* is the second novel in an intended quartet treating the confrontation between Islam and Christianity. The first novel, *Shadows of the Pomegranate Tree,* concerned the fall of Islam in Spain. *The Book of Saladin* is the story of the rise of Sultan Yusuf Salah al-Din's family and how Salah al-Din united the twelfth-century Islamic world for the liberation of Jerusalem from the Crusaders. The conquest and reconquest of Jerusalem has been the subject of many epics, although seldom seen through Islamic eyes.

This is very much a postcolonial book, one in which the Europeans not only invade a foreign land but are also barbarians with filthy habits, defilers of holy places, liars, and killers of women and children and especially of Jews. This is a novel shaped by modern sensibilities as well as facts. It is intended as an allegory for the next Islamic liberation of Jerusalem; Ali's introductory "Explanatory Note" alludes to its application to the present. The implications are that Arab leaders should stop quarreling among themselves; they must unite behind a single authority, or one ruler must have the single-mindedness, virtue, cunning, strength, and patience to bring about unification. (Ali is a politician, not a moralist.) The novel is also designed to show that the peoples of the region, such as the Jews, Copts, and other "people of the book," share a common culture, and tolerance, and were united behind Saladin's liberation of Jerusalem. Is Ali suggesting that while Western Christianity and European Jews (and the state of Israel) are alien to the region, those who have in the past lived under Islamic regimes should be accepted as brothers?

One of the main (invented) characters in the novel is Isaac Ibn Yakub, a Jewish scribe recommended to Saladin by Rabbi Musa Ibn Maymun (the famous Jewish philosopher Maimonides). Yakub becomes the Sultan's historian, entrusted by him to write the real history of his life and times in contrast to the literary pufferies of his official secretary and Islamic scholars. Eventually Yakub becomes part of Saladin's inner circle, even, toward the end of the book, his advisor. We are often reminded that Christians persecute Jews because of the Crucifixion. Other invented characters include two beautiful, intelligent women who provide the love story within the novel. One is a skeptic, a lesbian, raised by her father on the rationalism of the Andalusian philosopher Ibn Rushd (whose work is considered heretical by those who hold religious power). She seduces and educates the other woman, who has lost her true love and been made part of the harem. Besides lesbians in the harem, homosexuality is shown to have been commonplace at the time, although Ali's characters tolerate it more as amusing than as an alternative life-style.

Ali's prose can be careless, there are sentences that do not mean what he intends, and the narration can sound like a political editorial or a textbook summary. There are other flaws that make the novel feel like a middlebrow Book of the Month Club choice from the 1940s or 1950s; but once you get used to its clumsiness, it has the excitement of an old Hollywood epic.

Bruce King (review date winter 2001)

SOURCE: King, Bruce. Review of *The Stone Woman*, by Tariq Ali. *World Literature Today* 75, no. 1 (winter 2001): 111.

[*In the following review, King pans* The Stone Woman, *contending that Ali is not a "natural novelist" and that he lacks the ability to realistically tell a story.*]

The Stone Woman is the third installment in Tariq Ali's "Islamic Quartet." ***Shadows of the Pomegranate Tree*** (1999) concerned the collapse of Muslim Spain with the fall of Granada; ***The Book of Saladin*** (1998; see *WLT* 74:1, p. 245) told of the events leading to the reconquest of Jerusalem from the Crusaders; this new novel is a family saga set at a country home outside Istanbul at the end of the nineteenth century. The family has served the Sultan for centuries but now is critical of the clergy and awaits the end of the Empire and the birth of a new society that can compete with Europe. Some members of the family are part of an army plot to overthrow the Sultan and install a secular government. The conspirators, however, cannot agree on the relationship of Turkish nationalism to the many minorities that are part of the Ottoman Empire. (A Greek son-in-law has been killed by nationalists in a version of ethnic cleansing.)

The summer house was built as a place of exile for a former favorite and storyteller who was banished after criticizing the Sultan. Another member of the family was an eccentric who implicitly criticized the Sultan by pretending to be him and administering justice where it had otherwise been corrupted. The present generation feels cramped, impotent, like characters in a Chekhov play, and desires larger lives. As we learn about its members' lives and those of their elders, the truth is that despite the appearance of conventionality, their lives have been rich, even romantic.

Ali is not a natural novelist. It is difficult to take seriously such remarks as: "Salman is very depressed by the fact that the Empire has been irreparably decadent for three hundred years." His own politics can be seen in such lines as "What your philosophers call progress, my dear Baron, has created an inner drought in human beings . . . no solidarity between human beings. No belief in common except to survive and get rich." This is a novel in which "Uncle Memed cleared his throat. Salman smiled. Halil played nervously with his moustache."

Although his novels have impressive historical frames, Ali lacks the talent for making characters and conversations interesting, for dramatic excitement, suspense, and climax, for painting a lively imitation of life. His novels are galleries of stories: "My father assumed the broad and exaggerated tone of a village storyteller. 'As was his wont, the Sultan sent for . . .'" The characters confess most of their intimate life to the Stone Woman of the title, a rock which might be an ancient pagan monument. While Ali aims for a manner close to the period and place of his fiction, he lacks the ear to make it work.

Although hoping to dispel clichés about Islam, Ali is likely to reinforce stereotypes. That the Sultan, having chosen an heir, had his other children killed to prevent factions, I knew; I did not know that they were strangled with a silken cord so that common hands did not touch them. In each novel Ali has characters make pointed references to Islam as being the most tolerant religion in the world, especially toward Jews. Many readers will assume that the portrait of "Jo the Ugly," an American Jew with an immense pitted nose, is motivated by something other than tolerance: "He takes after his mother's brothers who are shysters and rogues, growing rich by robbing their own people"; "Who knows but the next hundred years might well be the years of people like Jo the Ugly."

Tariq Ali and David Barsamian (interview date November 2001)

SOURCE: Ali, Tariq, and David Barsamian. "Tariq Ali." *Progressive* 66, no. 1 (January 2002): 31-4.

[*In the following interview, originally conducted in November 2001, Ali discusses the relationship between the United States and Pakistan as well as the worldwide war on terrorism.*]

Tariq Ali was born in 1943 in Lahore, in what was then British-controlled India. He was educated in Pakistan and then at Oxford. His opposition to the military dictatorship in Pakistan during the 1960s led to permanent exile in Britain. He was active in the antiwar movement in Europe during the late 1960s.

Ali is a longstanding editor of *New Left Review* and has written more than a dozen books on history and politics. His forthcoming book is **The Clash of Fundamentalism: Crusades, Jihad, and Modernity.** He also has been working on two sets of novels. Three novels of the "Islamic Quintet" have been published by Verso: **Shadows of the Pomegranate Tree, The Book of Saladin,** and **The Stone Woman.** They portray Islamic civilization in a way that he says "run counter to the standard views." His "Fall of Communism" trilogy has seen the publication of **Redemption** and **Fear of Mirrors.** Ali's creative output extends to scripts for stage and screen. A short play of his on Iraq was recently performed at Cooper Union in New York. A veritable "all 'rounder," as they say in South Asia, he is currently working on an opera on Ayatollah Khomeini.

In late October, he was detained at the Munich airport. "The inspector's eyes fell on a slim volume in German that had been given to me by a local publisher," he said. "It was still wrapped in cellophane. In a state of some excitement, the inspector rushed it over to an armed policeman. The offending book was an essay by Karl Marx, *On Suicide.*" Ali said he was rudely instructed to repack his bag, minus the book, and was then taken to police headquarters at the airport. The arresting officer, Ali added, "gave me a triumphant smile and said, 'After September 11, you can't travel with books like this.' At this point, my patience evaporated."

Ali demanded to call the mayor of Munich, who had earlier interviewed him on the current crisis at a public event in the city. The threat of the call was sufficient, and Ali was allowed to continue on his journey.

Ali lives in London, and I spoke with him in late November by phone.

[*Barsamian*]: *A Pakistani general once told you, "Pakistan was the condom that the Americans needed to enter Afghanistan. We've served our purpose and they think we can be just flushed down the toilet." That was in the 1980s, when the United States and Pakistan funded and armed the mujahedeen to defeat the godless Soviet Union. Is the United States again using Pakistan as a condom?*

[Ali]: I think the Americans fished out the same condom but found it had too many holes in it. So they supplied a new one, and they've gone in again. But this time they couldn't go in with the Pakistani army, since the Pakistani army created the Taliban and propelled it to victory. It could hardly be expected to kill its own offspring. The U.S. forced the Pakistani army to withdraw its support, which it did, reluctantly. But it had to. Once Pakistani support was withdrawn from the Taliban, they collapsed like a house of cards, though one hardline faction will probably carry on in the mountains for a bit.

Most Americans may not know the history of Pakistani-U.S. support for the Taliban. In a talk you gave in late September, you said, "People are taught to forget history." What did you have in mind there?

In the West, since the collapse of communism and the fall of the Soviet Union, the one discipline both the official and unofficial cultures have united in casting aside has been history. It's somehow as if history has become too subversive. The past has too much knowledge embedded in it, and therefore it's best to forget it and start anew. But as everyone is discovering, you can't do this to history; it refuses to go away. If you try to suppress it, it reemerges in horrific fashion. That's essentially what's been going on.

It's a total failure of the Western imagination that the only enemy they can see is Adolf Hitler. This is something that actually started during the Suez War of 1956, what I call the first oil war. Gamal Abdal Nasser, the nationalist leader of Egypt, was described by British Prime Minister Anthony Eden as an Egyptian Hitler. Then it carried on like that. Saddam Hussein became Hitler when he was no longer a friend of the West. Then Milosevic became Hitler. Now Al Qaeda and the Taliban are portrayed as fascists. The implication strongly is that Osama bin Laden is a Hitler, even though he has no state power at all. It's just grotesque if you seriously think about it. In reality, the only player in this game who was soft on the Nazis was King Zahir Shah, who then sat on the Afghan throne. He hoped they would defeat the British in India, and he, having collaborated, might share part of the spoils!

But the reason they can get away with it is that history has been totally downplayed. We have populations now in the West with a very short memory span. One reason for this short memory span is that television over the last fifteen years has seen a big decline in the coverage of the rest of the world. History, when they do it, is ancient history, and they sensationalize even that. Contemporary history is virtually ignored on television. If you see what passes as the news on the networks in the United States, there's virtually no coverage of the rest of the world, not even of neighboring countries like Mexico or neighboring continents like Latin America. It's essentially a very provincial culture, and that breeds ignorance. This ignorance is very useful in times of war because you can whip up a rapid rage in ill-informed populations and go to war against almost any country. That is a very frightening process.

Contrast the last wars of the twentieth century with the first war of the twenty-first century.

One difference is that the previous wars were genuinely fought by coalition. The United States was the dominant power in these coalitions, but it had to get other people on its side. In both the Gulf War and in Kosovo, the U.S. had to get the agreement of other people in these alliances before it moved forward. The war in Afghanistan, the first war of the twenty-first century, shows the United States doing what it wants to do, not caring about who it antagonizes, not caring about the effects on neighboring regions. I don't think it's too bothered with what happens afterwards, otherwise it would be more worried about the Northern Alliance. The U.S. is telling the Northern Alliance to kill Taliban prisoners. It's totally a breach of all the known conventions of war. Western television networks aren't showing this, but Arab networks are showing how prisoners are being killed and what's being done to them. Instead, we're shown scenes that are deliberately created for the Western media: a few women without the veil, a woman reading the news on Kabul television, and 150 people cheering.

All these wars are similar in the way ideology is being used. It's the ideology of so-called humanitarian intervention. We don't want to do this, but we're doing this for the sake of the people who live there. This is, of course, a terrible sleight of hand because all sorts of people live there, and, by and large, they do it to help one faction and not the other. In the case of Afghanistan, they didn't even make that pretense. It was essentially a crude war of revenge designed largely to appease the U.S. public. In Canada in mid-November, I was debating Charles Krauthammer, and I said it was a war of revenge and he said, "Yeah, it was, so what?" The more hardline people, who are also more realistic, just accept this.

And the United States has perfected the manipulation. The media plays a very big, big role.

In what way?

During the Gulf War, journalists used to challenge government news managers and insisted they wouldn't just accept the official version of events. It seems that with the war in the Balkans and now this, journalists have accepted the official version. Journalists go to press briefings at the Ministry of Defense in London or the Pentagon in Washington, and no critical questions are posed at all. It's just a news-gathering operation, and the fact that the news is being given by governments who are waging war doesn't seem to worry many journalists too much.

The task does really devolve to alternative networks of information and education. The Internet has been an invaluable acquisition. I wonder how we would do without it. Information can be sent from one country to the other within the space of minutes, crossing channels, crossing oceans, crossing continents. But still, we can't compete with the might and power and wealth of those who dominate, control, and own the means of the production of information today. These are the five or six large companies that control and own the media, publishing houses, and the cinema.

Tony Blair has occupied center stage in the war on terrorism. In many ways he is even more visible than Bush. What accounts for Blair's enthusiasm for the war?

Blair does it to get attention. He does it to posture and prance around on the world stage, pretending that he is the leader of a big imperial power when, in fact, he's the leader of a medium-sized country in Northern Europe.

I think Clinton certainly liked using him. But the Bush Administration doesn't take him that seriously.

Noam Chomsky points out that Britain did not bomb Boston and New York, where major IRA supporters and financial networks are located.

I think Noam's right. But to just even raise the point goes to show that Britain isn't an imperial power and the United States is. The United States is now The Empire. There isn't an empire; there's The Empire, and that empire is the United States. It's very interesting that this war is not being fought by the NATO high command. NATO has been totally marginalized. The "coalition against terrorism" means the United States. It does not wish anyone else to interfere with its strategy. When the Germans offered 2,000 soldiers, Rumsfeld said we never asked for them. Quite amazing to say this in public.

In a recent article, you cited a poem by the tenth-century secular Arab poet al-Maarri:

> And where the Prince commanded, now the shriek,
> Of wind is flying through the court of state;
> "Here," it proclaims, "there dwelt a potentate,
> Who would not hear the sobbing of the weak."

Talk about "the sobbing of the weak."

The sobbing of the weak today is the sobbing of the victims of neoliberal policies. They consist of billions of people all over the world. These are the people who leave their countries. These are the people who cling onto the belly of a plane leaving Africa for Europe, not caring if they are killed in the process, and many of them are. This desperation is the result of globalization. The question is, will the weak be able to organize themselves to bring about changes or not? Will the weak develop an internal strength and a political strength to ever challenge the rulers that be? These are the questions posed by the world in which we live. People are increasingly beginning to feel that democracy itself is being destroyed by this latest phase of globalization and that politics doesn't matter because it changes nothing. This is a very dangerous situation on the global level, because when this happens, then you also see acts of terrorism. Terrorism emanates from weakness, not strength. It is the sign of despair.

Dear old al-Maarri was a great skeptic poet. He wrote a parody of the Koran, and his friends would tease him and say, "al-Maarri, but no one says your Koran." And he said, "Yes, but give me time. Give me time. If people recite it for twenty years it will become as popular as the other one." It was a good moment in Islam when people were actually challenging authority at every level. Very different from the world we live in now, incidentally.

And in this world, the United States is projecting a long war on terrorism. They're talking about it lasting for ten or fifteen years, and involving up to sixty countries. The Bush Administration reminds us almost on a daily basis that the war on terrorism is still in its earliest stages. What are the implications of that?

The main implication is a remapping of the world in line with American policy and American interests. Natural resources are limited, and the United States wants to make sure that its own population is kept supplied. The principle effect of this will be for the United States to control large parts of the oil which the world possesses. There are some people who say this war was fought because of oil. I honestly don't believe it. But that doesn't mean once they have sorted out the first phase of it, the war won't be used to assert or reassert U.S. economic hegemony in the region.

They want to do it in the Middle East, as well. A big problem in the Middle East is that the Iraqi state and Syrian state are potential threats to Israel just by the very fact they exist. Iraq also sits on a great deal of oil, and as that cutthroat Kissinger once said, "Why should we let the Arabs have the oil?" Since Israel is the central ally of the United States in the region, the U.S. would like to weaken the potential opposition. Attacking Iraq, and possibly even Syria, is one way to do that. This is a policy fraught with danger for those who carry it out because it totally excludes the reaction of ordinary people. Could there be mass explosions? And if there are, then you will see countries like Saudi Arabia going under. No one would weep if the royal family were overthrown, but they would probably if it were replaced by a U.S. protectorate or a U.S. colonial-type administration, or the U.S. disguised as the U.N. Other corrupt sheikdoms, like the United Arab Emirates, would crumble, as well. Then what will the U.S. do? Have the Israelis acting as guardians of oil in the whole region? That will mean a permanent guerrilla warfare. Or will they have American and European troops guarding these regions? That, too, would mean limited guerrilla warfare. The only way they'll be able to rule is by killing large numbers of people who live there.

What about Iraq?

If they attack Iraq in the next phase, it could create big problems for them. I'm sure that in Europe the anti-war movement would just mushroom. The Arab world could really explode. That is what their close allies in Saudi Arabia and Egypt are telling them: Do not attack Iraq. The coalition will break up, and even Turkey is saying that it will not be party to an attack on Iraq. Probably the plan is to create an independent state in a corner of Iraq, and then use that as a base to destroy Saddam Hussein. If they go down that route, the world then becomes a very unpredictable and very dangerous place. The one thing that it will not do is curb terrorism. It will increase terrorism, because the more governments you destroy, the more the people will seek revenge.

After flirting with neoisolationism, the U.S. is now deciding it wants to run the world. The U.S. should come out openly and say to the world, "We are the only imperial power, and we're going to rule you, and if you don't like it you can lump it." American imperialism has always been the imperialism that has been frightened of speaking its name. Now it's beginning to do so. In a way, it's better. We know where we kneel.

Mick Hume (review date 13 May 2002)

SOURCE: Hume, Mick. "Expect Blowback." *New Statesman* 131, no. 4587 (13 May 2002): 50-1.

[*In the following review, Hume compares and contrasts* The Clash of Fundamentalisms *with Gilles Kepel's* Jihad: The Trail of Political Islam.]

Like some dreadful progressive rock album of the 1970s, Tariq Ali's new book [*The Clash of Fundamentalisms*] seems likely to become better known for its cover than its contents. The cover is intended to illustrate what the author calls "the clash of fundamentalisms" by depicting George W Bush as a mullah and Osama Bin Laden as a US president. It succeeds only in illustrating, unintentionally, this messy book's own identity crisis, caught as it is between Ali's original plan for a history of Islam and his post-11 September attempt to tack on a theory of everything.

Declaring that he wants to "explain why much of the world doesn't see the [US] Empire as 'good'", Ali outlines how the terrorist attacks on New York and Washington were celebrated not only in the Arab world, but from Latin America to China. He does not mention the rabidly anti-American response from many of his friends on the liberal left in the west, who suggested that the US, and Wall Street in particular, had more or less got what it deserved—as if the office workers and firefighters killed in the twin towers had personally been starving Iraqi babies. This was the left-wing version of the same western self-loathing expressed by right-wing US evangelists, who claimed that 11 September was God's revenge on America for tolerating homosexuality and abortion.

Because nobody has claimed the attacks on America for a specific political cause, everybody has felt free to invent their own interpretation. Ali implies that, as the US is a "veteran imperialist power", this must have been a blow against imperialism. "The subjects of THE Empire had struck back", he says in awe, and this confirmed the "universal truth that . . . slaves and peasants do not always obey their masters".

Let us leave aside the question of whether some disaffected Saudi-born rich kids living and studying in western cities qualify as imperial subjects, slaves or peasants. Ali is saying that even if 11 September cannot be seen as a force for good, it was at least aimed against "the mother of all fundamentalisms: American imperialism". And he warns everybody in the west that, unless we make the world a more fair and equal place, we can expect further "blowback".

Ali has some interesting things to say about the history of Islam, but his central thesis about the present seems badly out of date. He claims that America's "war on terrorism" is simply a continuation of what the "Empire" has done over the past two centuries; the only thing to have changed is that the collapse of communism has deprived opponents of imperialism of a political alternative. So, he suggests, the world is trapped in "the clash between [an Islamic] religious fundamentalism . . . and an [American] imperial fundamentalism determined to 'discipline the world'".

In truth, reactions to 11 September have revealed a shortage of fundamental beliefs in both Washington and the Muslim world. Most people have demonstrated a distinct reluctance to stand up and fight for what are supposed to be their core principles. The few who do want to fight—the zealots of al-Qaeda, or the Israeli hard-liners—are marked by their isolation.

The traditional left might have lost its convictions in the post-cold-war world, but the leaders of the west also find it hard to maintain their old imperial certainty. Far from pursuing a fundamentalist crusade, Bush and Tony Blair have emphasised, time and again, that they are not fighting a war against Islam—which has served only to raise further questions about what they are fighting for.

There is a newly defensive mentality within the western camp, far removed from America's past belief in its own manifest destiny. The arm's-length conduct of the war in Afghanistan—bombing everything from a great height, coupled with a reluctance to gather intelligence on the ground—is shaped by the same uncertainty. Not that this makes it any less dangerous for those on the receiving end.

How do events in the Muslim world today fit into Ali's rigid framework of a clash of fundamentalisms? In a powerful new book, *Jihad*, the French professor Gilles Kepel argues that 11 September marked a new low for the fortunes of Islamic fundamentalism. "In spite of what hasty commentators contended in its immediate aftermath," he concludes, "the attack on the United States was a desperate symbol of the isolation, fragmentation and decline of the Islamist movement, not a sign of its strength and irrepressible might."

Kepel traces the rise of Islamist movements, through the Iranian revolution of 1979 to the victory of the Afghan mujahedin over the Soviet Union a decade later, and the dead-end into which they had turned by the mid-1990s, from Algeria to Iran, and Malaysia to Indonesia. Kepel identifies 11 September as a desperate provocation, designed to bring the military might of America down on Afghanistan and to rally the Muslim world to the cause of Bin Laden and the Taliban. In the event, however, it only demonstrated the incoherence of the few violent fundamentalists and their isolation from any wider Islamist movement. Why did the Muslim world fail to heed the call to jihad? "To begin with," Kepel writes, "no one has formally claimed responsibility for September 11, or articulated its purpose . . . apart from a desire to inflict damage on the United States, the goals of that cause remain vague."

Since 11 September, an informal global coalition has emerged, uniting everybody who hates western consumer society, from Islamic fundamentalists in the east to the anti-capitalist protesters and poets, whom Ali lauds, in the west. Although some aims of this coalition may appear progressive—for example, solidarity with the Palestinians—the sentiment behind it expresses a reactionary loss of faith in modern society and its achievements, and a conspiratorial view of capitalism.

In the end, Ali seems unable to come to terms with the changes of the present because he is trapped in his own idealised past, as a student activist who came to prominence through the protests against the Vietnam war. He imagines that US foreign policy is essentially the same today as it was in the 1960s—missing, ironically, the impact that defeat in Vietnam had on the imperial mindset.

Ali even claims that the anti-Vietnam movement marked "the high tide of American democracy". We might recall that America staged the world's first national democratic revolution, and abolished slavery after a bitter civil war. But for Ali, it seems that democracy peaked in an era when Americans elected Richard Nixon and Henry Kissinger by a landslide over the anti-war movement's candidate. Presumably, he means that the Vietnam years marked the high tide of Tariq Ali, and he appears to have been waiting for it to come in again ever since.

Richard Sennett (review date 7 June 2002)

SOURCE: Sennett, Richard. "They Mean Well." *Times Literary Supplement*, no. 5175 (7 June 2002): 6-8.

[*In the following review, Sennett compares and contrasts the central arguments of* The Clash of Fundamentalisms *with Fred Halliday's* Two Hours That Shook the World.]

What did the United States learn from September 11? The massacre has hardened the unilateralist arteries of the Government; many old scores from another era, such as isolating Cuba and North Korea or punishing Iran, are being settled today in the name of fighting terrorism. The American people remain angry, but many are increasingly bewildered by the world beyond America's borders. The plaint of ordinary Americans, "Why do they hate us?" may be naive, but it is well-meaning and deserves honest answers.

People who could do so have largely failed to provide these answers. Print journalists are reporting government spin as hard fact. The airwaves are filled with such shows as *The Military Diaries,* produced by R. J. Cutler, aiming to provide "militainment". American and British propaganda films from the Second World put out "Military Diaries" to explain to soldiers where they were going, what they would do there and why they were doing it. "Militainment", by contrast, focuses on feelings; *The Military Diaries* focus on what soldiers are eating, what music they are listening to, and how long it has been since they have had sex.

An unconscious elitism among the American press partly explains why they believe the people would be bored by something better. But, as the eminent television broadcaster Dan Rather has recently observed, his colleagues also fear the taint of seeming "un-American". In this, journalism reflects a more general collapse of the American Left after September 11.

In the first aftermath of the attack, discussions of the negative effects of American power may well have seemed mistimed. The reading public closed ranks against Susan Sontag, who immediately after the bombings, in a trenchant, brief *New Yorker* piece, connected American might to the murderous rage coming from abroad. The political scientist Chalmers Johnson, a sober and conservative analyst, was frequently vilified by people who had not read his book, *Blowback: The Costs and Consequences of American Empire* (reviewed in the *TLS* on July 27, 2001), as though he believed the infamous proposition, that "America had it coming". But the critical trauma continues: analyses of the irrationality of Islamic fundamentalism flourish, while discussions of the worldwide effects of American power remain timid.

The American Left has some cause to worry about proving itself a loyal opposition. An unease about seeming un-American can be traced partly to the Vietnam War, and before that to McCarthyism. The public at large recovered from the McCarthyite trauma more quickly than did intellectuals, for whom complicity—witting or unwitting—with a foreign, totalitarian power was a lasting, unresolvable issue. My generation still bears one domestic scar from the Vietnam era which will not heal; most young men in universities had the means to avoid military service, which meant that the poor and undereducated did the fighting abroad in our stead. These stains on the civic honour of the Left have diminished the capacity of certain elements to speak to others in good faith.

A more general impediment to reasoned critical debate about America's own role in our current troubles consists of the crossed destinies of American identity and religion. A majority of Americans believe in the physical existence of Hell, a large minority of Christians that they have personally come in contact with the Holy Ghost. This deep-seated religiosity has led Americans to support generously faith-based hospitals, schools and charity. Religion cements civil society, as government does not.

An inseparable faith in God and Country might seem to determine everything that Americans hold dear in the larger world. But the picture is more complicated. The general public from the September massacre onwards has drawn a firm line between Islam as such and terrorism—as, to his great credit, has the American President; one recent poll indicates that more than 70 per cent of the American public rejects the crude proposition that faith in Islam "leads to violent behavior". Attitudes towards Israel show a similar complexity. Many rightwing Americans, exemplified by the Revd Billy Graham (whose recorded conversations with President Nixon about the Jewish "stranglehold" on the US have recently been released), are both anti-Semites at home and stalwart defenders of Israel abroad. American Jews harbour far more mixed attitudes towards Israel itself than the pronouncements of our own religious leaders suggest, fearing that the passions of Jewish fundamentalists pose a threat to the long-term viability of Israel.

Still, Tariq Ali is right to entitle his new book *The Clash of Fundamentalisms*, as a way of naming the poles defining the current conflict, though I don't think he has rightly understood the American fundamentals of God and Country. The scion of an elite, secular, left-leaning Pakistani family, now a novelist and filmmaker working in London, Tariq Ali charts his own critical engagement with Islam and the forces of rigidity within it. The book comes in four parts: a broad-brush overview of the Islamic Enlightenment and its demise; more fine-painted inquiries into the relation between oil economics and religious movements in the Middle East; then politics and religion in Pakistan, Afghanistan and Kashmir; and finally, a short, sharp critique of the ways in which American foreign policy has disoriented the Islamic world.

The Clash of Fundamentalisms is urbane, highly intelligent and vividly written. One hopes this fine study will earn no fatwa; though he has remained secular, Ali is acutely conscious of how Islam can provide a sense of dignity and purpose for the poor. He presents the Koran as a set of propositions which have been worked out in different historical ways through the invention of institutions rather than the inspiration of individuals; what we term "fundamentalism" represents in part a reaction to the global breakdown of just those institutions which sustained the poor in the past.

But the other culture in the culture clash he depicts is made of very different ingredients. The American fundamentalism of God and Country is not simply clothing for global rule; it represents a religious experience which divides self and world, with few fixed, commanding institutions in between. From its Puritan origins, the contemporary historian Frances Fitzgerald has observed, American religious sentiment has been deeply personal and inward-turning. If the Puritan "City on a Hill" seemed constantly threatened by moral infection, crises of faith menaced individuals more than neighbourhoods within the divine city; personal conscience rather than church bureaucracies were the focus of belief.

Now, as at the beginning, the urgings of conscience can speak anywhere—to the Puritan wandering in the forest, and now to people listening to religious radio while driving. This personalizing of faith is why, for instance, many Americans who believe they have had personal contact with the Divine are led to that connection by analysing their own behaviour rather than through study of the Bible. When William James analysed the phenomenon of religious conversion a century ago, he thought the American inflection of becoming "twice-born" lay in the desire to transform oneself rather than in conformity to Truth. This is our fundamentalism, the fundamentalism of the person.

Fitzgerald promotes the study of foreign policy, as policy reflects directly this intensely personal religious vision. The religious logic of America's missile shield, for instance, she and her school trace to the City's fear of personal infection from without: moral violation has no *raison d'état*; thus, North Korea's nuclear powers loom larger in the consciousness of threat than does Russia's arsenal. Islamic fundamentalism, conceived as surrender of individual conscience to group rule, is particularly alien; adherence to dogmatic command runs exactly counter to the experience of inner transformation which ought to cut one free from the shackles of custom and institutions. Indeed, in nineteenth-century America, nativist Protestants questioned the "slavish" Catholicism of immigrants in terms eerily resonant of discussions about foreign fundamentalists today.

Of course, a real world exists "out there" (a revealing bit of American slang), and at moments of crisis, as in the two world wars, people have eventually responded to it. Nor is fundamentalism of the person simply egoistic individualism; it can lead to a genuine regard for others, but on distinctively American terms.

How this turn outwards now works in the minds of intellectuals becomes clear in a manifesto called "What We're Fighting For", written by David Blankenhorn, President of the Institute for American Values, and signed by otherwise strong critics of American society such as the philosophers Jean Bethke Elstain and Michael Walzer, the social scientists Francis Fukuyama and Robert Putnam. (The complete text is available on the Web at http://www.propositionsonline.com/html/fighting_for.html) This manifesto is not simple flag-waving, nor do Blankenhorn and his signatories preach "an eye for an eye". Their aim is to show that there are times when waging war is not only morally permitted, but morally necessary, as a response to calamitous acts of violence, hatred and injustice. This is one of those times.

To justify their position, they invoke those "American values [which] do not belong only to America, but are in fact the shared inheritance of humankind". They invoke an American version of religious faith as the most important of these values. While they recognize that "no religious tradition is spotless", still they reject what the manifesto calls "ideological secularism". (A footnote explains that they accept separating Church and State but are against "seeing the world based on rejection of religion or hostility to religion".) What they affirm is that religious faith is "an important dimension of personhood", and indeed the manifesto concentrates on defining its own authorial voice; while religion, like patriotism, might seem to imply a surrender or effacement of self, here the emphasis falls on "who we are".

What the manifesto does not clarify is how faith "as an important dimension of personhood" would lead to including North Korea in President Bush's "axis of evil". The document does not evaluate the ethics of actual American strategy in the Afghan region; rather, it insists on the sheer fact of moral agency. I can well understand waging war to destroy the madman Saddam Hussein's stock of biological and chemical weapons, but I cannot understand what my own personhood has to do with it.

The logic of "What We're Fighting For" consists in moving from "I believe" to "I am loyal to American values" to the conclusion that "waging war . . . is morally necessary". Absent from this logic, relegated to the limbo of secularism, is the conviction that we might discover normative ethical principles in the concrete relations of human beings to one another—admittedly an arduous economic, sociological and political task. The logic of faith surmounts all these stubborn particularities. "What We're Fighting For", despite its nuances and humanity, thus justifies Tariq Ali in calling the present moment a clash of fundamentalisms.

In making this criticism, I intend no comment on the faith of the authors of the manifesto. What is wrong is that the manifesto does little to illuminate the ethics appropriate to a superpower. Fred Halliday's *Two Hours That Shook the World* takes that issue on by setting out America's past complicity with its current moral enemies. Halliday, a British expert both on the Afghan region and the Middle East, is no knee-jerk anti-American. He sees real justice in the American campaign against Iraq a decade ago, though no divine justice involved; it was Saddam's chemical and biological arsenal which justified the war. He is equally hard on the Islamic elites; like Tariq Ali, he believes their renunciation of institutional responsibility for their peoples has helped create those economic and social conditions in which redemptive fundamentalism flourishes.

Time constraints of production make for a certain difficulty with this book. Though just published in the United States, it came out in Britain only a few months after the September massacre; the collection of Halliday's varied writings over many years is not entirely unified in focus. But an uncomfortable truth pervades the whole work. Halliday makes clear American complicity in the past with those who are now threats to its security—not complicity with evil but complicity with bad. "Strategic anti-Muslimism" is a policy he roots in the politics of oil, particularly the oil crisis of 1973, and in the end-game America played against the Soviet empire. Like any realpolitik practice, "strategic anti-Muslimism" has waxed and waned depending on circumstances, which a decade ago made the United States covertly Taleban-friendly. In a chapter on the internal politics of Saudi Arabia, Halliday examines America's laxity about the duplicities of the ruling family, elements of which have funded organizations that have in turn funded terrorism. An ethical foreign policy would, at the minimum, admit where and when one set of values is inevitably compromised by another.

At the heart of the book lies a more positive, and simple, ethical vision, in the masterful analysis that Halliday makes of terrorism perceived "from above" versus "from below". To recast his argument crudely, he distinguishes "terrorism", as a threat to the security of secure peoples, from "terrifying", the threat of power from above to those below. In this context, each major religion contains provision for discussion of just war, the conditions under which it is legitimate to use force, and of what kind of force it is legitimate to use.

For this reason, Halliday argues, the crude "identification of 'Islam' with 'terrorism' is a misuse of the latter term for polemical political purposes. . . . [It] confines discussion of terrorism only to Muslim states." The signers of "What We're Fighting For" do not dispute this—in principle. But they are not attentive to the sense in which those beyond the American pale might be terrified of its might, and the irrational consequences which follow, at the extreme, from hatred of one's own impotence.

It might be objected that there is no balm in Halliday's plain speaking for the families of the victims of September 11. Or again, that he asks too much in asking a people to be self-critical about its own strength. But he and Tariq Ali pose, in quite different ways, an urgent question: how can the integrity of secular politics be affirmed? The US, like most other Western democracies, has seen the legitimacy of the political process as well as of politicians nose-dive in the last generation. Cynicism about political ethics leaves only two options: retreat into spectacle—which could be called the Berlusconi Way, in which the spectacles of "militainment" would fit all too comfortably; or appeal to religion as a guide to politics.

The self-standing integrity of politics is a particularly urgent one for American intellectuals. Stained partly by histories of bad faith, and partly by an unconscious elitism, we too have ceased to be credible, critical, citizen voices for our own people. To regain that legitimacy by appealing to religious sentiment, by tapping into religious "personhood", is only to declare that intellectuals, too, are good Americans. Fred Halliday makes the straightforward point that American power has aroused "global inequality and global rancour". To which "What We're Fighting For" replies: we mean well. This amounts to a retreat from politics; it simply will not do.

Anthony Arnove (review date 8 July 2002)

SOURCE: Arnove, Anthony. "Islam's Divided Crescent." *Nation* 275, no. 2 (8 July 2002): 25-6.

[*In the following review, Arnove offers a generally positive assessment of* The Clash of Fundamentalisms, *but argues that the work would have been stronger if Ali had proposed alternatives to modern Islamism.*]

On September 23, 2001, midpoint between the horrific events of September 11 and the beginning of the war in Afghanistan, the *New York Times* ran an intriguing headline. "Forget the Past: It's a War Unlike Any Other," it advised, above an article by John Kifner noting that "Air Force bombers are heading toward distant airfields to fight a shadowy foe flitting through the mountains in a deeply hostile land already so poor and so ruined by two decades of war that [it] is virtually bereft of targets." It was a poor headline for an article that began by noting the long history of conflicts among great powers over control of Central Asia, but it was a message with a significant degree of resonance.

History was often being ignored in the heated discussions of the coming war and the attacks that provoked it, of course, but usually without anyone having to instruct us to forget it. Pundits and politicians alike could draw on a long tradition of keeping the public ill informed about the role of the United States in the world. And once the "war on terrorism" actually started, those who tried to speak about a context for the attacks of September, or of how the history of US intervention in the world had produced rage and frustration that could help fuel such actions, were accused of justifying terrorism.

In *The Clash of Fundamentalisms,* a riposte to Samuel Huntington's much-discussed "clash of civilizations" thesis, Pakistani writer and filmmaker Tariq Ali sets the ambitious goal of challenging such organized historical amnesia—"the routine disinformation or no-information that prevails today"—and of speaking forthrightly about many topics that have become unpopular or even heretical in the West, as well as within what he calls the House of Islam. "The virtual outlawing of history by the dominant culture has reduced the process of democracy to farce," Ali puts it in one chapter, "A short course history of US imperialism." In such a situation, "everything is either oversimplified or reduced to a wearisome incomprehensibility."

Whereas Huntington's "clash of civilizations" thesis posits a cultural conflict between Islamic and Western civilization, and sees religion as "perhaps the central force that motivates and mobilizes people," Ali argues that economics and politics, especially oil politics, remain central to the friction between Western powers and states in the so-called Islamic world, particularly in the Middle East. He rejects Huntington's identification of the West with "human rights, equality, liberty, the rule of law, [and] democracy," and he reminds us of the vast disparities that exist among cultures and nations within the Islamic world itself.

Few people are better disposed than Ali to serve as a guide to the neglected and distorted histories relevant to the conflict in Afghanistan, the broader "war on terrorism" now being fought on numerous fronts by the Bush Administration, and the intimately related conflicts in Pakistan, India and Kashmir, which have recently put the world on a heightened nuclear alert. Ali, a longtime editor of *New Left Review* and Verso books, is the author of three books on Pakistan and has deep personal and political connections to the region. In *The Clash of Fundamentalisms* he surveys a range of regional and historical conflicts that remain open chapters, including the creation of Israel and its ongoing occupation of Palestinian lands, the unfinished legacy of Britain's brutal partition of India in 1947 and the fallout from division of the world by the colonial powers. The book is an outstanding contribution to our understanding of the nightmare of history from which so many people are struggling to awake, and deserves serious engagement and consideration. Ali broadens our horizons, geographically, historically, intellectually and politically.

Despite his obvious hostility to religious modes of thinking—defending against religious orthodoxy in favor of "the freedom to think freely and rationally and [exercise] the freedom of imagination"—Ali has a sophisticated appreciation of the many contradictory movements and ideas that have organized themselves under the banner of Islam. He can debate Islamic doctrine with the most ardent purists while at the same time dispensing with the simplistic (and all too often racist) caricatures of Islam that pass for analysis in the West. In *The Clash of Fundamentalisms* he takes the reader on a necessarily schematic and selective history of Islam, though one wishes he had provided more signposts for those interested in further study than the scattered and inconsistent references included in this volume.

Ali writes here of his "instinctive" atheism during his upbringing in Lahore, Pakistan, and of being politicized at an early age. His experiences then helped him understand Islam as a political phenomenon, born of the specific historic experiences of Muhammad, who worked on a merchant caravan and traveled widely, "coming into contact with Christians and Jews and Magians and pagans of every stripe." Ali writes that "Muhammad's spiritual drive was partially fueled by socio-economic passions, by the desire to strengthen the communal standing of the Arabs and the need to impose a set of common rules," thus creating an impulse toward the creation of a universal state that remains an important element of Islam's appeal.

Ali offers a fascinating discussion of the Mu'tazilites, an Islamic sect that attempted to reconcile monotheism with a materialist understanding of the world, including a theory of the atomic composition of matter; some of its members also argued that the Koran was a historical rather than a revealed document. "The poverty of contemporary Islamic thought contrasts with the riches of the ninth and tenth centuries," Ali argues. But he is by no means backward looking in his own vision. He is particularly scornful of the mythical idealized past valorized by the Wahhabites in Saudi Arabia, the Taliban and other Islamic sects. "What do the Islamists offer?" Ali asks rhetorically: "A route to a past which, mercifully for the people of the seventh century, never existed."

Ali sees the spread of reactionary impulses within Islam in part as a response to "the defeat of secular, modernist and socialist impulses on a global scale." Various forms of religious fundamentalism, not only Islamic ones, have partially filled a void created by the failures of parties operating under the banner of secular nationalism and Communism in the Third World. These failures—his examples include Egypt and Syria—were connected to the limits of the nationalist leaderships themselves, especially their lack of democracy and suppression of religious movements by politicians seeking to preserve and extend their own power. But Ali also goes on to argue that "all the other exit routes have been sealed off by the mother of all fundamentalisms: American imperialism."

Consider, for example, the consequences of the US work to train and arm the Islamic forces in Afghanistan, the mujahedeen, to wage a holy war against the Soviet Union. A decade after the Soviets were expelled, the country "was still awash with factional violence," while "veterans of the war helped to destabilize Egypt, Algeria, the Philippines, Sudan, Pakistan, Chechnya, Dagestan and Saudi Arabia." The factional instability in Afghanistan, coupled with Pakistan's intervention, created the conditions that led to the Taliban's rise to power.

To discuss the US government's role in overthrowing the secular nationalist Mossadegh in Iran in 1953 and supporting the brutal Shah for decades; in operating through the intermediary of Pakistan's Inter-Services Intelligence units to back the mujahedeen in Afghanistan; in repeatedly downplaying serious human rights abuses by US "friends" such as Pakistan under Zia ul-Haq and Benazir Bhutto, whose governments actively sponsored the growth of the Taliban; and in lending support to groups like the Muslim Brotherhood in Egypt, Sarekat Islam in Indonesia and Jamaat-e-Islami in Pakistan is not merely a case of obsessing about past wrongs. As Ali argues persuasively, the past is indeed prologue.

Ali has a sharp mind and wit. His mode of history telling is lyrical and engaging, humane and passionate. He repeatedly points to the lessons learned by people in the course of struggle, challenging the pervasive view that people can be liberated by those other than themselves, setting out his differences with the advocates of "humanitarian intervention." Ali writes that Western intellectuals have been far too quick to support US-led military interventions such as the Gulf War and to provide a liberal veneer of respect to wars prosecuted only rhetorically in the name of human rights and democracy but actually motivated by traditional "reasons of state." Where other people see closed doors in history, he sees roads not taken and paths that remain to be pursued.

Yet Ali spends too little time enumerating what some of those alternate paths might be, especially for readers who are new to the history recounted in *The Clash of Fundamentalisms* (certainly a significant section of his readership, given the intense interest in Islam, Central Asia, the Middle East and US foreign policy that has been so much in evidence in recent months). In his final chapter, "Letter to a young Muslim," Ali provides a thoughtful challenge to his correspondent, but I fear he has not done enough to convince his reader to change allegiances. He has more to say about the weakness of Islamism than about any alternative vision of how a more just world might be achieved. What would a compelling agenda look like in an era when, as he notes, "no mainstream political party anywhere in the world even pretends that it wishes to change anything significant"? What might a radical secular program consist of today? How does one effectively mount a challenge to the claim that there is no alternative to American-style capitalism, or that attempts at fundamental change will reproduce the horrors of the Soviet Union?

Indeed, *The Clash of Fundamentalisms* would have been stronger if Ali had engaged this question more thoroughly. Though he expresses contempt for the bureaucratic and dictatorial regimes that confronted the United States during the cold war, at times he gives the Soviet bloc more credit than it deserves. To suggest that China and the Soviet Union were "striving for a superior social and economic system" is to give those regimes far too much credit, and in essence to maintain some illusion that Stalinist authoritarianism was a real alternative.

Ali at times repeats himself verbatim and gets a few details wrong (such as misdating Iraq's invasion of Kuwait in 1991, rather than 1990). None of this takes away from the importance of his argument that we are not living in a radically new epoch in history, but in a period with all too much continuity to the one before September 11.

Sara Powell (review date November 2002)

SOURCE: Powell, Sara. Review of *The Clash of Fundamentalisms*, by Tariq Ali. *Washington Report on Middle East Affairs* 21, no. 8 (November 2002): 102.

[*In the following review, Powell praises* The Clash of Fundamentalisms, *calling the work "a must read."*]

There's an old saying that you can't judge a book by its cover. With Tariq Ali's latest offering, however, many people do. You can't miss it: a picture of George Bush in Osama bin Laden's beard and turban, against a blood red background. As we have taken it to conferences throughout the summer, the cover has sold a lot of books, and generated even more double takes. (The back cover shows Bin Laden in a Bush suit and tie behind a presidential podium.)

But it's the interior of a book that counts, and what is enclosed between Bush and Bin Laden is a treasure that both men—and you—should read. Written in response to the terror attack on the U.S. in September of last year, Ali's *Clash of Fundamentalisms* is a refutation of Huntington's *Clash of Civilizations*, arguing instead that rival fundamentalisms—Islamism on one side, imperialism on the other—are the forces directing much of the world today. Both, Ali argues, must be opposed. To facilitate such opposition, he provides the historical context in which modern Islamism and U.S. imperialism arose.

Ranging widely throughout history to paint the background of the 9/11 attacks on the U.S., parts of this book may be redundant for some readers, but those who could learn nothing from it are few. Ali offers the reader a concise history of Islam: its origins, its remarkable expansion throughout most of Asia and part of Europe, Islamic dissenters, the Crusades, the Ottoman Empire and its decline that was concomitant with a massive rise in the power of the West, women in Islam, Wahhabism, and the role Islam (whether religious or political) played in the separation of Pakistan from India. That separation and its fall-out—the birth of Bangladesh and crisis over Kashmir incorporate elements of the background of U.S. imperialism with regard to Asia. As the recipient of U.S. aid while fighting the Soviet Union, and the recipient of U.S. wrath when ostensibly sheltering the 9/11 attackers, Afghanistan and its brief modern history also are addressed in the book.

Notably, Ali includes the rise of Zionism and the disastrous effects of its imposition on Palestinians and on the Arab world as a whole—particularly with regard to Arab/Muslim relations with the U.S.—as yet another area in which U.S. imperialism toward Asia plays a significant role. Reflecting Ali's leftist political roots, a common theme of U.S. ideological, political, economic and imperial conflicts with the U.S.S.R. runs throughout his commentary. While obviously not comprehensive. Ali's choice of topics reflects those most necessary to understand both the basic precepts of Islam and the roots of Islamism, as well as the formation of Western attitudes toward the Arab and Muslim worlds.

As the 9/11 attacks were most certainly carried out by Islamists, whether or not Bin Laden had anything to do with them (which Ali argues has not been proven), U.S. imperialism toward the Arab and Muslim worlds are Ali's chief concern. Nonetheless, he does provide a brief look at imperialist tendencies toward the rest of the world, starting with the earliest displacements of native Americans and running through the Korean and Vietnamese wars, as well as secretive forays into Latin American and African politics.

Ali concludes with thoughts on both the Sept. 11 attacks on the U.S. and on Islam. He rejects the notion that the former was an historical event of singular significance, arguing instead that it was a mere pinprick in the catalogue of atrocities humans have perpetrated against each other—including atrocities perpetrated by the U.S.—and that it would eventually be seen as such. Its real significance, Ali argues, is that 19 Muslim hijackers felt strongly enough about the U.S. to commit suicide in order to make the political statement of striking a blow at the U.S., and that the U.S. must address the question of why. Such a question leads Ali to his concluding remarks regarding Islam. In the chapter

"Letter to a Young Muslim," excerpted in the *London Review of Books*, Ali argues that Islam is overdue for a reformation of the kind Christianity underwent in the 16th century in order to prevent it reliving old battles.

Despite the density of information contained in ***Clash of Fundamentalisms*** (and occasional oblique references as the result of assumptions of knowledge on the author's part) Ali's narrative style—especially the charming autobiographical tidbits that personalize and humanize the history he writes—makes the book fun to read. The important and timely issues Ali addresses speak to those concerned about the present precarious state of the world. An appendix on the Arab-Israeli war, from a 1967 interview with Isaac Deutscher conducted by Alexander Cockburn, Tom Wengraf, and Peter Wollen in *The New Left Review*, and an index, round out the usefulness of the book as a text.

For those concerned for the state of humanity or bewildered by Sept. 11, for students of politics, history, and international relationships, for Muslims, Arabs, and Americans, and for fans of Tariq Ali's work, this book is a must read.

FURTHER READING

Criticism

Erol, Sibel. Review of *The Stone Woman*, by Tariq Ali. *Middle East Journal* 55, no. 2 (spring 2001): 340-42.

> Erol views *The Stone Woman* as a historical soap opera and describes the novel as superficial, contradictory, and unfulfilling.

Rhodes, Fred. Review of *The Clash of Fundamentalisms*, by Tariq Ali. *Middle East* (September 2002): 65.

> Rhodes praises *The Clash of Fundamentalisms*, noting that the work "blends history, literature, politics and autobiography to challenge the conformist culture of our times."

Smith, Jeremy. Review of *The Clash of Fundamentalisms*, by Tariq Ali. *Ecologist* 32, no. 5 (June 2002): 45-6.

> Smith evaluates the strengths and weaknesses of *The Clash of Fundamentalisms*.

Additional coverage of Ali's life and career is contained in the following sources published by the Gale Group: *Contemporary Authors,* **Vols. 25-28R;** *Contemporary Authors New Revision Series,* **Vols. 10, 99; and** *Literature Resource Center.*

Mary Daly
1928-

American critic, nonfiction writer, and autobiographer.

The following entry presents an overview of Daly's career through 2001.

INTRODUCTION

Among the most radical feminist scholars of the late twentieth century, Daly is known for basing her critical arguments on the academic traditions of theology and philosophy, rather than those of politics or economics. In works such as *The Church and the Second Sex* (1968) and *Beyond God the Father: Toward a Philosophy of Women's Liberation* (1973), Daly not only criticized the Catholic Church for demonizing women and relegating them to secondary roles but also denounced organized religion itself as the cornerstone of all oppressive patriarchal social institutions. In later works, such as *Gyn/Ecology: The Metaethics of Radical Feminism* (1978) and *Pure Lust: Elemental Feminist Philosophy* (1984), she shifted her focus to dissections of male-biased linguistic structures that perpetuate patriarchy, thus laying the foundation for a new feminist-oriented usage with the hope of fostering a women's revolution.

BIOGRAPHICAL INFORMATION

Daly was born on October 16, 1928, in Schenectady, New York, the only child of Frank and Anna Catherine Daly. Her parents were working-class Catholics, and Daly grew up as a devout member of the church. She enrolled at the College of St. Rose, where she earned a B.A. in English in 1950. Daly had been interested in philosophy and theology, but no degrees in either of those disciplines were offered at St. Rose at the time. Two years later, she earned her M.A. in English at Catholic University of America in Washington, D.C. Daly then entered the School of Sacred Theology at St. Mary's College in Notre Dame, Indiana, where she earned her Ph.D. in religion in 1954. Daly wanted to pursue a doctorate in Catholic theology, but such a degree was not then available to women anywhere in the United States. Daly learned that she could pursue the degree at the University of Fribourg in Switzerland, since the school was state-run and could not legally bar women from any course of study. For the next eleven years, Daly studied at Fribourg, earning a basic degree in sacred theology in 1960, a licentiate in sacred theology in 1961, a doctorate in sacred theology in 1963, and a doctorate in philosophy in 1965. In 1966 Daly took a job as an assistant professor of theology at Boston College. That same year, she published her first book, *Natural Knowledge of God in the Philosophy of Jacques Maritain* (1966), an academic analysis of the French philosopher. However, it was the publication of *The Church and the Second Sex* that first brought Daly widespread critical and popular attention. The book's strong criticism of the Catholic Church's attitudes toward women proved controversial, and Daly made several television appearances to further defend and expound her views. Her outspokenness angered some of the administrators at the Jesuit-run Boston College and, as a result, the following year she was denied both tenure and a promotion to associate professor. This action outraged many Boston College students and their demonstrations on Daly's behalf forced the administration to alter its position and eventually award tenure to Daly. Nevertheless, her future at Boston College remained unclear as the administration denied her promotion to full professorship in 1975 and 1989. In 1999 a male student at Boston College, with the backing of a conservative public-interest law firm, threatened to sue the college unless men were allowed to attend Daly's women's studies classes, which Daly had traditionally limited to women only. Before Boston College could officially respond, Daly requested that her next semester's classes be canceled and took a leave of absence. The college suspended Daly in 2000, prompting Daly to sue for violation of her tenure rights and breach of contract. The lawsuit was settled out of court in 2001.

MAJOR WORKS

An exhaustively researched and comprehensive history of the Catholic Church's alleged suppression of women, *The Church and the Second Sex* is a searing indictment of the Church as a fundamentally sexist and patriarchal institution. The book offers little in the way of suggested ecclesiastical reforms; instead, Daly argues that the Church's bias against women is an inherent result of its history and structure. However, in *Beyond God the Father,* Daly began to outline a feminist spiritual program that she believes could take the place of the current patriarchal religions, creating a foundation for a feminist theology. *Beyond God the Father* asserts that Christianity is based on a conception of God as a static, authoritarian, and—most importantly—male figure. Daly argues that this father figure has become the backbone of a system of symbols that men use to subjugate women. Furthermore, Daly claims that this religious subjugation legitimizes all other forms of social, racial, economic, and political oppression. *Beyond God the Father* calls for a feminist spiritual revolution—one that will replace the traditional concept of a male God with the existentialist-influenced conception of the divine as something readily available through the fullness of one's own being. Daly moved her focus outside the religious sphere with *Gyn/Ecology,* turning her critical attention to the issue of societal gender roles. The work's thesis states that women, after millennia of male domination, have unconsciously accepted a patriarchal ideal of femininity—an ideal that must be stripped away if women are to realize their full potential. In *Gyn/Ecology*'s central section, Daly delineates the results of this false ideal with a list of socially sanctioned abuses of women, including Chinese foot-binding, witch-burning, the Hindu suttee, and female circumcision. Daly points out that each of these imposed forms of mutilation is based on a male-created ideal of womanhood. In the book's final section, Daly demonstrates how women can use language to create a new definition of womanhood, giving once pejorative terms like "hag" and "crone" positive connotations while exposing the hidden patriarchal meanings of seemingly innocent or neutral terms. Daly further pursued this lexicographical project in *Pure Lust,* guiding the reader through three "realms." In the first realm, the ancient culture of the "Goddess" is examined; in the second, existing phallocentric conceptions are dismissed; and in the third, women are left free to create their own society. In each section, Daly discusses the patriarchal linguistic obstacles that she feels block women from fully realizing themselves as individuals. Daly's next work, *Websters' First New Intergalactic Wickedary of the English Language* (1987), is an expanded version of the linguistically oriented sections of her previous two works. Written with Jane Caputi and presented in dictionary form, the book reconstructs and redefines women's language through etymological investigation, alliterative wordplay, linguistic invention, and mythological association. In the autobiographical work *Outercourse: The Be-Dazzling Voyage: Containing Recollections from My Logbook of a Radical Feminist Philosopher* (1992), Daly recounts her youth, her education, her struggles with the Boston College faculty, and other personal matters, most notably the development of her critical ideals and the circumstances surrounding the writing of her previous works. Structured as a quasi-magical dialogue between Daly and a young radical feminist living in the year 2048, *Quintessence . . . Realizing the Archaic Future: A Radical Elemental Feminist Manifesto* (1998) offers a survey of social problems facing women in the 1990s, including the break-up of the second wave of the women's movement, the growing development of genetic engineering, society's over-reliance on technology, and the grip of postmodern theory on academia. *Quintessence* then presents a fictional history of the world from the 1990s to the year 2048, proposing that the women's movement will evolve into strong communities of like-minded women who, through intense devotion to each other and the ideals of radical feminism, will eventually cause the world's patriarchal institutions to crumble. In 2001 Daly published *The Gender Division of Welfare: The Impact of the British and German Welfare States,* a critical analysis of the modern institution of welfare, citing specific case studies and examples from the United Kingdom and Germany.

CRITICAL RECEPTION

Daly has acted as an important force in modern radical feminism, inspiring considerable critical debate, most of which has fallen along cultural and political lines. Certain aspects of her work, notably charges of essentialism and her historical ambivalence, have been hotly contested in feminist circles. One of Daly's most controversial positions has been her assertion that men are inherently inferior to women and should generally be excluded from the society of women. Many feminists have openly rejected this ideal, with some calling Daly blatantly sexist while others argue that it is within the power of individual men to reject patriarchal systems. Daly has also been criticized for her belief that the oppression of women by men is now, and has been throughout human history, the primary form of oppression, and that all other instances of oppression pale in comparison. This belief—and its corollary, that radical feminism is the single most important form of liberation ideology—has angered a number of activists and scholars who have charged Daly with both self-aggrandizement and shortsightedness. However, some of Daly's supporters have defended her by claiming that Daly is speaking metaphorically when comparing the oppression of women to other instances of oppression. They have also argued that Daly does not intend to denigrate other forms of oppression or liberation ideologies, and is simply speaking from within an admittedly outdated framework of 1960s-era radical politics. Many critics have agreed that Daly's analysis of language as a tool of oppression and liberation constitutes her greatest achievement, particularly in works such as *Pure Lust*. Nevertheless, some scholars have asserted that, by focusing entirely on the English language, Daly has framed feminism as an Anglocentric phenomenon. Others have criticized Daly's focus on redefining words as too limiting, arguing that she should focus instead on larger linguistic units of discourse. Daly's supporters have countered that Daly always defines words in the context of larger ideas, and that her focus on words—the basic units of meaning—rather than posing a limitation, allows her great analytical flexibility, since words are used in many different contexts.

PRINCIPAL WORKS

Natural Knowledge of God in the Philosophy of Jacques Maritain (nonfiction) 1966
The Church and the Second Sex (criticism) 1968; revised edition, 1985
Beyond God the Father: Toward a Philosophy of Women's Liberation (criticism) 1973; revised edition, 1985
Gyn/Ecology: The Metaethics of Radical Feminism (criticism) 1978; revised edition, 1990
Pure Lust: Elemental Feminist Philosophy (criticism) 1984; revised edition, 1992
Websters' First New Intergalactic Wickedary of the English Language [with Jane Caputi] (criticism) 1987
Outercourse: The Be-Dazzling Voyage: Containing Recollections from My Logbook of a Radical Feminist Philosopher (autobiography) 1992
Quintessence . . . Realizing the Archaic Future: A Radical Elemental Feminist Manifesto (criticism) 1998
The Gender Division of Welfare: The Impact of the British and German Welfare States (nonfiction and criticism) 2001

CRITICISM

Rosemary Radford Ruether (review date 10 November 1973)

SOURCE: Ruether, Rosemary Radford. "Theology by Sex." *New Republic* 169, no. 19 (10 November 1973): 24-6.

[*In the following review of* Beyond God the Father, *Ruether finds flaws in Daly's conception of women and her notion of castrating "phallic morality."*]

Mary Daly's new book [*Beyond God the Father*] is a bold effort to found a theology for the women's movement. Many will find this book startling and even repugnant. Mary Daly has little respect for orthodoxies, either Protestant or Catholic. She strives to break not only with orthodox theology, but also with the traditional logic and meaning of language, in order to reveal a new meaning over against the "insane sanity" of conventional rationality. For Dr. Daly, women are the ultimate outcasts of history, the submerged sexual caste within every class, nation and race. The liberation of women must break with established structures in a more radical way than any other movement.

How can such a theology call itself Christian? Dr. Daly maintains no pretense of continuity with the Judaeo-Christian tradition. For women, in her thought, there can be only one *regula fidei*—those forms of thought that vindicate the full personhood of women. By this standard the traditions of Judaism and Christianity are found wanting. This also means that feminist theology is open to the suppressed and forbidden traditions; the ancient mother and nature religions suppressed by patriarchy; the witches and heretics burned by Christians. Pre-patriarchal and anti-patriarchal traditions reveal themselves to be places of suppressed female autonomy and power and so gain authority as sources for feminist theology. Nevertheless Dr. Daly does not cut herself off from all traditional Christian theology. Indeed she chooses to vindicate, through a reinterpretation, the classical ontological theology of her Catholic heritage in Aquinas and Maritain.

Women should not imitate the inadequate liberation models of contemporary theology, including the apocalyptic model favored by black theology. Here liberation is seen as the victory of the oppressed over the oppressors. The women's movement is the one movement that cannot make murder the answer to oppression. Women and men are too closely bound to each other's survival to imagine that liberation for one can come about through the overthrow of the other. Rather, for Dr. Daly, the liberation model for women must be one of transformation and rebirth, the dissolution of both sides of a false antithesis to reveal a new androgynous humanity.

The male God must be rejected because "He" is not the true God, but an idol. He does the traditional work of idols: creating false consciousness, setting up false polarities, validating unjust rules of an oppressive society, making us look in the wrong places and ask the wrong questions about redemption. The true God is not "out there," nor even the God "who is not yet" so dear to theologians of hope. The true God is the power of Be-ing buried underneath our self-alienation, which is revealed in and through our reborn selves when we break the bonds of false consciousness and oppression. God is not "over against" humanity or even "nature," but the Be-ing through whom we come to be and which is manifest in our power to be when we open ourselves to It in joyful selfhood. The God of patriarchy is based on objective or "I-It" thinking, which found its basic model in the reduction of woman to the status of a "thing." Only the advent of woman as person can reveal that Be-ing which can found loving "I-Thou" relations between persons.

The death of God the Father also spells the repudiation of Christ. Christ was the symbol of the male as "God." At the same time Christ buttressed a slave ethic for those subjugated by patriarchy. Christ was the scapegoat who could be represented by the creators of the scapegoat, men. Women must be anti-Christ, not only to liberate themselves from slave ethics, but also to liberate the memory of Jesus "from enchainment to the role of 'mankind's most illustrious scapegoat' . . . so that Jesus can be recognizable as a free man."

Christology cannot be a redemptive model for women. But Dr. Daly does find prophetic dimensions in Mariology. In the doctrines of Mary's virginity, immaculate conception and assumption, Mariology pointed beyond Christolatry to the messianic concepts of the autonomy of women, the original unfallen nature of women, liberated from the male myth of the "curse of Eve," and the reintegration of the flesh and spirit in transcendent unity.

The women's movement is anti-church; it reveals the advent of a new androgynous humanity, a new liberated community of women with each other, men and women together, and finally as new cosmic covenant between humanity and nature. Nature itself must be liberated from its bondage to the phallic morality of rape and death.

This vision of the theological meaning of the women's movement is important and may well merit the identity that Dr. Daly gives it as being the "final cause." Yet there are disturbing contradictions in her analysis, certain oversimplifications that could subvert her best intentions.

First, it is questionable whether women should speak of themselves simply as an outcaste group. A more complex sociological analysis is needed about the meaning of women as a sexual caste *within every class*. This means that women of the élite classes, races and nations share the spoils of the masters. To call women of oppressed groups to negate their solidarity within their races and classes because these are patriarchal is to make an abstract analysis of woman's situation. Rather, women must integrate their struggle as women with their struggle as oppressed people, or with all other oppressed people. The abstract analysis of the women's movement that separates rather than unites women with all other struggles against oppression is precisely what is likely to lead the women's movement to remain unconsciously upper-class, Western and racist in its operations.

Secondly, to oppose "castration" to phallic morality is unfortunate. This "liberation symbol" contains that hidden violence that desires to "do unto others that which they have done unto you" which Dr. Daly at one point deplores. It seems that, in this language, she has been led astray by phallic consciousness. What she is reaching for is not well said by a word like "castration," but rather by a word that would symbolize our liberation from a morality that not only castrates women, but alienates men from their own potency. What we should seek is the "re-potentializing of everyone," in a dealienated way, so our creativity can become a reciprocal enhancement.

Thirdly, Dr. Daly's Mariology seems to have betrayed her into a notion of woman as the "innocent one" who has never been responsible for evil, except insofar as she has cooperated with male evil. Maleness becomes the sinful, broken world, while women contain the essence of the unfallen Eden which can be restored instantly by joining the women's movement. There is a docenticism about such salvation through change of consciousness that lacks a socioeconomic understanding of the structuring of women into the world of oppression that is necessary to give her liberation vision a "body." There is also a moral naiveté that essentializes woman's situation as the victim into a doctrine of woman as *natura pura*. If women are to grow up, they must learn not only to take power and act autonomously, but also that in so doing they too are capable of oppressing others. The liberation they seek cannot spring from the dreaming innocence of the premoral person, but the mature struggle for love, justice and peace by men and women who both know that they are capable of being divided against themselves and of destroying each other and the world.

Mary Jean Irion (review date 16 January 1974)

SOURCE: Irion, Mary Jean. "Wrenching Free of the Patriarchal Past." *Christian Century* 91 (16 January 1974): 46-7.

[*In the following review, Irion offers a positive assessment of* Beyond God the Father, *though notes shortcomings in Daly's lack of historical perspective.*]

The most searing and searching book yet to relate the movement for women's liberation to religion in America was published in autumn by Beacon. The author, Mary Daly, has been a leader in the movement for some time. Hers is truly a radical book, one with staying power that should outlast that of death-of-God-type radicalisms. Since her argument moves beyond church and Christianity, she will lose one set of friends as she picks up a new set of allies. Mary Jean Irion gives her a good hearing.

* * *

Beyond God the Father is a theological event growing out of the women's liberation movement. Like most revolutionary documents, it is honed on rage and cuts where it must—yet not without reason and faith in healing. If now and then a sharp edge sings with electric revenge, it also works toward finer patterns in religion and human relationships. The author holds that male interpretations of the universe have been untrue to reality and destructive of human potential, female and male; that creative eschatology can come only from the disenfranchised sex; and that the women's revolution "is an ontological, spiritual revolution, pointing beyond the idolatries of sexist society and sparking creative action in and toward transcendence." Thus she firmly grounds a mystical yet activist theology in the feminist movement.

This is certainly one of the most promising theological statements of our time, written in straightforward prose, strongly argued and copiously supported. Mary Daly, taking the scholarly route with doctorates in theology and philosophy, has come through a negation that male theologians (with the possible exception of Richard Rubenstein) have consistently refused, one way or another. She takes all the implications of radical theology seriously and begins the book free of God, Jesus, the Bible, the church, theological language, the Christian symbol system, the Omega Point and the theology of hope; she ends the book having done no sleight of hand to get any of it back. What miracle is reason! Free of fear, deceit, habit, guilt and confinement, free of all the hazards that institutional anxiety and scriptural pseudo-security have put in the way of fully creative humanism, theology stands here as did mathematics at the invention of zero: with a range of possibilities opening on infinity. The philosophical zero is not new, certainly, but it is new to theology; and now that this most conservative of all disciplines has acknowledged it, perhaps religion's moving day, long awaited, has arrived.

The author creates even as she destroys, experimenting with reversals and transformations on some traditional set pieces (Eve, Mary, Joan of Arc); but the result is the rescue of woman, not of the past. For the patriarchal past is inherently destructive of human values, threatening to undo us; we must wrench ourselves free. The method of liberation involves "a castrating of language and images that reflect and perpetuate the structures of a sexist world" and a renaming of self and world or God. This task requires great existential strength, for one must actualize the self in spite of the ever-presence of nothingness. Daly, like Tillich, calls people to courage, for in the willingness *to see* and *to be* is revelatory power. What will be revealed? "[The] becoming of the image of God," "the God beyond and beneath the gods who have stolen our identity." The new God is Be-ing: not noun, but verb. The future is absolutely open, and by participation in being, one affirms and goes beyond absence to presence—"not the presence of a super-reified something, but of a power of being which both is, and is not yet."

Not only theology but also women's liberation is considerably enriched by this book. Like the best of her revolutionary sisters, Dr. Daly holds that "the becoming of women implies universal human becoming"; she does not make woman-power the end but the means to a shared power that redeems man-the-master as well. Rejecting unisex, rejecting matriarchy in favor of a diarchal society, holding out the possibility of the psychologically androgynous person, the author avoids wild excess. Her position is defensible; "the sisterhood of man" is finally fair. Daly sees that sisterhood as, presently, "the final cause which draws life into its vision of human wholeness and significance," assuring the end of "phallic morality." She deepens the significance of women's liberation by giving it a religious dimension—something it has badly needed.

The usual muddles remain muddy. Where and what is evil? If oppression occasions such adventurous faith, why work to get rid of it? Is perfection desirable or not? But these are respectable mysteries.

There is, however, a serious historical weakness in the book: nowhere is significant account taken of classical humanism and the author's dependence upon it. She writes as if we have had a single-minded patriarchal system, when in fact humanism and Judeo-Christianity have been separate and contradictory strands in our heritage, even within the church. The disenfranchised Greek value system, dominated by Christian supernaturalism, has throughout the years formed an underground for human freedom. Its emphasis on the dignity and beauty of the human spirit, partially realized in Athens and later remembered in the Renaissance, is perhaps now being felt again, able to lift those early heights even higher.

For as **Beyond God the Father** runs away into the future with reason and passion at the full, leaving one symbol system behind, it is curving around back into a more ancient source, living out another symbol system. Mary Daly is Penelope and Odysseus; she is Telemachus and his bride-to-be. Homer, our civilization's original androgynous male, knew all about existential courage, the holy zero, and the true religion that any defunct supernaturalism struggles to reach. There is more importance in symbolic language, more of the past and the future in *now* than Dr. Daly accounts for. Her linear, end-oriented, social perspective can be freed to the curved space of the cosmos, where all is now, and now is all. Humanism is both means and end, inclusive; whereas feminism, I must believe, penned as it is in Judeo-Christian experience, has limited this book to a penultimate vision.

But the fact of inequality does require special attention to the disadvantaged part. **Beyond God the Father** should be widely read and discussed. Whether the church requires a further development of "women's theology" and whether society requires an increasing militancy in women depend upon the existential courage, the honesty and the clear speaking and acting of men. Let us see it in the church.

Doris Donnelly (review date 19 January 1974)

SOURCE: Donnelly, Doris. Review of *Beyond God the Father*, by Mary Daly. *America* 130 (19 January 1974): 39-41.

[*In the following review, Donnelly evaluates the strengths and weaknesses in* Beyond God the Father.]

Mary Daly usually does not tease. Coy she is not. Nor playful. Nor shy.

In fact, if ever there were a showdown at the O.K. Corral with those insecure, clerical, hierarchic types, nothing less than **The Church and the Second Sex**—her vastly knowledgeable and impeccably researched book detailing the history of ecclesial suppression of the feminine—would have qualified her as the one and only straight-from-the-hip champion of women-in-the-Church causes. And the odds on Professor Daly's mastery over her opposition would have been as secure as a Joe Frazier victory over Mortimer Snerd.

Something of a wonder, then, and a disappointment, that the bristling, forthright tone that so suited the expository style of her first book is too weak and anemic for her second women's lib book, **Beyond God the Father.** Like her first book, Mary Daly's newest is tough and punchy, but times and turf have changed so that rabid *aficionados* of books, articles and every *New York Times* Op-Ed piece on women's lib like me, who seethe with fury at sexist injustice or who revel in the occasional triumphs of our sisters' struggles toward becoming human, are now looking to other women, not for fighters, but for leaders; not for muscle, but for body; not for aggression, but for passion. And passion with a flesh-and-blood body is precisely what is missing from Mary Daly's book.

More than that, Daly teases us with insights that she hints at, toys with, but does not deliver on. Certainly, a patriarchal symbol system is inadequate, but what precisely is it that women can add to our understanding of the Deity that a one-sided masculine imagery lacks? Surely, a God who created both men and women should expect both men and women to tell us something about their Creator, but what, precisely, is reflected in God by women? In other words, the discussion has advanced, and we are no longer interested in repeating truisms; now comes the strenuous and creative encounter with the feminine force in creation. And Mary Daly tells us nothing new about the feminine, nothing new about who woman is—her sexuality—how woman is different so that the complementarity of an androgynous symbol system would make sense.

And more. "Why indeed must 'God' be a noun?" Daly asks. "Why not a verb—the most active and dynamic of all?" I suppose this may help some in their personal experience of God, in their prayer, in their moments of confusion at their own and God's identity when all seems hidden, but my own juices are left unstirred by God as either noun or verb, since God makes sense and gives meaning to both only as Person. And the connections that I would have to make to confront process theology and a static metaphysic juxtaposed with noun and verb imagery is simply an unnecessary and antiseptic cerebral exercise to me.

Similarly, I find Daly's strident position for abortion lacking in credibility. After continually evaluating and frequently repudiating a celibate, male-dominated ethical system, I am not about to canonize the optic of a woman who does not put her own womanhood in the experiences of marriage and childbirth on the line. Like Daly, I am appalled at the simple fact that a woman faced with an unwanted pregnancy virtually has only the choice of abortion or of giving birth and raising the child. Unlike Daly, however, and awed by medical doubts concerning the potential and rights of organisms that cannot support themselves, I would opt for the energies and monies of civilized people to be directed toward the discovery and implementation of other alternatives—not only toward more refined birth control education, but, more importantly, toward a healthy psychological acceptance of unwanted pregnancies, more freedom in the adoption process and a fundamental loving posture towards life.

Mary Daly has looked forward and backward with unabashed anger, an anger which has grown more apocalyptic with the passing of time. Time has not made anger irrelevant, just insufficient. We still do not have the feminist philosophy-theology book which looks inward with secure self-respect and outward with competent love. The tragedy is that anger held onto too long nurtures nothing but itself.

Margaret O'Brien Steinfels (review date 1 February 1974)

SOURCE: Steinfels, Margaret O'Brien. "Earthly Utopia or Armageddon?" *Commonweal* 99, no. 17 (1 February 1974): 442-43.

[*In the following review, Steinfels criticizes* Beyond God the Father, *noting Daly's "effort to decimate patriarchal religion, language, and ideas."*]

Earthly utopias, in books or in Vermont, are works of the imagination that allow us to fantasize alternative ways of living our lives and organizing the world. You are interested in a society of abundance, restraint, and civility, based on a credit card economy? See Edward Bellamy's *Looking Backward*. You are "into" common property, communal life, and connubial freedom? Check out John Humphrey Noyes' Oneida Community. You want a house without a kitchen? Read Charlotte Perkins Gilman's *Women and Economics*. But we need not dally in the 19th century; most radical writings of the last decade were excursions into the better way in a different world. And Mary Daly's *Beyond God the Father* is of this genre—Christianity without its stumbling blocks: God, Christ, sin, and salvation. It is a theological fantasy about religion freed from the patriarchal mentality.

Q. The patriarchal mentality—what is it? A. It is the outlook that sees all relationships as submissive, ultimately to an authoritarian God the father, and immediately to those dim shades of Him—men.

Q. What does the patriarchal mentality do? A. It makes women cringe. It idealizes women in the role of the victim, offering Jesus as a model of the sacrificial scapegoat, and makes of masochistic vices like "sacrificial love, passive acceptance of suffering, humility, meekness etc." virtuous behavior.

Q. What can we do about the patriarchal mentality? A. Destroy it. Since the image of God the father is merely the human attempt to describe "ultimate reality" or the divine, the destruction of that image is a legitimate point from which to begin a fantasy that would take us beyond God the father, a fantasy that would enlarge the place of the feminine in religion.

Fantasies liberate the imagination; what emerges often gives a new vision, a new way of seeing and understanding. Not unexpectedly fantasies about our highly imperfect world also liberate feelings of hostility, loathing and the desire to attack not just the immediate object of one's ire, in this case, the patriarchal mentality, but all that it has formed in the past, and touches in the present.

Beyond God the Father, which promises to be a fantasy about liberated men and women toward a truer understanding of the "ultimate reality," intermittently becomes a blind and ignorant assault on the sins and sinners of the past. The earthly utopia is frequently submerged, along with most of our already tenuous religious beliefs and symbols, in a wash of dubious arguments and spurious history. *Beyond God the Father* is, in fact, an unreadable book. Having read it, I find much of it unthinkable, and having thought about it, conclude that many of its positions are untenable. Those able to forage their way through the densest and darkest of prose, with as open a mind as possible and shield and buckler in place, will find themselves confronted by an enraged and furious theologian: Yahweh hath no fury like Mary Daly.

Many readers who make the journey will find a good deal that they agree with and, indeed, have read in other places. Women are oppressed. Mere human efforts to name God, be it God the father or the ground of being, are a kind of blasphemy. The use and abuse of Jesus as a carbon copy model has had its bizarre effects on women—and men. Yet it is not for these familiar complaints that Mary Daly's book was written, will be read, and should be criticized; it is for the distinctive and sweeping claims she makes. She is not a whimpering liberal interested in the reform of Christianity and the integration of women into its power structure. She is a militant feminist in the process of "calling forth" a new religion whose marching song will certainly be "Go Down, Moses." The new religion is to be informed and inspired by the liberating experience of radical feminism; its faith-experience grows out of living in "new time" and "new space" on the margins of patriarchal society; its mission is to call forth "new Being." Liberated women having transcended the basic form of oppression in our society—sexism—are physically and emotionally better prepared than men to rid society of, among other things, its burdensome patriarchal religious system which "oppresses women and corrupts men." This mantle of charismatic leadership is of the same cut and design as that worn by the prophets of other liberation theologies except that instead of capitalism, racism, militarism, etc., sexism is the enemy.

The effort to decimate patriarchal religion, language, and ideas proceeds from fantasy to fantasy—that is, from utopia to absurdity—amid talk of "ovarian insights," "scapegoat syndromes," "sisterhood as antichurch and cosmic covenant," "nonsaint," "methodicide," "Christocide," "bibliolatry," "phallic morality," and "the final cause: the cause of causes," feminism. Man alone does not live by words.

Nor should we, male or female, live by the Word. The big enemy in *Beyond God the Father* is, like father, like son, the former second person of the Blessed Trinity, the little man from Prague, that nefarious scapegoat, Jesus Christ. "The idea of a unique male savior may be seen as one more legitimation of male superiority. . . . To put it rather bluntly, I propose that Christianity itself should be castrated by cutting away the products of supermale arrogance: the myths of sin and salvation. . . ."

An earthly utopia or Armageddon? *Beyond God the Father* is a symptom of the madness which comes from resolutely following fantasies and ideas to their final and absurd ends. Ends, in this case, which embody the imperialistic notion that liberation from oppression, of whatever kind, is an experience that must be shared by anyone who wants to maintain their membership in the human race. It leads to those boyish games of whose is bigger, my oppression or yours. It builds a system which categorizes people according to the "saved" and the "damned," the "in" and the "out," the "worthy" and the "unworthy," the "liberated" and the "unliberated." It is as absurd as it is arbitrary. It is patriarchal.

Oppression is a relative condition. While it is right to rejoice with those who are liberated from oppression (even if, as is rarely admitted these days, it is self-oppression) it does not follow that they should become our political, religious, or cultural mentors—radical feminists, ultramontanes, reformed dope addicts and third world revolutionaries, included. It has never been clear why all the twitches one acquires in any liberation process fit one for anything but verdant, green pastures; or, why having found that 'I am as good as anyone else,' I must, therefore, be better than anyone else. Mark Twain once demonstrated how a belief in radical equality could be combined with an abiding skepticism when he snapped back to the anti-Semites of his day, "Jews are members of the human race; worse than that I cannot say of them." We victims of oppression (women, blacks, chicanos, children and, yes, men) can do nothing better than engrave on our pulsating egos the same statement for our own category.

And if the choice between religious leaders becomes a choice between a feminist, theology professor from Boston College and a carpenter's son from Galilee, I say stick with the working class.

Marie Augusta Neal (review date July 1976)

SOURCE: Neal, Marie Augusta. Review of *Beyond God the Father*, by Mary Daly. *Contemporary Sociology* 5, no. 4 (July 1976): 441-42.

[*In the following review, Neal compliments Daly's central argument in* Beyond God the Father.]

Attempting a radical critique of patriarchy, Mary Daly addresses the symbol system of liberation theologies and challenges male theologians to re-examine their language to see if they can say anything religious about transcendent being without relying on the unexamined assumptions of the holiness of patriarchy.

The book [*Beyond God the Father*], which was severely criticized by theologians and which cost the author her appointment to a full professorship at her university, appears regularly on the reading lists of major theologians who can handle the problem of God but cannot handle the challenge of Mary Daly. The serious theological reading that the book has received in the field of religion in the past two years makes it now a major datum for sociologists of religion who are examining the social construction of reality in cultural perspective and the linguistic legitimation of a given social order in societal perspective. To date, no one has been able to provide even the beginnings of a new language in which to talk about transcendence in a theologically satisfying way, even though many theologians acknowledge the substantive problems Mary Daly raises, namely that current language usage about God legitimates the oppression of women in modern society.

The central point of the book, the consideration of the error of the hypostatization of transcendence, seems alien to sociologists until Daly indicates that this process functions to legitimate the existing social, economic, and political status quo, in which women are victims along with other subordinate groups. It is at this point that the sociologist has reason to be interested, since much of what we write and observe does not demonstrate this legitimation, observable though it be. In this work, I think that she does put her finger on how the idols embedded in myths become "facts," and function as unexamined assumptions which victimize women.

Although the latter part of the book does not do as well in providing models for social change as the first part, sociologists of religion and of women will find the book informative. Anyone interested in seeing how the idea of transcendence can be elaborated, while traditional language and ideas of transcendence are ridiculed, will find the book interesting.

Virginia R. Mollenkott (review date 11 April 1979)

SOURCE: Mollenkott, Virginia R. "Against Patriarchy." *Christian Century* 96 (11 April 1979): 417-18.

[*In the following review of* Gyn/Ecology, *Mollenkott commends Daly's critique of patriarchal oppression, but objects to her judgmental and intolerant perspective.*]

Mary Daly, associate professor of theology at Boston College and leading philosopher-theologian of the radical feminist movement, proposed in her second book that feminists speak of God-as-a-Verb (***Beyond God the Father***, 1973). In ***Gyn/Ecology***, she repudiates the term "God" altogether, as representing "the necrophilia of patriarchy," and speaks only of the Goddess who "affirms the life-loving be-ing of women and nature." Because she says they reductionistically include and really exclude "gynocentric being/Lesbianism," she also rejects terms like "androgyny," "homosexuality," "humanism" and "human liberation."

Daly makes clear that she regards all Christian or Jewish feminists as mere reformists, "roboticized tokens" whose ineffectual efforts have been "actively promoted by the patriarchs." Asserting that orthodoxy's agenda is "toward the absolute elimination of all vestiges of real female presence," she considers Protestantism to be even more phallocentric than Catholicism:

> Having eliminated Mary, the Ghost of the Goddess, it sets up a unisex model, whose sex is male. Jesus . . . is male femininity incarnate. . . . He is the Supreme Swinging Single. . . . This christian demolition of the Goddess and mythic establishment of male divinity has paved the way for the technical elimination of women through the application of modern medicine, transsexualism, cloning, and other forms of genetic engineering.

The title, ***Gyn/Ecology***, refers to the cleansing and depolluting of the female Self which is necessary in order to escape from "the religious, technological, and medical Mafia" which substitutes a mask-like "femininity" for the real presence of real women. Mary Daly's thesis is that the "normal mode of existence of the patriarchal male" (by her definition, *every* male) is a sadomasochistic, split consciousness which is totally unable to relate to the inner mystery or integrity of the Other, and which has for centuries sapped women of their native strength. Daly underplays the role of male socialization and therefore denies the possibility of male transcendence of negative conditioning. Women can transcend theirs by becoming "Revolting Hags," but men are no concern of hers. She implies throughout that men are irrevocably inferior to women and therefore irrevocably intent on destroying women. Because she assumes that for men, biology is destiny, Daly is deeply sexist.

The real burden of ***Gyn/Ecology*** is to call all women to burn away "the false selves encasing the Self," and to spin cosmic tapestries out of the Goddess within. To do so, she says, it is necessary to pare away all myths, names, ideologies and social structures which cut off the flow of the Self's original movement.

Since obviously Christianity is in the forefront of what must be "pared away," it would be only too easy for Christian readers to conclude that ***Gyn/Ecology*** is simply a diatribe unworthy of their attention. Not so. Everyone concerned with social justice, male or female, ought to read at least the central portion of the book, "The Second Passage." In it Dr. Daly drops some of her maddening wordplay and supplies evidence for her conviction that recorded history is one long re-enactment of Goddess-murder through atrocities against women. There are harrowing chapters on Indian *suttee,* Chinese footbinding, African genital mutilation, European witchburnings, and American gynecology, concluding with a devastating cross-cultural comparison between Nazi medicine and American gynecological practices. Daly's analysis of the cool, dehumanizing "objectivity" of most scholars when they describe brutality to women is worth the price of the book.

Unfortunately, Daly herself is rather brutal in her contempt for male-to-female transsexuals, male homosexuals, lesbians who are not sufficiently "woman-identified," and more or less everybody who is not a radical/Lesbian feminist. Although her anger is fully justified when she is describing atrocities against women, she frequently manifests, even when describing people of goodwill, the judgmentalism and divisiveness that characterize human nature when we have forgotten our oneness with God's Spirit and therefore with all other beings. Because its author does not adequately distinguish between mere egocentricity and healthy self-affirmation in harmony with God as the inner and transcendent fountain of being, ***Gyn/Ecology*** fails to get to the heart of the matter. Nevertheless, Dr. Daly is voicing the most passionate challenge Christianity is likely to receive in many a year. Theologians, take note!

Marilyn Frye (review date August 1984)

SOURCE: Frye, Marilyn. "Famous Lust Words." *Women's Review of Books* 1, no. 11 (August 1984): 3-4.

[*In the following review of* Pure Lust, *Frye commends Daly's "exemplary iconoclasm," though expresses reservations concerning her treatment of race and her optimistic notion of natural harmony.*]

With **Pure Lust,** Mary Daly takes on once again that central and challenging project of a movement by women to liberate women: the work of creating new meaning. The project is challenging partly because it is "impossible"—as Alice told the rebel egg Humpty Dumpty, you can't just make words mean what you want them to mean. It is necessary because patriarchal meanings lock out the thought of woman as autonomous, yet women must be able to think themselves capable of surviving independence if they are to commit themselves to escape from servitude.

Much of Daly's work in **Pure Lust** is a scavenging through the systems of patriarchal meanings, picking up rags for a bag of semantic resources from which she and the rest of us Others can piece our new architextures of meaning. One mistake a reader can make is to reject or scorn the project if she finds Daly's own unfinished constructions displeasing to her taste or inadequate to her experience. The new meaning form, like a new art form, will arise in the different works of many creators, not by the fiat of one. Already in this book, Daly's own fabrications draw much more on the works of many different women from many different places and times than does the inventing in **Gyn/Ecology** (Beacon Press, 1978); the work is thoroughly literate and for the most part very subtly responsive to criticisms and reactions feminists have brought to her earlier work. But no one thinker or artist can invent for all of us, and I find, reading **Pure Lust,** that I want it to be received as an ordinary extraordinary work. It requires and deserves our ordinary thoughtful criticism; it needs to be appreciated within a context of many women's participation in other fundamentally similar projects of meaning-making. Though they are in some cases awesome and in some cases admirable, the new pictures Daly builds in **Pure Lust** do not entirely suit me. They do inspire and encourage me to rejoin the larger project with renewed vigor, and make more pictures of my own. As for the skills of rag-picking, Daly is certainly one of the craftiest among us. There is much to learn from her methods.

Alice was right: one cannot just make words mean whatever one might want them to mean. Words, taken singly and in isolation, are meaningless; so is any sort of symbol, image, or even narrative. What has meaning means something *to* someone, and to find something meaningful is to relate it to other things and other meanings—in fact, to all other things and other meanings within one's experience. If I choose to introduce a new word, I have to define it, explicitly or implicitly, in terms of words or concepts my interlocutors already know. Novel utterances can be interpreted because they fit the patterns, the regularities, in a semantic system. (The vast majority of utterances people make are novel: exactly that sequence of words with exactly that intonation has never before been produced.) The freshest new metaphor works only because it, reverberates through the existing net of meanings, "Novelty," understood as the creation of a symbol in-a-moment, out-of-nothing, never occurs. It is their connection with already-existing meanings that gives power to novel combinations.

The impossibility of arbitrary or "absolute" novelty in a culture and a symbol system underlies the meaning-making in **Gyn/Ecology** and in **Pure Lust.**

First, the Webster (one of Daly's most felicitous terms for women engaged in this enterprise) works with the elements of an existing language, in this case English, and an existing system of imagery and myth, in this case that of Euro-American christian-capitalist-commercial-scientific culture. The "new" vocabulary is made up of reassembled bits of the old; it has a certain familiar ring even as it sounds quite odd to the English-speaking ear of the woman cultured in that culture. (The "spinning voyagers" of **Gyn/Ecology** have many new names in **Pure Lust,** such as "Prudes," "Shrewds," and "Weirds.") The book is thick with dictionary definitions. Daly does not use the dictionary as an authority, but as a cultural artifact: a fairly comprehensive standard dictionary is a fairly comprehensive depository of the semantic resources for the inventions that are underway. (I have been known to complain that poets, who work with these same resources, do not have to work as hard as philosophers do because poets do not have to make everything explicit and philosophers do. My finding Daly's constant spelling out of explicit definitions somewhat tiresome is probably my punishment for such a cloddish complaint.)

Built into the project of making new meanings out of old is a political problem. For instance, some women have hoped to break through the barriers of meaning by connecting male-marked words like "judge," "officer" or "professor" with words like "woman," imagining we might generate new meanings by speaking in androgynous paradoxes. But this has yielded (in all but a few odd cases) just some not-very-new additions to the ranks of male-defined postures for women. Men have defined what positions a woman supreme court judge supports, what special value a female police officer has (she is especially good at handling domestic dispute calls and rape cases, of course), and lately, the special talent women professors have for teaching men how to "include" women in their "mainstream" curricula. Or, another example: naming God "She" or "The Great Mother." If nothing else changes, this does nothing at all but disguise the masculinity of God or heighten the pedestal on which the romanticized and hence degraded mother is confined. If the old meanings are still invoked, how can the new be radically new? Throughout this book, one of Daly's primary projects is to expose, analyze and immunize against such traps of assimilation and tokenism, against conversion to "male-ordered" "plastic feminism."

Second, patriarchal signs, symbols, images and myths were not invented out of nothing. They were constructed of the materials of an existing system. In the case of the "Western" culture which is the territory Daly is mainly working in, those earlier systems and symbols were woman-centered. The "new" patriarchal terms originally drew meaning and power from the interconnection of those symbols, which still vibrate and reverberate in, among and beneath them, even if very faintly or in layered disguise. To avoid being recaptured by phallocratic structures when we set out to make meaning, the "existing sources" we should draw on are those "original" symbols, images and myths out of which and upon which phallocratic systems have been constructed by processes of accretion, objectification, reversal, ossification, subtraction and attenuation.

If Daly's strategy can be summed up in any one word, that word is *Remember*. Her point is not that we should try to replicate some ancient matriarchy; it is that to avoid being captured in patriarchal male meanings, we should go back into their sources and backgrounds for our materials. *Pure Lust* is full of lessons in how to spot and read out the underlying or "original" semantics masked by the devices of patriarchal language, myth, image and theory. (And in the process of digging into the works of such characters as Aristotle, Aquinas, St. Paul, the popes Paul and Paul Tillich, as well as Freud and other towering figures of phallocracy, Daly provides a valuable education in "Western intellectual history" for any reader who has managed, in or out of the academy, to avoid the standard indoctrination.)

Pure Lust has three major sections which Daly calls Realms: Archespheres, Pyrospheres and Metamorphospheres. In the first of the three, she elaborates on the idea that patriarchal archetypes (she focuses especially on the Virgin Mary as the archetypical woman) are distorted and ossified constructions out of original images, those living, moving centers of meaning which she calls "Archimages" (rhymes with "rages"). One of the questions for radical feminism is this. How, if women are naturally powerful and patriarchal males are "impotent" (as Daly often says they are), could the latter ever have defeated the former? Part of the answer is given in this section, in discussions of how women are made self-defeating, self-annihilating when we buy in to the phallocratic archetypes. It is our own power that is turned against us, and this in turn helps explain why ideology, mythology and/or psychology are such large factors in the oppression of women, larger perhaps than in other sorts of oppression.

This first section ends with what was for me the single most suggestive and energizing statement in the book: "Womankind must once again discover Fire." The fire in question is passion. "Pyrospheres," the second section and for me the most accessible and the most powerful, is about passion and virtue.

Systems of meaning are not abstract independent "mental" constructions. They arise with and cannot exist apart from experience. To make meaning necessarily involves new construction of the speakers and thinkers as agents; for women who have been molded in patriarchy this means getting back into motion.

On Daly's account (she draws on Aristotle and the medievals here), true passions are motions. They are natural movements toward a perceived good or away from a perceived evil. They may be "potted"—dwarfed, contained, distorted, shallow-rooted. They may also simply be replaced, by "plastic" patriarchal passions or emotions which are "freefloating feelings resulting in more and more disconnectedness/fragmentation. Since they are characterized by the lack of specific and nameable causes, or 'objects' [what the emotion is about], they must be 'dealt with' endlessly in an acontextual way . . ."

The plastic passions she names are guilt, anxiety, depression, hostility, bitterness, resentment, frustration, boredom, resignation and fulfillment. As she says, plastic passions are endlessly preoccupying. They stiffen us into an oddly vague fixation on themselves and they fail to connect our process, as real passions would, with other people and the real world beyond themselves. They are "unnatural knots—snarls—of the spirit. Just as the fathers' lies are mind-bindings these feelings are will-bindings that twist the movements of women's appetites in upon themselves. Instead of spiraling outward, these snap backward, strangling the victim."

Daly's list and her descriptions of the plastic passions write several chapters of my own life, including some recent paragraphs on the defeats and future of radical feminism. Most particularly and vividly, she contributes to my understanding of the experience of white feminists who are caught up in an endless pseudostruggle against racism—or rather, as we say, "around" racism.

When white feminists are blocked or "fixed" against subtle and clearheaded analysis of white "woman's place" in racism and of the racial elements of the ties that bind white women to men, we seethe with these poisonous feelings (all of Daly's list at once, except perhaps for fulfillment, with the addition of despair and panic). That these feelings do not connect any process with any reality beyond themselves and are not really passions or e-motions at all, is recognized immediately by many feminist women of color who ask us, "Where is your rage?" White women are indeed victims of implanted auto-destructive mechanisms; race works in white women's lives as a kind of "biological determinism," constantly reinforcing our assimilation to white men; the fixation which keeps white women from touching all of this is *designed* to separate each of us from all other women. To name it all might release our rage. And the rage might liberate our "potted passions" too, thus liberating feminist women of color from the siege of white feminists' misdirected anger, distorted ambition and shallow righteousness.

In Daly's complex account of the "ultimate Taboo against Women-Touching women," she warns against thinking this has only to do with sexual touching, and argues that the taboo separates women in all ways from touching ourselves and each other. It enforces what she calls the "State of Separation" from which radical lesbian feminists mean to separate ourselves. I suspect that one reason white women shrink from naming and touching racism directly is that such naming and touching is part of what the Great Taboo forbids; it effectively precipitates white feminists into the morass of plastic passions. The taboo against touch may also explain why the folded-in attitude of confession which Daly deplores has seemed to be the only possible response to criticism of racist thinking or acting.

Daly tries to abscond with the word "race," punning it into a characterization of the running, spilling, rushing motion of the metamorphosis of the "Race of Women." I imagine she thought that grabbing the word and carrying it off like that would work as a way of breaking its negatively charged taboo power. I like the boldness of the move, but I do not think it works. As she says, it is only by touching the taboo object that we can break the spell. Her handling of the word "race" is not the taboo-breaking touch she wants; it seems to me to further remove the concrete problem of race and racism—and, in another sense, women of color themselves—from the range of white women's touch and capacity to be touched. When in *The Politics of Reality* I tried to recast the word "white," many of my friends thought that what I presented as a breakout was really only a flight. After much more work I think it is turning out that they were wrong about that. I am quite willing to be shown by Daly's further work that I am just as wrong to see her move with "race" as misdirected. For now, I am not buying it.

Where other women have spoken vaguely and timidly of "society," Daly speaks of the Phallic State, the State of Atrocity, the State of Separation, the State of Lechery, the State of Boredom, the dismembered state, and the sadostate. The political state she would see as a logical and noxious product of the more generic state named by these phrases. The word "state" is associated always in this work with the concept of *stasis,* the stationary, that which is not moving; all that is natural to women is characterized in terms of motion. The verb "to be" is taken as an active verb; Daly's conception of woman's being is developed entirely in terms of activities, processes, motions and movements and the qualities and modifications of motion and that which moves.

Motion may be traveling from one point to another in space, it may be change of attitude or shift of perception, it may be activity such as knitting, writing, or digging a hole. It may also be a thing's changing in such a way that it becomes a different thing than it was—a change of identity, a transformation. At the level of identity, motion is *metamorphosis,* the theme of the Third Realm, "Metamorphospheres." On Daly's account this "ontological movement" is what essentially characterizes everything that is alive, and for conscious and creative living things like us, the metamorphosis is conscious and creative.[1] But it can take place wholly or rightly only in the environmental condition of "statelessness." The enemies of women are individual patriots; the Enemy of Womankind and of life generally is that which impedes or stops motion. To be ourselves and not sick or dying, we must not be in a State.

Daly is consistently and wantonly anarchist. (She begins to convince me that radical feminism is essentially anarchistic.) To the believer in the state, there can be order, harmony and peace only if there is "social control," that is, force and coercion, somebody has to be in charge and that somebody has to have the power to make his decisions stick. For this belief to sound right, one has to make certain background assumptions about human and other nature (the sorts of assumptions made historically by Plato or by Hobbes). Daly does not make those assumptions; which is why her writing can seem both off-the-wall and highly impractical to some readers. Consistently with her anarchism, her worldview is both animistic and optimistic.

The universe being sounded in **Pure Lust** is conceived wholly in organic metaphors. The natural harmony Daly believes in—among women, in nature generally, and between any organism and the rest of nature—is like the harmony of the parts and functions of a healthy plant or animal. It is "natural" in the sense that it is not a result of art or management—it does not require anything like our familiar, mundane and desperate striving and struggling or human-like conscious preconception and planning. It just happens; that's the way plants and animals are. So also, on a cosmic scale, harmony happens. Her world is in every way alive and active, and originally, essentially, naturally happy. Some of Daly's readers have thought her pessimistic or "negative," because of her unexpurgated analysis of the malevolence and ugliness of patriarchy, its agents and their machinations. Not so. It is the contrast between the world women experience in patriarchy and the world as she believes it might be (and in some sense *is* . . . patriarchy is "unreal") that gives her hope and makes imagination possible. She knows in her crone's bones the possibility of happiness. If it were not for that, she would not write raging and funny books but collapse in the horror of what she knows. (For the record, her analyses of the motives and means of men in power almost all seem to me mind-bogglingly right.)

In the last footnote in the book, Daly acknowledges the contributions of many other creatures—birds, butterflies, horses—who have been valuable companions to her in the course of the writing. I understand that companionship; but I have also struggled with another curriculum, in the tutelage of slugs, root maggots, striped cucumber beetles, scab, mold, aphids and sturdy colonies of wild geraniums established amongst the infant carrots. Working in our garden, we fertilize and barricade, spray and sprinkle, disperse purely organic poisons and "biological controls," and with our fingers squash or rip out small beings whose identities are not known but who look to an educated eye like suspicious characters. All this in our efforts to preserve from predation and fatal competition what is to be a significant part of our supply of relatively unpolluted food for the year. As we work, acquiring in the process nasty sunburns and mosquito bites which will harass us out of our rest at night, my lover and I have been known ironically to incant the syllables *bi-o-phil-i-a* to the tune of the Hallelujah Chorus. These experiences provoke my chariness about Daly's concepts of *natural, biophilic, wild* and *real*, as indeed some of my experience of friendship among women has also done. Certain kinds and degrees of enthusiasms are not possible for me, even though my bones too sometimes speak of happiness.

At some points in the development of life on this planet some human animals entered a kind of existence in which concepts like *weed* and *pest* had application, and in which human bodies were tortured regularly by the work of tillage, human livelihoods threatened by two more days with or without rain. Now most of us who have the time and will to philosophize subsist on food produced by the tortured labor of other miserably exploited people and with the aid of tons of dangerous chemicals. How are we to imagine feeding and sheltering all of us without exploiting any of us, and without engaging in that perilous struggle with nature which is agriculture and horticulture? We cannot become a planet of communities of hunter-gatherers migrating through territories abundant with the food and weather we need. The point is not that fructarian grazing is the only correct and "biophilic" way to eat. What bothers me is that I do not have a useful, practical, ordinary understanding of "love of life" or of that "harmony" in which we want to be with plants and planets and with other animals—including each other.

I do not believe Daly's anarchic harmony is natural in the sense of requiring no straining and no deliberate invention. I merely believe it is possible. That sets for me the tasks of figuring out how to love life, how to understand the fact that in nature living things kill and eat other living things all the time, how to behave honorably, virtuously when another's vital motion would block mine—or mine hers—*et cetera*.

In *Pure Lust*, Mary Daly's contribution to such work is indirect. It comes in the form of exemplary iconoclasm (the shattering of the concept of *species*, for instance, is music to my ears), lessons in method that are more like art lessons than cooking lessons (no recipes are given), a prodigious new profusion of metaphors for mixing into conceptions of ourselves, and the renewing encouragement of Daly's own terrific vitality and inventiveness.

Note

1. This may provide the answer to the conundrum given by Carol Anne Douglas in her review of *Pure Lust* in *off our backs* (June, 1984) as to how Daly can be both an essentialist and an existentialist, both of which she seems to be.

Julia Penelope (review date December 1987)

SOURCE: Penelope, Julia. "Erratic, Ecstatic, Eccentric." *Women's Review of Books* 5, no. 3 (December 1987): 5-6.

[*In the following review, Penelope offers a positive evaluation of* Websters' First New Intergalactic Wickedary of the English Language.]

Have you ever stopped in the middle of an intense conversation to search for the "right" word? Have you ever found yourself in an emotionally charged situation in which your mind went blank, and hours, even days, later suddenly realized what you could have said? When it happens to me, I say that I'm "at a loss for words," and spend sleepless nights scratching at "I should have said's."

Typically, our English teachers encourage us to believe that these lapses are our fault, that the language has all the resources one could ever want, and that we are somehow lacking—in vocabulary, cleverness, wit. But in language, as elsewhere, form follows function. As a consequence of male meddling, the English we are taught is adequate only for talking about the world and living in the world as men conceive the world to be. Male language has messed with our minds. The worldview codified by the syntax and semantics of English is only one version of the world we move and act in, and not necessarily the most enlightened or intelligent version.

Why, for example, do sex-specific pairs of adjectives—*womanly/manly, feminine/masculine, girlish/boyish*—exist (and persist)? Because the categories legitimized by those adjectives help maintain the heteropatriarchy. Without the concepts of opposition, duality and sexuality imposed by the names, it would be harder to keep us in our place; the categories define the boundaries of permissible behaviors, limiting the ways we think of our Selves. What would it be like to grow up female without the word *feminine* in your vocabulary?

And what about concepts, experiences and behaviors that are utterly unspeakable in English? How can we use English to talk about our vision of a nonpatriarchal society? How can we conceive, and then describe, non-oppressive relationships? What we can't talk about we're likely to have trouble thinking about.

In English, men rule and women serve. English is a structured code that permits easy expression only of those concepts that follow the ruts made by male speakers and writers during the past thousand years. Women often find ourselves at a loss for words, but it isn't our linguistic competence that's lacking; it's the vocabulary of English, a vocabulary that seems infinitely flexible and hospitable to new words that name people, objects, events, actions, feelings and perceptions—as long as they validate, and are sanctioned by, the privileged male class.

Do women speak English? It's hard to tell. If we believe male historians and grammarians, the answer is a qualified "no." According to patriarchal research, women have gossiped, chatted, prattled, prated and nagged. Women who dared to Speak, to express themSelves, have been systematically ignored, erased, demeaned and disappeared by male chroniclers. There are 1,200+ terms for what men "do [to women] in bed," but Women's Liberation and Feminism have added only a few precarious words to the English vocabulary.

Words like *screw, fuck* and *slut* have a long if disreputable career and everyone knows what they mean. *Sexism*, in contrast, stretched by humanists to include the "plight of men," is virtually meaningless now, and only a few speakers have heard of *heterosexism*. Just the other day, a politically-aware and active Lesbian asked a friend of mine what "lookist" (she meant *looksist*) referred to. She thought it meant staring at a woman longer than was socially acceptable! No wonder we miscommunicate more often than not.

Women have been unable, or unwilling, to force the kinds of language change that would make English more accommodating to us. (For example, none of the neutral pronouns proposed by second-wave Feminists have been adopted in popular usage.) Nor have women had the opportunity to make conceptual "grooves," because our history is so discontinuous. There's an Aphra Behn here, a Hildegard of Bingen there, yonder a Mary Wollstonecraft, and Mary Daly down the road a ways. But they do not find an audience with the power to ensconce them in public memories, libraries and classrooms. In fact, their works are quite regularly and systematically "lost."

Can it be that the majority of English-speaking women have never felt constrained or limited by their language? If our contemporary situation is a reliable indicator, perhaps so, although. I'm reluctant to accept that. Most women seem content to go on using the distorted, misogynistic vocabulary of English, even going so far as to write elaborate justifications for perpetuating it. (Even Lesbians seem comfortable talking about sexual relationships in patriarchal terms, as "monogamous" or "nonmonogamous," in spite of the fact that terms and concepts alike are inapplicable.)

What are we to do if we refuse to remain perpetually "at a loss for words"? I think we have only two options: construct an entirely new language, as Suzette Haden Elgin has done,[1] or discover and develop the hidden layers of English in ways amenable to our political consciousness, as Mary Daly does.

The **First New Intergalactic Wickedary** gathers up the skeins of Mary's previous work, particularly the attention to language of **Beyond God the Father** and the linguistic discoveries and innovations of **Gyn/Ecology** and **Pure Lust.** The result is a cunning weaving that offers women an articulate, coherent network (Word-Web), a linguistic tapestry woven from the possibilities of our lives and the future we might make with them. The breadth and resonance of the vision are daring and convincing. Contrasting the Elemental reality of Websters, Hags, Spinsters and Crones with the elementary reality embedded in patriarchal English, Mary conjures Other ways of Be-ing and Becoming on the boundaries between masculist descriptions of how women "should" be and our experience as we know it. If it is true that how we speak reflects the way we think (and I think it is) the language of the **Wickedary** gives us a colorful, reliable map of a New World made visible, a world women create as we Speak.

The **Wickedary** is a Sin-thesis ("a going into, beyond") of Mary's Archaic ("Original") Work, bringing Words and Concepts from her earlier books together with New/

Archaic Discoveries from the Be-Wishing ("influencing in a Magical way by ontological Wishing") Background ("the Realm of Wild Reality").

> The Labyrinthine design of the *Wickedary* may appear twisted and contorted to those accustomed only to linear patterns such as graphs and charts. In fact, its order is organic and purposeful, and it can be compared to a flock of Wild fowl in flight. . . . They [the flight and cries of words/birds] also awaken the *Labyrinth* of the reader/hearer, that is, "the internal ear" (*Webster's*), which Websters understand to be the Elemental capacity for Hearing our way into and through these passages of the Background—the Wild reality hidden by the falsehoods of the patriarchal foreground.
>
> (from the Preface)

Like the work of Fore-bear Gertrude Steirr, Mary Daly's is a discovered language that is purposefully, radically unsettling. For this reason, re-viewing the *Wickedary* requires using the Background language of its Conjuring: the Radical Feminist perspective of her vision demands that we learn to read and write in an Other consciousness.

Patriarchal words "take on New/Archaic meanings when Heard within the context of **Websters' First New Intergalactic Wickedary of the English Language.**" The *Wickedary* is about Context, "the weaving together of words"; "connection of words, coherence" (*Webster's Seventh New Collegiate Dictionary*).

The *Wickedary* is Self-Contextualizing. It is a *Metadictionary,* a "Metapatriarchal dictionary, written by and for Wicked/Wiccan Websters"; a "dictionary that Gossips out the Elemental webs of words hidden in patriarchal dictionaries and other re-sources." Like patriarchal dick-tionaries, the definitions in the *Wickedary* assume a specific way of perceiving and comprehending the world. Whereas *Webster's* definitions describe how words mean in the "foreground" (the heteropatriarchal context), the *Wickedary* presents the coherence and meaningfulness of Weird Words Spoken and Heard among the Inhabitants of the Background. "The work of the *Wickedary* is a process of freeing words from the cages and prisons of patriarchal patterns."

How does context redefine and re-present a word? *Harpy,* for instance, an insulting judgment of a woman's character in a patriarchal context, like *Shrew* and *Hag,* becomes high praise when Spoken and Heard in the Super Natural Background:

> *Harpy in* ["a shrewish or depraved woman"—*Webster's*]: A Shrewish and Enraged woman, one who harps on Haggard themes. *Example* Susan B Anthony. . . .

The Birds/Words fly the coop!

Every respectable patriarchal word-list is sandwiched between two bunches of supplementary material, the Front Matter and the Back Matter. The Front Matter may consist of essays on such foreground topics as why publish yet another dick-tionary, a superficial "history" of the English language, correct spelling, pronunciation and suchlike. The Back Matter usually consists of geographical and biographical information and Tables of Measures. No one bothers to read the Front or the Back Matter, because they are Boring, tiresome justifications of male meddling with English. The Labyrinthine organization of the *Wickedary,* in contrast, invites leisurely browsing/dousing through each of its three Phases. Each Journeyer should travel at her own speed.

The First Phase spans five Preliminary Webs (Front Matter) which give the Reader a Sense of Direction as she enters the Magical Realm of Re-membering, engaging her Labyrinthine Sense ("the faculty of Hearing the difference between Real, Elemental Words and mere elementary terms"). In these Eye-opening essays Mary urges Readers to discover the Elemental Code within them. She invokes the Guides who accompany Wild Women on their Otherworld Journeying, an Awe-ful Assemblage. As we Re-member our connections with Other Elemental beings and acquire Volcanic Virtues, we prepare Our Selves to join the Tribe of Terrible Women, according to the Wicked Law of Attraction, Be-Musing great dreams, Be-Speaking changes, and Be-Laughing man-made pseudo-reality.

I couldn't resist the Call of the Wild. Gathering my Wits about me, I gleefully accepted Mary's invitation to embark on the Second Phase of this Journey, the three Word-Webs that comprise the Core of the *Wickedary.* These Weird ("earthy," "uncanny.") Wordlists chart the Background where the Race of Wild Women dwells and expose the stagnant, phallic consciousness of the patriarchal foreground ("Flatland"). Minding my Metamysterious Map, I Activized my Active Eyes and set off to Familiarize My Self with the Activities and Characteristics of the Background Inhabitants, to explore the Crone-logical Constellation of Haggard women (among them Sojourner Truth, Judy Grahn, Ma Rainey, Alix Dobkin, Emily Culpepper, Virginia Woolf, Alice Walker and Valerie Solanas).

As I traversed Word-Web One I was Amazed at the gaggle of terms and definitions that "Name Wild Reality and its patriarchal counterfeits from the perspective of those who choose the Background as our Homeland, . . . Living on the Boundary Between the worlds." These are the key words of the Outsiders' Society that release us to the Archespheres, "the Realm of true beginnings, where Shrews shrink alienating archetypes . . . uncovering the Archimage, the Original Witch within." This Word-Web distinguishes between

Biophilic Communication ("the natural communication among Elemental creatures—animals, plants, seas, the sun, the moon, the stars") and the use of the Biggest Lies (a "fundamental strategy of the Cockocratic State for breaking minds/spirits/senses."), between Tidal Demons ("Goddesses, Geniuses, Spirits") and tidy demons, the evil dispiriters . . . that fix the flow of women's creativity." Uplifted by Tidal Memory, my "Memory of the Deep Background," and my own Wonderlust ("strong and unconquerable longing for Elemental adventure and knowledge"), I spun into the Background:

Word-Web Two "introduces the reader to the Natives, their world view and customs, describes places of interest, and provides words and phrases necessary for communication in the Country of the Strange": the *Abecedarians*, Be-Spelling women who combine and recombine "the Elements of words in New ways, Hearing New Words into be-ing"; *Fore-Bears*, Foresisters "of Great Bears and Little Bears, honored by all Bearish Women"; and *Silly* ("Happy, Blessed, Graceful") *Quacks*, "quick, queenly" utterances, "the quintessential Elemental" cries of ducks.

These Super Natural Be-ings are given to such Batty behaviors as *Dis-ordering*—"Tidal Weaving and Reweaving; breaking through the tidy order/orders of Boredom"—and *Gossip*—exercising "the Elemental Female Power of Naming, especially in the Presence of other Gossips," taking part "in the festivity of word-play among Boon-Companions" and telling "like a Gossip," divining and communicating "the secrets of the Elements, the wisdom of the stars."

With so much to do, it was difficult to find time to brew even a tempest in a teapot, but I did succeed in attending several *Cat/astrophes,* events "precipitated by Catty Conspirators that [subvert] the patriarchal order or system of things," went *Con-Questing* with Amazon Argonauts, "adventuring into Uncharted/Unchartable Realms," and hung out with a bunch of "extraordinarily Strange, Eccentric" *Weirdies*. I skipped out on the Dryads, Furies, Familiars, Websters and Weird Sisters, and hopped on over to Word-Web Three to see what I could See.

Well, I probably don't need to tell you who the inhabitants of the foreground are: the usual gang of fools, frauds, gaffers, gaggers, snools and snotboys. There they all were, *snooking* ("prying about while sniffing and smelling") and *spooking* ("fabricating confusion"). The *pricks,* self-important members "of the thrusting throng," were eye-deep in their own *bull,* "the most solemn and respected form of discourse under patriarchy," leaving behind them a trail of *logocide,* "the systematic murder of logos (reason) in patriarchy, the State of Sleeping Death" and *verbicide,* "the systematic murder of words; the reduction of living words to the condition of mere noises echoing each other through the hollow world of the hollow men." Their *dick-speaking* and *flashing* ("compulsively" exposing their "inadequacies") were Boring and predicktable. There's not much to be said about patriarchal elementary intelligence that is Fascinating, but it's worth a Glance, because here you'll find, alphabetized, classified and defined, all the men and some of the women you know.

Abandoning Yahweh & Son and Yessir Professor to their own devices, I arrived at the Third Phase of the **Wickedary,** four "Deliberately Delirious essays designed to assist Wicked women to stray and stay off the tracks of trained responses and traditional expectations."

The essays of this "Back Matter" move from the analysis and description of the elementary terms of patriarchy to an explanation of the Real Acts of Be-Laughing, Nixing, Hexing and X-ing; they end by roaming into the Wild Realms beyond patriarchal space/time, travelling Widdershins, Counter-clockwise, away from the clockocracy. Here I found explicit descriptions of how man-handling abuses the English language. Mary exposes four patriarchal linguistic tactics. Reversal, the fourth tactic, for example, takes five forms: simple inversion (Ronald Reagan called "The Great Communicator"), reversals that take the elementary world as the model for natural phenomena (the prevalent metaphor that Elemental beings are machines), reversals that project patriarchal male qualities onto women and nature (attributing "penis envy" to women, calling other animals "predatory"), male reversals that appropriate women's capacities and qualities (*gynecologist*), and reversals by redundancy and contradiction ("weapons of life," "just war"). Naming these linguistic tricks and identifying the common varieties of foreground messages empowers women by showing how we can Be-Laugh Our Selves beyond their mind-binding (w)raps.

Some entries I expected to find but didn't. In **Gyn/Ecology** Mary discovered the tidy bifurcation of related words in patriarchal English, revealing how men had reserved control of *text, grammar* and *spelling* to themselves, leaving women the less prestigious and respectable realms of *textile, glamour* and *spells*. A similar pair of words, *Cosmic/cosmetic,* would have fit well in the **Wickedary.** Their significance dovetails neatly with the first three, and the point is implicit in the Metadictionary, where *Cosmic* occurs in several phrases. But when I turned to Word-Web Three, where I expected to find *cosmetic* between *consumer society* and *covert,* an appealing position for it, it wasn't there. Nor did I find the noun *friend* (from Old English *freond,* "free one") listed in Word-Web Two, an entry which would have elaborated the participial *Be-Friending* of Word-Web One. Too obvious? Overlookings? Lost notecards?

Many of the *Wickedary*'s entries are (surprisingly) adjectives or nouns. I found this disturbing because the Verb as concept is central to Mary's Metaethics, as is evident in the pages of the *Wickedary* itself. The phrase *Goddess the Verb* is defined as a "Metaphor for Ultimate/Intimate Reality, the constantly Unfolding Verb of Verbs in which all being participates . . . ," and *Being*, first introduced in **Beyond God the Father,** is similarly defined: "Ultimate/Intimate Reality, the constantly. Unfolding Verb of Verbs which is intransitive, having no object that limits its dynamism . . ." With so much ethical emphasis on verbiness, I wonder why entries like *Be-Musing, Be-Tidings, Prance of Life,* and *Metabeing,* to name a few, are entered in the *Wickedary* as nouns rather than verbs, treated as states rather than processes. Making them into verbs for Our Selves is easy enough, and I'm sure this will happen, but I'd like to know why Mary handled these entries as she did, especially when she's given us such powerful verbs as *Dragonize, Gorgonize* and *Eyebite/I-Bite*.

It's unfair to expect everything all at once, even from Mary Daly, and these omissions won't detract from the pleasures awaiting Other perusers of the *Wickedary*. There's enough word-weaving here to keep us Spinning until Mary's next book Aeromantically Activizes our Powers of Be-ing. I found my-Self Leafing/Leaping through for hours, discovering words I hadn't known existed (*depravation, maffick, fremitus*), words I'd known and used and but never looked up (*cheeky, dizzy, tough, jinx, apperception*) and what I think may be a hitherto hidden etymological relationship between Modern English *war* and Old English *wer,* the now obsolete word that once meant "male human being."

Because the *Wickedary* is erratic ("having no fixed course"), ecstatic ("causing to stand out") and eccentric ("out of the center"), its probabilities are Cosmic. It succeeds in a way that most books should, but don't: the information it provides is a springboard for the reader, Sparking her to discoveries and revelations of her own. Instead of working on this review, I was busy writing down: new words that Named themSelves: *Sinthesis, Nix-mister, nixonize.* It is a Starting/Sparking Place for all who've been itching to scratch lexical limitations.

Readers accustomed to the empty, meaningless, monotonous English of Reagan and the naughty/not-I windbags will find the *Wickedary* tough ("strong or firm in texture but flexible and not brittle"; "not easily chewed"; "characterized by severity or uncompromising determination"). But if you find that the Prancing, Frolicking phrases and sentences are making you dizzy and Brewing Brainstorms—you're experiencing Sylph-consciousness.

Note

1. Láadan means "the language of those who perceive," and it's a language structured specifically to enable women to talk about "chunks of reality" that matter to them but that "have not been given names of their own before." (This idea is the subject of Elgin's S/F novel, *Native Tongue*.) Having worked my way through both the grammar and dictionary of Láadan, I didn't find many "chunks of reality"-lexicalized that aren't already available to us in English. Notable exceptions include an expanded group of terms naming different kinds of "love," and a set of terms for describing several ways a heterosexual woman might feel about being pregnant, but the number of "encodings," as described in *Native Tongue,* is disappointingly small. Male violence, a variety of experience shared by a majority of women, is invisible in Láadan. There is no word for rape.

Jane Hedley (essay date spring 1992)

SOURCE: Hedley, Jane. "Surviving to Speak New Language: Mary Daly and Adrienne Rich." *Hypatia* 7, no. 2 (spring 1992): 40-62.

[*In the following excerpt, Hedley discusses Daly's attempt to depose male-defined language through etymological reconstructions and the invention of a new vocabulary for women, culminating in* Websters' First New Intergalactic Wickedary of the English Language.]

As radical feminists seeking to overcome the linguistic oppression of women, Rich and Daly apparently shared the same agenda in the late 1970s; but they approached the problem differently, and their paths have increasingly diverged. Whereas Daly's approach to the repossession of language is code-oriented and totalizing, Rich's approach is open-ended and context-oriented. Rich has therefore addressed more successfully than Daly the problem of language in use.

* * *

"For many women," Adrienne Rich explained in 1977, in her introduction to the collected poetry of Judy Grahn, "the commonest words are having to be sifted through, rejected, laid aside for a long time, or turned to the light for new colors and flashes of meaning: *power, love, control, violence, political, personal, private, friendship, community, sexual, work, pain, pleasure, self, integrity.* . . . When we become acutely, disturbingly aware of the language we are using and that is using us, we begin to grasp a material resource that women have never before collectively attempted to repossess" (*LSS* [*On Lies, Secrets, and Silence: Selected Prose 1966-1978*], 247).[1] The attempt to repossess language has been an important dimension of second wave feminism in the United States. For many feminists, this attempt has crystallized as "the great he/she battle" (Nilsen 1984): the struggle to discredit "generic he," along with a large set of nouns that are officially gender-neutral but have installed masculine gender as normative for entire categories of persons, and indeed for the human species as a whole. The he/she battle is for "equal opportunity," with an emphasis on the ways in which standard usage interferes with women's efforts to hold their own in public life and in the world of work.[2] Meanwhile, however, radical feminists have found it more important to stress that "the oppressor's language" interferes with women's ability to communicate and bond with one another. Thus, for example, in a poem called "Natural Resources" (1977), Rich announced:

> There are words I cannot choose again:
>
> *humanism*
> *androgyny*
>
> Such words have no shame in them, no diffidence before the raging stoic grandmothers:
>
> Their glint is too shallow, like a dye that does not permeate
>
> the fibers of actual life as we live it, now:
>
> (*FD* [*The Fact of a Doorframe: Poems Selected and New 1950-1984*], 262-63)

Here Rich expresses the conviction that an equal-opportunity agenda is not radical enough: gender-neutral usage cannot grasp the specificity of women's experience in the present, and it short-circuits the attempt to rescue a collective past from the oblivion to which the history of "mankind" has largely consigned women's lives.

In 1978, Mary Daly spoke in very similar terms of being engaged in an ongoing collective process of sifting and winnowing the words that feminist women would use to speak of important matters: "There are some words which appeared to be adequate in the early seventies, which feminists later discovered to be false words. Three such words . . . which I cannot use again are God, androgyny, and homosexuality" (Daly 1978, xi). Thus in 1977-78 Rich and Daly apparently shared the same agenda, as lesbian feminists whose "dream of a common language"—Rich's phrase, originally—gave direct expression to a politics of woman-bonding and woman-identification. "The crucible of a new language," Rich asserts in the Grahn introduction (1977), is *that primary presence of women to ourselves and each other* first described in prose by Mary Daly" (*LSS,* 250); meanwhile in *Gyn/Ecology* Daly hails Rich as a "boundary breaking poet and warrior" with whom she shares in an "uncommon quest for 'a common language'" (Daly 1978, xvii). Daly's "uncommon quest" would culminate ten years later in **Websters' First New Intergalactic Wickedary of the English Language.** Meanwhile, however, Rich was coming to understand her own relationship to language differently, and she would "survive to speak new language"[3] on very different terms.

There are two different ways of construing radical feminism, suggests the Australian feminist critic Meaghan Morris: as "a *politics* which works on whatever all women have in common" or as "a *theory* of the determining role played by sex over class, economic and cultural factors in the oppression of women" (Morris [1982] 1988, 46).[4] Ever since **Gyn/Ecology,** Daly's commitment to radical feminism in Morris's second sense has been unequivocal and unwavering: it has, if anything, strengthened in response to opposition from both inside and outside the feminist movement. In the 1970s Rich apparently shared this commitment: in "Compulsory Heterosexuality and Lesbian Existence" (1978), she argued that "the power men everywhere wield over women . . . has become a model for every other form of exploitation and illegitimate control" (*BBP* [*Blood, Bread, and Poetry: Selected Prose 1979-1985*], 68). But Rich explicitly distanced herself from this position during the 1980s: in "Notes toward a Politics of Location" (1984), she is outspokenly critical of "a form of [American] feminism so focused on male evil and female victimization that it . . . allows for no differences among women, men, places, times, cultures, conditions, classes, movements" (*BBP,* 221). The approach she favors in 1984 is one that would shelve the whole primacy question and broaden the feminist agenda by acknowledging that "most women in the world must fight for their lives on many fronts at once" (*BBP,* 218).

In one of Rich's earliest formulations of the problem both she and Daly have sought to address, we can begin to see how Rich's language radicalism would also come to differ from Daly's:

> This is the oppressor's language
> yet I need it to talk to you
>
> (*FD,* 117)

In this pair of lines from a poem dated 1968, the boldly totalizing generalization about language is very much in the spirit of Daly's project; yet Rich has framed that generalization as a particular instance of discourse. She uses the deictic words "This," "I," and "you" to stage the subjective experience of a particular woman, at a particular historical juncture, who is actively trying to communicate with someone else.[5] Rich's formulation thus calls attention to the two different modes in which language exists for us simultaneously: as a system of already encoded meanings and as ongoing, open-ended meaning-making activity.

From the outset, Daly's effort to repossess language has been code-oriented: "the oppressor's language" has presented itself to her as a totalizing system that must be modeled as such and completely dismantled. Her priorities are those of a systematic theologian for whom the power of words belongs primarily to their "cosmic" function—their power to name reality into being. Meanwhile Rich, though by no means indifferent to the cosmic power of words, has always been even more obsessed with their communicative function: in the foreword (1984) to her poetry collection *The Fact of a Doorframe,* she writes that her worst fear as a poet has always been "that these words will fail to enter another soul" (*FD*, xv). Rich's approach to the repossession of language has therefore always been context- or usage-oriented. And whereas Daly's "master trope"[6] is metaphor, the trope that uses the code against itself to produce semantic novelty through deviant predication, Rich favors metonymy, the trope of contexture, as she struggles to keep the language of her poetry grounded in "the actual world."[7]

Both Daly's code-oriented, "metaphoric" approach to the repossession of language and Rich's context-oriented, "metonymic" approach are "radical," in the sense that language itself is what they have sought to change.[8] Their difference exposes a tension that belongs to language itself in its dual existence as *langue* and *parole*—a code whose structures we internalize, but also the changing, context-sensitive medium of our dealings with one another.

WIELDING OUR LABRYSES: MARY DALY AND THE DEEP SPINNING POWER OF METAPHOR

Derived from the Greek *meta* (meaning after, behind, transformative of, beyond) and *pherein* (meaning to bear, carry), *metaphor* in the deepest sense suggests the power of words to carry us into a Time/Space that is after, behind, transformative of, and beyond static being—the status maintained by phallocracy.

(Daly 1973, xix)

Daly begins *Websters' First New Intergalactic Wickedary of the English Language* by explaining that "the word *webster,* according to *Webster's Third New International Dictionary of the English Language,* is derived from the Old English *webbestre,* meaning female weaver" (Daly and Caputi 1987, xiii). Under the entry for *Webster,* she credits Judy Grahn with this Discovery and cites *The Queen of Wands,* where Grahn engages in speculative etymology:

The word-weavers of recent centuries who have given us the oration of Daniel Webster and the dictionary listings of Merriam-Webster stem from English family names that once descended through the female line. Some great-grandmother gave them her last name, *Webster,* she-who-weaves.

(Quoted in Daly and Caputi 1987, 178)

This metaetymology models both the process whereby words can be said to have been stolen from women and the strategy Daly uses to repossess them: "a process of freeing words from the cages and prisons of patriarchal patterns" (Daly and Caputi 1987, 3).

In the *Wickedary,* weaving becomes the prototypical strategy of feminist lexicography. The book consists of a series of "Word-Webs"—"according to *Webster's* [Third International], the first meaning of web is 'a fabric as it is being woven on a loom . . .'" (Daly and Caputi 1987, xvii)—and Daly invites her readers to conceive of language itself as a fabric that was originally woven by women in conversation with one another. She cites conversations with other women as sources for some of her entries, to convey that she and her Cronies are once again actively engaged in language-making; and she stresses that the *Wickedary* itself is not, and could not be, finished. In the preface she explains that she has intended to model a certain "tension between incompletion and completion" (Daly and Caputi 1987, xviii)—between language as meaning making activity and language as system of signs.[9]

Daly's understanding of language is close to that of sociologist Peter Berger,[10] who treats language as the primary agent of what he calls "world-building." Human society, as theorized by Berger, is a "world-building enterprise," and language is the means by which the social world is constituted for its members as a meaningful order, or "nomos": "Every empirical language may be said to constitute a nomos in the making, or, with equal validity, as the historical consequence of the nomizing activity of generations of men [*sic*]" (Berger 1967, 20). From the perspective of nomos in the making, language is an ongoing, open-ended activity that expresses the human craving for meaning; but as the product of this activity, language "acts back upon" its producers and their descendants, imposing its conventions upon them as their patrimony. "The original nomizing act is to say that an item *is this,* and thus *not that.* As this original incorporation of the item into an order that includes other items is followed by sharper linguistic designations (the item is male and not female, singular and not plural, a noun and not a verb, and so forth), the nomizing act intends a comprehensive order of *all* items that may be linguistically objectivated" (Berger 1967, 20-21). Berger emphasizes that although the nomizing act is totalizing in its intention, in fact it never attains to totality: "just as there can be no totally socialized individual, so there will always be individual meanings that remain outside of or marginal to the common nomos" (Berger 1967, 20).

Like Berger, Daly regards language as the objectified consequence of an activity, but for Daly "the nomizing activity of generations of men" has been a conspiracy to uproot and stultify language. Dictionaries epitomize for Daly a whole set of cultural activities—including theology, metaphysics, gynecology, as well as lexicography—that have codified, in order to fix and perpetuate, the patriarchal status quo (otherwise known in Daly's writings as Stag-nation, or the State of the Living Dead). They have sought to legitimate pseudorealities—"civilization," "history," "God"—that alienate women from their own world-making powers. Dictionaries make a pretense of establishing the true senses of words by tracing them back to their earliest forms, but these etymologies have "no Originality in them": "appearing capable of taking us back to our roots or to first principles or sources, they in fact block access to Origins" (Daly and Caputi 1987, 244). Fortunately, however, this work of deracination has not entirely succeeded: thus *Webster's*, the *American Heritage Dictionary* and the *O.E.D.* "contain fragments of and clues to our own stolen heritage" (Daly and Caputi 1987, xxiii).

The **Wickedary** situates itself on the boundary of what Berger calls "the common nomos"; but whereas for Berger all that can be glimpsed beyond that boundary are individual meanings and the terrifying specter of "anomie," for Daly the boundary is a vantage-point from which women, collectively, can begin to Activize Original Be-ing. A Witch or Hag—Daly has used the *O.E.D.* to trace *Hag* back to a "prehistoric" West-Germanic compound with components akin to Old English *haga* "hedge" and Old German *dus* "devil"—is one who "haunts the Hedges/Boundaries of patriarchy, frightening fools and summoning Weird Wandering Women into the Wild" (Daly and Caputi 1987, 137). "Sitting on the Fence between the worlds," she "is engaged not only in Boundary Living but also in Boundary Breaking" (Daly and Caputi 1987, 267). The way that language can be enlisted for Boundary Living and Boundary Breaking is through the power of metaphor. "To a large extent," Daly explains, "metaphors are the language and the vessels of metapatriarchal Spiraling, that is, of Be-Witching" (Daly 1984, 404).

In her **Wickedary** entry under *Metaphors, Metapatriarchal,* Daly dissociates herself from the ornamental or figures-of-speech view of metaphor,[11] defining it in a way that is consistent with Suzanne Langer's account of metaphor and its role in language and with the work of more recent theorists of metaphor such as Max Black and Paul Ricoeur. According to Ricoeur, for example, metaphor produces semantic innovation through "deviant predication." We make a metaphor when we combine a subject and a predicate whose common or usual meanings clash in some important way. The predication thus produced is deviant, but if the metaphor succeeds it is also acceptable: its impertinence does not disappear but is overcome, since we have recourse to connotations or secondary semantic features of its crucial words. Metaphors thereby have the potential for enlarging the domain of what seems possible or can be thought: "*new* predicative meaning emerges from the collapse of . . . the meaning which obtains if we rely only on the common or usual lexical values of our words" (Ricoeur [1978] 1981, 232).

Metaphors thus live on the boundaries of conventional usage. When we speak of a dead or faded metaphor, we are citing a process whereby those boundaries have shifted: the conventional range of application of a particular expression has been extended through the assimilation of what had once been deviant, metaphorical applications. Suzanne Langer suggests that every new idea "evokes first of all some metaphoric expression. As the idea becomes familiar, this expression 'fades' to a new literal sense of the once metaphorical predicate, a more general use than it had before." This, Langer argues, is how language grows: metaphor is "the power whereby . . . new words are born and merely analogical meanings become stereotyped into literal definitions" (Langer 1942, 141). Langer's theory of language is based on a speculative account of its origins in a prediscursive human capacity for symbolic thinking: metaphor is for Langer not only the power whereby new words are born, but also the power of abstraction by which words as such were born in the first place, out of the sounds our prelinguistic forebears must have used to greet significant events.[12]

The process Langer treats as a positive or at least necessary one, insofar as it is central to the elaboration and maturation of languages, is assimilated by Daly to a process linguists call "pejoration," whereby words associated with women and their activities have, over time, become negatively stereotyped. "Like Langer, Shrews are aware of apparently faded metaphors, but . . . Shrewish analysis discovers a sexual politics of fading" (Daly 1984, 28). Daly is especially interested in words still used to denote women and their activities whose etymologies connect them with the elemental symbols of prediscursive thought, so that they seem to be etymologically linked to collective intuitions of Original Be-ing. Thus, for example, she reclaims the meaning of the word *spinster* not only by challenging the negative stereotype of the unmarried woman and restoring primacy to the word's original meaning, "a woman whose occupation is to spin" (Daly and Caputi 1987, 167), but also by attaching to that occupation a mythic dimension of meaning. She reminds us that in mythology the Fates are Spinsters (Daly 1978, 176): thus she discovers in this woman's occupation a presentational symbol for elemental cosmic process. *Spinning* becomes, in Daly's lexicon, a woman-identified synonym for world making: "Gyn/Ecological creation; Discovering the lost thread of connectedness within the cosmos . . ." (Daly 1978, 96). She regards the fading of the word's symbolic resonance as a semantic impoverishment and as evidence of a patriarchal conspiracy to divest language of its cosmic power. Restoring that power is a metaphoric process that gives the word *Spinster* several dimensions or levels of meaning: "When, for example, I say 'Spinsters Spin,' multi-leveled images of creation and change are evoked" (Daly 1984, 404).

In other instances, the work that metaphor does for Daly is critical rather than "cosmic." Thus, for example, she explains in the preface to her fourth book, **Pure Lust,** that its title has a double meaning. In lowercase, this phrase invokes the current, conventional meaning of *lust* and is used to Name the "life-hating lechery" that "assails women and nature on all levels"; at the same time, however, Daly reclaims a more positive definition, now obsolete, of lust—"intense longing or eagerness"—so that in uppercase, the phrase can be used to mean "simple sheer striving for abundance of be-ing" (Daly 1984, 2-4). The phrase **Pure Lust** thus becomes a double-edged "labrys": it refers to both the problem and its solution, the State of Bondage and the energy that will launch Wild Women into freedom. Just as with *Spinster,* the woman-identified definition of **Pure Lust** cites its more archaic, "original" meaning. In this case, however, Daly's strategy is to put the word's two meanings in conflict: she uses deviant predication to overcome the conventional, current meaning of *lust*; and deviance, as a feminist survival strategy, is thematized by the double definition.

Language can only do the consciousness-altering work Daly wants it to do insofar as words are used disruptively, jarringly, deconstructively: "Websters are aware that new words are new in the sense they are heard in an Other semantic context" (Daly 1984, 404). Thus many of Daly's neologisms are self-contextualizing compounds (*Nag-Gnosticism, Pure Lust*) that have metaphoric deviance built right into them, and she will often mix her metaphors, to keep them fade-resistant. In **Pure Lust** she explains that metaphoric predication is a safeguard against building a new prisonhouse on the ruins of the old one, which is what will happen if radical feminists begin "accepting Hag-identified new words as taken-for-granted labels" (Daly 1984, 404).

Long before Daly's linguistic project had emerged full-blown in the **Wickedary,** Meaghan Morris made a telling criticism of her whole approach to language. Writing for the Marxist journal *Intervention,* after Daly had made a controversial appearance in Sydney, Australia, in 1981, Morris accuses her of using language to create a self-enclosed speech community of the elect, and thereby largely ignoring the problem of "*language in use*" (Morris [1982] 1988, 30). Daly, Morris argues, appears to subscribe to the view that "there is a strength-potential in isolated signs which is sufficient to overcome the histories of their use":

> The word *race*, for example can be cheerfully put to 'new' political purposes by reviving the dictionary 'meanings' of rushing onwards, or of two tides meeting in a choppy sea—while the function of *race* in certain particular discourses, the history of those discourses, and the histories which those discourses have made and still make possible, remains . . . entirely beside the point.
>
> (Morris [1982] 1988, 42)

Morris takes issue with this position in no uncertain terms: "Unlike Mary Daly," she writes, "I do not believe that 'meanings' are in 'words,' but that meaning is produced in specific contexts of discourse" (Morris [1982] 1988, 32).

Morris's objection should not be taken to suggest that Daly is naive about how language works, or about how meaning is produced: as we have seen, her metaphoric feats rely on adroit manipulation of context. What Morris has recognized, however, is that Daly's discourse is *self*-contextualizing and auto-telic to a quite remarkable degree. This tendency is not nearly so pronounced in **Beyond God the Father** (1973), the first book she wrote after her conversion to radical feminism, as it is in **Gyn/Ecology,** where she undertook to expose and denounce "the totality of the lie which is patriarchy" (Daly 1978, 20), and in **Pure Lust,** which is structured to model an "Otherworld Journey of Exorcism and Ecstasy" (Daly 1984, x). In **Beyond God the Father** Daly was still making arguments. Here is a sample paragraph from that work, with italics added to highlight its discursive framework to the extent that Daly has made that framework explicit:

> A *qualitatively different understanding* of justice also *emerges when* the peculiar rigidities of the stereotypic male no longer dominate the scene. *Tillich has written of* transforming or creative justice, which goes beyond calculating in fixed proportions. *Unfortunately, he tries to uphold the idea that* "the religious symbol for this is the kingdom of God." *I suggest that* as long as we are under the shadow of a kingdom, real or symbolic, there will be no creative justice. *The transforming and creative element in justice has been intuited and dimly expressed by the term* "equity." *Aristotle defined this as* a correction of law where it is "defective owing to its universality." *What this leaves out is* the dynamic and changing quality of justice which does not presuppose that there are fixed and universal essences, but which is open to new data of experience.
>
> (Daly 1973, 128)

In this paragraph, Daly's linguistic usage is neither transgressive nor uncommon, and neither is her discursive procedure. The "qualitatively different understanding of justice" she seeks to establish is played off against classic formulations with which she disagrees but which afford a discursive context for her own. If the effort to redefine justice presages her growing interest in total renovation of the lexicon of "first philosophy," it nevertheless acknowledges and connects with the ways this concept has been understood within the tradition of Western metaphysics.

In **Pure Lust** Daly again cites Tillich's notion of "creative justice." Instead of paraphrasing Tillich, this time, she quotes him directly, after declaring that his formulation is "so alien to Pyrosophical awareness and analysis . . . that it will make a feminist's flesh crawl" (Daly 1984, 276). She sets up her quotation from Tillich as a separate block of text, suggesting that the reader try imagining a priest, rabbi, or minister reciting it to a woman who has been repeatedly battered by her husband. "What happens in such a case," Daly explains, is that "the woman is morally bullied [by Tillich's notion of creative justice] into forfeiting her right to judge . . . [and] breaking her own Naming process." We conclude that "Tillich's moral verbiage . . . is worse than useless" and that "*justice* is not an adequate name for that which Canny, Raging women create." Daly has already proposed that we substitute the woman-identified term *Nemesis*, and she now proceeds to explain why this would be desirable:

> The new psychic alignment of gynergy patterns associated with Nemesis is not merely rectifying of a situation which the term *unjust* could adequately describe. Nemesis is Passionate Spinning/Spiraling of new/ancient forms and connections of gynergy. It is an E-motional habit acquired/required in the Pyrospheres. It demands Shrewd as well as Fiery judgment and is therefore a Nag-Gnostic Pyrognostic Virtue. Nemesis is a habit built up by inspired acts of Righteous Fury, which move the victims of gynocidal oppression into Pyrospheric changes unheard of in patriarchal lore.
>
> (Daly 1984, 277)

What we should notice about this entire passage is not only that Daly is now unwilling to engage in dialogue with Tillich, but that her text's relationship to its hypothetical readers has also changed. Both Tillich's account of "creative justice" and her own celebration of Nemesis are proffered to the reader not as arguments, but as rival incantations. We are to imagine a priest or a rabbi reciting Tillich's text, and then, having repudiated his "moral verbiage," we are to enter into a "new psychic alignment of gynergy patterns" as Daly's verbal Pyro-technics burst upon us. In repudiating the moral verbiage of Tillich and his ilk, we not only disagree with him and reject his approach to the definition of justice, we leave his world for another—the world Daly's discourse weaves around us.[13]

Daly relies on what Roman Jakobson calls the "poetic function" of language (Jakobson [1960a] 1987) to set her discourse apart from the ordinary language of patriarchy and to strengthen its internal cohesiveness. The rhythms of her prose are often incantatory, and she makes lavish use of alliteration to "conjure the Chorus of Wild Racing Words" (Daly and Caputi 1987, xvii). These are poetic strategies that promote an iconic relation between sound and meaning, signifier and signified. Her neologizing compounds, her hyphenations and capitalizations, likewise call attention to the process of signification, forcing us to attend very carefully to the shapes of words. All of these strategies work together to foster the illusion that words do indeed possess their meanings intrinsically—that they have an inherent power or life of their own.[14] But this is only an illusion, one that Daly has to work very hard to create. In the preface to **Gyn/Ecology** she betrays this by claiming, with Humpty-Dumpty-ish bravado,[15] that the word she has coined for her title "says exactly what I want it to say"—and then taking three pages to explain what she wants it to say, in explicit defiance of the standard definition of *gynecology,* which she quotes from the *O.E.D.* The prominence and frequency of this kind of explicit word-definition is much greater in **Gyn/Ecology** than in Daly's earlier writings, and greater still in **Pure Lust,** the work that immediately predates the **Wickedary.** In **Pure Lust** it begins to seem as if word-redefinition had become the primary task of Elemental Feminist Philosophy.

As we proceed through Daly's writings chronologically we can thus, as it were, see the **Wickedary** coming. Despite her intention to model an open-ended, ongoing process of community-building through language, and despite the commitment to dialogue with other women that she often professes, Daly's "uncommon quest" has developed according to an inner logic of its own.[16] The **Wickedary** is full of "we"-statements, but the collectivity or community they invoke is internally generated by a proliferating series of epithets that reinforce one another in a circular fashion within the work itself: "*Webster's* do not use words, *we* Muse words"; "*Wild women* recognize *our* Guide Words . . ." (42); "*Wise women* . . . find here clues to *our* own liberation"; "*Wicked women* Announce *our* Departure from the State of Patriarchal Paralyis" (Daly and Caputi 1987, 24, 42, 284; italics added).[17] The women's community whose Naming process Daly champions in the **Wickedary** is an abstraction—not the agent but the figment of its prophetic exhortations. . . .

Whereas Daly's "uncommon quest" has resulted in a language that is so uncommon as to have no general currency, Rich's most recent writings suggest that she is no longer dreaming of a common language at all. Where she does call attention to particular words and their meanings, she emphasizes that a particular word has meant different things to the same person at different points in her life, or stages encounters in which differently located usages need to be respected. Her 1986 poem "Negotiations," for example, is addressed to a sister poet with whom, it seems, she has often angrily disagreed:

> Someday if someday comes we will agree
> that trust is not about safety
> that keeping faith is not about deciding
> to clip our fingernails exactly
> to the same length or wearing
> a uniform that boasts our unanimity
>
> (TP [*Time's Power*], 9)

Their hypothetical truce-day will not come, the speaker is suggesting, until she and her interlocutor have become more comfortable with their differences: thus, with respect to the words *truth* and *faith* her strategy here is not to formulate positive definitions, but by means of negative definitions to forestall premature closure.

Rich's career has followed a trajectory that is more or less the opposite of Daly's. Even as Daly's project of code-renovation has disclosed its totalizing intention more and more clearly, Rich has tried—more valuably, I think—to keep faith with the historical, material conditions of language in use. Perhaps the most important lesson she has for us is that there is no question of getting any word's meaning finally "right." Meanings are not "in" words, and the kind of usage-oriented change that Rich has consistently modeled for feminist readers is open toward the future as well as the past.

Notes

1. Where possible, in quoting from Rich's poems and prose writings, I will use abbreviations to refer the reader to three collections:

   LSS for *On Lies, Secrets and Silence: Selected Prose 1966-1978*; BBP for *Blood, Bread, and Poetry: Selected Prose 1979-1985*; FD for *The Fact of a Doorframe: Poems Selected and New 1950-1984*.

   Poems from *The Dream of a Common Language* (1978) and *A Wild Patience Has Taken Me This Far* (1981b) that were not reprinted in *FD* are referred to DCL and WP. Poems written after 1984 and published in *Time's Power* (1989) are referred to TP. The date that appears in my text will always, however, be the date Rich provides to establish when she wrote the poem or when she delivered or published the prose piece originally.

2. On the whole, American feminists have been more pragmatically interventionist than feminists working in the French intellectual tradition have been, as Betsy Draine (1989) points out. Their efforts have resulted in the adoption of guidelines for nonsexist usage by most of the major educational publishers in this country and by many organizations concerned with the teaching of English. For a bibliography of these guidelines, see Frank and Treichler (1989, 310-14).

3. This phrase is taken from "Transcendental Etude" (*FD*, 267), a 1977 poem I will be using later on to illustrate Rich's approach to the repossession of language.

4. For a brief account of the origins and development of radical feminism, see Eisenstein (1983, 125-35).

5. The gender of her interlocutor is not specified, but in view of the poem's date and her references to love-making between them I infer that Rich in this poem is still "trying to talk to a man."

6. This phrase was coined by Kenneth Burke (1941), whose suggestive discussion of metaphor and metonymy predates Jakobson's more precise linguistic analysis.

7. The classic discussion of metaphor and metonymy as opposed, complementary radicals of language is Jakobson ([1960b] 1987).

8. Within the British feminist movement, which has taken its bearings from a Marxist tradition of social and political analysis, the radical feminist approach is criticized for paying too little attention to the history of sexist usage within particular "discursive formations"; see, for example, Black and Coward ([1981] 1990).

9. I will argue later that the *Wickedary* cannot do this successfully. Because of its emphasis on code-refashioning, Daly's project is implicitly totalizing in its intention, despite her professed intention to model an ongoing communal process.

10. See Fiorenza (1983, 23), for whom Daly's writings afford a classic example of a "sociology of knowledge" approach to theology. Daly was apparently reading Berger in the early 1970s: she uses many of his key formulations in *Beyond God the Father* (1973), while calling attention to Berger's androcentrism. In *Gyn/Ecology* (1978), although she does not cite Berger, she uses his notion of "legitimation" to explain that the purpose of all major world religions is to shelter the male against anomie, and suggests that the symbolic message of all of them is "Women are the dreaded anomie" (Daly 1978, 39).

11. See Daly (1984, 25), where she approvingly cites Julian Jaynes's assertion in *The Origin of Consciousness in the Breakdown of the Bicameral Mind* that "metaphor is not a mere extra trick of language, as it is so often slighted in the old schoolbooks on composition; it is the very constitutive ground of language."

12. See Cassirer (1946), especially chapters 3 and 6. Langer is the English translator of *Language and Myth* and has built upon Cassirer's account of the origins of language.

13. Morris uses the "Dissembly of Exorcism" from *Gyn/Ecology* to make a similar point (Morris [1982] 1988, 40). My own example is chosen to highlight the way in which Daly's discursive posture has changed over time.

14. See Jakobson ([1976] 1987, 378): "Poeticity is present when the word is felt as a word and not a mere representation of the object being named or the outburst of emotion, when words and their composition, their meaning, their external and internal form, acquire a weight and value of their own instead of referring indifferently to reality." The *Wickedary* is full of explicit claims that words are living creatures or can be made to "come alive" (Daly and Caputi 1987, xvii).

15. On the subject of "feminist Humpty-Dumpties," see Cameron (1990, 11-12).

16. Morris recalls a telling moment from Daly's address in Sydney, when "the *we*-ness of the address was ruptured . . . by a woman who called out 'Mary, you're not speaking to *me* . . .'" (Morris 1988, 39).

17. I do not mean to accuse Daly of lying when she claims that her "we" in the *Wickedary* refers to other women who have helped her with the project in various ways (Daly and Caputi 1987, xxii), but rather to point out that the pronoun is manipulated in such a way as to take on a life of its own within the discursive system of the work itself.

References

The American Heritage Dictionary of the English Language: New College Edition. 1976. Ed. William Morris. Boston: Houghton Mifflin.

Benveniste, Emile. [1966] 1970. *Problems in General Linguistics,* trans. Mary Elizabeth Meek. Miami: University of Miami Press.

Berger, Peter. 1967. *The Sacred Canopy: Elements of a Sociological Theory of Religion.* New York: Doubleday.

Black, Maria, and Rosalind Coward. [1981] 1990. "Linguistic, Social and Sexual Relations: A Review of Dale Spender's *Man Made Language.*" *Screen Education* 39 (Summer); reprinted in *The Feminist Critique of Language: A Reader,* ed. Deborah Cameron. London and New York: Routledge.

Black, Max. [1954-55] 1981. "Metaphor." *Proceedings of the Aristotelian Society* n.s. 55: 273-94; reprinted in *Philosophical Perspectives on Metaphor,* ed. Mark Johnson. Minneapolis: University of Minnesota Press.

Burke, Kenneth. 1941. "Four Master Tropes." *Kenyon Review* 3: 421-38.

Cameron, Deborah. 1990. "Introduction: Why is Language a Feminist Issue?" In *The Feminist Critique of Language: A Reader,* ed. D. Cameron. London and New York: Routledge.

Cassirer, Ernst. 1946. *Language and Myth,* trans. Suzanne K. Langer. New York: Dover.

Daly, Mary. 1973. *Beyond God the Father: Toward a Philosophy of Women's Liberation.* Boston: Beacon Press.

———. 1978. *Gyn/Ecology: The Metaethics of Radical Feminism.* Boston: Beacon Press.

———. 1984. *Pure Lust: Elemental Feminist Philosophy.* Boston: Beacon Press.

Daly, Mary, and Jane Caputi. 1987. *Websters' First New Intergalactic Wickedary of the English Language.* Boston: Beacon Press.

Draine, Betsy. 1989. "Refusing the Wisdom of Solomon: Some Recent Feminist Literary Theory." *Signs* 15: 144-70.

Eisenstein, Hester. 1983. *Contemporary Feminist Thought.* Boston: G. K. Hall.

Fiorenza, Elizabeth Schussler. 1983. *In Memory of Her: A Feminist Theological Reconstruction of Christian Origins.* New York: Crossroad Press.

Frank, Francine Wattman, and Paula A. Treichler. 1989. *Language, Gender, and Professional Writing: Theoretical Approaches and Guidelines for Nonsexist Usage.* New York: Modern Language Association.

Gilbert, Sandra, and Susan Gubar. 1979. *Shakespeare's Sisters: Feminist Essays on Women Poets.* Bloomington: Indiana University Press.

Jakobson, Roman. [1960a] 1987. "Linguistics and Poetics." In *Style in Language,* ed. Thomas A. Sebeok. Cambridge MA: MIT Press; reprinted in *Language in Literature,* ed. Krystyna Pomorska and Stephen Rudy. Cambridge, MA.: Belknap Press.

———. [1960b] 1987. "Two Aspects of Language and Two Types of Aphasic Disturbances." In *Fundamentals of Language* [with Morris Halle], part 2. The Hague: Mouton; reprinted in *Language in Literature.* See Jakobson (1960a).

———. [1976] 1987. "What is Poetry?" Trans. Michael Heim. In *Semiotics of Art: Prague School Contributions,* ed. Ladislav Matejka and Irwin Titunik. Cambridge, MA: MIT Press, 1976; reprinted in *Language in Literature,* 368-78. See Jakobson (1960a).

Langer, Suzanne K. 1942. *Philosophy in a New Key.* Cambridge, MA: Harvard University Press.

Morris, Meaghan. [1982] 1988. "A-mazing Grace: Notes on Mary Daly's Poetics." *Intervention* 16; reprinted in Morris, *The Pirate's Fiancee: Feminism, Reading, Postmodernism.* London: Verso.

Nilsen, Alleen Pace. 1984. "Winning the Great He/She Battle." *College English* 46: 151-57.

The Oxford English Dictionary, 2d ed. 1989. Ed. J. A. Simpson and E. S. C. Weiner. Oxford: Clarendon Press.

Rich, Adrienne. 1978. *The Dream of a Common Language: Poems 1974-1977.* New York: Norton.

———. 1979. *On Lies, Secrets, and Silence: Selected Prose 1966-1978*. New York: Norton.

———. 1981a. "What Does Separatism Mean?" *Sinister Wisdom* 18 (Fall): 83-91.

———. 1981b. *A Wild Patience Has Taken Me This Far: Poems 1978-1981*. New York: Norton.

———. 1985. *The Fact of a Doorframe: Poems Selected and New 1950-1984*. New York: Norton.

———. 1989. *Time's Power: Poems 1985-1988*. New York: Norton.

Ricoeur, Paul. [1978] 1981. "The Metaphorical Process as Cognition, Imagination, and Feeling." *Critical Inquiry* 5: 143-59; reprinted in *Philosophical Perspectives on Metaphor*, ed. Mark Johnson. Minneapolis: University of Minnesota Press.

Carol Anne Douglas (review date January 1993)

SOURCE: Douglas, Carol Anne. Review of *Outercourse: The Be-Dazzling Voyage: Containing Recollections from My Logbook of a Radical Feminist Philosopher*, by Mary Daly. *Off Our Backs* 23, no. 1 (January 1993): 19.

[*In the following review, Douglas lauds Daly's frank and insightful portrayal of her life as a feminist scholar in* Outercourse.]

Looking back to *Outercourse: The Bedazzling Voyage*, logbook of radical feminist philosopher Mary Daly, is a good reminder of the obstacles faced by feminists in the late twentieth century. Daly is, of course, the feminist who reclaimed words such as spinster, hag, nag, and crone. Readers must remember that in the 20th century these terms had strong negative connotations to many people.

Readers will note many references to the Roman Catholic Church, which was the patriarchal religion in which ForeCrone Daly and quite a few other twentieth century feminists were raised. This church was organized in an ultra—hierarchical structure, with a central patriarch called the pope, at its head, For more background on Roman Catholicism, see *The Women's Encyclopedia of History*, under the entries for Daly, Mary; de la Cruz, Sor Juana; Hunt, Mary; Mary, the Blessed Virgin, representations of; and Raymond, Janice.

TOWARD SPINSTERHOOD

Daly tells of her voyaging through and beyond the church, after obtaining two doctorates in theology and one in philosophy; a difficult task for a working class woman with no money like Daly. At one point she was afraid she would be denied the doctorate in theology from the University of Fribourg in Switzerland because the university required all those who attained the degree to swear to reject "modernism," but she was saved by the patriarchs who decided to deny her permission to take the oath because that would give her the right to enter the male club of those privileged to teach theology at canonical institutions.

Daly apparently steered clear of men and traveled extensively in Europe, often with her mother, on very little money, enjoying herself hugely.

She then accepted a teaching position at Boston College, which was the former name of Mary Daly College. At that time, the college was run by an order of priests called Jesuits who were known as intellectuals but who persecuted ForeCrone Daly. When considering her for tenure, they actually said they were going to look only at the evaluations from male students! Many male students appreciated her brilliance, so she gained tenure, a decision the Jesuits no doubt regretted from then on as she moved beyond Catholicism and god and became a spinning spinster and, a revolting hag.

They punished her by denying her promotions and salary increases. At one point when she was on leave, one of her theology department colleagues told people calling to offer her speaking engagements that she was unavailable because she was having a mental breakdown.

However, Daly connected with enough Cronies to be able to withstand the harassment at Boston College. (By this time, she had come out as a lesbian.) When asked by a feminist in Ireland why she stayed at Boston College, Daly replied, "I choose to Stand my Ground." As both a student and a teacher (other than short-term courses and her many speaking engagements), Daly's entire career was spent in Catholic institutions; she doubted that secular patriarchal institutions would be fundamentally better.

Moreover, Daly retains a considerable attachment to the works of the Catholic theologian Thomas Aquinas, from which she spins off. I suspect she would gladly defend Aquinas as a spinning off place compared with, say, Marx.

A CAT AND A COW

Although her books ***Gyn/Ecology*** and ***Pure Lust*** expressed horrific and pervasive violence against women, Daly never ceases to enjoy life, to discover pleasure in words, friends, nature (especially her cat and cow familiars), and new feminist acquaintances in many places. Her balance between calling attention to horrors and nonetheless living joyously is truly A-mazing.

Sometimes one wonders whether her contemporaries always appreciated her playfulness. For instance, her discussion of the reflections of her preconceived spirit, in which she decided to be a female and communicated that decision to her mother-to-be, may have been a bit trying to some feminists at a time when women did not have assure rights to abortion. (And when abortion was still very common because women did not have complete control over the sexuality.)

As we know, a number of Daly's feminist contemporaries such as ForeCrone Audre Lorde criticized omission in *Gyn/Ecology* as racist. In *Outercourse,* Daly deals with this indirectly by summoning Susan B. Anthony as a character and giving Anthony a chance to apologize for the lack of understanding about race and class. (She also attempts chats with Harriet Tubman and Sojourner Truth, and has a vision of Spider Woman.) More directly, Daly says she regrets any pain her own omissions may have caused other women, particularly women of colors.

Anyone who has enjoyed ForeCrone Daly's other books will surely enjoy her *Outercourse.* Those who do not enjoy her work as much, perhaps because they come from different intellectual traditions, might nevertheless a least skim through *Outercourse* to understand where she came from as she spirals on. Certainly, anyone who is studying the twentieth century, particularly those focusing on the United States (that was in the days when there were nation states), should read *Outercourse.*

Sudie Rakusin, the amazing lesbian artist who illustrated Daly's *Wickedary* provides magnificent, animal-centered illustrations for each of the four spiral galaxies of *Outercourse.*

Carol J. Adams (review date March 1993)

SOURCE: Adams, Carol J. "Mary, Mary, Quite Contrary." *Women's Review of Books* 10, no. 6 (March 1993): 1, 3.

[*In the following review, Adams praises Daly's contribution to feminist theory and offers a favorable evaluation of* Outercourse.]

For anyone who has ever wanted to know more about the radical feminist philosopher behind *Beyond God the Father,* the Revolting Hag of *Gyn/Ecology,* the Nag-Gnostic philosopher of *Pure Lust* and the Conjurer of the *Wickedary,* here in one installment are the how, the why and the what of Mary Daly and her books. Through the medium of one woman's life—her own—Mary Daly invites us into the process of radical feminist philosophy.

Outercourse is big (at 477 pages, it is Daly's longest book); fascinating (describing travels and relations, travails and reflections); humorous (after recounting an especially insulting faculty meeting at Boston College, Daly comments "These men could not understand that they were giving me rich material for analysis"); and provocative (reminding us that women are the "touchable class," asking "While we wade knee deep in the blood of women shall I chat about Freud, Derrida, and Foucault?"). *Outercourse* takes risks, especially when it shares intimate moments of the sacred—a clover blossom announces to a young Mary Daly "I am," setting her on the path of becoming a radical feminist philosopher: "If a clover blossom could say 'I am,' then why couldn't I?"

Outercourse is above all inviting. While Daly's books are said to be difficult to read, *Outercourse* engages the reader on many levels, telling the story of a life (and a brilliant life at that), introducing the basic concepts contained in each of these previous "difficult" books, offering philosophical reflections and giving quotations from letters Daly received from ecstatic readers who found their own reality validated. The book relies on a certain vocabulary that has evolved to represent the sequence of insights of Daly's books. But it gently pulls the uninitiated into its logic and wordplay.

Outercourse expresses and enacts the major argument of *Beyond God the Father* (1973)—that the women's revolution is about participation in Be-ing. (Be-ing is hyphenated and capitalized to stress Daly's ontological position that Ultimate Reality is a Verb, an intransitive Verb.) *Outercourse* is a logical development from that starting-point: if through feminism we participate in Be-ing, then the story Daly will tell about her books and herself must contain both the autobiographical material that reflects her own participation in Be-ing and the philosophical arguments that accompany it.

The book also enacts (or as Daly would say, Realizes) another central tenet of Daly's Elemental Feminist Philosophy, which she described in *Pure Lust* as "a form of be-ing/thinking that is rooted in Metapatriarchal consciousness—consciousness that is in harmony with the Wild in nature and in the Self." This philosophy dissolves the dualism between "matter" and philosophy, consolidating both intuition and ecofeminism, the experience of the clover blossom and the European-trained scholar. Elemental Philosophy, Daly instructs through examples in *Outercourse,* is of the world. Thus she describes not only conversations, but also experiences with tornadoes and ancient "beehive structures," interactions with spiders who appear in cars, crabs crossing highways, a cow with a runny nose, and cats.

Outercourse will satisfy anyone curious about Mary Daly's life and her writings. We learn about her relationship with her mother Anna, her Catholic girlhood in upstate New York, the acquisition of degree after degree in her determined attempt to become a philosopher, the volcanic year in which she became a lesbian, her evolving ecofeminist consciousness, and about how all of her books—including **Outercourse**—came into being.

Mary Daly has always been in the process of interpreting herself. Practically from the moment she finished **The Church and the Second Sex** (1968), she has been revisi(ti)ng it: its writing and publication set in motion her separation from, as it brought her even closer (if only because of its reaction to her writings) to, the massive institution she scrutinized. As Daly has revisited earlier works, she has offered autobiographical groundings: notes about where she was, and where she is now.

This is the story of the journeys of a pirate, one who sees herself plundering from the patriarchy and smuggling treasures of archaic knowledge back to women. Since women under patriarchy have been vessels, Daly proclaims this is something that radical feminism must reverse. Thus the craft this pirate takes on her journey is truly a craft—as in a vessel—and also the craft of writing and witch/craft. "My True Course was and is Outercourse—moving beyond the imprisoning mental, physical, emotional, spiritual walls of patriarchy, the State of Possession."

Daly journeys from the foreground (the world of the patriarchy, the fatherland) to the Background, "the Homeland of women's Selves and of all other Others." Her voyage takes her through and over what she calls a "Subliminal Sea." Even when she felt like a cognitive minority of one, she writes, she realized that this did not mean she was alone: she had "subliminal knowledge of similar subliminal knowledge buried in other women." Letters she quotes from readers of her previous books echo with the sense of this subliminal knowledge. In response to **Beyond God the Father**, one woman wrote: "You took the top off my head. You electrified me. I felt as if—this may sound contradictory—I were *discovering* things for the first time and *recognizing* them as authentic, recognizing them as things I had so long felt myself." After reading the **Wickedary**, another woman exclaimed, "I am startled and thrilled to find words for my feelings."

To represent the movement of this pirate and her craft through the Subliminal Sea, from the foreground of patriarchy to the Background, Daly divides **Outercourse** into four "Spiral Galaxies." Each galaxy encompasses a certain time span in her life, and addresses the writing and themes of her books during that time. The First Galaxy—the time of growing up out of a Catholic girlhood, the acquisition of her seven higher degrees, the publication of **The Church and the Second Sex** and her experience of being denied tenure at Boston College—involves the effort to overcome *aphasia*, the "inability to Name Background reality as well as foreground fabrications and the connections among these." In the Second Galaxy—the time of the writing of **Beyond God the Father** and the Feminist postchristian introduction to **The Church and the Second Sex**—Daly encounters the demonic forces of elimination "who/which erase women's histories and our very lives" and overcomes *amnesia* (seeing beyond the "androcratic lies about women's history"). In the Third Galaxy, the time of **Gyn/Ecology, Pure Lust,** and the **Wickedary,** Daly confronts *apraxia* (the inability to Act as Radical Feminists), and moves into the Background present which is represented by the Fourth Galaxy.

Daly provides the answer to a question many have asked: why did she leave the church but stay in "academentia," since many see academia as even more oppressive? Her answer: she chooses "to Fight/Act (Stand my Ground) at that precise location on the Boundary between Background and foreground where the demonic patriarchal distortions of women's Archaic heritage are most visible and accessible to me."

Outercourse should draw at least three groups of readers. One group is those who have faithfully read Mary Daly for the past two decades, have been waiting for her next opus and asking her 'Where did your books come from?" In answering this question, Daly speaks also to the second group—those who have not yet encountered her writings—by inviting them into her spiraling thought, providing a way to engage with her other books. And those who have marginalized Mary Daly's radical feminist philosophy—arguing that it reiterates a manicheanism of its own, that it is essentialist, that it no longer works from within the belly of the beast—will meet a more complex individual than they have acknowledged, and may also refine their reading of her theory. All of these readers survive in what Daly calls the foreground now—a foreground she has always unerringly exposed: "the Age of Dis-memberment has arrived. the media men are excited, delighted. same old story, hate and gory. win an election. have an erection, selling polygrip and cars."

Daly does not attempt to pinpoint every step in her life, the beginning and end of every relationship, every story about each book's evolution. Despite being a philosophical autobiography, **Outercourse** seems to fall outside the burgeoning body of women's cross-genre writing which Diane Freedman characterizes as speaking "*of* as well as *from* the self."[1] While **Outercourse** speaks both of and from the self, the originating momentum for this speaking and the metaphysics that this speaking participates in feel different because of the unique way the grounding principle of ontology operates in Daly's thought and life. Daly is not so much reading her life as an example of her theory or writing in her own voice for the first time (she would, I am sure, say she has always written in her own voice), but placing herself philosophically within the ontological framework that her books provide in order to help elucidate these books. To bring her life more fully into her books, she embeds them in her own becoming and provides us with an understanding of the ontological significance of her experiences.

To write this review I began by digging out my notes from the Feminist Ethics class I took with Mary Daly during the 1974-75 school year. I find my notes on her revision of the deadly sins, including "processions—reification of process, stunting of female becoming" and "Male pride twists female pride into vanity, shame." Later in my notebook I find a list of the Boston College tenure board that turned Mary down for full professor in 1975. I drag down a book Mary assigned in class: *Rape: Victims of Crisis.* Yes, I remember correctly. She had pointed out the false naming of that title, and encouraged us to cross out "crisis" and write above it "men." I remember especially Mary joining a celebration of Susan B. Anthony's birthday I had planned at Radcliffe College, and a discussion we had about the adequacy of Anthony's slogan, "Failure is impossible," as a vision. Interestingly, it is this slogan that echoes on the last page of **Outercourse**.

Mary Daly's life is about Be-ing; she has challenged *aphasia* with Naming, *amnesia* with Knowing, *apraxia* with Acting. As a radical feminist philosopher she provides an analysis of ontology—what smashes female Be-ing in a patriarchal world and what enables it. From the moment in the 1970s when she realized the women's liberation movement was an ontological movement, in which women participate in their own becoming and being, she has, labrys-like, both named it and pushed it further. In the naming acts of her books, many women have experienced the creation of the ontological space for the discovery of their own authentic selves.

Daly reminds us that it does none of us any good to mince words, to be humble or hold back speaking the truth. In a sense, she demonstrates how "Failure is impossible" is not so much a slogan as a process. This is the story of **Outercourse**. No one knows it better than she: "We will do or die . . . or do *and* die. But we won't be defeated, ever."

Note

1. Diane P. Freedman, *An Alchemy of Genres: Cross-Genre Writing by American Feminist Poet-Critics* (Charlottesville, VA: University Press of Virginia, 1992). See also Diane P. Freedman, Olivia Frey and Frances Murphy Zauhar, eds., *The Intimate Critique: Autobiographical Literary Criticism* (Durham, NC: Duke University Press, 1993).

Cindy L. Griffin (essay date June 1993)

SOURCE: Griffin, Cindy L. "Women as Communicators: Mary Daly's Hagography as Rhetoric." *Communications Monographs* 60, no. 2 (June 1993): 158-77.

[*In the following essay, Griffin analyzes Daly's feminist philosophy of language and its application as an alternative mode of communication theory and rhetorical practice among women. According to Griffin, Daly elucidates the dichotomy between women's public and private discourse, embodied in a "foreground" of patriarchal oppression and a "background" of feminist authenticity and subversion.*]

In 1987, Spitzack and Carter suggested that, although women's visibility has increased in the communication discipline, the simple fact of their presence has not necessarily corresponded to increased knowledge about women's unique or distinctive forms of communication. While the study of women's communication may have become a part of the communication discipline in the 1990s, scholars who work in this area, for the most part, continue to attempt to understand and evaluate women's communication from traditional frameworks. The result is that women's communicative experiences and efforts, in their complex and myriad forms, tend to be distorted, devalued, and misunderstood. Adopting a feminist perspective on the study of women's communication, in contrast, would enable scholars to develop theories that better explain women's experiences and eloquence, challenging, if necessary, current knowledge about communication.[1] As Spitzack and Carter suggested, to do anything other than challenge these structures is to place research on gender and communication "back into the pre-established frameworks" that have offered little that is useful in understanding women's communication as unique, credible, and effective (p. 401). A feminist perspective, in addition, assists scholars in avoiding what Aptheker (1989) has labeled the "universal iconography" of "woman"—the illusion that all women, regardless of race, class, age, identity, and/or experiences are the same (p. 12). A feminist perspective toward women's communication, in sum, begins to explicate the many categories/structures of women's communication and to contribute to rhetorical scholarship by identifying and explaining these patterns.

Five areas regarding women's communication have emerged from previous feminist scholarship that suggest *topoi* from which to begin to expand and develop the conceptualization of women as communicators. The first *topos* concerns the nature of the oppression that perpetuates the silencing of women's voices and is raised by the research of Kurs and Cathcart (1983), Edson (1985), Endress (1988), Campbell (1989), Foss and

Foss (1991), Houston and Kramarae (1991), and Biesecker (1992). A second *topos* concerns various systems that contribute to the oppression of women and possible alternative world views that might empower and value women's communication. Questions regarding the nature of those rhetors who assume a stance of woman as communicator, a third *topos* of feminist scholarship, are raised by Campbell's (1973) research on the oxymoronic nature of the women's liberation movement, her two-volume work on women rhetors in history (1990), as well as the work of Japp (1985) and Solomon (1988). The fourth *topos*, the goals of women as communicators, is explored by Gearhart (1979) in her essay on communication as co-creation rather than persuasion. A fifth and final *topos* identifiable in previous research addresses the communicative strategies available to women who allow their voices to be heard within a framework that does not recognize women's perspectives as useful or important; this issue is raised by scholars such as Hancock (1972), Campbell (1986), Sheridan (1988), Williams (1990), and Houston and Kramarae (1991). While this list is by no means exhaustive, each of these researchers has made a significant contribution to the conceptualization of women as communicators and has offered at least one topic or construct with which to begin more comprehensive discussions of this notion.[2] A fully developed theory of women as communicators, however, has yet to be developed.

The theoretical writings of Mary Daly address these five feminist *topoi* by providing a more comprehensive feminist rhetorical perspective with which communication scholars can begin to examine public and private discourse.[3] Daly's perspective falls within the purview of what Jaggar (1983) and others would term a "radical" feminist rhetorical perspective. Such a perspective rests on three assumptions: (a) the oppression of women is at the root of all other systems of oppression and subordination; (b) important insights can be gained from women's own experiences of oppression; and (c) primary energy is devoted not to "organizing direct confrontations with 'the patriarchy'" but rather to "developing alternative social arrangements" (p. 104). Daly's perspective on women as communicators is revealed throughout her five books: **The Church and the Second Sex** (1985b), **Beyond God the Father: Toward a Philosophy of Women's Liberation** (1985a), **Gyn/Ecology: The Metaethics of Radical Feminism** (1978), **Pure Lust: Elemental Feminist Philosophy** (1984), and **Websters' First New Intergalactic Wickedary of the English Language** (Daly & Caputi, 1987). Each of these books challenges the roles and treatment of women in various cultural institutions, articulates what Daly calls "the potential of women's revolution" and the generation of "human becoming," and ventures into new realms of existence, language, and theorizing (1985a, p. 6).

Daly's perspective assists scholars in understanding a rhetorical duality that has yet to be articulated or addressed fully. It suggests that there is a rhetorical foreground in which women function as communicators and a rhetorical background to which women can aspire as communicators. While Foucault (1970, 1972) has identified a rhetorical *episteme*—a cultural code or structure of relations that dictates the language, perceptions and values of an age—that privileges certain voices and silences others, Daly's theory of women as communicators suggests that not only does the *episteme* of the foreground silence women's voices, but it works to misname or erase completely the perspectives and experiences of women. Articulating the nature of this duality reveals that the rhetoric within each realm—the foreground and the background—functions very differently. In the foreground, rhetoric oppresses and limits individuals and creates a state of ontological erasure for women; in the background, rhetoric transforms and facilitates for women the process of ontological affirmation. A theory of women as communicators, then, suggests that more than one rhetorical realm exists and that various realms serve different rhetors differently.

Daly's work also assists rhetorical scholars in incorporating and extending the work of feminist theorists such as Lakoff (1975, 1977, 1979), Fishman (1983), and Gilligan (1982) into theories of women's rhetorical forms and strategies. A theory of woman as communicator based on Daly's work disputes Lakoff's (1979) suggestion that women's special rhetorical characteristics grow out of a lack of self-confidence or a denial of responsibility. This theory also moves scholars beyond Fishman's (1983) claim that women perform the maintenance work of a conversation in mixed-sex pairs. Daly's theory suggests that women may, indeed, employ a kind of "women's language" and/or perform the maintenance work of conversation in the foreground, but in the background, this rhetoric is altered significantly. In the background, rhetoric is rooted in confidence in and responsibility to one's self and others, an attempt to construct rhetorical forms that represent women's experiences more fully and accurately, and an identification and emphasis on women's "personal identities" (Lakoff, 1977, p. 7). Daly's work also suggests that not only might background communicators answer to "different voices" ethically, as Gilligan (1982) argues, but that there are specific rhetorical strategies available to assist these rhetors in recognizing, maintaining, and even increasing their positions of interconnection to one another.

Daly's theory of women as communicators, in addition, offers concrete evidence of efforts directed toward rupturing the "phallocentrism" of the foreground as originally identified by Cixous (1976), Irigaray (1980, 1981), and Kristeva (1986). A comprehensive theory of women as communicators suggests that women listen to their bodies, experiences, marginality, histories, and differences and that they build a background of discourse based on these elements. As communicators, background rhetors re-connect with these characteristics, recognize the hidden and masked meanings of these forms and styles of being, and inscribe them into a language that is grounded in and informed by the valuing of women's diverse realities.

Finally, Daly's explication of the distinctive forms and styles of communication within the foreground and the background assist rhetorical scholars in understanding the dichotomy that has been perpetuated between "public" and "private" discourse. While attempts are made to keep these two spheres distinct, and scholarship has focused primarily on rhetoric as it occurs in the "public" realm and as it focuses on "public" topics, Daly's work provides a framework for exploring the intersection of these two realms. By articulating the various components of Daly's theory, rhetorical scholars can begin to develop and make use of new methods and strategies for assessing rhetoric that does not fit comfortably into either realm. Scholars can begin to assess rhetoric that incorporates both public and private topics and language with methods of analysis that offer insights into the nature and function of rhetoric that blends these two realms. Ursula Le Guin's (1989) "A Left-Handed Commencement Address," a speech that I analyze in this essay, is an example of such rhetoric. Le Guin's rhetoric does not fall neatly into the category of public or private; she makes use of both forms of address; and when judged by the standards of either form of address, Le Guin's speech seems inappropriate or poorly planned. Judged by Daly's perspective, however, the speech can be seen as a sophisticated combination of the two and a fairly remarkable piece of rhetorical discourse. Daly's theory, then, offers rhetorical scholars a model with which to begin further exploration into the implications of the public/private dichotomy as well as possible standards for evaluating and assessing rhetoric that blends or combines discourse from both realms.

I begin this paper by identifying within Daly's philosophical writings the constituent elements of a theory of women's rhetoric that develops throughout her work. I summarize Daly's theory according to the aspects identified and explored above: the nature of the world created by the patriarchy, the nature of the world created when women assume positions as communicators, the nature of the goals and processes of women as communicators, the principle rhetorical strategies available to women as communicators, and the natures of women as communicators. Daly's theoretical formulations then are applied to Le Guin's "A Left-Handed Commencement Address," in order to illustrate how Daly's theoretical perspective provides an alternative standard from which this speech may be judged perspicacious.

Finally, some suggestions for future applications of Daly's Hagographic rhetorical perspective are discussed.

NATURE OF WOMEN'S OPPRESSION: THE FOREGROUND

Daly's theoretical formulations of women as communicators do not offer scholars one grand theory designed to understand, predict, or explain fully every possible manifestation of women's communication. Daly's work is more consistent with Dance's (1978) discussion of the existence and even necessity of various theoretical explanations that enable scholars to formulate an understanding of a diverse, and frequently complex, phenomenon. Her theory represents what Gergen (1982) has identified as a generative theory—a theory "that unsettles common assumptions within the culture and thereby opens new vistas for action" (p. 133). As a generative theory, Daly's work challenges "that which is 'taken for granted'" and offers new avenues for understanding rhetorical phenomenon (Gergen, p. 109). Daly's theory can be understood by exploring the ways in which she challenges common assumptions about oppression, women's roles in society, and communication practices and forms.

Much of Daly's work focuses on the politics that oppress women: yet, within this emphasis is an explication and challenge of many of the assumptions that are embedded in research paradigms of communication researchers. Daly identifies the "foreground," a world or environment in which women are oppressed and silenced. The foreground reflects and supports a "male-centered" perspective, "where fabrication, objectification, and alienation" of women take place (Daly & Caputi, 1987, p. 76). In the foreground, men generally occupy the positions of power, and women are molded in and constrained to an existence that serves men's purposes. Daly describes the foreground as reflective of "sexual desire, especially of a violent, self-indulgent character," and as a false society—a "pseudosociety"—characterized by both an obsession with and an aggression toward women (1984, pp. 1-2). The foreground constructs and perpetuates a society that supports and worships the perspectives of men, drains women's energies, and reveals an inability on the part of humans to "reach beyond appearances" (1984, p. 49).

The foreground, characteristic of "science, theology, psychology, biology, and pornography," has as its purpose the obliteration of natural knowing and willing (1984, p. 50). This involves preventing women from existing in a state of "be-ing," which Daly defines as existing in this world in ways that connect women to the earth, to other women, and to themselves.[4] The foreground is informed by and perpetuated through the oppression and separation of women's selves from experience, is male centered and male controlled, and is the overriding condition in which women exist and to which women must respond. This state of "ontological impotence" offers only conditions of negation and experiences of erasure to women (1984, p. 36). The foreground is maintained and perpetuated by numerous strategies and constraints that function to keep women separated from their experiences and perspectives and, ultimately, unable to recognize their real selves (1978, p. 322).

Foreground Strategies of Constraint

Within the realm of the foreground, specific constraints are available to foreground rhetors to prevent women from emerging from the state of oppression and moving into a realm where their unique voices are heard and valued. These restrictions represent "entire conceptual systems . . . developed under the conditions of patriarchy" that "have been the products of males and tend to serve the interests of sexist society" (Daly, 1985a, p. 4). Foreground rhetors use these constraints to promote and advance the interests of the patriarchy, to perpetuate the oppression of women, and to control, objectify, alienate, silence, and/or erase women's perspectives and experiences. While the foreground offers women a kind of half-existence at best, particular methods of oppression are available, even imbedded into the structure of the foreground, that facilitate the objectification and silencing of women and their experiences.

Fixing women's images. One of the constraints Daly identifies provides foreground rhetors with a means for subtle and powerful control of women's images and identities. Similar to the theories of Lukács (1971), Hall (1985), and Spivack (1988), Daly articulates the process by which women's identities become fixed or reified so women have neither their own sense of self nor any freedom in constructing their identities. Daly calls this process the fixing of women's images, arguing that this constraint insures conformity of women within the foreground of oppression by the control of women's images and, as a result, control of their creativity. Not only does this control of images program certain behaviors and thoughts for women, but it has kept women focused eternally on appearance rather than intellect. Such fixed images freeze women into the position of beauty queen and a state of pseudo-exaltation (1985b, p. 60), subjected to threats of "unfeminine" if they do not conform to contrived standards of femininity set forth by the foreground.[5] In addition to this reification process, Daly identifies three other major constraints that are placed on women's existence and identity by the foreground.

Silencing and erasing women's voices. A second constraint operating in the foreground is the erasure and silencing of women's voices. Erasure and silencing are accomplished by instilling fear into the consciousness of women so that when they begin to speak out against the foreground, they either modify their responses to accommodate the foreground perspective or do not speak out at all. Examples of effective fear-instilling techniques that constrain women include the labeling of those who would challenge the foreground as man-haters, possessing "no sense of humor," "sick," "selfish," or "sexless" and the use and promotion of supposedly generic terms such as "he" or even "chairperson" (1978, pp. 18-20). Daly argues, as do many others, that the use of "he" to represent all people makes men visible and not women, simultaneously removing women's perspective from communication. Pseudo-generic terms like "person" or "people," according to Daly, make women "deceptively feel at home" in a language that continues to be male controlled (1978, pp. 18-19).

The foreground silencing of women is also illustrated in labels that are used to denigrate women—labels such as the term "spinster." In the foreground, the word "spinster" is commonly used as a deprecating term to identify an unmarried woman or a woman who seems unlikely to marry. There is, however, a definition for "spinster" that is seldom used and that is affirming rather than negating—"a woman whose occupation is to spin" (1978, p. 3). Taken out of the boundaries of the foreground definition, there is "no limit to the meaning of this rich and cosmic verb. A woman whose occupation is to spin participates in the whirling movement of creation" (1978, p. 3). Constrained by the foreground definition of the term, however, spinsters see and hear only the negative definition of this powerful word, and their creative powers are effectively silenced and erased.

Depreciation, particularization, spiritualization, and universalization. A third constraint used in the foreground entails clouding the issue of women's oppression in general. This constraint is perpetuated in four different ways—through depreciation, particularization, spiritualization, and universalization.[6] Depreciation involves asking the question, "Are you on that subject of women again when there are so many important problems—like war, racism, pollution of the environment?" (1985a, p. 5). With depreciation, the fact that sexism is "the basic structure underlying the various forms of oppression" is masked (1984, p. 320). Particularization occurs in the use of phrases such as, "Oh, that's Catholic problem," so that individuals are led to believe that patriarchy exists in only a few institutions (1985a, p. 5). Spiritualization is the refusal to look at facts of concrete oppression. With this technique, women are constrained by the proclamation, "in Christ there is neither male nor female" (1985a, p. 5). The effect of spiritualization is that even if there were no sex assigned to Christ, we are led to believe that there is no patriarchy anywhere else (1985a, p. 5). A final technique available for clouding the issue of the dominance of foreground perspectives is that of universalization, represented by the question, "But isn't the real problem human liberation?" As Daly suggests, "the words used may be 'true,' but when used to avoid confronting the specific problems of sexism they are radically untruthful" (1985a, p. 6).

Ritualistic violence toward women. While these four above noted constraints can be both subtle and powerful, a fourth strategy—ritualizing violence toward women—also is effective in that the symbolic and literal effects of this violence are masked and distorted. The very real and highly symbolic rituals of Indian suttee (1978, pp. 113-133), Chinese footbinding (1978, pp. 134-152), African genital mutilation (1978, pp. 153-177), and European witchburnings (1978, pp. 178-222) are examples of foreground violence enacted toward women, resulting in the restriction of women's activities and perspectives.[7] The ritualization of these acts serves to mask the depth and scope of the violence inherent in the acts and prevents the recognition of the commonalties among these rituals. The repetition of these symbolic rituals perpetuates the foreground violation of women, deceptively drawing the participants as well as the observers into "emotional complicity," training "both victims and victimizers to perform . . . their preordained roles" uncritically (1978, p. 109). Constrained in this ritualistic way, women cannot articulate their oppression easily, nor can they physically or mentally break out of these oppressive and dangerous situations.

Each of these constraints effectively insures conformity, silences the voices of women's deep selves, clouds the issue of women's oppression, and ritualizes the subordination of and violence toward women. On the surface, these techniques may appear as vastly isolated instances and vastly dissimilar practices. However, as Daly notes, rather than being unique, all of these techniques are "variations on the theme of oppression," and the "phenomenon," she explains, "is planetary" (1978, p. 111).

Foreground Communicators

The existence of a foreground—and the constraints operating within it—implies the existence of particular types of individuals characterized by a specific nature who will perpetuate this oppressive existence. Daly's theoretical formulation of the foreground identifies three types of individual oppressors: "Snools," "Fixers/Tricksters," and "corporate Big Brothers of Boredom" (1984, pp. 20-24). A "snool" can be defined as a "cringing person" and an "abject or mean-spirited" individual. Snools, feeling powerful and authoritative in the foreground, attempt "to reduce to submission" or to "cow" or "bully" those who do not abide by the rules of the foreground. Corporate Big Brothers of Boredom are the grim, depressing, bores of the foreground (1987, p. 186). Fixers/Tricksters are those individuals in the foreground who attempt to fix or block women's existences. Having blocked or fixed women's movement, a Fixer/Trickster then attempts to convince women that these identities are women's own creations (1984, p. 20). Snools, accompanied by the corporate Big Brothers of Boredom and the Fixers/Tricksters of identities and realities, "continually aim to freeze life" and to keep individuals "within the confines of bore-ocracy, using bore-ocratic details and mazes" (1984, pp. 20-23). In the foreground, snools rule by virtue of their powers of intimidation, privileged positions, and access to a language that adequately represents and describes their realities.

Snoolish, boring inhabitants of the foreground, however, are not strictly male. Women, too, comprise a portion of this group. These women are known as "Daddy's Girl[s]," "Self-loathing ladies," and "Fembots" (1978, pp. 8, 17). As snools, these women obey the rules of the foreground, responding like puppets when the strings of the foreground constraints are manipulated and pulled. There is, Daly suggests, only one rule for Daddy's Girls: "they must never laugh seriously at Father—only at his jokes" (1978, p. 17).

In addressing and illustrating the nature of the foreground, many previously unaddressed aspects of the politics that keep women oppressed surface. Not only does Daly address the reification of women's identities, but she identifies the subtle and pervasive strategies used in the foreground to interpellate women and to keep them unaware—even supportive—of this process. A theory of women as communicators must move far beyond this first step, however, and suggest ways in which women might begin their journey out of the foreground and into positions of ontological affirmation and self-identified communication. Daly's work enables rhetorical scholars to begin to describe the nature of the world created through this communication, the goals and processes of these communicators, the strategies women can use to create this world, and the natures of women as communicators.

Nature of the World Created by Women Communicators: The Background

Rather than remain in the foreground as objects of male oppression and constraints, Daly suggests that women can and do move outside this realm and create new ways of living, thinking, and be-ing. The world created by women as communicators, the Background, is one in which women reject the "mindless devastations" brought upon women by foreground myths and unrealities (1987, p. 264). Women are unsubdued in this world; they move contrary to the false standards imposed upon them by foreground rhetors and replace these standards with background reason and truths (1984, pp. 262-264). The nature of this world is one of Deviance and of moving the "Wrong Way, that is, contrary to customary procedures" (1987, pp. 268). The Background is a place in which women reject the notion of foreground female "docility" and obedience; they move beyond "patriarchal meanings/myths of good and evil" and create a world in which women are for each other and for themselves (1984, pp. 267-269). The Background is a world of "Self-creation" and of "Metamorphosing" women—women who are recasting their knowledge, language, and identities and who are actively supporting others who would engage in this journey (1984, p. 409). The world created by women as communicators, in sum, is a world out of control—a world out of the control of the foreground. While the foreground communicator may fear losing control, the Background communicator actively seeks this loss, challenging and transforming this control in order to understand women and women as communicators (1984, p. 410).

The nature of the world created by women as communicators implies a "universal human becoming" (1985a, p. 6). Yet, Daly recognizes that this world, with the recognition of the value of women, most likely will be considered "anti-male" (1978, p. 27). The cliche, she argues, "is not only unimaginative but deadeningly, deafeningly, deceptive," masking the potential of each individual, and fitting nicely into the foreground constraint of fear-instilling labels (1978, pp. 27-28). As communicators, women recognize the undermining effects of the foreground and its "anti-female" orientation (1978, p. 29). As communicators, women express a form of Outrage toward this oppression, and express their determination to name and transform this anti-female reality, creating a women-centered, women-identified reality.

The Nature of the Goals and Processes of Women Background Communicators

According to Daly, two primary goals exist for women as communicators in their responses to the foreground—transcendence and the generation of women's becoming. As communicators, Hags and Crones seek to move beyond the "idolatries of sexist society" and to encourage the transcendence of this state of existence (1985a, p. 6). Daly's notion of transcendence, however, is not the process of attempting to reconnect masculinity with femininity or vice versa. That form of transcendence, she suggests, rests "on the mistaken assumption that these 'halves' will make a whole" (1978, p. 387). Attempts to combine the foreground constructs of "masculinity" and "femininity" only result in "pseudo-integrity" and "pseudowholeness" because these "halves"—and even the idea that there are only two pieces of a whole human being—are foreground fabrications (1978, p. 387). The goals of the rhetor in the background are to transcend this dichotomy and to weave patterns of insight and knowledge that lead to women's becoming—the recognition of women as subjects living and creating life, altering the male-authored knowledge of the world, and weaving world/word tapestries of a new kind. These goals, then, are "metapatriarchal." They leave "reform" as well as re-forming behind, focusing instead on transforming our "Selves" and engaging in the process of "continual conversion of the previously unknown into the familiar" (1978, pp. 7-8).

Guided by these metapatriarchal goals, women as communicators make use of numerous strategies as they move into the realm of communicator—strategies that can be used to move beyond the foreground so women can create a world where their diverse voices can be heard. These strategies focus on the blasphemy of naming the oppressor as well as the actions of the oppressor, and on forms of communication by which women can move beyond the patriarchal construction of Self and into the Background, the realm of woman as subject/communicator.

Background Strategies of Women as Communicators

Engaged in the process of establishing themselves as ontologically whole and credible communicators, background communicators make use of various Outrageous styles of communication. As communicators, women break the rules and laws of the foreground, "figure out its meanings," and then develop alternative meanings, Background meanings that represent a world rich in women-centered and women-constructed realities (1984, p. 409). Background communicators attempt to change consciousness, behavior, and perceptions by upsetting unconscious traditional assumptions, and Daly identifies several techniques that are helpful in the process of creating an alternative to the dominant foreground rhetorical system. Like other theorists, Daly argues that reality is reflected in the prevailing social and linguistic structures of our time. But Daly moves beyond this perspective, suggesting that these structures represent the male-centered foreground. For women as communicators, alternative meanings to the foreground are developed by using techniques such as metaphors and redefinitions; alternative styles of capitalization; Spelling/Be-Spelling; Grammar/Sin-Tactics; and Spooking, Sparking, and Spinning.

Metaphor. Metaphors are tools to name change and challenge the foreground logic and, as such, are a necessary and natural component of the background.[8] Metaphors, according to Daly, "evoke action, movement. They Name/evoke a shock, a clash with the 'going logic,' and they introduce a new logic. Metaphors function to Name change, and therefore they elicit change." The metaphor, Daly reminds her readers, "is the very constitutive ground of language" (1984, p. 25). Background communicators use metaphors to move past the unnatural state of being that is representative of women's existence in the foreground and name the complex multiple meanings of life. In this way, Spinsters Spin past the Static State of the foreground and journey into new ways of being and communicating (1984, pp. 404-405).

Redefinition. The strategy of redefinition, which involves recognizing the "deceptive perceptions [that] were/are implanted through language—the all-pervasive language of myth"—can free women from these linguistic myths and assist them in moving into the realm of communicator (1978, p. 3). In employing this technique, women as communicators reinterpret words, take them out of their usual semantic field, and place them in the realm of women's creativity. Redefinition means that women really hear themselves and each other and, through this process, find new words to describe their experiences and their lives (1985a, p. 8). Daly does not suggest that background rhetoric is "an entirely different set of words" in the "material sense—that is, different sounds or combinations of letters on paper." Rather, she suggests that in background rhetorical strategies, words that are "identical with the old become new in a semantic context that arises from qualitatively new experience" (1985a, p. 8). Thus, for example, Hags and Crones use redefinitions not because Daly expects their's will be the final definitions of words, but rather because in so using them they will bring forth new meanings that have the power to transform old realities and reveal new ones.

Capitalization. Background communicators' capitalization of words is "capitally irregular, conforming to meaning rather than to standard usage" (1987, p. xxi). This strategy ensures that Background realities and foreground fabrications are properly named. Words such as "Websters," "Nag-Gnostic," and "Background" wear capitals to distinguish them from words in the foreground. Capitalizing "Boredom," in addition, indicates the official state produced by foreground "bores" and not only the feeling of boredom. Although confusing to foreground communicators, capitalization quickly makes sense to women who recognize the importance of naming realities for themselves.

Spelling/Be-Spelling. A fourth strategy available to background rhetors is that of Spelling/Be-Spelling. Daly suggests that this process involves changing the spelling of a word and engaging in a kind of "Archmagical Shape-shifting" by altering the physical form of the word (1987, p. 14). This technique, which is most effective when used in writing, releases the original magical powers of words, transforming the ways we respond to and interact with a word so that meanings that have been "masked and muted by man's mysteries" might be revealed (1987, p. 14). Women can engage in the process of Spelling/Be-Spelling in several ways: hyphens, slashes and irregular capitalization. Background rhetors, for example, can use hyphens to "Discover" new ways of knowing and understanding and allow new meanings to emerge, make use of slashes in order to "release ontological powers encased/encaged" within words, and borrow from the earlier strategy of irregular capitalization as exemplified by the term "Spelling/Be-Spelling" (1987, p. 14). Use of this strategy requires that women act as "Websters," weaving words and word-webs; Websters "break the boring rules of spelling imposed by snoolish schoolmasters" of the foreground (1987, p. 13).

Grammar/Sin-Tactics. Not only do Background communicators alter the spelling of words as they attempt to re-construct their identities and experiences, they commit what Daly calls the "Sin of Creative Dis-Ordering" of the foreground rules of "order" for words (1987, p. 30). Background rhetors recognize that "the arrangement of words is not merely a matter of . . . 'style'" but of naming one's own reality (1987, p. 30). This strategy involves asking, "who controls the ways in which words are put together?" Upon answering this question, rhetors work with and alter wording and pronoun choice, make use of slashes, hyphens, and the concept/term "Be-ing" as the Verb of un-limiting Self-communication in order to communicate more accurately. These grammatical alterations function to move women into positions of self-affirmation and existential courage by discovering the nature of words beyond the foreground. As a result of Daly's Sin-Tactical strategy, Background rhetors now can speak of foreground fabrications, the corporate Big Brothers of Boredom, and Bore-ocratic details and mazes. They can refer to Sister Spinsters, Hag-ocracies, and Journeying into Other worlds. Daly's own writing is filled with Sin-Tactical grammatical errors as she names and defines foreground rhetors as the language and image "shape-shifters of snooldom/fooldom" or suggests that women can create "Archaic arrangements" of words and meanings "without snoolish interruption and interference" in their own speaking and writing (1987, pp. 28-29). The goal of using the strategy of Grammar/Sin-Tactics, Daly explains, is to free words from the "paralyzing patterns" of the foreground and begin to form "magical metapatterns" based on background experiences and realities (1987, p. 24).

Spooking, Sparking and Spinning. As communicators, women focus their attention not only on language patterns and meanings or on the identification of the harm done to them by negative discourse or symbols, they also engage in a journey of becoming that involves connecting and re-connecting with others and themselves.

Having been spooked, which is to be frightened and silenced by the foreground and its myriad constraints, women, using Daly's strategy of Spooking, learn to Spook/Speak back. Daly's theory explains how women as communicators can detect the patterns of rhetoric that have erased and fragmented women and can speak "back at and beyond the spookers" (1978, pp. 318-322). As Spooking communicators, women challenge, for example, the legal system and its construction of women's identities (Hoff, 1991; MacKinnon, 1989; West, 1990); label pornography as a form of the modern witch craze (Dworkin, 1974, 1981; Griffin, 1981; Lederer, 1980); and raise issues of what makes a woman "attractive" (Cottin Pograbin, 1983; Freedman, 1986; Lakoff & Scherr, 1984; Steinem, 1982). In these challenges and other like them, women as communicators reveal the false identities constructed for them as well as the methods used to normalize these constructions.

To succeed in their process of speaking out, feminist communicators need energy. In Daly's theory, this energy is garnered by "Sparking" and involves building the fires of "female energy which both comprehends and creates who we are; that impulse in ourselves that has never been possessed by the patriarchy" (1987, p. 77). Sparking strategies involve building coalitions and "sisterhood" (Morgan, 1970); they entail a "resourcement" of our energies and identities (Gearhart, 1982) and the creation of a chorus of women who, as communicators, speak back to the foreground. Background rhetors need to recognize, however, that, at first, generating enough sparks for building fires of Female Friendship is difficult. This is because "patriarchal males, sensing the ultimate threat of Female Sparking," attempt to put these fires out whenever women start them (Daly, 1978, p. 320). Sparking, for example, occurs when women gather together, begin to discuss their experiences and knowledge, make sense of these outside the patriarchal framework and mindset and inside a background epistemology, and discover new ways of existing as whole human beings.

Spinning communicators take these new ways of existing and begin to make connections with others. Spinning involves weaving past the un-reality of the foreground and "dis-covering the lost thread of connectedness" that results from patriarchal perceptions; spinning rhetors, "whirling away in all directions" from the foreground, repair this thread and begin to built a web of connections to other women (1987, p. 96). Without Spinning, Daly explains, a woman as communicator may become "trapped in one of the blind alleys" of the foreground—she may become "fixated upon" the foreground rules for order (1978, p. 320). Spinning communicators, as they join with other Spooking and Sparking women create a network of women's realities. Spinning communicators, for example, can be found in the peace camps of Greenham Common,

establishing and operating women's health centers and networks, creating and running "safe houses" for women and children, and participating in alternative and non-hierarchical forms of spirituality. After Spooking and Sparking, Spinning rhetors create new worlds and new ways of existing that are for themselves, other women, and the planet.

The strategies of women as communicators, as most critics recognize, move contrary to the rules of the foreground, its practices, and its theories. These "Contrary-Wise" forms of communication, however, assist women as communicators in creating a world where their voices—diverse and complex—can be heard above and beyond the constraints/communicators of the foreground (1987, p. 113).

BACKGROUND COMMUNICATORS

Women can communicate authentically in the Background, the "homeland" in which women are able to achieve "ontological depth" and unlimited "Self-communication" (Daly, 1987, pp. 63, 64). In this realm, communication can be described as "exceeding normal or conventional bounds in thought, design, conception, execution, or nature." It also seems a bit extravagant, fantastic, and visionary, but this is only because, as yet, it cannot be explained by, as Daly herself suggests, "any known theories" (1987, p. 100). The following is a description of the unique traits, goals, strategies, and visions of the women communicators who move within the Background. These women cannot be grouped into one homogeneous category known as "Woman." Rather, they must be identified and understood by their multiple, highly complex, and ever changing communication styles and patterns.

In order for women to discover authentic, self-affirming, and women-centered forms and styles of communication, they must begin to define themselves in ways that have not been recognized within the foreground. This self-definition is a complex and diverse process, one in which women reach not a single definition or state of being but many kinds of be-ing (1987, p. 64). Daly describes the two kinds of be-ing that most fully exemplify this process of self-definition as "Hags" and "Crones." A "Hag" is most commonly defined as "a female demon," a "fury," or a "harpy." "Hag" also is defined as "an ugly or evil-looking old woman," referencing its former definition as "an evil or frightening spirit" (1978, pp. 14-15). Daly suggests that before we allow this word to sound too negative, however, we should move outside the constraints of the foreground and ask the relevant questions: "'Evil' by whose definition? 'Frightening' to whom?" (1978, p. 14) Considering the source, this foreground definition may be a compliment, for as Daly notes, "the beauty of strong, creative women is 'ugly' by misogynistic standards of 'beauty'" (1978, p. 15).

Hags exemplify the process of women's becoming outside the foreground because they embark on the journey of radical be-ing, seeking out, nurturing, and encouraging any creative enterprise that furthers women's process. In undertaking this journey, however, Hags become "haggard," a term commonly used in the foreground to "describe one who has a worn or emaciated appearance" (1978, p. 15). An obsolete definition of haggard, however, which Daly incorporates in her theoretical formulation, suggests that hags are communicators who are "untamed . . . 'intractable,' 'willful,' 'wanton' . . . wild in appearance." A haggard woman, then, can be defined as "a woman reluctant to yield to wooing"—one who is not "wooed" into compromise by traditional foreground rhetoric (1978, p. 15).

Haggard communicators, if they live long enough, become Crones—"the long-lasting ones" (1978, p. 16). These long-lasting rhetors have survived the life-threatening rhetoric of the foreground and are living to write/record/create the discourse of women as communicators (1978, p. 16). Crones act as Cronographers, recording from the Hag's perspective women's ways of be-ing, both past and present. These communicators recognize how they have been "tricked" by the "texts" of the foreground, find the courage to break out of the foreground constraints, and move into new ways of be-ing (1978, p. 6). As communicators, women recognize the illusion of the foreground, resist its summons and restrictions, and participate in the Journey of becoming. Background Communicators move past the foreground sense of reality and identity, creating a "Hag-ocracy," and affirming the complex processes of women as communicators (1978, p. 3).

Not only does Daly's work develop the dimensions of communication begun to be explored by feminist researchers—the nature of oppression, the goals and processes of women background communicators, the strategies available for developing women's voices, and the natures of women background communicators—but she articulates the unique characteristics of each of these elements. Daly's work, and this theory of communication, identify what might be labeled Hagography as rhetoric—women's communicative processes and patterns as they occur outside the patriarchal framework. As a result of Daly's Hagography, communication scholars might now begin to attend to very different sorts of communication phenomena and to use very different frameworks for analyzing these communicative events.

In order to illustrate some of these alternative frameworks and their application to a particular piece of feminist discourse, I now turn to an application of Daly's theory. In what follows, I apply Daly's theory of rhetoric to a speech given by Ursula Le Guin to the graduating class of Mills College, a private, all-women's college. In doing so, I illustrate how the Background framework Daly provides enables scholars to expand their critical tools and insights in their analysis and assessment of rhetoric.

An Illustrative Application of Daly's Hagographic Rhetoric to Ursula Le Guin's "A Left-Handed Commencement Address"

Ursula K. Le Guin is a distinguished author, feminist, and winner of numerous awards, including the National Book Award, Nebula, Hugo, Gandalf, and Kafka. She has written 16 novels and approximately 60 short stories and presented numerous public lectures. Of her work, Le Guin explains, "There is no more subversive act than the act of writing from a woman's experience of life using a woman's judgment" (1989, p. 177). In 1983, Ursula Le Guin delivered the commencement address to the graduating class of Mills College, titling it "A Left-Handed Commencement Address." Because of the nature of her address, the nature of the audience, and the various rhetorical strategies used by Le Guin, the speech offers rich data for rhetorical exploration. Le Guin's rhetoric combines elements of both public and private discourse and challenges patriarchal codes of conduct as well as rules for success. In her opening statement Le Guin thanked Mills College for offering her "a rare chance: to speak aloud in public in the language of women," acknowledging the existence of two rhetorical realms—women's and men's (p. 115). In the address, Le Guin touched on a variety of topics: power, failure, education, politics, relationships, children, careers, stereotypes, fears, and hopes. She compared success to failure and suggested that the two are intimately connected and she challenged her audience to have the courage to fail. In fact, she did not wish her audience success but, rather, the ability to live with failure and to live their lives free from domination.

When assessed through the lens of Daly's theory, Le Guin's speech exemplifies several of the patterns of communication articulated by that theory. As a rhetor, Le Guin speaks as a Hag—she is wild, risky, intractable and even unattractive to a foreground audience. She explains her choice to speak the language of women by stating boldly, "There is a Greek tragedy where the Greek says to the foreigner, 'If you don't understand Greek, please signify by nodding.' Anyhow, commencements are usually operated under the unspoken agreement that everybody graduating is either male or ought to be" (p. 115). Daly's conceptualization of the nature of women as communicators suggests that Le Guin, as a Hag, is reluctant to yield to the patriarchal code of audience adaptation—she will speak to the women of the audience even to the exclusion of the men. Le Guin's words are uncompromising and perhaps a bit unsettling to some audience members, yet, she maintains this posture throughout. She argues that intellectual tradition is male, the public tongue is male, and, perhaps women "have come a long way, baby, but no way is long enough. You can't even get there by selling yourself out: because there is theirs, not yours" (p. 115). Le Guin, in sum, confronts the foreground silencing of women, names women's experiences as one of exclusion and objectification, and sets the tone for her use of "women's language" throughout the address.

Le Guin goes on to suggest that women should not attempt to gain access to the foreground vision of postgraduation success, exemplifying Daly's thesis that the goals of women as communicators are different from those of the communicators operating in the foreground. She explains that women are "already foreigners" in this tradition and in society in general. "Women," she explains, "as women are largely excluded from, alien to, the self-declared male norms of this society" (p. 116). Her goal seems to be to create environments where women are free to craft their own futures. She encourages them to have children "only if" they want them. "Not hordes of them. A couple, enough" (pp. 115-116). She hopes they can build worlds of "weakness" for themselves and their children, and that they can ignore "words of power and talk about the battle of life" (p. 115). In effect, Le Guin is suggesting that the women in her audience step out of and away from the foreground—the society "where human beings are called Man, the only respectable god is male, and the only direction is up" (p. 116).

She reiterates her stance of woman as communicator, asking, "what if I talked like a woman right here in public? It won't sound right. It's going to sound terrible" (p. 115). Taking that risk, Le Guin continues to "talk like a woman" and to pursue her goal of constructing an alternative reality for women. At the same time, she engages in Daly's background strategy of redefinition. Le Guin states that what she hopes for her audience is not success and power: success "is somebody else's failure. . . . No, I do not wish you success. I don't even want to talk about it. I want to talk about failure" (p. 116). Failure is the "dark place. . . . the place that our rationalizing culture of success denies" (p. 116). We will all visit this place, she argues, and her goal is for her audience to "be able to live there," to "take responsibility for helplessness, weakness . . . the irrational and the irreparable, for all that is obscure, passive, uncontrolled, animal," and "unclean" (p. 117). As a woman as communicator, Le Guin exposes the unpleasant reality of foreground success, the concomitant oppression of women, and redefines "success" as "failure." Le Guin offers a new definition of success, one that recognizes the interconnection of individuals, the ability to live with ourselves as we encounter those aspects of existence that patriarchy has denied or rejected, and the valuing of that which has been assigned to women (p. 116).

Not only does Le Guin's rhetoric encourage her audience to move beyond the foreground of competition and power and into the Background, but it reflects many of the strategies available to women as communicators that Daly identifies. Le Guin takes her audience on a rhetorical journey into the Background by redefining key graduation themes—success and failure—and by reversing the implications of traditional metaphors. She alters the metaphor of darkness, for example, and suggests that darkness is the place that "nourishes" (p. 117). Darkness, Le Guin reasons, is the place "where no wars are fought and no wars are won," where one person does not have power over another (p. 117). She beckons her audience to leave the foreground and enter the darkness and the Background—to explore a different country than the one in which they have grown up—"to be at home there, keep house there, be your own mistress, with a room of your own" (p. 117). Le Guin's metaphor of darkness clashes with the logic of the foreground, which encourages us to avoid or escape the darkness, and offers a reversal of this frequently used metaphor suggesting, as Daly does, a need for change and/or transformation of the term and its meaning.

Le Guin also encourages her audience to participate in the strategies of Spooking and Sparking. She encourages her audience not to fall prey to what Daly labeled the "seductive summons" of the foreground. Le Guin admonishes her audience not to put on the masks of patriarchy and not to be fooled or tricked by foreground power games. She admonishes that, "if you put the mask on you'll have a hard time getting it off" (p. 116). Le Guin suggests that rather than putting on the masks of the foreground her audience members spook/speak back to "Machoman" (pp. 116-117). She encourages them to recognize the hazards of and leave behind "the so-called man's world of institutionalized competition, aggression, violence, authority, and power" (p. 116). She advocates Daly's strategy of Sparking explaining that if women "want to live as women, some separatism is forced upon us: Mills College is a wise embodiment of that separatism" (p. 116). She asks her audience to journey contrary to the foreground, to go beyond the "night side of our country," the side that has been despised by "Machoman" (p. 117). The sparking separatism of Mills College, Le Guin suggests, holds the potential for discovering the "day" side of women's country. The day side offers "high sierras, prairies of bright grass, we only know pioneers' tales about it, we haven't got there yet. We're never going to get there by imitating Machoman. We are only going to get there by going our own way, by living there" (p. 117). Le Guin's rhetoric articulates the need to spook/speak back to foreground messages that denigrate women's experiences and realities and reject these messages. Her rhetoric encourages women to consider and embrace new realms of existence and identity and to spark the fires of female togetherness in order to discover and spin into "the day side" of women's country.

Finally, Le Guin's address describes the nature of the world created by women as communicators—the state of deviance that Daly articulates in her theory. The image created by Le Guin's discourse is a world in which women live "not as prisoners, ashamed of being women, consenting captives of a psychopathic social system, but as natives" (p. 117). Women are at home in this world, "a world without the need to dominate, and without the need to be dominated" (p. 117). The world Le Guin describes is a world in which individuals look to the earth for blessing, not to the "sky full of orbiting spy-eyes and weaponry" (p. 117). The world created by Le Guin's rhetoric is a world where blessings come "from below" and "where human beings grow human souls" (p. 117).

Le Guin's commencement address, explained through the framework of women as communicators, becomes an intricate rhetorical document worthy of analysis and discussion, rather than an odd piece of rhetoric set aside or forgotten for lack of a proper critical/theoretical methodology. The address incorporates many of the elements formulated by Daly and employs many of the strategies available to Background rhetors. Le Guin assumes the stance of rhetorical "Hag," speaking against the foreground rules and constraints that she identifies and describes. She commits what Daly refers to as the "sin of ultimate blasphemy"—naming the "enemy" as male/Machoman. The strategies used in the address reflect many of those that Daly advocates women use as communicators: metaphors that clash with the going logic; redefinition; creative dis-ordering of rules and meaning; and Spooking and Sparking. Le Guin also describes the goals and the nature of the world created by women as they assume the stance of rhetors—goals and natures that differ greatly from the vision held out by the traditional intellectual community. Ultimately, she blurs the distinction between public and private discourse by discussing women's experiences, oppression, goals, and possibilities in a formal public setting. Furthermore, she uses what typically has been considered private language—the reciprocal, dialogic, and unguarded language that typifies women's discourse in the private realm—in the public realm. The result is a blurring of the distinction between public and private knowledge as well. Daly's theoretical framework assists critics in recognizing that Le Guin's rhetoric exposes foreground constraints and offers previously "unspeakable" background realities. As such, Le Guin's address calls into question the usefulness and function of making a firm distinction between these two realms of communication.

As this illustrative application of Daly's hagographic theory of women as communicators to Le Guin's commencement address revealed, Daly's theoretical formulations of foreground and Background frameworks and background strategies can greatly facilitate our analysis and appreciation of public and private discourse that otherwise might be dismissed as a fanciful but disorganized pastiche of comments. Likewise, Daly's theoretical formulations could add much to our understanding and appreciation of other rhetorical forms, including such "women's communication" genres as soap operas, harlequin romances, daytime audience-interaction talk shows, and the like.

Women as Communicators: Implications for Rhetorical Theory

This essay, which develops and describes a feminist rhetorical perspective of women as communicators, begins the process of articulating and exploring the rhetorical patterns and frameworks that exist in women's communicative styles and practices. A few of these patterns and frameworks—connections and interrelationships, for example—suggest traits and styles of interacting that typically are associated with women's roles. This may encourage some critics to label her theory as reinforcing stereotypical perspectives of women or even as a theory with essentialist underpinnings. This charge, however, runs counter to Daly's theory and her work. As Noddings (1990) explains, that "women and men have had different kinds of experience" and "our society's expectations and demands for their experience have differed" is obvious (p. 26). Daly's argument suggests not that women and men are innately different but, rather, that critics "have to work with difference—not essential difference, but experiential difference" (Noddings, 1990, p. 27).

The notion of Hagography as rhetoric, the process of dis-covering the variety of forms of women's communication and affirming those forms as they assist individuals in creating identities, functions not only as a generative theory but moves rhetorical scholars into the revisionist stage of the rhetorical tradition (Foss, Foss, & Trapp, 1991). At this stage, rhetorical constructs are reformulated so that they take into consideration women's diverse experiences and perspectives (pp. 284-287). Daly's theory, however, is more than revisionist and generative; it is highly political. Daly's work promotes the recognition of a rhetorical duality that informs and influences rhetorical practices in very different ways. Her theory reminds scholars that rhetoric that does not fit neatly into the foreground is usually relegated to the realm of non-rhetoric or, as Daly herself might suggest, non-sense. Daly's identification of the foreground and the Background assists women as communicators in challenging the ideologies that keep women oppressed and silenced (Moi, 1985) and in opening new pathways for understanding Background communication. Her theory also assists rhetorical scholars in recognizing that subjectives are continually created and recreated and that this is a process with no clear beginning or ending. According to Daly's theory, "subjectivity is an ongoing construction," a process that resembles a journey and "not a fixed point of departure or arrival from which one then interacts with the world" (de Laurentis, 1984, p. 159).

As Gergen (1982) suggests, developing theoretical perspectives that unsettle common assumptions requires, among other things, articulating the perspectives of those who do not share the majority view or interpretation, extending the "acceptable set of commonsense assumptions," and even searching "for an intelligible antithesis to commonly accepted understandings" (pp. 141-142). Daly's work as well as her radical feminist perspective urge rhetorical scholars to engage in this generative search, move contrary to the foreground, and begin to expand the base of acceptable assumptions regarding rhetorical phenomenon. Scholars are encouraged to move the Wrong Way—to explore in multiple directions and in multiple ways the rhetoric of other individuals who speak from outside the communication discipline. In so doing, rhetorical scholars begin to revise and expand the boundaries of the discipline and to explain more fully the diverse rhetorical phenomenon that are encountered daily. Revising and even re-creating some of the foreground sense-making structures for theory and criticism enables scholars to assess a wider variety of forms of communication with increased perspicuity as well as an increased awareness of the political nature of each rhetorical realm. Daly's feminist rhetorical perspective challenges some of the "truths" of the discipline and reminds rhetorical scholars that much is yet to be dis-covered in the realm of communication.

Notes

1. A useful and comprehensive definition and description of a feminist perspective and the feminist challenge to traditional research is offered in Foss & Foss (1989, 1991) and Foss, Foss, & Trapp (1991). Recognizing that the term feminist has numerous negative connotations, I offer the following definition for feminist that is consistent with both Daly's work and this research project. A feminist is an individual, usually a woman, who believes that women and men "should have equal opportunities for self-expression" and who works to secure these opportunities (Foss & Foss, 1991, p. 20). For other, similar, definitions of feminist and feminism, see Kramarae and Treichler (1985, pp. 158-161).

2. While scholars such as Spender, and Kramarae, for example, have made significant contributions to feminist theory, for the purposes of this essay, I have chosen to discuss those scholars who focus on feminist rhetorical theory specifically.

3. While Daly is not explicitly addressing Spitzack and Carter's notion of women as communicators and does not define herself as a communication theorist, she offers an increasingly detailed description of this concept throughout the work in which she focuses on communication and language. Thus, Daly's theoretical writings set the stage for discussion, elaboration, and modification of the idea of women as communicators and provide a useful alternative rhetorical critical frame for evaluating women's discourse.

4. Daly defines "be-ing" as "participation in the Ultimate/Intimate Reality" and as "the Final Cause, the Good who is Self-communicating, who is the Verb from whom, in whom, and with whom all true movements move," (1984, p. 2; c.f. 1985a, pp. xvii-xx; 1987, p. 64). For purposes of this essay, I have followed her use of this term throughout her books and attempted to reformulate her definition into lay terms that are more informative and helpful to this analysis.

5. Daly, of course, recognizes that women have seen "through the myths" and have been intellectually creative and productive. Her argument is, however, that even when women do break through these constraints, their work is hampered because they must struggle continually to dissipate the images under which they work as well as find ways to articulate their creativity so that will be heard (1985b, pp. 60-61).

6. Originally, in *Beyond God the Father* (1985a), Daly used the term "trivialization" rather than "depreciation." Since "Trivia" is one of the names for "the Triple Goddess," she no longer uses this term to mean the "depreciation/disparagement/belittling of the cause of women" (1984, p. 320n).

7. Daly received harsh criticism for her discussion of African genital mutilation by Lorde (1983). Lorde's criticism was directed at Daly's failure to "remember" images that are "dark and ancient and divine" in *Gyn/Ecology* and to incorporate fully the perspectives of women of color throughout her work (Lorde, 1983, pp. 94-97). Daly's fourth book, *Pure Lust* (1984), reflects her efforts to account for these "dark and ancient" images as does the *Wickedary* (Daly & Caputi, 1987).

8. Compare, for example, Daly's theory of metaphor with that of Burke (1969) or Weaver (1985). Burke suggests that a metaphor "is a device for seeing something in *terms* of something else. It brings out the thisness of a that, or the thatness of a this" (p. 503), while Weaver describes metaphor as "a means of discovery. . . . requiring only some form of parallelism. . . . leading us from a known to an unknown, but subsequently verifiable, fact of principle" (p. 203). Daly extends each of these perspectives, suggesting metaphors are not a means to express similarity but rather a means to articulate the need for change or transformation.

References

Aptheker, B. (1989). *Tapestries of Life: Women's Work, Women's Consciousness, and the Meaning of Daily Experience.* Amherst: University of Massachusetts Press.

Biesecker, B. (1992). "Coming to Terms with Recent Attempts to Write Women into the History of Rhetoric." *Philosophy and Rhetoric,* 25, 140-161.

Burke, K. (1969). *A Grammar of Motives.* Berkeley: University of California Press.

Campbell, K. K. (1973). "The Rhetoric of Women's Liberation: An Oxymoron." *Quarterly Journal of Speech,* 59, 74-86.

Campbell, K. K. (1986). "Style and Content in the Rhetoric of Early Afro-American Feminists." *Quarterly Journal of Speech,* 72, 434-445.

Campbell, K. K. (1989). "The Sound of Women's Voices." *Quarterly Journal of Speech,* 75, 212-258.

Campbell, K. K. (1990). *Man Cannot Speak for Her* (Vols. 1-2). Westport, CT: Praeger.

Cixous, H. (1976). "The Laugh of the Medusa." *Signs,* 1, 875-893.

Cottin Pogrebin, L. (1983, December). "A Feminist Wrestles with the Indisputable 'Fact' that Looks Do Count." *Ms.,* pp. 74-78, 109.

Daly, M. (1978). *Gyn/Ecology: The Metaethics of Radical Feminism.* Boston: Beacon.

Daly, M. (1984). *Pure Lust: Elemental Feminist Philosophy.* Boston: Beacon.

Daly, M. (1985a). *Beyond God the Father: Toward a Philosophy of Women's Liberation.* Boston: Beacon.

Daly, M. (1985b). *The Church and the Second Sex.* New York: Harper Colophon.

Daly, M. & Caputi, J. (1987). *Websters' First New Intergalactic Wickedary of the English Language.* Boston: Beacon.

Dance, F. E. X. (1978). "Human Communication Theory: A Highly Selective Review and Two Commentaries." *Communication Yearbook,* 2, 7-22.

de Laurentis, T. (1984). *Alice Doesn't: Feminism, Semiotics, Cinema.* Bloomington: Indiana University Press.

Dworkin, A. (1974). *Woman Hating.* New York: Dutton.

Dworkin, A. (1981). *Pornography: Men Possessing Women.* New York: Putnam.

Endress, V. A. (1988). "Feminist Theory and the Concept of Power in Public Address." In C. A. Valentine & N. Hoar (Eds.), *Women and Communicative Power: Theory, Research and Practice.* Annandale, VA: Speech Communication Association.

Edson, B. A. (1985). "Bias in Social Movement Theory: A View from a Female-Systems Perspective." *Women's Studies in Communication,* 8, 34-45.

Fishman, P. (1983). "Interaction: The Work Women Do." In B. Thorne, C. Kramarae, & N. Henley (Eds.), *Language, Gender and Society* (pp. 89-101). Rowley, MA: Newbury House.

Foss, K. A., & Foss, S. K. (1989). "Incorporating the Feminist Perspective in Communication Scholarship: A Research Commentary." In K. Carter & C. Spitzack (Eds.), *Doing Research on Women's Communication: Perspectives on Theory and Method* (pp. 65-91). Norwood, NJ: Ablex.

Foss, K. A., & Foss, S. K. (1991). *Women Speak: The Eloquence of Women's Lives.* Prospect Heights, IL: Waveland.

Foss, S. K., Foss, K. A., & Trapp, R. (1991). *Contemporary Perspectives on Rhetoric* (2nd ed.). Prospect Heights, IL: Waveland.

Foucault, M. (1970). *The Order of Things: An Archaeology of the Human Sciences.* New York: Pantheon.

Foucault, M. (1972). *The Archeology of Knowledge* (A. M. Sheridan Smith, Trans.). New York: Pantheon.

Freedman, R. (1986). *Beauty Bound.* Lexington, MA: Lexington.

Gearhart, S. M. (1982). "Womanpower: Energy Resourcement." In C. Spretnak (Ed.), *The Politics of Women's Spirituality: Essays on the Rise of Spiritual Power within the Feminist Movement* (pp. 195-206). Garden City, NY: Anchor/Doubleday.

Gearhart, S. M. (1979). "The Womanization of Rhetoric." *Women's Studies International Quarterly,* 2, 195-201.

Gergen, K. J. (1982). *Toward Transformation in Social Knowledge.* New York: Springer-Verlag.

Gilligan, C. (1982). *In a Different Voice: Psychological Theory and Women's Development.* Cambridge, MA: Harvard University Press.

Griffin, S. (1981). *Pornography and Silence: Culture's Revenge against Nature.* New York: Harper & Row.

Hall, S. (1985). "Signification, Representation, Ideology: Althusser and the Post-Structuralist Debates." *Critical Studies in Mass Communication,* 2, 91-114.

Hancock, B. R. (1972). "Affirmation by Negation in the Women's Liberation Movement." *Quarterly Journal of Speech,* 58, 264-271.

Hoff, J. (1991). *Law, Gender, and Injustice.* New York: New York University Press.

Houston, M., & Kramarae, C. (1991). "Speaking from Silence: Methods of Silencing and of Resistance." *Discourse and Society,* 2, 387-399.

Irigaray, L. (1980). "When Our Lips Speak Together." *Signs*, 6, 66-79.

Irigaray, L. (1981). "And the One Doesn't Stir without the Other." *Signs*, 7, 56-67.

Jaggar, A. M. (1983). *Feminist Politics and Human Nature*. Totowa, NJ: Rowman and Allanheld.

Japp, P. M. (1985). "Ester or Isaiah?: The Abolitionist-Feminist Rhetoric of Angelina Grimke." *Quarterly Journal of Speech*, 71, 335-348.

Kurs, K., & Cathcart, R. S. (1983). "The Feminist Movement: Lesbian-Feminism as Confrontation." *Women's Studies in Communication*, 6, 12-33.

Kramarae, C., & Treichler, P. A. (1985). *A Feminist Dictionary*. London: Pandora.

Kristeva, J. (1986). *The Kristeva Reader* (T. Moi, Ed.). New York: Columbia University Press.

Lakoff, R. T. (1975). *Language and a Woman's Place*. New York: Harper & Row.

Lakoff, R. T. (1977). "Language and Sexual Identity." *Semiotica*, 19, 119-130.

Lakoff, R. T. (1979). "Stylistic Strategies within a Grammar of Style." In J. Orasanu, M. K. Slater, & L. L. Adler (Eds.). *Language, Sex, and Gender* (pp. 53-78). New York: The New York Academy of Sciences.

Lakoff, R. T., & Scherr, F. L. (1984). *Face Value: The Politics of Beauty*. Boston: Routledge and Kegan Paul.

Lederer, L. (Ed.). (1980). *Take Back the Night: Women on Pornography*. New York: Bantam.

Le Guin, U. K. (1989). *Dancing at the Edge of the World: Thoughts on Words, Women, Places*. New York: Grove.

Lorde, A. (1983). "An Open Letter to Mary Daly." In C. Moraga & G. Anzaldua (Eds.). *This Bridge Called My Back: Writings by Radical Women of Color* (pp. 94-97). New York: Kitchen Table/Women of Color Press.

Lukács, G. (1971). *History and Class Consciousness: Studies in Marxist Dialectics* (R. Livingstone, Trans.). London: Merlin.

MacKinnon, C. A. (1989). *Toward a Feminist Theory of the State*. Cambridge MA: Harvard University Press.

Moi, T. (1985). *Sexual/Textual Politics: Feminist Literary Theory*. London: Methuen.

Morgan, R. (Ed.). (1970). *Sisterhood Is Powerful: An Anthology of Writings from the Women's Liberation Movement*. New York: Vintage.

Noddings, N. (1990). "Feminist Fears in Ethics." *Journal of Social Philosophy*, 21, 25-33.

Sheridan, D. (1988). "Empowering Women's Voice: Strategies of Norwegian Peacemaking Women." *Women's Studies in Communication*, 11, 37-49.

Solomon, M. (1988). "Ideology as Rhetorical Constraint: The Anarchist Agitation of 'Red Emma' Goldman." *Quarterly Journal of Speech*, 74, 184-200.

Spitzack, C., & Carter, K. (1987). "Women in Communication Studies: A Typology for Revision." *Quarterly Journal of Speech*, 73, 401-423.

Spivack, G. C. (1988). "Can the Subaltern Speak?" In C. Nelson and L. Grossberg (Eds.), *Marxism and the Interpretation of Culture* (pp. 271-313). Urbana: University of Illinois Press.

Steinem, G. (1982, April). "In Praise of Women's Bodies." *Ms.*, pp. 28-30.

Weaver, R. M. (1985). *The Ethics of Rhetoric*. Davis, CA: Hermagoras.

West, R. (1990). "Love, Rage and Legal Theory." *Yale Journal of Law and Feminism*, 1, 101-110.

Williams, M. R. (1990). *A Re-Conceptualization of Protest Rhetoric: Characteristics of Quilts as Protest*. Unpublished Doctoral Dissertation, University of Oregon, Eugene.

Krista Ratcliffe (essay date 1996)

SOURCE: Ratcliffe, Krista. "De/Mystifying Herself and Her Wor(l)ds: Mary Daly." In *Anglo-American Feminist Challenges to the Rhetorical Traditions: Virginia Woolf, Mary Daly, Adrienne Rich*, pp. 65-106. Carbondale: Southern Illinois University Press, 1996.

[*In the following essay, Ratcliffe provides an overview of Daly's radical feminist critique of patriarchal language and discusses the rhetorical strategies of intervention by which she exposes male oppression embedded in language and attempts to reclaim and liberate women's discourse from male domination.*]

> [T]his book is primarily concerned with the mind/spirit/body pollution inflicted through patriarchal myth and language at all levels.
>
> —Mary Daly, *Gyn/Ecology*

As a feminist philosopher, theologian, and political activist, Mary Daly is deeply concerned with Bathsheba's dilemma; however, she defines it in slightly different terms than does Woolf. Daly argues that the patriarchal categories constructed through language result in "a kind of gang rape" of a woman's mind and body ([***Beyond God the Father***] 152). In spite of (or perhaps because of) this jarring image, Daly also argues that a woman need not be doomed nor determined within these categories but may, instead, turn language back on itself and construct new categories while embarking on the journey of radical feminism. Such a journey—from twice-born Athena to thrice-born Athena,[1] from Righteous Truth to Sinister Wisdom, from Dutiful Daughter to Revolting Hag, from Spooking to Sparking to Spinning—has as its goal "the discovery and creation of a world other than patriarchy" (***Gyn/Ecology*** 1). Daly invokes this multidimensional journeying of radical feminism for herSelf and Others in her texts. But Daly's texts do more than just record three decades of an evolving radical feminist consciousness. Her critiques of myth, language, and ideology may also be read from the site of rhetoric and composition studies to extrapolate an Anglo-American feminist theory of rhetoric.

Since Daly first began writing in the 1960's, her mythic and linguistic critiques of patriarchy have gotten progressively more radical.[2] ***The Church and the Second Sex*** argues for equality of the sexes within the Church (6). ***Beyond God the Father*** argues for a new, unfolding definition of God that will create a space of "human becoming" (40). ***Gyn/Ecology*** argues for a radical feminist metaethics with which any woman can refute patriarchal history—for example, Indian suttee, Chinese footbindings, African genital mutilation, European witchburning, and American gynecology—and dis-cover her own history as well as its connections with other women's histories (xlvii). ***Pure Lust*** argues for an alternative to phallic lust in the form of a revisionary Pure Lust, which names the humor, hope, and harmony of women who challenge patriarchy (1-2). ***Websters' First Intergalactic Wickedary of the English Language*** by Daly and Jane Caputi offers a Metapatriarchal dictionary that creates new words and exposes sexist assumptions in old words by playing with etymological and metaphorical meanings (xiv-xv). As the culmination of all these works, the autobiographical ***Outercourse: The Be-Dazzling Voyage*** explores intersections of the personal, the philosophical, and the theological in radical feminist journeying.

Most importantly for rhetoric and composition studies, however, Daly's texts outline particular language strategies through which she finds her voice(s) and through which she hopes other women will find theirs. Daly's texts outline these strategies mostly in prefaces and introductions, forewords and afterwords, not only naming problems that will be explored but also identifying purposes and methods. In this way, her texts expose and critique insidious connections between myth, language, and the perpetuation of patriarchy. By examining Daly's critiques, by analyzing her own specific rhetorical strategies, and by exploring the differences between what she claims to do in her writing and what I read in her writing, I offer a rendering of her texts from the site of rhetoric and composition studies that articulates her contributions to this field. My purpose is to extrapolate an Anglo-American feminist theory of rhetoric that challenges the genderblindness of more traditional rhetorical histories, theories, and pedagogies.

To this end, I first locate Mary Daly as a rhetorical theorist. I then examine how her texts may be read as exposing a foreground rhetoric of patriarchal mystification and its strategies, which may be categorized into traditional rhetorical canons of invention, arrangement, style, memory, and delivery. In the majority of this chapter, however, I explore how Daly's texts may be read as conceptualizing a Background rhetoric of radical feminist de/mystification and as modeling its strategies; these Background strategies of Spinning, Disordering, Be-Spelling, Re-membering, and Be-Speaking are a feminist reversal of traditional rhetorical canons and, as such, imply revised concepts of a writing process and a rhetorical triangle. I conclude by posing theoretical and practical questions made possible by Mary Daly's Anglo-American feminist theory of rhetoric.

LOCATING MARY DALY AS A RHETORICAL
THEORIST

Mary Daly does not situate herself or her texts within a predominantly male tradition of Western rhetoric or even within a predominantly male tradition of Western scholarship.[3] While she acknowledges that a woman must enter patriarchal fields if she is ever to move beyond those fields, Daly's texts ultimately challenge such fields as well as their powerful traditions (***Gyn/Ecology*** 8). Daly clearly states why such challenges are needed: "Within a culture possessed by the myth of feminine evil, the naming, describing, and theorizing about good and evil has constituted a maze/haze of deception" (2). Daly identifies this maze/haze as patriarchy,[4] as the dominant ideology that cuts across all cultures, that encompasses everything, and that perpetuates itself through the good man speaking well about myth and language. She exhorts women to break through this maze/haze. Yet she rejects anti-intellectualism as a method, for she sees anti-intellectualism as a trap, an understandable but ultimately unproductive reaction against patriarchal education and scholarship that moronizes women (22). Instead, Daly calls for feminist scholarship that will enable feminism(s) to "become sensible" so that women can both think and feel themSelves becoming (23). The feminist scholarship that Daly models celebrates two moves: creating her own ideas through language yet being impeccably scholarly about doing so (***Pure Lust*** 412). The purpose of these scholarly moves is the liberation of myth and the liberation of language. Such liberation, Daly believes, has the potential to liberate women into radical feminism. To demonstrate how this theory of liberation locates Daly as a rhetorical theorist, I will critique her radical feminist concepts of Women, myths, and language function.

When talking about the liberation of women, Daly means *all* women. That is, she believes that because patriarchy "is itself the prevailing religion of the entire planet," it oppresses all of us regardless of our cultural location (***Gyn/Ecology*** 39). But Daly has been challenged for this seemingly uncomplicated use of the term *women,* and her texts have been attacked as separatist, essentialist, and racist. Because rhetorical theories ever circle around assumed definitions of subjectivity, Daly's claim and her critics' challenges deserve attention before we investigate her feminist theory of rhetoric.

Because Daly's feminism focuses on women's concerns, it is often charged with being a separatist ideology. Daly responds to this charge as follows: "The words *gynocentric be-ing* and *Lesbian* imply separation. This *is* what this book is about, but not in a simple way" (***Gyn/Ecology*** xlvi). That is, Daly is not a traditional separatist in terms of denying men the presence of women or women the presence of men, despite complaints that dismiss her as such because she has banned men from some of her classes. Daly interprets these complaints as male identified. Rather, Daly is a radical feminist separatist in her own terms; she encourages women to be present to one another, to identify ourselves in relation to each other instead of in relation to men. Within Daly's Woman-identified feminism, a radical feminist separatist is a be-ing who affirms "the flow of connectedness within each woman" and who works for a "feminist separation from the State of Separation" that is patriarchy (***Pure Lust*** 371-72, 373). Consequently, Daly spends little or no time talking about men, not because they cannot be liberated but because she figures plenty of other people will champion their cause (***Beyond*** [***Beyond God the Father***] 8, 172-74). From this position, Daly's feminism articulates how women can recognize and refuse their inferior status within patriarchy and achieve their own power within radical feminism. Daly's radical feminist separatist agenda has as its primary goal the transformation of a woman's Self and as its secondary goal the transformation of the social (***Gyn/Ecology*** 7). Within this logic, a radical feminist may exist with(in) the same time and space as patriarchy. Following a similar logic, Daly's feminist theory of rhetoric may be located within the rhetorical tradition(s) without being domesticated by it.

Because Daly's radical feminism focuses on women's Selves and on the powers of these Selves, it is often labeled essentialist. This charge is meant to dismiss Daly's intellectual power as naive by forcing her into the category of biological determinist. But Daly refuses such categorizing. She is not an essentialist in the Aristotelian sense; she does not believe that an irreducible essence defines a thing or a Self.[5] Neither is she an essentialist in John Locke's terms; she rejects his real and nominalist distinctions.[6] Instead, Daly redefines essentialism as a radical feminist concept.[7] This essentialism presumes an essence or a radical feminist Self that is always already in process, that is, the "Original core of one's being . . . that participates in Be-ing," which is the "Ultimate/Intimate Reality" or "Final Cause" (***Wickedary*** 95, 64). Within this theoretical framework, Daly's radical feminist Self is an essence in motion, a be-ing continually constructed through the interweavings of myth and language, a be-ing participating in Be-ing (***Pure Lust*** 160-61).[8] Thus, Daly is an essentialist, but in her own terms.

Because Daly's feminism focuses on the effects of patriarchy on all women, it has been accused of having an unacknowledged Euro-American focus. The most well-known challenge of this kind comes from Audre Lorde. On 6 May, 1979, she wrote a letter to Daly detailing her interpretation of ***Gyn/Ecology***; when she received no written reply, Lorde published her letter. In it, Lorde commends Daly for her "good faith toward all women" ("Open Letter" 67). She agrees with Daly that the oppression of women crosses all ethnic and racial boundaries; however, she argues that Daly's focus erases differences within this oppression (70). For example, Lorde concurs with Daly that too little has been written about African genital mutilation but also asks Daly to consider not just the similarities between African genital mutilation, Chinese footbinding, and American gynecology but also the differences: "To imply . . . that all women suffer the same oppression simply because we are women is to lose sight of the many varied tools of patriarchy" (67). Lorde concludes her letter with a thank-you for the insights that Daly has given her and an offering of her own insights as repayment (71). In many ways, Lorde's letter is offered as a gift because she had earlier decided never again to talk with white women about race; for Daly, however, she makes an exception.

In the introduction to the second edition of ***Gyn/Ecology***, Daly acknowledges Lorde's letter. Although she implies that Lorde has misunderstood her intent, she apologizes for the pain that any unintended receptions of her book might have caused: "I regret any pain that unintended omissions may have caused others, particularly women of color, as well as myself. The writing of ***Gyn/Ecology*** was for me an act of Biophilic Bonding with women of all races and classes, under all the varying oppressions of patriarchy" (xxxi). Although willing to apologize for unintended slights, Daly refuses to debate Lorde in published discourse, claiming that such debates hurt women's causes. And while I agree with Daly that women's wrangling over who is more oppressed is probably a counterproductive political move, I do not believe this is what Lorde intended.

Feminists may learn and grow from exchanging ideas, that is, from negotiating the very real differences between our intentions and our receptions.

The above challenges to Daly's texts should resonate for all of us as we consider her feminist theory of rhetoric. Although Daly rarely uses the word rhetoric, her critiques of patriarchal myth and language are indubitably rhetorical, for at the intersections of myth, language, and ideology we arrive at rhetoric.[9] When describing the rhetorical functions of such intersections, Daly establishes no easy cause and effect. Instead, she argues that our myths and language must change if patriarchy is to change and that patriarchy must change if our myths and language are to change. This claim does not posit a logical contradiction. Rather, it conceptualizes a complex, active cultural matrix within which a woman may employ language to (un)weave interweavings of patriarchal myth, language, and ideology within herSelf (*Gyn/Ecology* 389-424).

Daly's concerns about women and myth permeate her texts. Although strongly grounded in Western philosophy and Judeo-Christian theology, her texts define myth in the broadest sense of the wor(l)d. She is particularly concerned with how these myths metonymically re-present patriarchy. Her critiques of such re-presentations encompass different cultures,[10] yet the common denominator is that these critiques reimagine myths by dis-covering[11] women's perspectives, something that many traditional myths have either blindly or purposefully ignored. For example, the Neith myth is re-membered as the Libyan Triple Goddess whom the Greeks whitewashed into Athena (*Gyn/Ecology* 75, 88). Athena's myth is dis-covered as a Warrior goddess who must be born not only of Metis's womb, not only of Zeus's head, but also of her own words (13-14). Cinderella's myth is re-called as a young Oriental girl's being subjected to beautifying (read "eroticized") foot-bindings (151-52). Snow White's myth is un-covered as a young girl's being offered the same poisonous apple of patriarchy that the wicked stepmother has choked on all her life (44, 351). The Virgin Mary's myth is re-visioned as a young girl's being overwhelmed by a loving father's sexual advance (85). And the myth of the Trinity (the Father, Son, and Holy Ghost) is re-cognized as a patriarchal reversal of Trivia, the Triple Goddess who is manifested via Maiden, Mother, and Crone (75-79). Such antipatriarchal conclusions will no doubt disturb those who take less extreme positions. But this disturbing element is precisely why Daly's texts are worth reading. Demaris Wehr echoes this claim in her review of *Pure Lust*: "While such strong denunciations no doubt serve to deter adherents of these beliefs from reading [Daly's] work, I recommend they read [her texts] anyway. Why? Her powerful mind, her creative genius and her uncanny ability to put her finger on deep emotional, psychological and spiritual problems are ignored at our peril" (14). Moreover, Daly's metonymic critiques model a method that may be employed in a variety of contexts.

Of particular interest to rhetoric and composition scholars is the way Daly theorizes a tripled language function: that is, sign, symbol, and metaphor. She acknowledges that language functions as a sign system, with all the potential for free play that such a system entails. Without such play, feminists could not use old words in new ways. But she also insists on language's simultaneous symbolic function, which she believes both historicizes and invokes free play. She compares these functions of sign and symbol as follows: "Symbols, in contrast to mere signs, participate in that to which they point. They open up levels of reality otherwise closed to us and they unlock dimensions and elements of our souls which correspond to these hidden dimensions and elements of reality. . . . Of course, there can be no One Absolutely Right symbol for all Lusty women, for we belong to different tribes and have great individual diversity" (*Pure Lust* 25). Daly's problem with patriarchal symbols is obvious in her definition of them as "commonly flattened-out, frozen metaphors that have been captured, reduced, and reversed into one-dimensionality" (*Pure Lust* 405-6). Her solution to this problem is radical feminist de/mystification. This de/mystifying process exposes that symbols and their meanings are not eternally nor universally fixed; hence, they may be changed. Such a process also affirms the power of symbols for women in general and in particular, a move that enables Daly's concept of symbol to avoid the gender erasure that often occurs when people retreat into totalizing linguistic philosophy (all Americans speak the same language), totalizing feminism (all women are oppressed by language in the same way), or totalizing tokenism (a particular woman's problem with language is an exception, an aberration).

Although symbols function as metaphors within Daly's theory of language, metaphors possess more possibilities than mere symbolic function. More than stylistic dress laid onto thought, metaphors are the innate generative power of language that enables it to be used, consciously and unconsciously, to subvert the status quo. Daly defines the feminist agenda of this language function as follows: "[M]etaphors evoke action, movement. They Name/evoke a shock, a clash with the 'going logic' and they introduce a new logic. Metaphors function to Name change, and therefore they elicit change" (*Pure Lust* 25).[12] In turn, metaphors generate other metaphors, some of which Daly names metapatriarchal metaphors.[13] Such metaphors rupture the dominant logic(s) of patriarchy and propel "a woman further into the Wild dimensions of Other-centered consciousness—out of dead circles into Spiraling/Spinning motion" (405). Daly insists that metapatriarchal metaphors be seen not as fixed symbols, not as fixed abstractions, but as the never ending processual energy and motion that is radical feminism (407, 327-33) In this way, Daly conceptualizes a gendered language function that not only reflects reality but also continually (re)constructs it. It is this gendered function that separates Daly's theory of metaphor from humanist ones.

In Daly's theory the tripled language functions of sign, symbol, and metaphor occur simultaneously in two dimensions: the foreground and the Background. Daly defines *foreground* as the "male centered and monodimensional arena where fabrication, objectification, and alienation take place" (**Wickedary** 76). She defines *Background* as "the Realm of Wild Reality; the Homeland of women's Selves and of all Others" (63). Radical feminism, then, is a woman's newly created yet remembered journey from foreground to Background. It is a journey *from* the realm of patriarchy where meanings are frozen and reversed to a realm other than patriarchy where women may reconnect with unfrozen, a priori meanings that defy the patriarchal structure of language. Daly names this radical feminist process of Websters' moving from foreground to Background as Spinning (**Gyn/Ecology** 389-91).

Spinning is a be-ing's participation in the metaphoric drive of language in order to de/mystify gendered terms, phrases, claims, and actions. The passage below is a prime example of Daly's Spinning through writing. Through her wild and wicked feminist play with the word *paradise*, she challenges commonly accepted foreground meanings and discovers radical feminist Background ones:

> A primary definition of *paradise* is "pleasure park." The walls of the Patriarchal Pleasure Park represent the condition of being perpetually parked, locked into the parking lot of the past. A basic meaning of park is "game preserve." The fathers' foreground is precisely this: an arena where the wildness of nature and of women's Selves is domesticated, preserved. It is the place for the preservation of females who are the "fair game" of the fathers, that they may be served to these predatory Park Owners, and service them at their pleasure. Patriarchal Paradise is the arena of games, the place where the pleas of women are silenced, where the law is: Please the Patrons. Women who break through the imprisoning walls of the Playboys' Playground are entering the process which is our happenings/happiness. This is Paradise beyond the boundaries of "paradise." Since our passage into this process requires making breaks in the walls, it means setting free the fair game, breaking the rules of the games, breaking the names of the games. Breaking through the foreground which is the Playboys' Playground means letting out the bunnies, the bitches, the beavers, the squirrels, the chicks, the pussycats, the cows, the nags, the foxy ladies, the old bats and biddies, so that they can at last begin naming themselves.
>
> (*Gyn/Ecology* 7)

Many strategies employed in the above passage represent Daly's Spinning through writing, which uses language against itself, that is, uses foreground strategies to expose Background meanings. Toward this end, Daly employs several Ciceronian topoi. Definition enables her to redefine *paradise*, exposing how the foreground concept traps women and how the Background concept empowers them. Etymology enables her to unpack lost meanings of *paradise*, which further enhance her Background definition. Analogy, too, enables her to expand her definition of *paradise*, comparing it to a "park" and a "game preserve" in order to expose the penned-in animal status afforded to women in the foreground. Partition enables her to divide and define *game preserve* so that *game* suggests women and *preserve* suggests their disempowerment. Finally, effect enables her to explain how women are silenced, and difference enables her to demonstrate that women should name themselves. Likewise, Daly utilizes several figures to construct Background meanings. Metaphor allows her to expose *paradise* as a "Playboy's Playground." The alliteration of *ps* and *ss* allows her to construct a tone that is disdainful of the foreground. Polyptoton allows her to employ different forms of *preserve* to emphasize the static nature of the foreground. Paronomasia allows her to unpack *fair game* as both beautiful women and easy prey, exposing the animal status of women. Prosonomasia allows her to extend her metaphor and nickname men as "Playboys" and "Patrons."

By challenging patriarchal meanings, Daly's paradise passage and its strategies challenge the genderblindness of traditional logic and rhetoric. They also exemplify Daly's belief in language play: breaking through foreground meanings is a context-bound possibility, not simply a utopian desire. Although Daly acknowledges the limitations of such play for transforming the social, her wild and wicked Spinning is a deadly serious and revolutionary endeavor in that it possesses the potential to transform the Self.

Patriarchal scholarship diminishes the process of Spinning by capturing it in dictionaries and renaming it linguistic etymology. But according to Daly, other records also exist as deep Background feelings and ideas. These feelings and ideas are what Lorde challenges Daly to take even further: "Mary, I ask that you re-member what is dark and ancient and diving within yourself that aids your speaking" (69). It is to these ideas and feelings that Daly looks for inspiration; it is to them that she refers when traditional linguistic scholars accuse her etymologies of being "incorrect" or "far-fetched." She might agree that they are fetched from afar, but such far-fetched truths propel Daly's radical feminism. From this position in motion, Daly would not accuse foreground scholars in their own language of privileging the signified; she would accuse them of perpetuating the static premises of patriarchy. By exposing this play between foreground meanings and Background meanings, Daly unmasks how myth and language intersect in the foreground to perpetuate patriarchy. In other words, she un-covers the dominant rhetoric of patriarchy.

A RHETORIC OF PATRIARCHAL MYSTIFICATION

This dominant foreground rhetoric perpetuates the eighth deadly sin of deception (*Pure Lust* x).[14] The primary function of this deceptive rhetoric is to socialize women into the foreground, reinforcing its powerful ideology through the interweavings of myth and language. As such, this deceptive rhetoric constructs an inverted foreground culture that mystifies by reversing primary and derivative values (Burke, *Rhetoric of Motives* 104). Daly describes this foreground inversion as patriarchy's power to steal women's words and meanings (*Pure Lust* 86). In the following passage she exemplifies this claim: "Women's minds have been mutilated and muted to such a state that 'Free Spirit' has been branded into them as a brand name for girdles and bras rather than as a name of our verb-ing, be-ing Selves. Such brand names brand women 'Morons.' . . . Patriarchy has stolen our cosmos and returned it in the form of *Cosmopolitan* magazine and cosmetics" (*Gyn/Ecology* 5). Such foreground inversions of meaning are commonly perceived not as "mind-binding"[15] but as the "natural order of things" at the interwoven levels of the institutional, the personal, and the textual; as a result, women are discouraged from re-membering and un-covering possible Background meanings. The implications for women are enormous. They suffer not only from plastic and potted passions[16] but also from stifled and stilted speech. Shaped by genteel manners and customs, this speech, or "shallow verbiage," exists to flatter men and build their confidence; it pays no heed to a woman's repressed ideas and emotions (*Pure Lust* 18). Thus, a rhetoric of patriarchal mystification promotes what Daly calls the Big Lie.

This rhetoric, however, is not happenstance. It is driven by foreground methods. Within Western rhetorical traditions, these methods have been categorized into the canons of invention, arrangement, style, memory, and delivery. Although Daly does not couch her analysis in terms of the rhetorical traditions, her primary project may be read as identifying mystifying invention strategies, which she perceives to be particularly responsible for reproducing the continual stasis of the foreground.

The foreground's first mystifying invention strategy, trivialization, makes unimportant that which is important and succeeds when we fall prey to hierarchal, dichotomized thinking; for instance, antifeminists wondering why feminists are so concerned with women's problems when many other, more important troubles exist in our world, such as poverty, war, and racism. A second, particularization, focuses on only one aspect of an issue or event and succeeds when we neatly compartmentalize ourselves and our complex social matrix; for example, Anglo-Americans claiming or implying that race is only a concern for African Americans or Asian Americans. A third, spiritualization, is a form of particularization that separates mind, spirit, and body, and it succeeds when we ignore material influences on spirituality; that is, when the body is maimed to celebrate the soul. And a fourth, universalization, renders particular differences invisible by concentrating on the fictionalized whole, and it succeeds when we erase categories of difference, particularly gender, from our analyses; for example, claiming that we should focus on strategies of empowerment for all humans, not on particular strategies for Hispanic women (*Beyond* 5).

A fifth strategy, erasure, fosters a foreground forgetting of both mythic and linguistic events. Mythic erasure represses women's lives, stories, and meanings from traditions of history, literature, politics, theology, folklore, philosophy, and so on. Linguistic erasure represses women's words and their presence in grammatical constructions of language (*Gyn/Ecology* 8). Erasures succeed when the foreground remains unquestioned; for example, when literary canons composed predominantly of males are presented as the best that has ever been said and written. A sixth, reversal, inverts the hierarchal values assigned to binary oppositions; it also occurs on both mythic and linguistic levels. Mythic reversals coopt women's biological and social powers. Theological and mythological examples are Adam's giving birth to Eve and Zeus's giving birth to Athena; a philosophical example is Socrates' adopting conception and birthing as metaphors for his method of dialectic.[17] Linguistic reversals devalue language assigned to women; for example, our witchy connotation of *hag* mystifying its etymological root in *holiness* and our unquestioning use of *bunny, bitch, beaver,* and so on, mystifying our frequent association of animal names with women (14-17, 7). Daly conceptualizes subcategories of reversals: simple inversion (MX missiles as Peacekeepers), reversals that posit the elementary world as the model for natural phenomena (watches explaining a deistic cosmos), reversals that project male qualities onto women and nature (penis envy, predatory birds), and reversals by which patriarchal males appropriate capacities and qualities of women (philosophical midwifery) (*Wickedary* 239-58).

A seventh strategy, false polarization, posits false binary oppositions. Unlike some feminists, Daly does not reject the method of binary oppositions; in fact, she regularly employs them; for instance, foreground and Background. What she does attack, however, is the patriarchal presence assumed by the false positioning of binaries.

Such a strategy succeeds when we are afraid to name true positionings. Mythically, we see male-defined sexism (men holding the door open for women) being set up against male-defined feminism (women hating men) (**Gyn/Ecology** 8). The sexism is extremely conservative; the feminism, extremely radical. Such false positionings allow antifeminists to say, Gee, I hold open a door for a woman and she acts like this?—the result being that feminism(s) are easily dismissed. Linguistically, false binaries emerge as man/wife (which denotes differences in power and roles), madonna/whore (which limits women's options), and stud/wimp (which limits men's).

Divide-and-conquer, an eighth strategy, separates the oppressed to keep them from uniting and rebelling. Also occurring at mythic and linguistic levels, this strategy succeeds by turning women against each other, encouraging us to compete with one another rather than critique systemic oppressions. Mythic divide and conquer celebrates a token woman (whom Daly calls "twice-born Athena" or "Daddy's girl") as a positive role model for other women because she has played the game and pulled herself up by her bootstraps; ironically, the token's function is often to fill an unspoken quota and keep other women from attaining the same successful place. Linguistic divide and conquer is a form of particularization. It compartmentalizes our logic so that we separate, for example, logical and emotional appeals, thus effectively hiding (the existence and the validity of) their interconnectedness (**Gyn/Ecology** 8).

A ninth strategy, mummy words, entails using language to deaden the mind. This strategy succeeds when language remains invisible, when it is perceived as a tool that carries meaning rather than as an integral component in the construction of meaning. Daly cites the following examples: *civilization, mystery, custom, forefathers, history*—all of which are usually silent about women's actual social roles (**Wickedary** 243). Tenth, dummy words also imply a strategy of using language to deaden the mind; however, these words appear harmless so as to metaphorically mystify the danger of their referents. Again, this strategy succeeds when we allow language to remain invisible and do not question it. Daly cites these examples: *daughter* used as a radioactive decay product, *breeder* reactor, *air-breathing missile, artificial intelligence* (245). Eleventh, anti-biotic words imply a strategy in which dummy terms are so exaggerated that they deserve a separate category. Like mummies and dummies, anti-biotic words succeeds when their language is commonly accepted instead of exposed as the hyperbolic ironies they are. Daly notes the following example: acronyms like MAD (mutual assured destruction), names like *bomblet*, terms like *fallout, nuke, meltdown, deployment, and plutonium*, and code words like *disinformation* (character assassination) and *neutralize* (assassination) (246-47).

The Sado-Ritual Syndrome is the twelfth and most powerful strategy that patriarchy employs to relegate women to foreground stasis. Although the Syndrome occurs transculturally, it manifests itself differently: for example, Chinese footbinding, African and American genital mutilation, Indian widow burning, European witch burning, and so on. According to Daly, such rituals are perpetuated via men's and women's participation in the Sado-Ritual Syndrome's seven moves: obsessing about purity; erasing responsibility for atrocities performed in the name of a transcendent truth; catching on and spreading quickly; using women as scapegoats and "token torturers"; obsessing on order, repetition, and detail; accepting behavior that in other contexts would appear appalling; validating a ritual's existence through academic scholarship (**Gyn/Ecology** 130-35). The socializing function of this Syndrome keeps women from questioning their plight and imagining other possibilities. Because such patriarchal logic is inscribed within our bodies, this Syndrome is a powerful strategy for maintaining the status quo.

Although Daly discusses the remaining rhetorical canons in less detail, they also participate in constructing the foreground's rhetoric of patriarchal mystification. For example, she claims that foreground arguments are *arranged* in a "tidy" order, which she defines as "tracked, tamed, sanitized, routinized" (**Wickedary** 97); furthermore, she names the linear movement of this arrangement strategy "pure thrust" (221). Daly also claims that *styles* of such arguments too often invoke the noun-goddess and passive voice, thus deleting agency and direct action (86, 215). She further claims that such arguments construct a *memory* that allows only enough space for foreground memories; these memories perpetuate the "cock and bull story [of] patriarchal history, any highly respected account of the exploits of cocks and bullies which effectively erases the existence and history of women and all Others" (190). Finally, Daly claims that the *delivery* of these arguments occur either as consciousness razing or as recovering, that is, covering again (191, 222).

Within a rhetoric of patriarchal mystification, these five canons successfully mystify possible Background meanings by constructing foreground meanings that appear so clear, so precise, so logical, so normal, and so true that none of us think to question them. None of us can stand outside this rhetoric or its meanings because they are found at all levels of society: "from styles of grammar to style of glamour, from religious myth to dirty jokes, from theological hymns honoring the 'Real Presence' of Christ to commercial cooing of Coca-Cola as 'The Real Thing,' from dogmatic doctrines about the 'Divine Host' to doctored ingredient-labelling of Hostess Cupcakes, from subliminal ads to sublime art. Phallic myth and language generate, legitimate, and mask the material pollution that threatens to terminate all sentient life on this planet" (*Gyn/Ecology* 9). Within the foreground, the only option open to women is reacting, fighting on foreground turf in foreground terms (*Wickedary* 222). But Daly claims that such games cannot be won and that participation in them only further inflicts "mind/spirit/body pollution" upon a woman (*Gyn/Ecology* 9). For this reason, she offers an alternative to this foreground rhetoric of patriarchal mystification.

A Rhetoric of Radical Feminist De/Mystification

This Background rhetoric encourages and enables women to de/mystify foreground meanings and discover Background ones. Such a de/mystifying rhetoric is imperative if women are to unmask the eighth deadly sin of deception, which permeates every word we use (*Gyn/Ecology* 3). Daly describes this de/mystifying rhetoric in *Pure Lust*: "Breaking the bonds/bars of phallocracy requires breaking through to radiant powers of words, so that by releasing words, we can release our Selves" (4). She names the moves of this rhetoric *exorcism* and *ecstasy,* with *exorcism* entailing the (meta)physical dis-possessing of patriarchy and *ecstasy,* entailing the (meta)physical giddiness that emerges when women are released from foreground meanings (*Gyn/Ecology* 2; *Wickedary* 75). As such, a rhetoric of radical feminist de/mystification encourages and enables a woman to Spin between the foreground and Background, continually (un)weaving the intersections of patriarchal myth and language in order to create and dis-cover both herSelf and herWor(l)ds.[18]

This Background rhetoric depends upon language, namely, the possibilities of metaphor that Daly associates with the powers of magical conjuring:

> The Active Potency of the archimage, then, is transformative Power. This faculty, through which she "brings celestial forces to earth," is the power of healing broken connections. One way through which this is communicated is the transmission of Metaphoric words that transverse/pass across the fathers' archetypes, awakening the stifled *archai* with word-waves/wand-waves. The words/wands of Weird women also transverse the archetypes in the sense that they overturn and reverse them, reversing their reversals. For words are weapons, Labryses of Archimagical Amazons. Women participating in the biophilic powers of the Archimage also transverse in the "obsolete" sense of the term, which is "alter, transform," as we change our lives in the process of dis-spelling the archetypes.
>
> (*Pure Lust* 90)

This magical conjuring through metaphor manifests itself in many ways. Consider the slight of place that occurs when a woman is shifted from a "thing" noun to a "verbal" noun: instead of being a thing or object, she becomes a Namer or a Speaker, who has the power to "Name away the archetypes that block the ways/words of Metabeing" (86-87). In this way, magical conjuring both ruptures phallogocentric grammar and generates Daly's Elemental Feminist Philosophy. This Philosophy is a kind of be-ing and be-thinking that is grounded in a Metapatriarchal consciousness which presumes reason to be a function of instinct, intuition, and passion as well as mind (*Wickedary* 72).

Magical conjuring through metaphor is crucial to Daly's rhetoric of radical feminist de/mystification. It enables women to overcome both verbal violence and verbicide. While verbal violence degrades a woman semantically (*Gyn/Ecology* 358, 359-62), verbicide carefully kills words in order to rob them of meaning and reduce them to noise (*Wickedary* 233). The danger of verbicide is that it splits a woman from herSelf and creates in her an insecurity that results in amnesia, aphasia, and apraxis (*Pure Lust* 94). But Daly assures us that such states need not be permanent: "The remedy is unrelenting understanding that Stamina is stronger than the verbiage of the re-verberators, and that breathing/speaking forth Elemental words/actions is itself the creation and communication of Stamina, which is the living thread of conversation spun by Fates. . . . Naming our way beyond verbicide (which is deeply connected with gynocide) we are creators of our own fates—becoming Fates" (95). If a woman employs this remedy, she becomes patriarchy's worst fear: a castrator. For magical conjuring through metaphor implies the castration of language and images that construct and reflect patriarchy (*Beyond* 9; *Pure Lust* 166-69). In the process, magical conjuring creates new Elements—new hearing, new contexts, new speech, and new words—whose discursive powers can cast spells on the personal and the cultural.[19]

The first Element that Daly's Background rhetoric must conjure is a new hearing. In the last chapter of *Gyn/Ecology,* Daly concludes that the word was not the beginning, the hearing was (424). With this assertion, she challenges patriarchal obsessions with First Causes. She locates hearing (a human potential), not the Word (God's utterance), as the space where we can analyze Be-ing and Know-ing. This (meta) physical space is where women can question patriarchal ideology through myth and language:

> The essential thing is to hear our *own* words, always giving prior attention to our *own* experience, never letting prefabricated theory have *authority* over us. Then we can be free to listen to the old philosophical language (and all philosophy that does not explicitly repudiate sexism is old, no matter how novel it may seem). If some of this language, when heard in the context of female becoming is still worth hearing, we need not close our ears. But if we choose to speak the

same sounds they will be formally and existentially new words, for the new context constitutes them as such. Our process is *our* process.

(***Beyond*** 189)

Once this hearing is tapped and a radical feminist journey begun, other Elements necessary to Daly's Background rhetoric are also magically conjured. Once a woman hears differently, she must constantly negotiate between foreground and Background contexts. Because this process cannot be arrested, new hearing continually generates new contexts, that is, new movements between foreground and Background. Even when a woman uses old language, new contexts transform it into new speech (***Beyond*** 159). In turn, new speech generates questions as well as answers to these questions (8-9). As such, new speech is essential to Daly's rhetoric of radical feminist de/mystification. Without it, language becomes a trap; women, merely determined parrots. But a woman's employing new speech does not mean that she should imitate male-identified discourse (8). New speech leads to new words, and this process continually unfolds at all semiotic levels—in talk, in texts, in clothing style, in body language, and so on (***Gyn/Ecology*** 340; ***Wickedary*** 86). In this way, Daly's rhetoric of radical feminist de/mystification occurs in the presence of patriarchy.

Like its foreground reversal, Daly's Background rhetoric is not happenstance. It is driven by Background methodicide, which Daly defines as "deicide by means of asking Nonquestions, and Discovering, reporting, and analyzing Nondata" (***Wickedary*** 82). Methodicide is not the denial of method but rather the denial of foreground methods and the celebration of Background ones.[20] How does Daly's methodicide translate into practice? It encourages a woman to actively read and write against patriarchal myths and language that construct herSelf and her daily life. Because it occurs in the midst of systemic oppressions, methodocide has its limits; nevertheless, it can be invoked by a Self, whose limited conscious agency may trust its unconscious for assistance.

Methodocidal reading and writing presume that a woman can and should break the silence imposed by patriarchal structures of history, culture, society, and family (***Beyond*** 93). Breaking the silence, however, is not a simple talking cure, nor is it without consequences. Instead, it is a never ending process that breaks subject/object categories into intersubjective relations that continually (re)produce meanings beyond the hearing of patriarchal ears (152). It induces "the vertigo of creation," the dizziness associated with Spinning (***Gyn/Ecology*** 414-17). Methodocidal reading and writing also presume that patriarchal concepts like "natural" and "objective" must be challenged and that patriarchal arguments must be analyzed to determine how they focus only on certain facts, never questioning the assumptions or implications of these facts while ignoring other facts that may inform a woman's experience (***Beyond*** 107).

Daly advocates specific de/mystifying maneuvers for methodocidal reading and writing. These maneuvers, I argue, construct her Background rhetoric of radical feminist de/mystification. This rhetoric reverses the foreground canons of rhetoric and posits instead interwoven Background Non-canons of Spinning, Dis-ordering, Be-Spelling, Re-membering, and Be-Speaking.

SPINNING

The re-versing of invention, Spinning is the first of Daly's Background Non-canons. Neither *topoi* nor place, Spinning is the major metaphoric motion of Daly's Background rhetoric (***Gyn/Ecology*** 424). Daly defines Spinning as "Dis-covering the lost thread of connectedness within the cosmos and repairing this thread in the process" (***Wickedary*** 96). In the foreground, however, such Spinning is often deflected and deflated with the following results: "Our creativity is misdirected into misplaced rage against other women. It is traced into soap opera level aspects of 'relationships.' Under therapeutic treatment, it is tracked into psychobabble that closes off deep Memory. When academically trained, it repeats male theories. Groomed for professional excellence, it serves phallic institutions. 'Religious,' it worships a male god" (***Pure Lust*** 18). By moving Spinners toward the Background, Spinning exposes patriarchal socialization, reversing the foreground's deflection and deflation of Gyn/Ecological Creation and modeling this reversal for others (***Gyn/Ecology*** 404). But such an invention process is not easy: it requires repetitive practice, not just wishful thinking (***Pure Lust*** 261). To articulate the methods and possibilities of such an invention process, I have culled Daly's texts to identify different invention strategies, which may be read together as the Non-canon of Spinning that drives Daly's Background rhetoric.

The first type of Spinning is Daly's reversal of the seven-step Sado-Ritual Syndrome. As noted earlier, this Syndrome details how patriarchal rituals obsess on purity, erase responsibility, spread quickly, use women as scapegoats and as token torturers, promote compulsive orderliness and obsessive repetition, make the unacceptable acceptable, and justify themselves through scholarship (***Gyn/Ecology*** 130-35). But radical feminists may turn this Syndrome against itself, employing it as a de/mystifying strategy. Such de/mystifications may occur in interrelated reading and writing moves. In ***Gyn/Ecology*** Daly uses this Syndrome to read and write against cultural rituals such as widow burning and genital mutilation; in ***Pure Lust*** she employs this Syndrome to analyze and write against the effect of such atrocities on women's spirituality. This Syndrome could also be used to analyze Miss America pageants, *Cosmopolitan* covergirls, women in academia, and so on. And though Daly discusses this Syndrome in relation to patriarchy's atrocities against women, William Jones finds this analysis useful in demystifying patriarchy's ritualized oppression of African Americans.[21]

The second type of Spinning is Ludic Celebration. Daly defines this strategy as "thinking out of the experience of being; the free play of intuition in New Space" (***Wickedary*** 143). Ludic celebration begins with Laughing Out Loud, a strategy of "cracking the hypocritical hierarchs' house of mirrors [and] defusing their power of deluding Others" (142). This strategy not only breaks foreground logics but moves the Laugher into Background logics. Daly describes three types of Laughing Out Loud or Be-Laughing: Nixing, Hexing, and X-ing. Nixing is the re-fusal of absence and the assertion of presence (264). Hexing is the casting of Spells or Be-Wishing that breaks patriarchal boundaries (267-68). And X-ing is the naming of strange coincidences and synchronicities that are important to women's lives (269). These Ludic Celebrations are all "intertwined, interwoven wondrous workings/wordings that are Discovered and passed on" so that women can "keep a Silly Sense of Humor and regain a Sinful Sense of Direction" (263, 272).

A third type of Spinning is Be-Musing, "be-ing a Muse for oneSelf and for Other Muses [while] refusing Musing to a-Musing scribblers" (***Wickedary*** 65). In other words, a woman should refuse to serve as muses for others who drain her energy; instead, she should re-fuse herSelf and other Others who share her desire to de/mystify foreground meanings and un-cover Background ones. Such a move is neither simple nor easy, for it flies in the face of powerful socialization that asks women to be kind, nurturing, and supportive. But such a total woman, Daly argues, is really a "totalled woman" (232). Hence, Be-musing enables a woman to recognize her totalled foreground self as a false identity that covers her Background Self (95). Once Be-Musing occurs, the foreground self dis-covers the Background Self in a move that Daly names Realizing Presence.

A fourth type of Spinning, Realizing Presence refers to the Self's "active potency/power to create and to transform, to render present in time and space" (***Pure Lust*** 149). Despite her definition of Self as "the Original core," Daly is not a traditional humanist (***Wickedary*** 95); such a position is much too patriarchal for her. The Key distinction between Daly's Self and a humanist self lies in her definition of *Be-ing* as the "Ultimate/Intimate Reality, the constantly Unfolding Verb of Verbs which is intransitive, having no object that limits its dynamism" (64). As a part of this constant unfolding process of Be-ing, Daly's Self as be-ing is neither static nor unaffected by context. Instead, her Self as be-ing continually spins between foreground and Background, and "this Active Voicing . . . Spooks the spookers" (***Gyn/Ecology*** 340). Daly's Self exists as an active though not autonomous agent who is continually (re)constructed by patriarchal myth and language. While being (re)constructed, this Self may turn language on itself in order to unweave patriarchal ideology. Such a process frees the Background Self from foreground selflessness. Thus, Daly's Self is an agent who chooses herSelf and defines herSelf in relation to her own experiences, not only in relation to children or men (3-4).

Realizing Presence reverses two common foreground states: the presence of absence and the absence of Presence (***Pure Lust*** 149). The former refers to the lack of meaning in male-identified myths and ideologies, which manifests itself as mental and spiritual "bloat"; the latter refers to a missing substance and purpose, the absence of Self (147). Daly acknowledges that questions of presence and absence have dominated philosophical debates for centuries. Yet she also acknowledges that such questions have played out tragically in popular culture: the result is that a woman is robbed of her sense of Self and, hence, her confidence and ability to act. To reverse this phenomenon, Daly encourages us to Sin Big; because one etymology of the word *sin* is "to be," to Sin Big means to question foreground assumptions and refuse false ones, including the death of the author/speaker/writer/Spinner (151). The desired result is Realizing Presence, which can make a woman aware of herSelf, let her dis-cover Background meanings, and enable her to own the original power of her words (162).

Closely related is a fifth kind of Spinning, Realizing reason.[22] Daly defines this process as "both dis-covering and participating in the unfolding, the Self-creation, of reason," not as a transcendent truth but as an ongoing (meta) physical process; and she cites this strategy's most common manifestation in the repetition, the litany, of the sentence, "I just didn't realize . . ." (***Pure Lust*** 162). Bonnie Mann gives an example of Realizing reason when discussing how she uses ***Gyn/Ecology*** in her work with battered women; one woman named Barbara, when she first heard Daly's work read aloud, exclaimed, "Oh my god! I'm a radical feminist!" (xli).[23] In this instant, Barbara Realized reason by making connections between her particular experiences and those of other women.

Daly warns us that establishing particularization and universalization as a binary opposition creates a false opposition (***Pure Lust*** 322-25). Yet she posits them as active, interwoven principles of Realizing reason. The particular enables women to celebrate our diversity while the general provides structures within which such diversity flourishes. Respecting both the particular and the general, and not getting trapped in the general, is a great concern of Daly's:

> Not only are there ethnic, national, class and racial differences that shape our perspectives, but there are also individual and cross-cultural differences of temperament, virtue, talent, taste and of conditions within which these can or cannot find expression. There is, then, an extremely rich, complex Diversity among women and within each individual. But there is also above, beyond, beneath all this a Cosmic Commonality, a tapestry of connectedness which women as Websters/Fates are constantly weaving. The weaving of this tapestry is the Realizing of a dream which Adrienne Rich has Named "The Dream of a Common Language."
>
> (26-27)

In Daly's theory, this common language creates a space that is continually unfolding, a space in which logics of the general and particulars can exist.

By refusing stasis, Realizing reason assumes the unstoppable play of language between foreground and Background. As such, it breaks the logic of the foreground, exposing not only the existence of Background logic but also the multiplicity of this logic: "The expression 'Realizing reason' is doubled-edged. It is even multiple edged" (**Pure Lust** 162-63). Thus, Realizing reason is not the reification of a static logos within a determined cosmos, nor is it the celebration of an unknowable chaos within an unknowable cosmos; rather, it is the ongoing discovery and creating of logic(s) other than patriarchy (**Gyn/Ecology** 160-69). A particular strategy for Realizing reason is Be-Shrewing or "being a Shrewd Shrew," which reverses Aristotelian syllogistic logic (**Wickedary** 65): "Shrewdness was understood by Aristotle as 'a faculty of hitting upon the middle term [connecting link] instantaneously.' As he explained: It would be exemplified by a man who saw that the moon has her bright side always turned towards the sun, and quickly grasped the cause of this, namely that she borrows her light from him [*sic*]; or observed somebody in conversation with a man of wealth and divined that he was borrowing money, or that the friendship of these people sprang from a common enemy" (**Pure Lust** 267). Aristotle's syllogism is based on commonly accepted first principles and middle terms, what most people call common sense. Daly's shrewdness, however, is dependent on women's posing different first principles, different middle terms, different senses, and different contexts (269).

Daly's gendered challenge to Aristotle's logical syllogism has implications for the rhetorical enthymeme. In terms of individual socialization, Daly's challenge exposes how common assumptions privilege the power of the center. For example, such outsiders as women, minorities, and lower-class white males are encouraged to accept the economic structure of capitalism because they, too, may one day benefit from it; the odds of its happening, however, are never discussed. Conversely, Daly's challenge exposes how a focus on difference subverts the power of the center. Suppose the above-mentioned outsiders have no aspirations to climb a capitalistic ladder but rather prefer to pursue radical politics; as such, they might be accused of constituting clear and present dangers to our way of life. Nevertheless, they would exemplify how different principles and different senses may tear holes in the dominant ideology.

Daly's gendered challenge to Aristotle's enthymeme reveals the difficulty of communication between center and margins. Suppose a nonfeminist disagrees with a feminist claim, for example, that military women should fly jets in combat because they are as well-trained and capable as men. The nonfeminist could refute the major premise (i.e., ability and training are necessary for flying jets in combat) by invoking biological differences between men and women and by claiming that such differences affect either ability or training; or the nonfeminist could concede the major premise but supply a different middle term (e.g., combat necessitates special considerations for women in addition to their ability and training). Either way, the feminist claim is dismissed, and communication is closed down with a simple *because* clause. To move beyond such closure, the major premises, middle terms, and their underlying premises must be teased out; then they must be reimagined, articulated, questioned, and negotiated.

Context is the determining factor for deciding whether or not Be-Shrewing should be acted upon. Sometimes it is too draining, too time-consuming, too futile. Juanita Comfort speaks of picking her battles carefully, of choosing *not* to lay out the logic needed to educate a white professor who had refused to consider seriously the contributions of women within a certain literary period. Sometimes, however, Be-Shrewing is imperative. Deneen Shepherd speaks of carving a space for herself within academic discourse, challenging feminists (particularly, white feminists) to reconsider the place of personal narrative, the place of oral tradition as ways of knowing and being within academic discourse. As both Comfort and Shepherd make clear, deciding whether or not Be-Shrewing should be acted upon steals time. If the decision is no, time has still been spent considering the possibilities. If the decision is yes, even more time must be taken to remap premises, reconfigure logical stances, and painstakingly lay out claims and reasons. So the question is not whether Be-Shrewing costs time, but how much. Hence, Be-Shrewing slows political action.

A sixth kind of Spinning is Feminist Naming. Daly defines this strategy as "Truth-telling," or the "Original summoning of words for the Self, the world and ultimate reality" (**Wickedary** 83). Feminist Naming enables a woman to uncover Background meanings as she sees, feels, thinks, intuits them: "[It is a] deliberate confrontation with [the] language structure of our heritage [that] transcends the split between nonrational sounds of 'tongues' and the merely rational semantic games of linguistic analysis, for it is a break out of the deafening noise of sexist language that has kept us from hearing our own word" (**Beyond** 167).[24] Eight methods of Feminist Naming are outlined in **Gyn/Ecology**: (1) making up words—for example, *gyn/ecology,* (2) unmasking deceptive words—for instance, *recover,* which actually means to cover again, (3) unmasking hidden reversals—such as *glamour*'s referring to a witch's power, not merely a cosmetic trick, (4) inviting readers to see and hear words differently—for example, *de-light* or *re-verse,* (5) tracing etymologies—as in *text* and *textile,* which have the same root although they have evolved in different gendered directions, (6) considering multiple meanings of words—such as *spinster,* referring to an unmarried woman and to a radical feminist Spinner, (7) rejecting inauthentic words that obscure women's lives and their oppression—for instance, *chairperson,* and (8) listening to one's intuition and making personal decisions—such as Daly's decision not to use *herstory* (24). Despite its power, Feminist Naming does have limits. Sometimes we only know our truths by their absence, by a felt sense that has no name. Sometimes, even if we do have names for our truths, the common sense of the dominant culture dismisses them as unimportant.

Because Feminist Naming is synonymous with Truth-telling, Daly does not validate prevaricating as Quintilian does in his famous discussion about why good men tell lies (12.33-45). In Daly's theory, lying has three possible results: silencing the Self, assuming a privileged position over others (as in lying to them for their own good), or perpetuating the Big Lie of patriarchy. Not lying is an important political step for Daly, not only for establishing her own Background Self but also for directly challenging her readers' daily identification with commonly accepted foreground myths and languages To promote Truth-telling, Daly tells the truth about it: not lying has consequences (**Gyn/Ecology** 1-36). Nevertheless, Feminist Naming as Truth-telling serves several important (meta)physical functions. It enables a woman to confront false naming as a patriarchal tool of social control (**Beyond** 126). It enables her to conceptualize and articulate herSelf and the Background realm, (**Pure Lust** xii). And it enables her to reimagine deity as Be-ing. This latter move is imperative if the first two are to occur. For Feminist Naming is participating in Be-ing, "naming *toward* God [instead of] fixing names *upon* God, which [deafen] us to our potential for self-naming" (**Beyond** 33). Thus, Truth-telling takes on processual motion that lying tries to halt.

Daly's first Non-canon begins with exposing the Sado-Ritual Syndrome and culminates in the Play of Feminist Naming, which in turn generates more Syndrome exposures. And so goes radical feminist Spinning, proceeding in a Dis-ordering way.

DIS-ORDERING

The re-versing of arrangement, Dis-ordering is the second of Daly's Background Non-canons. Daly defines Dis-ordering by tracing its etymology to *order,* which derives from Latin terms that mean to warp and to weave; this warping and weaving is associated with "Tidal Weaving and Reweaving; breaking through the tidy order/orders of Boredom" (**Wickedary** 118). By playing with this warping and weaving metaphor, Daly refuses a fixed or formulaic foreground arrangement. Like Socrates, she offers no tidy introductions, narrations, proofs, refutations, or conclusions. Unlike Socrates, however, she describes Background Dis-ordering as Tidal, composed of gendered cosmic rhythms and interconnectedness (97). As such, Dis-ordering resembles a freewriting that de/mystifies patriarchal myth and language.

Daly's weaving metaphor implies that Dis-ordering is a process of constructing texts that is grounded in the particulars space and time of composing, whether that composing be reading or writing. This weaving metaphor also implies that Dis-ordering emerges as patterns that are simultaneously crafted and functional. Such claims are supported by her definition of *weaving* as an "Original activity of Websters: creating tapestries of Crone-centered creation; constructing a context which sustains Sisters on the Otherworld Journey"; and a "mode of Travelling: wending one's way through and around the baffles of blockocracy; crisscrossing and connecting with other Voyagers" (**Wickedary** 99-100). This definition simultaneously posits Dis-ordering as a process ("activity"), a product ("tapestries"), a space ("context"), a time ("Travelling"), and a recognition of intersubjectivity ("crisscrossing and connecting"). This definition challenges foreground arrangement patterns, whether classical schemes or their much diminished twentieth-century receptions like the five paragraph theme.

As demonstrated by Daly's own textual practice, the implications of Dis-ordering are multiple. First, it celebrates intertextuality. In many cases, Daly's forewords and afterwards are written years after the text's original publication; thus, they talk to and about the texts that follow, breaking down boundaries between time and space, reaffirming and rejecting earlier metaphors, methods, and claims. Likewise, subsequent books are conversations with and about her earlier texts. Second, Daly's Dis-ordering can break patriarchal logic for writers and readers. By jolting them with her claims and language play, she invites them to read and write differently, with more gender awareness. She is realistic, however, about the extent to which she can control the reception of her texts, as evidenced by the patriarchal reviews that she predicts for ***The Church and the Second Sex***.[25] Third, if Dis-ordering does not break patriarchal logic(s) for all her readers, at the very least it will alleviate Boredom, "the official/officious state produced by bores" (***Wickedary*** 186). Fourth, Dis-ordering re-fuses Spinning, generating ideas by taking writers and readers to a new space and time. For some, this new place is the Background; for others, it is a heightened awareness, or a vehement reaffirmation, of the foreground. Fifth, Dis-ordering merges subject and object, process and product, celebrating the journey while recognizing that each tapestry/text must be completed and used if only as a pattern for further Spinning. In these ways, Dis-ordering is neither a glib response to patriarchy nor a mere antiformalism.[26] Rather, it embodies radical feminist journeys and invites others to join (***Gyn/Ecology*** 23).

As discussed thus far, Spinning in a Dis-ordering fashion concentrates primarily on the voyager's attempt to de/mystify the foreground and discover her Background Self. But when Be-Spelling enters into play with Daly's first two Non-canons, it discloses how Spinning in a Dis-ordering fashion is not just done in a vacuum but encompasses innocent bystanders, enchanting those who happen to get caught up in the whirl.

BE-SPELLING

The re-versing of style, Be-Spelling is the third of Daly's Background Non-canons. A casting of charms and enchantment through language, Be-Spelling is listed in the ***Wickedary*** as the "ontological Shape-Shifting of words which awakens latent powers of be-ing in the Spell-speaker, in the hearer, and in the words themselves" (65). This definition reveals Be-Spelling's rhetorical functions, both communicative and socializing; the power of Be-Spelling is centered at the intersection of speaker, hearer, and language where it assumes a potency unrealizable at any one of the three points individually. That power may be channelled in "overthrowing dronedom/clonedom," that is, in throwing "the old order out of order" (19).

Be-Spelling functions at both conscious and unconscious levels, as exemplified by Daly's descriptions of her own textual practices. Her unconscious magical conjuring of metaphorical language is especially powerful for evoking an alliterative, incantatory quality in her prose: "[The words] seem to want to break the bonds of conventional usage, to break the silence imposed upon their own Backgrounds. They become palpable, powerful, and it seems that they are tired of allowing me to 'use' them and cry out for a role reversal. I become their mouthpiece, and if I am not always accurate in conveying their meanings, that is probably because I haven't yet learned to listen closely enough, in the realm of the labyrinthine inner ear" (***Gyn/Ecology*** 25). At other times, Daly's conscious magical conjuring is especially powerful for constructing, reflecting, and reinforcing her messages. In forewords, afterwords, introductions, explanatory notes, and prefaces, she discusses seven conscious Be-Spelling choices: spelling, grammar, word choice, pronoun usage, capitalization, punctuation, and sources. But whether unconscious or conscious, Be-Spelling choices do not culminate in static stylistic rules that all feminists should follow. Rather, these choices embody visual ruptures in texts that force writers and readers to become aware of, and reflect on, the foreground function of language. As such, these choices pose questions that each writer and reader must answer. Such a questioning process is necessary, Daly argues, if we are to recognize the ideological assumptions built into our foreground language practices.

To demonstrate Be-Spelling through her own writing, Daly cites seven particular strategies that expose links between words and magical conjuring. First, her Spellings are links that "open gateways, summon spirits, brew brainstorms, and Be-Speak Other worlds" (***Wickedary*** 13). Such Spellings invoke Dis-Spelling, "un-spelling/respelling the possessed words of phallocentric language [in order to release] the Original Magical Powers of Words" (118). Daly proposes three basic Spelling strategies: changing spellings so that words are seen differently (e.g., ***Gyn/Ecology*** instead of *gynecology*), changing contexts of spellings so that words are heard differently (e.g., the radical feminist un-covering of *spinster* as one who Spins), and spinning off so that words heard differently are written differently and thus seen differently (e.g., words in the ***Wickedary***) (14-18). The reasons for conjuring such Spellings are simple: patriarchal language and scholarship cannot convey women's Background energy (***Pure Lust*** 30). These Spelling strategies challenge the foreground assumption that correct spelling is indicative of intelligence yet extraneous to meaning; simultaneously, they expose the Background assumption that Spelling not only reflects but constructs a reader's and writer's Self.

Second, grammar is also a link between words and magical conjuring. Background grammar is the "harmonious interplay among the primal sounds of words; concordance of words Sounding and Resounding together in complex compositions, as they communicate manifold meanings" (***Wickedary*** 77). Linking *grammar* etymologically to *glamour*, Daly repudiates foreground meanings that reduce *grammar* to dull, dry, static studies and *glamour* to painted, airbrushed magazine covers. Instead, she uncovers their Background meanings of Be-Witching, or "breaking the rules/roles of boring bewitchingness" (66). When juxtaposed to Background Be-Witching, foreground grammar and glamour are exposed not as objective descriptions of language and beauty but as means of social control (24, 128). For example, Daly argues that foreground grammar deletes agency: passive voice mystifies accountability by erasing who or what performs as action; unattributed adjectives in such expressions as "*undesirable* behavior" suppress the agent's identity (i.e., *who* finds the behavior undesirable); and generic nouns such as *people* and *they* allow particular perpetrators to hide behind the general (**Gyn/Ecology** 324-26). In addition to deleting agency, Daly argues that foreground grammar deletes possibilities. That is, foreground grammar posits static categories and rigid rules of syntax, which Background grammar challenges with active verbs, active adjectives, and specific Naming that spooks the passive. Hence, Daly encourages a Spinning woman to play with the categories and rules of grammar, to practice Sin-tactics by making connections between seemingly unconnected information. Sin-tactics is a crucial strategy of Daly's Be-Spelling, enabling a Spinning woman to break patriarchal logic(s), rhetoric(s), silence(s), and taboo(s) (**Wickedary** 30).

Closely associated with Daly's concerns about spelling and grammar is her third Be-Spelling strategy, diction. She carefully deliberates over word choice not because words are politically correct but because they construct and reflect our be-ing in particular spaces and times. Words must be written and read both to expose old meanings in the foreground and to construct new meanings, New Words, in the Background: for example, what Daly calls *discrimination* in 1968 she might call *oppression* in 1975 (**Church** [**The Church and the Second Sex**] 14-15). Changes in time and space create different places in which people have different perspectives and words have different functions, hence Daly's interest in etymologies and Meta-etymologies (**Wickedary** xxiii). She employs them not only to expose Cronelogical meanings for Feminist Naming but also to invoke Be-Spelling enchantments, which she hopes will spark Spinning in herSelf and her readers (**Gyn/Ecology** 24). Thus, diction embodies more than a polite reflection of class status and educational achievement; in Daly's theory, it embodies a metaphoric, generative function.

Fourth, although pronoun usage is a type of word choice, Daly singles it out for individual mention as a Be-Spelling strategy. Pronouns pose particular problems because they perpetuate the dilemma of subject/object relations. Daly invokes her concept of intersubjectivity to resolve this dilemma theoretically and particular pronoun strategies to resolve this dilemma theoretically and particular pronoun strategies to resolve it linguistically. When considering third-person pronouns, Daly not only rejects the generic *he* but more interestingly questions the use of *they* when referring to women: *they* is an "objective" subject position that allows a woman to separate herself from other women. When contemplating first-person pronouns, Daly offers no easier choices: *I* conceals the writer's sex as does *we* (**Gyn/Ecology** 18-19). To solve this problem in the **Wickedary,** Daly and Caputi stipulate that we includes not only the coauthors but also other Background journeyers (xxii). Despite these strategies, Daly admits that no easy solutions or hard and fast rules exist: in the final analysis, context should determine pronoun selection (**Pure Lust** 31).

Fifth, Daly claims that her Be-Spelling strategy of capitalization reflects her meanings, not foreground ones or standard usage; yet she also discloses that the previous claim is not always true (**Wickedary** xxi). Nevertheless, patterns do emerge. Daly unfolds her capitalization logic as follows: "I consistently capitalize *Spinster,* just as one normally capitalizes *Amazon.* I capitalize *Lesbian* when the word is used in its woman-identified (correct) sense, but use the lower case when referring to the male-distorted version reflected in the media. *Self* is capitalized when I am referring to the authentic center of woman's process, while the imposed/internalizes 'self,' the shell of the Self, is in lower case" (**Gyn/Ecology** 25-26). Daly uses capital letters to distinguish **Wickedary** usage from standard usage, to emphasize foreground fabrications, to laugh at foreground seriousness, and to name Background meanings (xxi-xxii). Thus, her capitalization identifies for herSelf and her readers the differences between foreground and Background; it also forces readers to see and hear words in a different way.

Sixth, Daly's Be-Spelling strategy of punctuation is surprisingly standard. She puts quotations and dialogue in quotation marks; she emphasizes words being defined with italics; she ends sentences with periods and question marks; and she indicates possession with apostrophes. Her most subversive punctuation strategy involves the hyphen and the slash. With these marks, Daly regularly separates prefix and root, root and suffix as in *un-cover* or *re-cover, gyn/ecology* or *a/mazing.* In terms of signifieds, such strategies uncover foreground reversals; for instance, *un-cover* suggests that there was once a cover-up. These strategies also create Background meanings; for example, **Gyn/Ecology** suggests that women need to be saved. In terms of signifiers, however, such strategies provide a visual break in the language, a crossing out or slashing of foreground signifieds.

Daly's seventh Be-Spelling strategy, her use of sources, is an important political statement. As "the rebuttal of the rite of right re-search," Daly's feminist scholarship challenges patriarchal scholarship (**Gyn/Ecology** 23). To reverse standard foreground practices, Daly transvalues sources: her primary sources are women's experiences;

her secondary sources, men's texts from a variety of fields (27; ***Pure Lust*** 31). Unlike some feminists, Daly does not avoid using men's texts nor apologize for doing so; however, neither is she a disciple of these texts. Whether using them as proof or as springboards for thought, Daly is always aware of women's contributions to these texts (***Gyn/Ecology*** 27). Because of this awareness, Daly's sources invoke fleeting shadows in prefaces and dedications as well as forgotten episodes in women's history. In this way, her citation process is Woman identified.

As a feminist reversal of style, all of these Be-Spelling strategies are important to Daly's rhetoric of radical feminist de/mystification. The purpose of these strategies is to remind writers and readers of Virginia Woolf's claim that meanings do not reside in books and dictionaries but live in minds (***Wickedary*** 27). And within such minds, much is created and much is Re-membered.

Re-membering

The re-versing of memory. Re-membering is the fourth of Daly's Background Non-canons. It is Daly's answer to the Nietzschean question of how to create a memory for the human animal (***Gyn/Ecology*** 109; ***Pure Lust*** 169-78). Crucial to Daly's radical feminist journeys between foreground and Background, Re-membering entails "Re-calling the Original intuition of integrity; healing the dismembered Self" (***Wickedary*** 92-93). More than rote memorization, Re-memberings unpack foreground mystifications and reassemble them as Background de/mystifications. In this way, Re-memberings reverse foreground dismemberments of ourSelves and our wor(l)ds and posit new Background definitions. But such a defining process is not linear, with a neat beginning, middle, and end; instead, it folds back on itself in a never ending recursive motion. By citing specific texts to exemplify these definitions, Daly demonstrates how foreground memories and Background memories may exist simultaneously while taking their meanings from their immediate contexts.

So important is Re-membering to Daly's rhetoric of radical feminist de/mystification that she conceptualizes seven different types. The first, Memory, is "the power to Re-member; the power to transcend the categories of tidy time, to connect with the sources of instinctive, ecstatic knowledge" (***Wickedary*** 79); it puts fragmented members together into a web in which reason and instinct, seriousness and ecstasy construct a fuller knowledge than that which exists in the foreground. The second, Gynocentric Memory, is both the "Memory of a Gynocratic world that pre-existed patriarchy" and the "Crone-logical Memory: history that records/Re-calls events of central importance to women" (136). Merging history and prehistory, this memory is woman centered in its attempt to uncover the gaps, the white spaces, and the off-the-page spaces in (pre)history. The third, Elemental Memory, is the "faculty that Re-members Knowledge, emotions, and experiences beyond the fabricated elementary 'recollections' of the foreground" (80). Here Daly plays with foreground *elementary* and Background *Elemental,* defining the former as a lack of connection with the earth and the latter as the presences of this connection (73). Within an Elemental Memory, humans do not have dominion over the earth; instead, they understand their interconnectedness with the earth as well as the truths this interconnectedness bestows. The fourth, Tidal Memory, is the "Memory of the Deep Background, characterized by Tidal Rhythms of Re-membering"; because Daly posits *Elemental* as a synonym for *Tidal,* tidal memory can be read as a kind of Elemental Memory (97).

The fifth type of Re-membering, E-motional Memory, is an "Elementary Memory, stirring deep Passion, generating Movement out of the Fixed State" (***Wickedary*** 80). Neither static nor rational, E-motional Memory rides the rhythms of emotions and constructs a space for emotion and body language within Background logic(s) and rhetoric(s). By validating commonplace and commonsense meanings in a woman's life, E-motional Memory posits these meanings as valid proof. The sixth, Memory of the Future, is "active participation in Tidal Time; action that affects/effects the Future" (80). This memory makes both past and future possible in the present for individual be-ings and cultures. It also foregrounds the rhythmic, associative nature of memory and breaks down the affect/effect (subject/verb) dichotomy. Finally, the seventh, Metamemory, is "Deep, Ecstatic Memory of participation in Being that eludes the categories and grids of patriarchal consciousness . . . Memory beyond civilization" (81). Driven by Meta-etymologies and Meta-metaphors, Metamemory enables a woman to think beyond the foreground and Re-member her interconnectedness nature, other people, and the cosmos. Thus, a woman Re-members herSelf as a be-ing, a member of the ecological web that participates in Being.

Taken together, these Re-memberings do not question the process of categorizing; however, they do question the desire for static categories in patriarchal logic. As fluid Background categories, these Re-memberings blur boundaries and generate possibilities. Because these memories and their meanings are deeply rooted in our everyday words, Daly argues that we may discover them by analyzing not only language functions, nor only language use, but also the manner and context in which language functions and is used (***Pure Lust*** 152). Hence, Re-membering enables Be-Speaking, both verbal and textual.

BE-SPEAKING

The re-versing of delivery, Be-Speaking is the fifth of Daly's Background Non-canons. Daly defines Be-Speaking as "bringing about a psychic and/or material change by means of words; speaking into be-ing" (***Wickedary*** 65). As such, Be-Speaking becomes more than a list of simple tips for effective body language and enunciation; it becomes an integral gesture in the construction of power and knowledge that is rhetoric. According to Daly, this reversal of delivery has multiple possibilities within our culture, possibilities that include writing, painting, pottery, social work, marches, and scholarship as well as speaking (***Pure Lust*** 120). Within these multiple possibilities, each woman may contribute her particular talents, interests, and experiences.

Daly names three interwoven strategies—Raging, Be-Wildering, and Be-Thinking—as the main motions of "speaking into be-ing." Raging is not a developmental stage that must be resolved in order to progress to the next one; rather, it is a transforming force that presumes E-motion, especially anger, possesses the potential to unbind minds (***Gyn/Ecology*** xxxi). Raging reverses foreground repressed rage and enables us to keep women's loss of power within patriarchy constantly in the forefront of our thinking and acting. Although Raging can be misdirected, it can also be productively channeled into other Be-Speaking strategies, such as Be-Wildering and Be-thinking.

Be-Wildering takes the Self as well as Others farther into the Background when they follow the Call of the Wild (***Wickedary*** 66). Once this Call is discovered and Re-membered, Be-Wildering emerges as an exploratory gesture that challenges foreground logic and invites others to embark on radical feminist journeys by staying on the question. Be-Wildering does not pose simple questions nor provide easy answers. Rather, it enables us to tease out the blurrings of foreground categories as well as to question the categories themselves. Its purpose is to demonstrate that different ways of thinking/speaking/writing are neither craziness, nor wrong tracks, nor the sum total of raging hormones.

Because Raging and Be-Wildering are rhetorical strategies that lead to Background logic(s), they presume Be-Thinking, or thinking one's way farther into the Background with a warped logic (***Wickedary*** 65). By urging women to Re-call Original Questions, Daly Challenges the foreground's obsession with first causes; moreover, she exposes that questions should concern Final Causes, not first causes. Simply put, Final Causes are "The beginning, not the end of becoming"; as such, they provide the space of agency or Be-Speaking (76). Thus, Be-Speaking, invokes the mental, spiritual, and bodily be-comings of radical feminism.

With the process of Be-Speaking, we arrive back at Spinning. This movement exposes the interwoven nature of Daly's Non-canons. Because her rhetoric of radical feminist de/mystification is predominantly a generative rhetoric, Spinning occurs throughout all the Non-canons; that is, Spinning is both a cause and effect of Dis-ordering, Be-Spelling, Re-membering, and Be-Speaking. Daly's Non-canons are not linear motions, nor compartmentalized categories, nor simple causes and effects. Instead, Daly's Non-canons participate in continual be-ing—blurring, overlapping, and/or changing at particular moments of composing. For this reason, Daly's Background rhetoric of radical feminist de/mystification is a reversal of, not a counterpart to, the foreground rhetoric of patriarchal mystification. For Daly's Background rhetoric presumes a different mindset, a different process of seeing and hearing, a different set of assumptions about myth and language, and a different reading of their ideological implications for our-Selves and our wor(l)ds. Hence, her Background rhetoric posits her radical feminist concept of writing process.

DALY'S RADICAL FEMINIST HAG-OGRAPHY

Radical feminist writing processes must be articulated, Daly argues, because feminist processes "must become sensible (in actions, speech, works of all kinds) in order to become" (***Gyn/Ecology*** 23). Rather than beginning from a general premise of that which *should* be, Daly begins with her own feminist writing process, which presumes a metaphoric language function that enables the writer to break through foreground meanings into the Background. Daly names her feminist writing process "creative Hag-ography" and attributes it with several powers. It enables women to generate new Background thoughts and actions about women. it uncovers old thoughts and actions about women that have been denigrated or hidden over time. And it rebuts patriarchal methods of research in order to challenge the nature and value of foreground knowledge (23). Through these powers, Daly's radical feminist writing process participates in changing the personal, the textual, and the cultural. But this process requires the strength to stop repeating the same old patterns: that is, to Spin new ideas and ethics by reversing the old ones, to Dis-order old logics, to Be-spell our audiences, to Re-member ourSelves, and to Be-speak all of the above, not necessarily in that order (23). In turn, Daly invites other women and feminists to adapt their own versions of writing process for their own ends.

A particular kind of writer emerges through Daly's feminist writing process: the "Cosmic Writer is any Lusty woman who speaks the Words of her own being" and who, when such action is taken, is spurred to write more, Name more, and speak more (***Pure Lust*** 120, 173). Even though Daly acknowledges limitations in posing literacy as a solution to patriarchal oppression, she believes that most women have the power to articulate our own particular experiences, Naming them verbally if not in writing (174).[27] And even though she recognizes that the resulting consciousness will not erase nor even reform the social, she does believe that such a feminist literacy enables a Self to Be-Speak its way out of foreground meanings into Background ones (121). In this way, foreground speaking gives way to Background Speaking. Moreover, Daly insists that such Speaking cannot be seen as a one time experience but rather must be accepted as a continual journey. As such, this Naming/Wording/Speaking discovers, creates, and translates the radical feminist journey of weaving the self into the Self, a process that manifests itself throughout the body and on to the page (173).

For Daly, such weaving culminates not only in a radical feminist Self but also in a living text with radical feminist voices of its own. Daly describes her concept of text as follows: "It is by no means my contention that the task of feminist writers, or of any writer, is literally to 'transcribe' books that exist elsewhere. However, the intuition of a library and a community of scholars in another dimension seems to me inspired. For in true acts of creation one does participate in Other dimensions. Moreover, it is true that as we go about our work 'here' we are making our way 'there.' For in honest acts of creation deep Be-ing is disclosed. Such acts are carriers/Metaphors of Metabeing" (*Pure Lust* 120). This definition is in no way Platonic. "Other dimensions" refers not to Plato's transcendent and immutable forms of being, but rather to Daly's transcendent-and-immanent, always mutable process of be-ing within Be-ing. Thus, Daly's text is not a static reflection of a static truth, or a patriarchal essentialism. Instead, it is a constructed web of words that, in turn, constructs the Self as a text who reads and writes other texts. This constantly interchanging process constructs a new space in a new time, which is one of Daly's definitions of radical feminism.

Although Daly's ideal audience is receptive to this new space and new time, her Background rhetoric with its Background categories—Non-canons, writing process, writer, and text—leave her open to a plethora of criticism from unreceptive audiences, whether feminist or otherwise, whether academic or otherwise.[28] For example, poststructuralist (feminist) critics might argue that, by positing a priori meanings, Daly naively privileges the signified over the signifier. Materialist (feminist) critics might argue that, by positing a transcendent Be-ing in which Websters may participate, Daly naively assumes that patriarchal ideology and its power structures can be transcended by autonomous agents. Psychoanalytic (feminist) critics might argue that, by positing a material and spiritual Self who uses language for her own ends, Daly naively privileges consciousness. And African American critics might argue that, by positing gender as the dominant category of analysis, Daly naively dismisses the power differentials of race. Mary Daly, however, is anything but naive: she simply refuses to play within patriarchal logics and rhetorics. Instead, she Spins such criticisms to expose the gaps in them.

Daly recognizes such criticisms and models strategies for exposing their "logic" in a playful afterwords to *Pure Lust*. In this "Non-Chapter Thirteen: Cat/egorical Appendix," Daly narrates an academic journal representative's attempt to interview her, but instead of speaking for herSelf, Daly gives voice to her familiar, a feline named Ms. Wild Eyes whom the representative reluctantly agrees to interview in Daly's stead. The purpose of the interview is to identify, locate, or fix Daly's theory for the journal's constituency. The irony, of course, is that in attempting to fix Daly, the representative fixes himself. Using him to parody male-identified post-structuralist theories of language, Daly demonstrates that sexism is more deeply embedded in academia than are theoretical convictions about language (*Pure Lust* 412-15). For example, by preferring to talk with Dr. Daly instead of with her familiar, the representative seems to privilege autonomous agency, not heteroglossic discourse. By wanting to come straight to the point, he seems to desire clarity and presence, not play and absence, in language. By obsessing about her feminist invention process, he seems to prefer empirically-based theories of knowledge, not constructionist ones. By accusing her of insulting people (read "men"), he seems to promote a conspiracy of silence within the academy, not political action. By accusing her of biological determinism, that is, by interpreting be-ing and Be-ing as static concepts, he seems to defend the categories of phallogocentric culture, not their overlaps or gaps. By refusing her redefinition of Sin, he seems to champion fixed meanings, not multiple ones. And by ignoring her degrees in theology and philosophy and by trying to confine her to literature, he seems to reinforce a dichotomy between truth and fiction, not their blurrings. When at the end of the interview he still professes perplexity about Doctor Daly's work, Wild Eyes further confuses him with her own Background cat/egorical imperative: "What did you expect? Fuzzy foreground abstractions? We can't discuss metapatriarchal metapatterning Metaphor with just anyone . . ." (415).

While admittedly manipulating this representative as well as her "audience" in this NonChapter, Daly de/mystifies the rhetoric of patriarchal mystification as espoused by the journal representative so that the charges leveled against her are exposed as unconscious desires of academia. By refusing to participate in this rhetoric and its desires,[29] that is, by declining to debate the representative on his foreground turf and in his foreground terms, she forces him to be responsible for his own understanding of her Background turf and terms. If he so chooses, they have the possibility of communicating; if he does not, at least Daly has created her own Background space and time where her Self and be-ing are not dependent upon his language or logic. Daly's refusal to participate in his foreground rhetoric of patriarchal mystification is not simply the luxury permitted an Anglo-American, tenured professor; neither is her construction of a Background rhetoric of radical feminist de/mystification a universal theory. Rather, it is, for Daly, a means of Self-survival that allows her, and perhaps others, to flourish within the presence of patriarchy.

Inconclusive Musings

Mary Daly's Anglo-American feminist theory of rhetoric conceptualizes both the existence and strategies of a foreground rhetoric of patriarchal mystification and a Background rhetoric of radical feminist de/mystification with its accompanying concept of Hagography. The key to escaping from foreground rhetorics into Background ones is the socially transformative power of language. In Daly's theory, language may be employed to Spin ourSelves and our wor(l)ds, Dis-ordering and Be-Spelling so that we may Re-member Background meanings and Be-Speak them for ourSelves and for others.

But because no theory can explain and predict the actions and attitudes of every particular individual in every corner of the world, Mary Daly's feminist theory of rhetoric—being, among other things, white, middle-class, American, and lesbian—cannot but mystify as it demystifies. Because Daly's Anglo-American feminist theory of rhetoric cannot provide a totalizing theory, it should not be read as *the* answer to all women's problems; neither should it be dismissed out of hand. For Daly's feminist theory of rhetoric poses questions and possible answers about a multitude of our concerns: women and agency, the play of language, the construction of knowledge, the existence of de/mystified meanings, the conception of be-ing/Be-ing as a verb, the categories of foreground logic, the multeity of meanings, and the distinctions between truth and fiction, to name only a few. All these issues can subsequently inform feminist composition pedagogies.

Specifically, Daly's Anglo-American feminist theory of rhetoric invites continued conversations about the intersections of feminism with rhetoric and composition studies:

> 1. How does Daly's concept of Spinning, or Gyn/Ecological Creation, challenge Aristotle's concept of inventive topoi and multicultural concerns about invention?
>
> 2. How does Daly's concept of agency, which assumes a material and spiritual dimension, complicate the social constructionist theories of rhetoric and writing pedagogy that focus primarily on the material?
>
> 3. How does Daly's concept of conjuring through metaphorical language complicate Nietzsche's and subsequent deconstructionist theories of metonymic language function? And what are the implications for reading and writing pedagogy?
>
> 4. How does Daly's critique of patriarchal logic and its penchant for stable categories create a space in which Plato's and Descartes's charges against rhetoric may be refuted?
>
> 5. How does Daly's theologically grounded feminist theory of rhetoric, which focuses on both the word and The Word, challenge Kenneth Burke's rhetorical theory of logology and Logology?[30]

Chances are, most readers will not easily identify with Mary Daly's metaethics or her rhetorical strategies; on the other hand, they will not soon forget her powerful prose either. But whether or not we agree with her conclusions, whether or not we adopt her strategies, once we read Mary Daly, we are never quite the same (un)gendered readers or writers again. Throughout her texts, her goal is simple but not easily achieved: "Virginia Woolf knew of the need for a feminist tradition when she wrote of her hope for the eventual arrival of Shakespeare's sister. I hope for the arrival also of the sisters of Plato, of Aristotle, of Kant, of Nietzsche: sisters who will not merely 'equal them,' but do something different, something immeasurably more" (***Church*** 51). Mary Daly may not exactly be the Judith Shakespeare that Virginia Woolf imagines in *A Room of One's Own,* and she may have Spun beyond desiring to be Nietzsche's sister. Perhaps she can instead be read as the thrice-born Athena imagined in ***Gyn/Ecology,*** who is born into a particular culture not only through her mother's womb, not only through her father's brow, but also through her own words. Therein, I argue, lies the importance of Mary Daly's Anglo-American feminist theory of rhetoric: it conceptualizes a revisionary language theory and praxis through which a woman may participate in de/mystifying herSelf and her Wor(l)ds.

Notes

1. For the source of Daly's thrice-born Athena concept, see Nicholson.

2. For Daly's autobiographical accounts of her evolving radical feminism, see the "Autobiographical Preface to the 1975 Edition," *Church* 5-14; the 1990 "New Intergalactic Introduction," *Gyn/Ecology* xi-xliv; and, of course, her autobiography, *Outercourse.*

3. Daly claims that patriarchal scholarship is "writing that erases itself" and "even at its best, continues and participates in the Righteous Rites of female slaughter/erasure" (*Gyn/Ecology* 120). Also see 126, 133, 143-52, 170-77, 203-22, 288-92, 306-12.

4. Daly defines patriarchy as follows:
   > n 1: a society manufactured and controlled by males: FATHERLAND; society in which every legitimated institution is entirely in the hands of males and a few

selected henchwomen; society characterized by oppression, repression, depression, narcissism, cruelty, racism, classism, ageism, objectification, sadomasochism, necrophilia; joyless society, ruled by Godfather, Son, and Company; society fixed on proliferation, propagation, procreation, and bent on the destruction of all Life 2: the prevailing religion of the entire planet, whose essential message is necrophilia.

(*Wickedary* 89)

5. Aristotle discusses his definitions of essence in the *Metaphysics* (1.7.315-21). For critiques of this position, see Fuss xi, 71-72.

6. See Locke, 1.27-29, who defines real (or Aristotelian) essentialism as assuming an irreducible, unchanging essence and nominal essentialism as assuming that essence is a linguistic construction. For an extended discussion of feminism and essentialism, see Fuss.

7. For discussions of why feminisms should not attempt to redefine essentialism, see Judith Butler vii; and de Lauretis 267.

8. Daly distinguishes between Be-ing and be-ing as follows: Be-ing is the "Ultimate/Intimate Reality, the constantly Unfolding Verb of Verbs which is intransitive, having no object that limits its dynamism (*Wickedary* 64); be-ing is "actual participation in the Ultimate/Intimate Reality—Be-ing, the Verb" (65).

9. For an extended discussion of how rhetoric emerges at the intersection of myth, language, and ideology, see Burke, *Rhetoric of Motives* 101-10. This relationship is most evident, and applicable to Daly's project, in Burke's seventh definition of *ideology*: an "inverted genealogy of culture, that makes for 'illusion' and 'mystification' by treating ideas as primary where they should have been treated as *derivative*" (104).

10. Feminists have sometimes accused Daly of colonizing another culture's myths by viewing them from a Euro-American perspective. See Lorde, "Open Letter" 66-71.

11. To honor Daly's (theory of) language play, I use her spelling and punctuation when referring to her concepts. For example, I use the verb "dis-cover" purposely here to reflect Daly's meaning: "uncovering the Elemental Reality hidden by the hucksters, frauds, and framers of phallocracy; finding the treasures of women's Memory, Knowledge, History that have been buried by the grave diggers of patriarchal re-search" (*Wickedary* 118).

12. Influences on Daly's concept of metaphor include: Jaynes 48; Langer 14; Morton; Rich, *Dream*; Tillich 1.163; and the work of Julia Penelope (Stanley). See *Pure Lust* 25-30, 421).

13. Daly defines the term *metapatriarchal* as follows:

> [B]ecause the prefix *meta* has multiple meanings. It incorporates the idea of "postpatriarchal," for it means occurring later. It puts patriarchy in the past without denying that its walls/ruins and demons are still around. Since *meta* also means "situated behind," it suggests that the direction of the journey is into the Background. Another meaning of the prefix is "change in, transformation of." This, of course, suggests the transforming power of the journey. By this I do not mean that the women's movement "reforms" patriarchy, but that it transforms our Selves. Since *meta* means "beyond, transcending," it contains a built-in corrective to reductive notions of mere reformism.

(*Gyn/Ecology* 7)

14. In *Pure Lust* Daly identifies deception as the Eighth Deadly Sin, that is, "the most crucial one, which the fathers, of course, omit" (x). The other seven are Professions (pride); Possession (avarice); Aggression (anger); Obsession (lust); Assimilation (gluttony); Elimination (envy); Fragmentation (sloth) (x). In the Medieval period a debate arose as to whether the deadly sins should number seven or eight; like Daly, Gregory the Great championed lying, or deceit, as the eighth sin (Bloomfield 60-67).

15. Daly defines "mind-bindings" as "layers of crippling patriarchal thought patterns comparable to the footbindings which mutilated millions of Chinese women for over one thousand years: masterminded myths and ideologies meant to mummify the spirit and main the brain" (*Wickedary* 211).

16. Daly defines "plastic passions" as "those blobs in inner space which preoccupy and paralyze their victims—predominantly women—draining our energies, perverting us from the pursuit of Pure Lust" (*Pure Lust* 200); she defines "potted passions" as "feelings that fragment and distort the psyche, masking Passion, making Pyrognostic Lust incomprehensible" (206).

17. See duBois 169-83, who also analyzes this phenomenon in her feminist critique of classical philosophy.

18. For a critique of Daly's method, see Nye, who argues that Daly's Theory falls into the utopian trap of many Anglo-American radical feminisms because it assumes that something essentially female about women can be recovered and used to empower women (101). For other sides to this debate, see Spender 53-54, 165-71, 181-89, 228-29, and Penelope 35-38, 213, 218-23).

19. For an extended discussion of how Daly connects rhetoric and magic, see *Pure Lust* 79-123. Covino, *Magic* also explores the intersections of rhetoric and magic in Mary Daly's texts. For more on connections between rhetoric and magic, see Gorgias, who argues that two arts of witchcraft and magic are errors of the soul and deceptions of opinion; Burke, *Rhetoric of Motives* 40-42, 44; and *Rhetoric of Religion*; and Blankenship.

20. To unpack Daly's definition of *methodicide*, we need to examine the terms of her definition. *Nonquestions* are "genuinely Questing Questions; Canny Questions

frequently raised by women and erased by men and their henchwomen in the elementary schools of snooldom," a *snool* being a "normal inhabitant of sadosociety, characterized by sadism and masochism combined" (*Wickedary* 87, 227). And *nondata* are "information that is disruptive and disturbing to pedants and therefore banned from the categories and classifications of academented re-search, theory, and method" (86). Also see *Beyond* 7-12 and *Gyn/Ecology* 23-24. The debate about feminism and its relation to methodology has haunted the contemporary feminist movement; see Harding, *Feminism and Method* 1-14.

21. Dr. Jones is Professor of Theology at Florida State University.

22. To demonstrate how her concept of Realizing reason differs from foreground constructions of realism, Daly compares her concept to Platonic realism, Aristotelian realism, and nominalism (*Pure Lust* 160-61). Drawing on a "medieval tradition of 'theological ethics,'" Daly also locates reason as one of the eight "quasi—integral" parts of prudence (265-74).

23. The following is Barbara's explanation for why she suddenly saw herself as a radical feminist:

> I used to—when I'd go in the bookstore and I'd see books about radical feminism—I'd have this fear. And I'm a great reader, but oh I wasn't going to read that! And I always had this great fear that, oh, they would just be angry books. I don't know, I would have this awful fear. And then when Bonnie was reading stuff from *Gyn/Ecology* I thought, "God, why have I been so afraid of those books," . . . and if anything there's a connectedness. That *really* did help me, that really helped me because up until that point I felt like no other woman thought this way, that I was terribly radical and alone.
>
> (Mann xli)

24. Speaking in tongues, Daly argues, is evidence of psychological rebellion against strictures imposed by language (*Beyond* 166). For critical discussions of Daly's Feminist Naming, see Rich, "That Women Name Themselves" 10; and Reading.

25. The following are reviews that Daly predicts for her text: "I saw this coming in 1968," from a Conservative Catholic; "Despite her disclaimers, she still *belongs* to the Judeo-Christian tradition," from a Liberal Protestant Professor; and "She should join the Unitarian Universalists," from a Unitarian Universalist (*Church* 48).

26. For an opposing argument, see Fraser 93-100. In her critique of Kristeva's work on "avant-garde aesthetic production," Fraser argues that such language play, "irrespective of content," is indeed mere formalism (95).

27. For a discussion of the limits and possibilities of feminist naming, see Cameron, *Feminist Critique* 99-198.

28. For critiques of radical feminism and language theory as they apply to Daly, see Alcoff; Cameron, "Why Is Language" 12-20; Nye 95-103, 175, 178; Ruthven 36-50, 96; Weedon 6-7, 132-35.

29. Daly's maneuver is reminiscent of Callicles' move in Plato's *Gorgias*. Callicles refuses to participate in (and thus repudiates) the dialectical method; as a result, Socrates is forced into a rhetorical monologue, the very type of discourse that he purportedly most mistrusts.

30. Like Burke, Daly is intrigued by how language functions at the level of the word and "the Word," what Burke in *Rhetoric of Religion* calls logology and Logology. What Daly foregrounds is the gendered function: "Such extensions/incarnations of the collectively supreme patriarchal Word (Lie) in secular as well as sacral society requires the discrediting of women's own words, although patriarchally instilled delusions will be accepted from the mouths of women after these have been tested and corroborated. This follows the tradition of Christian gospel: The words of the women who has 'seen' the risen Christ were at first discredited, but the error of those who disbelieved the women was rectified when the reports were confirmed by male witnesses" (*Gyn/Ecology* 91).

Carol Anne Douglas (review date December 1998)

SOURCE: Douglas, Carol Anne. Review of *Quintessence . . . Realizing the Archaic Future: A Radical Elemental Feminist Manifesto*, by Mary Daly. *Off Our Backs* 28, no. 11 (December 1998): 14.

[*In the following review, Douglas praises Daly's optimistic world view, but finds* Quintessence *inferior to her previous works.*]

Readers in 2048 will like Mary Daly's new book, **Quintessence.** That's Daly's prediction, and the book is filled with comments from a radical feminist from that year who likes the book and conjures Daly back to discuss it.

Daly's faith in the future bespeaks her isolation, and the isolation of many radical feminists, in the present. She is rightly angry that some radical feminist books are no longer in print and numerous women's bookstores have gone out of business. But when Daly is angry, she is never simply angry. Always she finds joy as well as rage in radical feminist knowledge; always she leads beyond the anger to the joy.

Quintessence is the final element, beyond earth, air, water, and fire. She seeks it in a time when men are trying to find ways to use everything in the universe—

every plant, every star—for their purposes. Everything exists only to be used, they think. Daly is rightly horrified at this ethic of exploitation.

Daly writes of the scattering of radical feminists because they must disperse to find a living (especially those who teach college). This dispersion, a major cause of the feelings of isolation, she names a diaspora. The divisions among women she also calls a diaspora. I think the term is appropriate, not too strong. But she sees good in the dispersion of our ideas this creates. Similarly, remaindering of our books causes them to be sold at lower prices to women who might not be able to afford the original price, Daly notes. Her publisher has recently taken three of her books out of print.

If we feel despair, we must name it, not call it depression, which too easily suggests that it is an illness that can be treated, Daly writes. We must see that the condition of women under patriarchy is a state of despair. Seeing the hopelessness of reform under patriarchy can help us leap to hopefulness about going beyond it, she says. "In our Aloneness, Spinsters Rage Together," Daly says.

Daly sees grief as passive; she tries to transform it into rage, which can move us to creative action. We must have the Courage to Create, she writes. Out of despair, we may take Desperate Acts that will inspire change.

At the age of five, we are all philosophers, asking "Why?" until we are squelched, Daly writes. Citing an experiment, she says that if we hear that people are brilliant, we will start seeing them as brilliant and their performances will be brilliant. We should proclaim our Elemental Female Genius and believe in it, she writes.

The boundaries between feminist theory and fiction have always been hazy, and Daly deftly blurs them. In her vision, patriarchy crumbled around 2018 because of the powerful energies emanating from a few thousand radical elemental feminists. Men who did not decide to reject patriarchy just faded away, as did women who were too wedded to patriarchy. At this point, I almost wished this was entirely fiction, rather than theory, because I don't have enough of what Daly calls Hopping Hope to believe in this vision.

In around 2018, the Anonyma Network found/founded a lost continent, perhaps Atlantis, which they call the Lost and Found Continent. Women from all over the world flock to live there. Other radical elemental feminists live scattered across the world.

Daly is a little clearer in this book than in previous ones that men can reject patriarchy, and she names John Stoltenberg, author of *Refusing to Be a Man,* as one such man. Those men who reject patriarchy survive.

On the other hand, she praises Elizabeth Gould Davis, who wrote in *The First Sex* that Y chromosomes are defective and men are mutations. Daly wonders whether men's works saying that Y chromosomes are breaking down have been men's inspiration for cloning, or the fear that led to it.

Daly praises Simone de Beauvoir's *The Second Sex,* but finds more satisfying Davis's hypothesis that women are "the first sex." Daly does not believe that men have always been able to subordinate women. Her subtitle, Realizing the Archaic Future, suggests that the past—a distant, gynocentric past—provides the basis for the future, if we only recall it.

She believes that women once reproduced by parthenogenesis (without men), and her women of the future ponder this as an option.

Counting the women of the past and the future, and animals, radical elemental feminists are not a cognitive minority but a majority, Daly says.

Daly is horrified by the abuse of animals, which is growing to unimaginable dimensions. She cites researchers who expect to "create" a headless chicken to produce eggs. Those who do not believe that such abuse of animals will be turned on human beings are naive, she says. She criticizes "bioethicists" who say that cloning is acceptable as long as it doesn't involve human beings, but only (other) animals.

It's certainly understandable for Daly to be-longing for quintessence, which she describes as the ultimate harmonious integrity of the universe and Source of Ecstasy. She says that we can find the State of Natural Grace through many means, such as looking at a sunset, talking with a friend, or lovemaking.

Patriarchal religions are not the route to take us there, Daly says. It is understandable that women leaving Christianity because of its patriarchal form would turn to Eastern religions, but those also can be patriarchal, she notes, giving the example of the exiled Tibetan lamas who have secret subordinate women consorts.

But when she writes of angels as real, I cannot not follow. To me the idea that there are some beings who are all spirit suggests that there is a dichotomy between spirit and matter, and thus goes with those who suggests that animals have no spirit and who look upon matter as some lesser thing, rather than the essence of life. I am a materialist, but I know that we need to find sustenance for our cravings for meaning, and am glad that despite the miasma of contemporary patriarchy Daly can seek and help others seek quintessence.

I understand Daly's saying that the '90s make her want to time-travel; she also time-traveled in the '50s to Fribourg, Switzerland, where she studied theology, much of it medieval. The '90s have also made me want to time-travel and work on fiction set in the Middle Ages.

I admire Daly's body of work greatly, but I think this book is most likely to please those who already love Daly. For those who have not yet read her work, *Gyn-Ecology* is a better place to start.

Anyone who can transform despair to the passion to create deserves a great deal of respect.

Pamela Schaeffer (essay date 5 March 1999)

SOURCE: Schaeffer, Pamela. "Law Firm Forces Mary Daly's Hand." *National Catholic Reporter* (5 March 1999): 3.

[*In the following essay, Schaeffer recounts Daly's controversial academic career at Boston College and discusses the possibility of her early retirement in the face of a legal challenge brought by a male student denied admission to Daly's female-only class.*]

Feminist author Mary Daly's stormy 33-year career in the theology department at Boston College may be coming to an end. Her nemesis is a single male student who has demanded entrance to one of her women-only classes, challenging her 20-year policy of teaching men separately.

The student, Duane Naquin, is a pro bono client of the Center for Individual Rights, an aggressive, conservative, Washington-based public-interest law firm that has warned Boston College of a possible lawsuit on Naquin's behalf.

Rather than admit the student, Daly asked the university to cancel her spring semester classes. She is on paid leave and, saying she is effectively being forced to retire, is negotiating terms with the university. Daly said she is being "deprived of her right to teach freely."

Daly, who has often clashed with officials of the Jesuit school since she began teaching there in 1996, accused administrators of "caving in" to the law firm. The firm is engaged in a legal assault on affirmative action at universities around the country. In a recent fundraising letter, the center promise to devote "increased energy and resources" to fighting "radical feminism.

Daly, a self-proclaimed radical feminist, lesbian and "post-Christian," said she is deeply disappointed that Boston College had "buckled under to pressure from a right-wing group. They bully institutions," she said. Daly said she is confident Naquin had no interest in the content of her course in feminist ethics. She remains adamant about her women-only classroom policy.

FEDERAL LAW

"I am caught in a double bind," she said. "Either I go in and teach men who would ruin my classes, or I find a way to negotiate a solution."

Jack Dunn, director of public affairs at Boston College, said Daly's policy violates university policy and federal law. Administrators had not been swayed by the center's involvement and would have taken the student's side regardless, he said. Dunn said a second student had also challenged Daly's policy.

"Our position is that all the educational resources of the university are available to all students regardless of race or gender," he said. "Separate is inherently unequal."

"Federal law backs us, specifically Title IX," he said. "It would be wrong to make an exception." Dunn added, "Mary Daly has a unique perspective, and we think all students, including males, should be able to avail themselves of it."

Dunn said the university is not trying to push Daly out. "It was she rather than us who raised the issue of retirement," Dunn said.

Daly, who has published seven books but been denied full professorship at Boston College, has taught men separately since the late 1970s. She said she uses a time-tested "feminist strategy" of preserving a place where women can talk freely without the presence of men. She offers men separate instruction using the same books and materials as she uses in the class, she said.

Daly said her policy is not anti-male. Rather, she said, it derives from her discovery that women are less focused in her classes when men are involved, directing part of their attention to the way men are reacting to class material.

"I never refused to teach a male," she said. "But after I discovered how the dynamics changed in the classroom, I taught them separately." Usually, she said, just one or two men would be interested.

The university and its male students have tolerated Daly's policy over the years, although it has been one source of her intermittent clashes with school officials. Dunn said Daly's policy had stood because it had gone unchallenged by students. This year, though, Naquin, a senior at the university who signed up for Daly's introductory course in feminist ethics, wasn't buying it. Shortly after Daly explained her teaching policy to him, a letter arrived at Boston College from the Washington-based center threatening legal action unless Daly's classes were opened to men and its client, Naquin, was allowed to attend classes with women in Daly's spring semester course.

The letter was sent in mid-October to Jesuit Fr. William Leahy, president of Boston College, Daly said, but she was not informed of the center's involvement until late

December. "Boston College officials sat on it for two-and-a-half months. That didn't leave me time to strategize or consider my options," she said.

Daly said Naquin had lacked the required prerequisite for her course but had nevertheless been admitted by the theology department chair. She said she finds it shameful that Boston College would give in to pressure from "the right wing."

'DIVERSITY A HALLMARK'

"I am calling on Boston College to do the right thing and stand by faculty and students against assaults that would violate academic freedom," she said. "The right wing is trying to make this an issue of discrimination when it is about refusing to dumb down education and about the right and obligation of faculty not to be forced to accept students in their classes who are not qualified and do not have the prerequisites.

"One of the hallmarks of a great university is that it allows for diversity of methodology," she said.

Naquin refused to talk with *NCR*. The theology department chair, Donald Dietrich, said he was unable to discuss a legal matter and referred *NCR* to higher university officials. Terence J. Pell, senior counsel at the Center of Individual Rights, said he had "no comment" on the Boston College situation.

The Center for Individual Rights gained national recognition in 1996 when it won a case that signaled a halt to affirmative action polices and stunned higher education officials around the country. According to the U.S. Supreme Court ruling in that case, known as Hopwood v. State of Texas, the University of Texas Law School was barred from using racial quotas in deciding which applicants to admit but was allowed to consider an applicant's race as a "plus" among many other factors.

The center is behind lawsuits challenging race-based admission policies at the University of Michigan and the University of Washington. In late January, the center released a handbook instructing readers how to initiate lawsuits against institutions whose affirmative action policies allegedly violate the law. The handbook was advertised in campus newspapers at 14 major institutions. In its fundraising letter last fall, the center charged that the courts, "on practically every issue," had "ratified feminism's most extreme demands." Examples, the letter said, included holding employers liable for "sexual harassment the employers never knew about" and declaring all-male colleges to be unconstitutional.

In meetings with university administrators in late December, Daly, who turned 70 Oct. 16, decided that, rather than change her long-standing teaching practice and admit a male student who had already threatened to sue, she would ask the university to cancel her spring semester classes, go on paid leave and evaluate her options. One option, Daly said, is to work toward a retirement settlement with the university, although before the recent conflicts she had planned to teach indefinitely. "I want to stress that it was never my intention to retire at this time," she said.

Daly said she hopes to be compensated for what she describes as years of low salary due to conflicts with university officials. Further, she said, during her 33 years at Boston College, she has taken 14 years of unpaid leave to produce her books, resulting in a significant loss of retirement funds.

Daly declined to state the amount of her salary. In 1989, she earned $33,800. The average salary then for associates professors was $40,600. Daly said she had received few increases in the past 10 years.

Daly, who holds a master's degree in English from the Catholic University of America, a doctorate in religion from St. Mary's College, Notre Dame, and four degrees from the University of Fribourg, Switzerland, including doctorates in Sacred Theology and philosophy, was the first woman on the faculty of Boston College's theology department.

She points out that during her first three years of Boston College, from 1966 to 1969, she taught only men because women were not admitted to the school, except for nursing programs, until 1970. Daly was denied tenure in 1969, following publication of her book ***The Church and The Second Sex***. Daly describes that book as a mild exposition of the church's "misogyny."

STUDENT SUPPORT

Ironically, she points out, it was demonstrations by some 1,500 students, nearly all of them men, that saved her job. "Fifteen hundred of those young men marched and demonstrated for me in 1969," she said. "Some 2,000 professors and students signed a petition. That's how I got promotion and tenure." Now, she said, "one male student is trying to undo what they did." Daly was promoted to associate professor following those demonstrations, the rank she still holds.

Daly said her decision to cancel her spring semester classes had been difficult for other students. "I regret that," she said. The present situation had come as a "complete shock" after several years largely free of the conflicts of the past, she said. "I've been treated wrongly, and the students are deprived of my voice, a radical voice," she said.

She was denied full professorship in 1975 and again in 1989. The six-member promotion committee that rejected her application in 1989 said she was "undistinguished in every area, including teaching and publication." In 1979, following publication of her third book, *Gyn/Ecology: The Metaethics of Radical Feminism,* faculty members and administrators monitored her classes and students again demonstrated in her support.

Daly has contended that the university has punished her for pushing the boundaries of theology and philosophy while benefiting from her high profile. In an article she wrote for the Feb. 26/March 4, 1996, issue of *The New Yorker* magazine, she said Boston College had served as "my laboratory for the study of patriarchal tricks."

In the most recent controversy, a group of 14 female students demonstrated support for Daly in a letter published in the Feb. 15 issue of the campus newspaper, *The Heights*. The students described the impasse between Daly and university officials as "symptomatic of a much broader problem, that being a disrespect for and stifling of the multiplicity of perspectives crucial to academic freedom."

The students wrote, "Throughout her 33-year career at Boston College, Professor Daly has provided insight, inspiration and mentoring as a world-renowned philosopher/theologian and radical lesbian feminist. In refusing to support Professor Daly against the potential lawsuit threatened by the Center for Individual Rights, the administration is silencing Mary Daly and negating the very ideals that it proclaims invaluable."

Kate Heekin, one of the signers, said one class with Daly "absolutely changed my life." She added: "I consider it a tragedy that she's not teaching here anymore. I really do," Heekin said.

Heekin acknowledged, though, the difficulty of mobilizing broad support for Daly in the current academic environment. "I can't tell you how difficult it is to get even 20 women who have taken Mary Daly's classes and consider themselves pretty radical to mobilize," she said. "But there are about 10 of us, all seniors, who won't graduate without letting the university know we are not happy about this."

Megan Niziol, another signer, said Daly is "invaluable" as a professor. "She provides the environment to examine everything in your life in a way I had never done before," Niziol said.

Daly said she would use her leave to write a sequel to her most recent book, *Quintessence . . . Realizing the Archaic Future: A Radical Elemental Feminist Manifesto* (Beacon Press 1998).

Other titles of Daly's books, many of then notable for creative wordplay, are *Beyond God the Father: Toward a Philosophy of Women's Liberation*; *Pure Lust: Elemental Feminist Philosophy*; *Webster's First New Intergalactic Wickedary of the English Language*; and *Outercourse: The Be-Dazzling Voyage.*

Daly's work, though it has not earned her full professorship at a Boston College, is known internationally. "There are dissertations and books about my books," she said. She is frequently invited to speak at universities and conferences in the United States and abroad.

"The only place my work isn't recognized is at Boston College," she said.

Geraldine Moane (review date September-October 1999)

SOURCE: Moane, Geraldine. "Mary Daly's Radical Elemental Feminist Journey." *Women's Studies International Forum* 22, no. 5 (September-October 1999): 573-75.

[*In the following review, Moane praises Daly's accomplishment with* Quintessence, *arguing that the work "pushes her ontological analysis to new depths."*]

Quintessence is Mary Daly's seventh radical feminist book, published on the 30th anniversary of her first book, *The Church and the Second Sex* (Daly, 1968). *Quintessence* is also being published on the 25th anniversary of *Beyond God the Father* (Daly, 1973), and the 20th anniversary of *Gyn/Ecology* (Daly, 1978). It can be seen partly as a statement of Daly's most important ideas; this is implied in the subtitle of *Quintessence,* which names it as a 'Manifesto'. In a play on this abundance of anniversaries, *Quintessence* contains 'Cosmic Comments and Conversations' from the year 2048, the 50th anniversary of the first publication of *Quintessence.* These comments are written from the 'Lost and Found Continent' after the feminist revolution, and provide fascinating discussions and intriguing glimpses of 'an Archaic Future'.

Daly presents *Quintessence* as the third volume of a trilogy which also includes *Gyn/Ecology* (Daly, 1978) and *Pure Lust* (Daly, 1984). The trilogy charts what Daly calls 'the Metapatriarchal Journey of Exorcism and Ecstacy' (Daly, 1998, p. 15). *Quintessence* matches and may exceed the power of these earlier two books. It both reiterates the themes of the earlier volumes and elaborates many new themes. In *Quintessence,* Daly pushes her ontological analysis to new depths. Her greater focus on the patriarchal destruction of nature results in a devastating analysis of new technologies based on genetic manipulation, which she refers to as 'nectechnology'. She places connecting with the Wild and with Nature as the central focus—hence the subtitle of the book as a *Radical Elemental Feminist Manifesto.*

It may be helpful to first reiterate some of the themes from Daly's former works, which are gathered and expanded in *Quintessence*. The theme of the women's movement being an ontological movement as well as a cultural and political movement was presented clearly in *Beyond God the Father* (Daly, 1973). The view of radical feminism as a 'journey of becoming', involving both 'Exorcism and Ecstacy' was articulated more fully in *Gyn/Ecology* (Daly, 1978) and *Pure Lust* (Daly, 1984). In these books, Daly both exposed the mechanisms of patriarchy, particularly the atrocities against women and the various processes of mystification which resulted in what she called 'mindbindings', and offered a vision of a new way of being which involved overcoming the mindbindings ('Exorcism') and bonding with other women in a movement towards 'participation in be-ing' ('Ecstacy').

The analysis of patriarchy as a planetary system which involves an assault on women's spirits as well as minds and bodies was developed more fully in *Gyn/Ecology* (Daly, 1978), renowned for its exposure of atrocities which ranged from witchburning to genital mutilation. Here Daly also established her strength in 'cracking the codes' of Western mythology and language. That exposure opened Daly up to charges of racism by women of colour which motivated her to define her ground—of Western and Christian symbolism—more clearly, and also to be more inclusive and to acknowledge diversity in her later works. In *Pure Lust,* Daly (1948) focused again on Western and Christian mythology and discourse as vehicles for mystification and for the control of women. At the same time she highlighted their role in cutting women off from participation in be-ing, their connection with what she called 'Elemental Reality'. She also elaborated her view that necrophilia was a fundamental dynamic of patriarchy, associated with exploitation and destruction not only of women but of the environment.

The internal structure of the three books which form the trilogy centres around the exposure of patriarchy through analysis of what Daly terms *the deadly sins* (reversals of the seven deadly sins of Catholicism plus the unnamed sin of deception), and the elucidation of a transcendental vision of woman and nature-centered existence which is in harmony with the universe. *Quintessence* draws on *Gyn/Ecology* (Daly, 1978) and *Pure Lust* (Daly, 1984), and also on a further two books which, as she writes, intervened between *Pure Lust* and *Quintessence,* namely the *Wickedary* (Daly, 1987) and *Outercourse* (Daly, 1993). The *Wickedary* collected and defined the new words and phrases which Daly had used and also contained new words, phrases, illustrations, and essays. This vocabulary is used most effectively in *Quintessence* to clarify and embellish. *Outercourse* provided an intellectual autobiography, and moved Daly into exploring more esoteric ideas in 'the Fourth Spiral Galaxy', a realm where past, present and future are interconnected, where animals and foresisters are present, and where psychic and otherworldly phenomena manifest themselves. This is a realm which to an Irish reader is resonant of Celtic Mythology, a connection which Daly also makes.

Quintessence journeys in the realm of 'the Fifth Spiral Galaxy', seeking 'Universal and Cosmic Harmony' or 'Cosmic Integrity'. This is contrasted especially with fragmentation, and also with assimilation and elimination (the last three of the eight deadly sins). Fragmentation manifests itself in the separation of women from each other, from their own wisdom and history of resistance, from their vision of the future, from nature and their participation in be-ing. Women are separated from each other through the state of terror which is perpetuated through the myriad forms of violence against women. Examples of this in *Quintessence* include rape in war and its link to pornography in Bosnia-Hercegovina, and the condition of refugee women. Daly provides a moving exploration of the separation of women from each other, and more specifically, of the fragmentation in the women's movement, writing of the alienation, isolation, and disillusionment which this creates. Burning and erasing women's books are obvious manifestations of fragmentation, but Daly also offers a scathing analysis of post-modernism and the creation of 'Con-fusion' by academia and mass media.

Perhaps the most devastating of the atrocities documented in *Quintessence* are in the area of biotechnology, or 'nectechnology'. Daly provides up-to-date research and descriptions of biological technologies which up to recently were considered science fiction, offering this as a warning of the speed of proceedings in this area. In the case of cloning, for example, she exposes the deaths and deformities which accompany each "success", and makes the links between cloning and reproductive technologies. She foresees the use of adult women as incubators of genetically constructed fetuses who are referred to in the technical literature as 'Adam II'. She describes the formation of transgenic animals and plants, including the production of seeds which do not themselves reproduce and which can be patented. She notes that there have already been attempts to patent the cell lines of indigenous people. Additionally, she exposes the mindset—Man as God the creator—behind these technologies, and makes connections to nuclear technology, deforestation, colonisation of space, and other assaults on nature. Her hope is that the courage needed to confront these horrors will also fuel the 'Quest for Quintessence'.

The meaning of Quintessence is illuminated through an exploration of themes and concepts relating to the number 'five'. These include the fifth essence that permeates all nature in Medieval philosophy, the fifth province that is present through the four provinces of Irish mythology, and fifth element that unifies the other four. It is related to concepts from Daly's earlier works, such as 'Elemental Being', 'Pure Lust', and 'Final Cause', but it underlies and goes beyond these, placing them in a new light. Daly gets at the heart of 'Quintessence' in the word 'integrity', which names each individual woman's own integrity, and also her connection with the universal force or unifying principle ('Integrity') which provides coherence, the 'harmony of the spheres'. Her aim is to reach beyond what has been named and articulated and to bring into consciousness this mystical dimension. Through the book itself, the concept of 'Quintessence' becomes clearer as Daly and the reader catch glimpses of that which has been kept out of consciousness by the veils of mystification. **Quintessence** reaches for that which is beyond language and consciousness, which is elusive and ephemeral, yet which is at the core of existence.

Daly writes that the 'Quest for Quintessence' must be sustained in the face of the divisions and fragmentation which characterise the late 20th century. In Daly's view, this fragmentation can only be overcome by realising our connections with each other, with nature and with 'Elemental reality'. Here Daly urges women to make our presence felt, to believe in the potency of our words and deeds. Writing of 'Magnetic Presence' and 'Magnetic Courage', she argues that as radical feminists expand our courage and realise our universal connectedness, as we shout out loud and create nemesis, we can magnetise courage in other women, creating a field of Magnetic Courage. This will create Syn-Crone-icities, magnifying or amplifying the power, helping us to create a future that is Elemental. For Daly, the Radical Elemental Feminist journey is always double-edged, both confronting the atrocities of patriarchy and reaching for Quintessence. The goal is total subversion of the present order and the creation of a new context—'the Archaic Future'.

Between each of the five chapters in **Quintessence** which explore these and other themes are Cosmic Comments and Conversations. These take place on the Lost and Found Continent in the Biophilic Era. There is harmony between all forms of 'Elemental be-ing', created through a shifting of energy patterns by the magnetizing power of Radical Elemental Feminists. The narrator, named Annonyma (Annie), 'conjures' Mary Daly for conversations about her ideas and also about the women's movement and the post-patriarchal era. Here there is more informal elaboration, explanation, and debate on the themes from the five chapters. There is much discussion of the women's movement, where Daly expresses her faith in the 'Unquenchable Fire' in all women, regardless of whether it manifests itself in radical feminist acts. While Lost and Found Continent is presented as 'Fantastic', it plays on modern views of time, space and energy to provide further convincing arguments for the importance of every Radical Elemental Feminist act.

Daly's analysis is articulated through a metaphorical system which draws on transformations of Western discourse and, increasingly, the development of her own language and metaphors. The development of her own language and metaphors over the years has enabled her to more effectively evoke the vision for which she strives. For some, her language and metaphors are fascinating and inspiring, for others, difficult and inaccessible. At times, the universalising and ethnocentric elements of Western discourse appear, albeit in diluted form, as if they have migrated across the many transformations and leaps of imagination which Daly has made. Yet her central insights—that patriarchy is a system which involves an assault on spirit, mind and body; that women must resist, and always have and always will; that it is vital to connect with each other and with nature through a visionary or spiritual dimension—are shared by feminists from many different backgrounds. As Daly's work has progressed, she has developed her language and metaphors, especially through their elaboration in the **Wickedary** and their consistent use and expansion in **Outercourse,** so that their meanings are more fully accessible. Indeed **Quintessence** shimmers and sparkles through the treasure trove of new words and metaphors which Daly has crafted in the course of her journey.

This review could barely do justice to the richness, complexity, and power of **Quintessence.** Daly has charted a Radical Elemental Feminist journey which is profound and exhilarating. She has revisited her earlier works and carried her analysis of patriarchy and of Being to new depths and complexities. She has furthered our understanding of the links between the destruction of Nature and of women through her exposure of genetic technologies, pushing radical feminists to address the destruction of Nature with greater urgency. Her insistence on placing connection with Nature or with Elemental reality as central expands feminist visions in many ways. At a more personal level, she offers many thoughtful reflections on the changes in the women's movement over the last decades of the 20th century—and beyond, reflections which make **Quintessence** a very moving book. Through her exposure of patriarchy and her vision of 'Quintessence' Daly hopes to inspire the courage and the conviction in women to take action not only for now but for the future.

References

Daly, Mary. (1968). *The Church and the Second Sex.* Boston: Beacon Press.

Daly, Mary. (1973). *Beyond God the Father: Towards a Philosophy of Women's Liberation.* Boston: Beacon Press.

Daly, Mary. (1978). *Gyn/Ecology: The Metaethics of Radical Feminism.* Boston: Beacon Press.

Daly, Mary. (1984). *Pure Lust: Elemental Feminist Philosophy.* London: The Women's Press.

Daly, Mary. (1988). *Websters' First New Intergalactic Wickedary of the English Language,* conjured in cahoots with Jane Caputi. London: The Women's Press.

Daly, Mary. (1993). *Outercourse: The Be-Dazzling Voyage.* London: The Women's Press.

Daly, Mary. (1998). *Quintessence . . . Realizing the Archaic Future: A Radical Elemental Feminist Manifesto.* Boston: Beacon Press.

Daly, Mary. (1999). *Quintessence . . . Realizing the Archaic Future: A Radical Elemental Feminist Manifesto.* London: Women's Press.

Marsaura Shukla (review date winter 1999-2000)

SOURCE: Shukla, Marsaura. "Time Is on My Side." *Cross Currents* 49, no. 4 (winter 1999-2000): 550-57.

[*In the following excerpt, Shukla presents a favorable review of* Quintessence, *which the critic contrasts with Rosemary Radford Ruether's* Women and Redemption.]

The liquor store around the corner from my apartment has in its window a digital sign counting down in rapidly moving milli-seconds to the year 2000.[1] A friend of mine is developing a class on time and millennialism in the New Testament. The terrors of Y2K appear as a motif in television commercials for cars, insurance, soda-pop. As the twentieth century and the second millennium of the common era draw to a close, we all, in different ways, have time, history, and change on our minds. This cultural preoccupation forms a link between the otherwise very different books under review here. Mary Daly and Rosemary Radford Ruether each conjures her own vision of time as that in which the feminist project finds its "home." . . .

To turn from Ruether to Mary Daly's *Quintessence* is to shift "keys" dramatically. While Ruether makes some radical claims about the significance of history for feminist theology in her conclusion, hers is a fairly conventional presentation. She stands firmly in the recuperative tradition of feminist historiography, and the rhetorical force of her project derives from the conventions of such scholarship. Daly, as we have come to expect, is doing something very different. Whereas Ruether is engaged in a "retelling" of some of the stories that make up Christian history, Daly is engaged in a kind of "re-visioning," not only of history but of time itself.

The last line of *Quintessence* names the book a "Memory of the Future" (237). The paradoxical character of this description points to the complexity of Daly's play with the notions of time and history. This "play" begins on the cover and pervades the entire work. The text I read, published in 1998, announces on its cover that it is the "fiftieth anniversary edition," published in 2048 B.E. (Biophilic Era), of the "original" 1998 edition.

Quintessence is a "transtemporal" work, told in two voices: one, Mary Daly's, from 1998; and the second belonging to a woman living in 2048 who writes under the name of "Anonyma." These voices are interwoven throughout the book, with each chapter in Daly's voice being followed by a section of "cosmic comments and conversations with the author" reported in the voice of Anonyma ("Annie" for short). These conversations take place primarily between Annie and Mary Daly, whom Annie "invokes," but also include other women from 2048, like Kate, Annie's mother. The "invocation" is not a summoning of Mary Daly's "ghost." It is, rather, something like a physical transportation—Daly is "drawn out" of 1998 "into" 2048 *during* the time she is writing *Quintessence.* Thus the book is not simply (although it is partially) about the *passage* of time, a view of what Daly's work might "look" like fifty years from now. It is also a *product* of transtemporality, an "artifact" from a *different* time/space continuum.

The "cosmic comments and conversations" significantly complicate the sense of "time" that pervades *Quintessence* by rendering the 1998 of and to which Daly is speaking "the past," a past radically different from the "present" of 2048. In the intervening years, the world has become a new place. Annie reports this "history" to Daly in one of the early conversations:

> Wild Women and other Elemental creatures eventually achieved critical mass and acted to overthrow the moribund patriarchal rule. This Fierce Shifting of energy patterns was achieved with the help of our Sister the Earth, who vomited out many of the poisons that had sickened her. As she cleansed herself, there were many geographic and climatic changes.
>
> (61)

During this "Tremendous Transition," in 2018, the members of the Anonyma Network (a group of five thousand "Foresighted" women—Kate, Annie's mother, and her "Cronies") "Dis-covered" the Lost and Found Continent. In the "Gynocratic and Gynocentric" world of 2048, the Lost and Found Continent is a "joyous

Women's Space" and a "Power Center [generating] Elemental Energy," guarding against the "danger of slippage" back into patriarchy (66).

The idyllic world of the Lost and Found Continent is clearly meant both to contrast with the "necrophilic" mess of 1998 and to provide a "happy ending." The 1998 introduction to the "Manifesto" proclaims that "the writing of this book is a Desperate Act performed in a time of ultimate battles between principalities and powers. More than ever all sensate and spiritual life on this planet and anywhere within reach is threatened with extinction" (1). In the "cosmic comments and conversations" we learn that the worst-case scenario of extinction was avoided through the activism of the Anonyma Network and its radical feminist "Foresisters." Furthermore, we are shown that the war against patriarchy, waged by Daly in all her work, has been won, and on Daly's terms. As Kate says to Daly, "We're here to tell you that you Battle Axes won!" (191). At the risk of belaboring the point, Daly describes in another conversation the reaction of her friends every time she "returns" to 1998. "When I tell them about you they say 'So there *is* hope! There is a Future Sisterhood. We were right all along. We won't be defeated after all!' And that reawakens Vision and Courage" (233).

At the level of a projected "happy ending," **Quintessence** is easy to dismiss. This is in no small part due to the heavy-handed style in which the "cosmic comments and conversations" are written. Daly's (or perhaps I should say "Annie's") skill in constructing dialogue and narrative does not match her talent for manipulating language to create the "parodic" critiques and diatribes that characterize her work.² Yet, to read this book as nothing more than a flat-footed account of how the radical feminists will save and then rule the world would be to miss the point.

The "literary conceit" of **Quintessence** invites such a mistake by suggesting that the 2048 "cosmic comments and conversations" form the appropriate context within which to read the 1998 "manifesto" sections of the book. Such a reading, however, enacts precisely the preoccupation with the linear passage of time that Daly is working hard to resist and invites *us* to resist. When this "literary conceit" is *reversed,* and the "manifesto" sections of the book are read instead as the *context* for the "comments and conversations," it becomes clear that this book is not an empty exercise in "happy endings," but, rather, an attempt at transformation, at the *production* of "Transtemporality," a state that requires falling out of linear time. This project is named most clearly in the second part of the title of the book, "Realizing the Archaic Future," which "does not mean simply waking up and Seeing. It means working to open the Way for Transtemporal/Trans-spatial and Interspecies Bonding" (6).

The primary way in which Daly articulates the effects of patriarchy in her "Radical Elemental Manifesto" is as "diaspora," feeling "cut off from our Foresisters. . . . Severed from our own history," fearing "that our own Reality is being splintered/destroyed by agents of dividedness" (37). The Radical Feminist project requires that this state of diaspora be transformed into Positive Diaspora:

> Our participation in this transformative work requires that we break out of the dreary state of temporal as well as spatial diaspora. Temporal diaspora is the state of separation from our Real Present and therefore our True Past and Future. The institutions of patriarchy, most notably the media, foster this separation by embedding deadening archetypal images/molds into women, making us prisoners of archetypal deadtime (a.d.). Deviant Women dissolve these molds by performing Original Creative Acts, thereby participating in Background Time, which is Original/Archaic Time, beyond the stagnation/timelessness of patriarchetypes. By our successions of such acts we create a Real Future, which is an Archaic Future.
>
> (119, 121)

Daly's identification of the state of "temporal diaspora" and its "reversal," "Positive ['Transtemporal'] Diaspora," gathers together several threads from her earlier work. "Archetypal deadtime" is defined in **Wickedary** as "Timeless Time, lacking genuine movement, having no real past, present, or future,"³ and is associated with "tidy time," which is defined as "fathered time; measurements/divisions that cut women's Lifetimes/Lifelines into tidy tid-bits; dismembered time . . ." (**Wickedary,** 62). These are opposed to "Archaic Time," defined as "Original Creative Time . . ." (**Wickedary,** 97), and "Tidal Time," "Elemental Time, beyond the clocking/clacking of clonedom. . . . Time that cannot be grasped by the tidily man-dated world . . ." (**Wickedary,** 62). Within this web of oppositions, the "Archaic Future" is defined as the "direction of the movements of Archaic time," a "reality created through successions of Original Creative Acts/Actions" (**Wickedary,** 97).

The definitions in **Wickedary** draw a verbal "map" of an alternative time/space continuum, the paradoxical "transtemporality" of which is captured by the notion of an "Archaic ("Original, Primal, Primordial" [**Wickedary,** 62]) Future." In **Quintessence,** Daly takes the next step, that of *Realizing* ("[making] real. . . . [Bringing] into concrete existence" [**Wickedary,** 92]) this Archaic Future. The "cosmic comments and conversations" begin with an act of "invocation," but in that act the future is itself "invoked" for the reader. The dynamic relationship Daly sets up between the 2048 and the 1998 sections of the book, so that each is read in light of the other, is an attempt "to shift the meanings of Past, Present, and Future," to create a "counterflow of

Time" (199). ***Quintessence*** is an enactment of a different way of inhabiting time such that the "diaspora" of present is transformed.

> We have only to remove the blinders imposed in the pseudoworld of the foreground to See that these Future Women are Here Now. . . . This is indeed Intergalactic Travel. It is Transtemporal Diaspora that transforms temporal diaspora. Our Exile, Scattering, and Migration create an Outsiders' Society that is outside anything imaginable to microscopic/telescopic (re)visionaries. And it is Re-membering that makes it Real.

Through the "cosmic comments and conversations," Daly performs the "Here Now" of which she speaks. Her "Memory of the Future" is primarily an attempt to practice a transformed, re-membered present.

Daly has often been criticized for ignoring the historicity of women's knowledge and experience.[4] While ***Quintessence*** does not really answer these critiques, it does add a twist to the conversation. Both in the dis-membering of temporal diaspora and the re-membering of Transtemporal Diaspora, time/Time is the primary organizer of women's experience. Daly is asserting that it is from our sense of Past, Present, and Future that we get a sense of ourSelves.

Is time, as Mick Jagger claims, on my/our side? Both Ruether and Daly suggest that it is. Both, in different ways, approach the issue of identity and community within feminism through a "rehearsal" of history. Ruether rehearses history in the sense of recounting or relating facts. Daly's rehearsal is more performance driven. She is practicing, drilling, training for/in a "counterflow" of time. Yet both assert that some such "rehearsing" is an integral part of "performing" the future (Archaic or otherwise) of feminism.

Daly's notion of the problem of "diaspora" resonates with Ruether's sense of the necessity of locating and articulating the stories of women who acted as liberators. For Ruether too, a kind of "temporal diaspora" must be overcome—a diaspora that separates us from our "repressed plurality of identities" and, ultimately, stands as an obstacle to our becoming "fully christomorphic." For Ruether too, "re-membering makes it real." And yet "time" is conceived of differently by Daly and Ruether; as a result, the community into which we remember ourselves emerges differently in the work of each. The "pastness" of the past is all important to Ruether, both in the sense of its difference from the present and in its being *our* past, the forerunner of our present. To inhabit time so understood is to re-member ourselves into a "traditioned" community, a community that derives its future from precisely that which is *not* present. For Daly, on the other hand, linear time is that which we need to re-member ourselves out of. Time, correctly inhabited, is a Here Now, in which Past, Present, and Future are simultaneously experienced. The Past and Future gain their "Realness" from being Present. The community into which Daly calls us to re-member ourselves through this kind of overcoming of time is an "Outsider Society that is outside anything imaginable."

While both Ruether and Daly assert that we receive ourselves in/from time, the differences in their "rehearsals" raise the issue of identity. *How* time is on our side shapes *who* we are. How we chose to "rehearse" time shapes who we as "performers" of the future become.

Notes

1. I want to thank Susan Simonaitis and Karen Trimble Alliaume for their help with this review.

2. The notion of Daly's work as "parody" is developed by Mary McClintock Fulkerson [*Changing the Subject: Women's Discourses and Feminist Theology* (Minneapolis: Fortress, 1994) 299-354].

3. Mary Daly and Jane Caputi, *Websters' First Intergalactic Wickedary of the English Language* (Boston: Beacon, 1987), 62.

4. See, for example, Sheila Greeve Davaney, "Problems with Feminist Theory: Historicity and the Search for Sure Foundations" in *Embodied Love: Sensuality and Friendship as Feminist Values*. ed. Paula M. Cooey, Sharon A. Farmer, and Mary Ellen Ross (San Francisco: Harper & Row, 1987), 75-95.

Mary Daly and Catherine Madsen (interview date fall 2000)

SOURCE: Daly, Mary, and Catherine Madsen. "The Thin Thread of Conversation: An Interview with Mary Daly." *Cross Currents* 50, no. 3 (fall 2000): 332-48.

[*In the following interview, Daly discusses the abuses of patriarchal language, her conception of and contribution to radical feminism, the dangers of biotechnology, and her utopian vision of a patriarchy-free future world.*]

Perhaps a certain amount of disclosure is needed. I am, if not quite an ex-radical feminist, no longer a loyalist to radical feminism. My circumstances and my opinions would still look radical enough to anyone but another radical feminist, but I am no longer willing to worry what another radical feminist thinks of me. When I found that liberation meant confinement to an ever-narrowing circle of acceptable thought and behavior, I did not renounce liberation, but I decided at least to draw my own circle.

I am also a jaundiced observer of feminist theology. As promulgated in seminaries and religion departments, it seems to have lost the edge of insouciance that first made feminism interesting; the combined constraints of theological study and feminist collectivity seem not only to draw a circle but at times to enclose it with an electric fence that warns the mind against too much exploration. Original thought is stunted in such conditions. What feminist theology has not produced—cannot produce, as long as its main products are secondary source material and pastoral care—is a female Luther, a female Swift, a female Nietzsche, trenchant and scatological and fierce. Feminist theology can talk, in decorous academic prose, about the erotic in spirituality; it avoids a show of libido.

Mary Daly, of course, is made of more volatile stuff. As one of the originators of feminist religious thought, she is not bound by its subsequent limitations; at this point, in any case, she calls herself a philosopher and not a theologian at all. Beloved only daughter of working-class parents in upstate New York, victor over a Catholic educational system that prevented women from earning graduate degrees in philosophy, sole female student for seven years at the University of Fribourg, where she earned three doctorates, she has paid in full for the right to criticize patriarchal institutions as recklessly as she chooses. After the publication of *Beyond God the Father,* in which she called for an exodus of women from the Church, she was given tenure at Boston College only because of the protests of her students (at that time nearly all men). Much of her work since that time has consisted in blowing exuberant raspberries at the Vatican, Boston College, and the keepers of the patriarchal flame generally—who may have expected no better outcome from educating a woman, and must feel betrayed and vindicated by turns. For thirty-odd years she has hung on by a thread to the academy—a thread that has now been cut by Boston College, which has suspended her for her long-time policy of teaching only female students in the classroom (and male students in independent study). Whatever one thinks of her policy, the college's tactic is a little too transparently vindictive, as is the role of the Center for Individual Rights (the right-wing backers of the student who brought suit against Daly for discrimination). One does expect, however naïvely, of people who call themselves conservatives that they will have some sense of their own long-term interests. If they had been trying to prove Daly right—by demonstrating the power of a stripling boy to reduce an old woman to dishonor and poverty with the help of a male-controlled hierarchy—they could not have chosen a better tactic.

Daly's wordplay and "insufferable stubbornness" (her own phrase) have put her closely in the neighborhood of Luther, Swift, and Nietzsche. She has evolved a sort of intimate slang, alliterative and erratically capitalized, whose purpose is to burst the bubble of male dignity and make female deference ever more impossible: a rhodomontade of invective (snools, Stag-nation, cock-aludicrous, dick-tionary) that is either irresistible or intolerable, depending upon the reader. Her thinking is powered by the driving force of the syllogism, the high Thomist ecstasy of abstraction; it tars with a broad brush, but is always intellectual work. She incites her readers to great feats of boundary-breaking with epithets like "Positively Revolting Hags," "Nag-Gnostic Crones," "the Metapatriarchal Movement of Wayfaring Wayward Women." She is a proponent of parthenogenesis, in both its physical and intellectual forms—the creation of "unfathered works." It is heady stuff, especially for young women testing their intellectual powers for the first time or for women long frustrated in their search for feminist allies. The very intimacy of the language makes it unanswerable; one must meet it either with resistance or with conspiratorial glee.

As one who was long ago surfeited with feminist pride and who has exacting tastes in obscenity, I am inclined these days to resistance. I was grateful for *Beyond God the Father,* which gave me the immediate impetus to leave the Episcopal Church; I waited eagerly for *Gyn/Ecology,* which promised to be one of the more striking events on the feminist intellectual landscape. By the time of *Pure Lust* and the *Intergalactic Wickedary* I had begun to think that "ludic cerebration," to be cerebral enough (and even ludic enough) might need some self-critical element. Daly doesn't have a self-critical bone in her body—doubtless the best way to survive seven years' study as the only female at a Dominican institution—and the energy of radical feminism is, for her, genuinely self-renewing and self-sufficient without any pitfalls. When Daly is right she is very very right; I am particularly struck by her analysis of "aphasia, amnesia and apraxia" as the paralyzing results for women who are barred from thinking and speaking of their experience (something Freud noticed too but with a less thorough understanding). She traces very accurately the dumb despair of being forbidden to know one's powers, and the exhilaration of using them in spite of all prohibitions. But she is oblivious to one thing that matters very much: the tendency of revolutions to go wrong.

A disenchanted reader must be particularly careful to distinguish her disenchantment with the writer's actual work from her disenchantment with her enchantment. Daly is not to blame for the bloodthirsty enthusiasm with which I would once (at least in my daydreams) have overthrown patriarchy and punished its worst offenders, by ingenuities that I later discovered are in every small-time torturer's repertoire. She did not intentionally contribute to the painful and vicious infighting in the rank-and-file feminist movement of the late '70s and early '80s—a phenomenon that so perplexes her that in her recent book *Quintessence* she speculates it was caused by "man-made electromagnetic fields" (a hypothesis that cannot, however, account for similar breakdowns in the French Revolution and the Communist Party). She is a voice for genuine independence of mind—and a voice that can be heard by women outside the academy, where it is much more difficult to feel entitled to do intellectual work.

At the same time, her idiosyncratic language has done what idiosyncratic language will do and created a sect; it is extraordinarily easy for women to use her terms to dismiss other women as insufficiently radical. She has added heavily to the lexicon of female contempt for the male anatomy, an amusing pastime as long as one doesn't object to forming the habit of contempt. Her use of terms like "diaspora" and "the Race of Women"—for a sector of humanity whose presence is the precondition for anyone's existence, anywhere—is an attempt to bend historical and biological truths that do not easily bend. One can't explain to a totally committed person what it is to stand suddenly just outside the commitment: to see it comparatively, to recognize that the euphoric hopes and unheard-of liberties are becoming a new set of repressive boundaries, that the giddy bravado coming out of one's mouth has begun to sound like other forms of bravado one does not want to indulge. When I was thirty or so—an insignificant library clerk desperate with pent-up intellectual strivings that seemed to have no good outlet in "Womyn's Culture"—I encountered a book on the Nazi effort to delimit a German aesthetic; I recognized in one breath the parallels to my own earnest effort to develop a lesbian aesthetic, and woke to the prolonged intellectual hangover that anyone suffers who has given too much of herself to a political movement. One does not want, after a shift like that, to be invited into a conspiracy; one does not want to bolster one's serious love of a woman with sneering caricatures of men. One begins to mistrust altogether the impulse toward purity.

An interviewer who approaches Mary Daly with irreconcilable differences of temperament, ideology, and strategy does not get very far. She is famously impervious to critique: the Australian critic Meaghan Morris has written of her "preemptive disqualification" of critics as dupes or casualties of patriarchy—the "fembot," the "Painted Bird," the "token torturer." There is some justice in Daly's claim (elaborated below) that criticism arises from the envy of the analytical thinker for the free imagination—the envy of the Devourer for the Prolific, in Blake's terms. But the critical faculty is not, I think, exclusively the turf of the analytical thinker. Analytical thought can be a poor second to what the free imagination puts itself through on the way to doing its work. Consider the following exchange from one of the utopian sections of *Quintessence*, which alternate with the analytical sections (the "I" is Anonyma, a citizen of Lost and Found Continent fifty years in the future, and "Mary" is Daly herself):

> "Are there men and boys on the other continents?" [Mary] asked.
>
> "Yes," I said. "But since patriarchy is essentially finished, the implications of that change are enormous. . . . The world today is Gynocratic and Gynocentric. . . . The Earth's transformation has required that her inhabitants grow through profound psychic changes. Those who were not able to grow could not endure in the purity and strength of the New energy field. They simply withered away . . ."
>
> 'Are you saying that men who insisted on clinging to patriarchal beliefs and behaviors became obsolete and 'died off'?" asked Mary.
>
> "Yes, they rapidly became extinct," I said.
>
> "And what became of the patriarchally assimilated women who identified with the roles and rules of patriarchy?" asked Mary.
>
> I answered, "Those women who refused to release themselves from the phallocratic dependencies and habits that had been embedded in them under the old system were in effect refusing to evolve. So they also could not survive in the New energy field."

The free imagination—the imagination at work on a convincing fiction—might say: We are reading about death; is there any whiff of death in this passage? We are reading about *mass death*—a form of mass death that serves as the deliverance of our desperately overtaxed planet; is there any ambivalence among these survivors and beneficiaries of mass death? Does anyone mourn the dead? What does a death look like whose cause is the planet's retaliatory violence for violence committed on it? Is it really an advance for the indifferent, broad-shouldered earth to take up selective killing? The free imagination recoils from the impersonal *fait accompli* with a tidy moral lesson attached. If it's going to be like that, one might as well die with the phallocrats; it's as bad as the Rapture.

All that said, I liked Mary Daly. If, more or less inadvertently, she has replicated all the worst faults of the system she broke with—the massive ego-strength that permits no dissent, the elaborate logical scaffolding, the simultaneous unabashed reliance on miracles, the absolute lack of perspective—she has also brought with her all of its virtues: intelligence, good humor, persistence, the indefatigable demand for justice. What struck me most forcefully about her quickness of mind, her unassuming charisma, her mild, immovable purpose, was her essential innocence: it does not occur to her, it cannot be made to occur to her, that words may have consequences the writer doesn't intend. If, for myself, I consider that innocence well lost, there's still something moving about seeing someone who has it.

At one point in her life, Daly was fond of quoting a line from Peter Berger's *The Sacred Canopy*: "The subjective reality of the world hangs on the thin thread of conversation." It does; at moments during an interview that was generally at cross purposes, the threads twined and the world was suspended. Subjective realities are among the most difficult things on earth to bring into consonance. Perhaps one simply has to be grateful for all the consonance one can get.

[Madsen]: Some Europeans have told you that you think like a European. I'm curious what they meant.

[Daly]: Well, I studied there for seven years. That's the way I was trained. They're interested in analytic . . . *thought,* you know, and so much over here is empty babble! I don't know what else they meant. They loved **Pure Lust**—the analysis of Virtues and Vices, the scholastic terminology.

Having come back to the States after those seven years, and lived with the intellectual conditions here, what's your sense of what your work has accomplished for feminism and for philosophy?

That's not the way I think. I'm right in process, so I don't think of it as something that *has accomplished* but *is accomplishing.* I'm still doing it very vigorously, particularly in this battle against Boston College; I'm speaking all over the country. What I'm trying to do right now is wake women and others up to the right-wing backlash—the converging of conservative Catholicism and fundamentalism and all the rest, together with biotechnology, nectech [cloning, genetic manipulation, biological warfare]. All of that is stifling diversity and integrity, and so what I'm really working for is critical mass, a critical mass of feminists, ecologists . . . rebels . . . so there can be a survival of consciousness, a survival of biological and spiritual integrity, intellectual integrity. And it's been very exciting—radical feminism is really alive, it's just gone underneath. Like Harvard Divinity School, two nights ago—it was incredibly exciting when I spoke there, I could feel the mass shifting. The faculty weren't there, of course, but the students, and others who weren't from the school. . . .

So much of the way you go about your work is through examination of language—its misuses, its reversals, the need to "reverse the reversals" and recover truth and energy, the potential of radical feminist language to puncture patriarchal arrogance and pomposity through mockery and derision. I'm struck by the parallels between what you say about the deceptions of patriarchal language and something that George Steiner said in his 1959 essay "The Hollow Miracle" about the corruption of German by the Nazis:

> Languages are living organisms. . . . They have in them a certain life-force, and certain powers of absorption and growth. But they can decay and they can die. . . . Actions of the mind that were once spontaneous become mechanical, frozen habits (dead metaphors, stock similes, slogans). Words grow longer and more ambiguous. Instead of style, there is rhetoric. Instead of precise common usage, there is jargon. . . . All these technical failures accumulate to the essential failure: the language no longer sharpens thought but blurs it. . . . The language is no longer adventure (and a live language is the highest adventure of which the human brain is capable).

(she likes the quote): This is Rudolph Steiner?

George Steiner.

Oh, I don't know him.

He's a literary critic. So my question is this: As you work at unmasking decay and death in the common language, how do you guard against the same thing happening to your own language?

Doesn't seem to be happening. Because I keep inventing. I just don't think that way, see, about *guarding against.* I'm thinking about plunging ahead. All right, I think you guard against decay, in general, and stagnation, by moving, by continuing to move. And with courage. And courage is like—it's a *habitus,* a habit, a virtue: you get it by courageous acts. It's like you learn to swim by swimming. You learn courage by couraging. I often draw the Spiral Galaxy on the blackboard, and instead of stars there are Moments. So each Moment, a real Moment, is an act of courage, and that means that the world will speak back to you—and that Moment speaks to the next one, and the next one, and the next one.

OK, take the labrys: everything is double-edged. You "guard against" best by not even guarding—just by risking tremendously, and then you jump—Leap—into another sphere, or dimension.

Where do you think radical feminist language generally is in the greatest danger of losing its energy, and becoming a "mechanical frozen habit" or a kind of jargon?

See, this is where we have certain differences, because I never think of it that way. I don't mean to criticize you, I'm just giving my natural reaction, that "in danger of" or "losing" is kind of a negative take on it. My question is, how can we regenerate the energy of radical feminism? I don't think of the danger. Because I just refuse to acknowledge danger. Maybe that's crazy.

I think it's a difference, probably, in our positions. We're from different generations: you've been inventing radical feminism all this time, and I've been partly inventing it and partly seeing it come down already invented— seeing it adopted by other women my own age who were desperate for some kind of help in getting beyond where they were, and who sometimes clung on too tight to other women's formulations and used them in a doctrinaire way.

Well—there is a phenomenon, it bores me, but—of women in their thirties and forties—and I don't want to get into generationalism, because that's boring, I want communication among the generations—but, of "knocking down tall poppies," as they say in Australia, or trying to pick off this generation—mine—that was so alive in the '60s and '70s. I'm more alive than they are. And I think it happens when they're not able to create themselves. So this kind of envy—anger. . . . I never suffered from that. First of all because there was no living generation of feminists. I mean there was Virginia Woolf. And Simone de Beauvoir, just preceding. But getting back to your question, which was, where is radical feminism in the greatest danger of losing its energy and becoming a jargon? I almost wish there *were* a danger, the fact is that—See, that isn't the way it is, you keep inventing *new* words, you just keep moving. So I would say, how do we keep it alive? But that isn't even right, you keep alive by being alive, and by daring, and by listening.

See, it isn't hard for me, right now, to keep alive, because they're trying to kill me. It's perfectly obvious: I've been fired out the back door, they've taken away my tenure, I'm in danger of great poverty. They offered me this rotten little retirement agreement, I refused, and they lied and said that I *have* retired; the whole scenario is the most disgusting kind of rape scene, it's like a gang rape. And so I've decided, if they want me to be silent, I'll yell it from the rooftops. It's just made me freer, really. The more they do, the more I can expose. So I'm not in danger, because I'm not comfortable. I think the danger of a real radical feminist being comfortable is, like, nil. Don't you think so? A *radical* feminist.

Yeah; but I don't think that's my question.

Well, I don't know if I can meet your question.

Well—when **Gyn/Ecology** *came out, in the late '70s, the passage I turned out to be most grateful for was actually one of your side points; I put it on my refrigerator. "The Amazon Voyager can be anti-academic; only at her peril can she be anti-intellectual." That wasn't a message one heard very often in those days in radical feminism. It's not that intellect wasn't out there, but there was a kind of. . . .*

Leveling?

Exactly. And—well, for example, you're quite open about the usefulness of Aristotle and Aquinas to your own thinking.

Oh, I love that stuff. Yeah.

You don't let them get away with anything, but they were influences in your intellectual training.

They still are.

And still are, just as Virginia Woolf and Simone de Beauvoir and Matilda Joslyn Gage later became. My generation of radical feminists—I'm sorry to talk about generations; and of course *they can be transcended, but there is a common experience there—the women around me tended not to allow each other male intellectual influences, not without a lot of suspicion and* mea culpas *and apologies. As if the proper study of womankind is woman, and only woman, and only by means of women's works.*

No, I'll take it wherever I can get it. If there's an insight, I'll take it.

So the phenomenon of women decamping from radical feminism wasn't only—as is sometimes suggested—because they couldn't face the truth about women's condition, how terrible things are for women worldwide; at least that's not why I decamped, it was because I couldn't put up with this directive to be so incurious.

I never experienced that. It never hit me, absolutely. Maybe it was thrown at me, but. . . . Before radical feminism was actually a phrase used by anybody, I was one, I just didn't know the name. So I guess I was less susceptible to those [pressures].

It seems it should be a general truth, that once a woman's curiosity about women is roused, she can become curious about everything at a new level?

Yes.

There's this funny use of what have become radical feminist precepts to limit and hem in women's imaginations, it's very strange.

See, I haven't experienced that. Give me an example.

Well—I'm hesitant to put it this way, because people really aren't responsible for their disciples, but I've heard women quote you in the way other people use Catholic dogma, or Freudian psychology: it's this airtight little system in which they've got everybody figured out. It's a terrific contrast with the way you are, because your whole self-presentation, your speaking, your writing, your whole sense of the universe is bursting with joy: you're having a wonderful time. And this is so joyless—their eyes glaze over and they flip a switch, and this taped message comes out, You're-only-saying-that-because-you're-a-fembot-and-driven-by-Male-

Approval-Desire-et-in-saecula-saeculorum-Amen. *And they are not really looking at the woman they're analyzing, they're never really seeing her.*

It's a strange phenomenon to become this icon. There's nothing of *you* in it. *Read* my *books.*

The cost of discipleship. What do you think writers can do to discourage their readers from doing this?

I don't—see, again, there are a lot of problems I simply don't think about. Discourage—I try to *encourage* them to think for themselves. But if they won't crack the book open what can I do.

Or if they've cracked it open and they've memorized it like a catechism.

Yeah. Right. But—well, then they didn't get it. Because the last thing about it is—you know: *you don't memorize.* I don't care if they like my words, I love that if they like my words. But make up some of your own.

When feminists criticize your work, where do you think they're the most wrongheaded?

Maybe they focus too much on criticizing. You know, it seems to me that if you spend a lot of time criticizing rather than creating, that suggests a lack. I do have critiques of de Beauvoir, there are a lot of ways in which I think she's wrong. And I've written about it, but I don't spend a lot of pages on that; I respect her for what she's done. So I think a lot of that [focus on criticism] is just leaning on me, or on any village guru—and that's not what I ever want to be—leaning on me instead of branching out.

My intention, say, in writing **Gyn/Ecology** was to—truly for it to be a springboard, say for example the Second Passage [Daly's comparative analysis of Indian *Suttee,* Chinese footbinding, African genital mutilation, European witchburnings, and American gynecology, with an afterword on the influence of Nazi medicine on American gynecological practice]. And instead, *You didn't do it perfectly, there's something wrong with what you did about the African genital mutilation,* oh go to hell. It's just a springboard! *You* carry on, when you have specific knowledge.

Do you think the shape of academia has something to do with this, the fact that everybody's learning to do a certain kind of analytical, critical thought, and rather than producing creative work, they've got to produce analytical work?

Oh, yeah. It's what I call academentia. Everyone's supposed to look to authorities. And criticize. And so you have to break out of it—take what you can from it, but break out of it. I hate it. Sure, there was always the dream of the university, but look what's happened to me. It's perfectly logical.

No, we need a *diversity.* And with the backlash, this right-wing takeover, there'll be literally nothing. You know, the CIR, the Center for Individual Rights, which planted the boy in my class. . . . It's not even an issue, it's like changing the subject, to keep talking about discrimination; I don't discriminate. That's not discrimination. They are against gays and lesbians, radical feminists, blacks, all minorities, and blah blah, and having a voice. One monoculture, which is comparable to the monoculture being generated by bioengineering—which is a cleaned-up way of describing genetic mutation. But then that's typical of patriarchy, and its reversals, which is the most key concept: in everything "they" do, "they" meaning patriarchs and their henchwomen, and anyone who is imitative of them, they always are the reverse of what they claim to be. So *of course* in patriarchal education the mind is stultified. What else would you expect?

And law, oh God. The concept of reverse discrimination—the thing is that people buy it. And they don't seem to have the wits to untangle it. [They say] I've violated Title IX. What was Title IX *for*? But—*Oh, well, but you're discriminating.* . . . So I've found it very useful to do this diagram when I speak now, to show what happens. For example, there was this fellow at Lawrence Livermore laboratories, who was asked, "Why are you making weapons of death?" That's the genus, *weapons.* Then two subcategories, *weapons of death,* which is a redundancy, which leaves room for a contradiction: *weapons of life.*

You quoted that in—

That was in the **Wickedary.** And again: *rape.* "Forcible rape" is an absurd thing, it's redundant, and that leaves room for another kind of rape—

Consensual, maybe.

Yeah, or benign rape. So that diagram helps people see—I've just picked that up and found it useful recently, to make it clear what's going on. With "reverse discrimination" you have to change the word to a more apt word, which is *oppression.* The redundant thing would be to say "oppression of the institutionally powerless by the institutionally powerful"; of course that's who does it, they're the only ones who *can* do it. And then you get room for—oh, the opposite! Oppression of the institutionally powerful by the institutionally powerless. So a black guy can oppress white guys, et cetera. It's nonsense. But our minds have been so set to that, and it goes back to the myths—including the religious myths, even though we decry them. Like the Trinity: the Trinity is a model for cloning.

In Byzantine icons, the persons of the Trinity don't look different from each other: it's not an old guy with a beard and a young guy and a bird, it's three men who look identical.

In Fribourg, we spent months studying the Trinity. The idea was, there are two processions: the Father generates the Son, and he generates the Son by thinking of himself, but his thought is so perfect that it *is* himself, it is identical with himself, so they're consubstantial. Of course there's no time in this, because it's eternally happening. And so the Father generates the Son, and in the second spiration the Father and the Son love each other—of course they do, because they're the same guy masturbating—

And they produce! That's a good trick.

They spirate the Holy Spirit. But the thing is that it is a model of cloning, because it's total sameness. The same thing with Christ: Christ is a perfect clone. The incarnate Word. It's all there in Tibetan Buddhism too. With the Dalai Lama, they take this little boy, and take him away from his mother, and there's no matrilineal—he's the reincarnation of the previous one, and so it's cloning.

It's the mythos. And I think they are themselves uncomfortable to live out these myths, which they're constantly saying they don't believe, or they don't even mention because they didn't believe them—they *think*; but they're living them out, perpetually. So reversal is absolutely important. And I think more important than George Orwell's "doublethink"; he didn't go quite as far.

Thinking about Fribourg and all that inculcation of tradition, does anything ever jump out of your thought and suddenly announce itself as the residue of Catholic training and have to be rethought?

I think I've pretty thoroughly exorcised that. When I was studying, I loved it, and my curiosity drove me and drove me—and I still love it. But I think the real impetus was Pure Lust. [A partial definition: "pure Passion: unadulterated, absolute, simple, sheer striving for abundance of be-ing" (**Wickedary** 89).] I just wanted to *know*. I didn't want to become something, a priest or anything like that; I wanted to get it, I wanted to know. And of course I loved it. And it was by that desire to know that I was pushed ahead, it seems to me, to—YEAH. KNOW. I mean, just see it. It's inside out and upside down. And what pushed me to that, of course, was the speaking of feminism. Once feminism became a lived reality in community by the mid-'60s and early '70s I had all this baggage to work with. And it's really a very priceless thing I have, this treasure, I can always pull from it, and see more reversals.

What does that mean for its perpetuation in the future?

Perpetuation of—the original, or—?

Yeah, I mean, should somebody keep preserving the stuff?

I know, I've thought about that. Should anyone—actually, in my classes I have taught Thomas Aquinas, for fun. But not—not mocking him, really, because it's a great intellect. My students loved it. And then we talked about, well, what's happening. But actually to have something like Fribourg again, no . . . it would be acontextual. I think the only way is to have somebody like me teaching it—and undoing it.

The heretics and blasphemers maintaining orthodoxy.

Yeah. Right.

I like that.

In order to destroy it. "We had to destroy the village. . . ." We had to save it in order to destroy it.

That's a great reversal. [Laughter]

I do have to confess that when I read **Quintessence** *there was something that struck me as very Catholic. The deliverance of the planet from ecological disaster and patriarchal rule by women's psychic bonding, and the rapid, convenient reduction of the male population by Mother Nature without women having to get their hands dirty by murder or method—it all comes about because women adjust their minds to the proper understanding of the universe, and it's a miracle and doesn't have to be explained. Conform yourself to the true doctrine and the universe will take your side and rub out your enemies.*

Well—it's a leap of imagination. I was so sick of the '90s—so fed up with the '90s—that I wanted to jump, and this idea came into my mind and helped me to do that. It actually has turned out—I have a quote about Quintessence from the *New York Times,* this tiny article. . . . "The universe is expanding at an increasing rate, and the reason may be a force from another universe." They do think now there's another universe. "Dr. Andreas Albrecht, a cosmologist at the University of California at Davis, and his colleague Constantinos Skordis, have published a paper showing that a ubiquitous energy named quintessence could inflate the known universe like a balloon. 'Quintessence is a very ghostly thing,' said Dr. Nima Arkani-Hamed, who with his colleagues has presented evidence of how it might function within the ten dimensions predicted by superstring theory, which suggests that all matter is made from small vibrating strings." But the idea they got, that there's another world, the Otherworld Journey that I keep writing about—and that this other world is influencing this world now, I was trying to say that in *Quintessence*. And so that's fun too. Because there *are* parallels between the new physics and—and they love it, too, they love the parallels with Aristotelian philosophy.

Your students?

No, the scientists, the physicists. So—yeah, maybe it sounds Catholic, who cares. It's my thought; if that's a challenge, I don't know, I'd have to think about it. Well, why not make it quick and spontaneous: my sense was, terrible urgency—and I feel a terrible desperation; really, when Dolly came through, that exploded my brain. And then I started reading and reading about cloning, and genome theory, and all that. And I realized that *I don't want to live in the world they're making*. And there's no hope if you start with patriarchal premises. So I want to go back to the archaic past in order to get to the archaic future. So it is a kind of rapid transit, but then it is transtemporal. Why wouldn't it be rapid, everything *is* moving faster and faster.

I suppose so, but—the convenient disappearance of the patriarchs, and of males generally, just doesn't strike me as . . . sufficiently credible to give hope.

I know, your use of the word *convenient* gives your cynicism away. But—but why not? I mean, what it does is examine possibilities and new avenues of thought.

Well, why not is because of so many attempts at conveniently disappearing other populations in the twentieth century.

Well, I'm not disappearing them. It's just a possibility. It would be a wonderful one to me. Let it happen. Do you see any other way that patriarchy will disappear?

I don't know either. But if somebody put the tools in my hands to disappear them I wouldn't do it.

I don't think anyone would put the tools in my hands. No, I didn't have the women in *Quintessence* out killing them. But I do think there's something wrong with that life form, to be honest. You know, in the '70s we commonly called them *mutes* [short for *mutants*].

Yes, I remember that.

And there are articles that I've found on the Y chromosome as disappearing, both in German journals and American ones—that the Y chromosome is, perhaps it's taking a long time, but it's disappearing. The males obviously are terrified that they're going to disappear. So they have to clone. And I don't see that there would be any progress with male leadership, patriarchy—none. Nothing but the opposite. So of course I go wild: see what happens. But no, I'm not a killer. I'm not into killing. I think the earth, being female at core, will take care of it. Or else there's nothing but disaster here.

I guess I have more sympathy with Alice Walker's statement, "The good news is that Mother Nature is phasing out the white man. The bad news is that's who She thinks we all are."

But why would She have to think that? Would you object more to having just the males phased out than to having everyone phased out? Don't you think you would prefer to have a survival of really creative minds, a leap, an evolutionary leap? rather than just have us all go, because those guys are in control?

It's all hypothetical.

I don't want to die with them.

[*An inarticulate silence. The thin thread of conversation has, for the moment, snapped; unaskable questions tumble around in my head.*]

I'd—you know, I'd prefer to have intelligent people survive. If it were up to me. I wouldn't much care what sex they were.

Well, sure, in *Quintessence* I have a population of males. And I know intelligent males, males that I really like. But—the quote from Alice Walker suggests that we all have to go. I don't want to go.

No, I don't either.

So what are you going to do? Wait for them to . . . self-destruct? I'm in a hurry, so let it happen.

But if neither of us is willing to destruct them, then it's up to somebody else.

And I think there *are* somebody elses in the universe. Presences that are very very benevolent, and that wouldn't want evil to prevail. And I'm not equating male = evil, it's not that simple, there's evil in men and women, of course, but . . . I just have great . . . I do have hope, in the prevailing biophilia.

One more negative question; it's my nature.

I think so.

—Not negative at the outset, because I think there are certain parallels between your work as a philosopher and Nietzsche's, in the sense that Nietzsche is massively irreverent, and liberating, and was ignored during his lifetime in official philosophical circles—

We have *that* in common.

—but had a very excited unofficial following, and changed the intellectual landscape. But then people picked up Nietzsche's thought and twisted it and misused it; the idea of the Übermensch *was used horribly in a way he didn't intend.*

I doubt they were intelligent enough even to have read it. It maybe wasn't even the *misuse* of him; because it wasn't a use.

It seems entirely likely that it would have happened without him. But I also think of Yeats, and his disillusionment with Irish politics, and his lines in "Meditations in Time of Civil War":

> We had fed the heart on fantasies,
> The heart's grown brutal from the fare;
> More substance in our enmities
> Than in our love. . . .

History doesn't give us many examples of an idea being played out benignly and at its best. The state was supposed to wither away under socialism; it didn't. And so on. It's clear in **Quintessence** *how you would love to see your work being used by women in fifty years; how would you* not *want to see women using your work in fifty years?*

I don't care what they do. Because, for one thing, my idea of time is not as simple as it might appear. I think—I think our foresisters are here now. I don't believe in linear time. It would be nice to think that what I've done, what I'm doing, is a springboard for others to carry on. I think I'm going to carry on too, though. I'm not going to croak and say it's all over. So—it doesn't even matter to me if there's some adulation in the future or not. I don't give a damn, I just want to be alive and do what it is that I'm called to do. And I'm trying to do that.

Anne-Marie Korte (essay date 2000)

SOURCE: Korte, Anne-Marie. "Deliver Us from Evil: Bad versus Better Faith in Mary Daly's Feminist Writings," translated by Mischa F. C. Hoyinck. In *Feminist Interpretations of Mary Daly*, edited by Sarah Lucia Hoagland and Marilyn Frye, pp. 76-111. University Park: Pennsylvania State University Press, 2000.

[*In the following essay, Korte traces the development and contradictions of Daly's feminist theology and post-Christian critique of patriarchy, particularly as shaped by her reading of Simone de Beauvoir's* The Second Sex *and subsequent efforts to reconcile religious experience with the process of women's self-realization and transcendence.*]

Mary Daly's later writings tend to make late twentieth-century feminist readers uncomfortable. Her later works are sometimes praised for their poetic, visionary, or "destabilizing" style and imagery.[1] Far more often, though, these works are sharply criticized for containing essentialist and dualistic concepts of gender and ahistoric and undifferentiating analyses of patriarchy.[2] Why do scholars in women's studies so often choose Daly's works to expose faults and slips in radical feminist thinking? I believe this is mainly due to the many religious connotations and reminiscences that permeate her work. For what are we to think of "patriarchy as a worldwide religion," for example, or of invoking "elemental faith" to resist the "spells of male demons"?

Critiques of Daly's writings have repeatedly suggested that her controversial feminist concepts are related to her adherence to traditional theological and philosophical frameworks.[3] Indeed, classic Christian theology and philosophy undeniably inform Daly's feminist writings, and her later, so-called post-Christian, works are still rife with religious concepts and imagery, which is no doubt due to Daly's Roman Catholic upbringing and theological training. However, this angle offers little challenge as a research perspective, for it almost inevitably points to the question Did Mary Daly Really Leave Christianity?[4] At best, this question leads to contemplation of classic christian views of 'virtues' or 'passions' at the heart of Daly's later work. But more often than not, it calls Daly's credentials into question. The narrow scope of the "Did-She-Really" question precludes a more refined view of the complex role of religious faith in Mary Daly's oeuvre, a complexity which is the focus of this article.

That Daly's work is so well suited to what Teresa de Lauretis has called "upping the anti [*sic*] in feminist theory" is, I believe, closely connected to the problematic status of religious faith in the frameworks of critical Western science that feminist reflection draws upon.[5] I see feminism as a movement that, in a practical and political sense, strives for the emancipation and liberation of women, while at the theoretical level historifying and deeply problematizing gender. It is a movement that unmistakably continues to propagate the ideals of the Enlightenment.[6] The Enlightenment ideals intrinsic to the feminist agenda are emancipation, self-determination, democratization and (historic) relativization of (religious) traditions. These are all matters that encourage the processes of secularization. Philosopher Alice Jardine has suggested that feminism, with its battle against what are perceived as "false images" of women, may be seen as the final secularization of the West. Feminism "is necessarily bound to some of the most complex epistemological and religious contradictions of contemporary Western culture."[7] Feminism has prompted many women to distance themselves from religious traditions, but it has also engendered a passionate struggle to liberate and renew religious faith.

Quite early on, in **Beyond God the Father** (1973), Daly observed that it was far from evident to most feminists why one should care about God or religious faith at all.[8] But to her, as a theologian, these were all-important issues. Through all her writings, she has held a certain religious faith very dear. Although her theoretical frameworks and her language changed drastically, she described this faith in various contexts as "a passion for transcendence." In **Pure Lust,** for example, she wrote: "[O]ur struggle and quest concern Elemental participation in Be-ing. Our passion is for that which is most intimate and most ultimate, for depth and transcendence."[9] She is convinced that this passion for transcendence is of great importance for the continuing development of a feminist attitude and conduct.

As a feminist and a theologian, Mary Daly's position on religious faith changes through the course of her oeuvre. In this chapter, I explore these changes. With this approach, I hope to achieve two things. First, I aim to analyze the meaning of religious faith and theology in Mary Daly's work while avoiding the usual prejudices and interpretations applied to her work. To understand and value the role that religious faith plays in Daly's feminist writings, we need to raise issues that can deconstruct established modes of interpretation, such as "feminism versus traditional Western theology and philosophy," issues that can uncover conflicts and differences that resist subsumption into these standard approaches. Second, I will contribute to the discussion of what religious faith means to feminism. These two aims are interrelated; identifying the many, often contradictory, meanings of religious faith to feminism and to the women's movement may contribute to a (re)valuation of Mary Daly's feminist theological project—and vice versa.

Knowledge of God

Looking back on her college years in Fribourg, Switzerland (1959-67), Mary Daly described her experiences there as bizarre:[10] like Alice in Wonderland, she found herself in a totally clerical world, devoted to neoscholasticism—the study of Saint Thomas Aquinas's texts to defend Roman Catholicism against the philosophy of Modernity. However, Daly's de facto marginalized position in Fribourg—as a non-European, a layperson in the Roman Catholic church, and above all, as a (young) woman—must also have given her a certain intellectual advantage. She could engage in modern philosophy and liberal theological debate with relatively little to fear, because she was outside the Roman Catholic power structure and thus could not be punished for deviating from "official" views. Evidence of this relative freedom can be found in Daly's two neoscholastic dissertations dating from the early 1960s.[11]

In these studies, Daly not only showed her capabilities in neoscholastic "logic," but also gave voice to contemporary concerns in a remarkably strong and consistent way. But Daly did not attempt to reconcile Christianity and modernity on the level of neoscholastic discourse itself, as some other young Roman Catholic theologians tried to do at that time.[12] She alternated expressions of religious faith in an "Infinite Being" with skepticism toward the complacency of people who continued to speak in theological terms as though nothing had changed since the Middle Ages. Her notions of God, theology, and religious faith were neoscholastic. At the same time, she spoke for a new generation in the increasingly secular Western world: the men and women who were interested in religion, but uninspired—or even turned off—by traditional Christian language and logic. In this context, Daly also openly discussed the specific problems faced by women like herself. In the abridged version of her theological dissertation, Daly explicitly pointed out her own exceptional position as a woman striving for a theological doctorate.[13] In this publication, she also discussed the meaning of theology to "non-clerical people" and criticized the exclusion of women from higher theological education.[14]

In her theses, Daly argued in favor of "speculative theology," an inductive method based on "positive knowledge of God through creatures." Neither the explanation nor the proclamation of the content of biblical revelation *for* modern people, but rather gaining access to God oneself *from* the position of "modern man" formed her line of approach. By reflecting upon their own "sense of being," their self-awareness and their actual existence, human beings can grasp, by way of analogy, God's Being. According to Daly, this Thomistic view of theology was "fundamentally open to historic reality and to the experiential world." Daly hereby placed a remarkable emphasis upon the rational moment in theology. Unlike her young male colleagues who were increasingly coming to regard the immense abstractness of neoscholastic theology as a problem, she did not consider this to be an obstacle to the vitality or relevance of Thomistic theology.

I believe that Daly emphasized the rationality of theology because she reasoned from the position of all women and those laymen and modern believers who lack the philosophical and historical education necessary for independent theological reflection. In various ways, the emphasis on "speculative theology," on the rationality of theology, gives women the opportunity to participate in theology: "positive knowledge of God through creatures" supposes an understanding of theology in which nobody is excluded, either as a subject or as an object of theology. With these views, Daly was clearly thinking along different lines from those of most other advocates of women's emancipation in the Catholic church around that time. Daly's primary concern was not the equal access of women to ecclesiastical offices, but an autonomous, unmediated access to the "knowledge of God," for as many people as possible.[15]

FOR THE SAKE OF THEIR SOULS

Daly made a plea for speculative theology as positive knowledge of God through creatures and for participation in this theology by men and women who are not part of the clergy. In terms of content, this plea is akin to the sixteenth- and seventeenth-century humanist and emancipatory debates on opening up the study of theology to women. It was not until the twentieth century that women were admitted to theological studies at the university level, and Roman Catholic women had to wait until the 1960s before they were allowed in. However, many women did not see the importance of being permitted to study theology. It was especially their nonscholarly interaction with religion that earned them the praise of church and society. In her research on learned women in European history, historian Patricia Labalme concludes: "(Not until the twentieth century was there a female doctor of theology.) . . . The world of the university was beyond the reach of women. There was a world, however, always within the reach of women, the world of eternal truth. Piety might be a highroad to religious wisdom. . . . Religious endeavor both encouraged and limited the literary productivity of learned women. But none wrote on theology: that is for the Doctors, said St. Teresa.'"[16]

In the Middle Ages and Renaissance, there was a great respect for a number of women who gave voice to religious matters in the devotional, rather than the scholarly, genre. As a rule, these women belonged to religious orders and their orthodoxy was unquestioned. The church authorities emphatically promoted their prayers and visions, and in their introductions to these women's writings "invariably emphasized the woman's talents for prophesy, inspiration, Christian devotion, and genuine religiosity, not her acuity, erudition, or literary gifts."[17] The church stressed that these women were merely a vehicle of divine inspiration (something that many women were eager to corroborate) and that God had chosen the weak to confound the strong. This was how the phenomenon of lay and female mystical inspiration could be explained "away." Underlying this explanation is an ancient belief in women's abilities as mystics, prophets, and oracles and in their proclivity for religious fervor.

Women's access to theological studies did not become a public issue until the seventeenth century. It coincided with another question that divided academia at the time: the (in)dependence of philosophy and science from religious tradition (Descartes, Pascal, Spinoza). Sparked off by the Querelle des Femmes—the Renaissance polemics about "the nature of women"—women's participation in theology became the subject of debate. As a result of the humanist ideal and the Renaissance cult of erudition, women—often clergymen's daughters, sisters, or cousins—began entering the field of theology. Among scholars of theology, both in the Reformation and the Counter-Reformation, pleas were heard for opening the study of theology to women (Anna Maria van Schurman, Sor Juana Ines de la Cruz).[18]

Those who formulated these arguments, written mostly by women themselves, take the position that intellectual development and religious perfection go hand in hand. They therefore recommend the study of theology, but are clearly detached from the question of whether women should be able to practice a profession, acting as, for example, a clergy-woman or a teacher of religion. Studying theology would simply contribute to women's personal religious education and facilitate its transfer to children and other members of the family.[19]

The Enlightenment itself did not give rise to debates on whether women should be allowed to study theology. In religious terms, women seem to have felt more appreciated and included in counter-Enlightenment movements: Pietism and Romanticism. Religious women did not take Mary Wollstonecraft's and John Stuart Mill's rational feminist line. The nineteenth century saw wide acceptance of the idea that women were "by nature" religiously and morally superior, a notion held even by women themselves. As a result, women started to actively take part in congregations, missionary work, church-run social welfare work, and charities. This involvement also led to calls for admitting women to the ministry. However, the thought that women would become "better" people and Christians through education and studies, by developing their mental powers and enriching their minds, did not reappear in the nineteenth- and early twentieth-century discussion about women and theology.[20] In terms of content, Mary Daly's plea for speculative theology as positive knowledge of God through creatures is a continuation of the sixteenth- and seventeenth-century appeals for women to be allowed to study theology; according to these arguments, since women were given a brain they should not be denied "the bliss of understanding the highest, divine insights."

I think it is too reductive to attribute this point of view solely to Daly's Roman Catholic background. After all, some of Daly's contemporaries, including Roman Catholic women, were calling for allowing women into the priesthood. I think that Daly's humanist and emancipatory approach reflects a modern awareness of the value of higher education and that it is part of the belief in the American dream that must have been of great importance in Daly's Irish Catholic immigrant family. Daly's approach also shows her to be one of a new generation of well-educated Roman Catholics who had outgrown their traditional religious upbringing because of their academic education[21] and were looking for a more intellectual religious life. In addition, I think her neoscholastic education itself contributed to her point of view, since Thomistic theology presupposes "fides quaerens intellectum," religious faith that searches for insight.

Mary Daly's early writings criticize institutions, people, and (theological) ideas that hamper a "well-developed" and individual approach to God. However, Daly does not question religious faith as such. Her views on faith and theology are derived from the internal neoscholastic debate and do not confront or deal with the modern suspicion of religious faith that was highlighted by the Enlightenment. In her dissertations, Mary Daly manages to find a positive connection between the neoscholastic concepts of theology and religious faith, and women's and laypeople's emancipation. She continues this line in **Beyond God the Father** when she starts speaking about God as Be-ing and Verbing from a feminist perspective. She assumes a close and mutual link between "sense of being" and "knowledge of God," between "being" and "participation in Be-ing." "When women take positive steps to move out of patriarchal space and time, there is a surge of new life. I would analyze this as participation in God the Verb who cannot be broken down simply into past, present, and future time, since God is form-destroying, form-creating, transforming power that makes all things new."[22] In her later work, we find the same idea cloaked in the term "elemental faith," religious faith that promotes feminist awareness and women's independent action. But Daly's later writings contain numerous attacks on "patriarchal religion" and the "phallocratic belief system" that hampers women's ability to have faith in themselves. Modern suspicion of religious faith gained a firm foothold in Daly's later work and brought her to sharply demarcate and distinguish between "good" and "bad" faith. How did this change of viewpoint come about?

Exemplary

From an in-depth analysis of Mary Daly's oeuvre, I conclude that Simone de Beauvoir's existentialist feminism, and particularly her gendered concept of 'bad faith' must have had a major impact on Daly's concept of religious faith.[23]

As Daly said many times, Simone de Beauvoir's *The Second Sex* (1949) greatly influenced her feminist thinking.[24] However, in Daly's first feminist study, **The Church and the Second Sex** (1967), her resistance to Beauvoir's feminist analyses outweighed her admiration. She felt the need to dispute Beauvoir's feminist attack on the Roman Catholic church. But in repudiating Christianity in the name of women's autonomy, and accusing the Roman Catholic church of overt misogyny, Beauvoir had turned to historical facts, which Daly could hardly deny. Daly's only way out was to point to impending "historical changes" in the Roman Catholic church of the 1960s.[25]

At the same time, Daly discovered that Beauvoir had been inconsistent in her indictment of Christianity and the Roman Catholic church as active oppressors of women. In *The Second Sex*, Beauvoir made several references to women "achieving transcendence through religion." For example, she stated that the power of religious orders had brought women such as Teresa of Avila to "heights that few men ever reached."[26] Daly interpreted Beauvoir's remarks to mean that the church as a social institution could provide "the needed condition for a St. Teresa to rise above the handicap of her sex."[27] Daly also noticed Beauvoir's pronounced admiration for Teresa of Avila. Beauvoir praised Teresa for "living out the situation of humanity" in an exemplary fashion. "As for the psychological leverage which produced this phenomenon, Beauvoir does not explain further," Daly remarked. "The one indisputable fact is that Teresa of Avila was a Christian mystic."[28]

Daly was well aware of the discrepancy between Beauvoir's merciless portrayal of someone like the French mystic Marguerite Marie Alacoque—whom she described as neurotic, overemotional, and narcissistic—and her almost "lyrical" description of Teresa of Avila, whom she credited with "achieving transcendence." Daly seemed, however, not to be interested in exploring the reasons behind this discrepancy. In fact, she seemed only too happy to accept Beauvoir's suggestion that Teresa of Avila somehow took up an exceptional position in the ranks of Christian mystics. In **The Church and the Second Sex,** Daly turned Teresa into a precursor of modern Bible interpreters and of proponents of women's emancipation. "Apparently, as a consequence of mystical experience, Teresa's understanding rose above the common interpretation of Pauline texts concerning women," Daly concluded, echoing both Beauvoir's views and her language.[29]

Gendered Concept of Bad Faith

In contrast to Daly, I am very interested in possible reasons for the ambivalence in Beauvoir's views on Christian religion and women's autonomy, or "transcendence," as expressed in *The Second Sex*. Beauvoir wrote this comprehensive antiessentialist study with the intention of demythologizing opinions on women and "femininity" commonly held in her own social and intellectual milieu. She exposed and analyzed the androcentric bias with which women are classified as "the other" and as subordinate to men. She argued that this phenomenon pervaded not only the Western literary canon, but also myths, morals, and rituals worldwide. Beauvoir showed that both Western, Christian, "enlightened" civilizations and "primitive" cultures were rife with prejudice against women. Yet she also stressed the historical and contextual nature of "femininity"; in her view, women are not "feminine" by essence or nature. On the basis of many examples, she identified the social and psychological processes whereby women learn to act "feminine."

For a critical interpretation of these processes she turned to the central analytical frameworks of the existentialist philosophy that she and Jean-Paul Sartre had developed. *L'être et le néant* (1943), the first major product of their collaboration, and which appeared solely under Sartre's name,[30] described in great detail how individuals shrink from reaching their full potential and thus give up their freedom. Instead of striving to transcend a given situation, they cling to certain positions and states of mind that prevent them from taking their freedom and from "actualizing the self." This "inauthentic" or "self-deceptive" way of living was termed *mauvaise foi,* or bad faith.[31] But whereas *L'être et le néant* only discussed the individual factors that act as impediments to self-actualization, in *The Second Sex* Beauvoir argued that women's failure to achieve transcendence also had its roots in a shared social situation. Women's social position seemed to engender an almost inevitable, permanent condition of bad faith.

According to Beauvoir, women's position was characterized by the fact that they grow up, live, and make their choices in a world where men have cast them as the other. "They propose to stabilize her as object and to doom her to immanence since her transcendence is to be overshadowed and forever transcended by another ego which is essential and sovereign."[32] Beauvoir eventually linked this subjection to the other to women's reproductive role, or more precisely, to their complete immersion in the sustenance of life itself.

In terms of religion, *The Second Sex* also expands upon the frameworks of the existentialist philosophy set out in *L'être et le néant.* Although *L'être et le néant* firmly denounced religious faith (or, to be precise, God's existence) because of its incompatibility with the individual's radically infinite freedom,[33] Beauvoir's *The Second Sex* offered a far more complex view. Beauvoir endorsed the existentialist "rational" refutation of God's existence,[34] but also admitted—albeit with mixed feelings—that religious faith sometimes made women autonomous and helped them transcend the gender-related boundaries imposed on them. It is quite remarkable that religion was the only field where Beauvoir found examples of "self-actualized" women, as Mary Daly was quick to observe in 1967. Therefore, it seems appropriate to investigate in more detail why religious women such as Joan of Arc, Catherine of Siena, and Teresa of Avila were given such special status in *The Second Sex.*

RELIGION OF LOVE

In *The Second Sex,* there are two distinct trains of thought about women and religion. First and foremost, there is Beauvoir's main point of view: a strong conviction that religion affirms and legitimizes women's "immanence." She points to the blatant way in which Roman Catholicism achieves this: it provides saintly role models and uses symbols and rituals of kneeling and of women/mothers who are subservient to, and bow for, men/fathers representing God, the Almighty Father. Besides deepening women's dependency and powerlessness, religion also mystifies their fundamentally lower social status by granting them the illusion of transcendence. Christianity does this in a particularly ingenious way: ostensibly, it grants women an equal status: as creatures of God, both men and women possess eternal souls, bound to heaven. Simultaneously, Christianity, and particularly Roman Catholicism, offers women a magic universe filled with objects and activities to occupy their time and resign them to their fate: "Religion sanctions woman's self-love: it gives her the guide, father, lover and divine guardian she longs for nostalgically; it feeds her daydreams; it fills her empty hours. But, above all, it confirms the social order, it justifies her resignation, by giving her the hope of a better future in a sexless heaven. This is why women today are still a powerful trump in the hand of the Church; it is why the Church is notably hostile to all measures likely to help in woman's emancipation. There must be a religion for women; and there must be women, 'true women,' to perpetuate religion."[35]

But these mechanisms are at work not only in historical Roman Catholicism. According to Beauvoir, even contemporary Christianity has the same effect: "In modern civilisation which—even for woman—has a share in promoting freedom, religion seems much less an instrument of constraint than an instrument of deception. Woman is asked in the name of God not so much to accept her inferiority as to believe that, thanks to Him, she is the equal of the lordly male; even the temptation to revolt is suppressed by the claim that the injustice is overcome. Woman is no longer denied transcendence, since she is to consecrate her immanence to God."[36]

The second train of thought on women and religion in *The Second Sex* concerns the idea that (certain) women can achieve transcendence through religion. Both girls and adult women can gain autonomy through religious faith.[37] It is significant that, in this context, Beauvoir speaks of "mysticism" or "mystical experience" rather than religion. She is not interested in mysticism as a special religious experience, but rather as a special sort of erotic love. Beauvoir devotes an entire section to "the woman mystic."[38] This section forms the conclusion of an analysis of the ways in which women practice bad faith.[39] In Beauvoir's view, narcissism, erotic love, and mystical love have common characteristics. The gender specificity in how women forsake freedom lies in their rendering themselves—actually or imaginarily—totally dependent on men. Women practice a disastrous "religion of love":[40] a boundless devotion to divine men and masculine gods.[41]

> Love has been assigned to woman as her supreme vocation, and when she directs it toward a man, she is seeking God in him; but if human love is denied her by circumstances, if she is disappointed or overparticular, she may choose to adore divinity in the person of God Himself. To be sure, there have also been men who burned with that flame, but they are rare and their fervour is of a highly refined intellectual cast; whereas the women who abandon themselves to the joys of the heavenly nuptials are legion, and their experience is of a peculiarly emotional nature. Woman is habituated to living on her knees; ordinarily she expects her salvation to come down from the heaven where the males sit enthroned.[42]

Love of God can bring women to extremes of self-denial and self-abasement. Some female mystics even practiced automutilation, or physical self-neglect. But somehow this did not apply to Catherine of Siena and Teresa of Avila. In their cases, mystical experience rendered them autonomous; it empowered them and opened the gate to self-actualization in projects as important as those of men of power. "But the story of St. Catherine of Siena is significant: in the midst of a quite normal existence she created in Siena a great reputation by her active benevolence and by the visions that testified to her intense inner life; thus she acquired the authority necessary for success, which women usually lack."[43] Why are these women so exceptional? Why did Beauvoir consider them the only women to transcend their gender-specific boundaries and, what is more, to reach heights few men ever reached?

Resisting Subjection to Mortal Men

Beauvoir remained rather vague about the "self-actualization" of her great women mystics. She confined herself to stating that these women held their own against their male peers. I believe that Beauvoir's appreciation of these mystics' transcendence and self-actualization' is not based on an interest in their spiritual life or their actual social achievements. I think she held these women in high esteem because, as religious women, they were not bound by masculine authority, or at least they did not consider themselves to be. They did not recognize male authority and acted with amazing authority themselves.[44]

To Beauvoir, the importance of these mystics lay not only in their lack of ties to men, but also in their total lack of interest in men. In *The Second Sex*, one of Beauvoir's main concerns is the way in which women assent to their subjugation and objectification by men. In her quest for autonomy, independence, and self-actualization, the women mystics serve as paragons of womanhood, since they remained free of the bonds of earthly love and did not devote their entire lives to the sustenance of life itself.

Their unique status in Beauvoir's eyes results from her belief that the struggle for autonomy and the effort to resist subordination to men are intertwined with religious faith in a very concrete way. This link is evident not only in *The Second Sex*, but also in Beauvoir's *Memoirs* and other autobiographical texts. In one of the latter texts, there is an explicit reference to the direct link between the search for autonomy and self-awareness, and the experience of denying God's existence.[45] When asked in an interview what had made her aware of her position as a woman, Beauvoir answered by describing the time and place when she discarded her belief in God.[46] In interviews and in her *Memoirs*, Beauvoir confessed that her relation with Sartre had given her a fundamental security in life and a justification of her existence that she had previously only experienced in her relationship with her father and with God.[47] In *The Second Sex*, Beauvoir widened the scope of this interchangeability of father, God, and lover, and put the role they play in the process of "becoming a woman" in a wider context.

According to Beauvoir, a young girl's father "incarnates that immense, difficult, and marvelous world of adventure: he personifies transcendence, he is God." The girl's relationship with the eternal father is based on her relationship with her real father. All her life she may "longingly seek that lost state of plenitude and peace" that came from her father's affection. "The emotional concern shown by adult women toward Man would of itself suffice to perch him on a pedestal."[48]

The unique status of the women mystics in *The Second Sex* can be clarified by regarding the following two interrelated paradoxes as the core issues of Simone de Beauvoir's reflections on women and religion: (1) even women who have ceased to believe in God the Father may still put their faith in men as if they were gods; (2) by loving God "as a woman" women can radically break with their dependence on and subjugation to "mortal men." The first paradox describes Beauvoir's own position, while the second describes the position occupied by the great women mystics.

Joan of Arc

In ***The Church and the Second Sex***, Mary Daly steered clear of the hazardous topic of women's autonomy, love, and religion as explored by Simone de Beauvoir. Nevertheless, there are some indications that Daly did not miss Beauvoir's point after all and took good note of her conclusions and dilemmas. In the final chapter of *The Church and the Second Sex*, titled "The Second Sex and the Seeds of Transcendence," Daly assessed the results of her attempts to "disprove" Beauvoir's rejection of Roman Catholicism. She chose a curious epigraph for this chapter, a statement she borrowed from Joan of Arc: "I do best by obeying and serving my sovereign Lord—that is God."⁴⁹

This epigraph seemed to contradict all the issues Daly had presented and emphasized in the preceding chapters; she had previously argued in favor of a religious language that refrains from gendering God and had advocated total equality and "partnership" between men and women at all levels of church and society. Terms such as *obeying* and *serving* hardly fit into this scheme. However, the epigraph does make sense in light of Beauvoir's double paradox. It fits in well with the second paradox, which is that women could make a radical break with their dependence on men and their subordination to men, by loving God as a woman. By quoting Joan of Arc, Daly affirmed Beauvoir's argument, supporting autonomous religious women; and yet in the very same breath, she distanced herself from Beauvoir by declaring that she, Daly, did not need to turn her back on Christianity and the Roman Catholic church.

With this epigraph Daly confirms Joan of Arc's religious faith and autonomy toward earthly lords and sovereigns, as well as her own. Daly did not identify with the great women mystics, such as Teresa of Avila, whose outspoken, erotic mysticism Beauvoir had paid much attention to. By quoting Joan of Arc, Daly allied herself with a strong religious woman who was neither a member of a monastic order, nor involved in a (heterosexual) "mysticism of love." Joan of Arc was a sort of maverick: her autonomy was extreme and her actions were radical, as was her interpretation of a divine vocation. But unlike any of the other female mystics Beauvoir mentioned, Joan of Arc had had to pay a high price for her "radical transcendence": she was burned at the stake.

Daly later assessed this element of autonomy in her epigraph. In her 1975 **"Post-Christian Introduction"** to *The Church and the Second Sex,* she commented on her choice of epigraph (writing about herself in the third person): "It struck me as curiously fitting that the lead citation was from Joan of Arc. Joan had at least made a partial escape from patriarchy (as had Daly, in her own way.) . . . Of course, Daly's attention was focused not upon this ultimate "obeying and serving" but upon Joan's escape from the earthly masters."⁵⁰

PATRIARCHY AS A RELIGION

Simone de Beauvoir criticized Christian faith in general and Roman Catholicism in particular for having a negative impact on women's emancipation. Although Daly initially resisted this point of view, she eventually adopted it herself. I believe that she came to accept it precisely because Beauvoir had recognized that religious faith had an ambiguous impact—both positive and negative—on women's autonomy. Beauvoir's frame of reference allowed Daly her first opportunity to embrace modern criticism of religion in the name of feminism. This criticism, dating back to the Enlightenment, boils down to a renunciation of religious faith on the grounds that it, by definition, blocks people's autonomy. In this view, religious faith requires people to subject themselves to a higher being and to institutions claiming to represent this being. A concern of modern criticism of religion is to be free and protect human autonomy from the heteronomy intrinsic to religious faith in general and to institutionalized religion in particular.

As I mentioned before, existentialist philosophy strongly supported this criticism. It explicitly called any betrayal of one's own autonomy and self-actualization *mauvaise foi,* or bad faith. Daly took this modern criticism of religion much further: for example, to the point where she concluded that patriarchy as such was a religion. She put Beauvoir's remarkable comparison between (heterosexual) romantic love and religious faith as instruments of oppression at the core of her notion and critique of patriarchy. In a nutshell, Beauvoir had found that both love and religion force women to accept their status as the other in relation to men and to become "objects" instead of "realizing their potential." Deep veneration for divine men and masculine gods is women's particular—and particularly disastrous—form of bad faith.

Daly's later, rigorous critique of patriarchy in all its manifestations the world over is essentially an elaboration of this existentialist-feminist construction of gender-specific bad faith, culminating in the controversial thesis that "[p]atriarchy is itself the prevailing religion of the entire planet."⁵¹ In tracing the development of this thesis through Daly's writings, one finds that Daly, in her initial definition of patriarchy, mainly stressed the wider social processes responsible for the imbalance in power between the sexes.⁵² In ***Beyond God the Father*** (1973) Daly started to use the term patriarchy to describe a feminist analytical concept and defined patriarchy by comparing it to India's caste system:

> [T]here exists a worldwide phenomenon of sexual caste, basically the same whether one lives in Saudi Arabia or in Sweden. This planetary sexual caste system involves birth-ascribed hierarchically ordered groups whose members have unequal access to goods, services and prestige and to physical and mental well-being. Clearly I am not using the term "caste" in its most rigid sense, which would apply only to Brahmanic Indian society. I am using it in accordance with Berreman's broad description, since our language at present lacks other

terms to describe systems of rigid social stratification analogous to the Indian system.[53]

However, Daly's declaration that patriarchy is "the number one religion of the entire planet" is not a simple extension of her critical sociological observations about religion. In *Gyn/Ecology,* Daly worded her point of view as follows:

> Patriarchy is itself the prevailing religion of the entire planet, and its essential message is necrophilia. All of the so-called religions legitimating patriarchy are mere sects subsumed under its vast umbrella/canopy. They are essentially similar, despite the variations. All—from buddhism and hinduism to islam, judaism, christianity, to secular derivates such as freudianism, jungianism, marxism and maoism—are infrastructures of the edifice of patriarchy. All are erected as parts of the male's shelter against anomie. And the symbolic message of all the sects of the religion which is patriarchy is this: Women are dreaded anomie. Consequently, women are the objects of male terror, the projected personifications of "The Enemy," the real objects under attack in all the wars of patriarchy.[54]

Here, one of Beauvoir's observations is taken to the extreme: that women are turned into the other in relation to men, emphasizing that patriarchy functions and legitimizes itself in exactly the same way that religion does.

Daly presented a further development of her analytical concept of patriarchy as a religion in *Pure Lust* (1983). She wrote of a "phallocratic belief system" and a "universal religion of phallocracy" that prevents both men and women from believing in women's power and holiness.[55] The results are continued objectification and rape of women.

In discussing the effects of patriarchy as a religion, Daly pointed to Simone de Beauvoir's analysis of women's religious masochism. Beauvoir used the exalted and extreme acts of self-denial by the French Roman Catholic mystic Marguerite Marie Alacoque to exemplify how patriarchal religion fosters feelings of guilt and brings women to "masosadism."[56] According to Daly, Roman Catholicism is not unique in this respect; every type of patriarchal religion, in fact patriarchy as such, is guilty of the same. Continual objectification causes a nagging doubt at the core of woman's mind, identity, and self. Women consumed by this doubt are prone to masosadism in a "sadosociety." Neither they, nor anyone else, are able to believe in the power and holiness of women's lives.

Emerging Two-Track View of Religion

Simone de Beauvoir's ambivalence about the impact of religion on women's autonomy also offered Daly the opportunity to maintain her positive stance toward religious faith, based on a neoscholastic concept of God. Beauvoir's ambiguous views allowed Daly to remain a theologian and to develop her theological insights further. In *Beyond God the Father,* Daly processed Beauvoir's ideas in a way that is still quite similar to classical Christian theology. Daly sees feminist criticism of religion as criticism of idolatry—a well-respected and important Judeo-Christian point of view. This criticism of idolatry serves to liberate and innovate religion itself:

> The passive hope that has been so prevalent in the history of religious attitudes corresponds to the objectified God from whom one may anticipate favors. Within that frame of reference human beings have tried to relate to ultimate reality as an object to be known, cajoled, manipulated. The tables are turned, however, for the objectified "God" has a way of reducing his producers to objects who lack capacity for autonomous action. In contrast to this, the God who is power of being acts as a moral power summoning women and men to act out of our deepest hope and to become who we can be.[57]

In *Beyond God the Father,* feminist criticism of religion is inseparable from a dynamic interpretation of religious faith that supports feminism; these are two sides of the same coin. Later, when Daly renounced Christian theology altogether, feminist criticism of religion and feminist religious faith became increasingly separate topics in her work. From *Gyn/Ecology* onward, she voiced sharp criticism of any type of faith—religious or otherwise—that turns women into "objects under attack." At the same time, but on a different track, she continues to develop a thea-logy which supports women's autonomy and "self-realization."

In 1990, Iris Marion Young characterized Daly's *Gyn/Ecology* both as a repudiation of femininity along the lines of Beauvoir's brand of "humanist feminism" and as an example of the type of gynocentric feminism that Young considered the antithesis of humanist feminism. She regarded the two as irreconcilable because women either want to be like men or they do not, but they cannot dwell in between. Young therefore classified *Gyn/Ecology* as a transitional work: "In it Daly asserts an analysis of the victimization of women by femininity that outdoes Beauvoir, but she also proposes a new gynocentric language."[58]

I find Young's solution of calling *Gyn/Ecology* a transitional work rather inadequate. After all, the same "contradiction" is present in Daly's 1983 publication *Pure Lust* and other later writings. *Gyn/Ecology* is not an inconsistency in Mary Daly's work. I believe that it is consistent with Beauvoir's ambivalent view of religion in relation to women's independence. In *Gyn/Ecology,* Daly uses Beauvoir's gendered concept of bad faith to demonstrate how women are turned into the other and how, acting in bad faith, they turn themselves into objects and shrink from realizing their potential.

Daly's subsequent comparison of patriarchy to religion is still in keeping with Beauvoir's concept, but it provides Daly with a framework that allows her to do more than just analyze women's victimization and compliance: it also enables her to design strategies for resistance to and escape from patriarchy.

In line with Beauvoir's ambivalence toward religion, Daly starts to outline a "feminist faith" that supports this struggle. Basically, this faith is an unconditional affirmation of women's autonomy, transcendence, and self-actualization. Daly endorsed Beauvoir's finding that women have neither a history nor a religion of their own. She therefore reinvented this feminist faith by deconstructing patriarchal religious myths and imagery and reclaiming the fragments of women's lost or suppressed religious heritage in a gynocentric context. Daly's feminist faith is about establishing a subject position to counteract the objectification, silencing, and crushing of women. Hence, this faith both shapes, and is shaped by, a gynocentric language and context. Gynocentrism is necessary because women had been denied the power to name, as Daly concluded from her struggle with classic Christian discourse in **Beyond God the Father**. In Daly's post-Christian feminist writings this feminist faith manifests itself as an impressive amount of recaptured religious and mythical imagery rendered in an overwhelming, "scholarly" newspeak. In **Pure Lust,** Daly defined this feminist faith as "elemental faith." "Elemental" refers to all spiritual and material realities that have been attacked, suppressed, erased, or annihilated by the "phallocratic belief system."

Daly's seemingly contradictory combination of antiessentialist and gynocentric views can be accounted for by her ambiguous stance toward the role of religion in women's struggle for autonomy and "self-actualization." This brings her time and again to discern sharply between bad and good faith, between religion as an addiction ("opium") or a mystical experience (transcendence) and between religion's power to tempt women into total subjection or its role in empowering them to occupy a subject position. Her positive or affirmative view of religious faith enables her to emphasize women's subject position (gynocentrism), while her negative or critical view of religion allows her to put forward a cultural and religious critique (antiessentialism).

SUBJECTIVITY

Rather than exploring the (possibly contradictory) notions of gender and gender differences, I would like to focus on the various notions of subjectivity present in Daly's later writings. I think that this angle might best highlight Daly's unique significance as a theologian.

In Daly's later works, the affirmation of religious faith is used mainly to empower women as subjects. To describe what she means by such empowerment, Daly borrows terminology from her study of theology and philosophy (subject/object, self/other, being/nonbeing, being/Be-ing), as well as from popular psychology (power, energy, center, life, integrity, authenticity) and from her own, mythical female language (Hag, Crone, Spinster, Voyager, Witch, Goddess). Daly describes women's becoming subject first and foremost as self-realization, which raises the question of whether this is anything but an uncritical adoption of the androcentric notion of the autonomous self as embraced by existentialist philosophy.[59] Daly thought of many equivalents for women's "Self" and a variety of qualifications with reference to this self; these show us that Daly's notion of female self-awareness can be equated neither with self-determination ("being independent") nor with autonomy ("being free of foreign authority"). She speaks of the Self, the subject, being, presence, awareness, soul, source, force, integrity, wholeness, strength, centering, and so on.

Women's Self as evoked in **Gyn/Ecology** is characterized by the fact that it is not a given or state of being. It must (still) be actualized; it is a matter of becoming. Daly's point of departure is the absence and fragmentation of the Self. This point is further elaborated in **Pure Lust.** Here, Daly raises the question of to what extent women have "something of their own," a self, despite patriarchy's crushing and deadly effects. Some claim that women have nothing of their own; Daly disagrees.[60] She does not believe that women have been oppressed to the point where they have no self left. The problem is that they are obstructed from realizing this, from realizing their self. Among the obstacles are violence against women and "patriarchal lies," but Daly also mentions the lack of solidarity among women (violence among women, the token woman) and individual women's inner fragmentation ("patriarchy's presence in our own mind").

In **Pure Lust,** however, Daly provides a more profound exploration of women's lack of self-actualization. This text provides a consistent, multifaceted inquiry into what constitutes and reinforces inner cohesion. Daly discusses three aspects of inner cohesion: consciousness, power, and "lust/longing," or, in other words, identifying one's self, asserting the self and extending the self. These aspects are dealt with in three major parts or "Spheres" of **Pure Lust,** focusing on reason, passion, and lust, respectively. Daly also establishes a strong correlation between achieving inner cohesion and naming the self, the world, and God.[61]

But where exactly should we place this treatment of women's self that hinges on achieving and promoting inner cohesion? Is this a continuation of the androcentric philosophical notion of the autonomous subject, or a break with it? In some respects, Daly's approach resembles that of feminist philosophers such as Luce Irigaray, who aligned themselves with the poststructuralist attack on the dominant Western notion of the subject.[62] This resemblance is evident mainly in the importance assigned to the level of language, to deconstruction, to deviant readings and different semantic connotations in order to establish and affirm oneself as a woman.[63] Daly refers to Monique Wittig's works, but actually gives them a very different twist.[64] Wittig argues that it is impossible for women to say "I" in phallocentric discourse; Daly regards this as an example of the fragmentation of women's self-awareness. In line with Virginia Woolf, Daly believes this fragmentation is healed only in "moments of being," in epiphanous experiences during which an I is created when the severed parts of the individual suddenly and fleetingly come together.[65] Unlike the French feminist philosophers, Daly does not consider the unity and identity of the subject problematic as such. To her, rather, the main problem is the absence of focus and the lack of remembering; she considers the moments when women experience the constitution of a Self to be "revelations."

Daly's later writings contain two different and seemingly contradictory notions of subjectivity. In her criticism of patriarchy and religion, she argues that women need to construct an autonomous Self. But what she actually does and achieves and calls for in her writings, while naming, punning, and associating, constitutes a dismantling of this notion of subjectivity. She sings and associates, speaks in different voices, places herself outside any system, shows anger, pleasure, and analytical depth, draws on and cites Western theology, philosophy and mythology as well as contemporary culture; in so doing, she spins and weaves new tapestries of meaning. Insofar as Daly identifies and names her way of thinking, she provides new images of the Self as an intricate knot, consisting of many threads/links:[66] a thinking, feeling, listening and naming entity, which both integrates and reaches out, is self-supporting but also connected to others. These are concepts of the Self that are no longer caught in the opposition between the androcentric notion of the autonomous self and the criticism of this notion by feminists and French deconstructionists.

Daly is definitely not out to adopt this androcentric autonomous self, as she herself explains most lucidly in her treatment of the difference between her own "elemental feminist philosophy" and the androcentric ontology of Western philosophy and theology. Daly describes this ontology as follows: "The ontological question, the question of being-itself, arises in something like a 'metaphysical shock'—the shock of possible nonbeing. This shock often has been expressed in the question: 'Why is there something; why not nothing?'"[67] Daly considers the opposition generated in the second half of this ontological question unjustified: why would amazement about "being" be linked to bewilderment at the thought of "non-being"? Daly feels this automatic link points to a static notion of being, to a reified ontology which first and foremost sees being as the ability to stave off nonbeing. According to Daly, this idea reflects the position of phallic thinkers who sense the terror of the negation of everything that *is*—and therefore of their own, privileged position as well. The ontology that informs the primary questions of biophilic women is not based on this fear of nonbeing, but on the quest and longing for being (more).[68]

Daly posits a notion of subjectivity that resides in the tension between "being" and "Be-ing more." This tension does not arise from the shocking, distressing, or "impinging" experience of finiteness, individuality, and exclusiveness, but from the "unlocking," affirmative experience of "broadening," participation, and belonging.[69]

I believe that Daly derived this definition of subjectivity—which is not based on a modern, individualist, and androcentric opposition between autonomy and heteronomy—from premodern Thomistic religious ontology. This religious ontology assumes that there are various degrees of fullness or intensity of being. An increase in intensity means that people or matters are more involved in an all-transcending or encompassing reality: the fullness or completion of all that is in God. In this view, the way a being actualizes herself (more) is not by resisting or avoiding this all encompassing reality, but by opening herself up to this reality and knowing herself to be part of it.

Conclusions

Mary Daly's post-Christian writings have been interpreted in very different ways. On the one hand, her later work is often characterized as shying away from the actual ongoing conflicts, political issues, and difficult battles the women's movement faced after the euphoria of the first successes.[70] On the other hand, Daly's *Gyn/Ecology* formed the basis for Sonia Johnson's green, leftist political program for Johnson's U.S. presidential campaign in the early 1980s.[71] Daly's later work is interpreted as an unconditional and unmediated affirmation of "the feminine": the body, emotions, "the natural."[72] But Daly's later writings have also been interpreted as expressing a disdain for the actual lives of women and an overemphasis on rationality.[73] In the same vein, it has been concluded that immanence and "*Diesseitigkeit*" characterize the religiosity that Daly's work has testified to since *Beyond God the Father*,[74] while it has also been maintained that her work stresses transcendence.[75] Similarly, there are those who believe that Daly's writings since *Beyond God the Father* hinge on female spirituality and the rewriting of "matriarchal religious imagery,"[76] whereas others point to the fact that Daly, in her later writings, no longer identifies the divine with the female.[77]

I believe this polysemic ambiguity is characteristic of Mary Daly's later writings and that it is of little use to try to reduce her work to one unambiguous statement. I have shown that her work contains two widely divergent positions on religion, which are inspired by the ambivalent views of Simone de Beauvoir on religion's importance to the women's movement. I find Daly's work especially intriguing in those places where the positive and negative aspects of religion cause tension and friction. I have given an example of this by showing how Daly, as a theologian, remained faithful to a premodern notion of religious faith. This notion allows her to define subjectivity without getting caught in the modern androcentric opposition between autonomy and heteronomy in which the subject is represented as "the Self in juxtaposition with the Other" and as "the Self inferior or superior to the Other." Neoscholastic theology has provided her with another concept of subjectivity that, in some respects, better defines what happens when women occupy a subject position. This concept hinges on the absence of subjectivity and lack of inner cohesion rather than an opposition between Self and Other. It is more closely connected to Thomistic religious ontology than to modern androcentric existentialist ontology, which—through Sartre and Beauvoir—has also informed much of feminist theory.

Incidentally, I find Daly's work interesting not only because of these new feminist interpretations of her old, theological inheritance, but also because of her ongoing critical interpretations of Christian discourse. I choose the word interpretations because Daly reinterprets classical theological themes incorporated in texts of a postmodern signature—in itself an unusual mode for theological discourse. Daly's later writings are characterized by the use of more than one kind of logic and several voices directed at different readers.

As I mentioned earlier, some critics—such as Young—consider Daly's post-Christian writings a catalog of women's victimization. For example, her detailed descriptions in *Gyn/Ecology* of the atrocities that women all over the world are subjected to have been interpreted as an overstatement to prove women's victimization. However, I believe that Daly had something more in mind than proving that women are victims. I believe that *Gyn/Ecology* is Daly's multilayered way of revealing, reflecting, and meditating on physical violence against women. As such, this book discusses suffering, sin, evil, and (the hope of) salvation from a woman's perspective—a well-known theological track from an unusual angle.

It is remarkable that Daly's self-declared farewell to Christian theology and philosophy coincided with the introduction of the theme of violence against women in her writings. She had touched upon this theme earlier. In *Beyond God the Father*, she included it in her discussion of the necessity of replacing phallic morality. In her attempt to deconstruct androcentric Christian morality, she mentioned the unholy trinity of rape, genocide, and war as the three-headed monster to be faced and fought. To write of rape in the academic, theological context of 1973 was an act of true courage because Daly thereby presented herself as a professional theologian who openly took women's experiences seriously. However, the manner in which she dealt with the subject in *Beyond God the Father* was still very impersonal and abstract.[78]

In *Gyn/Ecology*, this had radically changed. Here, she described every physical detail of various, systematic acts of violence against women, such as rape, genital mutilation, foot-binding, widow-burning and hysterectomy. I read *Gyn/Ecology* primarily in light of this fascination with the violation of women's bodies. Feminist theologians have suggested that *Gyn/Ecology* is a women's tale of salvation or a female version of the Passion of Christ. Instead of Jesus, women are nailed to the cross. I agree that *Gyn/Ecology* deals with this central christian story, but I believe that it does so in a very profound and dialectical way. One of Daly's distinguishing characteristics is precisely that she rejects any direct or positive correlation between the Passion of Christ and women's suffering. She is truly scandalized by the suffering caused by violence. Therefore, she is shocked to the core by the fact that Christian theological discourse does acknowledge suffering due to physical violence in the case of Jesus—or God incarnate—but is often oblivious to women's suffering from physical violence. Christian theological discourse seems not only to be indifferent to women's suffering; it is also unable to recognize how the discourse itself propagates this suffering. It condones the hidden violence toward women that is central to many of its own religious images and parables. Therefore, a feminist reinterpretation of Christian passion stories does not suffice. The discourse needs to be altered by the inclusion of other stories of passion and resurrection, in particular of those who have been excluded from and hurt by androcentric theological discourse.

In her introduction to *Gyn/Ecology*, Daly stated that she had exchanged theology for ethics. According to her, *Gyn/Ecology* contains the "Meta-Ethics of Radical Feminism." However, besides it being a feminist exploration of ethics, I consider this book as much an extraordinary form of theology. Daly's self-confessed reversal to ethics seems to me an epistemological move inherent in a shift in feminist position. As Sandra Harding commented in a 1986 publication: "For feminists, it is a moral and political, rather than a scientific, discussion that serves as the paradigm of rational discourse."[79] In my opinion, *Gyn/Ecology* deals directly with the moral and political discussion that, from a feminist point of view, must be included into theological discourse, the main issue being "How can we ensure that women are done more justice?" rather than "What can we know about women?"

One might argue that this is precisely the point where theology turns into ethics. I disagree; the way in which **Gyn/Ecology** deals with "evil" is every bit as religious as it is ethical. One need only consider the book's central premise: the act of turning women into objects to be abused, or even destroyed, far too often goes unrecognized as fundamentally wrong or evil. And Mary Daly considers this, the deliberate obfuscation of what should be regarded as evil, one of the main "sins" of all patriarchal religions and societies. A call for ethics alone will not do, because ethics has been distorted by phallic morality. In this situation, "deliver us from evil" seems to be an indispensable prayer for women.

> Certainly, women have always cried and struggled for "justice." The thwarting of this longing and struggling gives rise to the birth pangs of radical feminist awareness. But only when the knowledge that something is not "right" evolves into uncovering the invisible context of gynocide and, beyond this, into active participation in the Elemental context of biophilic harmony and power can there be great and sustained creativity and action. To Name this active Elemental contextual participation, which transcends and overturns patriarchal "justice" and "injustice," Other words are needed. Nemesis is a beginning in this direction.[80]
>
> ... [U]nlike "justice," which is depicted as a woman blindfolded and holding a sword and scales, Nemesis has her eyes open and uncovered—especially her Third Eye. Moreover, she is concerned less with "retribution," in the sense of external meting out of rewards and punishments, than with an internal judgment that sets in motion a kind of new psychic alignment of energy patterns. Nemesis, thus Named, is . . . a relevant mysticism which responds to the tormented cries of the oppressed, and to the hunger and thirst for creative be-ing.[81]

Notes

1. See Catherine Keller, *From a Broken Web: Separation, Sexism, and Self* (Boston: Beacon Press, 1986), 207-12; Carol P. Christ, "Embodied Thinking: Reflections on Feminist Theological Method," *Journal of Feminist Studies in Religion* 5, no. 1 (1989): 7-15; Rita Nakashima Brock, *Journeys by Heart: A Christology of Erotic Power* (New York: Crossroad, 1989), 50; Sharon D. Welch, *A Feminist Ethic of Risk* (Minneapolis: Fortress Press, 1990), 1-10; Welch, "Sporting Power: American Feminism, French Feminisms, and an Ethic of Conflict," in *Transfigurations: Theology and the French Feminists,* ed. C. W. Maggie Kim et al. (Minneapolis: Fortress Press, 1993), 171-98; Mary McClintock Fulkerson, *Changing the Subject: Women's Discourses and Feminist Theology* (Minneapolis: Fortress Press, 1994), 46-47.

2. Audre Lorde, "An Open Letter to Mary Daly," in *Sister Outsider: Essays and Speeches* (Trumansburg, N.Y.: Crossing Press, 1984), 66-71; Hester Eisenstein, *Contemporary Feminist Thought* (London: Unwin Paperbacks, 1984); Beverly Wildung Harrison, *Making the Connections: Essays in Feminist Social Ethics,* ed. Carol S. Robb (Boston: Beacon Press, 1985); Chris Weedon, *Feminist Practice and Poststructuralist Theory* (Oxford: Basil Blackwell, 1987); Linda Alcoff, "Cultural Feminism Versus Post-Structuralism: The Identity Crisis in Feminist Theory," in *Feminist Theory in Practice and Progress,* ed. Micheline R. Balson et al. (Chicago: University of Chicago Press, 1989), 295-326; Jean Grimshaw, "Autonomy and Identity in Feminist Thinking," in *Feminist Perspective in Philosophy,* ed. Morwenna Griffiths and Margareth Whitford (Bloomington: Indiana University Press, 1988), 90-108; Morwenna Griffiths, "Feminism, Feelings, and Philosophy," in Griffiths and Whitford, *Feminist Perspectives in Philosophy,* 131-51; Elizabeth V. Spelman, *Inessential Women: Problems of Exclusion in Feminist Thought* (Boston: Beacon Press, 1988), 123-25; Amy Hollywood, "Violence and Subjectivity: *Wuthering Heights,* Julia Kristeva, and Feminist Theology," in Kim et al., *Transfigurations,* 81-108, especially nn. 14 and 108.

3. Rosemary Radford Ruether, *Sexism and God-Talk: Toward a Feminist Theology* (Boston: Beacon Press, 1983); Elisabeth Schüssler Fiorenza, *In Memory of Her: A Feminist Theological Reconstruction of Christian Origins* (London: SCM Press, 1983); Sheila Greeve Davaney, "The Limits of the Appeal to Women's Experience," in *Shaping New Vision: Gender and Values in American Culture,* ed. Clarissa W. Atkinson et al. (Ann Arbor: UMI Research Press, 1987), 30-48; Davaney, "Problems with Feminist Theory: Historicity and the Search for Sure Foundations," in *Embodied Love: Sensuality and Relationship as Feminist Values,* ed. Paula M. Cooey et al. (San Francisco: Harper and Row, 1988), 79-96; Ruth Großmaß, "Von der Verführungskraft der Bilder: Mary Daly's Elemental-Feministische Philosophie," in *Feministischer Kompaß, patriarchales Gepäck: Kritik konservativer Anteile in neueren feministischen Theorien,* ed. Ruth Großmaß and Christiane Schmerl (Frankfurt and New York: Campus Verlag, 1989), 56-116; Ellen T. Armour, "Questioning 'Woman' in Feminist/Womanist Theology: Irigaray, Ruether, and Daly," in Kim et al., *Transfigurations,* 143-70.

4. See also Ruether, *Sexism and God-Talk*; Mary Jo Weaver, *New Catholic Women: A Contemporary Challenge to Traditional Religious Authority* (San Francisco: Harper and Row, 1985); Großmaß, "Von der Verführungskraft der Bilder."

5. Teresa de Lauretis, "Upping the Anti [*sic*] in Feminist Theory," in *Conflicts in Feminism,* ed. Marianne Hir-

sch and Evelyn Fox Keller (New York: Routledge, 1990), 255-70.

6. The lasting impact of these Enlightenment ideals on feminism is evident in the prevalent categorization of feminist positions into the main political movements based on these ideals: liberal (or emancipatory) feminism, social (or sociological) feminism, and radical feminism (cultural criticism). See Ruether, *Sexism and God-Talk: Toward a Feminist Theology*, 214-34; Weedon, *Feminist Practice and Poststructuralist Theory* (Oxford: Basil Blackwell, 1987); Rosemary Tong, *Feminist Thought: A Comprehensive Introduction* (London: Routledge, 1989); Carolyn Merchant, "Ecofeminism and Feminist Theory," in *Reweaving the World: The Emergence of Ecofeminism*, ed. Irene Diamond and Gloria Feman Orenstein (San Francisco: Sierra Club Books, 1990), 100-105.

7. Alice A. Jardine, *Gynesis: Configurations of Woman and Modernity* (Ithaca: Cornell University Press, 1985), 100-101.

8. Mary Daly, *Beyond God the Father: Toward a Philosophy of Women's Liberation* (Boston: Beacon Press, 1973), 28-33.

9. Mary Daly, *Pure Lust: Elemental Feminist Philosophy* (Boston: Beacon Press, 1984), vii. See also Mary Daly, *The Church and the Second Sex* (London: Chapman, 1968), 223; and Daly, *Beyond God the Father*, 28-29.

10. Mary Daly, "Autobiographical Preface to the Colofon Edition," and "Feminist Postchristian Introduction," in Daly, *The Church and the Second Sex: With a New Feminist Postchristian Introduction by the Author* (New York: Harper and Row, 1975), 5-14, 15-51; Daly, "Vorwort zur deutschen Ausgabe von *Beyond God the Father*," in Daly, *Jenseits von Gottvater, Sohn & Co: Aufbruch zu einer Philosophie der Frauenbefreiung* (Munich: Frauenoffensive, 1980), 5-10; Daly, "New Archaic Afterwords," in Daly, *The Church and the Second Sex: With the Feminist Postchristian Introduction and New Archaic Afterwords by the Author* (Boston: Beacon Press, 1985), xi-xxx; Daly, "Original Reintroduction," in Daly, *Beyond God the Father: Toward a Philosophy of Women's Liberation; With an Original Reintroduction by the Author* (Boston: Beacon Press: Beacon Press, 1985), xi-xxix; Daly, "New Intergalactic Introduction," in Daly, *Gyn/Ecology: The Metaethics of Radical Feminism: With a New Introduction by the Author* (Boston: Beacon Press, 1991), xiii-xxxv; Daly, *Outercourse: The Be-Dazzling Voyage* (San Francisco: Harper, 1992).

11. Mary Daly, "The Problem of Speculative Theology: A Study in Saint Thomas" (Ph.D. diss., University of Fribourg, Switzerland, 1963); Daly, *Natural Knowledge of God in the Philosophy of Jacques Maritain* (Rome: Officium Libri Catholici, 1966).

12. Edward Schillebeeckx, "Het niet-begrippelijke kenmoment in onze Godskennis volgens Thomas van Aquino," *Tijdschrift voor Philosophie* 14 (1952): 411-53; Schillebeeckx, "Het niet-be-grippelijke kenmoment in de geloofsdaad: probleemstelling," *Tijdschrift voor Theologie* 3 (1963), 167-94; Schillebeeckx, *Openbaring en theologie* [Theologische Peilingen; 1] (Baarn: Nelissen, 1964). Johan Baptist Metz, *Christliche Anthropozentrik: Ueber die Denkform des Thomas von Aquin* (Munich: Koesel, 1962).

13. In the summary of her theological dissertation Daly states: "[The author] would like also to acknowledge her debt to all of the professors of the Faculty of Theology, who by opening for a woman the door to a doctorate in theology expressed openness of mind and spirit." Mary Daly, acknowledgments to *The Problem of Speculative Theology*, (Boston: Thomist Press, 1965). In her philosophical dissertation, Daly focused particularly on the philosophical and theological writings of women. Daly referred to the writings of Raissa Maritain—wife of Jacques Maritain, whose writings are the subject of her second dissertation, and to Raissa's role in her husband's philosophical development. Raissa Maritain, *Les grandes amitiés: Les aventures de la grâce*, vols. 1 and 2 (New York: Editions de la Maison Française, vol. 1, 1942; vol. 2, 1944); Maritain, *Situation de la poésie* [in cooperation with Jacques Maritain] (Paris: Desclée de Brouwer, 1948). Daly also praised Laura Fraga de Almeida Sampaic C. R. for her interpretation of Jacques Maritain's philosophical works, titled *L'intuition dans la philosophie de Jacques Maritain* (Paris: Vrin, 1963): "This enlightening and scholarly work is a most important aid to understanding Maritain's thought" (Daly, *Natural Knowledge of God*, 32 n. 76). Also, Daly favorably reviewed Sister M. Elisabeth I.H.M.'s publication "Two Contemporary Philosophers and the Concept of Being," *Modern Schoolman* 25 (1947/48), 224-37. "The author makes an interesting comparative analysis of Fr. Garrigou-Lagrange and Maritain" (Daly, *Natural Knowledge of God*, 20 n. 34). In addition, Daly pointed out yet another publication, by Sister Aloysius S.S.J., "The Epistemological Value of Sense Intuition," *Philosophical Studies* 5 (1955): 71-78.

14. Daly, *The Problem of Speculative Theology*, 41-47.

15. For a further elaboration of the central thesis of Mary Daly's theological dissertation about the importance and relevance of "speculative theology," based on (rational) "knowledge of God through creation," see Anne-Marie Korte, *Een passie voor transcendentie: Feminisme, theologie en moderniteit in het denken van Mary Daly* (*A Passion for Transcendence: Feminism, Theology, and Modernity in the Thinking of Mary Daly*) (Kampen: Kok, 1992), 55-59, 82-85.

16. Patricia H. Labalme, introduction to *Beyond Their Sex: Learned Women of the European Past,* ed. Labalme (New York: New York University Press, 1984), 3-4.

17. Katharina M. Wilson, ed., *Medieval Women Writers* (Manchester: Manchester University Press, 1984), xvii.

18. See Elisabeth Gössmann, ed., *Das Wohlgelahrte Frauenzimmer* [Archiv für philosophie- und theologiegeschichtliche Frauenforschung; 1] (Munich: Indicium, 1984); Gössmann, ed., *Eva—Gottes Meisterwerk* [Archiv für philosophie- und theologiegeschichtliche Frauenforschung; 2] (Munich: Indicium, 1985); Anna Maria van Schurman, *Opuscula Hebraea, Graeca, Latina, Gallica, Prosaica et Metrica* (Leiden: Ex Officina Elseviriorum, 1648); Beatriz Melano Couch, "Sor Juana Inés de la Cruz: The First Woman Theologian in the Americas," in *The Church and Women in the Third World,* John C. B. Webster and Ellen Low Webster, eds. (Philadelphia: Westminster Press, 1985), 51-57; Rosemary Radford Ruether and Rosemary Skinner Keller, eds., *Women and Religion in America,* vol. 2, *The Colonial and Revolutionary Periods* (San Francisco: Harper and Row, 1983), xv-xvi, 46, 65-68.

19. See Anne-Marie Korte, "Een gemeenschap waarin te geloven valt: Over de spirituele en de politieke betekenis van het geloof van vrouwen aan de hand van de 'ommekeer' van Anna Maria van Schurman en Mary Daly" (M.A. thesis, University of Nijmegen, The Netherlands, 1985), 41-57.

20. See Moltmann-Wendel, ed., *Frau und Religion,* 11-38; Rosemary Radford Ruether and Rosemary Skinner Keller, eds., *Women and Religion in America,* vol. 1, *The Nineteenth Century* (San Francisco: Harper and Row, 1981).

21. This issue was raised by Mary Daly herself in the short version of her theological dissertation. Mary Daly, *The Problem of Speculative Theology,* 41-43.

22. Daly, *Beyond God the Father,* 43.

23. Korte, *Een passie voor transcendentie,* 86-187.

24. Daly's first reference to Simone de Beauvoir appeared in a 1965 issue of *Commonweal,* a North American Roman Catholic journal: "Simone de Beauvoir, in *The Second Sex,* manifested a strange mixture of insight and understanding when she wrote that Mary kneeling for her own Son represents the supreme victory of the male over the female. Catholic readers, shocked by this, protest that Mlle. de Beauvoir simply does not understand. It may well be true that she does not have a sympathetic understanding of Catholic theology, but in fact she understands its abuses only too well. It is unfortunately not difficult to find examples in Catholic writings about women which manifest the vision of man-woman relationship which Simone de Beauvoir is talking about. (The tortured use of symbolism can be seen in Gertrud von le Fort's *The Eternal Woman,* which has sold hundreds of thousands of copies, as well as in countless other places.) We might well ask where the true culpability lies for Simone de Beauvoir's misunderstanding of Marian doctrine, and incidentally be grateful for her insight into the perversion thereof." Daly, "A Built-in Bias," *Commonweal* 81 (January 15, 1965): 509-10.

    In 1984, Daly wrote:

    > In the late 1940s the publication of Simone de Beauvoir's great feminist work, *The Second Sex,* made possible dialogue among women about their lives. For many years this work functioned as an almost solitary beacon for women seeking to understand the *connections* among the oppressive evils they experienced, for they came to understand the fact of otherness within patriarchal society.
    >
    > There were other feminist works in existence, of course, but these were not really accessible, even to the "educated" women. *The Second Sex* helped to generate an atmosphere in which women could utter their own thoughts, at least to themselves. Some women began to make applications and to seek out less accessible sources, many of which had gone out of print. Most important was the fact that de Beauvoir, by breaking the silence, partially broke the Terrible Taboo. Women were Touched, psychically and emotionally. Many women, thus re-awakened, began to have conversations, take actions, write articles—even during the dreary fifties. (Daly, *Pure Lust,* 374)

    See also Daly, *The Church and the Second Sex,* 56 and Daly, "Feminist Postchristian Introduction," 16.

25. Daly, *The Church and the Second Sex,* 192-223.

26. Simone de Beauvoir, *The Second Sex* (New York: Vintage Books, 1989), 130.

27. Daly, *The Church and the Second Sex,* 68.

28. Ibid., 69.

29. Ibid., 100.

30. Jean-Paul Sartre, *L'être et le néant: Essai d'ontologie phénoménologique* (Paris: Guillimard, 1943). For a recent critical study of Beauvoir and Sartre's collaboration, see Kate Fullbrook and Edward Fullbrook, *Simone de Beauvoir and Jean-Paul Sartre: The Remaking of a Twentieth Century Legend* (New York: Harvester Wheatsheaf, 1993).

31. Sartre, *L'être et le néant,* 93-108.

32. Beauvoir, *The Second Sex,* xli.

33. See also Jean-Paul Sartre, *L'existentialisme est un humanisme* (Paris: Nagel, 1946).

34. Beauvoir, *The Second Sex,* 632.

35. Ibid., 624.

36. Ibid., 621.

37. See ibid., 104; 622, 673-74, 673.

38. Beauvoir, "The Mystic," in *The Second Sex,* 670-78.

39. Beauvoir, "Justifications," in *The Second Sex,* 629-78.

40. Dorothy Kaufmann McGall has shown how Beauvoir in *Le deuxième sexe* outlines the pitfalls of romantic love for women by comparing it to religious devotion: "If every man, for Malraux and for Sartre after him, dreams of being God, woman, as Beauvoir portrays her in this chapter, dreams of being His beloved. For Beauvoir it is the woman most avidly seeking transcendence who is often most vulnerable to the religion of love. Denied the transcendence of action and adventure offered to the male, she seeks transcendence by losing herself in a man who represents the essential which she cannot be for herself." For the origins of this comparison Kaufmann refers to Beauvoir and Sartre's existentialist philosophy and to Beauvoir's personal history: her Catholic upbringing and her relation to her father, God, and Sartre. However, Kaufmann's reconstruction largely ignores the ambivalence in Beauvoir's comparison between love and religion. Dorothy Kaufmann McGall, "Simone de Beauvoir, *The Second Sex,* and Jean Paul Sartre," *Signs: Journal of Women in Culture and Society* 5, no. 2 (1979): 209-23, especially 216.

41. In *Die fröhliche Wissenschaft,* Friedrich Nietzsche ironically compared women's (heterosexual) love to religious faith, "the only faith women have." For a detailed analysis of the mainly Marxist and existentialist philosophical origins of Beauvoir's gendered comparison between heterosexual love and religious faith, see Korte, *Een passie voor transcendentie,* 149-54.

42. Beauvoir, *The Second Sex,* 670.

43. Ibid., 104.

44. See also ibid., 622.

45. Beauvoir herself considered religion a primary influence on her life and on her growing awareness of her position as a girl and a young woman. She stated that girls from southern Europe grow up with a religion that has an importance in their lives incomprehensible to women from an Anglo-American background. See "Une interview de Simone de Beauvoir par Madeleine Chapsal," in Claude Francis and Fernande Gontier, *Les écrits de Simone de Beauvoir: La vie—L'écriture. Avec en appendice: Textes inédits ou retrouvés* (Paris: Gallimard, 1979), 381-96.

46. "Une interview de Simone de Beauvoir," 383.

47. Dorothy Kaufmann McGall investigated Beauvoir's opinions on love and autonomy in light of her real life relationship with Sartre. She concluded: "Her ties to Sartre, however, have been as knotted and difficult in meaning as any tie to husband or family." Kaufmann McGall, "Simone de Beauvoir, *The Second Sex,* and Jean Paul Sartre," 223. For research on heterosexual and lesbian love in *The Second Sex,* see also Judith Butler, "Variations on Sex and Gender: Beauvoir, Wittig, and Foucault," in *Feminism as Critique: On the Politics of Gender,* ed. Seyla Benhabib and Drucilla Cornell (Minneapolis: University of Minnesota Press, 1987), 128-42; Jo-Ann Pilardi, "Female Eroticism in the Works of Simone de Beauvoir," in *The Thinking Muse: Feminism and Modern French Philosophy,* ed. Jeffner Allen and Iris Marion Young (Bloomington: Indiana University Press, 1989), 18-34; Toril Moi, *Feminist Theory and Simone de Beauvoir* (Oxford: Blackwell, 1990); Karin Vintges, *Filosofie als passie: Het denken van Simone de Beauvoir* (Amsterdam: Prometheus, 1992).

48. Beauvoir, *The Second Sex,* 287-90, especially 288.

49. Daly, *The Church and the Second Sex,* 220.

50. Daly, "Feminist Postchristian Introduction."

51. Mary Daly, *Gyn/Ecology: The Metaethics of Radical Feminism* (Boston: Beacon Press, 1978), 39.

52. The concept of religion Daly used in *Beyond God the Father* is derived primarily from critical sociologists such as Peter Berger and Herbert Marcuse. In their definition, religion's main function is to stabilize dominant social structures and to uphold norms and values that confirm the social status quo. Religious imagery and rituals make people "remember" and "internalize" the behavior expected of them. According to Daly, women in particular are socialized to consume and internalize religious images.

53. Daly, *Beyond God the Father,* 2.

54. Daly, *Gyn/Ecology,* 39.

55. Daly, *Pure Lust,* 31, 35-77; 170, 339.

56. Ibid., 57-66.

57. Daly, *Beyond God the Father,* 32.

58. Iris Marion Young, *Throwing Like a Girl and Other Essays in Feminist Philosophy and Social Theory* (Bloomington: Indiana University Press, 1990), 82.

59. Griffiths, "Feminism, Feelings, and Philosophy," 131-51; Weaver, *New Catholic Women*; Grimshaw, "Autonomy and Identity in Feminist Thinking," 90-108; Grimshaw, *Feminist Philosophers,* 146-61; Jean Grimshaw, "'Pure Lust': The Elemental Feminist Philosophy of Mary Daly," *Radical Philosophy,* no. 49 (1988): 25.

60. Daly, *Pure Lust,* 136-38.

61. The term "Self" ("Self is capitalized when I am referring to the authentic center of women's process" [Daly, *Gyn/Ecology,* 26]) is introduced in *Gyn/*

Ecology in close connection with a number of other, new expressions: gynocentric terms for God, consciousness and "living as a woman," namely "ultimate be-ing," "integrity of be-ing," and "gynocentric be-ing" (Daly, *Gyn/Ecology*, xi-xviii). This interrelatedness points to the fact that women's "Self" cannot be reduced to one of these three key notions; what is at stake is a *woman*'s affirmation of her self, which is related to all three of these aspects of Being. Compare the use of the term Self in the following instances:

> The finding of our original integrity is re-membering our Selves.
>
> (Daly, *Gyn/Ecology*, 39)
>
> The murder/dismemberment of the Goddess—that is, [of] the Self-affirming be-ing of women.
>
> (111)
>
> Our refusal to collaborate in this killing and dismembering of our own Selves is the beginning of re-membering the Goddess—the deep source of creative integrity in women.
>
> (111)
>
> The Goddess within—female divinity, that is our Selves.
>
> (111)

62. Luce Irigaray, *Speculum: De l'autre femme* (Paris: Minuit, 1974); Irigaray, *Ce Sexe qui n'en est pas un* (Paris: Minuit, 1977).

63. See for example Johanna Hodge, "Subject, Body, and the Exclusion of Women from Philosophy," in Griffiths and Whitford, *Feminist Perspectives in Philosophy*, 154, 167 n. 7.

64. See Daly, *Gyn/Ecology*, 19, 327, 350; Daly, *Pure Lust*, 177.

65. Virginia Woolf, *Moments of Being: Unpublished Autobiographical Writings*, edited, introduced, and annotated by Jeanne Schulkind (New York: University Press Sussex, 1976), 86-100.

66. Daly, *Gyn/Ecology*, 406.

67. Daly, *Pure Lust*, 159-60. Here, Daly refers to Paul Tillich, *Systematic Theology*, vol. 1 (London: Nisbet, 1953), 181.

68. Daly, *Pure Lust*, 30.

69. For descriptions of this ontological experience, Daly turns to Virginia Woolf's writings ("moments of being" as ontophanies [Daly, *Pure Lust*, 171-78]) and Sonia Johnson's work (the "breaking open process" as an epiphany [236-37]).

70. Jean Bethke Elshtain, "Feminist Discourse and Its Discontents: Language, Power, and Meaning," in *Feminist Theory: A Critique of Ideology* ed. Nannerl O. Keohane et al. (Chicago: University of Chicago Press, 1982), 135; Schüssler Fiorenza, *In Memory of Her*, 21-26.

71. Ynestra King, "Healing the Wounds," in *Gender/Body/Knowledge: Feminist Reconstructions of Being and Knowing*, ed. Alison M. Jaggar and Susan R. Bordo (New Brunswick: Rutgers University Press, 1989), 124, 136-37 n. 22.

72. Joan L. Griscom, "On Healing the Nature/History Split in Feminist Thought," in *Women's Consciousness, Women's Conscience: A Reader in Feminist Ethics*, ed. Barbara Hilkert Andolsen et al. (San Francisco: Harper and Row, 1985), 85-98.

73. Wildung Harrison, *Making the Connections*, 231; Weaver, *New Catholic Women*, 170-78.

74. Sallie McFague, *Metaphorical Theology: Models of God in Religious Language* (London: SCM Press, 1982), 155-59; Elisabeth Moltmann-Wendel, introduction to Moltmann-Wendel, ed., *Frau und Religion: Gotteserfahrungen im Patriarchat* (Frankfurt am Main: Fischer Taschenbuch Verlag, 1983), 14; Susan Brooks Thistlethwaithe, *Sex, Race, and God: Christian Feminism in Black and White* (New York, Crossroad, 1989), 16.

75. Brooke Williams, "The Feminist Revolution in 'Ultramodern' Perspective," *Cross Currents* 31 (1981): 311; Weaver, *New Catholic Women*, 176-77.

76. Großmaß, "Von der Verführungskraft der Bilder," 56-116; Anne Kent Rush, *Moon, Moon* (New York: Random House, 1976), 355.

77. Wanda Warren Berry, "Feminist Theology: The 'Verbing' of Ultimate/Intimate Reality in Mary Daly," in *Ultimate Reality and Meaning* 11, no. 3 (1988): 212-32; Korte, *Een gemeenschap waarin te geloven valt*, 162-65.

78. Daly, *Beyond God the Father*, 98-131. See also Korte, *Een passie voor transcendentie*, 284-90.

79. Sandra Harding, *The Science Question in Feminism* (Milton Keynes: Open University Press, 1986), 12.

80. Daly, *Pure Lust*, 275.

81. Ibid.

References

Alcoff, Linda. "Cultural Feminism Versus Post-Structuralism: The Identity Crisis in Feminist Theory." In *Feminist Theory in Practice and Progress*, edited by Micheline R. Balson et al., 295-326. Chicago: University of Chicago Press, 1989.

Allen, Jeffner, and Iris Marion Young, eds. *The Thinking Muse: Feminism and Modern French Philosophy*. Bloomington: Indiana University Press, 1989.

Aloysius, Sister, S.S.J. "The Epistemological Value of Sense Intuition." *Philosophical Studies* 5 (1955): 71-78.

Armour, Ellen T. "Questioning 'Woman' in Feminist/Womanist Theology: Irigaray, Ruether, and Daly." In *Transfigurations: Theology and the French Feminists*, edited by C. W. Maggie Kim et al., 143-70. Minneapolis: Fortress Press, 1993.

Atkinson, Clarissa W., et al., eds. *Shaping New Vision: Gender and Values in American Culture.* Ann Arbor: UMI Research Press, 1987.

Beauvoir, Simone de. *The Second Sex.* New York: Vintage Books, 1989.

Butler, Judith. "Variations on Sex and Gender: Beauvoir, Wittig, and Foucault." In *Feminism as Critique: On the Politics of Gender,* edited by Seyla Benhabib and Drucilla Cornell, 128-42. Minneapolis: University of Minnesota Press, 1987.

Christ, Carol P. "Embodied Thinking: Reflections on Feminist Theological Method." *Journal of Feminist Studies in Religion* 5, no. 1 (1989): 7-15.

Cooey, Paula M., et al., eds. *Embodied Love: Sensuality and Relationship as Feminist Values.* San Francisco: Harper and Row, 1988.

Daly, Mary. "Autobiographical Preface to the Colofon Edition," 5-14 and "Feminist Postchristian Introduction," 15-51. In Daly, *The Church and the Second Sex: With a New Feminist Postchristian Introduction by the Author.* Boston: Beacon Press, 1975.

———. *Beyond God the Father: Toward a Philosophy of Women's Liberation.* Boston: Beacon Press, 1973.

———. "A Built-in Bias." *Commonweal* 81 (January 15, 1965): 509-10.

———. *The Church and the Second Sex.* London: Chapman, 1968.

———. *Gyn/Ecology: The Metaethics of Radical Feminism.* Boston: Beacon Press, 1978.

———. *Natural Knowledge of God in the Philosophy of Jacques Maritain.* Rome: Officium Libri Catholici, 1966.

———. "New Archaic Afterwords." In Daly, *The Church and the Second Sex: With the Feminist Postchristian Introduction and New Archaic Afterwords by the Author,* xi-xxx. Boston: Beacon Press, 1985.

———. "New Intergalactic Introduction." In Daly, *Gyn/Ecology: The Metaethics of Radical Feminism: With a New Introduction by the Author,* xiii-xxxv. Boston: Beacon Press, 1991.

———. "Original Reintroduction." In Daly, *Beyond God the Father: Toward a Philosophy of Women's Liberation; With an Original Reintroduction by the Author,* xi-xxix. Boston: Beacon Press, 1985.

———. *Outercourse: The Be-Dazzling Voyage.* San Francisco: Harper, 1992.

———. *The Problem of Speculative Theology.* Boston: Thomist Press, 1965.

———. "The Problem of Speculative Theology: A Study in Saint Thomas." Ph.D. diss., University of Fribourg, Switzerland, 1963.

———. *Pure Lust: Elemental Feminist Philosophy.* Boston: Beacon Press, 1984.

———. "Vorwort zur deutschen Ausgabe von *Beyond God the Father.*" In Daly, *Jenseits von Gottvater, Sohn & Co: Aufbruch zu einer Philosophie der Frauenbefreiung,* 5-10. Munich: Frauenoffensive, 1980.

Diamond, Irene, and Gloria Feman Orenstein, eds. *Reweaving the World: The Emergence of Ecofeminism.* San Francisco: Sierra Club Books, 1990.

Eisenstein, Hester. *Contemporary Feminist Thought.* London: Unwin Paperbacks, 1984.

Elisabeth, Sister M., I.H.M. "Two Contemporary Philosophers and the Concept of Being." *The Modern Schoolman* 25 (1947/48): 224-37.

Elshtain, Jean Bethke. "Feminist Discourse and Its Discontents: Language, Power, and Meaning," In *Feminist Theory: A Critique of Ideology,* edited by Nannerl O. Keohane et al., 127-45. Chicago: University of Chicago Press, 1982.

Fraga, Laura de Almeida Sampaio C. R. *L'intuition dans la philosophie de Jacques Maritain.* Paris: Vrin, 1963.

Francis, Claude, and Fernande Gontier. *Les écrits de Simone de Beauvoir: La vie—l'écriture. Avec en appendice: Textes inédits ou retrouvés.* Paris: Gallimard, 1979.

Fullbrook, Kate, and Edward Fullbrook. *Simone de Beauvoir and Jean-Paul Sartre: The Remaking of a Twentieth Century Legend.* New York: Harvester Wheatsheaf, 1993.

Gössmann, Elisabeth, ed. *Eva—Gottes Meisterwerk.* [Archiv für philosophie- und theologiegeschichtliche Frauenforschung; 2]. Munich: Iudicium, 1985.

———. *Das Wohlgelahrte Frauenzimmer.* [Archiv für philosophie- und theologiegeschichtliche Frauenforschung; 1]. Munich: Iudicium, 1984.

Greeve Davaney, Sheila. "The Limits of the Appeal to Women's Experience." In *Shaping New Vision: Gender and Values in American Culture,* edited by Clarissa W. Atkinson et al., 30-48. Ann Arbor: UMI Press, 1987.

———. "Problems with Feminist Theory: Historicity and the Search for Sure Foundations." In *Embodied Love: Sensuality and Relationship as Feminist Values,* edited by Paula M. Cooey, 79-96. San Francisco, 1988.

Griffiths, Morwenna. "Feminism, Feelings, and Philosophy." In *Feminist Perspectives in Philosophy,* edited by Morwenna Griffiths and Margareth Whitford, 131-51. Bloomington: Indiana University Press, 1988.

Griffiths, Morwenna, and Margareth Whitford, eds. *Feminist Perspectives in Philosophy.* Bloomington: Indiana University Press, 1988.

Grimshaw, Jean. "Autonomy and Identity in Feminist Thinking." In *Feminist Perspectives in Philosophy*, edited by Morwenna Griffiths and Margareth Whitford, 90-108. Bloomington: Indiana University Press, 1988.

———. "'Pure Lust': The Elemental Feminist Philosophy of Mary Daly." *Radical Philosophy*, no. 49 (1988): 24-30.

Griscom, Joan L. "On Healing the Nature/History Split in Feminist Thought." In *Women's Consciousness, Women's Conscience: A Reader in Feminist Ethics*, edited by Barbara Hilkert Andolsen et al., 85-98. San Francisco: Harper and Row, 1985.

Großmaß, Ruth. "Von der Verführungskraft der Bilder: Mary Daly's Elemental-Feministische Philosophie." In *Feministischer Kompaß, patriarchales Gepäck: Kritik konservativer Anteile in neueren feministischen Theorien*, edited by Ruth Großmaß and Christiane Schmerl, 56-116. Frankfurt and New York: Campus Verlag, 1989.

Großmaß, Ruth, and Christiane Schmerl, eds. *Feministischer Kompaß, patriarchales Gepäck: Kritik konservativer Anteile in neueren feministischen Theorien.* Frankfurt and New York: Campus Verlag, 1989.

Harding, Sandra. *The Science Question in Feminism.* Milton Keynes: Open University Press, 1986.

Hilkert Andolsen, Barbara, et al., eds. *Women's Consciousness, Women's Conscience: A Reader in Feminist Ethics.* San Francisco: Harper and Row, 1985.

Hirsch, Marianne, and Evelyn Fox Keller, eds. *Conflicts in Feminism.* New York: Routledge, 1990.

Hodge, Johanna. "Subject, Body, and the Exclusion of Women from Philosophy." In *Feminist Perspectives in Philosophy*, edited by Morwenna Griffiths and Margareth Whitford, 152-68. Bloomington: Indiana University Press, 1988.

Hollywood, Amy. "Violence and Subjectivity: *Wuthering Heights,* Julia Kristeva, and Feminist Theology." In *Transfigurations: Theology and the French Feminists*, edited by C. W. Maggie Kim et al., 81-108. Minneapolis: Fortress Press, 1993.

Irigaray, Luce. *Ce Sexe qui n'en est pas un.* Paris: Minuit, 1977.

———. *Speculum: De l'autre femme.* Paris: Minuit, 1974.

Jaggar, Alison M., and Susan R. Bordo, eds. *Gender/Body/Knowledge: Feminist Reconstructions of Being and Knowing.* New Brunswick: Rutgers University Press, 1989.

Jardine, Alice A. *Gynesis: Configurations of Woman and Modernity.* Ithaca: Cornell University Press, 1985.

Kaufmann McGall, Dorothy. "Simone de Beauvoir. *The Second Sex,* and Jean Paul Sartre." *Signs: Journal of Women in Culture and Society* 5, no. 2 (1979): 209-23.

Keller, Catherine. *From a Broken Web: Separation, Sexism, and Self.* Boston: Beacon Press, 1986.

Kent Rush, Anne. *Moon, Moon.* New York: Random House, 1976.

Keohane, Nannerl O., et al., eds. *Feminist Theory: A Critique of Ideology.* Chicago: University of Chicago Press, 1982.

Kim, C. W. Maggie, et al., eds. *Transfigurations: Theology and the French Feminists.* Minneapolis: Fortress Press, 1993.

King, Ynestra. "Healing the Wounds." In *Gender/Body/Knowledge: Feminist Reconstructions of Being and Knowing,* edited by Alison M. Jaggar and Susan R. Bordo, 115-41. New Brunswick: Rutgers University Press, 1989.

Korte, Anne-Marie. "Een gemeenschap waarin te geloven valt: Over de spirituele en de politieke betekenis van het geloof van vrouwen aan de hand van de 'ommekeer' van Anna Maria van Schurman en Mary Daly." Master's thesis, Catholic University of Nijmegen, The Netherlands, 1985.

———. *Een passie voor transcendentie: Feminisme, theologie en moderniteit in het denken van Mary Daly (A Passion for Transcendence: Feminism, Theology, and Modernity in the Thinking of Mary Daly.)* Kampen: Kok, 1992.

Labalme, Patricia H., ed. *Beyond Their Sex: Learned Women of the European Past.* New York: New York University Press, 1984.

Lauretis, Teresa de. "Upping the Anti [*sic*] in Feminist Theory." In *Conflicts in Feminism,* edited by Marianne Hirsch and Evelyn Fox Keller, 255-70. New York: Routledge, 1990.

Lorde, Audre. "An Open Letter to Mary Daly." In *Sister Outsider: Essays and Speeches,* 66-71. Trumansburg N.Y.: Crossing Press, 1984.

McClintock Fulkerson, Mary. *Changing the Subject: Women's Discourses and Feminist Theology.* Minneapolis: Fortress Press, 1994.

McFague, Sallie. *Metaphorical Theology: Models of God in Religious Language.* London: SCM Press, 1982.

Maritain, Raissa. *Les grandes amitiés: Les aventures de la grâce.* 2 vols. New York: Editions de la Maison Française, vol. 1, 1942; vol. 2, 1944.

Maritain, Raissa. [in co-operation with Jacques Maritain]. *Situation de la poésie.* Paris: Desclée de Brouwer, 1948.

Melano Couch, Beatriz. "Sor Juana Inés de la Cruz: The First Woman Theologian in the Americas." In *The Church and Women in the Third World,* edited by John C. B. Webster and Ellen Low Webster, 51-57. Philadelphia: Westminster Press, 1985.

Merchant, Carolyn. "Ecofeminism and Feminist Theory." In *Reweaving the World: The Emergence of Ecofeminism*, edited by Irene Diamond and Gloria Feman Orenstein, 100-105. San Francisco: Sierra Club Books, 1990.

Metz, Johan Baptist. *Christliche Anthropozentrik: Ueber die Denkform des Thomas von Aquin*. Munich: Koesel, 1962.

Moi, Toril. *Feminist Theory and Simone de Beauvoir*. Oxford: Blackwell, 1990.

Moltmann-Wendel, Elisabeth, ed. *Frau und Religion: Gotteserfahrungen im Patriarchat*. Frankfurt am Main: Fischer Taschenbuch Verlag, 1983.

Nakashima Brock, Rita. *Journeys by Heart: A Christology of Erotic Power*. New York: Crossroad, 1989.

Pilardi, Jo-Ann. "Female Eroticism in the works of Simone de Beauvoir." In *The Thinking Muse: Feminism and Modern French Philosophy*, edited by Jeffner Allen and Iris Marion Young, 18-34. Bloomington: Indiana University Press, 1989.

Ruether, Rosemary Radford. *Sexism and God-Talk: Toward a Feminist Theology*. Boston: Beacon Press, 1983.

Ruether, Rosemary Radford, and Rosemary Skinner Keller, eds. *Women and Religion in America*. Vol. 1, *The Nineteenth Century*. San Francisco: Harper and Row, 1981.

———. *Women and Religion in America*. Vol. 2, *The Colonial and Revolutionary Periods*. San Francisco: Harper and Row, 1983.

Sartre, Jean-Paul. *L'être et le néant: Essai d'ontologie phénoménologique*. Paris: Gallimard, 1943.

———. *L'existentialisme est un humanisme*. Paris: Nagel, 1946.

Schillebeeckx, Edward. "Het niet-begrippelijke kenmoment in de geloofsdaad: Probleem-stelling." *Tijdschrift voor Theologie* 3 (1963): 167-94.

———. "Het niet-begrippelijke kenmoment in onze Godskennis volgens Thomas van Aquino." *Tijdschrift voor Philosophie* 14 (1952), 411-53.

———. *Openbaring en theologie*. [Theologische Peilingen; 1]. Baarn: Bilthoven, Nelissen, 1964.

Schüssler Fiorenza, Elisabeth. *In Memory of Her: A Feminist Theological Reconstruction of Christian Origins*. London: SCM Press, 1983.

Schurman, Anna Maria van. *Opuscula Hebraea, Graeca, Latina, Gallica, Prosaica et Metrica*. Leiden: Lugd. Batavor.: Ex Officina Elseviriorum, 1648.

Spelman, Elizabeth V. *Inessential Women: Problems of Exclusion in Feminist Thought*. Boston: Beacon Press, 1988.

Tillich, Paul. *Systematic Theology* Vol. 1. London: Nisbet, 1953.

Tong, Rosemary. *Feminist Thought: A Comprehensive Introduction*. London: Routledge, 1989.

Vintges, Karin. *Filosofie als passie: Het denken van Simone de Beauvoir*. Amsterdam: Prometheus, 1992.

Warren Berry, Wanda. "Feminist Theology: The 'Verbing' of Ultimate/Intimate Reality in Mary Daly." In *Ultimate Reality and Meaning* 11 no. 3 (1988): 212-32.

Weaver, Mary Jo. *New Catholic Women: A Contemporary Challenge to Traditional Religious Authority*. San Francisco: Harper and Row, 1985.

Webster, John C. B., and Ellen Low Webster, eds., *The Church and Women in the Third World*. Philadelphia: Westminster Press, 1985.

Weedon, Chris. *Feminist Practice and Poststructuralist Theory*. Oxford: Basil Blackwell, 1987.

Welch, Sharon D. *A Feminist Ethic of Risk*. Minneapolis: Fortress Press, 1990.

———. "Sporting Power: American Feminism, French Feminisms, and an Ethic of Conflict." In *Transfigurations: Theology and the French Feminists*, edited by C. W. Maggie Kim et al., 171-98. Minneapolis: Fortress Press, 1993.

Wildung Harrison, Beverly. *Making the Connections: Essays in Feminist Social Ethics*. Edited by Carol S. Robb. Boston: Beacon Press, 1985.

Williams, Brooke. "The Feminist Revolution in 'Ultramodern' Perspective." *Cross Currents* 31 (1981): 307-18.

Wilson, Katharina M., ed., *Medieval Women Writers*. Manchester: Manchester University Press, 1984.

Woolf, Virginia, *Moments of Being: Unpublished Autobiographical Writings*. Edited, introduced, and annotated by Jeanne Schulkind. New York: University Press Sussex, 1976.

Young, Iris Marion. *Throwing Like a Girl and Other Essays in Feminist Philosophy and Social Theory*. Bloomington: Indiana University Press, 1990.

Frances Gray (essay date 2000)

SOURCE: Gray, Frances. "Elemental Philosophy: Language and Ontology in Mary Daly's Texts." In *Feminist Interpretations of Mary Daly*, edited by Sarah Lucia Hoagland and Marilyn Frye, pp. 222-45. University Park: Pennsylvania State University Press, 2000.

[*In the following essay, Gray examines Daly's subversion of male-defined language and philosophy through the calculated use of metaphor, naming, and linguistic inventions, particularly as such strategies reveal Daly's view of language as fundamentally linked to the process of becoming.*]

> You are the icon of woman sexual
> in herself like a great forest tree
> in flower, liriodendron bearing sweet tulips,
> cups of joy and drunkenness.
> You drink strength from your dark fierce roots
> and you hang at the sun's own fiery breast
> and with the green cities of your boughs
> you shelter and celebrate
> woman, with the cauldron of your energies
> burning red, burning green.
>
> —Marge Piercy, "The Window of the Woman Burning"

In ***The Church and the Second Sex,*** originally published in 1968, Mary Daly took seriously the place of language in the social production of women and their experiences. She did this within a theological context. Her denunciation of the Eternal Feminine, an essentializing conception of women that held that women had a fixed, unchanging nature, was accompanied by a strong stand for a social constructionist perspective that was an attempt to refocus and rethink the idea of Woman. Her work was and remains blatantly political and strategic, a deliberate search to reconceive the ideas of Woman and divinity within her own divisive and destabilizing discursive framework.

Central to her concerns is her desire to create discourse(s) specific to women which represent their interests. Daly's explicit assumption is that language is not sex/gender neutral: rather, language is sex/gender specific. She maintains that all languages carry implicit symbolics and semantics. In Western societies, the symbolics and semantics of the dominant language are that of white, middle-class men who have created a master discourse. For such men, language serves the function of maintaining hegemonic masculinity with its associated power and sanctioned pseudoneutrality. On the whole, women accept this alleged neutrality. Daly claims, however, that women find themselves victims within this purportedly neutral system that seeks to define and name them. It is in this context that one should understand Daly's claim that women have had the power of naming stolen from them. And it is in this context that Daly elaborates the idea that language use is subversive: Daly's use seeks to overthrow the purported neutrality of patriarchal discourses and to claim a ground on which women can create their own sex-specific discourses.

Daly's subversive use of language is also strategic. By this I mean that she acknowledges that language always operates within sociopolitical contexts and that language is therefore implicitly perspectival. But she challenges men's discursive hegemony by making language work for her in an attempt to produce and initiate women's discourses. So, at one level, she uses the rules and plays of the master language with its apparently irresistible claim to neutrality as her own theological springboard. At another, she deliberately subverts that master language by undermining its foundations. She takes a pre-existing condition of language—that it is not neutral, but sexed/gendered and monopolizes those who are constituted within its sphere—and then she manipulates that condition in order to subvert its supposed neutrality. Daly's intention is to be divisive and to destabilize language to show that women and their experiences are produced through men's discursive practices, in which women cannot name for themselves. But she also intends to re-conceive language to enable women to name for themselves once more.

Note that Meaghan Morris, in writing about ***Gyn/Ecology,*** has argued that Daly uses language strategically.[1] When she uses the term "strategy"[2] Morris refers to the way in which Daly deploys "punning, alliteration, word-play, allegory, and the Great Metaphor of the Voyage"[3] to achieve her revolutionary ends. For Morris, however, Daly's strategy is unsuccessful. She maintains that Daly confines her critique to "a politics of subverting isolated signs, not one of transforming discourse" (71) or "language in use" (73).

What Morris means by 'discourse' is spelled out in her lengthy "digression on discourse" which she argues that Daly is concerned with semantics and not with contextual matters, "with the semantics of the said, rather than the enunciative strategies of saying." Her main claim is that Daly situates meanings *in words* instead of *in contexts* (74). Because Daly does this, then according to Morris, Daly fails to acknowledge that "a context—in particular, at least an image of an audience—plays a part in what is said and how it's said. Mary Daly's approach can imply quite the opposite: because you have 'true meanings' to articulate, you are likely to say the same thing in the same way in the same language in any circumstances to anyone to whom you accept to speak politically. It is then up to the audience to situate itself/themselves accordingly" (75).

On this view, Daly's preoccupation with nouns and their meanings renders hers a project that cannot be transformative, because *énonciation* should be the primary site of transformative discourse. To support her reading, Morris cites Pym's view of discourse as "'*constraints* on semiosis,' semiosis being defined as the production of meaning by signs *in continuous action* [*sic*]" (77; Morris' italics) and Benveniste's idea of discourse as the "'product of a speaking position'" (90).[4] Morris's stress then is on *énonciation,* the activity of language, what "everybody does every time that they open their mouths (to good or evil effect)."[5] In her view, Daly is not concerned with discursive action at all.

I am not persuaded by Morris's argument. It is not clear to me that Daly is unconcerned about either "speaking position" or the "production of meaning by signs in continuous action." Daly's desire to destabilize discourse is situated in her belief that patriarchy constitutes itself through the semantic position that Morris describes so well (and ascribes to Daly). Daly's focus on nouns, on radicalizing their meanings, depends for its success on *énonciation*: without a speaking position, without acknowledging that meaning is produced precisely as Morris suggests, there is little point to Daly's critique of the meaning/reference of nouns and discourse in general.[6]

Further, and this follows from what I have just claimed, Morris's contention about Daly's subverting isolated signs is strange given the post-modern culture in which she situates herself. Both Ferdinand de Saussure and Derrida argue that no sign can be isolated: that a sign is always a sign *within* a system and that to change one sign is to change the system as a whole.[7] I will argue, contrary to Morris, that Daly, cognizant of structural analysis, is successfully strategic and that her ontological concerns could not be articulated in any other way. Hence I will argue that Daly's is not a strategy of subverting isolated signs at all, but an attempt to displace supposedly neutral (but men's) discourse in order to produce a women's discourse, the function of which is to articulate women's Be-ing.[8] Punning, alliteration, wordplay, and allegory are all integral to the transformation of discourse and are not acts of terrorism against isolated linguistic signs: there can be no isolated aspects of, no isolated signs in, language. Daly's speaking position emerges from the oppression of women. Her choice of which aspects of language/discourse to subvert reveals a deep-seated commitment to producing new meanings by rethinking discourse as continuous activity.

Daly's early works, **The Church and the Second Sex** and **Beyond God the Father,** neither used nor appropriated language in a divisive and destabilizing manner. Daly's work with language begins in **Gyn/Ecology** and develops in earnest in the subsequent births of **Pure Lust, Wickedary,** and **Outercourse.** Daly's primary task in **The Church and the Second Sex** was to argue for the equality of women and men as church members, to expose the masculine bias of Christian theology, and to demonstrate the explicit iniquitous practical and psychological consequences that this theology had (and continues to have)[9] for women in the church. She saw the Catholic church as an oppressive, man-dominated institution which failed to reconcile its opposing views of women (as virgin and whore), but that used that opposition to revere, regulate, and revile the lives of its women adherents. In Daly's view, the movement to equality between women and men was anathema (70) to the church hierarchy, who resisted and opposed any change to the status of women within the church. "Those engaged in the struggle for the equality of the sexes have often seen the Catholic Church as an enemy. This view is to a large extent justified, for Catholic teaching has prolonged a traditional view of woman which at the same time idealizes and humiliates her" (107).

Informed as her work was by *The Second Sex* (107), her writing took on much of Simone de Beauvoir's critique of the socio-ontological arrangements that constitute, encompass, and entrap women. Indeed, Daly's book can be seen as a Catholic response to Simone de Beauvoir's critique of the Catholic church's oppression of women. Daly was keen to reveal the history and social circumstances of women in the church. With this disclosure would come an admission that women have been tied to immanence, tied to materiality and symbolized as the embodiment of temptation, lust, and sin. Daly was committed to arguing for some favorable outcomes once the problems were identified and acknowledged. With identification and acknowledgment, women could begin to overcome the historical and social contingencies that had cast them as secondary beings.

> The fundamental difference between Simone de Beauvoir's vision of the Church and women and that which motivated this book is the difference between despair and hope. For this reason our approach is fundamentally far more radical than that of the French existentialist. De Beauvoir was willing to accept the conservative vision of the Church as reality, and therefore has had to reject it as unworthy of mature humanity. However, there is an alternative to rejection, an alternative which need not involve self-mutilation. This is commitment to radical transformation of the negative, life-destroying elements of the Church as it exists today. The possibility of such commitment rests upon clear understanding that the seeds of the eschatological community, of the liberating humanizing Church of the future, are already present, however submerged and neutralized they may be. Such commitment requires hope and courage.
>
> (70)

Daly could, therefore, be seen as an apologist for the Truth that she believed the Catholic church manifested and revealed and this is a position quite contrary to Simone de Beauvoir's (172). However, there is a significant and fundamental point on which Simone de Beauvoir and Daly agree. Like Simone de Beauvoir (171), Daly attacked the essentializing notion of the Eternal Feminine, the Eternal Woman, the idea that there is a "fixed human nature" (155) peculiar to women. Daly's critics have wrongly argued that she does not persist with her exposure, that she ultimately retrieves an idea of feminine essence which revalorizes universalizing concepts of women. On this view, Daly retreats from her agreement with Simone de Beauvoir, and instead, revalorizes and reinscribes the Eternal Feminine in **Gyn/Ecology** and **Pure Lust.** Elisabeth Schüssler Fiorenza, for example, argues that Daly "brilliantly . . . uses an ontological-linguistic strategy to articulate such alterity. It is a process of Be-coming instantiated by the

Wild, Original, Self-actualizing woman who has made the leap from phallocracy into freedom, into the Otherworld of Be-ing" (155).

Schüssler Fiorenza argues that Daly reconstructs the category of Woman as a superior, natural category over and against Man. She describes Daly's position as just one of the many that come "dangerously close to reproducing in the form of deconstructive language traditional cultural-religious ascription[s] of femininity and motherhood, ascriptions all too familiar from papal pronouncements, which have now become feminist norms."[10] Schüssler Fiorenza's claim is strange, to say the least, when one considers Daly's complete refusal of fixed categorization and her vehement rejection of essentialism and the Eternal Feminine.

Note that Daly continually emphasizes the idea that Woman is in process, that women do not have a fixed, immutable nature. The (potential) creation of new Woman is the acknowledgment of that process. As social circumstances and conditions will change and change again, so too will women in their searches for Be-ing. The Otherworld Journey in which women should be engaged points to potentiality rather than actuality. So Daly is not appealing to the actuality of an Eternal, essential Woman at all. She is signposting the idea that women are in process, redefining their potentialities, re-claiming their own naming and thus their be-ing.

It should be stressed that in **The Church and the Second Sex** Daly extensively analyses and subsequently dismisses the concept of women's essence. Her reading identifies the Eternal Woman as the essential Woman: she is that which makes a woman truly Woman. It is this idea of essential womanhood that Daly passionately rejects. Daly remarks:

> The characteristics of the Eternal Woman are opposed to those of a developing, authentic *person,* who will be unique, self-critical, self creating, active and searching. . . . By contrast to these authentic personal qualities, the Eternal Woman is said to have a vocation to surrender and hiddenness; . . . Self-less, she achieves not individual realisation but merely generic fulfillment in motherhood, physical or spiritual. . . . She is said to be timeless and conservative by nature. She is shrouded in mystery because she is not a genuine human person.[11]

She argues that the Eternal Feminine and the Eternal Woman are symbols that operate at a normative level in society.[12] Hence the concepts of the Eternal Woman and the Eternal Feminine, although symbolic, are not merely descriptive. They *prescribe* how a woman ought to behave in order to count as a Woman. Women, on this account, are genuinely women by virtue of their "passive, dependent, totally relational"[13] qualities, which are embodied by the idea of the Eternal Woman. But, Daly maintains, these symbolic qualities are "radically opposed to female emancipation"[14] for they evince a perception of women that both describes and prescribes their individual natures as inferior human beings. Paradoxically, anything falling outside this model fails to count as a woman. The Eternal Feminine is, in other words, the essence of individual women: "The formula is very simple: once the *a priori* norms of femininity have been set up, all the exceptions are classified as 'defeminised.'"[15] Note the relationship, reminiscent of Plato, between the idea of universal Woman and individual women: one is an individual woman in virtue of participating in the ideal form of Woman.

So Daly argues that in a strong sense individual women were expected to derive the idea that they were women from the symbolic Eternal Feminine and the idea of "pure" or "brute" biological nature. The Eternal Feminine is an a priori given; women's sex remains a biological brute fact. Daly saw the Eternal Feminine as an evil which should be exorcised from the church as well as from the lives of women. While the grip of the Eternal Feminine persisted, little could be achieved for women. However, in highlighting the flawed nature of essential Womanhood, Daly resolved to launch on a project designed "to minimize biological differences"[16] in order to change how, and the conditions under which, women should be symbolized.[17] In this context, one must acknowledge that Daly's project was devoted to elaborating an idea of androgyny.

It is important to acknowledge that Daly was then concerned for women to remain within the church and that she believed that it would be possible to transform the church into the kind of institution in which women would have equality. For her the idea of androgyny suitably expressed the neutrality of the subject. Both women and men, if they were to throw off the shackles of essentializing theory, should see androgyny as an ideal. The last two chapters of **The Church and the Second Sex** are concerned with "some modest proposals" about how this might come about. Daly's optimism witnesses her belief in the liberal feminist commitment to full participation in the pre-established (sex-neutral) forms of hierarchical institutions. For her, acceptance of women as equal partners in an androgynous church would lead to the transformation of the institution itself, wherein "(m)en and women, using their best talents, forgetful of self and intent upon the work, will with God's help mount together toward a higher order of consciousness and being, in which the alienating projections will have been defeated and wholeness, psychic integrity, achieved."[18]

That meant that women and men must abandon the dominant image of women as the embodiment of the Eternal Feminine. In turn, that meant the traditional roles ascribed to women (in which the Eternal Feminine is honored) would need to be re-evaluated so that women could be given the freedom to move into new space(s). Daly contended that men also must go through a process of transformation and come to terms with the ways in which society had imposed values on, and expectations of, them. "The eternal masculine" traps and limits men as much as the Eternal Feminine has women.

> What is more the "eternal masculine" itself is alienating, crippling the personalities of men and restricting their experience of life at every level. The male in our society is not supposed to express much feeling, sensitivity, aesthetic appreciation, imagination, consideration for others, intuition. He is expected to affirm only part of his real self. Indeed, it may be that a good deal of the compulsive competitiveness of males is rooted in this half existence. . . . It is the nature of the disease, therefore, to inhibit the expansion of the individual's potential, through conditioned conformity to roles, and through a total identification of the individual with them.[19]

Thus although at the time of writing *The Church and the Second Sex* Daly had as her primary concern the liberation of women from archaic theory and the social practice built upon that theory, her concern was also for the liberation of all humans, women and men alike. She believed that women and men must fracture the stereotypes by which they are characterized and that the 'real'[20] self somehow exists apart from sexual identity. She took up this theme in *Beyond God the Father*, where she explored notions centered around androgynous being and in which she generated a trinity: language, transcendence, and androgyny. The relationship among these three is implicit: together they produce the ontological foundations for human becoming to ultimate, authentic Be-ing. Note that later, in *Gyn/Ecology*, Daly remarked that along with the terms 'God' and 'homosexuality', 'androgyny' is a term she will never use again. Daly situated these terms within the masculine paternal canon. They represent men's interests, not women's.

What I do want to emphasize here is that regardless of what patriarchal intellectual commitments Daly attacks and attempts to refute, her underlying commitment to women's liberation remains couched in terms of language and ontology. Daly uses the patriarchal centeredness of dominant language and ontology ingeniously, as we shall see.[21] Overwhelmingly, she appropriates and exploits patriarchal language and ontology to make political statements, to address what she considers to be socially and morally corrupt practices, and to redefine the enterprises of theology and philosophy. She reconstitutes language and ontology as her own Elemental Feminist Philosophy in *Gyn/Ecology* and *Pure Lust,* the works in which she develops her cosmic odyssey, her gynocratic vision.

In *Beyond God the Father* for example, Daly is very taken by the idea of process theology because it does not present us with a static world view. She obviously admires the work of Charles Hartshorne, who, she says, believes that "process is creative synthesis."[22] But she is dubious about the social worth of theory such as his and is also suspicious about that which is ready-made (man-made) and can apparently be readily appropriated by feminists. Her enterprise is to make new philosophy and create new language out of the experience(s) of women. "The essential thing is to hear our *own* words, always giving prior attention to our *own* experience, never letting theory have *authority* over us. Then we can be free to listen to the old philosophical language (and all philosophy that does not explicitly repudiate sexism is old, no matter how novel it may seem)."[23] Her endeavors, to create out of the old, to renegotiate the relation between ontology and language, should be seen in this light.

From the time of *Gyn/Ecology,* language is, categorically, the ontological groundwork of Daly's sex-specific women's discourse; in other words, language *becomes* ontology for Daly: language is the material out of which ontology is constructed, it is the being or *esse* of ontology. *Contra* Morris's argument, Daly's strategy involves more than isolating some signs. She seeks to highlight the idea that language and ontology are so related that language is a condition, not just for the articulation of ontology, but for the very possibility of ontology. For her then, the key to directly affecting change in women's lives is through radically re-viewing discourse. Daly's work with nouns begins this change. She is unequivocally committed to transforming discourse in an endeavor to create a space for women, in terms of language and ontology. Hence hers is subversive linguistic activity. By this, I mean that her strategy is to destabilize, refigure, and transform not only discourse, but the way in which one conceives of ontology and one's life, one's be-ing. But of necessity for Daly, the master discursive framework of patriarchal philosophy is the origin of her project.[24]

So what is the language/ontology relation which Daly affirms? There are three crucial, interconnected elements of Daly's work that elaborate her notion of the ontology/language relation. The first is the idea that women's meanings, the symbolization of their experiences and of women's discourses, must be produced out of existing discourses. The second is that naming is foundational to the creation of meanings; and the third is Daly's use of metaphor.

Daly argues that all language establishes and comes out of an ontologically committed context which is not neutral (as I argued earlier).[25] Put simply, language constructs ontology: language establishes the conditions of being. However, there is a reciprocal relationship involved here. Not only does language construct ontology, but the limits of language are set by our ontological understandings and commitments. Language is a condition for the construction of ontology, which in turn is a condition for language. For Daly, the production of be-ing, which participates in Be-ing, is grounded in displacing patriarchal meanings, in appropriating language, in acknowledging becoming, in shape shifting.[26] It presupposes an extant discourse. In a similar vein, Mark C. Taylor argues: "While philosophy's other always slips through the structures imposed by conceptual reflection, the unthought can only be evoked through the language of philosophy itself. The post-philosophical thinkers must strategically use language *against* language. 'In order to make the attempt of thinking recognizable and at the same time understandable for existing philosophy, it could at first be expressed only within the horizon of that existing philosophy and its use of current terms.'"[27]

Daly commits herself to using language against language: to looking at its etymological sources, using them, abusing them, drawing out their implications for women and doing that within the horizon, which necessarily must change, of existing philosophical and theological discourses. She is, therefore, engaged in a double project: exploring and using the present/past terrain of philosophy, while at the same time shifting the boundaries it imposes on itself and in particular upon women. The subverting of discourse is a strategy Daly deliberately embraces when she disfigures extant discourse in order to highlight the possibility of women's ontology/language. Hers is a political task that depends upon undermining (purportedly neutral) language. Daly understands language as a whole, as a dialogical, transformative means of achieving a radically altered society for women.[28] Given this kind of interpretation of Daly's work, Morris' allegation that Daly merely subverts isolated signs, rather than re-shaping discourse as a whole, should be seen as the dubious rendering that it is.

In the **Wickedary** Daly talks of elemental ontology, "the philosophical quest for Be-ing; rooted in the intuition that Powers of Be-ing are constantly Unfolding, creating, communicating; philosophy grounded in the experience of active potency to move beyond the foreground of fixed questions and answers and enter the Radiant Realms of Metabeing."[29] Such an understanding reinforces her belief that there is an intimate fundamental relation between language and ontology. Her term 'Meta-being', "(r)ealms of active participation in Powers of Be-ing, State of Ecstasy," is intended to convey the necessary conjunction of discourse and be-ing. For her Be-ing, "Ultimate/Intimate Reality, the constantly Unfolding Verb of Verbs which is intransitive, having no object that limits its dynamism; the Final Cause, the Good who is Self-communicating who is the Verb from whom, in whom, and with whom all true movements move,"[30] is an energizing process. 'It' is not fixed and determined as essence would be: the play of Be-ing scampers with delight in its boundlessness and constant shape changing.

This gives voice to the Heracleitan resonances we find in Daly's work. She stresses that language is primarily "performative/active/animate" activity, potentially alive with meaning. Her emphasis on process underscores her approach to language as an oceanic whole: vast, interrelated, and ever changing. On this basis, Daly proposes a re-orientation of language that will highlight the fluidity of verbs. And this brings us to the second element in her elaboration of the ontology/language relation.

In discussing the activity of naming which she understands as the locus of power, Daly argued:

> In order to understand the implications of this process it is necessary to grasp the fundamental fact that women have had the power of *naming* stolen from us. Women have not been free to use their own power to name themselves, the world, or God. The old naming was not the product of dialogue—a fact inadvertently admitted in the Genesis story of Adam's naming the animals and the woman. Women are now realising that the universal imposing of names by men has been false because partial. . . . To exist humanly is to name the self, the world and God.[31]

She identifies naming as a functional process which can oppress (as it has women) or liberate. In short, Daly believes that because men have named, they have controlled. Hence men have power. Language is therefore necessarily political: it provides the foundations for control and power. Language, then, has been, and continues to be, oppressive to women. In this sense, naming functions as a metonym for all of language.[32] Naming, in other words, is but one part of language. Yet the fact that naming plays such a decisive role in the productions of meanings and the construction of our worlds affirms the idea that the whole of language is engaged in some way with the process of naming. Naming—language as an activity that implies, and is implied by, discourse—is a prime mover in both the construction and understanding of Being. But, to reiterate, the concept of naming is not meant to be understood in a literal, narrow sense. Naming embraces the whole of discursive practice. In **Beyond God the Father,** Daly had denounced the monopolistic practice of naming in which men have engaged. She argued that what she calls "old naming" as a function of language has assumed an oppressive role within, and is constitutive of, patriarchal structures including discursive practice(s). So, Daly believed, "new naming" can creatively constitute a world in which all sexual oppression will disappear.

The power of naming, highlighted in **Beyond God the Father,** is a crucial feature of Daly's work in **Gyn/**

Ecology and by the time of *Pure Lust* had developed into a highly sophisticated network of critical exploration of language, play on words, neologism, and re-definition. But Daly re-orients what we might think of as 'usual' in the practice of naming. Predominantly, we associate naming with nouns: with sorting, categorizing. Daly is scathing about this practice and emphasizes the importance of verbs over nouns. This is where naming as a metonym becomes a clear strategic device for Daly. The shift from noun-naming to verb-naming swings naming to a new position within language. It is not just that one must find suitable nouns to use in naming: it is that with an emphasis on verbs and their open-endedness—the Heracleitian resonances to which I alluded above—the idea of new-naming becomes an idea of what all language is about: referring, expressing, disclosing, creating, and so on. In this sense, language is action, performance, process, being. Language is the embodiment of creation, the condition for the possibility of anything.

The stress on the role of verbs is no better highlighted than in Daly's discussion of the idea of God. In *Beyond God the Father* Daly argues: "Why indeed must 'God' be a noun? Why not a verb—the most active and dynamic of all? Hasn't the naming of 'God' as a noun been an act of murdering that dynamic Verb? And isn't the Verb infinitely more personal than a mere static noun? The anthropomorphic symbols for God may be intended to convey personality, but they fail to convey that God is Be-ing. . . . This Verb—the Verb of Verbs—is intransitive. It need not be conceived as having an object that limits its dynamism."[33]

Daly's concern with the term 'God' as a noun is not simply grammatical. 'God' either as a proper name or as a mere noun poses a problem for Daly because of her onto-theological concerns and mistrusts. That is to say, Daly ultimately refuses the androcentric term 'God', preferring instead 'Goddess'. This term however, is not intended to convey the idea of a female superperson with whom women might have a personal relationship. Instead, Daly's use is metaphorical. The term 'Goddess' represents potential, possibility: it evokes an idea of what women might become.

According to Daly, that God is construed as a fixed definable thing, that God is reified, is a Deadly Deception. Be-ing, with which she identifies the Goddess, is not a thing at all. In reifying, in making things into objects when that should not be the case, the Divine is essentialized, cast into rocklike solidity that does not change; but Be-ing should not and cannot be contained as nouns contain. (This is what patriarchy practices. Witness Daly's claim that 'God' "represents the necrophilia of patriarchy.")[34] Daly argues that reification is a masculine engagement with which she refuses to identify. According to her, the term 'God' and what it represents is irredeemably masculine. Daly also acknowledges the possibility of falling into the trap of reifying the Goddess, treating the Goddess as an object named by a noun as 'God' has been. But for her, 'Goddess', properly used, "affirms the life-loving be-ing of women and nature"[35] and is the embodiment of the Verb of verbs.

In refiguring the Divine in terms of concentrating on the "verbness of Be-ing," Daly is following a long theological tradition that situates discourse in ontology and ontology in discourse. The Old Testament story of the revelation of the Divine Name is enshrouded in cosmic mystery and linguistic difficulties:

> Moses then said to God, "Look, if I go to the Israelites and say to them, 'The God of your ancestors has sent me to you,' and they say to me, 'What is his name?' what am I to tell them?" God said to Moses, "I am he who is." And he said, "This is what you are to say to the Israelites, 'I am has sent me to you.'" God further said to Moses, "You are to tell the Israelites, 'Yahweh, the God of your ancestors, the God of Abraham, the God of Isaac and the God of Jacob, has sent me to you.' This is my name for all time, and thus I am to be invoked for all generations to come."[36]

Commentators on this biblical passage point out that there are etymological and interpretative worries concerning the text, both of which have bearing on Daly's concerns. Etymologically, they argue, *Yahweh* is archaically related to the Hebrew verb 'to be'. But they also acknowledge that it may be the causative 'he causes to be' or 'he brings into existence'.[37] In any case, the emphasis is on the activity (being, causing, or both) signified by the word. The interpretational question is, in part, one of how the word functions, for it apparently has a naming role.[38] What is pertinent for us is that the naming takes place through the use of the present indicative (a verb function), not through the isolation of properties, characteristics, or features (a noun function in terms of modification and qualification). In other words, God's pronouncement, "I am he who is," if we do take it to be a case of naming, is a verb-naming rather than a noun-naming. Needless to say, its origins and the rules of Hebrew grammar indicate that it is tied up with the verb 'to be' and hence is revelatory of God's Being (as Being).[39] Verb-naming according to Daly seeks not to reify, but to characterize the divine as active principle, as elemental, which is precisely what is happening in this Hebrew text.

The impetus for producing a peculiarly women's discourse lies precisely in theological quandaries such as that represented by the Yahweh debate. Daly uncovers the prejudice toward anthropomorphism that she maintains patriarchal use/discourse exhibits in its theological language. She realizes that language constitutes our understandings and conceptualizings, particularly because many of our concepts are "trapped" in nouns. By "playing around" with language, her intention is to create not only a conceptual shift, but an ontological shift: a shift that will make possible the discovery of the (metaphorical) Goddess in the experience of women.

Note that Mary Daly is concerned with "playing around." Much of her writing is a joyful playing with concepts, ideas, etymologies, and breaking up of syllables to re-emphasise new and different meanings. Daly's writing is the performance of that play. The divine is found not only in the deep and serious matters of the mind. The divine is found in unfolding the contorted layers of meaning that have fabricated women's lives as well as at times of bliss. Humor and play are restored to philosophy.

The mystery that is the divine is exposed in Yahweh's own playfulness, Yahwistic humor—I tell you who I am: I am. The Hebrew story, which historically speaking is assuredly counter-hegemonic and thus already antithetical to dominant Hebrew-inspired patriarchal conceptions of the divine, exhibits a deep religious bias toward acknowledging the Be-ing and mystery of divinity that falls outside noun-naming processes. So, in identifying noun-naming as a problem for "God," Daly reiterates part of a tradition that she puts superbly to work in her performing of feminist theology. The centrality of verbs, the stress on their processive function, signifies the open-endedness of Be-ing toward which women can move, marking the re-emergence of the Goddess. And this idea of the Goddess as Verb of Verbs should not be read through patriarchal modernist categories.

Daly's notion of the Goddess points "metaphorically to the Powers of Be-ing, the Active Verb in whose potency all biophilic reality participates."[40] Notice Daly's use of the word 'metaphorically' here. The recognition of this term and its cognates brings us to the third element in Daly's elucidation of the language/ontology relation: her use of metaphor. Just as naming functions as a metonym for the whole of language use and practice, so metaphor guides the explosion of language which occurs with the transference of energy from nouns to verbs. The role of metaphor becomes political. It is the means by which transcendence will be made possible. In other words, the Goddess is an expression of the possibility of women's transcendence, of women's gracious movement. Thus use of metaphor, the idea of the Goddess and transcendence are intimately linked.

Daly's chapter "Bewitching: The Lust for Metamorphosis" in **Pure Lust** contains a substantial elucidation of both the role and significance Daly wants to give metaphor. There, she argues that metaphors are not mere symbols nor mere abstractions. Metaphors are, as she notes in the **Wickedary,** "words that carry Journeyers into the Wild dimensions of Other-centred consciousness by jarring images, stirring memories, accentuating contradictions, upsetting unconscious traditional assumptions."[41] In **Pure Lust** she also maintains that the Great Mother is one of the "myriad possibilities for naming transcendence"[42] (and that some women can become fixated on images such as the Great Mother, an example of reification of the Goddess).

> A metapatriarchal metaphor "works" precisely to the extent that it carries a woman further into the Wild dimensions of other-centered consciousness—out of the dead circles into Spiralling/Spinning motion. Bewitching metaphors transmute the shapes of perception. They do this by jarring images, stirring memories, accentuating contradictions, upsetting unconscious traditional assumptions, evoking "inappropriate" laughter, releasing pent-up tears, eliciting gynaesthetic sensings of connections, arousing Dragon-identified Passions, inspiring acts of Volcanic virtue, brewing strange ideas.[43]

Daly's concern is with developing a metaphorical understanding of Woman and divinity that is open-ended. In this sense it is essential that one understands her project as non-literal. Daly situates herself within a tradition of metaphorical discourse of which she is simultaneously subversive.[44] She alleges: "Metaphors function to Name change, and therefore they elicit change. . . . Thus the very task of naming and calling forth Elemental be-ing requires metaphors."[45] For Daly, change necessitates the use of metaphor.[46]

The echo that rebounds in Daly's exegesis of metaphor resonates with the playfulness to which I alluded above. In using metaphor, one plays; that play constitutes performance, challenging and subverting the categories that subtend language. *Énonciation* occurs in the written text! For example, she speaks of women's bodies as "transmutable to and from energy" and of "[t]he spiration of the Archimage within Lusty women, who speak women's words, heals broken connections between words and their Sources, reconnecting women with their elemental origins."[47] As Daly showed in her analysis of essentialism, this is not the patriarchal way of thinking about women or their bodies. If women in patriarchy are lusty, they are whores; if there is spiration within women, it is the Word of God speaking to a (compliant) Virgin Mother to whom an announcement is made (that she will be the Mother of God). The change in metaphor brings about a change in thinking: Virgin Virtues do not revolve around the idea of submission; Virgin Virtues are "life affirming habits of Uncaptured/Unsubdued women";[48] to Gossip is "to exercise the Elemental Female Power of Naming, especially in the presence of other Gossips."[49]

Ironically, Daly's use of (seemingly stereotypical?) "female" metaphors tempts commentators to interpret Daly as essentialist. But Daly's metaphors appeal to the idea of women as constituted through their own language practices, which are not themselves neutral. This cannot be stressed enough, especially since the claim that there can be no sex-neutral subject is discussed widely in feminist literature and Daly's work highlights this assertion.[50] But there is a great deal of confusion about what is actually going on when feminist theorists call for a female subject and most of this confusion collapses into debates surrounding essentialism. In other words, the idea that there should or could be a female subject is almost always read as a reaffirmation of the idea of a female essence, even when a theorist taking such a stand identifies herself as a social constructionist and denounces essentialism. This is the case with Mary Daly and her critics.[51]

Rosi Braidotti, for instance, has maintained that Daly has a "conceptual tendency to naturalize the feminine"[52] and thus to reinstate essentializing notions of women. Braidotti's accusation stems from her analysis of Daly's (metaphorical) Goddess imagery, which she misreads as invoking essentialist images. Furthermore, she agrees with Morris, whom she interprets as accusing Daly of "re-naming at the level of lexicon, of the vocabulary, leaving unchanged the syntax of representation."[53] Let me revisit Morris, who writes: "One focus of Daly's interest in **Gyn/Ecology** is the possibilities offered by changing *particular words* (those items in the dictionary, ie. the available code—or *langue*—of patriarchal English). She de-constructs and de-forms them in their inert state as signs whose only context *is* the dictionary, and then puts them to work in the discourse. . . . Her strategy is to warp the words of the patriarchal dictionary, to bend the code back against itself until it snaps to their shrieks of derision" (her italics).[54]

To reiterate the point I made earlier in this essay, this interpretation charges that Daly deconstructs terms within language, without deconstructing the corpus, language in use, and her own speaking position. On this misreading, Daly valorizes Woman as she has been understood through the texts of Western philosophy, ascribing to Woman an essence that depends upon the implicit acceptance of the categories of Western thought. Morris's and Braidotti's readings of Daly are, however, literal rather than metaphoric. They fail to let Daly "mess with their minds,"[55] to let her metaphors dislodge patriarchal meanings and re-orient their thinking. They read her through a modernist lens.

Daly does not reinscribe Western philosophical ideas of Essential Woman at all. To recapitulate, her language is metaphorical and seeks to explore the previously unexplored: the possibility of women's discourse. It is important to stress that both Morris and Braidotti assume that Daly essentializes the Goddess and women because she boldly dismisses neutrality as a construction of patriarchy. It is possible that Morris and Braidotti do not recognize the link Daly makes between patriarchy and neutrality. However, that Daly holds that patriarchy constructs the idea of neutrality is apparent. Her rejection of androgyny, tied as it is to the idea of a gender-neutral "best possible subject," ("'John Travolta and Farrah Fawcett-Majors scotch-taped together'")[56] states her point sharply and shortly. Daly's underlying argument is always that language is sex specific: there is no gender-neutral sex and, therefore, there can be no gender-neutral language. Since language constructs subjectivities, identities, it follows that there can be no gender-neutral subject. The elimination of the idea of androgyny is couched in these terms.

Daly rejects androgyny; Morris and Braidotti revalorize neutrality. Braidotti's affirmation of neutrality in this text emerges when she argues: "So Daly falls into what I consider one of the worst traps besetting feminism today: the replacement of the masculine subject by the feminine subject. . . . The latent dogmatism in Daly's thought, quite as much as its reactionary nature, seems to me potentially dangerous for current feminism, insofar as it subverts the signs, not the codes."[57]

But Daly replies to her critics who choose the concept of neutrality over that of woman:

> Particularly insidious is the pseudo-feminist usage of the term *essentialist* to label and discredit all feminist writing that dares to Name and celebrate the Wild and Elemental reality of women who choose to think beyond the prescribed parameters of patriarchal mandates. . . . It elicits the patriarchally embedded Self-censor in women attempting to create in women-identified ways. . . . In other words, the expression of Original Powers and of the Ecstatic existential experience of women breaking free from patriarchal mind-bendings is stigmatized by the label "essentialist," leaving only the grimness of oppression as that which women have in common. Ultimately this reversal/usage functions to negate Hope for Life that transcends the illusion of inclusion in forever male-identified "humankind."[58]

The development of Woman's Be-ing, Elemental Woman's Be-ing, is dependent ultimately on the rejection of masculine discourse, men's discourse, commonly thought of as neutral discourse. Daly's intuition about the role of discourse is sound. Her belief is that the Divine, the Goddess, is mirrored through language practices and therefore the Divine is the mirror of women. The claim that discourse must be sex/gender specific, and that Daly is creating the context for meta-patriarchal discourse, is a superb strategy. But it is more than a strategy.

Earlier I remarked that a member of Daly's trinity in **Beyond God the Father** was the idea of transcendence. The relation between metaphor and transcendence is intimate. Indeed for Daly, metaphors are "the language/

vehicles of transcendent spiraling."[59] Metaphors promote transcendence: they embellish the possibilities for women to participate in Be-ing, to persist with the Journey. But what it means to transcend is elusive. And again, the idea of neutrality looms ominously, this time in the context of Simone de Beauvoir.

In her existentialist philosophy Simone de Beauvoir promoted the idea of transcendence, thought of as a peculiarly male interest. Man achieves transcendence in his own subjectivity, "the male recovers his individuality intact at the moment he transcends it."[60] Women do not achieve transcendence: they fail to develop as subjects, for they never transcend their own individuality. Women fail to create value: they make babies instead and remain immanent in the species.[61] This does not mean that women have no values. But it means that they subscribe to values that are produced externally to them and that are believed to be neutral.

Now, by appropriating men's discourse and developing the triadic relation between ontology and language, naming and metaphor, Daly shifts away from transcendence conceived of as a peculiarly men's project. She denies that women cannot achieve transcendence, cannot make their own values and seek their own autonomy. The play of metaphor evokes the Goddess. And it is in the Goddess, the Verb of Verbs, that transcendence moves to liberate. Transcendence thus becomes a function of women's process, of women's movement, and metaphor its expression. Transcendence is not to be reified, as a thing that can be defined. Transcendence is the process in which women are engaged as they name themselves, make and re-make themselves in performing their divinity, their participation in the Goddess. The language of transcendence and the Goddess is the language of metaphor. In Daly's hands, metaphor is the language of the Goddess, the language of divine politics, the language of Be-ing.

When one looks at the claim made against Daly—that she is essentialist because she launches a project that attempts to seek out Woman and that Daly's language betrays her—one wonders how closely her detractors have read her. Daly has not claimed to define, to categorize women. Daly works to find a way for women to become Wild, to be Lusty, to be Strong. Her belief that women can have no ontology, no being without women's language, recommends an analysis of the idea of Woman such as Daly has produced. If one can accept that women are on a Journey and that the Journey is within language, then the possibility of Elemental ontology opens before one. It is dangerous, the Journey, the Journey to ontology, for it is to be on the Outercourse, toward transcendence and Be-ing.

I have been arguing that Mary Daly's work is primarily directed towards the re-creation of women through the dis-membering and re-construction of discourse. I have argued that far from her project's being a mere changing of isolated signs as Morris has argued, Daly is concerned to produce a radically creative and subversive Woman's discourse. Implicit in that project is the development of an ethic that valorizes women without reinscribing real essentialist accounts (such as the Eternal Woman) of Woman. I have also argued, using Schüssler Fiorenza's terminology, that this strategy is ontological-linguistic, meaning that for Daly, a strong relationship exists between ontology and language, indeed that the two are so intertwined that language becomes ontology for Daly in the sense I have outlined above. She calls into question the idea that the dominant discourses of theology and philosophy are sex neutral. Because these discourses are masculine paternal discourses, Daly believes that women should develop their own language in which they can articulate their own be-ing. In other words, Daly seeks to re-vision the idea of women and their experiences, ontology and the divine. In so doing, she creates a politics of divinity that is not sex neutral but is an expression of women's transcendence because it involves the idea that women should reclaim the power of naming for themselves. Her work creates divinity as politics because she seeks to subvert hegemonic conceptions of language, the divine, and transcendence. In her work she seeks to subvert men's ownership of, and the imposition of boundaries on, the divine. Daly's work systematically defies the canons of men's theology and philosophy, within which is the myth of neutrality. While that myth preserves patriarchal—that is, masculine paternal—hegemony, women will not have the words with which they might name for themselves, a women's language. In new naming is new ontology, women's transcendence, and the Goddess. This is be-ing for women, Be-ing in women. This is women's participation in the Verb of Verbs. This is a women's politics of the divine. And this is Mary Daly's legacy to philosophy and theology.

Notes

1. Meaghan Morris, "A-mazing Grace: Notes on Mary Daly's Poetics," *Intervention* 16 (n.d.): 71-73.

2. Grosz and other commentators on Irigaray use the term "strategy" in discussing Irigaray's work. See Elizabeth Grosz, *Sexual Subversions: Three French Feminists* (St. Leonards: Allen & Unwin, 1989).

3. Morris, "A-mazing Grace," 73.

4. Morris here refers, in a footnote, to Pym's work, a 1980 honors thesis at Murdoch University, and notes that the definition was passed on to her by Anna Freadman.

5. Morris, "A-mazing Grace," 76.

6. One also might consider that in the early days of "second wave" feminism, there were howls of protest from women who realized that terms such as 'man'

and 'mankind' for instance, were meant to be inclusive and gender neutral. But in being inclusive, feminists argued, the terms denoted a disregard for the individuality and sexed subjectivity of women. There was, therefore, a push to subvert what might be thought of as "isolated signs" in the writing of public documents. The infamous replacement of "chairman" by "chairwoman" and then its replacement by "chairperson" and the introduction, in English, of the marriage-status-neutral term "Ms." for women, instead of the two choices "Miss" (unmarried woman) or "Mrs." (married woman) are examples of this practice of apparently subverting isolated signs. It is manifest however, that the subversion of isolated signs was, and is, only apparent. Such apparently minor changes have called attention to a problem endemic in many languages and have caused a rethinking of how particular nouns are used and when. I think that this is, in part, what Daly is addressing. I talk further about language neutrality later in this essay.

7. See Ferdinand de Saussure, "Course in General Linguistics" (1916), trans. Wade Baskin, in *A Critical and Cultural Theory Reader*, ed. Anthony Easthope and Kate McGowan, 8-13 (St. Leonards: Allen & Unwin, 1992): "[T]o consider a term as simply the union of a certain sound with a certain concept is grossly misleading. To define it this way would isolate the term from its system . . . Language is a system of interdependent terms in which the value of each term results solely from the simultaneous presence of the others" (8, 9); and Jacques Derrida, "Différence," in Easthope and McGowan, *A Critical and Cultural Theory Reader*, 108-32: "[T]he signified concept is never present in and of itself, in a sufficient presence that refers only to itself. Essentially and lawfully, every concept is inscribed in a chain or in a system within which it refers to the other, to other concepts, by the systematic play of differences" (115). See also Vincent Descombes, *Modern French Philosophy*, trans. L. Scott-Fox and J. M. Harding (Cambridge and New York: Cambridge University Press, 1980), chap. 3, "Semiology." His discussion of structural analysis, initially using Molière's "Le Bourgeois Gentilhomme" is particularly insightful here. See 82-100. Descombes also refers to Saussure's remark "'*In a language there are only differences,*'" going on to note, "That is why knowledge of any one element is conditional upon knowledge of the system," 87.

8. Daly uses the hyphenated forms Be-ing and be-ing to emphasize their "verbness" so that the reader will not be tempted to reify, as she might if she were to read them as nouns.

9. Although topics such as those raised by Daly about women and the church are commonplace discussion today, little in the sacramental life of the Catholic church (the official position of which remains as it has been for hundreds of years) has changed regarding the understanding and role of women. See John Paul II's apostolic letter *Ordinatio Sacerdotalis* (1994) for evidence of this

10. I have used the past tense here, in spite of the fact that this remains true of Catholic hierarchy and many devout men (and some women) Catholics. Arguments against ordination of women to the Catholic priesthood for example are based upon an assumed inferiority of women developed from Pauline texts in particular. The "different but equal" sentiments that condemn women to lesser positions of power in the church are also an example of this.

11. Daly, *The Church and the Second Sex*, 53.

12. Simone de Beauvoir, *The Second Sex*, trans. H. M. Parshley (London: Picador Books, 1949).

13. Daly, *The Church and the Second Sex*, 221.

14. In the "Post Christian Introduction" in *The Church and the Second Sex*, Daly speaks of the position she had taken in the first edition in terms of disownership. That is to say, she speaks of herself in the third person, dissociating from and critiquing the views of the earlier Daly.

15. See Simone de Beauvoir, *The Second Sex*, Part III, in particular her discussion of the Mother and the Virgin Mary, 170ff. It is beyond the scope of this essay, however, to explore in great depth the relationship between Simone de Beauvoir's work and Daly's.

16. Daly, *The Church and the Second Sex*, 70.

17. See in particular Daly's chapters "Demon of Sexual Prejudice: Exercise in Exorcism" and "Roots of the Problem: Radical Surgery Required" in *The Church and the Second Sex*, 166-91.

18. Ibid., 223.

19. Ibid., 193-94.

20. Throughout this essay, where the term 'reality' is obviously contested, I use single quotes. Where it is not necessarily contested, I omit the quotes.

21. The irony here is that according to Meaghan Morris, this very point was made by Layleen Jayamanne at what Morris calls "the Mary Daly event" in Sydney in 1981. But in that scenario, it is a point made against Daly, rather than for her. See Morris, "Amazing Grace," 70.

22. Daly, *Beyond God the Father*, 188.

23. Ibid., 189.

24. Nancy Fraser, discussing Foucault's work, also makes this point. She says: "Now, the fact that Foucault continues to speak (or at least to murmur) the language of humanism need not be held against him. Every good Derridean will allow that there is not, at least for the time being, any other language he could speak. . . . Foucault himself acknowledges that he

cannot simply and straightforwardly discard at will the normative associations with the metaphysics of subjectivity." Nancy Fraser, *Unruly Practices: Power, Discourse, and Gender in Contemporary Social Theory* (Cambridge, U.K.: Polity Press, 1989), 57.

25. See, for example, her discussion of titles and roles within a workplace context: "In women one notices 'accommodation attitudes,' that is, a self-abnegating and flattering manner that is almost 'second nature.' Conditioning to such accommodation attitudes is intensified by such customs as nonreciprocal first naming, common even when the boss (Mr. Jones, Father Jones, Professor Jones or Doctor Jones) is thirty years of age and the secretary, who is sixty, is called 'Sally.' A similar custom is reference by 'the boss' to 'Sally' as 'the girl' in the office. A young male 'executive assistant' doing essentially the same work as Sally, for a much higher salary, is of course not referred to as a '"boy."' See Daly, *Beyond God the Father*, 136.

26. Daly, "Be-witching: The Lust for Metamorphosis," in *Pure Lust*, especially 390ff.

27. Taylor's comment occurs in a discussion of Heidegger in Mark C. Taylor, "Cleaving: Martin Heidegger," in *Alt∇rity* (Chicago: University of Chicago Press, 1987), 42-43. In response to the interjector at the "Daly event" in Sydney in 1981, I would cite a claim such as this. Given that one grows up in a culture, how else can one speak except within its terms? Daly is challenging this and attempting to dissipate (a little) the boundaries. Taylor's quotation from Heidegger is Martin Heidegger, "Letter on Humanism," in *Basic Works*, ed. and trans. D. Krell (New York: Harper and Row, 1977), 235.

28. This point is reinforced in Daly, *Pure Lust*. See "On Lust and the Lusty," passim.

29. Daly, *Wickedary*, 86.

30. Ibid., 64.

31. Daly, *Beyond God the Father*, 8.

32. I thank Marilyn Frye for this insight.

33. Daly, *Beyond God the Father*, 33-34.

34. Daly, *Gyn/Ecology*, xi.

35. Ibid.

36. *Exodus* 3:13-15 New Jerusalem Bible (New York: Doubleday, 1985). The "I am has sent me to you" is the translation from the New Jerusalem Bible. For example, the sentence is also translated as "I am who I am." See RSV, Catholic ed. (Nelson, 1966).

37. New Jerusalem Bible, 85 n. g.

38. In the footnotes, the translators discuss the question of whether or not the intention of God is to give "his" name. They assume (not argue) that "he" does intend so doing and that is the context in which I am writing.

39. *Exodus*, New Jerusalem Bible, n. g.

40. Daly, *Pure Lust*, 26.

41. Daly, *Wickedary*, 82.

42. Daly, *Pure Lust*, 403.

43. Ibid., 405.

44. Ibid., 407-8.

45. Ibid., 25.

46. Ibid., 408.

47. Ibid., 91.

48. Daly *Wickedary*, 99.

49. Ibid., 133.

50. See Moira Gatens, "A Critique of the Sex Gender Distinction," in *A Reader in Feminist Knowledge*, ed. Sneja Gunew (New York: Routledge, 1991); and see Grosz, *Volatile Bodies*.

51. A recent example of this is in Lesley Instone's essay "Denaturing Women," in *Contemporary Australian Feminism* 2, ed. Kate Pritchard Hughes (South Melbourne: Addison Wesley Longman, 1997). Instone accepts Carlassare's diagnosis of Daly as essentialist, noting that Carlassare qualifies her position by arguing that Daly's essentialism is progressive rather than regressive. Such essentialism is strategic as it is "seen as contextual and emerging from specific historical and social situations" (155).

52. Braidotti, *Patterns of Dissonance*, 206.

53. Ibid.

54. Morris, "A-mazing Grace," 72.

55. Thank you to Sarah Hoagland for this expression.

56. Daly, *Gyn/Ecology*, xi.

57. Ibid., 207.

58. Daly, *Wickedary*, 251.

59. Ibid., 82.

60. Simone de Beauvoir, *The Second Sex*, 54.

61. Ibid., 54-56.

61. I would like to thank the following women for their encouragement and helpful discussions, insights, and editorial comments in relation to this paper: Marilyn Frye, Sarah Hoagland, Heather Thomson, Angela Bouris, Jan Preston-Stanley, Natalie Stoljar, Cynthia Freeland, and Philippa McLean.

References

Daly, Mary. 1973. *Beyond God the Father: Toward a Philosophy of Women's Liberation*. Boston: Beacon Press.

———. 1978. *Gyn/Ecology: The Metaethics of Radical Feminism*. London: Women's Press.

———. 1984. *Pure Lust: Elemental Feminist Philosophy*. Boston: Beacon Press.

———. 1985. *The Church and the Second Sex*. Boston: Beacon Press.

Daly, Mary, in cahoots with Jane Caputi. 1988. *Websters' First New Intergalactic Wickedary of the English Language*. London: Women's Press.

de Beauvoir, Simone. 1949. *The Second Sex*. Translated by H. M. Parshley. London: Picador Books.

Descombes, Vincent. 1982. *Modern French Philosophy*. Translated by L. Scott-Fox and J. M. Harding. New York: Cambridge University Press.

Easthope, Anthony, and McGowan, Kate, eds. 1992. *A Critical and Cultural Theory Reader*. St. Leonards: Allen & Unwin.

Fraser, Nancy. 1989. *Unruly Practices: Power, Discourse, and Gender in Contemporary Social Theory*. Cambridge, U.K.: Polity Press.

Grosz, Elizabeth. 1989. *Sexual Subversions: Three French Feminists*. St. Leonards: Allen & Unwin.

———. 1994. *Volatile Bodies: Toward a Corporeal Feminism*. Bloomington: Indiana University Press.

Gunew, Sneja, ed. 1991. *A Reader in Feminist Knowledge*. New York: Routledge

Heidegger, Martin. 1977. "Letter on Humanism," in *Basic Works*. Translated and edited by D. Krell. New York: Harper and Row.

John Paul II, 1994. *Ordinatio Sacerdotalis*. http://www.knight.org/advent.

Morris, Meaghan. N.d. "A-mazing Grace: Notes on Mary Daly's Poetics" *Intervention* 16. 70-92.

Piercy, Marge. 1990. *Circles on the Water*. New York: Alfred A. Knopf.

Pritchard Hughes, Kate, ed. 1997. *Contemporary Australian Feminism* 2. South Melbourne: Addison Wesley Longman.

Schüssler Fiorenza, Elizabeth. 1992. *But She Said: Feminist Practices of Hermeneutical Interpretation*. Boston: Beacon Press.

Taylor, Mark C. 1987. *Alt∇rity*. Chicago: University of Chicago Press.

Anne-Marie Korte (essay date 2000)

SOURCE: Korte, Anne-Marie. "Just/ice In Time: On Temporality in Mary Daly's *Quintessence*," translated by Mischa F. C. Hoyinck. In *Feminist Interpretations of Mary Daly*, edited by Sarah Lucia Hoagland and Marilyn Frye, pp. 418-28. University Park: Pennsylvania State University Press, 2000.

[*In the following essay, Korte discusses Daly's conception of time and her use of temporal disjunctions in* Quintessence *to escape patriarchal notions of absolute space/time.*]

At the brink of a new millennium, could there be a more fitting subject for Mary Daly, renowned for her "Be-Dazzling" leaps through time and space, to thematize than time? In her latest book, ***Quintessence . . . Realizing the Archaic Future*** (1998), Daly emphasizes time far more than in any of her earlier works. In the narrative as well as in the central concepts of this book, Daly plays with time, molds it, and explores the temporal dimension of all that exists "as far as it will go." In ***Quintessence,*** historical eras flash by and narrative points of view shift according to the flow and counterflow of time. Fortunately, there are enough historical references to provide the reader with some orientation. But the characters in ***Quintessence*** are no longer bound to one particular historical period. They "pop up" long before they were born or long after they have died, meeting each other in the Middle Ages, throughout the twentieth century, and even in the near future (from 1998 to 2048). About this last period, however, Daly discloses tantalizingly little. With a thirst for revelations about the near future, I raced through the book—but remained largely unsatisfied.

More revealing to me, however, turned out to be Daly's reflections on time. Interestingly, she bypasses "standard questions" in feminist thinking on time, abstaining from examining such well-known issues as linear versus cyclical time, objective (given) versus subjective (experienced) time or social versus biological time.[1] As I will show, the issue Daly primarily addresses is not so much how women perceive time, but rather which notions of time we must embrace to (be able to) do women justice.

In the sense that ***Quintessence*** relies on an incisively sketched difference between an oppressive past and a present full of hope, it reminded me of Daly's first feminist book, ***The Church and the Second Sex*** (1968). Clearly, and much more straightforwardly, that book also derived its narrative structure from the end of one era and the beginning of another. Its basic idea was that the world was on the brink of a new age that would bring great substantive change. Misogyny was portrayed as a thing of the past, an ancient horror about to be overcome. Depiction of the differences between past and present served to illustrate how far-reaching this transformation would be. Daly's plea for recognition and support of the impending era of "equality" and "partnership" was based on the hopeful signs of change she detected in the Roman Catholic church in the 1960s. Thirty years on, she no longer situates this qualitative difference in the present, but in the near future. Signs of hope can no longer be found in the here and now, but in the women who look back on our own time as history. Looking back from 2048 B.E. (Biophilic Era), the feminist renaissance is a historical fact and the 1990s appear to have been the dark ages of feminism.

This, I believe, is a fundamental element of Mary Daly's feminist approach to time. Expecting, or at least hoping for, changes that will manifest themselves as entirely new eras—this is a constant theme in Daly's writings. Large-scale thinking in terms of (new) ages is, in itself, a feature of modern Western consciousness of time. Daly's view of historical change, however, bears the unmistakably prophetic signs of the Judeo-Christian notion of time. Daly's great expectations are not the forthright product of a modern belief in progress. They are based on a critical assessment of the quality of present-day life, measured by norms and values that transcend the evidences of one's own time and place. Daly's point of departure is a vision of peace, justice, and beatitude on a cosmic scale—a vision that figures prominently in prophetic biblical texts. Here, cosmic vision and judgment of "one's own time" go hand in hand, demanding immediate conversion.

It is this perspective, I believe, that has informed Daly's feminist reflection on time from the very beginning. In *Beyond God the Father,* she starts urging women to adopt a critical stance toward all kinds of order that bear the stamp of patriarchy. To underscore this point, she again invokes the metaphor of the gloomy past and the radiant new era. To be caught up in patriarchal institutions is, according to Daly, "to be living in time past."[2] By contrast, women who choose not to be party to this any longer "are vividly aware of living in time present/future."[3] Daly localizes women's new awareness of time at the core of the new era: women's own time is situated at the edges of patriarchal time. "It *is* whenever we are living out of our own sense of reality, refusing to be possessed, conquered and alienated by the linear, measured-out, quantitative time of the patriarchal system. Women, in becoming who we are, are living in a qualitative, organic time that escapes the measurements of the system."[4] Daly called for a clear distinction between patriarchal time and "women's own time" or "Life-time."

At first glance, this view seems closely related to the feminist concept of "women's time" as explored by Julia Kristeva,[5] Heide Göttner-Abendroth,[6] and others. These authors have linked the way in which women perceive time to their bodily functions, to the nature of the tasks they usually perform (a day-to-day routine rather than long-term, goal-oriented projects), and to the systematic exclusion of women from language and science. Their explorations of how women experience time have generated conceptual distinctions such as linear versus cyclical time or objective (given) versus subjective (perceived) time. As part of the same debate, widely held concepts of time and historic periodization have come under fire. The criticism focuses on their failure to account for women's tasks and lifestyles. Women's cyclical, mimetic, fragmented, or interrupted perceptions of time are ignored, or even obscured.

In calling on women to distinguish between patriarchal time and women's time, however, Daly had something else in mind. She considers it a moral imperative for women to live on the edge of patriarchal institutions and to claim physical space/time for themselves. Rather than the perception of time, it is the value of time, of the quality of life realized with/in time, that is Daly's frame of reference. She disregards any link between women's perception of time and their biological functions and reproductive tasks. This is consistent with the way she has always ignored "characteristically female" physical experiences when tackling epistemological questions.

I believe that there is a very specific reason why Daly refuses to go along with these explorations of the "cyclical rhythms" of female corporeality. Cyclical notions of time have no positive appeal for her at all, as she made clear in the last chapter of *Beyond God the Father* (1973). There she stated her faith in the power of the women's movement to radically alter the history of humankind and the course of the entire universe. She argued that women's liberation will engender an unrivaled evolutionary impulse: a qualitative leap of cosmic proportions.[7] The nonbeing of women will be undone and oppression and domination in all its forms will be rooted out. Searching for terms and categories to adequately express this cosmic change, Daly reached the conclusion that most philosophical and theological representations of the future were simply inadequate for this purpose because they could not allow for a qualitative difference. They are closed systems, depicting the future as paradise regained and thereby stamping out any difference. The merging of all that exists with God, the absorption of the finite into the Infinite is seen as a return to the womb (*exitus-reditus*) rather than a move forward into a new Space/Time of "endless divergence."[8]

In my view, it is Daly's repellence of closed systems and of the *ewige Wiederkehr des Gleichen* (endless repetition of the same) that prompted her to go beyond simply criticizing patriarchal time or replacing it with women's time. Radical feminism requires disrupting and abandoning all accepted representations of time and space. With her own leap beyond the Christian and patriarchal era in 1975, Daly put her preaching into practice. The situation was too urgent to wait for all of humankind to take a qualitative leap. Daly stepped out on her own, to begin exploring and charting the new Space/Time herself.

Prophetic judgment of her own time has become a prominent feature of Daly's work. With *Quintessence* she has embraced the opportunity to deliver a feminist mission statement on the brink of the new millennium, and rightfully so. Admittedly, I would expect nothing less from this philosopher trained in theology. To write about the *eschata*, the last or ultimate things, is not only a providentially timed project but also a logical continuation of Daly's earlier works—which, as I have shown elsewhere, reinterpret the main theological issues from a radical feminist angle.[9] Eschatology, the last item on the theological agenda, deals with the final destiny of all that exists, in terms of both the universe as a whole and the fate of individual people. From a Christian perspective, the latter manifests itself as the resurrection of all individuals, including their bodily existence. This should be preceded by the Second Coming of Christ in an apocalyptic time of catastrophe, violence, and destruction, followed by a thousand-year reign of Christ. In my view, *Quintessence* provides a unique rereading of these issues.

Just like Daly's other post-Christian books, *Quintessence* criticizes its own present as an evil time, an era full of dangers and attacks on women and "all of their kind." But the call to depart from the existing era is expressed in new ways and gives rise to new reflections on the notions of time and space. Ever since *Gyn/Ecology*, Daly has characterized the detachment from the dangerous, perverted, and patriarchal present as the development of a critical distance. She illustrated this with the image of a (space) journey, a synchronous spiritual movement that allows the traveler to discover the depths and dynamic possibilities behind and beyond the reality of the present. One's inauthentic present life in the foreground directed by the fathers had to be exchanged for the authentic life of presence in the Background that women would control themselves. Daly put special emphasis on the idea that this life in the Background was "elsewhere," in other words, clearly distanced from here and now. But the metaphors used for imagining the necessary distancing, like traveling, moving, spinning, or hopping, also indicated a different temporal dimension of the Background. These metaphors suggest movements that "take their time," that have their own pace and intensity, and that make it possible to perceive and value one's own and one another's presence in other, maybe even multitemporal ways.

In *Quintessence*, these temporal dimensions of life in the Background are far more highlighted. At a future point of time, this life in the Background turns out to have been concretely realized. The new postpatriarchal age finally has arrived. Or so it seems, from the vantage point of the year 2048, on Lost and Found Continent, a special place on our own planet inhabited by a community of women who have managed to leave life-destroying patriarchy behind. We get glimpses of a multicultural group of women leading a life of paradise and extraordinary ecological awareness. The point of view in *Quintessence* alternates between 2048 and 1998, and sometimes the two perspectives blend. Mixing these two points of view also creates room to "realize" other moments in time.

Until now, Daly mainly explored shifts in historical time in the prefaces and epilogues to her writings. In *Quintessence* it has become the main focus. Temporal discontinuity is no longer primarily a way to depict the changes Daly herself in fact has experienced, such as abandoning Christianity or developing an increasingly radical feminist vision. These shifts in time are now also used to visualize substantive and much longed-for changes that have not happened yet.

In her previous books, Daly expressed qualitative changes as a detachment from the present or from the past which was once her present. To this end, she had her present-day self look back in amazement at the "prehistoric" writings of the earlier Mary Daly. This time, the present-day Daly and her work are "discovered" by a young, "future foresister," an inhabitant of the 2048 Lost and Found Continent who is surprised and upset at the situation of the 1990s, an era before her time. She is staggered by the insensitivity and ruthlessness of the people living then: why did they not recognize that they were perpetuating the wholesale destruction of life on earth? Why did the women do nothing about this? In order to answer these questions, she invokes Mary Daly, one of the few authors of the time who were studying this problem. Mary Daly appears before her in body and spirit. Together the two women reconstruct the obstacles that women faced in the horrible nineties. In those days, women were easily scared off and intimidated because of the serious sanctions against "aberrant" behavior. Women were manacled by religious fundamentalism and alternative religions. Moreover, there was a backlash against feminism itself. Many women were loath to associate with it, radical feminist literature was removed from the bookshops and pseudo-feminism, such as postmodern or French feminism, took over the universities. What is more, is it not possible that women suffered some form of slow physical numbing as a result of the large-scale poisoning of the earth?

Quintessence unfortunately does not explain how this process was stopped, although it is suggested that the earth itself ultimately and just in time revolted against its abuse. Increasing numbers of natural disasters and famines finally broke the life-destroying patriarchal hegemony. The fall of worldwide patriarchy has clear overtones of the apocalypse that precedes the Second Coming of Christ—in *Quintessence,* a Second Coming of Women, as Daly herself had prophesied in *Beyond God the Father.*[10] Yet, this apocalypse is discussed in very veiled terms—we are spared the details, to my relief and in clear contrast to the often unrestrained use of apocalyptic scenery in religious fundamentalism. It is also telling that the residents of Lost and Found Continent commemorate the plagues that visited the earth, but do not celebrate the final victory over patriarchy. They are well aware that patriarchy is tough to wipe out entirely and are wary of a possible resurgence. For that reason, they want to study the lives of their foresisters under the patriarchal order. They wish not only to mourn the injustice done to their sisters, but also to learn from the past.

In *Quintessence,* Mary Daly does not explore the perception of time in relation to women's day-to-day tasks or their physical functions. Nor does she discuss stress, or the feeling of "always being pressed for time," two experiences so characteristic of Western women's lives in the late twentieth century. When the Mary Daly character ends up in the Lost and Found Continent of the future, she is astonished by the clean air, the pure water, and the organic food, but makes no mention of a change in the pace of life. Nor does Daly comment on time as described by modern physics. Some see in Einstein's relative notion of time—that it is a function of place and movement, rather than linear and absolute—support for the feminist criticism of linear time. Despite such labels as Archaic Time or Original Time, Daly's own leaps and shifts in time do not result in a reclaiming of what other feminists characterize as "women's time," a primeval time in which birth and death, menstruation and pregnancy, sun and moon, mark the days, weeks, and years and divide them into rhythmic cycles.[11] It seems that for Daly, the importance of temporal discontinuity is that it grants distance from the present, the here and now we live in, in order to judge it. Temporal discontinuity constitutes difference, evokes and expresses the experience of a self that is not (any longer) undifferentiatedly immersed in the flow of time—a self that is capable of judgment.

To me, all of this raises the question of whether Mary Daly is interested in the phenomenon of time per se. After all, times and eras can be judged without any reflection on the concept of time as such, as the judgment might only have a bearing on the quality of life at a given time. So, must we conclude that Daly regards time merely as a given structure? Judging from the obvious passion and joy with which she employs temporal discontinuity, it seems more likely that she indeed considers time inherently significant. The shifting temporal point of view in *Quintessence* may provide the distance/difference necessary to judge the present, but it has other meanings too. The shifts in time also bring about encounters between completely different creatures, creating "elemental connections" that spark off renewal and change. In *Pure Lust,* Daly already used the term *synchronicity* (or in her own words, Syn-Crone-icities) to denote meetings at crossroads of species and souls, such as exchanges between women and cats or other sensitive beings. These encounters "convey a sense of harmony among apparently dissimilar Elemental phenomena."[12] In addition, she used the terms "Tide" or "Tidal Time" in the same sense.[13] To her, these are movements of the elements that can be experienced by those who leave patriarchal time/space and that can cause cosmic connections or "planetary communion." These connections are characterized by the crossing of boundaries. They make it possible to "pick up messages from an Other and better World."[14]

In *Quintessence,* Daly adds the temporal factor to these cross-border encounters. Flashbacks, foresight, and temporal contractions in which past, present, and future converge are quintessential moments in this type of meeting. Boundaries thought to be absolute, such as of time, place, species, or physical entity, are transgressed, while the boundaries of individual creatures are respected and remain intact. After all, Daly considers the violation of boundaries of individual creatures—or simply put, rape—the trademark of patriarchy, as is again stated in *Quintessence* where Daly displays the persistent terror of this violation, with examples ranging from the rape of women in the Bosnian civil war to biotechnological tinkering with humans and animals.

I believe that Daly assigns a positive meaning to time in the sense that she sees it as the dimension of extension and realization—a dimension women still have not claimed forcefully enough. Existing in time means more than endurance; it also means realizing volume, substance, and constancy. Time not only "makes difference," but is also the medium through which we can extend in all directions, reach, stand out, connect, be transformed, in short, become more without losing our contours and hence our concreteness as well as our limitations. While many Western theologies and philosophies regard time as a limiting factor at the level of the individual—time being directly linked to finiteness and death—Daly, at this level, seems to opt far more strongly for regarding time as the dimension of transformation and renewal.

In *Quintessence,* Daly develops promising images and concepts exploring the positive connotations of time as a facilitator of extension and realization. The epitome of this meaning of time is Quintessence, the book's guiding theme. To Daly, Quintessence denotes the completely different reality she yearns for. It is the opposite of the "soul-shrinking, stinking manmade mess that they have made of 'the globe' and everything else within reach."[15] Quintessence is a new way of expressing what Daly earlier called "Verb" and "Goddess," metaphors for "the Be-ing in which we live, love, create, and are."[16] Quintessence, she states, "is that which has drawn me on in my writing and searching. The Quest for Quintessence is the most Desperate response I know to the Call of the Wild. It means throwing one's life as far as it will go."[17]

The term Quintessence is derived from ancient Greek and Hellenistic philosophy and enables Daly to incorporate the space/time dimensions into her image of the ultimate reality in a far more explicit way than before. Quintessence is the last or highest essence, above the four elements of fire, air, water, and earth. It permeates all nature and is seen as the Spirit that gives life and vitality to the whole universe. Time and space, energy and matter, converge in this fifth or ultimate essence. It is in the context of this premodern metaphysical and mystical philosophy that Daly defines Quintessence as "the unifying Living Presence that is at the core of integrity and the Elemental connectedness of the Universe and that is the Source of our Power to Realize true Future—an Archaic Future."[18] Quintessence is "the Magnetizing Idea of the Good which is the Final Cause."[19] In sum, Quintessence enables extension and realization par excellence.

Daly's *Quintessence* makes clear that the feminist debate on time should neither be limited to the issue of how women experience time, nor left to those poststructuralist interpretations whose rejection of metaphysics inclines to foreclose any discussion of temporality related to the physical universe. Time should neither be reduced to subjective experience, nor be taken for granted—because too much is at stake. As is urged from Daly's writings, it is imperative that we also explore how time and our notions of time can realize justice.

Notes

1. See also Forman 1989b.
2. Daly 1973, 42.
3. Daly 1973, 42.
4. Daly 1973, 43.
5. Kristeva 1979, 5-19. See also Clément and Kristeva 1998.
6. Göttner-Abendroth 1989, 108-19.
7. Here, Daly's frame of reference is the cosmology developed by Pierre Teilhard de Chardin, a Roman Catholic geophysicist and philosopher, who envisaged evolution to arouse a continual improvement of the quality of the human mind.
8. Daly 1973, 193.
9. See Korte 1992, 339-41; "Deliver Us from Evil," in the present anthology.
10. Daly 1973, 95-97.
11. See, for example, Göttner-Abendroth 1989.
12. Daly 1984, 312-13.
13. Daly 1984, 290-91; Daly 1987, 231.
14. Daly 1984, 416.
15. Daly 1998, 4.
16. Daly 1998, 95.
17. Daly 1998, 4.
18. Daly 1998, 11.
19. Daly 1998, 102.

References

Briggs, Sheila. 1997. "A History of Our Own: What Would a Feminist Theology of History Look Like?" In Chopp and Davaney, 165-78.

Chopp, Rebecca S., and Sheila Greeve Davaney, eds. 1997. *Horizons in Feminist Theology: Identity, Tradition, and Norms*. Minneapolis: Fortress Press.

Clément, Catherine, and Julia Kristeva. 1998. *Le féminin et le sacré*. Paris: Stock.

Cooey, Paula M., Sharon A. Farmer, and Mary Ellen Ross, eds. 1988. *Embodied Love: Sensuality and Relationship as Feminist Values*. San Francisco: Harper and Row.

Daly, Mary. 1968. *The Church and the Second Sex*. London, Dublin and Melbourne: Geoffrey Chapman.

———. 1973. *Beyond God the Father: Toward a Philosophy of Women's Liberation*. Boston: Beacon Press.

———. 1975a. "Autobiographical Preface to the Colofon Edition," and "Feminist Post-christian Introduction." In *The Church and the Second Sex: With a New Feminist Postchristian Introduction by the Author*, 5-51. New York: Harper and Row.

———. 1975b. "The Qualitative Leap Beyond Patriarchal Religion." *Quest* 1 (Spring): 20-40.

———. 1978. *Gyn/Ecology: The Metaethics of Radical Feminism*. Boston: Beacon Press.

———. 1980. "Vorwort zur deutschen Ausgabe von *Beyond God the Father*." In *Jenseits von Gottvater, Sohn & Co: Aufbruch zu einer Philosophie der Frauenbefreiung*, 5-10. München: Frauenoffensive.

———. 1984. *Pure Lust: Elemental Feminist Philosophy.* Boston: Beacon Press.

———. 1985a. "New Archaic Afterwords." In *The Church and the Second Sex: With the Feminist Postchristian Introduction and New Archaic Afterwords by the Author,* xi-xxx. Boston: Beacon Press.

———. 1985b. "Original Reintroduction." In *Beyond God the Father: Toward a Philosophy of Women's Liberation, with an Original Reintroduction by the Author,* xi-xxix. Boston: Beacon Press.

———. 1987. *Websters' First New Intergalactic Wickedary of the English Language* [Conjured by Mary Daly in cahoots with Jane Caputi]. Boston: Beacon Press.

———. 1991. "New Intergalactic Introduction." In *Gyn/Ecology: The Metaethics of Radical Feminism, with a New Introduction by the Author,* xiii-xxxv. Boston: Beacon Press.

———. 1992. *Outercourse: The Be-Dazzling Voyage.* San Francisco: Harper.

———. 1998. *Quintessence . . . Realizing the Archaic Future: A Radical Elemental Feminist Manifesto.* Boston: Beacon Press.

Davaney, Sheila Greeve. 1998. "Problems with Feminist Theory: Historicity and the Search for Sure Foundations." In Cooey, Farmer, and Ross, 79-96.

Ermarth, Elizabeth Deeds. 1989. "The Solitude of Women and Social Time." In Forman 1989a, 37-46.

Forman, Frieda Johles. 1989a. "Feminizing Time: An Introduction." In Forman 1989b, 1-9.

———, ed. With Caoron Sowton. 1989b. *Taking Our Time: Feminist Perspectives on Temporality.* Oxford: Pergamon Press.

Garcia, Irma. 1989. "Femalear Explorations: Temporality in Women's Writing." In Forman 1989a, 161-82.

Göttner-Abendroth, Heide. 1989. "Urania-Time and Space of the Stars: The Matriarchal Cosmos Through the Lens of Modern Physics." In Forman 1989a, 108-19.

Korte, Anne-Marie. 1992. *Een passie voor transcendentie: Feminisme, theologie en moderniteit in het denken van Mary Daly (A Passion for Transcendence: Feminism, Theology, and Modernity in the Thinking of Mary Daly).* Kampen: Kok.

Kristeva, Julia. 1979. "Le temps des femmes." 33/44: *Cahiers de Recherche de Sciences de Textes et Documents* 5 (Winter): 5-19.

Lloyd, Genevieve. 1993. *Being in Time: Selves and Narrators in Philosophy and Literature.* London: Routledge.

Maïr Verthuy. "Hélène Parmelin and the Question of Time." In Forman 1989a, 94-107.

Stephen P. Jenkins (review date June 2001)

SOURCE: Jenkins, Stephen P. Review of *The Gender Division of Welfare: The Impact of the British and German Welfare States,* by Mary Daly. *British Journal of Sociology* 52, no. 2 (June 2001): 354-5.

[*In the following review, Jenkins praises Daly's "succinct and seductive" examination of modern welfare states in* The Gender Division of Welfare, *but laments the work's lack of post-1990 references.*]

[*The Gender Division of Welfare: The Impact of the British and German Welfare States*] makes a significant contribution to our understanding of the nature of contemporary welfare states, their relationships with families, markets, and outcomes for individuals. Distinctive features include reviews of earlier approaches, a new conceptual framework based on gender differentiation combined with a cross-national perspective, and the combination of theorizing and empirical work. The writing style is succinct and seductive.

Part I conceptualizes the relationships between gender and the welfare state. There is an useful critical survey of earlier frameworks, and persuasive argument in favour of a gendered approach and a cross-national perspective. Daly's own conceptual approach is a coherent development and integration of elements of earlier research rather than a radical departure. I concur with her desire to move away from typologies of welfare states towards better integration of micro-level outcomes, and her preference for two-country rather than many-country comparisons. Part II provides a comprehensive picture of the key characteristics of the British and German welfare states viewed through the lens of the conceptual framework. This focus is on policies for families and caring, risks covered, eligibility criteria, treatments of those entitled, and cash transfer systems. Part III examines the role of the welfare states (and the family) in the context of income redistribution, poverty, financial relationships within marriage and marital breakdown. It would be unfair to summarize the empirical findings in a few sentences (though there are no great surprises!). Indeed, pointing out "messy and stubborn practices encountered in social reality" is a part of the book's message—one with which I sympathize. The book concludes with thoughtful reflections on the utility of a gender approach to comparative welfare state analysis.

The enduring legacy of this book may be the analytical framework rather than the specific application. The main focus is on the mid-1980s, i.e. before Thatcherite and subsequent "reforms" to the British economy and welfare states, and before German reunification in 1989. (The discussion of later periods in the concluding chapter appears somewhat of an afterthought in comparison.) The introduction acknowledges this, stating none the less that "the mid-1980s suggests itself as an appropriate period from which to take stock of . . . postwar welfare state models." This may be so—but investigation of the impact of more recent changes (or whether things have in fact really changed) is likely to be of greater contemporary interest. Moreover there are few references later than the mid-1990s. Some unpublished research that is cited has long since appeared, and some notable recent research is not cited. One specific date issue: Daly's German sample—and hence empirical inferences—refer only to native Germans, i.e. "guestworkers" are not considered despite their importance in German society (they are over-sampled in her data source, so data availability is not an issue). It is important to note that the potential for quantitative cross-national research has markedly improved over the last decade, with substantial extensions to the collections of comparable data comprising the Luxembourg Income Study (http://lis/ceps.lu) and the Cross-National Equivalent Panel Data File (http://www.human.cornell.edu/pam/gsoep/equivfil.cfm). The latter also reminds me of an unwarranted side-swipe. Daly refers to "the latest fashion in poverty research, which searches after duration and movement . . . However none of the recent work on the dynamics of poverty gives cause to assume that the structures of poverty uncovered here would be any different to those found by dynamic analyses." One of the lessons of the last decade is indeed that, if one asks different questions, then one does get different (and complementary) answers to the standard cross-section-based approaches.

Overall, and despite some specific reservations, I thoroughly recommend this book as a worthwhile purchase for researchers, teachers, and students.

FURTHER READING

Criticism

Bahmueller, Nancy N., and Diane E. Bennekamper. "Be-ing in Womanspace." *Contemporary Psychology* 21, no. 7 (July 1976): 504.

Bahmueller and Bennekamper offer a positive assessment of *Beyond God the Father*.

Evans, Patricia M. Review of *The Gender Division of Welfare: The Impact of the British and German Welfare States,* by Mary Daly. *Canadian Journal of Sociology* 27, no. 2 (spring 2002): 269-72.

Evans lauds Daly's accomplishment in *The Gender Division of Welfare,* arguing that the work is "a welcome addition to the expanding scholarship on gender and welfare states."

Hanagan, Michael. Review of *The Gender Division of Welfare: The Impact of the British and German Welfare States,* by Mary Daly. *Journal of Social History* 35, no. 4 (summer 2002): 1021-23.

Hanagan praises *The Gender Division of Welfare,* noting that "Daly's study marks an important step in social science research."

Karagianis, Maria. "Mary, Mary, Quite Contrary." *Ms.* 9, no. 4 (June-July 1999): 56.

Karagianis provides an overview of Daly's legal battle to teach female students separately from men.

Maitland, Sara. "A New Psyche." *New Statesman* 109, no. 2809 (18 January 1985): 28.

Maitland compliments Daly's critique of male-defined language in *Pure Lust,* but finds shortcomings in her etymological equations and her disinterest in historical or social reality.

McNeil, Helen. "Hag-ography." *New Statesman* 99, no. 2559 (4 April 1980): 514-15.

McNeil praises the importance of the subject material in *Gyn/Ecology*, but criticizes Daly's polemical approach and linguistic imprecision.

Miller, Samantha, and Mark Dagostino. "No Boys Allowed." *People* (14 June 1999): 101.

Miller and Dagostino discuss the controversial legal case brought against Daly for denying male students admittance to her Boston College class.

Pollitt, Katha. "No Males Need Apply?" *Nation* 269, no. 6 (23-30 August 1999): 10.

Pollitt examines the legal dispute between Daly and Boston College, noting that she objects to both Daly's claim and the feminist support on her behalf.

Santoni, Ronald E. "Paean to Women." *Progressive* 38, no. 5 (May 1974): 59-60.

Santoni offers a positive assessment of *Beyond God the Father,* which he praises as a "brilliant and prophetic" book despite its shortcomings.

Sapiro, Virginia. Review of *Gyn/Ecology,* by Mary Daly. *Ethics* 90, no. 4 (July 1980): 611-13.

Sapiro compliments Daly's central argument in *Gyn/Ecology,* though cites flaws in her underlying Catholic perspective and her tendency toward description rather than analysis.

Sexton, David. "Nags, Shrews, and Snools." *Spectator* 254, no. 8172 (23 February 1985): 23.

Sexton provides an unfavorable review of *Pure Lust*.

Weil, Lisa. "Leaps of Faith." *Women's Review of Books* 16, no. 6 (March 1999): 21-2.

Weil offers a generally positive review of *Quintessence* despite misgivings over Daly's utopian optimism.

Youngs, Dale. "What's So Good about the Goddess?" *Christianity Today* (16 August 1993): 21.

Youngs discusses Daly's feminist theology and advocacy for goddess worship, which Youngs finds historically and theologically flawed.

Additional coverage of Daly's life and career is contained in the following sources published by the Gale Group: *Contemporary Authors,* **Vols. 25-28R;** *Contemporary Authors New Revision Series,* **Vols. 30, 62;** *Feminist Writers; Gay and Lesbian Literature,* **Ed. 1;** *Literature Resource Center;* **and** *Major 20th-Century Writers,* **Ed. 1.**

Slavenka Drakulic
1949-

(Also rendered as Slavenka Drakulić or Drakulič) Croatian novelist and essayist.

The following entry presents an overview of Drakulic's career through 2001.

INTRODUCTION

Drakulic is an internationally known novelist, essayist, and journalist who has explored the effects of communism and war on Eastern European women in both her fiction and nonfiction. Her work typically focuses on the domestic sphere and the individual rather that geo-political issues and traditional images of modern warfare. Although some have labeled Drakulic as a regional writer, her audiences have been primarily Western, partially due to the negative reactions of some Croatians to Drakulic's unflinching portrayal of her native region's cultural and political turmoil.

BIOGRAPHICAL INFORMATION

Drakulic was born on July 4, 1949, in Rijeka, Yugoslavia—now Croatia—to Ivan and Antonija Drakulic. Her father was an officer in the communist Federal Army and her mother worked for the communist government. Despite her parents' political affiliation, Drakulic became an outspoken critic of communism as well as an ardent feminist. She began working as a journalist, acting as the Eastern European correspondent for *Ms.* magazine and as a contributor to *Danas*, a major Croatian political journal. Drakulic has also written articles and reviews for publications such as *New Republic, The Nation,* and *Time* magazine as well as European newspapers such as *La Stampa, Frankfurter Allgemeine Zeitung, Dagens Nyheter,* and *Politiken.* In 1987 she participated in the International Writer's Workshop at the University of Iowa. Drakulic published her first novel, *Hologrami straha* (*Holograms of Fear*) in 1988, but her essay collection *How We Survived Communism and Even Laughed* (1991) was her first book to be written and published in English. Drakulic has one daughter, Rujana, from her first marriage. Rujana's father was Serbian and her mixed heritage would later cause both her and her mother difficulties when the Serbian-Croatian War broke out in June 1991. Rujana left the

country to avoid persecution while Drakulic spent time in Slovenia as a refugee. During this period, Drakulic began focusing her writing on the effects of war on families and individuals. She was awarded a Fulbright award in 1990, the 1992 Independent Foreign Fiction Award for *Holograms of Fear,* and an award from the Institute of Human Sciences in Vienna in 1994.

MAJOR WORKS

Holograms of Fear is Drakulic's most autobiographical and realistic novel, recounting the story of a Croatian woman suffering from kidney disease who must travel to New York to undergo a transplant. The dramatic thrust of the narrative is related during the woman's recovery, as she reminiscences about her past life in post-war Yugoslavia, her family, and a close friend who committed suicide. Drakulic explores mother-daughter relationships in the novel *Mramorna koza* (1989; *Marble Skin*) in which the protagonist carves an erotic statue of her mother entitled "My Mother's Body." When her mother sees the sculpture, she attempts suicide. As the daughter attempts to care for her mother, they are both forced to confront the painful events that have marred their relationship, particularly the daughter's abuse at the hands of her stepfather. In *The Taste of a Man* (1997), Tereza, a Polish literature student in New York, meets José, a visiting Brazilian professor of anthropology who is studying cannibalism. José and Tereza begin a passionate affair, despite the fact that José has a wife and child in Brazil. After José returns to Brazil to visit his family, Tereza becomes obsessed with their relationship and comes to a realization that she must possess José completely. Upon his return, Tereza murders José and consumes his flesh in an attempt to unite with him forever. *S: A Novel about the Balkans* (2000) opens in a Stockholm hospital where the protagonist, a woman named S., has just given birth to a son. Through flashbacks, Drakulic reveals that the baby was conceived as a result of S.'s rape by Serbian soldiers during the Serbian-Croatian War in 1991. The novel traces S.'s life as a half-Muslim teacher in a small Bosnian town, through her capture and torture by Serbian soldiers. Her confusion and sense of betrayal are heightened by the fact that she is also half-Serbian.

In addition to her fiction, Drakulic's nonfiction works show a firm focus on the ramifications of the social and political conflicts in Eastern Europe. In *How We Survived Communism and Even Laughed,* Drakulic traces communism's failure to meet the needs of women in Czechoslovakia, Poland, Bulgaria, and East Germany, using her own personal recollections and interviews with other Eastern European women. The essays focus on a wide range of subject material, from the oppression of women by communist governments to the domestic impact of shortages of material goods, such as the lack of toilet paper and tampons. *Sterben in Kroatian: Vom Krieg mitten in Europa* (1993; *The Balkan Express: Fragments from the Other Side of War*) collects essays that illuminate the gradual changes caused by the onset of war in the Balkan region from the spring of 1991 through May 1992. One of the most significant themes of the collection arises in the essay "Overcome by Nationhood" when Drakulic describes what it felt like to be stripped of all of her identification—including education, profession, and personality—and to be defined solely by her nationality. Drakulic argues that treachery becomes part of everyday life during wartime and that the label of nationalism can destroy individuality. In *Café Europa: Life after Communism* (1997), Drakulic examines the plight of Eastern Europe since the fall of communism in 1989, asserting that Eastern Europeans are viewed as second-class citizens by the rest of the world. She discusses why the region has refrained from embracing democracy and laments the cycle of recycling and rewriting history that occurs so frequently in Eastern Europe.

CRITICAL RECEPTION

Most critics have noted that Drakulic's work as a journalist exerts a definite influence on her fiction, though some have disagreed on whether or not the effect is positive. While several reviewers have commented that her journalistic background provides Drakulic with an eye for detail and a succinct prose style, others have argued that these qualities leave her novels flat, lacking full characterizations and well-developed plots. Drakulic's nonfiction has received more critical attention in the West than her fiction, attracting largely favorable reviews. However, much of Drakulic's nonfiction has not been published in her home country because of its frank and controversial look at the ethnic conflicts in the region. Some commentators have accused Drakulic of pandering to a Western feminist audience in her essays, claiming that her work routinely patronizes her fellow countrymen. Ivo Banac has asserted, "[t]he interest in Drakulic is the interest in East European ingenues—in the sort of deprived provincial girls who do laundry without household appliances and delight in soft, pink rolls of toilet paper as badges of civilized living." Nevertheless, many reviewers have found Drakulic's domestic focus on the effects of war and communism to be insightful and engaging. While discussing *The Balkan Express,* Anthony Borden has stated that, "Drakulic focuses on individual lives (often her own or those of her family), using the perversions that war forces onto everyday life to reveal the true complexity of the crisis and the enormity of the task of reconciliation."

PRINCIPAL WORKS

Hologrami straha [*Holograms of Fear*] (novel) 1988

Mramorna koza [*Marble Skin*] (novel) 1989

How We Survived Communism and Even Laughed (essays) 1991

Sterben in Kroatian: Vom Krieg mitten in Europa [*The Balkan Express: Fragments from the Other Side of War*] (essays) 1993

Café Europa: Life after Communism (essays) 1997

The Taste of a Man (novel) 1997

S: A Novel about the Balkans (novel) 2000; also published as *As If I Am Not There: A Novel about the Balkans*

CRITICISM

Melissa Benn (review date 24 January 1992)

SOURCE: Benn, Melissa. "Vogue Desire." *New Statesman and Society* 5, no. 186 (24 January 1992): 39.

[*In the following review, Benn discusses the domestic frame of reference of* How We Survived Communism and Even Laughed.]

I warn you. There is not much laughing in [*How We Survived Communism and Even Laughed.*] Originally commissioned as an essay in the US feminist magazine *Ms.*, Slavenka Drakulic, one of Yugoslavia's founding feminists, has written one of the first insider accounts of what it was like to be a woman under eastern European Communism. It is neither a comprehensive nor an academic study; more, a set of connected allusions, observations and recorded conversations.

For anyone used to those fictional and journalistic accounts of eastern Europe that concentrate on the shadowy state censor, the *samizdat* press, the professor-forcibly-turned-window-cleaner, Drakulic's resolutely domestic frame of reference is both shocking and exhilarating. Most of her action takes place not in the street or the office but in the post office queue, and, of course, the kitchen. Her first bold chapter heading says it all: "The Trivial is Political".

Above all, this is a book about *things*: about nylon stockings and soap, telephones and fur coats, tumble driers and toilet paper. (There is a whole chapter on the changing quality of toilet paper under communism.) It is also about food; people's dreams and glimpsed memories of proper pizzas, creamy chocolate, strawberries, that American bubble gum with the comic wrapping paper.

Drakulic is militant about the meaning of such items for those who have been deprived of them. She must be the first and only person to have begun a speech at a US Socialist Scholars' Conference by holding a tampon and sanitary towel aloft. "I have just come from Bulgaria where you cannot get these. Nor are they available in Poland or Czechoslovakia. Just think about it," she said. The audience was startled into applause, but, being mostly men, were more puzzled than roused.

It is implicit in her account that women are, literally, the guardians of longing. When her grandmother died, her wardrobe was crammed with white tulle and rancid oil, shampoo and outdated insulin, each of them a reminder of a shortage endured. Hers is a story reproduced a hundred thousand times.

Yet, in both east and west, a desire for the good things of life is too commonly called envy and emptied of political content. There is a wonderful description of how it feels, in this world of shortages, to hold a copy of *Vogue* in your hands. It is not just the images that wound—the impossibly beautiful women with their wondrous clothes—but the paper itself, the thick silkiness of it. "I hate it," says her Hungarian friend, Agnes. "It makes me so miserable I could almost cry."

Traditional socialists will find this book very difficult indeed, precisely because it explores the problem of shortages, the material world, in experiential terms. This was always feminism's fraught gift to "wider" politics; so be it. Where Drakulic fails to make the experiential leap herself is in a certain inability to imagine that western women might have a *Vogue* problem; that they, too, might have lived long lives of barely suppressed individualised rage and envy.

More than once, Drakulic's argument reminded me of the work of British feminist Carolyn Steedman, in particular a passage in her *Landscape for a Good Woman*. Steedman, writing of her mother's longing for the good things of life, says that there is in Britain, as yet, "no language of desire that presents what my mother wanted as anything but supremely trivial . . . and yet the borders of her exclusion were immense; her loss resolutely material."

Lindsey Hughes (review date 31 January 1992)

SOURCE: Hughes, Lindsey. "Out of Grandmother's Store Cupboard." *Times Literary Supplement*, no. 4635 (31 January 1992): 23.

[*In the following review, Hughes discusses* Holograms of Fear *in context of Drakulic's essays in* How We Survived Communism and Even Laughed.]

Images of death and decay haunt **Holograms of Fear,** a novel which focuses on a woman's thoughts before and after a kidney transplant operation in a hospital outside New York. The operation goes well, so why is she afraid? Why does the word "recovery" always appear in inverted commas? The answer emerges through flashbacks to the patient's home in Zagreb, to memories, tender and guilt-ridden, of her grandmother, mother and daughter, and of her own younger self growing up in post-war Yugoslavia, of fellow dialysis patients, including her father, and a woman friend who commits suicide, her indecisiveness embodied in a bowl of underwear left to soak overnight. The narrative shifts between countries and decades, and between the narrator's "two realities", her "two living halves multiplying like amoeba", as blood pulsates through veins or the tubes of a dialysis machine, drips from wounds and gushes from slashed wrists. Before the operation there is her sick self and her well self, which she tries unsuccessfully to keep apart; after it, there is a waking self and a "nightmare Me". She shuns mirrors in order to avoid the "terror of not recognising myself". The divisions are healed only in the closing pages. This is assured writing, even in translation, which works on many levels, not least that of political metaphor: the security of the hospital that no one can leave, but where the patients "never have to be responsible for anything"; the difficulty of freely drinking water, once strictly rationed under the regime of dialysis.

Slavenka Drakulić, a best-selling Croatian author and journalist, published her novel in 1987, too soon, it seems, to reflect today's fast-changing realities, but reading it in conjunction with her essays in **How We Survived Communism**—which covers the period from the 1950s to the present and includes a chapter on the anticipated outbreak of civil war in Yugoslavia—gives immediacy to the metaphors and reveals that much of the material in **Holograms** is autobiographical. I suspect that for many Western women who have travelled frequently in Eastern Europe one of the most hateful aspects of communist regimes is their neglect of the needs of women. Drakulić pulls few punches on this topic. In front of a scholarly audience in New York she holds up a Tampax and a sanitary towel (unavailable even today to many East European women) as symbols of communist failure: A smart American feminist who requests a "critical theory" of women's influence on "public discourse" in Yugoslavia is rebuked for asking the wrong questions. Drakulić warns against applying a First World ecological philosophy to Third World (ie, East European) women, to whom self-denial for the sake of "higher goals" is all too familiar. She seems to hint that, for now, feminism is as inappropriate as ecology in countries where it is hard simply to blame men, "because we all live in the same mess".

Men feature only incidentally, both in the essays and the novel, as does politics, which is likened to "a disease, a plague, an epidemic". Instead of political or sociological analysis, Drakulić deploys the "small everyday things" to create a powerful picture of what it felt and feels like to be a woman in Eastern Europe: a new washing machine decorated with an embroidered towel, shown off to guests but not used; hard, brownish "Golub" toilet paper; the peasant woman who fainted at the sight of twenty different kinds of sausage; a first banana consumed complete with skin; babies poisoned by imported milk powder sold past its sell-by date: "hundred-ways potato parties". Women talk about their lives, sitting amidst the steam from homemade soup (itself a symbol of "security") in tiny kitchen havens in Warsaw, Prague, Budapest, Bucharest and Zagreb, the streetlights outside shedding a "scant yellowish light"

in cities killed by decades of indifference to public space. The former USSR was not included in the author's itinerary, but Moscow and Petersburg could be added to her list of cities.

From these images emerges a powerful composite portrait, alternately harrowing and humorous, of East European women, which is enriched by constant cultural cross-references. Foreign sweet papers are like "messages from another world", a copy of *Vogue* is a "pebble from Mars", a fur coat in a New York junkshop—"an illusory ticket to your dreams". The collection ends with a description of grandmother's store cupboard, "a museum of communist shortages", the contents of which express distrust of the system more eloquently than any tapped phone conversation or dissident leaflet, and probably say more about communism than a dozen books by sociologists or political scientists.

Jenny Turner (review date 23 April 1992)

SOURCE: Turner, Jenny. "Self-Disclosing Days." *London Review of Books* 14, no. 8 (23 April 1992): 17-18.

[*In the following review, Turner analyzes the relationship between Drakulic's work and Western feminism, focusing on* Holograms of Fear *and* How We Survived Communism and Even Laughed *as well as Gloria Steinem's* Revolution from Within.]

'Courageous, poignant, superbly written in blood'; 'brave, funny, wise'; 'sensitivity, intelligence, grace . . . belies the huge internal struggle that leads to its poise'. **Holograms of Fear,** Slavenka Drakulic's first and largely autobiographical novel, is one of those tight, solipsistic, well-written memory-rambles about which there is nothing much to say. Ostensibly the story of the author's kidney transplant, it is in fact, as is sadly the convention with all too many 'literary' novels these days, a self-regarding show-tour of the fascinatingly sensitive inside of its author's own head. But women in general, and feminists in particular, are meant not only to love this sort of stuff, but to find it personally and politically useful. And this presumably is why North American feminist figureheads of the stature of Barbara Ehrenreich, Alice Walker, Gloria Steinem and Robin Morgan have given it their impeccably feminist imprimatur.

As North American feminist figureheads of great stature, Barbara Ehrenreich, Alice Walker, Gloria Steinem and Robin Morgan are all closely associated with New York's *Ms.* magazine, the flagship journal of international sisterhood; Slavenka Drakulic is *Ms.* magazine's East European correspondent. But to say that the *Ms.* pantheon puffs Drakulic because she is one of them is in itself not interesting: everybody knows that the one indisputable achievement of the contemporary women's movement is that it offers professional women the sort of networking and back-scratching opportunities their male cohorts get from clubbability and the Masons. What *is* interesting, however, is the impression one gets that the *Ms.* pantheon isn't puffing Drakulic's books just because she is one of them, or even because they feel sorry for her that she has had a hard time of it what with living in Yugoslavia and having had a serious kidney disease. These women actually seem to believe, in line with the great feminist 'the personal is political' trope, that because Drakulic's novel is deeply personal it must in some way be deeply politically useful as well.

Used slackly and sentimentally, the trope becomes a big, baggy repository for all sorts of slovenly thinking and self-deceiving bad faiths. It allows, for example, for the tiresome assumption that to engage in personal disclosure in a book, no matter how boring or silly your self-disclosures turn out to be, is somehow 'braver' and more 'honest' than writing a book which is interesting and clever. Gloria Steinem's own recently-published *Revolution from Within,* for example, was, as most reviewers pointed out, a boring and silly ragbag of personal revelation, friends-of-friends-type anecdote and casual bedtime reading in the literature of self-help—12-point programmes somehow taken to prove that sexism and racism, Emily Brontë and Auschwitz and Steinem's own romantic dalliance with a politically incorrect millionaire all have to do with lack of 'self-esteem'. But Gloria is so kind to everybody, smiles so sweetly on the cover, has exposed herself as such a well-meaning and vulnerable little thing that it is hard not to be kind to her in return.

What Steinem's writing persona seems just too nice and sweet to understand, however, is that all this be-nice-to-me-I've-had-a-real-self-disclosing-day stuff only works within the context of an unspoken feminist etiquette, and as such is as potentially dishonest, exploitative and even cruel as any other form of discourse. Like the British House of Commons with its Mr Speaker through whom all insulting remarks must be addressed, *Ms.*-type feminist etiquette demands that aggression, irritation, dislike, any feeling that seems a bit unsisterly, be mediated, sublimated, and signalled by diverse highly conventionalised means. The best that can come out of such an overmediated forum is a sentimental wall of sisterliness that uses many words to express very little of much interest or originality. At worst, it is an etiquette open to manipulation, abuse and filibuster in the hands of skilled operators pursuing their own hidden agendas. Women who go to feminist meetings will know exactly what I mean: newcomers ignorant of the etiquette generally spend a long time saying nothing, for fear of exposing themselves as incompetent in the conventions, and so feministically unsound. And by the time they've learned the lingo, they've generally learned how piss-easy it is to use kind and sisterly words to manipulate people, to guilt-trip them, to show them up and put them down.

Which leads us, by circuitous but, as I hope we will see, necessarily so routes, right back to Slavenka Drakulic. Drakulic's novel may be just a mediocre first novel, slightly interesting on what it is like to recover from a life-threatening illness, mostly uninteresting on everything else. But the essays she has collected in *How We Survived Communism and Even Laughed* are a different matter: an almost too rich and fascinating document of what can happen to international-feminist etiquette in the hands of a writer with secret agendas of her own, agendas which, in many cases, the writer herself doesn't appear to recognise.

As Barbara Ehrenreich dutifully points out, ***How We Survived Communism and Even Laughed*** is both 'the first ever grassroots feminist critique of Communism', and 'one of our [sic] first glimpses into real people's lives in pre-revolutionary Eastern Europe'. Both good reasons to take the book very seriously indeed. But Drakulic's book is also, as its British reviewers remarked, easy to dismiss as the outpourings of a sentimental, self-pitying, sanctimonious and self-deceiving woman who thinks that being a feminist allows her carte blanche to write and think as sloppily as she likes. In itself this is probably a fair comment, though one which could just as easily be applied to Gloria Steinem, Robin Morgan or anybody else, including you and me. But what makes Drakulic interesting is that she's a foreigner talking in the language of Western feminism, and so using Western feminist rhetoric with less sleight-of-hand than do Western writers to the manner born. As such, her book is not only about Eastern Europe, but also about how inadequate feminist language is in getting to grips with the awkward realities of our changing world.

How We Survived Communism . . . opens with a manifesto of feminist intent, promising an interest in 'trivia', because 'trivia' is what ordinary women's lives are all about. 'The trivial aspects, the small everyday things, were precisely what I wanted to see: how people ate and dressed and talked, where they lived. Could they buy detergent? Why was there so much rubbish all over the streets?' In theory this all sounds perfectly straightforward, but in practice it isn't. As an East European writing about Eastern Europe for an English-speaking (i.e. primarily US) general interest audience (i.e. one that may not be au fait with the *Granta* school of ex-dissident writing), Drakulic is involved in a delicate intercultural bridging operation This perhaps explains the bogus air that hangs around her book's very title, with its unconvincing invocation of 'we', its soggy emotive use of 'survived' and the upbeat bit about laughter. Drakulic is gamely trying to knee-jerk in time with *Ms.* magazine-type feministical correctness, because this seems to her to be what her readership wants and expects a woman writer to do.

'I wanted to take all these fragments of recent reality, as well as my own memories of life in a Communist country, and sew them back together.' Drakulic makes it easy for herself to sew together whatever she likes, as everything is already part of the same thing anyway. She locates herself and her writing within a strange and slippery historical framework: 'The end of Communism is still remote because Communism, more than a political ideology or method of government, is a state of mind.' Bulgaria, Russia or Slovenia, Catholic, Muslim or Orthodox, state journalist or state rubbish-collector, 1961, 1971, 1991: all cats are just as grey when languishing under a mysterious poison-cloud Communist 'state of mind'. East fuses with West, time fuses with place, subject fuses with object. Though few general-interest Western readers know or care enough about Eastern Europe to want to be bothered with such things as diversity, complexity or change, a neat little package with a handful of simple, grabbing truths in it is the sort of book everybody can buy and linger over. Timothy Garton-Ash has done it several times already, so why shouldn't she?

Warsaw, Sofia, Budapest, Prague, all cities in which women make soup and grumble about their menfolk in their overcrowded apartments, blur into a single East European patchwork of crumbling tower blocks, milkless cafeterias, overdarned stockings and miserable mustn't-grumble stoicism. The acquaintances to whom Drakulic is ostensibly giving voice and to whom she dedicates her book similarly blur into a sort of all-purpose Rentaslavenka figure, darning her thrice darned stockings, dyeing her hair bright red, spending her evenings in hopeless pipe-dreams of how pretty and feminine she could be if only she lived in the West. Presumably Drakulic writes so boringly and depressingly because she herself is bored and depressed by the everyday lifeworld of Eastern Europe. Not that she admits to it. 'For me,' she says, 'these women are the most beautiful in the world because I know what is behind the serious, worried faces, the unattended hair.' This is just a horrible orchestration of phoney emotion. All this slumming it round kitchen tables, all this 'sorrowful talk, as old as the smell of soup', all this we-this and we-that—one little word used so often to cover up huge gaps in sympathy and comprehension—it is all just utterly fake. When Drakulic talks about a girl she knows who jumped the Berlin Wall, about a woman friend who killed herself, about her own mother even, the intimacy feels forced, as though she is showing off about it.

The upshot is that Drakulic's written point of view comes to look very like that adopted by Western travel-writers, the sort who, labouring under the misapprehension that because they have 'travelled' in a country more than mere 'tourists' do, because they have sometimes even stayed in local houses and broken bread, they have become experts in that country's affairs. Foreign outsiders on this sort of trip perhaps can hardly be expected to be other than ignorant, thoughtless and hidebound by their own cultural preoccupations. But why should Drakulic feel she has to imitate them? In a book which professes to be about how material deprivation in Eastern Europe is dealt with from day to day as routine, is it necessary to observe that the jam jars, bottle-tops and so on that people collect knowing that they are bound to come in useful some day are things that 'normal people' throw away? In a world in which material deprivation and insecurity, political repression, even war are experiences known to most countries, what on earth does she mean by 'normal people'?

What Drakulic means, of course, is Westerners, and rich ones at that. And in a way, why shouldn't she? All she is doing is absorbing and reproducing Western media industry assumptions. One gets so used to reading feature-pages which assume that, if you're intelligent enough to read them at all, you must also be a homeowner who finds endless copy about restaurants and school fees interesting, that after a while one forgets to notice how bizarre is this equation of intelligence and curiosity with worldly wealth. But it is bizarre. And it takes a citizen from a poor country attempting to cater for this tacit norm to make you realise how very cruel it is as well. Drakulic's anthropological little adjectives aren't intended to describe or evoke, but to judge. They function as sneaky little signals, dropped into the text to remind us that although the writer may be from this miserable place, she herself is not of it. This isn't the language of any sort of edification, but the language of shame. Drakulic is ashamed of her family, her friends, her country, that they can enter the media paradise of the Western world, a realm which defines handsomeness and intelligence according to wealth, looking ugly and stupid. All she can do in such circumstances is to bracket herself off.

Every time she opens a copy of *Time* or *Newsweek,* she finds herself treated to yet more stories about what a mess her country is in, how it has always been in a mess and how it will always be in a mess, with little interview boxes about how all her countrymen ever dream about is slaughtering Serbs, getting a job in McDonald's or winning an audience with the Pope. And she knows Westerners well enough to know that few of us have enough grip on international affairs ever to question how or why such demeaning rubbish is constructed. It's no wonder that Drakulic comes to writing with the feeling that she has so much to prove.

The most illuminating parts of *How We Survived Communism* . . . are not those that deal with Eastern Europe in itself, but those that see Drakulic dealing with her felt relationship to her readership head-on. Here, for example, is Drakulic on the subject of a certain North American feminist who invites her to contribute a paper to a book she's editing—*Women in Eastern Europe: A Critical Theory Approach*: 'How easy, how incredibly easy it is for her; she even has an editor! . . . I can imagine her, in her worn-out jeans and fashionable T-shirt, with her trimmed black hair, looking younger than she is (aerobics, macrobiotics), sitting at her computer and typing this letter, these very words that sound so absurd that I laugh even more.'

The political climate which gave Drakulic the chance to write a book like *How We Survived Communism* . . . in the first place—the collapse of Communism as a 'system of government' in Eastern Europe, as 'a political ideology' worldwide—are part and parcel of a widespread retreat, in which Western feminism is itself very much involved, away from ideas to do with social collectivity in general. When Vaclav Havel and the other Charter 77 boys wrote their articles about Eastern Europe in the Eighties, it was open to them to mediate their ideas through collectivist concepts like 'civil society', 'popular rapprochement', 'democracy from below'. With Eastern Europe thrown with the rest of the world onto the mercy of the free market, such mediations come to seem irrelevant as everybody scrambles to get and then protect their own private niche. Whatever you ever thought of things like the globally transcendent value of feminist testimony, it is clear that such a concept can have no market currency unless you grab it for yourself. This is why Drakulic's sisterly rhetoric seems even more insincere than sisterly rhetoric has seemed before. All it is really about is Drakulic clinging to her own niche and bleating: 'Me, me, look at me!'

International-sisterhood-type thinking is premised on the conceit that the affinities between all forms of violence and injustice, from consumer capitalism to state socialism, from bottom-scouring toilet paper to fur coats, are simple and obvious and easily commensurable. This is not and has never been the case. And in the great confusion and suffering it manifests, Drakulic's book suggests also that nice kind feminism in its own way is also a medium capable of enacting its own special forms of violence and repression. If Gloria and her merry band really and truly care about the psychic and political fate of their international sisters, they're going to have to give up the gush and puff and acknowledge that sisterhood on its own means virtually nothing.

Amanda Mitchison (review date 29 January 1993)

SOURCE: Mitchison, Amanda. "Into the Dark." *New Statesman and Society* 6, no. 237 (29 January 1993): 47.

[*In the following review, Mitchison lauds* The Balkan Express *for vividly delineating a war's effects on everyday life.*]

Slavenka Drakulic's collection of autobiographical essays about the effect of the Yugoslavian war on everyday life [*Balkan Express: Fragments from the Other Side,*] is named after an excruciating train trip the author took from Vienna to Zagreb. She shares a compartment with two Yugoslavs. No one will speak for fear that their accent will disclose their ethnic origin, no one can take a newspaper out of their bag without revealing their allegiance. Even if the travellers did feel chatty, there is nothing to talk about except the war—an impossible, unacceptable subject for conversation between strangers.

So, as the train bumps along, the three passengers sit, knees jostling, looking out the window mutely. Yet, Drakulic observes, the silence which "verges on a scream" is a "good sign, a sign of our unwillingness to accept the war, our desire to distance ourselves and spare each other, if possible."

From a war that has been so noted for its brutality and horror, this approach may seem unexpectedly mild-mannered, almost drawing-roomish. There are no eyewitness reports of floating corpses in the river, no dens of torture, no barrels of babies' eyes—little of the common currency of war reporting.

Instead, Drakulic chronicles the smaller events which, between April 1991 and May 1992, illustrate the gradual shedding of normal life, the slow slipping into war. She notices that the word "slaughter" now slips off the television anchorman's lips with ease. She sees a gun tucked in the belt of a man at the bus stop. At the grocery store she hears a woman order: 16 kilos of oil, 20 kilos of flour, 20 kilos of sugar, 10 of salt.

Real life is always slightly at a slant for our expectations. When Drakulic opens a magazine and sees a photograph of a couple lying dead on the ground she finds she is fascinated, above all, by the crumpled, yellow packet of yeast by the woman's head. When the first bomb falls near Drakulic's flat in Zagreb, she freezes in her seat, and, overcome with a sense of heaviness, wonders why on earth she has just redecorated the bedroom with Laura Ashley wallpaper.

Just as in Anne Frank's Diary, despite the Holocaust, the teenager is obsessed with family squabbles and homework, Drakulic's attention to seemingly mundane matters accounts for the writing's verisimilitude. But there is also a self-conscious message: "Look, I'm one of you. I have an unexceptional urban, middle-class life—children, newspapers, visits to the cinema, shopping trips, television programmes. Now watch as I become something else . . . Let me show you the changes as the dark pressures of war take over."

Drakulic writes: "The war devours us from the inside, eating away like acid . . . it wrecks our lives . . . it spawns evil within us . . . we tear the living flesh of those friends who do not feel the same as we do . . ." Some of the most moving essays are Drakulic's attempts to explain astonishing acts of treachery: the nice, homeless young journalist who feels justified in informing on a friend in order to be given her apartment; the famous actress who defends the political autonomy of art and finds herself the focus of a hate campaign and is shunned by all her friends.

These cases are reported with the sympathy and understanding of someone who recognises her own complicity, her own tendency to humbug, and who explains how she too is implicated in these acts. In a heartrending letter to her daughter, Drakulic also acknowledges the responsibility of all her generation who saw what was happening in Yugoslavia, and simply buried themselves in their smaller, private concerns until it was too late.

The experience of civil war has been likened to having sex for the first time, or taking drugs. The individual, questioning his or her identity and worth, will never be quite the same again. For the hypersensitive, the entire world seems undermined. Emotions are heightened, skin is thinner, every drip of the bathroom tap or rumble of the central heating can suddenly become unbearably loud.

Inevitably, war also undermines our trust in the power of language, and the writer trying to convey this heightened internal reality must call on enormous powers both of expression and of restraint. That Drakulic accomplishes this balance—her "ice over a treacherous river"—is probably the greatest achievement in this wise, profound and original book.

Bettina Drew (review date 2 May 1993)

SOURCE: Drew, Bettina. "Broken Lives, Deadened Souls: Inside the Disintegrating Balkans." *Chicago Tribune Books* (2 May 1993): 6.

[*In the following review, Drew praises Drakulic's portrayal of the effects of war on the individual in* The Balkan Express.]

These powerful essays [in *The Balkan Express* which are] about the war in the former Yugoslavia . . . should be required reading for . . . anyone concerned about the barbarity being practiced in the Balkans. Pictures of life amid "the most horrible thing a human being can experience," they go beyond the numbing photographs and the political complexities that allow those distant from the conflict to turn the newspaper page.

"A war snaps your life in half," writes Slavenka Drakulic, a Croatian journalist and novelist who recently has reported on the systematic mass rapes and deliberate impregnations of Muslim women in the name of "ethnic cleansing" in Bosnia. "Yet you have to go on living as if you are a whole person. But . . . you are not—and never will be—a whole person again."

The Balkan Express chronicles the approach, arrival and reality of war from the spring of 1991 until May 1992. It is well known that the communist state kept a lid on centuries-old ethnic animosities. But at the same time, it reinforced the Yugoslav tendency to see World War II as heroic and meaningful, worth more than its million victims, and it discouraged citizens from becoming active, self-aware political beings.

When the Yugoslav state crumbled, it left behind no established democratic institutions to resolve conflicts. "Continuing to live with the same kind of totalitarian governments, ideology and yet untransformed minds," Drakulic writes, "it seems the people were unable to shoulder the responsibility for what was coming—or to stop it. War therefore came upon us like some sort of natural calamity, like the plague or a flood, inevitable, our destiny."

In her war-torn land, Drakulic is constantly struck by death in the midst of life: still-wet washing hanging outside a house destroyed by bombs, a roofless house whose exposed bedroom reveals blankets and pillowcases neatly in order, a puppy wandering the charred remains of a village. At a town at the front she is guided by a soldier who must confess to her the precise way in which the war made him a murderer. She listens to her mother's fears that they will tear down her father's gravestone because, though once a communist hero, even a dead member of the Federal Army is an enemy.

As the book progresses, it becomes fiercer, more relentless. In the essay **"If I Had a Son,"** Drakulic interviews a teenage soldier, imagining he is her son, listening to him tell her he will fight not for an ideal but simply because "they're killing my friends. They're killing them like dogs in the street and then dogs eat them because we can't get to them to bury them. How can I sit here and pretend that none of this is my business?"

Drakulic weaves into these essays her own reactions to the disintegration of her country: first, attempts at denial, then efforts to carry on normal routines, then flight to a peaceful village—but once there, church bells bring to mind the smoldering, broken church towers in some 60 villages in Croatia alone. Even Paris offers no escape: "a glimpse of shop window and then instantly a feeling of futility, remoteness, not belonging."

Perhaps most profoundly *The Balkan Express* shows how war erases individuals and reduces all people to a side, a nationality, a group. "Before, I was defined by my education, my job, my ideas, my character—and yes, my nationality too," Drakulic observes. "Now I feel stripped of all that. I am nobody because I am not a person any more. I am one of 4.5 million Croats."

Drakulic's collection of pre-war essays about Eastern Europe, *How We Survived Communism and Even Laughed*, was marked by a guarded optimism and even humor. Those qualities are gone in *The Balkan Express* because the writer herself has changed, and she knows it. Death has not been the worst that could happen in the war but rather "the separation of self from the body, the numbness of the inner being, extinction before death, pain before pain."

Once the idea of "otherness" takes hold, the unspeakable is possible, she painfully discovers when analyzing her anger at her daughter for giving their refugee friend Drazena a pair of high-heeled shoes. "The moment I thought Drazena ought not wear make-up or patent high-heeled shoes was the very moment when I myself pushed her into the group 'refugee'. . . . [T]hat she disappointed me by trying to keep her face together with her make-up and her life together with a pair of shoes, made me aware of my own collaboration with this war."

And so Drakulic comes to understand how Polish villagers near Nazi concentration camps got used to the screams from across the field. We are the war, she believes, for we carry within us the germ of the illness that reduces us to savages.

Buyers should ignore the insensitivity of commercial publishing in placing an attractive picture of Drakulic on the front cover, homage to the belief that a pretty woman can sell not only cars but even war. *The Balkan Express* is about the effects of war on peoples' souls. It is passionate defense of the individual, an important and timely book that deserves the widest possible audience.

Michael Ignatieff (review date 13 May 1993)

SOURCE: Ignatieff, Michael. "The Balkan Tragedy." *New York Review of Books* 90, no. 9 (13 May 1993): 3-5.

[*In the following review, Ignatieff traces the history of the current conflict in the Balkans using several recent works, including Misha Glenny's* The Fall of Yugoslavia, *Branka Magas's* The Destruction of Yugoslavia, *and Drakulic's* The Balkan Express.]

Since the summer of 1991, at least 50,000 people, most of them civilians, have been killed in the former Yugoslavia and at least a million more have been turned into refugees. After two-and-a-half years of fighting, a comprehensible explanation for the carnage still eludes most observers. The outside world's unspoken conviction, as it watches the unfolding savagery, is that all the parties must be, in differing degrees, insane. This belief comes in both simple and complicated forms, ranging from the sweeping finality of "they're all fucked," which I heard from a Canadian UN soldier trying to keep Serbs and Croats apart at an UNPROFOR checkpoint, to visiting journalists' speculation on the irrational strain throughout Balkan history.

The Balkans depicted in Robert Kaplan's recent book, *Balkan Ghosts: A Journey through History*,[1] for example, are a dark zone haunted by ghosts of violence and fanaticism. "Here men have been isolated by poverty and ethnic rivalry," he writes, "dooming them to hate. Here politics has been reduced to a level of near anarchy. . . ." The tone is familiar from better books, notably Rebecca West's *Black Lamb and Grey Falcon* (1941) and John Reed's *The War in Eastern Europe* (1916). The doom-laden approach purports to illuminate the present by delving into the past. In reality, it straightens out the meandering paths of the Balkan past into the more circumscribed tracks of destiny.

Nationalists everywhere turn the historical record into a narrative of self-justification. In the Balkans, the contestants have a particular interest in turning their history into fate, so that the past can then serve to explain away their hatreds. But there is no reason why outside observers should do the same.

Westerners often assert, for example, that the roots of the antagonisms in the Balkans lie in the fact that the Croats are Catholic, European, and Austro-Hungarian in origin, while the Serbs are essentially Orthodox, Byzantine Slav, with an added tinge of Turkish cruelty and indolence. The Sava and Danube rivers, which serve as borders between Croatia and Serbia, once demarcated the boundary between the Austro-Hungarian and Ottoman empires. If this historical fault-line is emphasized often enough, the conflict between Serbs and Croats can be seen as inevitable. Yet it is not how the past dictates to the present, but how the present manipulates the past which seems decisive in the Balkans. The Croats' insistence, for example, that they belong to Europe, because they once belonged to Austria-Hungary, is also a way of saying: we're not those backward Balkan Serbs.

In Croatia, Franjo Tudjman's ruling HDZ Party asserts that it is a Western-style political movement on the model of the Bavarian Christian Democrats. Actually, the Tudjman state resembles Milosevic's regime much more than either resembles a Western European government. They are both one-party states, democratic only in the sense that their leaders ratify their power by manipulating populist emotion.

Freud once argued that the smaller the difference between two people the larger it was bound to loom in their imaginations. This effect, which he called the narcissism of minor difference, is especially visible in the Balkans. An outsider who travels the highway between Zagreb and Belgrade is struck not by the decisive historical fault-line which falls across the lush Slavonian plain but by the opposite. Serbs and Croats speak the same language, give or take a few hundred words, and have shared the same village way of life for centuries. While one is Catholic, the other Orthodox, urbanization and industrialization have reduced the importance of religious differences. As Misha Glenny points out in *The Fall of Yugoslavia,* the war between Serbs and Croats in 1991 was not driven by irreducible historical or ethnic differences. Rather it was ignited by nationalist ideologues who turned the narcissism of minor difference into the monstrous fable that the people on the other side were genocidal killers, while they themselves were blameless victims. What is truly difficult to understand about the Balkan tragedy is how such nationalist lies ever managed to take root in the soil of a shared village existence. No more poignant proof of the intertwining of Croat and Serb ethnic tissue can be found than ethnic cleansing itself. When both sides began cleansing villages in 1991, they often dynamited or shelled every second house. It cannot be repeated too often that these people were neighbors, friends, and spouses, not inhabitants of different ethnic planets. Misha Glenny argues that it was precisely because they were brothers and recognized each other across the barricades that the fighting so often degenerated into atrocity, for example into horrible acts of facial mutilation.

In order for war to occur, nationalists had to convince neighbors and friends that in reality they had been massacring each other since time immemorial. But history has no such lesson to teach. The different sides were kept apart for much of their past in separate empires and kingdoms. The killing began only in 1928 with the assassination of Croat politicians in the Belgrade parliament. This in turn set off the slide into ethnic warfare during World War II. While the present conflict is certainly a continuation of the civil war of 1941-1945, this explains little, for one still has to account for the nearly fifty years of ethnic peace in between. These years were not merely a truce. Even sworn enemies on either side still cannot satisfactorily explain why the peace fell apart.

Moreover, it is a fallacy to regard the current conflict as the product of some uniquely Balkan viciousness. All of the delusions that have turned neighbors into enemies have been imports of Western European origin. Modern Serbian nationalism dates back to a Byronic style of national uprising against the Turks, while the nineteenth-century Croatian nationalist ideologue, Starcevic, derived the idea of an ethnically pure Croatian state indirectly from the German Romantics. The misery of the Balkan people does not derive from their home-grown irrationality, but from the pathetic longing to be good Europeans, that is, to import the West's most murderous ideological fashions. These fashions proved fatal in the Balkans, because the very idea of national self-determination could only be realized by destroying the multiethnic Balkan reality in the name of the violent dream of ethnic purity.

Even genocide is not some ghastly local specialty, but an import from the grand Western European tradition. Ante Pavelic's wartime Ustashe regime, which Serbs mistakenly regard as the true face of Croatian nationalism, couldn't have lasted a day in office without the armed backing of the German fascist regime, not to mention the tacit approval of that eminently European authority, the Catholic Church.

In effect, therefore, the "West" is making excuses for itself when it dismisses the Balkans as a subrational zone of intractable fanaticism; or when it insists that local ethnic hatreds were so rooted in history that their explosion into violence in 1991 was inevitable. On the contrary, the Balkan peoples had to be transformed from neighbors into enemies, just as the whole region had to be turned from a model of interethnic peace into a nightmare from the pages of Thomas Hobbes.

Mention of Hobbes should help to point us toward a more convincing explanation of the catastrophe. For as Hobbes understood, no emotion is more likely to generate ethnic and religious hatred than fear. By 1990, post-Titoist Yugoslavia had become a Hobbesian world, a state of nature in which the means of violence were too widely distributed to afford anyone safety, especially those who found themselves a minority in the successor republics. Interethnic accommodation depended on the existence of multiethnic state. When this disintegrated, society rapidly decomposed into its primary national elements, since these alone appeared to promise the Hobbesian minimum of security.

As Branka Magas, a Croatian historian who lives in London, observes, Tito's achievement was to create a state which accomplished the peaceful national unification of the six major peoples of the region. Multiethnic federalism was the only peaceful way such a unification could have been achieved. For Serbs or Croats to unify their nation would have required the forcible movement of populations, for as much as a quarter of the Croat and Serb populations had always lived outside the borders of their republics. Tito understood this and created an intricate ethnic balance which, among other things, reduced Serbian influence at the heart of the federal system in Belgrade, while promoting Serbs to positions of power in Croatia.

Tito's strategy, built as it was on a personal dictatorship, could not have survived beyond his death in 1980. Even by the early 1970s, his socialist rhetoric of "brotherhood and unity" was falling on deaf ears. In 1974, he compromised with nationalism, allowing the republics greater autonomy in a new constitution. By the end of his reign, however, the League of Communists, instead of counterbalancing the ethnic clientism among elites in the republics, was itself splitting up on ethnic lines.

This fragmentation was inevitable, given Tito's failure to allow the emergence of civic-rather than ethnic-based party competition. Had Tito allowed a citizens' politics in the Sixties or Seventies, a non-ethnic principle of political affiliation might have taken root. But as Milovan Djilas correctly foresaw, the great anti-Stalinist turned out to be a Stalinist in the end. By refusing to allow democracy, Tito only delayed his regime's collapse while guaranteeing that nationalism would be the only available language of political appeal for his successors. Tito always insisted his was a communism with a human face. In the end, his regime was no different from the other Communist autocracies of Eastern Europe. By failing to allow a non-ethnic political culture to mature, Tito insured that the fall of his regime turned into the collapse of the entire state structure. In the ruins, his heirs turned to the most atavistic methods of political mobilization in order to survive.

Ethnic difference itself was not responsible for the nationalist politics that emerged in the 1980s. Consciousness of ethnic difference, as Glenny argues, only turned into nationalist chauvinism when a discredited Communist elite began manipulating nationalist emotions in order to cling to power.

This is worth insisting upon since most outsiders assume that all Balkan peoples are incorrigibly nationalistic. In fact many of them lament the passing of Yugoslavia, precisely because it was a state which allowed them non-nationalistic ways of defining themselves. In a poignant and bitter essay, **"Overcome by Nationhood,"** which she includes in her fine collection ***The Balkan Express,*** Slavenka Drakulic describes what it was like, as an independent Croatian journalist in the late 1980s, to be engulfed by the rising clamor of nationalist rhetoric. Having always defined herself by her education, profession, gender, and personality, she found herself, in the maddened atmosphere of 1991, stripped of all defining marks of identity other than simply being a Croatian. All that mattered in Zagreb was whether one was supporting the nation. What is true of a courageous and independent Croatian intellectual cannot be less true of ordinary villagers. The language of nationalist pride and nationalist grievance only appeared to give voice to their fears and longings. In reality, it ended up imprisoning everyone in the fiction of "pure" ethnic identity.

As Misha Glenny shows, Serbia's Slobodan Milosevic was the first Yugoslav politician to break the Titoist taboo on popular mobilization of ethnic consciousness. With the unscrupulousness of a true demagogue, Milosevic portrayed himself both as the defender of Yugoslavia against the secessionist ambitions of the Croats and Slovenes and as the avenger of the wrongs done to Serbia by that very Yugoslavia.

For Branka Magas, the entire Yugoslav tragedy can be traced back to Milosevic's program, first set out in the 1986 Serbian Academy of Arts and Science Memorandum, to build a greater Serbia on the ruins of Tito's Yugoslavia. If the other republics would not agree to a new Yugoslavia dominated by the Serbs, Milosevic was prepared to incite the Serbian minorities in Kosovo, Croatia, and Bosnia-Herzegovina to rise up and demand Serbian protection. These minorities served as Milosevic's Sudeten Germans, the pretext and justification for his expansionary designs.

It is easy in retrospect to demonize the Serbs and to make it appear as if Milosevic was merely responding to the ethnic paranoia of both his domestic constituency and the Serbia diaspora. The reality is much more complicated. While there were Serbian nationalist extremists, like the Chetniks, still seething with resentment at Tito's campaign against Mihailovic during the Second World War, most urban Serbs in the early 1980s displayed little chauvinist paranoia and even less interest in their distant rural brethren in Knin, Pale, Kosovo, or Western Slavonia.

What needs to be explained, therefore, is why many ordinary Serbs' general indifference to the Serbian question turned into phobic anxiety that the Serbian diaspora was about to be annihilated by genocidal Croatians and fundamentalist Muslims. Magas argues as if Milosevic invented Serbian nationalism to serve his demagogic ends, but Serbian nationalism was not of Milosevic's making. It arose inevitably from the collapse of Tito's Yugoslavia. Once the multiethnic state disintegrated, every nationality outside a republic's borders found itself a national minority. As the largest such group, the Serbs felt particularly vulnerable.

Magas also argues as if the Croatian drive for independence was a protective response to Milosevic's expansionism. Misha Glenny's account rightly views Croatian nationalism as an independent force that bears some responsibility for the descent into tragedy. While both Croatia and Slovenia professed a willingness to live within a loosely federal Yugoslavia, in reality, by the late 1980s, the leaders of both republics were determined on independence. Croatians had a right to an independent state, but as Glenny points out, an independent Croatia aroused genuine fear in the 600,000-strong Serbian minority within its borders.

When Croatia set out on the path to independence in 1990, its new constitution described it as the state of the Croatian nation, with non-Croatians defined as protected minorities. While many Croats sincerely believed they were complying with European norms for the protection of minority rights, Serbs did not regard themselves as a minority but as a nation equal to the Croats. When the Croats revived the Sahovnica, the red and white checkered shield, as their new flag, Serbs took one look and believed the Ustashe had returned. The Sahovnica was both an innocently traditional Croat emblem and also the flag of the wartime regime which had exterminated a very large, if still undetermined, number of Serbs. When Serbs were dismissed from the Croatian police and judiciary in the summer of 1990, the Serbian minority concluded that they were witnessing the return of an ethnic state with a genocidal path.

Defenders of the Croatian position insist that these fears were exaggerated or manipulated by Milosevic. No doubt they were, but in the broader context of the collapse of the multiethnic Yugoslav state, Serbs had good reason to be afraid. (Glenny himself reported in these pages on the massacre of Serbs by right-wing Croats in the town of Gospic in the autumn of 1991).[2] This is the substance of Glenny's case, and while it has made his book unpopular in Zagreb, it is not anti-Croatian. It merely insists on showing, against the background of the general collapse of authority in the region, how each side's paranoia fed upon the other's.

As the BBC's Central European correspondent between 1989 and 1991, Glenny was uniquely placed to observe the disintegration of authority within Croatia's borders. He describes how in town after town the Serbian-Croatian war began with battles for control over the main seat of local power, the police station. In Serb villages like Borovo Selo, near Vukovar in Western Slavonia, the Croatian state dismissed local Serb policemen only to see them resurface as paramilitary vigilantes. When the Croats tried to restore control over Serbian areas, these paramilitary forces resisted and set up roadblocks at the entrance to their villages. With the Croats losing control of the Serbian areas of their state, the Yugoslav national army intervened, at first to restore order and then to smash the Croatian state altogether. Croatia then had no choice but to defend its national existence. It now finds a third of its national territory occupied by the rump state of Serbian Krajina and its supply routes to the Dalmatian coast blockaded by Serbian paramilitaries in Knin. The world's fitful attention is now turned on Bosnia. But the situation in Croatia is untenable and could explode into war at any time.

Glenny completed his book in June 1992, when the Bosnian war was still in its infancy. Yet in the chapter he devotes to Bosnia, he argues convincingly that it is not a separate drama, but a continuation of the primary struggle between Serb and Croat nationalist elites to establish ethnic states in the region. While Serbs have been rightly outlawed by the international community for their attempt to destroy the Bosnian state, the Croats have also been feeding on Bosnia's prostrate corpse. Croatia maintains both paramilitary and regular army units in Bosnia-Herzegovina and even otherwise liberal Croatians insist on their right to dismember the Bosnia-Herzegovina state, in order to guarantee the security of Dalmatia and south-central Croatia. As Misha Glenny recalls, Tudjman actually proposed to Milosevic in 1992 that they divide Bosnia between them. If Tudjman is now assisting Izetbegovic and the Muslims it is not in order to defend Bosnia's territorial integrity but merely to repel their common enemy.

From this it follows that the West may have made a mistake in singling out the Serbs for sanctions. At the least, Croatia should have been condemned, not for defending itself against invasion, but for its subsequent role in the dismembering of Bosnia.

When I talked with Milovan Djilas in Belgrade recently, he argued that the "satanization" of Serbia by the West had not undermined Milosevic or prevented him from aiding the Bosnian Serbs. Instead of blaming his regime for the long gas queues and the inflation, running at 200 percent per month, most Serbs in the streets blame the West. Even if economic chaos were to cause Milosevic to fall, his place might merely be taken by an even more odiously nationalistic demagogue.

Sanctions may be the minimum moral response to Serbian war crimes, but the West cannot suppose that they will be effective in stopping the war. Indeed the so-called "international community" has precious few cards left to play in the Balkans. It will not invade and protect citizens because no political leaders will take the risk. It cannot cut and run since its entire credibility is at stake. It cannot even impose a peace. At best it can only supervise a cease-fire once the disputants are sufficiently exhausted. Even then, peace keepers will have to stand on guard at the checkpoints, not for years but for decades.

The West's central dilemma is what position it should take toward the emerging order of ethnically cleansed micro-states which have taken the place of Yugoslavia.

Ethnic apartheid may be an abomination, but for the more than a million refugees who have fled or been driven from their homes, apartheid is the only guarantee of safety they are prepared to trust. The Vance-Owen plan is much condemned in Washington for appearing to reward the results of Serbian ethnic cleansing. But the innocent civilian victims in the area are indifferent to such scruples. For the West has failed to protect Sarajevo, where Muslim, Croats, and Serbs lived together in peace for centuries. The traumatized victims of this conflict are hardly likely to trickle back to the multiethnic communities they have left behind simply in order to vindicate our liberal principles.

Standing back from the catastrophe, one begins to see, with the help of Misha Glenny's fine book, that Western failures of policy were caused by something deeper than inattention, misinformation, or misguided good intentions. The very principles behind our policies were in contradiction. In the light-headed euphoria of 1989 our political leaders announced their support for the principle of national self-determination and for maintaining the territorial integrity of existing states, without realizing that the first principle contradicted the second. We insisted on the inviolability of frontiers, without making clear whether we also meant the frontiers between the republics within federal states like Yugoslavia. Most of all, we allowed guilt over our imperial past to lead us to evade our responsibilities for defining the terms of the postimperial peace. The Western Europeans and the US could have ended the cold war with a comprehensive territorial settlement in Eastern Europe, defining new borders, establishing guarantees of minority rights, and adjudicating between rival claims to self-determination. After Versailles, after Yalta, the collapse of the final empire in Europe gave us a third opportunity to define a durable peace for the whole continent. Yet so concerned were we to avoid playing the imperial policeman, so self-absorbed were we in the frantic late Eighties boom, that we let every local post-Communist demagogue exploit the rhetoric of self-determination and national rights to their own nefarious ends. The terrible new order of ethnically cleansed states in the former Yugoslavia is the monument to our follies as much as it is to theirs.

Notes

1. St. Martin's Press, 1993.
2. See *The New York Review*, January 30, 1992.

Anthony Borden (review date 17 May 1993)

SOURCE: Borden, Anthony. "'We are the War.'" *Nation* 256, no. 19 (17 May 1993): 672-74.

[*In the following review, Borden asserts that Drakulic's focus on the individual in* The Balkan Express *is important to understanding the war in that region.*]

A month into the shelling of Sarajevo, I interviewed a law professor at the university there. In retrospect it was a relatively hopeful period, before the worst atrocities occurred and the territory of Bosnia and Herzegovina was divided. It seemed terribly urgent then to talk about measures the international community could undertake, and the professor had several important proposals. Speaking by telephone from a safe place beneath a staircase, however, he emphasized how inappropriate and even hypocritical it was to discuss "high politics" at such a time.

The remark confused me. If "high politics" meant what the world could do to halt the nightmare, I had to disagree, and I dutifully plodded on in search of big answers to the big questions. A year later, however, with Sarajevo still besieged and a hitherto unimaginable range of atrocities well known, I now understand. For international politics—indeed the whole official peace process itself—is conducted on a rarefied level, with little necessary connection to or even impact on the events on the ground. It is all too easy to debate the power politics of Washington, Whitehall and the warlords in the Balkans while having scant idea of the lives of the people we profess to be concerned about.

The best corrective to this trap is the writing of journalist Slavenka Drakulić, in *The Balkan Express*, a new collection of articles about the war. Through short but deeply felt essays on everything from house paint and high-heeled shoes to point-blank murder, Drakulić tells the story of the Balkan crisis as people are living it. This is firsthand war reporting without body counts or strategic analyses; in-depth political commentary without the statements of presidents or the opinions of self-appointed experts. Drakulić focuses on individual lives (often her own or those of her family), using the perversions that war forces onto everyday life to reveal the true complexity of the crisis and the enormity of the task of reconciliation.

Drakulić's central theme, as she explains in an excellent new introduction to last year's *How We Survived Communism and Even Laughed* (her collection that includes several pieces originally published in *The Nation*), is the "special kind of loneliness which enters your soul in the middle of war." This emptiness breeds fear, and this fear brings the defensive mechanism of categorizing people into "us" and "the other." That dehumanizing step, in essence the identity politics of nationalism, is the real horror—after which, Drakulić explains, many cruelties become inevitable. It is then only a matter of degree from being rude to an old friend who has become a refugee to dropping a bomb into a basement where several of your enemies are cowering.

In the extraordinary title essay in *Balkan Express*, Drakulić describes a train ride from Vienna to Zagreb as a kind of nonstop journey into nightmare. Only a few years ago the trip would have been convivial, with passengers chatting in a friendly way, perhaps about their shopping, while passing through a broad space called Yugoslavia. Now the war is an inescapable "brand" on ex-Yugoslavs of all nationalities. In Vienna they feel uncomfortable. In the compartment on the train, all are terrified to speak, knowing the merest phrase will identify their "ethnic side." "In that moment the madness we are traveling towards might become so alive among us that we wouldn't be able perhaps to hold it back," she fears.

But suffering in welcome silence is not protection enough, as Drakulić comes across an article in the Belgrade daily *Borba* alleging a hideous war-time atrocity. "Report[ing] bestialities as the most ordinary facts," she writes, "gruesome pictures are giving birth to a gruesome reality; a man who, as he reads a newspaper, forms in his mind a picture of the testicles being drawn up from the well will be prepared to do the same tomorrow, closing the circle of death."

Contradicting the stereotype of hysterical Balkans intent on slaughtering one another, Drakulić describes hesitant killers, reluctant nationalists. One explanation is that she writes from Croatia during the defensive period; there is a notable lack of coverage of the treatment of Serb minorities in Croatia or of Croatian expansionism in Bosnia and, perhaps unavoidably, no writing about the situation for Serbs in Serbia. The pieces, with some very notable exceptions, are mainly about journalist colleagues, actors and other professionals; about herself, her mother and daughter; and about the looming presence of her late father, a former Partisan and army general.

But Drakulić's achievement is in describing the trickle-down effect of ethnic homogenization, showing how even the very liberal and highly educated elite cannot avoid the pull of nationalism. Sometimes the pressures are fairly obvious. In December, the leading Zagreb weekly *Globus* attacked Drakulić and four other writers as feminists, Marxists, Communists and, worst of all, Yugoslavs—in short, not adequately Croat. As Drakulić writes in a widely quoted piece:

> The war is . . . reducing us to one dimension. . . . Before, I was defined by my education, my job, my ideas, my character—and yes, my nationality, too—now I feel stripped of all that. I am nobody because I am not a person anymore. I am one of 4.5 million Croats. . . . The ideology of nationhood . . . has . . . been turned into something like an ill-fitting shirt. . . . You might not like [it]. . . . But . . . there is nothing else to wear. . . . And . . . perhaps it would be morally unjust to tear off the shirt of the suffering nation—with tens of thousands of people being shot, slaughtered and burned just because of their nationality. . . . Before this war started, there was perhaps a chance for Croats to be persons and citizens first, then afterwards Croats. . . . The last twelve months have taken away that possibility.

Drakulić does not try to provide the big answer; nor does she sound the by-now familiar (and well justified) alarms of a wider Balkan war. Instead she cautions that the deeper changes experienced by those in the region could infect the rest of Europe. "I don't know what the war is," she concludes,

> but I can see that it is everywhere. It is in a street flooded with blood . . . in Sarajevo. It is also in [our] not understanding it, in my unconscious cruelty towards [a refugee friend], . . . in the way it is growing within us and changing our emotions, our relations, our values. We are the war; we carry in us the possibility of the mortal illness that is slowly reducing us to what we never thought possible and I am afraid there is no one else to blame. We all make it possible, we allow it to happen.

War forces you to take sides, and if you don't oppose it, by design or default you are taking part in it.

Jerry Kisslinger (review date 14 June 1993)

SOURCE: Kisslinger, Jerry. "Portraits of Europe's Powder Keg." *New Leader* 76, no. 8 (14 June 1993): 17-19.

[*In the following review, Kisslinger compares and contrasts* The Balkan Express *to Robert D. Kaplan's* Balkan Ghosts.]

"Violence was, indeed, all I knew of the Balkans," Rebecca West wrote in *Black Lamb and Grey Falcon,* describing the stereotypes she held before ever visiting Yugoslavia. A half century later not much has changed. Western images of blood feuds, bombs and pistols in the waist find new confirmation in Croatia and Bosnia. We connect besieged Sarajevo with the assassination of Archduke Ferdinand in 1914, not the Olympics of 1984; hearing the name "Macedonia," we jump decades to the Balkan Wars or millennia to the conquests of Alexander. It is not hard to understand why, since except for a few folklorists and tourists, we have generally ignored this spectacularly complex region when it was at peace: The powder keg of Europe has only mattered when it exploded.

A small number of books have come out in response to the current tragedy in the Balkans. Misha Glenny's *The Fall of Yugoslavia* and Alex N. Dragnich's *Serbs and Croats* dealt with the political and historical background to the conflict. Now two journalists have published personal accounts of events in the region, one as an observer, the other as an insider.

In *Balkan Ghosts* Robert D. Kaplan, an American who has also written on the Middle East and Afghanistan, shares experiences gathered over a decade of reporting for the *Atlantic* and the *New Republic*. On its most ingenuous level, this is a Balkan travel book warmed by plum brandy and the author's self-described obsession with his subject. He moves us south from one end of the Balkans to the other, from Austria to the Asian aridity of Thrace. We stop at a rioting soccer stadium in Kosovo, on the flats of the Danube delta, in the smoke-coated intimacy of a Bulgarian journalists' club, and in the heady darkness of a Serbian monastery. We meet nuns, prostitutes, painters, priests, martyrs, opportunists, and alcoholics.

Kaplan vividly conveys both the unfamiliar landscape—the polluted Romanian countryside looks "as though someone had taken a billowing, yellow-green Oriental carpet and poured tar all over it"—and subtle ironies he encounters. In Transylvania, for instance, he finds a "coffee-house culture, even though there had been no coffee for many years." He reports as well on the forgotten back alleys of culture—on Saxons in Transylvania, Greeks in Albania, Turks in Bulgaria—giving voice to ethnic minorities deposited, like glacial moraine, by the retreat of empires.

But Kaplan's more ambitious subject is his impressionistic take on Balkan history. "The Balkans are a region of pure memory," he has written elsewhere, "a Bosch-like tapestry of interlocking ethnic rivalries where medieval and modern history thread into each other." Here he unweaves the basic strands of that tapestry: the trauma of Ottoman rule, the memories of medieval greatness that inspire revanchist ambitions in so many countries, the open wounds of World War II, and Communism's role in deep-freezing development. Above all, however, he presents an anecdotal cavalcade of larger-than-life characters, including Romania's Queen Marie and King Carol II, Serbia's St. Sava, the Macedonian rebel Gotse Delchev, Count Dracula, the Croatian Cardinal Stepinac, the Fascist Ion Antonescu, and Nicolae Ceausescu. These apparitions are the ghosts of the title, more foreground than background.

In sketching Balkan history, Kaplan goes heavy on Bosch strokes. "What does the earth look like in the places where people commit atrocities?" he asks, as if any place on earth were truly innocent. Mixed throughout his account are stories from the particularly brutal Balkan past—the excesses of the Ottomans, the violence of the Serbs and Albanians in Kosovo, and the horrors of World War II from the genocidal Croatian Ustashe state to the demise of Jewish Salonika to the rabidity of Romanian anti-Semitism in Bessarabia. The nadir of inhumanity is probably the 1941 pogrom of the *abator*, the slaughter-house where hundreds of Bucharest Jews were put through the stages of animal slaughter by Romanian Fascists.

As he extrapolates from these tales, Kaplan paints with a broad brush. For all his insightful interpretations along the way (such as his debunking the various myths about Greece, promoted by travel agents and classicists alike), he is too ready to portray the Balkans as a historical cauldron awash in gore, illicit sex and Eastern Orthodox incense—the haunted house of a violently dysfunctional family. One wishes for a less idiosyncratic sampling of Balkan figures. The author would similarly have been wise to avoid statements on "national character" and other sweeping generalizations about what he unblushingly calls "a time-capsule world: a dim stage upon which people raged, spilled blood, experienced vision and ecstasies."

When Kaplan refers to "the East" as a realm of "darkness, mystery, sadness, and irrationality," his orientalizing provokes us to ask whether the "enlightened" West—the home of Wounded Knee, the Hundred Years' War, the Spanish Inquisition, and Nazism—doesn't have *abators* of its own. The unusual cruelty of Balkan history may indeed help explain the current violence, but do these nations, however tangled their past at the border zone of continents and empires, really inhabit a different moral and historical universe? Kaplan is so anxious to prove they do that he even blames Nazism on Balkan thinking: It was in Vienna, "a breeding ground of ethnic resentments close to the Slavic World, that Hitler learned how to hate so infectiously."

An uncritical acceptance of other voices is equally distorting. Kaplan quotes without comment this characterization of the Balkans by the late New York *Times* correspondent C. L. Sulzberger: "It is, or was, a gay peninsula filled with sprightly people who ate peppered foods, drank strong liquors, wore flamboyant clothes, loved and murdered easily, and had a splendid talent for starting wars." Even Rebecca West, whose 1,200-page masterpiece on Yugoslavia is Kaplan's greatest inspiration, may have encouraged him to shoot from the hip on matters of national character. Almost every page of *Black Lamb and Grey Falcon* contains the kind of cultural generalizations that we can indulge in a British novelist of the 1930s but must read as absurdly patronizing in a reporter of the 1990s. Its over-reliance on earlier Western images of the Balkans, from Bram Stoker's *Dracula* to the film *Never on Sunday*, renders *Balkan Ghosts* unnecessarily derivative.

Dazzled by the nationalist and religious passions he has come upon, Kaplan embraces a view of politics in which ethnicity is all. This severely limits his treatment of the current conflicts. We get only the fuzziest sense of other factors, such as the manipulation of nationalism by leaders in both Belgrade and Zagreb, or the economic and political malaise that fueled ethnic tensions in the former Yugoslavia. Absent completely are the roles played by the West's early recognition of

Croatia and Slovenia, the inequitable arms embargo, and the world community's failure to face down aggression. Kaplan takes pains to "heartily condemn" the present violence, yet his lurid account makes it seem normal, if not inevitable. From Belgrade to Zagreb to Washington, those with an interest in fatalistically ascribing the war to "ancient hatreds" can read this book, nod their heads and pretend it simply had to happen.

Anyone comforted by that kind of demonization will have a harder time with **The Balkan Express** by the Croatian Slavenka Drakulić, who writes in an undeniably human first-person voice. She reminds us that "War is not a single act," it is "a head-spinning spiral of events and a gradual process of realization." The 18 beautiful and painful narratives in this slim collection trace her personal descent into the fighting in Croatia.

Drakulić's journey begins in April 1991, here in our world, where she has long been known as a contributor to the *Nation* and author of several books. Over Waldorf salad at the Harvard Club, she tries to explain the gathering storm to well-meaning friends. Her vain attempt to lay out alliances and territories on a napkin is a poignant symbol of the difficulty of clueing in Westerners.

Through the book's understated accounts, we watch her return to Zagreb and pass milestones of realization and denial, from her first glimpse of death in a newspaper photo, to her mother's advice, remembered across 50 years, on shopping in wartime ("Get salt!"), to her 20-year-old daughter's flight from the country. She learns the ache and shame of the refugee as she herself flees to Ljubljana, Vienna and Paris. And we see her draw close to the combat, visiting the front and meeting an adolescent who has learned to kill like a machine.

War erupts suddenly in these stories, forcing us to confront the normalcy of the life it destroys. When Drakulić's fork hangs in midair during the first air raids in Zagreb, some readers will be more surprised by the Cabernet and *pasta al bianco* on the table than by the bombs falling from above. Even in describing war photos she fixes on the recognizable remnants: the package of yeast next to a bloodied corpse, the clean wash still hanging next to an annihilated house. For this successful member of a post war generation raised on Titoist slogans of "Brotherhood and Unity," atrocities are anything but commonplace; again and again she articulates a shuddering horror at "the deep crimson hue of gore" imbuing her homeland, at the nationalistic furies that have been unleashed.

The war soon brings more complex troubles. "Death becomes a simple, acceptable fact," she writes, "but life turns to hell." In what may be her most touching essay, **"A Letter to My Daughter,"** Drakulić blames her own generation for failing to protect its sons and daughters from today's agony. In another, she discusses how the nationalism of the war creates ethical quandaries and intolerable demands for conformity; despite her skepticism, internal and external pressures move Drakulić reluctantly toward the kind of ethnically defined politics Kaplan takes for granted. She writes sympathetically of a Croatian actress whose insistence on performing in the Serbian capital leads to exile, and of a cosmopolitan professor whose protests against the "narrowing of human horizons that the war and nationalism have brought" makes her a pariah.

Above all, these essays convey a sense of violation. Drakulić describes a photo of a house that had its roof blown off. "The picture of this bedroom with two neat beds, helpless and exposed," she tells us, "looked like a picture of my own life: the perversity of war stripping away all intimacy." Thus bared, she probes the meaning of war in the minutiae of her personal life, in her own behavior as a daughter, friend, mother, and citizen.

In the title essay, she and two other passengers share a compartment on a train returning from Vienna to Zagreb. No one speaks because, she explains later, "speech implies categories, assumptions, meanings, understandings and misunderstandings," and may reveal them to be enemies. In **Balkan Express** she bravely breaks that silence. "In spite of everything," she writes in the Preface to this sad book, "I still believe in the power of words, in the necessity of communication." That faith alone is enough to challenge our assumptions, and to stir our compassion.

Andrea Ashworth (review date 30 July 1993)

SOURCE: Ashworth, Andrea. "Realm of the Senses." *Times Literary Supplement*, no. 4713 (30 July 1993): 20.

[*In the following review, Ashworth examines the themes, content, and style of* Marble Skin.]

Slavenka Drakulič is a mapper of fraught and forbidden territories. Having chronicled the recent Eastern European crises in her essay collections, **Balkan Express** and **How We Survived Communism and Even Laughed,** the Croatian writer has turned to fiction to explore the more intimate terrain of the female body. Her second novel, **Marble Skin,** marks her courageous foray into the literary no-man's-land of the sexual mother, a compelling figure of desire rather than maternal love. Crossing the frontiers of taboo, Drakulič plunges into the heart of incestuousness to expose the female psyche in its darkest and most fleshy aspects.

At the centre of the drama lies the marble mother, carved in erotic self-absorption and exposed to the gaze and the sticky fingers of the public. It is a labour of love and hatred, sculpted by a daughter desperate both to reach her elusive mother and to escape the tyranny of her perfect beauty by trapping it in marble. The real mother sees the sculpture and, recognizing the years of sexual conflict and stifled communication etched in its contours, tries to kill herself. With the force of her chisel, the daughter has broken through the marble skin to touch her mother and to wrench out a retribution for the incest and rape she once endured at the hands of her mother's husband.

First published in Yugoslavia in 1989, the book's scandalous subject-matter earned it an explosive reception. More provocative than the literal incest, however, is the shocking incestuousness of the writing, which melts the fine line between pleasure and pain, love and disgust, to reveal their disturbing closeness. The daughter is at once violent and tender in her yearning for the mother she finally kills in art. Whether caressing or lacerating, her obsessive desire is to touch, to immerse herself in her mother and her own emerging sexuality. Her thirst for female intimacy is satisfied only fleetingly in the rare and intoxicating moments when her mother brushes her hair or bathes her for the last time, before the faceless stepfather comes between them. For the most part, the mother remains distant and "terrifying in her absence", while the daughter gropes for impossible closeness through her mother's clothes, gestures, and even her husband. Pursuing her beneath the sheets, under her skin, and through her pores to her mucous membranes, the narrative takes us inside the mother and probes her most intimate thoughts and sensations.

While this visceral voyeurism offers tender insights (tasting inside the mouth or kissing the downy hairs behind the ear), it can also be suffocating. The narrative is relentless and penetrating, to the point of violating the mother: "she didn't know how to defend herself against the violence of a child's hands, rending her intimacy". The obsessive focus also robs her of her personality. It reduces both the mother and the other characters to glimpses of fragmentary detail, so that we are left sharing the daughter's frustration that "I honestly don't feel I have ever seen her closely, in her uniqueness. I have only seen gestures, curves, elements."

Though disturbing, the pervasive facelessness of *Marble Skin* imbues the novel with its overwhelming atmosphere of elusiveness and thirst. Whirling through dizzying shifts in perspective, the narrating "I" delves under the skins of the mother, the daughter and the stepfather to merge boundaries and identities in a "maelstrom of desire". Added to the abrupt leaps of tenses, this technique is at times more disconcerting than seductive. Eroticism is also undermined when sheer, fluid description is choked by the self-conscious explanation of the sculptor-narrator. The significance of the marble skin is too often driven home with a chisel-like "cold precision". Wielding more subtlety than force, however, Drakulič insinuates us into a heady realm of sensuous and sensual perception that blends touch, look, taste and smell. Searching the recesses of female sexuality, *Marble Skin* uncovers a breathtaking, subcutaneous world of knowing that is compelling if claustrophobic.

Susan P. Willens (review date fall 1993)

SOURCE: Willens, Susan P. Review of *The Balkan Express,* by Slavenka Drakulic. *Belles Lettres* 9, no. 1 (fall 1993): 59-60.

[*In the following review, Willens praises Drakulic's combination of narrative and journalism to describe the war in* The Balkan Express.]

Croat and Serb, Zagreb and Belgrade, Milosovic and Tudjman—newspapers and TV bombard us with new names as the former Yugoslavia collapses in gunfire and blood. ***The Balkan Express,*** by Slavenka Drakulic explains how this latest war in Europe feels from the inside, how it eats away the inner life: "The war is like a monster . . . it grabs you by the throat . . . overtakes the inner self until one can scarcely recognize oneself any longer." These 18 personal essays dramatize that terrible transformation.

At first, when the war begins to take shape, Drakulic comments philosophically about why her country has gone mad: "This society never had a proper chance to become a society not of oppressed peoples, but of citizens, of self-aware individuals with developed democratic institutions within which to work out differences, conflicts and changes, instead of by war. . . . War therefore came upon us like some sort of natural calamity, like a plague or a flood, inevitable, our destiny."

War brings the terrifying division between Serb and Croat, neighbor and neighbor, husband and wife. Demagogues fuel the hatreds. Unforgivable bombings, sieges, rapes force everyone to choose sides. Later, Drakulic notes the war mentality: her neighbors hoard, her daughter leaves for Canada with a stuffed animal from childhood in her suitcase, bombs begin to fall.

Still later in its awful progress, the war destroys sanity. Oppositions congeal; anyone who questions them is a traitor. The essay **"An Actress Who Lost Her Homeland"** traces the exile of one celebrity who refuses to accept the conflict. Finally come the refugees who need care when the war has exhausted those who should give it: "We are the war; we carry in us the mortal illness that is slowly reducing us to what we never thought possible."

By offering us her personal account of the Balkan war, Drakulic drops conventional journalism for a more appropriate form, half story and half essay. She keeps her journalist's eye trained on telling details, however: a refugee longs for frivolous high-heeled shoes, the Croatian president snubs a group of protesters, a church clock topples from its bombed tower, a teenage soldier becomes a practiced killer. She also records as honestly as possible the changes in her own feelings as the mythical monster of war enters and deforms her inner being.

Slavenka Drakulic, William Phillips, and others (interview date winter 1994)

SOURCE: Drakulic, Slavenka, William Phillips, and others. "Bosnia: Guilt by Dissociation? A Discussion with Slavenka Drakulic." *Partisan Review* 61, no. 1 (winter 1994): 60-79.

[*In the following interview, Drakulic discusses the political situation in the former Yugoslavia and possible solutions to the conflicts in the region.*]

[*Phillips*]: *I'm William Phillips, Editor of* Partisan Review. *We're glad to have with us tonight Slavenka Drakulic, one of the famous "five witches," the group of Croatian women writers recently denounced in a nationalist Croatian weekly for their dissident views. I want to introduce Edith Kurzweil, Executive Editor of* Partisan Review, *who will moderate the discussion and the questions after the talk.*

[*Kurzweil*]: *Many of you met Slavenka last year at our conference in Newark* ["*Intellectuals and Social Change in Central and Eastern Europe,*" Partisan Review *Fall 1992*] *and afterwards here in New York. In the meantime she has written yet another wonderful book, called* **The Balkan Express.**

[Drakulic]: I'm very happy to be here with you. I arrived just two days ago from Zagreb. As you know, there is a war only in some parts of Croatia, such as Dalmatia to the south, so I'm not exactly coming from the war zone, but I'm close enough; Zagreb is only about thirty miles from the war zone. I have chosen to tell you a story tonight which has to do with responsibility, one of the things we should talk more about. This story, the last one in **Balkan Express,** is called **"High-heeled Shoes."** It is a very personal and painful experience about how I myself became an accomplice of the war. You know, it's not enough to see only what's happening to other people; at some point I realized I had to look into the mirror and see what had happened to me and see how much I have been changed by what has been going on around me. I believe that if we look away from the war, believing it is only the politicians and the military power and the nations or the states who are responsible for it, then we are delegating our citizens' human and personal responsibility. It is this refusal to become engaged on an individual level that has allowed the war to go on. I think that each of us has to look into the mirror.

This story is about a friend of mine, a journalist, who left Sarajevo a year ago. When it was still possible to leave Sarajevo by normal means of transportation, she came to Zagreb with only a suitcase and her six-year-old daughter, And she brought clothes only for her daughter because she had planned to leave her with friends and go back herself to Sarajevo in a week. While in Zagreb, she saw on television footage showing that her house had been burned down; she couldn't go back there, because there was no longer a place to go back to. She asked for our help, and because she was a long-time friend everyone helped get her an apartment, gave her some money, assist with the child, get her clothes. One day she came to my house, because my daughter was to give her some clothes, and among the things she gave her were a pair of high-heeled shoes, black patent leather shoes that ladies wear to parties, very fashionable shoes. The moment I saw my daughter give her the high-heeled shoes, I said to her, "Why did you give her high-heeled shoes? She doesn't need them, she's a refugee." My daughter's reaction was very strong. She said, "Mother, just because she's a refugee doesn't mean that she needs to go out barefoot. She needs somehow to confirm her identity, and this is a good thing, to give her high-heeled shoes." Of course I became puzzled by my own reaction, and started to think about it, and this is where my, what shall I call it, vivisection began. I think that it has much to do with the projection of this war, with the media, with the prejudices, with the symbolic level of the war, and perhaps with what I call the image of this war. Of course all of you have seen these photos and images on television, all these peasants' faces, people poorly dressed, especially refugees, and women covered with scars, their peasant faces, their hands, the way they dress.

Here I will digress from the story and show you several photos, so that you can understand better what I am talking about when I say "the image of this war." Some of the photos are quite shocking, but I think that by now we all have become immune to them. This is precisely the problem I would like to address. The first photo is from a magazine cover page that was printed last year. The war in Croatia was more or less over, and the war in Bosnia already well on its way. It is a picture that somehow escaped my attention then, but later on I wrote another story entitled **"Three Little Hens,"** based on it. It's a picture of a dead man who is lying on the floor: his skull is open and there are three hens picking at his brain. This is a pretty dramatic photo, but we have seen even more dramatic ones, especially on television.

The second one appeared just a couple of weeks ago all over the world press. This is a blown-up picture of a woman who is hugging a skull. This third picture too is very meaningful for me. It's a cover of a slick, cultural, very highbrow magazine, which devoted a whole issue to the Balkans. One the cover they put a plain picture of two men and one woman. The woman has a dramatic expression of pain on her face, but you can't say which nationality any of them are or where it was taken. Are they Kurds, are they Serbs, are they Azerbaijanis? You can say only that they are peasants. Now you wonder why, after two years of war, the editors decided to put this picture on the cover of the Balkan issue. It's not depicting any kind of trauma, it's not of someone being beheaded or any such thing. It's just very revealing: it is how the world sees "the Balkans." The message is, "It is the peasants who are doing all this, you know." The problem is that since the very beginning, these kinds of pictures took over. The pictures clearly suggest cruelty, atrocities, savages, tribes, peasants, centuries-old hatreds; particular, complicated, strange. When I saw this cover page I said, "But this is not me, I don't belong to this, I don't identify with these people. I am urban, I have been living in a city all my life, I don't have anything to do with the peasants. Some other picture represents us, which other people, the people from the West, could identify with."

The photo in fact reinforces the underlying gap which has widened in spite of the Berlin Wall going down, in spite of Communism collapsing: East-West, developed-underdeveloped, city dwellers-peasants, civilization-savages. Of course the first reaction to these dramatic images a year ago, of concentration camps and dead bodies, was shock. This is one of the wars that has been covered the most-by the media; everything has happened in front of the television cameras. We have seen it all—every single atrocity. Saturation set in and became estrangement. For the West, it became less and less possible to find points of identification. Who are these savage and cruel people? What do they have in common with us? What do we have in common with them, when they are so obviously different? On the symbolic level, it was difficult to remove the barrier of "otherness." We, the civilized ones, can't understand what is going on there. Why all that killing? I think that all the pain and the suffering is somehow overshadowed by the images of cruelty and primitivism, sending a strong message and forming prejudices on the other side of the still-existing Berlin Wall. I'm purposely not talking about politics here, but rather about how political decisions were supported by the created images of the war, and by the problems of identification.

If we see the fighting nations are "different" and "special" and "violent," qualities which we very often would like to attribute for example to the Serbs, saying that they are genocidally evil—in other words, "different"—then the consequence is that no one is responsible for what is happening and for stopping the killings. Because if it is somehow built into this nation, then how could you possibly be expected to do anything about that? In short, the construction of the "otherness" is helping to create the indifference, the tolerance of massacres, ethnic cleansing, the repetition of history. By now, we should have learned one lesson about this war. It has the power to change the destiny of the Continent. Not because it could explode out of the borders of ex-Yugoslavia, but because the rules and principles for dealing with similar situations in Eastern Europe and the ex-USSR are being set right there and right now, and if we don't understand this, we don't understand anything about the ongoing war in the Balkans. No one can wash his hands of this war, no one can claim, "I don't know." There is no excuse for a single European state or nation, or even one person, to do nothing, to in fact become an accomplice to this war, and to the uncertain destabilized future of Europe.

Now let me go back to the story **"High-heeled Shoes."** As I said, I was quite puzzled by my own reaction, and then I started to think. I concluded that I somehow subconsciously and automatically put my friend into another category, into the category of "refugees." And I rejected my own responsibility. I delegated my own responsibility for a human being, for a friend of mine. I put her in an abstract category, and I delegated this responsibility to the Red Cross, to the State, to the Church, to the military; in other words, to the institutions. And in that way I think I betrayed my own friend. And what I recognized in myself is the process of creating "otherness," and I was very much frightened by it. I will read you the end of the story, because it's very difficult for me to *tell* you:

> Perhaps what I am also witnessing is a mechanism of self-defence as if there were a limit to how much brutality, pain or suffering one is able to take on board and feel responsible for. Over and above this, we are often confronted with more or less abstract entities, numbers, groups, categories of people, facts—but not names, not faces. To deal with pain on such a scale is in a way much easier than to deal with individuals. With a person you know you have to do something, act, give food, shelter, money, take care. On the other hand, one person could certainly not be expected to take care of a whole mass of people. For them, there has to be someone else: the state, Church, the Red Cross, Caritas, an institution. The moment one delegates personal

responsibility to the institution, the war becomes more normal, orderly, and therefore more bearable. The person not only relieves himself or herself of responsibility, but also of a feeling of guilt too; the problem is still there, but it is no longer mine. Yes, of course I'll pay the extra war-tax, I'll gladly give away clothing or food to Caritas or any responsible organization, instead of to the suspicious-looking individuals ringing the doorbell claiming that they are refugees. Because what if they are not real refugees—your help might get into the "wrong" hands and you'll never earn that place in heaven that you'd promised yourself at the outset. The moment I thought Drazena ought not wear make-up or patent high-heeled shoes was the very moment when I myself put her into the group "refugee," because it was easier for me. But the fact that she didn't fit the cliché, that she disappointed me by trying to keep her face together with her make-up and her life together with a pair of shoes, made me aware of my own collaboration with this war.

Now I think I understand what I couldn't understand before: how it happened that people who lived near German concentration camps didn't do anything, didn't help. In Claude Lanzmann's long documentary on the Holocaust, *Shoah*, there is a dialogue with one of the survivors from Chelmno, the place in Poland where Jews were first exterminated by gas, 400,000 of them.

"It was always this peaceful here. Always. Even when they were burning 2000 people—Jews—every day, it was just as peaceful. No one protested. Everyone went about his work. It was silent. Peaceful. Just as it is now," he said. . . .

I don't think our responsibility is the same—and I am not trying to equate the victims with those who murdered them in cold blood—all I'm saying is that it exists, this complicity: that out of opportunism and fear we are all becoming collaborators or accomplices in the perpetuation of war. For by closing our eyes, by continuing our shopping, by working our land, by pretending that nothing is happening, by thinking it is not our problem, we are betraying those "others"—and I don't know if there is a way out of it. What we fail to realize is that by such divisions we deceive ourselves too, exposing ourselves to the same possibility of becoming the "others" in a different situation.

The last time I saw Drazena she told me she was okay. She's staying in a friend's apartment until the autumn and freelancing for a local newspaper. Afterwards she will manage to find something else. She also told me that she is writing a war diary since that is the only way she can attempt to understand what is happening to her. "And what I find the most difficult to comprehend is the fact that there is a war going on," she said. "I still don't understand it. It's not that I expect a miracle to end this nightmare immediately. No, no. I mean, it is just hard for me to grasp that what is going on is the war. Do you know what a war is?" she asked, but I could tell from her look that she didn't really expect an answer.

. . . We are the war; we carry in us the possibility of the mortal illness that is slowly reducing us to what we never thought possible and I am afraid there is no one else to blame. We all make it possible, we allow it to happen. Our defense is weak, as is our consciousness of it. There are no them and us, there are no grand categories, abstract numbers, black and white truths, simple facts. There is only us—and, yes, we are responsible for each other.

And I also wanted to tell Drazena that she should go out and dance in her high-heeled shoes, if only she could.

Thank you.

Thank you very much, Slavenka. Who would like to start asking questions?

[*Deborah Solomon*]: *An obvious question is, what do you think the United States should do about the situation?*

[Drakulic]: The question is not so obvious. I'm not a politician, I'm a writer. But there are no simple answers. I can give you only my personal opinion. I think the United States shouldn't do anything on its own. If there is anything to be done, it should be done together with Europe. And both Europe and the United States are too reluctant to do anything. Forgive me for saying so, but I think wherever the United States has gone with force, there hasn't been a very brilliant outcome. So I'm very much afraid of intervening by bombing. A month ago, there were big talks about going in with planes and just bombing targets. Of course, I'm not an expert, but I think it is more important to set rules for the future, because obviously Yugoslavia, ex-Yugoslavia, the ex-Federation, with the new states emerging, and nationalism, and the war, may be the first place where this is happening, but it might not be the last one. So I think, if Europe, or the world for that matter, including the United States, doesn't set up very firm rules, the chaos will persist and recur. Europe and the United States should be asking questions like, should we allow changes of national borders? This is a big question. And how do we proceed? Do we proceed with force, or with some other measure? Are other measures, like sanctions, enough? What other kinds of pressures could be used? I think you can't make exemptions. You can't say, "Yes, now for this country, well, let's change the borders; let's divide Bosnia and Herzegovina among Croatia and Serbia, and give the Muslims some little enclave." What are you going to do then in the ex-USSR? They have nuclear arms, so maybe you are going to treat them differently, I don't know. I'm very pessimistic about the future of Europe. I would like to see a more consistent and more articulate politics towards the whole problem than just bombing, because after bombing, then what?

[*Philip Gourevitch*]: *My question has to do with your idea about the image of the war and the image of peasants and refugees and something that is "other," because I suspect that a lot of the media has traditionally conceptualized the image of the oppressed as the image of a peasant, and the image of the refugee looks a certain way. In contrast, if you see the image of someone dressed like you or like me, you think, "They're not doing so badly." Or you think of them the same way as you do in this country of rich people getting sent to jail, or in some way suffering or losing their homes: there is a certain public satisfaction in those images. And so I'm curious how you would suggest that one could effectively project the image of a suffering affluent person, a suffering familiar-looking person.*

The problem is that the overaccumulation of these images of "otherness" creates the effect of their being ignored, because you cannot identify with these people, their appearance, their problems. I have written a book where you *can* find points of identification with the Western world, so the people from the West could see that "this could happen to us." Out of four and a half million people in Croatia, four million didn't experience war directly. They haven't been bombed. Their children haven't been killed. Somehow the whole region of the Balkans has been cut off. And it was a clear message that it doesn't belong to Europe. The reaction to my book showed that people can identify much more easily when you show them that you are the same as they are, that there is no difference. And in that way you can somehow claim some responsibility, because if there is no understanding there can't be any responsibility. I'm not saying that the majority of the people there are not peasants. Of course the peasants are the ones who have been resettled and moved, who are the refugees. I'm describing the effect of this kind of journalism, though I'm not blaming journalists individually: we have to remember that forty of them have been killed in this war.

[*Kurzweil*]: *I'd just like to add one point. I think that your question itself points to the problem of being presented with images. The presenters, it seems, know a great deal more than what they show us; that adds to the construction of otherness Slavenka talks about. For us, it's at yet another remove.*

[*Gourevitch*]: *Remember that extraordinary image of the man who played the cello every day in Sarejevo? It was certainly a European image, I would say. And in terms of stirring a sense of responsibility in the West, I wonder whether that image really was more effective than the images of atrocity which at the same time make people "other" and also stir a greater sense of outrage. I'm just wondering really, I'm not challenging what you have pointed out.*

Okay, but have we seen any results of that outrage? What happened with all this outrage? Last year in August, images of concentration camps were projected for the first time, and nothing happened after that. There was the big story about tens of thousands of raped women, and nothing happened after that. So you have these worse and worse pictures projected; you have worse and worse atrocities committed; and the world is getting used to it. This is what I find so troubling, the phenomenon of getting used to it.

[*David Sidorsky*]: *On the one hand, your objection is to the difference, the otherness that we see as the Balkans as savagery. And you have evoked the metaphor of the Nazi genocide against the Jews, to describe what is going on. On the other hand, you say the war should be treated as if it were* not *singular: that there should be rules for dealing with it, so that we would know how to deal with similar future happenings in, for instance, the former Soviet Union. But if that's the case you're making, then what strikes one as missing is a defensible political analysis that asserts this is a war of a fairly similar, repeatable sort.*

As you say, it will repeat itself in Ossetia, in Azerbaijan, in many places. Namely, if you have a federation, and there is a secession which is disputed, and there are minorities who previously lived under a federation, then there is bound to be some sort of conflict. If Yugoslavia existed and a Serb population ruled, essentially, in Yugoslavia, with a Serb minority in Bosnia-Herzegovina, and there is a secession, then there is some need for some sort of solution on the political level. Croatia as an independent country has a solution; Slovenia had a solution. Bosnia-Herzegovina represents a very distinctive problem, and if one wants similarity, then at some point the political analysis comes; you suggested one part of it and dismissed it, that is to say, that there should be a Bosnian-Muslim autonomy. The Serbian population goes to Serbia, the Croatian population goes to Croatia. This, I understand, since you want rules for the future, is one formula of rules. There are others. There could of course be the insistence on the integrity of Bosnia-Herzegovina, with a Muslim majority, and no aggression from Serbia, or from Croatia, where the Croatian population is, if I understand the issue.

My point—this is just a logical point, I'm not an expert on Yugoslavia—is that to stress the otherness, to compare it inappropriately to the Nazi-Jewish experience, where there was no ethnic conflict over a territorial issue at all, is precisely to say this is not *similar. The similarity among all such issues has to do with the ethnic breakup of a federation, and this is, of course, exactly what you said about rules for what will happen in Georgia if North Ossetia and the Georgians wish to break up: what are the rules? But looking at the problem in this way, one stresses the political solution, or the political aspects of the problem; which, I gather, because of the demands you make on our sense of responsibility and emotional concern, you are not willing to address.*

I don't raise the political solution because I don't know what the ideal political solution is. I'm not a politician myself. I see my task as a writer who asks the questions, not one who gives the answers. If you understood me to say that it would be the best thing to divide Bosnia between Croats and Serbs and give Muslims the enclave, I didn't say that; I mentioned it, but it's not what I favor. I would put Bosnia temporarily under some kind of protectorate.

[*Istvan Deak*]: *In your beautiful reading something disturbs me: your analogy about the situation of the Poles, the Jews, and the Germans. I would see it differently. The Poles, in my opinion, are presented and shown in a very prejudiced way in Claude Lanzmann's documentary film,* Shoah. *Lanzmann was hunting for examples to show Polish anti-Semitism, and he questioned the least intelligent Polish peasants to prove that the Poles were anti-Semitic. Secondly, the Poles were totally unarmed, except for the resistance movement. The resistance movement itself was hunted down and ended up in concentration camps. The picture is not simply that there were Poles outside and Jews inside, because if the peasant Poles had not worked next to Auschwitz, there would have been Poles and not only Jews inside Auschwitz. There were hundreds of thousands of Poles in Nazi concentration camps who died.*

So I would say that the analogy that you make with today's situation perhaps is not quite right, because today's situation is absolutely insane, in that the United States and others could intervene. It's not that the Poles could have sacrificed themselves for the ghetto Jews but chose not to because they would have been killed. What makes the situation so difficult for us to understand and what makes us so exasperated is that it would be very easy for the Western powers to deal with Serbian aggression, and they are not doing it. And when you observe that United States intervention never has a positive outcome, I would say that it depends on what period you are talking about. It ended up quite successfully in World War Two, after it defeated Nazism. So that's why I wish you would either find another analogy, or explain to us why you think the situation is the same as with the Jews in Poland, that is, a world that is indifferent. The world's indifference today is far worse than the indifference of the Polish peasants.

Well, I wasn't especially attacking Polish peasants. I was talking about particular things in *Shoah*, simply because I think that the metaphor of the Jews is a very good one for every similar situation. It is a very good metaphor now for the Muslims, because they are losing territory and they are virtually exterminated in some parts. There are refugees, and what we'll see next is going to be a wave of Muslim terrorism, all over Europe. I think that the metaphor of Jews works very well for the fact that they have been exterminated people, so that regardless of where it occurred, were they Poles or were they in Croatia—we had the Jews being killed in Croatian concentration camps—the point is that people were standing there and didn't help. We see things happening to others, and we think it doesn't have anything to do with us. This is the essence of that metaphor. It doesn't really matter whether we are speaking about Jews and Poles or about Muslims or any other kind of otherness. Each of us could become a part of that otherness, in another situation. I wouldn't like you to take this so literally. I think there's always a Jew and always a community.

[*Dimitri Urnov*]: *You mentioned the repetition of the past, and we cannot but be concrete in talking about the past, and in taking some lessons out of it. What we have today is certainly an outcome of that remote past which repeats itself, but in what ways?*

I agree that part of this war in ex-Yugoslavia comes from the past, and it is somehow as if you had returned to the past, and as if it were a war of the living actually fighting the spirits of the dead of the Second World War. But I would say it is not only that, because I have lived in that country for forty-four years, and I know that we all lived in peace for a very long period of time. I see this war as having begun from the very top, not from the people, because in the ethnically mixed places like Vukovar, for example, we were not aware of any hidden conflicts. I would agree that the war began among the people, if it had in fact started five years ago, little by little, people fighting, and ethnic conflicts growing up to the point where the war started. But what I saw happening is just the opposite. I saw it happening at the very top. I saw the war being constructed, the idea of the war, the concept of the war, at a very high level, and then somehow in a spiral motion thrown down to the ground where it was almost impossible, much later on, to stop it, because when the first houses were burned, and the first people were killed, it was already done. I think it has very much to do with the fact that communism collapsed. You can't expect such a mammoth system, which existed for so many years and within which so many millions of people lived, to go away just like that.

Nationalism arose out of the collapse because as we know, historically, there was feudalism and after that communism, with no time in between for the development of a civil society and of the values of a democratic and liberal society. When, as it is popular to say, "the lid was lifted," you had two basic things that had always existed there: religion and the nation. And so, when the big system started to break down, people instinctively clung to the things that they knew. And this is one of the very important elements to remember, when you wonder how and why all of this nationalism was resurrected. Then, of course, the governments themselves perpetuated this kind of nationalism in order to stay in power. It was quite clear in the case of Milosevic. And I don't think that we have to have any doubts at this point about who started the war and how was it started in ex-Yugoslavia; it's all very well known. What is not known is that it was started at the very top.

[*Daniel Rose*]: *It's an American characteristic to think that for every question there must be an answer; for every problem, there must be a solution, however theoretical. And when the American public considers the events that are unfolding right before their eyes, they are disconcerted at not being able to imagine some kind of rational future for this society. That's one of the American problems; they just can't picture in which direction rational people can head. And we'd appreciate your comments on what you see as alternative futures, or as the prospects directly ahead.*

Whenever I travel abroad, one of the questions I am asked is, "What do you think the future is going to be?" Now, the difficult part of it is that this is the hardest question that could be put to us, because the word "future" has been erased from our life. Somehow we don't think about the future. Somehow we don't even conceive, we don't have imagination enough to imagine what kind of life we would even wish. There are several reasons for that. One is the fact that we have been living in a communist society, and in a communist society you have this feeling that this society is eternal; nothing is ever going to change. Of course it was an illusion, but you have been raised with the idea not to question, not to think, and just to let things go, and so the future basically doesn't exist as a concept.

The other fact is that with the war, you learn to live day by day, and you don't invest in the future, not even in your imagination. Not even our politicians are doing that. We all agree somehow deep down in ourselves, subconsciously, that this war is going to go on for quite some time. I was asked at the beginning, "How long do you think the war will go on?" I would say, "Well, at least five years," and everybody was kind of surprised. There is also political manipulation, because I think that the government we have now, or the governments in ex-Yugoslavia, both the Milosevic and Tudjman governments, are the type of governments that can exist only under the conditions of war, because it suits them very well. They don't even speak about the future. If they were to do so, for example in Croatia, the first question would be, "What kind of government do we want? What kind of democracy are we going to have?" These questions are not welcomed at the moment, because every question about the future is met with the answer: "We have a war. So let's not talk about democracy now, let's first solve this problem." So in short, the answer is, yes, I like the American way of assuming that for every problem there is a solution.

However, if there is a solution it's a long-term one, and it's very difficult to foresee the light at the end of the tunnel. For quite some time we'll have to deal with the problems we haven't solved. We haven't even solved the problem of the minority in Croatia, much less the Bosnian problem, which is a very burning question.

[*Phillips*]: *I gather that some intellectuals and writers behaved very badly in this situation. I wonder whether we're talking about a small number of writers and intellectuals, or most of them? How many behaved badly? I don't mean an actual count.*

I would say it's a very curious phenomenon. You will remember that at our conference Hans Magnus Enzensberger talked about intellectuals as bad people ["Intellectuals as Leaders," *PR* Fall 1992], and I quite agree with him. We concluded that intellectuals are not people of higher moral standards, and that it's rather dangerous to attribute higher moral standards to them. This is especially so when we are talking about intellectuals in Croatia and Serbia. In Serbia intellectuals actually elaborated the idea of "Greater Serbia" and helped the whole nationalist movement. It is a sad fact that its best writers actually went for all this. But Croatia is no better just because it's in a different position. Croatia is in a defensive war, so every single intellectual there is nationalist, but they believe they are nationalist for good reasons. So there are good and bad motivations. In general, before the war and during communist times we always had state writers; ninety-nine per cent of intellectuals and writers always went along with whatever politics there were or whoever ruled the country. There were very few independent individuals. It's the same now. So the intellectuals in both countries are "bad guys."

[*Elizabeth Dalton*]: *Your point about making people "other" is a very good one, but one has to recognize also that there is survival value in not getting totally sucked into the disaster next door. Yet I think you're mistaken if you think that in this country there is a feeling of indifference to the problem. The paradoxical side is that the more outraged people feel by the images on television, the more enthusiastic they are for military intervention, which you and many other people feel might well be disastrous. I think that wave has sort of passed a bit, but that feeling of moral outrage did lead President Clinton and many others to say we must bomb.*

I have seen that the feelings of the people sometimes are very different from their government's behavior; there is a huge gap between the two. Recently, I read in the *International Herald Tribune* that there has been a poll in several European countries about how to proceed in this conflict, and whether they should intervene with European forces or not, and in most countries there was a huge number, ranging from forty to sixty per cent of the populations, saying, "Yes, we are for intervention," while the governments were behaving very conservatively. So there is some kind of gap between what the people and what the governments really see as necessary. Maybe there is something wrong with Western democracy; perhaps people have no power to influence the governments. But I have seen that they are getting desensitized, anesthetized by these kinds of images. There are two sides of the media, of course; one is to bring the story out and to let the world know. But the question is, "What then?" What do you do with information? To inform may not be enough. I am just saying that we—intellectuals, writers, people in general—are not dealing enough with the moral issues, with the moral questions, with the questions of responsibility. I myself am puzzled why European intellectuals are not posing any of these questions. This war hasn't been an issue among European intellectuals at all. Intellectuals next door don't discuss it. They pretend not to understand, but I wonder if they want to understand what's going on. This puzzles me. I see it as closing your eyes, I see it as turning your head away. I am a bit bitter because I come from there. Maybe an insider's look into these problems is different from an outsider's position.

[Kurzweil]: *I want to follow up on that. Of course we all want the slaughter to stop. But can it be stopped with bombing? And, if it were to stop with bombing, where do we bomb? Do we know, can we even separate one population from another? After all, there are all these enclaves.*

Well, I think nothing could be won without ground troops engagement. I read an article by an expert who said that without two hundred and fifty thousand soldiers nothing could be solved at all, and who is going to put two hundred and fifty thousand soldiers in Bosnia? It's yet another issue.

[Phillips]: *You can get two hundred and fifty thousand troops, if the Europeans and the American government combine. The question is, as I see it, people are claiming that intervention wouldn't solve the problem. Now, I don't know the answer to that. You say you're not a politician, but you know more about it than we do. Do you think if America and the European nations send troops in it could stop the slaughter?*

Well, I suppose, yes. Someone has to stop it, but the problem is that it's an enormous number of soldiers, enormous sums of money, and the question is, why would someone do it?

[Joanna Rose]: *I have heard that there are Muslims, Turks, who are willing to go in with troops, but that the rest of the European countries do not want them to go in. There is money, there are troops, and there is a country willing to go in and help the Muslims in Bosnia. Well, is that a way of solving it?*

Yes, of course they would probably solve it, but we should also take a look into their interest in the whole issue. You need a political solution, a proper political solution for that, and without it I am afraid it can't work.

[Rose]: *It has to be troops you like, right?*

I think without combined forces under the auspices of the UN, nothing much could be done. And as we all know, the UN is a terribly bureaucratic organization, and it's terribly slow. God knows how many people will die before they do something. But as I said, we can have a think-tank about what should be and could be done there. I am very sorry if I disappointed you, but I don't have any political solution, any ready-made recipes, and I don't even see it as my task to do find them.

[Jack Diggins]: *You are puzzled about why intellectuals in the West have no response to this issue. I think it's mainly because a number of writers thought that communism was going to solve the problem of religion and nationality, but it has been a squalid failure. Many people felt that with the fall of communism, democracy would be able to take care of these issues, yet that doesn't seem to be able to do so. So everyone is at a loss, and there's nothing in the heritage of Western political thought to deal with these issues. We thought the Enlightenment would take care of it, but that hasn't happened: we thought modern technology and various other institutions would take care of these issues, but they didn't, and so we are at a loss. I also want to say, when you suggest that the problem starts at the top, I am really puzzled. To me, there was no problem while there was a top: there was an authoritarian system which kept a lid on this, and when that collapsed, the underlying problem of human hatred of people toward one another emerged. The elements of human animosity and human sinfulness and aggression can be manipulated, but I don't think they can be discounted.*

Yes. I want to answer the last part first, on why it was that when the lid was capped, we had an authoritarian society, and everything was quiet and in order. In Yugoslavia that was not the case, because the pressure wasn't strong enough to keep it under the lid; if there was anything boiling it would have been very obvious. The only thing we had was the Croatian Spring in 1971, and it was really a mild decentralization, not really a proper movement in the sense that Croatia wanted to secede. So I think that if we are speaking about lids and authoritarian pressure in a society, Yugoslavia is not a good example, because people really had started to live together, and there were a lot of mixed marriages, especially in Bosnia, about twenty to thirty percent of the children now are of mixed marriages. They have to take sides today; this is one of the saddest things about this war.

And I wouldn't really speak about hatred, except that I would say we have to be clear; it's not that nationalism didn't exist at all. I think that it was there all the time, but when I say that the war came from the top I mean that there were methods used to stir up emotions. It's not that everyone wasn't aware of what happened in the Second World War, that Serbs were killing Croats, Croats were killing Serbs, and so on, but it is like a disease. Under certain circumstances it develops and becomes an acute disease. Other than that it stays dormant, not necessarily developing into something malignant. This is the best metaphor that I can use for what is happening with nationalism in my country.

What I gather is that you are giving some kind of excuse for intellectuals because they are confused with this situation. Yes, I think they are confused, of course, I am confused myself, but this is not an excuse, because their task is to think about this, and to ask, and to argue, and to try to find some kind of solutions. However, you mentioned one very interesting point which I didn't: you said that communism contained the problems, and that we had hoped that democracy would solve them. Now, what is happening with democracy in Eastern Europe? Each representative of these new governments, and their new presidents, came and said, "Now, this is democracy. We are bringing you democracy." Democracy is like a gold medal. This is it. And what do you have? You have a democratic constitution, okay; you have a multiparty system, and you have free elections. There are the three institutions that you have." Yet these are no more than formalities, since all the parties are really working very much within the mentality of a one-party system. Then you say, "Well, this is giving democracy a bad name, it's somehow changing the concept of democracy itself, because they are using this word, this concept, and democracy is not really happening." So what you have is some kind of a backlash, even a danger that at some point people will say, "Oh, this is democracy? This is what we were fighting for? Excuse me, we are losing jobs, we don't have any security, there's an economic crisis, the people in government are the same people as before—in many countries, literally—so they are corrupt, they are just putting the money in their pockets."

Democracy is something that people have to take, that they have to build—slowly. And for people in Eastern Europe who have been living all their lives with a totalitarian mentality, it's very difficult. I have seen how it works. They are afraid to even start doing the little things—holding gatherings, forming ideas, citizens' groups—and thus it is going very slowly, because on the one hand you have very authoritarian governments, and on the other hand, the people don't have the feeling that they are citizens, that they are individuals, especially not in mass societies like nationalist ones.

[*Daphne Merkin*]: *You began earlier in the evening by saying that one of the problems with the media representation of the war is its focus on peasants, which reduces our perception of the population to an "other," other than ourselves, a view I don't particularly agree with. But what surprises me is, I understand American diffidence about intervening, but why are you diffident as an observer—not as a politician, which you said you are not, but as a writer and observer—about the American impulse to intervene, which is based precisely on the perception that these are not "others," but humans like ourselves? You did make one rather slighting remark about American intervention not always being successful, but as someone else pointed out, in fact it has been successful in major instances.*

In the Second World War, yes.

[*Merkin*]: *Counter-aggression is commonly the only way to stop certain kinds of aggression. So your diffidence puzzles me, more than American diffidence, and I wonder if you're resigned, more than you know—this is a question, or speculation—to the "otherness" of this war, its "in-house" quality. Is your equivocating when you were asked about American intervention in fact a reflection of your own sense that this is a rather insular, ongoing conflict that is not amenable to a dashing international assault? There's a certain resignation in what you are saying.*

Well, I have to say that if the message that you get is that this is an insular war and therefore I don't want America to intervene, that goes against everything I have ever written, which says, "We are as you are, and something should be done about that." So it's not insular. I see it as a European problem. Europe should be first to engage in solving this problem. But the problem with Europe is it thinks it's not part of Europe. So I think it's very important for America to do something, but not on its own. What I think should be done at this point is to find a principled solution for this kind of problem. What I understand is meant by intervention would be the bombing of certain strategic targets in Bosnia—Serbian supply lines and so on. This for me is not the solution. I think the solution should be more complete and more principled, and therefore I don't worry so much about "intervention yes or no," but "is this something that is going to contribute to the principal solution of the problem, which is in the first place a European problem?" What I'm saying is: bombing is not enough per se. Ground troops are necessary. This is what I understand from the analyses I have read.

Because this is a European problem and because this is a problem of principle, we should find, fight for, a principled solution at this point. It's not enough to speak only about intervention. This is the only action that I see as essential to take, apart from stopping the slaughter.

[Rose]: *You said that it is not for humanistic purposes that America would go to Bosnia. I have to defend my country. There is no other reason we would enter this situation except for humanistic purposes, because it is against every other interest of ours to enter for any other reason.*

But you are not entering it. I would love America to go in for purely humanistic reasons. Great! But it hasn't happened.

[Kurzweil]: *Let me interject some kind of explanation, something that I have watched for many, many years going back and forth between here and Europe. Americans are always, as Joanna Rose said, involved in the humanistic principle; ever since Wilson, they've been "making the world safe for democracy." Every time I've gone to Europe I've heard that America has intervened here and there because it has some imperialistic ends in mind, and this is a kind of clash of opinions, of principles, that is not understood from one side to the other, and we then continue it here in a national discussion.*

That is why these conflicts have to be solved as a joint project of America, Europe, NATO, and the United Nations. But it has to be a joint thing, not only the Americans going in. I am sorry if I sound very disappointingly conservative on that issue, but I do really think that if America pushes Europe into doing something and they do something together, fine. Yet in my view this is essentially a European problem. The Europeans have to solve it because they are going to have enormous problems in the future if they don't sort this out.

[Phillips]: *Why don't the European countries, in your opinion, want to do anything?*

Because they are fighting among themselves. There is this problem of France and Britain and Germany, and they have their own conflicts about the war, how to solve it and who is for what kind of solution.

[Phillips]: *Well, they could just stop the slaughter. Why not?*

If it would be so easy and simple, they would do it, probably.

[Phillips]: *I'm not sure.*

[Kurzweil]: *I think you're being naive.*

It's also very sad and disappointing to see all these big forces fighting among themselves about who should do what and who should send troops and how much money is needed, while people are being killed every day. This is the biggest frustration of all. And this is where you feel you can't do anything about it.

[Phillips]: *I don't think that's quite an accurate picture of why America is not doing as much as it should. Let me start by saying that I'm struck by your remark that American intellectuals have done very little about the situation in presenting some kind of united group attitude and demanding some kind of action. Now, somebody said that that's because intellectuals are confused. Well, intellectuals are often confused: it doesn't seem to prevent them from doing things. For instance, they protested the Vietnam War, and they were confused at the time; and they supported World War Two, and they were also confused at that time. So I don't think confusion is the reason. I think that what has happened here is that the Clinton Administration can't make up its mind what to do because it's afraid of public opinion. There's a certain amount of public opinion that's simply isolationist, but there's another sector of public opinion, which seems to be supported by military experts, asserting that no intervention will help unless it's so enormous that it can't be undertaken. And the reason given is that the situation in the former Yugoslavia is so complex that no military action can disentangle the various forces and stop the slaughter. I think that's one reason why many of us have hesitated to take a bold and positive stand. Now, what do you think? Is there any truth in this argument that the situation is so complex that intervention by Americans alone or Americans with European troops won't do any good? Is that a false argument?*

I think it's a false argument. I think that a proper number of troops and proper military action could stop it, but I think it has to go along with other measures to solve the problem, to be very simple on that point.

[Sidorsky]: *I'd like to support your hesitation about intervention from the United States, but on different grounds, because I agree entirely with Joanna Rose that the only grounds for American intervention is what would be called humanitarian intervention. And indeed it's precisely that, because the intervention would have to be so large that you're speaking about significant casualties. The Serbs are going to fight back; they're going to kill people. And then, too, people pay a price for humanitarian intervention without any national interest—that's usually a compelling reason why people say countries should intervene only where there is a national interest—unless they are part of a large consort of nations, usually the case with humanitarian interven-*

tion, in which situation you assume that the casualties would be minimal.

The second comment has to do with your reference to a "principled solution." There is no principled solution in one sense of the word "principle," because there are only two principles here, federation and secession. Now, you do not wish, I assume, to force a refederation: you supported the Croatian unilateral secession, you support Slovenia's unilateral secession, presumably you support Bosnia-Herzegovina's unilateral secession. The alternative then is to accept the principle of secession, and never cross boundaries against a seceded state. Someone should have taught this to the Union vis-a-vis the Confederacy.

[Jan Kavan]: *I'm not sure if I agree with your explanation that Europe is not going in with a resolution to stop the slaughtering simply because the European powers, Britain, France, Germany and so on, cannot agree among themselves on the solution. I think that's probably one aspect, but in fact in the majority of the meetings among the foreign ministers of the EC, there was a prevailing consensus that, first, they don't have a proper political solution, other than that they have different ones which would clash; and secondly, and primarily I think, they don't want to risk losing the lives of their own soldiers, because that would go down badly with public opinion, again since they don't have a national interest in Bosnia-Herzegovina. They have an interest as Europeans to keep Europe stable and secure, which is in fact also in the United States' interest. The United States has, obviously, humanistic moral motivation, but that is not its only motivation. It is in the interest of the United States to have a stable and secure Europe, and it has a responsibility as the world's remaining superpower to help. The objection of the Europeans was that Americans offered to lift the embargo, to help the Muslims defend themselves and to bomb certain strategic targets, but they were not prepared to commit American troops, risk American lives, until a peaceful solution could be agreed upon. And once again, the Europeans felt that this would endanger the lives of their own soldiers. I agree with you that bombing alone would not solve the problem but exacerbate it.*

I think that, as David Sidorsky mentioned, federation and secession are both principles, but they are far from the only ones. The other one is to find out whether it's possible any longer to have a multinational, multi-ethnic unit, which, after all, Bosnia-Herzegovina was. At that time, the government argued that it was one of the few regions left in the former Communist Europe which had managed to have a functioning multi-ethnic and multinational society. Is that in any way possible now?

I'm grateful that you pointed out one of the essential issues, the hesitation of America and Europe to put the lives of their soldiers at risk, and rightly so. But on the issue of other kinds of solutions, it comes down to the question, "Is it possible for a multi-ethnic state like Bosnia to exist, or does it really have to divide into cantons and provinces, ethnically cleansed in this or that way?" Whether we are dealing with the federation or with secession or with the possibility of a multi-ethnic community, we must address the question of the borders and the question of the minorities. If we are speaking about nation-states, then we have to define the borders and minorities. Of course, the most substantial difference is whether this happens with a war or without war. The problem with the war is that while we discuss and try to find the solutions, it goes on. And in the face of it I, both as a writer and as a person who lives there, feel quite helpless.

[Kurzweil]: *Slavenka, thank you very much.*

Helena Cobban (essay date spring 1994)

SOURCE: Cobban, Helena. "Jean, Slavenka, and the Tea Party for Sanity." *Antioch Review* 52, no. 2 (spring 1994): 270-85.

[*In the following essay, Cobban discusses the effects of war on women portrayed in works by Drakulic and Jean Said Makdisi.*]

An accident of history, really, that brought this nice young man, untested in foreign affairs, to the presidency of the republic at a time when the United States is in a position of unequaled supremacy in world politics. Decisions that he makes—on Bosnia, Somalia, Cambodia, wherever—can rip apart the fabric of whole nations.

What does Bill Clinton know of war?

Forests of print have addressed this question, and enough electronic wizardry to boost a message to the edge of the universe. But that discourse was always dominated by men—fighting men in uniforms, political men reading opinion polls, think tank men fine-tuning the game of grown-up bullyboys called "deterrence." But put all of these specialists together in a room, and the picture you get of this thing called "war" is still incomplete. Locked outside, but more deserving of entry than ever before, are people with a different view of war: those who are not its producers but, perforce, its consumers (and who thereby are consumed by it). Themselves products of two great developments of this century of ours—the inclusion of massed civilian populations in the target sets of warriors, and the spread of mass education—some of these civilian war consumers can today describe war in a way that is more complete than any previous description. Especially the women among them.

Move over, Les Aspin. Move over, all you Clausewitz wannabes with your Rube Goldberg "models" of this or that form of warfare. Move over, warrior-poets of glory or of anguish. Make room for experts like these: Jean Said Makdisi, a college teacher and mother who chronicled sixteen years of war in Lebanon in her book *Beirut Fragments* (1990); and Slavenka Drakulic, a journalist and mother who chronicled the first year of the present Balkan wars in **The Balkan Express: Fragments from the Other Side of War** (1993).

These women might both have put into their titles a word, *fragments,* that implies a tentativeness of experience or discourse. But each book builds an overwhelming, thoughtful, and undeniably true picture of what war does to societies at the end of our century.

Never mind the generals. Compared with these women, what does Bill Clinton know of war?

Should we arrange a tea party perhaps? Invite Jean, Slavenka, and Bill. Do you think he's ever been to their countries? Maybe he visited "Yugoslavia" in 1969, on the trip when, most famously, he went to Moscow. I was in Yugoslavia in 1970: I got off the train in Slavenka's home-town, Zagreb, and hitchhiked down to the coast. Then in 1974, I went to work as a correspondent in Lebanon. I "covered" and lived the war there from 1975 through 1981; had my first two children there; knew, like Jean Makdisi, the special terrors of raising children inside a war zone. I knew, as Slavenka would, the particular difficulty that a mother can have in dealing, as a journalist, with topics impossible to speak of.

This is how Slavenka described an interview she was supposed to conduct with a survivor from the Croatian city of Vukovar, which had recently fallen to the Serbs. Ivan was nineteen. He had fought along-side the city's defenders, but had then been forced to withdraw from it with his mother and five younger siblings. His father was lost—either dead or captured. Slavenka talked to Ivan in Zagreb:

> I knew he was waiting for me to ask him questions, but I was at a loss for words. I didn't know what to ask him, caught by surprise. His face was so unbearably young that it undid me in a way. This is a story that cannot be written, I thought, not the story of this child who has lost his friends, his house, his father, even the war itself. . . . He could be my son, I thought, and could not stop thinking of it. . . . The more talkative and open he became, the more I withdrew. I felt guilty.

Yes, these two women would be good to invite to my tea party. We'll have Bill sitting there—I hope our trees don't set off his allergies. I think we should invite Hillary, too; maybe she can do some cultural interpretation for us.

Why a tea party? Well, you might think of the Boston Tea Party, not a true tea party at all, of course, but it did mark a transition to a hopeful new order. You might think of the Mad Hatter's Tea Party, a total up-ending of existing logics and systems of argument. Or you might think of this tea party, encountered by Jean when, in the midst of Israel's punishing 1982 bombardment of Beirut, she went with her husband to visit some friends:

> For an instant I thought I was hallucinating, but soon I was laughing in delight. There on the lawn she had set up a table on which was spread afternoon tea. There was a teapot with a crocheted tea cosy, the kind you buy at church bazaars; there were porcelain teacups, silver sugar tongs and teaspoons, embroidered linen napkins, and a little silver dish with biscuits. Both she and her sister, whose house had become uninhabitable because of the bombings, were wearing long, fashionable cotton kaftans. They were neatly groomed and freshly lipsticked. . . .
>
> "I can't believe this," I said. "I feel as if I'm dreaming. How do you do it?"
>
> "My dear, I would go mad if I didn't. . . . What do you want me to do? Die? When I must, I will. Meanwhile, every afternoon I have my tea."

So, a tea party for sanity, amidst the craziness and killings of the new world disorder! Held here, in Washington D.C., capital city of the planet, and quite a killing ground in its own right. What could make more sense?

As the guests arrived, I would make sure each was well seated. Then I would preside over the ritual of pouring the tea, using the silver teapot bequeathed me by my Aunt Katie; and I would find out who drinks their tea with lemon, with milk, or with sugar. Perhaps at this point, already, Jean and Slavenka would start right on in, sharing with each other and the rest of us their considerable insights into one of our era's most troubling processes: the dividing up of people into confining ethnic or religious boxes.

In Lebanon, the enforced dividing was attempted along both sectarian and "national" lines. The Maronite Christian militias fought hard to create and enlarge enclaves free of both Palestinian and (Lebanese) Muslim presence. "Cleansing" (*tantheef*) was their word for this process from the beginning of the fighting in 1975. (In Arabic, as in English, "cleansing" has a close but usually unmentioned relationship with the more purely military term "mopping-up.") In vast parts of the beautiful land of Lebanon, the Maronite campaign tore through a long-established coexistence, setting neighbor against neighbor, friend against friend, in a process of seemingly inexorable violence. The same process has now torn apart previously diverse communities in the former Yugoslavia—there, breaking communities up along lines of imputed ethnicity. Saddest of all, to anyone who has experienced Beirut, is the attempted destruction in Sarajevo of the idea of peaceable coexistence among the residents of a single, gloriously diverse modern city.

In Lebanon and in Yugoslavia, the deadly process of group homogenization hastens and has been hastened by war. Here is how this process feels to Jean, a Protestant Christian and a Palestinian, married to a (Christian?) Lebanese, who in the 1970s and 1980s were raising their three sons in Muslim-dominated West Beirut:

> I have felt repeatedly that religion has worked rather like the stamp with which cattle are branded. I have seen it so many times in the movies. The cowboy chases the steer relentlessly. He throws a noose over the animal's head. . . .
>
> And so we are all, like it or not, branded with the hot iron of our religious ancestry. . . .
>
> And how does the brand work? How does one fall into the clutches of that cowboy holding the hot iron? How does one feel as it sizzles into the flesh? I have felt it. . . .

Here, a marvelous discovery, is the very same metaphor in the hands of Slavenka, a Croat formerly married to a Serb, by whom she has one daughter, now in her twenties: "War is like a brand on the brows of Serbs who curse Croat mothers, but it is also a brand on the faces of Croats leaving a country where all they had is gone."

In January 1992, the day before the European Community gave formal recognition to Croatia, Slavenka wrote an essay called **"Overcome by Nationhood."** By then, her new country had been racked for some months already by fighting between Croats and ethnic Serbs backed by neighboring Serbia. Slavenka wrote: "Along with millions of other Croats, I was pinned to the wall of nationhood—not only by outside pressure from Serbia and the Federal Army but by national homogenization within Croatia itself. That is what the war is doing to us, reducing us to one dimension: the Nation." But neither of these women allows herself to indulge in abstract moralizing. Slavenka explained with engaging honesty how she, too, felt drawn into this identification with the national idea by the horrors of the war:

> Right now, in the new state of Croatia, no one is allowed not to be a Croat. And even if this is not what one would really call freedom, perhaps it would be morally unjust to tear off the shirt of the suffering nation—with tens of thousands of people being shot, slaughtered and burned just because of their nationality. It wouldn't be right because of Vukovar, the town that was erased from the face of the earth. Because of the attacks on Dubrovnik.

While Slavenka felt herself becoming sucked into the system of ethnic categorization, for Jean no such option has ever, in the Lebanese context, been available. The complicated warp and woof of her personal reference groups has precluded it. Jean also actively resists the idea of closed sectarian identities in strong and wrenchingly effective language:

> Although I am, by this definition at least, a Christian, I think of Islam as part—a large part—of my heritage and revere it as such. . . . I am the child in equal measure of Christianity and Islam, but, to my great discomfort, the marriage made between them in my historical background is threatened. I do not wish to choose between them. Yet the choice is being made for me by elements over which I have no control. . . . The situation I find myself in is like that of watching the rape of my own past, two legs of one body being forced apart to the eternal shame of victim and violator.

Is there something special about women, and our lives, that gives us a special, recognizable set of attitudes towards and insights into war? For years, I thought not. I was a successful war correspondent, after all; I got my stories on the front pages of major newspapers when I was only twenty-three. I reveled in proving myself as good as (better than!) my colleagues who were men. I hated signs of what I considered squeamishness in myself. I felt embarrassed in 1976 when, being taken by Falangist militia guides around Tel al-Zaatar, a Palestinian refugee camp that the Falangists had just the day before captured, I found I could take in every detail of the tour, the bodies squished this way and that by the trucks of Falangist looters, the body of a pregnant mother with her belly split terrifyingly, casually, open, and so on, until—when our Falangist guides invited us into a basement where they promised "lots more bodies"—*I found I could not go on.*

So there I sat. In a little dusty courtyard in the middle of that stinking, dried-out wasteland. In the strangely reassuring company of three crumpled bodies of tiny supplicating old people. And I pondered the words with which Falangist military boss Bashir Gemayel had prefaced our tour: "I am proud of what you are going to see there."

Like that. No attempt to invoke the thin pretense with which I have heard other commanders respond to rumors of atrocity: The heat of the battle . . . a few excesses . . . dealt with promptly by commanders on the spot. . . . Bla bla, perhaps, but at least, a recognition that these things should not be crowed about, should be prevented or kept hidden, are acts deserving of shame.

Heat of battle / animals in heat / killing and pornography.

But here I was. The tour carefully arranged. The declaration pridefully asserted. And I knew that words could never, in their standard journalistic arrangement, adequately "cover" this "story."

(Within six years, U.S. diplomats were trumpeting pudgy Bashir as their great white hope for the healing of Lebanon. In 1982, with U.S and Israeli backing, he was elected president of Lebanon. Before he could be inaugurated, he was assassinated. His followers, well trained, immediately carried out another, equally horrific series of atrocities in the camps at Sabra and Shatila. No one can claim this was unexpected. Our press coverage from 1976 did at least accurately convey the facts, if not the full moral import, of the event.)

In 1980, at the start of another war, my husband at the time was covering the Iranian front, and I was covering the Iraqi front. Our two preschoolers were with the nanny in Beirut. Came a telex: "There is fighting in your neighborhood, and one of the militias has put a sniper on the roof of your building." Did I stay on in Iraq, where the "story" was excellent? No, I didn't. Could I cover the story in Beirut, where the politics were intriguing? No, I couldn't. All I could think of as I raced back across the desert to Beirut was an image of my beautiful children, held up bleeding, dead, as I had seen so many other children taken from bombed-out buildings.

Nowadays, I consider such an attitude towards the horror of war to be authentic, and relevant. It is an important part of the human experience. It was not a part that fit into the standard conventions of journalism of that day—or of our present day. It is an attitude that women have more frequently than men, given our roles as nurturers. Men sometimes have it, too, I know. But none of us is heard: the hegemony that (male) power-based thinking exercises over the political echelon seeps into nearly every corner of the public discourse, forcing women who want to participate to do so on those terms. For some years now, I have been a member of both the International Institute for Strategic Studies, and an American-based networking group called Women in International Security. Most of the talented, ambitious women in these groups shy away from any discussion of whether women have a special attitude towards war. Their role models are Jeane Kirkpatrick or Margaret Thatcher: women who have spectacularly made it in a male-ordered world.

But I think it would be good to engage our tea party guests in a serious discussion of whether women have a special, and perhaps especially constructive, attitude towards violence and war. It's an important discussion, one that has particular relevance in this era of wars against civilians—and at this point, when the United States may become sucked into violence in the Balkans, as is already happening in Somalia. Let these two wonderfully wise women from Lebanon and Croatia help us further the discussion.

Partly, it is these women's ability to operate within both the public and the private worlds, and to see and muse upon the connections between them, that gives their writing its particular attitude and effectiveness. Jean attended school in very Church of England schools in Cairo, in the fifties. So she is probably familiar with the English tea-time custom of eating the piece of plain buttered bread before moving on to the jams, the jellies, the cakes, fruit breads, or scones. At our tea party, the conversation would probably keep threatening to run away with us; the chirping of Minton cups being replaced on their saucers would die away, the tea remain half-drunk, morsels of cake left uneaten on the plates—while Jean and Slavenka trade their impressions of the dualisms of war.

Slavenka writes with exasperation of the impossibility, when dining with admirers at the Harvard Club in Cambridge, of conveying to them the complexities of the Balkan situation. She then imagines the following scene, which draws its power from the cool precision of its domestic detail:

> I can easily imagine the face of a Bush, a Kohl or a Major, at first eagerly paying attention to the report given by an expert consultant who comes from this part of the world over the plate of clear bouillon and then perhaps some light plain-cooked white fish, only to shake his head wearily at the end of the dinner, lifting a silver spoon of slightly quivering creme caramel, admitting that he cannot understand, not fully, that madness, the Balkan nightmare.

Jean writes of her war that,

> It seemed simple at first, and limited, but gradually grew in complexity to encompass every aspect of life and thought, even as it grew geographically and in intensity. Expanding ripples of conflicts in a lake of violence caused parallel ripples in my own existence, and sent me, reeling, fragmented portions of consciousness.
>
> Gradually, I . . . found myself overcome by the effort to manage both the inner and outer battles. Almost every aspect of the war I had fought out in my own heart. Whenever I heard the argument of one side expounded, I could immediately anticipate the other; and one without the other would seem simplistic, false. I could therefore accept and reject simultaneously all the arguments of the war, while at the same time categorically rejecting the war itself.

The connections between the public and private worlds are not the only connections that these women are able to help us see. Another kind of connection, particularly relevant for the era we have entered, is that between different cultures. Both, of course, are represented here in languages that are not their native tongues: How privileged we English speakers are, to have these writers communicate with us (and so beautifully!) in our own language. But the most important cultural divide they bridge, as in Slavenka's introductory essay on the Harvard Club, is that between cultures torn by war and those that do not know how blessed they are with peace.

In December 1991, Slavenka once again left Zagreb, this time for Paris:

> I walked down brightly lit streets . . . and I could hardly feel my own weight. It seemed to me I was almost floating, not touching the pavement, not touching reality; as if between me and Paris there stretched an invisible wire fence through which I could see everything but touch and taste nothing—the wire that could not be removed from my field of vision and that kept me imprisoned in the world from which I had just arrived. . . . In a Europe ablaze with bright lights getting ready for Christmas I was separated from Paris by a thin line of blood: that and the fact that I could see it, while Paris stubbornly refused to.

While Slavenka rails especially against a Europe that has turned its back on the Balkans, Jean reserves her special anger for the arms dealers of the world:

> I ponder, for the ten thousandth time since this damnable war began, on the happiness of the manufacturers and salesmen of arms and ammunition. Every roar, whistle, and crash translates itself in my mind to the sound of a cash register, the tinkle of champagne glasses, and the hum of conversation at a very expensive restaurant somewhere. The glisten of shrapnel, the smoke billowing out of someone's ruined home, the rumble of the big guns, are all echoed in my imagination as the glitter of jewelry, the smoke of cigars lazily puffed out of appreciative lips, and the rolling of drums for a hip-swinging, carefree dance. . . .

In addition to their ability to make sense of, and connections between, two or more different worlds, what marks these two writers as particularly female is the way they experience war as mothers. (Perhaps, too, their writing gains extra poignancy from their special concern as mothers of "mixed-parentage" children.)

Some of Jean's most anguished writing deals with the conflict she experienced when the Israeli army cast a deadly noose of siege around West Beirut. Should she defy the attackers by staying in her own home, as every fiber of her cried out to do? Or should she give in to the urgings of her husband, Samir, echoed within the parental part of herself, and take her sons out of the besieged portion of the city to safety?

> My husband insisted. Like so many Lebanese, he had learned the lesson of Palestine and so he would stay; but for the safety of our children, I must take them and go. I argued; I pleaded; I fought; but he prevailed. Would I, he had shouted, would I take the responsibility if our children were burned like those we had seen on television the night before? The sight of those little burned bodies had made him vomit. I had not had the courage even to look at them.
>
> I could not find a counterargument. "You take them; I'll stay," I had tried feebly. I had no right to condemn the children. I felt shame, humiliation, rage, as I packed in the dark. . . . My anger was a wheel with a hundred spokes. . . .

Jean took her sons out of the siege, and waited with them in a friend's house in the hills nearby. The agony of being outside the tortured city was intolerable; and when her husband later found a way to come out and join her for a few days' visit, he learned firsthand how hard her situation was. The three boys—the youngest was eleven—were eager to return. So, like many others who had previously fled, the whole family walked back into their besieged hometown.

Jean's descriptions of the psychology of a city under siege and constant bombardment from land, sea, and air should be required reading for all politicians whose military are urging this "solution" to any problem:

> All of my previous hesitancy evaporated: Here was no doubt at all. This was one battle in which I felt I could unquestioningly take sides. All the criticisms that I had of the PLO's conduct in Lebanon—and there were many—receded, for it fought directly and gallantly, against the overwhelming force of the Israelis. Such courage as I possessed, such imagination, such idealism, such historical sense were all mobilized, focused on the necessity of resistance, which became to me the most meaningful political act of my life.

But the siege, and the daily, deadly bombardments carried on for weeks and weeks. They brought Jean to an even more terrifying view of her parental responsibilities:

> Eventually, exhaustion filtered insidiously through the stoicism. I remember the haggard look on every face, the circles under the eyes, the weight everyone lost. We were the living among the dead and the dying, never knowing when we would be called to join their ranks, and so we took on the look of the dead. . . . The death machines worked; hardly anything else did. I remember raw, wordless fear, actual terror, gnawing at the bravest people, weakening them. And watching the children: my young son taking my hand and placing it over his pounding heart to show me; his thirteen-year-old brother sitting very still, very quietly, but very close to me, whispering on August 4, "Mummy, we're going to die today; for sure, we're going to die."

A few days later, she once again put her parenting self first, and, shortly before the mid-August ceasefire finally took effect, she took the boys out of the city.

By the time Slavenka started writing the essays in this collection, in April 1991, her daughter, Rujana, was, by contrast to Jean's boys, just about grown up. In summer 1991, Rujana left Zagreb to go visit Slavenka's ex-husband in Canada, and she only reappeared in Zagreb the following spring. Slavenka thanks God that she has no sons. "To have a son in wartime is the worst curse that can befall a mother," she wrote to her daughter in April 1992. (This was before most of us learned what some Serbian fighters were doing to Bosnian daughters in their "cleansing" campaign.)

Because she is a mother and a gifted writer, Slavenka has a sympathetic imagination that enables her to imagine that any of the young men waging this war might have been her son. Here is more of her reaction to nineteen-year-old Ivan, the survivor from Vukovar:

> He could be my son, he is four years younger than my daughter, I thought, again disturbed by his youth, and looked down at my hands, at the floor. . . .
>
> While I watch him light his cigarette with a resolute gesture, slightly frowning as if trying to look older, I again feel horror pierce me like a cold blade: really, what if this were my own son? What would I tell him—not today at this table when the war is almost behind us, but in the early summer of 1991 in Vukovar? What would I have done, if one day he came to me and simply said, "Mama, I'm going"? Of course, I wouldn't ask where he was going, that would have been clear by then, it could mean only one thing, going to fight in the war. I wouldn't even be surprised, perhaps I would have expected it. . . . But I would nevertheless tell him not to go, because this is not his war. . . . Forget it, I'd say, no idea is worth fighting for. But it's not an idea that this is all about, he'd say, I don't give a damn about ideas, about the state, about independence or democracy. They're killing my friends, they're killing them like dogs in the street and then dogs eat them because we can't get to them to bury them. . . .

The dialogue that follows is a quietly explosive master text of moral philosophy. But if we were discussing this issue of "what is war"—for mothers, for anybody—at our tea party, I would hope that the guests had already read, as well, the next essay in Slavenka's collection, **"What Ivan Said."** Ivan, asked to help load a pile of corpses onto a truck: "I couldn't do it, I just stood by. As soon as I got there, I began to vomit. People, dead people, rotting, decaying, flies coming out of their mouths. . . ." Ivan, watching his friends beat a local Serb to death. Ivan, killing a man for the first time, close up. Ivan, deciding with his friend not to kill two advancing Serbian soldiers because they were conscripts, not volunteers:

> One of them almost shot my brother, then my brother returned fire and shot him. The other one threw himself on the ground. . . . When he gave himself up, we saw he was really just a kid. . . . We felt sorry for him, he was born in 1972, like me.

This is powerful stuff, as journalism and also in the context of the greater human story. I believe that Slavenka's ability, as a mother and as a writer, to reach out to Ivan in the full dimension of his humanity was an essential ingredient in her success in getting this story. When I was in Beirut, I interviewed several young fighters from different sides of the war. But I was still fairly young, myself. I was speaking to them more from a sense of horror at what it was that they felt they had to do, than from the sense that Slavenka conveys so strongly: of the terrible sadness a mother might feel, on learning that they have done these things.

Another part of these women's testimony speaks to the power of domestic and personal orderliness to restore a larger sense of orderliness to a life turned inside out by crisis and war. I have felt some of this in my own life: there were years of internal and external chaos when my most powerful personal mantra was "When in doubt, fold clothes." So perhaps, when we need a change of mood at the tea party, we can trade some stories along this general theme.

We need not ask Jean to repeat the story of the tea party amidst chaos that was the exemplar for our own gathering. But as I ask my children to fetch the guests' cups for a refill, we could ask her to recall the day when, in the middle of the Israeli siege, she found her friend S emerging "triumphantly" from the working salon of a resourceful hairdresser. Or she might recall the numerous occasions she refers to in her book when, following yet another hideous series of events, she takes special pains over her appearance. Like this time, in April 1989, after she had spent several nights in the parking-garage-shelter with no electricity:

> I woke up at 7:30. It was quiet outside. I showered and dressed, choosing my clothes carefully. I chose a dark blue skirt and a sweater and a white blouse, polished my black shoes, and fixed my hair. In patching up my appearance, in choosing particularly neat and orderly clothes, I felt I was undoing the humiliation of my rat-like state last night.

Slavenka's friend Drazena would probably appreciate that account. Drazena came to Slavenka's house after fleeing from the siege in Sarajevo. Slavenka's daughter, Rujana, insisted that, among the other things they were giving Drazena, it was a good idea to give her a pair of black patent leather high-heeled shoes. At first, Slavenka thought that a daft idea; Drazena would need "sensible" footwear to trek around looking for an apartment and a job. But Rujana stood her ground, and persuaded her mother that having the emotional lift of elegant shoes might be precisely what Drazena needed.

Slavenka recounts this discussion with her usual, most engaging candor. She then develops her theme by musing how easy it is to start judging people by the categories into which they fall ("refugee") rather than by who they are as persons:

> What I am starting to do is to reduce a real, physical individual to an abstract "they"—that is, to a common denominator of refugees, owners of the yellow certificate. From there to second-class citizen—or rather, non-citizen—who owns nothing and has no rights, is only a thin blue line. I can also see how easy it is to slip into this prejudice as into a familiar pair of warm slippers, ready and waiting for me at home. . . .
>
> Now I think I understand what I couldn't understand before: how it happened that people who lived near German concentration camps didn't do anything, didn't help.

High-heeled shoes, warm slippers: once again, domestic images, and the contrasts between them, are skillfully invoked to convey truths of existential human import.

Slavenka might tell us, too, about the Laura Ashley wallpaper that she had bought at the beginning of July 1991, when the Yugoslav Federal Army dropped the first bombs on Slovenia:

> I had been wanting to redecorate my bedroom for ages, but went to buy the paper only after I heard the news about the attack. . . . I was aware that I was doing it in spite of the war, perhaps as a symbolic gesture of faith in a future when putting up new wallpaper would make sense.

And Jean might counter by explaining, as she did two or three times throughout her book, how important it was to her after times of particular stress to work out her frustrations in house-cleaning. House-cleaning, that is, as the persistent, quiet, and hopeful response to all the militiamen's attempts to sow the chaos and disruption of their form of "cleansing."

Then Jean might recall the first time her apartment received a direct hit from heavy artillery. The whole family had been waiting out the attack in the underground garage of their building. After it subsided, she went up to check the apartment:

> Front door doesn't open. Wrong keys? After a little struggle, lock gives way. I have an impression of total whiteness. Strange, I think to myself, when did Samir have time to cover everything with white sheets? Funny: I don't own enough white sheets to cover everything. . . .
>
> Realization dawns. Those are not white sheets, but dust. The place is a shambles. Everything is white and broken. Real fear now. This is death. Not something to be read about in the newspapers, but something that has come into my house, that has violated my life, my territory, my being. . . .

But Jean resolved that she would stay in Beirut. That was March 1976. She stayed through another eight months of intense internal fighting that year; then through five years of continued sporadic fighting, some of it very violent. (I left Beirut with my children in early 1981.) She stayed through most of the Israeli siege of 1982, then through the chaotic years of internal warfare that followed. In the last dated entry in her book, in February 1990, she recorded that her apartment had received another direct hit.

I believe that Jean is still in Beirut. In spring 1990, she wrote:

> Time has been wasted; years have passed; loneliness and emptiness have encroached. I have had my youth ushered into middle age by war. My children's—all the children's—childhood was lived in its shadow. My youngest son was four when the war began; now he is in university.

Women's lives can be described as having their own rhythms, with each initiation into a new stage being marked by its own rituals and meaning. First menstruation, first romantic love, marriage, first intercourse, first childbirth; the nursing and raising of children, and sending them off into the world; developments in the world of friends, the maturing of a marriage, the passing of older generations. The rhythm of these events (which may not always happen in the same order) has in our time been overlaid with other acts of transition: graduations from various stages of education; first full-time job, then promotions or other changes in our careers; moves from one community to another; perhaps a divorce. As for war, in the past it was often present in women's lives, against the background of the traditional transitions. But generally, in the past, women's experience of war was vicarious, mediated through either their male family members or its general impact on their communities.

In this century, women and children in settled civilian communities have become the direct targets of war, however far they might be from a battlefront: from the first tentative forays into aerial bombardment of cities in the First World War, to the development of a whole doctrine, "counter-value targeting," that held massed civilian populations to be a plausible target in the "massive retaliation" of nuclear deterrence. What has happened, *is* happening, to women and families in Beirut, Croatia, and Bosnia, is just a simple extension of this thinking.

So perhaps we can start to look at women's lives in new ways, constructing the dimensions of our experience not just on the basis of how many children we have, or the stage we've reached on the job ladder, but also by examining our lives through the lens of war. In this context, Jean has to emerge the veteran. Not just in surviving the eighteen years of Beirut's war, but in the intensity of some of those experiences, and the thoughtful, articulate way in which her writing tries to make sense of them, mark this woman as one who can give wisdom to us all.

> Those who are outside looking in see only the war. For us, there are people, friends, life, activity, production, commitments, a profound intensity of meaning. . . .
>
> Most important of all, there has been a sense of community so powerful as to compensate for the difficulties of life. I have felt, over the years, in spite of the depression, the fear, and the doubts, a sense of privilege at having shared this impossible fragment of history with so many good people. We have looked evil in the face; we have spoken to wicked men; we have asked ourselves the questions that most people are spared; and we have understood that the lines between goodness and evil are sometimes broad and clear, sometimes thin and invisible. We have done these things together.
>
> We have understood our own and each other's limitations in a way that has made us all more tolerant of humanity. There are, for instance, no more illusions left

in any of us about bravery and stoicism, about who can stand how much and for how long. We have seen each other crack under the pressure of events, each one in his own way, each one at his own time and for his own reason; we have seen each other lose dignity, seen each other shake in humiliating fear. We used to laugh at these weaknesses but no longer do so. We have seen ourselves and each other under a microscope for years, naked blobs of humanity on glass slides scrutinized through the merciless lens of history, and nothing any of us does surprises the rest anymore. We understand and accept our own and our friends' limitations.

Some of the profoundest insights that Jean draws from her experience of war are related to her gathering renunciation of violence:

> Familiarity, they say, breeds contempt. Familiarity with violence breeds contempt—for what? People? Life? Nature? Goodness? Beauty? Prayer? God himself? For me, familiarity with violence has bred contempt for violence, and only for that, for I have seen what it has accomplished and it is nothing to be proud of....
>
> In the name of causes come the scream of children, the wails of mothers, the smoke of a burned land. In the name of humanity comes the merciless inhumanity of air raids, tanks, machine guns, and throats slit from ear to ear gushing blood.
>
> And in the midst of this orgy of violence, this dance of death, this saturnalia of killing, what is there to do but refuse it? Put it down, this refusal, if you will, to sentimental bourgeois finickiness, and dismiss it with contempt. I have no answer, except to say that I have seen what I have seen.

Slavenka shares Jean's passion for nonviolence. In July 1991, she wrote a moving essay about the World War II pistol that her father had kept hidden away in a closet at home and showed to his two children only once, hiding from them, along with the pistol, memories of the terror of war that continued to prey on his mind. Then, moving to her present situation, the writer adds:

> While I shop for dog food in a store selling hunting equipment, where they also sell guns, an old man comes in offering to sell a lady's pistol for 1000 DM. He puts it down on the counter, small and shiny like a silver toy. All of a sudden, I felt a strong urge to possess it, to buy it, to have it—me, too. Why not, I think, I am alone, defenseless and desperately frightened. My desire lasts only a second, but I realize that in that moment the jaws of war have finally closed around my fragile life.... Like my father's, my life is now breaking in two.

And even Jean, while pronouncing a nonviolent manifesto, does so with huge empathy for those who are not able to. In the passage about her attitude towards those who defended Beirut in 1982, she expressed clear support for people using forceful means to defend their home-town. And she even seriously questioned whether, under each and every circumstance like those she has seen, she would abstain from acts of personal cruelty:

> What do all these acts of unimaginable cruelty mean? ... I want to know whether I can escape the apparently inescapable conclusion that it is in the nature of the beast, that any of us could do it, that I could do it. Could I, if pushed far enough, yet do it?
>
> I have not seen my baby's body mangled in the dust or my fiancee's raped body lying bloody in the street, legs wide apart and eyes blank. I have not seen my father dishonored in death or my mother's nakedness exposed to the world. I have not seen my beautiful, strong, young husband reduced to unidentifiable bits of flesh.... And since I haven't, I no longer dare say that I would not do such cruel things as have been done.
>
> Besides, is there a difference between killing people by pressing a button as you soar through the sky and killing people while you see terror on their faces?

Slavenka might reply to this question that yes, from the point of view of the killer, there is a difference: in her interview with Ivan, he spells out how much harder it is to kill someone when you can see his face. But both women would probably agree that, from the point of view of the victims and their survivors, there probably isn't any difference at all.

The atmosphere at our tea party has become quite serious. We are talking, after all, about questions at the core of human existence and purpose. Jean might bring some of her points home, for the Americans present, by expanding her reflection on what she describes as the "generalized rage" of the young men with guns. Perhaps, she writes, they wield them, "to vent a bottomless anger with a world that has done them no good and, when they shoot, aim at their own dissatisfaction as much as at any more precise target."

In her introductory essay, this thoughtful, experienced survivor of the war zone warns:

> Outsiders look at Beirut from a wary distance, as though it had nothing to do with them; as though, through a protective glass partition, they were watching with immunity a patient thrash about in mortal agony, suffering a ghastly virus contracted in forbidden and faraway places. They speak of Beirut as if it were an aberration of the human experience: It is not. Beirut was a city like any other and its people were a people like any other. What happened here could, I think, happen anywhere.

So these women—whose depth of experience of war and breadth of sympathetic imagination have allowed them to conclude that there are circumstances under which anyone, even you or I, dear reader, might submit to the brand of a confining, imposed identity, and that there are circumstances under which anyone, even you or I, might commit atrocities—are also telling us that there are circumstances under which any societies, even yours and mine, might fall apart. That's a serious thought to ponder. Not just in Croatia, Mogadishu, or Tadjikstan. But here in Washington D.C., too.

Come to think of it, never mind Bill Clinton. We could just have Hillary at the tea party. And have a far-reaching discussion between women about society, evil, social breakdown—and the wars, and threats of wars, in all of our cities.

Elinor Murray Despalatović (review date fall 1994)

SOURCE: Despalatović, Elinor Murray. Review of *Sterben in Kroatien: Vom Krieg mitten in Europa*, by Slavenka Drakulic. *Slavic Review* 53, no. 3 (fall 1994): 927-28.

[*In the following review, Despalatović contends that Drakulic is at her best when describing the "underside" of the war in Croatia in* The Balkan Express.]

[*Sterben in Kroatien: Vom Krieg mitten in Europa*] is the German edition of the collection of essays known in this country as **The Balkan Express: Fragments from the Other Side of the War** (1993). The essays were originally written in Croatian and English. The English version contains two additional essays (**"My Father's Pistol"** and **"A Bitter Capuccino"**). Drakulić is a well-known Croatian journalist who, in addition to publishing articles in *Danas,* the major independent Croatian political journal, has been a regular contributor to *The New Republic, New Statesman and Society, The Nation* and *Time.* Her earlier book of essays, **How We Survived Communism and Even Laughed,** ends just before war broke out in Croatia. **Sterben in Kroatien** is about life in Croatia in the middle of war.

Drakulić is not an ordinary Croat; she comes from the communist establishment. Her father, an army officer, fought with the partisans and she was raised in a household which was Croatian in form; both parents were Croats but Yugoslav and communist in orientation. Slavenka Drakulić's former husband was a Serb. In the first essay, **"Ein Brief an meine Tochter,"** she explains that at the time they married such things were not important. Their daughter is half Croatian and half Serbian at a time when the two nations are at war. In the last decade of communist Yugoslavia, Slavenka Drakulić became an outspoken anti-communist, a leading feminist writer and an internationally known journalist. She was in London when war broke out in Slovenia. Her daughter fled abroad as war reached Croatia and Drakulić herself spent a short time then in Slovenia as a "refugee." With the coming of war, the world Drakulić knew, imperfect as it may have been, was shattered and the new was alien to her. Perhaps that is why hers is a voice more appreciated abroad than in her own country: she stands at an emotional distance from independent Croatia.

Drakulić observes the war in Croatia as one would a natural disaster. She is haunted by the images of families killed while going about daily chores, boys forced to take up arms, friendships broken. She writes many of the essays from abroad, well aware that few there understand the intricacies of the Croatian war and that the repeated horrors of war become "boring" to outsiders. She laments that the illusion of freedom within communist Yugoslavia, seen in the ability to shop abroad and to travel freely, blinded people to the need to organize politically for post-communism. Although there is one standard war report and an interview with a boy who fought at Vukovar in the Croatian National Guards, Drakulić is at her best when she writes of what one might call the "underside" of the war. She describes her mother's worry that "they" will despoil her husband's grave because it has a red star, her own momentary irritation that a colleague from Sarajevo, who is now a refugee, wears high-heeled shoes, and that a young ambitious journalist who had been apartment "sitting" for a couple who were living and working in Belgrade tried to steal the apartment. Drakulić is consistently negative about the present Croatian government and in one essay describes Croatian President Franjo Tudjman calmly ignoring a demonstration of refugees from Vukovar as he sits in his favorite Zagreb cafe.

There is nostalgia in this book for a Yugoslavia which was large and prosperous, where nationality did not matter, where children chanted praises to "brotherhood and unity" and where there was peace.

Liliana Brisby (review date 19 October 1996)

SOURCE: Brisby, Liliana. "Another False Dawn." *Spectator* 277, no. 879 (19 October 1996): 52-3.

[*In the following review, Brisby points out inconsistencies in Drakulic's* Café Europa: Life after Communism, *but argues that "her critique is well worth listening to."*]

In **How We Survived Communism and Even Laughed,** a collection of essays published a decade ago, Slavenka Drakulic had a marvellous title which unfortunately she failed to live up to. The book was rather humourless and survival was irritatingly viewed mainly from a consumerist perspective: there was more about the miseries of not having proper lavatory paper than about the humiliations of being treated like a sheep by the communist rulers. As the daughter of one of Tito's partisan generals in a country reaping the benefits of the 1948 break with Stalin, she used her frequent travels to the West to train her keen journalistic eye on the contrasting experiences of women on both sides of a disintegrating Iron Curtain. Part of a cynical and apolitical post-war generation, she did not believe in Marxism but was ideological in her espousal of militant feminism to the point of denying her small daughter the coveted Barbie doll.

Ten years on, her new batch of short essays focuses on life in Eastern Europe after the fall of communism. No longer a struggling single mother, but happily married to a gentle Swedish journalist, with a well-stocked home in Sweden and a summer house in Croatia, the author finds that the gulf between the two halves of Europe persists. Despite growing privatisation, a free market and the lifting of censorship, she sees a lasting legacy of communism in the inability of East Europeans to grow up and practise democracy—'they do not know how to be free and are not ready for responsibility'. Instead, they are willingly mobilised behind their rediscovered and often rewritten past, clinging to nationalist ideals and myths which lead to the old mistakes, back to Balkanisation rather than to the Westernisation they aspire to. Real democracy still eludes them.

While there is little to quarrel with in the author's general observations, the charm of her writing, now as before, is to be found in the arresting details, and revealing paradoxes gleaned as she ranges over the spectrum of post-1990 change from Albania to Czechoslovakia. Revolution is seen in small everyday things: sounds, looks, smells, images. Would anyone else have spotted that in Budapest, as in no Western capital, you can buy sweets in a shop called Bonbonnière Hemingway? In Zagreb a beautiful cinema, once named 'the Balkan', has been rechristened 'the Europa', encapsulating what people want to be, not what they are. In Sofia, where a smile is at a premium, the Café Wien's meticulous recreation of an elegant Viennese ambience produces 'a Brechtian alienation effect', as do the depleted 'supermarkets' and the humble Café Hollywood in Bucharest.

Drakulic's habit of looking at the state of personal hygiene and public lavatories as a litmus test of the surviving heritage of Communism and the faltering advance of democracy leads to a comic act of symbolic resistance followed by serious reflection. Having relieved herself in the gleaming bowl of the pink and gold kitsch bathroom in the sumptuous villa of Ceausescu's daughter,

> I understood that a civilised democratic society has a very slim chance of taking root in countries where a normal clean bathroom with running hot water, toilet paper and soap was a luxury reserved for dictators.

True, as far as it goes.

Not being political, Drakulic puts her faith for the future in responsible individualism. But in confessing that she has remained an incorrigible hoarder of cheap consumer goods and that she expresses her opposition to the appalling shortages and soaring prices under post-communist dispensations by becoming 'a "professional" East European smuggler' of foreign goods, she gets entangled in contradictions which her life in the West has not resolved.

Nevertheless, her critique is well worth listening to, especially with regard to her native Croatia. Her merciless lampooning of General Franco Tudjman is just, and her refusal to be swept away by the prevailing nationalist tide is worthy of respect. However, her condemnation of the crimes of the fascist wartime leader Ante Pavelic and the horrors of the extermination camp at Jasenovac ('our own, local, home-made little Auschwitz') would have carried even more weight if paralleled by a more acute political indictment of communism.

In asking rather diffidently whether Eastern Europe, too, has something to contribute to the West it longs to join, Drakulic mentions the model of the moral politician represented by Vaclav Havel. This seems to me to hit the nail on the head: for the most heartening thing about communism's collapse was its ultimate failure to win by way of fear and opportunism. In the end, the dissident voices of courageous men and women of principle could not be silenced.

Christopher Merrill (review date 16 February 1997)

SOURCE: Merrill, Christopher. "Breaking Away." *Los Angeles Times Book Review* (16 February 1997): 11.

[*In the following review, Merrill offers a positive assessment of* Café Europa, *praising the collection as insightful and engaging.*]

"Life, for the most part, is trivial," Slavenka Drakulic announced in ***How We Survived Communism and Even Laughed,*** her first collection of essays published in English. "But trivia is political." The wit and candor with which she explored in those pages the relationship between political authority and the trivia of daily life in the former Yugoslavia earned her a spirited readership in the West. Here was a fresh and, more important, reliable guide to a land—*terra incognita,* for many—about to lay claim to the world's attention.

True, the Communist system had fallen apart, but the habits of thinking inculcated in its citizenry persisted, often in the guise of virulent nationalism. When fighting broke out in Yugoslavia, first in Slovenia, then in Croatia and then, most tragically, in Bosnia-Herzegovina, Drakulic chronicled "the other, less visible side of war"—the ways in which war changes one's values, perceptions and thinking.

In ***The Balkan Express: Fragments from the Other Side of the War,*** she described, in poignant terms, how the war stripped Yugoslavs of their individuality and plunged the land into ever-accelerating cycles of destruction and despair.

In her latest collection of personal essays, *Café Europa: Life after Communism,* Drakulic uses a wider lens to focus on the general plight of Eastern Europeans seven years after the revolution. The Croatian writer, newly married to a Swedish journalist, now divides her time between Zagreb and Vienna, and what she discovers shuttling between her homes, as well as in travels to Bucharest, Budapest, London, Prague, Sofia, Stockholm, Tel Aviv and Tirana, is that she can neither escape her past nor pretend that Eastern Europeans are anything other than second-class citizens. Writing in English, in a supple and felicitous manner. Drakulic suggests how very far she and her countrymen have yet to go to create a civil society. "Even I, in my own head, have not made the definite step from 'them' to 'me,' from communism to democracy," she admits.

Civil society, she realizes, will not begin of its own accord. "Individual responsibility, including the responsibility for oneself, is an entirely new concept here," she writes, yet it is crucial to the development of democracy. She illustrates the continuing failure to recognize the connection between individual behavior and democratic ideals in a variety of ways, none more humorously than in her essay on bad teeth: "As absurd as it may sound, in the old days one could blame the Communist Party even for one's bad teeth. Now there is no one to blame, but it takes time to understand that."

Drakulic tells her "short half-stories, half-essays," as she describes her style of reportage, through revelatory details—a hotel clerk's refusal to smile, the number of new businesses with Western names, the amount of mud in the city streets.

In Tirana, for example, once her eye becomes accustomed to the concrete bunkers lining the road—some of the more than 600,000 "pillboxes" built to protect Albanians from a Western invasion—she notices the mangled remains of greenhouses the Albanians wrecked during their revolution. It turns out that they destroyed everything associated with the Communist state—factories, schools, hospitals and monuments to their hated dictator, Enver Hohxa. Drakulic explains their anger as a function of the bunkers, whose "only purpose was to create and perpetuate fear. If you live surrounded by them, when freedom finally comes, that fear turns into hatred and aggression. You could even call it the 'pillbox effect.'"

Café Europa is full of such insight; and if there is a limitation to Drakulic's method it resides in her occasional refusal to ask the larger questions these insights demand—questions she never ducks when it comes to references to her homeland. For example, though she sympathizes with the Albanians' desire to erase even the material aspects of their past, she is not so forgiving of her countrymen's propensity to rewrite history. To her horror, Croatia's "independent" fascist past is now cause for celebration: Street names are changed to honor members of the Ustasha, the Nazi puppets who committed vicious atrocities during World War II, their crimes against humanity played down or denied. And the Croatian people, she asserts, are engaged in a conspiracy of silence about the ways in which their government "is more or less discreetly establishing a direct link with the 1941-45 period, thus rehabilitating fascism." This is why Drakulic admires the Germans: They at least had the strength not to erase their Nazi past.

The most moving essay here, **"My Father's Guilt,"** is indeed a meditation on memory. On a visit to her father's grave, the writer notices that her mother has taken to covering up the star carved into his tombstone, signifying his membership in the Communist Party. He was by turns an opponent of fascism, a partisan and a high-ranking officer in the Yugoslav National Army—marks against him in Croatia today. But the writer believes that it is no better to forget Croatia's communist history than it is to resurrect and celebrate its Ustasha past: "It is all part of our identity and our growing up as individuals, as citizens, as a nation. It is essential if we decide that we don't want to repeat the same mistakes that brought us where we are now—to the war."

The war, in fact, is the most visible sign of the divisions the writer discerns between Eastern Europeans and Western Europeans. That she can find in every European capital "a hotel, a cinema, a bar, a restaurant, a cafe or a simple hole in the wall, named, for our desire, Europa" does not mean that Western Europeans have accepted their neighbors. Drakulic vividly portrays the distances between them during a meal with a family of Bosnian refugees in Stockholm. The refugees do not belong to Swedish society and all that remains of their former lives is the food they share with her.

How can it be, she wonders, that after 50 years of peace another genocidal war broke out in Europe? And why did Europeans watch the war, paralyzed? "Should we not, must we not ask, then, what is Europe after Bosnia?" America, too, for that matter. *Café Europa* is literary journalism of the highest order.

Kate Bingham (review date 11 April 1997)

SOURCE: Bingham, Kate. "Strangers in a City." *New Statesman* 126, no. 4329 (11 April 1997): 49.

[*In the following review, Bingham lauds Drakulic's narrative skill in* The Taste of a Man *and discusses the novel's major themes.*]

There is much to admire in [*The Taste of a Man*] Slavenka Drakulic's chilling tale of all-consuming passion, not least the skill with which she measures out the desperate paradox that lies at its very heart. Remorseless in their detail, her descriptions are simultaneously erotic and objective. Celebratory in tone, *The Taste of a Man* is also a heartfelt, if unrepentant confession. Its themes are exile, social taboos and obsessive love.

José and Tereza are strangers in the city. He is a Brazilian anthropologist with an interest in cannibalism, who has a wife and child in Sao Paulo. She is a Polish literature student and, nominally, a poet. They have nothing in common except, paradoxically, their differences: at first, "the fact that we were not each speaking our own language made it easier, rather than more difficult, to strike up a conversation."

As in the story of Sylvia Plath's first physical encounter with Ted Hughes, she bites him, drawing blood. Three days later he moves into her apartment. Soon, however, "José and I could barely rely on any language other than that of the body, precisely because we lacked a common language." Their relationship is forced on to an exclusively physical plane. And, ultimately, it proves fatal.

Single-mindedness and clarity of purpose are all-important when choosing to kill the one you love. Tereza's account explores the intricate memory-triggers and thought processes leading to her final decision. It is in these that the real tension of the story lies.

In spite of its willingness to describe the unimaginable, there are few surprises in this novel.

In the controlled, dispassionate voice of a true obsessive intent on rationalising her behaviour, Tereza, narrator and chief protagonist, introduces the story with a chapter devoted almost entirely to house-cleaning.

This leaves little room for doubt in the reader's mind that a truly terrible crime has recently taken place in her now-spotless New York apartment. Still, one can't help staying with it out of a sense of grisly expectation and in this Drakulic does not disappoint.

Liesl Schillinger (review date 10 August 1997)

SOURCE: Schillinger, Liesl. "Hungry for His Love." *Washington Post Book World* (10 August 1997): 5.

[*In the following review, Schillinger asserts that the theme of Drakulic's* The Taste of a Man *is the loss of identity that occurs when a person is consumed by love.*]

In her book *The Balkan Express,* a collection of sensitive and subversive reflections on the war in her native Yugoslavia, Slavenka Drakulic wrote that the worst aspect of war was not its carnage, or its chaos, but its relentless way of alienating people from who they used to be before the war, of estranging them from themselves. Just before Christmas in 1991, in the aftermath of the massacres in Vukovar, the author sat, impassive, in a bath in a Parisian hotel, recollecting brutal photographs of the atrocity, and watching impassively as blood seeped out of a cut in her finger. Squeezing the cut, watching the blood ooze, she wrote:

> This body was no longer mine. It had been taken over by something else, taken over by the war. I had thought that the death of the body was the worst thing that could happen in war; I didn't know that worse was the separation of self from the body, the numbness of the inner being, extinction before death, pain before pain.

Now, in the novel *The Taste of a Man,* her third, Drakulic again explores the terrifying possession that comes when a person is consumed by a larger, inexorable force; this time, love. Again we see a woman in a tiled bathroom at Christmastime, watching blood pinken the water as she struggles to remember who she is. Again we read language, almost in the same words, of the annihilation of self, the usurpation of the body by the other. But this time the blood the woman sees belongs not to herself, but to the man she has murdered—a man she loved, and the man in whom she had invested her identity so wholly that rather than lose him she chose to kill him, cut him up and, in short, eat bits of him, in order to rebuild herself via the grim communion. Drakulic's narrator, Tereza, reflects:

> On the surface, that is what I did. I took his life, I killed him. . . . But that is not at all what this is about: it is about the possibility of prolonging life, about a way of allowing us to stay together. Jose's death was merely a necessary detail, an unavoidable step towards achieving union; a means, not an end.

In other words, to paraphrase My Lai, she had to destroy the union in order to save it. Usually, one would hate to give so much away in a review; but here, Drakulic's relentless foreshadowing, which peekaboos from the dedication page all the way to the bloody end, guarantees that anyone who reads the first five pages cannot possibly doubt the nature of the unappetizing feast that awaits them. At any rate, the point of the book, one guesses, is not so much the story as its telling, and love has precious little to do with it.

There are those who will want to see *The Taste of a Man* as a straightforward story of obsessive love; and indeed, the book does inhabit the male-female-wife love triangle that has been so convenient to romantic tragedy and comedy immemorially. If you choose to read the book this way, and if you have a fondness for

"Fatal Attraction"-type sexual jealousy stories, a thoroughgoing indifference to the psyche of the male character in such a triangle, and a hearty taste for hacksaws, you can be satisfied with the novel on those points alone. Tereza, a Polish graduate student at New York University, falls headlong in love with Jose, a married Brazilian visiting professor, who is at work on a book about cannibalism. A smorgasbord of ghoulish teasers pop out from every corner: The book opens with Tereza fanatically scouring blood out of the floorboards; the couple meets when Tereza, by a "chance happening," lunges for Jose's copy of *Divine Hunger,* a book about his pet subject, "the geographic distribution of exo-cannibalism and endo-cannibalism. At the time," Teresa declares (can we be blamed if we doubt her?), "nothing in the world could have interested me less than a study of cannibalism." But funnily enough, the subject keeps recurring, at dinner parties, at art exhibitions and wherever else the two of them wander. "At their first tryst they lunch off each other's shoulder blades, Tereza mistaking Jose for a "roast joint" a la Sylvester eyeing Tweetybird, and for small talk, they discuss the manner in which the subjects of the film "Alive!" snacked off slivers of their doomed co-passengers' bodies in order to survive. They love, he dies, she has interior monologue.

Much as Fassbinder's remarkable film *The Marriage of Maria Braun* served as an allegory of the whorish compromises post-War Germany had to make to ensure its survival, Drakulic's novel serves, one guesses, as an allegory for semi-Post-War Yugoslavia (sic), which continues to devour what it loves—its own people—under the unhealthy illusion that by doing so, it can be restored. As Jose explains to Tereza, describing the consoling grace that allowed the survivors of the "Alive!" crash in the Andes to violate the human flesh taboo. "Up there in those heights there were no obstacles between them and God. The moment they believed that God wanted them to stay alive by eating the corpses of their friends, it all became so simple." In *The Taste of a Man,* Drakulic has written a grotesque; a cannibalistic fable that makes love war, and takes no prisoners.

Cynthia Simmons (review date summer 1998)

SOURCE: Simmons, Cynthia. Review of *Café Europa: Life after Communism,* by Slavenka Drakulic. *Slavic and East European Journal* 42, no. 2 (summer 1998): 343-45.

[*In the following review, Simmons compares Drakulic's oeuvre to the works of Dubravka Ugresic and asserts that* Café Europa *is both informative and entertaining.*]

Café Europa is the Croatian journalist Slavenka Drakulić's third book of essays on life in post-Communist (now ex-) Yugoslavia. *How We Survived Communism and Even Laughed* (New York, 1992) brought the author to the attention of American readers. Lecturing on the first book in this "series," she amused audiences by holding up a tampon as a symbol of why communism was destined to fail—its inability to provide citizens with the basic requisites of modern existence. She also lamented the intractability of communism in Eastern Europe, even after its formal demise, as a "state of mind." Another book of short essays appeared the following year. *The Balkan Express: Fragments from the Other Side of War* (New York, 1993) was perhaps the most accessible journalist's take on the various human sides to the Yugoslav wars. She interviewed Bosnian refugees and Croatian soldiers. Anyone who followed the war closely will recall the incident in **"Love Story,"** when a young Sarajevan couple (the Bosnian Serb Boško and Bosnian Moslem Admira) were gunned down while trying to flee besieged Sarajevo for Belgrade, even though their safe passage had been agreed to by both sides. In *Café Europa* Drakulić revisits some of the issues concerning newly independent countries in Eastern Europe that she discussed in the previous books and comments as well on the realities of (let us hope) post-war ex-Yugoslavia.

It is an unfortunate irony that the two women writers who have been most successful in conveying to Western (especially American) readers the commonplace tragedies of the Yugoslav debacle and the perspectives of the victims of the conflicts—Drakulić and the writer and Slavist Dubravka Ugrešić—suffered recriminations and, to varying degrees, persecution in their native Croatia for their "cosmopolitanism," that is, their rejection of virulent nationalism. Ugrešić published a book of essays on the war from her vantage point in the United States (she lost her teaching position at the University of Zagreb), *Have a Nice Day* (New York, 1994), followed by the award-winning lament for her homeland *Kultura laži (antipolitički eseji)* (*Culture of Lies [Antipolitical Essays],* Zagreb, 1996), which will be published in English this year. Ugrešić's name appears in a review of Drakulić's book for several reasons. These women, coevals and former residents of Zagreb, by virtue of their celebrity and eventual notoriety, appear to have become indistinguishable in the public consciousness. This is understandable when one considers the uncanny way in which they at times appear to be in sync, or in dialogue. They have both discussed in their works their mothers' vacillation over whether to remove the red star from their husbands' (and the writers' fathers') graves, because service in the Partisans or the Yugoslav Army became a source of suspicion or shame after Croatia's succession from Yugoslavia. And they have likewise both analyzed the West from the perspective of Eastern Europe: the reduction of individuals to a monolithic mass of "Eastern Europeans" that begins with their first meeting with a Western border guard, the culture of Western advertising, and the perky phatic language that is required in a service economy—our "Have a nice day!" Yet there are significant differences. Drakulić's prose conveys a sense of immediacy and the presence of the writer as an eyewitness and participant. This contrasts to Ugrešić's pensiveness and her philosophical and literary recontextualization of events.

In *Café Europa,* Drakulić is most engaging when she takes us where few people are allowed to go, whether literally or figuratively. Her piece on Albania, **"The Pillbox Effect,"** may be edifying even for Slavists, for whom many of the other revelations of this book come as no surprise. The author describes her first reaction when landing in Tirana to the hundreds of defensive "pillboxes" around the airport, which only confirms the image of Albania as a virtual prison. Drakulić reminds us of the rampant destruction that ordinary citizens inflicted on their own country's infrastructure after the revolution. The author attributes this mayhem to the public's attack on all that they equated with the government—and that would have been everything. However, her suggestion that this destruction occurred because Western television advertising promised Albanians a whole new world once they were out from under Hoxha's rule seems less plausible.

Drakulić reveals much of herself personally; at times she is confessional. In **"To Have or Have Not,"** she questions her habit of carrying loads of goods back to friends and relatives in Croatia, even now when almost everything is available there, if expensive. She recalls the original reasons for this practice—there was less to buy in Yugoslavia, and it was the duty of the person traveling "abroad" to compensate the less fortunate at home. Yet now she is irritated that attitudes have not changed. The person living abroad is not necessarily more fortunate, but those in Croatia still feel more needy and entitled.

Drakulić's generalizations on the current status of "Westernization" in Eastern Europe will not be news to specialists, but she travels widely and offers glimpses of the process in various locales. In Prague, there is still no sense of the connection between work and pay. Capitalism means only the former scheming to get money, but now without rules. In Sofia, hotel receptionists still equate service with servitude and treat hotel guests with contempt—they are determined to preserve their pride despite their position. Several pieces deal with Croatia's rush to resurrect, rather than atone for, its Fascist past. The title essay **"Café Europa"** treats the ambivalent attitude of Eastern Europeans toward the West. Capital cities all have their version of a European café, but their vision of the Europe that denies them their geographical membership in the continent is just that—an ideal that cannot be realized or even approached without drastic cultural changes.

Presumably Drakulić wrote *Café Europa* in English. It is pleasantly idiomatic, yet still in serious need of an editor. The English is too often ungrammatical, and occasionally confusing (in the last sentence on page 84, surely both clauses should not be negative—Croatia *was* able to erase its Fascist past), or nonsensical ("the uniform of an army officer . . . complete with a sable" [71]). More disturbing is the rare occasion when the author seems to write carelessly. In the touching essay with which the book concludes, **"Bosnia, or What Europe Means to Us,"** Drakulić recounts a visit to a Bosnian refugee family in Stockholm. She muses over the differences between them and herself—superficial matters like names and ways of preparing food—and the more important similarities—45 years of shard history, their Slavic race, not to mention their basic humanity. She regrets the Western European nations' neglect of their formerly shared homeland, which they justified "with the very convenient theory of the 'ancient hatred' of peoples of the Balkans" (211). Yet on the very next page, when discussing the myth of "Europe" that Eastern Europeans devised, Drakulić employs the same orientalist stereotype that she deplores: "Because for us, the people from the Balkans, the biggest fear is to be left alone with each other. We have learned better than others what you do to your own brother" (212). Certainly the author was referring to the latest atrocities, "brother" was intended metaphorically, and this reviewer is hyper-sensitive. Yet we must be that careful.

Café Europa is a now humorous, now poignant glance at the growing pains of Eastern Europe. Drakulić entertains and informs. Her book is welcomed by those who are invested in any way in the fates of these nations and who strive to remind the world of their continuing existence.

Dina Iordanova (review date fall 1998)

SOURCE: Iordanova, Dina. Review of *The Taste of a Man,* by Slavenka Drakulic. *Slavic and East European Journal* 42, no. 3 (fall 1998): 568-88.

[*In the following review, Iordanova notes flaws in* The Taste of a Man, *but asserts that Drakulic's concurrent interests in writing essays on civil causes and erotic novels makes her career interesting.*]

[In *The Taste of a Man,*] Teresa—a Polish post-doc in literature and a poet, and Jose—a Brazilian visiting scholar, meet by accident at the New York Public Library where Jose is doing research for a book on a 1980s incident of cannibalism in the Peruvian Andes. They engage in a passionate love affair, soon move in together, and intensely enjoy each other before their life schedules take them back to the places they came from and to the people they left behind. Jose is a married man; his wife calls at some point to let him know she is pregnant, and Jose flies away for a week to see her. Alone in New York, Teresa realizes that she has become so devoted to Jose that she just cannot bear losing him. She gradually grows obsessed with the idea of possessing him fully, and comes to think that the only way to keep him is to kill him. She plans his death, then carries out the plan, then eats bits of Jose's flesh, and spends several days in dismembering his decomposing body and getting rid of the body parts. Then she takes an airplane and leaves for Warsaw.

This straightforward story is told in a way that makes it look rather complex—mostly in flashbacks in which Teresa, busy cleaning blood stains, recounts the relationship and reveals an elaborate world of past and present relationships and interactions. The preoccupation with disease and death in their bodily aspect is characteristic for Drakulic's fiction (this is her third novel, following **Holograms of Fear** and **Marble Skin**). Cannibalism is only one of the many dimensions that consumption in general takes in **The Taste of a Man**—another one is eating (there are numerous references to traditional Brazilian and Polish dishes, detailed descriptions of cooking and eating at restaurants), and a third one consists of references to the body of Christ, quite relevant considering that the protagonists are Catholic. It seems that the plan to consume the body of the lover is at least partially induced by the nature of Jose's own macabre studies. Throughout the book there are scattered references to well-known incidents of cannibalism, and the text itself triggers parallels to works like the Brazilian film *How Tasty Was My Little Frenchman*, or Peter Greenaway's *The Cook, The Thief, His Wife and Her Lover* and his more recent *Pillow Book*, where the consumption of the body of the beloved one is represented as a superior level in a love relationship.

Drakulic is conscious of the expanding universe in which races and cultures mix in a global post-modern copulation, a blend that only lately has come to be of interest to Slavic writers. **The Taste of a Man** is a novel which integrates several dominant trends, characteristic of today's cosmopolitan fiction writing. The first one is the concern with explorations of the body; a second is the preoccupation with the erotic; and a third is the interest in experiences of displacement. One cannot expect, however, that this novel will be trend-setting itself. Challenging the boundaries of sensuality is the main feature of **The Taste of a Man,** and Drakulic deserves praise for being as daring as she is. Yet, the eroticism is not as intense as one could expect, and occasionally looks like an imitation of Erica Jong. Teresa's obsession remains insufficiently explored, and the detailed gut-wrenching description of ritualistic dismemberment commands the attention of the author more than the psychological motivation of her heroine.

Another shortcoming is the lack of a full-blooded male protagonist. Jose is somehow not quite present in the book. Before becoming a decomposing dead body, he was supposed to be an exciting individual, but in fact he remained a stereotypical exotic presence with nothing much impressive besides his Brazilian olive-colored skin. He was never alive enough to make the reader understand what in him incited the passion that led to his killing and consumption.

Born in 1949, Drakulic now enjoys acknowledgment as an international columnist, writing for *The New Republic* (USA), *La Stampa* (Italy), *Dagens Nyheter* (Sweden), *Frankfurter Rundschau* (Germany), and *The Observer* (UK). Her collections of essays are much better known than her fiction (**How We Survived Communism and Even Laughed, Balkan Express, Café Europa**). Endorsed by internationally known feminists, she often speaks for all East European women. Her articulate commitment to cross-cultural interpretation and understanding has made her a major voice from the former Yugoslavia. Drakulic has proven to be a courageous and blunt woman, for which she has gained as much admiration as criticism.

From the photograph on the cover of **The Taste of a Man,** Drakulic looks straight at the reader with an enigmatic smile. Yes, obviously she enjoys being controversial. Yes, she is an outspoken essayist who is known for her commitment to civil society causes. But she is also a "sexual persona," preoccupied with recording the experiences of intense eroticism and dynamic cosmopolitanism. This should not eclipse her vocal defense of Bosnian women or blasting of Croatian nationalism, however. While some may question the compatibility of these two lines of literary output, I prefer to see these two aspects of Drakulic as the most intriguing and promising feature in her work. She will most likely continue to provoke and surprise us.

Valerie Jablow (review date March 2000)

SOURCE: Jablow, Valerie. "No Place Like Home." *Women's Review of Books* 17, no. 6 (March 2000): 1-3.

[*In the following review, Jablow discusses Drakulic's* S: A Novel about the Balkans *and Dubravka Ugresic's* The Museum of Unconditional Surrender.]

If truth, as the saying goes, is the first casualty of war, the second surely is the idea of home. In their native Croatia, Slavenka Drakulić and Dubravka Ugrešić have paid an enormous price for their literary survival. Both were born in 1949, when Yugoslavia and its republics were just picking themselves up after the Nazi occupation during World War Two. Both grew up under Tito's brand of communism. Both became leading writers of nonfiction as well as fiction that challenged the status quo in their homeland. As such, both moved in a circle of intellectuals, admired and feared for their subversive potential in a state where media control and antifeminism were the norm.

But as the war in Yugoslavia—the most recent one, not the centuries' worth of others waged on its soil and subsumed in history—erupted nearly ten years ago, both Drakulić and Ugrešić faced new challenges. Both watched in horror as Croatian streets were renamed after Nazi sympathizers from Croatia's World War Two alliance with Germany. Both found themselves on a list of "anti-Croatian" writers put out by the ruling nationalist party of the newly independent state. What their home was, and is, has never been harder to write about—or accept. Since 1993, in fact, Ugrešić has remained in more or less permanent exile.

Given their commonalities, it's not surprising that Drakulić's and Ugrešić's latest novels delineate the unspeakable effects of the recent European war on identity, home and self from the point of view of women who experienced it. Indeed, readers have come to expect their insight into often forbidden subjects, whether surviving communism, nationalism, or hatred of women. But focusing on such commonalities obscures why Drakulić and Ugrešić are avidly read in many countries (even if, sadly, not much in their homeland): they are excellent writers who have added immensely to European literature and thought over the last twenty years. As different in their approaches and styles as ever, they ensure that silence on the former Yugoslavia will never be deserved or lasting.

We first meet S., the protagonist of Drakulić's fourth novel of the same name [*S: A Novel about the Balkans*], in a Stockholm hospital in 1993. There, she has given birth to a son conceived by rape—specifically, rape by Serbian soldiers in Bosnia at the height of the war in 1992. Gradually, we learn the harrowing details of why she is there and how, as Drakulić unfolds events from the previous year. She is Muslim, daughter of a Muslim father and Serbian mother. She is 29 years old, unmarried, and has a sister who lives with their parents in Sarajevo. She herself is a teacher in a small, mostly Muslim, village in Bosnia. When Serbian soldiers in early summer 1992 force the Muslim villagers to a concentration camp, she is disbelieving: how could this be happening and to her, half Serb, of all people? Given only a few minutes to leave and not even beginning to understand what it means, she takes her two best possessions, a red summer dress and a pair of never-worn Italian shoes. The shoes, notes Drakulić with perfect poignancy, still smell of fine leather.

Thus a nightmare begins. After several villagers are killed outright, the rest are bused to a deserted warehouse complex in the middle of a forest. It is a so-called exchange camp, but clearly the only exchange intended here is with death. Through S.'s eyes, we see the face of human cruelty and suffering: the guards "amenable to bribes," the necessity of selfishness in a new world where food, medicine and safety are coveted luxuries, the bloodstains on concrete floors that the prisoners themselves must clean. The younger women, including S., stay in a darkened cell called the "women's room." There, they slowly descend into madness, awaiting the repeated, personalized hatred that has come to signify this war: rape and torture of women.

Drakulić has reduced the names of all the Yugoslav characters down to single letters. She gives place names the same treatment, and the perpetrators of the violence themselves speak in bursts of short, angry words. It's a wonderful conceit: under such circumstances, language, that civilizing force, can no longer function. Like the fancy shoes and dress that S. is forced to use here as her pillow, the contents of civilization have utterly lost their meaning.

Given the graphic nature of what she describes, it is much to Drakulić's credit that she pulls this off with such a engagingly told story. Ironically, in this, probably her best work of fiction yet, her training as a journalist serves her exceptionally well. In March 1993, for instance, she reported in *The Nation* on Bosnian Muslim women in a refugee camp outside Croatia's capital, Zagreb. Many, she noted, were too ashamed to talk of the rapes and other tortures they had endured. Still, each was able to document in her own way the horrors that she saw, elements of which Drakulić clearly fictionalized here to powerful effect. This is no newspaper account or simple dramatization: you are indeed there.

As in Drakulić's previous novels, the lack of spoken dialogue creates a sense of emotional interiority. Released from the camp to the "freedom" of a refugee camp in Zagreb, for instance, S. finds out that she is pregnant from being raped and cannot obtain an abortion:

> Her body lies in the bed like an inanimate object, an empty bellows or shopping bag. Nothing has changed in her departure from the camp. Her body is still in their power, even more so now. Only now does S. understand that a woman's body never really belongs to the woman. It belongs to others—to the man, the children, the family. And in wartime to soldiers. Five months. A distant and remote verdict has condemned her to this condition from which there is no escape, S. feels as if someone has returned her to the camp, to the "women's room." She has been betrayed. This is war, inside her, in her own womb. And they are winning.
>
> (p. 156)

The novel's denouement, in Sweden, is both heartrending and the weakest part of the book. But that apparent contradiction is not entirely Drakulić's fault: after all, what resolution can there possibly be to losing one's identity and family, one's home? S. reflects on the hospital-issued gown her newborn is clothed in, with the Swedish words for "public property" stamped on it. Those words, she sees, are "a symbol of fate. Only just born and already he belongs to somebody else, not to himself." Sadly, after years of "ethnic cleansing," intolerant nationalism and European misunderstanding and indifference, this experience promises to be one of the more enduring products of that war.

The war in the former Yugoslavia is also the subject of *The Museum of Unconditional Surrender*, but this bald statement doesn't do justice to Ugrešić's creation. Written between 1991 and 1996, as Yugoslavia and its citizens were being fragmented into relics, the novel is itself a series of fragments—diary, letters, stories, even a wartime recipe—that together create a moving meditation on the effects of war and exile on identity and what we know as home. This untraditional format is only what we have come to expect from Ugrešić's fiction: in her previous novel, *Fording the Stream of Consciousness* (1993), for instance, she played on names, languages and literature to create a fantastical world based loosely on the banalities of a literary conference.

In this novel, Ugrešić has set the stakes much higher than in anything she has done previously. Her middle-aged narrator may be, as some have speculated, a portrait of the author—Yugoslav herself, born to a Yugoslav father and Bulgarian mother, in exile from her work as a teacher and translator of Russian literature in Zagreb. No matter. Known to us only as Bubi (her mother's endearment), the narrator travels through her experiences as an exile, living in Berlin with other exiles from the former Yugoslavia. But this is no mere skipping down Yugoslavia's memory lane (what cynics call "Yugonostalgia"). Ugrešić uses Bubi's history and that of her mother, along with an extended essay on photography as a basis for memory and future, and quotations from other writers and artists in exile (including Josef Brodsky, Vladimir Nabokov and the fictional characters she creates), as a kind of palimpsest of war. The effect is stunning: Ugrešić slowly persuades us that the Yugoslavia-rending war was not the singular event we desperately want to believe it is, but a cataclysm linked to all wars in Europe this century, from the cold war back to the first world war, through which Yugoslavia was carved into being.

The novel briefly takes us into the present of the narrator's Berlin exile, only to delve into her past in the former Yugoslavia. We meet her mother, who left Bulgaria after World War Two and fell in love with a handsome Yugoslav sailor, Bubi's father. Though he dies in the 1970s, we never actually see the father directly. Like so much in their family life, he's viewed only through the photographs that literally burst out from the family closet and that her mother hides from Bubi. This chaos is not a matter of bad housekeeping. After all, in the small, sooty town where Bubi grows up, where after the deprivation of World War Two scraps of cloth served as clothes and soup was made from the only ingredients available, fat and water, identity is yet another possession that may be taken, depending on who's in power. Indeed, the disintegration of the former Yugoslavia, and the ousting of its Communist patrons, presents Bubi's mother with a particular challenge:

> In 1991 . . . Mother gathered my father's old medals . . . into a heap, put them into a plastic bag—as though they were human remains—saying sadly: "I don't know what to do with these . . . What if someone finds them?" . . . I believe that it was then that she looked for the first time at [his] moist gravestone and suddenly noticed the five-pointed star (although it had always been there, at her request) and perhaps for the first time she had the thought . . . that it might be possible to paint out the five-pointed star carved into the stone.
>
> (pp. 22-23)

As a sort of crossroads for East and West, Europe and Asia, Berlin is the stage of four of the novel's seven sections. In its streets and cafes, and most particularly the numerous flea markets of that once-divided city, refugees and exiles from all over the former Yugoslavia cross paths. Even more than a source of cash for impoverished immigrants, Berlin's flea markets act as living memory banks:

> The Turk sits in the cab of his truck surveying his territory: a scattered heap of old books, records, albums, photographs. . . . Things last longer than people. Albums outlive their owners. A prolonged life hides in an old coat, in a senseless object which meant something to someone and which will again mean something to someone else. That is how souls migrate. Here refugees from Bosnia meet. They enquire after souls: who is from where, does anyone know what's become of so and so, where is such and such now . . . They exchange news. They gather according to their towns and villages. Along the way they buy some small thing which will help their little refugee room look like home.
>
> Here, in Gustav-Meyer Allee, on Saturdays and Sundays, the country that is no more, Bosnia, draws its map once again in the air, with its towns, villages, rivers and mountains. The map glimmers briefly and then disappears like a soap bubble.
>
> (p. 230)

If a book as purposely decentered as this can be said to have an emotional core, Ugrešić has provided it in a funny and singularly fantastic event. The narrator and her friends, all women and teachers from throughout the former Yugoslavia, get together for one last time to "throw cards"—their euphemism for playing with tarot cards. Of course they don't know it will be the last time, for Yugoslavia has not yet been destroyed. Besides enormous political consequences, the war had mundane ones as well—for instance, eliminating the easy travel between Sarajevo, Belgrade and Zagreb that these friends, happily, normally, took for granted along with their identity as Yugoslavs. During this last session, the women find they have a strange guest in their midst. He's nothing less than a lonesome male angel, who manages to touch their spirits and homes with a bit of humor and happiness that the breakup of their country, and circle, will soon deny.

Not surprisingly, given the fragmentary design of the book, one of the most painful moments occurs offhandedly, in a letter one of her Yugoslav friends writes to Bubi. The friend lists all the places he visited before the war that destroyed not only a political entity but memory and the idea of home. He concludes simply: "Those are all the cold, melancholy, objective images (or more precisely: verbal photographs) from a past life in a former country which it will never again be possible to connect into a whole."

As we learn late in the book, there was a "real" Museum of Unconditional Surrender, which closed in Berlin in 1994, a small relic of communist East Berlin. As both Ugrešić and Drakulić testify, the museum and its contents will live on in the hearts and minds of those who have indeed lost more than a country. "Remembering is actually an act of love," says one of Bubi's Berlin friends. In a war with no winners, that may be the most important lesson of all, and we are lucky to have writers like Ugrešić and Drakulić to provide it.

Radmila J. Gorup (review date summer 2000)

SOURCE: Gorup, Radmila J. Review of *As If I Am Not There: A Novel about the Balkans*, by Slavenka Drakulic. *World Literature Today* 74, no. 3 (summer 2000): 669-70.

[*In the following review, Gorup complains that* As If I Am Not There *is overly concerned with ideology and lacks sufficient plot and characterization.*]

Now the tumor is beside her, as if transformed by some miracle into a child. It is difficult for S. to accept. She has never thought of it as a child, only as a disease, a burden she wished to get rid of, a parasite she wanted removed from her organism." So ruminates S., the protagonist of [*As If I Am Not There,*] the newest novel by Slavenka Drakulić. Drakulić, a Croatian journalist and writer, is familiar to the U.S. reading audience as the author of three novels (**Holograms of Fear, The Taste of a Man,** and **Marble Skin**) and several nonfiction works, including **How We Survived Communism and Even Laughed** (1992) and **Balkan Express** (1993).

It is March 1993 in a Stockholm hospital where S., the novel's unnamed principal character, has just given birth to a baby conceived in a rape camp in Bosnia. The mother feels only revulsion for the child. For nine months she considered it a burden, a tumor growing inside her, and she could not wait to rid herself of it. She welcomes the labor pains. Recalling how Bosnian women in a Zagreb refugee camp killed a baby, S. does not even want to look at her own child.

This beginning prepares the reader for the bland prose of the novel, in which Drakulić, in her own words, abandons the documentary technique in order to "give voice" to rape victims unable to describe their own suffering. Ten months earlier, S. was taken together with thousands of others to a prison camp, where they were subjected to unspeakable acts of terror. While the majority of men were shot, young attractive women were used by soldiers as sex slaves.

S., a twenty-nine-year-old school-teacher in a small village in Bosnia, half-Serb and half-Muslim, is herself taken to one such notorious "women's room." However, she soon catches the eye of the camp commander, who, unlike her regular abusers, is clean-shaven and sober. She welcomes the change, because she is determined to survive her ordeal and bear witness to it. After six months, scarred but alive, S. is among the first exchange prisoners. Resettled in Sweden, she begins the difficult task of reassembling her life.

Regardless of the author's noble intentions, nothing is more upsetting than a fiction writer with a mission. The plot of *As If I Am Not There* quickly develops into a flat-footed narrative which chronicles, in black and white, the events of S.'s six-month ordeal. Drakulić does not do a convincing job of depicting either events or characters. Rather than allowing S.'s character to develop, the author uses S. to illustrate her own political ideas. History is simplified, an image seen on CNN or a story told in the *New York Times*. Everything is clearcut, charged with an effect in mind. The author never stops to elaborate, explain, emphasize. As a result, characters and their feelings are muted.

As If I Am Not There is a journalistic enterprise thinly disguised as a novel. Summaries of women's experiences given through "indirect narrative" are reminiscent of actual press coverage of the rapes in Bosnia. The world of the novel is divided into "good guys" and "bad guys." Occasionally a "bad" character is presented with some vestiges of humanity, like the woman who brings food to the "women's room" or the young soldier who initially addresses S. formally. However, that quickly evaporates. "They," the Serbs, are all brutes; everyone else is good.

Ideology and fiction are a dangerous mix. The black-and-white depiction was supposed to have gone out of vogue with the demise of social realism. Whereas the reading of the newest novel by Dubravka Ugrešić, which deals with the same time period, was a pure joy, the perusal of *As If I Am Not There* was altogether unsatisfying.

Noemi Marin (essay date fall 2001)

SOURCE: Marin, Noemi. "Slavenka Drakulic: Dissidence and Rhetorical Voice in Postcommunist Eastern Europe." *East European Politics and Societies* 15, no. 3 (fall 2001): 678-97.

[*In the following essay, Marin examines Drakulic's role as a marginalized Balkan critic, commending her "rich narratives of postcommunist and communist times."*]

What the communist regimes in Eastern and Central European countries left for posterity are scars of oppression. In spite of communist appeals and propaganda, for decades people fought to reinforce democratic values, freedom, and human rights within and beyond these countries' borders. Moreover, due to communism's oppressive politics, some of the most eloquent representatives of civil societies chose expatriation and dissidence as a political, cultural, and rhetorical way to articulate democratic beliefs from behind the Iron Curtain.[1]

Solzhenitsyn, Kundera, Milosz, Cioran, and Eliade are among well-known expatriates who identify themselves as writers of resistance from communist Eastern and Central Europe.[2] According to their accounts, expatriation and dissidence mark them forever, being both their stigma and their redemption. A marginalized "condition" remains a constant part of their disrupted discourse.[3] Joseph Brodsky,[4] in his appeal to other exiled writers, defines the problem of exile and dissidence as a linguistic confluence joining discourse, questions of identity, and legitimacy of voice, a rhetorical "pendulum" oscillating between moments of "expulsion" into the "capsule" of one's native language, and "the necessity of telling about oppression."[5]

After 1989, the discursive scene in Eastern and Central Europe takes a cultural, political, and rhetorical turn, offering detailed and controversial perspectives on the civil and civic transformations in process in this part of the world.[6] Emerging from the *samizdat* arena and advocating political change, voices of democracy like Václav Havel, George Konrád, and Adam Michnik, for example, provide insight on the turmoil of transition from communism, on nationalism, and on the difficult political venues these countries face on their road to democracy.[7]

It would be easy to think that, once communism was over-thrown and new societies were emerging, writers of dissent from this part of the world were freed from turmoil. Not so. Critical intellectuals are and remain confronted with ontological, political, and rhetorical questions of identity and public voice. Their dissidence implies an inherent conflict, for participants fighting communism or communist ghosts cannot simply throw off one identity and assume another. Rhetorically, these public anticommunist writers carry a double problem throughout their discourse. For, while dissidents speak to the necessity of democratic values and civil society, in doing so, they communicate from their condition of marginalization and resistance.

Such dissident intellectuals bring to the discourse their personal experiences of living in the margins, of recuperating rhetorical voice in the public arena, and of moral responsibilities of democratic existence after the fall of communism. Dissidence, then, becomes a significant rhetorical site for multiple investigations of public discourse. While continuing to advocate civil societies, democratic intellectuals revisit their experiences through discourse and, thus, rhetorically create new definitions of resistance and democratic identity in novel sociocultural contexts. Significantly, dissident intellectuals continue to voice their presence in the public arena, bringing to their audiences appeals for democratic values.[8]

Once communism was defeated, could critical rhetors of resistance's powerful appeals for democracy in the public arenas of their countries fall silent? Do public intellectuals continue to have rhetorical power? Can they change the collective discourse of communist values into individual involvement in creating civil societies? And in their discursive processes, how can these advocates of democracy reaffirm the need for civil society while legitimizing their own rhetorical voice through language?

Slavenka Drakulić is a writer from the Balkans, one of the critical intellectuals whose life in the margins posits significant rhetorical and political problems. A Croat and also a former Yugoslav, a European who lives part of her time in Eastern Europe and the rest on the western side of the continent, a civic voice with two homes and no land, an advocate of democracy, Drakulić brings to the rhetoric of resistance a unique and intriguing perspective on the relationship between marginalization and discourse. For Drakulić, the chaos of the Balkans starts in 1990 and from then to present times, her search for rhetorical voice in a democracy never stops. Drakulić experiences dissent in postcommunist Eastern Europe, in her native Croatia. Although 1989 represents the "end" of the communist era, for some critical intellectuals in the Balkans, exile and dissent remain political, cultural, and ethnic realities.

An unsettled voice, Drakulić offers in her writings in the 1990s rich narratives of postcommunist and communist times in a country once called Yugoslavia.[9] For this Croat journalist with dangerous ideas of anti-nationalist resonance, issues of political power remain to be redefined by the rhetorical, cultural, and political identity present in her discourse.[10] Why, then, does a critical intellectual in postcommunist Croatia continue to resist the public arena of nationalist and neo-communist practices? How can Drakulić recapture her legitimacy once her native land is no longer in the realm of political oppression?

Focusing on the discourse of this important voice in postcommunist Eastern Europe, this study argues that critical writers as rhetors recapture rhetorical identity by transforming the condition of dissidence into rhetorical strategies of public legitimation. Thus, the study explores Slavenka Drakulić's discourse of resistance from a rhetorical perspective. The critical examination proposes an insight into Drakulić's rhetorical strategies to legitimize resistance and transform discourse. Specifically, I argue that Drakulić's rhetorical strategies to reconstruct her legitimate voice in and through discourse assist her creation of an important rhetorical action: namely to reevaluate the cultural and political salience of collective and individual responsibility in the creation of civil society in Eastern Europe.

Accordingly, the research examines first Drakulić's dissident rhetoric and her strategies of redefinition in discourse before and after 1989 in Eastern Europe. Second, it explores her rhetorical strategies of redefinition utilizing as a case study an essay I consider representative for the rhetorical legitimation of Drakulić's voice in the public arena. Third, the study investigates this critical intellectual's strategies of legitimation in light of collective and individual responsibilities in postcommunist discourse.

Voices of Dissidence: Novel Critical Questions on Rhetorical Action

Before examining how Drakulić's strategic resistance regains power and legitimation through a language of dissent, let us visit certain assumptions used in this rhetorical exploration. *Identity* or *voice,* key terms I use interchangeably throughout the study, constitutes the speaker's rhetorical power in discourse. The inherent premise for using *identity* or *voice* in this analysis is that exile and dissidence test a rhetor's powers as a speaker. Identity constitutes in my view a dynamic inherent dimension of the rhetor's reinvention of self in response to exile and dissidence. *Identity* for such a rhetor comprises of revisitation of the traditional *ethos,* while transforming itself, at the same time, into a *relational* construction of the speaker within the cultural, political, and social context of his or her dissidence or exile. It is toward this rhetorical reinstantiating of voice that I gear my examination of Slavenka Drakulic's position as a rhetor of resistance.

In addition, while proposing a rhetorical investigation of the speaker's powers in discourse, this study acknowledges the role *culture* plays rhetorically in discourse.[11] By interpellating contextual and constitutive forces in discourse, speakers of resistance create cultural discourse as they invoke salient relationships between context and voice in their rhetorical appeals to democratic views. In this sense, culture becomes a dynamic rhetorical concept that transforms speakers, audiences, and critics. Culture as a rhetorical dimension reveals how expatriation and dissent force critical intellectuals from Eastern and Central Europe into a rhetorical crisis, into the silence of non-participation in public discourse. Hence, in order to explore Drakulic's appeals, the significant rhetorical issue of her reinvention of voice becomes the speaker's negotiation of identity against political power in specific cultural discourse. This exploration, then, proposes a notion of rhetoric that *interpellates* the rhetor and his or her culture through discourse.

Slavenka Drakulic: How Many Lives in the Margins?

From a rhetorical perspective, Slavenka Drakulić presents an interesting and atypical case in dissident literature. Unlike other critical intellectuals coming to terms with their existence in limbo for a long time, her identity as an expatriate is relatively new (only eight years) and not total.[12] And unlike fellow Croatian feminist, Dubravka Ugrešić, a voluntary exile, Drakulić refuses to acknowledge such an identity in her writings.[13] Relatively *new* in experiencing dissent and marginalization, Drakulić *refuses* to consider her political status of *persona non grata* either a definitional or a definitive experience. More important, from a rhetorical, and I might add, political standpoint, Drakulić cannot remain silent when facing post-1989 neo-communist practices.

Slavenka Drakulić reconstructs her dissident identity in two accounts, ***The Balkan Express*** and ***Café Europa,*** published outside of her country. Drakulić's discourse on postcommunist Eastern Europe reveals a rhetor in conflict with forced displacement as a refugee during the Balkan war, vehemently resisting the realities of nondemocratic practices in her native land. Writing from the margins, her discourse always already engages the *other* discourse (pun intended) on Croatian realities. For, in contrast to Drakulić's articulations, the official account in Croatia offers an explanation for the casualties of an absurd war, providing a rationale for authoritarian politics or nationalistic "fantasies of salvation" (to borrow the title from Tismaneanu's recent work on the complex political realities in the area).[14]

Drakulić's life, identity, and rhetorical powers carry a "before and after 1989" narrative. Before 1989, she is settled as a critical intellectual and journalist in the former Yugoslavia, publishing in one of the most important newspapers in Zagreb, *Danas*.[15] Unlike most dissidents from Eastern Europe, Drakulić's life in the margins of political opposition remains without political consequences.[16] Able to publish actively in magazines and newspapers in the West,[17] Drakulić has a passport in hand and the freedom to travel in both Western and Eastern Europe, enjoying, as she acknowledges, a "much higher standard of living and greater freedom . . . than did [those people in] the rest of the communist states."[18]

After the 1989 revolutions, expecting a civil democracy to follow in the Balkans, Drakulić carries a bewildered voice. History, it seems, has a different political experience in store for this land. The fall of the communist regime brings with it the disintegration of the six federal republics called, once upon a time, Yugoslavia.[19] All of a sudden, the war in the Balkans between Serbia and Croatia, and later between Serbia and Bosnia-Herzegovina, presents a different reality, a reality of battles, nationalist claims, and civil unrest. Her homeland, Croatia, is proclaimed independent in January 1992. As a new state, Croatia posits a novel political and cultural question, since "no one is allowed *not* [my emphasis] to be a Croat."[20] Drakulić, Ugresić, and many other critical voices charge that Croat independence and Tudjman's nationalist and authoritarian regime do not bring a civil society and freedom in the country.[21] Can it be that the political transformation of Croatia remains a skeptical scene with no guarantees for a democracy?[22]

Leaving the experience of refugees in the Balkan war aside,[23] in the hope of a brighter future, Drakulić finds out that her right to speak up against the government is denied in the Croatian media in the name of nationalistic cleansing of the public arena.[24] Hence, the year 1993 marks a rhetorical, political, and cultural turn for Slavenka Drakulić. Her questioning of the regime, her writings in the domestic and international press prove uncomfortable for the new authorities.[25] If Croatia is a democratic regime, asks Drakulić, why is the discourse of political resistance and dissidence not allowed in the new public arena? And why is the media controlled by the nationalist frenzy of Tudjman's rhetoric? Can it be that communist practices are back with a vengeance, only under a different name in this new state?[26]

The response to her critique is dramatic. Called a "witch" in an article entitled "Croatian Feminists Rape Croatia," she is expelled from the press in her country.[27] Hunted, together with four other women writers for her "anti-war, anti-nationalistic, and individual standpoint,"[28] Drakulić crosses the *cultural* borders of exile, becoming a persona non grata in Tudjman's Croatia.[29] A "traitor of the Croatian people," Drakulić is forced to enter life in the margins of discourse, this time, on feminist charges.[30]

One could say, then, that Drakulić exists rhetorically and politically in more than one marginalized discourse, namely in the realm where women's voices are barely audible in a male-oriented culture.[31] Thus, harassed in the media, unable to present her opinions in the new public arena, her public voice is silenced.[32] In postcommunist Croatia, Drakulić becomes a political dissident.

Publicly banned, Drakulić loses her public and professional identity in Croatia, as her collaboration with the newspaper *Danas* ceases.[33] A critical intellectual, a witch, and a feminist, her main offense was her overt criticism of "nationalist homogenization and the non-democratic new regime."[34] Oblivion is her punishment.[35] The only way Drakulić is present in the Croat press is in well-articulated attacks against her.[36] Drakulić explains that: "*they* [my emphasis] publish only criticism towards my writings."[37]

And yet, Drakulić resists her *non grata* status, mentioning her publications in Croatia in 1995 in *Feral Tribune*, one of the very few opposition newspapers.[38] For the most part, however, Drakulić remains with no readership in her homeland, no presence in the Croatian media, expatriated, and yet refusing to accept her new political status. What happens, then, to her rhetorical redefinition of identity in response to dissidence?

Drakulić repositions herself as a critical writer and rhetor in search of civil societies throughout Eastern Europe. Drakulić moves away, fighting old enemies like communism and authoritarian regimes, relentlessly promoting individual responsibilities to create democratic societies, a view she articulates in her collection of essays *Café Europa: Life after Communism*, in 1996. A voice of resistance on a mission to reveal the horrid traces of communism, Drakulić travels Central and Eastern Europe in search of answers for her own vocabulary of democracy. Touring the trails of postcommunist change in Europe, she never forgets her marked life in the margins, as an Eastern European.[39] Drakulić remembers: "I know, they know, and the police officers know that barriers exist and that citizens from Eastern Europe are going to be second-class citizens still for a long time to come, regardless of the downfall of communism or the latest political proclamations. Between us and them there is an invisible wall."[40]

In response to her own role as a dissident journalist away from her readership and from the public arena of her homeland, Drakulić invokes her identity in relation to the linguistic and cultural dimensions of the communist *past* and the postcommunist *present*. Thus, time and grammar become her counterpart context in which she recreates her voice of resistance against nationalism and the authoritarian regime in Croatia. "Introduction: First-Person Singular," the very first essay of her writings on postcommunism in Eastern Europe, reveals Drakulić's rhetorical strategy to reconstitute the dissident voice through the cultural powers of language.[41] Therefore, as she recaptures her identity as a public intellectual in postcommunist Eastern Europe, how does the speaker articulate a voice of democracy through her discourse of resistance?

THE OLD PARADIGM IN CROATIA: RESISTING MEMORIES OF COMMUNISM

In **"Introduction: First-Person Singular"** Drakulić offers a rhetorical account of her symptomatic political opposition to the still-communist Croatia. The writer recaptures rhetorical force as a speaker of dissent in relation to the cultural and political metaphor of "we" and "I." This simple contrastive paradigm aligns the writer's voice with discursive counterparts in communist and neo-communist times in Croatia and the Balkans.[42] Especially for Eastern European writers, pronouns represent strategic choices to invoke cultural walls of exclusion that words create in circumstances of dissent.[43]

Presenting herself as a political and rhetorical user of pronouns, Drakulić captures the rhetorical tensions that "I" versus "we" carry in the new political, cultural, and social Eastern Europe. More important, the author provides reflexive and reflective meanings to the cultural and political dyad "I" versus "we," turning it into a powerful appeal for democracy. Her claims not only address her audiences back home, but also all people aware of communist ideologies of past or present times. Rhetorically, her strategic relation between "I" and "we" becomes a cultural and political move to differentiate two conceptual cultural identities: communist versus dissident. In the discursive process, Drakulić reconstitutes herself as a promoter of democratic values in Eastern Europe, opposing anew communist practices. Objecting strongly to any communist and neo-communist experiences, Drakulić provides a powerful account of political ostracism before and after the so-called fall of the Iron Curtain in the Balkans. And in doing so, Drakulić reinvents her discourse as a grammar of dissidence, to paraphrase Burke.[44]

Empowering her voice as the grammatical voice of the singular "I," Drakulić asserts her dissident identity as a threat for any communist and neo-communist public sphere.[45] For, both in past and in present political contexts in Croatia as her homeland and her cultural point of reference, "the first-person singular" is "exiled from public and political life," turning it into a voice of dissidence.[46]

Similarly, Drakulić explores how the first-person pronoun constitutes a rhetorical gauge exposing the cultural and political barriers between the author and communist or neo-communist times in Croatia. Drakulić articulates resistance by juxtaposing a rhetorical action of saying no as a definition of the "I" against communist contexts:

> How does a person who is a product of a totalitarian society learn responsibility, individuality, initiative? By saying "no." But this begins with saying "I," thinking "I" and doing "I"—and in public as well as in private. Individuality, the first-person singular, always existed under communism, it was just exiled from public and political life and exercised in private.[47]

Individuality is the locus for her voice of dissent, the "I" represents the rhetorical impetus for her identity of difference, her *rejective* terra firma, her own outside.[48] The negation implies more than a rhetorical tension marking the grammatical distinction between first-person pronouns in singular and plural form. In this discursive relationship, Drakulić affirms her own voice of resistance against the "safe, anonymous 'us'" of the collective brought about by communism.[49]

Rhetorically, this dyad transforms Drakulić into an outsider, a critical voice isolated from life as part of "we," apart from the mass mentality of possible nationalistic or neo-communist views. Thus, Drakulić turns the cultural relationship between "I" and "we" into a rhetorical and political locus of conflict, into the very nexus of her voice of dissent. Strategically, as she refuses the "we," Drakulić recaptures the communist times as part of her resistance. Accordingly, the strategic play of pronouns as cultural and political articulations become the rhetorical locus for the author's own voice in discourse. For, when looking at "we," Drakulić remembers that:

> I hate the first-person plural. But it is only now . . . that I realize how much I hate it. My resistance to it is almost physical, because more than anything else, to me it represents a physical experience. I can smell the scent of bodies pressed against me in a I May parade. . . . I can feel the crowd pushing me forward, all of us moving as one, a single body—a sort of automatic puppet-like motion because no one is capable of anything else.[50]

For Slavenka Drakulić, the first-person plural constitutes her enemy, personifying everything communism means or has ever meant. Memories triggered by the plural pronoun remind her of the ideology and propaganda pressed on the populations. Remembering mandatory participation in popular and populist events in communism, the writer reacts to the transformation of people into "a single body," a "puppet-like" group. As the first-person plural gets personified and rhetorically transformed into communist cultural discourse, Drakulić vehemently rejects the public sphere of the collective, responding as a promoter of individualism (equating, culturally, in this part of the world, democratic freedom of speech), and thus, the dissident voice.

After all, this writer is ostracized precisely because she continues to say "I," remaining excluded and in disagreement with the popular and more collective government of present-day Croatia.[51]

In order to bring this criticism to present-day Croatia, the writer invokes another rhetorical strategy—a temporal comparison of past and present, a powerful reminder of the political and social significance of the year 1989 in the area. Delineating in this grammatical dyad the rhetorical identities of communist versus democratic participants in society, Drakulić posits herself within different times to emphasize her political opposition through discourse. Once again, using language and grammar as rhetorical and cultural invocations of dissent, Drakulić turns the past tense into a rhetorical strategy in order to reject the communist ideology of Eastern or Central Europe. Thus, thinking of the past, Drakulić recalls that she "grew up with 'we' and 'us' in the kindergarten, at school, in the pioneer and youth organizations, in the community, at work."[52] In addition, as a journalist and a critical intellectual, the author reminisces on the political dangers of using the first-person singular, on the problems a speaker like herself faces in and through the language of individuality in a not-yet-democratic society.[53]

> Writing meant testing out the borders of both language and genres, pushing them away from editorials and first-person plural and towards first-person singular. The consequences of using the first-person singular were often unpleasant. You stuck out; you risked being labeled an "anarchic" element (not even a person), perhaps even a dissident. For that you would be sacked, so you used it sparingly, and at your own risk. This was called self-censorship.[54]

Here, her discursive resistance becomes a rhetorical strategy of opposition to and resistance against communism and its haunting ghosts, a call to reclaim individual responsibility in creating democratic life in Eastern Europe. Depicting the life dictated by the "we" of communist times, Drakulić delineates clearly the fluid insider and outsider position of any professional in the communist media before (and after) 1989.[55] In communist times in Eastern Europe, whenever a person attempted to speak out against the regime, that individual became an outsider, "an 'anarchic' element," or "even a dissident."[56]

Of course, the fall of communism in 1989 should have changed all that. Drakulić denies that it did in Croatia. With this strategic move, her indictment of the neo-communist regime takes shape. Blaming the war on the collective mentality of nationalism, Drakulić relentlessly criticizes the political, cultural, and rhetorical consequences of such a mind set. For, she argues, "that hideous first-person plural" infects "20 million-bodied mass swinging back and forth," making them follow "their leaders into mass hysteria."[57] Thus, the rhetorical relationship between time and identity helps her to reconstitute herself against both past and present communist *times* in Croatia.

Drakulić transforms her rhetorical voice from that of a critical intellectual of past communism to that of the present dissident living in the outside. As an advocate of democracy, her individual voice can no longer be heard in the new Croatia. Left without readership in her homeland, Drakulić explains how the communist past and neo-communist present call forth in discourse identities like hers. As in communist times, individual citizens "had no chance to voice his [her] protest or his [her] opinion, not even his [her] fear" in the postcommunist Balkans:

> He could only leave the country—and so people did. Those who used "I" instead of "we" in their language *had to escape* [my emphasis]. It was this fatal difference in grammar that divided them from the rest of their compatriots. As a consequence of this "us," no civic society developed. . . . As under communism, individualism was punished—individuals speaking out against the war, or against nationalism, were singled out as "traitors,"[58]

Accordingly, exile, particularly her own unacknowledged expatriation, is interconnected with dissidence, within the user of "I," within the action of saying no. Drakulić has not so much distanced herself from her Balkan homeland, as she has from pre-1989 communism. In her view, and not only hers, it appears that the Croat regime has not thrown off the communist past; and therefore, those who dissent remain distanced between their democratic dreams and the realities of 1989 and beyond. Thus, locating herself in an account on present neo-communist and nationalist practices, the writer emphasizes that, like her own case, critical voices of antinationalism *remain* singled out, ostracized as traitors, forced to leave their homeland.[59]

In other words, even if Drakulić does not explicate her own status in the essay, she acknowledges that people who use the first-person singular continue to live as dissidents and expatriates in countries like hers, after 1989. As the writer links her political agenda to her right of freedom of speech, Drakulić sees the "fatal difference in grammar" as a conflicting relationship between her identity and the present regime in Croatia. A "traitor" in and through her rhetorical action, Drakulić experiences and articulates marginalization and dissent.[60] The relationship Drakulić constructs between voice and past-present communist practices starts in language, accruing rhetorical and sociocultural force. "Introduction: First-Person Singular" becomes her grammatical, rhetorical, and cultural discourse of resistance, capturing an unsettled identity determined to fight (yet again) neo-communist practices in Eastern and Central Europe

INDIVIDUALISM: A NECESSARY STRATEGY IN POSTCOMMUNIST RHETORIC

Can, then, a rhetoric of dissidence offer novel relationships between individualist and collective perspectives in the public sphere of Eastern Europe? I argue that Drakulić's rhetoric of dissent assists postcommunist discourse in creating a democratic public sphere. More important, Drakulić's rhetorical and cultural contribution emphasizes the role of individualist and collectivist discourse in a democracy. Norman Manea, a well-known dissident from Romania, supports similar views, explaining the meaning of "I" as a political threat to communist regimes:

> It is hard to believe that in a totalitarian society the "I" could survive, and yet inferiority was a mode or resistance, however unavoidably imperfect. It [the "I"] acted as a center for our moral being, as a means of respiration from the corrupting aggressiveness of the environment; as a hope, however uncertain, for the integrity of conscience. The "I" persists, even in the totalitarian environment . . . the site of struggle between the centripetal necessity to preserve a secret, codified identity and the centrifugal tendency towards liberation.[61]

An unsettled and unsettling rhetor, Drakulić does not intend to solve the critical, cultural, and rhetorical problem between the two strategic appeals. Not satisfied with a simple contradictory relationship between the communist and the postcommunist appeals embedded in the individualist or collectivist nouns and pronouns, Drakulić layers multiple and complex rhetorical loci for such strategic usage, precisely to remind, evoke, and invoke the political, cultural, and social power of "I" versus "we."

Accordingly, by collapsing identity along the past and the postcommunist realities of her country, Drakulić reconstitutes her voice as a speaker rejecting nationalist and neo-communist practices in the Balkans. In other words, the "I" versus "we" rhetorical strategy allows Drakulić to respond to "otherness."[62] Drakulić turns the paradigm of individualism and collectivism into a dynamic trope of communist and postcommunist existence. For Drakulić, language becomes the main repository of the cultural and political connotations for former communist regimes.

Recalling abusive usages of language in communism and contrasting them with the powers of civic rights in a democracy, the Croat dissident recaptures legitimacy for her own rhetoric of resistance. In recent electronic correspondence with the author, Drakulić continues to remind audiences of the rhetorical role of "we" as collective enemies of the democratic, individualistic voice of postcommunist discourse.[63] The Croat writer articulates with these rhetorically sensitive pronouns a locus for an identity free of communism, calling audiences enthymematically to join a freed paradigm of political discourse in Eastern Europe.

WHERE NOW? ARE WE DONE WITH DISSIDENTS AND EXILE IN POSTCOMMUNIST TIMES?

As argued here, I consider Drakulić's appeals for democratic discourse extremely important for all scholarship on contemporary public discourse. In my view, critical intellectuals' reinvention of voice in Eastern Europe reveals important rhetorical, cultural, and sociopolitical perspectives on resistance and democracy in a world at the beginning of a new millennium. Ten years after the Eastern and Central European revolutions and the demise of communism, the discourse of such cultural and political luminaries continues to be questioned or revered, challenged or challenging, as these societies change toward civil arenas of democracy.[64] After 1989, the discourse on nationalism, on difference and tolerance, and on ethnic cleansing raises questions for the new Europe, for western, central, and eastern democratic communities altogether.

What is happening in the Croatian public sphere, after Tudjman, after a new president, Stipe Mesic, and a new prime minister, Ivica Racan, won the elections early in 2000?[65] Croatia has chosen a new government, a new public discourse, and new expectations for a democratic life in Eastern Europe. Even Drakulić recognizes that some members of the new Croatian parliament are as much part of the democratic intellectuals group as she is.[66] Thus, can one say that critical intellectuals have finally completed their political and rhetorical role for democratic discourse in the area?

In a recent interview, Drakulić clarifies that the political changes in Croatia are bringing new alliances—some intellectuals "who were for Tudjman" are now "shifting towards the new government," a government with "more of a democratic potential," yet where opportunism rules. The (former) dissident warns (again) that: "Croatia—as was Yugoslavia—is still a society with very small margins for intellectuals to be independent."[67]

In this novel context, what happens to dissidence, to voices of resistance and to the "I" versus "we" mind set? Leaving the persona *non grata* status, after eight years of dissent and a decade of postcommunism. Drakulić agrees that the "nationalist 'we' that ruled the public sphere is not dominant any longer." And yet, Slavenka Drakulić immediately adds that, in spite of all changes, "no power likes independent minds, people who think independently . . . So you are always on the margin of society, even if your friends are in the government."[68]

Most likely, Drakulić's rhetorical identity of resistance is needed more than ever in the discourse of democracy in Eastern Europe. Her articulations of voice against the social, political, rhetorical and cultural past remain necessary in a public arena waiting to be freed from oppression.

Notes

1. Tismaneanu offers an extensive definition of civil societies for Eastern and Central Europe: "[C]ivil society can thus be defined as the ensemble of grassroots, spontaneous, nongovernmental (although not necessarily antigovernmental) initiatives from below that emerge in the post-totalitarian order as a result of a loosening of state controls and the decline as the ideological constraints imposed by the ruling parties. KOR or more recently, the 'Orange Alternative' semi-anarchist group in Poland; Charter 77 in Czechoslovakia; various forms of dissident activities in the Soviet Union; the 'Peace and Human Rights Initiative' in the GDR; and all the independent peace and human rights activities, including the underground presses, samizdat publications, and the flying universities as they existed especially in Hungary and Czechoslovakia in the 1980s, can be considered components of the growing civil society" (See Vladimir Tismaneanu, *Reinventing Politics Eastern Europe from Stalin to Havel* [New York: Free Press, 1992] 170-71).

2. Some of these dissidents' works that deal specifically with exile and anticommunist ideas are Aleksandr I. Solzhenitsyn, *The Gulag Archipelago, 1918-1956 An Experiment in Literary Investigation,* trans. Thomas R. Whitney (New York: Harper and Row, 1974); Milan Kundera, *Milan Kundera and The Art of Fiction: Critical Essays,* ed. Aaron Aji (New York: Garland, 1992); Czeslaw Milosz, *The Captive Mind,* trans. Jane Ziclonko (New York: Vintage, 1981); Emile M. Cioran, *Temptation to Exist,* trans. Richard Howard (Chicago, Ill.: Quadrangle, 1970); and Mircea Eliade, *1937-1960, Exile's Odyssey,* trans. Mac Linscott Ricketts (Chicago, Ill.: University of Chicago Press, 1988).

3. Joseph Brodsky calls "exile" a condition. See Joseph Brodsky. "The Condition We Call Exile." in *Altogether Elsewhere: Writers on Exile,* ed. Marc Robinson (San Diego, Cal.: Harcourt Brace, 1994) 3-12.

4. Brodsky reveals the exiled authors' urgent motivation to act, rhetorically in my view, through language and speak up against communism. Brodsky writes in "The Condition" that: "our [exiled writers] greater value and greater function lie in our being unwitting embodiments of the disheartening idea that a freed man is not a free man; that liberation is just the means of attaining freedom and is not synonymous with it" (11).

5. Brodsky, "The Condition," 9-11.

6. J. F. Brown, *Hopes and Shadows: Eastern Europe After Communism* (Durham, N.C.: Duke University Press: 1994); and Vladimir Tismaneanu, *Fantasies of Salvation: Democracy, Nationalism, and Myth in Post-Communist Europe* (Princeton, N.J.: Princeton University Press, 1998).

7. An extensive body of literature on communist and postcommunist changes reflects also the other, the political context and significance of exilic or dissident action in Eastern and Central Europe. See Stanislaw Baranczak, "Before the Thaw The Beginning of Dissent in Postwar Polish Literature (The Case of Adam Wazyk's 'A Poem for Adults')." *East European Politics and Societies* 3 (1989): 10-15; Miklos Haraszti, *The Velvet Prison: Artists under State Socialism* (New York: Basic Books, 1987); Vaclav Havel, *Summer Meditations,* trans. Paul Wilson (New York: Vintage, 1993); Ferenc Feher and Agnes Heller, *Hungary 1956 Revisited: The Message of a Revolution—A Quarter of a Century After* (London: George Allen and Unwin, 1983); Gale Stokes, ed., *From Stalinism to Pluralism: A Documentary History of Eastern Europe since 1945* (New York: Oxford University Press, 1991); Michael Kennedy, "An Introduction to Eastern European Ideology and Identity in Transformation," in Michael Kennedy, ed., *Envisioning Eastern Europe: Postcommunist Cultural Studies* (Ann Arbor: University of Michigan Press, 1994), 1-46; Tony Judt. "Nineteen Eighty-Nine: The End of Which European Era?" *Daedalus* 23:3 (1994): 1-19; George Kolankiewiez, "Elites in Search of a Political Formula," ibid., 143-57; Steven Lukes, "Principles of 1989: Reflections on Revolution," in Kenneth W. Thompson, ed., *Revolutions in Eastern Europe and the U.S.S.R., Promises vs. Practical Morality* (Lanham, Md.: University Press of America, the Miller Center Series, 1995), 149-65; Andrei Sakharov, "Our Understanding of Totalitarianism," in Peter J. S. Duncan and Martyn Rady, eds., *Towards a New Community: Culture and Politics in Post-Totalitarian Europe* (London: University of London, 1993), 3-15; Tismaneanu, *Reinventing Politics*; and Katherine Verdery, *National Identity under Socialism: Identity and Cultural Politics in Ceausescu's Romania* (Berkeley: University of California Press, 1991).

8. I use interchangeably the terms "critical intellectuals," "public intellectuals," "democratic intellectuals," and "dissidents." In the body of literature on Eastern and Central Europe in communist and postcommunist times, scholars, mentioned previously use the terms interchangeably as well, emphasizing such critical voices' *political, social, and cultural function* of *dissidence* under communist regimes.

9. Slavenka Drakulić, *How We Survived Communism and Even Laughed* (New York: Norton, 1991); Slavenka Drakulić, *The Balkan Express: Fragments from the Other Side of War* (New York: Harper Collins, 1993); and Slavenka Drakulić, *Café Europa: Life after Communism* (New York: Penguin, 1996).

10. Throughout her writings in the 1990s, Drakulić has not changed her perspective on the communist and

neo-communist political situation in her country. Drakulić repeatedly claims that in Croatia "communism is not gone. Briefly, the new political leaders [Franjo Tudjman] used democracy to establish their authoritarian system, much alike one-party system during communism" (Slavenka Drakulić, e-mail to the author, 1 February 1999).

11. A singular definition of "culture" can be a difficult operational concept for this study, as the discourse of dissidents from Eastern and Central Europe reveals different dimensions of communist and postcommunist culture. However, a basic definition of "culture" stemming from the intercultural research in communication can function as an operational assumption for this research. Accordingly, Dodd defines culture as "a holistic set of values, interrelationships, practices, and activities shared by a group of people, influencing their views on the world" (See Carley H. Dodd, *Dynamics of Intercultural Communication,* 5th ed. [Boston, Mass.: McGraw-Hill, 1998], 36).

12. George Konrád and Andrei Codrescu, for example, had been experiencing alienation for 16 and 25 years respectively. See George Konrád, *The Melancholy of Rebirth: Essays from Post-Communist Central Europe, 1989-1994* (San Diego, Cal.: Harcourt Brace, 1995), ix; and Andrei Codrescu, *The Hole in the Flag: A Romanian Exile's Story of Return and Revolution* (New York: Avon, 1991), 11-77.

13. Dubravka Ugresić, another persona non grata, acknowledges her political fate. Leaving Croatia, Ugresić comments that: "soon I shall be *voluntarily* joining that ocean of (willing and unwilling) refugees who are knocking at the doors of other countries in the world" (See Dubravka Ugresić, *The Culture of Lies: Antipolitical Essays,* trans. Celia Hawkesworth [University Park: Pennsylvania State University Press, 1998], 85).

14. Vladimir Tismaneanu, *Fantasies of Salvation: Democracy, Nationalism, and Myth in Post-Communist Europe* (Princeton, NW.: Princeton University Press, 1998).

15. Robert Kaplan retells his encounter with Slavenka Drakulić in Zagreb. He writes about her as a settled voice of opposition, identified as "a Zagreb journalist who writes in Croatian for *Danas* (*Today*), a local magazine, and in English for *The New Republic* and *The Nation*" (See Robert Kaplan, *Balkan Ghosts: A Journey Through History* [New York: Vintage, 1994], 3-29, 6).

16. According to her own description in "A Chat with my Censor," Drakulić wrote articles on cultural politics or on Albanians in the province of Kosovo prior to the fall of communism, in 1988. See Slavenka Drakulić, "A Chat with my Censor," in *How We Survived Communism and Even Laughed* (New York: Norton, 1991), 77-82, 78.

17. Drakulić has been a contributing editor at *The Nation* since 1986. She also publishes often in *The New Republic,* the *Los Angeles Times,* and the *New York Times.* For example, see Slavenka Drakulić. "Voting Their Fears in Croatia," *New York Times* 21 June 1997, A21.

18. Continuing her explanation, Drakulic expands on the benefits a passport could bring to the Yugoslav population: "We had refrigerators and washing machines when others did not, and could travel abroad, see American movies, buy a graduation dress in Milan or spend our summer holidays in Greece or Spain. Yes, essentially it is a comparison between prison cells, but the comfort of your cell makes a lot of difference when you are imprisoned" (See Drakulić, "My Father's Guilt," in *Café Europa,* 143-60, 149). Also, Drakulić repeatedly acknowledges her different status in comparison with the rest of Eastern and Central Europeans in the 1980s. She explains that: "[H]aving a Yugoslav passport meant that you could travel both to the West, and to the East, and the USSR was the only country in the communist bloc that I did not visit" (See Drakulić, "Why I Never Visited Moscow," in *Café Europa* 22-32, 28).

19. See Marcus Tanner, "'Comrade Tito Is Dead,'" in *Croatia: A Nation Forged in War* (New Haven, Conn. Yale University Press, 1997), 203-11; and Tismaneanu, "Vindictive and Messianic Mythologies: Post-Communist Nationalism and Populism," in *Fantasies,* 65-88.

20. Drakulić "Overcome by Nationhood," in *Balkan,* 52.

21. Tanner notices the authoritarian practices similar to communist ones. Mixing nationalist vision with the legacy of communist politics. Tudjman's regime raises many questions in the international arena regarding freedom of speech and freedom of speech. In addition, the 1996 "free" elections constitute yet one more remainder of the communist practices in the public arena. Tanner states that: "[A]longside the disturbing new habit of judging everyone in Croatia's history on the simple basis of whether they were *dr zavnorvorm* (state-building) or not, there were other signs that Tudjman and the HDZ had a *decidedly skewed view on democracy* [my emphasis]" (See Marcus Tanner, "Postscript: Freedom Train." *Croatia,* 299-305, 303)

22. Both Ugresić and Drakulić present doubt in terms of the political future of the new Croatian state. See Ugresić, *Culture,* 49-55; and Drakulić, *Balkan,* 53-60.

23. Drakulić, "On Becoming A Refugee," in *Balkan,* 29.

24. Tanner presents the problem of liberated media in Tudjman's new political arena: The new government were soon determined to control the media almost as much as the old Communists, and much more so than the Racan-era Communists had been. The new HDZ bosses were strong nationalists with an intolerant streak. Milovan Sibl, director of the new Croat-

ian news agency Hina, was typical of the group. "Many of these journalists are of mixed origins," he scoffed, referring to the anti-HDZ press, "one Croat parent, one Serb. How can such people provide an objective picture of Croatia? . . . The only place you can read the truth about President Tudjman is in Hina news" (See Tanner, *Croatia*, 221-41, 230).

25. The 1996 elections in Croatia appear, according to the western press, to have been tainted by nationalist politics. See Chris Hedges. "In Croatia's Capital. Politics and Democracy Don't Mix Well." *New York Times,* 2 May 1996, A10.

26. Tanner, *Croatia,* 299-305.

27. Martha Halpert, reporting on the fifty-ninth International PEN Congress held in Zagreb in 1993, writes in *Partisan Review* about this incident. "The guests from abroad focused on an article, published in the private tabloid *Globus* last December 11th, which denounced five outspoken female Croatian writers as "witches." . . . Two of the brutally attacked women. Slavenka Drakulić and Dubravka Ugresić . . . are members of PEN" (See Martha Halpert. "The Fifty-ninth International PEN Congress." *Partisan Review* 3 [1993]: 450-52, 452).

28. Halpert, "The Fifty-ninth International PEN," 452.

29. Dubravka Ugresić, partner in "crime" with Drakulić and others, presents the Croat political discrimination on feminist basis, as she offers more quotes from the same article appeared in the Croatian press. The accusations are mostly warranted by these women's feminist actions, depicted as follows: "In 'democratic' Croatia, those women have been proclaimed 'traitors,' 'women who conspire against Croatia,' 'a serious danger,' 'women who sell their homeland for their own gain,' 'amoral beings,' 'a group of unhappy, frustrated women' . . . and finally 'witches,'" (Ugresić, *Culture,* 124).

30. Drakulić, e-mail with the author, 18 February 1999.

31. Rada Ivekovic is another of the "witches" who suffered discrimination and had to become a voluntary exile. See Rada Ivekovic. "Women, Nationalism, and War: 'Make Love Not War.'" *Hypalm* 8:4 [1993]: 113-27.

32. Drakulić writes that "the new political leaders used democracy to establish their authoritarian system, much alike one party system during communism. If you write this, however, *you become an enemy of the system, i.e. a dissident* [my emphasis]. You cannot get a job, you are harassed in the media, etc. which all happened to me. So you have to go abroad in order to survive!" Drakulić even calls herself an "enemy of the state" Personal correspondence with (Drakulić, e-mail to the author, 1 February 1999).

33. After 1992, the liberated media becomes a problem for the Tudjman's political arena. Determined to control it, the new government returns to the old practices of communist censorship. Press releases continue to report abusive and authoritarian measures taken against journalists. Similar instances are mentioned in the articles: "CPJ Protests Journalist Trial in Croatia," *Editor and Publisher,* 12 October 1996: 25; and "Jail Time for Croat Journalists." *Editor and Publisher* 2 May 1998: 48.

34. Drakulić, e-mail to the author, 18 February 1999.

35. From 1993 on, the writer admits it becomes "impossible to publish anything in Croatia." Drakulić, e-mail to the author, 18 February 1999.

36. A sample of such an attack is published by C. Michael McAdams, "C. Michael McAdams Responds to Michiko Kakutani's *New York Times* Review of Slavenka Drakulić's *Ghost of Communist Past.*" *The Zatedmear,* 9 April 1997. A reprint of a position signed by C. Michael McAdams, University of San Francisco, this attack is just one of his vehement responses sponsored by the Croatian Information Services. His recent *Croatia; Myth and Reality: The Final Chapter* intends precisely to rectify all cultural and political misconceptions related to Croatia. See C. Michael M. Adams, *Croatia, Myth and Reality: The Final Chapter* (Arcadia, Ca.: CIS Monographs, 1997).

37. Drakulić, e-mail with the author, 18 February 1999.

38. Drakulić publishes *The Taste of a Man* in Croatia in 1995. Drakulić, e-mail to the author, 18 February 1999.

39. Married to a well-known Swedish journalist, Richard Swartz, Drakulić can use both Western and Eastern European identities. She mentions in one of the essays that identities in intercultural marriages reveal the cultural and political barriers between Eastern and Western Europe. See Drakulić, "Buying a Vacuum Cleaner," in *Café,* 109-18.

40. Drakulić, "Invisible Walls Between Us," in *Café,* 21.

41. Drakulić "Introduction: First-Person Singular," in *Café Europa* 1-6.

42. In my correspondence with Drakulić, the author overtly states that "communism is not gone" in Croatia. This is the reason I refer to *neo*-communist and *post*-communist times as synonymous terms for the Croat political situation after 1989. Personal correspondence with Drakulić, e-mail to the author, 1 Feb. 1999.

43. Most of the Eastern and Central European dissident writers refer in their writings to the cultural difference between "we" and "they," implying the political and sociocultural dichotomy between official and underground discourse in communist times. Baranczak, when analyzing dissidence, refers to this important rhetorical strategy in yet another dissident's discourse, Miklos Haraszti; see Stanislaw

Baranczak, "The State Artist." *Breathing Under Water: And Other East European Essays* (Cambridge, Mass.: Harvard University Press, 1990) 87. George Konrad makes use of the same strategy in "15 March: A Colorful Day," *Melancholy of Rebirth*, 130-36.

44. Kenneth Burke, *A Grammar of Motives* (Berkeley: University of California Press, 1969).

45. Drakulić, "Introduction," 3.

46. Konrad writes about identical cultural and political delineations in grammatical form between official and underground arenas in communist Hungary. The famous dissident writes that: "[L]ooking backward, we must keep in mind that communist censorship did more than prohibit; it affirmed, affirmed all manner of things. Moreover, it did so in exalted tones and as often as not in the *first-person plural* [my emphasis]" (Konrad, *Melancholy*, 90).

47. Drakulić, "Introduction," 3-4.

48. In a similar way, playing against each other the cultural with the political connotations of pronouns in Eastern Europe, Codrescu writes that in Romania "we knew why we existed, why we were 'us' and not 'they' . . . why the world was the way it was" (5). (See Andrei Codrescu, *The Disappearance of the Outside: A Manifesto for Escape* [Reading, Mass.: Addison-Wesley, 1990], 1-37).

49. Drakulić, "Introduction," 4.

50. Drakulić, "Introduction," 1-2.

51. Drakulić, "Introduction," 2.

52. Drakulić, "Introduction," 2.

53. Drakulić was never a member of the Communist party. See Drakulić, "My Father's Guilt," in *Café*, 143-60.

54. Drakulić, "Introduction," 2-3.

55. Baranczak refers to similar rules of censorship in the Polish press under communism. See Stanislaw Baranczak, *Breathing Under Water*, 61-67.

56. Drakulić, "Introduction," 3.

57. Ibid.

58. Ibid.

59. Ibid.

60. Ibid.

61. Norman Manea, "Common Historical Roots." *Partisan Review* 4 (1992): 577.

62. According to Drakulić, the powers of language, the strategy of "naming them, by reducing them to the other" in discourse lead to horrors like the killings of Jews in World War or the ethnic cleansing in the Balkans (144). The author reacts precisely against the refusal of Croatian audiences to reflect on their cultural and political discourse, when naming "the other." For, continuing to use such vocabulary, places audiences as complacent participants in the discourse of war (See Drakulić. *Balkan*, 144-45).

63. Drakulić, e-mail to the author, 18 February 1999.

64. Most recently, Tismaneanu reiterates the importance of critical intellectuals in Eastern and Central European post-1989 discourse. See Vladimir Tismaneanu, "Fighting for the Public Sphere: Democratic Intellectuals under Postcommunism." in eds., *Between Past and Future: The Revolutions of 1989 and Their Aftermath* Sorin Antohi and Vladimir Tismaneanu, (Budapest: Central European UP, 2000) 153-75.

65. A large number of reports in the press cover the changes in Croatia, like "Croatia: All Change in Croatia." *The Economist*, Jan 8, 2000, v. 354, 8152, 46: "Croatian Elections," *Europe*, February 2000, S3; or "Croatia—Edgy Start," *The Economist*, 8 April 2000, v. 355, 8156, 56.

66. Drakulić agrees that "yes, some of my friends are in the government, and this government has more of a democratic potential. But I do not see that . . . yesterday's dissidents play any role" in the new Croatian public sphere. (Personal Correspondence with Drakulić, e-mail to the author, 26 July 2000).

67. Drakulić, e-mail to the author, 26 July 2000.

68. Drakulić, e-mail to the author, 26 July 2000.

FURTHER READING

Criticism

Banac, Ivo. "Misreading the Balkans." *Foreign Policy* 93 (winter 1993): 173-82.

Banac explores the change in Drakulic's writing between *How We Survived Communism and Even Laughed* and *The Balkan Express*.

Dobbs, Michael. "Profits and Loss." *Washington Post Book World* (23 March 1997): 8.

Dobbs praises Drakulic as a social critic in *Café Europa*, although he finds faults with her prose style.

Dunlap, Lauren Glen. Review of *How We Survived Communism and Even Laughed*, by Slavenka Drakulic. *Belles Lettres* 8, no. 1 (fall 1992): 19.

Dunlap examines how Drakulic uses everyday objects to illuminate the political situation in Eastern Europe in *How We Survived Communism and Even Laughed*.

Omang, Joanne. "The Cost of Survival." *Washington Post Book World* (19 March 2000): 9.

> Omang discusses the major themes of *S.* and asserts that "Drakulic's purpose is unabashedly journalistic and educational."

Phillips, Andrew. "Balkan Brutality." *Maclean's* 106, no. 29 (19 July 1993): 45, 47.

> Phillips evaluates the strengths and weaknesses of the essays in *The Balkan Express*.

Rocawich, Linda. Review of *How We Survived Communism and Even Laughed*, by Slavenka Drakulic. *Progressive* 56, no. 12 (December 1992): 38-9.

> Rocawich discusses *How We Survived Communism and Even Laughed* in light of the war which broke out in Croatia after its publication.

Additional coverage of Drakulic's life and career is contained in the following sources published by the Gale Group: *Contemporary Authors,* **Vol. 144;** *Contemporary Authors New Revision Series,* **Vol. 92; and** *Literature Resource Center.*

Carolyn Heilbrun
1926-

(Full name Carolyn Gold Heilbrun; has also written under the pseudonym Amanda Cross) American novelist, critic, essayist, nonfiction writer, short story writer, and biographer.

The following entry presents an overview of Heilbrun's career through 2002. For further information on her life and works, see *CLC,* Volume 25.

INTRODUCTION

Whether writing under her real name or under the pseudonym Amanda Cross, Heilbrun has earned widespread respect for her feminist theories, her frank perspective on academic life, and her series of highly literate murder mysteries. Once best known for her detective novels, Heilbrun has entered the canon of feminist scholarship with works such as *Writing a Woman's Life* (1988) and *Hamlet's Mother and Other Women* (1990). Critics have noted the interplay between Heilbrun's scholarly work and fiction, particularly her use of her mysteries to illustrate aspects of her critical theory.

BIOGRAPHICAL INFORMATION

Heilbrun was born on January 13, 1926, in East Orange, New Jersey, the only child of Archibald and Estelle Gold. In 1945 she married James Heilbrun, a professor of economics, with whom she has three children. She attended Wellesley College, graduating with a B.A. in 1947. Heilbrun then enrolled at Columbia University, earning an M.A. in 1951 and a Ph.D. in 1959. She taught at Brooklyn College for one year before returning to Columbia in 1960, where she taught for over three decades. Heilbrun became a full professor of English in 1972, later serving as the Avalon Foundation professor in the humanities from 1986 to 1992. She resigned from her Columbia professorship in 1992, citing sexual discrimination as her reason for leaving. She has since lectured and taught at several universities, including Swarthmore College and Yale University. In 1964 Heilbrun published her first mystery novel *In the Last Analysis,* written under the pseudonym Amanda Cross. Her Amanda Cross detective novels have received a number of awards such as the Mystery Writers of America Scroll in 1964 and the Nero Wolfe Award for Mystery Fiction in 1981. She served as a Guggenheim fellow in 1965, a Rockefeller fellow in 1976, and a Radcliffe Institute fellow in 1976. From 1982 to 1984 she was a member of the executive board of the Mystery Writers of America and, from 1976 to 1979 and 1982 to 1984, Heilbrun was a member of the executive council of the Modern Language Association of America, serving as the president in 1984. She has also contributed essays and articles to several publications including the *New York Times Book Review, Shakespeare Quarterly, Saturday Review,* and *Texas Quarterly.*

MAJOR WORKS

In 1957, in her first published essay "The Character of Hamlet's Mother," Heilbrun signaled the themes she would refine and amplify throughout the next five decades, both in her fiction and nonfiction. "Hamlet's Mother" asserts that middle-aged and elderly women can still be sexual and vibrant individuals, criticizing literary scholars for misunderstanding and maligning the true nature of Queen Gertrude's lust in Shakespeare's *Hamlet*. Heilbrun later expanded on this thesis in the essay collection *Hamlet's Mother and Other Women*. Heilbrun continued her exploration of human sexuality in her first major work of literary criticism, *Toward a Recognition of Androgyny: Aspects of Male and Female in Literature* (1973), which posits that the condition of androgyny—defined as a refusal to accept sexually dictated gender roles—can free the individual from society's prescribed expectations of male and female identity. In *Reinventing Womanhood* (1979) Heilbrun gathers examples of female literary characters who, by their refusal to sacrifice independence for the conventional "happy ending," serve as role models for contemporary women. In cooperation with Margaret R. Higgonet, Heilbrun coedited *The Representation of Women in Fiction* (1983), a collection of critical essays by female scholars such as Susan Gubar, Elizabeth Ermarth, and Nancy K. Miller that attempts to reexamine how women have been portrayed in literary texts. *Writing a Woman's Life* offers an examination of women's biographies and autobiographies, discussing a diverse range of works on notable women including George Eliot, Elizabeth Barrett Browning, Gertrude Stein, and Margaret Thatcher. In 1995 Heilbrun collaborated with Gloria Steinem to write the authorized biography *The Education of a Woman: The Life of Gloria Steinem*, combining a history of contemporary feminism with the life story of the high-profile feminist activist. The essays in *The Last Gift of Time: Life beyond Sixty* (1997) reflect on a desire that originated during Heilbrun's adolescence to commit suicide at the age of seventy, offering a candid and emotional look at the negative and positive aspects of the aging process. Heilbrun's *When Men Were the Only Models We Had* (2002) reflects on her admiration of such male critics as Clifton Fadiman, Lionel Trilling, and Jacques Barzun, while lamenting the rampant sexism she experienced in academia.

Writing under the name Amanda Cross, Heilbrun has published a series of mystery novels focusing on Professor Kate Fansler, an amateur sleuth and academic who teaches Victorian literature at a large uptown university. Fansler is portrayed as an independent and thoroughly modern heroine, with many of her adventures set against the backdrop of the intensely political world of university academia. *In the Last Analysis* revolves around Fansler helping a psychiatrist friend to clear himself of a murder charge after a patient is found dead in his office. The situation allows Fansler to deliver her strong opinions by way of witty literary allusions—her ability to quote appositely on every occasion becomes a hallmark of her style—while imaginatively reconstructing the murder scene. In *The James Joyce Murder* (1967) Fansler returns from doing research in the country to assist her young nephew who is accused of killing a neighbor. As Heilbrun further developed her feminist critical theory in works such as *Reinventing Womanhood*, several of the Amanda Cross mysteries began to take on a more political and socially conscious tone, particularly by focusing on the institutional sexism found in many American universities. A female graduate student is murdered in *The Question of Max* (1976) after she threatens her college's male literary-critical hegemony. In *Death in a Tenured Position* (1981) Fansler investigates the death of the first woman tenured in the women's studies program at Harvard University, with suspicion falling on the victim's faculty colleagues. *An Imperfect Spy* (1995) opens with the suspicious death of a woman faculty member at a conservative law school. In 1998 Heilbrun published *The Puzzled Heart*, in which Fansler's husband Reed is kidnapped by a group opposed to her feminist stance. The ensuing investigation forces Fansler into an extended examination of her personal and professional relationships. Fansler acts as an advisor to a new amateur detective, Estelle "Woody" Woodhaven, in *Honest Doubt* (2000). Both women investigate the murder of Charles Haycock, a disliked Alfred Tennyson scholar at a small New Jersey college. Throughout the novel, Fansler guides the exasperated Woody through the labyrinth of academic politics. Heilbrun has also published a collection of short stories, *The Collected Stories of Amanda Cross* (1997), which presents nine short mysteries most of which feature Kate Fansler as the protagonist.

CRITICAL RECEPTION

For her works of critical theory, Heilbrun has been consistently lauded for her ability to take complex feminist concepts and translate them into accessible language. Reviewers have praised her emphasis on women's writing and the role of women in literature, describing her analysis as erudite, engaging, and insightful. Though some scholars have derided Heilbrun's unswerving feminist perspective, others have applauded her use of fictional and autobiographical examples to expound on her central arguments. Heilbrun's Amanda Cross mysteries have attracted considerable attention for their complex plotting and positive female role models, despite some critical debate about detective fiction's sustainability as a genre for feminists. Additionally, many critics have complimented *Death in a Tenured Position* and *An Imperfect Spy* for raising important questions about the treatment of women by academic and literary institutions. However, some reviewers have questioned the validity of Heilbrun's biography of Gloria Steinem, *The Education of a Woman*, arguing that her collaboration and friendship with the feminist activist caused Heilbrun to focus on the more positive aspects of Steinem's life and career.

PRINCIPAL WORKS

The Garnett Family (nonfiction) 1961
In the Last Analysis [as Amanda Cross] (novel) 1964
The James Joyce Murder [as Amanda Cross] (novel) 1967
Christopher Isherwood (criticism) 1970
Poetic Justice [as Amanda Cross] (novel) 1970
The Theban Mysteries [as Amanda Cross] (novel) 1971
Toward a Recognition of Androgyny: Aspects of Male and Female in Literature (criticism) 1973
The Question of Max [as Amanda Cross] (novel) 1976
Reinventing Womanhood (essays and criticism) 1979
Death in a Tenured Position [as Amanda Cross] (novel) 1981
The Representation of Women in Fiction [editor; with Margaret R. Higgonet] (essays and criticism) 1983
Sweet Death, Kind Death [as Amanda Cross] (novel) 1984
No Word from Winifred [as Amanda Cross] (novel) 1986
Writing a Woman's Life (essays) 1988
A Trap for Fools [as Amanda Cross] (novel) 1989
Hamlet's Mother and Other Women (essays and criticism) 1990
Players Come Again [as Amanda Cross] (novel) 1990
The Education of a Woman: The Life of Gloria Steinem (biography) 1995
An Imperfect Spy [as Amanda Cross] (novel) 1995
The Collected Stories of Amanda Cross [as Amanda Cross] (short stories) 1997
The Last Gift of Time: Life beyond Sixty (essays) 1997
The Puzzled Heart [as Amanda Cross] (novel) 1998
Women's Lives: The View from the Threshold (lectures) 1999
Honest Doubt [as Amanda Cross] (novel) 2000
Edge of Doom [as Amanda Cross] (novel) 2002
When Men Were the Only Models We Had: My Teachers Barzun, Fadiman, and Trilling (nonfiction) 2002

CRITICISM

Sara Hudson (review date spring 1984)

SOURCE: Hudson, Sara. Review of *The Representation of Women in Fiction*, edited by Carolyn Heilbrun and Margaret T. Higonnet. *Southern Humanities Review* 18, no. 2 (spring 1984): 185-88.

[*In the following excerpt, Hudson considers the utility and readability of the critical essays collected in* The Representation of Women in Fiction.]

The Representation of Women in Fiction is a collection of feminist criticism. In the first of a two-part Introduction, Carolyn Heilbrun celebrates the devotion of the 1981 meeting of the English Institute to a program on women in fiction which, she notes, marks a break in the traditional (marginal) role allotted to women on the past thirty-nine programs of the Institute. Three of the six essays in this collection were presented as Institute papers: "Fictional Consensus and Female Casualties," by Elizabeth Ermarth; "The Birth of the Artist as Heroine: (Re)production, the *Künstlerroman* Tradition, and the Fiction of Katherine Mansfield," by Susan Gubar; and "Writing (from) the Feminine: George Sand and the Novel of Female Pastoral," by Nancy K. Miller. Of the remaining three essays, one was also presented as a paper, "Liberty, Sorority, Misogyny," by Jane Marcus; the other two were written for this collection: "Herself Against Herself: The Clarification of Clara Middleton," by J. Hillis Miller; and "*Persuasion* and the Promises of Love," by Mary Poovey. There is one common ground on which the majority of these essays rest, and that is the nineteenth century, which has been thus far—and by far—the best of hunting grounds for feminist criticism, just as Virginia Woolf continues to be its most important ancestor. Woolf plays a part, more or less important, in three of the six essays.

In the second part of the Introduction, Margaret Higonnet analyzes the new literary history, which is being shaped "in part by feminist studies of the representation of women" and altered by the retrieval of a "past that had no status." Making use of two major categories of feminist criticism proposed in part by Elaine Showalter ("Feminist Criticism in the Wilderness," *Critical Inquiry*, Winter, 1981), Higonnet assigns the essays by Gubar, Marcus, and Poovey to the category of "historical revisionism." The second category "emphasizes structural or semiotic modes of analysis." The trendy essays in this category are certainly more difficult to take in, and some readers, myself included, will be grateful to Higonnet for providing a summary of each essay. Even so, there may be trouble, as the following portion of Higonnet's account of Nancy Miller's essay makes (un)clear:

> Women's figures help define and (dis)integrate the multiple heterogeneous structures that we call literary texts. The richness of these relationships is suggested by Nancy Miller's essay deciphering George Sand's *Valentine* and exploiting topological and stylistic analysis along lines that bear comparison to Gaston Bachelard and Mikhail Bakhtin, as well as Michael Riffaterre. . . . One question raised by defining woman as a function within a system of signs is whether we are dealing with signifier, signified, or both. An evacuation of identity appears to be one consequence of seeing woman as Otherness, *altérité*. She may be given positive value as the mystery of the ineffable and the *néant* that permits affirmation of (masculine) being, or she may retain the negative value of a mere empty

void. The ambivalence of woman as signifier can be taken as the basso continuo of our topic.

And for a flavor of the essay itself, consider this sample, or rather, imagine listening to it:

> This passage permits us, I think, to differentiate among three chronotopic valorizations of desire in a sexual and textual economy: masculinist (in its extreme, libertine) discourse, which valorizes the time of possession (and possession as penetration); feminizing discourse, which seeks a loving negotiation with the feminine (Saint-Preux enamored in the hour after; ultimately, Roland Barthes); and finally a feminine-feminist discourse, which indirectly or directly valorizes the hour that precedes and essentially *precludes* possession (though not enjoyment, which becomes *jouissance* minus penetration.)

I obviously find the essays by Gubar, Marcus, and Poovey more digestible and hence more useful; but perhaps I will take uneasy refuge in one of Mrs. Hopewell's favorite sayings: "It takes all kinds to make the world."

Charles Champlin (review date 20 May 1984)

SOURCE: Champlin, Charles. "Two Women with the Kiss of Death." *Los Angeles Times Book Review* (20 May 1984): 6.

[*In the following excerpt, Champlin argues that the strength of* Sweet Death, Kind Death *is Heilbrun's portrayal of academic life.*]

There are those who swear by another of the murderous angels, the academic who signs herself Amanda Cross. She is in the English tradition in a sense, recalling the work of other academics (like Michael Innes, who is in reality Prof. J. I. Stewart). The speech of characters is rich with epigram and literary allusions and reads as if it were being written rather than said.

Cross has the added appeal of writing as a vigorous feminist whose academic heroine, Kate Fansler, treats her husband as a minor adjunct of some limited usefulness in certain legal situations but who can trade citations (one of Martin Buber for two of Stevie Smith) in a way that makes life a perpetual High Table.

In her latest, ***Sweet Death, Kind Death*** (from a Stevie Smith poem), Cross sends Kate off to a small college where another academic woman has seemingly weighted herself with rocks and walked into the campus lake to drown. Unlikely.

It is a good enough puzzle, although as always in Cross' books, the strength is in the incidental music about academic life—the bitchery, the treacheries large and small born of ruthless politicking, and the ceaseless, unending, interminable high-arch talk.

My trouble—I'm not an enthusiast—is that Cross' expository prose and her dialogue merge indistinguishably into a continuum of small, set-off phrases like a dotted line across a map.

I quote, truly, at random, expecting, not improbably, that even more heavily perforated examples could be found, and admitting, not less improbably, that one could even unearth a lonely, defiantly uninterrupted sentence, if only, as Al Smith once remarked in conversation, we should live so long:

> "AT&T has," Kate pointed out, "provided us with means of speaking across distance. Do you, in the throes of your Humpty Dumpty complex, again suspect eavesdroppers?"
>
> Yes, but only at the lower late-night rate.

As Rendell understands, pace is all, and a feeling of blood in the veins and fear in the heart.

Not all mysteries are created equal.

Maureen T. Reddy (review date December 1986)

SOURCE: Reddy, Maureen T. "She Done It." *Women's Review of Books* 4, no. 3 (December 1986): 8.

[*In the following excerpt, Reddy delineates the role of contemporary feminism in Heilbrun's series of mystery novels, written under the pseudonym Amanda Cross.*]

There seem to have been few feminist mysteries between 1935 and 1964, the year that Amanda Cross's first book, ***In the Last Analysis,*** appeared. Perhaps they passed rapidly out of print? Were written but not published? Since 1964, Cross has produced a total of eight mysteries, all featuring amateur detective Kate Fansler. Like her creator, who is actually Carolyn Heilbrun, the widely respected feminist scholar, Kate is a professor of English at Columbia University with a fine appreciation of the absurd.

The most recent Cross mystery owes a great deal to *Gaudy Night*: concerned less with crime and punishment than with the ways in which character, particularly female character, is shaped, ***No Word from Winifred*** is an unusual mystery novel. Although the ostensible object of Kate's investigation is a missing woman named Winifred, the real subjects of the book are women's changing social position and women's relationships with each other; in some ways, this book is about the effect of twenty-odd years of contemporary feminism on women's lives. Cross places Kate on the cusp of two eras. In her forties, she now has a circle of feminist colleagues, but is old enough to have been educated exclusively by men and to have seen this as the norm. (When she learns that Winifred, her "honorary aunt," and the aunt's closest friend all once wanted to be boys, Kate easily sympathizes and explains the desire to her uncomprehending niece Leighton as an almost universal fantasy among young girls who discovered early that all freedom was denied them due to their sex.)

Combining an investigation of a mystery with an investigation of social conditions is becoming an Amanda Cross trademark. Two of her recent books, **Death in a Tenured Position** and **Sweet Death, Kind Death,** are more sophisticated in their political analyses than is **No Word from Winifred,** and are also more compelling as mysteries. In **Death in a Tenured Position,** Kate investigates the death of the first woman hired as a professor by Harvard's English department; in **Sweet Death, Kind Death,** she investigates a feminist professor's apparent suicide at a women's college that is resistant to women's studies; in both, the central crime and the social criticism are more convincingly interwoven than in this most recent book.

The exploration of expanding possibilities for women in **No Word from Winifred** is most interesting but also most confusing in the sections on female friendship. At times Kate seems to celebrate the endurance of bonds between women and the relatively new phenomenon of female collegiality (one cannot be collegial without colleagues), but at others she seems caught in a 1950s time warp. For instance, in the midst of a discussion of women's powerful connections with each other, Kate says to a woman (a professor who has just left her husband and moved, with two small children, from New York to California, where she has a university appointment),

> That's the way it is with women . . . We're separated each into her own home, each feeling a monster if she isn't happy every minute with the company of her small children and her microwave oven. Women need to talk to each other—sometimes, I think it's more important than the ERA—talk to each other honestly, discover we're none of us unique monsters.
>
> (p. 158)

Now, suburban imprisonment remains an issue for many women, but it is patently not an issue for these two particular women; the conversation rings false.

Cross seems anxious to work certain messages into **No Word from Winifred**; although I sympathize with the political impulse, it often causes the novel to go awry, especially since many of the messages are trite (such as the idea that plainly dressed women are not necessarily lesbians and that lesbians are often very chic). Well, yes, but so what? This sort of thing may be the deliberate effect of Cross's aiming at a wide audience, but it makes Kate seem absurdly naive.

Abigail McCarthy (review date 2 December 1988)

SOURCE: McCarthy, Abigail. "Women Who Step Forward: Fasting & the Politics of Carmel." *Commonweal* 18, no. 21 (2 December 1988): 647-48.

[*In the following review, McCarthy applies Heilbrun's ideas in* Writing a Woman's Life *to several case studies, including political activist Carol Fennelly's fasting campaign and the dispute at the Morristown Carmel convent.*]

I recently reviewed Carolyn Heilbrun's *Writing a Woman's Life* (W. W. Norton) for another publication. It is a thought-provoking little book about the depiction of women in biography and autobiography. As is often the case with books with interesting theses, or with ideas which interact with my own, I find it coloring my thought about events in the news.

Columbia professor Heilbrun holds that the truthful telling of a woman's life—even the self-telling (and even the authentic living of it)—has been impossible until very recently because of the age-old view of woman's role. "Anonymity, we have long believed, is the proper condition of women," she says. To be a woman has meant "to put a man at the center of one's life and to allow to occur only what honors his prime position. Occasionally women have put God or Christ in the place of a man; the results are the same: one's own desires and quests are always secondary." Women have not been allowed ambition, self-realization, or the acquisition of power except under some disguise or other.

This was in my mind as I watched and read the news reports of Carol Fennelly, member of the Community for Creative Nonviolence, who narrowly escaped death from fasting during the last six weeks of the presidential campaign. She is the long-time companion and coworker of Mitch Snyder, activist for the homeless, who has survived several such life-threatening fasts. As the result of one (during which he was supported by prominent government wives and film personalities) he extracted from President Reagan himself the promise of the renovation of a government building as a model shelter. The campaign fast was another attempt to focus attention on the homeless. It culminated in a march on the Capitol led by Snyder and Cher among others—by that time Carol Fennelly was too weak to join them.

Whatever we may think of the tactic of fasting to make or gain a point—at its best it is a kind of spiritual blackmail and, used too often, may promote callousness—it has sometimes been very effective, at least in the short run. To fast almost to death must require great courage, a strong will, steadfastness, and devotion to a cause—all traits exhibited by Carol Fennelly. But why, I wondered, did she join the fast herself this time after being a supportive figure for many years, nursing Mitch Snyder through one crisis after another, and content to act as his spokeswoman?

Fennelly says it was because it was time for women, especially mothers like herself, to step forward in the cause of the homeless. They must do so because the plight of homeless children is dire—they are living their whole lives in shelters, abandoned cars, slum-like motel rooms. Thus she felt she had to act. Sympathetic newspeople saw it a bit differently. They reported her as "stepping out from the shadow of Mitch Snyder" and asserting leadership for women in the cause. The impulse to personal accomplishment and leadership is almost always, Heilbrun asserts, depicted in the self-telling of women's stories, as the response to a spiritual call "to an accomplishment and an achievement in no other way excusable in a female self."

Fennelly's story recalls another thesis of Heilbrun's—that women seeking spiritual achievement discover themselves through identification with some "other." "Identity is grounded through the relation to the chosen other." Certainly Fennelly became an activist as a follower of Snyder. There are very interesting parallels here in the stories of saintly women. But here I would quarrel with Heilbrun about her use of the word "occasionally" in saying that occasionally women have put God or Christ in the place of a man in their lives. Literally hundreds and thousands of women have done so and many lived lives of heroic accomplishment as a result. If one is to reexamine the telling of women's lives, the stories of the saints, canonized or not, are a wonderfully fertile source of exploration.

Actually a very good start at exploring this source has already been done by Phyllis McGinley in *Saint-Watching*. She limned strong women like Bridget of Sweden, Catherine of Siena and Mère Jahouvey. She also included a fascinating and sophisticated study of the attachments between many men and women saints—"the comradeship between men and women geniuses." She lists such famous pairs as Benedict and Scholastica, Paula and Jerome, Clare and Francis of Assisi, Jeanne de Chantal and Francis de Sales, Vincent de Paul and Louise de Marillac, etc. And in not all of them is the woman the follower. In every case, however, McGinley argues that each one of the pair would have been less without the other. A second look at the women's stories in these pairs is now due.

Another theme of Heilbrun's is that the part other women play in any one woman's story is seldom told. She thinks of this omission primarily in terms of women's friendships and of supportive groups of women. Still another theme is the issue of power and control in women's lives. Exactly because they bring these two themes together, it would seem to me that the study of religious communities, only recently initiated by women historians, is another very fertile source. These communities, like women's colleges and women's organizations, may be subcultures, but their study will illuminate the stories of women.

The above was borne home to me by the headlines about the disputes at the Morristown Carmel where five nuns barricaded themselves in the infirmary in protest against their new superior. Shades of St. Teresa sent to be prioress at the convent of the Incarnation! "When . . . she entered the choir, an angry group attempted to bar her way. Some cried out against her; others for her. The pandemonium was increased when some of her supporters attempted to sing the *Te Deum* and the rest shouted them down" (Peers, *Mother of Carmel*). When we think of the further insights into the politics of Carmel, of which we catch glimpses in the story of Thérèse of Lisieux, we can only wonder, as Heilbrun evidently does, whether women would really prefer, as many claim they do, "a world without evident power or control." It is worth looking into.

Marian Sandmaier (review date January 1989)

SOURCE: Sandmaier, Marian. "Outlaw Stories Empower & Inspire." *New Directions for Women* 18, no. 1 (January 1989): 20.

[*In the following review of* Writing a Woman's Life, *Sandmaier commends Heilbrun's contention that women need to chronicle the true stories of their lives as well as the female experience as a whole.*]

In 1968, novelist and memoirist May Sarton published *Plant Dreaming Deep,* an exquisitely beautiful meditation on the experience of buying her own home and living alone. The reviews were approving; her readers rapturous. And then Sarton did something extraordinary: She rewrote the story of those bravely told years of aloneness and called it *Journal of a Solitude*: now a furious, pain-charged account of struggle and survival. The year was 1973. The mask was lifted; the pretense over.

The publication of Sarton's twice-told tale marks a genuine watershed in women's autobiography, contends Carolyn T. Heilbrun in her passionately argued, revelatory book, ***Writing a Woman's Life.*** It was, she says, the first deliberate attempt to set the record straight on a woman's own experience: to reject the blandly passive, culturally sanctioned stories women have been permitted to tell about themselves—or have told about them in biography—and to expose to the world one's anger, dreams of power and the unapologetic struggle to set the course of one's life.

Outlaw Stories Needed

Women need many, many more of these outlaw stories, these clandestine records of feeling and doing, as models for their own still difficult, harshly judged journeys toward autonomy, says Heilbrun, who is the Avalon Foundation. Professor in the Humanities at Columbia University and the author of two other ground-breaking books of feminist analysis.

Heilbrun makes a convincing case that such "new plots" serve as crucial sources of inspiration as well as detailed road maps for destinations still officially closed to women. Yet until recently, women have been deprived of such hopeful narratives, offered instead autobiographies and biographies of women that traced the only acceptable female plot—one driven by a need for male love and approval and untainted by a yen for power in the public domain. As surely as fairy tales and myth, Heilbrun contends, "these stories have formed us all."

Heilbrun draws on a vast knowledge of 19th and 20th century literature to illustrate how women's lives have been systematically distorted for public consumption. One telling example: Although the life of medieval scholar and detective novelist Dorothy Sayers was marked by what Heilbrun calls "a profound sense of vocation," her authorized biography by James Brabazon reads like a brave but sad compromise. "Life robbed (Dorothy Sayers) of most of the ordinary human experiences of satisfactory emotional relationships, sexual and parental. No wonder she had to fall back on the intellect." It is the Brabazon interpretation, of course, not the Heilbrun revision, that is the most widely read version of Sayers' experience.

What's perhaps more disturbing than biographical bias is that women themselves—regardless of the enormity of their accomplishments—have rarely dared to publicly tell the true stories of their lives. Read the autobiographies of Jane Addams, Emma Goldman, Golda Meir or Eleanor Roosevelt, and you will find these extraordinary leaders taking pains to deny their own "unwomanly" power, pointing instead to luck or others' generosity or a vague "call to service" to explain their dazzling achievements. But pour over their journals and letters—documents never intended for public scrutiny—and very different women emerge: ambitious, managerial, plainly exhilarated by their impact on worlds beyond kitchen and nursery.

The self-protective instincts of these women were not misplaced. Heilbrun amply documents the punishment meted out to women who have dared to tell their "unacceptable" stories. When Anne Sexton began writing poetry about her own physical experience of femaleness, for instance, one male reviewer fumed: "It would be hard to find a writer who dwells more insistently on the pathetic and disgusting aspects of bodily experience . . ." When poet Adrienne Rich published the searingly honest *Of Woman Born* in 1975—in which she admitted that women at times may hate their own children—even some women reviewers denounced the book as bitter and sick, effectively ghettoizing it as a "radical feminist" book. Yet Rich took her risks willingly, noting in her book that only when women are able to share their "private and often painful experience" will they understand the universality of their oppression and find the fearlessness to live authentic lives.

And this willingness, Heilbrun reminds us, is not only the mandate of a few poets and famous women with book contracts. "Women," she writes, "must turn to one another for stories; they must share the stories of their lives and their hopes and their unacceptable fantasies . . . We must begin to tell the truth, in groups, to one another. Modern feminism began that way and we have lost, through shame or fear of ridicule, that important collective phenomenon." She is right on target, and this eloquent book makes one understand why in a fresh and compelling way.

Emily Toth (review date February 1989)

SOURCE: Toth, Emily. "Questioning the Quest." *Women's Review of Books* 6, no. 5 (February 1989): 11.

[*In the following excerpt, Toth praises the eloquence, honesty, and wit of the essays in* Writing a Woman's Life.]

And certain motives are still not seen as appropriate for women, Carolyn Heilbrun points out brilliantly in ***Writing a Woman's Life***. The romance and marriage plot is still the accepted narrative for a woman's story; the quest narrative of ambition—like Lorin Jones' single-minded concentration on her art—is much harder to shape when the life at the center is a woman's. Polly's first impulse, once she learns that Lorin Jones didn't care about anything except her painting, is to portray her as spiteful, sly and selfish—the usual condemnations for a woman who puts her own dreams first.

Let's look at it another way, says Heilbrun in these eloquent essays. Why do women who are public achievers not present themselves as powerful? Women like Ida Tarbell and Jane Addams, she says, have written their autobiographies as if they were passive agents of destiny, as if their causes, like seducers, sought and courted them. But their letters show that the women were actually powerful and tireless fighters to change the world. Did Tarbell, Addams and their sisters see ambition as the dirtiest of female secrets? As Heilbrun notes, the ambitious and passionate George Sand was in her day described as a "great man." In the constricted terms available for women, there was no way to describe a woman who succeeded at both love and work.[1]

Narratives of women's lives in the past have emphasized their relations with men, and we've all read narratives of women's sacrifices, endless variations on "she was a success on the job, but a failure as a woman." Even grocery-store tabloids offer love, motherhood and loneliness as the only possible roles for women: famous stars like Linda Evans are alleged to be longing for the children they never had, and Elizabeth Taylor is always unhappy in love, for life is lonely at the top.

Men, in short, have tried to sell us a very skewed version of what is in our own interests—and few writers remind us of this as deftly as Heilbrun does. Young womanhood, we're told, is the season when the world is open to us: we're at the height of our beauty, and therefore of our power. (As Gloria Steinem has pointed out, this is why college women often have trouble believing that women are oppressed.) Only the quest for a suitable husband is presented as romantic or exciting, and this is a sly ploy, says Heilbrun: "Women are allowed this brief period in the limelight" in order to "encourage the acceptance of a lifetime of marginality." Marriage has to be portrayed through a romantic haze, to make it "attractive to its female half" and therefore "useful to its patriarchal supporters."

There are, Heilbrun points out, a few marriages that don't kill women's possibilities: Virginia and Leonard Woolf's marriage was "revolutionary," for both put work at the center. While "the compulsion to find a lover and husband in a single person has doomed more women to misery than any other illusion," Heilbrun says, the Woolfs managed a much more interesting variation: they always surprised each other. But for most of us, the most interesting possibilities come later in life, and only if a woman escapes "the temptation of the conventional woman's life." In the past, being a "fallen woman" was one escape route, although it was not celebrated as such: it's rarely said that George Eliot not only benefited from living in sin, but also was blessed in being neither beautiful nor maternal. She had the chance to create her own life.

Writing a Woman's Life is a delight to read, for Heilbrun never hesitates to talk straightforwardly about forbidden subjects—such as women's anger and desire for power. She celebrates both, because they give us strength, and she also gives generous credit to other women, especially Nancy K. Miller, who have helped hone her ideas. Our greatest source of knowledge and power is consciousness-raising with other women, she says (and I agree).

Moreover, it's with other women that we can begin to chart rich new narratives for women's lives. Writing itself can be an act of self-creation, an "awakening" that often takes place for women in early middle age. The new, uncharted quest plot replaces the tired old marriage plot as women discover their real talents, their real selves. Heilbrun describes how she came to be "Amanda Cross," writer of detective fiction a fascinating glimpse into her own self-creation (and wonderful material for Heilbrun's own biographers. I hope there'll be many).

But what is most inspiring about *Writing a Woman's Life* is Heilbrun's celebration of growing old for women. The older we get, she points out with relish, the less we need to care what "they" think. We become much freer to ignore rules, including beauty standards: as they aged, Elizabeth Cady Stanton and Margaret Mead chose to be fat and felt fine. (Similarly, Alison Lurie's Polly says to hell with diets and high heels.) Past 50, we worry less and less about catering to others' needs, and the last third of life is best marked by "laughter," the "spontaneous recognition of insight and love and freedom."

Heilbrun, as always, is clever and memorable, full of passages to underline and quote One of my favorites: "Lord Peter Wimsey once said that nine-tenths of the law of chivalry was a desire to have all the fun. The same might well be said of Patriarchy." Through her writings in the last two decades, she has mentored all of us: I read her reviews so I can share in her wisdom and her laughter. And in *Writing a Woman's Life,* she is telling me that I'm still on the right track. Now I am one of the women who can, as she has, "make use of our security, our seniority, to take risks, to make noise, to be courageous, to become unpopular."

I resolve to do just that.

Note

1. Personally, I've always enjoyed Andre Maurois's claim that after sex, Sand would get out of bed and continue writing her novels, while her men lay wrung-out and groaning. (Confession. I just made up "wrung-out and groaning," as my own contribution to Sand's biographical legend—but Sand did leave her lovers in bed while she wrote every day, eight hours a day.)

Linda Simon (review date 10 February 1989)

SOURCE: Simon, Linda. "Biography beyond Gender." *Christian Science Monitor* 81, no. 53 (10 February 1989): 13.

[*In the following review, Simon derides the lack of sympathy for men as well as the narrow focus of Heilbrun's thesis in* Writing a Woman's Life.]

In her latest book, *Writing a Woman's Life*, feminist scholar Carolyn Heilbrun asserts that in telling the story of a woman's life, whether in autobiography or biography, that story must be shaped to fit a male narrative—a linear progression of experiences ending in worldly success. There are only a few narratives available to women—the marriage narrative, for example—and except for these, women are bereft of a story.

Like many other feminist critics, Heilbrun draws on a small population of women to support her views. Sylvia Plath, for one, and Virginia Woolf, Colette, and George Sand. Eudora Welty annoys Heilbrun because she is too sentimental and nostalgic. "I do not believe in the bittersweet quality" of Welty's memoir, *One Writer's Beginnings,* Heilbrun writes. "Nostalgia, particularly for childhood, is likely to be a mask for unrecognized anger." Ida Tarbell's autobiography, *All in the Day's Work,* also fails to reveal anger, according to Heilbrun.

Women who do not reveal anger are, in Heilbrun's view, repressing the true quality of their lives. But men who reveal anger, distress, or suffering are likewise not to be believed.

There is a curious lack of empathy in Heilbrun's reading of men's lives. These lives, she says, are "easy" and "inevitable." She claims that T. S. Eliot's life reads as if it were a tale from the Hardy Boys adventure series. "Men tend to move on a fairly predictable path to achievement," she writes; "women transform themselves only after an awakening."

I do not know many lives that fit her summary; if one looks at writers like Ezra Pound, Eugene O'Neill, Tennessee Williams, or even Truman Capote, one does not see easy lives.

Heilbrun's thesis suffers from a narrow focus. The women she, examines are white, middle-class, well-educated, 19th- or 20th-century writers. She calls for new criteria for the lives of women, but such criteria cannot be generated from this sample. Instead, Heilbrun and other feminist critics must ask themselves if the criteria they wish to apply to women are true across cultural and historical lines. Furthermore, they need to ask themselves if the patterns they see in the telling of women's lives for any particular period were also true in the telling of men's lives at that time.

When Heilbrun refers to Ida Tarbell, for example, she fails to consider the biography of one of her contemporaries, Elizabeth Gurley Flynn, another social activist. Flynn's autobiography, *The Rebel Girl,* bristles with the indignation one would expect from its inflammatory title. Heilbrun, I think, would be well satisfied by the anger expressed in its pages. And yet the autobiography of Ray Stannard Baker, one of Tarbell's closest colleagues, is a work that is as much a "public" telling of a life as that of Tarbell, as reticent and reserved.

When Heilbrun complains that Tarbell's book is what it is because she had no model for a woman's story, I wonder why Tarbell, who forged her own career quite aggressively, who began as a biographer, who invented, with a handful of other writers, the "literature of exposure," would suddenly, at the end of her life, have needed to emulate other writers' works. There is, I would argue, something else going on in the writing of a life besides the creation of a narrative influenced by gender.

Heilbrun's interest in the telling of lives seems more than academic. Much of this slim volume is given over to anecdotes from her childhood and youth, to revelations about her authorship of mystery novels under the pseudonym Amanda Cross, to hints about the quality of her marriage.

These autobiographical explorations are far more interesting, and seem far more authentic, than the sweeping statements Heilbrun makes about other women's lives. Too often she veers from discussing the telling of lives to criticizing the life as it was led (as with Welty), and too often her conclusions seem unsubstantiated.

Feminist criticism is moving intrepidly from fiction to nonfiction, but it must move cautiously, taking into consideration the complexities that distinguish each life from every other, male or female. To argue against Heilbrun's thesis is not to dismiss the work of many feminist critics—Phyllis Rose, for example, in her more temperate and illuminating collection of essays, *Writing of Women*—who have sought ways to understand the differences between women's and men's lives and to interpret an individual's behavior. But this book does not further that work. It pushes it backward.

Linda Simon (review date winter 1990)

SOURCE: Simon, Linda. "The Shape of Women's Lives." *Michigan Quarterly Review* 29, no. 1 (winter 1990): 133-39.

[*In the following review of* Writing a Woman's Life, *Simon examines Heilbrun's assertions about the problems and constraints of the genres of female biography and autobiography.*]

Biography and autobiography present quite enough problems for critics and scholars even when we do not consider the gender of the subject. What, after all, happens in the process of distilling a life into the pages of a book? How do we perceive the theme and plot of an individual's life? What questions do biographers ask of sources to help them understand a life as it was lived? What criteria should we apply when evaluating a biography or autobiography as a work of literature or history?

These problems are compounded when we decide to compare the biographies and autobiographies of women with those of men; and, inevitably, the lives of women with the lives of men. What is the difference—is there a difference—in the shape of women's and men's life stories?

It is this last question that complicates the whole enterprise of feminist literary criticism, whether focused on fiction, poetry, or such non-fiction as biography and autobiography. There are many reasons for differences in texts: cultural, historical, sociological, psychological reasons, that have nothing to do with gender. But examining textual differences according to gender presupposes an assumption that not all feminist critics share: that there is an essential definition of maleness and womanness that transcends historical and cultural context.

Those who subscribe to such a definition would have us seek patterns of behavior that distinguish all men from all women. Whether women are artists, journalists, scientists, social activists, entertainers, mystics, mothers, pioneers, socialites, gymnasts—it does not matter how a woman defines her identity, these critics say, in order to examine the text of her life; it only matters whether the individual is a woman. A middle eastern woman, veiled and shrouded, therefore, has more in common with Emma Goldman, say, than does John Reed. A fifteenth century British noblewoman has more in common with Grace Paley, for example, than with Henry VI. And, these critics assert, ways that women choose to relate their lives have some consistency throughout female experience.

As improbable as these assertions may seem, they have formed the basis for some past work on women's biography and autobiography and they have been revived by Carolyn Heilbrun in her latest reflection on the subject, *Writing a Woman's Life*.

The title itself is confusing. A woman's life story, after all, may be written by a biographer (male or female) or by the woman herself. Those projects are distinct from their conception, and the resulting texts cannot be discussed as if they were interchangeable. One, biography, is a work of history; the other, a primary source upon which histories may be based. One, biography, bears the burden of recording verifiable evidence; the other, of inventing a text that translates felt experience into a work of literature.

The biographer aligns with the reader in examining a life as a text. She "reads" a life for theme, patterns, and plot. She serves as mediator between sources about her subject and the reader, allowing the reader to enter the subject's historical context. A biographer draws her conclusions from a legacy of words: diaries, letters, legal documents, memoirs of friends or lovers or enemies, transcripts of interviews. She cannot be certain of anything that has not been documented as some form of text.

The autobiographer, on the other hand, is both subject and source, I and eye. Her task is to assert a consistent identity, much as the novelist does in creating the protagonist of a tale. Whatever the autobiographer's motivation—to be remembered, to set the record straight, to give testimony to an existence that would otherwise be obliterated by death, to fulfill public expectations for juicy gossip—she creates a text that the biographer may one day read as one source, among many, in examining a life. The autobiographer is able to draw upon undocumented sources—feelings and memories—and select from them. She is not constrained to place herself within a context, to explain anything, to defend her behavior.

Biographers have pressures from the marketplace that place constraints on the shape of their work. They are, as a rule, never so famous as their subject. But biographers do gain status in the literary community according to their subject. If I am writing about T. S. Eliot, I am more important, as a biographer, than if I am writing about the American poets Louis Zukofsky or Lorine Niedecker. I will have an easier job finding a publisher. My book will be reviewed in more journals. I will be invited to speak at more author's hours at local libraries.

If I am compelled, out of sympathy with their lives, to write about Zukofsky or Niedecker, I need to justify to potential publishers why that person's life will result in a marketable book. I will have to persuade an editor that my subject had alliances with interesting people; led a life filled with action and tension; travelled to colorful places; produced work that was defined by others (recognizable critics, for example) as successful. If I can find instances of insanity, alcoholism, disease (preferably venereal), and adultery, so much the better.

If I am fortunate enough to find a publisher who will commission a biography of Niedecker, I will be fulfilling expectations about biography in general, not about women's biography in particular, when I set out to write.

The assumptions of the genre itself have changed throughout history. In the nineteenth century my subject would have been a public figure whose life was informed by exemplary values. The resulting biography would have confirmed the prevailing view that the world in general and western culture in particular was moving energetically toward betterment. Life, by definition, was linear, whether it was the life of a man or a woman.

As we move into the twentieth century, however, no longer are we interested in relating the tales of exemplary lives, but of flawed lives. Modern psychological theories have given biographers permission to delve into the depths, the underside, the dark corners of human experience, and to tell a story of success (our subjects are, at some level, successful or they would not be visible) threatened at every moment by failure. Modern biography is the search for vulnerability.

Autobiography has different constraints from the marketplace. An autobiography may be poetic and impressionistic and still be taken seriously. The autobiographer does not have to sell veracity or thorough documentation to find a publisher. She merely has to present a good story, with the same requirements that might make a good novel. She does not have to be famous—in the past year we have seen autobiographies by such women as Eva Hoffman, Mary Morris, Mary Kay Blakely, Nancy Mairs—women who are not likely subjects of a biography, but are published because they have created, in their text, an interesting character.

I take this time to distinguish between biography and autobiography because if we want to consider seriously the issue of life plots, it is autobiography that is our primary source; it is autobiography that is free of the constraints of publishing and marketing that shape most biography; it is autobiography that defines itself as invented life.

Heilbrun's reading of autobiographies leads her to conclude that women are bereft of a story of their own. But her reading is curiously selective. She cites the autobiography of Ida Tarbell, for example, to prove that women refuse to disclose their feelings of aggression and anger when they tell about their lives, but she fails to cite others, such as the autobiography of Elizabeth Gurley Flynn, a contemporary of Tarbell, and like her involved in social activism and reform, whose book bristles with the indignation one would expect from its inflammatory title, *The Rebel Girl.* Nor does Heilbrun compare Tarbell's work with other such "public" autobiographies as Ray Stannard Baker's *American Chronicle.* Baker, a colleague of Tarbell, was also a muckraker, but not so well-known as she, then or now. When Heilbrun complains that Tarbell's book is what it is because she had no model for a woman's story, I wonder why Tarbell, who forged her own career aggressively, who began as a biographer, who invented, with a handful of other writers, the "literature of exposure," would suddenly, at the end of her life, have needed to emulate other writers' work.

I would argue, instead, that Tarbell, who wrote her life story because she needed money, was responding to her readers' expectations for a book that focused on her work as a journalist and her central role as a major force in the country's political history. Heilbrun would like us to believe that the same criteria apply to Tarbell and Flynn, but not to Baker; but the *kind* of autobiography a writer chooses affects the telling of the tale, and that choice is not necessarily gender-based.

Take Gertrude Stein, for example, whose *Autobiography of Alice B. Toklas* has been examined by feminist critics as if it were an authentic effort to explore her identity, and lamented as a work that bows to patriarchal conventions. But Stein was writing for fame and fortune, at the suggestion of friends with publishing connections, to perpetuate the legend of herself as the center of a Parisian community of writers and artists. All the time she was writing, she complained in her *real* work—those serious, hermetic volumes that Yale University published after her death—about the whole enterprise of commercial publishing. She did not mean *The Autobiography* to reflect the reality of her life plot. That plot was explored, in all its tortuous circumlocutions, in the hermetic works.

Yet critics such as Heilbrun do not allow for different aims and motivations in writing one's life story. Instead, they recall the lives of a small circle of unhappy women—Sylvia Plath, of course, and Virginia Woolf—to generate criteria about the telling of lives for the rest of women, in all cultures, through all time. It is as if sweeping theories about the telling of men's lives were constructed from the life stories of Gerard de Nerval (who, the story goes, walked his lobster through the streets of Paris) or Wittgenstein, who seems to have been a trifle rigid.

Heilbrun veers from criticizing the writing of a life to evaluation of the life as it was lived. She complains about Eudora Welty because she is a proud southern lady whose memoir, *One Writer's Beginnings,* is to Heilbrun's taste too sentimental and nostalgic. "I do not believe in the bittersweet quality" of the book, Heilbrun tells us. "Nostalgia, particularly for childhood, is likely to be a mask for unrecognized anger." I think such an assessment is irresponsible, but Heilbrun insists that all women are restively squirming to lace themselves into ill-fitting corsets of life.

Impatient as she is with Welty for her cultivated femininity, she is equally impatient with Willa Cather, who at times assumed male dress and pseudonyms. Cather, Heilbrun says, "could neither fit, within the expectations of her sex, into a life that allowed the enactment of her dreams, nor discover in the public sphere a place where she could be wholly herself." Other feminist critics, however, have not seen Cather's life as so miserably circumscribed. Phyllis Rose, for example, in her more temperate and illuminating collection of essays, *Writing of Women,* grants, with more generosity, Cather's right to choices that served to liberate her from the provincialism that stifled many other American writers—male as well as female. "This writer we think of as Middle Western spent most of her life in the East. She chose to be a New Yorker. She was the hard-driving editor of a successful magazine and didn't start writing fiction full time until she was forty. Her literary ties were to Europe. The girl next door of American letters hated small-town America, rejected heterosexuality, and distrusted the family as the enemy of art. "It is time," Rose says, "to establish Willa Cather's complexity and her stature as a writer."

Heilbrun, in her effort to help forge a new direction in feminist criticism, ignores the complexities that distinguish each life from every other, male or female. Her approach, based as it is on the belief in a generalized female experience, is shared by many other feminist critics. But this belief is being questioned publicly now in such works as *Inessential Woman,* by Smith College philosophy professor Elizabeth Spelman.

Feminist theory, Spelman sees, has evolved from many disciplines, most significantly from psychology, sociology, literature, and history. Yet the women on whom writers have based their work have been, for the most part, white and middle-class. They have been educated far beyond most women in the world. They have access—unusual for other cultures and other times—to goods, services, support systems, and one another.

This homogeneity disturbs Spelman. "Is it really possible," she asks, "for us to think of a woman's 'womanness' in abstraction from the fact that she is a particular woman, whether she is a middle-class black woman living in North America in the twentieth century or a poor white woman living in France in the seventeenth century?"

To explore this issue, Spelman takes a close look at two seminal works in feminist theory: Simone de Beauvoir's *The Second Sex* and Nancy Chodorow's *The Reproduction of Mothering.* In both works, she finds that a lack of recognition of the differences in race and class weakens each author's generalizations about consistencies in the behavior of women, about sexism, and about alternatives possible in women's lives. De Beauvoir, she notes, resists the idea that there is some "essence" of womanhood common to all females and urges her readers to look at the lives that women lead in order to draw conclusions about gender. But at the same time, de Beauvoir insists that "woman"—no matter who or where—"lacks the sense of the universal," and instead sees the world as "a confused conglomeration of special cases."

When describing relationships between men and women, de Beauvoir ignores the influence of race or class. Spelman cautions us to remember that power is based not only on gender. "To refer to the power 'all men have over all women,'" she writes, "makes it look as if my relationship to the bank vice president I am asking for a loan is just like my relationship to the man who empties my wastebasket at the office each night."

Unlike de Beauvoir, Nancy Chodorow evolves theory from a universal human experience: parenting, and she claims that the relationship between mother and child is therefore universally consistent. Drawing upon Freud (who himself based his theories on women of a particular Viennese class), she concludes that girls see their mothers as extensions of themselves, while boys see her as the "Other" with whom they can never identify. This early relationship then sets a pattern that establishes all future relationships, causing women to invest themselves in their connections with others, and men to seek power over others.

Besides raising questions about the connections men do make in their public and private lives, Spelman also questions Chodorow's assumption that women necessarily identify with one another and value a strong sense of community with other women. How, then, Spelman asks, do some women become racist?

"There are no short cuts through women's lives," Spelman concludes. It is very good advice for feminist critics, and Bella Brodzki and Celeste Schenck would agree. Their collection of essays, *Life/Lines,* breaks new ground in our understanding of the range of life plots available to women as they transform their experiences into literature.

Although Heilbrun herself defends her interest in "privileged" women in one of these essays, other contributors examine the life stories of women from a variety of backgrounds and cultures. There are essays on blacks, native Americans, Latin Americans, lesbians, medieval and Renaissance women, and a turn-of-the-century Egyptian feminist. Autobiography as genre is defined broadly to include poetry, fiction, and film. And other contextual considerations, besides gender, are explored. So, in discussing Native American autobiographies, British writer Helen Carr pays close attention to the motivations and assumptions of the anthropologists who collected the testimonies. Nellie McKay, writing about Zora Neale Hurston, does not exclude race and cultural context from her study; to illuminate Hurston's work, she even compares it to the autobiography of Frederick Douglass. It is rare, indeed, to set male autobiography beside female and to question differences; but *Life/Lines* is an unusual book in its scope and aim.

What makes the collection so refreshing, when set against Heilbrun's book or Estelle Jelinek's *Women's*

Autobiography, is the editors' uncompromising commitment to diversity and their recognition that gender "is no longer the only situating category of interest" for many feminist critics. "As we see it," Brodzki and Schenck tell us, "this vigilant stance can help us to push beyond the mere overturning of binary oppositions, the implications of which are as crucial for male as for female readers and critics of autobiography. The establishment of a separatist female tradition, even feminist critics have warned, carries the danger of reverse reification. Autobiography can thus provide male and female readers with fertile ground for reseeding, along newly drawn feminist lines, contemporary ideas about selfhood."

Life/Lines will serve as a strong model for future collections and studies that explore textual representations of lives. Perhaps even men's lives will be included in such studies, persuading male and female readers that such exemplary autobiographers as St. Augustine, Benjamin Franklin, and Henry Adams do not represent the range of male experience as much as they do not represent female experience. It is the variety of human experience, after all, that interests those of us who look to autobiography for intellectual and spiritual enlightenment.

Lawrence E. Mintz (review date summer 1992)

SOURCE: Mintz, Lawrence E. "Review Essays." *Journal of Popular Culture* 26, no. 1 (summer 1992): 165-71.

[*In the following review of* Writing a Woman's Life, *Mintz compliments Heilbrun as an astute and provocative feminist scholar.*]

In the 1960s and 1970s feminist scholars voiced a concerted objection to the patriarchal bias in western intellectual thought. Because scholarship has been dominated by male voices, telling all stories from a male point of view, they argued, women's experience has been ignored, devalued, or wrongly interpreted. Feminist scholars insisted that we listen to women as they tell their own stories, so that we would have a balanced view of human experience. It sounded reasonable enough, but for almost three decades, feminist scholars have been wrestling with an intellectual puzzle: if we accept the argument that western knowledge is flawed by a fundamental patriarchal bias, how can we find informants who will have resisted the patriarchal consciousness, informants who will have viewed their own experience with a female mind's eye? In short, how can a woman tell her own story if she has been indoctrinated with a male point of view?

The first answer was to look at women's experience "objectively," and so in the first wave of feminist scholarship, social scientists frequently led the way.

Like the cliometricians who described slavery by measuring calories and space, feminist sociologists determined means and norms to describe women's experience. But this was not a universally satisfying solution. Anyone who has experienced a feminist consciousness-raising group realizes that objective statistics lack the transformative power of personal narratives—storytelling. In c-r groups, participants recognize details of their own lives in the graphic personal storytelling of other women. Although this storytelling has been ridiculed by detractors as narcissistic self-indulgence, many feminist scholars have insisted on the validity of personal narratives as evidence. At the same time, they have struggled to develop theories and methods for collecting, evaluating, analyzing, editing, and using them.

Literary critics have held a prominent place in recent feminist scholarship because they examine stories by and about women. Carolyn Heilbrun is one of the most astute practitioners of the craft. In her most recent book, ***Writing a Woman's Life,*** Heilbrun tells her own story. As a young girl, she says, "I was profoundly caught up in biography because it allowed me to enter the world of daring and achievement. But I had to make myself a boy to enter that world." For girls and women, romances have been the major available narrative model. In romances, women seem to be the center of the story for that brief time when they withhold themselves; when they accept the man as the center of their lives, the story ends.

> Women are allowed this brief period in the limelight—and it is the part of their lives most constantly and vividly enacted in a myriad of representations—to encourage the acceptance of a lifetime of marginality. And courtship itself is, as often as not, an illusion: that is, the woman must entrap the man to ensure herself a center for her life. The rest is aging and regret.
>
> (21)

Heilbrun argues that limiting the life stories available to women will limit the way women can envision living their lives. Heilbrun believes that stories have a greater effect than day-to-day living.

> What matters is that lives do not serve as models; only stories do that. And it is a hard thing to make up stories to live by. We can only retell and live by the stories we have read or heard. We live our lives through texts.
>
> (3)

Having persuasively stated her thesis, Heilbrun turns to the lives of exceptional women to explore alternative life narratives in a series of speculative essays. Using Dorothy Sayers's writings and life, she examines the quest theme—a theme traditionally reserved for men—in women's biography. Reminding us of Hannah Arendt's words, that "if we do not know our own history, we are doomed to live it as though it were our private fate," Heilbrun looks at women poets who expressed their anger in the autobiographical, "confessional" mode: Levertov, Cooper, Kizer, Kumin, Sexton, Rich, and Plath. Heilbrun shows us alternate stories about marriage and friendship; she suggests that, contrary to most women's expectations, aging can allow women to "stop being female impersonators" and begin living their own lives. And she briefly explores her own reasons, as a young college professor, for creating an alter ego, Amanda Cross, who writes detective stories about Kate Fansler, a gutsy and questing woman detective.

The book suggests that there are some women who have led lives that we might profitably emulate: women who married for equitable companionship rather than passion, women for whom female friendship is a support in their forays into the public world. It is a small book, easily read, but also provocative.

Stacey Vallas (review date September 1992)

SOURCE: Vallas, Stacey. Review of *Hamlet's Mother and Other Women,* by Carolyn Heilbrun. *English Language Notes* 30, no. 1 (September 1992): 72-3.

[*In the following review, Vallas asserts that* Hamlet's Mother and Other Women *demonstrates Heilbrun's significant role in the progress of literary and gender studies.*]

Carolyn Heilbrun begins her **Writing a Woman's Life** (1988): "There are four ways to write a woman's life: the woman herself may tell it, in what she chooses to call an autobiography; she may tell it in what she chooses to call fiction; a biographer, woman or man, may write the woman's life in what is called a biography; or the woman may write her own life in advance of living it, unconsciously, and without recognizing or naming the process." **Hamlet's Mother and Other Women,** a collection of Heilbrun's essays, reviews, and addresses spanning the years 1957 to 1988, also explores these modes of biography as well as the construction of female character by male artists and critics—in short, the multiplicitous means of "writing" women's lives. As the volume's title suggests, with its joining of a fictional female character with "other women," both fictive and actual, and with its substitution of "women" for the expected "essays," Heilbrun is interested in pursuing the connections between fiction and lived experience, between the models and narratives imagined for women in literature and in life. "Out of old tales," she asserts, "we must make new lives."

In **"What Was Penelope Unweaving?"**—an inspired and inspiring regional MLA keynote address—Penelope serves as a figure for such a revisionary practice. For Heilbrun, Penelope is "without a story" in the sense that all women, having been confined to the plot of courtship, marriage, and motherhood—having identified themselves primarily in the light, or shadow, of male desire—are without their own stories. But unlike so many female characters, Penelope finds herself, for a time at least, "in a rare position of autonomy and choice" to unweave the old story and invent a new one. At the heart of each of these essays is this feminist concern with the struggle "to become the subject of one's own life."

While the voicing of untold stories and the invention of new scripts—of mothers and daughters, of female friendship, of women in equal partnership with men, of the questing woman artist, of female middle age—is a common thread throughout, this collection demonstrates the impressive heterogeneity of Heilbrun's interests and knowledge. In the section **"Exemplary Women,"** she ranges from Margaret Mead to Freud's daughters (literal and figural) to Vera Brittain and Winifred Holtby to Woolf's complex relationship to the work of Joyce. Included in **"Literature and Women"** are essays on May Sarton's autobiographies (*To the Lighthouse, Little Women*) and transformations in the English novel's representation of marriage. **"Feminism and the Profession of Literature"** is comprised of lectures and addresses Heilbrun gave in the late '70s and '80s, while a final section examines the workings of class and gender in detective fiction, both defining the particular contours of this popular genre and challenging any rigid dichotomy between it and "real novels."

In many ways this volume traces not only a history of Heilbrun's discerning and varied work as a critic, teacher, MLA president, author and reader of detective fiction, but also a history of second-wave feminism within the profession of literature. The titular essay, **"The Character of Hamlet's Mother,"** was Heilbrun's first publication, opens the volume, and alone comprises its first section. While all the other pieces were written between 1973 and 1988, this article appeared in 1957. It is dated but illuminating precisely for this reason. One can sense that Heilbrun knows she is advancing what will be deemed a radical, suspect, even ridiculous argument: that Gertrude, though "passion's slave," is intelligent, insightful, and gifted with language. Meticulously and persuasively marshalling evidence, Heilbrun demonstrates what now, of course, seems self-evident—that the queen is far from a slothful, shallow, and dull creature—but what at the time was the charting of new interpretive possibilities. In her reading of Gertrude, Heilbrun calls into question conventional assumptions about gender, reframing how the relationship between a women's sexuality and identity might be viewed. This essay and the others which continue this work—and continue to refine the terms of the feminist project—mark how transformed the terrain of literary studies has been in the last three decades and how significant a role their author has played in that transformation.

Lillian S. Robinson (review date July 1995)

SOURCE: Robinson, Lillian S. "Postmurderism." *Women's Review of Books* 12, nos. 10-11 (July 1995): 32.

[*In the following review, Robinson notes the dislocation of structure and content in* An Imperfect Spy.]

The distinguished feminist critic Carolyn Heilbrun has been publishing mystery novels under the pseudonym Amanda Cross since 1964. So it was by design that, in 1991, the names of both Heilbrun and Cross appeared on the program of a Texas conference called "Feminist Practice: Representation of Women in Law and Literature." (I was on the same panel as Cross.)

Ten years earlier, in Cross's *Death in a Tenured Position,* Professor Kate Fansler, tired of teaching *Middlemarch* ("even *Middlemarch*") at her Columbia-like university, took off for Harvard to untangle the events surrounding the appointment, mistreatment and death of the first tenured woman in that institution's English Department. Now, in 1995, Fansler is still tired of teaching *Middlemarch*—tireder, perhaps, since there's not even an "even," this time. So, in *An Imperfect Spy,* she takes a busman's holiday to teach a seminar at a reactionary local law school. And what is the topic of this seminar? None other than "Women in Law and Literature." Intertextuality being the name of the game in this novel (which relies on significant references to *Tess of the d'Urbervilles,* John Le Carré's Smiley novels and *Harriet the Spy*), I cried out, "I been there before," but in delighted recognition, and without the least desire to light out for the territory.

After some thirty years, I thought I knew what to expect of an Amanda Cross novel, especially since growth and change in the continuing characters is one of those things. In this sense, *An Imperfect Spy* does not disappoint. We get the usual mix of characters: not only Kate and her husband, Reed Amhearst (who is—I warn you—in mid-mid-career crisis), but the familiar group of pompous academic men who are complicit in crimes against women, and the witty, literate women who resist them. Two recent deaths at Schuyler Law School bring up issues concerning gender in the academy (Schuyler's first tenured woman, the object of ill-treatment by her colleagues, might also have been helped—by them?—to her death) and in the larger world with which the academy interacts (another law professor's battered wife is in prison for his murder). There are some male students at least as vicious as their teachers, as well as some of both sexes whose consciousness gets raised.

But *An Imperfect Spy* differs from its predecessors in both its design and its content. Structurally, the narrative breaks the expected, essentially nineteenth-century pace and sequence. We learn important pieces of the plot too late or too soon or, somehow, obliquely, and there are so many red herrings that if you removed them, there would hardly be a plot left. Similarly, the feminist issues are brought in rather perfunctorily. If the reader isn't already and unequivocally on the side of battered women, this novel's treatment of the problem is not likely to prove convincing. Even the male students' sexist campaign against Kate, because we learn about it at second hand and after the fact, fails to ignite appropriate indignation.

Because these developments violated my entrenched expectations, I was unsure at first what to make of them. I now think that what is going on is not inept construction, much less unconcern about dramatizing women's issues. Rather, *An Imperfect Spy* is The First Postmodern Amanda Cross Novel. It's not just Kate Fansler who's tired of *Middlemarch,* it's Carolyn Heilbrun. And what she's doing about it is making another kind of novel, dislocating the familiar elements that she brings over into the new form. The dislocation is provocative in two senses of the word—at once stimulating and annoying, with the former winning out. I'm eager to see where the experiment takes her next.

Gayle Feldman (essay date 11 September 1995)

SOURCE: Feldman, Gayle. "Heilbrun on Steinem, Steinem on Heilbrun." *Publishers Weekly* 242, no. 37 (11 September 1995): 25-6, 30.

[*In the following essay, Feldman explores the collaboration between Heilbrun and Gloria Steinem, which resulted in* The Education of a Woman: The Life of Gloria Steinem.]

She's the woman who told the world, "This is what 40 looks like," and made many yearn to look just like that.

She's been treated as an icon—and as a pinup. For years, her life has been picked over for public delectation.

There was the childhood spent alternately on the road or in a bathing suit at the lakeside resort her family struggled to run; the years from 10 through 17, after her parents' divorce, taking care of a mother whose mind wandered in and out of reality; the escape to Smith College and the life of the 1950s "good girl"; the sojourn in India, long before it became fashionable to do so; her discovery of journalism, and journalism's discovery in the '60s of a miniskirted "darling," who was condescended to as a sexy career girl or treated seriously—as an honorary man; the early '70s feminist epiphany and founding of *Ms.*; and the past quarter-century living as gadfly extraordinaire for causes great and small. Not to mention two bestsellers along the way—*Outrageous Acts and Everyday Rebellions* (Holt, 1983) and *Revolution from Within* (Little, Brown, 1992).

Gloria Steinem, this is your life. Well, sort of. For however much that life has seemed to be carried out and dissected in public, there is a part of Steinem that has remained elusive even to those close to her. Now, Carolyn Heilbrun, no slouch herself in the feminist pantheon—author of the classic **Writing a Woman's Life** (Norton) as well as the Amanda Cross mysteries, and former Avalon professor at Columbia University—is trying to lift the curtain a little more, in **The Education of a Woman: The Life of Gloria Steinem,** which was written with Steinem's full cooperation—although without any right of approval.

With a 40,000-copy first printing, the biography is the lead title in this first year of the reincarnated Dial Press. Heilbrun will be going on a five-city tour and doing further promotion from New York; and Steinem's cooperation is extending even to a few interviews on the book's behalf. Thus, during one week in August, *PW* spent an afternoon with Steinem and an afternoon with Heilbrun, being "educated" as to the nature of the two women's lives and the book that comes from their commingling.

Despite a few similarities—Steinem is 61, Heilbrun is 69; both graduated from seven sisters schools in the 1950s—the two couldn't be more unalike. Steinem lives alone on several floors of a Manhattan brownstone, in rooms darkened by draperies and damask, where the memories of a vagabond life take object form, spilling over onto every table, every corner, every wall.

Heilbrun lives across town, facing the western edge of Central Park in a prewar block whose very solidity seems to speak of long decades of married life, in rooms where order and neatness are intensified by the light of the large picture windows.

But if you ask either what she hopes for **The Education of a Woman,** their answers are remarkably consonant. Heilbrun first: "We live in a time when all the pressure is to go back, for women to live a conventional, prescribed life. The backlash against feminism is fundamentalism, and it is very widespread.

"I'd like people to read this book and say that this is a different life from the kind most women lived in those years. It shows that there are other ways for women to live. But this life is exemplary only in its possibilities—this is what *one* woman's education could look like."

For Steinem, "what's remarkable about Carolyn is that here is a woman who married young, had children and an academic career and yet never condemns me for living a different life, and I'm someone who's been frequently condemned. We both hope this book will be of use to female readers trying to figure out that there are as many ways to live as there are individual women.

"It's possible this may be one of the few, or the only biography of a contemporary woman that doesn't interpret her worth in terms of the presence or absence of a husband and children. The self-willed moments of moving forward toward one's true self—those are usually missing from women's biographies, which tend to show how women survived adversity rather than how they were self-directed.

"Carolyn's use of my life as the peg for larger insights was for me the high point in the emotional roller coaster of reading the book. For example, there was her insight about the conventional male division of life into public and private—with 'public' being work and 'private' being family—so that men who leave public life often say, with varying degrees of sincerity, that they want to spend more time with their family. But for women, the division is usually into 'others' and 'self.' At some point later in life, women often take a turn away from others toward the self—whether or not they have husbands and children. In a way, this was as true for me after 50 as it is for many women whose children are grown. It seems to be a pattern that is deeper than different life choices."

But of the reading experience, in terms of seeing her life set out before her, Steinem says: "I'm not sure I can answer the question whether it seems to me it is my life I am reading. When I read it, it plunges me into the events and I lose track."

One thing is sure, though. Steinem has always maintained that she intended to write the story of her life one day but admits, "I wasn't ready to do an autobiography. It felt like going back, and I wanted to go forward. But I've come away from this feeling it's possible for me to write that book. The experience of this book will help draw me away from being a reporter. I don't have to explain the externals because Carolyn has done it."

Ironically, Heilbrun's biography started—so many do these days—as an attempt by Steinem to hold on to her own life. As Steinem recalls, "It was 1988 or '89 and I was consulting for Random House at the time. I had never met Carolyn, but I had always admired her work, and at one of the Random House meetings, I wondered about whether we couldn't get her to do a biography of P. D. James.

Meanwhile, over a number of years I'd been approached by people about doing my biography. I remember saying plaintively to friends, 'Can't I get the legal rights to my own life?' Several juvenile biographies had already been done, and when I voiced my complaints, friends told me, 'All you can do is cooperate with someone you respect.'

So when P. D. James said no, I offered myself to Carolyn as a consolation prize, and I was amazed when she said yes. It seemed to me I should be writing *her* biography [at least two biographies of Heilbrun are indeed in the works]. I've given up on the legal rights to my own life [another Steinem biography is currently being written by Sydney Stern for Carol Publishing]. When others have asked for my cooperation, I've said that I don't have the time or the will to put into it. But part of what I've learned from Carolyn is that there's never *a* biography—there are many.

Heilbrun says, "I suspect I've always wanted to write a biography of a woman. I had written biographical studies of men, but biography has changed an enormous amount, and it's not easy to find a subject who's had a life that's satisfactory and at the same time is making a genuine contribution and is also a feminist. Others have asked me to do their biographies and I've said no. So many women are anti-Semitic, homophobic, racist. Steinem didn't seem any of those.

Doing her biography seemed a chance to use an academic approach and at the same time write something that was readily accessible. For example, what academics have discovered about gender and sexuality needs to be read by intelligent people everywhere. The essential point for me was to think what I could do with her life, and as I went along, the life became even more interesting than I had expected.

For example, Gloria had the courage to live apart from socialization, which she escaped to a great extent—that's a tendency of women who have lived exceptional lives. She didn't go to school [as a younger child], and this escape from normal socialization can also be a really dramatic response to a mother whose life was unhappy.

Steinem's mother, Ruth, was, unusually for the 1920s, a college graduate. Even more unusually, she worked full-time as a newspaper journalist while also managing a house, raising a baby (Gloria's older sister Susanne) and coping with a financially irresponsible husband, until her first nervous breakdown in 1930, four years before Gloria was born.

By the time Steinem was 10, her parents had divorced and her mother's mind was lost in a web of fears and voices and unreality. Although many years later, with enlightened professional help, Ruth achieved a fragile equilibrium, Gloria Steinem spent her adolescence trapped in Toledo, Ohio, living in squalor, taking care of her mother on her own (her sister was by then away in college). But, as Heilbrun explains in the book, instead of indulging in the dreams of the "socialized" young girl, which would have had her rescued by a man, Steinem's fantasies always placed herself as the rescuer.

She was determined to get out, and, growing up in a working-class neighborhood, was determined not to be a "victim" like so many of the women she saw around her. One of the exit routes she explored was a beauty pageant. And, interestingly, one of the areas on which biographer and subject disagree most concerns Steinem's celebrated beauty. Heilbrun makes much of Steinem's appearance throughout the book. As she told *PW*, "Gloria takes for granted a body in which she is wholly comfortable, and she isn't realistic about her looks. But what I had to learn was that looks could be a burden, too."

But according to Steinem, "Carolyn's emphasis on my appearance is not the way I feel about myself. For example, when I entered that pageant at 16, it was the only game in town. It seemed to me the only way of getting out of Toledo. She talks about the pageant, but not about the impact of losing. It was very crushing to one's self-worth. I cried and felt this way of getting out of my neighborhood was lost to me. Moreover, I had lied about my age to get in at all."

Another area of sensitivity between biographer and subject is the treatment of *Ms.* magazine. According to Heilbrun, "anytime I said anything critical about *Ms.*, she was very unhappy, or thought it was unfair." Steinem finds Heilbrun's take on the magazine's history as "very critical. It's a question of proportion and context."

Another part of the book that is "quite painful" for Steinem is the section on *Revolution from Within*: "Carolyn writes very critically about it, and clearly didn't like it very much. It's also painful to see the coverage of [the affair with Mort] Zuckerman. It seems to loom larger than in life. Neither one of us was wrong. I was simply infatuated with someone I made up."

Nevertheless, although "sometimes painful," Steinem found the experience of working with her biographer on the whole "often surprising and gratifying and illuminating. It's good for a writer to be a subject. But I wish she had traveled with me. She's too accustomed to dealing with dead authors and texts!"

Both agree that Heilbrun learned a lot through the process, especially about what it is like to live life in the glare of the media spotlight. As Steinem puts it, "Carolyn hadn't paid a great deal of attention to the popular media before this enterprise. My own indignation has been worn down over the years. I've come to expect that complexity gets simplified into labels. But it was interesting to watch Carolyn's indignation as she encountered the media coverage compared to the real event." Heilbrun says simply, "I discovered there are two different realities: the media and real life."

Steinem was able to open most doors for her biographer—but not all. She and the late Jacqueline Onassis had been friends, sometimes going to the movies together in the afternoon. Heilbrun recalls, "there was a lovely letter from Jackie to Gloria that I wanted to use, but the lawyers for the estate said that they would go to the full extent of the law if I even tried to paraphrase it."

Facing publication, Steinem says, "there is not the same level of anxiety I experienced with my own books, but I'm still nervous and fearful, particularly for Carolyn. I feel I'm something of a lightning rod for ill will that may wash over on her." Heilbrun seems sanguine, however: "I always expect controversy. All the people who have hated Steinem will say I was taken over by her."

In the end, what does Heilbrun make of the education of a woman? "My sense of it is that a woman goes on developing through her whole life—the older she gets, the more she learns and changes. Men are more radical in youth; women in age. Maybe there are things we all have to have in our lives, but we don't all have to do everything at the same time."

And what of Steinem? What does she make of this "education" based on her life? "I'd emphasize the 'a' in the subtitle. The more individual the truth, the better chance you have of being useful to others. And for me, Carolyn's book has helped me to let go. I can't control it, and that's all right. I suppose you need to live in the present as much as possible and do what feels true."

Marion Winik (review date 8 October 1995)

SOURCE: Winik, Marion. "Heilbrun for the Defense." *Los Angeles Times Book Review* (8 October 1995): 2, 7.

[*In the following review, Winik contends that* The Education of a Woman *"reads like a biography written by the subject's feminist-academic-maiden-aunt—too careful, too dry and too doting."*]

When I heard that Carolyn Heilbrun had written a biography of Gloria Steinem [***The Education of a Woman***], I was excited. Heilbrun's book ***Writing a Woman's Life*** has been required reading in women's studies classes since its publication in 1988 as a pioneering framework for understanding the lives of "women who write their own scripts." As Steinem is undoubtedly one such woman, this seemed an inspired pairing of biographer and subject.

Indeed, the "serious" parts of Steinem's story are well-told: her difficult, poverty-stricken childhood with a mentally ill mother and a lovable but irresponsible father; the formation of her ideas during a post-college year spent in India; the evolution of her feminism in the '60s and '70s, and the trials and tribulations of *Ms.* magazine are presented cogently and insightfully, as are the personal changes she went through when she reached the age of 50. But Gloria Steinem is a feminist icon because of the colorful life she's led and the fun she's had, as well as what she has had to overcome. Heilbrun's careful telling of Steinem's life is a respectable choice, but one that leaves some of us frustrated that the "juicier" parts of the story are covered in less detail.

Steinem offers her biographer a public and private world peopled with celebrities, set in the vibrant spheres of publishing and politics, laced with scandalous incidents, from the rescue of Linda Lovelace to an affair with millionaire Mort Zuckerman. This is a woman who went underground as a Playboy Bunny for an article in *Show* magazine, who staged a demonstration at her 25th class reunion at Smith College, who ran on a ticket with Norman Mailer and Jimmy Breslin for comptroller of the city of New York. She is known not only for her politics, but for her "look," her personal style and her wit, which has made its mark from the White House, where she helped Ted Sorenson add humor to JFK's speeches, to the newsstands of Manhattan, where readers devoured her '70s City Politic columns for *New York* magazine with titles such as "Kissing with Your Eyes Open: Women and the Democrats."

This seems to be the material for a pretty racy book, but that is clearly not the book Heilbrun wanted to write. In fact, she sees Steinem as a victim of prurient interest in her unconventionality, her looks and her private life on the part of both the shallow-minded, sensationalist dogs of the American media on the one hand and the jealous, relentlessly PC meanies of the feminist movement on the other. And she makes it her business to take Steinem's side in every one of these battles, to plead the case even where Steinem herself backed down, victim of her own relentlessly conciliatory nature. (This combination of, "I don't care what you think"/"Oops, don't be mad at me" is one Heilbrun rightly identified as a burden of our gender; a good object lesson for all of us.) But the resulting story is yet another one-dimensional portrait, this time not by way of media sensationalism but of revisionist goody-goodyism. ***The Education of a Woman*** reads like a biography written by the subject's feminist-academic-maiden-aunt—too careful, too dry and too doting.

Heilbrun is fascinated by the way Steinem's femininity is set at cross-purposes with her feminism, her famous beauty causing trouble with everyone from ego-maniac rivals, such as Betty Friedan, to sexist pigs, such as Screw magazine Publisher Al Goldstein, to patriarchal old farts at the Woodrow Wilson Center, a research institute affiliated with the Smithsonian. It was an ongoing disappointment for Steinem, one with which her biographer sympathizes, to have the press focus so relentlessly on her appearance. For example, Heilbrun tells us about a 1971 article in the *Miami Herald* that described Steinem as "blessed with a hard-to-beat combination of brains, beauty and charm." It further noted that she "believes her good looks have been more of a hindrance than a help in her success . . . and feels women are more interested than men in sex." Heilbrun's comment is that "reporters were still picking out the salacious bits [of their interviews with Steinem] to report."

Personally, I don't see the salaciousness, and wish only that Heilbrun would have seen fit to share these views about men, women and sex, which today are so respectable you can take courses on them in college. As Heilbrun acknowledges, one of the many interesting things about Steinem is her love life. She never married, but she did have a series of romances with well-known and/or interesting men such as film director Robert Benton; Tom Guinzberg, publisher and former editor of the Paris Review; director Mike Nichols; Franklin Thomas (president of the Ford Foundation), and Assistant Atty. Gen. Stan Pottinger, virtually all of whom claim to love her to this day. Unfortunately, for those who would like to know more about this astonishingly successful career in serial monogamy and who wouldn't mind a few prurient details along the way, the accounts of these relationships are disappointing, partly because they emphasize politics over feeling, partly because they tread so carefully around the privacy of this cast of living characters.

For example, Heilbrun notes that "Steinem met Rafer Johnson at the 1968 convention; this was the first of her 'romantic friendships' with a black man. Many of the activist black men she met were, she found, more sensitive to the dangers and oppression of sexism than their white male counterparts." Oh god, we're thinking, is this really all we're going to hear about this? Nor does this theory do much to explain her '68 affair with football-player-turned-actor Jim Brown, who, Heilbrun reports, included an account of his affair with Steinem in his "sex-stuffed" 1989 autobiography. For a moment, I wished I was reading that book.

In telling us about a widely reprinted photograph of Steinem and Henry Kissinger and her accompanying jest, "I am not now nor have I ever been a girlfriend of Henry Kissinger," Heilbrun tells us: "This picture and the rumors it produced would haunt Steinem forever." Oh, please. Is it really so haunting? Or if it was then, do we have to solemnly agree with that view today?

Steinem has suffered because, by being sexy, by being photographed with Kissinger, by having an interesting love life, by putting Wonder Woman on the cover of *Ms.* magazine—she violated the movement's idea and the media's idea of how a feminist should look and act in the '70s and '80s. She felt bad about this, tried to downplay it, and even retreated from it as her life went on. Her biographer continues this scramble for acceptability. One cannot help but feel that if Heilbrun would just get off the defensive, a more powerful Steinem would emerge. One finally is not sure whether Steinem was so battered by the forces of political correctness that she became boring in her attempt to placate critics, or whether Heilbrun is doing it to her out of an urge to respect her privacy. And one wishes, at least for a moment, that no matter how tough it was for Gloria to be a babe in the feminist movement, we would take a moment out to admit that it's really not so bad to have great legs.

Perhaps the most confusing thing about this book is the ending, where Heilbrun sums up Steinem's contribution to feminism in these words: "To the media and those who live in its light, Steinem is, to various degrees, an enigma, and, perhaps inevitably, a paradox. But to the many thousands she has helped or encouraged or rescued, she is, like the mythical Kilroy of World War II, essential and ubiquitous. Steinem was here."

Is it just me, or is that a pretty backhanded compliment?

Vivian Gornick (review date 6 November 1995)

SOURCE: Gornick, Vivian. "What Feminism Looks Like." *Nation* 261, no. 15 (6 November 1995): 544-46.

[*In the following review, Gornick maintains that one of the major thematic concerns of* The Education of a Woman *is the impact of Steinem's beauty and femininity on her life and career.*]

The first woman astronaut went up into space and, standing on the ground, her mother cried, "God bless Gloria Steinem!"

The women's movement, in a moment of disarray, needed an enemy within, and it cried, "Gloria Steinem!"

Asked in a small city why she had never married, Steinem said for the television cameras, "I wanted women to see that you could not marry, and still have an interesting life." In the studio people applauded wildly.

A few years ago, watching her drift through a roomful of intellectual women—it was not her crowd, she could find no easy place to touch down—I heard a scientist ask, "What exactly is it that she *does*?" and a critic replied, "It's not what she does, it's what she arouses in others."

Gloria Steinem belongs to a generation of feminists that includes Kate Millett, Ellen Willis, Betty Friedan and Susan Brownmiller, yet she alone became its enduring emblematic figure. She is to feminism what Yasir Arafat is to the Palestinians: an incarnation, a figure of powerful suggestiveness, a projection in the popular imagination of all in our cause that glimmers, and all that grieves. After twenty-five years of the most sophisticated politicking in feminist history, the glamorous woman among us is the one who, more than any other, continues to hold the inner attention of depressed housewives, expectant schoolgirls, angry waitresses and restless academics.

If you should turn in the crowd and ask, Why? the answer you're likely to get is, "Because she's beautiful, and she's not threatening," or "She's beautiful, and she's made herself vulnerable," or "She's beautiful, and . . ." fill in the blank, it doesn't actually matter what comes next. The answer always astonishes. I am moved when I hear it. Moved and appalled and sobered. "She's beautiful. She could have been *anything*. And she became a feminist." Indeed, an incarnation. To contemplate Steinem's image in the world is to gaze steadily into the meanness of our everlasting anxiety, the gravity of our uprising. Steinem herself understands this better than anyone: from the inside out. And perhaps Carolyn Heilbrun does too, as her new biography, **The Education of a Woman,** is remarkably absorbed by the question of Gloria's looks.

Steinem was born sixty-one years ago in the Midwest into a family whose drift toward the margin was steady. She was smart, and she was pretty. Like millions before and after, she thought pretty would be the passport to another life, but as it turned out it only meant "coming in second in beauty contests in Toledo, Ohio." An older sister rescued her, took her to Washington, D.C., to finish high school. Then came a scholarship to Smith College. After Smith she knew how to do the world.

A couple of years out of college she came to New York to find an exciting job. Fit for nothing in particular and connected to no one at all, luck failed to rescue her. But a curious job in Cambridge came her way. Through the good offices of a man she'd met in India (she had spent a year there on a student fellowship), she went to work for the Independent Research Service, a foundation that "encouraged" young Americans to attend the International Communist Youth Festivals being held in Europe. The year was 1959. The money was coming from the C.I.A. This Steinem did not know, but even if she *had* known, she would have taken the job. Not that she was a baby cold warrior, not at all; it was rather that she had no real politics, she only knew that she loved *doing* politics. That, and being close to men in power, kept her in the Service until 1962 when, with new savvy and sufficient connections, she hit New York running.

Not pretty enough to come in first in a beauty contest, the future founder of *Ms.* was very pretty for a girl journalist around town. In no time at all she was writing for the slicks, interviewing the famous, sleeping with the powerful. She became known for whom she knew. An article about her in *Newsweek* in 1965 stated, "Gloria Steinem . . . is as much a celebrity as a reporter and often generates news in her own right. . . . She has dated Ted Sorensen and Mike Nichols, discussed the poverty program at lunch at the White House, and makes opening nights (and the women's pages the next day). . . . Her subjects often become her most vociferous fans. 'She's the smartest, funniest, and most serious person I know,' says Nichols, 'and she looks great.'"

When I read this paragraph recently in Heilbrun's book, I recalled an early-seventies piece in which famous men Steinem knew were interviewed about her newly declared feminism. John Kenneth Galbraith, trying to explain Gloria's success, attributed it to "brains, comic perception and extremely good looks." Good looks was a factor? "I have to be honest," he said.

I remembered myself all those years ago, staring at that sentence; remembered going cold inside; remembered looking at her picture and thinking, No wonder your face is opaque, your body controlled, your style unreadable. Necessary weapons, if it's Galbraith with whom you need to be seen. It was tempting then to think of Steinem, How different the game she's been playing is from that of the rest of us, how hidden its terms, how complicated its bounty. But I must have quickly corrected myself because I also remember thinking, This woman says something none of the rest of us are going to say. It's not the words, it's the presentation.

I had always been struck by the absence of expressiveness in Steinem's face, coupled with the steady patience of her voice repeating its simple feminist message. The face was neither unintelligent nor insincere, it simply betrayed no signs of inner life. It was a face that had been carefully put together—and not yesterday, either; a face behind whose eyes one could never get; a face modeled not by nature but by will. What she was saying, coming out of *that* face, was her offering to feminism. The entire performance urged, "Mark me well, listen and look, the two go together."

More than twenty years later the face is remarkably unchanged, as are the words and the listeners. They flock to her, still, by the thousand, and often one sees on their faces the penetrating stare of first recognitions. As Steinem talks one hears repeatedly the inevitable murmur of "She's so beautiful," but in the crowd stand countless women who also came in second in a beauty contest in Toledo, Ohio, and also needed to command the attention of the local Man of Power. The women who might have become Steinem, but instead became Thelma and Louise. These women listen intently to her, their faces as knowing as her own. To them Steinem speaks directly, and tirelessly. She is famous—and justly so—for her kindness, her devotion, her unfailing response to the women who remind her of her own young self; famous as well for repeating in speech after speech what other feminists stopped repeating fifteen years ago. It isn't just that she knows there are women out there waiting to hear the fundamentals for the first time; it's that she herself is still mesmerized by her own message. She can taste in her mouth the iron she tasted thirty years ago, in that first moment when she "got it," when she saw herself as she was seen in the world.

Steinem once wrote a book about Marilyn Monroe, with whom she identified. Of this identification Heilbrun writes, "Monroe believed she existed . . . only because men saw her with delight. . . . Steinem recognized [her] conviction that she was invisible, except when seen by others. . . . About the same time she was writing the Monroe book, she began to wonder if that insight might not describe her own situation as well."

Marilyn Monroe was one of the great examples of a woman both gratified and imprisoned by that in herself which aroused fantasy in others. It was the loneliness in her that compelled, the peculiar, haunting nature of it. That loneliness is there in all of us, but in Monroe it created a vacancy that, somehow, became erotically inviting. It is into this vacancy that projection inevitably moves. Why, exactly, the phenomenon occurs in some and not in others is hard to know. It is the mystery of "star quality." A quality there in Monroe the Sexpot, as it is there in Steinem the Feminist. Two pretty girls who believed what every woman in the world believed: that to be beautiful was to be free of shame, conflict and humiliation.

Carolyn Heilbrun's biography does not penetrate the mystery; it celebrates the incarnation. Heilbrun, like all right-minded feminists, yearns for the spirit of revolutionary feminism to be alive, fully fleshed and walking about once more. Out of that longing she wrote this book. Because of her book I wrote this piece. Steinem's life, Heilbrun's book, my reflections—together they form a document of sorts. Evidence of the ongoing need in my generation of feminists to keep sifting through the history, trying to puzzle out better how we came to be the women who made a powerful piece of politics out of one's "own hurt feelings."

Wini Breines (review date December 1995)

SOURCE: Breines, Wini. "Career Feminist." *Women's Review of Books* 13, no. 3 (December 1995): 8-9.

[*In the following review, Breines criticizes* The Education of a Woman, *arguing that the biography is "strangely transparent, an unmessy narrative of Steinem's admirable life with little attention to depth, complications, or contradictions."*]

Carolyn Heilbrun writes Gloria Steinem's life [in *The Education of a Woman*], as an uncomplicated story. Steinem was born into a white lower-middle-class family in 1934 in Toledo, Ohio. She spent many years parenting her seriously troubled mother, eventually went to Smith College, traveled in India and returned to the US to become a journalist. She is independent, has had many lovers but never married or had children; as Heilbrun points out, she is an uncommon woman whose life has been determined only by herself. (Heilbrun argues that in this Steinem is more radical than many feminists who have chosen the security of marriage and children.) Steinem has always had sympathy for the underdog and has unselfishly committed herself to causes larger than herself. In 1969 she became, or understood that she was, a feminist, and has devoted her life to feminism ever since.

Steinem appears to have been unusually ambitious and energetic in the pursuit of power and celebrity, albeit for good causes, but Heilbrun never considers ambition as a motive. Steinem's experiences, encounters and accomplishments are narrated as if her motives were consistently clear and good-hearted. Is this one more woman downplaying another woman's ambition in order to present her as acceptably feminine, with no desire for power, recognition and authority? Perhaps unsurprisingly, one of Heilbrun's themes is the centrality of Steinem's femininity to the success of her feminism.

The story Heilbrun tells is strangely transparent, an unmessy narrative of Steinem's admirable life with little attention to depth, complications, or contradictions. Her well-known disconnectedness from her inner self is reproduced by her biographer: Heilbrun does not probe deeply or analytically into Steinem's personality, or, for that matter, her relationship to the women's movement; she positions herself as a sympathetic friend or referee, supportive and uncritical. *The Education of a Woman* reinforces a picture of a full but unreflective life.

For me, reading *The Education of a Woman* raised two thorny issues that the US women's movement of the 1970s grappled with. (Heilbrun seems untroubled by them; her instinct is to defend Steinem from criticism.) The first is the relationship of the women's movement to Steinem, a woman whom the media recognizes as a leader (in Heilbrun's words, "the most famous feminist in the country, if not the world"), a woman who founded *Ms.* magazine—a great achievement and tool for second-wave feminism—a woman who is in the news when feminism is in the news. The second issue, which expands upon the first, is why the internecine struggles between different wings and personalities of the women's movement were so bitter. Writing about such issues is risky in this period of cruel and deadly attacks on feminism's achievements and on women themselves, but to a student of second-wave feminism they call out for attention.

To locate myself in this discussion: I am a first-generation women's liberation movement participant. I was an activist in the New Left and antiwar movements and a member of Bread and Roses, a socialist feminist Boston-based organization that was part of the youthful radical wing of the women's movement. Today I am an academic. Steinem, for me, was and is remote, a media figure, a liberal. I have never seen her or heard her speak. Heilbrun writes convincingly about Steinem's tireless dedication to feminism, her energetic establishment of and commitment to *Ms.* and women's issues, her compassion, conciliatory nature and fair play, her significance. I do not doubt all this, nor that Steinem has persuaded thousands of women to become feminists—although what that means is contested, and relevant for this discussion.

In fact, Steinem reminds me of Allard Lowenstein, murdered in 1980 by a mentally ill student he had mentored—another tireless, nationally prominent, liberal organizer of the same generation, in his case for civil rights, against the war in Vietnam and for a liberal anti-communist Democratic Party. Frenetic, uncentered, with minimal domestic life, through public speaking and personal interaction they both charged the lives of people with whom they came in contact. And because they were liberals who worked the media and were anointed as leaders, both continue to inspire mixed feelings in those who worked hard and quietly for years with no recognition. Radicals in particular have been critical of both Lowenstein's and Steinem's politics.

Analyses of the civil rights, New Left and women's movements have underscored their democratic inclinations towards anti-authoritarian and anti-hierarchical relationships and organizational forms that often took shape as hostility to leadership.[1] Based on their experiences in American institutions and earlier movements, young feminists were suspicious that individuals would abuse power and authority. They wanted all women to feel empowered and equal; sisterhood meant rejecting hierarchy. Numerous women felt they had not been treated as equals in the civil rights, New Left and Black Power movements, and in their own movement(s) they tried to ensure that no one individual dominated, whether in consciousness-raising or activist groups.

In that political context, Steinem was controversial. Both her visibility and politics disturbed radical and youthful feminists. In Heilbrun's words,

> For the women who were coming out of the left to organize the feminist movement, and to Betty Friedan, Steinem seemed . . . a late arrival on the scene. That she was also the one the media anointed because she was "feminine", . . . glamorous, . . . and . . . nonthreatening was to cause a good deal of ill feeling among feminists who had arrived earlier, pledging their lives, their fortunes, and their sacred honor when the movement was young.
>
> (p. 187)

An irritatingly repetitive theme is that Steinem's beauty separated her from the rest of us (reinforcing the idea that feminists are ugly), that her heterosexual desirability confused mainstream critics and feminists alike: how could you be sexy, beautiful, feminine and a feminist? (Duh.) Heilbrun argues that the "aura of frivolity," associated with Steinem would reassure millions of women teetering on the edge of feminism that one did not have to eschew elegance or 'femininity,' or, above all, men, to be for 'women's lib.'" She does not find problematic Steinem's combinations of public sexiness and commitment, high living and sympathy for the underdog, her talent for "getting over" with the media and for downplaying feminist political differences. Like her subject, she seems to believe that appealing to the lowest common denominator is the way to bring women into the women's movement and that women's similarities outweigh their differences. But if this is ever true, it never lasts for long. Class, race, ethnic, generational, sexual preference and political differences always eventually surface.

Steinem has worked within the system, defining a feminism that, according to Heilbrun—who contrasts Steinem's politics to radical "structureless" feminism and Betty Friedan's "upper-middle-class" feminism—was palatable to most American women; in that way she kept "the feminist cause in the forefront of the national consciousness." But Steinem raised the hackles of radical women in the trenches organizing rape crisis and day care centers, fighting for abortion law reform, abortion counseling and clinics, and simultaneously trying to reorder their lives according to new ideas about gender that provoked questions about compatibility with men and sexual preference.

Not that Steinem was against these projects. But her links to and comfort with powerful men—to power perhaps—her jet-setting, celebrity and inclination to work within the system led many to question her authenticity. While Heilbrun suggests that Steinem's contradictions were the very qualities that made her a persuasive feminist, for many young radical feminists they spawned only mistrust.

Because she assumes that Steinem's choices were consistently justifiable and well-intentioned, Heilbrun feels no need to wonder whether this hostility was deserved. But the conflicts were and are real, and they raise an issue that goes beyond Steinem's particular case: how did women in the white women's movement treat one another when they disagreed? There is a good deal of evidence that feminists were no less sectarian or more kind toward those they considered their enemies than men have been. Often they (we) behaved as though feminists with different politics, but with whom we basically agreed about the problems women faced in American society, were the real enemies.

Why? In a chapter entitled **"Trashing"** (taking its title from Jo Freeman's essay of the same name), Heilbrun tells the story of the New York radical feminist group Redstockings' accusation that Steinem had worked for the CIA when she organized anti-communist students to go to international youth festivals in the 1950s. Heilbrun represents Steinem as a victim of vicious attacks, "accusations . . . without substance and often ridiculous"; but this dismisses an important issue. Many people, like Steinem and Allard Lowenstein, consciously or not, were enmeshed in Cold War politics. Liberal student and youth activism, for example the National Student Association, *was* funded during the Cold War by the CIA and other government agencies.

Heilbrun asks "why, as their frustration and anger mounts, women attack one another rather than the establishment . . ." Among her answers are that radical women wanted publicity for themselves or their groups, believed Steinem watered down feminism to a politically unacceptable level, never got the credit they felt was their due, and were critical of any woman who stood out. Some of this is undoubtedly true: political differences existed and were significant for how one understood sexism, racism and heterosexism and the strategies that resulted. And as an individual Steinem *had* managed to acquire a degree of power and efficacy that less well-connected feminists could only dream of.

My interest is not in whether those accusations were true or not, but in how this bitterness was replicated in numerous other hostilities between groups of movement women. I do not want to belittle conflicts between those who embraced diverse political ideologies, analyses, strategies and goals. Nevertheless, like Heilbrun I do find the furious suspicion of other women disturbing. And I admit that my uneasiness may be due to the sense of siege women are experiencing in the 1990s. It feels important now to submerge differences in the face of the backlash, whereas in the heady days when feminism was new and feminists were feeling powerful, political differences among us seemed crucial.

But why would women activists be different from men? Am I replicating Heilbrun's focus on Steinem's niceness, holding women to a different political standard, worried that women *should* be nice to one another? Men attack each other out of frustration, anger and ideological purity. We know it is very difficult to create alternative psychological and social patterns. Radical social movements have divided over apparently minor differences, producing dogmatism as if by magic, with individuals and groups close in political perspective turning on one another with as much energy as they do on those in power.

Is this more characteristic of left-wing social movements? Consider, for example, the last years of SDS or the struggles between Black Panthers and Ron Karenga's group, US. Radical marginality appears to encourage sectarianism. Finally, though, maybe Heilbrun and I are both worrying about the wrong question. Mainstream politics always includes infighting and verbal assaults, but it's never characterized as cruel sectarianism when Republican politicians attack one another.

Working in the last several years with Alexander Bloom on *Takin' It to the Streets: A Sixties Reader* (Oxford University Press, 1995), a collection of original documents from the movements of the 1960s, I found that some white feminists of my generation who had been active in the late 1960s and early 1970s seemed more bitter as a group than, say, white New Left men. There was contentiousness and suspicion about reprint permissions, about who had written what and who had gotten and should get credit for particular essays or manifestos. I sensed feelings of disappointment and bitterness, perhaps because these women had not received more recognition or because they were disappointed their worlds had not changed more. Expectations were so high during the late 1960s and early 1970s, it was inevitable that the women's movement that has changed so much is blamed for not changing more. (Conservatives blame it for precisely the opposite.) Terrible disappointment and blaming or accusing other feminists of, for example, betrayal or ambition, need to be better understood. They are deeply connected to early feminists' feelings of hope, love and marginalization.

There is no doubt that Gloria Steinem is of enormous importance to the feminist movement, that she has worked tirelessly on behalf of feminism, that in the public eye her name, along with Betty Friedan's, is often synonymous with second-wave white feminism. But it seems too soon to write a serious biography. And Heilbrun's book is evidence of this; laboriously, even defensively, she reproduces a narrative Steinem herself has largely told. A more analytical biography would have helped us to get a better grip on the political messiness that Steinem's life embodies and provokes.

Note

1. See for example Wini Breines, *The Great Refusal. Community and Organization in the New Left* (Philadelphia: Rutgers University Press, 1989); Jo Freeman, *The Politics of Women's Liberation* (New York: David McKay Co., 1975); Todd Gitlin, *The Sixties: Years of Hope, Days of Rage* (New York: Bantam Books, 1987); Edward P. Morgan, *The 60s Experience: Hard Lessons about Modern America* (New York: Philadelphia: Temple University Press, 1991).

Florence King (review date 29 January 1996)

SOURCE: King, Florence. "The Mud Turtle's Progress." *National Review* 48, no. 1 (29 January 1996): 62-4.

[*In the following review, King offers a negative assessment of* The Education of a Woman, *asserting that Heilbrun's inability to objectively portray her subject is "maddening."*]

The parable of the mud turtle comes at the end of this hagiographic book, but it so perfectly illustrates the feminist blind spot of both biographer and subject that I shall start with it.

Here is how Gloria Steinem claims she learned to respect the right to self-determination:

During a science field trip in college, she found a turtle beside a road. Afraid that it would get run over, she picked it up and carried it back into the woods where it would be safe—only to be told by her professor that it had probably taken the turtle weeks to reach the muddy shoulder where she wanted to lay her eggs, but now, thanks to Miss Steinem's help, she would have to start all over again.

"It was a lesson Steinem never forgot," writes Carolyn G. Heilbrun.

Really? Coulda fooled me. Miss Steinem has made a career of meddling in women's egg-laying habits and taking them where she thinks they ought to be. Now, in what is tactfully known as post-feminism, they are faced with the task of starting all over again.

Writing a biography [*The Education of a Woman*], of a still-living subject whose friends, enemies, and lovers are still alive is a delicate operation, but Carolyn G. Heilbrun is eminently qualified to jump in with both feet. The author of *Writing a Woman's Life*, she is widely regarded as the leading expert on female biography. She is also a salted-in-the-shell feminist who used to teach at Columbia until the "boys' treehouse gang," as she calls male English professors, drove her away. "Women who speak out," she reminds us, "usually end up punished or dead." Note that "usually." Both Miss Heilbrun and Miss Steinem have flourished like the green bay tree.

Gloria Steinem was born in 1934 into a solid middle-class Toledo family, but her father's wild financial schemes and her mother's nervous breakdowns landed them in not-so-genteel poverty. After her parents divorced, she lived with her increasingly delusional mother in a ratty apartment and attended a working-class high school, earning extra money tap dancing at the Lion's Club. These gritty experiences shaped her politics. Years later, watching Chicago police beat up protestors at the 1968 Democratic Convention, she said, "Those cops are the boys I went to high school with."

Life improved in 1951 when her older sister institutionalized their mother and took Miss Steinem to live with her in Washington, where she entered the city's elite public school, Western High in Georgetown. No more tap dancing for Babbitts; secure in her improved social status, she became a swimming instructor at the segregated city's Negro pool. Lady Bountiful on the half shell.

To pay her tuition at Smith, the family sold a piece of property they had managed to hang onto. She graduated in 1956 and won a Chester Bowles fellowship to study in India, spending half of the $1,000 stipend en route on an abortion in London. Avoiding all Westerners, she sought out "the real India," her solo trek through remote regions facilitated by railroad cars reserved for women only. She went completely native; dyed her hair black, wore saris—and had a karma reading. It said she had "lived in Bengal in a previous incarnation, and that she had done something disastrous to have been born in the United States."

When she returned to New York, the guilt she had felt in India at being pulled in a tonga (rickshaw) by another human being made her resolve to ride in the front seat of cabs, but she soon gave it up for reasons not hard to imagine.

She conquered male-dominated publishing like a Marxist Scarlett O'Hara. Her best early writing had a Nellie Bly flair, especially her 1963 exposé of Playboy Clubs, "A Bunny's Tale," but even the worshipful Miss Heilbrun admits that *The Beach Book* was "clearly not a book any serious publisher in his right mind would have agreed to." But Viking's Tom Guinzberg was not in his right mind, he was in Miss Steinem's bed. We aren't sure where John Kenneth Galbraith was, but he wrote the introduction to her sandy anthology, explaining that he did so because "I like the girl who put it together." Sold with a sun screen inside the cover, *The Beach Book* contained suggested fantasies: "You have just dealt a crushing defeat in public debate to (choose one: William Buckley Jr., Hugh Hefner, David Susskind, Ayn Rand), who is being laughed off the stage."

But she was never frivolous for long. Given some stock in *New York* magazine, she used it as collateral to bail women out of prison to get abortions when the prison hospital refused to perform them. Even more earnestly, she told a new bride: "You married that man? I would have stopped you; he's another conservative central European."

When she founded *Ms.* she vowed to run "a communal, cooperative, nonhierarchical, democratic" magazine patterned on the "strict structurelessness" of early radical feminism. Nobody had a title and there was no masthead, just an alphabetical list of "workers" with the now-famous Miss Steinem buried under S. This egalitarian code was broken when a worker's mother said, "I saw your boss on television."

Private offices with doors were verboten; everyone worked in a communal room which also served as the nursery for single mothers on the staff. Editorial duties were assigned by lot; all the workers read all the copy and everyone got to express an opinion, including the receptionist. When a reviewer panned Kate Millett's book some workers didn't want to run the review because it might hurt Miss Millett's feelings; another warned, "Kate might have a nervous breakdown" unless they cut the mean parts.

By 1979 *Ms.* had lost so much money that Miss Steinem had to file for nonprofit status. This enabled her to get a $300,000 grant from the Ford Foundation. Whether it helped that she had had an affair with Ford Foundation president Franklin Thomas is not known.

Her last important lover was real estate tycoon Mortimer Zuckerman, whose limo made her feel so guilty that she asked him to replace it with a van. Normally she would not have slept with a man who believed in trade with countries whose embassies she picketed, but he knew how to break down her resistance: he told her he had had an emotionally deprived childhood. It worked. She decided to "help" him, telling herself, "Once happy, he would give all his money to the poor." He didn't—nor did he get rid of the limo.

The only enjoyable parts of this book are the quoted passages by other writers. Miss Heilbrun herself is maddening. Three examples will suffice.

Miss Steinem's gullibility in business matters: "Those who despise all group hatreds, all racial and sexual stereotypes, are more easily duped."

Miss Steinem takes up feminism: "Like Paul after his vision on the road to Damascus, but like him in no other way, she decided to go forth and speak, to spread the message."

Miss Steinem today: "She has, furthermore, shocked many people in frankly stating that her sexual drive has diminished."

What is so shocking about a woman of 61 saying that? It's the only sensible thing she's ever said.

Cathy Young (review date 31 May 1996)

SOURCE: Young, Cathy. "Pretty-Power." *Times Literary Supplement,* no. 4861 (31 May 1996): 11.

[*In the following review of* The Education of a Woman, *Young argues that Heilbrun's biased view of her subject compromises the biography as a serious study of Steinem's life and work.*]

If there is one person whose name has been a symbol of American feminism in the past twenty years, it is Gloria Steinem. As journalist, activist and bestselling writer, Steinem has been a charismatic and controversial figure. Many, from the movement veteran Betty Friedan in the 1970s to dissidents like Christina Hoff Sommers today, have criticized her for promoting a gender-war ideology (though in the 1970s, some radicals also attacked her as too bourgeois). Others, more sympathetic to her politics, have been troubled by her recent plunge into New Age-flavoured pursuits such as inner healing and building self-esteem.

Now comes a lengthy, frankly partisan biography of Steinem whose author, the writer and academic Carolyn Heilbrun, is somewhat controversial in her own right (in 1992, announcing her voluntary retirement from Columbia University, she criticized the university as a male bastion where she felt beleaguered). Heilbrun chronicles Steinem's difficult childhood, plagued by poverty and her mother's mental illness; her entry into a more privileged world as a student at prestigious Smith College; her early career as a journalist-cum-glamour girl; her romances, some of them with rich and famous men like the publisher Mortimer Zuckerman; and her activism and writing after her conversion to feminism, including the history of *Ms.* magazine.

"To the media and those who live in its light, Steinem is, to various degrees, an enigma and, perhaps inevitably, a paradox", writes Heilbrun. ***The Education of a Woman*** highlights many contradictions in Steinem's life. A critic of the traditional family, she never lived in one. Her father was not a stable provider but a feckless dreamer; her mother was talented but fragile and "sometimes crazy"; her parents separated when she was ten. (To Heilbrun, this suggests that a home environment at odds with conventional notions of the family is best suited for producing "a loving and passionately engaged human being".) An activist who spoke of unequal opportunities for women, she herself was quite successful in the pre-feminist 1960s—but was often treated with condescension as "a pretty girl who writes".

There is, finally, the paradox of "a feminist in a miniskirt". While Steinem's name is linked to a movement that has railed against the treatment of women as sex objects, her looks, which age has barely withered, have always been part of her public image. Heilbrun, who seems rather too preoccupied with her subject's appearance, surely exaggerates when she calls Steinem "the epitome of female beauty", but she was good-looking enough to go undercover as a Playboy bunny for a famous magazine assignment. Heilbrun concludes that despite Steinem's habit of "underplaying . . . if not denying" her attractiveness, she undoubtedly appreciated—"in however ambivalent a manner"—its value as an asset at the start of her career, and consciously used its effect later on as a living refutation of the stereotypes of feminists as hairy Amazons or ugly spinsters who could not get a man. In Heilbrun's words, Steinem proved that women "had the right to assume power without sacrificing sexuality."

The Education of a Woman tells an entertaining enough story, offering some juicy anecdotes about celebrities who have crossed Steinem's path and painting an often colourful picture of the life of the left-wing intelligentsia in the 1960s and of the women's movement in the 1970s and 80s. But as a serious analysis of Steinem's life and work, the book is hopelessly compromised by Heilbrun's adoration of her heroine, whom at one point she likens to Gandhi and of whom she gushes, "On the part of many women as well as men, Steinem has inspired lust or passionate desire."

Too often, the biography reads more like a valentine. Heilbrun does permit herself some critical remarks about Steinem's books, pointing out the banality of the self-help ideas articulated in Steinem's self-esteem work, *Revolution from Within*. But any detail that might be seen as less than appealing is explained away or glossed over. Thus, the episode in which Steinem told a writer for *Vanity Fair* that her former flame Zuckerman had never given money to *Ms.*—prompting Zuckerman to submit records of his donations and threaten a suit—is blamed on the magazine's negligence in fact-checking, but the issue of Steinem's apparent disingenuousness never comes up.

A committed leftist, Heilbrun even shows remarkable tolerance towards Steinem's work in 1959 for a CIA-backed foundation set up to send young Americans to International Communist Youth Festivals to counter Soviet influence ("these events must be seen in their historical context"); one suspects that her attitude would be quite different in the case of someone she admired less. And certain aspects of Steinem's activism, which even Heilbrun perhaps finds too embarrassing, are simply omitted—such as her involvement in the largely discredited cause of so-called recovered memories of childhood sexual abuse.

Steinem's alliance with anti-pornography extremists cannot be evaded altogether, but Heilbrun tries to paper over the significance of the pornography debate in feminism, blithely asserting that "much of the disagreement could be cured by information"—for instance, "the antipornography groups are not advocating censorship, but activism and social pressure, and they are not 'antisex' but in favour of differentiating pornography from erotica, like rape versus sex". But this is really *mis*information, since the activists want any woman offended by pornography to be able to sue its producers and distributors, and some of their leaders, like Andrea Dworkin, essentially equate all heterosexual intercourse with rape.

Here, at least, Heilbrun acknowledges the possibility of legitimate disagreements within feminism. Elsewhere, feminists whose views differ from Steinem's are reduced to caricatures (Katie Roiphe is said to have found "fame and fortune by blaming the rape victim"), and women who criticize Steinem are assumed to have nefarious motives: they are threatened by a combination of "such looks and such radical and feminist ideals", or they "ach[e] for the publicity Steinem seemed able so easily to evoke".

Ultimately, the purpose of this impassioned tribute is not just a celebration of Steinem but a defence of what she stands for today: a brand of feminism that rejects the institutions of Western societies as thoroughly "patriarchal", sees women as living in a state of siege, and often uses "male" as a pejorative (Heilbrun comments on the need for environmentalism "on a planet hideously misused by male ambitions of domination, exploitation, and arrogance", as if women did not use technology). Steinem has undoubtedly played an important role, helping to bring attention to women's issues at a time when legitimate feminist ideas were not taken very seriously by the media. But the direction she represents has reached an impasse, and is being challenged by a new generation of independent-thinking women who reject both anti-feminist traditionalism and gender-war feminism. So far, Steinem and Heilbrun have responded by name-calling—a sign of weakness if ever there was one.

Annette Zilversmit (review date January 1998)

SOURCE: Zilversmit, Annette. "Free at Last." *Women's Review of Books* 15, no. 4 (January 1998): 10-11.

[*In the following review, Zilversmit praises the essays in* The Last Gift of Time *as courageous and inspiring looks at the process of aging.*]

"Not to change one's life is not to keep living," wrote Virginia Woolf. To open with a quote from Woolf is appropriate for a review of Carolyn Heilbrun's moving memoir-reflection [***The Last Gift of Time***]. It is obviously appropriate for those who know this feminist's writing on Virginia Woolf, who shattered the "appropriate" for women with her life and art. It is appropriate because Heilbrun's direct but supple prose is sp(l)iced with quotations from other authors, mostly women, offering what critic Laura Levitt has called "textual embraces."

But this Woolfian aphorism is necessary as well as appropriate, because, in spite of what the book's title seems to suggest, this collection of essays is not the smooth continuing saga of the life and thought of a pioneer feminist mover during her seventh decade; it reflects the changing, the "re-imagining" once more of a woman's life that until 1992 looked like the fulfillment of Heilbrun's own directives as set down in her 1979 book ***Reinventing Womanhood***.

By her 66th year, Heilbrun had been a professor for more than thirty years in Columbia University's English Department, where few women and certainly no Jewish woman had been appointed before. She had written several books of feminist criticism and literary history (all still in print and still read by a wide audience) and she was enjoying a "long, extended, mostly satisfying marriage" that had produced three children. And (where she fit it in is hard to fathom) she was the creator, under the name of Amanda Cross, of ten mystery novels, and promising more.

Having checkerboarded time and place successfully in all those roles, admittedly with struggle and anxiety (especially about being a mother, as she reveals in this book), Heilbrun had no intention of changing her life. Believing, as she had written in ***Reinventing Womanhood,*** that "[w]omen must continue to invade the domains of power in order to change institutions as we know them, in order to offer places to other women . . . and to do justice to themselves," she had not planned on leaving her position. But she also did not plan to meet the depth of resistance toward feminism in her own department. Though she chooses not to give details of the final frustrating months, she epitomizes the situation in the words of an eminent male colleague, who declared in the student newspaper that one of the ten worst books he had ever read was by Adrienne Rich.

In the spring of 1992, as an act of protest (dramatic enough to be covered in the *New York Times*), Heilbrun resigned her tenured, and by now endowed, professorship. Having always feared the loss of her university affiliations and structures, she was "shocked" at how immediately relieved she was never to have to enter that "poisonous atmosphere" again. Understanding suddenly "how privileged Victorian women must have felt when they took off the stays and dresses that inhibited motion and flexed their bodies and moved their muscles," she finds that she "had entered a life unimagined previously, of happiness, impossible to youth or to the years of constantly being needed at home and at work."

The achievement of that transition, the reinvention of a woman's life after a long professional career, was not easy. How Heilbrun reached her present balance of "activity and serenity" outside the academy is the plot of this memoir. She begins by admitting that this transition was easier than her climb up "the slippery academic ladder," where no stories, even oral ones, from the rare women faculty, were there to guide her. She acknowledges she now enjoys (I would say has earned) many advantages: a long-time partner, an ample pension, and city and country homes. But the greatest difference from her academic past is, she writes, the chamber of women's voices she now surrounds herself with—newly-made women friends and colleagues, daughters, long-lost cousins and, most of all, the many contemporary women writers, especially American poets, she reads and writes.

When Heilbrun finds the bitter and disillusioned memoirs of the well-known journalist and novelist, Doris Grumbach, who only mentions male colleagues, she confirms that "the intimacy [of women's voices] helped make [my] sixties my happiest decade." In her essay-portrait of the now seventy-year-old poet Maxine Kumin, she expands: "We read . . . as women read about women who have braved the terrors and hopes we share, at least to some degree. Courage in women always catches me up, moves me to compassion, and the desire [to offer other women] succor, sustenance, if possible."

Not by any means a self-help book, ***The Last Gift of Time*** is filled with gentle (sometimes not so gentle) proddings, disarmingly frank insights and lessons learned as Heilbrun re-maps what may be the last part of an achieving woman's life. Untethered from unsupportive colleagues, she finds the first of her "few but insistent desires"—total solitude. What she thinks she wants is that "room," in this case a house, of her own.

"To be alone," she discovers, "if one has not been doomed to aloneness is a temptation so beguiling that it carries with it the guilt of adultery, and the promise of consummation." And her first essay in this book, **"The Small House,"** tells of her search for that space, and a surprising discovery once she inhabits it. She wittily recreates her wrangles with realtors who refuse to believe that she wants no swimming pool, large grounds, or old trees. But having found a spare barn-like structure and spent half a day there alone, she welcomes back her (luckily not very loquacious) husband, gives him a study downstairs (hers is up), and concludes that what she truly wanted was "a house where the only noise was mine and his."

With space chosen and time taken, Heilbrun faces in *Time* her greatest challenge—how to fill them. Even this productive scholar "for whom work is the essence of life" has to decide how to make her new life satisfying. As she listens to two "muses," one an erotically charged male, the other a female English writer, she makes her most serious wrong turn. Hearing in one ear Sylvia Townsend Warner urging "the aging" to undertake something difficult and new and "re-root" themselves, and in the other Andrew Marvell, warning his coy mistress of too little "world enough and time," Heilbrun seduces herself into spending the first years of her retirement writing the biography of activist feminist Gloria Steinem. Yet with the publication of *The Education of a Woman* in 1995, to respectable, if mixed, reviews, she confesses she has wasted (her) time and spent her world with a non-introspective woman whom she still respects, but who, she acknowledges, provided no "sub-texts" for her literary soul.

The remaining twelve essays reflect the more careful use of her time and world. They are the richest part of the book both in substance and craft. Two of the best, **"A Unique Person"** and **"An Unmet Friend,"** are evocative portraits of May Sarton and Maxine Kumin, the first of whom Heilbrun actually befriended for many years before her death, the second very much alive, but one of those "unmet friends" she wants to preserve that way. Heilbrun has analyzed and praised their writings else where; here she highlights the courageous changes each woman writer made at crucial points in her career, moves both inspiring and cautionary for Heilbrun herself.

Sarton is admired for leaving the literary social circles of New York for desolate country houses, there to write of the joys and ravages of solitude. But after drawing Sarton with her wounds and woundings, her never-forgotten bad reviews and her inconsiderateness to those who did love her, Heilbrun concludes that, ironically, she with "husband, children, parents, and work" has been able "to bask" more fully in the solitude she carefully planned than this poet of solitary life who was always beckoning and berating lovers and friends. She cites Kumin for surrendering the security of a suburban Boston life, taking a reluctant husband and children to live on a horse farm so that she could write more deftly her "women's poetry" of animals, love and loss. Although this is the only writer she calls her "alter ego," Heilbrun also knows that, unlike Kumin, she could never be the constant attendant of animals and domesticity.

Fortified by inscribing these "exemplary" women, Heilbrun moves into high gear herself, pronouncing on a wide range of subjects. Annoyed in "Sex and Romance" that middle-aged writers like Marilyn French and Doris Lessing still have heroines who yearn for sexual passion, she asks whether "if we could discover a word that meant 'adventure' and did not mean 'romance,' we in our last decades [would not connect] yearning and sex." Resigned, though quite affectionately, to her own less than romantic, essentially intractable husband, she wonders in **"Living with Men"** why women bother with them at all.

Grounding some of these more jaunty pieces are intimations of mortality and some unfinished business. Perhaps the most poignant excursion is the unexpected return in **"The Family Lost and Found"** to that part of her self which has been problematic in many of her writings—that of being a Jew. Having identified closely with a women's tradition, first in *Writing a Woman's Life* (1988) and now in this latest book, Heilbrun is challenged to confront her other "outsider" position when cousins of her father's sisters (whom she claims not to have known about) read about her resignation from Columbia in the newspaper and arrange to meet her. Her immigrant father had severed himself from his family and religion once he became socially and financially successful; now she ponders her willed forgetfulness: "Which was stranger, that I never knew my father's family, or that I never wondered why?" The reunion leads to new recoveries, but Heilbrun still leaves much unresolved.

But it is the irresolutions and the points of contention (and agreement) I have as I read Heilbrun that remind me of what has always made reading her so bracing and pleasurable. For all her polished prose, the tone is always conversational, the "we" used frequently. Heilbrun is always challenging (women) readers to make more sense of their lives, "to catch courage" from reading other women's writings. Coming upon this book as I was myself trying to decide whether to continue as chair of a contentious English department, I caught that courage and made my decisions. For those inoculated by present contentment, reading this long-time feminist's charting of her last years will be no less than inspiring. For others, more exposed and conflicted, *The Last Gift of Time* may be that saving dose of courage.

Perspectives in Psychiatric Care (review date April-June 1999)

SOURCE: Review of *The Last Gift of Time,* by Carolyn Heilbrun. *Perspectives in Psychiatric Care* 35, no. 2 (April-June 1999): 2, 36.

[*In the following review, the critic offers a positive assessment of* The Last Gift of Time, *praising the collection as entertaining and insightful.*]

May Sarton's readers will remember Carolyn Heilbrun as Sarton's friend and critic. I also remember a scathing article Heilbrun once wrote in the *New York Times Magazine* about sexism in the English department at Columbia University. Heilbrun is a well-known feminist writer and biographer of Gloria Steinem.

As the title suggests [***The Last Gift of Time***], this book is a collection of essays about life after 60. For those of us around this age, or working with patients around this age, it will strike many familiar chords. In the preface, Heilbrun cites several other recent books about women aging. These include Doris Grumbach's *Coming into the End Zone* as well as Sarton's last four journals: *At Seventy: A Journal*; *Endgame: A Journal of the Seventy-Ninth Year*; *Encore: A Journal of the Eightieth Year*; and *At Eighty Two: A Journal.* Heilbrun sees her senior years as more blessed than those of Grumbach and Sarton. She credits her close friendship with women as an advantage over Grumbach, who lived in a world of male writers. As for Sarton, Heilbrun characterizes her as a very troubled, volatile woman.

In the first essay, Heilbrun describes a house she buys to escape both New York City and the big country house she and her husband own and use to entertain their grown children and friends. Though she buys the house seeking solitude, her husband follows her and settles in, not wanting to be in the big house without her. Having lived a long marriage, they settle for solitude together.

Next, she buys a dog, Bianca, and learns to amble in her walks with her, for she no longer has to hurry.

> My desire for Bianca, and my pleasure in her was rewarding, as many seemingly odd choices can be rewarding, if at a price. Of course there is always a price. But the fear of paying it, I convinced myself before giving in to my need for a dog, is the highest price of all.
>
> (p. 35)

In the essay on time, Heilbrun quotes Grumbach's description in *Extra Innings: A Memoir* of meetings in academia:

> All the things I disliked most about academic meetings in the old days were present in this one: the fraudulent surface of civility, the undercurrent of prearranged and determined agendas, the rude disregard of a woman chairman by male members of the executive committee accustomed to dominating every moment of their privileged lives, their loud (or contrivedly too soft) and always obtrusive voices carrying every question and insisting on every answer. My humiture was intense. I came away feeling sick, tired, discouraged, and angry at myself for spending four days of my diminishing supply of time in this absurd way.
>
> (p. 38)

Heilbrun was shocked at how little she missed academia after retiring from Columbia, and how much she savored the gift of time she'd finally earned.

> I entered into a period of freedom, and only past sixty learned in what freedom consists: to live without a constant, unnoticed stream of anger and resentment, without the daily contemplation of power, always in the hands of the least worthy, the least imaginative, the least generous.
>
> (p. 39)

An essay on e-mail discusses the possibility of keeping in touch with old friends and students without the inconvenience of calling them when they weren't prepared to talk, or searching for pens, paper, and mailboxes.

> I hope it is now obvious that e-mail is especially suited . . . to those of us no longer revolving our days around the working world. It reaches into our privacy without invading it, an astonishing accomplishment; it connects us with those with whom the possibility of connection might have remained unexpected; it offers us welcome without the necessity of social arrangements; it inspires us to confidences and the practice of wit.
>
> (p. 68)

I was especially enticed by the essay about May Sarton, **"A Unique Person."** Along with the recent biography of Sarton (Peters, 1997), this essay does not paint a flattering portrait. In an attempt to present her strengths as well as her weaknesses, Heilbrun acknowledges Sarton's contributions to the women readers of her journals: "By writing of her own life, she illuminates theirs" (p. 72). Her attraction is seen as "an ability intensely to experience every moment and to convey that intensity in such a way as to enrich the lives of more sober folk" (p. 88).

One of the most entertaining essays for me was **"On Not Wearing Dresses."** "Oh, the triumph of saying in one's sixties that one will never wear panty hose again" (p. 132). I was pleased to finally see something I wrote years ago in this journal (Lego, 1981) echoed in her words, ". . . without social and cultural restraints individuals will be sexually attracted to other individuals based not on their sex (meaning gender) but on the strength of their personal appeal" (p. 134). Heilbrun is heartened by signs that women of all ages are becoming more interested in comfort than desirability. ". . . at least some women will wish to be judged by qualities other than their dress, their ability to appear thin and helpless, their success in inspiring male lust" (p. 136).

Married for many years and working in a male-dominated department, Heilbrun has strong opinions about men. In **"Living with Men"** she writes that statements should not be made about "all men," with two exceptions: All men, she believes, have an inability to accept the unconscious to change anything other than their appearance. In addition ". . . if you aren't doing what they want, they aren't going to love you no matter how nice you are" (p. 172). I found myself taking exception to these generalizations as, I suspect, many nurse psychotherapists will. She philosophically concludes ". . . if one is married to a man, this is what is to be expected on the debit side, just as if you have a cat as a pet, you expect the furniture to get clawed" (p. 123).

As nurse psychotherapists who have just gained reimbursement for Medicare clients, we will soon find our caseloads filled with patients over 60. I found Heilbrun's ideas and experience reverberated with my own, my friends', and the aging patients I now see. As she writes,

> The greatest oddity of one's sixties is that if one jumps for joy, one always supposes it is for the last time. Yet this supposition provides the rarest and most exquisite flavor to one's later years. The piercing sense of "last time" adds intensity, while the possibility of "again" is never effaced.
>
> (p. 55)

Works Cited

Grumbach, D. (1993). *Extra Innings. A Memoir.* New York: Norton.

Lego, S. (1991). "Beginning Resolution of the Odeipal Conflict in a Lesbian Who Is about to Become a "Parent" to a Son." *Perspectives in Psychiatric Care,* 19 (3-4), 107-11.

Peters, M. (1997). *May Sarton. A Biography.* New York: Knopf.

Sarton, M. (1984). *At Seventy. A Journal.* New York: Norton.

Sarton, M. (1992). *Endgame. A Journal of the Seventy-Ninth year.* New York: Norton.

Sarton, M. (1993). *Encore. A Journal of the Eightieth Year.* New York: Norton.

Sarton, M. (1996). *At Eighty Two. A Journal.* New York: Norton.

Sarah Emsley (review date autumn 1999)

SOURCE: Emsley, Sarah. Review of *Women's Lives: The View from the Threshold,* by Carolyn Heilbrun. *Dalhousie Review* 79, no. 3 (autumn 1999): 425-27.

[*In the following review, Emsley compliments Heilbrun's portrayal of the challenges that women face in the modern world in* Women's Lives, *but concludes that the work's conclusion is incomplete and unsatisfying.*]

Carolyn G. Heilbrun's **Women's Lives** is composed of the four Alexander lectures she delivered at the University of Toronto in 1997. The University of Toronto Press summary and introduction to Heilbrun's lectures (i-ii) lists her as part of "a line of distinguished scholarly work with such previous lecturers as Walter Ong, Robertson Davies, and Northrop Frye," but then goes on to suggest that "Heilbrun, within this distinguished genealogy, reworks the very notion of the line, creating a new pattern of writing and approaching literary culture."

Heilbrun does challenge the notion of linearity as a model of successful literature. invoking in her second chapter, **"The Evolution of the Female Memoir,"** Susan Winnett's argument in an article on "Women, Men, Narrative, and the Principles of Pleasure," which asks "Is there . . . always the same 'master plot' imitating linear male sexuality, or do some narratives reflect female sexual experience?" (Heilbrun 33). Heilbrun says that "Women may be said to have neither a path nor a linear rise and fall; rather, their sexual experience may be defined as a series of circles, a rhythm that may appear to men, and to those of us taught to think like men, unfamiliar, repetitive, and declining to proceed to a single, ordained finale" (34). In her rhetoric in these lectures, Heilbrun says, she herself resists the male, linear pattern, and returns to some points in a seemingly repetitive but in fact intentionally circular way.

After explaining her own lecturing style, she draws attention to a number of moments when she creates circular patterns, such as when she reminds readers in Chapter Three, **"Embracing the Paradox,"** that she has already discussed Cathy Davidson's memoir *Thirty-Six Views of Mount Fuji* in the first lecture (71). But while asserting the validity of the circular narrative, Heilbrun simultaneously undermines her own argument by placing these intentional repetitions in parentheses, thus marginalizing the very method she seeks to defend. For example, she says in another parenthetical argument on the next page, "(Let me pause here to make a quite irrelevant and yet to me significant point about the liminality of current professional female nomenclature . . .)," and she then discusses the fact that many women academics are known by a married name that often belongs to a former husband. She argues that women should instead claim a name that will be their own for their entire professional and personal lives. This discussion of names is surely not incidental or unnecessarily repetitive in a chapter on the formation of women's identities. The parentheses may be intentional, but to claim that an issue she feels strongly about is "quite irrelevant" detracts from Heilbrun's defence of digression, repetition, and circularity as valid forms of female narrative.

Women's Lives circles through, among other things, questions of women's beauty or relative lack of it in relation to their intellectual and artistic success, women's lived experience of dissent from convention and the challenge of writing about that experience, the tensions between mothers and daughters over what constitutes a useful and fulfilled life, and the necessity of continuing the struggle to recognize and value women's lives and potential. Heilbrun writes clearly and passionately of the challenges women confront daily through their lives, and she urges readers to celebrate the idea that women are on the threshold of possibilities. The condition of liminality, she writes, is a "threshold experience" that offers choices and challenges: "to be in a state of liminality is to be poised upon uncertain ground, to be leaving one condition or country or self and entering upon another. But the most salient sign of liminality is its unsteadiness, its lack of clarity about exactly where one belongs and what one should be doing, or wants to be doing" (3). **Women's Lives** celebrates that state of liminality as possessing a transformative power for the direction of women's lives. What the book doesn't do, however, is talk much about the consequences of the choices women eventually must and do make.

Liminality may be liberating, but it is not eternal. It can indeed be exciting and energizing to imagine the power to make new choices, to create new patterns, and to live in a different way, but ultimately those choices, patterns, and lives are made, and then women have to live with them. Heilbrun says that "the place of feminism, and women within it . . . is a place that is amidst, among, atwixt, rooted nowhere but in the realm of questioning, experiment, and adventure, and as it questions everything, it uses what it finds befitting" (98). But how do women determine what is befitting? Heilbrun doesn't address this question, and at this point she avoids circling back to her first and most prominent example of a woman who created her own unconventional life and thus flourished as an artist—George Eliot, who with her well-known belief in the peremptory and absolute nature of moral duty would be unlikely to sympathize with a way of life that involves experiment without context or standards. Heilbrun argues that "in the higher reaches of academic feminist theory, the state of necessary in-betweenness is understood and valued" (98), which may be true, but academic feminism as Heilbrun outlines it nevertheless has a specific, decided, even linear goal: "Feminism, in literature as in life, has either moved women, or tried to move them, from the margins closer to the centre of human experience and possibility or has made evident their absence from that centre" (3).

Liminality and circularity are useful and exciting, sites of tensions, debate, and the opening up of possibility, but they are not ends in themselves. Heilbrun's argument for the value of women's liminal condition is important and interesting, but just as she undermines the value of circularity in her lectures by deriding some of her own points as irrelevant or as mere digressions, her case for the central importance of liminality in women's lives eclipses the consequences of the choices women make as a result of the very freedom that liminality gives them. These consequences are hinted at in the last paragraph of the book, where, after suggesting that the conventional place of women "will always be attractive to those who would rather be safe than sorry," Heilbrun concludes that "the threshold, on the contrary, is the place where as women and as creators of literature, we write our own lines and, eventually, our own plays" (102). Following the conventional path of women's lives means rehearsing a drama others have acted before us; living on the threshold of experience means improvising and revising action, practising lines and writing new ones. The view from the threshold, however, is of the plays women will write, no longer hovering at the margin or the threshold in a condition of uncertainty and obscurity, but central to fully lived human life. The threshold is a valuable intermediate step, a place where women can practise, but it is not the place where they will write their own plays. Although Heilbrun doesn't say this explicitly, she implies that women won't live liminal lives at the threshold forever, because after rehearsing and improvising, they will need to move to writing from the centre, if possible. This book needs a sequel.

Carolyn Dever (essay date summer 2000)

SOURCE: Dever, Carolyn. "The Feminist Abject: Death and the Constitution of Theory." *Studies in the Novel* 32, no. 2 (summer 2000): 185-206.

[*In the following essay, Dever comments on the state of feminism through an exploration of the relationship between academic and personal life in Marilyn French's* The Women's Room *and Heilbrun's* Death in a Tenured Position.]

> The corpse (or cadaver: *cadere*, to fall), that which has irremediably come a cropper, is cesspool, and death; it upsets even more violently the one who confronts it as fragile and fallacious chance.
>
> —Julia Kristeva, *The Powers of Horror*[1]

When Ginny Babcock, the wealthy, white, Southern protagonist of Lisa Alther's *Kinflicks* (1976), moves from Cambridge to Vermont to live in a women's collective with her lesbian lover Eddie, she soon grows impatient with the pieties of her liberationist friends. That impatience swiftly yields poetic justice, however, as Ginny's irritants are hoisted, jointly and severally, by their own petards. First falls Laverne, best known for her close relationship with an enormous vibrator; Ginny writes, "Just then there was a scream and a sizzling sound from upstairs, and all the lights went out."[2] Putting out the electrical fire, Ginny and her friends find Laverne, charred and apparently dead, lying under a sleeping bag. They resuscitate her, and when the ambulance arrives, the driver inspects Laverne's prostrate body: "Folding down the sleeping bag another turn, he rolled out one of her knees and discovered raw burned patches on the insides of her thighs. With a frown, he noticed an electrical cord. As he pulled on it, Laverne's vibrator popped out of her . . . The doctor held the phallus-shaped vibrator, turned it over, sniffed it, scratched his head. It had a big crack all the way up it. Laverne had apparently achieved her goal of the Ultimate Orgasm" (p. 332).

Laverne survives the trauma but leaves the commune to take up life in a convent; this is either a retirement or a retreat, depending on one's perspective on her pursuit of the Ultimate Orgasm. The next victim is not so lucky, however. Ginny's lover Eddie seeks revenge on freewheeling snowmobilers who trespass on the commune's property. In defense of that property, and hoping to entrap the trespassers, she erects a thin, nearly invisible piece of wire along the property line. But in a hysterical rage against Ginny, Eddie herself steals one of those snowmobiles and shoots across the snowy meadow:

> But just before Eddie reached the pond, Ira's Sno Cat appeared to hesitate slightly. The next instant, Eddie's head flew off her shoulders and bounced and spun across the ice like a crazed basketball. I watched with utter appalled disbelief: What I had just seen couldn't possibly have happened! Ira's Sno Cat coasted to a stop, and Eddie's headless body rolled off the seat and onto the ice with a dull plunk.
>
> (P. 335)

Most shocking for Ginny about this death is its very cleanness: there was no blood spilled as Eddie's head and body were severed far more precisely than even the adjective "surgical" might suggest. And if Eddie's decapitation underscores the flimsy logic of her feminist commitment, dying as she does in defense of private property, Laverne's self-inflicted injury suggests the dangers inherent in appropriating the phallus, especially when that phallus comes equipped with an electrical cord.

Soon thereafter Ginny leaves the commune to marry Ira Bliss, the owner of the snowmobile on which Eddie met her demise. Thus ends Ginny's radical feminist phase, and with the death of Eddie and the claustration of Laverne, thus ends the novel's engagement with non-heterosexual eroticism of any sort. Eddie's wire boundary would in the end prove brutally efficient as the commune becomes its own structure of feminist containment, securely detached from the world at large.

My purpose in this essay is to suggest that such episodes of violent death serve a profoundly constitutive, boundary-establishing function within feminist novels produced in the U.S. during the late 1970s and the early 1980s. Death acts as the invisible wire that kills Eddie, marking a distinction between feminist survivors and feminist scapegoats, marking a distinction, too, as it does here in the most graphic of terms, between the feminist mind and the feminist body. Indeed, as Eddie's death most gruesomely suggests, the mind-body divide is a core concern for feminist fictions of this period, and in the novels on which I will focus, Marilyn French's *The Women's Room* (1977) and Amanda Cross's **Death in a Tenured Position** (1981), it is thematized through the negotiation of protagonists' academic careers and their complex, often contradictory, personal lives. Indebted to *The Group*, Mary McCarthy's 1963 novel that follows a group of Vassar undergraduates into the world, feminist novels of the late 1970s exploit a university context in an attempt to fathom the intersection of the feminist mind and the feminist body, and, in the process, to develop a critique of the misogyny endemic within institutions. Among the many novels featuring university settings are *Kinflicks*, *The Women's Room*, **Death in a Tenured Position,** Rita Mae Brown's *Rubyfruit Jungle* (1972), Marge Piercy's *Small Changes* (1972), Erica Jong's *Fear of Flying* (1974), and Alice Walker's *Meridian* (1976). My particular interest in *The Women's Room* and **Death in a Tenured Position** involves their setting in English Departments, and thus their engagement with overlapping concerns, specifically, the intersection of aesthetic practices and feminist social action. Characters' intellectual concern with literature, with instabilities of meaning, the construction of women's literary ancestry, and the far reaches of aesthetic sublimity, exists in marked contrast with the "here and now" of their own fictional lives and the bodies which they inhabit, encounter, and for which they clean.

The contrast of mind and body, of academy and "real life," represents a standoff between feminism, in theory—that is, feminism as an idealized, abstracted, oftentimes academic pursuit—and feminism in practice, which involves difficult demands of the body, of dirt, of pleasure, of the daily degradations and humiliations that put theory to the test, find it wanting, and work to fine-tune its generalizing assumptions. In the early 1980s, feminism "became secure and prospered in the academy while feminism as a social movement was encountering major setbacks in a climate of new conservatism," writes Jane Gallop in *Around 1981*.[3] Among other factors involved in the increasing academicization of U.S. feminism in the early 1980s were recent translations, and thus the new availability, of texts by French poststructuralists including Derrida, Cixous, Irigaray, Kristeva, and Lacan. This critical context contributed to the acceleration of a shift in U.S. feminist theories from a primarily Marxist critical paradigm to one that depended increasingly on a psychoanalytic model. Thus intervening at an extremely sensitive moment in feminist history, novels of this period locate themselves at the intersection of academic and more generally social concerns; from that juncture, they present theories of their own about the means by which feminist ideals might operate in the context of material praxis.[4]

In 1981, Carolyn Heilbrun, then a professor of English at Columbia University who writes detective novels under the name Amanda Cross, published ***Death in a Tenured Position***. This novel is part of a series that features the protagonist Kate Fansler, an independently wealthy, WASP-ish, feminist English professor at a major university in New York City, who happens to solve murder mysteries in her spare time. I want to emphasize the categories of identity that Cross rather aggressively attaches to her detective, not simply to suggest that Fansler is a surrogate for Cross/Heilbrun, but rather to emphasize the fact that Fansler, by virtue of her identity, symbolizes a series of mainstream, bourgeois feminist values: like many of her counterparts, including Isadora Wing of Jong's *Fear of Flying*, Fansler is a New Yorker, financially invulnerable due to her possession of a trust fund, heterosexual, white, well-educated, and because of her own personal experiences, concerned with sexual chauvinism. Kate Fansler's feminist politics run deep but not radical; early in ***Death in a Tenured Position***, she encounters the lesbian separatist Joan Theresa and becomes painfully conscious of the legibility of her appearance: "The raincoat Kate had hung up was a fashionable raincoat. Her shoes, though flat, were fashionable shoes. Her panty hose covered shaved legs. Her suit, ultra-suede, was worn over a turtleneck knit, and on her jacket was a pin: a gold pin. Kate was dressed for the patriarchy."[5] "'My clothes,'" says Kate to Joan Theresa, "'make my life easier, as yours make your life easier'" (p. 10). Upper-class, educated, and a feminist, Kate Fansler's very liminality enables her to achieve the symbolic translations necessary to accommodate both feminist and "patriarchal" agendas. She is intelligent, attractive, and desirable, and in fictional worlds, the material and especially sartorial tokens of middle-class respectability are a central mechanism through which feminist agendas are transmitted to a mass-market readership. Later in the novel, Kate jokingly accuses her friend Sylvia of becoming "'one of those awful women's libbers'" (p. 26). Sylvia's response: "'You betcha. I eat bras; my favorite is 34B, pink, lightly sizzled. I will eat one soon if the waiter doesn't come. Shall we have it with white wine or red?'"

This novel's lightly satirical detachment from radical politics belies the fact that it contains the spectrum of feminist possibilities in characters that range from commune-dwelling lesbian separatists, to the gentler feminism of Kate and Sylvia, to the brutal misogyny of its villains and of its victim. And indeed, as both a detective and, suggestively, as an academic, Kate will need the protective coloring of her wealth and conventional style, for the novel's mystery goes right to questions of institutional authority: ***Death in a Tenured Position*** concerns first the career crisis, then the death of Janet Mandelbaum, the first female professor of English at Harvard University.

If Columbia University's English Department was symbolically central to the women's movement because of the scandal surrounding Kate Millett's publication of *Sexual Politics* in 1970,[6] Harvard's English Department emerges even more powerfully as the emblem of patriarchal privilege paradoxically surrounded by Cambridge, the heart of youth culture and a center of the antiwar movement. The juxtaposition of Harvard's backwardness and the progressive enclave of Cambridge is fruitful within popular literatures of the women's movement, a dichotomy deployed not only by Cross, but also by Alther, Piercy in *Small Changes,* and most famously, by French in *The Women's Room*. Cross and French alike frame their fictions through the observation that there is almost literally no place for women at Harvard, an architectural critique that symbolizes implicit institutional misogyny. Both novels focus on what Lacan calls "urinary segregation," borrowing on bathroom politics in order to make a point about gendered ideologies that follow from entrenched social conventions of sexual difference.[7]

French's novel opens with Mira peering into the mirror in an obscure Harvard "ladies' room"—"She called it that, even though someone had scratched out the word *ladies*' in the sign on the door, and written *women*'s underneath"[8]—while Cross's Janet Mandelbaum is found dead in the English Department men's room. True to the larger lavatorial motif, the professional politics of misogyny represented through these women's encounters with the university focuses on bodily implications; the insistence in an academic context on women's bodies suggests that the body is profoundly inescapable, untranscendable even in the loftiest of contexts. In Cross's novel, a young Harvard English professor writes to a friend of his department's mandate to hire a woman, implicitly equating the male-separatist enclave of the academy with the politics of the old-boys' room: "Of course, they are all worried about menopause—it is absolutely all they can think of when a woman threatens to penetrate their masculine precincts—how revealing language is" (p. 1). And when Kate Fansler first considers coming to Janet Mandelbaum's assistance at Harvard, she recalls Henry James, who "wrote a novel in the 1890s in which a young woman shows an admirer around Harvard, pointing out each of the buildings and remarking that there is no place for women in them; Harvard hasn't changed much since. Little more than ten years ago, women could not use many of the libraries" (p. 14).

For French, too, the architectural exclusion of women from Harvard only underscores a more widespread pattern of exclusion justified by the putative uncontainability of the female body. Linking the scatological implications of bathrooms with libraries, Val, the most radical of Mira's graduate student friends (and the one who is ultimately—predictably—punished for her radicalism with death) argues similarly that Harvard discriminates against women for "sanitary" considerations: "'You let women through the front doors and what will they do? Splat splat, a big clot of menstrual blood right on the threshold. Every place women go they do it: splat splat. There are little piles of clotty blood all over Lamont Library now. There are special crews hired just to keep the place decently mopped down'" (p. 304). Val's fantasy of the library's contamination caricatures misogynistic fears about the uncontainability of women's bodies, even as it suggests that patriarchal institutions—the library, the university—are insufficiently fortified to effect that containment at all.

Emily Martin argues that women have used sex-segregated bathrooms as "backstage areas" and spaces in which they could constitute their own "solidarity and resistance" to the containment of their bodies in the public sphere of the workplace.[9] *The Women's Room,* from its title to its conclusion, is intensely aware of the possibilities and the dangers of such resistance. Although bathrooms themselves in this novel tend to be spaces of women's isolation, anxiety, and panic, the collegial community that the women in Mira's circle succeed in constructing serves as the kind of "women's room" Virginia Woolf imagines in *A Room of One's Own,* its own site of subversion from within. But for some the inescapable, inevitably visceral embodiedness of women is the stuff of the most treacherous anxiety dreams, presenting a conundrum that is as frightening as it is liberatory. Reflecting Val's imagery, the graduate student Kyla has the following dream prior to her oral exam:

> She dreamt she was in the room where orals were held, a wood-paneled room with small paned windows and a broad shining table. The three men who were to examine her were sitting at one end of the table quarreling as she walked in. She had just stepped inside the door when she spied the pile in the corner. Instantly she knew what it was, but she was incredulous, she was so ashamed, she moved nearer to check it out. It was what she thought. She was horrified. Those stained sanitary napkins, those bloody underpants were hers, she knew they were hers, and she knew the men would know it too. She tried to stand in front of them, but there was no way she could conceal them. The men had stopped quarreling, they had turned to face her, they were peering at her . . .
>
> (P. 410, ellipses in original)

In a startling moment of unconscious identification, Kyla aligns herself, and her fears for and about herself, with the misogynistic establishment: she, like her examiners, fears the uncontainable bloody excesses of the female body, and for Kyla such a fear of bodily betrayal is at once embarrassing and professionally disabling. Her body's secrets refuse to remain contained in the other space of the women's room; in Kyla's deepest anxiety, her body refuses to collude with "the men" over the open secret of its femaleness, and simply reiterates the fear that her examiners will fail to perceive Kyla's mind within the insistent context of her uncontrollable body.

"Menstrual blood," writes Julia Kristeva, "stands for the danger issuing from within identity (social or sexual); it threatens the relationship between the sexes within a social aggregate and, through internalization, the identity of each sex in the face of sexual difference."[10] For Val, for Kyla, for Janet Mandelbaum, their bodies signify sexual difference even as their vocational ambitions lay claim to a pretense of gender neutrality; the well-trained mind should, in theory anyway, neutralize the ideological effects of a binary-sex model. Like Cross, French deploys the ostensibly abstract intellectual politics of the university in order to undercut the ascetic assumptions of disembodiedness implicit within the life of the mind, foregrounding instead the painful struggle feminists faced in the effort to reconcile the body politics of academic labor with more abstract claims of aesthetics and the intellectual sphere. By forcing the reconciliation of the abstract and the material, such bodily degradations help to constitute the borderlines of the feminist subject, even as they expose the very vulnerability of that subject-position by modeling the most spectacular, even mortal, implications of its failure.

Kristeva suggests that the degradations of the abject help to serve a constitutive function: mediating within the binary pair "subject" and "object," the abject becomes recognizable through the act of expulsion, through the putting-out that, in one stroke, constitutes and maps the boundary line between in and out. The constitutive function of the body, and especially of the abjectified corpse, in novels of the women's liberation movement expresses "feminist subjectivity" as a singular and a collective enterprise by modeling the serious implications of its failure. Bodily humiliation signifies the risks feminist subjects undertake: "as in true theater, without makeup or masks, refuse and corpses *show me* what I permanently thrust aside in order to live," writes Kristeva.

> These body fluids, this defilement, this shit are what life withstands, hardly and with difficulty, on the part of death. There, I am at the border of my condition as a living being. My body extricates itself, as being alive, from that border. Such wastes drop so that I might live, until, from loss to loss, nothing remains in me and my entire body falls beyond the limit—*cadere,* cadaver. If dung signifies the other side of the border, the place where I am not and which permits me to be, the corpse, the most sickening of wastes, is a border that has encroached upon everything.[11]

Within Kristeva's theoretical model, produced in 1980 at the very transitional moment negotiated within these novels, the category crisis staged in the expulsion of the abject involves the psychic processes through which not only subjectivity but subjectivity as a gendered category is constituted: "The abject confronts us . . . with our earliest attempts to release the hold of *maternal* entity even before existing outside of her, thanks to the autonomy of language. It is a violent, clumsy breaking away, with the constant risk of falling back under the sway of a power as securing as it is stifling."[12] As Kristeva suggests, the power politics of boundary-formation are delicate: the nascent subject, shuttling between the predicament of maternal claustration and its patriarchal obverse, autonomy, finds herself called upon to reconcile the irreconcilable, in a context in which her very survival is on the line. The double bind that characterizes Kristeva's emerging subject recapitulates the predicament of the mature but would-be feminist subjects of Cross's and French's novels, and in all three cases, the subject-formation at stake involves the conundrum of femininity; how might female, and indeed, *feminist,* subjectivity come into being, caught as it is between the annihilating codes of maternity on one side and the equally dangerous patriarchal sphere on the other? The corpses of Janet Mandelbaum and, later in *The Women's Room,* of Val, Mira's heartiest, most joyously embodied feminist friend, exist in these novels as abjectified objects against which a feminist subject expresses the extremes of her own enterprise. In one sense, and paradoxically perhaps, such feminist corpses act the role of good mother: they play dead, and accordingly constitute themselves as unresistant objects to be inscribed with meaning from the outside by those who profit from their loss. But more disturbingly, they also serve the function of the scapegoat: because the abject have been punished so brutally for their failings, the feminist subjects constituted in their wake are damaged goods, made timid and conciliatory by their awareness of the thin line they walk, by the mortal dangers implicit within the apparently paradoxical construct "autonomous woman."[13]

The result is a form of bodily self-loathing inflicted by the academy, a misogynistic institution which stands in the way of women's access to the life of the mind, to aesthetic worlds, and to the professional prestige and livelihood that are presumed to follow upon academic success. Hence **Death in a Tenured Position,** a novel that presents its own ambivalence about the first woman to achieve the professional success that universities—and the culture for which they stand—would deny to the general population of women. Janet Mandelbaum was selected strategically to join the Harvard faculty, more perhaps because of her antipathy toward feminism than for the excellence of her scholarship. Janet rails against the expectation that she, as the token woman, will lobby for the greater good of women: "all the women—students, assistant professors, administrators—seem to think I should rally to some woman's cause: women's studies, the problems of women at Harvard, welcoming women to the graduate program, to Radcliffe—as though there were only one sex in the universe. Why should I be more interested in the women than the men? I'm interested in good seventeenth-century scholars; the sex is irrelevant" (p. 45). She continues later, "'I honestly do think that if women have the ability and are willing to pay the price they can make it. I did'" (p. 46). Along those lines, Joan Theresa, lesbian separatist and radical feminist, argues that not only was Janet never a feminist, "'She was never a *woman,* professionally speaking'" (p. 12), and Kate Fansler agrees: "'I assumed that was why Harvard had taken her. She had also had a hysterectomy, when young, and therefore could be guaranteed not to have a menopause, during which all women go mad, as everyone knows.'"

Stripped of her "woman" credentials because she does not identify with woman-centered political causes and implicitly because she lacks that fundamental equipment for hysteria, the womb, Janet Mandelbaum is nonetheless punished—by misogynists, by feminists, by herself—because she is a professional woman. The first instance of this punishment occurs in the context of a rather improbable crisis, in which a graduate student slipped Janet a drugged cocktail; when she passed out, he placed her limp body in the ornamental bathtub located in the Harvard English Department men's bathroom. He then telephoned Joan Theresa's commune and warned them that one of the "sisters" was in trouble. The idea, apparently, was to suggest that Janet, who would appear to know the lesbian separatists who came to her rescue, would be tarred with the same brush, would be taken for a lesbian herself; this produces crisis not only for Janet, but for the rescuing lesbian, Luellen, who is in a custody battle for her children. Sylvia muses on the illogic of this plot: "'The point however, is that *they* thought they could discredit Janet by getting her involved with that all-women commune in Cambridge. Perhaps add another suspicion to her deteriorating reputation. But they were fools. They united two groups who would never, otherwise, have anything to do with each other: the woman-identified and the male-identified'" (p. 30, italics in original).

Kate Fansler was initially called to Harvard to intervene informally on Janet's behalf, and the women's commune, too, has something at stake in her presence in Cambridge: Luellen hopes Kate will testify in her custody battle, and Kate realizes that "'a judge would take my word about whom to give the children to because of the way I dress'" (p. 87). As Sylvia suggests, the commune women are the polar opposite of antifeminist Janet Mandelbaum, but as the novel's plot suggests, they remain united in several concerns common to them as women: they both need the help of mainstream feminist Kate Fansler; they are similarly degraded and publicly humiliated in an intellectual (and homophobic and misogynistic) context because of their bodies and what their bodies suggest about their sexuality. But while Kate suspects the entire Harvard faculty is capable of murdering its first tenured woman professor in order to "scotch the whole scheme" of female faculty (p. 106), in the end, quite chillingly, it is not one of the suspects but rather Mandelbaum herself who acted in violence.

Kate Fansler's investigation into Mandelbaum's murder represents an attempt to locate violent hatred of Mandelbaum either in the radical feminist fringe or in the misogynist Harvard faculty, each of which has something to gain by her death. But it is ultimately revealed that Mandelbaum died by her own hand, and in the course of this investigation, that everyone is guilty—the Harvard English Department for its closed-minded loathing of her; her friends Kate and Sylvia for isolating her, for giving her "no community" (p. 187); her lesbian feminist "sisters" for turning their back on a woman in need: "'She belonged nowhere, poor Janet'" (p. 181). Mandelbaum's chosen symbolic gesture was to commit suicide in the office of the English Department chairman; her colleague Clarkville, discovering the body, moves it from the office to the men's room (where it has already been discovered once) in a misguided attempt at concealment. Because Mandelbaum's body "'was in a position with the legs drawn up,'" putting it "'on the toilet in the stall may have seemed, under the circumstances, the logical thing'" (p. 166), and Clarkville, chivalrous to the end, chooses the men's room in order to spare the English Department's secretaries the shock of discovering Mandelbaum dead.

The circumstances of Mandelbaum's death, the ensuing cover-up, and its discovery, decisively reiterate the scatological motif. But this time, Mandelbaum herself, although a prominent scholar, was responsible for placing her own body in a suggestive position. The novel ultimately punishes Mandelbaum, exchanging her embrace of scholarly asceticism for a conclusive gesture toward her body's status as material and as grotesque. Why, though, despite its indictment of everyone from radical feminists to vicious misogynists for failing to accept Mandelbaum's person and politics, must this novel conclude with a revelation of her suicide? This text turns on the death of a woman. And despite the belated regrets of most of its characters, there is enormous hostility directed toward Janet Mandelbaum, whether because she is female or because she is not feminist. The message implicit in a novel whose protagonist speaks for the feminist mainstream is that while there might be no room for women at Harvard now, there will be eventually—but there is no room for women such as Janet Mandelbaum, whether by her own choice or the choice of feminists, within the women's movement. Kate Fansler represents a new feminist orthodoxy here, a middle ground available to women who fall somewhere between the radical feminism of Joan Theresa and the borderline misogyny of Janet Mandelbaum; vaguely skeptical of both, Kate looks on more in sorrow than in anger as both are punished for their occupation of the fringes.

Death in a Tenured Position is set in an English Department, and it exploits its setting in order to foreground not only questions of professionalism, politics, and sexuality relevant to the women's movement, but also questions of aesthetics. In this it is paradigmatic of popular feminist fictions from this period, which consistently emphasize the importance of beauty, creativity, and in that vein, education, as fundamental to feminist social action. These texts suggest that the desire for aesthetic and erotic pleasure, as well as the liberal feminist egalitarian impulse, can be addressed through the cultivation of the analytical tools found in the university, while the cultivation of the mind, as Cross's novel suggests, represents the possibility of circumventing the gross bodily implications of femininity. As fictional texts, these novels clearly have much at stake in underscoring the importance of fictional and literary works to a larger feminist project. But the consistent representation of aesthetic concerns within the aggressively professional context of the academy—Janet Mandelbaum's investment in George Herbert, for instance, concerns career more than pleasure—equates the cultural valuation of the sublime with a kind of bourgeois careerism. An academic career is potentially feminist and also quite democratically accessible to smart women with the proper training. The university, paradoxically, symbolizes both the most rigidly entrenched of patriarchal institutions and a context in which feminist political interventions might take hold. In this it stands somewhat optimistically for the potential of bourgeois feminism to transform the world.

Feminist fictions emphasize the profound importance of class issues to the women's movement through their concern not only with the class status of women, but also with the fluid class boundaries available through education. The sense in which they remain conventional narratives, then, underscores the nature of the fictional intervention into feminist practice, addressing central questions of the women's movement while putting a premium on the human cost of the difficult decisions these central questions require. These are novels in which female characters agonize over the double binds that characterize their lives, and in which every decision, one way or the other, has negative implications. Just as Kate Fansler serves a crucial mediating function between the extremes of radical lesbian feminism and rigid misogyny, these narratives, too, operate in terms of mediation. They construct an implicit readerly identification for white, middle-class, heterosexual women, and through the trials of their white, middle-class, usually heterosexual protagonists, they model strategies for the accommodation of feminist principles of equality within essentially conventional lives.[14] In the context of such narratives of identification, the topos of violent death persists as a sign of abjection that, through the purifying, almost excretory function, exposes the outermost limits—and the frightening risks—of the feminist project.

Marilyn French's *The Women's Room* is the most fully realized of various attempts to work through the conflicts created by cultural expectations for women, and as in most feminist novels, feminism is a positive possibility within otherwise annihilating choices. French follows her protagonist Mira through girlhood, adolescence, marriage, life as a suburban housewife and mother, divorce, graduate school, and ultimately—and not optimistically—to a lonely existence as a junior-college instructor of English literature in a town isolated on the coast of Maine. This is not a happy ending, but Mira is introspective and intact at the novel's conclusion, no mean feat considering the extent to which her ostensibly "normal" and certainly conventional life experiences are represented in terms of their ability to inflict psychic and even physical damage, despite Mira's reasonably protected status as an open-minded, intelligent, middle-class, well-educated white woman. She is not a woman living in poverty like the lesbians in **Death in a Tenured Position** and Piercy's *Small Changes* who must fight the system that would take away their children; nor does she experience overt misogyny and certainly nothing like racial discrimination or hatred. Rather, Mira is a woman who suffers because she is a member of the cultural mainstream, even the cultural ideal, an intelligent, thinking, sensitive woman living in the post-war U.S.; her suffering is acute and its damage genuine.

Mira's predicament leaves her split, more knowingly than Janet Mandelbaum, between body and mind, between the grotesque implications of her material existence and the possibilities held forth in the act of intellection. It is not possible for Mira to reconcile these claims. Accordingly, her feminism, however abstract it gets, never fully escapes the most degraded bodily implications of patriarchy in terms ranging from the cleaning of toilets to rape at knifepoint. *The Women's Room* is a novel set largely in a university context, but it opens in the bathroom of that university, and French is meticulous in situating the more abstract ideological concerns of the women's movement within the material context of women's lived experience: university, bathroom.

Mira, an acutely intelligent child, first found that intelligence disrupted by menstruation: "The problem was sex . . . At the end of her fourteenth year, Mira began to menstruate and was finally let in on the secret of sanitary napkins. Soon afterward, she began to experience strange fluidities in her body, and her mind, she was convinced, had begun to rot. She could feel the increasing corruption, but couldn't seem to do anything to counter it" (p. 14). With menstruation comes the beginning of sexual desire, and Mira's introduction to the entire consumer economy of womanhood. Suddenly the intellectual emphases of her private life give way to ideas of romantic love, but as a teenager, she swiftly learns that her participation in romance means that she must forsake not only physical but also mental independence: left alone one night in a bar, she drinks too much, dances with a number of teenage boys, and comes dangerously close to being gang-raped by them.

> Other girls went to bars, other girls danced. The difference was she had appeared to be alone. That a woman was not marked as the property of some man made her a bitch in heat to be attacked by any male, or even by all of them at once. She was a woman and that alone was enough to deprive her of freedom no matter how much the history books pretended that women's suffrage had ended inequality, or that women's feet had been bound only in an ancient and outmoded and foreign place like China. She was constitutionally unfree.
>
> (P. 35)

Having been introduced to the consumer culture of womanhood, Mira soon learns, violently, that she is its chattel. And significantly, as this quote should demonstrate, the feminist praxis modeled by *The Women's Room*, with its title's allusion to Woolf's peroration for women's intellectual freedom in *A Room of One's Own*, is more concerned with the subtle sexism of white, middle-class heterosexual culture than with interventions at the level of formal law.

Like the women of Woolf's text, Mira's intelligence, her private life of the mind, is her only path of escape from the insidious degradations of middle-class femininity. But mind is inextricable from body, and Mira's body, as she so rapidly learns, represents a problem in a culture that would see it only in terms of a man's ownership: "Mira understood—what young woman does not?—that to choose a husband is to choose a life. She had not needed Jane Austen to teach her that. It is, in a sense, a woman's first, last, and only choice. Marriage and a child make her totally dependent on the man, on whether he is rich or poor, responsible or not, where he chooses to live, what work he chooses to do" (p. 26). As Virginia Woolf suggests and French reiterates repeatedly, women are a social class, and as a class, they are generally poor. This point is represented particularly acutely given the novel's normative middle-class context and its version of heterosexual marital convention, for Mira's perception that her future physical well-being depends on her choice of husband presupposes certain assumptions about that husband's earning power; in contrast, in *Rubyfruit Jungle* (1972), Rita Mae Brown's lesbian protagonist Molly Bolt, working outside the presumption that her life is coextensive with her marriage, tells a story of economic self-sufficiency that originates in a childhood of constant poverty.

For the women of Mira's suburban adult lifestyle, on the other hand, "work" is tied to the body and detached from the monetary economy of wages; they are in a secondary relationship to earning power, and the power relations of their marriages reflect the equation of money and control. "Women see men as oppressors, as tyrants, as an enemy with superior strength to be outwitted. Men see women as underminers, slaves who rattle their chains threateningly, constantly reminding the men that if they wanted to, they could poison his food: just watch out" (p. 68). Women's work involves the bearing of and caring for children, tasks that further alienate them from "ownership" of their bodies and that impose a form of exhaustion that drains their intelligent minds; when Mira first gets pregnant, "She saw the situation as the end of her personal life. Her life, from pregnancy on, was owned by another creature" (p. 48). The narrator interposes here with a commentary on Mira's "unnatural" response to her predicament: "What is wrong with this woman? you ask. It is Nature, there is no recourse, she must submit and make the best of what she cannot change. But the mind is not easily subdued. Resentment and rebellion grow in it—resentment and rebellion against Nature itself. Some wills are crushed, but those that are not contain within them, for the rest of their days, seeds of hate. All of the women I know feel a little like outlaws." Feminism for Mira represents the fomenting of rebellion in her mind against the captivity and ownership registered on her body. Because of the differences between male and female bodies, "Women and men. They played by different rules because the rules applied to them were different. It was very simple. It was the women who got pregnant and the women who ended up with the kids" (p. 216). The material implications of women's lack of access to money and men's access to freedom are dire for women and children; after Mira's divorce and the mid-life divorces of several of her friends, the narrator writes, "If you want to find out who all the welfare mothers are, ask your divorced male friends. It sounds easy, you know, going on welfare. But apart from the humiliation and resentment, you don't really live very well. In case you didn't know. Which is unpleasant for a woman, but sends her into fits when she looks at her kids" (p. 230).

The indignities, petty humiliations, and injustices represented in *The Women's Room* are the by-product of "normal" American life, and in her exposé of the quotidian, French locates "women's liberation" at and as the heart of middle-class concerns. French's critique of marriage represents a logical progression from material degradation to larger epistemological questions, and the novel's more esoteric academic analyses of inequality suggest that experience and epistemology are inextricable. Feminist praxis begins, for French, for Mira, at home: "But for women especially, the new washing machine or dryer or freezer really was a little release from slavery. Without them, and without the pill, there would not be a woman's revolution now" (p. 72). Indeed, the liberatory implications of labor-saving devices have been central to bourgeois feminism, from Friedan's *The Feminine Mystique* (1963), with its analysis of affluent women's boredom, through more contemporary debates about day care.[15] In *The Women's Room*, labor-saving devices represent an avenue out of the endlessly self-replicating implications of dirt generated by human bodies. "All my life,' the narrator comments, "I've read that the life of the mind is preeminent, and that it can transcend all bodily degradation. But that's just not my experience. When your body has to deal all day with shit and string beans, your mind does too" (p. 46). From this point on, the phrase "shit and string beans" is the novel's refrain, representing the physical and mental captivity entailed in housewifery, and particularly in the raising of small children and the maintenance of the affluent suburban household. Mira, living the "American Dream" and trying to "get her mask on straight" (p. 151), is explicit about the most hideous aspects of middle-class womanhood: "Down on her hands and knees in one of the endless bathrooms, she would tell herself that in a way she was fortunate. Washing the toilet used by three males, and the floor and walls around it, is, Mira thought, coming face to face with necessity. And that was why women were saner than men, did not come up with the mad, absurd schemes men developed: they were in touch with necessity, they had to wash the toilet bowl and floor" (p. 150).

For Mira and women like her, the "necessity" of dealing with "shit and string beans" is a universal among women, and this novel suggests a related universality of female oppression, even if the presence of options in this context, such as cleaning help, appliances, and even access to birth control, locates this form of protest firmly in the middle of the middle class. "Everybody should clean up their own vomit," Mira thinks. "Everybody should clean up the toilet they use" (p. 227). But in Mira's world, everybody doesn't—women do. And even in the most openly feminist contexts, behavioral expectations based on gender roles are stubborn; theory and practice remain at odds with one another. To the suggestion of universal "selflessness," to men and women equally bearing the expectations of the other, the narrator replies:

> It was a rhetorical solution. Because the fact is that everyone doesn't act in both roles and probably can't and not everyone would be willing to accept that and so the whole thing seemed to me as if we'd been talking about the street plan and architecture of heaven. In fact, it didn't make much sense even for us to insist that men and women both should be selfless, because although we were all in graduate school, all of us took the female role at home . . . And we were supposed to be "liberated" . . . I mentioned this, and Isolde sighed. "I hate discussions of feminism that end up with who does the dishes," she said. So do I. But at the end, there are always the damned dishes.
>
> (P. 60)

Someone is always stuck doing the dishes, and the question of cleaning up afterwards is allegorized outward in this novel to suggest its centrality for both feminist practice and theory. "Women always have to clean up their own messes," thinks Mira (p. 246), and the rage provoked by such debasement is the fire behind feminist theoretical passions. After a theoretical argument, Kyla, Mira's graduate school colleague, bursts out: "'Oh, Mira!' . . . 'Why do you always have to bring us down to the level of the mundane, the ordinary, the stinking, fucking refrigerator? I was talking about ideals, nobility, principles . . . 'And she leaped up and charged across the room and threw herself on Mira and hugged her, kept hugging her, saying, 'Thank you, oh, thank you, Mira, for being so wonderful, so awful, for always remembering the stinking, filthy refrigerator!'" (p. 241).

As Kyla's outburst indicates, the "evidence of experience" proves a powerful polemical tool within *The Women's Room*: pragmatism emerges as the inescapable groundwork to more esoteric flights of feminist fancy.[16] "For here, underneath all the intellect, the abstraction, the disconnection, were the same old salt tears and sperm, the same sweet blood and sweat she'd wiped up for years. More shit and string beans" (p. 304). Mira's return to school following her divorce occurs as an attempt to transcend the "real" implications of everyday existence: "It was a new life, it was supposed to revitalize you, to send you radiant to new planes of experience where you would get tight with Beatrice Portinari and be led to an earthly paradise. In literature, new lives, second chances, lead to visions of the City of God" (p. 147). But typically within the genre of feminist realism, Mira quickly realizes that the formal conventions of representation fail to accommodate her own lived experience, with the result that "shit and string beans" continue to preoccupy her daily life. The narrator writes:

> The problem with the great literature of the past is that it doesn't tell you how to live with real endings. In the great literature of the past you either get married and live happily ever after, or you die. But the fact is, neither is what actually happens. Oh, you do die, but never at the right time, never with great language floating all around you, and a whole theater full of witnesses to your agony. What actually happens is that you do get married or you don't, and you don't live happily ever after, but you do live. And that's the problem.
>
> (Pp. 148-49)

Marriage in French's novel rarely guarantees happiness, and life without happiness is in effect a living death. And this novel, consistent with its dark aesthetic vision, is pragmatic about the implications of Mira's feminist struggle. She gets her Ph.D., true, from the same Harvard English Department that effectively kills Janet Mandelbaum, but she does not turn into Mandelbaum, much less Kate Fansler, reaping the material and intellectual benefits of a scholarly life. Mira, an older graduate, settles into a job at a very isolated small college in Maine. So despite the fact that she opts out of marriage and more children with her lover Ben in favor of her intellectual freedom, she winds up a solitary eccentric wandering the rocky shores of Maine all winter long.

But employed, and living on her own terms, Mira is alive. She is friends with her adolescent sons and occasionally even enjoys her life as a teacher. If Mira represents the feminist mainstream, French paints a bleak picture of the implications of acting on a commitment to personal freedom; typically pragmatic, she underscores the sense in which every decision carries its price, and Mira's integrity costs her human relationships. On the other hand, however, this novel, like so many others of this historical moment, articulates a feminist mainstream through the sharp contrast with the feminist radical fringe. And occupation of that radical fringe is, as is so often the case, lethal.

In French's novel, Mira's most radical friend is Val, who with her daughter Chris constitute a family unit that is presented as idyllic: it is open, fluid, accepting, political, welcoming, a household of women who practice a utopic, user-friendly version of the feminism with which the novel's more conventional women struggle. Chris, however, goes off to college and is raped, and their ensuing trip through the justice system brings Chris and Val down to the level of degradation, humiliation, and debasement that is the more common experience of women in patriarchal culture. This radicalizes Val to a degree that the novel represents as understandable but untenable; Chris and Val conclude that any male attention is rape, that the legal system is complicit with the rapist, and that Chris is fighting for her right to exist in a world of men. Representing an extreme version of the separatist rhetoric of anti-porn and other radical feminist groups, Val declares, "'Whatever they may be in public life, whatever their relations with men, in their relations with women, all men are rapists, and that's all they are. They rape us with their eyes, their laws, and their codes'" (p. 462).

The novel rejects this position implicitly.[17] Mira is the mother of two sons and thus typically represents the feminist struggle for equality without separatism, and at this moment, she feels "liberated" through her pursuit of her scholarly work: scholarship, she believes, "did not seem slavery to her but freedom. For the first time, she understood what graduate school had been all about: it was designed to free her for this. She did not have to worry over every detail; she had enough knowledge to make certain statements, and enough awareness of how to get knowledge to find out how to make others. That was liberating. She was free to be as methodical as she chose, in a work that seemed significant. What more could she ask?" (p. 475). If knowledge is Mira's ticket to liberation, then political action is Val's, for Val becomes a political activist, indeed, an extremely radical feminist, as a result of her daughter's rape.[18] And for this decision she pays the price of death, no mere poisoning as in Janet Mandelbaum's case, but a brutally graphic and public destruction of her body and all that it stands for: as Val participates in a protest, police shoot so many bullets into her body that it explodes.

"'There are no words,'" someone says at her funeral (p. 496), and unlike Mira, whose choice in the mind-body binary places her on the side of the mind, Val surpasses the contingencies of materiality; because she exploded, she is containable neither in body nor in words:

> No words to wrap her body in like a shroud, like clean white sanitized bandages, around and around and around until she was all clean and white and sanitized and pure, her blood dried, her mass of exploded flesh covered, her stink deodorized, and she sanitary, polite, acceptable for public notice, a mummy propped on a table for public ceremony, its very presence a promise, a guarantee that she will not rise up in rage with hair wild on her head, a knife in her hand, screaming, "No! No! Kill before you accept!"

The novel does not deal with Val's death with any real explicitness, nor does it pursue the implications of the cause in which she died: Val and her group were trying to rescue a young black woman, Anita Morrow, who had been raped, and who stabbed her rapist in self-defense. The rapist, "from a respectable white family," died, and Anita Morrow was charged with murder. The prosecution claimed she was a prostitute, but like most of the female characters in this novel, she was a university student who "wanted to be an English teacher" (p. 492), although the media represented her as uneducable. Eventually, "Anita Morrow was found guilty of murder on grounds of illiteracy" (p. 493)—as if illiteracy were a crime.

This murder case introduces an important new tension late in the novel: the suggestion that education and the upward mobility that it purchases are the prerogative of middle-class white women alone underscores a certain complacency within Mira's analysis of the class politics of gender difference. Anita Morrow, Val, and Chris are punished for declarations of rage and selfhood that are significantly more extreme than the world, including the world of the protagonist Mira, is willing to handle. And in the context of the novel's dark representation of feminist life choices, the injustice of these concluding events is clear, even as their overarching message is still more clear: there is an ineradicable danger to life as a radical feminist, and in the bourgeois worlds of mainstream feminism, radical life-choices are conventionally punished either by humiliating ridicule or by death. Radical life-choices, in other words, put the body on the line, and by underscoring its material vulnerabilities, they realize the danger ever present within female resistance. The protections afforded within this equation are various, for some lives—Anita Morrow's, for example—are always already in danger; the concept of "choice" for Anita Morrow involves only the degree to which she might dare to resist a system which is implicitly constructed to resist her. Mira's place on the scale of privilege is quite high, but even her choices, reasonably moderate though they are, strand her on the rugged coast of Maine. And Val was forced by circumstance and by violence to choose a life for which there is no place at all in the world. This caused her body to be shattered to bits all over the street, in the name of legal justice.

The fictional texts of the mainstream women's movement are decidedly anxious about feminist rage and feminist activism, and they represent an ideal of bourgeois feminism as a decidedly cerebral endeavor. Characters such as Alther's Ginny or Jong's Isadora Wing, whose trust funds enable them to try on roles, jobs, and sexualities without material consequences, enable a parody of the double bind Marilyn French represents as agonizing and inextricable: more abstract theoretical approaches to sexual discrimination emerge subtly as the property of the "straight," of the white, heterosexual middle classes. Amanda Cross's series detective Kate Fansler is certainly represented as a feminist, but short of coming to the rescue of a colleague in crisis at Harvard, her more conventional mode of feminist action is her eternal presence as "'The Token Woman'" (p. 5) on any number of university committees. The ubiquitousness with which feminist novelists in the late 1970s situate their characters' political activities within universities is symptomatic of a larger set of agendas pertaining to the brand of feminist action they represent: feminism is an individual concern, is a movement connected with the achievement of personal career and intellectual goals facilitated by education, and relies on a logic of metonymy, suggesting that what is good for one woman will be good for women more generally. In this context, radical individualism becomes its own form of activist intervention; Ginny Babcock leaves the commune to marry Ira Bliss, and later still, she leaves Ira, rolling her "Sisterhood is Powerful" T-shirt into a knapsack and striking out after new adventures.

Serving the practical aims of consolidation in death, the feminist abject is occasionally recapitulated in further service to the feminist subject. At the end of Jong's *Fear of Flying,* in a moment of crisis, the protagonist and first-person narrator Isadora Wing reads a notebook she kept in the early days of her present marriage: "I sat very quietly looking at the pages I had written. I knew I did not want to be trapped in my own book."[19] What follows is an anxiety dream that is at once liberatory and anomalous, that ruptures the terminologies of psychological, intellectual, narrative, and sexual entrapment that constitute Isadora's "own book"—her diary as well as the novel *Fear of Flying.* Isadora dreams of walking up the steps of Columbia's Low Library to receive her college diploma, her three "husbands" watching from the audience, and encountering lesbian novelist Colette at the lectern, "only she was a black woman with frizzy reddish hair glinting around her head like a halo." Colette says:

> "There is only one way to graduate . . . and it has nothing to do with the number of husbands."
>
> "What do I have to do?" I asked desperately, feeling I'd do anything.
>
> She handed me a book with my name on the cover. "That was only a very shaky beginning," she said, "but at least you *made* a beginning."
>
> I took this to mean I still had years to go.
>
> "Wait," she said, undoing her blouse. Suddenly I understood that making love to her in public was the real graduation, and at that moment it seemed like the most natural thing in the world. Very aroused, I moved toward her. Then the dream faded.
>
> (P. 290)

Jong's novel continues for two more chapters of *denouement* in which Isadora considers a reunion with her husband. But despite the structural centrality and psychological importance accorded this dream, the novel never refers back to it, nor attempts to elucidate its implications.

Why does *Fear of Flying* reach its climax in and through these terms? Somehow "Colette," racial and erotic exotic, is a profoundly useful, if alien, object of desire to the rampantly heterosexual, white, New Yorker Isadora Wing.[20] The novel that begins with the notorious fantasy of the "Zipless Fuck" (p. 11) concludes with a commencement that reestablishes the boundaries of sexual transgression: "Very aroused, I moved toward her. Then the dream faded." Interracial, transnational, exhibitionist lesbian sex is tied up here with the goal of successful authorship, both registering in the realm of "academic" achievement: Isadora's book represents a form of ongoing coursework, whereas "making love to [Colette] in public was the real graduation." But, again, "the dream faded," the erotic encounter between Isadora and Colette relegated, again, to the realm of the unsaid.

The love that dare not speak its name speaks volumes for Isadora Wing, whose Colette-fantasy consolidates a number of crucial—and troublesome—identity categories within the women's movement. Colette is a white Frenchwoman turned into a red-haired African-American; she is a lesbian and an academic; she is a literary figure, access to whose fictions, in practical terms, presupposes a certain achievement of literacy. And "making love to her in public was the real graduation," for Isadora Wing the key to escaping the conventional *Bildung* of her life thus far, the "graduation ceremony" that leads Isadora to the brink of an independent, self-determined identity.

In her deployment of Colette, Jong, like other feminist novelists of this period, forges a strategic connection between pleasure and knowledge, linking women's unleashed eroticism both to the concept of their intellectual freedom and also to formal institutional structures of the academy—Columbia's Low Library; a graduation ceremony. Knowledge is not only power; it is power rooted in pleasure; the realization of the creative and the beautiful; the construction of a feminist counterculture utopia right in the belly of the patriarchal beast itself. But perhaps the most common critique of the women's liberation movement in the late 1970s and the early 1980s focuses on what feminism leaves out. The argument that feminists, and feminist theories, construct white, middle-class, heterosexual women's experiences as normative recapitulates the politics of abjectification modeled by fictional deaths. In both cases, the mainstream constitutes itself through an act of violent expulsion, through a philosophical decapitation symbolically rendered, like Eddie's, through self-contradiction, through the failure to perceive the invisible boundaries that feminists have established and, however unconsciously, that they continue to patrol.

"Here it is not only a question," writes Judith Butler, "of how discourse injures bodies, but how certain injuries establish certain bodies at the limits of available ontologies, available schemes of intelligibility . . . [H]ow is it that the abjected come to make their claim through and against the discourses that have sought their repudiation?"[21] How, in other words, do the dead reawaken? Or, more appropriately perhaps, how do they expose themselves as the always already there, as the ghosts on whose very animating alterity feminist theories of animation, and of alterity, rely? In this context, Isadora Wing's transformative dream is as efficient as it is revealing of the profoundly constitutive role of the un-dead feminist. Colette, ghost, is the token black woman; lesbian; feminist literary ancestor; import from the prestigious context of French high culture. This leads to a new form of liberation: Isadora Wing, intensely aroused, responds sexually to Colette. And then she and her novel together walk away from this encounter; in the last scene Isadora is contemplating reunion with her husband. By reawakening the dead Colette, and by apostrophizing her in the name of categories of identity under erasure in this novel, Jong reveals the contingencies to which Isadora Wing's ultimate liberation, her release from entrapment within the generic confines of the fictional real, are indebted. Literally, figuratively, politically, Colette's outrageously overdetermined alterity serves an authorizing, even constitutive function for Isadora, for this novel, and for the witty, urbane feminist subject canonized in its graduation ceremony. Isadora forgets, but the novel reminds us, that it is Colette who confers the degree. And then she is gone.

Notes

1. Julia Kristeva, *The Powers of Horror: An Essay on Abjection*, trans. Leon S. Roudiez (New York: Columbia Univ. Press, 1982), p. 3.
2. Lisa Alther, *Kinflicks* (New York: Plume, 1996), p. 331. All quotations refer to this edition, and page numbers will be cited parenthetically in the text.
3. Jane Gallop, *Around 1981: Academic Feminist Literary Theory* (New York: Routledge, 1992), p. 10.
4. For an argument concerning "une fiction théoretique," or Nicole Brossard's notion of "fiction/theory" as it occurs in formally experimental feminist and lesbian novels, see Teresa de Lauretis, "Sexual Indifference and Lesbian Representation," *The Lesbian and Gay Studies Reader*, ed. Henry Abelove, Michèle Aina Barale, and David M. Halperin (New York: Routledge, 1993), pp. 141-58.
5. Amanda Cross, *Death in a Tenured Position* (New York: Ballantine Books, 1981), p. 10. All quotations refer to this edition, and page numbers will be cited parenthetically in the text.
6. *Time*, August 31, 1970 and December 14, 1970. I discuss this episode, and its implications, at length in the introduction to my current book project, *Feminism, In Theory: The Practice of Abstraction*.
7. Jacques Lacan, "The Agency of the letter in the unconscious," in *Écrits: A Selection*, trans. Alan Sheridan (New York: Norton, 1977), p. 151.
8. Marilyn French, *The Women's Room* (New York: Ballantine Books, 1988), p. 1. All quotations refer to this edition, and page numbers will be cited parenthetically in the text.
9. Emily Martin, *The Woman in the Body: A Cultural Analysis of Reproduction* (Boston: Beacon Press, 1987), p. 97.
10. Kristeva, *The Powers of Horror*, p. 71.
11. Ibid., p. 3, italics in original. See Martin, *The Woman in the Body*, pp. 45-50, for an analysis of the cultural and economic construction of menstrual blood as a form of waste.
12. Ibid., p. 13, italics in original. Kristeva argues later that women's use of the abject involves not mastery but the reiteration of an external patriarchal authority: "When a woman ventures out in those regions it is usually to gratify, in very maternal fashion, the desire for the abject that insures the life (that is, the sexual life) of the man whose symbolic authority she accepts" (p. 54).
13. On the constitutive function of the scapegoat, see René Girard, *Violence and the Sacred*, trans. Patrick Gregory (Baltimore: The Johns Hopkins Univ. Press, 1977). On the gendered politics of abjection, see Judith Butler, "Bodies That Matter," in *Bodies That Matter* (New York: Routledge, 1993).
14. For a feminist theory of readerly response and identification, see Janice Radway, *Reading the Romance: Women, Patriarchy, and Popular Literature* (Chapel Hill: Univ. of North Carolina Press, 1984).
15. Betty Friedan, *The Feminine Mystique* (New York: W. W. Norton Co., 1963). Of the many critiques of Friedan's class- and race-blind theory of gender, bell hooks's is perhaps the most influential; she writes: "[Friedan] did not discuss who would be called in to take care of the children and maintain the home if more women like herself were freed from their house labor and given equal access with white men to the professions. She did not speak of the needs of women without men, without children, without homes. She ignored the existence of all non-white women and poor white women. She did not tell readers whether it was more fulfilling to be a maid, a babysitter, a factory worker, a clerk, or a prostitute, than to be a leisure class housewife . . . She made her plight and the plight of white women like herself synonymous with a condition affecting all American women. In so doing, she deflected attention away from her classism, her racism, her sexist attitudes towards the masses of American women" (*Feminist Theory: From Margin to Center* [Boston: South End Press, 1984], pp. 1-2).

16. Joan W. Scott, "The Evidence of Experience," in Abelove, et al., pp. 397-415. Scott's post-poststructuralist critique of the experiential as an authoritative epistemological form provides an interesting theoretical foil to the very serious authority granted experience in theoretical and fictional works of the late 1970s.

17. For an analysis of critical responses to the question of men in *The Women's Room,* see Lisa Marie Hogeland, *Feminism and Its Fictions: The Consciousness-Raising Novel and the Women's Liberation Movement* (Philadelphia: Univ. of Pennsylvania Press, 1998), pp. 90-93.

18. On the cost of Val's "failed activism," and on the surprising infrequency of feminist fictional representations of activism, see Hogeland, *Feminism and Its Fictions,* p. 107.

19. Erica Jong, *Fear of Flying* (New York: Signet, 1995), p. 288. All quotations refer to this edition, and page numbers will be cited parenthetically in the text.

20. On Colette's mixed-race heritage, see Judith Thurman, *Secrets of the Flesh: A Life of Colette* (New York: Knopf, 1999).

21. Butler, *Bodies That Matter,* p. 224.

Publishers Weekly (review date 6 November 2000)

SOURCE: Review of *Honest Doubt,* by Amanda Cross. *Publishers Weekly* 247, no. 45 (6 November 2000): 74.

[*In the following review, the critic asserts that the plot in* Honest Doubt *draws from many autobiographical elements of Heilbrun's own life.*]

In her 13th Kate Fansler novel (after ***The Puzzled Heart***), Cross lets her mask of pseudonymity slip [in ***Honest Doubt***], building her plot and characters out of the myriad impressions of vicious, small-minded academic infighting she has amassed as the real-life Carolyn C. Heilbrun, Columbia University humanities prof and past president of the Modern Language Association. Introducing a new investigator, heavy, mid-30ish, motorcycle riding PI Estelle "Woody" Woodhaven, Cross pulls Fansler onto the sidelines to serve as charming adviser in a murder case set at insular, fictitious Clifton College in New Jersey. When Charles Haycock, a reactionary Tennyson scholar, drops dead at a Christmas party, poisoned via an overdose of heart medicine placed in his private bottle of Greek retsina, Woody is hired by Clifton's English department to find the killer. Soon she turns to Fansler in despair at academicians' double-talk. In a gentle, courtly style that rubs off awkwardly on the much-younger Woody, college professor Fansler shares her rueful insights into the bias and petty tyrannical oldboying that has mired contemporary academia in irrelevance and mediocrity. As wry and charming as Fansler is, however, Woody's exasperation soon rubs off on the reader. Virtually all the characters Woody interviews end up spouting off about what a dull and noxious little bog Clifton College is. All agree that the dead man was so sexist and such a nut that the world is better off without him. Alas, the redoubtable Cross has produced a kind of mystery emeritus, a meandering reflection on a kind of cultural crime that cannot be satisfyingly solved.

Daphne Merkin (review date November-December 2001)

SOURCE: Merkin, Daphne. "A Fantasy of Empowerment." *New Leader* 84, no. 6 (November-December 2001): 43-5.

[*In the following review of* When Men Were the Only Models We Had, *Merkin praises the work's scholarship, commenting that Heilbrun "affords us an inside look at the conflicted and not always straightforward route she took in carving out a piece of intellectual turf to call her own."*]

Since the beginning of post-Gutenbergian time, when the first young woman with a writerly gleam in her eye looked up from her loom and gazed pensively into space instead of attending to her weaving, it has been hard for both men and women to reconcile intellectual aspirations with the demands of domesticity—not to mention the perceived imperatives of femininity. Yeats may have famously ruminated on the inherent conflict between ordinary preoccupations and the single-mindedness of an artistic calling in his poem "The Choice"—"The intellect of man is forced to choose / Perfection of the life, or of the work"—but until fairly recently this was presumed to afflict mainly those of the male persuasion. There can be little doubt that historical role models for socially well-adapted brainy women have ever been in short supply, as opposed to the many cautionary instances of lonely bluestocking or alcoholic poetess types.

I can remember as a graduate student in the English Department at Columbia University nervously imagining myself growing old and gray and brittle among the stacks, and the gratitude I felt when I came upon the example of Madame de Staël's lively literary salons or George Eliot's unconventional, late-blooming love life. But then again these women struck me as the more remarkable for managing to have it all, even from the vantage point of the liberated '80s. In Clare Boothe Luce's famously bitchy play, *The Women,* currently enjoying a revival on Broadway, some of the more cutting (and less dated) remarks are at the expense of women whose fate it is to be thought clever—made by one of their own, a successful but loveless lady novelist. Far better, we in the audience are left to infer, to be a woman saddled with a head filled with straw.

How much have things changed for our daughters in the postfeminist world we live in? Are the preponderance of young girls still socialized the way they have traditionally been—that is, say, safer to be cute than smart? (Certainly one night of watching *Dawson's Creek* or Britney Spears' new video "I'm a Slave for U" with my 12-year-old daughter would convince anyone that popular culture is sending out its same old constricting and sexually segregated message: She who gets the boy wins. End of story.) These are but a few of the questions that came to mind while reading Carolyn G. Heilbrun's *When Men Were the Only Models We Had: My Teachers Barzun, Fadiman, Trilling.*

Heilbrun taught in the English Department at Columbia for more than three decades and has written, among other books, *Toward a Recognition of Androgyny* and *Writing a Woman's Life*; she is also the author of a best-selling series of detective novels under the pen name Amanda Cross. Her new work is a meditation on professional mentorship—or, more properly, a signal lack of mentorship—and how it came to be that a young woman in otherwise admirable possession of her senses found herself stuck in a holding pattern, first as a graduate student and then a professor of literature in search of an academic "father" who was nowhere to be found.

The book opens like a fairy tale to be read aloud at bedtime, an improbable yet captivating story from long ago and far away: "Once upon a time there were three men who exemplified, without knowing it, my ideal life. All of them became famous as writers, influential thinkers and public figures. Their names are Clifton Fadiman, Lionel Trilling and Jacques Barzun. . . . Although one of them never knew of my existence, the second ignored it, and the third treated me with formal kindness, without them I would have had no concrete model in my youth of what I wanted to become. Indeed, until I was past 40 they remained my guides. It is hardly too much to say they were my motivation, my inspiration, my fantasy."

Those words would be of interest coming from any woman whose level of accomplishment would seem to suggest that she considered herself the equal of any man. But they are particularly striking coming from Heilbrun, who early on embraced the antipatriarchal ideology of the emerging women's movement and made her mark as a critic with a keen nose for the stratagems and subversions of gender.

In *Writing a Woman's Life*, Heilbrun wrote perceptively about the obstacles strewn in the path of a woman who wishes to inhabit diverse and often equally demanding roles without giving short shrift to any. And she pointed to the delicate marital balance achieved by Leonard and Virginia Woolf as one worth emulating: "Despite all the criticism that Woolf scholars in America have leveled against Leonard, and the scorn that Woolf critics in England have leveled against them both for their social position and class, these two had a revolutionary marriage, which I would define simply as one in which both partners have work at the center of their lives. . . ." Given the sorts of authoritative judgments she has become known for, it is all the more to Heilbrun's credit that she affords us an inside look at the conflicted and not always straight-forward route she took in carving out a piece of intellectual turf to call her own.

Heilbrun was a Columbia graduate student during the '50s, when men ruled the academic roost. ("No books by women," she observes, "were studied in the honors courses.") Already married, she was, as she tells it, "merely putting my toe in," not intending to go further than a master's. But Lionel Trilling's lectures, tracing the innately double-edged nature of human desires through novels like Henry James' *Princess Casamassima,* convinced her to go on to doctoral studies: "He spoke as a prophet—no less dramatic a word will suffice. He made acceptable what we believed, but had thought improper to believe."

It was in a graduate seminar co-taught by Trilling and the historian Jacques Barzun, who were close friends as well as colleagues, that Heilbrun learned how to write "readable, clear, elegant prose" and discovered the passion for "the life of the mind" that fueled her own desire to enter the field. Both professors were attentive and hard-working; each annotated Heilbrun's paper "as no other paper I wrote in graduate school was ever marked, perhaps ever read. The respect they showed for us," she writes, "was invigorating, and full of the promise of what an academic life might afford."

Significantly, that "promise" was conveyed even though Trilling and Barzun deigned to include only one novel by a woman—Charlotte Brontë's *Jane Eyre*—in their seminar. It undoubtedly helped that the two men were constitutionally courteous, if a bit remote—the one described as "distant and disdainful," the other as "distant" and "cool." Heilbrun went on to pave a lifelong friendship with Barzun But it is Trilling—"self-enclosed" in his aloofness and essentially inhospitable to intellectual ambition in women—who really makes the blood rush to her cheeks, notwithstanding (or perhaps because of) his ungenerous views.

The genteelly-mannered author of *The Liberal Imagination* had "no use for Virginia Woolf" and thought women in fiction, in contrast to male characters, "seldom exist . . . as genuine moral destinies." Nor does Heilbrun overlook the fact that although Trilling was famous for cultivating disciples (who worshiped his every word, and would continue to do so after his death), there were no female students among them. She readily concedes that Trilling's lofty conception of engaged yet dispassionate scholarship offered scant hope to women aspirants: "Never once in anything he said did Trilling admit women to the fellowship of learning. Men were what it was all about, men struggling for some assurance—these were the actors in Trilling's drama."

Still, whatever his flaws, Trilling was the male presence who inspired Heilbrun as none other and who remained forever out of grasp. He is, in a manner of speaking, the Boy That Got Away, not as a sexual object so much as an idealized (i.e. older and wiser) alter ego, a kindred spirit with whom she shared certain cultural values, an appreciation of the uses of the double negative, and a psychological outlook based on an acceptance of the ubiquity of ambivalence. (She quotes Trilling's charming and profound rejoinder to Richard Sennett's accusation, as reported by Sennett in the *New Yorker*, that he was too much of an equivocator—"always in between" positions. "Between," Trilling replied, "is the only place to be.")

The chapters Heilbrun devotes to Clifton Fadiman—whom she encountered only in his writings and through his radio show, *Information Please*—are, for me, the least persuasive. In part this is because he does not quite fit into the book's larger trajectory, and in part because the thinking in these sections feels less shaped by personal reflection and more pressed into the service of a post facto feminist agenda.

Heilbrun first came upon the *New Yorker* critic and longtime Book-of-the-Month Club judge when, as a 15-year-old, she disagreed with his scornful assessment of Jane Austen ("Even before graduate school, I knew that Jane Austen was in no way genteel"). But she attributes her youthful appreciation of James to a volume of his stories that Fadiman published in 1945. "I thought then," she writes, "and I still think, that this was . . . a remarkably advanced and incisive introduction to the Master." She goes on to recount how her initial enthusiasm for Fadiman faded over the years as she realized that he exhibited a casual yet consistent misogyny in his reviews of writing by women. He is included as one of Heilbrun's "three musketeers," I suppose, because he, like Trilling and Barzun, was an unwitting influence, and because his career incarnated one of her ideals, holding out the possibility of writing high-level criticism aimed at "the nonacademic intelligent reader."

As perhaps befits a work by a woman who looked in vain for a male mentor, the true hero of **When Men Were the Only Models We Had** is a heroine, and a somewhat surprising one at that: the writer Diana Trilling, Lionel's formidable wife, to whom posthumous tribute is offered. She had discounted Diana as a figure of stature for much of her lifetime, both on the basis of her ferocious, harridan-like reputation—"all I heard of her left the impression that she was carping, demanding, exacting, unworthy of Lionel"—and a disgusted perusal of Diana's *Claremont Essays,* published in 1964.

Heilbrun belatedly discovers an unsuspected affinity with her when she is asked to review Diana's portrait of her marriage to Trilling, *The Beginning of the Journey*. Impressed by Diana's ability to empathize with people very different from herself, and with her willingness—"unlike anyone else in her circle, from Lionel to Hannah Arendt"—to reconsider her views, Heilbrun goes back and re-reads Diana's earlier books in the light of her new appreciation of Diana's own struggles to establish herself as an intellectual presence while still accepting her "wifely role." While at pains to keep her distance from some of Diana's opinions—notably on feminism and McCarthyism—Heilbrun ends up respecting her for her willingness to "allow the truth about women's lives to enter into her writing."

When Men Were the Only Models is full of wonderful insights and revealing anecdotes, yet what sets it apart from other "look back in mellowness" narratives is the author's tone of almost inadvertent honesty. Without ever addressing directly the issue of how she herself navigated the academic status quo, Heilbrun drops enough clues for the reader to form an impression that her strategies for implementing her own ambition included a hefty dose of surface compliance with "male rule." Hers was the way of a good girl with a hankering for subversion, rather than of an out-and-out rebel.

Heilbrun demonstrates throughout a disconcerting ability to go along with the intellectual fashions of the times until it was safe to do otherwise. Although she was, by her own account, quietly ahead of the curve in her convictions about Virginia Woolf's literary greatness, she kept these feelings to herself as late as 1964, when she admitted having been captivated by Woolf's writings "in secret." One wonders whether she would have discovered Diana Trilling a bit sooner had she not adopted the habit of conformity.

Finally, though, what makes Heilbrun's account so moving is the unrequited romance that informs it. Her book is a love story of sorts, more Jamesian even than anything Henry James could have written, about a woman living in a chronic state of longing for the affirming male glance that never comes. Even now, as a woman in her 70s looking back with a mixture of incredulity and fondness at the misogynistic attitudes she was willing to swallow in her younger days, and professing to a "disenchantment" with Lionel Trilling, Heilbrun is still capable of describing his effect on her as a graduate student in near-rapturous terms: "Trilling's lectures," she writes, "seemed to hold the key to salvation, and salvation, for me as for him, is what I hoped to find in literature. . . ."

Hers is a fantasy of intellectual empowerment that will strike a chord with many readers—never to be fully renounced so much as permanently suspended in imaginative recall: "Like the perfection of the man one did not marry," Heilbrun writes toward the end of her book, "of the life one did not choose, of the child one did not have, the dream remains unchallenged by reality."

Jeffrey Hart (review date January 2002)

SOURCE: Hart, Jeffrey. "A Lost Lady." *New Criterion* 20, no. 5 (January 2002): 65-8.

[*In the following review of* When Men Were the Only Models We Had, *Hart provides a scathing indictment of Heilbrun's book, asserting that 'we witness the melancholy sight of a mind in ideologically induced disintegration.'*]

This is an extraordinary book [**When Men Were the Only Models We Had**], I am relieved to say. If Mr. Kurtz had kicked free of the earth, as Conrad wrote, the Columbia English professor Carolyn Heilbrun has kicked free at least from common sense and immensely shared human experience. The "woman's movement," she tells us, struck her as an overwhelming and liberating development. She appears here to be interested in absolutely nothing except the situation of women as she sees it. I called this book extraordinary, not intending that as a celebration. If the emotions and ideas that inform it came to prevail generally, life would not be worth living.

When you know that she has written a book on androgyny, you understand that we are in serious trouble. In 1997 she published **The Last Gift of Time: Life beyond Sixty.** She reflected on turning sixty, not wearing clothes that are distinctively female, and gaining a lot of weight as if deliberately to destroy whatever attractiveness she might have had. The age sixty moment causes her to consider committing suicide, though these days sixty is hardly the end of the line. You would think she had just turned ninety instead of sixty. It is entirely plausible, on the evidence of this book, that for Heilbrun life itself has lost its savor. Her emotions have been so wrenched out of shape by feminist dogma that she cannot present to the readers of her books a recognizable shared world.

Heilbrun has been married and is a mother, but she is awfully sour on marriage. In **When Men Were the Only Models We Had,** she observes that

> Unrealistic fantasy explains why so many novels in the past ended with wedding bells. The marriage did not have to be endured by readers, only by the participants, and then it was not to be overseen. Hope was all that mattered, that and the experience, *at least in novels* [italics added], of "being in love."

That first sentence says that a happy marriage is an "unrealistic fantasy." This amounts to moral and intellectual treason against an enormous amount of actual human experience. Her use of the synecdoche "wedding bells" has a sneering quality. The next sentence says that marriage is something to be "endured." Sometimes, maybe. But you can move out. She knows that the woman is the victim in marriage. The third sentence says that "being in love" is an experience that happens "in novels," whereas in the actual world it is one of the most overwhelming of human experiences. She sneeringly encloses the phrase "being in love" within quotation marks, as if it were a fiction or an illusion. I suppose for her androgyny is a superior condition. Planet Earth calling Carolyn Heilbrun: Romeo and Juliet are angry. (You would also gather from these sentences that novels do not, or seldom at least, depict unfortunate marriages. If that is what is implied, the notion is preposterous. Start with *Middlemarch*.)

Evident in this book are the destructive forces that have divided the once-powerful Columbia English Department into bitter and dysfunctional factions. She herself acknowledges the bitterness within the department. In fact, Columbia has had to bring in Professor Jonathan Arac from the University of Pittsburgh to serve as chairman and try to patch things back together. The hope is that Arac can talk with people who refuse to talk with each other. I gather that this is a first in the history of the American university. But the feuding Columbia professors have been unable to agree on appointments, promotions, requirements, and so forth because of ideological furies. Professor Edward Said, himself a fanatic in his own right, has been driven to ask his colleagues to calm down and start teaching literature again. Fat chance.

For decades, the freshman Humanities I-II course has been the jewel of Columbia's undergraduate liberal arts education. Students and alumni have almost unanimously testified to its value. I myself taught it for six years (1956-62). It begins with the *Iliad* in the Fall of Freshman year and travels through established classics and selections from the Old and New Testaments, ending with an important novel—when I taught it, *Crime and Punishment*. The faculty teaching the course met for lunch once a week at the Faculty Club on Morningside Drive to exchange ideas. These were often brilliant occasions.

Sourpuss will have none of that. She writes:

> When I, however, joined the Columbia faculty, as a woman I was not allowed to teach the so-called honors courses in the college, though I longed to. I cannot resist noting here that decades later, it afforded me much amusement when the young women now teaching the honors courses, Contemporary Civilization and Humanities (CC and LIT-HUM, as they were dubbed), hated almost every minute of it, evidence of the sharp change in the department since the days when those honors courses had been revered.

The expression "sharp change" is a risible understatement. The Humanities I-II course was justly revered, I might add. I am skeptical about Heilbrun's statement that she was not assigned a section of that course because she is a woman. Professor Marjorie Hope Nicolson, a major eminence, was chairman of the graduate English Department.

There are many reasons for not assigning a particular individual to Humanities I-II. Reading this book, I am certain Heilbrun's classroom discussion would have been a destructive travesty. The sentences I have just quoted drip with resentment and venom. "So-called" honors courses? In fact they *were* called honors courses, part of a core curriculum. And how about those "young women" who "hated almost every minute" of teaching Homer, Plato, Exodus, Job, Sophocles, Thucydides, Dante, Shakespeare, Voltaire, Molière, Goethe, Dostoyevsky? Who were these "young women"? Clearly, they were unsuited to be professors of literature, since they "hated" teaching some of the best things ever written. They surely belonged in the Department of Abnormal Psychology, not as teachers, to be sure, but as objects for scientific study.

What pathology blinded them to the best that has been thought and said and split the Columbia English Department? Pretty clearly, they were radical feminists who were bored by great literature, "hated" it even, and instead wanted to teach their gripes. Harold Bloom has called this faction the "party of resentment." To permit one of these vipers into an academic department of literature was an act of tragic folly.

Heilbrun has here a nasty little chapter entitled "From WASPS and Dryden to Jews and Freud." I note her treatment of Mark Van Doren, one of the great classroom teachers in the history of Columbia College. I took his course called "The Narrative Art," one of the most profound and thoughtful courses offered: Homer, the Bible, Dante, Cervantes, Kafka. His books *The Noble Voice* (on epics) and *Shakespeare* are still powerful, vital critical efforts. His first major work, *John Dryden*, remains the best book on Dryden, and was reviewed with great admiration in the *Times Literary Supplement* by none other than T. S. Eliot. Not bad for a Ph.D. dissertation.

Heilbrun seems to think that Mark Van Doren became a star at Columbia because he had the right WASP background and connections. This is reductive nonsense. Probably he did have such connections. His brother Carl was in the History Department. But his M.A. thesis on Thoreau had been published and without a doubt he deserved his appointment and his eminence because of merit.

Heilbrun seems to have an irresistible desire to turn herself into an intellectual disaster area. She writes: "I . . . sat in on Van Doren's Shakespeare's lectures and can remember nothing at all except a general ambiance of pleasantness." This is but one of her many epiphanies of disgraceful self-revelation. Van Doren's lectures on Shakespeare were luminous. Hers was a mind losing active cerebral cells.

The arch-villain of this book, absurdly enough, is Lionel Trilling. (He was already the model for a murderer in her 1970 mystery novel *Poetic Justice,* written under the pen name Amanda Cross.) Two other figures, Clifton Fadiman and Jacques Barzun, make cameo appearances. She never met Fadiman, but admired his relaxed prose style, and he is marginally in this book because Heilbrun thinks he undervalued writers who were women. I judge that Fadiman is here as stuffing, to make a book out of her attack on Lionel Trilling. She has nothing but praise for Jacques Barzun, and he did, according to her, respect the possibility of achievement for women. But his impeccable politeness was to her a distancing wall. Life sometimes is really hard. Her multitude of gripes and whines soon becomes Marie Antoinettish.

Her main gripe here, among a cavalcade of somewhat lesser gripes, is that Trilling and Barzun were not familiar enough with her, either as a graduate student or as a colleague. "They knew each other well; me they scarcely knew at all." She did not seek intimacy in a sexual sense. She wanted informality, exchanges of ideas, appreciation, and she met with formal manners, she thinks, of course, because she is a woman. She was excluded from their "club" as she puts it.

Now I had a somewhat parallel career to Heilbrun's at Columbia. I took the famous Barzun-Trilling seminar, as she did, while a graduate student and a member of the English Department. I knew Barzun and Trilling, but they were thirty years older than I, had gone to

Columbia together as young men, and had been friends for decades. Social intimacy such as Heilbrun desired was out of the question. Exchanging jokes, let along personal revelations, was not something desired. These older men, formal but also relaxed, were friendly and interested. Still, such comradeship as she wanted would have falsified our relative positions Unlike the needy Heilbrun, I experienced their formality as a form of honesty.

Trilling did not mix with the younger professors over cocktails, though he did have me and others to the Trilling apartment for drinks and talk, sometimes dinner. He engaged me to give his son Jim tennis lessons. I had Lionel and Diana to dinner at the West Side Tennis Club. I remember that on one occasion at the Trillings' apartment I spotted a large cockroach running around and said "Gregor." Lionel said "No one throw an apple," but Diana was furious, saying we should not joke about the great Kafka. But despite such fun he was still Lionel Trilling, and I was still only trying for importance and achievement.

Barzun and Trilling, professionally speaking, were immensely powerful. I had little power. It would have been absurd for them to treat me as if I were thirty years older than I was, as if my meager achievement were somehow comparable to theirs. Formality is a good way to recognize the disparities of power. It is more authentic than some sort of false "intimacy." You don't slap the President of the United States on the back.

About Trilling's literary criticism Heilbrun is now to a considerable degree dismissive. In the real world, Trilling at his best ranks among the great literary critics who have written English. Heilbrun does not admire his somewhat mandarin prose style, a mixture of the Oxford style of Newman and Arnold plus something of the distinction-making delicacy of Henry James. She prefers Fadiman. But at its best Trilling's prose is an inspired instrument.

She thinks, with some reason, that he considers men more important than women in a power sense. Surely that was a product of his time and place. I myself think his *Liberal Imagination* is a mixture of great essays and potboilers to fill out a book. It is remarkable that he can write about Dreiser without acknowledging the greatness of *Sister Carrie* and *An American Tragedy*. And his defence of Mark Twain's ending to *Huckleberry Finn* strikes me as silly. As Heilbrun says, graduate students today do not pay much attention to him, but that is their loss. Does any civilized person care much about Paul de Man or Jacques Derrida? Flies of a summer.

Heilbrun records that when she was a graduate student Trilling advised her to drop her monocular feminist obsession. That was excellent advice. In this book we witness the melancholy sight of a mind in ideologically induced disintegration. Her mental lens is befogged. She has lost the ability to see the object as in itself it actually is, certainly the preliminary to reasonable discourse. She is a tragedy that has happened, unless, in a tough-minded way, you may regard her as a comedy without laughter. She is besotted by feminism. Trilling also supported her for tenure at Columbia. He must have been tired or intimidated. To use a term he liked and she would hate, it would have been "manly" to send her packing.

FURTHER READING

Criticism

Gerrard, Nicci. "Who Cares Whodunnit?" *New Statesman and Society* 3, no. 88 (16 February 1990): 38.

Gerrard praises *A Trap for Fools,* noting that the work "possesses amiability and zest."

Grumman, Joan. Review of *The Representation of Women in Fiction,* edited by Carolyn Heilbrun and Margaret T. Higonnet. *Modern Fiction Studies* 30, no. 2 (summer 1984): 425-28.

Grumman argues that *The Representation of Women in Fiction* successfully illustrates the progress of women's literary studies.

Manos, Nikki Lee. "Heilbrun's Apologia." *Belles Lettres* 6, no. 3 (spring 1991): 23.

Manos maintains that in *Hamlet's Mother and Other Essays* Heilbrun writes clearly and elegantly, which, she asserts, should prompt others to explore and celebrate women's writing.

McCarthy, Abigail. "Alternate Destinies and Imagined Identities." *Washington Post Book World* 18, no. 45 (6 November 1988): 5-6.

McCarthy states that the primary aim of *Writing a Woman's Life* is to "help by examining women's lives anew and suggesting new ways they might be written."

Mesic, Penelope. "Steinem's Lives: Exploring the Growth of a Celebrated Feminist." *Chicago Tribune Books* (8 October 1995): 3, 5.

Mesic lauds Heilbrun's complex portrait of Gloria Steinem in *The Education of a Woman.*

Review of *Edge of Doom,* by Amanda Cross. *Publishers Weekly* 249, no. 39 (30 September 2002): 53.

The critic praises *Edge of Doom*'s "literary wit and classy conversation," but laments the novel's lack of action and plot detail.

White, Jean M. "Mysteries." *Washington Post Book World* 14, no. 25 (17 June 1984): 6.

White provides an unfavorable assessment of *Sweet Death, Kind Death.*

Additional coverage of Heilbrun's life and career is contained in the following sources published by the Gale Group: *Beacham's Encyclopedia of Popular Fiction: Biography and Resources,* **Vol. 1;** *Contemporary Authors,* **Vols. 45-48;** *Contemporary Authors New Revision Series,* **Vols. 1, 28, 58, 94;** *Contemporary Literary Criticism,* **Vol. 25;** *Contemporary Popular Writers; Feminist Writers; Literature Resource Center; Mystery and Suspense Writers;* **and** *St. James Guide to Crime & Mystery Writers.*

The Bluest Eye

Toni Morrison

(Born Chloe Anthony Wofford) American novelist, nonfiction writer, essayist, playwright, and children's writer.

The following entry presents criticism on Morrison's novel *The Bluest Eye* (1970) through 2000. For further information on her life and complete works, see *CLC*, Volumes 4, 10, 22, 55, 81, and 87.

INTRODUCTION

Morrison's first novel, *The Bluest Eye,* examines the tragic effects of imposing white, middle-class American ideals of beauty on the developing female identity of a young African American girl during the early 1940s. Inspired by a conversation Morrison once had with an elementary school classmate who wished for blue eyes, the novel poignantly shows the psychological devastation of a young black girl, Pecola Breedlove, who searches for love and acceptance in a world that denies and devalues people of her own race. As her mental state slowly unravels, Pecola hopelessly longs to possess the conventional American standards of feminine beauty—namely, white skin, blonde hair, and blue eyes—as presented to her by the popular icons and traditions of white culture. Written as a fragmented narrative from multiple perspectives and with significant typographical deviations, *The Bluest Eye* juxtaposes passages from the Dick-and-Jane grammar school primer with memories and stories of Pecola's life alternately told in retrospect by one of Pecola's now-grown childhood friends and by an omniscient narrator. Published in the midst of the Black Arts movement that flourished during the late 1960s and early 1970s, *The Bluest Eye* has attracted considerable attention from literary critics—though not to the same degree as Morrison's later works. With its sensitive portrait of African American female identity and its astute critique of the internalized racism bred by American cultural definitions of beauty, *The Bluest Eye* has been widely seen as a literary watershed, inspiring a proliferation of literature written by African American women about their identity and experience as women of color.

PLOT AND MAJOR CHARACTERS

Ignoring strict narrative chronology, *The Bluest Eye* opens with three excerpts from the common 1940s

American elementary school primer that features the All-American, white family of Mother, Father, Dick, and Jane. The first excerpt is a faithful reproduction, the second lacks all capitalization and punctuation marks, and the third dissolves into linguistic chaos by abandoning its spacing and alignment. This section is interrupted by an italicized fragment representing the memories of Claudia MacTeer, the principal narrator of *The Bluest Eye.* As an adult, Claudia recalls incidents from late 1941 when she was nine years old living in Lorain, Ohio, with her poor but loving parents and her ten-year-old sister, Frieda. Claudia's friend, Pecola Breedlove, is an emotionally impaired African American girl who comes from a broken home. The rest of *The Bluest Eye* divides into four separate time sequences, each named for a season of the year and each narrated by Claudia. Interspersed throughout the text are fragments in the voice of an omniscient narrator that discuss Pecola's obsessive desire for blue eyes and her parents,

Pauline and Cholly; each fragment is introduced with different lines from the Dick-and-Jane primer. In "Autumn," Claudia begins her narrative as the MacTeers take in a boarder, Mr. Henry Washington. At the same time, Pecola comes to live with the MacTeer family after Cholly burns down his family's house. Recounting their typical girlhood adventures, Claudia particularly remembers the onset of Pecola's first menses. The omniscient narrator intermittently interrupts with descriptions of the Breedlove's household, noting how the parents are unable to hide the violence of their relationship in the presence of Pecola and her brother Sammy. In the midst of the hostilities, Pecola constantly prays for blue eyes, believing that if she only had blue eyes, life would be better. In "Winter," Claudia recalls the arrival at school of Maureen Peale, a lighter-skinned, wealthy black girl with green eyes whom the girls both hate and admire. When a group of boys harasses Pecola, Maureen temporarily befriends Pecola, but eventually turns on her, calling the darker-skinned and deeply hurt Pecola "ugly." The omniscient narrator again interrupts and describes an incident involving Pecola and Geraldine, a socially mobile middle-class African American woman who loves her blue-eyed cat more than she loves her own son, Louis Junior. When Pecola is wrongly blamed for the cat's death, Geraldine quietly calls her a "nasty little black bitch." Claudia opens the "Spring" sequence of *The Bluest Eye* with disparate memories about Henry Washington fondling Frieda's breasts, his subsequent beating and eviction by Mr. MacTeer, and a visit to Pecola's apartment. The omniscient narrator's descriptions of Pauline and Cholly's history predominate the rest of this section. The narrator relates events from Pauline's early life, her marriage, and how she became a maid for an affluent, white family. The narrator next recounts Cholly's traumatic childhood and adolescence. Abandoned almost at birth, he is rescued by his beloved Aunt Jimmy, who later dies when he is sixteen. After her burial, Cholly is humiliated by two white hunters who interrupt his first sexual encounter with a girl named Darlene. He flees to Macon, Georgia, in search of his father who is miserably mean and wants nothing to do with his son. Crushed by this encounter, Cholly eventually meets and marries Pauline and fathers her children. Years later, in Lorain, a drunken Cholly staggers into his kitchen, and overcome with lust, brutally rapes and impregnates Pecola. "Spring" concludes with a story about Soaphead Church, a self-proclaimed psychic and mystic, who counsels an unattractive black girl who wishes she had blue eyes. In "Summer," Claudia resumes her narration, recalling how the gossip spreads regarding Pecola being pregnant with Cholly's baby. Near the end of the novel, Pecola finally narrates a story about her conversation with an imaginary companion concerning her new blue eyes and whether they are "the bluest eyes" in the world. In the last section of *The Bluest Eye* Claudia remembers meeting Pecola after Cholly's baby is delivered stillborn and accounts for the whereabouts of Sammy, Cholly, and Pauline.

MAJOR THEMES

In *The Bluest Eye,* the opening excerpt from the Dick-and-Jane primer juxtaposed with the experiences of African American characters immediately sets the tone for Morrison's examination of a young black girl's growing self-hatred: American society tells Pecola happy, white, middle-class families are better than hopeless, black, working-class families. Victimized in different degrees by media messages—from movies and books to advertising and merchandise—that degrade their appearance, nearly every black character in the novel—both male and female—internalizes a desire for the white cultural standard of beauty. This desire is especially strong in Pecola, who believes that blue eyes will make her beautiful and lovable. At the same time, every African American character hates in various degrees anything associated with their own race, blindly accepting the media-sponsored belief that they are ugly and unlovable, particularly in the appalling absence of black cultural standards of beauty. In a sense, Pecola becomes the African American community's scapegoat for its own fears and feelings of unworthiness. Unlike Claudia, who possesses the love of her family, Pecola has learned from her appearance-conscious parents to devalue herself. She endures rejection by others who also value "appearances" and who ultimately share the same symptoms that characterize Pecola's insanity. Besides exposing the inherent racism of the American standard of beauty, *The Bluest Eye* also examines child abuse in terms of the violence that some African American parents subconsciously inflict on their children by forcing them to weigh their self-worth against white cultural standards. Cholly's rape of Pecola in effect culminates the psychological, social, and personal depreciation by white society that has raped Cholly his entire life. As his surname implies, Cholly can only breed, not love, and his brutal act against his daughter produces a child who cannot live. Finally, Pecola's longing for blue eyes speaks to the connection between how one is seen and how one sees. Pecola believes that if she had beautiful eyes, people would not be able to torment her mind or body. Her wish for blue eyes rather than lighter skin transcends racism, with its suggestion that Pecola wants to see things differently as much as to be seen differently, but the price for Pecola's wish ultimately is her sanity, as she loses sight of both herself and the world she inhabits.

CRITICAL RECEPTION

Regarded by modern literary critics as perhaps one of the first contemporary female bildungsroman, or coming-of-age narratives, *The Bluest Eye* initially received modest reviews upon its publication in 1970. Commentators later claimed that they neglected the work because Morrison was unknown at the time. Since then, however, *The Bluest Eye* has become a classroom staple, and scholarship on the novel has flourished from a number of perspectives. A recurring discussion has focused on the novel's ability to replicate African American vernacular patterns and musical rhythms. Many critics have approached the novel in the context of the rise of African American writers, assigning significance to their revision of American history with their own cultural materials and folk traditions. Others have considered the ways *The Bluest Eye* alludes to earlier black writings in order to express the traditionally silenced female point of view and uses conventional grotesque imagery as a vehicle for social protest. Scholars also have been attracted to *The Bluest Eye* by its deconstruction of "whiteness" along racial, gender, and economic lines, while feminists have equated the violence of the narrative with self-hatred wrought by a wide range of illusions about white American society and African American women's place in it. In addition, some have examined the influence of environment on the novel's characters, identifying stylistic affinities with literary naturalism. Others have offered Marxist interpretations of the novel's formal aspects in terms of the ideological content of its representation of African American life. Acknowledging Morrison's achievement in the novel, critics have generally acclaimed *The Bluest Eye* for deconstructing a number of literary taboos with its honest portrayals of American girlhood, its frank descriptions of intraracial racism or "colorism" in the African American community, and its thoughtful treatment of the emotional precocity of prepubescent girls.

PRINCIPAL WORKS

The Bluest Eye (novel) 1970
Sula (novel) 1973
The Black Book [editor] (nonfiction) 1974
Song of Solomon (novel) 1977
Tar Baby (novel) 1981
Dreaming Emmett (play) 1986
Beloved (novel) 1987
Jazz (novel) 1992
Playing in the Dark: Whiteness and the Literary Imagination (essays) 1992
Rac-ing Justice, En-gendering Power: Essays on Anita Hill, Clarence Thomas and the Construction of Social Reality [editor and author of introduction] (essays) 1992
*The Dancing Mind (speech) 1997
Paradise (novel) 1998
The Big Box [with Slade Morrison; illustrations by Giselle Potter] (juvenilia) 1999
I See You, I See Myself: The Young Life of Jacob Lawrence [with Deba Foxley Leach, Suzanne Wright, and Deborah J. Leach] (juvenilia) 2001
Book of Mean People [with Slade Morrison; illustrations by Pascal Lemaître] (juvenilia) 2002

*This work contains the text of Morrison's 1996 acceptance speech for the National Book Foundation Medal for Distinguished Contribution to American Letters.

CRITICISM

Keith E. Byerman (essay date June 1982)

SOURCE: Byerman, Keith E. "Intense Behaviors: The Use of the Grotesque in *The Bluest Eye* and *Eva's Man*." *CLA Journal* 25, no. 4 (June 1982): 447-57.

[*In the following essay, Byerman compares the use of grotesque literary conventions in* The Bluest Eye *and Gayl Jones's* Eva's Man, *highlighting its suitability to African American literature as a vehicle for social protest.*]

At the end of Toni Morrison's *The Bluest Eye,* the little black girl Pecola, a victim of incest, is pictured talking to herself in a mirror about her imaginary blue eyes. At the end of *Eva's Man,* by Gayl Jones, Eva is describing, in increasing incomprehensible terms, her poisoning and castrating of the man with whom she lived. Both of these female characters are the central figures of the novels under discussion, and each is, in literary terms, a grotesque. But such figures are not being used by Morrison and Jones just to shock or entertain; rather, they use these bizarre characterizations to examine the even greater grotesqueries of American society. Pecola epitomizes the American obsession with whiteness, while Eva, in a slightly different way, exemplifies the society's fixation on sexual dominance. The novels develop, then, a grotesque within a grotesque and serve to show the particular appropriateness of the grotesque in black literature that is also social criticism.

The grotesque as a literary convention has two aspects that can be found in the fiction under discussion. Flannery O'Connor has described one of these by saying of grotesque characters: "They seem to carry an invisible burden; their fanaticism is a reproach, not merely an eccentricity."[1] Frederick J. Hoffman, in discussing the Gothic and grotesque in Southern writing, comments that "one thing is expectedly true: in a society where intensities of behavior are frequent, the 'gothic' is a kind of norm. . . . There are frightening and often puzzling details, which the reader finds difficult to fit into context, so he concludes that they are 'grotesque'. . . ."² As shall be seen, this social element is the most basic theme of the two novels. The supposed normalities of American life are shown to be absurd and ominous distortions.

The second aspect has to do with the reader's reactions to grotesque literature. The grotesque appeals to something in us that is pre-rational, that defies our intellectual categories. Unlike other writing that is concerned with the beautiful and the realistic, the grotesque is deliberately extravagant, distorted, violent, and ugly. We find it, nonetheless, strangely attractive as well as repulsive. Michael Steig has said that "the grotesque involves the arousing of anxiety by giving expression to infantile fears, fantasies and impulses. . . ."³

Such a reaction must be created by Jones and Morrison because the social elements they are talking about are themselves pre-rational. It is assumed by these writers that the reader shares the attitudes toward sexuality and race that they are criticizing. The moral visions of the novels can only be understood if these attitudes can be brought into question at the level at which they exist. Therefore, the incest, narcissism, murder, and castration of the books reach beneath the usual level of reader response to give a particular kind of shock of recognition.

In *The Bluest Eye* and *Eva's Man,* then, the social manifestations of the grotesque described by O'Conner and Hoffman are combined with the psychological ones mentioned by Steig. Morrison describes a social situation so distorted by the myth of whiteness that it produces a child, Pecola, who is so obsessed by the blue-eyed beauty of Shirley Temple that she creates a self-contained reality that cannot be penetrated even by rape and incest. Jones shows us a society so fixated on the domination of women that Eva can liberate herself only by biting off the penis of her lover. We as readers are forced to consider not only the absurdity of idolizing a blue-eyed child and protecting the sexual vanity of a preadolescent boy, but also the horror when these absurdities lead to murder, incest, and schizophrenia.

The world of *The Bluest Eye* is clearly one that has a distorted sense of color. All the blacks in the book feel insecure and even inferior because of their skin tone. The narrator says of Pecola's family, the Breedloves:

> It was as though some mysterious all-knowing master had given each one a cloak of ugliness to wear, and they had each accepted it without question. The master had said, "You are ugly people." They had looked about themselves and saw nothing to contradict the statement; saw, in fact, support for it leaning at them from every billboard, every movie, every glance. "Yes," they had said. "You are right." And they took the ugliness in their hands, threw it as a mantle over them, and went about the world with it.⁴

The significant point here is that such a burden is accepted without direct coercion. There are few white characters in the novel to impose the view. The ideological hegemony of whiteness is simply too overwhelming to be successfully resisted. No alternative source of valuation is provided for these characters. As a case in point, the narrator Claudia serves as a contrast to the Breedloves and especially to Pecola. Though much less passive and more aware of her black identity, Claudia, too, must eventually accommodate herself to the dominant view. When little, she has the disturbing habit of tearing apart the white dolls she is given as gifts. "But the dismemberment of dolls was not the true horror. The truly horrifying thing was the transference of the same impulses to little white girls. . . . To discover what eluded me: the secret of the magic they weaved on others" (p. 22). The magical secret points us toward the nonrational basis of the social belief. Claudia's bizarre response seems an almost reasonable treatment of this complex of ritual and superstition. She seeks understanding where only unthinking faith is tolerated. She changes, however:

> When I learned how repulsive this disinterested violence was, that it was repulsive because it was disinterested, my shame floundered about for a refuge. The best hiding place was love. Thus the conversion from pristine sadism to fabricated hatred, to fraudulent love. It was a small step to Shirley Temple. I learned much later to worship her, just as I learned to delight in cleanliness, knowing even as I learned, that the change was adjustment without improvement.
>
> (p. 22)

Claudia, the strongest character in the book, cannot defy the myth and is even made to feel guilty for her childhood doubts. Knowing full well that the myth is a lie, she must nonetheless bow before its idol.

Pecola, in sharp contrast, never has any uncertainties about the gospel according to Shirley. She is portrayed throughout as a true believer who wants only to be like her idol. Every scene in which she appears is used to demonstrate her lack of self-esteem and her passiveness in the face of this American dream. Whites, lighter-skinned blacks, and dark-skinned blacks who redirect their self-hatred, all make her feel her unworthiness. She responds by seeking out a presumed medium who, she believes, can provide her with the emblem of whiteness, blue eyes. In her last scene, she sits in her room talking to an imaginary friend about the precise intensity of the blueness, about whether she, in truth, now has America's bluest eye.

But this rather pathetic obsession is made horrifying when we realize that, during this time, Pecola has conceived and miscarried a baby as a result of rape by her father. This reality is only on the fringes of her consciousness, and we must depend on Claudia and an omniscient narrator to provide us with the details.

What we learn is that the father himself has been victimized, in terms of sexuality, by the same whiteness that destroyed his daughter. Abandoned by his father and mother, Cholly has had no opportunity to develop any self-esteem. What little might have existed was destroyed when his first attempt at lovemaking was interrupted by white men who ridiculed him. This assault on his being saps him of his manhood, both physically and psychologically. He turns his anger against himself and the black girl with him since there is nothing he can do to the men who caused the trauma. Such a feeling of powerlessness only reinforces his self-hatred.

His rage eventually turns into alcoholism and repeated conflict with his wife, who seems to him, simply by being his wife, to be a constant reminder of his ineffectiveness. He would love her, but because love imposes responsibility, he tries to hate her.

This same love-hate complex applies to his children. Moments before the incest, he sits watching Pecola:

> Guilt and impotence rose in a bilious duet. What could he do for her—ever? What give her? What say to her? What could a burned-out black man say to the hunched back of his eleven-year-old daughter? If he looked into her face, he would see those haunted, loving eyes. The hauntedness would irritate him—the love would move him to fury. How dare she love him? Hadn't she any sense at all?
>
> (p. 127)

Somehow he wants her to be responsible for the misery of his life. He expects her to reinforce his self-hatred by despising him. The fact that she loves him only intensifies his despair. Such a reaction is to be expected from what we know of him. But what follows is not. In the midst of this emotional confusion, he sees Pecola make a slight gesture that reminds him of her mother in better days. A surge of tenderness causes him to move nearer his child. This protective gesture then is confused by his hatred, and he sexually assaults her. When she becomes pregnant, he abandons the family.

Pecola's reaction is to substitute the sweet world of Shirley Temple for her own bitter one. She escapes, but we as readers cannot. We are left in a state of the grotesque. On the one hand, we are repulsed by Cholly's action and sympathetic to his victim. On the other, we have been made to see that he is himself a victim of the society that condemns him. Because we have been introduced to his way of thinking and suffering, we verge on understanding his action and sharing his confusion. Both of these responses, repulsion against the action and attraction to the actor, are mutually necessary for the grotesque to work in this scene.

Similarly, Pecola leaves us with an ambiguous feeling. We are sorry for her victimization, but we know that she has entered a realm where her suffering will seldom come into her consciousness. That realm is, for us, both silly and pathetic. At a deeper level, Claudia has captured the impact of this particular grotesqueness by pointing out the Christ-like nature of her friend:

> All of us—all who knew her—felt so wholesome after we cleaned ourselves on her. We were so beautiful when we stood astride her ugliness. Her simplicity decorated us, her guilt sanctified us, her pain made us glow with health, her awkwardness made us think we had a sense of humor. Her inarticulateness made us believe we were eloquent. Her poverty kept us generous. Even her waking dreams we used—to silence our own nightmares. And she let us, and thereby deserved our contempt. We honed our egos on her, padded our characters with her frailty, and yawned in the fantasy of our strength.
>
> (p. 159)

Pecola is a grotesque Messiah: she gives the world not grace but the illusion of relief from intolerable circumstances. She is sacrificed so that others may live with the perversions of society. She is a grotesque within a grotesque. She is unquestionably mad, but where in *The Bluest Eye* is there any sanity?

In *Eva's Man,* the madness of the central character is also readily apparent; but, significantly, the effect is to create an optimistic ending. Eva's act, though violent, is a way of resisting the oppression she has had to suffer. If Pecola is a suffering Christ, Eva is an avenging angel. Her crime is a symbolic liberation from the particular grotesqueness of her society.

The burden of color in *The Bluest Eye* becomes the curse of sexuality in *Eva's Man.* Domination in this book is exercised by men, of whatever color. Women are the ones who are victimized. Virtually every woman in the novel suffers some attack on her integrity. Just as Pecola was educated in color inferiority, so Eva goes through a long training in sexual politics. Every aspect of her society—family, folklore, friendships, marriage—is presented as infused with sexuality. Eva can no more escape the omnipresent phallus than Pecola could the ubiquitous blue eyes.

The family in this case seems almost normal. The mother is concerned that her daughter learn's proper social behavior, including the protection of her virtue. The father is a strong, authoritative figure who seems to deserve the respect he receives from Eva. But this situation is complicated by the presence of two other characters, Miss Billie and Tyrone. Miss Billie is the mother's closest friend, but her conversations are always related to the sexual aggressiveness of the men in the neighborhood. Thus the mother's teaching about chastity is complemented and contradicted by a sex education that demystifies and yet encourages sexuality. The primary lesson learned by Eva is that men are obsessed with sex.

Little in the book refutes this assertion. Tyrone is the mother's friend, though Eva, who narrates, can find no evidence of promiscuity. But Tyrone's attitude toward the child Eva is different. He finds her attractive, and despite her youth, he repeatedly attempts to seduce her.

This activity ends only when the father discovers what he believes to be the unfaithfulness of his wife. What is taught to Eva, however, is not the expected lesson. He waits until he has occasion to return home early and finds the "lovers" together. He then quietly dismisses Tyrone and focuses his hostility on his wife. Eva describes the scene:

> Then it was like I could hear her clothes ripping. I don't know if the gentleness had been for me, or if it had been the kind of gentleness one gets before they let go. But now he was tearing that blouse off and those underthings. I didn't hear nothing from her the whole time. I didn't hear a thing from her.
>
> "Act like a whore, I'm gonna [f——] you like a whore. You act like a whore, I'm gonna [f——] you like a whore."
>
> He kept saying that over and over. I was so scared. I kept feeling that after he tore all her clothes off, and there wasn't anymore to tear, he'd start tearing her flesh.[5]

What is important about this episode is not the obvious double standard, nor even the verbal and physical abuse; rather, it is the lesson taught Eva. It reinforces in a violent way what Miss Billie had said. The father, a figure of respect, becomes so obsessed that he punishes a woman Eva believes to be innocent instead of the man who she knows from her own experience is guilty. To the extent she believes her father, she must feel that she, too, can never be innocent, since Tyrone found her attractive. To the extent that she disapproves of her father's action, she realizes that no man is to be trusted in sexual matters. It is little wonder that she does not tell her father of Tyrone's real offenses.

This process of education is strengthened by the folklore of the community. In the most prominent case, Miss Billie tells the story of the queen bee. She is a woman who is cursed: each of the men she loves dies. The community holds her somehow responsible, even though she seems merely the victim of bad luck. When she falls in love again, she commits suicide rather than let another man die. Such a story only reinforces the view that women are by nature sinful, that they are responsible for the evil in the world. Original sin, in some cosmic way, has attached itself to the female gender. Eva is thus further encouraged to believe that a woman can never be innocent, even if she has done nothing.

This psychological training is complemented by her physical encounters with male companions. In addition to the trouble she has had with Tyrone, as a little girl she must deal with the sexually precocious Freddy. Although too young for intercourse, he is obsessed with the sexual act and substitutes a dirty popsicle stick for a penis when he play-acts a rape on Eva. When she tries to get advice about how to cope with his aggressions, Miss Billie only laughs and calls him a healthy young rooster. When another man later grabs for her crotch and she cuts his hand with a knife, she is the one put in jail for assault. Even the protection of her physical being is a matter of no consequence to her society. If she resists sexual encounters, then she is labelled silly or criminal. If she even appears to submit, then she will be labelled a whore.

She attempts to adapt herself to the distortions of her society despite her doubts. She marries James, a father figure, and moves with him to a new home. She becomes aware of his possible obsessiveness when he refuses to allow a telephone to be installed in the house, because, he says, he does not want her lovers calling. He reaches the high point of his madness when she repeats the mistake of her mother. A boy from the college she attends visits her one afternoon, and James comes home to find them talking. He then reenacts the violence of her father. Sending the boy away, he stares at her:

> He was just sitting there, real hard, and then he just reached over and grabbed my shoulder, got up and started slapping me. "You think you are a whore, I'll treat you like a whore. You think you a whore, I'll treat you like a whore."
>
> Naw, he didn't slap me, he pulled up my dress and got between my legs.
>
> "Think I can't do nothing. [f——] you like a damn whore." Naw, I'm not lying. He said, "Act like a whore, I'll [f——] you like a whore." *Naw, I'm not lying.*
>
> (p. 163)

This confrontation serves to convince Eva that her gender is indeed her destiny, that she cannot delude herself that she can be different from her mother. But she is in fact different from both her mother and the queen bee, both of whom resign themselves to their condition. Unlike Pecola, Eva cannot accept the myth of her society.

When she next encounters a man who would rob her of her humanity, she strikes out. Her relationship with Davis begins ambiguously. He initiates it with a comment that is a refrain in the book. When she asks why he is interested in her, he says that something in her eyes told him what she wanted. This reading of the eyes is a presumption of all the men that meet Eva. What is read, of course, is sexual desire. Davis is another obsessed man.

Despite this fact, she returns to the apartment with him, though she knows that she cannot give what he wants, since she is menstruating. Two things are clear at this point. One is that Eva differentiates between sexuality and sexual domination. She makes the point several times that she enjoys intercourse, and she only resists the assumption that women are nothing other than their sexual organs. The second point is that she is not deluded into thinking that Davis must be, finally, the "right man." The fact of her period makes it possible to test his perception of her.

He fails the test. Although he is kind and not initially insistent, he objectifies her to a greater extent than any other man. He will not allow her to leave the room or to comb her hair. He loses patience and takes her despite her condition. He also remains indifferent to her sexual preferences and concerns himself only with demonstrating his prowess. He will not listen to her story, and at one point, he mistakenly calls her Eve rather than Eva.

She does not this time tolerate her own reification. She first poisons him, and then, when he is dead, she indulges in sexual play with the body which culminates in her biting off his penis. This scene is comparable in shock effect to the rape of Pecola. But Gayl Jones uses hers to suggest complex possibilities by attaching mythic associations to it. When Eva arrives, she is bleeding from her period. Later, she comments that she has a pain in her side. At one point, she says that she feels as though there were large rusty nails in her hands. This Christ imagery is completed when, after the murder, she pictures herself being told by a man that her breasts are loaves of bread. Furthermore, Davis's misnaming of her has a strange appropriateness. At the moment of the castration, she relates her action to the biting of an apple. She is, in the light of these symbols, an Eve-Messiah who sacrifices another for both salvation and knowledge. She has gotten revenge for the death of the queen bee and the humiliation of her mother. But she has done this by symbolically liberating all women from the guilt attributed to them and by pointing to the true root of all evil.

She is mad, of course. And men put her in a prison for the criminally insane. Her incarceration replicates the confinement of her father's home, James's home, and Davis's apartment, all of which were clearly institutions for the insane. But in this case there is a kind of freedom in knowing that her resistance has made it possible to escape men. Her liberation is epitomized in the sexual attentions she receives from Elvira, her cellmate. Eva has nightmares, and her crime and situation are abnormal by all conventional standards. But this abnormality only serves to intensify the awareness that the society she has offended is an even greater obscenity.

The Bluest Eye and *Eva's Man*, though very different, are alike in their use of the conventions of the grotesque. Each involves some sort of obscenity that shocks our sensibilities. The incest of Morrison's book is outdone by the necrophilia and castration of Jones's. Each gives us central characters who are shown to be insane. But each also goes further, for the real grotesqueness in both is revealed to be primarily in the fictional worlds of the books. And these worlds are our world. The two black female characters, in their suffering, act as vehicles for criticizing America's treatment of blacks and women. The grotesque is an especially appropriate form for this commentary because it takes what is considered normal and twists it so that it loses its familiar qualities and becomes alien to us as the observers. In the case of these two novels, the normalities of American life, sex, and race are exaggerated to reveal their basic destructive absurdity. The actions and mental states of the heroines are clearly a function of the distortions and perversions of their worlds. Eva and Pecola respond to their impossible situations in ways that are unacceptable, and each of them enters a kind of prison. But we as readers are made to understand that the real horrors are still loose in the world.

Notes

1. *Mystery and Manners,* ed. Sally and Robert Fitzgerald (New York: Farrar, Straus and Giroux, 1961), p. 44.

2. *The Art of Southern Fiction: A Study of Some Modern Novelists* (Carbondale: Southern Illinois University Press, 1967), p. 118.

3. "Defining the Grotesque: An Attempt at Synthesis," *Journal of Aesthetics and Art,* 29 (1970), 258.

4. Toni Morrison, *The Bluest Eye* (New York: Simon and Schuster, 1972), p. 34. All further references to this work will be cited in the text.

5. Gayl Jones, *Eva's Man* (New York: Random House, 1976), p. 37. All further references to this work will be cited in the text.

Madonne M. Miner (essay date 1985)

SOURCE: Miner, Madonne M. "Lady No Longer Sings the Blues: Rape, Madness, and Silence in *The Bluest Eye*." In *Conjuring: Black Women, Fiction, and Literary Tradition,* edited by Marjorie Pryse and Hortense J. Spillers, pp. 176-91. Bloomington: Indiana University Press, 1985.

[*In the following essay, Miner links oral storytelling traditions to the process of self-defnition in* The Bluest

Eye, *exploring the intersections between Pecola's narrative and mythic accounts of Greek goddesses Philomena and Persephone.*]

Robert Stepto begins a recent interview with Toni Morrison by commenting on the "extraordinary sense of place" in her novels. He notes that she creates specific geographical landscapes with street addresses, dates, and other such details.[1] His observations certainly hold true for Morrison's first novel, **The Bluest Eye,** set in a black neighborhood in Lorain, Ohio, in 1941. Reading **The Bluest Eye,** I feel as if I have been in the abandoned store on the southeast corner of Broadway and Thirty-fifth Street in Lorain where Pecola Breedlove lives, as if I have been over the territory traversed by the eleven-year-old black girl as she skips among tin cans, tires, and weeds.

Morrison's skill in creating this very specific place accounts, in part, for my sense of the strangely familiar, the uncanny, when I read her novel—but only in part. While reading, I am familiar not only with Pecola's neighborhood but also, in a more generalized way, with Pecola's story. The sequence of events in this story—a sequence of rape, madness, and silence—repeats a sequence I have read before. Originally manifest in mythic accounts of Philomela and Persephone, this sequence provides Morrison with an ancient archetype from which to structure her very contemporary account of a young black woman. In the pages which follow I want to explore intersections between these age-old myths and Morrison's ageless novel.

For an account of Philomela, we must turn to Ovid, who includes her story in his *Metamorphoses* (8 A.D.). According to the chronicler, this story begins with an act of separation: Procne leaves her much-loved sister, Philomela, to join her husband, Tereus, in Thrace. After several years, Procne convinces Tereus to make a trip to Athens and escort Philomela to Thrace for a visit. In Athens, Tereus barely manages to curb the lust he feels for Philomela. He caresses her with his eyes, watches possessively as she kisses her father good-bye, and uses each embrace, each kiss,

> . . . to spur his rage, and feed his fire;
> He wished himself her father—and yet no less
> Would lust look hideous in a father's dress.[2]

Arriving in Thrace, Tereus drags Philomela into a dark wood and rapes her. The virgin calls out the names of father, sister, gods, but to no avail. Having indulged his lust, Tereus prepares to leave this "ringdove . . . with bloodstained plumes still fluttering" when she dares cry out against his sin:

> "I'll speak your deed, and cast all shame away.
>
> My voice shall reach the highest tract of air,
> And gods shall hear, if gods indeed are there."[3]

Tereus cannot tolerate such sacrilege against his name, so he perpetrates yet another rape: with pincers he

> . . . gripped the tongue that cried his shame,
> That stammered to the end her father's name,
> That struggled still, and strangled utterance made,
> And cut it from the root with barbarous blade.[4]

Deprived of speech and lodged in "walls of stone," Philomela weaves the tale of her plight into a piece of fabric, which she then sends to Procne. When Procne learns of her sister's grief and her husband's treachery, she determines upon a most hideous revenge; she slays the son she has had with Tereus and feeds his remains to the unsuspecting father. While Ovid's story ends with this feast, popular mythology adds yet another chapter, transforming Philomela into a nightingale, damned forever to chirp the name of her rapist: tereu, tereu.

Obviously, male-violating-female functions as the core action within Philomela's story. Under different guises, this violation occurs several times: first, when Tereus ruptures the hymen of Philomela; second, when Tereus ruptures the connecting tissue of Philomela's tongue; and, finally, when he enters her body yet again ("Thereafter, if the frightening tale be true, / On her maimed form he wreaked his lust anew"[5]). With each act Tereus asserts his presence, his sensual realm, and denies the very existence of such a realm (encompassing not only sensuality, but the senses themselves) to Philomela. As if to reinforce the initial violation, Tereus, following his act of rape, encloses Philomela in silence, in stone walls. He thereby forces her to assume externally imposed configurations instead of maintaining those natural to her.

If man-raping-woman functions as the most basic "mythemic act"[6] in Philomela's story, the most basic mythemic *inter*-act involves not only this pair, but another: father and sister of the rape victim. When, for example, Ovid notes that Tereus, lusting for Philomela, "wished himself her father," and when the chronicler describes Philomela, in the midst of the rape, calling out her father's name (for help, of course, but for what else?) he sets the act of violence within a familial matrix. Thus, we cannot limit consideration of this act's motivations and ramifications to two individuals. Interestingly enough, however, just as the basic mythemic act (man raping woman) robs the woman of identity, so too the mythemic interact; dependent upon familial roles for personal verification ("mother of," "sister of," "wife of"[7]) the female must fear a loss of identity as the family loses its boundaries—or, more accurately, as the male transgresses these boundaries.

Having noted the most important structural elements in Philomela's story, we cross an ocean, several centuries and countless historical, racial, and class lines before coming to the story of Pecola. Despite obvious contextual differences between the two stories, structural similarities abound. Individual mythemes from Philomela's story appear, without distortion, in that of Pecola. First, in various ways and at various costs, the female figure suffers violation: by Mr. Yacobowski, Junior, Bay Boy and friends, Cholly, Soaphead. Second, with this violation a man asserts his presence as "master," "man-in-control," or "god" at the expense of a young woman who exists only as someone to "impress upon." Third, following the violation/assertion, this woman suffers an enclosure or undesirable transformation; she cowers, shrinks, or resides behind walls of madness. Finally, the most characteristic example of violation/assertion/destruction occurs within the family matrix; Cholly Breedlove rapes his own daughter, violating a standard code of familial relations. We now might look more closely at individual instances of mythemes structuring the Pecola story.

An early, and paradigmatic, example of male transgression and subsequent female silence occurs in the "See the Cat" section. Junior, a tyrannical, unloving black boy, invites a rather credulous Pecola into his house, ostensibly to show her some kittens; like Philomela, Pecola has no idea of the dangers involved in trusting herself to a male guide. Once inside, engrossed in admiration of the furnishings, she forgets about Junior until he insists that she acknowledge him:

> She was deep in admiration of the flowers when Junior said, "Here!" Pecola turned. "Here is your kitten!" he screeched. And he threw a big black cat right in her face.[8]

Pecola immediately responds to this unexpected penetration by sucking in her breath; metaphorically she draws herself inward. She then attempts to flee, but just as Tereus confines Philomela behind stone walls, Junior confines Pecola behind the wall of his will:

> Junior leaped in front of her. "You can't get out. You're my prisoner," he said. His eyes were merry but hard. . . . He pushed her down, ran out the door that separated the rooms, and held it shut with his hands.
>
> (pp. 73-74)

Male realms expand as those of the female suffer an almost fatal contraction.

Junior does not actually rape Pecola. Morrison, however, duplicates the dynamics of the scene between Junior and Pecola in a scene between Cholly and Pecola, where rape *does* occur. Eleven-year-old Pecola stands at the sink, scraping away at dirty dishes, when her father, drunk, staggers into the kitchen. Unlike Tereus and Junior, Cholly does not carry his victim into foreign territories; rather, Pecola's rape occurs within her own house, and this fact increases its raw horror (Morrison denies us the cover of metaphor and confronts us directly with a father's violation of his daughter). As Morrison explains, several factors motivate Cholly, but the two thoughts floating through his besotted brain immediately prior to his penetration of Pecola point, once more, to his desire for confirmation of his presence. First, a gesture of Pecola's, a scratching of the leg, reminds him of a similar gesture of Pauline's—or, more accurately, reminds him of *his own* response to this gesture. He repeats his response, catching Pecola's foot in his hand, nibbling on the flesh of her leg, just as he had done with Pauline, so many years before. Of consequence here is not Pecola's gesture, but Cholly's belief that he can regain an earlier perception of himself as young, carefree and whimsical by using this girl/woman as medium. When Pecola, however, unlike the laughing Pauline, remains stiff and silent, Cholly shifts to a second train of thought, a second stimulus to self-assertion: "The rigidness of her shocked body, the silence of her stunned throat, was better than Pauline's easy laughter had been. The confused mixture of his memories of Pauline and the doing of a wild and forbidden thing excited him, and a bolt of desire ran down his genitals, giving it length" (p. 128). Thus, on a literal level, Cholly expands as Pecola contracts:

> The tightness of her vagina was more than he could bear. His soul seemed to slip down to his guts and fly out into her, and the gigantic thrust he made into her then provoked the only sound she made—a hollow suck of air in the back of her throat. Like the rapid loss of air from a circus balloon.
>
> (p. 128)

As in the episode with Junior, Pecola sucks inward, but without positive effect; like a deflating circus balloon, she *loses* the benefits of lifegiving oxygen and the power of speech.

To enforce this silence, Cholly need not cut off Pecola's tongue or imprison her behind stone walls. The depresencing of Pecola Breedlove takes a different form from that of Philomela. Upon regaining consciousness following the rape, Pecola *is* able to speak; she tells Mrs. Breedlove what has happened. But as Mrs. Breedlove does not want to hear and does not want to believe, Pecola must recognize the futility of attempted communication. Thus when Cholly, like Tereus, rapes a second time, Pecola keeps the story to herself; in silence this eleven-year-old girl steps across commonly accepted borders of reason and speech to enter her own personal world of silence and madness. Pecola's "self" becomes so crazed, so fragmented, that it conducts conversations with itself—and with no one else:

> "How come you don't talk to anybody?"
>
> "I talk to you."
>
> "Besides me."

"I don't like anybody besides you. . . ."

"You don't talk to anybody. You don't go to school. And nobody talks to you."

(p. 153)

Of course, when Pecola comments that her mirror image does not engage other people in conversation, she engages in self-commentary; "I" and "you" are one and the same. Tragically, even when combined, this "I" and "you" do not compose one whole being. Claudia's description of the mutilated Pecola leaves no doubt that she no longer exists as a reasonable human being; like Philomela-turned-nightingale, the "little-girl-gone-to-woman" undergoes a transformation:

> The damage done was total. . . . Elbows bent, hands on shoulders, she flailed her arms like a bird in an eternal, grotesquely futile effort to fly. Beating the air, a winged but grounded bird, intent on the blue void it could not reach—could not even see—but which filled the valleys of the mind.
>
> (p. 158)

Silent, isolated, insane: Pecola cannot escape.

In depicting the effects of rape on one young woman, Morrison sets into motion a series of associations that take their cue from gender. Men, potential rapists, assume presence, language, and reason as their particular province. Women, potential victims, fall prey to absence, silence, and madness.[9] An understanding of the powerful dynamics behind this allotment of presence/absence, language/silence, reason/madness along sexual lines contributes to an understanding of the painful truths contained in Philomela's story, in Pecola's story, and in the story of yet another rape victim: Persephone. While clearly related to the Philomela myth, that of Persephone differs in certain details which, when brought to *The Bluest Eye*, prompt an even richer reading of the novel. Before engaging in an application of Persephone's story to that of Pecola, however, we might look at three different renditions of the Persephone myth, each of which may advance our understanding of the way Persephone's and Pecola's stories intersect mythopoetically.

Homer sets a springtime mood of warmth, gaiety, youthfulness, and beauty as he begins his rendition of Persephone's story:

> Now I will sing / of golden-haired Demeter,
> the awe-inspiring goddess,
> and of her trim-ankled daughter,
> Persephone,
> who was frolicking in a grassy meadow.[10]

When Pluto, god of the underworld, abducts the "trim-ankled" young woman (and surely it is not mere coincidence that Morrison specifies Pecola's ankles as a stimulant to Cholly's desire) this mood changes abruptly; in terror, the virgin shrieks for her father, Zeus. While noting that Persephone directs her shrieks to her father, Homer also comments on the virgin's hopes relative to her mother:

> Still *glimpsing* the earth,
> the brilliant sky,
> the billowing, fish-filled sea
> and the rays of the sun,
> Persephone vainly hoped *to see* her mother again.[11]

Homer establishes a causal connection between rape and the loss of a particular *vision*. He further substantiates this connection in Demeter's response to her daughter's rape, a punitive response which involves Demeter's changing the world so that its occupants will no longer see fruits and flowers:

> She made that year
> most shocking and frightening
> for mortals who lived on the nourishing earth.
> The soil did not yield a single seed.
> Demeter kept them all underground.[12]

The goddess imposes a sensual deprivation on mortals parallel to the sensual deprivation suffered by her daughter (note that *The Bluest Eye* opens with a statement of similar deprivation: "Quiet as it's kept, there were no marigolds in the fall of 1941"). By the end of the hymn, Demeter and Pluto reach a compromise; half of the year Persephone resides with her mother and the flowers grow; during the other half, Persephone remains with Pluto and the earth produces no fruits.

James Frazer, in *The Golden Bough*, relates another version of the Persephone story. In substance, Frazer comes very close to Homer; in detail, however, the two diverge, and Frazer's details reverberate in *The Bluest Eye*. First, Frazer provides more specifics about Persephone's "frolic"; the young woman gathers "roses and lilies, crocuses and violets, hyacinths and narcissuses in a lush meadow."[13] Individual flowers in Frazer's catalog call forth associations of importance to *The Bluest Eye*: the virginal lily, bloody hyacinth (taking its color from the slain youth, Hyacinthus, beloved of Apollo) and narcotic Narcissus (taking its name from the self-enclosed youth, Narcissus, capable of seeing only himself).[14] The mythic situation itself, flower picking, finds an analog in the novel as Pecola, on her way to the candy store, peers into the heads of yellow dandelions. Second, Frazer's more detailed description of Persephone's abduction and underworld residence might serve as metaphoric description of Pecola's state of mind following her rape: "the earth gaped and Pluto, Lord of the Dead, issuing from the *abyss*, carried her off . . . to be his bride and queen in the *gloomy subterranean world*."[15] Finally, when Frazer concludes the story, he notes that although the "grim Lord of the

Dead" obeys Zeus's command to restore Persephone to Demeter, this Lord first gives his mistress the seed of a pomegranate to eat, which ensures that she will return to him. Tereus and Cholly also "give seeds" to women, thereby ensuring that the women never will be able to reassume their previously experienced wholeness.

In a very recent reworking of the Persephone story, Phyllis Chesler focuses most intently on the fate of this myth's female characters. Because she places women's experiences at the center of her version, Chesler begins with a chapter of the story which does not appear in Homer and Frazer: Persephone menstruates. Further, Chesler specifies the nature of certain acts and relationships that her male counterparts choose to obscure; she identifies rape as rape, fathers as fathers:

> One morning Persephone menstruated. That afternoon, Demeter's daughters gathered flowers to celebrate the loveliness of the event. A chariot thundered, then clattered into their midst. It was Hades, the middle aged god of death, come to *rape* Persephone, come to carry her off to be his queen, to sit beside him in the realm of *non-being* below the earth, come to commit the first act of violence earth's children had ever known. Afterwards, the three sisters agreed that he was old enough to be Persephone's *father*. Perhaps he was; who else could he be? There were no known male parents . . . and thus they discovered that in shame and sorrow childhood ends, and that nothing remains the same.[16]

Morrison, like Chesler, pays attention to female rites of passage; she includes a description of Pecola's first menstruation, an experience which bonds Pecola to her adopted sisters, Claudia and Frieda. Also like Chesler, Morrison insists on the paternal identity of the rapist (Pecola need not shriek the name of father as Philomela and Persephone do; father is right there) and emphasizes that the rape act brings one entire way of life to a close ("nothing remains the same"). This rapport between Chesler's Persephone and Morrison's Pecola surfaces in conclusions to the stories as well. Chesler writes:

> Persephone still had to visit her husband once each year (in winter, when no crops could grow), but her union with him remained a barren one. Persephone was childless. Neither husband nor child—no stranger would ever claim her as his own.[17]

Pecola's fate runs along strikingly parallel lines. Despite the offerings and incantations of Claudia and Frieda, Pecola miscarries and remains childless. Grown people turn away, children laugh, and no stranger attempts to share Pecola's world.

Structurally, the stories of Philomela, Persephone, and Pecola share the same blueprint: violated by a male relative, a young virgin suffers sensual loss of such an extreme that her very identity is called into question. In one brutally explicit scene Ovid conveys the terror of Philomela's sensual loss—Tereus severs his sister-in-law's tongue and deprives her of speech. As chroniclers of this same basic female experience, Homer, Frazer, and Chesler also must convey the terror of sensual loss. In their versions, however, *sight* rather than speech assumes priority, and they convey the terror of deprivation not in one explicit scene, but by depicting the ramifications of an altered vision. Of course, this particular emphasis encourages yet further consideration of the Persephone myth and Morrison's novel, the very title of which suggests an interest in the way vision structures our world. This interest, reflected in the novel's title (what does it mean to see through "the bluest eye"?) and in sectional titles (how does one "see mother," "see father"?) springs naturally from Morrison's more fundamental interests how does the world see a young black girl? how does a young black girl see a world? and finally, what are the correspondences between presence/absence, vision/nonvision, male/female?

As described by various psychologists and psychoanalysts,[18] the processes of identity construction and personal integration involve an extremely sensitive and constantly shifting balance between seeing and being seen—so that, for example, only after an infant sees itself reflected in the mother's eyes (that is, given a presence) can the infant, through its own eyes, bestow a presence on others. Throughout **The Bluest Eye,** Morrison provides several examples of the ways sex and race may prompt a dangerous distortion of this visual balance. An early instance of this distortion, and subsequent personal disintegration, occurs during an exchange between Pecola and Mr. Yacobowski, white male proprietor of a candy store on Garden Avenue.[19] Pecola enjoys her walk to Mr. Yacobowski's store. Many times she has seen that crack in the walk, this clump of dandelions. Having seen them, she grants them a reality, a reality which redounds to include Pecola herself:

> These and other inanimate things she saw and experienced. They were real to her. She knew them. . . . She owned the crack . . . she owned the clump of dandelions. . . . And owning them made her part of the world, and the world part of her.
>
> (p. 41)

Such a happy rapport between viewer and vision is short-lived, however. When Pecola enters the candy store and comes under Mr. Yacobowski's eyes, her existence, as well as the existence of her world, become matters of doubt. Mr. Yacobowski *does not see* her:

> Somewhere between retina and object, between vision and view, his eyes draw back, hesitate, and hover. At some fixed point in time and space he senses that he need not waste the effort of a glance. He does not see her, because for him there is *nothing to see*
>
> (pp. 41-42, my italics)

In effect, this scene parallels previously described rape scenes in the novel: male denies presence to female. Pecola cannot defend herself against this denial: "she looks up at him and sees the vacuum where curiosity ought to lodge. And something more. The total absence of human recognition—the glazed separateness" (p. 42). Nor can she defend her world; walking home, she rejects dandelions she formerly has favored. They, like Pecola herself, certainly will not satisfy standards that the blue eyes of a Mr. Yacobowski may impose:

> Dandelions. A dart of affection leaps out from her to them. But they do not look at her and do not send love back. She thinks "They are ugly. They are weeds."
>
> (p. 43)

Before contact with this white male, Pecola creates belief in both a world and a self; following contact with Yacobowski, her conjuring powers impaired, she abandons the effort.

A second example of visual distortion finds Pecola face to face with Geraldine, one of those "brown girls from Mobile and Aiken" able to construct inviolable worlds by imposing strict boundaries between the acceptable and the unacceptable, the seen and the unseen. Unlike Mr. Yacobowski, Geraldine does *look* at Pecola, but, like Yacobowski, Geraldine does not *see* Pecola; she sees only a series of signs, a symbolic configuration. Thus, when Geraldine returns home and discovers a shrieking son, a frying feline on the radiator, and an unfamiliar black girl in her living room, she responds by distancing herself from Pecola. With no qualms whatsoever she relegates the young girl to the general category of "black female who is an embarrassment to us all", or, "black female whom we would prefer to keep out of sight":

> She looked at Pecola. Saw the dirty torn dress, the plaits sticking out of her head, hair matted where the plaits had come undone, the muddy shoes with the wad of gum peeking out from between the cheap soles, the soiled socks, one of which had been walked down into the heel of the shoe. She saw the safety pin holding the hem of the dress up.... She had seen this little girl all of her life.
>
> (p. 75)

Pecola, for Geraldine, serves as symbol of everything ugly, dirty, and degrading. Physically as well as symbolically, Geraldine must negate Pecola, must deny the ragged eleven-year-old access to her world. The woman who does not sweat in her armpits or thighs, who smells of wood and vanilla (pp. 70-71) says to Pecola, *quietly* says to Pecola: "'Get out.... You nasty little black bitch. Get out of my house!'" (p. 75). In other words, get out of my world, out of the vision I construct before and about me. Pecola leaves. As she leaves, she hangs her head, lowers her eyes; incapable of defending herself against visual distortion, Pecola attempts to deny vision altogether. But, even here, she fails: "she could not hold it [her head] low enough to avoid seeing the snowflakes falling and dying on the pavement" (p. 76). These snowflakes, falling and dying, suggest the visual perimeters of Pecola's world. In an earlier comment, Morrison generalizes as to the nature of these perimeters: "She would see only what there was to see: the eyes of other people" (p. 40). As these eyes do not see her, or see her only as a sign of something other, Pecola loses sight of herself.

Although Pecola's encounters with Mr. Yacobowski and Geraldine serve as the most complete and sensitively drawn examples of visual imbalance, they merely reenforce a pattern of imbalance begun much earlier in Pecola's life—for that matter, begun even before Pecola sees the light of day, while she is in Pauline's womb. During the nine months of pregnancy, Pauline spends most afternoons at the movies, picking up an education in white values of beauty and ugliness. Morrison describes this education as yet another violation of male on female, white on black. There, in a darkened theater, images come together, "all projected through the ray of light from above and behind" (p. 97). This ray of light resembles a gigantic eyeball (apologies to Emerson) which defines the boundaries of existence and which, of necessity, projects a white male vision. Having absorbed these silver-screen values, Pauline conjures up "a mind's eye view" of her soon-to-be-born child more in keeping with white fantasy than black reality. Upon birth, Pecola gives the lie to this view, and Pauline expresses her disappointment:

> So when I seed it, it was like looking at a picture of your mama when she was a girl. You know who she is, but she don't look the same.... Head full of pretty hair, but Lord she was ugly.
>
> (p. 99)

As various psychologists attest, the mother's gaze is of primary importance in generating a child's sense of self. Tragically, Pauline looks at her infant daughter and then looks away.

Morrison's novel contains repeated instances of Pecola's negation as other characters refuse to see her. *The Bluest Eye* also provides numerous instances of Pecola's desire to hide her own eyes, thereby refusing to acknowledge certain aspects of her world. Morrison articulates this desire for self-abnegation most explicitly in a postscript to her description of a typical fight between family members in the Breedlove home. Mrs. Breedlove hits Cholly with a dishpan, Cholly returns the blow with his fists, Sammy strikes at Cholly while shouting "you naked fuck," and Pecola covers her head with a quilt. The quilt of course cannot completely block out this scene, so Pecola prays that God will make her disappear. Receiving no response from the man in the sky, she does her best on her own:

She squeezed her eyes shut. Little parts of her body faded away. Now slowly, now with a rush. Slowly again. Her fingers went, one by one; then her arms disappeared all the way to the elbow. Her feet now. Yes, that was good. The legs all at once. It was hardest above the thighs. She had to be real still and pull. Her stomach would not go. But finally it, too, went away. Then her chest, her neck. The face was hard too. Almost done, almost. Only her tight, tight eyes were left. They were always left.

Try as she might, she could never get her eyes to disappear. So what was the point? They were everything. Everything was there, in them.

(p. 39)

These paragraphs forcefully convey Pecola's desire and her notion of how she might realize it. If Pecola were to *see* things differently, she might *be seen* differently; if her eyes were different, her world might be different too.[20] As Morrison deals out one ugly jigsaw piece after another, as she fits the pieces together to construct Pecola's world, we come to understand the impulse behind Pecola's desire, as well as its ultimate futility. When boys shout at her, "'Black e mo Black e mo Ya daddy sleeps nekked'" (p. 55), Pecola drops her head and covers her eyes; when Maureen accuses her of having seen her father naked, Pecola maintains her innocence by disclaiming, "'I wouldn't even look at him, even if I did see him'" (p. 59); when Maureen attacks her yet again Pecola tucks her head in "a funny, sad, helpless movement. A kind of hunching of the shoulders, pulling in of the neck, as though she wanted to cover her ears" (p. 60). By covering ears, eyes, and nose Pecola attempts to shut out the testimony of her senses. Reminded of her own ugliness or that of her world, she repeatedly resorts to an elemental self-denial.

Pecola quavers when Mr. Yacobowski and Geraldine refuse to acknowledge her. She shrinks in fear when Maureen and Bay Boy insist on acknowledging her ugliness. Quavering and shaking, Pecola *does* maintain a hold on her world and herself—until Cholly smashes her illusions about the possibility of unambivalent love in this world. Throughout the novel, Pecola ponders the nature of love, pursues it as a potentially miraculous phenomenon. On the evening of her first menstruation, for example, she asks, "'How do you do that? I mean, how do you get somebody to love you'" (p. 29). And, after a visit to Marie, Poland, and China, Pecola ponders, "What did love feel like? . . . How do grown-ups act when they love each other? Eat fish together?" (p. 48). When Cholly rapes his daughter, he commits a sacrilege—not only against Pecola, but against her vision of love and its potential. Following the rape, Pecola, an unattractive eleven-year-old black girl, knows that for her, even love is bound to be dirty, ugly, of a piece with the fabric of her world. Desperate, determined to unwind the threads that compose this fabric, Pecola falls back on an early notion: the world changes as the eyes which see it change. To effect this recreation, Pecola seeks out the only magician she knows, Soaphead Church, and presents him with the only plan she can conceive. She asks that he make her eyes different, make them blue—blue because in Pecola's experience only those with blue eyes receive love: Shirley Temple, Geraldine's cat, the Fisher girl.

In its emotional complications, Soaphead's response to Pecola's request resembles Cholly's response to Pecola's defeated stance; both men move through misdirected feelings of love, tenderness, and anger.[21] Soaphead perceives Pecola's need and knows that he must direct the anger he feels not at her, but rather at the God who has encased her within black skin and behind brown eyes. But finally, when Soaphead decides to "look at that ugly black girl" and love her (p. 143), he violates her integrity in much the same way Cholly violates her body when he forces open her thighs. Prompted by the desire to play God and to make this performance a convincing one, Soaphead casts Pecola in the role of believer. Thus, although he *sees* Pecola more accurately than other characters do, he subordinates his vision of her to his vision of self-as-God. He later boasts in his letter "To He Who Greatly Ennobled Human Nature by Creating It":

> I did what you did not, could not, would not do. I looked at that ugly little black girl, and I loved her. I played You. And it was a very good show!
>
> (p. 143)

Of course, the script for this show sends Pecola into realms of madness. Even Soaphead acknowledges that "No one else will see her blue eyes" (p. 143), but Soaphead justifies himself first on the grounds that "she will love happily ever after" and then, more honestly, on the grounds that "I, I have found it meet and right to do so" (p. 143). In other words, Soaphead's creation of false belief is not necessarily right for Pecola, but for himself. Morrison substantiates this assessment of Soaphead's creation a few pages later, when she portrays its effect on Pecola. Imprisoned now behind blue eyes, the schizophrenic little girl can talk only to herself. Obviously, this instance of male-female interaction parallels earlier scenes from the novel: "rape" occurs as Soaphead elevates himself at the expense of Pecola.

In *The Raw and the Cooked* Lévi-Strauss observes: "There exists no veritable end or term to mythical analysis, no secret unity which could be grasped at the end of the work of decomposition. The themes duplicate themselves to infinity."[22] Although the stories of Philomela, Persephone, and Pecola do not form a composite whole, each of them, with its varied and individual emphases, contributes to a much larger woman's myth, which tells of denial and disintegration, which unveils the oft-concealed connections between male reason, speech, presence and female madness, silence, absence. As a young black woman, Pecola assumes an especially poignant position in this growing complex of mythic representations; she is absent (and absenced) in relation to the norms of male culture and in relation to the norms of white culture. Ultimately, I read Pecola's story as a tragic version of the myth; this twentieth-century black woman remains behind blue eyes, an inarticulate, arm-fluttering bird. But I cannot read **The Bluest Eye** as tragedy; Claudia, our sometimes-narrator, *speaks,* as does Morrison, our full-time novelist. Thus, although the novel documents the sacrifice of one black woman, it attests to the survival of two others—a survival akin to that of Philomela or Persephone—filled with hardship, but also with hope.

Notes

1. Robert Stepto, "'Intimate Things in Place': A Conversation with Toni Morrison," in *The Third Woman,* ed. Dexter Fisher (Boston: Houghton Mifflin, 1979), p. 167.

2. A. E. Watts, trans., *The Metamorphoses of Ovid* (Berkeley: University of California Press, 1954), p. 131.

3. Watts, p. 133.

4. Ibid., p. 133.

5. Ibid., p. 133.

6. I take this term from Claude Lévi-Strauss. For an explanation of Lévi-Strauss's *modus operandi* see Robert Scholes, *Structuralism in Literature* (New Haven: Yale University Press, 1974), pp. 68-74.

7. "From her initial family upbringing throughout her subsequent development, the social role assigned to the women is that of serving an image, authoritative and central, of man: a woman is first and foremost a daughter/a mother/a wife." Shoshana Felman, "Women and Madness: The Critical Phallacy," *Diacritics* 5 (1975), p. 2.

8. Toni Morrison, *The Bluest Eye* (New York: Pocket Books, 1979), p. 73. I will include all further page citations from Morrison's novel within the body of my text.

9. An observation from Shoshana Felman about Balzac's short story "Adieu" condenses many of the associations described. Felman notes: "the dichotomy Reason/Madness, as well as Speech/Silence, exactly coincides in this text with the dichotomy Men/Women. Women as such are associated both with madness and with silence, whereas men appear not only as the possessors, but also as the dispensers, of reason, which they can at will mete out to—or take away from—others. . . . Masculine reason thus constitutes a scheme to capture and master, indeed, metaphorically RAPE the woman" (p. 7).

10. Penelope Proddow, trans., *Demeter and Persephone, Homeric Hymn Number Two* (Garden City, N. Y.: Doubleday, 1972), n.p.

11. Ibid., my italics.

12. Ibid., n.p.

13. Sir James George Frazer, *The Golden Bough* (New York: Macmillan and Company, 1950), p. 456.

14. According to Frazer, in the original Homeric myth Persephone, drawn by the sight of narcissues, moves beyond the reach of help. The choice of this particular plant as lure is of interest not only because of the Narcissus myth, but also because of recent psychoanalytic readings of this myth. These readings stress the importance of a child's progression through a stage of narcissistic self-love and suggest that this progression can occur only with the help of a mother-figure who assures the child of external love.

15. Frazer, p. 456.

16. Phyllis Chesler, *Women and Madness* (New York: Avon Books, 1973), p. xiv.

17. Ibid., p. xv.

18. See, for example, D. W. Winnicott, "Mirror-role of Mother and Family in Child Development," in *The Predicament of the Family,* ed. Peter Lomas (New York: International University Press, 1967), pp. 26-33; Heinz Lichtenstein, "The Role of Narcissism in the Emergence and Maintenance of a Primary Identity," *International Journal of Psychoanalysis* 45 (1964), pp. 49-56.

19. Why specify "Garden Avenue"? Perhaps Morrison wants to suggest that Pecola's experience is the twentieth-century urban counterpart to Persephone's experience in an actual garden?

20. "If she looked different, beautiful, maybe Cholly would be different, and Mrs. Breedlove too. Maybe they'd say, 'Why look at pretty-eyed Pecola. We mustn't do bad things in front of these pretty eyes'" (p. 40).

21. Compare, for example, Cholly's response (pp. 127-28) to that of Soaphead (p. 137).

22. Lévi-Strauss, *The Raw and the Cooked* (New York: Harpers, 1969), p. 5.

Ruth Rosenberg (essay date winter 1987)

SOURCE: Rosenberg, Ruth. "Seeds in Hard Ground: Black Girlhood in *The Bluest Eye.*" *MELUS* 21, no. 4 (winter 1987): 435-45.

[*In the following essay, Rosenberg discusses several aspects of* The Bluest Eye *that differentiate Morrison's novel from earlier fictional accounts of African Ameri-*

can girlhood, including descriptions of first menses and mother-daughter interactions, "colorism," and the emotional precocity of pre-adolescent girls.]

Little black girls learned their lessons in self-authentication from autobiographies of such artists as Mahalia Jackson, Maya Angelou, and Bessie Smith, which explained how, in spite of immense obstacles, one might fashion a self.[1] When Sherley Anne Williams was a troubled twelve-year-old in the fifties, she searched, in vain, through the shelves of her junior high school library for some fictionalized depiction of her own problems. Because she found nothing there that would speak to her difficulties, she says, she *"was led, almost inevitably . . . to the autobiographies of women entertainers—Eartha Kitt, Katherine Dunham, Ethel Waters. The material circumstances of their childhood were so much worse than mine; they too had had to cope with early and forced sex and sexuality, with mothers who could not express love in the terms that they so desperately needed. Yet they had risen above this, turned their difference into something that was respected in the world beyond their homes. I, in the free North, could do no less than endure"* (196).

Black girls did not exist as far as the publishers of school anthologies were concerned. Barbara Dodds Stanford writes that "'Whites Only' could have been stamped on almost every literature series for high school students published before 1965" (3). Nancy Larrick, who studied 5,206 children's books published between 1962 and 1964, claims that only 349 of those thousands of books include even one black child either in the illustrations or the text. Of that 6.7 percent which do show a black child, all but a small fraction are "set outside the United States or before World War II. Quite clearly, the books used in American schools were primarily by and about white, Anglo-Saxon, middle-class people" (84-85).

It was this absence of fictionalized characters with whom she could identify that started Sherley Anne Williams *"on the road to being a writer"* (195). At some point, in virtually every interview with a black woman writer, comes a similar admission. The consistent response to the question of why she became an author is that she could not find the books that she needed. Alice Walker has said that she was forced "to write all the things *I should have read*" ("Saving the Life That Is Your Own" 157).

Toni Morrison was a precocious reader as a child, but it was not until she discovered the Russian novelists that she found herself spoken to. Otherwise, she felt herself shunted to the sidelines. She mourned for "'the people who in all literature were always peripheral—little black girls who were props, background, these people were never center stage, and those people were me'" (Strouse 54). Asked why she had written *The Bluest Eye* (1970), she responded, "'I was interested in reading a kind of book that I had never read before. I didn't know if such a book existed, but I had just never read it in 1964 when I started writing *The Bluest Eye*'" (Parker 252).

Working out of her memory of what Lorain, Ohio, had been like in 1940, she reconstructed her own childhood. Placed center stage are three little girls: the book's narrator, Claudia Macteer, 9; her sister Frieda, 10; and their friend Pecola Breedlove, 11. It is an initiation story so unlike any other that had been done before that Toni Cade Bambara says her students have difficulty dealing with it. Among other things they fail to appreciate the traumatic aspects of the first menses because the onset of menstruation is not something that is valued in our culture. As Bambara notes, "The initiation or rites of passage of the young girl is not one of the darlings of American literature. The coming of age for the young boy is certainly much more the classic case. I wonder if it all means that we don't put a value on our process of womanhood" (Guy-Sheftall 247).[2]

Morrison renders not only the terror and the mystery of that initial bleeding, but also the older sister's competence in handling it. As Pecola stands with the blood trickling down her legs, her eyes rimmed with fear, asking if she's going to die, Frieda explains, "'That's ministratin''" (25), and dispatches Claudia for some water to clean the steps. The younger sister's resentment at missing whatever important things are going on in the bushes with a white rectangle of cotton is vented against the prying girl from next door who then screams out that they are "'playing nasty'" (27). Mrs. Macteer runs out, pulling a switch from the bush and whipping Frieda with four stinging cuts on the leg. About to punish Pecola, too, she notices "the white tail" and the "little-girl-gone-to-woman pants" (28) and hugs them both. That Claudia still does not comprehend what is happening becomes evident in her panic as she listens outside the bathroom and hears the water gushing into the tub. When she asks if Pecola is being drowned, Frieda answers, "'Oh, Claudia. You so dumb. She's just going to wash her clothes and all'" (28). Later that night as they sleep together, they "were full of awe and respect for Pecola. Lying next to a real person who was really ministratin' was somehow sacred" (28). Claudia needs her sister to interpret her experience for her. The children are forced to rely on each other for information, since adults make themselves so inaccessible.

The child's intense curiosity is not responded to verbally. Adults demand deference and fend off questions. They maintain a social distance between themselves and their children through non-reciprocal conversations. Claudia says, "Adults do not talk to us—they give us directions. They issue orders without providing information" (12). Communication is a hierarchically structured, one-way transmission. Claudia observes that "we didn't initiate talk with grownups; we answered their questions" (22). Another strictly enforced rule, in the forties at least, was the insistence upon terms of respect. A child had to address her mother as "Ma'am."

A new boarder's arrival in the Macteer household provides another occasion to instruct the children about their place. Their status, it is impressed upon them, is a little lower than that of the furniture: "Frieda and I were not introduced to him—merely pointed out. Like, here is the bathroom; the clothes closet is here; and these are my kids" (16).

Parents express their concern through the strict annihilation of any vestige of impropriety, through lashing out. Each season brings a change in whipping style for the Macteer girls: "They beat us differently in the spring. Instead of the dull pain of a winter strap, there were these new green switches that lost their sting long after the whipping was over. There was a nervous meanness in these long twigs that made us long for the steady stroke of a strap or the firm but honest slap of a hairbrush" (78).

Since parental concern manifests itself in this way, an act of translation is required to read the love latent in it. Claudia shows her ability to realize that she is loved during an illness—the vehicle of her understanding being the pair of rough hands that smear salve on her chest. In an interview with Robert Stepto, Morrison confirms this belated realization, so beautifully inscribed in her first novel: "'And when they punished us or hollered at us, it was, at the time, we thought, so inhibiting and so cruel, and it's only much later that you realize that they were interested in you,'" that "'they cared'" (214). Claudia's recognition that she is loved must come through her other senses because it is never told to her. Expressions of maternal concern are seldom verbalized in *The Bluest Eye*; rather, they are beaten into the child, inscribed on her skin. It was this maternal attitude that Sherley Anne Williams had, as a girl, hoped to find expressed in fiction by black women and whose absence fixed her determination to write about the issue. Only in black women's autobiographies did she find how others coped "with mothers who could not express love in the terms . . . [children] so desperately needed."[3]

Certainly nine-year-old Claudia does not feel coddled, and her claims for attention are never overtly acknowledged: ". . . if we cut or bruise ourselves, they ask us are we crazy. When we catch colds, they shake their heads in disgust at our lack of consideration" (12-13). Put to bed with a cough, Claudia is scolded and begins to cry because "my mother's anger humiliates me; her words chafe my cheeks" (14). She is not reassured verbally: "No one speaks to me or asks how I feel" (13). Only later does she realize that the rough hands that rub salve on her chest are expressing concern; that love, even when it cannot be heard, can be smelled and tasted. Having made that recognition, she learns to inhale the love that coats her chest, along with the salve (14).

How important a service Toni Morrison rendered in this depiction becomes evident when one contrasts it with Richard Wright's fictionalization of the mother-child interaction in *Black Boy*. As Ralph Ellison has explained, Wright mistook "gestures of protection" for "blows of oppression." He failed retroactively to interpret his mother's whippings as does the girl who narrates Morrison's novel. "One of the Southern Negro family's methods of protecting the child," writes Ellison, "is the severe beating—a homeopathic dose of the violence generated by black and white relationships. Such beatings as Wright's were administered for the child's own good . . . by the mother. . . . the cruelty is also an expression of concern, of love" (85-86, 91).

Wright's Richard needed Ellison to reinterpret what might be construed as "maternal sadism" as "an expression of concern." Morrison's Claudia is able to effect this translation for herself because she internalizes an image of what it means to be a mother. As Alice Walker has argued metaphorically in another context, black women need to know both history and "herstory," because "to know ourselves as we are, we must know our mothers' names" (*In Search of Our Mothers' Gardens* 276).

Another aspect of *The Bluest Eye* that differentiates it from earlier fictional representations of little black girls is the novel's radical repudiation of "colorism."[4] Afro-American fiction is rife with light-skinned heroines. The protagonist of Harriet E. Wilson's *Our Nig* (1859), for example, is a mulatto. William Wells Brown's *Clotelle, or the Colored Heroine* (1867) is about a quadroon whose appearance gives no evidence "that a drop of African blood coursed through her veins." Emma Dunham Kelly's *Megda* (1891) has a white-skinned Afro-American heroine, as does Frances Ellen Watkins Harper's *Iola LeRoy, or Shadows Uplifted* (1893). Even Janie, in Zora Neale Hurston's *Their Eyes Were Watching God* (1937), is described as having light skin.

Nothing was more damaging to a dark-skinned girl than such valorization of what she could never be. Among the devastating passages in Afro-American autobiographies that testify to the irreparable damage done is Maya Angelou's recollection in *I Know Why the Caged Bird Sings* (1970) of a persistent childhood fantasy that she might one day wake up blonde and blue-eyed, not ugly and black. Gwendolyn Brooks's *Report from Part One* (1972) tells how she came to feel that she was of less worth than a "high-yellow" child, a theme that Brooks had presented earlier in her novel *Maud Martha* (1951). Because being dark meant never being considered beautiful, being other became a canonical part of black women's literature. "In almost every novel or autobiography written by a black woman," writes Mary Helen Washington, "there is at least one incident in which the dark-skinned girl wishes to be either white or light-skinned with good hair" (xv). So inherent is this "colorism" that one critic of children's literature has asserted that differentiations of skin color are what distinguish "culturally conscious" books from "inauthentic" ones: "Gradations in skin color," observes Rudine Sims, "are almost automatically part of an Afro-American's description of another Afro-American" (70).[5]

Thematically, *The Bluest Eye* consists of a stipulative definition which radically redefines beauty. The Macteer sisters hate Maureen, a new girl in school to whom everyone else defers reverentially. Claudia wants "to kick her" and plots "accidental slammings of locker doors on her hand" (54). Described by Morrison as "a high-yellow dream child with long brown hair braided into two lynch ropes" (52), Maureen has a hair style which underscores the "sinister quality of such beauty, at the same time acknowledging the white ancestor responsible for those ropes" (de Weever 406).

Claudia's ability to survive intact and to consolidate an identity derives from her vigorous opposition to the colorist attitudes of her community. She fights "to counteract the universal love of white baby dolls, Shirley Temples, and Maureen Peals" (148). In marked contrast to Pecola Breedlove's surrender to Western values, Claudia refuses to be tamed into conventional behavior and smashes the Shirley Temple doll that is imposed on her at Christmas. Allowing Pecola's submission to the messages transmitted by her culture to be presented from the viewpoint of a nine-year-old who energetically resents them permits Morrison to expose their insidiousness. The socialization patterns thoughtlessly transmitted from mother to daughter, from Pauline Breedlove to Pecola, are fatal to that child's self-esteem, but Claudia, who is bent on self-definition, will mature into someone who has control of her destiny.[6]

The process of bequeathing self-hatred is symbolized in the name Mrs. Breedlove has given her daughter. As Maureen Peal explains to Pecola, it came, like Mrs. Breedlove's "education in self-contempt" (97), from the movies:

> "Pecola? Wasn't that the name of the girl in *Imitation of Life*?"
>
> "I don't know. What is that?"
>
> "The picture show, you know. Where this mulatto girl hates her mother 'cause she is black and ugly."
>
> (57)

The point being made in this onomastic interplay is that Mrs. Breedlove learned to devalue herself through commercialized fantasies and is teaching her daughter a similar sense of unworthiness. Alice Walker quotes an article from *The Black Scholar* which calls this "psychic annihilation," letting "whites turn blacks on themselves."[7]

Ineluctably, the implications of Pecola's name work themselves out in her stunted imitation of a life. Acting on her conviction that her teachers ignore her, her schoolmates despise her, and her parents quarrel because she is ugly, she decides to transform herself. "Each night, without fail, she prayed for blue eyes. Fervently, for a year she had prayed" (40). She ingests penny candy to become the picture on the wrapper, the smiling white face with its "blue eyes looking at her out of a world of clean comfort. . . . To eat the candy is somehow to eat the eyes, eat Mary Jane. Love Mary Jane. Be Mary Jane" (43). She consumes the blue eyes on the Shirley Temple mug with her gaze, drinking in three quarts of milk to swallow its whiteness. Pecola's mother impresses on her daughter the fact that she prefers the pink-and-white, blue-eyed Fisher girl to her own child. Determined to change her eyes so that she too will be lovable, Pecola finds a faithhealer, Soaphead Church, who promises them to her because he is "wholly convinced that if black people were more like white people they would be better off."[8] The price she pays for them is her own sanity: She wanders through the town dump, babbling about how blue the eyes are that no one else can see.

Pecola's childhood is cancelled one Saturday afternoon when, at the age of twelve, she is raped by her father and left unconscious on the kitchen floor. Such things were not much mentioned in the fifties, when Sherley Anne Williams had looked in vain for a book about "forced sex" and had been too embarrassed to ask the librarian,[9] but Toni Morrison portrays the pedophiles that prey on little girls: Henry Washington, the boarder who is thrown out of the Macteers' house for "fingering" Frieda, and Soaphead Church, who is notorious for his sexual molestations. While Pecola retreats into delusion, those with the toughness and resiliency to defend themselves develop the inner strength needed to survive. As Claudia says, "We had defended ourselves since memory against everything and everybody" (149).

Frieda's coping skills are demonstrated when she disperses the gang of boys taunting Pecola in the schoolyard. She threatens Woodrow Cain with some information she has stored up from overheard adult conversations, and he slinks away, not wanting to be exposed as a bed wetter. This success in rescuing their friend emboldens the Macteer girls to try another strategy to save Pecola's unborn baby—"We did not think of the fact that Pecola was not married; lots of girls had babies who were not married. And we did not dwell on the fact that the baby's father was Pecola's father too; the process of having a baby by any male was incomprehensible to us—at least she knew her father. We thought only of this overwhelming hatred for the unborn baby" (148). But the marigold seeds they plant on behalf of Pecola's baby fail to sprout, and because they fail to save the baby's life, they avoid Pecola.

The girls' guilty self-recriminations form the prologue and the epilogue, for it has not occurred to them that the earth itself might have been "unyielding." It is this "hard ground" that the novel explores—a world that permits the foreclosure of childhood, that imposes a premature adulthood. The sociologist Joyce A. Ladner calls the pubescent black girl "emotionally precocious" because she has had either vicarious or personal experience of violence. Having been either a victim or a witness of aggression, she learns strategies of defending herself more vigorously than someone who has never been so vulnerable. Although these preadolescents have encountered harshness and cruelty, they "develop survival skills enabling them to cope with the world."[10]

In centering her story on an ordinary girl who is taught by her colorist culture that she is ugly, Toni Morrison portrays the cruel ground which forecloses Pecola's longing to be loved. The passage from the school primer which opens *The Bluest Eye* represents the "all-white world of children's books" which the novel challenges. The little MacTeer sisters, who tell Pecola's story, raise their voices in defense of what is black. Their penetrating vision sees, in Pecola's womb, "the baby that everybody wanted dead, and s[ee] it very clearly. It was in a dark, wet place, its head covered with great O's of wool, the black face holding, like nickels, two clean black eyes, the flared nose, kissing-thick lips, and the living, breathing silk of black skin" (148).

Defiantly alone in their protective impulses toward the unborn baby, they assume a maternal role toward it which is far beyond their capacities to fulfill. Their touching efforts to make a miracle on its behalf and their celebration of its blackness, which no one in their "unyielding" community shares, enhance the book's poignancy.

The protagonist, Pecola, seen through the eyes of a fastidious, middle-class neighbor, seems "dirty." The neighbor's gaze reveals the girl's

> torn dress, the plaits sticking out on her head, hair matted where the plaits had come undone, the muddy shoes with the wad of gum peeping out from between the cheap soles, the soiled socks, one of which had been walked down into the heel of the shoe. She saw the safety pin holding the hem of the dress up. . . . She had seen this little girl all her life. . . . Hair uncombed, dresses falling apart, shoes untied and caked with dirt.
>
> (75)

Toni Morrison's gaze reveals to the reader that Pecola is a little girl who has always been on the periphery. She presents us with Pecola's innocence and tragedy. The authorial stance of *The Bluest Eye* is epitomized in the disingenuous voices of its narrators: "We had dropped our seeds in our own little plot of black dirt" (9).

Notes

1. To assess the importance of autobiography as a genre in Afro-American letters, see Brignano. Stephen Butterfield explains how autobiography can be "both an arsenal and a battleground": ". . . if you are never able to take who you are for granted, and the social order around you seems deliberately designed to rub you out, stuff your head with little cartoon symbols of what it wants or fears you to be, and mock you with parodies of your highest hopes, then *discovering who you really are* takes on the dimensions of an epic battle with the social order" (284, emphasis added).

2. Bambara's own "The Girl's Story" also deals with this issue. "In almost every household that I can think of when I was growing up," says Bambara, "the onset of the menstrual period was mysterious and frightening, and totally without information and totally without support from the immediate household" (Guy-Sheftall 246).

3. Morrison would probe this painful problem again in her second novel, *Sula* (1974). When Hannah Peace asks her mother Eva if she has ever loved her, even the question is repudiated by the mother as "an evil wondering." Critic Mary Helen Washington provides useful insights into this incident: "Eva's plain, hostile answer is, 'No. I don't reckon I did. Not the way you thinkin',' and she accuses Hannah of thinking evil for even asking such a question. Later, she feels the need to explain that 'No,' but the rest of her answer is so brutal that the love behind it is almost unrecognizable: '. . . what you talkin'' bout did I love you girl. I stayed alive for you can't you get that through your thick head or what is that between your ears heifer? [sic]' This is the love of a woman who battled her way through life in order to keep her kids from starving. . . . She did not have anything left over to play around with them or teach them games or be silly with them and so her strength actually seems like a kind of cold indifference. . . . Eva takes care of her children, but she does so without physical affection or tenderness" (xxii).

4. "Colorism," according to Alice Walker, is a form of self-hatred, manifested in celebrations over "the birth of a 'golden' child" or the urgings to marry a "high-yellow" in order "to lighten up the race" (*In Search of Our Mothers' Gardens* 290, 311). "The structured colorism of the black middle class . . . is camouflaged by the promise of 'upward mobility,' i.e., proximity to, imitation of, and eventual merger with

(or, as Chestnutt wrote, 'absorption into') the white middle class" (310).

5. Sims also notes that, in an effort to evoke positive associations, these color descriptions are often presented in food-related imagery.

6. Some of the best contemporary criticism of Afro-American letters is coming from Germany. Berndt Ostendorf says that the function of black art is "to put people in control of their personal destinies. Black art is a form of externalizing the wounds of historically conditioned socialization patterns. These have to be objectified and isolated as art before they can be successfully transcended" (32). That Alice Walker, for one, has assumed this Blakean task is evident throughout her interview with Claudia Tate, particularly in her remarks on the responsibilities of her black readership.

7. "'. . . certainly every Afro-American is descended from a black black woman. What then can be the destiny of a people that pampers and cherishes the blood of the white slaveholder who maimed and degraded their female ancestor? What can be the future of a class of descendants of slaves that implicitly gives slaveholders greater honor than the African women they enslaved?'" (*In Search of Our Mothers' Gardens* 295).

8. Toni Morrison told Robert Stepto that, "with Soaphead, I wanted, needed someone to give the child her blue eyes. Now she was asking for something that was just awful—she wanted to have blue eyes and she wanted to be Shirley Temple, I mean, she wanted to do that white trip because of the society in which she lived and, very importantly, because of the black people who helped her want to be that. (The responsibilities are ours. It's our responsibility for helping her believe, helping her come to the point where she wanted that.) I had to have someone—her mother, of course, made her want that in the first place—who would give her the blue eyes . . . wholly convinced that if black people were more like white people they would be better off" (223).

9. What, asks Williams, did the white writers whose works she encountered in the library "know about being black, being on welfare, being solicited for sex by older black men in the neighborhood . . . ?" (195). Sonia Sanchez, too, has observed that, when she was twelve or thirteen, she had "mostly read white writers. No one gave me any literary work by black writers to read. . . . That's really a terrible commentary on education" (Tate interview 147). In the same interview, Sanchez recounts how she had to defend herself against sexual molestation in the corner store in Harlem when she was nine (138-39). Maya Angelou tells in *Caged Bird* of her rape at the age of eight. Mary Burger calls black adolescents "Child-Women": "The Black woman's need to grow up fast, bypassing a leisurely childhood, emanates from harsh environmental conditions" (111).

10. Ladner 62, 65. "An eight-year-old girl has a good chance of being exposed to rape and violence and her parents will be powerless to protect her" (62).

Works Cited

Bambara, Toni Cade. "The Girl's Story." *The Sea Birds are Still Alive*. New York: Random, 1977. 152-65.

Brignano, Russell C. *Black Americans in Autobiography: An Annotated Bibliography of Autobiographies and Autobiographical Books Written since the Civil War*. Durham: Duke UP, 1974.

Burger, Mary. "Images of Self and Race in the Autobiographies of Black Women." *Sturdy Black Bridges: Visions of Black Women in Literature*. Ed. Roseann P. Bell, Bettye J. Parker, and Beverly Guy-Sheftall. Garden City: Anchor, 1979. 107-22.

Butterfield, Stephen. *Black Autobiography in America*. Amherst: U of Massachusetts P, 1974.

de Weever, Jacqueline. "The Inverted World of Toni Morrison's *The Bluest Eye* and *Sula*." *CLA Journal* 22 (1979): 402-14.

Ellison, Ralph. *Shadow and Act*. New York: Random, 1964.

Guy-Sheftall, Beverly. "Commitment: Toni Cade Bambara Speaks." *Sturdy Black Bridges: Visions of Black Women in Literature*. Ed. Roseann P. Bell, Bettye J. Parker, and Beverly Guy-Sheftall. Garden City: Anchor, 1979. 230-49.

Ladner, Joyce A. *Tomorrow's Tomorrow: The Black Woman*. New York: Anchor, 1971.

Larrick, Nancy. "The All-White World of Children's Books." *Saturday Review* 11 Sept. 1965: 63-65, 84-85.

Morrison, Toni. *The Bluest Eye*. New York: Holt, 1970.

Ostendorf, Berndt. *Black Literature in White America: Studies in Contemporary Literature and Culture*. Totowa: Barnes, 1982.

Parker, Bettye J. "Complexity: Toni Morrison's Women—An Interview Essay." *Sturdy Black Bridges: Visions of Black Women in Literature*. Ed. Roseann P. Bell, Bettye J. Parker, and Beverly Guy-Sheftall. Garden City: Anchor, 1979. 251-57.

Sims, Rudine. *Shadow and Substance: Afro-American Experience in Contemporary Children's Fiction*. Urbana: NCTE, 1983.

Stanford, Barbara Dodds, and Karima Amin. *Black Literature for High School Students*. Urbana: NCTE, 1973.

Stepto, Robert B. "Intimate Things in Place: A Conversation with Toni Morrison." *Chant of Saints: A Gathering of Afro-American Literature, Art, and Scholarship*. Ed. Michael S. Harper and Robert B. Stepto. Urbana: U of Illinois P, 1979. 213-29.

Strouse, Jean. "Toni Morrison's Black Magic." *Newsweek* 30 Mar. 1981: 52-57.

Tate, Claudia. "Alice Walker." *Black Women Writers at Work*. New York: Continuum, 1983. 175-87.

———. "Sonia Sanchez." *Black Women Writers at Work*. New York: Continuum, 1983. 132-48.

Walker, Alice. *In Search of Our Mothers' Gardens: Womanist Prose*. New York: Harcourt, 1983.

———. "Saving the Life That Is Your Own: The Importance of Models in the Artist's Life." *The Ethnic American Woman: Problems, Protests, Lifestyles*. Ed. Edith Blicksilver. Dubuque: Kendall/Hunt, 1979.

Washington, Mary Helen, ed. *Black-Eyed Susans: Classic Stories by and about Black Women*. Garden City: Anchor, 1975.

Williams, Sherley Anne. "In Honor of Free Women." *Midnight Birds: Stories by Contemporary Black Women Writers*. Ed. Mary Helen Washington. Garden City: Anchor, 1980. 193-98.

Michael Awkward (essay date 1988)

SOURCE: Awkward, Michael. "Roadblocks and Relatives: Critical Revision in Toni Morrison's *The Bluest Eye*." In *Critical Essays on Toni Morrison,* edited by Nellie Y. McKay, pp. 57-68. Boston: G. K. Hall & Co., 1988.

[*In the following essay, Awkward considers the ways Morrison has incorporated and manipulated the works of earlier African American writers in* The Bluest Eye *in order to express and validate specific types of African American female experiences whose cultural significance those texts often deny.*]

In **"Rootedness: The Ancestor as Foundation,"** Toni Morrison insists that ancestors play an essential role in individual works in the Afro-American canon. She states:

> It seems to me interesting to evaluate Black literature on what the writer does with the presence of the ancestor. Which is to say a grandfather as in Ralph Ellison, or a grandmother as in Toni Cade Bambara, or a healer as in Bambara or Henry Dumas. There is always an elder there. And these ancestors are not just parents, they are sort of timeless people whose relationships to the characters are benevolent, instructive and protective, and they provide a certain kind of wisdom.[1]

Despite the apparent optimistic assurance of this statement, Morrison is well aware that "the presence of the ancestor" is not always viewed by the Afro-American writer as "benevolent, instructive and protective."

Indeed, she argues—just a few sentences following the above declaration that the works of Richard Wright and James Baldwin exhibit particularly identifiable problems with the ancestor. For Morrison, Wright's corpus suggests that he "had great difficulty with that ancestor," and Baldwin's that he was "confounded and disturbed by the presence or absence of an ancestor."[2]

Morrison's singling out of Wright and Baldwin as figures in whose works ancestors represent troubling presences (or absences) is not, it seems to me, a random act. For, as Morrison is well aware, the Wright-Baldwin personal and literary relationship represents the most fabled *intertextual* association in Afro-American letters. Baldwin's attacks on his acknowledged precursor Wright[3] offer intriguing Afro-American examples of what Harold Bloom has termed "the anxiety of influence." In "Alas, Poor Richard," for example, Baldwin says of his method of creating canonical space for his own perceptions of Afro-American life: "I had used [Wright's] work as a kind of springboard into my own. His own was a roadblock in my road, the sphinx, really, whose riddles I had to answer before I could become myself."[4]

An intertextual reading of Morrison's first novel, *The Bluest Eye* (1970), suggests that the works of older Afro-American writers also represented "roadblocks" in her journey to artistic selfhood. Specifically, Morrison's novel contains clear evidence of her (sometimes subtle) refigurations of Baldwin's discussion of Wright in "Many Thousands Gone" and the Trueblood episode in Ellison's *Invisible Man*. As we shall see, such revisionary acts, as well as her complex manipulation of her novel's prefatory primer, provide Morrison with the means of giving authentication and voice to specific types of black and feminine experiences whose validity and significance these texts—by overt and covert means—deny.

I

In "The Structuring of Emotion in Black American Fiction," Raymond Hedin astutely discusses Morrison's manipulation of the contents of **The Bluest Eye**'s prefatory primer. Hedin says:

> Morrison arranges the novel so that each of its sections provides a bitter gloss on key phrases from the novel's preface, a condensed version of the Dick and Jane reader. These phrases . . . describe the [American] cultural ideal of the healthy, supportive, well-to-do family. The seven central elements of Jane's world—house, family cat, Mother, father, dog, and friend—become, in turn, plot elements, but only after they are inverted to fit the realities of Pecola's world.[5]

Morrison employs the primer not only as prefatory material to the text proper, but also to introduce the chapters of *The Bluest Eye* that are recounted by the novel's omniscient narrative voice. The seven epigraphic sections are, as Hedin implies, thematically tied to the chapters which they directly precede.

For example, the chapter which introduces the Breedlove family to the reader is prefaced by the primer's reference to Jane's "very happy" family:

HEREISTHEFAMILYMOTHERFATHER
DICKANDJANETHEYLIVEINTHEGREEN
NANDWHITEHOUSETHEYAREVERYH[6]

But the family presented in the subsequent pages of the novel is the very antithesis of the standardized, ideal (white) American family of the primer. The reader learns, in fact, of the Breedloves' utter failure to conform to the standards by which the beauty and happiness of the primer family (and, by extension, American families in general) are measured.

But it is possible to make further claims for Morrison's employment of the primer as epigraph. In her systematic figuration of an inversive relationship between pretext (the primer) and text (her delineation of Afro-American life), the author dissects, *deconstructs*, if you will, the bourgeois myths of ideal family life. Through her deconstruction, she exposes each individual element of the myth as not only deceptively inaccurate in general, but also wholly inapplicable to black American life. The emotional estrangement of the primer family members (an estrangement suggested by that family's inability to respond to the daughter Jane's desire for play) implies that theirs is solely a surface contentment. For despite Hedin's suggestion that this family is represented as "healthy" and "supportive," it appears to be made up of rigid, emotionless figures incapable of deep feeling.

Morrison manipulates the primer in such a manner I believe, in order to trope certain conventions prominently found in eighteenth-, nineteenth-, and early twentieth-century Afro-American texts. The convention that Morrison revises here is that of the authenticating document, usually written by whites to confirm a genuine black authorship of the subsequent text (for example, William Lloyd Garrison's preface to Frederick Douglass's *Narrative*). The Afro-American critic Robert Stepto has suggested that the manipulation of such white pretextual authorization of the black voice has had a significant influence in the development of the Afro-American narrative. The Afro-American narrative moves, as Stepto suggests in *From behind the Veil*, from white authentication of blackness to, with the examples of Ralph Ellison and Richard Wright, black self-authentication.[7] Morrison's manipulation of *The Bluest Eye*'s prefatory primer signals, it seems to me, another step in the development of the Afro-American narrative as conceived by Stepto. Morrison returns to an earlier practice—of the white voice introducing the black text—to demonstrate her refusal to allow white standards to arbitrate the success or failure of the black experience. Her manipulation of the primer is meant to suggest, finally, the inappropriateness of the white voice's attempt to authorize or authenticate the black text or to dictate the contours of Afro-American art.

The Bluest Eye's first-person narrator, Claudia, performs a similar act in rejecting white criteria of judgment when she is able to view her childhood, which she had formerly conceived in a vocabulary of pain and degradation, as being characterized by "a productive and fructifying pain" and filled with the protective, "sweet," "thick and dark" love of a mother "who does not want me to die."[8] Like Nikki Giovanni's persona in "Nikki Rosa," Claudia discovers that despite the difficulties of poverty in an opulent America, "all the while I was quite happy."[9]

Claudia's achievement of a positive reading of her childhood, however, is not unproblematic, to be sure. Perhaps the most poignant (and certainly the most charged in an intertextual sense) of the incidents that result in her ability to reread her own life is her attempt to understand the rationale for standards that insist on white physical superiority. Claudia's efforts to comprehend the myth of white physical superiority while attempting, at the same time to hold on to her views of her own people's beauty and cultural worth, exposes hers as a situation "betwixt and between" that the anthropologist Victor Turner has labeled liminality or marginality. Marginals, according to Turner,

> are simultaneous members (by ascription, optation, self-definition, or achievement) of two or more groups whose social definitions and cultural norms are distinct from, and often even opposed to, one another.[10]

To begin to resolve such social ambiguity, Turner argues, it is necessary that the marginal seek both the origin and an understanding of the often self-aggrandizing myths of the "more prestigious group."[11] The questing marginal must seek to understand the origins of myths, "*how* things came to be *what* they are."[12] Consequently, adults' gifts of white dolls to Claudia are not pleasure-inducing toys, but, rather, signs (in a semiotic sense) that she must learn to interpret correctly. Such interpretation requires mining the dolls' surfaces—pink skins, blue eyes, blond hair—a literal search for sources:

> I had only one desire: to dismember [the doll]. To see of what it was made, to discover the dearness, to find the beauty, the desirability that had escaped me, but apparently only me. Adults, older girls, shops, magazines, newspapers, window signs—all the world had agreed that a blue-eyed, yellow-haired, pink-skinned doll was what every girl child treasured. "Here," they said "this

is beautiful, and if you are on this day 'worthy' you may have." ... I could not love it. But I could examine it to see what it was that all the world said was lovable.[13]

Claudia's search for the source of white beauty, however, is not confined solely to dolls. She says that the impulse to dismember white dolls gives way to "The truly horrifying thing":

> ... the transference of the same impulse to little white girls. The indifference with which I could have axed them was shaken only by my desire to do so. To discover what eluded me: the secret of the magic they weaved on others. What made people look at them and say, "Awwwww," but not for me? ...
>
> If I pinched them, their eyes—unlike the crazed glint of the baby doll's eyes—would fold in pain, and their cry would not be the sound of an icebox door, but a fascinating cry of pain.[14]

Claudia's somewhat sadistic dismemberment of white dolls and her subsequent torture of white girls are meant to recall, it seems to me, Bigger Thomas's axed mutilation of the dead body of Mary Dalton (presented by Wright as a symbol of young white female beauty) in *Native Son*.[15] Morrison's refiguration of Wright's scene, as we shall see, is her means of adding her voice to the discourse surrounding Bigger's murder, the most renowned of which belongs to James Baldwin.

Claudia's impulses lend nominal weight to Baldwin's claim in "Many Thousands Gone" that "no Negro living in America ... has not ... wanted ... to break the bodies of all white people and bring them low."[16] But while Baldwin suggests that such violent urges are "urges of the cruelest vengeance" and motivated by "unanswerable hatred,"[17] Claudia's acts are motivated in the main by a need to locate the source of white beauty that is not immediately apparent to her. Baldwin believes that, in general, the Afro-American refusal to give in to such urges and "smash any white face he may encounter in a day" results from a noble embrace of humanity. He states:

> the adjustment [from rage to accommodation] must be made—rather, it must be attempted, the tension perpetually sustained—for without this he [the Afro-American] has surrendered his birthright as a man no less than his birthright as a black man. The entire universe is then peopled only with his enemies, who are not only white men armed with rope and rifle, but his own far-flung and contemptible kinsmen. Their blackness is his degradation and it is their stupid and passive endurance which makes his end inevitable.[18]

For Baldwin, such "adjustment" allows the Afro-American to claim (or reclaim) his humanity, and to demystify and devillainize whites and to love his own people.

Claudia's adjustment, on the other hand, has significantly different causes and consequences:

> When I learned how repulsive this disinterested violence [directed toward white girls] was, that it was repulsive because it was disinterested, my shame floundered about for refuge. The best hiding place was love. Thus the conversion from pristine sadism to fabricated hatred to fraudulent love. It was a small step to Shirley Temple. I learned much later to worship her ... , knowing, even as I learned, that the change was *adjustment without improvement*.
>
> (my emphasis)[19]

Claudia's "conversion" is motivated not by an embrace of humanity, but rather by "shame." The questing marginal's quandaries about the origins of this standard remain unanswered. She learns only to feel ashamed of the curiosity that led to her "disinterested violence," and that her failure to accept without question the standards of white America is considered "repulsive."

Claudia terminates her search for the source of white myths of superiority and replaces the violent urges she had previously directed at whites with "fraudulent love." But the suppression of violent urges by Afro-Americans has significantly different implications for Morrison than for Baldwin. For Morrison, the Afro-American's humanity is not what is at stake, and "fraudulent love" of whites, the ultimate result of this rejection of violence, is not better or more authentically human. It is only different, only "adjustment" (an intentional repetition of Baldwin's terminology, it would appear) "without improvement." Hence, Morrison suggests, in her subtle rejection of Baldwin's reading of Bigger Thomas's humanity, that the adjustment of which the older writer speaks can lead to the devaluation of the authentically black.

II

We have seen how the revisionist impulses of *The Bluest Eye* plainly demonstrate Morrison's view of the terms in which a truly healthy black art and life are possible. Her provocative revision of Ellison suggests most clearly her view that energetic rejection of male (mis)representations of women is necessary for a faithful and responsible depiction of women's lives. I believe that at the heart of *The Bluest Eye*'s delineation of an incestuous encounter between Pecola and her father is Morrison's intertextually charged revision of the Ellisonian depiction of incest in the Trueblood episode of *Invisible Man*.

The Breedlove family in Morrison's text possesses a parodic relation to Ellison's incestuous clan. This relation is initially suggested in the names of the respective families. Ellison's designation suggests that the sharecropper and his family are the true (genuine) "bloods" (an Afro-American vernacular term for culturally immersed blacks). The Breedloves' name, however, is bestowed with bitter irony: theirs is a self-hating family in which no love is bred. In both texts the economically destitute families are forced to sleep in dangerously close(d) quarters. In *Invisible Man*, cold winters—and a lack of money with which to purchase fuel—force the nubile Matty Lou into bed between her still-procreative parents. In the case of ***The Bluest Eye***, Pecola sleeps in the same room as her parents, a proximity that necessitates her hearing the "Choking sounds and silence" of their lovemaking.[20]

Further, there are stark similarities between mother and daughter in both texts that contribute to the incestuous act in both cases. In a discussion of the Trueblood Episode in Ralph Ellison's *Invisible Man*, Houston Baker argues that the daughter Matty Lou is her mother "Kate's double—a woman who looks just like her mother and who is fully grown and sexually mature."[21] And Cholly Breedlove's incestuous lust is awakened by Pecola's scratching of her leg in a manner that mirrored "what Pauline was doing the first time he saw her in Kentucky."[22]

It is possible, with the above evidence in place, to begin to suggest the specifics of what seems to me to be Morrison's purposefully feminist revision of Ellison. Read intertextually, ***The Bluest Eye*** provides—as I shall demonstrate below—an example par excellence of what the feminist critic Annette Kolodny has called revisionary reading [that] open[s] new avenues for comprehending male texts."[23]

In *The Resisting Reader*, Judith Fetterley argues that the reading of the Western canon's overwhelmingly male (and decidedly phallocentric) texts has encouraged women's agreement with the inscribed antifemale slant of the works. Having been taught to accept the phallocentric as indisputably universal, the woman reader unconsciously internalizes the often misogynistic messages of male texts. Fetterley insists that a female must, in order to participate successfully as a woman in the reading experience, "become a resisting rather than an assenting reader and, by this refusal to assent, . . . begin the process of exorcizing the male mind that has been implanted" in women.[24] The removal of the male implant results, for Fetterley, in "the capacity for what Adrienne Rich describes as re-vision, 'the act of looking back, of seeing with fresh eyes, of entering an old text from a new critical direction.'"[25] Feminist revision, according to Fetterley, offers the terms of a radically altered critical enterprise and the liberation of the critic: "books will . . . lose their power to bind us unknowingly to their designs."[26]

Houston Baker's "To Move without Moving" is an excellent example in support of Fetterley's view of the (sometimes dangerously) persuasive powers of texts.

For in this essay, we can observe the power of texts quite literally to bind even the most intellectually nimble readers/critics to their designs. Baker has exhibited, in a stunning reading of the economics of female slavery and the figuration of a community of female slaves in Linda Brent's *Incidents in the Life of a Slave Girl*,[27] his awareness of the ways in which feminist theory can help illuminate literary texts. This sensitivity to feminist concerns is, unfortunately, missing from his reading of Ellison. Instead, Baker's essay mirrors the strategies by which Trueblood (and Trueblood's creator) validates male perceptions of incest while, at the same time, silencing the female voice or relegating it to the evaluative periphery.

Baker begins his reading by citing Ellison's discussion in the essay "Richard Wright's Blues" of "The function, the psychology, of artistic selectivity."[28] This function, according to the novelist, "is to eliminate from art form all those elements of experience which contain *no compelling significance* (my emphasis).[29] Ellison's words provide a means to discuss the shortcomings of his own and Baker's treatments of the subject of incest. For Ellison's statement, situated as it is in Baker's essay, leads to an inquiry as to why neither Ellison's text nor Baker's critique of it treat the female perspective on, and reaction to, incest as containing "no compelling significance."

In the case of the novel, Trueblood's incestuous act is judged almost exclusively by men, from the black school administrators who wish to remove the sharecropper from the community to Trueblood's white protectors who pressure the administrators to allow the sharecropper to remain in his house and who "wanted to hear about the gal [Matty Lou] lots of times."[30] They form, as it were, an exclusively male-evaluate circle which views Trueblood's act as either shamefully repugnant or meritoriously salacious.

Except for the mother Kate's memorably violent reaction, the female perspective on Trueblood's act is effectively silenced and relegated to the periphery in Trueblood's recounting of the story. Never in the sharecropper's rendering of the story are Matty Lou's feelings in the foreground or even actually shared with the reader. Further, Trueblood is well aware of the silent scorn that the women who help Kate attend to the unconscious Matty Lou bear for him. When he returns home after an exile precipitated, in his view, by the inability of others to distinguish between "blood-sin" and "dream-sin," he orders the scornful community of women that has formed in response to his "dirty lowdown wicked dog" act off his property: "There's a heap of women here with Kate and I runs'em out."[31] Having effectively run out the openly critical female community and silenced, by means of his abominable act, his wife and daughter, Trueblood is able to interpret his act in an extremely self-serving way, untroubled by the radically incompatible perspectives of women. Thus he can, despite his belief that he is a good family man, fail to see the bitter irony in his own assessment of his family situation: "Except that my wife and daughter won't speak to me, I'm better off than I ever been before."[32]

From a feminist perspective, Baker's reading of the Trueblood episode proves as problematic as the sharecropper's own because he, too, relegates the woman's voice to the evaluative periphery and sketches his own circle of males to justify and validate Trueblood's act. Baker asserts that one of the dominant themes of *Invisible Man* is "black male sexuality"[33] and invokes male social thinkers to suggest the accuracy of this reading vis-à-vis the Trueblood episode. And while statements from Clifford Geertz and Freud help Baker to substantiate points about the uncontrollability of phallic energy and about Trueblood's dream signalling a historical regression,[34] they fail, because they invoke worlds in which women are indisputably at the mercy of the phallic and legislative powers of men, to allow the critic to consider the response of the victim to her father's act.

And though Baker makes a valiant effort to endow the hastily considered Matty Lou with positive qualities, viewing her—along with her mother—as one of the "bearers of new black life,"[35] she remains in the critic's interpretation of the episode—as she does in the sharecropper's narration—simply an absence. While Baker's essay adds immeasurably to our understanding of Ellison's art, it fails, unfortunately, to consider the subsequently silenced victim of Trueblood's unrestrained phallus. Only by failing to grapple seriously with the implications of Trueblood's representation of Matty Lou's state following the incestuous act—"Matty Lou won't look at me and won't speak a word to nobody"[36]—can Baker conceive of the consequences of the taboo-breaking act as generally beneficial.

Unlike Baker's reading of the Trueblood episode of *Invisible Man* in which incest is conceptualized as material and tribal gain, Morrison's revision depicts it as painfully devastating loss. Actually, Morrison's reading of Ellison's text must be remarkably similar to Baker's, for in refiguring Trueblood in the character of Cholly Breedlove, she surrounds her creation with images consistent with Baker's conception of the Ellisonian character as majestic Afro-American vernacular artist free from social restraints. Morrison says:

> Only a musician would sense, know, without even knowing that he knew, that Cholly was free. Dangerously free. Free to feel whatever he felt—fear, guilt, shame, love, grief, pity. Free to be tender or violent, to whistle or weep. . . . He was free to live his fantasies, and free even to die, the how and when of which held no interest for him. . . .[37]

It was in this godlike state that he met Pauline Williams.[38] Only an Afro-American artist with the blues sensibility that Baker argues for Trueblood can organize and transform into meaningfully unified expression the utter chaos of Cholly's life. But Morrison—the remarkably skilled craftsperson who does transform Cholly's life into art—provides the blues song that is *The Bluest Eye* with a decidedly feminist slant. For while Ellison furnishes his depiction of incest with a vocabulary of naturalism and historical regression that permit it to be read in relation to undeniably phallocentric sociocultural interpretations of human history, Morrison's representation is rendered in startlingly blunt terms.

Trueblood's presence inside his sexually inexperienced daughter's vagina is described in ways that suggest a significant symbolic import. The sharecropper's dream of sexual contact with a white woman while in the home of an affluent white man necessarily brings to mind images of lynching and castration of black men because of the threat of black male sexuality. Consequently, Trueblood's actual presence inside his daughter assumes less of an importance in the text than his dream encounter with an unnamed white woman. Morrison, however, provides her depiction of incest with no such historically symbolic significance:

> [Cholly's] mouth trembled at the firm sweetness of the flesh. He closed his eyes, letting his fingers dig into her waist. The rigidness of her shocked body, the silence of her stunned throat, was better than Pauline's easy laughter had been. The confused mixture of his memories of Pauline and the doing of a wild and forbidden thing excited him, and a bolt of desire ran down his genitals, giving it length, and softening the lips of his anus. Surrounding all of this lust was a border of politeness. He wanted to fuck her—tenderly. But the tenderness would not hold. The tightness of her vagina was more than he could bear. His soul seemed to slip down to his guts and fly out into her, and the gigantic thrust he made into her then provoked the only sound she made—a hollow suck of air in the back of her throat.[39]

Cholly is far from the majestic figure that Baker argues for Trueblood during his efforts to "move without movin'" in his daughter's vagina. And though Morrison does give the incestuous male figure the capacity for sympathy—citing, for example, the "border of politeness" that accompanies his lust—Cholly's "wild," "confused" act lacks the inscribed symbolic weight of Trueblood's transgression. While the sharecropper's inability to withdraw from his daughter's vagina represents, according to Baker, Trueblood's "say[ing] a resounding 'no' to the castratingly tight spots of his existence as a poor farmer in the undemocratic south,"[40] the tight sexual space represents for Cholly the forbidden area that must be forcibly entered and exited. The text of *The Bluest Eye* informs us: "Removing himself from her was so painful to him he cut it short and snatched his genitals out of the dry harbor of her vagina."⁴¹

Morrison finally seems to be taking Ellison to task for the phallocentric nature of his representation of incest that marginalizes and renders as irrelevant the consequences of the act for the female victim. Morrison writes her way into the Afro-American literary tradition by bringing to the foreground the effects of incest for female victims in direct response to Ellison's refusal to consider them seriously. So while the victims of incest in both novels ultimately occupy similarly asocial, silent positions in their respective communities, Morrison explicitly details Pecola's tragic and painful journey, while Ellison, in confining Matty Lou to the periphery, suggests that her perspective contains for him "no compelling significance."

While the criticism of *The Bluest Eye* has correctly demonstrated Morrison's revisionary intentions vis-à-vis its prefatory primer, it has failed to chart its refigurations of such key texts as Baldwin's and Ellison's. The stunning success of Morrison's revisionist gestures is on a par with Baldwin's efforts to clear away the roadblock to his entry into the Afro-American literary tradition, Richard Wright. But unlike Baldwin, Morrison locates her disputes with ancestors primarily within fictional texts. As a result, she is able to create a first novel that represents an important revisionary moment in Afro-American letters, one in which like no novel before it with the exception of Zora Neale Hurston's *Their Eyes Were Watching God*,⁴² nationalist and feminist concerns combine to produce what Morrison elsewhere has called a "genuine Black . . . Book."⁴³ Morrison's revisionary gestures, it seems to me, create canonical space for subsequent black *and* feminist texts such as Ntozake Shange's *For Colored Girls,* Gloria Naylor's *The Women of Brewster Place,* and Morrison's own *Sula,* as well as for the rediscovery of Hurston's classic novel. *The Bluest Eye,* then, has served to change permanently the overwhelmingly male disposition of the Afro-American literary canon.

Notes

1. Toni Morrison, "Rootedness: The Ancestor as Foundation," in *Black Women Writers (1950-1980),* ed. Mari Evans (New York: Doubleday, 1984), 343.

2. Ibid.

3. James Baldwin, "Everybody's Protest Novel," and "Many Thousands Gone," in *Notes of a Native Son* (New York: Bantam, 1955), 9-17, 18-36; Baldwin, "Alas, Poor Richard," *Nobody Knows My Name* (New York: Dial, 1961), 181-215.

4. Baldwin, "Alas, Poor Richard," 197.

5. Raymond Hedin, "The Structuring of Emotion in Black American Fiction," *Novel* 16, no. 1 (Fall 1982): 50.

6. Toni Morrison, *The Bluest Eye* (New York: Washington Square Press, 1970), 34.

7. See Robert Stepto, *From behind the Veil* (Urbana: University of Illinois Press, 1979).

8. Morrison, *Bluest Eye,* 14.

9. Nikki Giovanni, "Nikki Rosa," *Black Feelings, Black Talk, Black Judgement* (New York: Morrow Quill, 1970), 59.

10. Victor Turner, *Dramas, Fields, and Metaphors* (Ithaca, N.Y.: Cornell University Press, 1974), 233.

11. Ibid.

12. Ibid.

13. Morrison, *Bluest Eye,* 20.

14. Ibid., 22.

15. See Richard Wright, *Native Son* (New York: Harper and Row, 1940), 90-92.

16. Baldwin, "Many Thousands Gone," 30.

17. Ibid.

18. Ibid.

19. Morrison, *Bluest Eye,* 22.

20. Ibid., 49.

21. Houston Baker, "To Move without Moving: Creativity and Commerce," in *Blues, Ideology, and Afro-American Literature* (Chicago: University of Chicago Press, 1984), 185.

22. Morrison, *Bluest Eye,* 28.

23. Annette Kolodny, "A Map of Rereading," in *The New Feminist Criticism,* ed. Elaine Showalter (New York: Pantheon, 1985), 55.

24. Judith Fetterley, *The Resisting Reader* (Bloomington: Indiana University Press, 1978), xxii.

25. Ibid.

26. Ibid., xxii-xxiii.

27. See Baker, "To Move without Moving," 50-56.

28. Houston Baker, "Richard Wright's Blues," in *Shadow and Act* (New York: Vintage, 1964), 94.

29. Ibid., 93.

30. Ralph Ellison, *Invisible Man* (New York: Vintage, 1952), 52.

31. Ibid., 66.

32. Ibid., 67.

33. Baker, "To Move without Moving," 180.

34. For Baker's discussion of Geertz and Freud (and others), see *Blues, Ideology, and Afro-American Literature,* 17-84.

35. Baker, "To Move without Moving," 185.

36. Ellison, *Invisible Man,* 66.

37. Morrison, *Bluest Eye,* 125-126.

38. Ibid.

39. Ibid., 128.

40. Ibid., 187.

41. Ibid., 128.

42. For a discussion of the nationalist and feminist dimensions of Hurston's masterwork, see Michael Awkward, "The Inaudible Voice of It All: Silence, Voice, and Action in *Their Eyes Were Watching God,*" in *Feminist Criticism of Black American Literature, Studies in Black American Literature,* vol. 3 (Greenwood, Fla.: Penkevill, 1986).

43. Toni Morrison, "Behind the Making of *The Black Book,*" *Black World,* February 1974, 89.

Trudier Harris (essay date 1988)

SOURCE: Harris, Trudier. "Reconnecting Fragments: Afro-American Folk Tradition in *The Bluest Eye*." In *Critical Essays on Toni Morrison,* edited by Nellie Y. McKay, pp. 68-76. Boston: G. K. Hall & Co., 1988.

[*In the following essay, Harris examines the influence of African American folk traditions in* The Bluest Eye *with respect to the relation between communal patterns of survival and coping and the shaping of individual character.*]

The Bluest Eye is not only the story of the destructive effects of inter- and intraracial prejudice upon impressionable black girls in the midwest; it is also the story of Afro-American folk culture in process. Through subtle and not-so-subtle ways, Toni Morrison suggests that the vibrancy of the folk culture persists through the fortunes and misfortunes of the characters, and it serves to baptize them into kinship with each other. From folk wisdom to the blues, from folk speech to myths and other beliefs, Lorain, Ohio, shares with historical black folk communities patterns of survival and coping, traditions that comfort in times of loss, and beliefs that point to an enduring creativity.

The setting mirrors perhaps one of the greatest beliefs in black communities during and after slavery—that the North is a freer place for black people economically and socially. It does not matter that Lorain, Ohio, is just a shade north of south, or that Pauline Breedlove has only come from Kentucky, a couple of hundred miles away; it is still relevant that the city is north of where she was, that it holds out to her the traditional expectations of existence above the Mason Dixon line. It was irrelevant that some blacks arrived in the North and found conditions hardly better than the ones they thought they were escaping in the South. These migrants felt they had to hold out the promise to their relatives and friends in the South even if the promise had failed them. So tales circulated about how wonderful things could be "up North." Then, too, the myth was reinforced in those blacks who tamed the concrete jungle, acquired good jobs, and sent their children to school well clothed. In time they formed a middle class, separated from the hordes of their still-migrating sisters and brothers.

For Pauline and Cholly Breedlove, the myth of the North is temporarily a reality. For awhile, in Ohio, they have a house and the money they need. But Pauline's restlessness and Cholly's drinking eventually lead them to the triangular storefront house that comes to epitomize their economic and mental state. When Pauline loses a tooth and gives up trying to imitate white movie heroines, she resigns herself to poverty and ugliness. When her children are born, she conditions them to see the North as the nightmare into which her dream has turned. In short, her trading of myth for reality becomes detrimental to her whole family; even when the mythical images were those of the distorting silver screen, Pauline could believe that the promise of the North could be fulfilled. Once she loses faith in the possibility for change, she gives up beliefs that have tied her to historical black communities as well as to prevailing folk traditions. Giving up reflects, in part, her ultimate transference of identification from blacks to whites, as illustrated in her worship of the "little pink-and-yellow" Fisher girl. Her severing of ties to the folk culture in turn short circuits any connections she could pass on to Pecola that would aid her in reconnecting to that culture.

In general, Morrison's characters adhere to many folk beliefs, superstitions, and signs common to historical communities. This is especially true of beliefs surrounding sickness and death. For example, the novel opens with Claudia's remembrances of her mother's treatment for colds when she was growing up: a massage with Vicks salve, a bit to swallow, neck and chest wrapped in a "hot flannel." All were designed to induce sweating, which was believed to be effective in reducing fevers. In black communities where doctors were expensive or scarce, home remedies and items that could be purchased without prescription were relied on. Wrappings frequently became preventive medicine; children warded off colds and other ailments by wearing roots held on by flannel applied under their dresses and shirts. The belief extends to some of the older women in Morrison's community. Cholly's Aunt Jimmy wears her asefetida bag "around her neck";[1] other older women in the community "wrapped their heads in rags, and their breasts in flannel" (110). For them, belief in natural cures is a way of life, and they are not willing to part with their practices.

The specifics of these details are less important than that they show how people in such communities *cared* for each other, a caring that is in stark contrast to most of the characters in *The Bluest Eye*. Where such caring touches the lives of the characters, as with Claudia and with Cholly when Aunt Jimmy was alive, there is a positive influence upon behavior. When such caring disappears, as with Cholly after Aunt Jimmy's death, or was never available, as with Pecola, disastrous results ensue. Thus, through these sometimes casual references, Morrison offers a part of the pattern of black interaction that sustains against the dissolution represented by Pauline's refusal to mother her children, Geraldine's distortion of the notion of family, and Cholly's destructive abuse of his daughter.

The emphasis upon caring applies to the cures offered Aunt Jimmy during her illness. While they do not save her, they illustrate a variety of beliefs and convey the altruistic concern absent from many relationships in the novel. Taken ill after a camp meeting during a rainstorm, Jimmy is told: "Don't eat no whites of eggs," "Drink new milk," "Chew on this root" (108). Refusing such advice, Jimmy does not get better until M'Dear, the local healer, is brought in. "A competent and decisive diagnostician," M'Dear is usually called in when all the "ordinary means" of curing illnesses have failed. She determines that Jimmy has caught a cold in her womb and advises her to "drink pot liquor and nothing else" (108). Jimmy does well until a neighbor decides that she is strong enough to eat a peach cobbler; the next morning Cholly finds her dead. Since the community believes M'Dear "infallible," Jimmy could only have died from eating the peach cobbler. With the logic of the beliefs that guide their cures and preventions, the women rationally conclude that deviation from the advice (drink pot liquor) that had shown itself effective led to Jimmy's death. In their minds the peach cobbler was not blameless, or Jimmy's condition irreversible. A natural cure had been put into effect, and the natural flow was interrupted by the introduction of an alien element. That alien element was responsible for the death. The women accept that with the same stoicism that they combat the waywardness of their husbands and children and the racism of whites.

Their belief in and the very description of M'Dear is also reminiscent of historical folk communities where local healers, or conjurers, or hoodoo doctors usually had distinctive physical characteristics or deformities that set them apart from others in the community. Newbell Niles Puckett, in his study of conjuration in the South,[2] emphasized that many of the conjurers had one blue eye and one black eye, were extremely dark skinned, might be crippled or walked with a cane, and that they frequently lived apart from the rest of the community. M'Dear "was a quiet woman who lived in a shack near the woods" (108). Her power and the confidence the community has in her are reflected in her physical characteristics. Cholly expects her to be "shriveled and hunched over" because he has heard that "she was very, very old": "But M'Dear loomed taller than the preacher who accompanied her. She must have been over six feet tall. Four big white knots of hair gave power and authority to her soft black face. Standing straight as a poker, she seemed to need her hickory stick not for support but for communication" (108). The preacher's accompaniment lends power to M'Dear's authority, for in this realm of belief, the secular and the sacred come together. M'Dear's place in the community is as secure, or more so, than the preacher's; her practical status as midwife lends credence to, if not actual tolerance for, her other areas of expertise. Her ties to the community, despite her seeming outsider status, provide another contrast to Pecola, who, severed from those traditions that could incorporate her, merely remains outside the bonds of caring.

The community that believes in M'Dear's powers and in the killing power of peach cobbler also has its share of other folk beliefs and entertainments. Blue Jack, the old man who befriends Cholly after he quits school, is an active tradition bearer of various kinds of tales: "Blue used to tell him old-timey stories about how it was when the Emancipation Proclamation came. How the black people hollered, cried, and sang And ghost stories about how a white man cut off his wife's head and buried her in the swamp, and the headless body came out at night and went stumbling around the yard, knocking over stuff because it couldn't see, and crying all the time for a comb. They talked about the women Blue had had, and the fights he'd been in when he was younger, about how he talked his way out of getting lynched once, and how others hadn't" (106). The story about the headless woman ties in to many tales of decapitation that circulate in oral tradition, those that are legendary in form, that is, told for true, and those that are etiological in form, explaining, for example, how the jack-o-lantern came into existence.

Blue becomes a folk hero to Cholly, and, long into adulthood, after he has killed three white men and become his own legend, Cholly remembers the good times he has had with Blue. The veneration comes as much from the stories Blue has told as from his admiration of Blue's life—carefree and without responsibilities to anyone. It also comes from the fact that Blue has been one of the few people, besides Aunt Jimmy, who cared for Cholly, who responded to him as a human being, rather than as a phallic symbol, a "nigger," or a burden. No such model exists for Pecola; even the prostitutes who befriend her are equally alienated from the community.

Elements of folk speech, like the folktales and folk heroes are also relevant to the novel. Metaphors comparable to those Zora Neale Hurston uses in *Jonah's Gourd Vine* (1934) occur intermittently, making contrasts between the characters like Geraldine, who deny any ties to folk roots, and those who are closer to the selves inherent in their blackness, such as Claudia's mother. When Mrs. MacTeer exclaims that she has "as much business with another mouth to feed as a cat has with side pockets" (23), she exhibits philosophical ties with black people who express their conditions in metaphoric language that is arresting in its vividness. Pauline Breedlove's observation that it is as "cold as a witch's tit" (35) in her house is also a familiar folk expression. When Miss Marie notes that Pecola, on a visit to her house, is without socks, she describes her "as barelegged as a yard dog" (44), a comparison that again evokes the folk creativity that draws similes and metaphors from animals and the natural world. Such expressions tie these characters to historic folk communities even if they should later, as Pauline does, choose to reject most of those bonds of kinship.

Other traditions relevant to the shaping of black character are nicknaming and name calling, which again reflect patterns of caring and incorporation into community. Pauline is pained that she does not have a nickname and blames it on the family's pity for her, for the "slight deformity" she suffers, left from a nail puncture in her foot when she was two years old. Nicknaming is an old and venerated tradition in the black community, and not having been given one, Pauline felt excluded. Without that special favor bestowed upon her, and without being teased or having anecdotes told about her, Pauline "never felt at home anywhere, or that she belonged anyplace" (88). In their studies of nicknames in black communities, scholars have focused on the tremendous value they have, the special recognition they bestow upon an individual for a feat accomplished, a trait emphasized, or a characteristic noticed. Without a nickname, Pauline feels unclaimed by her family in any special way. When the rich white family for which she works in Ohio assigns her a nickname—Polly—it serves in part to explain Pauline's attachment to them: "they gave her what she never had" (101) and thereby claim her attention and her loyalty more so than anyone in her family had done. The white family tells anecdotes about her, of how they could "never find anybody like Polly," of how "she will *not* leave the kitchen until everything is in order," and of how she is ultimately the "ideal servant" (101). A perversion of the functions nicknames serve in black communities, Pauline, as Polly, illustrates the potential identity-shaping purpose such naming provides. She desperately clings to her relationship with the Fishers, but fails to see in her daughter a similar need to be claimed in a special way. Pecola's formal name, reminiscent of movies and books, suggests distance rather than claiming.

To be called "out of one's name," as Bernice Reagan has asserted in some of her research on naming, can be just as negatively powerful as a nickname can be positive.[3] The person so defamed is denied a confirming identity, and thereby suffers a lack comparable to what Pauline feels for not being singled out. The school children who shout names at Pecola shame her and use her features as a way of denying her admission into their society. When the boys circle her in a ritual of insult and shout "Black e mo Black e mo Ya daddy sleeps nekked" (55), Pecola becomes the victim who invites further abuse because she suffers visibly. The game is tantamount to a rite of separation. In the process, Pecola is given another opportunity to view her status as an outsider. Her rescue by Maureen Peal, Claudia, and Frieda is only temporary, because Maureen indulges Pecola only in an effort to discover if the insult the boys have shouted about her father is really true. Unsatisfied, the light-skinned Maureen draws a circle of acceptance around herself that excludes the other three girls: "I *am* cute! And you ugly! Black and ugly black e mos. I *am* cute!" (61). Conscious of her unattractiveness and her color, Pecola seems to disappear where she stands, unable to join Claudia and Frieda in returning insults to Maureen, or to appreciate that they are fighting for her. She senses too strongly rejection at an irredeemable level. Children, teachers, neighbors, and other adults have confirmed what her mother concluded upon her birth: that Pecola will never be an insider in the black community and cannot possibly hope for acceptance beyond it. All combine to reinforce Pecola's belief that the only escape for her is to become beautiful through obtaining the bluest eyes of all, ones that will dazzle everyone into loving her.

Her belief in what blue eyes will accomplish for her is just as strong as some of the folk beliefs expressed in the novel. Belief is the single most important factor in conjuration as in Christianity, the two systems to which Pecola is most frequently exposed. Her prayers to God to make her disappear are predicated upon the belief that such a feat is possible. Her giving of the poisoned meat to the old dog is similarly predicated upon the belief that, if a reaction occurs, her wish for blue eyes will be granted. Hope for a magical transformation underlies both desires, and Pecola's belief in the possible transformation ties her to all believers in sympathetic magic. Her conviction that the blue eyes have been granted her may be viewed as insanity, but it simultaneously fits the logic that has led to that final reward. It is no stranger than the community women's belief that Jimmy has died from eating a peach cobbler. Belief is the single most important element in both outcomes.

Pecola's basic wish for blue eyes ties her to all believers in fairy tales and other magical realms. It is Cinderella wanting to be transformed from char girl to belle of the ball, or Sleeping Beauty waiting a hundred years for the prince to awaken her. It is the classic tale of the ugly duckling turned beautiful swan, of the beast transformed through love and caring into the beautiful prince, of Sir Gawain's pig lady turned into a dazzling woman. While Pecola seems doomed whatever she does—if she resorts to fantasy, she is considered crazy, and if she tries to live in the real world, there is no place for her—her desire for blue eyes ties her to many heroines of fairy tales, and to many young girls who have wished for features other than the ones they have. While many of the latter desires are no more than passing fancies, Pecola's is more intense because she is never given the opportunity, in any realm (home, school, playground), to see anything positive in herself as she is. The patterns of caring and incorporation hinted at in some of the occurrences in the novel never reach her strongly enough to reshape her opinion of herself.

Belief in magical realms or in the power to make present conditions seem magical is also seen in the desire of Claudia and Frieda to influence Pecola's fate by planting the marigolds correctly. They hope, as Pecola does with the offering to the dog, to bring about a kind of sympathetic magic, to create a space and circumstances in which Pecola will have a healthier future. When they fail, they blame themselves for not performing the rites correctly, for not having the right amount of belief. Destined to live in the realistic world, which promises a sane future for them, Claudia and Frieda are encouraged to put aside their childish beliefs. Diverging into a different world, Pecola makes the transition into fantasy, into a world from which Claudia's and Frieda's destinies have effectively and happily shut them out.

Beliefs that are adhered to over long periods of time and repeated occurrences can be defined as rituals. One of these operative in Morrison's novel is the ritual surrounding the funeral of Aunt Jimmy; certainly the funeral itself is a ritual, but so too is the traditional gathering of neighbors, relatives, and friends immediately after the death. They come as if in a dance, to perform the movements that custom and tradition have assigned to them. First, they must prepare for the burial. Then, they prepare food for those who come from near and far. They, and the relatives, must divide the belongings of the loved one and see that those left homeless are provided for. Since Cholly has never witnessed the ceremonies surrounding a funeral, he gets an education simultaneously with our witnessing of the unfolding of a tradition. The ladies of Jimmy's generation take over: they "cleaned the house, aired everything out, notified everybody, and stitched together what looked like a white wedding dress for Aunt Jimmy" (111). They also manage to get clothes for Cholly to attend the funeral, and they ensure that all of his physical needs are met.

After the traditional viewing of the body, and the "tearful shrieks and shouts" (113) of the mourners, the processional moves to the cemetery. Although the funeral is not depicted in detail, Morrison captures its emotional intensity in the metaphoric language of classic tradition:

> It was like a street tragedy with spontaneity tucked softly into the corners of a highly formal structure. The deceased was the tragic hero, the survivors the innocent victims; there was the omnipresence of the deity, strophe and antistrophe of the chorus of mourners led by the preacher. There was grief over the waste of life, the stunned wonder at the ways of God, and the restoration of order in nature at the graveyard.
>
> (113)

The funeral serves to return order to a community disrupted by death. Like all rituals, it provides a functional release, a pattern into which grief can be shaped, for the entire community.

After the "thunderous beauty of the funeral," the funeral banquet is "a peal of joy"; it is "the exultation, the harmony, the acceptance of physical frailty, joy in the termination of misery. Laughter, relief, a steep hunger for food" (113). It is the sign that things can continue without the departed one, and it serves to put the grieving for her in the perspective of the larger force of ongoing life. Concerns return to the practical—who will take Cholly and what relatives will get which of Aunt Jimmy's belongings.

With the ritual over, the "accounts settled," and the spectacle completed, the individual families return to their own homes, content in the knowledge that they have played well the roles that tradition and custom have assigned to them. Now, comparable to Janie's burying of Tea Cake in Zora Neale Hurston's *Their Eyes Were Watching God*,[4] there are only the tales to be told, the stories carrying the memories of what happened at Jimmy's funeral, about how well she was "laid out" and how much her family and friends appreciated her. In death, as in life, the pattern of caring that eludes Pecola is a recurring strand in the novel, one that has touched Cholly and Pauline, but from which they have become disconnected in their pursuit of clothes and alcohol.

Jimmy's death provides for one kind of traditional ritual of caring and continuation. Another tradition Morrison draws upon in the novel is that of the blues. In many ways *The Bluest Eye* is similar to Ralph Ellison's *Invisible Man*[5] in its very theme and structure: "What did I do to be so black and blue?" Conscious of it or not, that question must reverberate in Pecola's mind throughout her adventures in the novel. Again and again, she is confronted with people who emphasize to her that she must "stay back" because of her blackness. Again and again, she is "boomeranged" over the head with the knowledge that little black boys do not want to "haul no coal" or be identified with a "stovepipe blonde" and that most of her friends, family, and neighbors believe that "white is right." She lives the blues twenty-four hours a day, through each of the long minutes drawn out in each of those hours. Mrs. MacTeer can sing about "hard times, bad times, and somebody-done-gone-and-left-me-times" (24) and about "trains and Arkansas" (78); and Poland can sing about "blues in [her] meal-barrel / Blues up on the shelf" (44), but Pecola can give both of them lessons in living the blues. The ugliness that she believes is hers is just as blues-inducing as those levees breaking to release floodwaters in the Mississippi Delta. At least there was release from floods, and perhaps the pantry can be replenished, but Pecola's ugliness is there to stay. The potential for release from her state of the blues will never be fulfilled because the world around her does not believe that relief is her just due; it will always convey to her that the blues is her permanent condition, not a temporary state from which she can reasonably anticipate escape.

Her adventures, like those of her father, would "become coherent only in the head of a musician" (125), or in the structural composition of a novel that resembles a blues creation. Yet the blues are a way for people to touch their pain and that of others, to sing of what, in any given instance, is but an individualized account of collective suffering. But Pecola is unable to articulate the pain she feels or channel it through the form of the blues. Like her belief in fantasies derived from outside the black community, her state of the blues is familiar, but she has no model for it to serve as a way of connecting her to the community rather than cutting her off from it.

Pauline and Cholly Breedlove have both come into contact with forms of Afro-American culture used to tie black people to each other in caring, sharing ways. Yet their move to the North parallels a dissolution in their abilities to use the forms to which they have been exposed for any sustaining purposes. Thus they break the chains of continuity in culture and can only produce children who are outside that which had the potential to nurture them. Pecola and Cholly must therefore exist in a world of fragmentation, in a world where Mrs. MacTeer and Poland might show signs of the more sustaining Southern black culture, but which they cannot effectively transmit to the Breedlove children. They, like other characters in their isolated existences in the novel, are tied together by cultural forces stronger than all of them, but the strands of that cultural net keep breaking away from Pecola to slip her back into a sea of confusion about herself and about her place in the world of Lorain, Ohio.

Notes

1. Toni Morrison, *The Bluest Eye* (New York: Pocket Books, 1972), 105. Subsequent references to this source appear in the text in parenthesis.

2. Newbell Niles Puckett, *Folk Beliefs of the Southern Negro* (Chapel Hill: University of North Carolina Press, 1926).

3. Bernice Reagan, "We Are 'Girl,' 'Chile,' 'Lady,' That and 'oman,' 'Hussy,' 'Heifer,' 'A Woman'; or, Naming That Imprisons and Naming That Sets You Free," Unpublished paper presented at the Annual Meeting of the Modern Language Association, Washington, D.C., 27 December 1984.

4. Zora Neale Hurston, *Their Eyes Were Watching God* (Philadelphia: J. B. Lippincott, 1937. reprint, Urbana: University of Illinois Press, 1978).

5. Ralph Ellison, *Invisible Man* (New York: Random House, 1972).

Thomas H. Fick (essay date spring 1989)

SOURCE: Fick, Thomas H. "Toni Morrison's "Allegory of the Cave": Movies, Consumption, and Platonic Realism in *The Bluest Eye*." *Journal of the Midwest Modern Language Association* 22, no. 1 (spring 1989): 10-22.

[*In the following essay, Fick analyzes the themes, structures and characters of* The Bluest Eye *in relation to Western literary and philosophical traditions, as primarily represented in T. S. Eliot's* The Wasteland *and Plato's "Allegory of the Cave," and their significance to African American economic and social conditions.*]

Toni Morrison's first novel, *The Bluest Eye* (1970), is an unusually effective exploration of racism in twentieth-century American in part because of the place it gives to central legacies of Western civilization. Like Ralph Ellison, whose *Invisible Man* draws on Emerson and Whitman as well as folklore, Morrison recognizes the importance of Western literature and philosophy to the Afro-American experience in America; in some ways *The Bluest Eye* stands opposed to more hermetic work like Alice Walker's *The Color Purple*, which despite its many strengths does not come to terms with the intellectual and economic foundations of racism and whose portrayal of character and personal growth suffers accordingly.[1] Morrison's characters are more convincing and ultimately more moving than Walker's because they operate in a world shaped by a complex and sometimes repressive cultural heritage. In *The Bluest Eye* this heritage is primarily represented by T. S. Eliot's *The Waste Land* and Plato's "Allegory of the Cave" in Book VII of *The Republic*.[2] These two important moments in Western culture provide specific thematic and structural elements in the novel; in a larger sense they suggest Morrison's belief in the close relationship between intellectual traditions and particular economic and social conditions.

Eliot's contribution in *The Bluest Eye* is the more apparent because it operates on the level of imagery as well as theme and structure. In the prologue the narrator Claudia MacTeer remembers when she and her sister Frieda planted marigold seeds in a childish rite they hoped would guarantee the health of their twelve-year-old friend Pecola's baby. If the seeds sprout, they think, the baby will thrive. But no seeds sprout, the baby dies, and Pecola spends her life "plucking her way between the tire rims and the sunflowers, between Coke bottles and milkweed, among all the waste and beauty of the world."[3] Only much later does Claudia understand that it isn't her fault, that "the entire country was hostile to marigolds that year" (160). *The Bluest Eye* is framed by the narrator's brooding recollection of a wasteland, and the seasons which title the major sections—"Autumn," "Winter," "Spring," and "Summer"—mark off a parody of rebirth and growth. In "the thin light of spring" (127) Pecola Breedlove is raped by her drunken father (a cruel sort of breeding indeed), and in summer, pregnant, she goes mad after the equivalent of Eliot's Mme Sosostris works a phony spell to give her blue eyes.

The echoes of Eliot's *Waste Land* are important for thematic and structural reasons and for what they reveal about Morrison's interest in literary tradition. The central conceptual presence in *The Bluest Eye,* however, is Plato's "Allegory of the Cave." This is initially difficult to see because the idea and image of the wasteland is everywhere directly present in the novel while Plato's allegory operates through the analogy of the cinema. Movies are the centrally destructive force in the novel not only because of the values they present—perfect white bodies and romantic love—but because of the way they present them: as flawless Archetypes above and outside the shadowy world of everyday life. For Morrison, that is, the message *and* the medium are almost equally dangerous: as we shall see, the cinema reproduces the structure of Plato's allegory in terms appropriate to a technological and capitalist society and provides the focus for an exploration of the complicity between Platonic realism, racism, and a culture of consumption. In order to understand the centrality of Platonic "realism" as it is embodied in the cinema, however, we first need to understand what personal, cultural, and artistic issues this version of realism engages.

The Bluest Eye is an angry book but it is also an orderly one, perhaps because in Afro-American literature a careful structure is frequently used to contain and shape the anger that might otherwise be construed as lack of control.[4] A reasonable place to begin, then, is with the blue eyes of the title, the blue eyes Pecola Breedlove thinks will introduce harmony and love into her fragmented and emotionally barren life. For Pecola, change has become a matter of survival: her father is a drunk, her mother's love goes to a white child, and the whole world tells her she is ugly. On the most obvious level her desire for blue eyes is a response to an ideal of beauty that takes specific form in the Shirley Temples, Hedy Lamarrs, Ginger Rogerses, and unnamed models whose blond hair, blue eyes, and white skins dominate the landscape of American life, "leaning from every billboard, every movie, every glance" (34). Blue eyes epitomize everything desirable in white American culture, but Pecola's longing for this cosmetic change expresses her deeper need to reform the world by reforming the way she sees it, a transcendental rather than existential imperative: "It had occurred to Pecola some time ago that if her eyes, those eyes that held the pictures, and knew the sights—if those eyes of hers were different, that is to say, beautiful, she herself would be different" (40).

As this quotation suggests, like many children Pecola asks questions that are disconcerting for both their naiveté and their insight. She poses one such question at the age of eleven: "'How,'" she asks Frieda and Claudia, "'do you get somebody to love you?'" (29). The children don't know, but the narrative provides a number of exemplary answers: the neighborhood whores' caustic camaraderie, her parents' desperate fights, the sterile "nesting" of bourgeois black women, and most destructively Pecola's rape by her own father.[5] But there is another question Pecola wants answered even more, for without an answer "love" has no meaning: the conditions of her own and the world's reality. This is the question she silently poses to Marie, one of the three whores who, besides Claudia and Frieda, are her only friends: "Pecola looked and looked at the women. Were they real? Marie belched, softly, purringly, lovingly" (49). Marie's answer is clear and unambiguous because its sheer physicality avoids the abstractions such a question is likely to evoke, but the primary emphasis of the passage is on sight, not sound—on the intensity of Pecola's "looking." The connection between sight and reality tells us as much about Morrison's commitment to the mode of realism as it does about Pecola. As a mode realism has been characterized by its emphasis on sight: as Jeffrey Mehlman remarks, "excellence of *vision* is the distinguishing mark of realism" and Edwin Cady finds that the principal American realists share a common concern with sight.[6] To "look and look," therefore, is to accept the world's immediate existence, as Pecola does when she accepts the whore's insistent presence, but to look with eyes other than one's own is to falsify both self and world.[7] Pecola's wish for blue eyes is not only a wish to match the ideal of the white child, it is also a rejection of right seeing, of the premises of realism for those of romance.

In fact, like many of the classic examples of realism from Flaubert's *Madame Bovary* to Clemens's *Huckleberry Finn* the themes and structure of Morrison's novel center on an explicit antagonism to the forms and motives of romance. Tom Sawyer's extravagant dedication to the conventions of romantic fiction counterpoint Huck Finn's sound heart and empirical instincts. Huck tests Tom's assertions both intentionally—for example by rubbing a lamp to see if the promised genie will show—and unintentionally by becoming involved with the real-life counterparts of Tom's fictional heroes. The Shepherdson-Grangerford feud shows Huck that Tom's "authorities" are dead wrong when it comes to chivalric ideals: codes of honor lead to murder not glory. *The Bluest Eye* follows a similar structure of ironic counterpoint. The novel's epigraph is a "Dick and Jane" children's story that serves as an ironic commentary on the MacTeers's and Breedloves's daily lives: "Here is the house. It is green and white. . . . Here is the family. Mother, Father, Dick, and Jane live in the green-and-white house. They are very happy," and so forth. Each segment of this story is used as a section "title" to introduce its counterpart in 1940s racist America: the green and white house of Dick and Jane introduces the Breedloves's "irritating and melancholy" (30) storefront apartment; the strong and smiling father is a bitter drunk; the happy family is poor and miserable.[8] The commitment to realist discourse implied in this ironic juxtaposition is made explicit in the characterization of Pecola's friendly whores. Marie, China, and Poland "did not belong to those generations of prostitutes created in novels, with great and generous hearts, dedicated, because of the horror of circumstance, to ameliorating the luckless, barren life of men, taking money incidentally and humbly for their 'understanding.'" Instead, they are "whores in whores' clothing" (47-8).

In *The Bluest Eye,* however, the opposition between real and ideal is more profound than in *Huckleberry Finn*. The obsession with romance and chivalry that Clemens blamed on Sir Walter Scott does not depend on an alternative sense of the real, but on a belief that some actions and attitudes are better than others. Despite their literary origins, that is, notions of chivalry are thoroughly social: Tom Sawyer is not only an aficionado of pirate oaths but a consummate politician, able to read and use others' expectations and desires. Morrison, on the other hand, is interested in antithetical senses of the real, in different *ways* of locating value in the world rather than in the different values alone. The "Dick and Jane" primer is important not only because it provides a particular set of expectations of modes of behavior (as Scott provides a number of paradigmatic scenarios for Tom Sawyer) but because it locates these expectations and behaviors in a realm of immutable Archetypes—equivalent to the Platonic idea of the "real"—in contrast with which this transient world is only an imitation. Compared to the world of green and white houses, strong, smiling fathers and happy mothers, Claudia's and Pecola's world is but an *Imitation of Life,* to cite the title of a movie that one character admires extravagantly.[9]

The novel centers on one successful and several unsuccessful efforts to move beyond Platonic "realism" toward an understanding and acceptance of the physical world's primacy. The first section, narrated from the young Claudia's point of view, introduces the detailed and imperfect particulars of daily life from the limited perspective of a child. Here, as in each of young Claudia's subsequent sections, typography recapitulates ontology: the right margins are "unjustified"—as ragged and as honest as the perceptions of a young girl.[10] The house is "old, cold, and green . . . peopled by roaches and mice" (12) and the first impression is of a world as starkly opposite Dick and Jane's as possible. Adults, young Claudia tells us, "do not talk to us—they give us directions. They issue orders without providing information. When we trip and fall they glance at us; if we cut or bruise ourselves, they ask us are we crazy" (12). But these are the impressions of a child; like their counterparts in the "Peanuts" comic strip the adults in *The Bluest Eye* are remote, unintelligible, and nearly invisible. Further, the uncertainty we as readers feel about the true proportions of love and neglect in Claudia's life duplicates the ambiguity mark of a world where emotions, like relationships, are mutable rather than absolute (as they are for Dick and Jane). In fact, we find out that love is not absent but "thick as Alaga syrup" (14). The adults are simply too preoccupied with scavaging coal and making ends meet to be the endlessly smiling paragons of a story book.

Unlike the monotonous rhythm of Dick and Jane's prose world, young Claudia's narrative modulates through a number of moods and ends with Pecola's question about love, a question which has been partially answered in the equivocal—because human—terms of the just-concluded section. Love is dynamic rather than static, a process rather than a magic formula. The primary focus, however, is on Claudia's commitment to right seeing—the reverse of Pecola's desire for new, impossibly blue eyes and all that they imply about value in literature as in life. Even as a child Claudia is determined to understand the "beauty, the desirability" (20) of America's cultural icons: Shirley Temple and the white dolls constructed in her image. Though fueled by hate for the icons that usurp her family's admiration, Claudia is rational and resolutely empirical in her quest for understanding. She tears apart her Christmas present of a white doll, looking for its beauty: "Remove the cold and stupid eyeball . . . take off the head, shake out the sawdust, crack the back against the brass bed rail, it would bleat still. The gauze back would split, and I could see the disk with six holes, the secret of the sound. A mere metal roundness" (21). Young Claudia is an empiricist among metaphysicians, unable to believe there is value above and beyond what can be found in the immediate world; she lays the groundwork for the older Claudia's rejection of romance for realism. For Christmas, she remembers, "I did not want . . . to possess any object. I wanted rather to feel something," and feeling is a matter of contact, of specific things and places: "The lowness of the stool made for my body, . . . the smell of lilacs, the sound of the music, and, since it would be good to have all of my senses engaged, the taste of a peach . . ." (21).

At the opposite pole from Claudia's world of sense and feeling is the celluloid world of transcendent beauty and health, Dick and Jane in the age of McLuhan. References to movies and movie stars punctuate the narrative, forming an insistent counterpoint to Claudia's quest for authenticity in experience. The MacTeers's boarder, Mr. Henry, delights in calling the young girls Greta Garbo and Ginger Rogers; Pecola drinks three quarts of milk just to see Shirley Temple's picture on the mug; black women have their hair styled like Hedy Lamarr's; Betty Grable's name looms large on theatre marquees. Movies convey an adult version of Dick and Jane's ideal world, but in *The Bluest Eye* the emphasis is not just on the particular scenes, formulae, or characters—that special hairdo or inflection—but on the medium itself. To understand the importance of the cinema, therefore, we need to consider method as well as content, the how as much as the what of its deception.

By co-opting individual sight and replacing it with the camera's apparent omniscience a movie can bestow false authority on its images and offer a nicely framed, repeatable world totally unlike young Claudia's. But it is a mistake to think of the cinema only as cultural shorthand for twentieth-century escapism; its appearance in *The Bluest Eye* serves to recall an older and more intellectually distinguished precursor. The cinema functions almost precisely like the famous cave in Plato's *The Republic,* as a brief summary of the allegory will show. Socrates asks us to imagine people living from childhood in a cave, chained by leg and neck with their backs to the only entrance. Behind them is a fire with a parapet in front of it "like the screen at a puppet show, which hides the performers while they show their puppets over the top."[11] Objects are carried by men behind the parapet so that the fire projects the objects' shadows on the wall of the cave in front of the chained viewers. Obviously, Socrates says, the captives would think the shadows are the sole reality, and if one of the people crossing behind them spoke, the echo would make the sound seem to come from the projected shadow. He concludes, "In every way, then, such prisoners would recognize as reality nothing but the shadows of those artificial objects."[12] But the shadows are still shadows; the "real" lies outside the cave, in the immutable Archetypes represented by the objects carried between the fire and the cave wall. This allegory is an accurate though technologically unsophisticated description of the cinema: celluloid takes the place of Socrates's hand-carried objects, and a projector the place of his fire.[13] In each case the effect is the same: the screen shows the shadow of a perfect world, the "real" world of which ours is merely an imitation. But while Socrates imagines the possibility that through rigorous mathematical preparation one will be able to face the "real" (i.e., ideal) world itself, Morrison sees the very notion of a Platonic real as centrally false and destructive. The characters who measure themselves against advertisements and movies are captives not because they are ignorant of the world above and behind, but because they believe that there is such a world.

Pauline Breedlove is the cinema's primary victim, and her story gives shape and context to Pecola's more general tragedy. As a child in Alabama Pauline had cultivated the pleasures of ordering her small world, but she is an artist without the means to realize her creative impulses: "She missed—without knowing what she missed—paints and crayons" (89). When her marriage to Cholly deteriorates she has little else to do but go to the movies, where she is introduced to romantic love and physical beauty, "the most destructive ideas in the history of human thought": "She was never able, after her education in the movies, to look at a face and not assign it some category in the scale of absolute beauty, and the scale was on absorbed in full from the silver screen" (97). The notion of absolute beauty commits Pauline to think of her world as a shadow, a projection of the perfect world where "'white men [take] such good care of they women, and they all dressed up in big clean houses'" (97). The consequences of Pauline's immersion in a world of absolutes are intensely personal. In order to embrace the Platonic real she must repudiate the temporal and conditional, the transient physical world whose most insistent manifestation is the body itself. Indeed, the cinema offers a neo-religious physical perfection whose ultimate source is not the Bible but a technologized Republic: "There the flawed became whole, the blind sighted, and the lame and halt threw away their crutches" (97). But in the long run the body cannot be denied, as Pauline discovers one day in the Dreamland Theatre when, coiffed like Jean Harlow, she bites into a candy bar and breaks off a rotten tooth. In contrast with the absolutes of physical beauty and romantic love the pleasures of body and emotion can only seem disappointingly transient and flawed.

The lost tooth climaxes a long process that began with a tiny spot of decay, but personal hygiene is hardly at issue here. As the narrator comments, "even before the little brown speck, there must have been the conditions, the setting that would allow it to exist in the first place" (93). In context, these conditions are social and institutional rather than narrowly hygienic they recall the opening image of a wasteland that breeds only decay and rape. Thus while Pauline's experience in the movies can usefully be read as a general warning to dreamers it is also something more. As Marcia Westkott argues in "Dialectics of Fantasy," "Fantasy not only opposes real conditions, but also reflects them. The opposition that fantasy expresses is not abstract, but is rooted in the real conditions themselves, in concrete social relations."[14] In **The Bluest Eye** the real conditions are those of American consumer culture, the continuing "gilded age" that began after the Civil War and replaced physical slavery with other forms of mastery.[15] Try as she might, Pauline cannot be Jean Harlow, and the sense of inadequacy that comes from this failure is part of her tragedy. Even more troubling, however, is the sort of ideal that she does achieve: freedom in the 1940s means fulfilling a role that perfects the antebellum position of blacks. As her personal life falls apart she divides her time between the movies and her employer's family, where she becomes the "queen of canned vegetables," "reign[ing]" over cupboards stacked high with food" (101). Her skin glows "in the reflection of white porcelain, white woodwork, polished cabinets, and brilliant copperware" (86). Finally she becomes "an ideal servant" (100), trading personal authenticity for a stereotype in the guise of an Archetype. Pauline's decline from person to "reflection" illustrates how the means of slavery have been internalized. The captive is held most obviously by her commitment to images from movies; even more fundamentally, however, she is bound by this medium's operative assumption that human existence is but an "imitation of life."

William Carlos William's poem "To Elsie" can help us understand the particularly American context of Pauline Breedlove's tragedy. Williams made "no ideas but in things" the battle-cry of his aesthetic program, and his prose and poetry are an extended response to the notion of Platonic realism, especially as it is worked out in twentieth-century consumer culture. He is the poet of the local and the physical, of body and place; what "depends" upon the white chickens beside the red wheelbarrow in Williams's best known poem is quite simply poetry itself. Whether dancing naked in front of the mirror ("Danse Russe"), indulging his indiscriminate nose ("Smell"), or simply eating cold plums ("This Is Just to Say") Williams is intent on recovering what we have lost pursuing abstractions. "To Elsie" is one of the clearest statements of his commitment to the immediate against the transcendental. Like Pauline Breedlove, Elsie is an exemplary rather than exceptional figure, "expressing with broken / brain the truth about us."[16] Cut off from peasant traditions, unable to see the beauty of the peasant world, she addresses herself to dreams of cheap finery,

> as if the earth under our feet
> were
> an excrement of some sky
>
> and we were degraded prisoners
> destined
> to hunger until we eat filth. . . .[17]

Like Morrison, Williams sees us as prisoners in a twentieth-century version of Plato's cave, dismissing our world as excrement while straining after a transcendent but meretricious ideal. Both believe that to free ourselves from these chains we need, like Claudia, to have "all of [our] senses engaged" (21) in the discovery of the local and immediate. But most of all we need to see straight, through our own eyes: to trust and respect the angle of vision that makes each imperfect world, and makes it valuable.

Pecola's trip to buy candy early in the novel concisely explores these needs. When Pecola sets out for Mr. Yacobowski's store she is filled with affection for herself and her immediate world: the "sweet, endurable, even cherished irritation" (40) of the coins in her shoe; the dandelions that others call ugly "because they are so many, strong, and soon" (41); the Y-shaped crack in the worn-smooth concrete so perfect for skating. These are "the familiar and therefore loved images" of her world:

> These and other inanimate things she saw and experienced. They were real to her. She knew them. They were the codes and touchstones of the world, capable of translation and possession. She owned the crack that made her stumble; she owned the clumps of dandelions. . . . And owning them made them a part of the world, and the world a part of her.
>
> (41)

But at the candy store she can't make Mr. Yacobowski see what she wants—"the angle of his vision, the slant of her finger, makes it incomprehensible to him" (42). Pecola has once again been told that the way she sees is wrong, and that her world—the immediate, the local, and the sensual—is worthless, even unreal. It is not surprising, then, that on the way home she finds the world beneath her feet has turned to excrement: she looks at the dandelions and discovers "'They *are* ugly. They *are* weeds'"; she trips on the sidewalk crack (no longer her friend) and "anger stirs and wakes in her" (43). The world has changed because Mr. Yacobowski denies her perspective, and because as a consequence Pecola, like Elsie, has been forced to deny the particular in herself—the special conditions of her own loves and hates.

As Pecola's experience suggests, *The Bluest Eye* is as critical of economic and political systems, of the underlying "concrete social relations" that generate fantasy, as it is of fantasy itself.[18] The essentially political and economic origins of Pecola's self-betrayal are represented in the exchange of the "sweet, endurable, even cherished" feel of her money—more sensation than specie—not for an equivalent feeling but for a consumable image of the ideal. Her transaction reverses the terms of Claudia's economy: feelings are exchanged for things, rather than things for feelings. Specifically, Pecola wants "Mary Janes" because each wrapper has the picture of a young girl, "blond hair in gentle disarray, blue eyes looking at her out of a world of clean comfort," and she devours the Mary Janes because to do so "is somehow to eat the eyes, eat Mary Jane. Love Mary Jane. Be Mary Jane" (43). Like the earlier milk-drinking binge (three quarts to see Shirley Temple on the mug), her action points to a confederation of the ideal with an economy of consumption. Eating Mary Janes is a strictly capitalist magic: by ingesting the product she hopes to ingest what advertising associates with it, and certainly an appeal to this magic is at the root of advertising's power.[19] In other words, the idea of a transcendent reality is no longer a matter of philosophical debate but of immediate commercial application, as the shift from cave to cinema clearly suggests. Capitalism appropriates the idea of Platonic reality in order to inspire a demand for products that is both insatiable and predictable since both qualities are essential for a smoothly functioning system. Only economic chaos can result when some want dandelions and others marigolds, when the common is as valuable as the exceptional, or when values and demand vary from region to region, class to class. Modern consumer capitalism is made possible by locating or even more commonly creating stable markets, as recent work on the institutional matrix in the publishing industry has effectively illustrated.[20] In short, in *The Bluest Eye* capitalism is presented as redefining the image of a bound and shackled audience in the "Allegory of the Cave": Socrates's observers become the captives of an economic system which appropriates the ideal in the name of profit.

In a novel concerned with racism, of course, captivity has a special resonance, and *The Bluest Eye* is profoundly concerned with the shifting forms of "slavery" in America. Slavery can be most simply defined as a commodification of the body: men become objects of commerce, as Harriet Beecher Stowe recognized when she wished to subtitle *Uncle Tom's Cabin* "The Man That Was a Thing." When we look for signs of racism in *The Bluest Eye* we are most quickly drawn to those made familiar by works like *Uncle Tom's Cabin* whose explicit message is the visible dehumanization of blacks: segregation, lynching, poor paying jobs, racial stereotyping. But even Stowe's novel deals with more than the cruder forms of Southern slavery. As Richard Slotkin demonstrates, the paternalistic slave-owning economy shared important qualities with the paternalistic factory system in the North,[21] a point Stowe also makes when she has Augustine St. Clare, her spokesperson, quote his plantation-owning brother: "'he says, and I think quite sensibly, that the American planter is "only doing, in another form, what the English aristocracy and capitalists are doing by the lower classes;" that is, I take it, appropriating them, body and bone.'"[22] Shortly after the publication of *Uncle Tom's Cabin* Herman Melville made the same connection in "The Paradise of Bachelors and the Tartarus of Maids," a powerful and topical short story which portrays the exploitation of white, unmarried women in a Northern paper mill.[23] When the balance of power definitively changed from agrarian to industrial society (and from South to North) after the Civil War, this form of economic and psychological captivity extended its domain to the Southern blacks who began to join the ranks of white workers in the North. Finally, as labor laws progressively eliminated the conditions Stowe and Melville wrote about advertising stepped in, blurring the line between "captivity" and "captivating" by internalizing the means of bondage for blacks and whites.

The journey of the Breedlove family South to North, from pre-industrial America to consumer society, recapitulates this temporal and economic change in geographic terms. The contrasting experiences of rural, Southern-reared Cholly and his Northern-born daughter are especially instructive. As an adolescent in the South Cholly is interrupted during his first sexual encounter by white hunters, who make him give a dehumanizing sexual performance at gunpoint: "'Come on, coon. Faster. You ain't doing nothing for her'" (117). But this gut-wrenching scene belongs to a polemical tradition whose very familiarity can distract us from the more subtle but related influences at work in the North—the sorts of performances and responses required of those who buy into the premises of a consumer society. The crude white masters of the South are replaced by invisible systems of mastery dedicated to maximizing profit through a process equally dehumanizing. In the sections of the novel set in Ohio, Morrison portrays Pecola's violation of self in imagery that recalls Cholly and his companion's violation at the hands of the hunters. The incident at the candy store, for example, draws its power from the conflation of sex and consumption: when Pecola eats her Mary Janes she experiences "nine lovely orgasms" (43), one for each candy. Sexual love is one of the most profound and private expressions of individuality, but for both Cholly and Pecola sex assumes a public aspect: for Cholly a spectacle, and for Pecola a form of packaged masturbation. In each case human beings are defined not in terms of their feelings but as performers and consumers respectively, and in each case the results are nearly the same: anger is displaced from its real target. When Cholly is surprised by the hunters he directs his hate not at the powerful white men, since doing so "would have consumed him, burned him up like a piece of soft coal" (119), but at his adolescent partner. Similarly, after buying the candy and tripping on the cracked sidewalk Pecola experiences a moment of cathartic anger: "There is a sense of being in anger. A reality and presence. An awareness of worth. It is a lovely surging". (43). Her anger's unspoken target is not the beloved crack but Mr. Yacobowski and all those who devalue her world; unfortunately the momentary clarity of vision, the discovery of reality and worth, cannot hold against the attraction of "blue eyes [in] a world of clean comfort" (43). Instead of turning her anger outward as Claudia does, she turns it self-destructively inward and celebrates her surrender to external definition with the orgiastic pleasures of consumption.

The story of Pecola's idealism and destruction has an unexpected but important precursor in F. Scott Fitzgerald's *The Great Gatsby*, an American classic that can help us locate **The Bluest Eye** in a long tradition of works about the American dream. Both novels focus on protagonists who at bottom believe not so much in the reality of an ideal as in the ideal nature of reality, a Platonic reality in the service of consumption. As Nick Carraway tells us, Jay Gatsby "Sprang from his Platonic conception of himself. . . . [and] he must be about his Father's business, the service of a vast, vulgar, and meretricious beauty."[24] Race, sex, and opportunity rather than values account for his success and Pecola's failure. Despite his criminal business practices, that is, Gatsby believes in a world of absolutes where Daisy Buchanan, her voice "full of money" (120), survives in splendid and virginal youth just as he last saw her; this is a glitzy adult version of Pecola's Dick and Jane world where time, lust, and ambiguity seem to play no part. In each case the protagonist is confronted with violent proof of the world's disorder and transience. Gatsby breaks up "like glass"[25] against Tom Buchanan's brutal malice and the evidence of Daisy's imperfection; Pecola is raped by a father who has not learned how to love. One is murdered—a symbolic suicide—and the other goes mad.

In its concise duality Pecola's family name, Breedlove, summarizes the problems posed by each novel: how can one reconcile the claims of body and spirit in a secular world, how can one be in and of the world without becoming brutalized by physical impulses, enthralled by the ideal, or exploited by those who would make use of both? Cholly Breedlove shows the depth of this problem when he rapes Pecola: confused, caught between disgust and love, "he wanted to fuck her—tenderly" (128). The rape, like his name, is an oxymoron whose two terms, at least for Cholly, cannot be conjoined. But **The Bluest Eye** does not end in despair; both anger and community offer a way to redeem the waste land, although each has its own dangers.[26] Anger can provide a "sense of being" and "an awareness of worth" (43), but it becomes lethal if displaced from its rightful target: Claudia remains sane by confronting racist society directly and through her retrospective narrative, while Pecola goes mad because she fights herself. A community, on the other hand, can support and comfort, as we see in young Claudia's first section. But when Pecola's drama has played itself out this same community takes the pregnant girl as a scapegoat whose defects define their virtues; as Claudia says, "We were so beautiful when we stood astride her ugliness. Her simplicity decorated us, her guilt sanctified us, her pain made us glow with health" (159). Personal and collective health begins with the effort at self-recovery exemplified in the narrative, which is itself a shaping and refinement of Claudia's anger at the white dolls, but it ends in a recognition of human interdependency. Finally, **The Bluest Eye** asks us to consider *how* as well as *what* we see, both as individuals and as a society. The wasteland will be fully redeemed only when all its members see with their own eyes, when they are no longer held captive, like a contemporary version of Plato's audience, by the idea that "reality" is a consumable absolute, a product independent of local commitments and personal loyalties.

Notes

1. Trudier Harris, for example, argues that *The Color Purple* leaves the reader "equally skeptical about accepting the logic of a novel that posits so many changes as a credible progression for a character. Such total change of life-style, attitudes, and beliefs . . . asks more of the reader than can be reasonably expected" ("From Victimization to Free Enterprise: Alice Walker's *The Color Purple*," *Studies in American Fiction* 14 (1986), 16.

2. Gerry Brenner has recently discussed Morrison's treatment of Western mythology in *Song of Solomon*. See *Song of Solomon*: Morrison's Rejection of Rank's Monomyth and Feminism," *Studies in American Fiction* 15 (1987), 13-24.

3. Toni Morrison, *The Bluest Eye* (New York: Pocket Books, 1970), p. 159. Future references will be cited in the text.

4. Raymond Hedin argues that anger has been problematic for black writers because of racist attributions of brutishness and lack of control. As a consequence,

Hedin says, black writers have paid special attention to structure in their fiction: "Emphasis on form implicitly conveys the rationality of the writer; and that context of rationality allows him to express his anger, or the anger of his characters, without suggesting an overall lack of control" ("The Structuring of Emotion in Black American Fiction," *Novel* 16 [1982], 37). Hedin discusses *The Bluest Eye* briefly on pages 49-50. For a discussion of the novel as a female *Bildungsroman* see Joanne S. Frye, *Living Stories, Telling Lives* (Ann Arbor: U of Michigan P, 1986), 97-102. Frye argues that "The general problem for Claudia's self-definition is a version of the conflict between submission and self-assertion, which is the problem of all female authorship" (99). But this application of Sandra Gilbert and Susan Gubar's influential thesis in *The Madwoman in the Attic* (New Haven: Yale UP, 1979) seems less useful than Hedin's approach because it minimizes the special circumstances of black authorship in America.

5. Morrison comments that "all the time that I write, I'm writing about love or its absence" (Jane S. Bakerman, "The Seams Can't Show: An Interview with Toni Morrison," *Black American Literature Forum* 12 [1979], 60).

6. Jeffrey Mehlman, *Revolution and Repetition: Marx/Hugo/Balzac* (Berkeley: U of California P, 1977), 124; Edwin H. Cady, *The Light of Common Day: Realism in American Fiction* (Bloomington: Indiana UP, 1971), 5.

7. Many critics have discussed vision and the relationship between seeing, subjectivity, and objectification in *The Bluest Eye*. Frye comments that for Pecola the need "to *see*, to participate in the culture's image of what life ought to be . . . become the negation of her subjectivity" (102). Cynthia A. Davis, on the other hand, analyzes *The Bluest Eye* in terms of Sartre's Existential doctrines: "human relations revolve around the experience of 'the Look,' for being 'seen' by another both confirms one's reality and threatens one's sense of freedom" ("Self, Society, and Myth in Toni Morrison's Fiction," *Contemporary Literature* 23 [1982], 324).

8. For a concise discussion of the child's reader in *The Bluest Eye* see Phyllis Klotman, "Dick-and-Jane and the Shirley Temple Sensibility in *The Bluest Eye*," *Black American Literature Forum* 13 (1979), 123-25.

9. Maureen Peal, the "high-yellow dream child" (52) who is everyone but Claudia and Frieda's favorite, mentions this 1934 movie starring Claudette Colbert because (in Maureen's selective synopsis) it is about a beautiful mulatto girl named Pecola who "'hates her mother' cause she is black and ugly but then cries at the funeral'" (57). In the movie Pecola's mother gives her pancake recipe to her white employer, who parlays it into a fortune.

10. Throughout the novel the margins reflect different narrators and points of view. The sections with ragged right margins are narrated primarily from young Claudia's point of view, although the language is the adult narrator's; sections with justified right margins are narrated by the older Claudia from an omniscient point of view. I will use "young Claudia" whenever I need to distinguish the narrator of the childhood sections from the omniscient narrator (the adult Claudia).

11. Plato, *The Republic of Plato*, trans. Francis Macdonald Cornford (1941; rpt. New York: Oxford UP, 1967), 228.

12. Plato, 229.

13. L. Chauvois points out that in fifth- and fourth-century Greece puppet theaters formed a sort of "cinéma populaire," and that Plato's allegory of the cave is a transposition of this extremely popular form of national amusement. See L. Chauvois, "Le 'cinéma populaire' en Grèce au temps de Plato et sa projection dans l'allégorie de la 'caverne aux idées,'" *Revue Générale des Sciences Pures et Appliquées,* 74 (1967), 193-5. In the notes to his translation of *The Republic* Cornford remarks that "A modern Plato would compare his Cave to an underground cinema" (228n).

14. Marcia Westkott, "Dialectics of Fantasy," *Frontiers: A Journal of Women Studies,* 2 (1977), 1. Quoted in Alfred Habegger, *Gender, Fantasy, and Realism in American Literature* (New York: Columbia UP, 1982), 7.

15. For a discussion of the black emigrant's experience of reification in the North see Susan Willis, "Eruptions of Funk," in *Black Literature and Literary Theory,* ed. Henry Louis Gates (New York: Methuen, 1984), 263-83.

16. William Carlos Williams, "To Elsie," in *The Collected Earlier Poems of William Carlos Williams* (New York: New Directions, 1951), 271.

17. Williams, 272-3.

18. The political thrust of Morrison's novels is apparent to every sensitive reader. As Morrison explained in a recent interview, "I am not interested in indulging myself in some private, closed exercise of my imagination that fulfills only the obligation of my personal dreams—which is to say yes, the work must be political" (Toni Morrison, "Rootedness: the Ancestor or Foundation," in *Black Women Writers [1950-1980]: A Critical Evaluation,* ed. Mari Evans [Garden City, NY: Anchor Doubleday, 1984], 343).

19. Susan Willis points out that candy is often associated with capitalism in Morrison's fiction (228n).

20. Richard H. Brodhead, *The School of Hawthorne* (New York: Oxford UP, 1986), 48-66; Janice A. Radway, *Reading the Romance: Women, Patriarchy, and Popular Literature* (Chapel Hill: U of North Carolina P, 1986, 19-46.

21. Richard Slotkin, *The Fatal Environment: The Myth of the Frontier in the Age of Industrialization, 1800-1890* (New York: Atheneum, 1985) 138-58.

22. Harriet Beecher Stowe, *Uncle Tom's Cabin*, ed. Kathryn Kish Sklar (New York: The Library of America, 1984), 269. Gillian Brown argues that "in the name of domesticity, *Uncle Tom's Cabin* attacks not only the patriarchal institution, but nineteenth-century patriarchy: not only slave traders, but the system and men that maintain 'the one great market' upon which trade depends" ("Getting in the Kitchen with Dinah: Domestic Politics in *Uncle Tom's Cabin*," *American Quarterly*, 36 [1984], 511).

23. For an excellent introduction to nineteenth-century American racism see Carolyn Karcher, *Shadow Over Promised Land: Slavery, Race, and Violence in Melville's America* (Baton Rouge: Louisiana State UP, 1980), 1-27.

24. F. Scott Fitzgerald, *The Great Gatsby* (New York: Charles Scribners Sons, 1925), 99.

25. Fitzgerald, 148.

26. Morrison's cautious optimism comes from a belief in the power of the local and individual; in this she resembles William Carlos Williams, who found Eliot's *The Waste Land* "the great catastrophe to our letters" because it ignored "the elementary principle of all art, in the local conditions" (*The Autobiography of William Carlos Williams* [New York: Random House, 1951], 146, 174.). Williams's response to Eliot is "Spring and All," a poem rooted in the sense of place. In reworking the image of the waste land Morrison strips it of abstraction: at the end of the novel Pecola is living among very real Coke bottles, tire rims, and milkweed.

Vanessa D. Dickerson (essay date 1989)

SOURCE: Dickerson, Vanessa D. "The Naked Father in Toni Morrison's *The Bluest Eye*." In *Refiguring the Father: New Feminist Readings of Patriarchy,* edited by Patricia Yaeger and Beth Kowaleski-Wallace, pp. 108-27. Carbondale: Southern Illinois University Press, 1989.

[*In the following essay, Dickerson analyzes the "doubled" identity of fathers—characterized as at once both "familiar" and "unknowable" to their daughters—in* The Bluest Eye, *focusing on the way Cholly's familiarity with Pecola causes not only his daughter's demise but also his own.*]

In Toni Morrison's ***The Bluest Eye*** (1970), the nine-year-old narrator Claudia McTeer and her ten-year-old sister Frieda lie in bed one night and peer at their naked father who "pass[es] the open door of [their] room":

We had lain there wide-eyed. He stopped and looked in, trying to see in the dark room whether we were really asleep or was it his imagination that opened eyes were looking at him? Apparently he convinced himself that we were sleeping. He moved away, confident that his little girls would not lie open-eyed like that, staring, staring. When he had moved on, the dark took only him away, not his nakedness. That stayed in the room with us. Friendly-like.

(60)

These lines are busy with meaning. On the one hand, they point up the father's insistence on the innocence of his daughters. On the other hand, they intimate the vulnerability of McTeer himself: the lines suggest that for the father the gaze of his daughters would constitute some exposure or violation of his self. Incredulous and suspicious, the father resists the reality of the incident; silent and wide-eyed, the girls grant the significance of the encounter as they acknowledge a difference between a "him" that the darkness takes away, removes, or obscures, and a "nakedness" that is "friendly-like."

Understandably, McTeer refuses to see the open-eyed presence of his daughters because their gaze is an assertion of female selfhood, which threatens the personal power of McTeer. By looking at "him" the girls show a curiosity and a boldness, which the patriarch Noah found so presumptuous and disrespectful as to warrant anathema (Gen. 10:18-29). By denying the gaze of his daughters, McTeer, like this biblical figure, both restricts Frieda and Claudia's access to and understanding of a masculine self that is rendered awesome because it is remote and obscure, and also limits the knowledge, growth, and empowerment of the girls themselves by disallowing the part of his daughters that may be curious about sexuality. While McTeer refuses to acknowledge this dimension of his girls, the daughters perceive two sides to the father—the "him" or self that is in the shadows—that is, the self that the dark obscures, the self they cannot see or know directly—and the nakedness of a physical self revealed, a self they can see and interpret as familiar, if not intimate, companionable, if not congenial, knowable, if not open: "friendly-like."

The phrase "friendly-like" takes the relationship between McTeer and his daughters out of the realm where the father is the "big and strong" (7) parent who acts as the lawgiver and the benevolent keeper of his biological charges to a place where the children feel they are not confronting a seemingly infallible, inscrutable other, but rather an adult they recognize as vulnerable, warm, primal, accessible. Frieda and Claudia construe the nakedness of their father as "friendly-like" because when he is naked he is less dignified and distant, less concealed, less adulterated, more natural. Cloaked by the darkness, McTeer symbolically adds one more layer to the personal, social, psychological complexities that already separate child and adult. To put it another way, the clothed adult is a complicated, often formidable—if not intimidating text for which the child lacks the analytical skills. "Adults," announces Claudia who perceives grown-ups as enigmatic and obscure, "do not talk to us—they give us directions. They issue orders without providing information" (12). Claudia describes the father who denies the possibility that his daughters would stare at his nakedness, the shadowy father who insists that he remain unseen, unknown, hidden. But she also admits, "The edge, the curl, the thrust of their emotion is always clear to Frieda and me. We do not, cannot, know the meanings of all their words, for we are nine and ten years old. So we watch their faces, their hands, their feet, and listen for the truth in timbre" (16). Naked, the body becomes a primer that the child can more easily decipher.

In *The Bluest Eye,* the children, those readers of the truth in adult hands, faces, feet, and voices, also give us the key we need to understand the most provocative father in the novel, Cholly Breedlove, who rapes his eleven-year-old daughter Pecola at the height of "lust and despair," states of genitals and of mind engendered in his own unneat primerless childhood. Toni Morrison writes in awe of a character she herself finds it difficult to fathom: "The pieces of Cholly's life could become coherent only in the head of a musician. Only those who talk their talk through the fold of curved metal, or the touch of black-and-white rectangles and taut shins and strings echoing from wooden corridors, could give true form to his life" (125).[1] It is not only this jazz musician of Morrison's specification, but also the more primal musician of her suggestion, the child, that can give us the clues needed to piece together the episodes of Cholly's being. Indeed, the explanation for Cholly's tender rape lies fittingly enough in the afterschool chant of "uncorrigival" (56) black schoolboys who taunt Pecola one day after school. "Black e mo Black e mo," they incant, "Ya daddy sleeps nekked" (55).

While these boys provide the key to Cholly's unstorybooklike improvised fatherhood, the girls—Pecola, Maureen, Frieda and Claudia—pick up the reference to nakedness that the boys so quickly drop and worry it until it begins to yield meaning. It is Frieda and Claudia's frank and shameless encounter with their own father's nakedness that enables us to define the truth of Cholly's nakedness. The scene in which McTeer stands naked before his daughters introduces, as we have seen, the figure of two fathers—one, the "him" that passes into the darkness, is obscure, distant, dignified, jealous of his power, a lawgiver; the other, the father with the "friendly-like" nakedness that remains before the girls and the reader, is warm, exposed, spontaneous, physical. Unlike Claudia and Frieda's father, who survives, Morrison suggests, because he is able to be the obscured and the naked father, Pecola's father, even more the victim of unpropitious personal, social, and economic conditions, is cast out. He lives the life of the naked father. In a society controlled by traditional white patriarchs, Cholly, denied the opportunity to protect, provide, and command, becomes not just confused and frustrated, but desperately extreme in his spontaneity, passions, physicality, weakness—his nakedness. In *The Bluest Eye,* Morrison portrays the conditions under which a naked father such as Cholly is created and shows how such a nontraditional father operating in a traditional Dick-and-Jane society ruins himself and his own.

Cholly Breedlove's childhood is vexed by bitter-sweet exposure and overexposure. When he is only a helpless four-day-old, his mother compromises his existence when she leaves him on a junk heap, "Down in the rim of a tire under a soft black Georgia sky" (105). The ugliness of the junk heap is not mitigated by the soft black Georgia sky, rather the two are juxtaposed forever like the ebony and ivory of a keyboard in Cholly's life. Fifteen years later, when Cholly has his first sexual experience, he suffers a more blatant exposure that undercuts the ecstacy of the moment. Heady with the "thunderous beauty of [Aunt Jimmy's] funeral" and the "exultation" of the funeral banquet (113), Cholly, who has set out with a small group of youths to a wild vineyard, finds himself alone and about to experience his first sexual encounter with one Darlene. However, just as Cholly, astride Darlene, feels "an explosion threaten" (116), two white men out coon hunting interrupt the lovemaking with their eyes, lamps, flashlights, and laughter.

> "Hee hee hee heeeee." The snicker was a long asthmatic cough.
>
> The other raced the flashlight all over Cholly and Darlene.
>
> "Get on wid it, nigger," said the flashlight one.
>
> "Sir?" said Cholly, trying to find a buttonhole.
>
> "I said, get on wid it. An' make it good, nigger, make it good."
>
> (117)

As the "flashlight [makes] a moon on his behind" (117), Cholly, having lost the thrust of his desire, fakes "with a violence born of helplessness" (117) the moves of intercourse. The two white men have spotlighted Cholly's nakedness, vulnerability, and powerlessness, and in doing so have put a junk heap beneath his soft Georgia sky. The dissonance is jarring as the pleasurable excitement of coition collides with the painful make-believe of coition performed for two white men, as love slides into hate. Cholly feels deeply the degradation of having this very private act of affirming his manhood turned into a sideshow, into the spectacle of two animals rutting in the woods.

Unable to shield Darlene or himself from the snickering, guntoting, coon hunting, white men, Cholly transfers his hatred to the weakest player in "the drama" (117), the one who lies beneath him literally and figuratively: "He hated her. He almost wished he could do it—hard, long, and painfully, he hated her so much. The flashlight wormed its way into his guts and turned the sweet taste of muscadine into rotten fetid bile. He stared at Darlene's hands covering her face in the moon and lamplight. They looked like baby claws" (117).

This hatred is no more or less than the inversion of Cholly's desire to protect Darlene from exposure. But since he "had not been able to protect, to spare, to cover [her] from the round moon glow of the flashlight" (119), he opts to save something of himself by hating Darlene. Since hating the hunters "would have destroyed him" (119), he must degrade and reduce Darlene. She has proffered him a thing as fruity as muscadine, but under the light of the white men her gift has soured. The pitiful hands she uses to cover her face so that she cannot see or be seen become "claws," but significantly those of a small, helpless baby.

This reference to Darlene's babylike helplessness recalls Cholly's own helplessness as an abandoned infant at the same time that it points up his inability to protect not only Darlene but himself from the violation of the white man. In fact Cholly's hatred of Darlene is also self-hatred. For in her he senses the dawning of his own parental nakedness. That is, unable to protect, to fight, to hide, Cholly cannot manifest the patriarchal prowess, benevolence, or obscurity (after all, his backside is literally exposed) that is traditionally associated with maleness and manhood. Like Darlene he is accessible, weak, and naked. And to be thus naked is to share not only the tenderness and the plight of the female, but also to share a role traditionally assigned to her. The naked male is feminized, if not humanized.[2]

It follows, then, that Cholly, revolted by his identification with the femininity of nakedness, goes in search of his father. What Cholly finds strips him of any illusions he entertains about a relationship with that parent. He does see in his parent his own eyes, mouth, and head; however, instead of a man as tall as the black father who had broken open the watermelon at the July picnic, he finds a man shorter than himself and going bald at that. Instead of a man as sympathetic as Blue, one who is willing to share the heart of life with his son just as Blue had shared the heart of the watermelon, instead of the dignified, firm, but benevolent patriarch, he finds a man impatient, insensitive, unapproachable, and hard. The father made present is flawed and alien, the bastardization of the inscrutable father, the diametrical opposite of the naked father.

In the wake of these painful discoveries, Cholly reveals how tender and vulnerable he really is when "he soil[s] himself like a baby," goes down to the river where, "finding the deepest shadow under the pier . . . [he] crouched in it [the river] behind one of the posts . . . [and] remained knotted there in the fetal position, paralyzed, his fist covering his eyes, for a long time" (124). The fetal position and the paralysis of this scene recall Cholly the infant deserted on the junk heap and Cholly the teenager momentarily paralyzed by the flashlight of the white men. Smelling himself just as he had smelled the white men in the woods, just as he had "inhaled a rife and stimulating man smell" (121) among the black gamblers, young Breedlove "takes off his pants, underwear, socks, and shoes" and washes all but these last in the river" (125).

Having thus regressed, Cholly lets his thoughts return to one of the first females who helped define his passage from childhood to manhood:

> Suddenly he thought of his Aunt Jimmy, her asafetida bag, her four gold teeth, and the purple rag she wore around her head. With a longing that almost split him open, he thought of her handing him a bit of smoked hock out of her dish. He remembered just how she held it—clumsy-like, in three fingers, but with so much affection. No words, just picking up a bit of meat and holding it out to him. And then the tears rushed down his cheeks to make a bouquet under his chin.
>
> (125)

Up to this point, Cholly's feelings for Aunt Jimmy have been as confused as those he later has for Darlene. Aunt Jimmy has saved Cholly from death on a junk heap; however, Cholly has wondered whether it "would have been just as well to have died" (105) on that junk heap. Some of Cholly's ambivalent feelings about his mother-aunt are mirrored in the character of the aunt as Morrison presents her. For example, Aunt Jimmy subsumes the manly role of the rescuer and provider as well as the womanly role of the nurturer. The feminine role of nurturer finally characterizes the aunt for Cholly (he is nearly split open with a recognition of love when he remembers her "just picking up a bit of meat and holding it out to him"); as her androcentric name suggests, she has not only been aunt and mother to Cholly, but also Jimmy and father.

Aunt Jimmy, then, embodies both a remoteness, firmness, and maleness, and a tenderness, weakness, and femaleness that Cholly finds difficult to accept. When Cholly smells the old asafetida bag that Aunt Jimmy wears to ward off sickness and infirmity, when he sees the purple rag (not kerchief) she uses to cover and protect her hair, and when he is made to sleep with her for warmth in the winter, he has mixed feelings of pity and revulsion about the smell of that asafetida bag, about the sight of that purple rag, and finally about the sight of Aunt Jimmy's nakedness, of her old, wrinkled breast sagging in her nightgown (105). Cholly has misgivings about the vulnerability these things ultimately signal.

The pity Cholly has felt for his Aunt Jimmy intimates an identification with the aunt. And it becomes clear elsewhere in the novel that the experiences of a maturer Cholly will bear some resemblance to those of all the Aunt Jimmy's of Cholly's childhood. For like these old black women he too "had grown, [e]dging into life from the back door" (109). He too had taken orders from the white men. And he too had knelt by the riverbank. But the difference between Cholly and these old black women is indeed "all the difference there was" (110). Listening to the chatter of these old women, hearing the lullaby of their grief (110), the child Cholly can at best only revision the thing that most strikingly sets him apart from them and validates his man-life. "In a dream his penis changed into a long hickory stick, and the hands caressing it were the hands of M'Dear" (110). This childhood dream identifies Cholly's penis as the one thing that does not allow him, like the old black women, to "walk the roads of Mississippi, the lanes of Georgia, the fields of Alabama unmolested" (110). His penis marks a manhood that the Southern white man openly and continually flouts or denies. In this way Cholly's penis is simultaneously his rod of affliction and of self-validation. The transformation of Cholly's penis into a hickory stick that M'Dear caresses also points to another association that will in part help account for Cholly's rape of Pecola. For the hickory stick that M'Dear carries when Cholly first sees her is used "not for support but for communication" (108). The dream suggests, then, that Cholly will use his stick-penis to communicate.

From start to finish, Cholly's communications and relations with women are problematic. Aunt Jimmy's love for Cholly, clumsy and unspoken, is nevertheless and eventually communicated. Cholly, however, never manages to express clearly to Aunt Jimmy what he feels. Dead, she can never receive the bouquet of tears that token his love for and loss of her. Similarly, after the trauma Cholly and Darlene both experience under the glare of the white man's flashlight, Cholly's communications with Darlene are strangled when he turns to her: "We got to get girl. Come on!" (118). Cholly's confusion and fear of vulnerability coupled with the growing desire to move from adolescence to manhood further qualify Cholly's relations with the female as he opts, if not for the role of the traditional male who is firm, in control, a protector of women, then for the "strong black devil" (106) who is defiant, daring, bad, a user of women.

In a rite de passage with three unnamed prostitutes, Cholly proves himself the mighty disposer of women, a male reminiscent of the "woman-killer" Blue, whom Cholly had so admired and yet had found an unapproachable father figure (119). In the encounter with the prostitutes, an event that quickly follows Cholly's memories of his dead aunt, Cholly puts aside the weakness, tears, and love he begins to feel by the Georgia riverside for the kind of power and obscurity that sex in a brothel affords him. Here, Cholly takes back "aimlessly" (125) a manhood from women who remain unnamed because they are dwarfed by Cholly's need to affirm his male self. In the transaction, these women are used to satisfy his hunger. And yet what Cholly receives from this incident, Morrison suggests, is equivocal in value as he does not get anything as substantial as Aunt Jimmy's smoked hock or even Darlene's grapes. From the prostitute he takes "lemonade in a Mason jar," "slick sweet water" (125).

Having received this unsubstantial libation from a Mason jar, Cholly sets out on the road to a godlike freedom too extreme to result in good for himself or others. The man Pauline meets and marries has experienced a freedom that ultimately accentuates his nakedness:

> Only a musician would sense, know, without even knowing that he knew, that Cholly was free. Dangerously free. Free to feel whatever he felt—fear, guilt, shame, love, grief, pity. Free to be tender or violent, to whistle or weep. Free to sleep in doorways or between the white sheets of a singing woman. Free to take a job, free to leave it. He could go to jail and not feel imprisoned, for he had already seen the furtiveness in the eyes of his jailer, free to say, "No, suh," and smile, for he had already killed three white men. Free to take a woman's insults, for his body had already conquered hers. Free even to knock her in the head, for he had already cradled that head in his arms. Free to be gentle when she was sick, or mop her floor, for she knew what and where his maleness was. He was free to drink himself into a silly helplessness, for he had already been a gandy dancer, done thirty days on a chain gang, and picked a woman's bullet cut of the calf of his leg. He was free to live his fantasies, and free to die, the how and the when of which he had no interest for him. In those days, Cholly was truly free. Abandoned in a junk heap by his mother, rejected for a crap game by his father, there was nothing more to lose. He was alone with his own perceptions and appetites, and they alone interested him.
>
> (125-26)

The "godlike" freedom that reveals itself in these lines is neither the genuine nor the conventional thing. The force here represented is not that of a lawgiving, unbending, inscrutable godlike Yaweh. Cholly's acts tend to invert those of the patriarchy. For Cholly, the law becomes lawlessness; firmness can quickly turn to meanness, order passes into confusion. The freedom posited in these lines is one of contradiction, of paradox, of extremity, of heavenly tenderness and hellacious murder. Cholly's liberation is here exposed as a liberation of detachment and worthlessness: "there was nothing more to lose." Having no real power, no real possessions, no relationship, Cholly is naked. Having no real power, Cholly is subjected to prison, insults, bullets, and rejection. Having no real possessions, he is cut adrift as he moves from one place to another. Having no real relationship, he is "alone with his own appetites and perceptions."

As we have seen, Cholly's appetites and perceptions have in the course of his move from childhood to manhood shifted from smoked hock to slick sweet water, from love to sex. In his marriage to Pauline, Cholly tries to have the smoked hock, the love, the traditional Dick-and-Jane idea. He even tries to realize that which can more firmly establish the male's place in a patriarchal society—fatherhood. However, "having no idea of how to raise children, and having never watched any parent raise himself, he could not even comprehend what such a relationship should be. Had he been interested in accumulation of things, he could have thought of them as his material heirs; had he needed to prove himself to some nameless 'others,' he could have wanted them to excel in his own image and for his own sake" (126-27). The problem is that as a father Cholly has been stripped by his past of the possibilities of material accumulation and of social standing. Poor and black, renting a storefront because of a poverty that "was traditional and stultifying" (31), Cholly Breedlove and his family cannot indulge the "hunger for property, and for ownership" (18) that drives other blacks like the Peals, the Geraldines, and the McTeers (18). Cholly's modest attempts to buy his family and himself some of life's amenities are thwarted by whites who, in control of money and materials, take advantage of the helplessness and powerlessness visited upon black men in American society who, like Cholly, suffer deprivation of the goods and experiences by which manhood is signified.[3] Thus when Cholly buys a new sofa that is delivered to his house with split fabric, it becomes, as the delivery man tells Cholly, "Tough shit, buddy. *Your* tough shit" (32).

The "joylessness" (32) of paying for something that is damaged marks a social impotence that is accentuated by the presentation of other fathers in the novel. The white male in Morrison's novel, for example, usually realizes the idea of the powerful but somewhat distant if not inscrutable provider. Morrison encourages this notion of remoteness and obscurity with her purposefully brief representations of the white fathers in the novel. At most the reader learns that these patresfamilias have money, which equals power, or they have possessions, land, and servants, which also amount to power and control. Though these often unnamed white men tend not to be physically present in the novel (and we can never know them or even McTeer as intimately as we do Cholly), their presence is very definitely felt as the heads of households of "power, praise, and luxury" (101). As the Dick-and-Jane text with its own brief mention of the father suggests, these obscure figures are the ideal patriarchs, the father against which society measures Cholly. At the top of a hierarchy of color and money is Mr. Fisher, a well-to-do white father who commands a household in which Pauline finds "beauty, order, cleanliness and praise" (101). At the very bottom is Cholly, a poor renting black father whose household is characterized by ugliness, cold, and strife. The distance between this naked black father and the white ideal of fatherhood looms insurmountable.

While Cholly in no way resembles the white patresfamilias in the novel, Morrison's multiple imaging of black fatherhood shows that he is both unlike and like his black contemporaries especially in his relations with his daughter. Cholly is most unlike the father of "the high-yellow dream child" (52), Maureen Peal. A black approximation of Mr. Fisher, Mr. Peal is able to secure the financial well-being of his daughter. According to the McTeer girls, Maureen "was rich . . . as rich as the richest of the white girls, swaddled in comfort and care" (52). The fine patent-leather shoes, fluffy sweaters, brown velvet coat trimmed in white rabbit fur, kelly-green knee socks, and money with which Peal outfits his daughter help reinforce, if not foster, her sense of self-esteem and beauty: "I *am* cute! And you ugly!" she screams to "the three black girls [Claudia, Frieda, and Pecola] on the curbside, two with their coats draped over their heads, the collars framing the eyebrows like nuns' habits, black garters showing where they bit the tops of brown stockings that barely covered the knees" (61).

Pecola is finally the strongest foil to the confident daughter of Mr. Peal. For Cholly Breedlove has neither genetically nor financially created a doll-like child, a storybook Jane, or a Polly Fisher. In one of her most unconfident and vulnerable moments, Cholly's daughter, a representative of his fatherly accomplishments, stands in a "dirty torn dress, the plaits sticking out on her head, hair matted where the plaits had come undone, the muddy shoes with the wad of gum peeping out from between the cheap soles, the soiled socks, one of which has been walked down with the heel of the shoe . . . a safety pin holding the hem of the dress up" (75).

The McTeer girls are not without slack in their own worn stockings (54); however, Morrison suggests that though their father shares some of Cholly's weaknesses, his is not so starkly impotent or naked. We can never know McTeer as well as we know Cholly. The circumstances of his childhood and his entry into manhood are not given; Morrison textually obscures and reveals McTeer. For us, then, as well as for his children, a side of him remains in shadow. We glimpse him only when we hear of his nakedness and again when he turns the lecherous boarder, Mr. Henry, out of his house for making lewd advances to Frieda (80).

Yet one of the most sustained though oblique commentaries on Cholly's fatherhood comes through the portrayal of McTeer in a poetic interlude that commences the section of the novel called "Winter." Here Claudia McTeer pays tribute to a father who, like Cholly, cannot swaddle his girls in luxury, but a father, who unlike Cholly, is not so naked as to turn physically his frustration at his condition upon his daughters. Claudia writes:

> My daddy's face is a study. Winter moves into it and presides there. His eyes become a cliff of snow threatening to avalanche; his eyebrows bend like black limbs of leafless trees. His skin takes on the pale, cheerless yellow of winter sun; for a jaw he has the edges of a snowbound field dotted with stubble; his high forehead is the frozen sweep of the Erie, hiding currents of gelid thought that eddy in darkness. Wolf killer turned hawk fighter, he worked night and day to keep one from the door and the other from under the windowsills. Vulcan guarding the flames, he gives us instructions about which doors to keep closed or opened for proper distribution of heat, lays kindling by, discusses qualities of coal, and teaches us how to rake, feed, and bank the fire. And he will not unrazor his lips until Spring.
>
> (52)

The first part of this tribute to McTeer describes a parental figure reminiscent of the white patriarchs whom Cholly can never be or emulate. With skin that "takes on the pale, cheerless yellow of winter sun," father McTeer is identified not only with the coldness and whiteness of a season, but also with the remoteness of the traditional white father. A cheerless face given to "avalanche" and "currents of gelid thought" requires study, as it is formidable, grim, and reticent—the face of the stern, unreadable "him" obscured by the dark.

As Claudia continues the description of her daddy, and that cold parent warms up, as it were, with images of heat that lead toward a spring, the father depicted comes to resemble Cholly especially as he assumes the role and blackness of the Vulcan. Vulcan, the lame keeper of the flames, is a more human and frail form than the wintry one Claudia first pictures. In his blackness and vulnerability, Vulcan is also a figure closer to the black devil with which Cholly had identified as a youth.[4] Nevertheless, as the description progresses, it becomes clear that even as a Vulcanlike figure, McTeer's warmth, his nakedness is still governed by the wintriness of the obscured parent we hear of in the opening lines. He never completely exposes himself to his daughters as Cholly finally does. When McTeer opens up enough to talk to his offspring, he teaches, directs, and instructs them about the blackness of coal and about warmth, and thus remains the lawgiver and the supervisor. In other words, the unrazored slash in McTeer's face becomes a mouth as he moves from the role of wintry, remote patriarch to the role of the communicative, less aloof, father who is not so almighty and invincible as not to worry "night and day" about food, shelter, and warmth. And in his difficulties, his troubles, and his nakedness, McTeer is able to remain distant enough to give what comfort and care he can to his children in a way that is not so extreme as to devastate them. He has that degree of nakedness that his daughters need to feel loved and secure instead of defiled and brutalized.

McTeer does what Cholly Breedlove has not, can not: "Wolf killer turned hawk fighter, he [McTeer] worked night and day to keep one from the door and the other from under the windowsills." This is to say that McTeer has kept hunger from the door and the cold from the windowsills. Cholly, so repeatedly unmanned by a society and by personal relationships that have allowed him comparatively no respect, no money, no voice, has been worsted in the struggle of the father to provide care and comfort. He has suffered a defeat that negates his ability to act conventionally—that is, within a patriarchal circle of commerce. Therefore instead of "guarding the flames" Cholly does not bother to fetch the coal his wife needs to warm the house and prepare the food. Rather, he burns down the house and puts his family outdoors. Finally when spring comes and Cholly unrazors his mouth—that is, when he tries to speak to his child—he rapes her.[5]

The actual rape (which is preceded by a rush of seemingly contradictory emotions) is the culmination of Cholly's own deflowered life, his own weakness and powerlessness, his own nakedness. Without money, without authority, without dominion, without education, Cholly looks at the hunched back of his child and perceives in the "clear statement of her misery . . . an accusation" (127). Here is the same accusation with its accompanying guilt, pity, and revulsion that Cholly felt when, caught with his pants down, he could not shield Darlene. "He wanted to break her neck [Pecola's, as presumably he had Darlene's]—but tenderly. Guilt and impotence rose in a bilious duet. What could he do for her—ever? What give her? What say to her? What could a burned-out black man say to the hunched back of his eleven-year-old daughter?" (127) As Cholly casts about for something to lay hold of that will confirm his manhood and his fatherhood, it is apparent that he has a strong desire to communicate with his child, to relieve her of the burden of unhappiness; however, he feels stripped and exposed as he so often has been in the past.

When Cholly, "reeling drunk" (127), sees his young, helpless, hopeless daughter, he sees in her the focal point for poignant feelings predominant in childhood events, such as the picnic with Blue and his encounter with his father. But more important, he experiences feelings codified in his relationship with the significant females in his life. Cholly's mixed feelings for Aunt Jimmy, his interrupted experiment with Darlene, his marriage to Pauline, and presumably his knowledge of his rejecting mother generate varying degrees and combinations of the "revulsion, guilt, pity, then love" (127) that lead up to Cholly's violation of Pecola. The questions that run through Cholly's mind before he crawls "on all fours" toward his daughter are questions that pertain to all the women who have cared for Cholly Breedlove. "How dare she love him? Hadn't she any sense at all? What was he supposed to do about that? Return it? How? What could his calloused hand produce to make her smile? What of his knowledge of the world and of life could be useful to her? What could his heavy arms and befuddled brain accomplish that would earn him his own respect, that would in turn allow him to accept her love?" (127).

Pecola at this point is not just Cholly's offspring, she is Cholly's everywoman. She is the woman who can open her legs and thereby testify to Cholly's manhood, and yet when he cannot protect that same woman that he himself is victimizing, she becomes the one who undercuts that testimony; she is implicated in the degradation and the denial of his manhood. She is a human baby with claws. Cholly's ambivalence, contradiction, and befuddlement are underscored in questions that reveal an almost indignant desire to help and to please his child and a simultaneously anxious need to aggrandize himself (to "earn him his own respect" and allow him to accept her love?).

Cholly, of course, answers these questions, which lay bare his feelings of worthlessness and degradation, by offering (for the rape is, in his mind, both a violation and a gift, a tender fuck) the knowledge and the power that is naturally his, the knowledge and the power that has ever been begrudgingly and mythically granted the black male, that of sexuality. And in the wake of Cholly's carnal gift to his daughter is the wholesale carnage of his life and hers, of their potential and hope. Pecola, despairing of a white "heavenly, heavenly Father" (141) who will grant her the bluest eyes, unwittingly sacrifices an old dog Bob at the altar of another of the black fathers imaged in the novel Soaphead Church.[6] Pecola loses her baby and her sanity. Even the marigolds that Claudia and Frieda superstitiously plant to insure the life of Pecola's baby die. Cholly's "touch was fatal," writes Claudia, "and the something he gave her filled the matrix of her [Pecola's] agony with death" (159).

Claudia goes on to explain that Cholly had really loved Pecola, loved her enough to be the only one "to give something of himself to her." Cholly is not the obscured paterfamilias who hides himself from his daughter. Unlike the partially naked McTeer who denies the gaze of his daughters, Cholly bares himself: he gives Pecola complete access to his masculine self. However, while Cholly thus acknowledges the sexual side and power of his daughter, his nakedness is not "friendly-like," because it is finally unmitigated by any reference to others or to a reachable, sociable idea of fatherhood.

Unleashed in its social meaning, friendly nakedness becomes fiendish in the havoc wreaked upon the child. The gift Cholly gives his daughter is poisoned by the starkness of Cholly's very self, which has been warped by personal experience, social and economic conditions and circumstances that have stripped him of the capacity to share in a tradition inimical to that self. As Claudia puts it, "Love is never any better than the lover," and "the love of a free man is never safe. There is no gift for the beloved. The lover alone possesses his gift of love. The loved one is shorn, neutralized, frozen in the glow of the lover's inward eye" (159-60).

Shorn, and neutralized, himself, Cholly's love for his child is the love not only of a man who is free, but also of one who is so naked he is consequently dispossessed. And in the extreme nakedness of abandonment, degradation, poverty, and confusion there is no friendliness for children; there is only the waste and barrenness of aborted fatherhood. With its worship of whiteness, maleness, and power, and its high valuation of land, wealth, and acquisitions, with its hatred and exclusion of blackness and its fierce disdain of femaleness, frailty, and want, Western society has warped black fatherhood and consequently sacrificed the children.

The magic, the miracle of Morrison's novel is the survival, if not the transcendence, of a black father like McTeer who, in spite of the stress of being a black man in a white paternalistic culture, is able to foster in his children a feeling of security and a good sense of self. The saddest reality in the novel is the naked father like Cholly who, distressed unto madness by his total segregation from purportedly godly ideals of manhood and fatherhood, raises children who cannot see, and so deny the value and beauty of their selves and wish for the bluest eye.

Notes

1. In her analysis of *The Bluest Eye,* Barbara Christian notes the musical qualities of the novel's form (*Black Women Novelists: The Development of a Tradition, 1892-1976* [Westport: Greenwood, 1980], 138-53).

2. The ways in which Cholly's humanity is undercut are worth noting. Mrs. McTeer straightaway refers to Cholly as "that old Dog Breedlove" (Toni Morrison, *The Bluest Eye* [New York: Washington Square Press, 1970], 17). Claudia explains, "Cholly Breedlove, then, a renting black, having put his family outdoors, had catapulted himself beyond the reaches of human consideration. He had joined the animals; was, indeed, an old dog, a snake, a ratty nigger" (19). Later on we find Cholly sniffing the air like an animal to identify the scents of white men and the black gamblers (116, 121). And finally before he rapes his daughter, he gets down on all fours and crawls toward her like an animal.

3. Susan Willis (*Specifying: Black Women Writing, The American Experience* [Madison: University of Wisconsin Press, 1987]) offers an interesting insight

into the ways in which black men have maintained themselves when she writes, "Historically, gambling and bootlegging have afforded black men the opportunity to deal in a money economy without being employed by the economy" (12). When Cholly finds his father, that parent is gambling. When Cholly moves north with Pauline he quickly finds work in the steel mills of Lorain, Ohio. By the end of the novel Cholly has succumbed to the bootleggers, if he has not become one. Frieda notes that he is "always drunk" (*Bluest Eye*, 81), and he dies in a workhouse.

4. According to Thomas Bulfinch (*Mythology*, abbr. Edmund Fuller [New York: Dell, 1959]), in one account of the titans, Vulcan (Hephaestos), son of Jupiter and Juno, was born lame; Juno, dissatisfied with Vulcan's deformity, flung him out of the heavens. In another account, Vulcan's lameness results from his fall.

This reference to Vulcan links McTeer with Cholly. Though a crippled potentate, Vulcan was also the celestial artist. Morrison hints at Cholly as a frustrated artist of sorts when she insists that his psyche and life are the stuff of jazz musicians. Vulcan, in his smithy with all its attendant blackness and heat, is also reminiscent of the devil in his workshop. The devil is, of course, a figure with which young Cholly at one point openly identifies. Significantly, Cholly's understanding of the devil is not traditional or conventional. Cholly's devil is that opposite of the patriarchal devil. "He wondered if God looked like that [the black father at the picnic]. No, God was a nice old white man, with long white hair, flowing white beard, and little blue eyes that looked sad when people died and mean when they were bad" (106). Cholly's devil is a strong black man, caring and accessible. The black devil-father wants, as Cholly sees it, to split open the world (watermelon) and give its red guts (sustenance, good things) to the blacks who need it. Quite the opposite of the obscured, distant father, the devil-father stands so close that Cholly "felt goose pimples popping along his [own] arms and neck" (106). Cholly here is describing a version of the naked father. As Cholly in his own nakedness performs apparently devilish acts in the novel, it becomes clear that in the weakness and vulnerability of the naked father is also included the idea of the fallen father. This is to say that the naked father is fallen in the sense that he has fallen away from the white patriarchal idea, and fallen in the sense that acts in which he engages mark his weakness, his powerlessness to resist temptation, his sin, and finally fallen in the sense that he is pushed away or dispossessed. A tabular schema of this assertion follows:

1st father—"obscured"	2nd father—"naked"
Yaweh	devil
inscrutable	exposed
powerful	weak (or fallen)

5. In his *Fingering the Jagged Grain: Tradition and Form in Recent Black Fiction* (Athens: University of Georgia Press, 1985), Keith Byerman writes that Cholly attempts to deal with "self-hatred and oppression by becoming as evil as possible.... Behind this 'bad-nigger' persona lies a history of distortions of principal relationships and rituals of life." In various ways society has so conditioned and controlled Cholly, Byerman perceptively observes, that the effect has been one of "denying him a socially acceptable means of expressing authentic human emotion." Byerman goes on to note that Cholly "is incapable of appropriate fatherly behavior because he has had no parents" (187-89). I contend that this want only partly accounts for Cholly's inappropriate behavior. What Cholly needs most is covering and the protection that may come out of love, consistency, sustenance, and equality in any significant personal and social relationships. For indeed, such covering provides the space, the time, and the wherewithal to integrate and affirm a culturally constructed self.

6. Mr. Henry, but especially Elihue Micah Whitcomb, alias Soaphead Church, are part of Morrison's device of multiple imaging. These two characters are not biological fathers per se, rather they are father figures. Mr. Henry, a fatherly figure who lives with the McTeers, is soon cast out of that household when he gets too friendly with Frieda McTeer. Soaphead Church, whose attentions to Pecola are not physical, though they are very damaging, emerges as a more interesting fatherlike character. A self-appointed instrument of God (138), a type of Father Divine who had "dallied with the priesthood in the Anglican Church" (130), Soaphead Church, as his name suggests, is a pseudo-father whose relations with "his daughters"—that is, the young black girls who visit him—connect him to Cholly Breedlove. Morrison deliberately and carefully links Soaphead to Cholly to drive home further her point about how Western standards of fatherhood or fatherliness can be distorted or perverted in black fathers who live in a society that has historically, socially, and economically pushed them toward complete vulnerability. In his letter to the "heavenly, heavenly Father" of white patriarchy, Soaphead essentially locates his weakness and the beginning of his trouble in the history of his West Indian family, which has sought to whiten itself:

> We in this colony took as our own the most dramatic, and the most obvious, of our white masters' characteristics, which were, of course, their worst. In retaining the identity of our race, we held fast to those characteristics most gratifying to sustain and least troublesome to maintain. Consequently we were not royal but snobbish, not aristocratic but class-conscious; we believed authority was cruelty to our inferiors, and education was being at school. We mistook violence for passion, indolence for leisure, and thought recklessness was freedom. We raised our children and reared our crops; we let infants grow, and property develop. Our manhood was defined by acquisitions. Our womanhood by acquiescence. And the smell of your fruit and the labor of your days we abhorred.
>
> (140)

In trying not only to be white, but also to adopt the white standards, the Whitcombs are falsified and weakened.

Soaphead's father, a bad version of the white Yawehlike paterfamilias inflicts upon young Elihue not only "the precision of his [the father's] justice and the control of his violence" (133), but also "his theories of education, discipline, and the good life" (133). But "for all his exposure" to the fathers of "the Western world"—Christ, Hamlet, Gibbon, Othello, Dante—Soaphead only learns "the fine art of self-deception" and hatred (133). These two inculcations help lead Elihue to, among other things, his preference for little girls, the members of humanity whom he finds "least offensive" because they "were usually manageable and frequently seductive" (132). The little girls are just as vulnerable as he, if not more so, and so he identifies with these children in his sick way.

Soaphead Church himself is every bit as destructive as Cholly Breedlove when he insists that he felt that he was being "playful" and "friendly" when he "touched their [the little girls'] sturdy little tits and bit them—just a little" (142). Soaphead's characterization of his deeds as "playful" is his perverted rendering of the lines in the Dick-and-Jane primer: "See Father. He is big and strong. Father, will you play with Jane? Father is smiling. Smile, Father, smile" (7). A bogus parent, Soaphead is neither big nor strong, though magical powers are attributed to him. Were he a little boy, his actions may possibly be construed as innocent exploratory play; however, the play of this "father" is not, as he declares, innocent. His play is abuse and victimization. Soaphead's description of his actions as "friendly" is not the "friendly-*like*" (my italics) warmth and nurturing that Claudia and Frieda sense in the presence of their naked father who denies, as it were, the tacit and full-blown realization of "friendly" (that is, unlike Cholly and Soaphead, McTeer dismisses the possibility of ever physically manifesting friendliness to his daughters).

Like Cholly, this false father Church gives to Pecola a gift no better than himself. The parallels between Cholly and Soaphead are telling. The caresser of little girls, Soaphead never touches Pecola. Instead, like a fairy godfather, he grants her wish for the bluest eyes. While he, a self-deceived and deceiving father figure, passively gives Pecola a lie that leads her to madness. Cholly Breedlove, a more confused than deceived father, violently gives Pecola his physical self, a gift that has propelled her not only toward Soaphead's gift of insanity, but also toward exile and death.

Finally, Soaphead voices an important indictment against white patriarchy and how it has excluded and injured black lives when he writes:

> You said, "Suffer little children to come unto me, and harm them not." Did you forget about the children?
> Yes. You forgot. You let them go wanting, sit on road shoulders, crying next to their dead mothers. I've seen them charred, lame, halt. You forgot, Lord. You forgot how and when to be God.
> That's why I changed the little black girl's eyes for her, and I didn't touch her; not a finger did I lay on her.... I did what You did not, could not, would not do: I looked at that ugly little black girl, and I loved her. I played You. And it was a very good show!
>
> (143)

The truth here is that Yaweh has not been kind to the children, especially to the daughters like Pecola who have black fathers in white society who cannot recreate Yaweh in themselves, cannot manage a mite of the power to protect, provide, and comfort. In Soaphead's cry for the children is a cry interestingly enough for both Cholly and for Soaphead himself. For both these men are in some sense reduced to children; that is, in as far as their manhood has been denied or undercut in society, they remain children who have urges to "play" in particular with those who are at least as weak and exposed as they are—the little girls.

Shelley Wong (essay date summer 1990)

SOURCE: Wong, Shelley. "Transgression as Poesis in *The Bluest Eye*." *Callaloo* 13, no. 3 (summer 1990): 471-81.

[*In the following essay, Wong isolates a two-fold process in Morrison's narrative method in* The Bluest Eye *that transgresses conventional boundaries of signification and then reconfigures the material to form a new order of signification.*]

In the opening pages of ***The Bluest Eye,*** Toni Morrison writes that since the "why" of Pecola and Cholly Breedlove's situation is "difficult to handle, one must take refuge in how" (9). This admission, hardly the admission of a lack of technique or craft, is, instead, Morrison's admission that she is interested in, not questions of final causes, but questions of process, questions about how process comes to be shut down. Not surprisingly, then, ***The Bluest Eye*** opens with a tuition in closure. In a passage rendered in the style of the Dick and Jane series of primers, the novel lays bare the syntax of static isolation at the center of our cultural texts:

> Here is the house. It is green and white. It has a red door. It is very pretty. Here is the family. Mother, Father, Dick and Jane live in the green-and-white house. They are very happy. See Jane. She has a red dress. She wants to play. Who will play with Jane? See the cat. It goes meow-meow. Come and play. Come play with Jane. The kitten will not play. See Mother. Mother is very nice. Mother, will you play with Jane? Mother laughs. Laugh, Mother, laugh. See Father. He is

big and strong. Father, will you play with Jane? Father is smiling. Smile, Father, smile. See the dog. Bowwow goes the dog. Do you want to play with Jane? See the dog run. Run, dog, run. Look, look. Here comes a friend. The friend will play with Jane. They will play a good game. Play, Jane, play.

(7)

With the exception of Jane, each character—Mother, Father, Dick (who is absent from the narrative after the first mention of his name), the dog and the cat—maintains himself in a self-enclosed unity, "each member of the family in his own cell of consciousness" (31). The short, clipped sentences accentuate their discreteness. Each of their respective actions—again, with the exception of Jane—is marked by an intransitive verb: "laugh, smile, run," and the conventional sound signatures ascribed to cats and dogs—"meow-meow" and "bowwow." While the verbs "laugh," "smile," and "run" can function as transitive verbs, they do not do so in this passage. These verbs—including "see"—are also imperatives, suggesting the presence of, though never naming, the controlling authority that directs both the reader and the characters of the story. Only Jane (and the unnamed "friend"), who "wants to play," expresses a desire, or a capacity, to engage a world beyond the self. The family is purportedly "very happy." However, the laughing and smiling, seen in the context of the characters' atomized condition, seem not to express joyful affirmation but, rather, almost scornful repudiation. They refuse to play.

In an interview, Morrison commented that she had "used the primer, with its picture of a happy family, as a frame acknowledging the outer civilization. The primer with white children was the way life was presented to black people" (LeClair 28-29). The lesson of this passage in fact goes well beyond acknowledging or presenting white bourgeois values—it goes as far as enacting the very conditions of alienated self-containment which underlie those values. We might note, for instance, that the "house" precedes the "family" in order of both appearance and discussion. In this scheme of things, human relations are preempted by property and commodity relations. The space of ownership engulfs the time of human development and fellowship. The body of human relationships is drawn into the marketplace of being, an essentially timeless space which fosters a frightening commensurability between people and units of exchange, a commensurability which renders family members falsely individualized moments of a social and material whole. In the school of bourgeois economics, the child's first lesson in cultural literacy teaches the primacy of the singular and the discrete. The lesson works against memory and history, and collapses the structure of desire and *communitas,* while simultaneously promoting the desirability of discrete repetition, the wish to be always equal to some measure of ideality divorced from one's own physical and spiritual needs.

The primer passage itself is subsequently repeated twice (though with quite another lesson in mind): the first time without punctuation or capitalization, and the second time without punctuation, capitalization, or spaces between words or sentences. Again, in an interview, Morrison offers a reason for this particular arrangement: "As the novel proceeded I wanted that primer version broken up and confused, which explains the typographical running together of words" (LeClair 29). The brevity and the apparent simplicity of this explanation belie the dynamic complexity of a formal practice. "Broken up" means broken into pieces, ceasing to exist as a unified whole. "Confused" means mixed indiscriminately, blurred, from the Latin root *confundere* meaning "to pour together." Out of this seeming contradiction, it is possible to locate a two-fold process which marks the trajectory of Morrison's narrative practice—i.e., the practice of taking apart and then pouring back together to form the ground of a' new order of signification.

Formal considerations notwithstanding, some critics have read these typographical arrangements as symbolic representations of three different kinds of family situations. The first typographically "correct" version formally represents the ideal (or close to ideal) American family typified in the novel by the white Fisher family (Pauline Breedlove's employers), or the aspiring black bourgeois household of Geraldine, Louis, and Louis Junior. The second version is then associated with the family of the young narrator, Claudia MacTeer, a family admitting of some "disorder," but which "still has some order, some form of control, some love" (Ogunyemi 112). The final run-on version is said to depict the "utter breakdown of order among the Breedloves" (Ogunyemi 112).[1]

What these critics have overlooked, however, in their rush to establish thematic equivalencies, is the actuating potential of Morrison's formal textual strategies. They focus on the facts of the story but do not attend to the technique through which the story is told. The omission is problematic because while the story itself may fall within the thematic bounds of bleakness, the way in which it is told can constitute a means of resistance to both personal despair and cultural oppression. By omitting punctuation and capitalization, Morrison begins to break up—and down—conventional syntactic hierarchies, conventional ways of ordering private and public narratives.

The practical effect of this omission is to force one to reevaluate the cultural signposts which give the measure to one's life. By also omitting conventional spacing between words and sentences and breaking lines without respect for the integrity of the word, Morrison collapses those measures altogether, forcing one to pick one's way through a welter of potential signification. The progressive elimination of markers and the running together of words at once defamiliarizes and refamiliarizes the signifying terrain. In refusing the terms of the dominant culture's patterning of experience, one is in a position to restate the familiar, that is, to retrace the particular contours of one's own experience, to regain the practice of one's own narrative. This refusal of ready-made terms, and the responsibility it entails, plays itself out through other art forms, such as music—in particular, jazz. Some time ago, in answer to an interview question, the jazz pianist Thelonious Monk offered the following:

> Jazz and freedom go hand in hand. That explains it. There isn't anything to add to it. If I do add something to it, it gets complicated. That's something for you to think about. *You* think about it. *You* dig it.
>
> (Monk)

The refusal of the dominant culture's ready-made terms also challenges that culture's monopoly of meaning. The singular authority of the self-contained word threatens always to hypostatize and monopolize the very process of signification itself. As Morrison notes in conversation:

> It's terrible to think that a child with five different present tenses comes to school to be faced with those books that are less than his own language. And then to be told things about his language, which is him, that are sometimes permanently damaging. He may never know the etymology of Africanisms in his language, not even know that "hip" is a real word or that "the dozens" meant something. This is a really cruel fallout of racism. I know the standard English. I want to use it to help restore the other language, the lingua franca.
>
> (LeClair 27)

It is indeed a fallout of racism, but it is also a fallout of a way of organizing social and economic relations. It is a fallout of what one Chinese American writer has called—and called into question—a "Christian esthetic of one god, one good, one voice, one thing happening, one talk at a time," in short, an ideology and an aesthetic of authoritarian closure (Chin xxviii).

The single image of the ideal, the single meaning of the word, command either silence or mute repetition, and produce people "who know not what they do / but know that what they do / is not illegal" (Loy 127). Against a contemporary mood wherein, as Morrison notes, "everybody is trying to be 'right'" (LeClair 27), *The Bluest Eye* launches a critique of received norms of beauty and morality. The novel accomplishes this, in part, through its structural affinity with jazz, in particular, with a jazz practice which insists on overstepping conventional boundaries. Working out of an aesthetic of transgression, such music is frequently misunderstood, and mistaken for the stammered expression of past and/or present oppressions. When Theodor Adorno condemns jazz for its perpetuation of slave rhythms, its integration of "stumbling and coming-too-soon into the collective march-step" (128), he mishears the music because he conflates "slave"—black American in bondage—with "slavish"—being imitative, submissive, or spineless. Adorno considers jazz's incorporation of slave rhythms to be black America's self-mocking responses to, and affirmation of, past and present oppressions. For Adorno, syncopation involves the "coming-too-soon" into an enforced march-step, the self-lacerating eagerness which rushes headlong into servitude. But syncopation is not always a matter of being ahead of the beat; syncopation can also involve dragging the beat, resisting the received measure by deliberately working behind the beat. While acknowledging other critics' ideas concerning the transformative power of "stumbling," Adorno nevertheless refuses to concede the idea's actuality. Had he known Monk's music, for example, he could have seen that the "stumbling," the sometimes rapid and unexpected rhythmic shifts, are not ways of reflecting or accommodating victimage but are, instead, ways of negotiating a cultural minefield. To stumble the way Monk stumbles is to recognize the constant necessity of picking one's way through that minefield, refusing to be pinned down by the enemy, to be where the enemy expects you to be, or to be caught within the range of their oppressive cultural instrumentation. It can be a terrifying freedom—the freedom to be blown apart by a careless step, by an extravagant hubris. But at the same time, "stumbling" remains one of the few honest motions left in a world that demands a collective march-step. Decrying the tendency amongst young people today to give themselves up to a totally administered existence (LeClair 28), Morrison peoples her novels with characters such as Cholly Breedlove in *The Bluest Eye* and Sula and Ajax in *Sula* who try to resist such pervasive administration:

> They are the misunderstood people in the world. There's a wildness that they have, a nice wildness. It has bad effects in a society such as the one in which we live. It's pre-Christ in the best sense. It's Eve. When I see this wildness gone in a person, it's sad. This special lack of restraint, which is a part of human life and is best typified in certain black males, is of particular interest to me.... Everybody knows who "that man" is, and they may give him bad names and call him a "street nigger"; but when you take away the vocabulary of denigration, what you have is somebody who is fearless and who is comfortable with that fearlessness. It's not about meanness. It's a kind of self-flagellant resistance to certain kinds of control, which is fascinating. Opposed to accepted notions of progress, the lockstep life, they live in the world unreconstructed and that's it.
>
> (Tate 125-26)

The word "unreconstructed" is crucial here, for it points up and elaborates on that two-fold process characterizing both Morrison's use of the primer passage and an analogous jazz practice. An "unreconstructed" world suggests a world that has, first of all, been taken apart and then not—or not yet—put back together in any definitive sense of a final unity. The world unreconstructed refuses the matter-of-factness with which the administered world fixes a permanent name to an object, choosing instead to remain plural and fissiparous, requiring constant naming and constant articulation. Whether that articulation evolves into the blues, jazz, or other modes of formal expression, the impulse behind it is to express the mutable extravagance of materiality and to eschew the restraining paucity of all forms of ideality. In blues and jazz, improvising becomes a way of keeping the world open to its own potentiality. Jazz articulates meaning through attention to the particulars of the moment, to the work under hand, rather than through any strict adherence to received, and preconceived, notions of the bar or the line. Musicians such as the pianist Cecil Taylor or the alto saxophonist Ornette Coleman have, in their early work, even called into question the very notion of tonal centers:

> [The resulting music is] in many cases atonal (meaning that its tonal "centers" are constantly redefined according to the needs, or shape and direction, of the particular music being played, and not formally fixed as is generally the case . . .).
>
> (Jones 226)

> [Through jazz improvisation] music and musician have been brought, in a manner of speaking, face to face, without the strict and often grim hindrances of overused Western musical concepts; it is the overall musical intelligence of the musician which is responsible for shaping the music.
>
> (Jones 227)

The improvised piece, if it is to be articulate, requires not only attention to the immediate complex of sound and feeling being worked out but, also, attention to the total field of composition, to the "*total area* of its existence as a means to evolve, to move, as an intelligently shaped musical concept, from its beginning to end" (Jones 226).

"Intelligence," I might note, takes its etymological cue from an agricultural vocabulary, from the Latin for "gleaning," the gathering together of meanings. Much of Morrison's writing comes back repeatedly to this concern with her characters' abilities to gather meaning from the ragtag details of a life. Pauline Breedlove "liked, most of all, to arrange things," but that impulse was never able to find an appropriate outlet: "she missed—without knowing what she missed—paints and crayons" (*TBE* [*The Bluest Eye*] 88-89). In Morrison's second novel, *Sula*, we find Sula Peace without a way to perform herself in the world:

> [Sula's] strangeness, her naivete, her craving for the other half of her equation was the consequence of an idle imagination. Had she paints, or clay, or knew the discipline of the dance, or strings; had she anything to engage her tremendous curiosity and her gift for metaphor, she might have exchanged the restlessness and preoccupation with whim for an activity that provided her with all she yearned for. And like any artist with no art form, she became dangerous.
>
> (121)

Similarly, for Cholly Breedlove in *The Bluest Eye,* the inability to articulate the disparate moments of a life results in a hysteria of freedom:

> The pieces of Cholly's life could become coherent only in the head of a musician. Only those who talk their talk through the gold of curved metal, or in the touch of black-and-white rectangles and taut skins and strings echoing from wooden corridors, could give true form to his life. Only they would know how to connect the heart of a red watermelon to the asafetida bag to the muscadine to the flashlight on his behind to the fists of money to the lemonade in a Mason jar to a man called Blue and come up with what all that meant in joy, in pain, in anger, in love, and give it its final and pervading ache of freedom. Only a musician would sense, know, without even knowing that he knew, that Cholly was free. Dangerously free.
>
> (125)

Cholly was free in the sense that he was not bound by responsibility (or response-ability) to anyone but himself. Having been "abandoned in a junk heap by his mother, rejected for a crap game by his father, there was nothing more to lose" (126). For Cholly, in this "godlike state" (126), the world remained unreconstructed. Having lost all measures of relatedness to others, he was free to remake, or free to not make at all, his own ties to the world. In this sense, the unreconstructed narrative of his life resembles the third primer passage where all hierarchies, all conventional ordering has been collapsed. Using the analogy of a tape recording played back at high speed, or a film shown in fast motion, the seeming absence of cultural markers requires one either to create new orders of signification or to risk losing one's way altogether. In a nation which has historically insisted upon some people "shar[ing] all the horrors but none of the privileges of our civilization" (Algren ix), what passes for cultural measures can, when taken up by the disinherited, quickly be revealed as a hysteria of mismeasure.

For Cholly, the inability to ground himself in new measures results in despair. Initially unfitted, by way of race and class, for the dominant culture's patterning of experience, and then fitted too tightly into the "constantness, varietylessness, [and] sheer weight of sameness" (126) of his marriage, Cholly was soon smothered by his own "inarticulate fury and aborted desires" (37).

"Only in drink was there some break" (126) from the relentless routinization of body and soul. The weight of sameness, the tyranny of repetition—at home and at the mill—destroys for him the sense of time as a generative, forwarding process. The destruction, however, actually begins much earlier than his marriage. Cholly's abandonment by his parents radically disconnects him from the time of family. Later, the interruption and the frustration of his first sexual encounter by two white hunters further highlights his separation from the world of generative and reproductive time. This intrusion of the white world maintains a historical precedent in slavery. The slave trade had disrupted generative, and genealogical, time by breaking up families and by rendering family members commodities, that is, by reducing the ever-changing, ever-proliferating body to the status of exchangeable homogeneous units. Nowhere in this novel is this legacy of slavery—the disfigurement of human relationships by the marketplace—more ironically stated than in Morrison's decision to locate a family by the name of "Breedlove" in a converted (and poorly converted at that) storefront.

In the Breedloves' lives, repetition as the time of "flesh on unsurprised flesh" (38), as the copying of a static ideal, or as the submission to slave or factory time, results only in a stopped narrative, an arrested history. Pecola's rape too is, in one concrete sense, an arrested history. As Cholly moves to rape her, Pecola's "shocked body" (128) startles Cholly out of the miasma of routinized desire that was his marriage, setting in motion a "confused mixture" (128) of his memories of his first encounter with Pauline and his hatred for Darlene, the young girl who had witnessed his humiliation in front of the white hunters. Pecola's "shocked body" excites him, perhaps because it recalls for him a time before the freezing of his bodily imagination. Thus, while trying to break out of the stultifying confines of his quotidian existence by doing "a wild and forbidden thing" (128), Cholly succeeds only in copying those two earlier moments. In turning back process through raping his own daughter, Cholly breaks with and thwarts genealogical time. Within this context, their baby cannot possibly live, for nothing can issue from a stopped narrative.

The pathos of the Breedloves' lives lies in their complete alienation from each other and from the world; locked in their individual cells of consciousness, they are unable to give birth to each other, unable to bring each other into the world of generative time. In *The Bluest Eye,* Morrison allows the reader to see how the Breedloves arrive at their atomized conditions. The subsequent revelation points up how a metaphysics, a socioeconomic system, a society and a community, can interact in a mutual frenzy of blind ideality to mutilate people, particularly girls and women. The destructiveness of culturally sanctioned closures is implicit in the very title of the novel, where the "eye" is decidedly singular. There can, after all, only be one bluest eye, not a pair of eyes that are the bluest in the world, but a single eye. The impossibility of Pecola's wish is rooted in the singularity of the superlative. In order to achieve the bluest eye, she has to sacrifice the other—the result, self-mutilation. Pecola's subsequent derangement, the splitting up of her psyche and the splitting off of herself from the world, provides the only route to the superlative.

The Bluest Eye emerges as the indictment and the uncrowning of a social and economic order which upholds and implements a metaphysics of isolate unity. The world of discrete facts spawned by such a metaphysics refuses the ambivalence of the material world; it refuses to acknowledge the mutuality of material being that reveals itself in a newborn baby whose eyes "all soft and wet," are a "cross between a puppy and a dying man" (100); in a dog who coughs the "cough of a phlegmy old man" (139); in men who are dogs (15, 128); in cats who take the place of men (70); in an old woman who "yelps" like a dog (144); in a pregnant woman who "foals" (99); in a young girl who "whinnies" when she begins to menstruate (25); in all the ways that the material body asserts its transformative possibilities in an unfinished world of metamorphosis:

> The unfinished and open body (dying, bringing forth and being born) is not separated from the world by clearly defined boundaries; it is blended with the world, with animals, with objects . . . it represents the entire material bodily world in all its elements.
>
> (Bakhtin 27)

In confusing, in running together, the usually discrete states of birth and death and the discrete orders of humans and animals, Morrison breaks down the false and isolating solidity of self-contained identities and, at the same time, answers with an emphatic "No" Soaphead Church's question to God: "Is the name the real thing then? And the person only what his name says?" (*TBE* 142). In refusing the fixed identity of word and object, Morrison begins the work of decentering the logos itself. Through Soaphead's address to God, Morrison reveals the inanity at the center of the authoritarian word:

> Is that why to the simplest and friendliest of questions "What is your name?" put to you by Moses, You would not say, and said "I Am Who I Am." Like Popeye? I Yam What I Yam? Afraid you were, weren't you, to give out your name? Afraid they would know the name and then know you? Then they wouldn't fear you?
>
> (142)

One way Morrison breaks open the secretive, evasive nature of the solitary word is by acknowledging the physicality of words themselves. Words are not dead letters on the page but live sounds in the mouth and in the ear. She pays careful attention to not only the connotations of words, but also to the cadences of the language itself. Through the repetition of words, images, and grammatical structures, she affirms and enacts the resonance of materiality. To repeat in this way is not to yearn after the exactness of a copy but, rather, to follow up the traces of a family resemblance. In *The Bluest Eye,* Morrison uses the repeated phrase in much the same way a musician uses a riff—i.e., as a way of grounding, without prescribing, the entire composition; it is as much a point of departure as it is a point of return. On one level, the riff bears structural affinities with the rhetorical device of anaphora, a device which Morrison uses throughout the novel. Anaphora literally means "a bringing again" and refers to the practice of beginning successive sentences or clauses with the same word or sound. Each "bringing again" of the concrete word or sound offers another look, another hearing, another context, and another shifting around and gathering of meanings. "Truth" is to be found, not in semantics alone, but also in "timbre" and cadence (16).

For Morrison, language is material; language "is the thing that black people love so much—the saying of words, holding them on the tongue, experimenting with them, playing with them" (LeClair 27). The same could be said of a jazz musician's relationship to the musical phrase, particularly in the practice of the riff-solo sequence, the riff, here, being the occasion of collective playing which launches the individual musician on his own solo improvisation. The musician will take up the phrase and play with it, extending it and turning it over and over again until he extracts from it all the meaning that his own desires and questionings can call up. In Morrison's writing, the riffing frequently takes the form of a kind of rhyming, not of sounds necessarily (though this is often the case), but of occasions. This rhyming manifests itself temporally and spatially. In temporal terms, the novel is composed in such a way that it continually folds back on itself, replaying certain themes, images, or words. When we encounter Maureen Peal in the "Winter" section of the novel, we realize that her appearance had in fact been prepared for in the "Autumn" section, when Pecola, savoring the thought of eating Mary Jane candies, feels a "peal of anticipation unsettl[ing] her stomach" (41). The sonic rhyme in "peal" signals the occasional rhyme—both the eating of the Mary Jane candies and the appearance of Maureen Peal in midwinter promise false springs. Maureen is the "disrupter of seasons" (52), and for Pecola, the Mary Janes will ultimately be the disrupters of generative time, the seasonal time of the body. The repetition also throws us forward into Pecola's later encounter with Soaphead. There, on the verge of achieving the much desired transubstantiation, of achieving the beauty and the popularity of a Maureen Peal, Pecola's stomach is unsettled by the odor of the poisoned meat and by Bob's subsequent death throes.[2]

In spatial terms, Morrison rhymes by distributing human and animal characteristics amongst her characters in such a way that the human and animal worlds are unmistakably linked through a shared materiality. When humans "nest" and dogs cough like old men, and when a "high-yellow dream child" has a "dog-tooth" and another girl "whinnies" in fear, the hierarchical boundaries between the human and the animal are no longer absolute and human pretensions to the contrary are exposed as self-delusions.

In her writing, Morrison dethrones isolate unity and, instead, articulates the connectedness of people, animals, objects, and words—in short, all the manifestations of material being. The very act of articulating—of "making [one's] own patchwork quilt of reality—collecting fragments of experience here, pieces of information there" (*TBE* 31)—becomes a means of survival. For some of Morrison's characters—such as Mrs. MacTeer and Poland, one of the three whores who live in the apartment above the Breedloves—the blues provide a means to gather and to transmute the pain of daily existence. Mrs. MacTeer, Claudia tells us, "having told everybody and everything off . . . would burst into song and sing the rest of the day," singing about "hard times, bad times, and somebody-done-gone-and-left-me times" (23-24). In his essay, "Richard Wright's Blues," Ralph Ellison writes this:

> blues is an impulse to keep the painful details of and episodes of a brutal experience alive in one's aching consciousness, to finger its jagged grain, and to transcend it, not by the consolation of philosophy but by squeezing from it a near-tragic, near-comic lyricism.
>
> (90)

Ellison's choice of the word "transcend" seems to jar against the rest of his observation, and in its place, I would insert the word "transform," for the blues do not rise above the pain but bear witness to it and make it livable. Morrison's own writing stems from a similar impulse. After Soaphead has performed Pecola's miracle, he writes a letter to God. As he prepares to do so, he reaches for a "bottle of ink [that] was on the same shelf that held the poison" (139). The juxtaposition of the ink and the poison is far from gratuitous. The literal poison on the shelf here merely underscores the novel's repeated concern with a metaphorical poisoning which works through the American culture industry's projection—from the movie screen, from Mary Jane candy wrappers, and from Shirley Temple mugs—of a single image of ideal beauty, one that is decidedly white and devoid of any "dreadful funkiness" (68). The writing-out of pain remains inseparable from the cause itself.

There are those, however, without the means to transform their experience. The criminal failure to be equal to the dominant culture's image of beauty, to be equal to any imposed measure of ideality, leaves Morrison's characters scrambling for refuge in what are often destructive alibis. When it becomes known that Cholly has raped his own daughter, and that she is pregnant as a result of it, the black community's response ranges over disgust, amusement, shock, titillation, and outrage. Their moral outrage, while purportedly based on the violation of the incest taboo, is also clearly based on the violation of culturally sanctioned standards of beauty: "Ought to be a law: two ugly people doubling up like that to make more ugly. Be better off in the ground" (148). Any child of Cholly and Pecola's was "bound to be the ugliest thing walking" (148), and it would be better, for all concerned, if the baby didn't live to remind them of their own tenuous relationship to white America's standards of beauty. The baby doesn't live. And the community's alibi, created to deflect their own complicity in its death and in Pecola's psychological death, remains intact:

> All of us—all who knew her—felt so wholesome after we cleaned ourselves on her. We were so beautiful when we stood astride her ugliness. Her simplicity decorated us, her guilt sanctified us, her pain made us glow with health, her awkwardness made us think we had a sense of humor. Her inarticulateness made us believe we were eloquent. Her poverty kept us generous. Even her waking dreams we used—to silence our own nightmares. And she let us, and thereby deserved our contempt. We honed our egos on her, padded our characters with her frailty, and yawned in the fantasy of our strength.
>
> And fantasy it was, for we were not strong, only aggressive; we were not free, merely licensed; we were not compassionate, we were polite; not good, but well behaved. We courted death in order to call ourselves brave, and hid like thieves from life. We substituted good grammar for intellect; we switched habits to simulate maturity; we rearranged lies and called it truth, seeking in the new pattern of an old idea the Revelation and the Word.
>
> (159)

"Quiet as it's kept" (9), the narrator tells us at the beginning of the novel, leaving us to anticipate the "big lie [that] was about to be told" (LeClair 28). From that moment on, the novel bears witness to the lie that is closure itself. In bearing witness, Morrison will tell the tale of "who survived under what circumstances and why" (LeClair 26). Through the telling, the dominant culture's monologue on itself will be challenged and ruptured by the lingua franca of ambivalent materiality itself. In this sense, the telling becomes a liberating pedagogy. In commenting on her function as a writer, Morrison says:

> I write what I have recently begun to call village literature, fiction that is really for the village, for the tribe . . . [my novels] ought to identify those things in the past that are useful and those things that are not; and they ought to give nourishment.
>
> (LeClair 26)

According to the tenets of an older Platonic tradition of rhetorical theory, the function of the rhetorician was to move the soul of another in order that the soul begin to move itself. In more recent terms, the American poet Charles Olson has formulated another conception of that function for the contemporary writer: "he who can tell the story right has actually not only, like, given you something, but has moved you on your own narrative" (38). In bearing accurate witness to the "big lie," Morrison has reopened the tale of the tribe, reopened for the members of her tribe and for her readers the points of entry to a private and a public narrative. Telling and freedom go hand in hand, we can hear Morrison saying—"*You* dig it."

Notes

1. A similar reading of this primer passage can be found in Klotman, (123-25).

2. In conversation with Claudia Tate, Morrison has spoken of what I have referred to as a rhyming of occasions in terms of "omens": "you don't know what's going to happen at the time the omens occur, and you don't always recognize an omen until after the fact, but when the bad thing does happen, you somehow expected it" (Tate, 124-25).

Works Cited

Adorno, Theodor. *Prisms*. Trans. Samuel and Shierry Weber. Cambridge, Mass.: MIT Press, 1981.

Algren, Nelson. *Never Come Morning*. 1942. New York: Harper, 1963.

Bakhtin, Mikhail. *Rabelais and His World*. Trans. Helene Iswolsky. Bloomington: University of Indiana Press, 1984.

Chin, Frank. *The Chickencoop Chinaman/The Year of the Dragon*. Seattle: U of Washington P, 1981.

Ellison, Ralph. *Shadow and Act*. 1953; 1964. Toronto: New American Library of Canada Limited, 1966.

Jones, LeRoi. *Blues People*. New York: Morrow Quill Paperbacks, 1963.

Klotman, Phyllis. "Dick-and-Jane and the Shirley Temple Sensibility in *The Bluest Eye*." *Black American Literature Forum* 13 (Winter 1979): 123-25.

LeClair, Thomas. "The Language Must Not Sweat." *New Republic,* 184 (21 March 1981): 25-29.

Loy, Mina. *The Last Lunar Baedeker*. Highlands: The Jargon Society, 1982.

Monk, Thelonious. In Martin Williams, liner notes, *The Smithsonian Collection of Classical Jazz*. Smithsonian Institute, 1953.

Morrison, Toni. *Sula*. 1973. New York: New American Library, 1982.

———. *The Bluest Eye*. New York: Washington Square Press, 1970.

Ogunyemi, Chikwenye Okonjo. "Order and Disorder in Toni Morrison's *The Bluest Eye*." *Critique: Studies in Modern Fiction* 19 (1977): 112-20.

Olson, Charles. *Muthologos: The Collected Lectures and Interviews*. Ed. George Butterick. 2 vols. Bolinas: Four Seasons Foundation, 1978.

Tate, Claudia, ed. *Black Women Writers at Work*. New York: Continuum Publishing Co., 1983.

Doreatha Drummond Mbalia (essay date 1991)

SOURCE: Mbalia, Doreatha Drummond. "*The Bluest Eye*: The Need for Racial Approbation." In *Toni Morrison's Developing Class Consciousness*, pp. 28-38. Selinsgrove, Mass.: Susquehanna University Press, 1991.

[*In the following essay, Mbalia traces the narrative development of racism as the primary focus of* The Bluest Eye *in order to account for the novel's structural limitations.*]

In *The Bluest Eye*, Toni Morrison's emphasis is on racism. Specifically, she investigates the effects of the beauty standards of the dominant culture on the self-image of the African female adolescent. The role of class, the primary form of exploitation experienced by African people that will become the focus of later works, is only relevant insofar as it exacerbates that self-image. Of the three main characters—all African female adolescents—it is Pecola Breedlove who is the primary focus. It is she who is most affected by the dominant culture's beauty standards because it is she who is the poorest and, consequently, the most vulnerable. Thus, even with this early work, Morrison is conscious of the role economics plays in the African's having a wholesome self-image. For it is the Breedloves' fight for survival that weakens the family structure and makes the family members more vulnerable to the propaganda of the dominant culture. Still, it is clear that in *The Bluest Eye* Morrison regards racism as the African's primary obstacle. Describing the Breedloves, she writes: "Although their poverty was traditional and stultifying, it was not unique. But their ugliness was unique."[1] This comment demonstrates that in the late 1960s, when this novel was written, Morrison's level of consciousness about the primary cause of the nature of the African's oppression in the United States as well as in the rest of the world was considerably weak, for she not only subordinates the role of economics to racism, but also neglects to show a causal relationship between them, that an exploitive economic system gives rise to racist ideology.

The thesis of the novel is that racism devastates the self-image of the African female in general and the African female child in particular.[2] Toni Morrison's emphasis is on the society, not the family unit. According to her, the African's self-image is destroyed at an early age as a result of the ruling class's (i.e., the European capitalist class's) promotion of its own standard of beauty: long, stringy hair, preferably blond; keen nose, thin lips; and light eyes, preferably blue. By analogy, if the physical features of the European are accepted as the standard of beauty, then the African must be ugly. This is the type of logic that the Breedloves use to convince themselves of their ugliness:

> They had looked about themselves and saw nothing to contradict the statement; saw, in fact, support for it leaning at them from every billboard, every movie, every glance. "Yes," they had said. "You are right." And they took the ugliness in their hands, threw it as a mantle over them, and went about the world with it.[3]

Although Morrison clearly and correctly understands that the concept of beauty is a learned one—Claudia MacTeer learns to love the big, blue-eyed baby doll she is given for Christmas; Maureen Peal learns she is beautiful from the propaganda of the dominant society as well as from the African adult world; and Pauline Breedlove learns from the silver screen that every face must be assigned some category on the scale of absolute beauty—Morrison does not yet understand that this concept will change depending on the racial makeup of the dominant class. That is, her immature class consciousness at this point in her writing career precludes her understanding of three important facts: first, that the ruling class, whether of European, African, or Asian descent, possesses the major instruments of economic production and distribution as well as the means of establishing its socio-cultural dominance (i.e., all forms of media including books, billboards, and movies); second, that possessing such means, the ruling class uses and promotes its own image as a measurement of beauty for the entire society; and third, that the success of this promotion ensures the continual dominance of this ruling class.

Although her class analysis is immature at this point, Morrison is at least conscious of a limited role that economics plays in the exploitation of African people. For example, Morrison begins *The Bluest Eye* with a page and a half of one passage repeated in three different ways. Each of the passages reflects the three primary families in the novel: the Dick-Jane primary reader family, the MacTeer family, and the Breedlove family. The first family is symbolic of the ruling class; it is an economically stable family. Both the MacTeers and the Breedloves symbolize the exploited class although the Breedloves are less economically stable than the MacTeers. In fact, the spacing of the passages reflects the varying economic levels of these families. Although the MacTeers are poor, the father works and provides some shelter, food, and clothing for the economic survival of the family. On the other hand, the Breedloves are dirt poor, and it is the extent of their poverty that strips them of their sense of human worth and leaves them more vulnerable to the cultural propaganda of the ruling class. Their house, significantly a run-down, abandoned store, reflects no stability. The family members come and go like store patrons, having no sense of family love and unity. That Morrison takes the time to describe and explain the poor economic conditions of the Breedlove family, and the effects of these conditions on it, reflects her awareness of the class question. At least she informs the reader that the MacTeers and Breedloves do not suffer simply because of racism, but because of poverty as well.

Additionally, Morrison reveals her class consciousness by exploring the intraracial prejudices caused by petty bourgeois Africans, those who aspire for the same goals and aspirations of the ruling class. In *The Bluest Eye,* she creates three "minor" African families who, because they benefit economically, politically, and/or socially from the exploitation of their own people, disassociate themselves from poor Africans and associate themselves with the ruling class.

One such family is the Peals. Although the reader is introduced to only one member of this family, Maureen, her appearance, behavioral patterns, and remarks about the nature of her family's "business" offer sufficient glimpses of the Peals to reflect their class interests. Physically, Maureen looks and dresses like a little European-American girl, the storybook Jane or the child actress Shirley Temple. Her hairstyle, "long brown hair braided into two lynch ropes that hung down her back" resembles that of little European girls. In fact, the description of her hair as lynch ropes clearly associates her with the African's oppressors.[4] Her "high-yellow" complexion and her clothes make this association even more pronounced. She wears "Kelly-green knee socks," "lemon-drop sweaters," "brown velvet coat trimmed in white rabbit fur, and a matching muff."[5]

Socially, Maureen's behavior patterns reflect the way in which some within the dominant class relate to poor African people. She pities Pecola when she is humiliated by Bay Boy and Junie Bug, and she humors Claudia by speaking to her on one occasion after neglecting her on many others. Economically, the Peal family appears to make money by exploiting the race issue. They initiate suits against European-American establishments (e.g., Isaley's ice cream store in Akron) that refuse to serve Africans. Although, according to Maureen, her "family does it all the time,"[6] apparently these suits are benefitting financially no other African family but the Peals.

Still, Morrison is more interested in developing the skin-color conflict (race) than the class conflict (capitalism). For the emphasis in the Peal section is on "unearned haughtiness," Maureen's physical appearance. She looks like the doll that Claudia has had to learn to love; she is the person whom the teachers smile at encouragingly, the parents talk to in honey-coated voices, the boys leave alone; she is Shirley Temple; she is Jane. Moreover, Maureen's last appearance in the novel is clearly associated with the question of intraracial prejudice based on skin color. When Maureen is verbally attacked by Claudia, she responds by using the same dehumanizing name calling that Bay Boy used against Pecola: "I *am* cute! And you ugly! Black and ugly black e mos. I *am* cute!"[7] Clearly, Maureen sees herself as superior because she looks more like her oppressors.[8]

By disassociating itself from the African community, the second family—Geraldine, Louis, and Louis Junior—also reflects ruling class aspirations. The family members consider themselves to be *colored,* a term that for them signifies some nebulous group of Africans who are neither European nor African: "Colored people were neat and quiet; niggers were dirty and loud."[9] So Louis Jr. plays with European-American children; his hair is cut short to deemphasize its woolliness; his skin is continually lotioned to keep him from revealing his ashy Africanness. When Geraldine sees Pecola, she is reminded of everything she has sought to escape—everything associated with the poor, struggling African masses: their physical appearance, their behavioral patterns, their lifestyle, and their speech patterns. Her calling Pecola, a little girl of ten, a "nasty little black bitch" and commanding her to "get out of my house" illustrate the extent of Geraldine's isolation from her people and her association with her oppressors. Perhaps even more significant is the fact that she showers love on her black cat, but not her "black" son. Clearly, for her, the blue eyes of the cat make it easier to love the animal than her own son. All in all, her thoughts, words, and actions parrot those of the ruling class.

The third family, the Elihue Micah Whitcombs, are so obsessed with the physical appearance of Europeans that they jeopardize their mental stability by intermarrying to maintain some semblance of whiteness. They are grateful that their ancestor, a decaying British nobleman, chose to whiten them, and they enthusiastically separate themselves "in body, mind, and spirit from all that suggested Africa" while developing "Anglophilia."[10]

They are, in fact, convinced of DeGobineau's hypothesis that "all civilizations derive from the white race, that none can exist without its help, and that a great society is great and brilliant only so far as it preserves the blood of the noble group that created it."[11] Not only do the Whitcombs strive for the "whiteness" of the ruling class, but they imitate the exploitive nature of this class as well; they exploit their own people, the Africans who live in the West Indies: "That they were corrupt in public and private practice, both lecherous and lascivious, was considered their noble right."[12]

Clearly, Morrison's class consciousness, however weak, is reflected in her condemnation of these families who share the class aspirations of their oppressors. All suffer from what Kwame Nkrumah called the crisis of the African personality—Africans so bereft of their own national identity that they exhibit distorted, even psychopathic, behavioral patterns. Morrison is certainly aware of this crisis, for in this work as in later ones, she harshly criticizes those characters who divorce themselves from the African community. In fact, she considers this petty bourgeois sector of the African population the living dead, a buffer group between the ruling and the oppressed classes who are always portrayed as abnormal in some sense. In *The Bluest Eye*, Geraldine lavishes love on her black cat, but withholds it from her son; the Whitcombs become a family of morons and perverts. Quite appropriately, Elihue is donned Soaphead Wilson by the community for he is a pervert who is incapable of healthy love. Instead, he loves worn things and little girls; Pecola is both worn (loss of virginity) and a little girl.

Morrison's characterization of these three "minor" families—the Peals, the "Geraldines," and the Whitcombs—certainly substantiates the premise that she does possess some class consciousness even in this first novel. However, that these are not major families in the novel indicates that her class consciousness is decidedly weak. Moreover, even though Morrison is conscious of the role class aspirations play in these minor families, she often discusses these aspirations as if they were intraracial prejudices based on skin color rather than class conflicts. That is, her discussions of class conflicts are couched within, and thus over-shadowed by, her discussions on racial prejudices. Indeed, it is interesting to note that just as Africans in the United States in the 1960s and early 1970s viewed the primary enemy of African people as "the white man," so does Morrison, writing *The Bluest Eye* in the late 1960s, see the issue as one of European versus African. However, as she continues to think about, write about, and experience the ongoing oppression of African people despite the gains of the Civil Rights Movement, she will become more conscious of the fact that capitalism, not racism, is the African's greatest enemy.

It is interesting to surmise that the limited focus on the issue of class as the primary problem confronting African people in *The Bluest Eye* and the primary focus on racism as the major concern may be dialectically related to the novel's inorganic structure. The structural limitations of the novel can be gleaned through the many artificial props that Morrison relies on to help her develop her theme. First, she includes two prefaces, one to inform the reader of the conflict in the novel, the other to present the outcome. The first preface, extracted from the Dick-Jane primary reader, presents the three dominant families that will be contrasted in the novel: the Dick-Jane family, the MacTeers, and the Breedloves. Each is represented by one of the three storybook passages that Morrison places at the beginning of the novel to give the reader his or her first clue as to the economic and social well-being—or lack thereof—of the families. The structure of the first passage, representing the Dick-Jane household, is correct according to the double spacing and punctuation requirements of a standard typewritten passage. The next passage lacks the traditional structure of the first. It is single spaced. Representing the MacTeer household, it signifies neither the ideal nor completely chaos. Rather, it reflects a struggling household, one that manages to survive despite its economic hardships. The third passage is completely devoid of spacing and punctuation. Its words are run together, reflecting the chaos found in the Breedlove household. Therefore, just as the second two passages are presented to enable the reader to compare and contrast them with the first, so the MacTeer and Breedlove families are presented to enable the reader to compare and contrast their condition in society with that of the standard or ideal European-American family, the Dick-Jane family. The structural layout of the passages enhances the theme that as Africans born in a racist society, neither the MacTeers nor the Breedloves enjoy the benefits of America that their European counterparts do.

The second preface, the marigold page, presents the outcome of the novel—the unfortunate and irreparable demise of Pecola Breedlove in particular and of the Breedlove family in general. It also reveals the reason for this demise; the infertile soil of Lorain, Ohio, symbolic of the United States, precludes the healthy, normal growth of the marigolds, symbolic of African-American people.

Another prop used by Morrison to help her tell her story is the use of three different levels of time. First, the reader is introduced to a present that exists outside of the novel proper, the present of the adult Claudia. Second, the reader is given a glimpse of the future within the context of the novel, the marigold preface. Third, the story proper actually begins in the present on page twelve. However, by page seventeen, with the introduction of Pecola, and certainly by page thirty, with the description of the Breedlove's store house, the reader does not know what time period exists. Does Pecola come to live with the MacTeers after the Breedlove's abandoned store house is burned, or does Cholly burn some other, prior dwelling place, and then the Breedloves move into the abandoned store? Such questions arise because of Morrison's clumsy handling of time throughout the novel. She is not yet skilled in structuring plots.

The use of names of seasons to indicate the major parts of the novel also aids Morrison in telling her story. By beginning the novel with autumn, she informs us that the world of the novel is topsy turvey. Spring usually symbolizes the beginning of things, the time of birth and rebirth. Autumn, in contrast, is the time of death and decay. Summer, commonly associated with life in full bloom, ripeness, is a time of death, life in its final moments. These seasonal divisions aid the reader in understanding the fundamental decadence of life for the African living in the United States. They help tell Morrison's story of the warped psyche of an adolescent African female living in a racist society.[13]

A fourth structural crutch is Morrison's reliance on a series of passage chapter headings primarily to let the reader know that the Breedlove family will be the focus of the chapters and, secondarily, to let the reader know what specific aspect of the family will be the focus. For example, chapter 2, the first section that concerns the Breedloves, has as its heading a run-together passage describing the house of Dick and Jane. By using this particular passage as the heading, Morrison informs the reader that the contents of the chapter will be devoted to a description of the Breedlove house. When a heading includes all the members of the Dick-Jane family, as in chapter 3, the reader knows that all the Breedloves will be discussed. Admittedly, Morrison has created an interesting and unique structural device. Still, these headings do in fact simplify her task as a writer, for she can rely on them to help organize her material, i.e., to help develop the plot of **The Bluest Eye**. In later works, such devices are omitted because they are unnecessary. Moreover, they distract the reader from concentrating on the narrative itself. In later works, Morrison demonstrates her developed consciousness, her developed writing ability, and her developed confidence by relying only on the narrative to tell her story. In other words, the act of writing itself helps her class consciousness develop, and her developed class consciousness enhances her writing skills. The two are dialectically related.

Morrison's reliance on three narrators—Claudia the child, Claudia the adult, and an omniscient narrator—is problematic as well.[14] For instance, as narrator, Claudia the adult at times ascribes her adult feelings and adult analytical ability to Claudia the child. The reader is amazed, for instance, that a nine-year-old can understand that U.S. capitalist society is to blame for creating the standard of beauty: "And all the time we knew that Maureen Peal was not the Enemy and not worthy of such intense hatred. The *Thing* to fear was the *Thing* that made her beautiful, and not us."[15] For most, this realization does not come until adulthood. Phyllis Klotman attempts to offer a logical explanation for this shift in point of view from the child to the adult Claudia when she writes: "The narrative voice shifts . . . when the author wants us to have a more mature and objective view of the characters and their situations. . . . There is not only a progression in Claudia's point of view from youth to age, but also from ignorance to perception."[16] Contrarily, Morrison's narrative structure is more illogical than logical since Claudia the child thinks like an adult at times and a child at others. There is not what Klotman refers to as "a progression in Claudia's point of view." Throughout the novel, the reader constantly asks the following question: Is Claudia, the adult narrator, looking back on her childhood and telling the story, or is she telling the story as a nine-year-old participant and an adult observer?

The use of the omniscient narrator adds to this narrative confusion and awkwardness. It is the omniscient narrator who tells the Breedlove's story; Claudia, the child and/or adult, relates the events within the remaining chapters. What prevents the reader from being totally confused by this arrangement is the inclusion or omission of chapter headings. Chapters without headings are told by Claudia; those with headings are told by the omniscient narrator. However, this understanding of Morrison's narrative structure does not rid it of its awkwardness. On the contrary, the division of the story in such a way contributes to the reader's impression that Morrison, at this early stage in her writing career, must rely on artificial or external textural devices to organize her material.

Just as there are organization weaknesses between chapters, so are there weaknesses within chapters. In interviews with both Jane Bakerman and Robert Stepto, Morrison admits that she had difficulty with the Pauline Breedlove section of the novel. Unable to have either of her three narrators—the omniscient narrator, the adult Claudia, or the child Claudia—tell Pauline's story, Morrison is forced to use italics to symbolize Mrs. Breedlove's own thoughts. Morrison admits this writing weakness to Bakerman:

> When I wrote the section in **The Bluest Eye** about Pecola's mother, I thought I would have no trouble. First I wrote it out as an "I" story, . . . then I wrote it out as a "she" story. . . . I was never able to resolve that, so I used both. The author said a little bit and then she said a little bit. But I wish I had been able to do the "I" thing with her. I really wanted to.[17]

To Robert Stepto, she says: "I sort of copped out . . . because I used two voices."[8]

Having to oscillate between Pauline's thoughts within italics and the omniscient narrator's comments within a single chapter is only one instance of Morrison's inability to make her text cohere. The introduction of Pecola is another. At the end of one paragraph, Morrison completes a discussion of Mr. Henry Washington, the MacTeer's new boarder. At the beginning of the next, Pecola is introduced by the following nebulous statement: "She slept in the bed with us."[19] There is no transition from the discussion on Mr. Henry to that on Pecola. Neither is there a legitimate stylistic reason for this textual gap since for the reader it creates confusion, not clarity.

Too, there is at least one chapter—the Geraldine-Junior chapter—that seems superfluous to the rest of the text because it is not clearly integrated with the other chapters. Unlike the Maureen Peal section, which clearly helps to explain the effects of racism within the African race, and unlike the Soaphead Wilson section, which is relevant in providing the conditions under which Pecola imagines she has blue eyes, the Geraldine-Junior section seemingly does not advance the plot of *The Bluest Eye*. At first glance, it appears merely as a repetition of an already established fact: Pecola has an all-consuming desire to have blue eyes. However, it actually moves beyond repetition by relating the circumstances under which Pecola becomes convinced that she can be "black" and have blue eyes and, by convincing her of this fact, helps to seal her fate. But for Morrison to use an entire chapter to make this point (and then to make it so unclearly) is a mark of her undeveloped writing skills.

Later works evidence a symbiosis between text and structure, for as Morrison better understands capitalism/imperialism—the exploitation of one class of people by another class—she will structure her text to represent the type of economic system that condemns exploitation and promotes collectivism: socialism. Thus, by the time she writes *Tar Baby*, her story will be told equally by all of the main characters in the novel as well as by the omniscient narrator. Each will have the opportunity and the responsibility to contribute to the organic whole. And by the time she writes *Beloved*, she will so expertly manipulate past, present, and future as to demonstrate to African people that there is no significant difference between the quality of their life now and that experienced in slavery. This devotion to creating a dialectical relationship between text and structure will, in turn, point the way to the solution: collectivism.

Notes

1. Toni Morrison, *The Bluest Eye* (New York: Washington Square Press, 1970), 24.

2. Toni Morrison's decision to use an African female as protagonist reflects her interest in gender oppression as well as race and class oppression. In fact, all three forms of oppression are explored in each of Morrison's works. However, their primacy varies depending on the author's level of consciousness. In *The Bluest Eye*, sexism, like class exploitation, plays a secondary role to race oppression. Morrison does make clear, however, that the African female is the most vulnerable to capitalist propaganda in the United States, for it is the female in general who, in the United States, has often had her worth measured in terms of beauty rather than character or accomplishment. Also, Morrison's concern with gender oppression is reflected in the rape of Pecola. Pecola's rape and subsequent pregnancy further isolate her from society and, therefore, hasten her flight into insanity.

3. Morrison, *The Bluest Eye*, 34.

4. The Harlem Renaissance poet and novelist, Jean Toomer, made clear this association between the European female's hair and lynching in his short poem, "Portrait in Georgia":

> Hair—braided chesnut, coiled like a lyncher's rope.
> Eyes—fagots
> Lips—old scars, or the first red blisters,
> Breath—the last sweet scent of cane
> And her slim body, white as the ash of black flesh after flame.

Toni Morrison, student of African literature and former English major and teacher, is certainly aware of Toomer's poem. Her point that Maureen Peal's hair resembles lynch ropes is intended to remind the reader of this poem and thus to elicit feelings of apprehension and ugliness rather than beauty.

5. Morrison, *The Bluest Eye*, 53.

6. Ibid., 57.

7. Ibid., 61.

8. Keith E. Byerman's comment on the skin-color conflict in *The Bluest Eye* reflects the extent of Morrison's emphasis on race: "Morrison describes a social situation so distorted by the myth of whiteness that it produces a child, Pecola, who is so obsessed by the blue-eyed beauty of Shirley Temple that she creates a self-contained reality that cannot be penetrated even by rape and incest." "Intense Behaviors: The Use of the Grotesque in *The Bluest Eye* and *Eva's Man*," *CLA Journal* 25 (June 1982): 448. Also Chikwenye Ogunyemi's insightful statement on the significance of the novel's title emphasizes the issue of race as Morrison's thematic concern: "The bluest eye can be a pun on 'the bluest I,' the gloomy ego, the black man feeling very blue from the psychological bombardment he is exposed to from early life to late. The novel is, then, a blues enunciating the pain of the black man in America

and an attempt to grapple with the pain which is sometimes existential. The superlative 'bluest' implies that the other groups are 'blue' and 'bluer'—and, of course, the black race is the 'bluest.'" "Order and Disorder in Toni Morrison's *The Bluest Eye*," *Critique* 19, no. 1 (1977): 114.

9. Morrison. *The Bluest Eye*, 71.

10. Ibid., 132.

11. Ibid., 133.

12. Ibid., 133.

13. According to Barbara Christian, "Morrison's use of the inversion of the truth is sifted. So that the seasonal flow of birth, death and rebirth is inverted in the human society." Christian, "Community and Nature," 74.

14. The structural problems of the text have led some critics such as Jacqueline DeWeever to believe that there is only one narrator. According to DeWeever, "Claudia tells the story from her point of view, presenting the world of three little black girls. DeWeever, "The Inverted World," 404.

15. Morrison, *The Bluest Eye*, 62.

16. Phyllis R. Klotman, "Dick-and-Jane and the Shirley Temple Sensibility in *The Bluest Eye*," *Black American Literature Forum* 13, no. 4 (Winter 1979): 123-24.

17. Bakerman, "'The Seams Can't Show,'" 59.

18. Stepto, "'Intimate Things in Place,'" 222.

19. Morrison, *The Bluest Eye*, 7.

John Bishop (essay date summer 1993)

SOURCE: Bishop, John. "Morrison's *The Bluest Eye*." *Explicator* 51, no. 4 (summer 1993): 252-55.

[*In the following essay, Bishop comments on the ironic implications of Pecola's name in* The Bluest Eye *with respect to ideals of beauty.*]

Many writers have noted the importance of names (and the act of naming) in Toni Morrison's novels but, surprisingly, no one in print has noted the ironies surrounding the name of Pecola Breedlove, the central character of *The Bluest Eye*.[1]

"I just moved here. My name is Maureen Peal. What's yours?"

"Pecola."

"Pecola? Wasn't that the name of the girl in *Imitation of Life*?"

"I don't know. What is that?"

"The picture show, you know. Where this mulatto girl hates her mother 'cause she is black and ugly but then cries at the funeral. It was real sad. Everybody cries in it. Claudette Colbert too."

"Oh." Pecola's voice was no more than a sigh.

"Anyway, her name was Pecola too. She was so pretty. When it comes back, I'm going to see it again."

(56-57)[2]

As many have remarked, white cinematic icons—blue-eyed, pale-skinned Shirley Temple is their main representative—shape the self-images of the novel's black community in general and the Breedlove family in particular. The book's single reference to a specific film, then, invites comparison between the story in the novel and the story on the screen. (Since the novel is set seven years after the movie's 1934 release, the twelve-year-old Pecola could not have been named for the girl in the film.) Maureen's accurate but incomplete summary of the film, based on Fannie Hurst's 1933 bestseller, illustrates her—and her community's—adoption of Hollywood's image of beauty: "black" is "ugly," "mulatto" is "pretty," and, by extension, Shirley Temple is prettier still. Maureen's reference to the film illustrates how white cultural values shape the black community's idea of physical beauty—an idea that Morrison's narrator deems one of "the most destructive ideas in the history of human thought" (97).

More telling is the connection between Aunt Delilah, the mother in the film, and Pecola's mother Pauline. Like Delilah, Pauline—herself a credulous consumer of Hollywood images—is a domestic servant for a white family, a woman for whom "[a]ll the meaningfulness of her life was in her work" (102). By invoking *Imitation of Life,* Morrison registers Pauline's fantasy of the good life as it is lived by her cinematic counterpart: to be loved by, and to live with, the white family that employs her; to have a beautiful (i.e., light-skinned) daughter; to enrich the family by her skill in cookery (pancakes, in the film); and to be martyred by her ungrateful child. Some of these things she manages to accomplish, working for an "affectionate, appreciative, and generous" family whose patriarch remarks, "I would rather sell her blueberry cobblers than real estate," and cultivating a sense of her own persecution, bearing her husband "like a crown of thorns and her children like a cross" (100-01). But Pauline's life falls short of her fantasy, and her awareness of the discrepancy exacts a tragic price:

She became what is known as an ideal servant, for such a role filled practically all of her needs. . . . More and more she neglected her own house, her children, her man—they were like the afterthoughts one has just before sleep, . . . the dark edges that made the daily life with the Fishers lighter, more delicate, more lovely. Here she could arrange things, clean things, line things up in neat rows. . . . Pauline kept this order, this beauty, for herself, a private world, and never introduced it into her storefront, or to her children.

(100-02)

It is in relation to her daughter that the contrast between Pauline and Delilah is most telling. Once an avid movie-goer, Pauline has imbibed Hollywood's implicitly white version of beauty: "[s]he was never able, after her education in the movies, to look at a face and not assign it some category in the scale of absolute beauty, and the scale was one she absorbed in full from the silver screen" (97). Far from being the light-skinned and "so pretty" daughter who "passes" for white in the film, Pecola is repeatedly described as "black" and "ugly" or both at once (34; 39; 61; 75; 140-43; 159). Her own mother, to whom she is "like a black ball of hair," puts it flatly: "Lord she was ugly" (99; 100). By invoking the film, Morrison thus indicates Pecola's failure to measure up—in the eyes of Hollywood, of Maureen Peal, and her own mother—to the "so pretty" mulatto daughter of the film.

Most significant, however, is the hitherto unnoticed discrepancy in Maureen Peal's account of the film: the name of "the girl in *Imitation of Life*" is not, in fact, "Pecola," but "Peola."[3] The irregularity is appropriate because it denotes Pecola's failure to be like her cinematic double: she spends "long hours looking in the mirror, trying to discover the secret of the ugliness that made her ignored and despised at school . . ." (39). Maureen Peal's mistake has a larger relevance as well, for in Morrison's novels the act of (mis) naming signifies the community's power to deny individual autonomy and to use people for its own ends. The appropriation of her name is another token that Pecola is the novel's scapegoat, raped by her father and blamed by the community. The misnaming puts her in company with the book's other outcasts: the prostitute Miss Marie, known to all (save Pecola) as "The Maginot Line," and the quack mystic Elihue Whitcomb, dubbed "Soaphead Church."

Finally, one must note the phonic play created by the missing *c* of "Peola." The book's very title, as others have observed, is a pun: Pecola's consciousness disintegrates (she becomes the "bluest I") because she wishes in vain for those "bluest eyes" that would make her face—and her life—like one in the movies.[4] Pecola has inscribed in her name the discrepancy that makes that dream impossible. Morrison makes clear that the community has failed to save Pecola, and this failure is figured as blindness:

The gray head of Mr. Yacobowski looms up over the counter . . . [H]e looks toward her . . . [H]is eyes draw back . . . [H]e senses that he need not waste the effort of a glance. He does not see her, because for him there is nothing to see. How can a fifty-two-year-old white immigrant store-keeper with the taste of potatoes and beer in his mouth, his mind homed on the doe-eyed Virgin Mary, . . . see a little black girl? Nothing in his life suggested that the feat was possible, not to say desirable or necessary.

(41-42)

They cannot see Pecola because only the pretty, pale Peola is deemed worth of notice—they do not *c* the real girl. Pecola's final madness, marked by an interior dialogue between two halves of her fractured consciousness, one with blue eyes and one without, is the final marker of the damage done by her (and her mother's) vain wish to reconcile the "black and ugly" Pecola with her impossible fantasy self, the Peola of the silver screen.

Notes

1. See, for instance, Karen F. Stein, "'I didn't even know his name': Names and Naming in Toni Morrison's *Sula*," *Names: Journal of the American Name Society* 28.3 (September 1980): 226-29; Lucinda K. MacKethon, "Names to Bear Witness: The Theme and Tradition of Naming in Toni Morrison's *Song of Solomon*," *CEA Critic* 49 (winter 1986-summer 1987) 199-207; Linda Buck Myers, "Perception and Power Through Naming: Characters in Search of a Self in the Fiction of Toni Morrison," *Explorations in Ethnic Studies* 7.1 (1984): 39-55; and Ruth Rosenberg, "'And the Children May Know Their Names': Toni Morrison's *Song of Solomon*," *Literary Onomastic Studies* 8 (1981): 195-219.

2. Toni Morrison, *The Bluest Eye* (New York: Pocket Books, 1970). Subsequent page references are to this edition.

3. Thomas H. Fick, in "Movies, Consumption, and Platonic Realism in *The Bluest Eye*" (*MMLA* 22 [spring 1989]: 10-22), mentions *Imitation of Life* in passing, but repeats Maureen Peal's mistake—calling the daughter in the film "Pecola."

4. The pun is made more evident by the jacket copy for the book's first edition in 1970, in which each *i* is dotted in blue ink. I am indebted to C. O. Ogunyemi ("Order and Disorder in Toni Morrison's *The Bluest Eye*," *Critique* 19.1 [1977]: 113) for this observation.

Harihar Kulkarni (essay date summer 1993)

SOURCE: Kulkarni, Harihar. "Mirrors, Reflections, and Images: Malady of Generational Relationship and Girlhood in Toni Morrison's *The Bluest Eye*." *Indian Journal of American Studies* 23, no. 2 (summer 1993): 1-6.

[*In the following essay, Kulkarni interprets Pecola's fate in* The Bluest Eye *through Jacques Lacan's theory of the mirror stage of psychosexual development, tracing the origin of Pecola's sense of inferiority to Pauline's self-image.*]

The Bluest Eye is Toni Morrison's *The Waste Land.* Like Eliot, she too, in a limited sense, presents bleak, wastelandish human conditions characterized by grotesque environment which, like the earth of 1941, is unyielding. She brings into focus a place that fosters an underground invisibility and barrenness, composed of an imaginary cultural dissolution and fraught with brutal discrimination that strains human comprehension and stuns our conscience; where the "soil is bad for certain kinds of flowers. Certain seeds it will not nurture, certain fruit it will not bear, . . . and the victim had no right to live" (Morrison 1970:160).[1] The Lorain of 1941 is almost an industrial incarnation of the wastelandish underground where blacks like Cholly and Pauline Breedlove are pathetically relegated to a hidden, self-diminutive existence, "festering together in the debris of a realtor's whim" (p. 31), little more than compost for the capital growth of others. Hopelessly fragmented under the weight of various horrors typical of black life in America, the Breedloves remain buried as deep as the failed sacrificial marigold seeds planted by Claudia and Frieda MacTeer. Displaced from daylight, they remain invisible to the moted blue eyes of the Euro-American culture, yet ironically enough, such blue eyes are what dark Pauline and her eleven-year-old girl child Pecola obsessively long for. Morrison digs into the malady of black existential conditions characterized by a grotesque quality which, as Anderson (1976: 24) defines it, is

> the moment one of the people took one of the truths to himself, called it his truth, and tried to live his life by it, he became a grotesque and the truth he embraced became falsehood.

The novel presents black persons who become grotesque by embracing the generationally inherited white culture and its value structure as their own.

The existential gloom and grotesqueness, then, could be attributed not to nature but rather to the misappropriated images of a Eurocentric cultural mirror inviting a renunciation of one's own true self and the natural resistance of one's own black reflection.

Offering a critique of mirrors and reflections, Jacques Lacan (1977:3) notes that "the mirror image could seem to be the threshold of the visible world." For instance, an infant takes delight in testing mirror images and verifies the hypothesis of an emergent cohesive self. Culture, however, encourages cases of mistaken identities as one grows, since only certain images appear to have a chance for recognition by others. In ***The Bluest Eye,*** black girlhood assumes tragic propensities when it borrows identity models from the mandates of white culture and from the malevolent parental mirrors as well. Now, to seize upon and maintain a foreign image—inappropriative mental image of the self—seals the individual in the wastelandish soil of psychic underground, a terrain characterized by grotesque isolation and fragmentation: Pecola Breedlove's fate precisely.

Jacques Lacan envisages the mirror stage as having a clear function in growth because it gives form to the disembodied image of the earliest months of life. This specular image both verifies and alienates the self or, in the process of recognizing oneself, it even enables identification of another as potentially compatible. Such an identification, thinks Lacan (*ibidem*), leads to "the larger question of the meaning of beauty as both formative and erogenic." This linkage of beauty to sexual and social fulfillment stands central to Morrison's discourse of disaffection.

Like many other contemporary black women writers such as Maya Angelou, Gwendolyn Brooks and Paule Marshall, Morrison too believes in the anxiety black girls/women feel about what their mirrors tell them. She holds that girls growing up black and female in a white society often experience the malady of internalizing the belief that an aesthetically pleasing image is what constitutes the necessary precondition for receiving love and security. If the cultural or patriarchal voice in the mirror emanates unkind messages about women's self-evaluation, it has still unkinder things to transmit to black females who are barred even from becoming "women" in the traditional sense. A preoccupation with overcoming this devaluation consumes Pecola and Pauline Breedlove. At the root of such preoccupation, almost an obsession with both of them, is something deeper and more fundamental, some emotional component which operates actively. Although Pecola spends "long hours . . . looking in the mirror, trying to discover the secret of the ugliness, the ugliness that made her ignored or despised . . ." (p. 39) everywhere, it is not merely the white beauty that she is looking for, but an existential harmony which that beauty symbolizes. Her search is for the security of a loyal mirror, for its total acceptance which, as Pecola presumes, can easily be found in the preoedipal unity of the mother-daughter symbiosis. For Pecola, an approving mirror is equivalent to an approving mother. Basing her argument on Lacan's theory of the mirror stage, Winnicott (1971:12) notes that the child looking upon the mother's face, sees himself or herself: "In other words, the mother is looking at the baby and what she looks like is related to what she sees there." The child, however, loses its sense of worth if it sees the mother mirror governed only by "moods or, worse still, the rigidity of her defenses" (*ibidem*).

Such malevolent reflections are exactly what Pecola sees. From the beginning, Pauline Breedlove's mirror reflects to her daughter her own sense of inferiority which, in turn, Pecola radiates back to her. This mother-daughter mirror reflects images of sometimes-self and sometimes-other in their struggle to know who each is, an effort which runs generationally. The reverence for whiteness, which is Pecola's most valued possession, is passed on to Pauline through the intergenerational mirror by *her* mother. Pauline seeks her own missing mother as she looks at Pecola. She tells Pecola: "So when I seed it [the baby], it was like looking at a picture of your mama when she was a girl. You knows who she is, but she don't look the same" (p. 99). Pauline's mother worked as a maid for a white family, and by internalizing its mores, allowed herself to be encased in the glass coffin. The intergenerational mirror has already fractured Pauline's psyche and placed her beyond redemption. She resists any concept of internal wholeness based on cultural autonomy, believing that salvation will come from outside. By escaping into the world of white acquescience, dark Pauline believes that she has been refined when she has actually been weakened through "psychological paralysis."

The Fisher house is a place where she retains the illusion of being among the fairest in the land. A white movie theater is no mere place, but some religious shrine signifying wholeness and vision. To Pauline, it is a place where "the flawed became whole, the blind sighted, and the lame and halt threw away their crutches" (p. 97). She represents a self that exudes nothing but mania for all that is white, and lovelessness for everything that is her own. She reflects what Lacan (1977:4) calls a "primordial Discord" to her daughter. The image that Pecola returns weighs her mother's fantasies even more. She stands as a constant reminder of Pauline's blackness and limitations. To Pauline, the newborn Pecola is no more than a mere "black ball of hair" (p. 98), something that causes sheer disappointment. It was better to hold an image of Pecola than to embrace the real girl. Pauline clearly embodies the damages of what Morrison calls "an enslavement of the sense" (Clark 1980:51). "In equating physical beauty with virtue, she stripped her mind, bound it, and collected self-contempt by the heap" (p. 97), explains Claudia.

Morrison provides textual ambivalence by portraying the world of relationship in the MacTeer family. As opposed to Pauline's, the mirror that Mrs. MacTeer holds out to her daughter is the one which Demeter held out to Persephone. She provides Claudia enough sustenance and security to allow her to develop a voice that surfaces from the crisis of adolescence and blackness. In spite of the stress and tension that she encounters in white society, Mrs. MacTeer displays "love, thick and dark as Alga syrup . . . sweet, musty, with an edge of wintergreen in its base—everywhere . . ." (p. 14). The voices of her mirror transform Claudia's blues into sweet, exotic songs. Claudia narrates:

> She would sing about hard times, bad times, and somebody-done-gone-and-left-me times. But her voice was so sweet and her singing-eyes so melty I found myself longing for those hard times, yearning to be grown without "a thin di-i-ime to my name. . . ." Misery colored by the greens and blues in my mother's voice took all of the grief out of the words and left me with a conviction that pain was not only endurable, it was sweet.
>
> (p. 24)

Having not been succumbed to the societal indoctrination, Mrs. MacTeer sustains her daughter's gaze. Unlike Pecola, Claudia longs to express her knowledge based on a strong sense of relationship as well as on internal wholeness. She possesses a faculty she inherited from the well-guarded African "nommo" of her mother which, as Karla Holloway (1987:41) defines, embodies a power which "can be destructive or sustaining—but its power seems to be held best by women who have remembered its creative potential." It is this power of the Demeterian mirror that enables Claudia to resist the notion of white superiority and to feel connections with her own community. She informs us: "We felt comfortable in our skins, enjoyed the news that our senses released to us, admired our dirt, cultivated our scars, and could not comprehend this unworthiness" (p. 62).

In Claudia, one finds what Lacan calls a perfect "dialectical synthesis" of the internal self and the external reality. She feels whole and happy and embodies the spirit of her community so much so that Morrison (1984:341) thinks of her as a reflection of "the community or the reader at large, commenting on the action as it goes ahead . . . a choral note." The symbiosis with self and community is what Claudia has inherited from the positive reflections of her maternal mirror. Winnicott (1971:118) notes:

> When a family is showing concern over a period of times, each child derives benefit from being able to see himself or herself in the attitude of the family as a whole.

By mirroring one another, the MacTeer family, especially the mother, endows her daughter with a sense of identity and selfworth, something that Pecola does not know. It is through the correct mirror of mother that Claudia has gained a valuable insight into the mechanism of "ideological environment." She has a resentful realization that

> adults, older girls, shops, magazines, newspapers, window—all the world had agreed that a blue-eyed, yellow-haired, pink-skinned doll was what every girl child treasured.
>
> (p. 20)

Like Pecola, she has not learnt to "tame her anger down." Rather, Claudia feels, and rightly so, that "anger is better. There is a sense of being in anger . . . An awareness of worth" (p. 43).

In contrast, Pauline is no Demeter nor Pecola a Persephone signifying a nurturing ground of authentic being. Pecola, therefore, can harbor no such resentment. Owing to her mother's flawed mirror, she allows the ideological apparatus to be inserted into the fabric of her consciousness and get her psyche hopelessly fragmented. To her, eating the penny candy is the only way to salvation. She sees on the candy wrapper a

> [S]miling white face. Blond hair in gentle disarray, blue eyes looking at her out of a world of clean comfort. The eyes are petulant, mischievous. To Pecola they are simply pretty. She eats the candy, and its sweetness is good. To eat the candy is somehow to eat the eyes, eat Mary Jane. Love Mary Jane. Be Mary Jane.
>
> (p. 43)

Adulation of "Pretty blue eyes . . . Blue sky eyes. Blue-like Mrs. Forrest's blue blouse eyes. Morning-glory-blue-eyes. Alice-and-Jerry-blue-storybook-eyes" (p. 40) is Pecola's sole obsession, signifying an existential anathema which is passed on to her through the malevolent cultural mirror of her mother. Pauline's culture invites this obsession, tempts Pecola with it, and systematically poisons her life that finds no relief.

As a girl child growing up black and female in a hostile society, Pecola easily observes Pauline's self-distaste, gazes at her mother, her approving mirror, and buries herself through stunting complicity. Commenting on the attachment theory, psychologist Robert Karen (1990:49) observes that proper relationship with the mother provides impetus for growth to young children, who during their mirror stage life, try out various behaviors on their caretakers: "A sense of reciprocity—the agency of a friendly mirror—influences growth." Karen adds that some mirrors are not so accommodating, and "nature's intentions could go awry . . . if the environment failed them." In Pecola's case, there is no reciprocity, but only a self-surrendering complicity resulting out of her need for survival which demands total adaptation to her mother's needs in failed environments. Carol Gilligan (1989:25) thinks that adolescent girls possess a natural ability for spontaneity, even in anger, and "repeatedly . . . emphasize the need for open conflict and voicing disagreement." Pecola's volatile environments dissolve all such possibilities of spontaneity, leaving only dreary complicity, which, according to Winnicott (1971:147) ". . . is not authenticity but rather the creation of self that only appears to be authentic." In other words, Pecola creates a false identity which is invented as "a defence against that which is unthinkable" (*ibidem*). In her case, there is nothing more "unthinkable" than a father's rape and a "dangerously poised" mother. It is this complicity that leads Pecola to her ultimate doom. "Her need for friendship and acceptance is finally met by her split personality" (Gaston 1980:210). Madness and isolation become her private, safe mirror that no one can shatter. Gilligan (1989:26) maintains that girls can be liberated and made to feel whole if women "can stay in the gaze of girls. . . ." Pauline's sustenance of that gaze could have enabled Pecola, in the Lacanian sense, to see the mature and positive other of her species and redeem her life. But only to be looked upon negatively and having nothing or nobody to look up to creates a disjointed self-image and thrusts her headlong into the dismal abyss of life-consuming isolation and madness.

The discordance of Pecola's girlhood could be attributed not only to Pauline and her flawed mirror but also to Cholly and his mirror-free life. "Abandoned in a junk heap" (p. 126) by his mother who "wasn't right in the head" (p. 105), "rejected for a crap game by his father" (p. 126), and later by Aunt Jimmy, Cholly remains blind to proper relationships with others. Without a father, mother or school where one would have some moral and social instruction, Cholly's perceptions and behavioral pattern were decidedly shaped by libertinism. In the absence of a guiding mirror,

> Cholly was free. Dangerously free. Free to feel whatever he felt—fear, guilt, shame, love, grief, pity. Free to be tender or violent, to whistle or weep. Free to sleep in doorways or between the white sheets of a singing woman. Free to take a job, free to leave it.
>
> (p. 125)

He is left with no one from whom to distinguish himself, no woman to recognize as unlike himself. Nancy Chodorow (1987:13) maintains that the male must reject his "primary femaleness," as the discovery and rejection of this is "important to men to have a clear sense of gender difference." Even Jean Strouse (1974:7) echoes the same opinion when she remarks that ". . . much of what we call 'masculine' behavior . . . is evidence of the constant struggle to fight off this primary feminine identification." In the absence of a strong, primary relationship with a female, Cholly cannot distinguish "me" from "not me," the object-relating which provides foundations for all relationships. For him, therefore, the distinctions between self and other remain constantly blurred. His libidinous desires assume anarchic shape and remain ungoverned by taboos. In the absence of proper role models, "he floated aimlessly" (p. 119) and did "what he felt at the moment" (p. 127). Ostensibly a child of chaos, he makes others lives chaotic.

Devoid of mirrors reflecting primary identification, Cholly's sense of self is not only wavering but even fraught with simplistic notions that life is just a matter of light over darkness, power over powerless, and male over female, or father over daughter, to be precise. He destroys Pecola by raping and impregnating her, shatters the cohesiveness of her self, and violates her reflective image, permanently transforming her into a big contaminated Other. Writing about daughters in seduction, Winnicott (1971:52) observes that "in seduction some external agency exploits the child's instincts and helps to annihilate the child's sense of existing as an autonomous unit." Cholly's rape robs Pecola's existing sense of autonomy by forcing her to gaze into the same mirror he himself was forced to gaze into during his childhood days. The brutal patriarchal encounter removes Pecola from the sense that granted distinctions between self and other, between appropriativeness and the forbidden just as her father was removed in the early phase of his life. She remains without a cultural place in patriarchal society when she tries to achieve Oedipal love for her father. She is left to collect the garbage of life by seeking a pathetic regression to the previous generation, to her father's beginnings on a junk heap. She comes to symbolize, as Claudia puts it, "all of our waste which we dumped on her and which she absorbed" (p. 159). Pecola becomes an emblem of inversion, of waste, of all rubbish that no one really wants. The voice of patriarchy shatters her semi-tranquil mirror, ruins the world of her relationships, and finally produces conditions of isolation, psychic derangement and silence in Pecola's life.

Toni Morrison describes *The Bluest Eye* as a novel "about one's dependency on the world for identification, self-value, and feeling of worth" (Gaston 1980:197). Generational dependency as the only base for identification is what constitutes the real malady for the Breedlove family. The parental mirror causes psychic annihilation in Pecola's life, and shatters the cohesiveness of her self, leaving no context of the past or hope for a future. The forerunner of Jadine Childes, Pauline Breedlove generates subterrean diabolical chaos in Pecola's life by introducing her to the destructiveness of a culturally sanctioned mirror symbolized by the "eye" that is decidedly singular and the "bluest" in the world. Subsequently, Pecola's wish, rooted in the singularity of the superlative, causes psychic devastation, splitting her psyche and splitting her own self from the world as well. As opposed to Pauline's intergenerational dependency, Cholly's pseudo-Bohemianism characterized by a chaotic disconnectedness leaves Pecola in a permanent disjuncture with the outer and inner world, causing total dislocation of self, mind and body. Thus, tragic entrapment becomes the only sign structure signifying Pecola's existence. As Gilbert and Gubar (1979:37) put it:

> To be caught and trapped in a mirror rather than a window . . . is to be driven inward, obsessively studying self-images as if seeking a viable self. [This inward search] is necessitated by a state from which all outward prospects have been removed.

Having been offered the Lacanian "primordial Discord" at the social and familial level, whatever little inward search Pecola can make uncovers only an illusory and imitative self, a distorted, discordant version of the real thing, or a self that is hopelessly fragmented, making her life, to use loosely T. S. Eliot's phrase, a "heap of broken [self] images." With all of her "outward prospects" snatched away, she is emotionally abandoned as if only isolation and madness, with its freedom to invent conducive voices and reflections, can restore that "viable self." Grotesque mirrors and malevolent reflections coupled with dark images encase Pecola in a jar of mental illness, and finally seal her off in the glass coffin where, like millions of other black-eyed Susans, she is condemned to dwell eternally.

Note

1. All further references to this book are indicated by page numbers only.

Works Cited

Anderson, Sherwood. 1976. *Winesburg, Ohio*. Harmondsworth: Penguin Books.

Chodorow Nancy. 1987. "Gender, Relation, and Difference in Psychoanalytic Perspective" In Eisenstein and Jardine: 3-19.

Clark, Norris. 1980. "Flying Black: Toni Morrison's *The Bluest Eye, Sula*, and *Song of Solomon*." Minority Voices 4:2:51-61.

Eisenstein, Hester and Alice Jardine. 1987. Editors. *The Future of Difference*. New Brunswick, New Jersey: Rutgers University Press.

Evans, Mari. 1984. Editor. *Black Women Writers (1950-1980): A Critical Evaluation*. New York: Anchor/Doubleday.

Gaston, Karen Carmean. 1980. "The Theme of Female Self-Discovery in the Novels of Judith Rossner, Gail Godwin, Alice Walker, and Toni Morrison." Doctoral Dissertation, Auburn University.

Gilbert, Sandra and Susan Gubar. 1979. *The Madwoman in the Attic: The Woman Writer and the Nineteenth Century Literary Imagination*. New Haven: Yale University Press.

Gilligan, Carol et al. 1989. Making Connections: *The Relational Worlds of Adolescent Girls at Wimma*. New York: Wimma Willard School Press.

Holloway, Karla F. C. and Stephanie A. Demetrakopoulos. 1987 *New Dimensions of Spirituality: A Biracial and Bicultural Reading of the Novels of Toni Morrison* New York: Greenwood Press.

Karen, Robert. 1990. "Becoming Attached." *The Atlantic* 265:2:35-70.

Lacan, Jacques. 1977. *Ecrits: A Selection*. Translated by Alan Sheridan. New York: W. W. Norton.

Morrison, Toni. 1970. *The Bluest Eye.* New York: Washington Square Press.

———. 1984. "Rootedness: The Ancestor as Foundation." In Evans: 339-345.

Strouse, Jean. 1974. *Women and Analysis: Dialogues on Psychoanalytic Views of Femininity.* New York: Grossman.

Winnicott, D. W. 1971. *Playing and Reality.* New York: Basic Books.

Jane Kuenz (essay date fall 1993)

SOURCE: Kuenz, Jane. "*The Bluest Eye*: Notes on History, Community, and Black Female Subjectivity." *African American Review* 27, no. 3 (fall 1993): 421-31.

[*In the following essay, Kuenz shows the relationship between images of mass culture and identity development by focusing on its detrimental effects on the subjectivity of the African American female characters in* The Bluest Eye.]

In Toni Morrison **The Bluest Eye,** the Breedloves' storefront apartment is graced overhead by the home of three magnificent whores, each a tribute to Morrison's confidence in the efficacy of the obvious. The novel's unhappy convergence of history, naming, and bodies—delineated so subtly and variously elsewhere—is, in these three, signified most simply and most crudely by *their* bodies and *their* names: Poland, China, the Maginot Line. With these characters, Morrison literalizes the novel's overall conflation of black female bodies as the sites of fascist invasions of one kind or another, as the terrain on which is mapped the encroachment and colonization of African-American experiences, particularly those of its women, by a seemingly hegemonic white culture. **The Bluest Eye** as a whole documents this invasion—and its concomitant erasure of specific local bodies, histories, and cultural productions—in terms of sexuality as it intersects with commodity culture. Furthermore, this mass culture and, more generally, the commodity capitalism that gave rise to it, is in large part responsible—through its capacity to efface history—for the "disinterestedness" that Morrison condemns throughout the novel. Beyond exemplifying this, Morrison's project is to rewrite the specific bodies and histories of the black Americans whose positive images and stories have been eradicated by commodity culture. She does this formally by shifting the novel's perspective and point of view, a narrative tactic that enables her, in the process, to represent black female subjectivity as a layered, shifting, and complex reality.

The disallowance of the specific cultures and histories of African-Americans and black women especially is figured in **The Bluest Eye** primarily as a consequence of or sideline to the more general annihilation of popular forms and images by an ever more all-pervasive and insidious mass culture industry. This industry increasingly disallows the representation of any image not premised on consumption or the production of normative values conducive to it. These values are often rigidly tied to gender and are race-specific to the extent that racial and ethnic differences are not allowed to be represented. One lesson from history, as Susan Willis reiterates, is that "in mass culture many of the social contradictions of capitalism appear to us as if those very contradictions of capitalism appear to us as if those very contradictions had been resolved" ("I Shop" 183). Among these contradictions we might include those antagonisms continuing, in spite of capitalism's benevolent influence, along the axes of economic privilege and racial difference. According to Willis, it is because "all the models [in mass cultural representation] are white"—either in fact or by virtue of their status as "replicants . . . devoid of cultural integrity"—that the differences in race or ethnicity (and class, we might add) and the continued problems for which these differences are a convenient excuse *appear* to be erased or made equal "at the level of consumption" ("I Shop" 184). In other words, economic, racial, and ethnic difference is erased and replaced by a purportedly equal ability to consume, even though what is consumed are more or less competing versions of the same white image.

There is evidence of the presence and influence of this process of erasure and replacement throughout **The Bluest Eye.** For example, the grade school reader that prefaces the text was (and in many places still is) a ubiquitous, mass-produced presence in schools across the country. Its widespread use made learning the pleasures of Dick and Jane's commodified life dangerously synonymous with learning itself. Its placement first in the novel makes it the pretext for what is presented after: As the seeming given of contemporary life, it stands as the only visible model for happiness and thus implicitly accuses those whose lives do not match up. In 1941, and no less so today, this would include a lot of people. Even so, white lower-class children can at least more easily imagine themselves posited within the story's realm of possibility. For black children this possibility might require a double reversal or negation: Where the poor white child is encouraged to forget the particulars of her present life and look forward to a future of prosperity—the result, no doubt, of forty years in Lorain's steel mills—a black child like Pecola must, in addition, see herself, in a process repeated throughout **The Bluest Eye,** in (or as) the body of a white little girl. In other words, she must not see *herself* at all. The effort required to do this and the damaging results of it are illustrated typographically in the repetition of the Dick-and-Jane story first without punctuation or capitalization, and then without punctuation, capitalization, or spacing.

Perhaps one function of the mass deployment of these stories was in fact to raise hopes for a better future in order to counteract the oppressiveness of the present and, in the process, to delimit the chance of dissatisfaction or unrest and encourage unquestioning labor at the same time. If so, it also tempts, as these tactics always do, the opposite conclusion: The comparison of their lives to Dick and Jane's seemingly idyllic ones will breed, among those unaccounted for in mass culture's representations, resentment and class consciousness instead. That this is not the result for most of the characters in *The Bluest Eye,* as it is not for most people in general, bespeaks the extent to which mass culture has made the process of self-denial a *pleasurable* experience.[1] Indeed, as I hope to show later, this process is explicitly sexual in *The Bluest Eye* and offers, particularly for women, the only occasion for sexual pleasure in the novel.

As noted above, interaction with mass culture for anyone not represented therein, and especially for African-Americans, frequently requires abdication of self or the ability to see oneself in the body of another. The novel's most obvious and pervasive instance of this is in the seemingly endless reproduction of images of feminine beauty in everyday objects and consumer goods: white baby dolls with their inhumanly hard bodies and uncanny blue eyes, Shirley Temple cups, Mary Jane candies, even the clothes of "cream child" Maureen Peal, which are stylish precisely because they suggest Shirley Temple cuteness and because Claudia and Frieda recognize them as such. But Claudia and her sister can recognize "the *Thing* that made [Maureen] beautiful and not [them]" (62) only in terms of its *effects* on other people. Despite knowing that they are "nicer, brighter," they cannot ignore how "the honey voices of parents and aunts, the obedience in the eyes of [their] peers, the slippery light in the eyes of [their] teachers" (61-62) all pour out to the Maureen Peals of the world and not to them. From the responses of other people to girls like Maureen and others for whom Shirley Temple is the model, the sisters learn the *fact* of their own lack, variously identified as ugliness or "unworthiness," if not the essence of it. "What was the secret?" Claudia asks, "What did we lack? Why was it important? And so what?" (62)

Claudia's body, much more so than her sister's, has yet to be completely socialized in the process Frigga Haug calls "female sexualization." By this, Haug means both the production of femininity through the competent performance of feminine skills (including how to hold, move, and dress the body) and the reproduction of subordination within and on women's bodies as evidenced in the gradual "sexualization" of various body parts (for example, hair or legs) as girls mature. This process—inevitably modified, as *The Bluest Eye* indicates, by both race and class—results in bodies that are always the site of multiple discourses circling around and ultimately comprising what we call "femininity" or, as it is generally construed, "the sexual." Claudia's confusion about the source of her failure to arouse "honey voices" and "slippery light" indicates that, though she is catching on quickly, she has yet to experience her body as the alienated entity Haug describes. She is still at the level of sensation, not prohibition or enforced definition: Instead of "asking the right questions" about her sister's near molestation, for example, Claudia wants to know what it feels like to have breasts worth touching and to have them touched (79).

The innocence of this question parallels the delight with which Claudia revels in her own body's myriad substances and smells. While women like Geraldine are quick to dispatch with "funk" wherever it "crusts" (68), Claudia is fascinated with her own body's sometimes graphically nauseating materiality: She is captivated by the menstrual blood her sister hurries to wash away; she studies her own vomit, admires the way it "[clings] to its own mass, refusing to break up and be removed" (13); she abhors the "dreadful and humiliating absence of dirt [and] the irritable, unimaginative cleanliness" (21) that accompanies it; she remembers the year recounted in the novel as a time when she and Frieda "were still in love with [themselves and] . . . felt comfortable in [their] skins, enjoyed the news that [their] senses released to [them], admired [their] dirt, cultivated [their] scars, and could not comprehend this unworthiness" (62) that distinguishes them from Maureen and is already overwhelming Pecola.

The older Claudia attributes this ease with her body to her youth and admits that she eventually succumbs to the pleasures of dominant discourse and its definitions of "femininity." Speaking of Shirley Temple, she says, "Younger than both Frieda and Pecola, I had not yet arrived at the turning point in the development of my psyche which would allow me to love her" (19). She goes on explicitly to equate "worshiping" Shirley Temple with "delighting" in cleanliness (22). *The Bluest Eye* suggests that this "development"—the sexualization of Claudia's body (changes both in it and in how she experiences it) and the simultaneous transformation of her psyche is learned and achieved through commodities like the Shirley Temple cups that proscribe appearance and behavior in accordance with the images they project. Claudia learns to "love" Shirley Temple when she learns to identify herself *as* Shirley Temple, as a complete person—limited as that is for women in our culture to some variation of "the sexual." Moreover, femininity and "the sexual" can be produced and reproduced as *commodities,* as Pecola's belief that she can simply acquire blue eyes indicates. The mass dissemination of these images of femininity in American society was and is among the primary mechanisms by which women are socialized and sexualized in this country. It is no accident that Morrison links many of these images of properly sexualized white women to the medium of film which, in 1941, was increasingly enabled technologically to represent them and, because of the growth of the Hollywood film industry, more likely to limit the production of alternate images.

* * *

The effect of the constant circulation of the faces of, for example, Ginger Rogers, Gretta Garbo, Jean Harlow, and, again, Shirley Temple is to reintroduce and exaggerate, as it does for Pauline Breedlove, "the most destructive ideas in the history of human thought" (97)—romantic love and physical beauty, each defined according to what they exclude and each destructive to the extent that they are made definitionally unavailable. After waiting out two pregnancies in the dark shadows of the silver screen, Pauline "was never able . . . [again] to look at a face and not assign it some category in the scale of absolute beauty" which she had "absorbed in full" from the movies (97). Among these faces to which she can't help but assign a pre-determined value is her own, ironically made less acceptable by her Jean Harlow hairstyle because of the rotten tooth that contradicts it. In spite of the hope implicit in naming her after a fair character in a movie itself called *Imitation of Life*,[2] Pecola, too, is, according to her mother and apparently everyone else," '*ugly*'" (100). The consequences of this estimation, repeated as it is continually throughout Pecola's life, are, of course, obvious: When others—Mr. Yacobowski, her teachers, etc.—cannot or will not see her, then she ceases to be seen at all or sees herself in the iconographic images she can attain only in madness.

The horror of the industry responsible for generating and continuing these repeated, static, and unattainable images is not just that, in the process of appropriating standards of beauty and femininity for white women, it does not allow alternate images and standards to coincide—though such is certainly horrible—but that in so doing it also co-opts and transforms a history of communal and familial relationships it cannot otherwise accommodate. This co-optation was facilitated by the migration of African-Americans in the first half of this century and the end of the last to Northern, usually industrial, towns like Lorain, a process that accelerated the separation of families and friends as it removed them farther from whatever common culture existed in the rural South (Willis, *Specifying* 83-109). In the absence of a network of community members ready to step in—as Aunt Jimmy's family and friends do—and make it their business to look after each other, blacks up north who feel isolated from their past and alienated in their present are more likely to look elsewhere for self-affirming context.

As Pauline Breedlove's history bears out, the culture industry is always quick to provide its notion of what this context should be and thus assure the dependence necessary for its own continued existence, even, indeed especially, at the expense of alternate cultural forms. Although she has few fond memories of her childhood, it is her early married life in Lorain that Pauline remembers as the "'*lonesomest time of my life.*'" She is simply not prepared for the kinds of changes not prepared for the kinds of changes wrought by her transplantation north:

> *I don't know what all happened. Everything changed. It was hard to get to know folks up here, and I missed my people. I weren't used to so much white folks. The ones I seed before was something hateful, but they didn't come around too much. . . . Up north they was everywhere—next door, downstairs, all over the streets—and colored folks few and far between. Northern colored folk was different too. Dicty-like. No better than whites for meanness. They could make you feel just as no-count, 'cept I didn't expect it from them.*

(93)

From this seemingly fragmented and hostile community, Pauline turns to day jobs in the homes of "nervous, pretentious" people and to the movies. Her attachment to the former is due in part to the fact that at the Fishers she can exercise the artistic sensibility that otherwise cannot find expression. As a child in Alabama and especially Kentucky, Pauline "liked, most of all, to arrange things. To line things up in rows—jars on shelves at canning, peach pits on the step, sticks, stones, leaves. . . . She missed—without knowing what she missed—paints and crayons" (88-89). But it is not until her job at the Fishers that Pauline can again "arrange things, clean things, line things up in neat rows. . . . [At the Fisher's] she found beauty, order, cleanliness, and praise. . . . It was her pleasure to stand in her kitchen at the end of a day and survey her handiwork" (101). Moreover, her job with the Fishers provides her with the semblance of acceptance and community she cannot find or create in her own home and neighborhood. They have given her the nickname she never had as a child and tell small anecdotes about her. Mr. Fisher says, "'I would rather sell her blueberry cobblers than real estate'" (101). Finally, it is easier for Pauline to ignore the fact that both the name and the anecdotes are condescending and exemplative of her subordinate, and ultimately outsider, status in the Fisher household (as evidenced when Claudia feels "the familiar violence" rise at the little pink girl's question" 'Where's Polly?'" [86]) than to do without the "power, praise, and luxury" (101) she finds there.

The other place she finds this "power, praise, and luxury" is, of course, the movies, and, unfortunately, it is to them that Pauline turns for help and validation rather than the few black women she has met in Lorain who, "with their goading glances and private snickers," were merely "amused" by her and her loneliness (94).[3] It is at the movies that Pauline learns to equate "physical beauty and virtue," where she "stripped her mind, bound it, and collected self-contempt by the heap." As she watches "'*white men taking such good care of they women, and they all dressed up in big clean houses*'" (97), Pauline finds it increasingly difficult to return to her own life and, as a result, "more and more . . . neglected her house, her children, her man" (101). Like the Dick-and-Jane story, Pauline's movies continuously present her with a life, again presumably ideal, which she does not now have and which she has little, if any, chance of ever enjoying in any capacity other than that of "the ideal servant" (101).[4] In the absence of alternate images which might validate and endorse a kind of virtue not tied to physical beauty or ones offering competing definitions of beauty itself, *and* in the absence of a network of family and friends, especially women friends, whose own lives would provide a differing model and the context in which to erect her own, Pauline succumbs to the "simple pleasure" of "black-and-white images projected through a ray of light" and "curtailing freedom in every way" (97).

Images projected on the screen and mass-produced items curtail freedom in other, less obvious and brutal ways as well, although the effects can be due as much to what is *not* seen or experienced as to what is. Claudia, for example, fosters a brutal hatred for her white baby dolls not just because they don't look like her but because the gift of them is supposed to replace and somehow improve upon what she would really prefer for Christmas: the *experience* of sitting "on the low stool in Big Mama's kitchen with [her] lap full of lilacs and [listening] to Big Papa play his violin for [her] alone" (21). Instead of family interaction—and the touching, playing, and ritual storytelling that might accompany it—Claudia is supposed to pretend to be the mother of this "thing" dressed in "starched gauze or lace" and sporting a "bone-cold head" (20).

Similarly, Claudia hates Shirley Temple well enough because her socks stay up, but what really gets her is the presence in the films of Bojangles. This is the outrage: the rewriting of either a historical moment (the Civil War) or interpersonal relationship (an orphaned child and benevolent older friend) with her part edited or bleached out so that those few images of African-American life afforded space on the big screen are put there not as evidence or proof of the experience itself, but as a tactic for further erasure, denial, or revisioning of just that experience. Instead of the ideologically opportune sight of an older black man "soft-shoeing it and chuckling" harmlessly, aimlessly, with a little white girl, the world should be seeing *her*, Claudia, socks around her ankles, "enjoying, sharing, giving a lovely dance thing" (19) with *her* friend, uncle, daddy Bojangles.

It does not, however, and Morrison signals the effects of these oversights—of supplanting or having supplanted both one's appearance and one's history and culture—repeatedly in **The Bluest Eye** in details of sexuality, especially women's but, as the lifestories of Cholly and Soaphead indicate, not exclusively so. Mr. Henry, for example, when first moving into the MacTeers' home, greets Claudia and Frieda with, "'You must be Greta Garbo, and you must be Ginger Rogers'" (17), thus reducing them to type in a kind of objectification which, in part, will make it easier for him later to molest Frieda. He follows this greeting with a gift of money, a gesture repeated later when he wants them out of the house so he can entertain two of the more colorful "members of [his] Bible class" (65), China and the Maginot Line. The exchange of money and the objectification of women as types converge here in such a way as to align his interaction with the two women and with Frieda and Claudia under the heading of prostitution.

* * *

The incident with Mr. Henry suggests one way the mass circulation of images of "femininity" negatively affects women in the area of sexuality by negatively affecting the attitudes and thus behavior of the people with whom they interact. **The Bluest Eye,** however, documents further the effect of those images on women themselves *on the level of the body* and in terms of how they understand and experience their own sexuality. For Pauline, for example, sexual pleasure depends entirely on the ability to "'*feel a power*'" (103) that comes from a sense of herself as desirable. In bed with Cholly, she thinks,

> *I know he wants me to come first. But I can't. Not until he does. Not until I feel him loving me. Just me. . . . Not until I know that my flesh is all that be on his mind. . . . Not until he has let go of all he has, and give it to me. . . . When he does, I feel a power. . . . I be strong enough, pretty enough, and young enough to let him make me come.*
>
> (103)

Unfortunately, Pauline defines strength, beauty, and youth solely in the terms she's learned from film; thus, as the possibility of ever attaining them is foreclosed, so too is sexual pleasure. Confident that "'*my Maker will take care of me*,'" (104), Pauline reassures herself that "'. . . it don't make no difference about this old earth,'" (104), thus hoping to cash in on one dream in exchange for relinquishing another.

Sexual pleasure is no longer even a consideration for Geraldine and the other "sugar-brown girls" who have lost "the dreadful funkiness of passion . . . of nature . . . of the wide range of human emotions" (68) almost as a consequence of moving north and away from family and towns like Mobile, Aiken, and Nagadoches, whose names "make you think of love" (67) if the girls themselves do not. Geraldine's desire to eschew inappropriate manifestations of black American culture by maintaining the "line between colored and nigger" (71) and thus to effect a bland respectability is connected in her portrait with a body that can give itself only "sparingly and partially": "She stiffens when she feels one of her paper curlers coming undone from the activity of love. . . . She hopes he will not sweat—the damp may get into her hair" (69).

Geraldine's concern is focused on her hair, that part of her appearance which, along with her fair skin, she can control and adapt most easily to standards of white beauty. One is reminded at this point of Pauline and her Jean Harlow hairstyle or China who, with a flick of the wrist, converts herself from one feminine type to another: One minute she has the "surprised eyebrows" and "cupid-bow mouth" of a starlet, the next the "Oriental eyebrows" and "evilly slashed mouth" (49) of a *femme fatale*. Pecola, however, whose ugliness "came from conviction," has no such physical qualities capable of altering and thus redeeming what she and her family perceive as her "relentlessly and aggressively" ugly appearance (34). Pecola, in fact, is *all* sign: To see her body is to know already everything about her or at least everything her culture deems important about her.

The depiction of her sexuality is thus correspondingly total: Pecola gets off eating candy—nothing new here, except that, for her, orgasm takes the form of a curious transubstantiation and, ultimately, transformation: "To eat the candy is somehow to eat the eyes, eat Mary Jane. Love Mary Jane. Be Mary Jane" (43). Unlike Claudia who cannot yet, in the words of Susan Willis, "imagine herself miraculously translated into the body of Shirley Temple so as to vicariously live white experience as a negation of blackness" ("I Shop" 174), Pecola not only can, but, from this denial of self and substitution of the store-bought image, actually gets in the process "nine lovely orgasms with Mary Jane" (43). Whatever pleasurable resources Pecola's own body may harbor are available to her now—and this at the early age of eleven—only to the extent that, like her mother, she can experience them as the alienated effects of another woman's body.

Most of the time, however, she cannot do this and, rather than reconcile herself, as her mother has, to the prospect of greater glory and bigger rainbows in the next world, Pecola opts instead to make a life of her own erasure and annihilation. As her parents and brother fight in the next room, she prays to God to "'make me disappear'" and then performs the meditation to do so:

> She squeezed her eyes shut. Little parts of her body faded away. Now slowly, now with a rush. Slowly again. Her fingers went, one by one; then her arms disappeared all the way to the elbow. Her feet now. . . . The legs all at once. It was hardest above the thighs. She had to be real still and pull. Her stomach would not go. But finally it, too, went away. Then her chest, her neck. The face was hard, too. Almost done, almost. Only her tight, tight eyes were left. They were always left.
>
> (39)

The inability to make her eyes go away prompts Pecola's final disappearing act: The ugliness of her entire body is dissolved in and absolved by the blue eyes only she and her new "friend" can see. Her breakdown at the end of the novel is the last in a series of instances in which boundaries marking the space between inside and outside, self and other, sense and nonsense are broken, removed, or simply no longer perform their tasks. As the novel's prefatory Dick-and-Jane story turns from order to chaos with the gradual removal of punctuation and spacing, so too does the erasure of Pecola's body and sexuality lead to her madness and isolation.

* * *

It seems to me that it is at this point that we can begin to make sense of Morrison's notion of "disinterested violence" which she introduces first with Claudia and elaborates upon in her depiction of the three prostitutes, Cholly, and, by implication, the black community in Lorain, Ohio. After systematically destroying her baby dolls in order to "discover the dearness, to find the beauty, the desirability that had escaped [her]" (20) and then, finding this tactic unproductive, transferring "the same impulses to little white girls," Claudia "learned how repulsive this disinterested violence was, that it was repulsive because it was disinterested" (22). Michael Awkward argues that what Claudia feels is "repulsive" here is her own "failure to accept without question the standards of white America" (72), a reading which, while it has a lot of general application in the novel, seems to misdirect the focus of this passage. Claudia's self-in-crimination is, it seems to me, more in response to her failure to *feel enough* for her white victims, to have the interest that would make her actions meaningful. Willis claims that Claudia's realization "that violence against whites runs the risk of being 'disinterested' . . . suggests that white people are little more than abstractions . . . [that] all are reified subjects" ("I Shop" 174). What Claudia realizes is that her violence cannot help but be disinterested, since even the little girls she thinks she wants to dismember are finally only representatives to her of the system she resents and wants to dismantle. "Disinterestedness," then, is the result of not seeing individual people and how their actions combine in ways affecting you; "disinterested violence," the prelude to "adjustment without improvement" (22), is possible precisely when the specificity of bodies, places, and histories is erased, as it is by commodity culture and those living under its aegis.

Though charming in their own way, China, Poland, and the Maginot Line are also condemned in *The Bluest Eye* for just this kind of refusal to take into account difference and history:

> Except for Marie's fabled love for Dewey Prince, these women hated men, all men, without shame, apology, or *discrimination*. They abused their visitors with scorn *grown mechanical from use*. Black men, white men, Puerto Ricans, Mexicans, Jews, Poles, whatever—all were inadequate and weak, all came under jaundiced eyes and were the recipients of their *disinterested wrath*.
>
> (47-48; emphasis added)

Neither their hatred for men and the "mechanical" violence it spawns[5] nor Marie's love for Pecola, however, has much effect on either their own standing in the community or Pecola's life. Any power moves they think they are making by indiscriminately hating all men are probably negated by the fact that they do not take into account differences in race and class, factors supremely affecting their position *vis á vis* men, especially in their profession. Their kindness to Pecola is similarly disinterested in that, by failing to see *her* and her situation clearly, the three, in the words of Michele Wallace, "fail to understand victimization or the fact that [she] is in danger" (65).[6]

This failure is finally the community's as a whole, a fact Morrison repeatedly suggests by illustrating the extent to which as a group it too has "absorbed in full" dominant standards of value and beauty with little or no inspection of or reflection on the effects to itself or to its individual members. In her conversation with friends, Mrs. MacTeer jokes about "'Aunt Julia . . . still trotting up and down Sixteenth Street talking to herself'" (15). The significance of this remark is not really apparent until the depiction of Pecola's breakdown is complete, and we are presented with a similar image of Pecola "walking up and down, up and down, her head jerking to the beat of a drummer so distant only she could hear" (158). Lorain sees Aunt Julia as "'that old hag floating by in that bonnet'" whom the County will not "'take'" and whom the sight of will "'scare the living shit out of you'" (15). One of the women attributes Aunt Julia's fate to senility, but the designation "*still trotting*" implies she has been out there a while. Their inability or refusal to make sense of her actions, to put them in context, foreshadows their eventual scapegoating of Pecola and suggests that the town has an undiagnosed and unexamined history of producing women like Pecola, that her experience—and the extremity of it—is not an isolated instance.

Morrison characterizes Cholly's disinterestedness as the condition of being "dangerously free. Free to feel whatever he felt—fear, guilt, shame, love, grief, pity. Free to be tender or violent" (125). Her depiction of him traces the source of this freedom to his loss of mother, father, community, and home and to the feeling that the history of people and events extends as far as his interest in them:

> . . . Cholly was truly free. Abandoned in a junk heap by his mother, rejected for a crap game by his father, there was nothing more to lose. He was alone with his own perceptions and appetites, and they alone interested him.
>
> (126)

Paradoxically, this is a state that allows him to see Pecola more clearly than probably anyone else in the book (with the exception of the adult Claudia) and to love her in spite of what he sees, but does not allow him to interact with her in any form other than "reactions based on what he felt at the moment." Cholly sees his daughter washing dishes and sees also, in her stooped frame, "an accusation" against him. Unlike others in town, though, he sees "her young, helpless, hopeless presence" (127) and "loved her enough to touch her, envelop her, give something of himself to her" (159) where no one else would.

In the four examples cited above, disinterestedness is occasioned specifically by the inability to place people and events into contexts that would flesh out experience and thus make obvious the limitations of present actions or beliefs. It becomes steadily more difficult for characters in *The Bluest Eye* to do this because they are either separated from the supportive networks that would encourage it and (or as a result) because their placement in American culture does not sanction accurate representations of what that context would be. The result is a community of individuals who are, at times, painfully alienated from each other as each is divided within him- or herself. Pecola's split consciousness at the end of the novel is a literal representation of this doubleness[7]; it affects other characters also as distortions or denials of self, but denials and distortions approved and fostered in popular iconographic representation.

* * *

An explicit formal project of *The Bluest Eye,* then, is to rewrite the specific stories, histories, and bodies of African-Americans which are quickly being made invisible in commodity culture and which, if written, will make disinterestedness and its unproductive or damaging results impossible. Morrison acknowledges this project in so many words when she says she wrote *The Bluest Eye* because she wanted to read the story it would tell. The novel's shifting focus and point of view, its willingness to let different people speak and *not* to reconcile contradictory explanations and claims where they arise is indicative of Morrison's preference for telling all sides of Pecola's story rather than hammering home one of them. In this, she is like other black women writers who, according to Mae Henderson, "through their intimacy with the discourses of other(s) . . . weave into their work competing and complementary discourses—that seek to adjudicate competing claims and witness concerns" (23). It would be to miss the point, then, to read *The Bluest Eye* looking to assign blame. One of the great virtues of the book is its capacity to empathize and to allow its readers to empathize—something not possible in the absence of history and context—with all of its characters, perhaps especially those who seem most irredeemable: Cholly, Soaphead Church, Pauline.

Finally, though, since *The Bluest Eye* and this project of representing African-Americans focuses most specifically on the histories and bodies of black women, the novel's alternating perspective reproduces formally *their* complicated subjectivity in particular. As she shifts from young girl to older woman to black man to omniscient narrator, Morrison seems to move her examination of Pecola's life back and forth from the axis of race to that of gender. This process allows her in turn to move through the story as both insider and outsider in what Mae Henderson calls a "contestorial dialogue" involving "the hegemonic dominant and subdominant or [after Rachel Blau Du Plessis] 'ambiguously (non) hegemonic' discourses" (20). At one point Morrison writes as a black person among other black people speaking to a white audience, at others as a woman among women speaking to men. The movement between these positions allows Morrison to "see the other, but also to see what the other cannot see, and to use this insight to enrich both our own and the other's understanding" (36). Of course these categories can be separated only artificially since, as Valerie Smith notes, "the meaning of blackness in this country shapes profoundly the experience of gender, just as the conditions of womanhood affect ineluctably the experience of race" (47). By doing so here, however, Toni Morrison enables the reader to witness structurally the complexity of black female subjectivity as she writes it back into a culture whose social and economic mechanisms would otherwise try to write it out.

Notes

1. For more on this analysis of mass culture see, among many others, Adorno and Horkheimer's work in Arato and Gebhardt, Fredrick Jameson, or Tonia Modleski.

2. I take it, then, that Maureen's guess is correct, that Pauline does name Pecola after the movie's black daughter and even then getting it wrong: The daughter's name is Peola, not Pecola.

3. It is not the case, however, that the kind of community support Pauline needs is simply unavailable in Lorain. When Cholly burns their apartment, for example, Pauline's own daughter Pecola is taken in immediately by the MacTeers and, in spite of Mrs. MacTeer's raving about the amount of milk Pecola drinks, is cared for as a matter of course.

4. Morrison's reference to *Imitation of Life,* then, is quite specific and damning: Both versions of the film finally take as a given the black woman's status as servant in the white woman's household. A recent television screening of the original version was introduced optimistically as the story of two women who must "hide their friendship" by masquerading as mistress and maid. While Sirk's version problematizes as it foregrounds the story's racial thematics, it counteracts much of its own insightfulness by concluding with an image of the fair-skinned black daughter being reincorporated into the white family, sans mama and the "problems" her definite blackness presented.

5. "On one occasion the town well knew, they lured a Jew up the stairs, pounced on him, all three, held him up by the heels, shook everything out of his pants pockets, and threw him out of the window" (48).

6. Wallace also argues that "in distinct contrast to the variety of maternal images in the book, these women neither nurture nor protect children" and that, by including them in the text, Morrison "seems to question the self-involvement of traditional modes of black female creativity, as well as [pose] a general critique of more recent feminist strategies of 'man-hating' and 'self-love'" (65). I am not sure what exactly she means by "the self-involvement of traditional modes of black female creativity," but I think the characterization of the three prostitutes is more complex and ultimately more endearing than Wallace admits. When it comes time to name who "loves" Pecola, for example, the narrator—now definitively Claudia—cites Cholly and the Maginot Line.

7. Awkward argues that Pecola's "schizophrenia" is a "coded intertext of W. E. B. Du Bois's discussion of a Black 'double consciousness' in *The Souls of Black Folk*" (12).

Works Cited

Arato, Andrew, and Eike Gebhardt, eds. *The Essential Frankfurt School Reader.* New York: Continuum, 1982.

Awkward, Michael. *Inspiriting Influences: Tradition, Revision, and Afro-American Women's Novels.* New York: Columbia UP, 1989.

Haug, Frigga, ed. *Female Sexualization: A Collective Work of Memory.* Trans. Erica Carter. London: Verso, 1987.

Henderson, Mae Gwendolyn. "Speaking in Tongues: Dialectics, Dialectics, and the Black Woman Writer's Literary Tradition." Wall 16-37.

Jameson, Fredric. "Reification and Utopia in Mass Culture." *Social Text* 1 (1979): 135-48.

Modleski, Tonya. *Loving with a Vengeance: Mass-Produced Fantasies for Women.* New York: Routledge, 1984.

Morrison, Toni. *The Bluest Eye.* New York: Washington Square, 1970.

Smith, Valerie. "Black Feminist Theory and Other Representations of the Other." Wall 38-57.

Wall, Cheryl A., ed. *Changing Our Own Words: Essays on Criticism, Theory, and Writing by Black Women.* New Brunswick: Rutgers UP, 1989.

Wallace, Michele. "Variations on Negation and the Heresy of Black Feminist Creativity." *Reading Black, Reading Feminist: A Critical Anthology.* Ed. Henry Louis Gates, Jr. New York: Meridian, 1990. 52-67.

Willis, Susan. "I Shop Therefore I Am: Is There a Place for Afro-American Culture in Commodity Culture?" Wall 173-95.

———. *Specifying: Black Women Writing the American Experience.* Madison: U of Wisconsin P, 1987.

Edmund A. Napieralski (essay date fall 1994)

SOURCE: Napieralski, Edmund A. "Morrison's *The Bluest Eye.*" *Explicator* 53, no. 1 (fall 1994): 59-62.

[*In the following essay, Napieralski compares and contrasts the narrative elements of* The Bluest Eye *with those of the classical myth of Oedipus.*]

In addition to the popular myths that she uses in ***The Bluest Eye*** to criticize society—the Dick and Jane Story and Pauline Breedlove's Dreamland Theatre—Toni Morrison also incorporates characters, incidents, and themes that recall classical myth. In her article, "Lady Sings the Blues," Madonne M. Miner has explained how Pecola's rape by her father recalls Philomela's by Tereus and Persephone's by Pluto (176). Pecola's story—her tragic failure to find her truth, to find her happiness in knowing who she is and her worth to herself and others—recalls also the tragedy of *Oedipus the King.* In ***The Bluest Eye,*** however, the myth appears in a peculiar and distorted fashion. Raymond Hedin has pointed out that central elements of the Dick and Jane world—"house, family, cat, Mother, Father, dog, and friend"—become "inverted to fit the realities of Pecola's world" (50). Much the same can be said about the myth of Oedipus and the world of ***The Bluest Eye.***

First, the novel's setting recalls Sophocles' play. Barrenness envelops Lorain, Ohio, in 1941: Claudia, a choral character, says, "We thought, at the time, that it was because Pecola was having her father's baby that the marigolds did not grow . . . seeds shriveled and died" (3). Although not, on the surface at least, as serious as the plague gripping Thebes, it is a barrenness nonetheless—metaphorical as well as literal—that is somehow connected to incest, a sin that from the beginning of humankind has been thought to pollute the earth. Moreover, the novel progresses through chapters or episodes named after the seasons—Autumn through Summer—that provide the backdrop of a planting and harvesting cycle appropriate to the sacrifice of a scapegoat.

The Oedipus story takes further shape in the lives of Pecola's parents, Cholly and Pauline Breedlove. As Jocasta mocked the truth of oracles, Pauline also rejects facts of her life, first for the fantasy of the Dreamland Theatre, and then for the imitation of life she lives with her white employers, the Fishers. As Jocasta had originally abandoned Oedipus as a child and had virtually denied his existence, Pauline denies and ultimately deserts her own daughter.

Abandonment has also crippled the life of Cholly Breedlove: "When Cholly was four days old, his mother wrapped him in two blankets and one newspaper and placed him on a junk heap by the railroad" (103). Cholly is rejected a second time, as a teenager, when he travels to Macon in search of his father. Samson Fuller resents this strange boy's intrusion on his dice game and brutally turns him away, leaving Cholly to soil himself and weep like a baby. Cholly's virtual denial of his relationship to his daughter in his rape of Pecola becomes understandable—though certainly not excusable—against this background. Cholly, the victim of a mother and father's rejection, becomes the victimizer in a worse abandonment.

Valerie Smith in *The Southern Review* noted that throughout her fiction Morrison demonstrates the "interconnectedness of past and present" (723). In ***The Blu-***

est Eye, that interconnectedness appears as a family curse, a relentless and recurring pattern or design characteristic of Greek tragedy generally and of *Oedipus the King* in particular. Pieces of this pattern reach an awful climax in Cholly's rape of Pecola, an act that follows immediately the flashback to his own rejection by his father. Overcome by conflicting emotions of guilt, pity, love, revulsion, and fury, Cholly watches Pecola standing at the sink, "one foot scratching the back of her calf with her toe" (127). The gesture reminds him of that time in the past in Kentucky when he saw his wife-to-be for the first time—Pauline, with one foot pierced as a result of a childhood accident. In short order, abandonment, betrayal, and a crippling both figurative and literal from the past and the present gather in a fate-filled moment to destroy Pecola. After the rape she awakes from a faint, "trying to connect the pain between her legs with the face of her mother looming over her" (129).

Although Oedipus at first appears to belong to a family and to Thebes, he is, like Pecola, an outsider, alienated and apart—someone, as Claudia explains, who is a "case," "outdoors." Oedipus seeks answers about his identity from oracles, family, and servants; Pecola looks for her place too, but in her case from a variety of inadequate models and helpers: Shirley Temple, Mary Janes, Maureen Peal, Geraldine, a trio of whores. None provides helpful answers or even clues to who she is or should become. After the rape by her father, however, Pecola does seek out her own seer, her own Teiresias—Soaphead Church.

Morrison devotes considerable space in the novel to describing the background, personality, and theology of Soaphead Church—"Reader, Adviser, and Interpreter of Dreams." As adviser and interpreter he appears to perform functions similar to those Teiresias did for the people of Thebes: "People came to him in dread, whispered in dread, wept and pleaded in dread" (136).

Soaphead Church, however, whose real name—Elihue Micah Whitcomb—mocks the Jewish prophets, mocks in his behavior as well the seer of Sophocles' tragedy. Instead of the piety of Teiresias, he exhibits arrogance and disrespect in the letter he addresses "TO HE WHO GREATLY ENNOBLED HUMAN NATURE BY CREATING IT." Instead of exercising power to do good as Teiresias tries to, he abuses his position to lead Pecola not to salvation but to damnation. Teiresias tries to dispel Oedipus' illusion and to lead him to see truth and to experience self-knowledge. Soaphead Church, on the other hand, leads Pecola to lies, self-delusion, and madness. "I, I have caused a miracle," he boasts in his letter to God. "I gave her the eyes. I gave her blue, blue, two blue eyes. . . . No one else will see her blue eyes. But she will. And she will live happily ever after" (144). Unlike Teiresias who is physically blind but spiritually enlightened, Soaphead Church is spiritually blind and even self-deluded.

Differences in the behavior and experiences of Oedipus and Pecola are also striking. On the one hand, Oedipus blinds himself in a fit of grief and guilt. He laments his condition, but sees the truth, claims an identity. He also gains stature by bravely accepting the exile he had decreed as further punishment for himself. On the other hand, Pecola who sees with what she believes to be blue eyes is really blind. She has no claim to an identity and wholeness but has instead been divided in two, inside and outside the mirror. Pecola also becomes an exile: "walking up and down, her head jerking to the beat of a drummer so distant only she could hear" (162). For Pecola, no victory, only defeat. No plague is lifted.

Several critics of her fiction have remarked on Morrison's use of myth and on the tension her writing explores between universal myths and the unique experience of black people. Terry Otten, for example, notes that "For Morrison, the artistic struggle involves achieving the balance between writing a truly black literature and producing a fiction that in Faulkner's phrase 'grieves on universal bones'" (2). In her study of *The Bluest Eye, Sula,* and *Song of Solomon,* Cynthia Davis claims that these works testify to Morrison's developing use of mythic structure and to her attempt "to combine existential concerns compatible with a mythic presentation with an analysis of American society" (334)

In *The Bluest Eye,* Morrison seems less interested in depicting universal experience than in using myth to grieve over American society in general and black American experience in particular. The plague that ravages the landscape and infects people in the world of the novel and generation after generation is racism. Racism denies truth, freedom, justice, and the opportunity to experience identity and dignity. The tragic victim is neither a king nor even one little girl but an entire people. The question of responsibility, of fate and free will, hovers over Sophocles' play. At the end of *The Bluest Eye* the question of responsibility also remains to challenge us. Who or what is, after all, responsible for the soil that is bad for certain kinds of flowers, for seeds it will not nurture, for fruit it will not bear?

Works Cited

Davis, Cynthia A. "Self, Society, and Myth in Toni Morrison's Fiction." *Contemporary Literature* 23 (1982): 323-342.

Hedin, Raymond. "The Structuring of Emotion in Black American Fiction." *Novel* 16 (1982): 35-54.

Miner, Madonne M. "Lady No Longer Sings the Blues: Rape, Madness, and Silence in *The Bluest Eye*." *Conjuring: Black Women, Fiction, and Literary Tradition*. Ed. Marjorie Pryse and Hortense J. Spillers. Bloomington: Indiana U P, 1985. 176-191.

Morrison, Toni. *The Bluest Eye*. New York: Holt, Rinehart and Winston, 1970.

Otten, Terry. *The Crime of Innocence in the Fiction of Toni Morrison*. Columbia, Missouri: U of Missouri P, 1989.

Smith, Valerie. "The Quest for and Discovery of Identity in Toni Morrison's *Song of Solomon*." *The Southern Review* 21 (1985): 721-732.

Mark Ledbetter (essay date 1995)

SOURCE: Ledbetter, Mark. "Through the Eyes of a Child: Looking for Victims in Toni Morrison's *The Bluest Eye*." In *Literature and Theology at Century's End*, edited by Gregory Salyer and Robert Detweiler, pp. 177-88. Atlanta, Ga.: Scholars Press, 1995.

[*In the following essay, Ledbetter examines the characteristics of the victims in* The Bluest Eye *and the reader's response to them, investigating the ethical dimensions of writing and reading the novel.*]

> . . .
> And then last night, I tiptoed up
> To my daughter's room and heard her
> Talking to someone, and when I opened
> The door, there was no one there . . .
> Only she on her knees, peeking into
>
> Her own clasped hands
>   Imamu Amiri Baraka (LeRoi Jones)[1]

INTRODUCTION

Desperation characterizes the victim. The victim will do most anything to avoid his fated end, which is disappearance. Victims are a lost people; they are victims because they are neither heard nor seen. To posture any sense of "real" presence is to no longer be a victim.

"Otherness" characterizes desperation.[2] A tremendous mystery—awe inspiring, even religious—embodies acts of desperation. The desperate act is always described by the voyeur with the phrase, "Why did she do that?" The irony, here, is that the voyeur, too, is desperate to see and, therefore, to know and to experience the mystery, however horrible, of the observed "other." As a result, she becomes victim, too, of the unanswered question, "Why?"

Violence characterizes otherness. Victims in an ethic of reading and writing are those persons desperate to be heard and seen (note the passive voice) and whose alternative to a literal disappearance from the human story, is to commit desperate acts of violence to themselves, even to those whom they love, in order to create a world that, while not of their choosing, is at least of their making. In this world, the victims are seen and heard. The voyeur is implicated into the lives of the victims, for the violence violates the sensibilities of the observer, who knows, because of this violation, that he has encountered otherness, a moment beyond human control and definition and so physically and emotionally scarring, that he must embody this moment in order to define his existence.

The voyeur is characterized by need, the need to control a situation by surreptitiously looking at and into the world around him. The voyeur is not simply the "peeping-Tom" variety, but also the reader of newspapers and the follower of fire engines. And yet perhaps the most persistent voyeur is the reader of literature. This voyeur, the reader of literature, experiences an ethical moment when she is blinded, at least temporarily, when the object of her sight, the text, looks back at her. With this "returned gaze" comes the moment of implication. Narrative's victim(s) is discovered when the text "looks back," and the reader (voyeur), in turn, blinks.

At this moment, the text's ethical dimensions reveal themselves, and the victim is named. Writer and reader, as well as characters in the text, must choose from a discourse inherently ethical and one which encourages responsible reflections, if not actions. What are my connections with narrative's victims, particularly the violence they experience and the violence they cause me? In response to such a question, I suggest that personal violation, beyond our control and as a result of our observing the body violence to narrative's victims, is a claim of human community. Personal violation is the moment of silence, where writer and reader become victims themselves, and is a silence out of which come questions of, Complicity? Empathy? Naivete? Ignorance?, questions which Levinas might call "the rumbling within silence,"[3] questions which make reader and writer profoundly aware that no one is immune from the disease of victimization. There are only pained victims and anesthetized victims, but there are only victims.

THE DESPERATE VICTIM

Thus, I begin the application of theory to practice with a brief essay on discovering and naming the victim. I believe that this exercise is critical to any argument concerning the ethical dimensions of writing and reading, particularly the suggestion that such an ethical enterprise involves making heard and hearing silenced voices. I turn, now, to a novella by Toni Morrison, ***The Bluest Eye***, and ask, "Who are society's victims?"

Desperate acts of violence by text, character, and reader provide intimately profound moments of ethical reflection in Morrison's *The Bluest Eye*. Remember, desperation characterizes the victim. Characters are desperate for love and will choose freely to violate society's most strictly-held moral codes, as well as to inflict violence on their own bodies, in order to be loved. The text itself reveals a language of desperation, fragmented by the nature of the story it tells and violently interrupting any attempt, on the part of reader or writer, to create a neat or romantic closure to the narrative. The reader is desperate to avoid the pain that comes from seeing the world through an abused child's eyes, and to avoid the moral impotence that comes with knowing that another victim has vanished from the human story, violently lost to a world dark and silent, "right before our [your] very eyes".[4]

The Bluest Eye is the story of black America in the South during 1941, pre-civil rights legislation. African Americans were shunned and denied opportunities by the powerful white community. This disease of prejudice and hatred infected the African American community itself, where a disenfranchised people, struggling to "make ends meet" economically, as well as create a stable social community, find little time to develop a family life that gives love and nurture to the individual members. Through physical and emotional violence, family members forge a world of love, however seemingly perverted and mutated, given the one thing they possess: their bodies.

The painfully constant theme in *The Bluest Eye* is that desperation forces the victim to victimize others and even the self. Victimization has a vicious circuity in the community of the hopeless and the helpless, and more often than not requires not merely the unpredictable act or event, by the narrative and/or characters, to break free from the victim's cycle but more so a horrifyingly indecipherable, if not shockingly inhuman, act or event by the narrative or characters. These acts or events are the moments in narrative where the text confronts the voyeur, the reader, the "me" of the narrative, and forces "me" to blink. Roles are reversed; I am being read, and ethical reading begins.

The Bluest Eye has many such moments. Cholly, the father, rapes his daughter, an act that horrifies and excites him and is his last and only claim on/to love. Mrs. Breedlove rejects her own child—a violence to maternity—yet calls the daughter in the white family for whom she works, "baby," in a vain attempt to construct a family life that she will never know. Pecola, the daughter, longs for blue eyes, a sign of acceptance in the white person's world. Everyone loves a blue-eyed child. When her wish is not granted by God, she blinds herself—physically?—certainly mentally, turning inward to the dark world of the victim where she can define love on her own terms and leaving the blue glaze of her mutilated or crazed eyes to look upon her victimizing world.

II THE DESPERATE TEXT

The text, at first glance, attempts to gloss the world of the victims. *The Bluest Eye* is not about victims, suggest the epigrams of the early chapters; rather, the world is victim-less. Each chapter begins with the world of the Dick and Jane primer, indeed, an Edenic life where all the people "are very happy" (7). But the Dick and Jane story has nothing to do with the African Americans' story of victimization, and language becomes desperate. The narrative tries three times to construct the story of the friends and the nice house, of Dick, Jane, their parents, and the dog.

> Here is the house. It is green and white. It has a red door. Here is the family. Mother, Father, Dick, and Jane live in the green-and-white house. They are happy...See the dog run. Run, dog, run. Look, look. Here comes a friend.
>
> Here is the house. it is green and white. It has a red door. Here is the family. Mother, Father, Dick , and Jane live in the green-and-white house. They are happy...See the dog run. run, dog, run. Look, look. Here comes a friend.
>
> HereisthehouseItisgreenandwhiteIthasareddoorHereisthefamilyMotherFatherDickandJaneliveinthegreenandwhitehouseTheyarehappySeethedogrun RundogrunLooklookHerecomesafriend.

Each time, the story refuses to be told in its entirety, until the language of the story crumbles in on itself, violated by an inability to approximate the harsh realities of a world, a world of victims, that will never live with such security or happiness.

The narrative is divided into chapters by the names of the four seasons, beginning with Autumn, an odd beginning for most of us, a sort of "in-the-middle" existence, but which seems appropriate for the life of the victim. The victim-less text would end or begin with Spring, a time of rebirth and new beginnings. The language within each chapter of the text violates the season which names it. Autumn is not a season with leaves of beautiful colors, as one might expect, but rather a season of a child's sickness, coughed-up on her bed, and the colors of fall are used to describe her vomit. "The puke swaddles down the pillow onto the sheets—green-gray, with flecks of orange" (13).

"Winter," says the young narrator, "tightened our heads with a band of cold and melted our eyes" (52). The winter should be expectant and should not hold you tightly in its moribund grip. The child's winter should be playful, and the primary emotion should be anticipation. Yet the only "epiphany" the young children have in *The Bluest Eye*'s winter is to discover a reason to hate someone "better-off" than they are: "we discovered that she had a dog tooth" (53).

Spring echoes autumn and winter with references to death. The text violates itself. Desperate to name lives that will change, like the seasons, naturally and for the good, the language reminds us that there are no seasons in the lives of victims. Pecola is raped by her father. Ironically, his last name is Breedlove; she carries his child. Spring is incestuous for the victim; it breeds on the familiar, violating her purity and offering only the false hope of birth.

Summer is "the season of storms" (146). Summer is the most frightening because it represents the "*Moirai* of our small lives" (146). Pecola is summer's child and is fated to be victim. In the summer, Pecola's child by her father dies before the pregnancy completes term. The victim has no sense of completion to her life. Acquiescing to the world's claim that "the victim had no right to live" (160), Pecola disappears into a world, violent and silent and sadly alone.

Seasonal change is seductive; its newness offers hope to those of us at liberty to define ourselves in its beauty and predictability. Yet for the victim, the seasons serve as metaphor for the old adage, "what goes around, comes around." Indeed, in *The Bluest Eye,* the seasons represent lack of change, a violation of nature's narrative, which should suggest that with each season something other than the status quo awaits us. The victim discovers that there are no seasons in her life, only *a* season of silence, which is characterized by frustration, pain, and a lack of control over her life.

Thus, the language of the text violently turns on itself, refusing to allow the victim to go unnoticed. Dick and Jane stories, as well as the pleasant and sensual changes of the season, are seductive, and they appeal to the person who neither knows desperation nor runs the risk of disappearing from the human story. But these master plots fail to tell the story of language's victims. Yet Morrison's language, like all language, has the power to invoke the other. In *The Bluest Eye,* this language of "otherness" is the language of victim. The victims in an ethic of reading and writing stand as an other against the master plot. When the master plot encounters the story of victim, an other, the victim-less and romantic story, like the tale of Dick and Jane, crumbles. The victim is revealed.

III THE DESPERATE CHARACTER

The wish of the victim often reflects the depth of her desperation. Victims wish not only for those things they are denied but also for those things which they can never have, much like a one-armed person wishing to grow another arm. The inability to fulfil that wish, regardless of its impossible nature, leads to the desperate act that is often violent and serves, at a level of distortion, if not perversion, to meet the requirements of the wish and to horrify the seemingly "normal" observer of the desperate act.

I suggest that the "wish" is Levinas's notion of "obsession," which is "irreducible to consciousness, even if it overwhelms it." This wish or obsession is, in Levinas's terms (which I think reflects Morrison's text's intentions), the victim's last grasp at "freedom," an almost pre-reflective wish or obsession to be other than she is.[5] In this obsession exists the desperate act, which culminates all previously "failed" acts to free oneself from being the victim. The desperate act, in an attempt to be other, creates an otherness that violates all traditional or normal expectations of what those of us who control narrative's master plots consider to be human and humane and challenges our definitions.

The Breedlove family has wishes. Pauline Breedlove wishes for a house and a family like the one for whom she is a servant. "Power, praise, and luxury were hers in this household" (101). Life here is ordered and neat. Finding satisfaction in this white family's household, "she stopped trying to keep her own house" (101). She establishes an intimate connection with the family. They give her "what she had never had—a nickname—Polly" (101). "She is the ideal servant" (101). Yet Mrs. Breedlove's wish can never have fulfillment. She is the "ideal servant." Her wish is to be the "ideal" mistress of her own house, yet she is neither white nor monied and her wish is bound to fail.

We are not aware of the desperate nature of her wish until she denies the maternity of her own child to act as the mother of the white child for whom she is a servant. By laying claim to the white family's daughter, she attempts to lay claim to their lives. The irony is that in the same motion with which she dismisses her daughter, she is valuing the role of daughter in the family life.

Pecola spills a blueberry pie on the white family's floor, or as Mrs. Breedlove says, "my floor" (87). Pecola is slapped to the floor and abused verbally. The family's little girl, "in pink," starts crying. Sending her own child out the door, she begins to call the white child "baby," and when asked who the other child was, she will not say that Pecola is her daughter, only "don't worry none" (87).

While I may not condone physical violence as the appropriate punishment for children, I am not horrified by the violent act of mother striking daughter. I am moved to reflect on a moment of violence in which mother denies the identity of her daughter. This desperate act, a result of what Langston Hughes calls, "a dream deferred," reveals a moment of ethical reflection that names Mrs. Breedlove not a bad mother, but rather a victim of racial prejudice certainly, but perhaps more so of a world that has lied to her, the "ideal servant," and told her that she could ever be other than a victim, an otherness she exposes to us—the violence of a mother dis-owning her daughter—causing further, more profound, ethical reflection about the lies we tell to those whom we control and in turn encourage the victim to tell herself.

Cholly Breedlove's wish is less easy to define but is as poignant as Mrs. Breedlove's, and the wish's denial leads to a violent act even more horrifying than familial rejection. Cholly wants to be wanted by a family. There was a time, before the whiskey, when Mrs. Breedlove wanted him to take her away from her poverty, and she wanted him sexually. "But it ain't like that anymore. Most times he's thrashing away inside me before I'm woke, and through when I am" (104). Their love for each other is equalled only by their hate. "She needed Cholly's sins desperately" (37), and for Cholly, she was one of the few things abhorrent to him that he could touch and therefore hurt (37). In desperation, the victim hurts the one whom he loves the most. Loved ones are the most convenient, and ironically, because victims are drawn to a community of pained others, they make themselves available to one another.

Cholly's life is a series of failed communities. "Abandoned in a junk heap by his mother, rejected for a crap game by his father, there was nothing more to lose. He was alone with his own perceptions and appetites, and they alone interested him" (126). What the world will not give, Cholly is prepared to take. He will be impotent no longer, the male victim's final words before an act of desperation.

Cholly rapes his daughter. The voyeur is repulsed by the violence. Cholly is overwhelmed with ambiguity. "He wanted to break her neck—but tenderly . . . What could he do for her—ever? What give her? What say to her" (127)? The language is that of the poor boy proposing to the rich girl; then, he reminds us that she is "his eleven-year-old daughter" (127). Suddenly remembering the first time he saw his wife, Cholly takes his daughter. Now he wants "to fuck her—tenderly" (128). Pecola becomes the victim's victim.

Cholly disappears from the text, the ever possible, even probable, fate of the victim. The crime of incest, one of Freud's original taboo's, demands serious judgement. And I make no apologies for a society where "our manhood was defined by acquisitions. Our womanhood by acquiescence" (140). And yet I am moved by the narrator's argument for sympathy. "Cholly loved her. I'm sure he did. He, at any rate, was the one who loved her enough to touch her, envelop her, give something of himself to her. But his touch was fatal" (159). The victim is left without choice, no romantic option between loss of integrity with life or maintained integrity with death. Loss of integrity and death go hand and hand for the victim. Cholly, emasculated by society, asserts his manhood on a girl-child, losing his integrity and a place in the narrative. The victim disappears.

Pecola Breedlove's wish is the most desperate of all wishes. She, a young black girl, wishes to have blue eyes. To have blue eyes, "Pretty blue eyes . . . Morning-glory-blue-eyes" (40), will make her world, now torn and violent, whole and peaceful. "Cholly would be different, and Mrs. Breedlove too. Maybe they'd say, 'Why, look at pretty-eyed Pecola. We mustn't do bad things in front of those pretty eyes'" (40). Unlike Claudia, a young girl her age, who can distinguish between the possible and the impossible and who "destroyed white baby dolls" (22), quite aware that she did not have access to their privilege, Pecola wishes for the blue eyes of the young white girls. Seduced by her obsession, she is seemingly ignorant of the fact that such a change cannot happen.

"Each night, without fail, she prayed for blue eyes" (40). To be seen is the victim's most profound desire and is why Pecola wants blue eyes. She sees the world clearly with the eyes she has, and what she sees with crystal clear sight is that the world ignores a young black girl. The storekeeper, "does not see her, because for him there is nothing to see. . . . Nothing in his life even suggested that the feat was possible, not to say desirable or necessary" (42). The face of the victim is blank and indistinguishable.

Of course the world reminds her, all the time, that blue eyes are favorites. Shirley Temple has blue eyes. Even the "Mary Jane" candy she buys has a young girl, "blond hair in gentle disarray, blue eyes looking at her out of a world of clean comfort" (43), and depicts a life denied her. The sky, where the white families live, is "always blue" (84).

When a "Reader, Adviser, and Interpreter of Dreams" (130) arrives in town, Pecola comes to him. After all, his card reads, "If you are overcome with trouble and conditions that are not natural, I can remove them" (137). The dilemma is interesting. Pecola believes that her dark eyes are unnatural; she is a victim of society's rhetoric that describes beautiful and powerful people. Rhetoric, to be successful, need not be true, only persuasive, which is rhetoric's own inherent perniciousness. Though Pecola's eyes are very natural, the white world's rhetoric has won; rhetoric's best audience is desperate people.

This false prophet convinces Pecola that her eyes will turn blue; he convinces himself that her request is "logical" (137), "an ugly little girl asking for beauty. . . . A little black girl who wanted to rise up out of the pit of her blackness and see the world with blue eyes" (137). The promise is a lie, and the lie is devastating. "To rise up out of the pit of her blackness," may be the most evil statement in Morrison's text. The phrase's horror is that it embodies both truth and lie. Pecola's blackness is a "pit," not of her own making but no less depthful and restraining. And yet, what world would ask her to rise out of her blackness? For the victim, the right, true, and beautiful world is always other, and leaves the victim no choice but to become like the world or to vanish, silently.

Pecola's eyes turn blue. "A little black girl yearns for the blue eyes of a little white girl, and the horror at the heart of her yearning is exceeded only by the evil of fulfillment" (158). Does she blind herself or does she go crazy? The text says that, "She . . . stepped over into madness" (159). Whether Pecola's eyes become blue from the blue-like glaze of the physically blind or whether she simply turns inward, creating a world of her own in which her eyes are blue, I think, does not matter. From either perspective, the violation of this young girl's mind/body, her eyes, is both painful and unsettling.

Pecola spends her time now in conversation with herself, creating a fictitious friend who confirms that her blue eyes are beautiful. "What will we talk about? *Why, Your eyes.* Oh, yes. My eyes. My blue eyes. Let me look again. *See how pretty they are.* Yes. They get prettier each time I look at them. *They are the prettiest I've ever seen*" (156).

The victim may either disappear, like Cholly, or create a world frightening and other, if she is to continue to exist. Pecola creates the world of other. This new world violates the sensibilities of those persons who chose to look upon it or who fall under Pecola's gaze. Those persons of her world, other victims, are "frightened" when they see her (158). Their world may, by necessity, become like hers. Others, who see her "blue eyes" know that they have "failed" her (158). Victims exist because there are those who victimize. Pecola's life, "among the garbage and the sunflowers" (160), where she "flailed her arms like a bird in an eternal grotesquely futile effort to fly" (158), indicts her observer, calling us either to be a participant in her world or the cause of it.

IV The Desperate Reader

The frightening implication of the rhetoric that describes a victim is the loss of freedom. The victim is not free to be other than victim. In fact, to be other than victim is to lose one's power of mystery and awe, is to lose otherness. The empathetic observer of society's victims is not free to free the victim from her bondage, whether economic, religious, racial, sexual, or otherwise. The reader of texts, who sees and hears the victims of those texts, is violated by a moral powerlessness, discovering, as in **The Bluest Eye,** that "it's too late . . . it's much, much, much too late" (160) for Mrs. Breedlove, Cholly, and Pecola.

The admission of powerlessness is the reader's desperate act, a moment of confession, when he reveals a personal victimization and, therefore, a oneness with the text's victims. Perhaps, this moment is narrative's ethic, for if we all become victims, then there are no victims.

Such an idealistic moment does not deny difference, in race, gender, or economic status, the differences between us which produce victims. I am looking only for a moment of complicity and community, where distinctions are erased. Differences will/should remain, as a cause for celebration and, more important, perhaps, as the revealer of victim. For as long as there is difference, there will be victims. So, what is left for the desperate reader? I think that an ethic of reading and writing reminds the reader that he should take a turn as victim.

To choose to be victim is the one powerful freedom that the reader, privileged, ever omniscient, has. But readers only make such a choice out of desperation, and readers only reach such desperate moments when they are violated by the violence of the text, by moments shocking to and discordant with our everydayness: a father wants love, a wholesome desire, and so he rapes his daughter; a child wants blue eyes, and (because?) she's black, so she steps "over into madness" (159) to gain them.

The victim's world, through a child's eyes, is a violent and horrifying moment, a moment that should so awaken our anesthetized existences, as readers, that narrative as an ethical event is one of many givens in the critical process called reading. In fact, I think that narrative is the one certain and predictable event in which an ethic is implied because reader and writer, by their very actions, *choose* to participate in a community, a narrative community, where society's victims are most profoundly and uncomfortably presented back to the very society which creates them.

Narrative has the power to hear the voices of the young Pecolas say, "Please God, . . . make me disappear" (39), and to describe her disappearance: "she squeezed her eyes shut. Little parts of her body faded away. . . . Only her tight, tight eyes were left. They were always left" (39). Perhaps most important, narrative has the power to force our gaze upon her gaze, those blue eyes, and know who the victim is.

Notes

1. Imamu Amiri Baraka, "Preface to a Twenty Volume Suicide Note," ed. Arna Bontemps, *American Negro Poetry* (New York: Hill & Wang, 1974), pp. 178-9.

2. I would describe my use of "Otherness" here, if not in agreement with, certainly influenced by Emmanuel Levinas in an essay called "Time and the Other." He describes the other by saying: "its hold over my existing is mysterious. It is not unknown but unknowable, refractory to all light. But this precisely indicates that the other is in no way another myself, participating with me in a common existence. . . . We recognize the other as resembling us, but exterior

to us; the relationship with the other is a relationship with a Mystery." Ed. Sean Hand, *The Levinas Reader*, (Oxford: Blackwell, 1989), p. 43.

3. See Levinas's "There is: Existence without Existents," in Hand, *A Levinas Reader*, p. 28.

4. Toni Morrison, *The Bluest Eye* (New York: Washington Square Press, 1970), p. 58. All future references are to this text and are parenthetically referenced in the essay.

5. See Levinas's "Substitution" in Hand, *A Levinas Reader*, pp. 88-92.

Lynn Scott (essay date 1996)

SOURCE: Scott, Lynn. "Beauty, Virtue and Disciplinary Power: A Foucauldian Reading of Toni Morrison's *The Bluest Eye*." *Midwestern Miscellany* 24 (1996): 9-23.

[*In the following essay, Scott correlates Michel Foucault's theories about the workings of power in modern societies with Morrison's exploration of American racism in* The Bluest Eye, *demonstrating Morrison's contention that racism has less to do with exclusion than with the pressure to assimilate to cultural ideals of beauty and virtue.*]

> In that young and growing Ohio town whose side streets, even, were paved with concrete, which sat on the edge of a calm blue lake, which boasted an affinity with Oberlin, the underground railroad station, just thirteen miles away, this melting pot on the lip of America facing the cold but receptive Canada—What could go wrong?
>
> (*The Bluest Eye*, 93)

Set in a small, industrialized, Midwestern town on the eve of World War I, *The Bluest Eye* explores the relationship of a variety of black families and individuals to each other as well as to the larger white community from which they are marginalized by racism. The locale is important. Neither the rural south, nor a large northern ghetto, Lorain, Ohio affords an intimate microcosm of caste and class, both within and without the black community. The narrator's question, "what could go wrong?", is both rhetorical and ironic.

The population of Lorain is described as ethnically disparate and fluid. While segregation is still legal, blacks are not allowed in Lake Shore Park, much of the community is integrated. Black and white children attend the same school, frequent the same stores, and even live next door to each other. Yet the "integration" of this Midwestern community does not result in the cultural mixing implied by the metaphor of a "melting pot." The term "melting pot," like so many names and labels in Morrison's work, ironically belies the characters' experience. In fact, the community is marked by sharp social stratification, fragmentation, and radical instability for its most marginal members. Claudia MacTeer, whose first person narration frames the novel, uses a different metaphor to describe the social relations of her world; it is a "garment" rather than a "pot" and her position in this garment is the "hem," the struggling periphery of life. Claudia's perspective, especially her resistance to oppression, is linked to her position in the social fabric, a fabric held together by an externally imposed cultural ideal; an ideal that her narrative deconstructs.

Michel Foucault's analysis of the link between power and knowledge is useful in engaging the analysis of racism that Toni Morrison develops in this novel. In particular his concepts of "genealogy," "discourse" and "disciplinary power" are relevant to questions of method and theme in *The Bluest Eye*. "Genealogy" is the term Foucault used to describe his historical method. Unlike traditional approaches, genealogy does not set forth a developmental or progressive view of history, nor does it view events as historically inevitable. Foucault used this method to reveal the relationship between discourses and the disciplinary structures employed by social institutions to control bodies and actions. Paul Bove summarizes Foucault's concept of discourse as "an institutionalized system for the production of knowledge in regulated language" (53). In other words, knowledge and truth are constituted in discourse, and discourse is both constituted by and constituting of institutions. It is the function of genealogy to unmask discourse by showing its association with the subjugating effects of power.

> . . . genealogy lets us confront how power constructs truth-producing systems in which propositions, concepts, and representations generally assign value and meaning to the objects of the various disciplines that treat them.
>
> (Bove 57)

The Bluest Eye is suggestive of a genealogy in several respects. The novel affirms that events can't be traced back to single origins, that history is circuitous, and most importantly that the purpose of historical reflection is not to romanticize the past, or to justify the present, but to unmask structures of power. Like Foucault, the narrator of *The Bluest Eye* wishes to explore the how of her story, not the why. After the primer introduction, Claudia tells the ending of the story she is about to relate. By making the end known in the beginning, she directs the reader away from the suspense of what happens and away from the representation of events as a linear cause and effect sequence. Claudia concludes her introduction by claiming: "There is really nothing more to say—except why. But since why is difficult to handle, one must take refuge in how" (9). The difficulties of finding a determinate cause are put aside for a more functional description. Morrison's genealogical approach in *The Bluest Eye* is appropriate to her purpose of unmasking the claims to truth in the discourses of western beauty and bourgeoise morality. The novel is an exploration of how images of physical beauty and moral virtue are disseminated through popular culture, the school, the family and the community, and how they *combine* to serve a system of racial and sexual oppression.

The Dick and Jane passage, which opens the novel and reappears in parts as chapter headings, represents, in Foucauldian terms, the norm or standard against which all subjects of a discipline are measured. By opening the novel with this passage Morrison links the two most important institutions that discipline young bodies, the family and the school. For young children literacy means acquiring a discourse that normalizes family relationships. Dick and Jane readers represented the American family as a white, middle class, harmonious unit. In the novel the three black families are distributed in a hierarchical relation to the story book family. The idea of the school as a disciplining institution whose effects are extended to the family is carried through in the characterization of Geraldine, whose orderly and beautiful house appears to place her family closest to the story book model. Geraldine, like others of her class, had learned "how to get rid of the funkiness" in "land-grant colleges" and "normal schools" (68). Her domestic skills were acquired in the Home Economics Department where she learned how to make souffles (70-71). Further down the pyramid are the MacTeers, who lack social status, but are successful in their struggle to survive the harsh climate and contingencies of life. The Breedloves in their disorder, violence and suffering are at the bottom and represent the greatest distance from the norm. While the Dick/Jane family may have little if anything to do with the characters' experience, it remains a powerful construct through which they learn to evaluate their lives. In showing literacy to be a force of subjugation, Morrison revises the slave narrative tradition that links literacy to freedom.

In the epigraph to the novel the Dick/Jane passage is repeated first without any punctuation and second without any space between letters. This dismembering of language has its corollary in Claudia's desire to dismember white baby dolls and little white girls in order to discover "the secret of the magic they weaved on others" (22). The secret, however, is not to be found in the language, the object, or even the person that transmits the images of normalization. "Doll's we could destroy, but we could not destroy the honey voices of parents and aunts. . . ." Maureen Peal, a "high yellow dream child" screams at Claudia: "I *am* cute! And you ugly! Black and ugly," and Claudia considers the "wisdom, accuracy, and relevance" of Maureen's words (61). Claudia realizes the "truth" of these words is a constructed truth, but its source of power eludes her.

> And all the time we knew that Maureen Peal was not the Enemy and not worthy of such intense hatred. The *Thing* to fear was the *Thing* that made *her* beautiful and not us.
>
> (62)

In Foucauldian terms the invisible "thing" that Claudia fears, the "thing" that includes some and excludes others, that ranks and classifies individuals, that creates asymmetries according to a standard of beauty is an entire disciplinary structure, a mode of power. The norms and hierarchies of disciplinary power are maintained by a continual surveillance, where "subjects are presented as objects to the observation of a power that [is] manifested only by its gaze" (*Discipline and Punish* 188). While power makes its subjects visible, it remains invisible:

> Disciplinary power . . . is exercised through its invisibility; at the same time it imposes on those whom it subjects a principle of compulsory visibility. In discipline it is the subjects a principle of compulsory visibility. In discipline it is the subjects who have to be seen. Their visibility assures the hold of the power that is exercised over them. It is the fact of being constantly seen, of being able always to be seen, that maintains the disciplined individual in his subjection.
>
> (*Discipline and Punish* 187)

Maureen Peal may not be "the Enemy," but she manifests the gaze of an invisible power, a power that is implicit in the body of Shirley Temple, of white baby dolls, of Mary Jane Candy wrappers, of Jean Harlow and all the other symbols of western beauty that gaze on the characters of *The Bluest Eye*. Foucault describes surveillance as "an uninterrupted play of calculated gazes" that functions not only "from top to bottom, but also to a certain extent from bottom to top and laterally" (177). Thus surveillance is carried out by individuals who are themselves under surveillance and inscribed in the same disciplinary system as the objects of their surveillance. Maureen identifies blackness as the mark of visibility which makes Pecola, Claudia and Frieda less than herself. The passage is just one instance in the novel where we see the normalizing gaze coming from within the black community. Maureen Peal provides an example of Foucault's analysis of the individual as produced by power. While Maureen uses her power to exclude and repress, she is ultimately a product of the same power she exercises. Because she identifies with the subject position created by the discourse of western beauty, one can see her as fabricated by power as well as exercising it.

The power of the gaze and the trap of visibility are important motifs throughout *The Bluest Eye*. The opening section "Autumn" is framed by two scenes where

Claudia describes and resists the gaze of her white neighbor, Rosemary Villanucci. At the beginning of "Autumn" Rosemary is sitting in her father's Buick "eating bread and butter." She tells Claudia and Frieda that they can't come in. Claudia narrates, "We stare at her, wanting her bread, but more than that *wanting to poke the arrogance out of her eyes . . .*" (emphasis mine 12). The mixture of anger with jealous desire in Claudia's response suggests the difficulty of resistance; the desire for the other's place acknowledges the other's power. Rosemary's eyes reappear at the end of "Autumn" in the menstruation scene:

> . . . I saw a pair of fascinated eyes in a dough-white face. Rosemary was watching us. I grabbed for her face and succeeded in scratching her nose. She screamed and jumped back.
>
> "Mrs. MacTeer! Mrs. MacTeer!" Rosemary hollered. "Frieda and Claudia are out here playing nasty! . . ."
>
> (27)

Pecola experiences puberty under the surveillance of a white gaze that measures her distance from the norms of physical beauty and virtue and view her as an object of fascination. Under Rosemary's gaze the categories of blackness and sexuality are linked to moral corruption implied by the term, "nasty." Pecola becomes the object of a prurient interest. Rosemary's gaze constitutes a matrix of racial and sexual oppression that is repeated in the scene where the school boys, encircle Pecola and chant: "Black e mo. Yadaddsleepsnekked" (55). The circle is the prison of a discourse that equates, blackness, ugliness and sin; Pecola, trapped within this circle becomes the visible expression of the boys' "exquisitely learned self-hatred" (55). Pecola "covers her eyes" in a gesture of shame and a characteristic attempt to protect herself from the violating gaze of others by "disappearing."

Yet, it is important to note that both of these scenes are followed by a temporary reprieve for Pecola. Once Mrs. MacTeer understands the situation, "her eyes were sorry," and she tells Rosemary to go home, "the show is over" (28). Pecola is taken into the bathroom to be washed; outside the door Claudia and Frieda can hear the restorative music of their mother's laughter. In the second episode Frieda comes to Pecola's rescue by hitting one of the boys over the head and breaking the circle. The progressive victimization of Pecola does not occur without interruption. Both the MacTeer family and the three prostitutes offer Pecola alternate spaces for development, yet, finally, these spaces are not adequate to save Pecola from madness. The pervasive tone of loss in the novel stems not from the lack of resistance, but from its failure to disrupt the system of power that can finally bend even the desire for love and the impulse for freedom to its own ends.

There is an evident similarity between Pecola's initiation into womanhood and her father, Cholly's initiation into manhood. At age fourteen Cholly's first sexual experience in a dark pine forest is interrupted by two white men who shine bright lights on the couple and force Cholly to perform at gun point: "Get on wid it, nigger . . . an make it good" (117). Under the gaze Cholly can only "simulate what had gone on before" (117). Powerless to resist the hunters and overcome by hatred and shame, Cholly transfers these emotions to the girl beneath him. The significance of a private sexual act is literally constructed under a public gaze. For both Pecola and her father the trap of visibility functions at the site of sexually formative experience; both are seen by white eyes who construct black bodies as objects of vicarious pleasure.

Cholly Breedlove's love for Pauline, however, is not determined by his adolescent humiliation. Initially, Cholly and Pauline are "young, loving and full of energy" (92). Their brief romance is another space in the novel where the gaze does not operate. While Morrison certainly does not idealize these characters' southern beginnings, it is not until they come to Lorain, in search of work and a better standard of living, that their personalities and their marriage disintegrate. The pressures they face are described in cultural and commercial terms. Pauline's isolation increases through the loss of community.

> I missed my people. I weren't used to so much white folks. The ones I seed around before was something hateful, but they didn't come around too much. I mean, we didn't have too much truck with them. Just now and then in the fields, or at the commissary. But they want all over us. Up north they was everywhere—next door, downstairs, all over the streets—and colored folks few and far between. Northern colored folk was different too. Dicty-like. No better than whites for meanness. They could make you feel just as no-count, 'cept I didn't expect it from them. That was the lonesomest time of my life.
>
> (93)

Pauline begins to straighten her hair, buy new clothes and wear make-up, hoping that other women will "cast favorable glances her way" (94). The couple begin, what is to become, a constant quarrel over money, so in order to pay for the expense of fashioning herself appropriately, Pauline turns her love for domestic labor into a cash benefit. She goes to work in white women's homes, neglecting her own. After their children are born, the Breedloves move into a converted store where the furnishings are "conceived, manufactured, shipped and sold in various states of thoughtlessness, greed and indifference" (31). The store/home symbolizes a conflation of commercial and domestic space revealing the extent to which the Breedlove's private lives have been thoroughly interpenetrated by market values. The mass-marketed furniture symbolizes the Breedlove's ethical and spiritual decline. The "ugly" Breedloves are on display in their store; created by the subjugating gaze of others, they are ironic products of their desire to assimilate into an alien community. In the south Cholly experiences the gaze of the white hunter as an abrupt and cruel rupture; in the north the gaze is diffuse, omnipresent and commercial.

While *The Bluest Eye* is about the power of gazes to subjugate, it is also about the necessity of re-visioning. Nowhere is this more clear than the climatic scene where Cholly rapes Pecola. The reader, who has been led to condemn the classifying and voyeuristic gazes of Maureen Peal, Rosemary Villanucci, Geraldine and the rest, is challenged to view Cholly's abhorrent act as a result of complex, tangled motivations, and to empathize with the father as well as the daughter. In an interview with Claudia Tate, Toni Morrison stated that she prepared her readers for this scene in order to get them to really *look at it.*"

> I tell you at the beginning of *The Bluest Eye,* on the very first page what happened, but now I want you to go with me and look at this, so when you get to the scene where the father rapes the daughter, which is as awful a thing, I suppose, as can be imagined, by the time you get there, it's almost irrelevant because I want you to *look* at him and see his love for his daughter and his powerlessness to help her pain. By that time his embrace, the rape, is all the gift he has left.
>
> (125)

In the very long paragraph that leads up to the rape Cholly is watching Pecola as she washes dishes with her back to him. This scene presents a sharp contrast to the previous and subsequent sightings of Pecola. When the store owner, Mr. Yacobowski's eyes encounter Pecola, there is a "vacuum . . . a total absence of human recognition" (42). When Geraldine looks at Pecola she sees an intruder, "a nasty little black bitch" who brings disorder to her home (75). In contrast to these other cursory and dismissive gazes, Cholly's gaze lingers; it discovers Pecola's sorrowful existence, her "whipped," unhappy look. Then his gaze turns back against itself forcing Cholly to look inward to experience his own failure. Feeling "revulsion, guilt, pity, then love" (127) as he looks at his daughter, Cholly experiences the anger and guilt of a father who has nothing to give a child. Pecola never turns around, but Cholly precedes to imagine his daughter's gaze upon him: "If he looked into her face, he would see those haunted, loving eyes. The hauntedness would irritate him—the love would move him to fury. How dare she love him? Hadn't she any sense at all?" (127) What finally triggers the rape, is Pecola's small gesture with her foot that reminds Cholly of his original love for Pauline and fills him with "softness . . . a tenderness, a protectiveness" (128). Because Pecola never turns around to meet her father's gaze, the reader must view the scene through the rapist's eyes alone and acknowledge that an act of destruction originated in an impulse of love. By constructing Cholly's motivations in this way, Morrison ironically reflects on Pecola's desire to be loved. Love is de-romanticized. Love can not transcend the disciplinary structures that subjugate bodies.

By constructing Cholly's motives as complex and by comparing his life to that of a blues musician, the novel also reflects on the link between discourse and power. Foucault discusses how the human sciences (sociology, psychology, etc.) use language to extend disciplinary methods. In feudal society the chronicle of a person's life "formed part of the rituals of his power" (*Discipline and Punish* 191). But in modern society individual lives are frequently described for the purpose of increasing social control and domination. Surveillance in modern disciplinary systems occurs in part through the documentation of people's lives in language (especially the lives of children, the sick, and criminals).

> This turning of real lives into writing is no longer a procedure of heroization; it functions as a procedure of objectification and subjection.
>
> (*Discipline and Punish* 192)

To the extent that characters in many realistic and, especially, naturalistic novels often represent psychological or sociological types, such fiction is an adjacent literary discourse to the discourses of the human sciences. Morrison's departure from realistic technique and style, especially her mode of characterization, is instrumental to her purpose of exposing the way racism is perpetuated through a subjugating discourse.

Compare, for example, the difference between Morrison's description of Cholly and Richard Wright's description of Bigger Thomas. In the final section of *Native Son* the reader views Bigger through Max's lengthy Marxist analysis that explains Bigger's actions as a direct consequence of social forces over which he had no control. Bigger is analyzed as a case of psychopathology created by racism. Max's words create a mirror by which Bigger comes to know himself. While Wright, through Max, makes Bigger very describable in language, Morrison pointedly tells her readers that Cholly can *not* be described in language: "The pieces of Cholly's life could become coherent only in the head of a musician" (125). Words, finally, can not fully express the paradoxes of Cholly's life, while music, particularly the blues, is a medium that might give form to the combination of joy and pain, love and hate that make up Cholly's character and experience. This distrust of language is consistent with a Foucauldian analysis of discourse. Morrison creates characters that resist psychological or sociological labels by employing a lyrical, non-realistic style that challenges her readers to view not only events and characters, but cultural values in unexpected ways.

By describing Cholly as a "free" man," the narrator de-romanticizes freedom in the same way she has de-romanticized love. Cholly is free simply because he is not bound to the moral codes of his community. He is neither the heroic individual who exposes social injustice by placing himself in opposition to society, nor is he the criminal whose actions threaten social destruction. In other words, Morrison breaks apart the opposition between society and freedom, the formula of so many narratives of emancipation. The discourse of "freedom" like that of "love" can not be detached from the lives of disciplined bodies. Cholly's "freedom" as well as the society's "morality" are *both* functions of social control, of the power that subjugates bodies. Cholly's status as outsider, his violation of the moral code, make him a delinquent in the eyes of the community. Foucault describes the production of delinquency and the moralization of the lower classes as the primary methods of de-politicizing crime, keeping the lower class divided among themselves and thus subjugated to power (*Discipline and Punish* 257-292). The ritualized violence of Pauline and Cholly's marriage suggest that "morality" and "freedom" are placed in opposition in a discourse that serves existing power relations. Pecola, rejected by her mother and raped by her father, is the victim of this opposition.

As just suggested, Pauline's position in the disciplinary structure is drawn in counterpoint to Cholly's. Her character clearly illustrates how the discourses of beauty and virtue create "intelligible" and "useful" bodies. Drawing from Foucault, Susan Bordo defines the "intelligible body" as our cultural and aesthetic conceptions of the body, and the "useful body" as the practice that is used to achieve these norms (25-26). Bordo stresses the importance of visual images in the creating of the intelligible feminine body: "With the advent of movies and television, the rules for femininity have come to be culturally transmitted more and more through the deployment of standardized visual images." As a result femininity has become a matter of constructing an "appropriate surface presentation of the self" (Bordo 17). In *The Bluest Eye* Pauline receives her "education in the movies," where she learns "to equate physical beauty with virtue," and to assign every face she looks at a "category in the scale of absolute beauty" (97). Pauline, who from childhood liked to "arrange things" and "line things up in rows" (88), is one of Morrison's artists without an art form: "She missed—without knowing what she missed—paints and crayons" (89). Her education in the movies provides her with a culturally acceptable system of creativity. Pauline does her hair up like Jean Harlow and tries to, in Bordo's words, construct the "appropriate surface presentation of the self."

She fails. After losing a front tooth, Pauline "settled down to just being ugly" (98). But Pauline is characterized by her ability to make use of her "defects." She learns to wear her ugliness "as an actor does a prop: for the articulation of character, for support of a role she frequently imagined was hers—martyrdom" (34-5). If she can't be beautiful, she will be virtuous. "She came into her own with the women who despised her, by being more moral than they" (100). Pauline is the consummate performer always able to find a role in the scheme of things, a place within the disciplinary system. As Foucault would say, she "assumes responsibility for the constraints of power; [she] makes them play spontaneously upon [herself]; [she] inscribes in [herself] the power relation in which [she] simultaneously plays both roles; she becomes the principle of [her] own subjection" (*Discipline and Punish* 202-203). Pauline's position as the "ideal servant" in the white family represents her availability as an agent of and for power. "Power, praise and luxury were hers in this household. They even gave her what she had never had—a nickname—Polly" (101). As Pauline rises in the esteem of the white family she works for, her own family disintegrates. Her daughter, Pecola is the victim of the Manichean dialectic of Pauline's double life. That Pecola comes to represent the blackness her mother detests is implied in one of the novel's most painful scenes where Pecola spills the pie of "blackish blueberries" (86) in the kitchen of the white family.

Pecola, not surprisingly, is named by her mother for a character in a movie, although she seems to be unaware of the origin of her name until Maureen Peal points it out. However, the dark Pecola does not resemble the "pretty . . . mulatto" girl in *An Imitation of Life* (57), and Mrs. Breedlove finds her daughter ugly from day one. Given a name which only serves to mark her distance from the norm of beauty, it is hardly surprising that Pecola blames her miserable home and school life on her own "ugliness." Pecola finds that teachers and other adults avoid looking at her. Underlying the absence or vacancy on their gaze is "distaste," a distaste she associates with her blackness, a distaste "lurking in the eyes of all white people" (42).

Pecola tries to escape the brutality of her life by making her body disappear. During her parents' fights she closes her eyes (as she did when surrounded by the school boys) and succeeds in making all her body parts fade away, except for her eyes. She comes to believe that the secret of "the ugliness that [makes] her ignored or despised" is in the eyes (39). Thus, Pecola prays to God for a miracle, for blue eyes:

> It had occurred to Pecola some time ago that if her eyes, those eyes that held the pictures, and knew the sights—if those eyes of hers were different that is to say beautiful, she herself would be different.
>
> (40)

Pecola's desire for blue eyes is doubly significant. It not only represents her wish to be loved by looking like the little white girls so prized in her culture, it also represents a tacit knowledge of how power works. Eyes are the organ of sight and Pecola, named, ironically, after an image on the silver screen, is the victim of a power that values and classifies bodies according to norms established and disseminated by visual images. It seems appropriate, therefore, that the "eye" comes to represent "I." Pecola believes that if she can change her eyes, she can change herself, or more importantly the way others perceive her with their eyes. Pecola's desire then reveals not only her culture's racism, it reveals her culture's *method* of perpetuating racism.

Soaphead Church, a West Indian Anglophile, a misanthrope revolted by the human body, and a man who likes to play God, transforms Pecola's desire into a pathological "reality." At the end of the novel Pecola's isolation from the community is complete. She lives in a fantasy world where she has blue eyes and spends her days in silent conversation with an imaginary "friend." Susan Bordo argues that "pathology as embodied protest" is a motif in feminist literature. Pecola's desire for blue eyes can be viewed as this type of "unconscious, inchoate, and counterproductive" protest. Like the anorexics that Bordo describes, Pecola has pursued the ideals of her culture "to the point where their destructive potential is revealed for all to see" (Bordo 20-21). Pecola's fate is the logical extreme of the culture's values inscribed on the black body. Like the anorexics, Pecola's pursuit of her culture's image of the body beautiful is a way to seek power, but her experience of power is a self-destructive, dangerous illusion. Soaphead Church believes that his gift to Pecola will allow her to "live happily ever after" (143). The reader sees otherwise in the concluding section where Pecola in conversation with her "friend" agonizes over whether or not her eyes are blue enough. The normalizing gaze turned inward is relentless and Pecola has become thoroughly imprisoned by it.

Even Claudia, who wants Pecola's baby to live, who scratches Rosemary's eyes, and who disassembles white baby dolls, is not immune from worshipping whiteness. The retrospective point of view allows Claudia to describe both her resistance and the way in which it is folded back and made available for discipline. The attraction of Shirley Temple for both Frieda and Pecola eludes Claudia because she is younger than they. Claudia states that she "had not yet arrived at the turning point in the development of [her] psyche which would allow [her] to love [Shirley Temple]" (19). The turning point comes when Claudia experiences shame over her own violence directed at little white girls

> When I learned how repulsive this disinterested violence was, that it was repulsive because it was disinterested, my shame floundered about for refuge. The best hiding place was love. Thus the conversion from pristine sadism to fabricated hatred, to fraudulent love. It was a small step to Shirley Temple. I learned much later to worship her, just as I learned that the change was adjustment without improvement.
>
> (22)

"Maturity" requires that Claudia adopt a discourse of virtue. Even though Mrs. Breedlove, Pecola and Claudia respond to power differently, at some point each is motivated by shame—shame over a lost tooth, shame over "blackness," shame over one's own violent response to the things and people that embody the norm. Shame inscribes each character in a discourse of virtue that reinforces cultural norms. Thus, Morrison clearly shows how closely associated the discourses of beauty and virtue really are and how they act together to reinforce one another.

The Bluest Eye exposes a power that classifies and subjugates bodies, that produces different subjectivities within its discourse, and that is disseminated by a normalizing gaze which turns its subjects into agents of power. In short, there is a close resemblance between Foucault's understanding of the workings of power in modern society and Morrison's understanding of racism. While both writers emphasize the difficulties involved in resisting power, they seem to suggest that an analysis of how power works is the first step toward change. In *The History of Sexuality, Vol. 1* Foucault writes:

> We must make allowance for the complex and unstable process whereby discourse can be both an instrument and an effect of power, but also a hindrance, a stumbling-block, a point of resistance and a starting point for an opposing strategy. Discourse transmits and produces power; it reinforces it, but also undermines and exposes it, renders it fragile and makes it possible to thwart it.
>
> (101)

Foucault goes on to describe how the discourses of the human sciences which increased social control over sexuality, also made possible the emergence of a "reverse discourse." He describes, specifically, how homosexuality "began to speak in its own behalf" by using the same vocabulary and categories that had condemned it to demand its legitimacy (101).

Similarly, the black empowerment movement reversed the discourse of white supremacy: "Black Power" and "Black is Beautiful" became nationally heard slogans in the late sixties. Morrison stated that she wrote **The Bluest Eye** between 1965 and 1969 "during great social upheaval in the life of black people." Just as Claudia is telling a long kept secret, Morrison saw her novel as a "public exposure of a private confidence." ("Unspeakable Things Unspoken," 20). **The Bluest Eye** exposes a community enthralled by the value of whiteness, and the narrator's angry response. As such it not only critiques the past, but provides a genealogy for the reverse discourse on race that emerged in the sixties. Claudia's childhood resistance to a culture enamored by western models of beauty is more visceral than articulate, but it marks an opening for change. The existence of a reverse discourse in the culture that produced the novel informs the more sophisticated narrative voice that modulates Claudia's childhood memories. By setting the novel in Lorain, Ohio, a locale where the schools and some neighborhoods are racially mixed, and by writing the novel at a time after the legal battle against segregation had been won, Toni Morrison challenges her readers to reconsider the nature of racism. The traditional "protest novel" focuses on the injustice of race-based exclusion that results from legal or de-facto segregation. Morrison has revised this text, by exploring racism less as a problem of exclusion, than as a problem of pressure to assimilate to destructive cultural values.

Works Cited

Bordo, Susan R. "The Body and the Reproduction of Femininity: A Feminist Appropriation of Foucault." *Gender/Body/Knowledge: Feminist Reconstructions of Being and Knowing.* Ed. Alison M. Jagger and Susan R. Bordo. New Brunswick, NJ: Rutgers UP, 1989. 13-33.

Bove, Paul A. "Discourse." *Critical Terms for Literary Study.* Eds. Frank Lentricchia and Thomas McLaughlin. Chicago: University of Chicago Press, 1990. 50-65.

Foucault, Michel. *Discipline and Punish: The Birth of the Prison.* Trans. Alan Sheridan. New York: Vintage Books, 1979.

———. *The History of Sexuality Volume 1: An Introduction.* Trans. Robert Hurley. Pantheon Books: New York, 1978.

———. "Nietzche, Genealogy, History." *Language Counter-Memory, Practice: Selected Essays and Interviews.* Trans. Bouchard and Simon. Ithaca, New York: Cornell University Press, 1977. 137-164.

———. *Power/Knowledge: Selected Interviews and Other Writings,* 1972-1977. Trans. Gordon, Marshall, Mepham, and Soper. New York: Pantheon Books, 1980.

Morrison, Toni. *The Bluest Eye.* New York: Washington Square Press, 1970.

———. "Unspeakable Things Unspoken: The Afro-American Presence in American Literature" *Michigan Quarterly* 28 (1988): 1-34.

Tate, Claudia. *Black Women Writers at Work.* New York: Continuum, 1983.

Allen Alexander (essay date summer 1998)

SOURCE: Alexander, Allen. "The Fourth Face: The Image of God in Toni Morrison's *The Bluest Eye*." *African American Review* 32, no. 2 (summer 1998): 293-303.

[*In the following essay, Alexander explores Morrison's representation and allusions to a deity in* The Bluest Eye, *contrasting Western notions of the divine with African perceptions of the same, which traditionally associate the deity with evil in this world.*]

Religious references, both from Western and African sources, abound in Toni Morrison's fiction, but nowhere are they more intriguing or perplexing than in **The Bluest Eye**. And of the many fascinating religious references in this novel, the most complex—and perhaps, therefore, the richest—are her representations of and allusions to God. In Morrison's fictional world, God's characteristics are not limited to those represented by the traditional Western notion of the Trinity: Father, Son, and Holy Ghost. Instead, God possesses a fourth face, one that is an explanation for all those things—the existence of evil, the suffering of the innocent and just—that seem so inexplicable in the face of a religious tradition that preaches the omnipotence of a benevolent God.

Is Morrison's introduction of this fourth face into her fiction, then, a means of depicting evil, a redesigned Satan, if you will? It is true that in Morrison's fiction the fourth face at times is portrayed as a reservoir of evil—for example, when the people of the Bottom in **Sula** believe "that the fourth explained Sula" (118), who for them is a manifestation of evil—but the fourth face is much more than a rationalization for all that ails humanity. When Morrison's references to God are taken in their totality, it becomes quite clear that her depiction of the deity is an attempt to humanize God, to demonstrate how God for her characters is not the characteristically ethereal God of traditional Western religion but a God who, while retaining certain Western characteristics, has much in common with the deities of traditional African religion and legend.[1]

Though Morrison's model of God owes much to African tradition, a major part of her portrait is dedicated to exposing how traditional Western notions about God affect her characters. If **The Bluest Eye** can in any way be characterized as an initiation story, then a major portion of a character's initiation involves discovering the inadequacy of Western theological models for those who have been marginalized by the dominant white culture. But many of Morrison's characters, unlike Richard Wright in *Black Boy* and James Baldwin's John Grimes in *Go Tell It On the Mountain,* fail to follow Baldwin's admonition in *The Fire Next Time* to recognize the religion of the white majority for what it is and to "divorce [themselves] from all the prohibitions, crimes, and hypocrisies of the Christian church" (67). In Morrison's oeuvre, the characters who blatantly attack the norms of white society—for example, Guitar Bains in *Song of Solomon*—often seem ridiculously ignorant of their own heritage (Guitar does not know the reasoning behind Malcolm X's choice of last name [160]), and consequently their philosophy retains some of white culture's worst characteristics—witness the violence and genocidal hatred of the Seven Days. Sula is a character who certainly rejects the norms of society, but it is not clear exactly which society—white or black, or both—she is rejecting. And then in *The Bluest Eye* there is the sad case of Pecola Breedlove, who falls prey to the false notions of white superiority espoused not only by the white community but also by her mother and Soaphead Church.

Though the traditional theological models of white society may adversely affect others of Morrison's characters, Pecola is by far the one character whose life seems most vulnerable to the whims of those who have bought into the Western tradition. At every turn Pecola is confronted with attitudes and images based on the myth of white superiority that reinforce her tendency toward self-hatred. When Pecola encounters Mr. Yacobowski, a white man whose religious sensibility, "honed on the doe-eyed Virgin Mary," is alien to the world she inhabits, she is struck by "the total absence of human recognition" on his face (42). But such blatant expressions of racial inequality are not limited to the white characters, who are noticeably few and far between. Geraldine, a black woman who is said to have suppressed her racial identity by getting rid of "the dreadful funkiness of passion, the funkiness of nature, the funkiness of the wide range of human emotions" in order to appease the white man's "blunted soul" (68), treats Pecola as not only a nuisance or blight, as does Mr. Yacobowski, but as a threat to the "sanitized"—i.e., anti-black—environment that she has constructed around her son. As Pecola is thrown out of Geraldine's house, she sees a portrait of an Anglicized Jesus "looking down at her with sad and unsurprised eyes" (76), an image of a God who seems either incapable of helping her or complicit in her suffering.

With this portrait of Jesus, Morrison introduces us to one of the shortcomings of the Western model of God, namely the problem of how a supposedly omnipotent and loving God can allow the existence of evil and suffering. Morrison reintroduces this model of an inadequate God, of a deity incapable of alleviating or unwilling to rectify the injustices of human society, as she recounts Cholly Breedlove's childhood. At a church picnic, Cholly watches the father of a family raise a watermelon over his head to smash it on the ground and is impressed with the man's god-like stance, which he sees as the opposite of the unimpressive white image of God: "a nice old white man, with long white hair, flowing white beard, and little blue eyes that looked sad when people died and mean when they were bad" (106).

Although this white image of God is woefully inadequate for Cholly, who, at least during this period of his life, embraces his African heritage, it is an image to which Pauline Breedlove clings, even at the expense of her daughter's psychic well-being. Pauline, though she has not enjoyed the quasi-middle-class lifestyle that Geraldine believes is the result of having suppressed her racial identity, still looks to white society—through films produced for and religion constructed around the tastes of the white majority—to provide the guidelines for her manner of living. Her acceptance of her poverty and suffering, reflected in her belief that "'it don't make no difference about this old earth' "because" 'there is sure to be a glory'" (104), echoes the teachings of slave masters, who manipulated biblical passages to stifle dissatisfaction among those they oppressed. Pauline has bought into the Western notion of linear history, an outlook that emphasizes the future and belittles the past.[2]

Pauline has also adopted the Western theological tradition of either—or thinking, of believing that the differences between good and evil, righteous and unrighteous, believer and nonbeliever, are clearly demarcated. This ethical orientation is reflected in her belief that she is "an upright and Christian woman, burdened with a no-count man, whom God wanted her to punish" (37),[3] and she rationalizes that her antipathy toward Cholly is sanctified by her God, for "Christ the Judge" demands that she make her husband pay for his transgression. Yet Pauline cannot think of "Christ the Judge" and "Christ the Redeemer" simultaneously because such a linkage does not fit the severely drawn categories of good and evil that she has inherited from the dominant white culture. To her way of thinking, "Cholly was beyond redemption" (37). Pauline's religion, built upon such a rigid and unforgiving foundation, cannot tolerate the notion that a man like Cholly could be a blend of both good and bad, that he, quite simply, could be human. Consequently, she never recognizes God's fourth face. She remains as detached from this concept as she does from her family and heritage. Pauline's belief system, whose either—or design requires its adherents to judge others, often by impossible standards, leads her to leave behind those persons, including her family members, whom she feels fail to measure up to her standards. She thus becomes an extreme individualist, a person cut loose from her cultural moorings.[4]

Though Pauline is not the only African American character in Morrison's fiction to try to mold herself in an image that she thinks will be more acceptable to white society (Jadine from *Tar Baby* and Ruth Foster from *Song of Solomon* are two obvious examples, as are Soaphead Church and Pecola in *The Bluest Eye* and Helene Wright in *Sula*), her name, which may be a direct reference to Pauline theology, and her central role in the psychological disintegration of Pecola make her perhaps Morrison's most identifiable example of this type. And one chief reason that she so aptly fills this role is her vision of God, which is so antithetical to the fourth-face image that is more central to her heritage. Pauline's adoption of the white society's notion of an ethereal God who judges humans from an alien perspective contrasts with a strain in African American thought that has sought to put a human face on God. As Major J. Jones points out in his study *The Color of God*, this African-influenced theological outlook envisions God as "neither threat nor rival" to humans. Instead, "God is . . . the very basis or ground of the creature's fullest possible self-realization. . . . Black religious experience . . . is about being and becoming more human under God" (22).

Since this outlook suggests that one's humanity is inextricably linked to God, it follows that such an orientation would lead one to believe that perhaps the connection runs both ways, that God cannot be fully God, or at least a God to humanity, without also being in some sense human. This concept is not completely alien to Western theology, for the Christian faith itself depends on the notion of God becoming a man in the form of Jesus, but, as Jones concludes, and as Morrison suggests in her fiction, the West has lost its connection—through various factors, including, no doubt, Pauline influences on Christian theology—to this fundamental idea of a link between God and humanity. Consequently, in white society God has been molded into an otherworldly presence who, despite Christ's role as redeemer of fallen humanity, regards human weakness, in the form of sin, as something disconnected from the divine.

Within the African tradition we see a substantially different representation of God. In African folklore God is often depicted as having very human-like qualities, not only regarding his appearance but also his personality and abilities. Whereas the Western tradition pictures God as a stoical figure who demands perfection from his creation because of his own perfection, African storytellers have given God a human face, portraying him as a lovable character with a sense of humor and a streak of fallibility. Julius Lester in his renditions of traditional African folk tales characterizes God as "an amateur" (13) who is trying his best "to make the world look a little prettier" (3) but who doesn't "know what he's doing half the time" (23). This folksy God, a God who is seen not only as the creator but also as the ancestor of humanity and who consequently possesses many of the characteristics of his imperfect creation (Sawyerr 95), is a far cry from the West's omnipotent, infallible God who despises human frailty.

There is little doubt, given Morrison's characterization of Pauline, that the author sees the values of white religion as inappropriate and ultimately self-defeating guides for her African American characters. Though she does not present us with a character in *The Bluest Eye* who, like Baldwin's John Grimes, is suspicious of the trappings of white religion, including those characteristics that have been absorbed by African American Christianity, she does portray characters who embrace these trappings, such as Pauline and Geraldine, as less than admirable figures. In contrast to John Grimes, who senses that his parents' church has lost something of value because it has moved too far away from its African roots, Pauline chooses her church precisely because it is a place "where shouting [i]s frowned upon" (100), a sanctuary from the passion that she so despises. But ultimately both John and Pauline suffer from their association with these churches. John comes to regard the church as a source of darkness and oppression and thinks of God as a "monstrous heart" (217) that consumes his joy and stunts his passion for life. Pauline divorces herself from her African American heritage and in the process loses the closest manifestation of that tradition: her family. Obviously neither Baldwin nor Morrison sees a movement from an African to a Western sensibility as an appropriate step for a productive and authentic life.

The question, then, arises: How does Morrison demonstrate the qualities of an African-inspired vision of God in her fiction? Of course, no serious reader of Morrison's work would begin an analysis with the assumption that there is a simple, clear-cut answer to any question regarding her richly complex work, and her portrayal of an African religious sensibility offers no exception. Her selection of the fourth face of God image underscores her commitment to demonstrating that this sensibility is inherently attuned to the notion that God is much larger than the image to which the divine has been confined by Western theology. And a significant part of that largeness is built on the belief that God is in some way responsible either as an active participant or a willing spectator—in the tragedies that befall human beings.

Such an idea is certainly not foreign to the Western theological tradition, which is constructed on the foundation of a Judaic faith that sees God as many things, from protector to the engine behind catastrophe. But in the Judaic tradition, there is typically a reason behind God's decision to punish humans—namely, their defiance of divine laws. In contrast to this belief that tragedy can ultimately be explained by human transgression, traditional African religions tend to understand tragedy as something that happens regardless of what humans have or have not done.

This association of God with the existence of evil is a common element among several of the many variations of traditional African religions.[5] E. Thomas Lawson notes that within the Zulu tradition evil is not seen as "an independent, autonomous power" but as a force that draws its strength from three positive powers: the God of the Sky, the ancestors, and medicine (27). K. A. Busia finds a similar belief among the Ashanti, for whom nature is populated by the "malignant spirits of fairies and forest monsters" who "are subservient to the Supreme Being, from whom ultimately they all derive their power" (qtd. in Sawyerr 100).

Within the belief systems of many African peoples God's kinship to evil far surpasses that of a source of origin. Evil not only derives its power from God but is allowed to flourish by God. Harry Sawyerr, who in the preface to his study *God: Ancestor or Creator?* stresses the difficulty of studying the African concept of God because of the vastness of the continent and the diversity of its population, nevertheless feels comfortable asserting that within African belief systems "the general well-being of man, as well as his distress, are freely attributed to God" (ix) He supports this contention with evidence from his study of the Yoruba, for whom "evil forces seem to be more subject to the ultimate control of God. They can and often do destroy human life, but not without the permission of God" (49). This notion that evil exists because God allows it to was noted over two hundred years ago by Olaudah Equiano. In his autobiography, published in 1789, Equiano recalls traditions he learned as a child in Africa, and he writes that his people believed that God "governs events, especially our deaths or captivity" (27). This same idea can be found in the work of Zora Neale Hurston, who introduced into her fiction characters like Janie and Tea Cake of *Their Eyes Were Watching God* who combine an African sensibility with a belief that "all gods dispense suffering without reason" (138). Janie and Tea Cake, caught in the destructive path of a hurricane, wonder if God "meant to measure their puny might against His" (151). And later as she watches Tea Cake suffer from a rabid dog's bite, Janie concludes that "God would do less than He had in His heart" (169).

However, there is also a strain of African belief that sees God not as the source or master of evil but as a participant in the universe's struggle against malignant forces. According to J. B. Danquah, the Akan—a cultural group which includes the Ashanti—believe that "Nana, the principle that makes for good, is himself or itself participator in the life of the whole, and is not only head" (88). Since God (Nana) is thus viewed by the Akan as a part of creation rather than as a being apart from it, they see "physical pain and evil . . . as natural forces which the Nana, in common with others of the group, has to master, dominate and sublimate" (88-89). Within this framework of belief, God and humans are part of the same community, working together, like the people of the Bottom in *Sula*, against evil, not in a futile effort to eliminate it but in order to outlast it (118).

African perspectives on the existence of evil are multiple and varied, but one idea that seems to link them is that an explanation for the presence of evil is unnecessary. Evil is a real presence in the lives of African peoples, yet it is precisely because of the weight of evil on them that they steer away from metaphysical speculations about it. As James Cone, writing from an African American Christian perspective, contends, ". . . black reflections about suffering have not been removed from life but involved in life, that is, the struggle to affirm humanity despite the dehumanizing conditions of slavery and oppression" (183).

One African folk tale that illustrates this African belief that evil is not a riddle to be solved but a reality with which one must deal is the story of a woman who, after her family has died, goes in search of God in order to find an explanation for the tragedy that has beset her. As she searches the world for God, she encounters people who question her motives, for they contend that "'Shikakunamo [the Besetting One] sits on the back of everyone of us and we cannot shake him off!' "She ultimately fails in her quest,' 'and from that day to this, say the Africans, no man or woman has solved the riddle of this painful earth'" (McVeigh 48-49).

Morrison deftly works a similar sense of tragedy into *The Bluest Eye*, though one could well argue that in her fiction it is based as much on the inadequacy of the Western model of God as on African traditions. Though there is no shortage of suffering characters in the novel, the Breedloves, like the woman troubled by Shikakunamo, or like Job in the Old Testament, seem uniquely chosen to wear the mantle of divine retribution: "It was as though some mysterious all-knowing master had given each one a cloak of ugliness to wear. . . ." The fact that they see support for the cloak "leaning at them from every billboard, every movie, every glance" is an indication of just how much what white society values has distorted their own self-image, so much so that each accepts the ugliness "without question" (34). But even though the Breedloves' pitiful circumstances seem to be largely attributable to human action, both in the form of a racist society and their own personal shortcomings, the odds are so great against them that it appears that the hands of "some mysterious all-knowing master" are holding them back, or perhaps choking the life out of them in the same way that those hands strangle the life from "a tuft of grass [that] had forced its way up through a crack in the sidewalk, only to meet a raw October wind" (48). In the world of the Breedloves, it seems that much more than human forces are working against them, that, in fact, "the earth itself might have been unyielding" to their survival (9).

If, then, God is, in Morrison's cosmology, the agent behind much human suffering, do her characters' attitudes suggest that they respond to their plight in a way reflective of the African sensibility toward tragedy reflected in the tale of the woman seeking Shikakunamo? This is not the case with Pauline and Pecola, both of whom approach their pain in ways more in line with the values of white culture. Pauline molds her lifestyle to correspond to what the dominant culture. Pauline molds her lifestyle to correspond to what the dominant culture applauds. And Pecola withdraws into herself, "peeping out from behind the shroud very seldom, and then only to yearn for the return of her mask" (35), which she puts aside only after believing she has acquired a feature—blue eyes—that she identifies with the happiness that eludes her. Pauline and Pecola, in effect, attempt to deal with their circumstances by altering their sense of reality, not by attempting to maintain their authenticity as meaningful members of a larger community. They seem willing to exchange their personhood, and consequently their heritage, for models of themselves that only strengthen in their minds the cultural norms that make them hate their true selves.

In contrast to Pauline and Pecola, Cholly, though he is in many ways as tragic a figure as they are, seems to see the life-affirming values of his heritage, an insight that he discovers most memorably while thinking about the image of God while watching the man smash the watermelon at the church picnic:

> It must be the devil who looks like that—holding the world in his hands, ready to dash it to the ground and spill the red guts so niggers could eat the sweet, warm insides. If the devil did look like that, Cholly preferred him. He never felt anything thinking about God, but just the idea of the devil excited him. And now the strong, black devil was blotting out the sun and getting ready to split open the world.
>
> (107)

The image that Cholly relishes is one that embraces the fourth face, one that portrays God as much more than the pallid, antiseptic God envisioned by white society. Cholly's God is dynamic, complex, unpredictable, exciting, dangerous.[6]

The notion that God can be dangerous, something other than the benevolent grandfather figure that has been pre-eminent in the Western mind, might be unsettling, but Cholly appears to welcome the idea, perhaps because such an image seems much more realistic in a world that does not give the impression of being controlled by an omnipotent and loving deity. He sees this representation of God reaffirmed at his Aunt Jimmy's funeral, where "there was grief over the waste of life, the stunned wonder at the ways of God, and the restoration of order in nature at the graveyard" (113). Here, the concept of evil, of pain and suffering and those things that appear to contradict that which affirms goodness and life, is not an alien thought, nor is it something that overwhelms the funeralgoers and forces them into a state of nihilistic apathy.[7] In contrast to the Western approach to the existence of evil, which has been marked by attempts to sequester or destroy it, these people, drawing from their African Americans in general, "that evil has a natural place in the universe" and consequently "they are not surprised at its existence or horrified or outraged" (Parker 253).

Is there, then, no limit to the amount of evil one can tolerate without lashing out? Is not what happens to Pecola, particularly at the hands of her father and Soaphead Church, so horrific and outrageous that some response against it is necessary? For Pecola, unfortunately, there is no one to respond but herself, and her lack of response—what some might call her acceptance of her situation—cannot be attributed to the African sensibility of which Morrison has spoken. Pecola has become so disconnected from her heritage that her movement toward insanity is instead an indictment of the white cultural framework that has become her guidepost for living.

But Morrison does not intend for us to conclude that the African sensibility toward tragedy is one of complacent and powerless acceptance. To the contrary, she suggests that the correct stance for one to take with regard to tragedy is not passively to give in to its inevitability but, like the people of the Bottom in *Sula,* to be actively engaged with it so that it can be "dealt with, survived, outwitted, triumphed over" (118). Yet Pecola is ill-equipped to outwit and triumph over her tragic situation. She lacks the cultural rootedness or the intestinal fortitude to outlast the forces that work to annihilate her personhood. And in the end she accepts as her destiny the destruction of her true being in favor of an insanity-induced self-image that validates in her mind the inherent inferiority of her heritage.

The instrument that finally pushes Pecola over the edge is Soaphead Church, a character who not only rejects his African heritage but who also relinquishes his identity as a human being in favor of the self-generated delusion that he is in some sense a god. He is a hater of humanity, a self-professed misanthrope whose "disdain for people" ironically "led him into a profession designed to serve them," that of a "Reader, Adviser, and Interpreter of Dreams" (130). However, he "serves" others not out of a spirit of generosity but because of a selfish desire to assert his power over the innocent and weak. Into the lair of this preyer on humanity walks Pecola, who stands little chance of withstanding Soaphead. Instead of sexually molesting her, as he has been fond of doing to other girls, Soaphead assaults her psyche, taking from her any knowledge of her true identity.

But is Soaphead totally to blame for Pecola's demise? From his seemingly peculiar perspective he is not, but is his view of the world really all that unique? It would be easy to conclude, given Morrison's consistently negative appraisal of Western theological models, that Soaphead, who is easily Morrison's most detestable character in a novel that is replete with them, represents the worst side of white religion. Such a conclusion makes even more sense when one considers how Soaphead, following the path the West has laid down for God, severs himself from humanity. In this sense he could be seen as an allegorical figure. But Morrison is much too complex a writer to introduce such an obviously allegorical character into her work, and there is evidence in the text that suggests that Soaphead, far from being solely a human likeness of the white God, actually embraces a theological perspective that is not far removed from that of the fourth-face notion of African tradition. Like the people of the Bottom, he believes that, "since decay, vice, filth, and disorder were pervasive, they must be in the Nature of Things," that "evil exist[s] because God had created it." But he also departs from the African perspective, rejecting the notion that evil is part of God's nature and instead believing that the deity "made a sloven and unforgivable error in judgment: designing an imperfect universe" (136). His adoption of this idea suggests that he still embraces the Western notion of dualism, the belief that good and evil exist as separate forces. His explanation for the existence of evil, then, is not far removed from that of Western theologians who have struggled with the apparently contradictory notion that evil exists in spite of the presence of an omnipotent and benevolent God. Yet Morrison, ever conscious of complicating Soaphead's character, once again undercuts any idea that we might have regarding his one-to-one connection to any theological tradition, revealing that he sees God as something less than omnipotent, as a power so weak and incompetent that "Soaphead suspected that he himself could have done better" (136).

In the final analysis Soaphead's theology is schizophrenic, leaping back and forth between Western and African traditions, between different notions of the physical and metaphysical. His perspective is thus an anticipation of what will happen to Pecola, whose idea of self will teeter on the edge between reality and a reality-induced fantasy, a delusion that may have been locked into place by Soaphead but one for which the community surrounding her—her family and friends and the messages thrust at her by white society—is also culpable. Pecola becomes the ultimate tragic figure, who, in the words of Claudia MacTeer, took "all of our waste which we dumped on her and which she absorbed" (159). In this sense she becomes a Christ figure, one who takes on the ugliness (sin) of the world around her and consequently absolves others of their feelings of inferiority (guilt). But Morrison's final image of God is an aborted one: Unlike Christ, there is no resurrection for Pecola. In her world, "it's much, much, much too late" to keep hope alive (160).[5]

Although there is no clear affirmation of life in **The Bluest Eye,** the possibility of hope though it seems far removed from the lives of the characters, remains for those who can rediscover the value of their heritage and reject the notion that they can succeed only if they adopt the norms of white society. The experiences of Pauline and Pecola suggest that it is impossible for a character to adapt to white society without also sacrificing one's true self. In order to adapt, both Pauline and Pecola have to embrace the Western concept of dualism—of believing that life is divisible, that good is distinguishable from evil, that the past, present, and future are disconnected. The failure of these two characters to retain their authenticity, to be who they truly are, suggests "that half a reality is insufficient for anyone" (Lepow 364).

In contrast to the efforts of Pauline and Pecola to separate themselves from their heritage, there are characters who seem to have an understanding that their lives in the past and the present have value. For example, the three prostitutes—China, Poland, and Miss Marie—who live above the Breedloves offer a counterpoint to Pauline, showing Pecola that their lives, no matter how much they are despised by others, have meaning because the women define themselves rather than relying on the judgments of outsiders. They make no pretensions about being anything other than "whores in whores' clothing" (48) and thus provide Pecola with a contrast to her mother, who tries to change who she is in order to fit white society's dictates. Whereas Pauline has done her best to squelch her own and her daughter's taste for the passion of life, the prostitutes, with their large appetites for the sensual, whether it be in the form of sex or food, show Pecola that the physical is a realm to be embraced rather than shunned. Marie makes even the disgusting seem beautiful to Pecola, who witnesses her belching "softly, purringly, lovingly" (49). That love might be associated with such physical crudeness is an idea that Pecola could never have gotten from her mother. And it is Pecola's failure to embrace the image Marie provides that ultimately makes her susceptible to Soaphead's trap, for he exploits her tendency to divorce physical reality from her identity.

Much like the prostitutes, Mr. and Mrs. MacTeer seem largely unconcerned with fulfilling any roles prescribed by outside influences. They do not pamper their children the way that Pauline, trying to emulate the whites for whom she works, pampers "the little girl in pink" (87). Mrs. MacTeer often speaks harshly to her daughters, but Claudia realizes that "love, thick and dark as Alaga syrup" (14), fills her home. Their father also proves his love through actions rather than words, standing as

"Vulcan guarding the flames" of the home fires (52). Though Claudia and Frieda do not always understand the words of their parents, they understand "the edge, the curl, the thrust of their emotions" (16). Unlike Pecola, who must face Pauline's and Soaphead's acts of deception, Claudia and Frieda have the advantage of living with adult role models who place more value on action than image. Mr. and Mrs. MacTeer are soundly grounded in reality. Consequently, they are not drawn to the false ideals peddled by Hollywood and Madison Avenue which so distort Pauline's self-image.

Cholly, though there are aspects of his character that put him "beyond the reaches of human consideration" (18), has experienced and appreciated the value of his heritage through individuals like Aunt Jimmy. He provides Pecola with yet another alternative to her mother, acting as a physical foil to Pauline's movement toward an image-driven existence. When Pecola recalls the sound of her parents making love, she remembers being appalled by Cholly's groans, yet as "terrible as his noises were, they were not nearly as bad as the no noise at all from her mother" (48-49). As imperfect as Cholly is, he is still more genuine than Pauline. His rape of Pecola is reprehensible, but he does not rape her mind the way that Pauline and Soaphead do. Claudia senses that Cholly really loves Pecola: "He, at any rate, was the one who loved her enough to touch her, envelop her, give something of himself to her" (159). The fact that this one gift given to Pecola is in reality a sexual assault on her body underscores just how horribly brutal her life is.

But perhaps the character who holds the most promise for living an authentic existence is Claudia, whose telling of the story is a sign in itself that she has come to recognize the value of rediscovering the past. It is Claudia, after all, who seems to be most in touch with reality, for she is the one who reconstructs it for the reader. Claudia understands that those who try to measure their world with black-and-white scales and to find easy solutions to the drudgery of daily life are doomed to lose not only their grounding in their heritage but also their grounding in reality. Ultimately, the price such a person pays is the loss of one's self. When Claudia observes her parents, she recognizes that their authenticity is not based on the literal meaning of the words they speak but in the way they are spoken: "Sometimes their words move in lofty spirals; other times they take strident leaps, and all of it is punctuated with warm-pulsed laughter—like the throb of a heart made of jelly" (16). The story she gives us is not one that allows us to march straight toward the truth, for such a path would oversimplify a world that is so full of evil and so far beyond explanation that it need not be explained—it can only be "dealt with, survived, outwitted, triumphed over" (*Sula* 118). Claudia's narrative, which has a circular and, some might say, elusive quality to it, is in itself a reflection of the image that is so central to her heritage: the fourth face of God.

Notes

1. Any serious student of Western and African religions knows that the conceptualizations of God within fairly similar theological traditions can differ dramatically. My intent in this essay is not to examine the competing models within closely related traditions but to explore how Morrison presents the differences between general models of two distinctly different traditions: the Western and the African.

   Though my study is limited to the images of God present in *The Bluest Eye*, other studies have dealt with this topic in relation to some of Morrison's other novels. See Vashti Crutcher Lewis for a comparison of Shadrack's role in *Sula* to that of "a divine river spirit" or "a West African Water priest who represents and speaks for a river god" (92). See Janice M. Sokoloff for an examination of Eva Peace's god-like role in *Sula*. And see Lauren Lepow for an exploration of Valerian's role in *Tar Baby* as "the image of a white man's god" (368) and an analysis of the religious connotations of Son's name.

2. Maxine Lavon Montgomery has made this same point with regard to the people of the Bottom in *Sula*, arguing that "Western linear history" is "a distorted version of reality that keeps the townsfolk reaching out in vain for a future that persistently eludes their grasp" (128).

3. Patricia Hunt discusses *Sula*'s parabolic qualities, which she sees as part of Morrison's critique of either-or thinking.

4. As Trudier Harris has pointed out, Pauline's separation from the African American community is underscored by her "attachment to the rich white family for which she works in Ohio when they assign her a nickname—Polly" (20). Harris contends that Pauline's acceptance of the nickname is a subversion of the tradition of nicknaming that has been a central feature of the African American community.

5. Though most scholars argue that African traditional religions tend to associate evil with God in some way, at least one writer, Gwinyai H. Muzorewa, concludes that "African traditional religion holds that all good comes from God and that evil was not created by God" (19).

6. The contrasting images of a white and a black God envisioned by Cholly are part of a larger pattern of inversion present throughout the novel. See Jacqueline de Weever for a discussion of this pattern in *The Bluest Eye* and *Sula*.

7. According to John S. Mbiti, in many African religions God "is brought into the picture primarily as an attempt to explain what is otherwise difficult

for the human mind" (45). In contrast to Western religious traditions, within which the existence of evil is typically blamed on the sinful nature of humans and a spiritual being who stands in conflict with a benevolent God, practitioners of African religions tend not to divorce God from the problem of evil.

8. Pecola's symbolic connection to Christ and her failure to triumph over her circumstances is illustrative of Morrison's drive to stress the failure of white theological models for her African American characters. Deborah Guth has uncovered this same theme in *Beloved* in which "the hostile dialogic interaction between" Christian symbols and the circumstances of African American characters "leads to a total polarization that exposes the terrible inadequacy of the Christological model to contain or clarify the teleology of black historic reality" (90).

Works Cited

Baldwin, James. *Go Tell It on the Mountain*. 1953. New York: Dell, 1985.

———. *The Fire Next Time*. 1962. New York: Dell, 1988.

Cone, James H. *God of the Oppressed*. San Francisco: Harper, 1975.

Danquah, J. B. *The Akan Doctrine of God: A Fragment of Gold Coast Ethics and Religion*. 2nd ed. London: Frank Cass, 1968.

de Weever, Jacqueline. "The Inverted World of Toni Morrison's *The Bluest Eye* and *Sula*." *CLA Journal* 22 (1979): 402-14.

Equiano, Olaudah. *The Life of Olaudah Equiano*. 1789. London: Dawsons of Pall Mall, 1969.

Guth, Deborah. "'Wonder What God Had in Mind': *Beloved*'s Dialogue with Christianity." *Journal of Narrative Technique* 24.2 (1994): 83-97.

Harris, Trudier. *Fiction and Folklore: The Novels of Toni Morrison*. Knoxville: U of Tennessee P, 1991.

Hunt, Patricia. "War and Peace: Transfigured Categories and the Politics of *Sula*." *African American Review* 27 (1993): 443-59.

Hurston, Zora Neale. *Their Eyes Were Watching God*. 1937. New York: Harper, 1990.

Jones, Major J. *The Color of God: The Concept of God in Afro-American Thought*. Macon: Mercer UP, 1987.

Lawson, E. Thomas. *Religions of Africa: Traditions in Transformation*. San Francisco: Harper, 1984.

Lepow, Lauren. "Paradise Lost and Found: Dualism and Edenic Myth in Toni Morrison's *Tar Baby*." *Contemporary Literature* 28 (1987): 363-77.

Lester, Julius. *Black Folktales*. New York: Grove, 1969.

Lewis, Vashti Crutcher. "African Tradition in Toni Morrison's *Sula*." *Phylon* 48 (1987): 91-97.

Mbiti, John S. *African Religions and Philosophy*. 2nd ed. Oxford: Heinemann, 1989

McVeigh, Malcolm J. *God in Africa: Conceptions of God in African Traditional Religion and Christianity*. Cape Cod: Claude Stark, 1974.

Montgomery, Maxine Lavon. "A Pilgrimage to the Origins: The Apocalypse as Structure and Theme in Toni Morrison's *Sula*." *Black American Literature Forum* 23 (1989): 127-37.

Morrison, Toni. *The Bluest Eye*. 1970. New York: Washington Square P, 1972.

———. *Song of Solomon*. 1977. New York: Plume, 1987.

———. *Sula*. 1973. New York: Plume, 1982.

Muzorewa, Gwinyai H. *The Origins and Development of African Theology*. Maryknoll: Orbis, 1985.

Parker, Bettye J. "Complexity: Toni Morrison's Women—An Interview Essay." *Sturdy Black Bridges: Visions of Black Women in Literature*. Ed. Roseann P. Bell, Parker, and Beverly Guy-Sheftall. New York: Anchor, 1979. 251-57.

Sawyerr, Harry. *God: Ancestor or Creator?* London: Longman, 1970.

Sokoloff, Janice M. "Intimations of Matriarchal Age: Notes on the Mythical Eva in Toni Morrison's *Sula*." *Journal of Black Studies* 16 (1986): 429-34.

Carl D. Malmgren (essay date spring 2000)

SOURCE: Malmgren, Carl D. "Texts, Primers, and Voices in Toni Morrison's *The Bluest Eye*." *Critique: Studies in Contemporary Fiction* 41, no. 3 (spring 2000): 251-62.

[*In the following essay, Malmgren studies the multicultural and polyphonic structures of* The Bluest Eye *with respect to the novel's concern with victimization and its causes.*]

The Bluest Eye represents a remarkable undertaking, especially for a first novel. In terms of formal features, it might be described as a kind of narratological compendium. For one thing, the novel incorporates several different forms of textuality. It opens with three different versions of its epigraphic "master" text, several lines drawn from an elementary school primer. That is followed by an italicized "overture," introducing the primary narrator, Claudia MacTeer, and the dominant motifs of the work—victimization and its causes:

> It was a long time before my sister and I admitted to ourselves that no green was going to spring from our seeds. Once we knew, our guilt was relieved only by fights and mutual accusations about who was to blame.
>
> (5)

The body of the novel is composed of two related kinds of texts, variously interspersed: four seasonal sections, narrated in the first person by Claudia MacTeer; and seven primer sections (employing various narrational situations), so named because each section is set off by an epigraph taken from the master primer. The end is a kind of coda, beginning "So it was" (204), in which Claudia reviews the outcomes of the narrative and rehearses its lessons. Linda Dittmar praises the architectonics of the novel as "a brilliant orchestration of a complex multiformed narrative" (140).

Texts and Voices

The novel is not only multitextual; it is also polyphonic. The seasonal sections are in the first person, but even they are double-voiced, aware of the difference between the experiencing "I" and the narrating "I." In places Claudia speaks as the nine-year-old girl going through the experience, ignorant, for example, as to what "ministratin'" is (28). Elsewhere, she switches to an adult perspective on the incident being narrated: "We trooped in, Frieda sobbing quietly, Pecola carrying a white tail, me carrying the little-girl-gone-to-woman pants" (31). And sometimes she speaks from the moment of the enunciation itself: "But was it really like that? As painful as I remember? Only mildly" (12).

The primer sections are, if anything, even more ambitious, in that they eventually make use of the full spectrum of what Stanzel terms "narrative situations."[1] The narrator assumes authorial position and privilege when she gives the reader a lecture on the lifestyles and values of the "sugar-brown Mobile girls" (82):

> They go to land-grant colleges, normal schools, and learn to do the white man's work with refinement: home economics to prepare his food; teacher education to instruct black children in obedience; music to soothe the weary master and entertain his blunted soul. Here they learn the rest of the lesson begun in those soft houses with porch swings and pots of bleeding heart: how to behave.
>
> (83)

From the same position, she reviews the history of the Breedlove's storefront apartment (33-37); in the following primer section, she moves successively through the minds of the members of the Breedlove family during a violent morning confrontation (39-46).

The primer sections devoted to Pauline and Cholly Breedlove and to Soaphead Church are, in large part, narrated figurally, with Pauline, Cholly, and Soaphead as the centers of consciousness. Those sections focus on the what and how of their featured protagonists' experiences. But even those sections are multivocal. Those figural presentations are frequently qualified by authorial interpolations or commentary; the Pauline section, for example, begins with the following explanation of her feeling of unworthiness:

> The easiest thing to do would be to build a case out of her foot. This is what she herself did. But to find out the truth about how dreams die, one should never take the word of the dreamer. The end of her lovely beginning was probably the cavity in one of her front teeth. She preferred, however, to think always of her foot.
>
> (110)[2]

What follows is figural narration, a recounting of Pauline's perspective on the events of her life. To make that experience even more immediate, however, the narration shifts several times to quoted and italicized first-person dramatic monologue. Pauline speaks aloud, apparently to a Lorain neighbor, deputy for the reader:

> That was the last time I seen real June bugs. These things up here ain't june bugs. They's something else. Folks here call them fireflies, Down home they was different. But I recollect that streak of green. I recollect it well.
>
> (112)

In the space of a few pages, the narration shifts from authorial to figural to first person. In addition, the Soaphead Church primer section contains, in entirety, a formal and pedantic letter that Soaphead writes to God after his encounter with Pecola. And the last primer section consists of a schizoid dramatic dialogue between Pecola and her imaginary second self in which the two of them rhapsodize about the blueness of Pecola's eyes.

A number of critics have called attention to the multiple narrations (and multiple narrators) in the novel. Arguing that "the possibility of a bystander really being able to tell the whole story is implicitly obviated by the novel's shift in narrators," Demetrakopoulos stipulates at least three narrators: Claudia, "the omniscient point of view," and Pecola (35). Samuels says that Claudia "retells the story with the assistance of other, external narrators" (25). Dittmar argues that "Claudia covers a lot of ground, but she is not the novel's pivotal consciousness. She is a narrator, not the narrator" (143). The critical consensus seems to be that there are two main speakers, Claudia in the seasonal sections, and an authorial persona elsewhere. The authorial persona supplies the master primer text and uses it epigraphically and assumes the privilege of rendering the dramatic monologues of Pauline and Pecola in the primer sections

(Gibson 21, 25, 30; Holloway 40; Byerman 450). In her afterword to the novel, Morrison herself refers derogatorily to her narrational doubleness, saying that it made a "shambles" of her text: "I resorted to two voices, [. . .] both of which are extremely unsatisfactory to me" (215).

I argue (pace Morrison) that strong evidence, textual and biographical, exists to suggest that a single narrator, Claudia MacTeer, has composed the texts and created the voices and that my reading adds an important dimension to the meaning of the text.[3] As noted above, Claudia's first person seasonal sections are double-voiced, shifting back and forth between the perspective of the nine-year-old and that of an older and wiser adult. The passage in which Claudia discusses her evolving relationship to white baby girls indicates the distance between these two perspectives:

> If I pinched them, their eyes—unlike the crazed hint of the baby doll's eyes—would fold in pain, and their cry would not be the sound of an icebox door, but a fascinating cry of pain. When I learned how repulsive this disinterested violence was, that it was repulsive because it was disinterested, my shame floundered about for refuge. The best hiding place was love. Thus the conversion from pristine sadism to fabricated hatred, to fraudulent love. It was a small step to Shirley Temple. I learned much later to worship her, just as I learned to delight in cleanliness, knowing, even as I learned, that the change was adjustment without improvement.
>
> (23)

Here is a discerning adult making nuanced discriminations. We know that she is significantly removed from the time of the events she recounts because her narration rehearses and implicitly repudiates (and therefore comes after) a love for Shirley Temple that itself came "much later" than her original hatred and sadism.

The text gives us no way to date Claudia's enunciation or to specify her adult age, but she has the mature voice and perspective of someone looking back from a distance, someone, say, in her mid-to-late thirties. ***The Bluest Eye*** was published in 1970, when Morrison was thirty-nine years old. Like Claudia, Morrison was born in Lorain, Ohio; like Claudia, she would have been nine years old in 1940-41, the year in which the events of the novel take place. Those similarities suggest that Claudia MacTeer is Morrison's persona in the novel, her fictional "second self." Indeed, Morrison states in the afterword that the novel had a autobiographical origin, that Pecola was based on a real-life elementary school classmate who, out of the blue as it were, confided that she wanted blue eyes (209).

That is the (suspect) argument from biography, the old mimetic shibboleth about Art and Life being intimately related. But no substantial textual evidence supports that connection. As the passage above suggests, Claudia's seasonal sections demonstrate that she has the talent and insight to make the kind of discriminations that characterize the text as a whole and that she has the stylistic resources to rise to the lyricism found in various places in the novel.[4] Most important, the Claudia sections articulate an ideological project that is carried out in great detail elsewhere in the novel: the critique of cultural stereotypes imposed by the dominant white culture. In terms of theme, then, the novel is seamless, univocal.[5] In addition, Claudia is singled out as the MacTeer sister blessed with Imagination (just as Frieda is marked as the Executive, the one who makes decisions). In the "Autumn" section, for example, the girls are bored, and Claudia supplies an extensive list of possible activities for them: looking at Mr. Henry's girlie magazines or Bible, threading needles for the blind lady, searching through trash cans, making fudge, or eavesdropping at the Greek hotel (26-27). When the sisters are afraid that Frieda is "ruined" after she has been molested by Henry the roomer, Claudia comes up with the solution to their problem by concocting a highly fanciful line of "reasoning" that includes fat people, the three prostitutes, whiskey, and Cholly Breedlove (101-02). Those episodes reinforce the connection between Morrison and Claudia by suggesting that Claudia has the imaginative resources to invent alternatives, to impersonate various characters, to create fictional worlds.

The novel begins with Claudia's voice: "Quiet as it's kept, there were no marigolds in the fall of 1941. We thought, at the time, that it was because Pecola was having her father's baby that the marigolds did not grow." The second paragraph specifies that "we" comprises "my sister and I" (5). The novel ends with Claudia speaking for a more generalized "we": "We are wrong, of course, but it doesn't matter. It's too late. At least on the edge of my town, among the garbage and the sunflowers of my town, it's much, much, much too late" (206). Occam's razor should dictate that what comes between the beginning and end belongs to her as well.

The problem is that the primer sections, which make up about two-thirds of the novel, refuse to say "I." They contain almost no reference to the speaker's person,[6] certainly no explicit identification of that authorial speaker as the grown-up Claudia MacTeer; therefore, no apparent linkage is evident between the primer sections and the seasonal sections. In addition to the thematic continuity I have mentioned there are other connections. For example, the substance, rhetoric, and syntax of part of Soaphead Church's letter to God is echoed in Claudia's coda to the novel. Soaphead indites (and indicts):

> In retaining the identity of our race, we held fast to those characteristics most gratifying to sustain and least

troublesome to maintain. Consequently we were not royal but snobbish, not aristocratic but class-conscious; we believed authority was cruelty to our inferiors, and education was being at school. We mistook violence for passion, indolence for leisure, and thought recklessness was freedom.

(177)

Claudia reprises (and embellishes):

And fantasy it was, for we were not strong, only aggressive; we were not free, merely licensed; we were not compassionate, we were polite; not good, but well-behaved. We courted death in order to call ourselves brave, and hid like thieves from life. We substituted good grammar for intellect; we switched habits to simulate maturity; we rearranged lies and called it the truth.

(205-06)

It is as if Claudia took the condemnation of African Americans she voiced in the persona of Soaphead Church and brought it to bear on the victimization of Pecola Breedlove.

More convincing than the rhetorical and stylistic echo is the explicit repetition of substantive commentary. In the cat primer section, Geraldine returns to her tidy home to find Pecola there and sees in the little girl only anathema:

She had seen this little girl all of her life. [. . .] Hair uncombed, dresses falling apart, shoes untied and caked with dirt. [Little girls like this] had stared at her with great uncomprehending eyes. Eyes that questioned nothing and asked everything. Unblinking and unabashed, they stared up at her. The end of the world lay in their eyes, and the beginning, and all the waste in between.

(91-92)

In the coda, Claudia repeats that summary view of Pecola, but with a significant addition; she speaks elegiacly of Pecola wandering on the edge of town, "plucking her way between the tire rims and the sunflowers, between Coke bottles and milkweed, among all the waste and beauty of the world—which is what she herself was" (205).

But the most compelling evidence of linkage connects the primer section devoted to Cholly Breedlove with Claudia's coda. Having rehearsed Cholly's history, the primer section asserts that it would take a jazz musician to render the essence of Cholly's being, "its final and pervading ache of freedom. Only a musician would sense, know, without even knowing that he knew, that Cholly was free. Dangerously free. Free to feel whatever he felt—fear, guilt, shame, love, grief, pity" (159). The speaker continues for some lines detailing the contours and extent of Cholly's freedom and then links the "god-like state" of freedom Cholly enjoys to both his marriage to Pauline and his rape of his daughter. In her coda to the novel, Claudia insists that, despite what he did to her, Cholly loved his daughter, but that his touch was fatal because "love is never any better than the lover," and "the love of a free man is never safe" (206). By using that epithet for Cholly and connecting it to his crime against his daughter, Claudia rehearses the argument spelled out in Cholly's primer section and makes it her own. Because we can link Claudia directly to the cat, Soaphead, and Cholly sections, it is possible to conclude that *The Bluest Eye* is entirely her composition, her achievement. Indeed, we can say that the eye in the title contains a multiple pun: it is at once the eye longed for by Pecola Breedlove, and the 'I' that authorizes the novel as a whole, the "bluest I" that witnesses Pecola's fate, Claudia MacTeer.

Primers and Voices

At the very beginning of her narration, Claudia spells out why she is composing *The Bluest Eye*; she wants to figure out what happened to the marigolds she and her sister planted in the fall of 1941: "It was a long time before my sister and I admitted to ourselves that no green was going to spring from our seeds. Once we knew, our guilt was relieved only by fights and mutual accusations about who was to blame" (5). The marigolds are, of course, metonymically and metaphorically connected to Pecola, so Claudia is asking "who is to blame" for what happened to Pecola, for her tragic fate. The end of the overture acknowledges that this is not an easy question to answer: "There is really nothing more to say—except why. But since why is difficult to handle, one must take refuge in how" (5). What follows is the first seasonal section, "Autumn."

Claudia tells us that she must begin with how in order to get at why.[7] Can we link those basic narrative questions with the shape her narrative takes? I have noted that the seasonal sections, narrated by a foregrounded first person, Claudia MacTeer, are quite different from the primer sections. She begins each section with a present tense epitomization of the season being recalled: "Nuns go by quiet as lust" (9); "My daddy's face is a study. Winter moves into it and presides there" (61); "The first twigs are thin, green, and supple" (97); "I only have to break into the tightness of a strawberry, and I see summer" (187). In each section, she then relates in detail one or two of her experiences during that season, partly from the perspective of a nine-year-old, who believes, for example, that drinking alcohol will keep her sister Frieda from being "mined". These sections have irregular margins.[8] The entire set-up—a first-person narrator, entries keyed to a particular time of year, the present tense, the perspective of the experiencing "I," and irregular margins—suggests a particular narrative form, the diary.

The diary is a "primitive" narrative form, specifically intended to recount the how of experience. A diarist is someone who records events and is at the mercy of the seasons, the times, time. The seasonal sections, or diary entries, tell us what happened at that particular time. That Claudia uses seasons and not dates to identify the entries indicates, however, that the entries are retrospective, and therefore both selective and shapely. They are selective in that each of them focuses on encounters between the MacTeer sisters and Pecola Breedlove during that fateful year; shapely insofar as each encounter involves some kind of violence—verbal, emotional, physical—perpetrated against Pecola. The seasonal sections give us, in sum, an intimate, personal view of the how of Pecola's victimization.

The novel's epigraph consists of three versions of lines from the Dick-and-Jane primer—one regular, one without capitals or punctuation, and one without capitals, punctuation, or spacing. The standard critical reading of the three versions is that the first represents the life of white families, orderly and "readable"; the second, that of the MacTeer family, confused but still readable; and the last, that of the Breedlove family, incoherent and unintelligible.[9] The primer sections of the novel use portions of that third version as "titles," lines keyed to material presented in that section. The first primer section, for example, dealing with the history and condition of the Breedlove's seedy storefront apartment, begins

HEREISTHEHOUSEITISGREENANDWH
ITEITHASAREDDOORITISVERYPRETT
YITISVERYPRETTYPRETIYPRETTYP

(33)

Subsequent sections use as epigraphs primer lines describing Dick and Jane's family, the cat, Mother, Father, the dog, and a friend of Jane's. The section following the epigraph focuses on that figure in Pecola's life but relates tales of misery that are an ironic counterpoint to the fairy-tale world depicted in the primer itself. Cumulatively the sections render in great detail the loveless "Breedlove version" of the primer text.

In terms of voice, however, the primer sections are very different from the seasonal sections. The authorial narrator here refuses to say "I," except when impersonating one of her characters. She keeps her material at a distance from herself. The Soaphead Church section, for example, begins "Once there was an old man" (164)—as if to signal her objectivity and control. From a magisterial position, she reviews and highlights the biographies of Geraldine, Pauline, Cholly, and Soaphead. Narrationally, she ranges from authorial commentary to figural presentation to dramatic monologue. She even supplies the text of Soaphead's letter to God and the script of Pecola's schizoid "dialogue" with herself. She employs a wide spectrum of novelistic techniques and practices—including justified right-hand margins—to explain what happened to the members of the Breedlove family. The conclusion would seem to be that diaries can tell us how or what, but only novels, and the narrative resources belonging to them, can tell us why.[10] Diaries render the experience of victimization; novels explain it. The absence of 'I' in the primer sections can be taken as a sign of the unwillingness of the magisterial authorial persona to call undue attention to herself. To answer the question why, the novelist must go beyond the personal and diaristic. She must become im-personal if she is to rise to true impersonation. To make sense of what happened to Pecola, Claudia MacTeer has to call upon all her talents as a novelist.

The novelistic primer sections treat extensively those in Pecola's immediate family or those who come into immediate contact with her (Geraldine, Soaphead). They dwell upon the members of the African American community who act directly on her, implying that they are responsible for her fate, because they have embraced and internalized a set of values and ideas imposed upon them by the dominant white culture.[11] Accepting an essentialist view of beauty that consigns them to invisibility and condemns them to self-hatred, they become the "instruments of [their] own oppression" (Gibson 21). Claudia very clearly makes that indictment of her race at several places in her narrative. An early example is her summary remarks about the Breedlove family:

> You looked at them and wondered why they were so ugly; you looked closely and could not find the source. Then you realized that it came from conviction, their conviction. It was as though some mysterious all-knowing master had given each one a cloak of ugliness to wear, and they had each accepted it without question. The master had said, "You are ugly people." They had looked about themselves and saw nothing to contradict the statement; saw, in fact, support for it leaning at them from every billboard, every movie, every glance. "Yes," they had said. "You are right."
>
> (39)[12]

Leveling the same charge against Pecola's classmates (65), Maureen Peal (73-74), Geraldine (83-87), Pauline (122), Soaphead (168), and others, Claudia suggests that almost no one in the black community is able to resist that particular interpellation by the dominant white culture.

This near-total capitulation to white values, in combination with Pecola's awful victimization, leads many critics to see the novel as terribly bleak—in the words of Demetrakopoulos, "one of the darkest works I have ever read" (31). Commenting in the afterword on Claudia's conspiratorial opening words—"Quiet as it's kept"—Morrison herself says that the novel involves the "disclosure of secrets," that "something grim is about to be divulged," namely "a terrible story about things one would rather not know anything about" (212, 213). Dittmar worries that "the microcosm Morrison locates in her Ohio town includes few venues for anger directed beyond the black community and almost no potential for regeneration within it," and concludes that the novel "does indeed seem overwhelmingly pessimistic, given its relentless piling up of abuses and betrayals" (140). Byerman argues that the "ideological hegemony of whiteness is simply too overwhelming to be successfully resisted" and specifies that even "Claudia, the strongest character in the book, cannot defy the myth" (449, 450).[13]

But if Claudia is the single narrator and the narrative is entirely her composition, then she has indeed resisted the power of "white mythology."[14] In the first seasonal section, Claudia relates how, when she was a little girl, she dismembered white dolls to find out what made them beautiful and therefore lovable—to discover the essence of Beauty. All she found was sawdust (21). The text composed by the adult Claudia, *The Bluest Eye,* carries on the same discovery procedure on a grander scale; it undertakes the deconstruction and demystification of the ideology that makes those dolls beautiful: "And all the time we knew that Maureen Peal was not the enemy and not worthy of such intense hatred. The *Thing* to fear was the *Thing* that made her beautiful, and not us" (74, emphasis in original).

In that respect, Claudia's use of the Dick-and-Jane primer as master text represents a brilliant choice, for a primer is a basic tool of ideological indoctrination; it introduces readers to and inculcates the correct values,[15] As one critic notes, "the act of learning to read or write means exposure to the values of the culture from which the reading material emanates. [. . .] One cannot simply learn to read without being subjected to the values engraved in the text" (Gibson 20). The same logic adheres, of course, to reading the text that is *The Bluest Eye*; one cannot read it without being subjected to Claudia's discovery of "the unreality or emptiness behind the facade of [the white] construction of femininity" (Munafo 8). In that respect, her text constitutes a counterprimer, designed "to counteract the universal love of white baby dolls, Shirley Temples, and Maureen Peals" (*The Bluest Eye* 190); it critiques and thus dismembers the values and iconography fostering that love.

Claudia suggests in the coda that her narrative originates partly in guilt and betrayal, that she and the other members of the black community "assassinated" Pecola by scapegoating her or by turning their backs on her. Her narrative tries to make up for that betrayal. If we compare the lines from the primer mastertext to the epigraphs for the primer sections, we discover that a silencing has taken place; there is no primer section for the following epitext lines: "See Jane. She has a red dress. She wants to play. Who will play with Jane?" Jane (Pecola) has been effectively eliminated, erased, silenced. The eye is proverbially the window to the soul, to all that is unique, irreplaceable, essential, but Pecola's eye/I is not her own; it belongs to the dominant culture. As a result, she identifies herself with a lack, with what she has not. She is, in effect, self-less and invisible. As one critic notes, "Morrison's novel contains repeated instances of Pecola's negation as other characters refuse to see her" (Miner 187). Because she cannot speak for or defend herself, she is literally and figuratively silenced almost throughout the text, condemned to an "imitation of life." As Morrison suggests in her afterword, the novel is built on a "silence at its center: the void that is Pecola's 'unbeing'" (215).

The Bluest Eye is itself the text that counterpoints the missing primer lines. It makes "Jane" visible and gives her a kind of being; it is the attempt of Claudia/Morrison to make the silence speak, to give voice to the voiceless. As a child, Claudia herself is silenced: she notes that adults do not talk to children; they give them orders (10). Growing up means acquiring a voice, joining the world of discourse, something that Pecola is prohibited from doing. In a sense, then, Claudia makes up for her betrayal by lending her voice to Pecola, by speaking her through her story. In so doing, by giving a present to the absent, Claudia makes the absent present.

That line of argument recalls a basic idea that the narrative calls into question, the idea that beauty is an essence, that it is present to itself (Walther 777). Morrison's novel not only critiques that idea, but it also transvalues it. Claudia invites readers to imagine the very real beauty of Pecola's unborn baby, with "its head covered with great O's of wool, the black face holding, like nickels, two clean black eyes, the flared nose, kissing-thick lips, and the living, breathing silk of black skin" (190). As Munafo notes, "[t]his affirming vision of Pecola's unborn baby asserts black presence and reinscribes blackness as beautiful" (9). More important, Claudia insists over and over that we acknowledge Pecola's own beauty. At one point Claudia notes the pleasure that Pecola's smile gives her (106); elsewhere she frets that Pecola would never know her own beauty (46-47).[16] Claudia's narrative exists, the coda informs us, to reveal "all the waste and beauty of the world—which is what she [Pecola] herself was. All of our waste which we dumped on her and which she absorbed. And all of our beauty, which was hers first and which she gave to us" (205). *The Bluest Eye* renders both the waste and the beauty.

Notes

1. I am referring, in traditional terms, to point of view. I use Stanzel's nomenclature because it is more exact

2. Insofar as the implied author assumes the right to insert this kind of commentary throughout the primer sections, we can say that their narrational dominant is authorial.

3. Klotman notes in passing that Claudia is the sole narrator, but she does not develop that line of argument (123-24). Smith claims that Claudia narrates "the preschool primer with which the novel begins," but that an "ostensibly omniscient narrator" recounts the subsequent primer sections (124). She does not explain why Claudia narrates one but not the others. Harris begins by suggesting that Claudia is the single narrator: "As storyteller, it is Claudia's job to shape the past so that it provides coherent meaning for the present audience" (16); "[a]s multivoiced narrator, Claudia must make sense of what has ravaged the community" (22). Later, she retreats from that position, referring casually to "the parts of the novel Claudia narrates" (24) and saying that Claudia "occasionally gets help from some of the members of her community" (23).

4. Claudia's memory of being ill in the Autumn section: "But was it really like that? As painful as I remember? Only mildly. Or rather, it was a productive and fructifying pain. Love, thick and dark as Alaga syrup, eased up into that cracked window. I could smell it—taste it—sweet, musty, with an edge of wintergreen in its base—everywhere in the house. [. . .] And in the night, when my coughing was dry and tough, feet padded into the room, hands repinned the flannel, readjusted the quilt, and rested a moment on my forehead. So when I think of autumn, I think of somebody with hands who does not want me to die" (12).

5. Klotman says that "education by school and society is the dominant theme of *The Bluest Eye*" (123).

6. I could find only one use of first-person pronominal forms in the primer sections (other than in direct discourse). It occurs in the Pauline section: "So she became, and her process of becoming was like most of ours" (126). The speaker is also clearly present in the following passage, which serves to date her enunciation in a way similar to Claudia's: "So fluid has the population in that area been, that probably no one remembers longer, longer ago, before the time of the gypsies and the time of the teenagers when the Breedloves lived there, nestled together in the storefront" (34). Like Claudia, the speaker remembers that time very well.

7. Smith argues that both Claudia and the novel dodge the question why: "*The Bluest Eye* does not undertake to explain, for example, why black Americans aspire to an unattainable standard of beauty; why they displace their self-hatred onto a communal scapegoat; how Pecola's fate might have been avoided" (124). I argue that Claudia and her book answer all these questions.

8. Dittmar is the only critic who notes the uneven margins, connecting them with orality, but not with a specific narrative form: "While such margins may serve to suggest the text's informal, possibly spoken origins, the mere use of this unusual device is attention-getting, especially given its recurrent suspension and re-introduction" (141).

9. See Ogunyemi 112, Klotman 123, Wong 472. Wong argues that the primer lines depict each character as "maintain(ing) himself in a self-enclosed unity" and thus enact "the very conditions of alienated self-containment which underlie [white bourgeois] values" (471, 472).

10. Structurally, the number of primer sections increases in the latter half of the novel, as if, having made the how of Pecola's victimization clear, the narrative chooses to focus on the why.

11. The argument that "by acting in 'Bad Faith,' Pecola remains responsible, in the final analysis, for what happens to her" (Samuels and Hudson-Weems 15) is, therefore, flat-out wrong.

12. In her afterword, Morrison warns specifically "against the damaging internalization of assumptions of immutable inferiority originating in an outside gaze" (210). See, in this regard, Guerrero; and Miner, 184-88.

13. Cf. Dittmar: "Individual characters may not participate in [positive] change; certainly Claudia, for all her adult retrospection, provides no empowerment" (142).

14. Cf. Rosenberg: "Claudia's ability to survive intact and to consolidate an identity derives from her vigorous opposition to the colorist attitudes of her community" (440); and Munafo: "Claudia says no [to the idea of whiteness], and in so doing she retains a sense of self-affirmation" (9).

15. Powell also argues that the primer is "a highly significant beginning," but for a different reason: "it points to the fact that all Afro-American writers have, willingly or not, been forced to begin with the Master's language. The Dick-and-Jane reader comes to symbolize the institutionalized ethnocentrism of the white logos" (749).

16. In her afterword, Morrison describes her response to the classmate who wanted blue eyes as follows: "although I had certainly used the word 'beautiful,' I had never experienced its shock—the force of which was equaled by the knowledge that no one else recognized it, not even, or especially, the one who possessed it" (209).

Works Cited

Byerman, Keith E. "Intense Behaviors: The Use of the Grotesque in *The Bluest Eye* and *Eva's Man*." *College Language Association Journal* 25.4 (June 1982): 447-57.

Demetrakopoulos, Stephanie A. "Bleak Beginnings: *The Bluest Eye*." Holloway and Demetrakopoulos 31-36.

Dittmar, Linda. "'Will the Circle Be Unbroken?': The Politics of Form in *The Bluest Eye*." *Novel: A Forum on Fiction* 23.2 (Winter 1990): 137-55.

Gibson, Donald. "Text and Countertext in Toni Morrison's *The Bluest Eye*." *LIT: Literature, Interpretation, Theory* 1.1-2 (1989): 19-32.

Guerrero, Edward. "Tracking 'The Look' in the Novels of Toni Morrison." *Black American Literature Forum* 24.4 (Winter 1990): 761-73.

Harris, Trudier. *Fiction and Folklore: The Novels of Toni Morrison*. Knoxville: U of Tennessee P, 1991.

Holloway, Karla F. C. "The Language and Music of Survival." Holloway and Demetrakopoulos 37-47.

Holloway, Karla E. C. and Stephanie A. Demetrakopoulos. *New Dimensions of Spirituality: A Biracial and Bicultural Reading of the Novels of Toni Morrison*. Contributions in Women's Studies, Number 84. New York: Greenwood, 1987.

Klotman, Phyllis. "Dick-and-Jane and the Shirley Temple Sensibility in *The Bluest Eye*." *Black-American Literature Forum* 13.4 (Winter 1979): 123-25.

Miner, Madonne M. "Lady No Longer Sings the Blues: Rape, Madness, and Silence in *The Bluest Eye*." *Conjuring: Black Women, Fiction, and Literary Tradition*. Ed. Marjorie Pryse and Hortense J. Spillers. Bloomington: Indiana UP, 1985. 176-91.

Morrison, Toni. *The Bluest Eye*. 1970; rpt. New York: Plume, 1994.

Munafo, Giavanna. "'No Sign of Life': Marble-Blue Eyes and Lakefront Houses in *The Bluest Eye*." *LIT: Literature, Interpretation, Theory* 6.1-2 (1995): 1-19.

Ogunyemi, Chikwenye Okonjo. "Order and Disorder in Toni Morrison's *The Bluest Eye*." *Critique* 19.1 (1977): 112-20.

Powell, Timothy B. "Toni Morrison: The Struggle to Depict the Black Figure on the White Page." *Black American Literature Forum* 24.4 (Winter 1990): 747-60.

Rosenberg, Ruth. "Seeds in Hard Ground: Black Girlhood in *The Bluest Eye*." *Black American Literature Forum* 21.4 (Winter 1987): 435-45.

Samuels, Wilfred D. and Clenora Hudson-Weems. *Toni Morrison*. Boston: Twayne, 1990.

Smith, Valerie. *Self-Discovery and Authority in Afro-American Narrative*. Cambridge: Harvard UP, 1987.

Stanzel, Franz. *Narrative Situations in the Novel: "Tom Jones," "Moby Dick," "The Ambassadors," "Ulysses."* Trans. James P. Pusack. Bloomington: Indiana UP, 1971.

Walther, Malin LaVon. "Out of Sight: Toni Morrison's Revision of Beauty." *Black American Literature Forum* 24.4 (Winter 1990): 775-89.

Wong, Shelley. "Transgression as Poesis in *The Bluest Eye*." *Callaloo* 13 (1990): 471-81.

FURTHER READING

Criticism

Alwes, Karla. "'The Evil of Fulfillment': Women and Violence in *The Bluest Eye*." In *Women and Violence in Literature: An Essay Collection,* edited by Katherine Anne Ackley, pp. 89-104. New York: Garland Publishing, 1990.

> Alwes equates the violence in *The Bluest Eye* with self-hatred caused by Pauline's and Pecola's illusions about white American society and their places in it.

Bloom, Harold, ed. *Toni Morrison's "The Bluest Eye": Modern Critical Interpretations*. Philadelphia: Chelsea House, 1999, 270 p.

> Bloom presents previously published criticism of *The Bluest Eye,* offering various perspectives on the diverse issues raised by the novel.

Cormier-Hamilton, Patrice. "Black Naturalism and Toni Morrison: The Journey Away from Self-Love in *The Bluest Eye*." *MELUS* 19, no. 4 (winter 1994): 109-27.

> Cormier-Hamilton examines the influence of environment on the characters of *The Bluest Eye* from a "black naturalistic" perspective, highlighting differences between traditional uses of naturalism and African American approaches to naturalism, which are shown to rely upon a protagonist's struggles with self-awareness and self-realization.

Dittmar, Linda. "'Will the Circle Be Unbroken?': The Politics of Form in *The Bluest Eye*." *Novel: A Forum on Fiction* 23, no. 2 (winter 1990): 137-55.

> Dittmar discusses the formal aspects of *The Bluest Eye* as a function of ideology, specifically highlighting the novel's displacement of "social pathology and failed human values into the black community."

Doughty, Peter. "A Fiction for the Tribe: Toni Morrison's *The Bluest Eye*." In *The New American Writing: Essays on American Literature since 1970,* edited by Graham Clarke, pp. 29-50. New York: St. Martin's Press, 1990.

Doughty studies *The Bluest Eye* within the context of the development of black women's writing since the 1970s when African American writers began revising their history with the materials and narrative traditions of their own culture.

Earle, Kathryn. "Teaching Controversy: *The Bluest Eye* in the Multicultural Classroom." In *Approaches to Teaching the Novels of Toni Morrison,* edited by Nellie Y. McKay and Kathryn Earle, pp. 27-33. New York: Modern Language Association of America, 1997.

Earle advises instructors teaching *The Bluest Eye* in multicultural settings, concerning not only the novel's racial issues but also its sexual component.

Heinze, Denise. *The Dilemma of "Double-Consciousness" in the Novels of Toni Morrison.* Athens: University of Georgia Press, 1993, 198 p.

Heinze analyzes Morrison's oeuvre through 1992 with sections devoted to *The Bluest Eye* concerning such themes as aesthetics, familial relations, social status, and metaphysics.

McKay, Nellie Y., and Kathryn Earle, eds. *Approaches to Teaching the Novels of Toni Morrison.* New York: Modern Language Association of America, 1997, 179 p.

McKay and Earle present essays that outline effective strategies to teach each of Morrison's novels, including *The Bluest Eye,* addressing such topics as racial and identity issues raised by her works, literary and historical contexts, stylistic and narrative techniques, and theoretical approaches for classroom situations.

Moses, Cat. "The Blues Aesthetic in Toni Morrison's *The Bluest Eye.*" *African American Review* 33, no. 4 (winter 1999): 623-36.

Moses identifies the themes and rhetorical structures of *The Bluest Eye* with the conventions of blues music, discerning a female subjectivity in the character of Claudia that relates to the African American oral tradition of "testimony" in the blues aesthetic.

Munafo, Giavanna. "'No Sign of Life'—Marble-Blue Eyes and Lakefront Houses in *The Bluest Eye.*" *LIT: Literature Interpretation Theory* 6, nos. 1-2 (April 1995): 1-19.

Munafo illuminates the racial, gender, and economic implications of Morrison's deconstruction of "whiteness" in *The Bluest Eye.*

Portales, Marco. "Toni Morrison's *The Bluest Eye*: Shirley Temple and Cholly." *Centennial Review* 30, no. 4 (fall 1986): 496-506.

Portales examines Morrison's characterizations of Pecola and Cholly in *The Bluest Eye,* focusing on the cultural forces that shape their respective identities.

Wren, James A. "Morrison's *The Bluest Eye.*" *Explicator* 55, no. 3 (spring 1997): 172-76.

Wren presents a medical autopsy of Aunt Jenny's death in *The Bluest Eye* in light of folk remedies.

Yancy, George. "The Black Self within a Semiotic Space of Whiteness: Reflections on the Racial Deformation of Pecola Breedlove in Toni Morrison's *The Bluest Eye.*" *CLA Journal* 43, no. 3 (March 2000): 299-319.

Yancy explores the symbolic values of "whiteness" as it functions within the life of Pecola in *The Bluest Eye,* focusing on both the character's psychological and bodily "ugliness" and the inherent distortions of "whiteness" itself.

Additional coverage of Morrison's life and career is contained in the following sources published by the Gale Group: *African American Writers,* Eds. 1, 2; *American Writers Supplement,* Vol. 3; *Authors and Artists for Young Adults,* Vols. 1, 22; *Beacham's Encyclopedia of Popular Fiction: Biography and Resources,* Vol. 2; *Black Literature Criticism,* Vol. 3; *Black Writers,* Eds. 2, 3; *Concise Dictionary of Literary Biography, 1968-1988; Contemporary Authors,* Vols. 29-32R; *Contemporary Authors New Revision Series,* Vols. 27, 42, 67; *Contemporary Literary Criticism,* Vols. 4, 10, 22, 55, 81, 87; *Contemporary Novelists; Contemporary Popular Writers; Dictionary of Literary Biography,* Vols. 6, 33, 143; *Dictionary of Literary Biography Yearbook,* 1981; *DISCovering Authors; DISCovering Authors: British Edition; DISCovering Authors: Canadian Edition; DISCovering Authors Modules: Most-studied, Multicultural, Novelists, Popular Fiction and Genre Authors; DISCovering Authors 3.0; Exploring Novels; Feminist Writers; Literature and Its Times,* Vols. 2, 4; *Literature Resource Center; Major 20th-Century Writers,* Eds. 1, 2; *Modern American Women Writers; Novels for Students,* Vols. 1, 6, 8, 14; *Reference Guide to American Literature,* Ed. 4; *St. James Guide to Young Adult Writers; Something about the Author,* Vol. 57; *Short Stories for Students,* Vol. 5; and *Twentieth Century Romance and Historical Writers.*

How to Use This Index

The main references

> Calvino, Italo
> 1923-1985 .... CLC 5, 8, 11, 22, 33, 39,
> 73; SSC 3, 48

list all author entries in the following Gale Literary Criticism series:

AAL = *Asian American Literature*
BG = *The Beat Generation: A Gale Critical Companion*
BLC = *Black Literature Criticism*
BLCS = *Black Literature Criticism Supplement*
CLC = *Contemporary Literary Criticism*
CLR = *Children's Literature Review*
CMLC = *Classical and Medieval Literature Criticism*
DC = *Drama Criticism*
HLC = *Hispanic Literature Criticism*
HLCS = *Hispanic Literature Criticism Supplement*
HR = *Harlem Renaissance: A Gale Critical Companion*
LC = *Literature Criticism from 1400 to 1800*
NCLC = *Nineteenth-Century Literature Criticism*
NNAL = *Native North American Literature*
PC = *Poetry Criticism*
SSC = *Short Story Criticism*
TCLC = *Twentieth-Century Literary Criticism*
WLC = *World Literature Criticism, 1500 to the Present*
WLCS = *World Literature Criticism Supplement*

The cross-references

> See also CA 85-88, 116; CANR 23, 61;
> DAM NOV; DLB 196; EW 13; MTCW 1, 2;
> RGSF 2; RGWL 2; SFW 4; SSFS 12

list all author entries in the following Gale biographical and literary sources:

AAYA = *Authors & Artists for Young Adults*
AFAW = *African American Writers*
AFW = *African Writers*
AITN = *Authors in the News*
AMW = *American Writers*
AMWR = *American Writers Retrospective Supplement*
AMWS = *American Writers Supplement*
ANW = *American Nature Writers*
AW = *Ancient Writers*
BEST = *Bestsellers*
BPFB = *Beacham's Encyclopedia of Popular Fiction: Biography and Resources*
BRW = *British Writers*
BRWS = *British Writers Supplement*
BW = *Black Writers*
BYA = *Beacham's Guide to Literature for Young Adults*
CA = *Contemporary Authors*
CAAS = *Contemporary Authors Autobiography Series*
CABS = *Contemporary Authors Bibliographical Series*
CAD = *Contemporary American Dramatists*
CANR = *Contemporary Authors New Revision Series*
CAP = *Contemporary Authors Permanent Series*
CBD = *Contemporary British Dramatists*
CCA = *Contemporary Canadian Authors*
CD = *Contemporary Dramatists*
CDALB = *Concise Dictionary of American Literary Biography*
CDALBS = *Concise Dictionary of American Literary Biography Supplement*
CDBLB = *Concise Dictionary of British Literary Biography*

CMW = *St. James Guide to Crime & Mystery Writers*
CN = *Contemporary Novelists*
CP = *Contemporary Poets*
CPW = *Contemporary Popular Writers*
CSW = *Contemporary Southern Writers*
CWD = *Contemporary Women Dramatists*
CWP = *Contemporary Women Poets*
CWRI = *St. James Guide to Children's Writers*
CWW = *Contemporary World Writers*
DA = *DISCovering Authors*
DA3 = *DISCovering Authors 3.0*
DAB = *DISCovering Authors: British Edition*
DAC = *DISCovering Authors: Canadian Edition*
DAM = *DISCovering Authors: Modules*
   DRAM: *Dramatists Module;* ***MST:*** *Most-studied Authors Module;*
   MULT: *Multicultural Authors Module;* ***NOV:*** *Novelists Module;*
   POET: *Poets Module;* ***POP:*** *Popular Fiction and Genre Authors Module*
DFS = *Drama for Students*
DLB = *Dictionary of Literary Biography*
DLBD = *Dictionary of Literary Biography Documentary Series*
DLBY = *Dictionary of Literary Biography Yearbook*
DNFS = *Literature of Developing Nations for Students*
EFS = *Epics for Students*
EXPN = *Exploring Novels*
EXPP = *Exploring Poetry*
EXPS = *Exploring Short Stories*
EW = *European Writers*
FANT = *St. James Guide to Fantasy Writers*
FW = *Feminist Writers*
GFL = *Guide to French Literature,* Beginnings to 1789, 1798 to the Present
GLL = *Gay and Lesbian Literature*
HGG = *St. James Guide to Horror, Ghost & Gothic Writers*
HW = *Hispanic Writers*
IDFW = *International Dictionary of Films and Filmmakers: Writers and Production Artists*
IDTP = *International Dictionary of Theatre: Playwrights*
LAIT = *Literature and Its Times*
LAW = *Latin American Writers*
JRDA = *Junior DISCovering Authors*
MAICYA = *Major Authors and Illustrators for Children and Young Adults*
MAICYAS = *Major Authors and Illustrators for Children and Young Adults Supplement*
MAWW = *Modern American Women Writers*
MJW = *Modern Japanese Writers*
MTCW = *Major 20th-Century Writers*
NCFS = *Nonfiction Classics for Students*
NFS = *Novels for Students*
PAB = *Poets: American and British*
PFS = *Poetry for Students*
RGAL = *Reference Guide to American Literature*
RGEL = *Reference Guide to English Literature*
RGSF = *Reference Guide to Short Fiction*
RGWL = *Reference Guide to World Literature*
RHW = *Twentieth-Century Romance and Historical Writers*
SAAS = *Something about the Author Autobiography Series*
SATA = *Something about the Author*
SFW = *St. James Guide to Science Fiction Writers*
SSFS = *Short Stories for Students*
TCWW = *Twentieth-Century Western Writers*
WLIT = *World Literature and Its Times*
WP = *World Poets*
YABC = *Yesterday's Authors of Books for Children*
YAW = *St. James Guide to Young Adult Writers*

Literary Criticism Series
Cumulative Author Index

20/1631
See Upward, Allen

A/C Cross
See Lawrence, T(homas) E(dward)

Abasiyanik, Sait Faik 1906-1954
See Sait Faik
See also CA 123

Abbey, Edward 1927-1989 .... **CLC 36, 59**
See also ANW; CA 45-48; 128; CANR 2, 41; DA3; DLB 256, 275; MTCW 2; TCWW 2

Abbott, Lee K(ittredge) 1947- .... **CLC 48**
See also CA 124; CANR 51, 101; DLB 130

Abe, Kobo 1924-1993 ..... **CLC 8, 22, 53, 81; SSC 61; TCLC 131**
See also CA 65-68; 140; CANR 24, 60; DAM NOV; DFS 14; DLB 182; EWL 3; MJW; MTCW 1, 2; RGWL 3; SFW 4

Abe Kobo
See Abe, Kobo

Abelard, Peter c. 1079-c. 1142 ..... **CMLC 11**
See also DLB 115, 208

Abell, Kjeld 1901-1961 .... **CLC 15**
See also CA 191; 111; DLB 214; EWL 3

Abish, Walter 1931- .... **CLC 22; SSC 44**
See also CA 101; CANR 37, 114; CN 7; DLB 130, 227

Abrahams, Peter (Henry) 1919- .... **CLC 4**
See also AFW; BW 1; CA 57-60; CANR 26; CDWLB 3; CN 7; DLB 117, 225; EWL 3; MTCW 1, 2; RGEL 2; WLIT 2

Abrams, M(eyer) H(oward) 1912- .. **CLC 24**
See also CA 57-60; CANR 13, 33; DLB 67

Abse, Dannie 1923- .... **CLC 7, 29; PC 41**
See also CA 53-56; CAAS 1; CANR 4, 46, 74; CBD; CP 7; DAB; DAM POET; DLB 27, 245; MTCW 1

Abutsu 1222(?)-1283 .... **CMLC 46**
See Abutsu-ni

Abutsu-ni
See Abutsu
See also DLB 203

Achebe, (Albert) Chinua(lumogu) 1930-
. **BLC 1; CLC 1, 3, 5, 7, 11, 26, 51, 75, 127, 152; WLC**
See also AAYA 15; AFW; BPFB 1; BW 2, 3; CA 1-4R; CANR 6, 26, 47; CDWLB 3; CLR 20; CN 7; CP 7; CWRI 5; DA; DA3; DAB; DAC; DAM MST, MULT, NOV; DLB 117; DNFS 1; EWL 3; EXPN; EXPS; LAIT 2; MAICYA 1, 2; MTCW 1, 2; NFS 2; RGEL 2; RGSF 2; SATA 38, 40; SATA-Brief 38; SSFS 3, 13; TWA; WLIT 2

Acker, Kathy 1948-1997 .... **CLC 45, 111**
See also AMWS 12; CA 117; 122; 162; CANR 55; CN 7

Ackroyd, Peter 1949- .... **CLC 34, 52, 140**
See also BRWS 6; CA 123; 127; CANR 51, 74, 99; CN 7; DLB 155, 231; HGG; INT 127; MTCW 1; RHW; SUFW 2

Acorn, Milton 1923-1986 .... **CLC 15**
See also CA 103; CCA 1; DAC; DLB 53; INT 103

Adamov, Arthur 1908-1970 .... **CLC 4, 25**
See also CA 17-18; 25-28R; CAP 2; DAM DRAM; EWL 3; GFL 1789 to the Present; MTCW 1; RGWL 2, 3

Adams, Alice (Boyd) 1926-1999 . **CLC 6, 13, 46; SSC 24**
See also CA 81-84; 179; CANR 26, 53, 75, 88; CN 7; CSW; DLB 234; DLBY 1986; INT CANR-26; MTCW 1, 2; SSFS 14

Adams, Andy 1859-1935 .... **TCLC 56**
See also TCWW 2; YABC 1

Adams, (Henry) Brooks 1848-1927
.... **TCLC 80**
See also CA 123; 193; DLB 47

Adams, Douglas (Noel) 1952-2001 . **CLC 27, 60**
See also AAYA 4, 33; BEST 89:3; BYA 14; CA 106; 197; CANR 34, 64; CPW; DA3; DAM POP; DLB 261; DLBY 1983; JRDA; MTCW 1; NFS 7; SATA 116; SATA-Obit 128; SFW 4

Adams, Francis 1862-1893 .... **NCLC 33**

Adams, Henry (Brooks) 1838-1918
.... **TCLC 4, 52**
See also AMW; CA 104; 133; CANR 77; DA; DAB; DAC; DAM MST; DLB 12, 47, 189; EWL 3; MTCW 1; NCFS 1; RGAL 4; TUS

Adams, John 1735-1826 .... **NCLC 106**
See also DLB 31, 183

Adams, Richard (George) 1920- .. **CLC 4, 5, 18**
See also AAYA 16; AITN 1, 2; BPFB 1; BYA 5; CA 49-52; CANR 3, 35; CLR 20; CN 7; DAM NOV; DLB 261; FANT; JRDA; LAIT 5; MAICYA 1, 2; MTCW 1, 2; NFS 11; SATA 7, 69; YAW

Adamson, Joy(-Friederike Victoria)
1910-1980 .... **CLC 17**
See also CA 69-72; 93-96; CANR 22; MTCW 1; SATA 11; SATA-Obit 22

Adcock, Fleur 1934- .... **CLC 41**
See also CA 25-28R, 182; CAAE 182; CAAS 23; CANR 11, 34, 69, 101; CP 7; CWP; DLB 40; FW

Addams, Charles (Samuel) 1912-1988
.... **CLC 30**
See also CA 61-64; 126; CANR 12, 79

Addams, Jane 1860-1935 .... **TCLC 76**
See also AMWS 1; FW

Addams, (Laura) Jane 1860-1935
.... **TCLC 76**
See also AMWS 1; CA 194; FW

Addison, Joseph 1672-1719 .... **LC 18**
See also BRW 3; CDBLB 1660-1789; DLB 101; RGEL 2; WLIT 3

Adler, Alfred (F.) 1870-1937 .... **TCLC 61**
See also CA 119; 159

Adler, C(arole) S(chwerdtfeger) 1932-
.... **CLC 35**
See also AAYA 4, 41; CA 89-92; CANR 19, 40, 101; CLR 78; JRDA; MAICYA 1, 2; SAAS 15; SATA 26, 63, 102, 126; YAW

Adler, Renata 1938- .... **CLC 8, 31**
See also CA 49-52; CANR 95; CN 7; MTCW 1

Adorno, Theodor W(iesengrund) 1903-1969
.... **TCLC 111**
See also CA 89-92; 25-28R; CANR 89; DLB 242; EWL 3

Ady, Endre 1877-1919 .... **TCLC 11**
See also CA 107; CDWLB 4; DLB 215; EW 9; EWL 3

A.E. .... **TCLC 3, 10**
See Russell, George William
See also DLB 19

Aelfric c. 955-c. 1010 .... **CMLC 46**
See also DLB 146

Aeschines c. 390B.C.-c. 320B.C. .. **CMLC 47**
See also DLB 176

Aeschylus 525(?)B.C.-456(?)B.C. . **CMLC 11, 51; DC 8; WLCS**
See also AW 1; CDWLB 1; DA; DAB; DAC; DAM DRAM, MST; DFS 5, 10; DLB 176; LMFS 1; RGWL 2, 3; TWA

Aesop 620(?)B.C.-560(?)B.C. .... **CMLC 24**
See also CLR 14; MAICYA 1, 2; SATA 64

Affable Hawk
See MacCarthy, Sir (Charles Otto) Desmond

Africa, Ben
See Bosman, Herman Charles

Afton, Effie
See Harper, Frances Ellen Watkins

Agapida, Fray Antonio
See Irving, Washington

Agee, James (Rufus) 1909-1955 .... **TCLC 1, 19**
See also AAYA 44; AITN 1; AMW; CA 108; 148; CDALB 1941-1968; DAM NOV; DLB 2, 26, 152; DLBY 1989; EWL 3; LAIT 3; MTCW 1; RGAL 4; TUS

Aghill, Gordon
See Silverberg, Robert

Agnon, S(hmuel) Y(osef Halevi) 1888-1970
.... **CLC 4, 8, 14; SSC 30**
See also CA 17-18; 25-28R; CANR 60, 102; CAP 2; EWL 3; MTCW 1, 2; RGSF 2; RGWL 2, 3

Agrippa von Nettesheim, Henry Cornelius
1486-1535 .... **LC 27**

Aguilera Malta, Demetrio 1909-1981
.... **HLCS 1**
See also CA 111; 124; CANR 87; DAM MULT, NOV; DLB 145; EWL 3; HW 1; RGWL 3

Agustini, Delmira 1886-1914 .... **HLCS 1**
See also CA 166; HW 1, 2; LAW

Aherne, Owen
See Cassill, R(onald) V(erlin)

Ai 1947- .... **CLC 4, 14, 69**
See also CA 85-88; CAAS 13; CANR 70; DLB 120; PFS 16

Aickman, Robert (Fordyce) 1914-1981
.... **CLC 57**
See also CA 5-8R; CANR 3, 72, 100; DLB 261; HGG; SUFW 1, 2

Aidoo, (Christina) Ama Ata 1942- .... **BLCS**
See also AFW; BW 1; CA 101; CANR 62; CD 5; CDWLB 3; CN 7; CWD; CWP; DLB 117; DNFS 1, 2; EWL 3; FW; WLIT 2

Aiken, Conrad (Potter) 1889-1973 .. **CLC 1, 3, 5, 10, 52; PC 26; SSC 9**
See also AMW; CA 5-8R; 45-48; CANR 4, 60; CDALB 1929-1941; DAM NOV, POET; DLB 9, 45, 102; EWL 3; EXPS; HGG; MTCW 1, 2; RGAL 4; RGSF 2; SATA 3, 30; SSFS 8; TUS

Aiken, Joan (Delano) 1924- .... **CLC 35**
See also AAYA 1, 25; CA 9-12R, 182; CAAE 182; CANR 4, 23, 34, 64; CLR 1, 19; DLB 161; FANT; HGG; JRDA; MAICYA 1, 2; MTCW 1; RHW; SAAS 1; SATA 2, 30, 73; SATA-Essay 109; SUFW 2; WYA; YAW

Ainsworth, William Harrison 1805-1882
.... **NCLC 13**
See also DLB 21; HGG; RGEL 2; SATA 24; SUFW 1

Aitmatov, Chingiz (Torekulovich) 1928-
.... **CLC 71**
See Aytmatov, Chingiz
See also CA 103; CANR 38; MTCW 1; RGSF 2; SATA 56

Akers, Floyd
See Baum, L(yman) Frank

Akhmadulina, Bella Akhatovna 1937-
.... **CLC 53; PC 43**
See also CA 65-68; CWP; CWW 2; DAM POET; EWL 3

Akhmatova, Anna 1888-1966 ... **CLC 11, 25, 64, 126; PC 2**
See also CA 19-20; 25-28R; CANR 35; CAP 1; DA3; DAM POET; EW 10; EWL 3; MTCW 1, 2; RGWL 2, 3

Aksakov, Sergei Timofeyvich 1791-1859
.... **NCLC 2**
See also DLB 198

Aksenov, Vassily
See Aksyonov, Vassily (Pavlovich)

Akst, Daniel 1956- .... **CLC 109**
See also CA 161; CANR 110

Aksyonov, Vassily (Pavlovich) 1932-
.... **CLC 22, 37, 101**
See also CA 53-56; CANR 12, 48, 77; CWW 2; EWL 3

Akutagawa Ryunosuke 1892-1927 .. **SSC 44; TCLC 16**
See also CA 117; 154; DLB 180; EWL 3; MJW; RGSF 2; RGWL 2, 3

Alain 1868-1951 .... **TCLC 41**
See also CA 163; EWL 3; GFL 1789 to the Present

Alain de Lille c. 1116-c. 1203 ...... **CMLC 53**
See also DLB 208

Alain-Fournier .... **TCLC 6**
See Fournier, Henri-Alban
See also DLB 65; EWL 3; GFL 1789 to the Present; RGWL 2, 3

Al-Amin, Jamil Abdullah 1943- .... **BLC 1**
See also BW 1, 3; CA 112; 125; CANR 82; DAM MULT

Alanus de Insluis
See Alain de Lille

Alarcon, Pedro Antonio de 1833-1891
.... **NCLC 1**

Alas (y Urena), Leopoldo (Enrique Garcia) 1852-1901 .... **TCLC 29**
See also CA 113; 131; HW 1; RGSF 2

Albee, Edward (Franklin III) 1928-
..... **CLC 1, 2, 3, 5, 9, 11, 13, 25, 53, 86, 113; DC 11; WLC**
See also AITN 1; AMW; CA 5-8R; CABS 3; CAD; CANR 8, 54, 74; CD 5; CDALB 1941-1968; DA; DA3; DAB; DAC; DAM DRAM, MST; DFS 2, 3, 8, 10, 13, 14; DLB 7, 266; EWL 3; INT CANR-8; LAIT 4; LMFS 2; MTCW 1, 2; RGAL 4; TUS

Alberti, Rafael 1902-1999 .... **CLC 7**
See also CA 85-88; 185; CANR 81; DLB 108; EWL 3; HW 2; RGWL 2, 3

Albert the Great 1193(?)-1280 ...... **CMLC 16**
See also DLB 115

Alcala-Galiano, Juan Valera y
See Valera y Alcala-Galiano, Juan

Alcayaga, Lucila Godoy
See Godoy Alcayaga, Lucila

Alcott, Amos Bronson 1799-1888 ... **NCLC 1**
See also DLB 1, 223

Alcott, Louisa May 1832-1888 .... **NCLC 6, 58, 83; SSC 27; WLC**
See also AAYA 20; AMWS 1; BPFB 1; BYA 2; CDALB 1865-1917; CLR 1, 38; DA; DA3; DAB; DAC; DAM MST, NOV; DLB 1, 42, 79, 223, 239, 242; DLBD 14; FW; JRDA; LAIT 2; MAICYA 1, 2; NFS 12; RGAL 4; SATA 100; TUS; WCH; WYA; YABC 1; YAW

Aldanov, M. A.
See Aldanov, Mark (Alexandrovich)

Aldanov, Mark (Alexandrovich)
1886(?)-1957 .... **TCLC 23**
See also CA 118; 181

Aldington, Richard 1892-1962 .... **CLC 49**
See also CA 85-88; CANR 45; DLB 20, 36, 100, 149; LMFS 2; RGEL 2

Aldiss, Brian W(ilson) 1925- .... **CLC 5, 14, 40; SSC 36**
See also AAYA 42; CA 5-8R; CAAE 190; CAAS 2; CANR 5, 28, 64; CN 7; DAM NOV; DLB 14, 261, 271; MTCW 1, 2; SATA 34; SFW 4

Aldrich, Bess Streeter 1881-1954
.... **TCLC 125**
See also CLR 70

Alegria, Claribel 1924- ... **CLC 75; HLCS 1; PC 26**
See also CA 131; CAAS 15; CANR 66, 94; CWW 2; DAM MULT; DLB 145; EWL 3; HW 1; MTCW 1

Alegria, Fernando 1918- .... **CLC 57**
See also CA 9-12R; CANR 5, 32, 72; EWL 3; HW 1, 2

Aleichem, Sholom .... **SSC 33; TCLC 1, 35**
See Rabinovitch, Sholem
See also TWA

Aleixandre, Vicente 1898-1984 .... **HLCS 1; TCLC 113**
See also CANR 81; DLB 108; EWL 3; HW 2; RGWL 2, 3

Aleman, Mateo 1547-1615(?) .... **LC 81**

Alencon, Marguerite d'
See de Navarre, Marguerite

Alepoudelis, Odysseus
See Elytis, Odysseus
See also CWW 2

Aleshkovsky, Joseph 1929-
See Aleshkovsky, Yuz
See also CA 121; 128

Aleshkovsky, Yuz .... **CLC 44**
See Aleshkovsky, Joseph

Alexander, Lloyd (Chudley) 1924- .. **CLC 35**
See also AAYA 1, 27; BPFB 1; BYA 5, 6, 7, 9, 10, 11; CA 1-4R; CANR 1, 24, 38, 55, 113; CLR 1, 5, 48; CWRI 5; DLB 52; FANT; JRDA; MAICYA 1, 2; MAICYAS 1; MTCW 1; SAAS 19; SATA 3, 49, 81, 129, 135; SUFW; TUS; WYA; YAW

Alexander, Meena 1951- .... **CLC 121**
See also CA 115; CANR 38, 70; CP 7; CWP; FW

Alexander, Samuel 1859-1938 .... **TCLC 77**

Alexie, Sherman (Joseph, Jr.) 1966-
.... **CLC 96, 154; NNAL**
See also AAYA 28; CA 138; CANR 95; DA3; DAM MULT; DLB 175, 206, 278; MTCW 1; NFS 17

al-Farabi 870(?)-950 .... **CMLC 58**
See also DLB 115

Alfau, Felipe 1902-1999 .... **CLC 66**
See also CA 137

Alfieri, Vittorio 1749-1803 .... **NCLC 101**
See also EW 4; RGWL 2, 3

Alfred, Jean Gaston
See Ponge, Francis

Alger, Horatio, Jr. 1832-1899 ... **NCLC 8, 83**
See also CLR 87; DLB 42; LAIT 2; RGAL 4; SATA 16; TUS

Al-Ghazali, Muhammad ibn Muhammad
1058-1111 .... **CMLC 50**
See also DLB 115

Algren, Nelson 1909-1981 .... **CLC 4, 10, 33; SSC 33**
See also AMWS 9; BPFB 1; CA 13-16R; 103; CANR 20, 61; CDALB 1941-1968; DLB 9; DLBY 1981, 1982, 2000; EWL 3; MTCW 1, 2; RGAL 4; RGSF 2

Ali, Ahmed 1908-1998 .... **CLC 69**
See also CA 25-28R; CANR 15, 34; EWL 3

Ali, Tariq 1943- .... **CLC 173**
See also CA 25-28R; CANR 10, 99

Alighieri, Dante
See Dante

Allan, John B.
See Westlake, Donald E(dwin)

Allan, Sidney
See Hartmann, Sadakichi

Allan, Sydney
See Hartmann, Sadakichi

Allard, Janet .... **CLC 59**

Allen, Edward 1948- .... **CLC 59**

Allen, Fred 1894-1956 .... **TCLC 87**

Allen, Paula Gunn 1939- ... **CLC 84; NNAL**
See also AMWS 4; CA 112; 143; CANR 63; CWP; DA3; DAM MULT; DLB 175; FW; MTCW 1; RGAL 4

Allen, Roland
See Ayckbourn, Alan

Allen, Sarah A.
See Hopkins, Pauline Elizabeth

Allen, Sidney H.
See Hartmann, Sadakichi

Allen, Woody 1935- .... **CLC 16, 52**
See also AAYA 10; CA 33-36R; CANR 27, 38, 63; DAM POP; DLB 44; MTCW 1

Allende, Isabel 1942- .. **CLC 39, 57, 97, 170; HLC 1; WLCS**
See also AAYA 18; CA 125; 130; CANR 51, 74; CDWLB 3; CWW 2; DA3; DAM MULT, NOV; DLB 145; DNFS 1; EWL 3; FW; HW 1, 2; INT CA-130; LAIT 5;

LAWS 1; LMFS 2; MTCW 1, 2; NCFS 1; NFS 6; RGSF 2; RGWL 3; SSFS 11, 16; WLIT 1
Alleyn, Ellen
See Rossetti, Christina (Georgina)
Alleyne, Carla D. .... CLC 65
Allingham, Margery (Louise) 1904-1966 .... CLC 19
See also CA 5-8R; 25-28R; CANR 4, 58; CMW 4; DLB 77; MSW; MTCW 1, 2
Allingham, William 1824-1889 .. NCLC 25
See also DLB 35; RGEL 2
Allison, Dorothy E. 1949- .... CLC 78, 153
See also CA 140; CANR 66, 107; CSW DA3; FW; MTCW 1; NFS 11; RGAL 4
Alloula, Malek .... CLC 65
Allston, Washington 1779-1843 ...... NCLC 2
See also DLB 1, 235
Almedingen, E. M. .... CLC 12
See Almedingen, Martha Edith von
See also SATA 3
Almedingen, Martha Edith von 1898-1971
See Almedingen, E. M.
See also CA 1-4R; CANR 1
Almodovar, Pedro 1949(?)- .... CLC 114; HLCS 1
See also CA 133; CANR 72; HW 2
Almqvist, Carl Jonas Love 1793-1866 .... NCLC 42
Alonso, Damaso 1898-1990 .... CLC 14
See also CA 110; 131; 130; CANR 72; DLB 108; EWL 3; HW 1, 2
Alov
See Gogol, Nikolai (Vasilyevich)
Alta 1942- .... CLC 19
See also CA 57-60
Alter, Robert B(ernard) 1935- ...... CLC 34
See also CA 49-52; CANR 1, 47, 100
Alther, Lisa 1944- .... CLC 7, 41
See also BPFB 1; CA 65-68; CAAS 30; CANR 12, 30, 51; CN 7; CSW; GLL 2; MTCW 1
Althusser, L.
See Althusser, Louis
Althusser, Louis 1918-1990 .... CLC 106
See also CA 131; 132; CANR 102; DLB 242
Altman, Robert 1925- .... CLC 16, 116
See also CA 73-76; CANR 43
Alurista .... HLCS 1
See Urista, Alberto H.
See also DLB 82
Alvarez, A(lfred) 1929- .... CLC 5, 13
See also CA 1-4R; CANR 3, 33, 63, 101; CN 7; CP 7; DLB 14, 40
Alvarez, Alejandro Rodriguez 1903-1965
See Casona, Alejandro
See also CA 131; 93-96; HW 1
Alvarez, Julia 1950- .... CLC 93; HLCS 1
See also AAYA 25; AMWS 7; CA 147; CANR 69, 101; DA3; DLB 282; MTCW 1; NFS 5, 9; SATA 129; WLIT 1
Alvaro, Corrado 1896-1956 .... TCLC 60
See also CA 163; DLB 264; EWL 3
Amado, Jorge 1912-2001 . CLC 13, 40, 106; HLC 1
See also CA 77-80; 201; CANR 35, 74; DAM MULT, NOV; DLB 113; EWL 3; HW 2; LAW; LAWS 1; MTCW 1, 2; RGWL 2, 3; TWA; WLIT 1
Ambler, Eric 1909-1998 .... CLC 4, 6, 9
See also BRWS 4; CA 9-12R; 171; CANR 7, 38, 74; CMW 4; CN 7; DLB 77; MSW; MTCW 1, 2; TEA
Ambrose, Stephen E(dward) 1936-2002 .... CLC 145
See also AAYA 44; CA 1-4R; 209; CANR 3, 43, 57, 83, 105; NCFS 2; SATA 40, 138

Amichai, Yehuda 1924-2000 . CLC 9, 22, 57, 116; PC 38
See also CA 85-88; 189; CANR 46, 60, 99; CWW 2; EWL 3; MTCW 1
Amichai, Yehudah
See Amichai, Yehuda
Amiel, Henri Frederic 1821-1881 .. NCLC 4
See also DLB 217
Amis, Kingsley (William) 1922-1995
.... CLC 1, 2, 3, 5, 8, 13, 40, 44, 129
See also AITN 2; BPFB 1; BRWS 2; CA 9-12R; 150; CANR 8, 28, 54; CDBLB 1945-1960; CN 7; CP 7; DA; DA3; DAB; DAC; DAM MST, NOV; DLB 15, 27, 100, 139; DLBY 1996; EWL 3; HGG; INT CANR-8; MTCW 1, 2; RGEL 2; RGSF 2; SFW 4
Amis, Martin (Louis) 1949- ... CLC 4, 9, 38, 62, 101
See also BEST 90:3; BRWS 4; CA 65-68; CANR 8, 27, 54, 73, 95; CN 7; DA3; DLB 14, 194; EWL 3; INT CANR-27; MTCW 1
Ammons, A(rchie) R(andolph) 1926-2001
... CLC 2, 3, 5, 8, 9, 25, 57, 108; PC 16
See also AITN 1; AMWS 7; CA 9-12R; 193; CANR 6, 36, 51, 73, 107; CP 7; CSW; DAM POET; DLB 5, 165; EWL 3; MTCW 1, 2; RGAL 4
Amo, Tauraatua i
See Adams, Henry (Brooks)
Amory, Thomas 1691(?)-1788 .... LC 48
See also DLB 39
Anand, Mulk Raj 1905- .... CLC 23, 93
See also CA 65-68; CANR 32, 64; CN 7; DAM NOV; EWL 3; MTCW 1, 2; RGSF 2
Anatol
See Schnitzler, Arthur
Anaximander c. 611B.C.-c. 546B.C. .... CMLC 22
Anaya, Rudolfo A(lfonso) 1937- ..... CLC 23, 148; HLC 1
See also AAYA 20; BYA 13; CA 45-48; CAAS 4; CANR 1, 32, 51; CN 7; DAM MULT, NOV; DLB 82, 206, 278; HW 1; LAIT 4; MTCW 1, 2; NFS 12; RGAL 4; RGSF 2; WLIT 1
Andersen, Hans Christian 1805-1875
.... NCLC 7, 79; SSC 6, 56; WLC
See also CLR 6; DA; DA3; DAB; DAC; DAM MST, POP; EW 6; MAICYA 1, 2; RGSF 2; RGWL 2, 3; SATA 100; TWA; WCH; YABC 1
Anderson, C. Farley
See Mencken, H(enry) L(ouis); Nathan, George Jean
Anderson, Jessica (Margaret) Queale 1916-
.... CLC 37
See also CA 9-12R; CANR 4, 62; CN 7
Anderson, Jon (Victor) 1940- .... CLC 9
See also CA 25-28R; CANR 20; DAM POET
Anderson, Lindsay (Gordon) 1923-1994
.... CLC 20
See also CA 125; 128; 146; CANR 77
Anderson, Maxwell 1888-1959 .... TCLC 2
See also CA 105; 152; DAM DRAM; DFS 16; DLB 7, 228; MTCW 2; RGAL 4
Anderson, Poul (William) 1926-2001
.... CLC 15
See also AAYA 5, 34; BPFB 1; BYA 6, 8, 9; CA 1-4R, 181; 199; CAAE 181; CAAS 2; CANR 2, 15, 34, 64, 110; CLR 58; DLB 8; FANT; INT CANR-15; MTCW 1, 2; SATA 90; SATA-Brief 39; SATA-Essay 106; SCFW 2; SFW 4; SUFW 1, 2

Anderson, Robert (Woodruff) 1917-
.... CLC 23
See also AITN 1; CA 21-24R; CANR 32; DAM DRAM; DLB 7; LAIT 5
Anderson, Roberta Joan
See Mitchell, Joni
Anderson, Sherwood 1876-1941 . SSC 1, 46; TCLC 1, 10, 24, 123; WLC
See also AAYA 30; AMW; BPFB 1; CA 104; 121; CANR 61; CDALB 1917-1929; DA; DA3; DAB; DAC; DAM MST, NOV; DLB 4, 9, 86; DLBD 1; EWL 3; EXPS; GLL 2; MTCW 1, 2; NFS 4; RGAL 4; RGSF 2; SSFS 4, 10, 11; TUS
Andier, Pierre
See Desnos, Robert
Andouard
See Giraudoux, Jean(-Hippolyte)
Andrade, Carlos Drummond de ..... CLC 18
See Drummond de Andrade, Carlos
See also EWL 3; RGWL 2, 3
Andrade, Mario de .... TCLC 43
See de Andrade, Mario
See also EWL 3; LAW; RGWL 2, 3; WLIT 1
Andreae, Johann V(alentin) 1586-1654
.... LC 32
See also DLB 164
Andreas Capellanus fl. c. 1185- ... CMLC 45
See also DLB 208
Andreas-Salome, Lou 1861-1937 .. TCLC 56
See also CA 178; DLB 66
Andreev, Leonid
See Andreyev, Leonid (Nikolaevich)
See also EWL 3
Andress, Lesley
See Sanders, Lawrence
Andrewes, Lancelot 1555-1626 .... LC 5
See also DLB 151, 172
Andrews, Cicily Fairfield
See West, Rebecca
Andrews, Elton V.
See Pohl, Frederik
Andreyev, Leonid (Nikolaevich) 1871-1919
.... TCLC 3
See Andreev, Leonid
See also CA 104; 185
Andric, Ivo 1892-1975 .... CLC 8; SSC 36; TCLC 135
See also CA 81-84; 57-60; CANR 43, 60; CDWLB 4; DLB 147; EW 11; EWL 3; MTCW 1; RGSF 2; RGWL 2, 3
Androvar
See Prado (Calvo), Pedro
Angelique, Pierre
See Bataille, Georges
Angell, Roger 1920- .... CLC 26
See also CA 57-60; CANR 13, 44, 70; DLB 171, 185
Angelou, Maya 1928- .. BLC 1; CLC 12, 35, 64, 77, 155; PC 32; WLCS
See also AAYA 7, 20; AMWS 4; BPFB 1; BW 2, 3; BYA 2; CA 65-68; CANR 19, 42, 65, 111; CDALBS; CLR 53; CP 7; CPW; CSW; CWP; DA; DA3; DAB; DAC; DAM MST, MULT, POET, POP; DLB 38; EWL 3; EXPN; EXPP; LAIT 4; MAICYA 2; MAICYAS 1; MAWW; MTCW 1, 2; NCFS 2; NFS 2; PFS 2, 3; RGAL 4; SATA 49, 136; WYA; YAW
Angouleme, Marguerite d'
See de Navarre, Marguerite
Anna Comnena 1083-1153 .... CMLC 25
Annensky, Innokenty (Fyodorovich) 1856-1909 .... TCLC 14
See also CA 110; 155; EWL 3
Annunzio, Gabriele d'
See D'Annunzio, Gabriele

Anodos
See Coleridge, Mary E(lizabeth)
Anon, Charles Robert
See Pessoa, Fernando (Antonio Nogueira)
Anouilh, Jean (Marie Lucien Pierre)
1910-1987 .... **CLC 1, 3, 8, 13, 40, 50; DC 8**
See also CA 17-20R; 123; CANR 32; DAM DRAM; DFS 9, 10; EW 13; EWL 3; GFL 1789 to the Present; MTCW 1, 2; RGWL 2, 3; TWA
Anthony, Florence
See Ai
Anthony, John
See Ciardi, John (Anthony)
Anthony, Peter
See Shaffer, Anthony (Joshua); Shaffer, Peter (Levin)
Anthony, Piers 1934- .... **CLC 35**
See also AAYA 11, 48; BYA 7; CA 21-24R; CAAE 200; CANR 28, 56, 73, 102; CPW; DAM POP; DLB 8; FANT; MAICYA 2; MAICYAS 1; MTCW 1, 2; SAAS 22; SATA 84; SATA-Essay 129; SFW 4; SUFW 1, 2; YAW
Anthony, Susan B(rownell) 1820-1906
.... **TCLC 84**
See also FW
Antiphon c. 480B.C.-c. 411B.C. ... **CMLC 55**
Antoine, Marc
See Proust, (Valentin-Louis-George-Eugene-)Marcel
Antoninus, Brother
See Everson, William (Oliver)
Antonioni, Michelangelo 1912- .... **CLC 20, 144**
See also CA 73-76; CANR 45, 77
Antschel, Paul 1920-1970
See Celan, Paul
See also CA 85-88; CANR 33, 61; MTCW 1
Anwar, Chairil 1922-1949 .... **TCLC 22**
See Chairil Anwar
See also CA 121; RGWL 3
Anzaldua, Gloria (Evanjelina) 1942-
.... **HLCS 1**
See also CA 175; CSW; CWP; DLB 122; FW; RGAL 4
Apess, William 1798-1839(?) .... **NCLC 73; NNAL**
See also DAM MULT; DLB 175, 243
Apollinaire, Guillaume 1880-1918 ...... **PC 7; TCLC 3, 8, 51**
See Kostrowitzki, Wilhelm Apollinaris de
See also CA 152; DAM POET; DLB 258; EW 9; EWL 3; GFL 1789 to the Present; MTCW 1; RGWL 2, 3; TWA; WP
Apollonius of Rhodes
See Apollonius Rhodius
See also AW 1; RGWL 2, 3
Apollonius Rhodius c. 300B.C.-c. 220B.C.
.... **CMLC 28**
See Apollonius of Rhodes
See also DLB 176
Appelfeld, Aharon 1932- .. **CLC 23, 47; SSC 42**
See also CA 112; 133; CANR 86; CWW 2; EWL 3; RGSF 2
Apple, Max (Isaac) 1941- .. **CLC 9, 33; SSC 50**
See also CA 81-84; CANR 19, 54; DLB 130
Appleman, Philip (Dean) 1926- .... **CLC 51**
See also CA 13-16R; CAAS 18; CANR 6, 29, 56
Appleton, Lawrence
See Lovecraft, H(oward) P(hillips)
Apteryx
See Eliot, T(homas) S(tearns)

Apuleius, (Lucius Madaurensis)
125(?)-175(?) .... **CMLC 1**
See also AW 2; CDWLB 1; DLB 211; RGWL 2, 3; SUFW
Aquin, Hubert 1929-1977 .... **CLC 15**
See also CA 105; DLB 53; EWL 3
Aquinas, Thomas 1224(?)-1274 ... **CMLC 33**
See also DLB 115; EW 1; TWA
Aragon, Louis 1897-1982 .... **CLC 3, 22; TCLC 123**
See also CA 69-72; 108; CANR 28, 71; DAM NOV, POET; DLB 72, 258; EW 11; EWL 3; GFL 1789 to the Present; GLL 2; LMFS 2; MTCW 1, 2; RGWL 2, 3
Arany, Janos 1817-1882 .... **NCLC 34**
Aranyos, Kakay 1847-1910
See Mikszath, Kalman
Arbuthnot, John 1667-1735 .... **LC 1**
See also DLB 101
Archer, Herbert Winslow
See Mencken, H(enry) L(ouis)
Archer, Jeffrey (Howard) 1940- .... **CLC 28**
See also AAYA 16; BEST 89:3; BPFB 1; CA 77-80; CANR 22, 52, 95; CPW; DA3; DAM POP; INT CANR-22
Archer, Jules 1915- .... **CLC 12**
See also CA 9-12R; CANR 6, 69; SAAS 5; SATA 4, 85
Archer, Lee
See Ellison, Harlan (Jay)
Archilochus c. 7th cent. B.C.- .... **CMLC 44**
See also DLB 176
Arden, John 1930- .... **CLC 6, 13, 15**
See also BRWS 2; CA 13-16R; CAAS 4; CANR 31, 65, 67; CBD; CD 5; DAM DRAM; DFS 9; DLB 13, 245; EWL 3; MTCW 1
Arenas, Reinaldo 1943-1990 . **CLC 41; HLC 1**
See also CA 124; 128; 133; CANR 73, 106; DAM MULT; DLB 145; EWL 3; GLL 2; HW 1; LAW; LAWS 1; MTCW 1; RGSF 2; RGWL 3; WLIT 1
Arendt, Hannah 1906-1975 .... **CLC 66, 98**
See also CA 17-20R; 61-64; CANR 26, 60; DLB 242; MTCW 1, 2
Aretino, Pietro 1492-1556 .... **LC 12**
See also RGWL 2, 3
Arghezi, Tudor .... **CLC 80**
See Theodorescu, Ion N.
See also CA 167; CDWLB 4; DLB 220; EWL 3
Arguedas, Jose Maria 1911-1969 ... **CLC 10, 18; HLCS 1**
See also CA 89-92; CANR 73; DLB 113; EWL 3; HW 1; LAW; RGWL 2, 3; WLIT 1
Argueta, Manlio 1936- .... **CLC 31**
See also CA 131; CANR 73; CWW 2; DLB 145; EWL 3; HW 1; RGWL 3
Arias, Ron(ald Francis) 1941- .... **HLC 1**
See also CA 131; CANR 81; DAM MULT; DLB 82; HW 1, 2; MTCW 2
Ariosto, Ludovico 1474-1533 . **LC 6, 87; PC 42**
See also EW 2; RGWL 2, 3
Aristides
See Epstein, Joseph
Aristophanes 450B.C.-385B.C. .... **CMLC 4, 51; DC 2; WLCS**
See also AW 1; CDWLB 1; DA; DA3; DAB; DAC; DAM DRAM, MST; DFS 10; DLB 176; LMFS 1; RGWL 2, 3; TWA
Aristotle 384B.C.-322B.C. .... **CMLC 31; WLCS**
See also AW 1; CDWLB 1; DA; DA3; DAB; DAC; DAM MST; DLB 176; RGWL 2, 3; TWA

Arlt, Roberto (Godofredo Christophersen)
1900-1942 .... **HLC 1; TCLC 29**
See also CA 123; 131; CANR 67; DAM MULT; EWL 3; HW 1, 2; LAW
Armah, Ayi Kwei 1939- ...... **BLC 1; CLC 5, 33, 136**
See also AFW; BW 1; CA 61-64; CANR 21, 64; CDWLB 3; CN 7; DAM MULT, POET; DLB 117; EWL 3; MTCW 1; WLIT 2
Armatrading, Joan 1950- .... **CLC 17**
See also CA 114; 186
Armitage, Frank
See Carpenter, John (Howard)
Armstrong, Jeannette (C.) 1948- .... **NNAL**
See also CA 149; CCA 1; CN 7; DAC; SATA 102
Arnette, Robert
See Silverberg, Robert
Arnim, Achim von (Ludwig Joachim von Arnim) 1781-1831 .... **NCLC 5; SSC 29**
See also DLB 90
Arnim, Bettina von 1785-1859 .... **NCLC 38, 123**
See also DLB 90; RGWL 2, 3
Arnold, Matthew 1822-1888 .... **NCLC 6, 29, 89; PC 5; WLC**
See also BRW 5; CDBLB 1832-1890; DA; DAB; DAC; DAM MST, POET; DLB 32, 57; EXPP; PAB; PFS 2; TEA; WP
Arnold, Thomas 1795-1842 .... **NCLC 18**
See also DLB 55
Arnow, Harriette (Louisa) Simpson
1908-1986 .... **CLC 2, 7, 18**
See also BPFB 1; CA 9-12R; 118; CANR 14; DLB 6; FW; MTCW 1, 2; RHW; SATA 42; SATA-Obit 47
Arouet, Francois-Marie
See Voltaire
Arp, Hans
See Arp, Jean
Arp, Jean 1887-1966 ...... **CLC 5; TCLC 115**
See also CA 81-84; 25-28R; CANR 42, 77; EW 10
Arrabal
See Arrabal, Fernando
Arrabal, Fernando 1932- .. **CLC 2, 9, 18, 58**
See also CA 9-12R; CANR 15; EWL 3; LMFS 2
Arreola, Juan Jose 1918-2001 .... **CLC 147; HLC 1; SSC 38**
See also CA 113; 131; 200; CANR 81; DAM MULT; DLB 113; DNFS 2; EWL 3; HW 1, 2; LAW; RGSF 2
Arrian c. 89(?)-c. 155(?) .... **CMLC 43**
See also DLB 176
Arrick, Fran .... **CLC 30**
See Gaberman, Judie Angell
See also BYA 6
Arriey, Richmond
See Delany, Samuel R(ay), Jr.
Artaud, Antonin (Marie Joseph) 1896-1948
.... **DC 14; TCLC 3, 36**
See also CA 104; 149; DA3; DAM DRAM; DLB 258; EW 11; EWL 3; GFL 1789 to the Present; MTCW 1; RGWL 2, 3
Arthur, Ruth M(abel) 1905-1979 .... **CLC 12**
See also CA 9-12R; 85-88; CANR 4; CWRI 5; SATA 7, 26
Artsybashev, Mikhail (Petrovich) 1878-1927
.... **TCLC 31**
See also CA 170
Arundel, Honor (Morfydd) 1919-1973
.... **CLC 17**
See also CA 21-22; 41-44R; CAP 2; CLR 35; CWRI 5; SATA 4; SATA-Obit 24
Arzner, Dorothy 1900-1979 .... **CLC 98**
Asch, Sholem 1880-1957 .... **TCLC 3**
See also CA 105; EWL 3; GLL 2

Ash, Shalom
See Asch, Sholem
Ashbery, John (Lawrence) 1927- . **CLC 2, 3, 4, 6, 9, 13, 15, 25, 41, 77, 125; PC 26**
See Berry, Jonas
See also AMWS 3; CA 5-8R; CANR 9, 37, 66, 102; CP 7; DA3; DAM POET; DLB 5, 165; DLBY 1981; EWL 3; INT CANR-9; MTCW 1, 2; PAB; PFS 11; RGAL 4; WP
Ashdown, Clifford
See Freeman, R(ichard) Austin
Ashe, Gordon
See Creasey, John
Ashton-Warner, Sylvia (Constance) 1908-1984 .... **CLC 19**
See also CA 69-72; 112; CANR 29; MTCW 1, 2
Asimov, Isaac 1920-1992 .... **CLC 1, 3, 9, 19, 26, 76, 92**
See also AAYA 13; BEST 90:2; BPFB 1 BYA 4, 6, 7, 9; CA 1-4R; 137; CANR 2, 19, 36, 60; CLR 12, 79; CMW 4; CPW; DA3; DAM POP; DLB 8; DLBY 1992; INT CANR-19; JRDA; LAIT 5; LMFS 2; MAICYA 1, 2; MTCW 1, 2; RGAL 4; SATA 1, 26, 74; SCFW 2; SFW 4; SSFS 17; TUS; YAW
Askew, Anne 1521(?)-1546 .... **LC 81**
See also DLB 136
Assis, Joaquim Maria Machado de
See Machado de Assis, Joaquim Maria
Astell, Mary 1666-1731 .... **LC 68**
See also DLB 252; FW
Astley, Thea (Beatrice May) 1925- . **CLC 41**
See also CA 65-68; CANR 11, 43, 78; CN 7; EWL 3
Astley, William 1855-1911
See Warung, Price
Aston, James
See White, T(erence) H(anbury)
Asturias, Miguel Angel 1899-1974 ... **CLC 3, 8, 13; HLC 1**
See also CA 25-28; 49-52; CANR 32; CAP 2; CDWLB 3; DA3; DAM MULT, NOV; DLB 113; EWL 3; HW 1; LAW; LMFS 2; MTCW 1, 2; RGWL 2, 3; WLIT 1
Atares, Carlos Saura
See Saura (Atares), Carlos
Athanasius c. 295-c. 373 .... **CMLC 48**
Atheling, William
See Pound, Ezra (Weston Loomis)
Atheling, William, Jr.
See Blish, James (Benjamin)
Atherton, Gertrude (Franklin Horn) 1857-1948 .... **TCLC 2**
See also CA 104; 155; DLB 9, 78, 186; HGG; RGAL 4; SUFW 1; TCWW 2
Atherton, Lucius
See Masters, Edgar Lee
Atkins, Jack
See Harris, Mark
Atkinson, Kate 1951- .... **CLC 99**
See also CA 166; CANR 101; DLB 267
Attaway, William (Alexander) 1911-1986
.... **BLC 1; CLC 92**
See also BW 2, 3; CA 143; CANR 82; DAM MULT; DLB 76
Atticus
See Fleming, Ian (Lancaster); Wilson, (Thomas) Woodrow
Atwood, Margaret (Eleanor) 1939- . **CLC 2, 3, 4, 8, 13, 15, 25, 44, 84, 135; PC 8; SSC 2, 46; WLC**
See also AAYA 12, 47; BEST 89:2; BPFB 1; CA 49-52; CANR 3, 24, 33, 59, 95; CN 7; CP 7; CPW; CWP; DA; DA3; DAB; DAC; DAM MST, NOV, POET; DLB 53, 251; EWL 3; EXPN; FW; INT CANR-24; LAIT 5; MTCW 1, 2; NFS 4, 12, 13, 14; PFS 7; RGSF 2; SATA 50; SSFS 3, 13; TWA; YAW
Aubigny, Pierre d'
See Mencken, H(enry) L(ouis)
Aubin, Penelope 1685-1731(?) .... **LC 9**
See also DLB 39
Auchincloss, Louis (Stanton) 1917- . **CLC 4, 6, 9, 18, 45; SSC 22**
See also AMWS 4; CA 1-4R; CANR 6, 29, 55, 87; CN 7; DAM NOV; DLB 2, 244; DLBY 1980; EWL 3; INT CANR-29; MTCW 1; RGAL 4
Auden, W(ystan) H(ugh) 1907-1973
..... **CLC 1, 2, 3, 4, 6, 9, 11, 14, 43, 123; PC 1; WLC**
See also AAYA 18; AMWS 2; BRW 7; BRWR 1; CA 9-12R; 45-48; CANR 5, 61, 105; CDBLB 1914-1945; DA; DA3; DAB; DAC; DAM DRAM, MST, POET; DLB 10, 20; EWL 3; EXPP; MTCW 1, 2; PAB; PFS 1, 3, 4, 10; TUS; WP
Audiberti, Jacques 1900-1965 .... **CLC 38**
See also CA 25-28R; DAM DRAM; EWL 3
Audubon, John James 1785-1851
.... **NCLC 47**
See also ANW; DLB 248
Auel, Jean M(arie) 1936- .... **CLC 31, 107**
See also AAYA 7; BEST 90:4; BPFB 1; CA 103; CANR 21, 64, 115; CPW; DA3; DAM POP; INT CANR-21; NFS 11; RHW; SATA 91
Auerbach, Erich 1892-1957 .... **TCLC 43**
See also CA 118; 155; EWL 3
Augier, Emile 1820-1889 .... **NCLC 31**
See also DLB 192; GFL 1789 to the Present
August, John
See De Voto, Bernard (Augustine)
Augustine, St. 354-430 ..... **CMLC 6; WLCS**
See also DA; DA3; DAB; DAC; DAM MST; DLB 115; EW 1; RGWL 2, 3
Aunt Belinda
See Braddon, Mary Elizabeth
Aunt Weedy
See Alcott, Louisa May
Aurelius
See Bourne, Randolph S(illiman)
Aurelius, Marcus 121-180 .... **CMLC 45**
See Marcus Aurelius
See also RGWL 2, 3
Aurobindo, Sri
See Ghose, Aurabinda
Aurobindo Ghose
See Ghose, Aurabinda
Austen, Jane 1775-1817 ..... **NCLC 1, 13, 19, 33, 51, 81, 95, 119; WLC**
See also AAYA 19; BRW 4; BRWC 1; BRWR 2; BYA 3; CDBLB 1789-1832; DA; DA3; DAB; DAC; DAM MST, NOV; DLB 116; EXPN; LAIT 2; LMFS 1; NFS 1, 14; TEA; WLIT 3; WYAS 1
Auster, Paul 1947- .... **CLC 47, 131**
See also AMWS 12; CA 69-72; CANR 23, 52, 75; CMW 4; CN 7; DA3; DLB 227; MTCW 1; SUFW 2
Austin, Frank
See Faust, Frederick (Schiller)
See also TCWW 2
Austin, Mary (Hunter) 1868-1934
.... **TCLC 25**
See Stairs, Gordon
See also ANW; CA 109; 178; DLB 9, 78, 206, 221, 275; FW; TCWW 2
Averroes 1126-1198 .... **CMLC 7**
See also DLB 115
Avicenna 980-1037 .... **CMLC 16**
See also DLB 115
Avison, Margaret 1918- .... **CLC 2, 4, 97**
See also CA 17-20R; CP 7; DAC; DAM POET; DLB 53; MTCW 1
Axton, David
See Koontz, Dean R(ay)
Ayckbourn, Alan 1939- .... **CLC 5, 8, 18, 33, 74; DC 13**
See also BRWS 5; CA 21-24R; CANR 31, 59; CBD; CD 5; DAB; DAM DRAM; DFS 7; DLB 13, 245; EWL 3; MTCW 1, 2
Aydy, Catherine
See Tennant, Emma (Christina)
Ayme, Marcel (Andre) 1902-1967 .. **CLC 11; SSC 41**
See also CA 89-92; CANR 67; CLR 25; DLB 72; EW 12; EWL 3; GFL 1789 to the Present; RGSF 2; RGWL 2, 3; SATA 91
Ayrton, Michael 1921-1975 .... **CLC 7**
See also CA 5-8R; 61-64; CANR 9, 21
Aytmatov, Chingiz
See Aitmatov, Chingiz (Torekulovich)
See also EWL 3
Azorin .... **CLC 11**
See Martinez Ruiz, Jose
See also EW 9; EWL 3
Azuela, Mariano 1873-1952 . **HLC 1; TCLC 3**
See also CA 104; 131; CANR 81; DAM MULT; EWL 3; HW 1; LAW; MTCW 1, 2
Ba, Mariama 1929-1981 .... **BLCS**
See also AFW; BW 2; CA 141; CANR 87; DNFS 2; WLIT 2
Baastad, Babbis Friis
See Friis-Baastad, Babbis Ellinor
Bab
See Gilbert, W(illiam) S(chwenck)
Babbis, Eleanor
See Friis-Baastad, Babbis Ellinor
Babel, Isaac
See Babel, Isaak (Emmanuilovich)
See also EW 11; SSFS 10
Babel, Isaak (Emmanuilovich) 1894-1941(?)
.... **SSC 16; TCLC 2, 13**
See Babel, Isaac
See also CA 104; 155; CANR 113; DLB 272; EWL 3; MTCW 1; RGSF 2; RGWL 2, 3; TWA
Babits, Mihaly 1883-1941 .... **TCLC 14**
See also CA 114; CDWLB 4; DLB 215; EWL 3
Babur 1483-1530 .... **LC 18**
Babylas 1898-1962
See Ghelderode, Michel de
Baca, Jimmy Santiago 1952- ...... **HLC 1; PC 41**
See also CA 131; CANR 81, 90; CP 7; DAM MULT; DLB 122; HW 1, 2
Baca, Jose Santiago
See Baca, Jimmy Santiago
Bacchelli, Riccardo 1891-1985 .... **CLC 19**
See also CA 29-32R; 117; DLB 264; EWL 3
Bach, Richard (David) 1936- .... **CLC 14**
See also AITN 1; BEST 89:2; BPFB 1; BYA 5; CA 9-12R; CANR 18, 93; CPW; DAM NOV, POP; FANT; MTCW 1; SATA 13
Bache, Benjamin Franklin 1769-1798
.... **LC 74**
See also DLB 43
Bachelard, Gaston 1884-1962 ..... **TCLC 128**
See also CA 97-100; 89-92; GFL 1789 to the Present
Bachman, Richard
See King, Stephen (Edwin)

Bachmann, Ingeborg 1926-1973 ..... **CLC 69**
See also CA 93-96; 45-48; CANR 69; DLB 85; EWL 3; RGWL 2, 3

Bacon, Francis 1561-1626 .... **LC 18, 32**
See also BRW 1; CDBLB Before 1660; DLB 151, 236, 252; RGEL 2; TEA

Bacon, Roger 1214(?)-1294 .... **CMLC 14**
See also DLB 115

Bacovia, George 1881-1957 .... **TCLC 24**
See Vasiliu, Gheorghe
See also CDWLB 4; DLB 220; EWL 3

Badanes, Jerome 1937- .... **CLC 59**

Bagehot, Walter 1826-1877 .... **NCLC 10**
See also DLB 55

Bagnold, Enid 1889-1981 .... **CLC 25**
See also BYA 2; CA 5-8R; 103; CANR 5, 40; CBD; CWD; CWRI 5; DAM DRAM; DLB 13, 160, 191, 245; FW; MAICYA 1, 2; RGEL 2; SATA 1, 25

Bagritsky, Eduard .... **TCLC 60**
See Dzyubin, Eduard Georgievich

Bagrjana, Elisaveta
See Belcheva, Elisaveta Lyubomirova

Bagryana, Elisaveta .... **CLC 10**
See Belcheva, Elisaveta Lyubomirova
See also CA 178; CDWLB 4; DLB 147; EWL 3

Bailey, Paul 1937- .... **CLC 45**
See also CA 21-24R; CANR 16, 62; CN 7; DLB 14, 271; GLL 2

Baillie, Joanna 1762-1851 .... **NCLC 71**
See also DLB 93; RGEL 2

Bainbridge, Beryl (Margaret) 1934-
...... **CLC 4, 5, 8, 10, 14, 18, 22, 62, 130**
See also BRWS 6; CA 21-24R; CANR 24, 55, 75, 88; CN 7; DAM NOV; DLB 14, 231; EWL 3; MTCW 1, 2

Baker, Carlos (Heard) 1909-1987
.... **TCLC 119**
See also CA 5-8R; 122; CANR 3, 63; DLB 103

Baker, Elliott 1922- .... **CLC 8**
See also CA 45-48; CANR 2, 63; CN 7

Baker, Jean H. .... **TCLC 3, 10**
See Russell, George William

Baker, Nicholson 1957- .... **CLC 61, 165**
See also CA 135; CANR 63; CN 7; CPW; DA3; DAM POP; DLB 227

Baker, Ray Stannard 1870-1946 .. **TCLC 47**
See also CA 118

Baker, Russell (Wayne) 1925- .... **CLC 31**
See also BEST 89:4; CA 57-60; CANR 11, 41, 59; MTCW 1, 2

Bakhtin, M.
See Bakhtin, Mikhail Mikhailovich

Bakhtin, M. M.
See Bakhtin, Mikhail Mikhailovich

Bakhtin, Mikhail
See Bakhtin, Mikhail Mikhailovich

Bakhtin, Mikhail Mikhailovich 1895-1975
.... **CLC 83**
See also CA 128; 113; DLB 242; EWL 3

Bakshi, Ralph 1938(?)- .... **CLC 26**
See also CA 112; 138; IDFW 3

Bakunin, Mikhail (Alexandrovich)
1814-1876 .... **NCLC 25, 58**
See also DLB 277

Baldwin, James (Arthur) 1924-1987
.... **BLC 1; CLC 1, 2, 3, 4, 5, 8, 13, 15, 17, 42, 50, 67, 90, 127; DC 1; SSC 10, 33; WLC**
See also AAYA 4, 34; AFAW 1, 2; AMWR 2; AMWS 1; BPFB 1; BW 1; CA 1-4R; 124; CABS 1; CAD; CANR 3, 24; CDALB 1941-1968; CPW; DA; DA3; DAB; DAC; DAM MST, MULT, NOV, POP; DFS 15; DLB 2, 7, 33, 249, 278; DLBY 1987; EWL 3; EXPS; LAIT 5; MTCW 1, 2; NCFS 4; NFS 4; RGAL 4; RGSF 2; SATA 9; SATA-Obit 54; SSFS 2; TUS

Bale, John 1495-1563 .... **LC 62**
See also DLB 132; RGEL 2; TEA

Ball, Hugo 1886-1927 .... **TCLC 104**

Ballard, J(ames) G(raham) 1930- .... **CLC 3, 6, 14, 36, 137; SSC 1, 53**
See also AAYA 3; BRWS 5; CA 5-8R; CANR 15, 39, 65, 107; CN 7; DA3; DAM NOV, POP; DLB 14, 207, 261; EWL 3; HGG; MTCW 1, 2; NFS 8; RGEL 2; RGSF 2; SATA 93; SFW 4

Balmont, Konstantin (Dmitriyevich)
1867-1943 .... **TCLC 11**
See also CA 109; 155; EWL 3

Baltausis, Vincas 1847-1910
See Mikszath, Kalman

Balzac, Honore de 1799-1850 .. **NCLC 5, 35, 53; SSC 5, 59; WLC**
See also DA; DA3; DAB; DAC; DAM MST, NOV; DLB 119; EW 5; GFL 1789 to the Present; LMFS 1; RGSF 2; RGWL 2, 3; SSFS 10; SUFW; TWA

Bambara, Toni Cade 1939-1995 .... **BLC 1; CLC 19, 88; SSC 35; TCLC 116; WLCS**
See also AAYA 5, 49; AFAW 2; AMWS 11; BW 2, 3; BYA 12, 14; CA 29-32R; 150; CANR 24, 49, 81; CDALBS; DA; DA3; DAC; DAM MST, MULT; DLB 38, 218; EXPS; MTCW 1, 2; RGAL 4; RGSF 2; SATA 112; SSFS 4, 7, 12

Bamdad, A.
See Shamlu, Ahmad

Banat, D. R.
See Bradbury, Ray (Douglas)

Bancroft, Laura
See Baum, L(yman) Frank

Banim, John 1798-1842 .... **NCLC 13**
See also DLB 116, 158, 159; RGEL 2

Banim, Michael 1796-1874 .... **NCLC 13**
See also DLB 158, 159

Banjo, The
See Paterson, A(ndrew) B(arton)

Banks, Iain
See Banks, Iain M(enzies)

Banks, Iain M(enzies) 1954- .... **CLC 34**
See also CA 123; 128; CANR 61, 106; DLB 194, 261; EWL 3; HGG; INT 128; SFW 4

Banks, Lynne Reid .... **CLC 23**
See Reid Banks, Lynne
See also AAYA 6; BYA 7; CLR 86

Banks, Russell 1940- ... **CLC 37, 72; SSC 42**
See also AAYA 45; AMWS 5; CA 65-68; CAAS 15; CANR 19, 52, 73; CN 7; DLB 130, 278; EWL 3; NFS 13

Banville, John 1945- .... **CLC 46, 118**
See also CA 117; 128; CANR 104; CN 7; DLB 14, 271; INT 128

Banville, Theodore (Faullain) de 1832-1891
.... **NCLC 9**
See also DLB 217; GFL 1789 to the Present

Baraka, Amiri 1934- ... **BLC 1; CLC 1, 2, 3, 5, 10, 14, 33, 115; DC 6; PC 4; WLCS**
See Jones, LeRoi
See also AFAW 1, 2; AMWS 2; BW 2, 3; CA 21-24R; CABS 3; CAD; CANR 27, 38, 61; CD 5; CDALB 1941-1968; CP 7; CPW; DA; DA3; DAC; DAM MST, MULT, POET, POP; DFS 3, 11, 16; DLB 5, 7, 16, 38; DLBD 8; EWL 3; MTCW 1, 2; PFS 9; RGAL 4; TUS; WP

Baratynsky, Evgenii Abramovich 1800-1844
.... **NCLC 103**
See also DLB 205

Barbauld, Anna Laetitia 1743-1825
.... **NCLC 50**
See also DLB 107, 109, 142, 158; RGEL 2

Barbellion, W. N. P. .... **TCLC 24**
See Cummings, Bruce F(rederick)

Barber, Benjamin R. 1939- .... **CLC 141**
See also CA 29-32R; CANR 12, 32, 64

Barbera, Jack (Vincent) 1945- .... **CLC 44**
See also CA 110; CANR 45

Barbey d'Aurevilly, Jules-Amedee 1808-1889
.... **NCLC 1; SSC 17**
See also DLB 119; GFL 1789 to the Present

Barbour, John c. 1316-1395 .... **CMLC 33**
See also DLB 146

Barbusse, Henri 1873-1935 .... **TCLC 5**
See also CA 105; 154; DLB 65; EWL 3; RGWL 2, 3

Barclay, Bill
See Moorcock, Michael (John)

Barclay, William Ewert
See Moorcock, Michael (John)

Barea, Arturo 1897-1957 .... **TCLC 14**
See also CA 111; 201

Barfoot, Joan 1946- .... **CLC 18**
See also CA 105

Barham, Richard Harris 1788-1845
.... **NCLC 77**
See also DLB 159

Baring, Maurice 1874-1945 .... **TCLC 8**
See also CA 105; 168; DLB 34; HGG

Baring-Gould, Sabine 1834-1924 . **TCLC 88**
See also DLB 156, 190

Barker, Clive 1952- .... **CLC 52; SSC 53**
See also AAYA 10; BEST 90:3; BPFB 1; CA 121; 129; CANR 71, 111; CPW; DA3; DAM POP; DLB 261; HGG; INT 129; MTCW 1, 2; SUFW 2

Barker, George Granville 1913-1991
.... **CLC 8, 48**
See also CA 9-12R; 135; CANR 7, 38; DAM POET; DLB 20; EWL 3; MTCW 1

Barker, Harley Granville
See Granville-Barker, Harley
See also DLB 10

Barker, Howard 1946- .... **CLC 37**
See also CA 102; CBD; CD 5; DLB 13, 233

Barker, Jane 1652-1732 .... **LC 42, 82**
See also DLB 39, 131

Barker, Pat(ricia) 1943- ...... **CLC 32, 94, 146**
See also BRWS 4; CA 117; 122; CANR 50, 101; CN 7; DLB 271; INT 122

Barlach, Ernst (Heinrich) 1870-1938
.... **TCLC 84**
See also CA 178; DLB 56, 118; EWL 3

Barlow, Joel 1754-1812 .... **NCLC 23**
See also AMWS 2; DLB 37; RGAL 4

Barnard, Mary (Ethel) 1909- .... **CLC 48**
See also CA 21-22; CAP 2

Barnes, Djuna 1892-1982 ... **CLC 3, 4, 8, 11, 29, 127; SSC 3**
See Steptoe, Lydia
See also AMWS 3; CA 9-12R; 107; CAD; CANR 16, 55; CWD; DLB 4, 9, 45; EWL 3; GLL 1; MTCW 1, 2; RGAL 4; TUS

Barnes, Jim 1933- .... **NNAL**
See also CA 108; 175; CAAE 175; CAAS 28; DLB 175

Barnes, Julian (Patrick) 1946- .... **CLC 42, 141**
See also BRWS 4; CA 102; CANR 19, 54, 115; CN 7; DAB; DLB 194; DLBY 1993; EWL 3; MTCW 1

Barnes, Peter 1931- .... **CLC 5, 56**
See also CA 65-68; CAAS 12; CANR 33, 34, 64, 113; CBD; CD 5; DFS 6; DLB 13, 233; MTCW 1

Barnes, William 1801-1886 .... **NCLC 75**
See also DLB 32

Baroja (y Nessi), Pio 1872-1956 ...... **HLC 1; TCLC 8**
See also CA 104; EW 9

Baron, David
See Pinter, Harold
Baron Corvo
See Rolfe, Frederick (William Serafino Austin Lewis Mary)
Barondess, Sue K(aufman) 1926-1977 .... CLC 8
See Kaufman, Sue
See also CA 1-4R; 69-72; CANR 1
Baron de Teive
See Pessoa, Fernando (Antonio Nogueira)
Baroness Von S.
See Zangwill, Israel
Barres, (Auguste-)Maurice 1862-1923 .... TCLC 47
See also CA 164; DLB 123; GFL 1789 to the Present
Barreto, Afonso Henrique de Lima
See Lima Barreto, Afonso Henrique de
Barrett, Andrea 1954- .... CLC 150
See also CA 156; CANR 92
Barrett, Michele .... CLC 65
Barrett, (Roger) Syd 1946- .... CLC 35
Barrett, William (Christopher) 1913-1992 .... CLC 27
See also CA 13-16R; 139; CANR 11, 67; INT CANR-11
Barrie, J(ames) M(atthew) 1860-1937 .... TCLC 2
See also BRWS 3; BYA 4, 5; CA 104; 136; CANR 77; CDBLB 1890-1914; CLR 16; CWRI 5; DA3; DAB; DAM DRAM; DFS 7; DLB 10, 141, 156; EWL 3; FANT; MAICYA 1, 2; MTCW 1; SATA 100; SUFW; WCH; WLIT 4; YABC 1
Barrington, Michael
See Moorcock, Michael (John)
Barrol, Grady
See Bograd, Larry
Barry, Mike
See Malzberg, Barry N(athaniel)
Barry, Philip 1896-1949 .... TCLC 11
See also CA 109; 199; DFS 9; DLB 7, 228; RGAL 4
Bart, Andre Schwarz
See Schwarz-Bart, Andre
Barth, John (Simmons) 1930- .. CLC 1, 2, 3, 5, 7, 9, 10, 14, 27, 51, 89; SSC 10
See also AITN 1, 2; AMW; BPFB 1; CA 1-4R; CABS 1; CANR 5, 23, 49, 64, 113; CN 7; DAM NOV; DLB 2, 227; EWL 3; FANT; MTCW 1; RGAL 4; RGSF 2; RHW; SSFS 6; TUS
Barthelme, Donald 1931-1989 . CLC 1, 2, 3, 5, 6, 8, 13, 23, 46, 59, 115; SSC 2, 55
See also AMWS 4; BPFB 1; CA 21-24R; 129; CANR 20, 58; DA3; DAM NOV; DLB 2, 234; DLBY 1980, 1989; EWL 3; FANT; LMFS 2; MTCW 1, 2; RGAL 4; RGSF 2; SATA 7; SATA-Obit 62; SSFS 17
Barthelme, Frederick 1943- .... CLC 36, 117
See also AMWS 11; CA 114; 122; CANR 77; CN 7; CSW; DLB 244; DLBY 1985; EWL 3; INT CA-122
Barzun, Jacques (Martin) 1907- .... CLC 51, 145
See also CA 61-64; CANR 22, 95
Bashevis, Isaac
See Singer, Isaac Bashevis
Bashkirtseff, Marie 1859-1884 ..... NCLC 27
Basho, Matsuo
See Matsuo Basho
See also RGWL 2, 3; WP
Basil of Caesaria c. 330-379 .... CMLC 35
Bass, Kingsley B., Jr.
See Bullins, Ed

Bass, Rick 1958- .... CLC 79, 143; SSC 60
See also ANW; CA 126; CANR 53, 93; CSW; DLB 212, 275
Bassani, Giorgio 1916-2000 .... CLC 9
See also CA 65-68; 190; CANR 33; CWW 2; DLB 128, 177; EWL 3; MTCW 1; RGWL 2, 3
Bastian, Ann .... CLC 70
Bastos, Augusto (Antonio) Roa
See Roa Bastos, Augusto (Antonio)
Bataille, Georges 1897-1962 .... CLC 29
See also CA 101; 89-92; EWL 3
Bates, H(erbert) E(rnest) 1905-1974 .... CLC 46; SSC 10
See also CA 93-96; 45-48; CANR 34; DA3; DAB; DAM POP; DLB 162, 191; EWL 3; EXPS; MTCW 1, 2; RGSF 2; SSFS 7
Bauchart
See Camus, Albert
Baudelaire, Charles 1821-1867 .... NCLC 6, 29, 55; PC 1; SSC 18; WLC
See also DA; DA3; DAB; DAC; DAM MST, POET; DLB 217; EW 7; GFL 1789 to the Present; LMFS 2; RGWL 2, 3; TWA
Baudouin, Marcel
See Peguy, Charles (Pierre)
Baudouin, Pierre
See Peguy, Charles (Pierre)
Baudrillard, Jean 1929- .... CLC 60
Baum, L(yman) Frank 1856-1919 . TCLC 7, 132
See also AAYA 46; CA 108; 133; CLR 15; CWRI 5; DLB 22; FANT; JRDA; MAICYA 1, 2; MTCW 1, 2; NFS 13; RGAL 4; SATA 18, 100; WCH
Baum, Louis F.
See Baum, L(yman) Frank
Baumbach, Jonathan 1933- .... CLC 6, 23
See also CA 13-16R; CAAS 5; CANR 12, 66; CN 7; DLBY 1980; INT CANR-12; MTCW 1
Bausch, Richard (Carl) 1945- .... CLC 51
See also AMWS 7; CA 101; CAAS 14; CANR 43, 61, 87; CSW; DLB 130
Baxter, Charles (Morley) 1947- ..... CLC 45, 78
See also CA 57-60; CANR 40, 64, 104; CPW; DAM POP; DLB 130; MTCW 2
Baxter, George Owen
See Faust, Frederick (Schiller)
Baxter, James K(eir) 1926-1972 ...... CLC 14
See also CA 77-80; EWL 3
Baxter, John
See Hunt, E(verette) Howard, (Jr.)
Bayer, Sylvia
See Glassco, John
Baynton, Barbara 1857-1929 .... TCLC 57
See also DLB 230; RGSF 2
Beagle, Peter S(oyer) 1939- .... CLC 7, 104
See also AAYA 47; BPFB 1; BYA 9, 10; CA 9-12R; CANR 4, 51, 73, 110; DA3; DLBY 1980; FANT; INT CANR-4; MTCW 1; SATA 60, 130; SUFW 1, 2; YAW
Bean, Normal
See Burroughs, Edgar Rice
Beard, Charles A(ustin) 1874-1948 .... TCLC 15
See also CA 115; 189; DLB 17; SATA 18
Beardsley, Aubrey 1872-1898 .... NCLC 6
Beattie, Ann 1947- .... CLC 8, 13, 18, 40, 63, 146; SSC 11
See also AMWS 5; BEST 90:2; BPFB 1; CA 81-84; CANR 53, 73; CN 7; CPW; DA3; DAM NOV, POP; DLB 218, 278; DLBY 1982; EWL 3; MTCW 1, 2; RGAL 4; RGSF 2; SSFS 9; TUS

Beattie, James 1735-1803 .... NCLC 25
See also DLB 109
Beauchamp, Kathleen Mansfield 1888-1923
See Mansfield, Katherine
See also CA 104; 134; DA; DA3; DAC; DAM MST; MTCW 2; TEA
Beaumarchais, Pierre-Augustin Caron de 1732-1799 .... DC 4; LC 61
See also DAM DRAM; DFS 14, 16; EW 4; GFL Beginnings to 1789; RGWL 2, 3
Beaumont, Francis 1584(?)-1616 . DC 6; LC 33
See also BRW 2; CDBLB Before 1660; DLB 58; TEA
Beauvoir, Simone (Lucie Ernestine Marie Bertrand) de 1908-1986 ... CLC 1, 2, 4, 8, 14, 31, 44, 50, 71, 124; SSC 35; WLC
See also BPFB 1; CA 9-12R; 118; CANR 28, 61; DA; DA3; DAB; DAC; DAM MST, NOV; DLB 72; DLBY 1986; EW 12; EWL 3; FW; GFL 1789 to the Present; LMFS 2; MTCW 1, 2; RGSF 2; RGWL 2, 3; TWA
Becker, Carl (Lotus) 1873-1945 .... TCLC 63
See also CA 157; DLB 17
Becker, Jurek 1937-1997 .... CLC 7, 19
See also CA 85-88; 157; CANR 60, 117; CWW 2; DLB 75; EWL 3
Becker, Walter 1950- .... CLC 26
Beckett, Samuel (Barclay) 1906-1989
. CLC 1, 2, 3, 4, 6, 9, 10, 11, 14, 18, 29, 57, 59, 83; SSC 16; WLC
See also BRWR 1; BRWS 1; CA 5-8R; 130; CANR 33, 61; CBD; CDBLB 1945-1960; DA; DA3; DAB; DAC; DAM DRAM, MST, NOV; DFS 2, 7; DLB 13, 15, 233; DLBY 1990; EWL 3; GFL 1789 to the Present; LMFS 2; MTCW 1, 2; RGSF 2; RGWL 2, 3; SSFS 15; TEA; WLIT 4
Beckford, William 1760-1844 .... NCLC 16
See also BRW 3; DLB 39, 213; HGG; LMFS 1; SUFW
Beckham, Barry (Earl) 1944- .... BLC 1
See also BW 1; CA 29-32R; CANR 26, 62; CN 7; DAM MULT; DLB 33
Beckman, Gunnel 1910- .... CLC 26
See also CA 33-36R; CANR 15, 114; CLR 25; MAICYA 1, 2; SAAS 9; SATA 6
Becque, Henri 1837-1899 .... NCLC 3
See also DLB 192; GFL 1789 to the Present
Becquer, Gustavo Adolfo 1836-1870 .... HLCS 1; NCLC 106
See also DAM MULT
Beddoes, Thomas Lovell 1803-1849 . DC 15; NCLC 3
See also DLB 96
Bede c. 673-735 .... CMLC 20
See also DLB 146; TEA
Bedford, Denton R. 1907-(?) .... NNAL
Bedford, Donald F.
See Fearing, Kenneth (Flexner)
Beecher, Catharine Esther 1800-1878 .... NCLC 30
See also DLB 1, 243
Beecher, John 1904-1980 .... CLC 6
See also AITN 1; CA 5-8R; 105; CANR 8
Beer, Johann 1655-1700 .... LC 5
See also DLB 168
Beer, Patricia 1924- .... CLC 58
See also CA 61-64; 183; CANR 13, 46; CP 7; CWP; DLB 40; FW
Beerbohm, Max
See Beerbohm, (Henry) Max(imilian)
Beerbohm, (Henry) Max(imilian) 1872-1956 .... TCLC 1, 24
See also BRWS 2; CA 104; 154; CANR 79; DLB 34, 100; FANT

Beer-Hofmann, Richard 1866-1945
.... TCLC 60
See also CA 160; DLB 81
Beg, Shemus
See Stephens, James
Begiebing, Robert J(ohn) 1946- ...... CLC 70
See also CA 122; CANR 40, 88
Behan, Brendan 1923-1964 .... CLC 1, 8, 11, 15, 79
See also BRWS 2; CA 73-76; CANR 33; CBD; CDBLB 1945-1960; DAM DRAM; DFS 7; DLB 13, 233; EWL 3; MTCW 1, 2
Behn, Aphra 1640(?)-1689 . DC 4; LC 1, 30, 42; PC 13; WLC
See also BRWS 3; DA; DA3; DAB; DAC; DAM DRAM, MST, NOV, POET; DFS 16; DLB 39, 80, 131; FW; TEA; WLIT 3
Behrman, S(amuel) N(athaniel) 1893-1973
.... CLC 40
See also CA 13-16; 45-48; CAD; CAP 1; DLB 7, 44; IDFW 3; RGAL 4
Belasco, David 1853-1931 .... TCLC 3
See also CA 104; 168; DLB 7; RGAL 4
Belcheva, Elisaveta Lyubomirova 1893-1991
.... CLC 10
See Bagryana, Elisaveta
Beldone, Phil "Cheech"
See Ellison, Harlan (Jay)
Beleno
See Azuela, Mariano
Belinski, Vissarion Grigoryevich 1811-1848
.... NCLC 5
See also DLB 198
Belitt, Ben 1911- .... CLC 22
See also CA 13-16R; CAAS 4; CANR 7, 77; CP 7; DLB 5
Bell, Gertrude (Margaret Lowthian) 1868-1926 .... TCLC 67
See also CA 167; CANR 110; DLB 174
Bell, J. Freeman
See Zangwill, Israel
Bell, James Madison 1826-1902 .... BLC 1; TCLC 43
See also BW 1; CA 122; 124; DAM MULT; DLB 50
Bell, Madison Smartt 1957- .... CLC 41, 102
See also AMWS 10; BPFB 1; CA 111, 183; CAAE 183; CANR 28, 54, 73; CN 7; CSW; DLB 218, 278; MTCW 1
Bell, Marvin (Hartley) 1937- ...... CLC 8, 31
See also CA 21-24R; CAAS 14; CANR 59, 102; CP 7; DAM POET; DLB 5; MTCW 1
Bell, W. L. D.
See Mencken, H(enry) L(ouis)
Bellamy, Atwood C.
See Mencken, H(enry) L(ouis)
Bellamy, Edward 1850-1898 ..... NCLC 4, 86
See also DLB 12; NFS 15; RGAL 4; SFW 4
Belli, Gioconda 1949- .... HLCS 1
See also CA 152; CWW 2; EWL 3; RGWL 3
Bellin, Edward J.
See Kuttner, Henry
Belloc, (Joseph) Hilaire (Pierre Sebastien Rene Swanton) 1870-1953 .... PC 24; TCLC 7, 18
See also CA 106; 152; CWRI 5; DAM POET; DLB 19, 100, 141, 174; EWL 3; MTCW 1; SATA 112; WCH; YABC 1
Belloc, Joseph Peter Rene Hilaire
See Belloc, (Joseph) Hilaire (Pierre Sebastien Rene Swanton)
Belloc, Joseph Pierre Hilaire
See Belloc, (Joseph) Hilaire (Pierre Sebastien Rene Swanton)

Belloc, M. A.
See Lowndes, Marie Adelaide (Belloc)
Belloc-Lowndes, Mrs.
See Lowndes, Marie Adelaide (Belloc)
Bellow, Saul 1915- ...... CLC 1, 2, 3, 6, 8, 10, 13, 15, 25, 33, 34, 63, 79; SSC 14; WLC
See also AITN 2; AMW; AMWR 2; BEST 89:3; BPFB 1; CA 5-8R; CABS 1; CANR 29, 53, 95; CDALB 1941-1968; CN 7; DA; DA3; DAB; DAC; DAM MST, NOV, POP; DLB 2, 28; DLBD 3; DLBY 1982; EWL 3; MTCW 1, 2; NFS 4, 14; RGAL 4; RGSF 2; SSFS 12; TUS
Belser, Reimond Karel Maria de 1929-
See Ruyslinck, Ward
See also CA 152
Bely, Andrey .... PC 11; TCLC 7
See Bugayev, Boris Nikolayevich
See also EW 9; EWL 3; MTCW 1
Belyi, Andrei
See Bugayev, Boris Nikolayevich
See also RGWL 2, 3
Bembo, Pietro 1470-1547 .... LC 79
See also RGWL 2, 3
Benary, Margot
See Benary-Isbert, Margot
Benary-Isbert, Margot 1889-1979 ... CLC 12
See also CA 5-8R; 89-92; CANR 4, 72; CLR 12; MAICYA 1, 2; SATA 2; SATA-Obit 21
Benavente (y Martinez), Jacinto 1866-1954
.... HLCS 1; TCLC 3
See also CA 106; 131; CANR 81; DAM DRAM, MULT; EWL 3; GLL 2; HW 1, 2; MTCW 1, 2
Benchley, Peter (Bradford) 1940- . CLC 4, 8
See also AAYA 14; AITN 2; BPFB 1; CA 17-20R; CANR 12, 35, 66, 115; CPW; DAM NOV, POP; HGG; MTCW 1, 2; SATA 3, 89
Benchley, Robert (Charles) 1889-1945
.... TCLC 1, 55
See also CA 105; 153; DLB 11; RGAL 4
Benda, Julien 1867-1956 .... TCLC 60
See also CA 120; 154; GFL 1789 to the Present
Benedict, Ruth (Fulton) 1887-1948
.... TCLC 60
See also CA 158; DLB 246
Benedikt, Michael 1935- .... CLC 4, 14
See also CA 13-16R; CANR 7; CP 7; DLB 5
Benet, Juan 1927-1993 .... CLC 28
See also CA 143; EWL 3
Benet, Stephen Vincent 1898-1943 . SSC 10; TCLC 7
See also AMWS 11; CA 104; 152; DA3; DAM POET; DLB 4, 48, 102, 249; DLBY 1997; EWL 3; HGG; MTCW 1; RGAL 4; RGSF 2; SUFW; WP; YABC 1
Benet, William Rose 1886-1950 .... TCLC 28
See also CA 118; 152; DAM POET; DLB 45; RGAL 4
Benford, Gregory (Albert) 1941- .... CLC 52
See also BPFB 1; CA 69-72, 175; CAAE 175; CAAS 27; CANR 12, 24, 49, 95; CSW; DLBY 1982; SCFW 2; SFW 4
Bengtsson, Frans (Gunnar) 1894-1954
.... TCLC 48
See also CA 170; EWL 3
Benjamin, David
See Slavitt, David R(ytman)
Benjamin, Lois
See Gould, Lois
Benjamin, Walter 1892-1940 .... TCLC 39
See also CA 164; DLB 242; EW 11; EWL 3

Benn, Gottfried 1886-1956 . PC 35; TCLC 3
See also CA 106; 153; DLB 56; EWL 3; RGWL 2, 3
Bennett, Alan 1934- .... CLC 45, 77
See also BRWS 8; CA 103; CANR 35, 55, 106; CBD; CD 5; DAB; DAM MST; MTCW 1, 2
Bennett, (Enoch) Arnold 1867-1931
.... TCLC 5, 20
See also BRW 6; CA 106; 155; CDBLB 1890-1914; DLB 10, 34, 98, 135; EWL 3; MTCW 2
Bennett, Elizabeth
See Mitchell, Margaret (Munnerlyn)
Bennett, George Harold 1930-
See Bennett, Hal
See also BW 1; CA 97-100; CANR 87
Bennett, Gwendolyn B. 1902-1981 ...... HR 2
See also BW 1; CA 125; DLB 51; WP
Bennett, Hal .... CLC 5
See Bennett, George Harold
See also DLB 33
Bennett, Jay 1912- .... CLC 35
See also AAYA 10; CA 69-72; CANR 11, 42, 79; JRDA; SAAS 4; SATA 41, 87; SATA-Brief 27; WYA; YAW
Bennett, Louise (Simone) 1919- .... BLC 1; CLC 28
See also BW 2, 3; CA 151; CDWLB 3; CP 7; DAM MULT; DLB 117; EWL 3
Benson, A. C. 1862-1925 .... TCLC 123
See also DLB 98
Benson, E(dward) F(rederic) 1867-1940
.... TCLC 27
See also CA 114; 157; DLB 135, 153; HGG; SUFW 1
Benson, Jackson J. 1930- .... CLC 34
See also CA 25-28R; DLB 111
Benson, Sally 1900-1972 .... CLC 17
See also CA 19-20; 37-40R; CAP 1; SATA 1, 35; SATA-Obit 27
Benson, Stella 1892-1933 .... TCLC 17
See also CA 117; 154, 155; DLB 36, 162; FANT; TEA
Bentham, Jeremy 1748-1832 .... NCLC 38
See also DLB 107, 158, 252
Bentley, E(dmund) C(lerihew) 1875-1956
.... TCLC 12
See also CA 108; DLB 70; MSW
Bentley, Eric (Russell) 1916- .... CLC 24
See also CA 5-8R; CAD; CANR 6, 67; CBD; CD 5; INT CANR-6
Beranger, Pierre Jean de 1780-1857
.... NCLC 34
Berdyaev, Nicolas
See Berdyaev, Nikolai (Aleksandrovich)
Berdyaev, Nikolai (Aleksandrovich) 1874-1948 .... TCLC 67
See also CA 120; 157
Berdyayev, Nikolai (Aleksandrovich)
See Berdyaev, Nikolai (Aleksandrovich)
Berendt, John (Lawrence) 1939- .... CLC 86
See also CA 146; CANR 75, 93; DA3; MTCW 1
Beresford, J(ohn) D(avys) 1873-1947
.... TCLC 81
See also CA 112; 155; DLB 162, 178, 197; SFW 4; SUFW 1
Bergelson, David 1884-1952 .... TCLC 81
See Bergelson, Dovid
Bergelson, Dovid
See Bergelson, David
See also EWL 3
Berger, Colonel
See Malraux, (Georges-)Andre
Berger, John (Peter) 1926- .... CLC 2, 19
See also BRWS 4; CA 81-84; CANR 51, 78, 117; CN 7; DLB 14, 207

Berger, Melvin H. 1927- .... CLC 12
See also CA 5-8R; CANR 4; CLR 32; SAAS 2; SATA 5, 88; SATA-Essay 124

Berger, Thomas (Louis) 1924- . CLC 3, 5, 8, 11, 18, 38
See also BPFB 1; CA 1-4R; CANR 5, 28, 51; CN 7; DAM NOV; DLB 2; DLBY 1980; EWL 3; FANT; INT CANR-28; MTCW 1, 2; RHW; TCWW 2

Bergman, (Ernst) Ingmar 1918- .... CLC 16, 72
See also CA 81-84; CANR 33, 70; DLB 257; MTCW 2

Bergson, Henri(-Louis) 1859-1941
.... TCLC 32
See also CA 164; EW 8; EWL 3; GFL 1789 to the Present

Bergstein, Eleanor 1938- .... CLC 4
See also CA 53-56; CANR 5

Berkeley, George 1685-1753 .... LC 65
See also DLB 31, 101, 252

Berkoff, Steven 1937- .... CLC 56
See also CA 104; CANR 72; CBD; CD 5

Berlin, Isaiah 1909-1997 .... TCLC 105
See also CA 85-88; 162

Bermant, Chaim (Icyk) 1929-1998 . CLC 40
See also CA 57-60; CANR 6, 31, 57, 105; CN 7

Bern, Victoria
See Fisher, M(ary) F(rances) K(ennedy)

Bernanos, (Paul Louis) Georges 1838-1948
.... TCLC 3
See also CA 104; 130; CANR 94; DLB 72; EWL 3; GFL 1789 to the Present; RGWL 2, 3

Bernard, April 1956- .... CLC 59
See also CA 131

Berne, Victoria
See Fisher, M(ary) F(rances) K(ennedy)

Bernhard, Thomas 1931-1989 .... CLC 3, 32, 61; DC 14
See also CA 85-88; 127; CANR 32, 57; CD-WLB 2; DLB 85, 124; EWL 3; MTCW 1; RGWL 2, 3

Bernhardt, Sarah (Henriette Rosine) 1844-1923 .... TCLC 75
See also CA 157

Bernstein, Charles 1950- .... CLC 142,
See also CA 129; CAAS 24; CANR 90; CP 7; DLB 169

Berriault, Gina 1926-1999 ...... CLC 54, 109; SSC 30
See also CA 116; 129; 185; CANR 66; DLB 130; SSFS 7,11

Berrigan, Daniel 1921- .... CLC 4
See also CA 33-36R; CAAE 187; CAAS 1; CANR 11, 43, 78; CP 7; DLB 5

Berrigan, Edmund Joseph Michael, Jr. 1934-1983
See Berrigan, Ted
See also CA 61-64; 110; CANR 14, 102

Berrigan, Ted .... CLC 37
See Berrigan, Edmund Joseph Michael, Jr.
See also DLB 5, 169; WP

Berry, Charles Edward Anderson 1931-
See Berry, Chuck
See also CA 115

Berry, Chuck .... CLC 17
See Berry, Charles Edward Anderson

Berry, Jonas
See Ashbery, John (Lawrence)
See also GLL 1

Berry, Wendell (Erdman) 1934- .. CLC 4, 6, 8, 27, 46; PC 28
See also AITN 1; AMWS 10; ANW; CA 73-76; CANR 50, 73, 101; CP 7; CSW; DAM POET; DLB 5, 6, 234, 275; MTCW 1

Berryman, John 1914-1972 . CLC 1, 2, 3, 4, 6, 8, 10, 13, 25, 62
See also AMW; CA 13-16; 33-36R; CABS 2; CANR 35; CAP 1; CDALB 1941-1968; DAM POET; DLB 48; EWL 3; MTCW 1, 2; PAB; RGAL 4; WP

Bertolucci, Bernardo 1940- ...... CLC 16, 157
See also CA 106

Berton, Pierre (Francis Demarigny) 1920-
.... CLC 104
See also CA 1-4R; CANR 2, 56; CPW; DLB 68; SATA 99

Bertrand, Aloysius 1807-1841 .... NCLC 31
See Bertrand, Louis oAloysiusc

Bertrand, Louis oAloysiusc
See Bertrand, Aloysius
See also DLB 217

Bertran de Born c. 1140-1215 .... CMLC 5

Besant, Annie (Wood) 1847-1933 ... TCLC 9
See also CA 105; 185

Bessie, Alvah 1904-1985 .... CLC 23
See also CA 5-8R; 116; CANR 2, 80; DLB 26

Bethlen, T. D.
See Silverberg, Robert

Beti, Mongo .... BLC 1; CLC 27
See Biyidi, Alexandre
See also AFW; CANR 79; DAM MULT; EWL 3; WLIT 2

Betjeman, John 1906-1984 ..... CLC 2, 6, 10, 34, 43
See also BRW 7; CA 9-12R; 112; CANR 33, 56; CDBLB 1945-1960; DA3; DAB; DAM MST, POET; DLB 20; DLBY 1984; EWL 3; MTCW 1, 2

Bettelheim, Bruno 1903-1990 .... CLC 79
See also CA 81-84; 131; CANR 23, 61; DA3; MTCW 1, 2

Betti, Ugo 1892-1953 .... TCLC 5
See also CA 104; 155; EWL 3; RGWL 2, 3

Betts, Doris (Waugh) 1932- ... CLC 3, 6, 28; SSC 45
See also CA 13-16R; CANR 9, 66, 77; CN 7; CSW; DLB 218; DLBY 1982; INT CANR-9; RGAL 4

Bevan, Alistair
See Roberts, Keith (John Kingston)

Bey, Pilaff
See Douglas, (George) Norman

Bialik, Chaim Nachman 1873-1934
.... TCLC 25
See also CA 170; EWL 3

Bickerstaff, Isaac
See Swift, Jonathan

Bidart, Frank 1939- .... CLC 33
See also CA 140; CANR 106; CP 7

Bienek, Horst 1930- .... CLC 7, 11
See also CA 73-76; DLB 75

Bierce, Ambrose (Gwinett) 1842-1914(?)
.... SSC 9; TCLC 1, 7, 44; WLC
See also AMW; BYA 11; CA 104; 139; CANR 78; CDALB 1865-1917; DA; DA3; DAC; DAM MST; DLB 11, 12, 23, 71, 74, 186; EWL 3; EXPS; HGG; LAIT 2; RGAL 4; RGSF 2; SSFS 9; SUFW 1

Biggers, Earl Derr 1884-1933 .... TCLC 65
See also CA 108; 153

Billiken, Bud
See Motley, Willard (Francis)

Billings, Josh
See Shaw, Henry Wheeler

Billington, (Lady) Rachel (Mary) 1942-
.... CLC 43
See also AITN 2; CA 33-36R; CANR 44; CN 7

Binchy, Maeve 1940- .... CLC 153
See also BEST 90:1; BPFB 1; CA 127; 134; CANR 50, 96; CN 7; CPW; DA3; DAM POP; INT CA-134; MTCW 1; RHW

Binyon, T(imothy) J(ohn) 1936- ..... CLC 34
See also CA 111; CANR 28

Bion 335B.C.-245B.C. .... CMLC 39

Bioy Casares, Adolfo 1914-1999 .. CLC 4, 8, 13, 88; HLC 1; SSC 17
See Casares, Adolfo Bioy; Miranda, Javier; Sacastru, Martin
See also CA 29-32R; 177; CANR 19, 43, 66; DAM MULT; DLB 113; EWL 3; HW 1, 2; LAW; MTCW 1, 2

Birch, Allison .... CLC 65

Bird, Cordwainer
See Ellison, Harlan (Jay)

Bird, Robert Montgomery 1806-1854
.... NCLC 1
See also DLB 202; RGAL 4

Birkerts, Sven 1951- .... CLC 116
See also CA 128; 133, 176; CAAE 176; CAAS 29; INT 133

Birney, (Alfred) Earle 1904-1995 ..... CLC 1, 4, 6, 11
See also CA 1-4R; CANR 5, 20; CP 7; DAC; DAM MST, POET; DLB 88; MTCW 1; PFS 8; RGEL 2

Biruni, al 973-1048(?) .... CMLC 28

Bishop, Elizabeth 1911-1979 .... CLC 1, 4, 9, 13, 15, 32; PC 3, 34; TCLC 121
See also AMWR 2; AMWS 1; CA 5-8R; 89-92; CABS 2; CANR 26, 61, 108; CDALB 1968-1988; DA; DA3; DAC; DAM MST, PCET; DLB 5, 169; EWL 3; GLL 2; MAWW; MTCW 1, 2; PAB; PFS 6, 12; RGAL 4; SATA-Obit 24; TUS; WP

Bishop, John 1935- .... CLC 10
See also CA 105

Bishop, John Peale 1892-1944 .... TCLC 103
See also CA 107; 155; DLB 4, 9, 45; RGAL 4

Bissett, Bill 1939- .... CLC 18; PC 14
See also CA 69-72; CAAS 19; CANR 15; CCA 1; CP 7; DLB 53; MTCW 1

Bissoondath, Neil (Devindra) 1955-
.... CLC 120
See also CA 136; CN 7; DAC

Bitov, Andrei (Georgievich) 1937- .. CLC 57
See also CA 142

Biyidi, Alexandre 1932-
See Beti, Mongo
See also BW 1, 3; CA 114; 124; CANR 81; DA3; MTCW 1, 2

Bjarme, Brynjolf
See Ibsen, Henrik (Johan)

Bjoernson, Bjoernstjerne (Martinius) 1832-1910 .... TCLC 7, 37
See also CA 104

Black, Robert
See Holdstock, Robert P.

Blackburn, Paul 1926-1971 .... CLC 9, 43
See also BG 2; CA 81-84; 33-36R; CANR 34; DLB 16; DLBY 1981

Black Elk 1863-1950 .... NNAL; TCLC 33
See also CA 144; DAM MULT; MTCW 1; WP

Black Hawk 1767-1838 .... NNAL

Black Hobart
See Sanders, (James) Ed(ward)

Blacklin, Malcolm
See Chambers, Aidan

Blackmore, R(ichard) D(oddridge) 1825-1900 .... TCLC 27
See also CA 120; DLB 18; RGEL 2

Blackmur, R(ichard) P(almer) 1904-1965
.... CLC 2, 24
See also AMWS 2; CA 11-12; 25-28R; CANR 71; CAP 1; DLB 63; EWL 3

Black Tarantula
See Acker, Kathy

Blackwood, Algernon (Henry) 1869-1951
.... **TCLC 5**
See also CA 105; 150; DLB 153, 156, 178; HGG; SUFW 1

Blackwood, Caroline 1931-1996 .. **CLC 6, 9, 100**
See also CA 85-88; 151; CANR 32, 61, 65; CN 7; DLB 14, 207; HGG; MTCW 1

Blade, Alexander
See Hamilton, Edmond; Silverberg, Robert

Blaga, Lucian 1895-1961 .... **CLC 75**
See also CA 157; DLB 220; EWL 3

Blair, Eric (Arthur) 1903-1950 ... **TCLC 123**
See Orwell, George
See also CA 104; 132; DA; DA3; DAB; DAC; DAM MST, NOV; MTCW 1, 2; SATA 29

Blair, Hugh 1718-1800 .... **NCLC 75**

Blais, Marie-Claire 1939- ... **CLC 2, 4, 6, 13, 22**
See also CA 21-24R; CAAS 4; CANR 38, 75, 93; DAC; DAM MST; DLB 53; EWL 3; FW; MTCW 1, 2; TWA

Blaise, Clark 1940- .... **CLC 29**
See also AITN 2; CA 53-56; CAAS 3; CANR 5, 66, 106; CN 7; DLB 53; RGSF 2

Blake, Fairley
See De Voto, Bernard (Augustine)

Blake, Nicholas
See Day Lewis, C(ecil)
See also DLB 77; MSW

Blake, Sterling
See Benford, Gregory (Albert)

Blake, William 1757-1827 ...... **NCLC 13, 37, 57; PC 12; WLC**
See also AAYA 47; BRW 3; BRWR 1; CDBLB 1789-1832; CLR 52; DA; DA3; DAB; DAC; DAM MST, POET; DLB 93, 163; EXPP; LMFS 1; MAICYA 1, 2; PAB; PFS 2, 12; SATA 30; TEA; WCH; WLIT 3; WP

Blanchot, Maurice 1907- .... **CLC 135**
See also CA 117; 144; DLB 72; EWL 3

Blasco Ibanez, Vicente 1867-1928
.... **TCLC 12**
See also BPFB 1; CA 110; 131; CANR 81; DA3; DAM NOV; EW 8; EWL 3; HW 1, 2; MTCW 1

Blatty, William Peter 1928- .... **CLC 2**
See also CA 5-8R; CANR 9; DAM POP; HGG

Bleeck, Oliver
See Thomas, Ross (Elmore)

Blessing, Lee 1949- .... **CLC 54**
See also CAD; CD 5

Blight, Rose
See Greer, Germaine

Blish, James (Benjamin) 1921-1975
.... **CLC 14**
See also BPFB 1; CA 1-4R; 57-60; CANR 3; DLB 8; MTCW 1; SATA 66; SCFW 2; SFW 4

Bliss, Reginald
See Wells, H(erbert) G(eorge)

Blixen, Karen (Christentze Dinesen) 1885-1962
See Dinesen, Isak
See also CA 25-28; CANR 22, 50; CAP 2; DA3; DLB 214; LMFS 1; MTCW 1, 2; SATA 44

Bloch, Robert (Albert) 1917-1994 ... **CLC 33**
See also AAYA 29; CA 5-8R; 179; 146; CAAE 179; CAAS 20; CANR 5, 78; DA3; DLB 44; HGG; INT CANR-5; MTCW 1; SATA 12; SATA-Obit 82; SFW 4; SUFW 1, 2

Blok, Alexander (Alexandrovich) 1880-1921
.... **PC 21; TCLC 5**
See also CA 104; 183; EW 9; EWL 3; LMFS 2; RGWL 2, 3

Blom, Jan
See Breytenbach, Breyten

Bloom, Harold 1930- .... **CLC 24, 103**
See also CA 13-16R; CANR 39, 75, 92; DLB 67; EWL 3; MTCW 1; RGAL 4

Bloomfield, Aurelius
See Bourne, Randolph S(illiman)

Blount, Roy (Alton), Jr. 1941- .... **CLC 38**
See also CA 53-56; CANR 10, 28, 61; CSW; INT CANR-28; MTCW 1, 2

Blowsnake, Sam 1875-(?) .... **NNAL**

Bloy, Leon 1846-1917 .... **TCLC 22**
See also CA 121; 183; DLB 123; GFL 1789 to the Present

Blue Cloud, Peter (Aroniawenrate) 1933-
.... **NNAL**
See also CA 117; CANR 40; DAM MULT

Bluggage, Oranthy
See Alcott, Louisa May

Blume, Judy (Sussman) 1938- .. **CLC 12, 30**
See also AAYA 3, 26; BYA 1, 8, 12; CA 29-32R; CANR 13, 37, 66; CLR 2, 15, 69; CPW; DA3; DAM NOV, POP; DLB 52; JRDA; MAICYA 1, 2; MAICYAS 1; MTCW 1, 2; SATA 2, 31, 79; WYA; YAW

Blunden, Edmund (Charles) 1896-1974
.... **CLC 2, 56**
See also BRW 6; CA 17-18; 45-48; CANR 54; CAP 2; DLB 20, 100, 155; MTCW 1; PAB

Bly, Robert (Elwood) 1926- ...... **CLC 1, 2, 5, 10, 15, 38, 128; PC 39**
See also AMWS 4; CA 5-8R; CANR 41, 73; CP 7; DA3; DAM POET; DLB 5; EWL 3; MTCW 1, 2; PFS 6, 17; RGAL 4

Boas, Franz 1858-1942 .... **TCLC 56**
See also CA 115; 181

Bobette
See Simenon, Georges (Jacques Christian)

Boccaccio, Giovanni 1313-1375 .. **CMLC 13, 57; SSC 10**
See also EW 2; RGSF 2; RGWL 2, 3; TWA

Bochco, Steven 1943- .... **CLC 35**
See also AAYA 11; CA 124; 138

Bode, Sigmund
See O'Doherty, Brian

Bodel, Jean 1167(?)-1210 .... **CMLC 28**

Bodenheim, Maxwell 1892-1954 ... **TCLC 44**
See also CA 110; 187; DLB 9, 45; RGAL 4

Bodenheimer, Maxwell
See Bodenheim, Maxwell

Bodker, Cecil 1927-
See Bodker, Cecil

Bodker, Cecil 1927- .... **CLC 21**
See also CA 73-76; CANR 13, 44, 111; CLR 23; MAICYA 1, 2; SATA 14, 133

Boell, Heinrich (Theodor) 1917-1985
.... **CLC 2, 3, 6, 9, 11, 15, 27, 32, 72; SSC 23; WLC**
See Boll, Heinrich
See also CA 21-24R; 116; CANR 24; DA; DA3; DAB; DAC; DAM MST, NOV; DLB 69; DLBY 1985; MTCW 1, 2; TWA

Boerne, Alfred
See Doeblin, Alfred

Boethius c. 480-c. 524 .... **CMLC 15**
See also DLB 115; RGWL 2, 3

Boff, Leonardo (Genezio Darci) 1938-
.... **CLC 70; HLC 1**
See also CA 150; DAM MULT; HW 2

Bogan, Louise 1897-1970 ...... **CLC 4, 39, 46, 93; PC 12**
See also AMWS 3; CA 73-76; 25-28R; CANR 33, 82; DAM POET; DLB 45, 169; EWL 3; MAWW; MTCW 1, 2; RGAL 4

Bogarde, Dirk
See Van Den Bogarde, Derek Jules Gaspard Ulric Niven
See also DLB 14

Bogosian, Eric 1953- .... **CLC 45, 141**
See also CA 138; CAD; CANR 102; CD 5

Bograd, Larry 1953- .... **CLC 35**
See also CA 93-96; CANR 57; SAAS 21; SATA 33, 89; WYA

Boiardo, Matteo Maria 1441-1494 ...... **LC 6**

Boileau-Despreaux, Nicolas 1636-1711
.... **LC 3**
See also DLB 268; EW 3; GFL Beginnings to 1789; RGWL 2, 3

Boissard, Maurice
See Leautaud, Paul

Bojer, Johan 1872-1959 .... **TCLC 64**
See also CA 189; EWL 3

Bok, Edward W. 1863-1930 .... **TCLC 101**
See also DLB 91; DLBD 16

Boker, George Henry 1823-1890
.... **NCLC 125**
See also RGAL 4

Boland, Eavan (Aisling) 1944- . **CLC 40, 67, 113**
See also BRWS 5; CA 143; CAAE 207; CANR 61; CP 7; CWP; DAM POET; DLB 40; FW; MTCW 2; PFS 12

Boll, Heinrich
See Boell, Heinrich (Theodor)
See also BPFB 1; CDWLB 2; EW 13; EWL 3; RGSF 2; RGWL 2, 3

Bolt, Lee
See Faust, Frederick (Schiller)

Bolt, Robert (Oxton) 1924-1995 ...... **CLC 14**
See also CA 17-20R; 147; CANR 35, 67; CBD; DAM DRAM; DFS 2; DLB 13, 233; EWL 3; LAIT 1; MTCW 1

Bombal, Maria Luisa 1910-1980 ... **HLCS 1; SSC 37**
See also CA 127; CANR 72; EWL 3; HW 1; LAW; RGSF 2

Bombet, Louis-Alexandre-Cesar
See Stendhal

Bomkauf
See Kaufman, Bob (Garnell)

Bonaventura .... **NCLC 35**
See also DLB 90

Bond, Edward 1934- .... **CLC 4, 6, 13, 23**
See also BRWS 1; CA 25-28R; CANR 38, 67, 106; CBD; CD 5; DAM DRAM; DFS 3, 8; DLB 13; EWL 3; MTCW 1

Bonham, Frank 1914-1989 .... **CLC 12**
See also AAYA 1; BYA 1, 3; CA 9-12R; CANR 4, 36; JRDA; MAICYA 1, 2; SAAS 3; SATA 1, 49; SATA-Obit 62; TCWW 2; YAW

Bonnefoy, Yves 1923- .... **CLC 9, 15, 58**
See also CA 85-88; CANR 33, 75, 97; CWW 2; DAM MST, POET; DLB 258; EWL 3; GFL 1789 to the Present; MTCW 1, 2

Bonner, Marita .... **HR 2**
See Occomy, Marita (Odette) Bonner

Bonnin, Gertrude 1876-1938 .... **NNAL**
See Zitkala-Sa
See also CA 150; DAM MULT

Bontemps, Arna(ud Wendell) 1902-1973
.... **BLC 1; CLC 1, 18; HR 2**
See also BW 1; CA 1-4R; 41-44R; CANR 4, 35; CLR 6; CWRI 5; DA3; DAM MULT, NOV, POET; DLB 48, 51; JRDA; MAICYA 1, 2; MTCW 1, 2; SATA 2, 44; SATA-Obit 24; WCH; WP

Booth, Martin 1944- .... **CLC 13**
See also CA 93-96; CAAE 188; CAAS 2; CANR 92

Booth, Philip 1925- .... CLC 23
See also CA 5-8R; CANR 5, 88; CP 7; DLBY 1982

Booth, Wayne C(layson) 1921- .... CLC 24
See also CA 1-4R; CAAS 5; CANR 3, 43, 117; DLB 67

Borchert, Wolfgang 1921-1947 .... TCLC 5
See also CA 104; 188; DLB 69, 124; EWL 3

Borel, Petrus 1809-1859 .... NCLC 41
See also DLB 119; GFL 1789 to the Present

Borges, Jorge Luis 1899-1986 .. CLC 1, 2, 3, 4, 6, 8, 9, 10, 13, 19, 44, 48, 83; HLC 1; PC 22, 32; SSC 4, 41; TCLC 109; WLC
See also AAYA 26; BPFB 1; CA 21-24R; CANR 19, 33, 75, 105; CDWLB 3; DA; DA3; DAB; DAC; DAM MST, MULT; DLB 113; DLBY 1986; DNFS 1, 2; EWL 3; HW 1, 2; LAW; LMFS 2; MSW; MTCW 1, 2; RGSF 2; RGWL 2, 3; SFW 4; SSFS 17; TWA; WLIT 1

Borowski, Tadeusz 1922-1951 .... SSC 48; TCLC 9
See also CA 106; 154; CDWLB 4; DLB 215; EWL 3; RGSF 2; RGWL 3; SSFS 13

Borrow, George (Henry) 1803-1881 .... NCLC 9
See also DLB 21, 55, 166

Bosch (Gavino), Juan 1909-2001 ... HLCS 1
See also CA 151; 204; DAM MST, MULT; DLB 145; HW 1, 2

Bosman, Herman Charles 1905-1951 .... TCLC 49
See Malan, Herman
See also CA 160; DLB 225; RGSF 2

Bosschere, Jean de 1878(?)-1953 .. TCLC 19
See also CA 115; 186

Boswell, James 1740-1795 .. LC 4, 50; WLC
See also BRW 3; CDBLB 1660-1789; DA; DAB; DAC; DAM MST; DLB 104, 142; TEA; WLIT 3

Bottomley, Gordon 1874-1948 .... TCLC 107
See also CA 120; 192; DLB 10

Bottoms, David 1949- .... CLC 53
See also CA 105; CANR 22; CSW; DLB 120; DLBY 1983

Boucicault, Dion 1820-1890 .... NCLC 41

Boucolon, Maryse
See Conde, Maryse

Bourget, Paul (Charles Joseph) 1852-1935 .... TCLC 12
See also CA 107; 196; DLB 123; GFL 1789 to the Present

Bourjaily, Vance (Nye) 1922- ...... CLC 8, 62
See also CA 1-4R; CAAS 1; CANR 2, 72; CN 7; DLB 2, 143

Bourne, Randolph S(illiman) 1886-1918 .... TCLC 16
See also AMW; CA 117; 155; DLB 63

Bova, Ben(jamin William) 1932- .... CLC 45
See also AAYA 16; CA 5-8R; CAAS 18; CANR 11, 56, 94, 111; CLR 3; DLBY 1981; INT CANR-11; MAICYA 1, 2; MTCW 1; SATA 6, 68, 133; SFW 4

Bowen, Elizabeth (Dorothea Cole) 1899-1973 ..... CLC 1, 3, 6, 11, 15, 22, 118; SSC 3, 28
See also BRWS 2; CA 17-18; 41-44R; CANR 35, 105; CAP 2; CDBLB 1945-1960; DA3; DAM NOV; DLB 15, 162; EWL 3; EXPS; FW; HGG; MTCW 1, 2; NFS 13; RGSF 2; SSFS 5; SUFW 1; TEA; WLIT 4

Bowering, George 1935- .... CLC 15, 47
See also CA 21-24R; CAAS 16; CANR 10; CP 7; DLB 53

Bowering, Marilyn R(uthe) 1949- ... CLC 32
See also CA 101; CANR 49; CP 7; CWP

Bowers, Edgar 1924-2000 .... CLC 9
See also CA 5-8R; 188; CANR 24; CP 7; CSW; DLB 5

Bowers, Mrs. J. Milton 1842-1914
See Bierce, Ambrose (Gwinett)

Bowie, David .... CLC 17
See Jones, David Robert

Bowles, Jane (Sydney) 1917-1973 .... CLC 3, 68
See Bowles, Jane Auer
See also CA 19-20; 41-44R; CAP 2

Bowles, Jane Auer
See Bowles, Jane (Sydney)
See also EWL 3

Bowles, Paul (Frederick) 1910-1999 .... CLC 1, 2, 19, 53; SSC 3
See also AMWS 4; CA 1-4R; 186; CAAS 1; CANR 1, 19, 50; CN 7; DA3; DLB 5, 6, 218; EWL 3; MTCW 1, 2; RGAL 4; SSFS 17

Bowles, William Lisle 1762-1850 .... NCLC 103
See also DLB 93

Box, Edgar
See Vidal, Gore
See also GLL 1

Boyd, James 1888-1944 .... TCLC 115
See also CA 186; DLB 9; DLBD 16; RGAL 4; RHW

Boyd, Nancy
See Millay, Edna St. Vincent
See also GLL 1

Boyd, Thomas (Alexander) 1898-1935 .... TCLC 111
See also CA 111; 183; DLB 9; DLBD 16

Boyd, William 1952- .... CLC 28, 53, 70
See also CA 114; 120; CANR 51, 71; CN 7; DLB 231

Boyle, Kay 1902-1992 .... CLC 1, 5, 19, 58, 121; SSC 5
See also CA 13-16R; 140; CAAS 1; CANR 29, 61, 110; DLB 4, 9, 48, 86; DLBY 1993; EWL 3; MTCW 1, 2; RGAL 4; RGSF 2; SSFS 10, 13, 14

Boyle, Mark
See Kienzle, William X(avier)

Boyle, Patrick 1905-1982 .... CLC 19
See also CA 127

Boyle, T. C.
See Boyle, T(homas) Coraghessan
See also AMWS 8

Boyle, T(homas) Coraghessan 1948- .... CLC 36, 55, 90; SSC 16
See Boyle, T. C.
See also AAYA 47; BEST 90:4; BPFB 1; CA 120; CANR 44, 76, 89; CN 7; CPW; DA3; DAM POP; DLB 218, 278; DLBY 1986; EWL 3; MTCW 2; SSFS 13

Boz
See Dickens, Charles (John Huffam)

Brackenridge, Hugh Henry 1748-1816 .... NCLC 7
See also DLB 11, 37; RGAL 4

Bradbury, Edward P.
See Moorcock, Michael (John)
See also MTCW 2

Bradbury, Malcolm (Stanley) 1932-2000 .... CLC 32, 61
See also CA 1-4R; CANR 1, 33, 91, 98; CN 7; DA3; DAM NOV; DLB 14, 207; EWL 3; MTCW 1, 2

Bradbury, Ray (Douglas) 1920- ... CLC 1, 3, 10, 15, 42, 98; SSC 29, 53; WLC
See also AAYA 15; AITN 1, 2; AMWS 4; BPFB 1; BYA 4, 5, 11; CA 1-4R; CANR 2, 30, 75; CDALB 1968-1988; CN 7; CPW; DA; DA3; DAB; DAC; DAM MST, NOV, POP; DLB 2, 8; EXPN; EXPS; HGG; LAIT 3, 5; LMFS 2; MTCW 1, 2; NFS 1; RGAL 4; RGSF 2; SATA 11, 64, 123; SCFW 2; SFW 4; SSFS 1; SUFW 1, 2; TUS; YAW

Braddon, Mary Elizabeth 1837-1915 .... TCLC 111
See also BRWS 8; CA 108; 179; CMW 4; DLB 18, 70, 156; HGG

Bradford, Gamaliel 1863-1932 ..... TCLC 36
See also CA 160; DLB 17

Bradford, William 1590-1657 .... LC 64
See also DLB 24, 30; RGAL 4

Bradley, David (Henry), Jr. 1950- ... BLC 1; CLC 23, 118
See also BW 1 3; CA 104; CANR 26, 81; CN 7; DAM MULT; DLB 33

Bradley, John Ed(mund, Jr.) 1958- .... CLC 55
See also CA 139; CANR 99; CN 7; CSW

Bradley, Marion Zimmer 1930-1999 .... CLC 30
See Chapman, Lee; Dexter, John; Gardner, Miriam; Ives, Morgan; Rivers, Elfrida
See also AAYA 40; BPFB 1; CA 57-60; 185; CANR 7, 31, 51, 75, 107; CPW; DA3; DAM POP; DLB 8; FANT; FW; MTCW 1, 2; SATA 90, 139; SATA-Obit 116 SFW 4; SUFW 2; YAW

Bradshaw, John 1933- .... CLC 70
See also CA 138; CANR 61

Bradstreet, Anne 1612(?-1672 ..... LC 4, 30; PC 10
See also AMWS 1; CDALB 1640-1865; DA; DA3; DAC; DAM MST, POET; DLB 24; EXPP; FW; PFS 6; RGAL 4; TUS; WP

Brady, Joan 1939- .... CLC 86
See also CA 141

Bragg, Melvyn 1939- .... CLC 10
See also BEST 89:3; CA 57-60; CANR 10, 48, 89; CN 7; DLB 14, 271; RHW

Brahe, Tycho 1546-1601 .... LC 45

Braine, John (Gerard) 1922-1986 .... CLC 1, 3, 41
See also CA 1-4R; 120; CANR 1, 33; CD-BLB 1945-1960; DLB 15; DLBY 1986; EWL 3; MTCW 1

Braithwaite, William Stanley (Beaumont) 1878-1962 .... BLC 1; HR 2
See also BW 1; CA 125 DAM MULT; DLB 50, 54

Bramah, Ernest 1868-1942 .... TCLC 72
See also CA 156; CMW 4; DLB 70; FANT

Brammer, William 1930(?-1978 ..... CLC 31
See also CA 77-80

Brancati, Vitaliano 1907-1954 ...... TCLC 12
See also CA 109; DLB 264; EWL 3

Brancato, Robin F(idler) 1936- .... CLC 35
See also AAYA 9; BYA 6; CA 69-72; CANR 11, 45; CLR 32; JRDA; MAICYA 2; MAICYAS 1; SAAS 9; SATA 97; WYA; YAW

Brand, Max
See Faust, Frederick (Schiller)
See also BPFB 1; TCWW 2

Brand, Millen 1906-1980 .... CLC 7
See also CA 21-24R; 97-100; CANR 72

Branden, Barbara .... CLC 44
See also CA 148

Brandes, Georg (Morris Cohen) 1842-1927 .... TCLC 10
See also CA 105; 189

Brandys, Kazimierz 1916-2000 .... CLC 62
See also EWL 3

Branley, Franklyn M(ansfield) 1915-2002
.... **CLC 21**
See also CA 33-36R; 207; CANR 14, 39; CLR 13; MAICYA 1, 2; SAAS 16; SATA 4, 68, 136

Brant, Beth (E.) 1941- .... **NNAL**
See also CA 144; FW

Brathwaite, Edward Kamau 1930-
.... **BLCS; CLC 11**
See also BW 2, 3; CA 25-28R; CANR 11, 26, 47, 107; CDWLB 3; CP 7; DAM POET; DLB 125; EWL 3

Brathwaite, Kamau
See Brathwaite, Edward Kamau

Brautigan, Richard (Gary) 1935-1984
.. **CLC 1, 3, 5, 9, 12, 34, 42; TCLC 133**
See also BPFB 1; CA 53-56; 113; CANR 34; DA3; DAM NOV; DLB 2, 5, 206; DLBY 1980, 1984; FANT; MTCW 1; RGAL 4; SATA 56

Brave Bird, Mary .... **NNAL**
See Crow Dog, Mary (Ellen)

Braverman, Kate 1950- .... **CLC 67**
See also CA 89-92

Brecht, (Eugen) Bertolt (Friedrich) 1898-1956 ... **DC 3; TCLC 1, 6, 13, 35; WLC**
See also CA 104; 133; CANR 62; CDWLB 2; DA; DA3; DAB; DAC; DAM DRAM, MST; DFS 4, 5, 9; DLB 56, 124; EW 11; EWL 3; IDTP; MTCW 1, 2; RGWL 2, 3; TWA

Brecht, Eugen Berthold Friedrich
See Brecht, (Eugen) Bertolt (Friedrich)

Bremer, Fredrika 1801-1865 .... **NCLC 11**
See also DLB 254

Brennan, Christopher John 1870-1932
.... **TCLC 17**
See also CA 117; 188; DLB 230; EWL 3

Brennan, Maeve 1917-1993 .. **CLC 5; TCLC 124**
See also CA 81-84; CANR 72, 100

Brent, Linda
See Jacobs, Harriet A(nn)

Brentano, Clemens (Maria) 1778-1842
.... **NCLC 1**
See also DLB 90; RGWL 2, 3

Brent of Bin Bin
See Franklin, (Stella Maria Sarah) Miles (Lampe)

Brenton, Howard 1942- .... **CLC 31**
See also CA 69-72; CANR 33, 67; CBD; CD 5; DLB 13; MTCW 1

Breslin, James 1930-
See Breslin, Jimmy
See also CA 73-76; CANR 31, 75; DAM NOV; MTCW 1, 2

Breslin, Jimmy .... **CLC 4, 43**
See Breslin, James
See also AITN 1; DLB 185; MTCW 2

Bresson, Robert 1901(?)-1999 .... **CLC 16**
See also CA 110; 187; CANR 49

Breton, Andre 1896-1966 . **CLC 2, 9, 15, 54; PC 15**
See also CA 19-20; 25-28R; CANR 40, 60; CAP 2; DLB 65, 258; EW 11; EWL 3; GFL 1789 to the Present; LMFS 2; MTCW 1, 2; RGWL 2, 3; TWA; WP

Breytenbach, Breyten 1939(?)- .... **CLC 23, 37, 126**
See also CA 113; 129; CANR 61; CWW 2; DAM POET; DLB 225; EWL 3

Bridgers, Sue Ellen 1942- .... **CLC 26**
See also AAYA 8, 49; BYA 7, 8; CA 65-68; CANR 11, 36; CLR 18; DLB 52; JRDA; MAICYA 1, 2; SAAS 1; SATA 22, 90; SATA-Essay 109; WYA; YAW

Bridges, Robert (Seymour) 1844-1930
.... **PC 28; TCLC 1**
See also BRW 6; CA 104; 152; CDBLB 1890-1914; DAM POET; DLB 19, 98

Bridie, James .... **TCLC 3**
See Mavor, Osborne Henry
See also DLB 10; EWL 3

Brin, David 1950- .... **CLC 34**
See also AAYA 21; CA 102; CANR 24, 70; INT CANR-24; SATA 65; SCFW 2; SFW 4

Brink, Andre (Philippus) 1935- .... **CLC 18, 36, 106**
See also AFW; BRWS 6; CA 104; CANR 39, 62, 109; CN 7; DLB 225; EWL 3; INT CA-103; MTCW 1, 2; WLIT 2

Brinsmead, H. F(ay)
See Brinsmead, H(esba) F(ay)

Brinsmead, H. F.
See Brinsmead, H(esba) F(ay)

Brinsmead, H(esba) F(ay) 1922- ..... **CLC 21**
See also CA 21-24R; CANR 10; CLR 47; CWRI 5; MAICYA 1, 2; SAAS 5; SATA 18, 78

Brittain, Vera (Mary) 1893(?)-1970
.... **CLC 23**
See also CA 13-16; 25-28R; CANR 58; CAP 1; DLB 191; FW; MTCW 1, 2

Broch, Hermann 1886-1951 .... **TCLC 20**
See also CA 117; CDWLB 2; DLB 85, 124; EW 10; EWL 3; RGWL 2, 3

Brock, Rose
See Hansen, Joseph
See also GLL 1

Brod, Max 1884-1968 .... **TCLC 115**
See also CA 5-8R; 25-28R; CANR 7; DLB 81; EWL 3

Brodkey, Harold (Roy) 1930-1996 . **CLC 56; TCLC 123**
See also CA 111; 151; CANR 71; CN 7; DLB 130

Brodskii, Iosif
See Brodsky, Joseph

Brodsky, Iosif Alexandrovich 1940-1996
See Brodsky, Joseph
See also AITN 1; CA 41-44R; 151; CANR 37, 106; DA3; DAM POET; MTCW 1, 2; RGWL 2, 3

Brodsky, Joseph . **CLC 4, 6, 13, 36, 100; PC 9**
See Brodsky, Iosif Alexandrovich
See also AMWS 8; CWW 2; EWL 3; MTCW 1

Brodsky, Michael (Mark) 1948- .... **CLC 19**
See also CA 102; CANR 18, 41, 58; DLB 244

Brodzki, Bella ed. .... **CLC 65**

Brome, Richard 1590(?)-1652 .... **LC 61**
See also DLB 58

Bromell, Henry 1947- .... **CLC 5**
See also CA 53-56; CANR 9, 115, 116

Bromfield, Louis (Brucker) 1896-1956
.... **TCLC 11**
See also CA 107; 155; DLB 4, 9, 86; RGAL 4; RHW

Broner, E(sther) M(asserman) 1930-
.... **CLC 19**
See also CA 17-20R; CANR 8, 25, 72; CN 7; DLB 28

Bronk, William (M.) 1918-1999 .... **CLC 10**
See also CA 89-92; 177; CANR 23; CP 7; DLB 165

Bronstein, Lev Davidovich
See Trotsky, Leon

Bronte, Anne 1820-1849 ... **NCLC 4, 71, 102**
See also BRW 5; BRWR 1; DA3; DLB 21, 199; TEA

Bronte, (Patrick) Branwell 1817-1848
.... **NCLC 109**

Bronte, Charlotte 1816-1855 ...... **NCLC 3, 8, 33, 58, 105; WLC**
See also AAYA 17; BRW 5; BRWR 1; BYA 2; CDBLB 1832-1890; DA; DA3; DAB; DAC; DAM MST, NOV; DLB 21, 159, 199; EXPN; LAIT 2; NFS 4; TEA; WLIT 4

Bronte, Emily (Jane) 1818-1848 .. **NCLC 16, 35; PC 8; WLC**
See also AAYA 17; BPFB 1; BRW 5; BRWC 1; BRWR 1; BYA 3; CDBLB 1832-1890; DA; DA3; DAB; DAC; DAM MST, NOV, POET; DLB 21, 32, 199; EXPN; LAIT 1; TEA; WLIT 3

Brontes
See Bronte, Anne; Bronte, Charlotte; Bronte, Emily (Jane)

Brooke, Frances 1724-1789 .... **LC 6, 48**
See also DLB 39, 99

Brooke, Henry 1703(?)-1783 .... **LC 1**
See also DLB 39

Brooke, Rupert (Chawner) 1887-1915
.... **PC 24; TCLC 2, 7; WLC**
See also BRWS 3; CA 104; 132; CANR 61; CDBLB 1914-1945; DA; DAB; DAC; DAM MST, POET; DLB 19, 216; EXPP; GLL 2; MTCW 1, 2; PFS 7; TEA

Brooke-Haven, P.
See Wodehouse, P(elham) G(renville)

Brooke-Rose, Christine 1926(?)- .... **CLC 40**
See also BRWS 4; CA 13-16R; CANR 58; CN 7; DLB 14, 231; EWL 3; SFW 4

Brookner, Anita 1928- . **CLC 32, 34, 51, 136**
See also BRWS 4; CA 114; 120; CANR 37, 56, 87; CN 7; CPW; DA3; DAB; DAM POP; DLB 194; DLBY 1987; EWL 3; MTCW 1, 2; TEA

Brooks, Cleanth 1906-1994 .... **CLC 24, 86, 110**
See also CA 17-20R; 145; CANR 33, 35; CSW; DLB 63; DLBY 1994; EWL 3; INT CANR-35; MTCW 1, 2

Brooks, George
See Baum, L(yman) Frank

Brooks, Gwendolyn (Elizabeth) 1917-2000
.... **BLC 1; CLC 1, 2, 4, 5, 15, 49, 125; PC 7; WLC**
See also AAYA 20; AFAW 1, 2; AITN 1; AMWS 3; BW 2, 3; CA 1-4R; 190; CANR 1, 27, 52, 75; CDALB 1941-1968; CLR 27; CP 7; CWP; DA; DA3; DAC; DAM MST, MULT, POET; DLB 5, 76, 165; EWL 3; EXPP; MAWW; MTCW 1, 2; PFS 1, 2, 4, 6; RGAL 4; SATA 6; SATA-Obit 123; TUS; WP

Brooks, Mel .... **CLC 12**
See Kaminsky, Melvin
See also AAYA 13, 48; DLB 26

Brooks, Peter (Preston) 1938- .... **CLC 34**
See also CA 45-48; CANR 1, 107

Brooks, Van Wyck 1886-1963 .... **CLC 29**
See also AMW; CA 1-4R; CANR 6; DLB 45, 63, 103; TUS

Brophy, Brigid (Antonia) 1929-1995
.... **CLC 6, 11, 29, 105**
See also CA 5-8R; 149; CAAS 4; CANR 25, 53; CBD; CN 7; CWD; DA3; DLB 14, 271; EWL 3; MTCW 1, 2

Brosman, Catharine Savage 1934- ... **CLC 9**
See also CA 61-64; CANR 21, 46

Brossard, Nicole 1943- .... **CLC 115, 169**
See also CA 122; CAAS 16; CCA 1; CWP; CWW 2; DLB 53; EWL 3; FW; GLL 2; RGWL 3

Brother Antoninus
See Everson, William (Oliver)

The Brothers Quay
See Quay, Stephen; Quay, Timothy

Broughton, T(homas) Alan 1936- ... **CLC 19**
See also CA 45-48; CANR 2, 23, 48, 111

Broumas, Olga 1949- .... **CLC 10, 73**
See also CA 85-88; CANR 20, 69, 110; CP 7; CWP; GLL 2

Broun, Heywood 1888-1939 .... **TCLC 104**
See also DLB 29, 171

Brown, Alan 1950- .... **CLC 99**
See also CA 156

Brown, Charles Brockden 1771-1810
.... **NCLC 22, 74, 122**
See also AMWS 1; CDALB 1640-1865; DLB 37, 59, 73; FW; HGG; LMFS 1; RGAL 4; TUS

Brown, Christy 1932-1981 .... **CLC 63**
See also BYA 13; CA 105; 104; CANR 72; DLB 14

Brown, Claude 1937-2002 . **BLC 1; CLC 30**
See also AAYA 7; BW 1, 3; CA 73-76; 205; CANR 81; DAM MULT

Brown, Dee (Alexander) 1908- . **CLC 18, 47**
See also AAYA 30; CA 13-16R; CAAS 6; CANR 11, 45, 60; CPW; CSW; DA3; DAM POP; DLBY 1980; LAIT 2; MTCW 1, 2; SATA 5, 110; TCWW 2

Brown, George
See Wertmueller, Lina

Brown, George Douglas 1869-1902
.... **TCLC 28**
See Douglas, George
See also CA 162

Brown, George Mackay 1921-1996 . **CLC 5, 48, 100**
See also BRWS 6; CA 21-24R; 151; CAAS 6; CANR 12, 37, 67; CN 7; CP 7; DLB 14, 27, 139, 271; MTCW 1; RGSF 2; SATA 35

Brown, (William) Larry 1951- .... **CLC 73**
See also CA 130; 134; CANR 117; CSW; DLB 234; INT 133

Brown, Moses
See Barrett, William (Christopher)

Brown, Rita Mae 1944- .... **CLC 18, 43, 79**
See also BPFB 1; CA 45-48; CANR 2, 11, 35, 62, 95; CN 7; CPW; CSW; DA3; DAM NOV, POP; FW; INT CANR-11; MTCW 1, 2; NFS 9; RGAL 4; TUS

Brown, Roderick (Langmere) Haig-
See Haig-Brown, Roderick (Langmere)

Brown, Rosellen 1939- .... **CLC 32, 170**
See also CA 77-80; CAAS 10; CANR 14, 44, 98; CN 7

Brown, Sterling Allen 1901-1989 ..... **BLC 1; CLC 1, 23, 59; HR 2**
See also AFAW 1, 2; BW 1, 3; CA 85-88; 127; CANR 26; DA3; DAM MULT, POET; DLB 48, 51, 63; MTCW 1, 2; RGAL 4; WP

Brown, Will
See Ainsworth, William Harrison

Brown, William Wells 1815-1884 ..... **BLC 1; DC 1; NCLC 2, 89**
See also DAM MULT; DLB 3, 50, 183, 248; RGAL 4

Browne, (Clyde) Jackson 1948(?)- .. **CLC 21**
See also CA 120

Browning, Elizabeth Barrett 1806-1861
.... **NCLC 1, 16, 61, 66; PC 6; WLC**
See also BRW 4; CDBLB 1832-1890; DA; DA3; DAB; DAC; DAM MST, POET; DLB 32, 199; EXPP; PAB; PFS 2, 16; TEA; WLIT 4; WP

Browning, Robert 1812-1889 .... **NCLC 19, 79; PC 2; WLCS**
See also BRW 4; BRWR 2; CDBLB 1832-1890; DA; DA3; DAB; DAC; DAM MST, POET; DLB 32, 163; EXPP; PAB; PFS 1, 15; RGEL 2; TEA; WLIT 4; WP; YABC 1

Browning, Tod 1882-1962 .... **CLC 16**
See also CA 141; 117

Brownmiller, Susan 1935- .... **CLC 159**
See also CA 103; CANR 35, 75; DAM NOV; FW; MTCW 1, 2

Brownson, Orestes Augustus 1803-1876
.... **NCLC 50**
See also DLB 1, 59, 73, 243

Bruccoli, Matthew J(oseph) 1931- .. **CLC 34**
See also CA 9-12R; CANR 7, 87; DLB 103

Bruce, Lenny .... **CLC 21**
See Schneider, Leonard Alfred

Bruchac, Joseph III 1942- .... **NNAL**
See also AAYA 19; CA 33-36R; CANR 13, 47, 75, 94; CLR 46; CWRI 5; DAM MULT; JRDA; MAICYA 2; MAICYAS 1; MTCW 1; SATA 42, 89, 131

Bruin, John
See Brutus, Dennis

Brulard, Henri
See Stendhal

Brulls, Christian
See Simenon, Georges (Jacques Christian)

Brunner, John (Kilian Houston) 1934-1995
.... **CLC 8, 10**
See also CA 1-4R; 149; CAAS 8; CANR 2, 37; CPW; DAM POP; DLB 261; MTCW 1, 2; SCFW 2; SFW 4

Bruno, Giordano 1548-1600 .... **LC 27**
See also RGWL 2, 3

Brutus, Dennis 1924- .. **BLC 1; CLC 43; PC 24**
See also AFW; BW 2, 3; CA 49-52; CAAS 14; CANR 2, 27, 42, 81; CDWLB 3; CP 7; DAM MULT, POET; DLB 117, 225; EWL 3

Bryan, C(ourtlandt) D(ixon) B(arnes) 1936-
.... **CLC 29**
See also CA 73-76; CANR 13, 68; DLB 185; INT CANR-13

Bryan, Michael
See Moore, Brian
See also CCA 1

Bryan, William Jennings 1860-1925
.... **TCLC 99**

Bryant, William Cullen 1794-1878
.... **NCLC 6, 46; PC 20**
See also AMWS 1; CDALB 1640-1865; DA; DAB; DAC; DAM MST, POET; DLB 3, 43, 59, 189, 250; EXPP; PAB; RGAL 4; TUS

Bryusov, Valery Yakovlevich 1873-1924
.... **TCLC 10**
See also CA 107; 155; EWL 3; SFW 4

Buchan, John 1875-1940 .... **TCLC 41**
See also CA 108; 145; CMW 4; DAB; DAM POP; DLB 34, 70, 156; HGG; MSW; MTCW 1; RGEL 2; RHW; YABC 2

Buchanan, George 1506-1582 .... **LC 4**
See also DLB 132

Buchanan, Robert 1841-1901 ..... **TCLC 107**
See also CA 179; DLB 18, 35

Buchheim, Lothar-Guenther 1918- ... **CLC 6**
See also CA 85-88

Buchner, (Karl) Georg 1813-1837
.... **NCLC 26**
See also CDWLB 2; DLB 133; EW 6; RGSF 2; RGWL 2, 3; TWA

Buchwald, Art(hur) 1925- .... **CLC 33**
See also AITN 1; CA 5-8R; CANR 21, 67, 107; MTCW 1, 2; SATA 10

Buck, Pearl S(ydenstricker) 1892-1973
.... **CLC 7, 11, 18, 127**
See also AAYA 42; AITN 1; AMWS 2; BPFB 1; CA 1-4R; 41-44R; CANR 1, 34; CDALBS; DA; DA3; DAB; DAC; DAM MST, NOV; DLB 9, 102; EWL 3; LAIT 3; MTCW 1, 2; RGAL 4; RHW; SATA 1, 25; TUS

Buckler, Ernest 1908-1984 .... **CLC 13**
See also CA 11-12; 114; CAP 1; CCA 1; DAC; DAM MST; DLB 68; SATA 47

Buckley, Christopher (Taylor) 1952-
.... **CLC 165**
See also CA 139

Buckley, Vincent (Thomas) 1925-1988
.... **CLC 57**
See also CA 101

Buckley, William F(rank), Jr. 1925-
.... **CLC 7, 18, 37**
See also AITN 1; BPFB 1; CA 1-4R; CANR 1, 24, 53, 93; CMW 4; CPW; DA3; DAM POP; DLB 137; DLBY 1980; INT CANR-24; MTCW 1, 2; TUS

Buechner, (Carl) Frederick 1926- .... **CLC 2, 4, 6, 9**
See also AMWS 12; BPFB 1; CA 13-16R; CANR 11, 39, 64, 114; CN 7; DAM NOV; DLBY 1980; INT CANR-11; MTCW 1, 2

Buell, John (Edward) 1927- .... **CLC 10**
See also CA 1-4R; CANR 71; DLB 53

Buero Vallejo, Antonio 1916-2000 . **CLC 15, 46, 139; DC 18**
See also CA 106; 189; CANR 24, 49, 75; DFS 11; EWL 3; HW 1; MTCW 1, 2

Bufalino, Gesualdo 1920(?)-1990 .... **CLC 74**
See also CWW 2; DLB 196

Bugayev, Boris Nikolayevich 1880-1934
.... **PC 11; TCLC 7**
See Bely, Andrey; Belyi, Andrei
See also CA 104; 165; MTCW 1

Bukowski, Charles 1920-1994 ... **CLC 2, 5, 9, 41, 82, 108; PC 18; SSC 45**
See also CA 17-20R; 144; CANR 40, 62, 105; CPW; DA3; DAM NOV, POET; DLB 5, 130, 169; EWL 3; MTCW 1, 2

Bulgakov, Mikhail (Afanas'evich) 1891-1940
.... **SSC 18; TCLC 2, 16**
See also BPFB 1; CA 105; 152; DAM DRAM, NOV; DLB 272; EWL 3; NFS 8; RGSF 2; RGWL 2, 3; SFW 4; TWA

Bulgya, Alexander Alexandrovich 1901-1956
.... **TCLC 53**
See Fadeev, Aleksandr Aleksandrovich; Fadeev, Alexandr Alexandrovich; Fadeyev, Alexander
See also CA 117; 181

Bullins, Ed 1935- . **BLC 1; CLC 1, 5, 7; DC 6**
See also BW 2, 3; CA 49-52; CAAS 16; CAD; CANR 24, 46, 73; CD 5; DAM DRAM, MULT; DLB 7, 38, 249; EWL 3; MTCW 1, 2; RGAL 4

Bulosan, Carlos 1911-1956 .... **AAL**
See also RGAL 4

Bulwer-Lytton, Edward (George Earle Lytton) 1803-1873 .... **NCLC 1, 45**
See also DLB 21; RGEL 2; SFW 4; SUFW 1; TEA

Bunin, Ivan Alexeyevich 1870-1953 . **SSC 5; TCLC 6**
See also CA 104; EWL 3; RGSF 2; RGWL 2, 3; TWA

Bunting, Basil 1900-1985 ..... **CLC 10, 39, 47**
See also BRWS 7; CA 53-56; 115; CANR 7; DAM POET; DLB 20; EWL 3; RGEL 2

Bunuel, Luis 1900-1983 .. **CLC 16, 80; HLC 1**
See also CA 101; 110; CANR 32, 77; DAM MULT; HW 1

Bunyan, John 1628-1688 .... **LC 4, 69; WLC**
See also BRW 2; BYA 5; CDBLB 1660-1789; DA; DAB; DAC; DAM MST; DLB 39; RGEL 2; TEA; WCH; WLIT 3

Buravsky, Alexandr .... CLC 59
Burckhardt, Jacob (Christoph) 1818-1897
.... NCLC 49
See also EW 6
Burford, Eleanor
See Hibbert, Eleanor Alice Burford
Burgess, Anthony . CLC 1, 2, 4, 5, 8, 10, 13, 15, 22, 40, 62, 81, 94
See Wilson, John (Anthony) Burgess
See also AAYA 25; AITN 1; BRWS 1; CDBLB 1960 to Present; DAB; DLB 14, 194, 261; DLBY 1998; EWL 3; MTCW 1; RGEL 2; RHW; SFW 4; YAW
Burke, Edmund 1729(?)-1797 .... LC 7, 36; WLC
See also BRW 3; DA; DA3; DAB; DAC; DAM MST; DLB 104, 252; RGEL 2; TEA
Burke, Kenneth (Duva) 1897-1993 .. CLC 2, 24
See also AMW; CA 5-8R; 143; CANR 39, 74; DLB 45, 63; EWL 3; MTCW 1, 2; RGAL 4
Burke, Leda
See Garnett, David
Burke, Ralph
See Silverberg, Robert
Burke, Thomas 1886-1945 .... TCLC 63
See also CA 113; 155; CMW 4; DLB 197
Burney, Fanny 1752-1840 ...... NCLC 12, 54, 107
See also BRWS 3; DLB 39; NFS 16; RGEL 2; TEA
Burney, Frances
See Burney, Fanny
Burns, Robert 1759-1796 . LC 3, 29, 40; PC 6; WLC
See also BRW 3; CDBLB 1789-1832; DA; DA3; DAB; DAC; DAM MST, POET; DLB 109; EXPP; PAB; RGEL 2; TEA; WP
Burns, Tex
See L'Amour, Louis (Dearborn)
See also TCWW 2
Burnshaw, Stanley 1906- ...... CLC 3, 13, 44
See also CA 9-12R; CP 7; DLB 48; DLBY 1997
Burr, Anne 1937- .... CLC 6
See also CA 25-28R
Burroughs, Edgar Rice 1875-1950
.... TCLC 2, 32
See also AAYA 11; BPFB 1; BYA 4, 9; CA 104; 132; DA3; DAM NOV; DLB 8; FANT; MTCW 1, 2; RGAL 4; SATA 41; SCFW 2; SFW 4; TUS; YAW
Burroughs, William S(eward) 1914-1997
.... CLC 1, 2, 5, 15, 22, 42, 75, 109; TCLC 121; WLC
See Lee, William; Lee, Willy
See also AITN 2; AMWS 3; BG 2; BPFB 1; CA 9-12R; 160; CANR 20, 52, 104; CN 7; CPW; DA; DA3; DAB; DAC; DAM MST, NOV, POP; DLB 2, 8, 16, 152, 237; DLBY 1981, 1997; EWL 3; HGG; LMFS 2; MTCW 1, 2; RGAL 4; SFW 4
Burton, Sir Richard F(rancis) 1821-1890
.... NCLC 42
See also DLB 55, 166, 184
Burton, Robert 1577-1640 .... LC 74
See also DLB 151; RGEL 2
Buruma, Ian 1951- .... CLC 163
See also CA 128; CANR 65
Busch, Frederick 1941- .. CLC 7, 10, 18, 47, 166
See also CA 33-36R; CAAS 1; CANR 45, 73, 92; CN 7; DLB 6, 218
Bush, Barney (Furman) 1946- .... NNAL
See also CA 145

Bush, Ronald 1946- .... CLC 34
See also CA 136
Bustos, F(rancisco)
See Borges, Jorge Luis
Bustos Domecq, H(onorio)
See Bioy Casares, Adolfo; Borges, Jorge Luis
Butler, Octavia E(stelle) 1947-
.... BLCS; CLC 38, 121
See also AAYA 18, 48; AFAW 2; BPFB 1; BW 2, 3; CA 73-76; CANR 12, 24, 38, 73; CLR 65; CPW; DA3; DAM MULT, POP; DLB 33; MTCW 1, 2; NFS 8; SATA 84; SCFW 2; SFW 4; SSFS 6; YAW
Butler, Robert Olen, (Jr.) 1945- ..... CLC 81, 162
See also AMWS 12; BPFB 1; CA 112; CANR 66; CSW; DAM POP; DLB 173; INT CA-112; MTCW 1; SSFS 11
Butler, Samuel 1612-1680 .... LC 16, 43
See also DLB 101, 126; RGEL 2
Butler, Samuel 1835-1902 .... TCLC 1, 33; WLC
See also BRWS 2; CA 143; CDBLB 1890-1914; DA; DA3; DAB; DAC; DAM MST, NOV; DLB 18, 57, 174; RGEL 2; SFW 4; TEA
Butler, Walter C.
See Faust, Frederick (Schiller)
Butor, Michel (Marie Francois) 1926-
.... CLC 1, 3, 8, 11, 15, 161
See also CA 9-12R; CANR 33, 66; DLB 83; EW 13; EWL 3; GFL 1789 to the Present; MTCW 1, 2
Butts, Mary 1890(?)-1937 .... TCLC 77
See also CA 148; DLB 240
Buxton, Ralph
See Silverstein, Alvin; Silverstein, Virginia B(arbara Opshelor)
Buzo, Alexander (John) 1944- .... CLC 61
See also CA 97-100; CANR 17, 39, 69; CD 5
Buzzati, Dino 1906-1972 .... CLC 36
See also CA 160; 33-36R; DLB 177; RGWL 2, 3; SFW 4
Byars, Betsy (Cromer) 1928- .... CLC 35
See also AAYA 19; BYA 3; CA 33-36R, 183; CAAE 183; CANR 18, 36, 57, 102; CLR 1, 16, 72; DLB 52; INT CANR-18; JRDA; MAICYA 1, 2; MAICYAS 1; MTCW 1; SAAS 1; SATA 4, 46, 80; SATA-Essay 108; WYA; YAW
Byatt, A(ntonia) S(usan Drabble) 1936-
.... CLC 19, 65, 136
See also BPFB 1; BRWS 4; CA 13-16R; CANR 13, 33, 50, 75, 96; DA3; DAM NOV, POP; DLB 14, 194; EWL 3; MTCW 1, 2; RGSF 2; RHW; TEA
Byrne, David 1952- .... CLC 26
See also CA 127
Byrne, John Keyes 1926-
See Leonard, Hugh
See also CA 102; CANR 78; INT CA-102
Byron, George Gordon (Noel) 1788-1824
.... NCLC 2, 12, 109; PC 16; WLC
See also BRW 4; CDBLB 1789-1832; DA; DA3; DAB; DAC; DAM MST, POET; DLB 96, 110; EXPP; LMFS 1; PAB; PFS 1, 14; RGEL 2; TEA; WLIT 3; WP
Byron, Robert 1905-1941 .... TCLC 67
See also CA 160; DLB 195
C. 3. 3.
See Wilde, Oscar (Fingal O'Flahertie Wills)
C. 3. 3.,
See Wilde, Oscar (Fingal O'Flahertie Wills)
Caballero, Fernan 1796-1877 .... NCLC 10
Cabell, Branch
See Cabell, James Branch

Cabell, James Branch 1879-1958 ... TCLC 6
See also CA 105; 152; DLB 9, 78; FANT; MTCW 1; RGAL 4; SUFW 1
Cabeza de Vaca, Alvar Nunez 1490-1557(?)
.... LC 61
Cable, George Washington 1844-1925
.... SSC 4; TCLC 4
See also CA 104; 155; DLB 12, 74; DLBD 13; RGAL 4; TUS
Cabral de Melo Neto, Joao 1920-1999
.... CLC 76
See Melo Neto, Joao Cabral de
See also CA 151; DAM MULT; LAW; LAWS 1
Cabrera Infante, G(uillermo) 1929-
.... CLC 5, 25, 45, 120; HLC 1; SSC 39
See also CA 85-88; CANR 29, 65, 110; CDWLB 3; DA3; DAM MULT; DLB 113; EWL 3; HW 1, 2; LAW; LAWS 1; MTCW 1, 2; RGSF 2; WLIT 1
Cade, Toni
See Bambara, Toni Cade
Cadmus and Harmonia
See Buchan, John
Caedmon fl. 658-680 .... CMLC 7
See also DLB 146
Caeiro, Alberto
See Pessoa, Fernando (Antonio Nogueira)
Caesar, Julius .... CMLC 47
See Julius Caesar
See also AW 1; RGWL 2, 3
Cage, John (Milton, Jr.) 1912-1992
.... CLC 41
See also CA 13-16R; 169; CANR 9, 78; DLB 193; INT CANR-9
Cahan, Abraham 1860-1951 .... TCLC 71
See also CA 108; 154; DLB 9, 25, 28; RGAL 4
Cain, G.
See Cabrera Infante, G(uillermo)
Cain, Guillermo
See Cabrera Infante, G(uillermo)
Cain, James M(allahan) 1892-1977 . CLC 3, 11, 28
See also AITN 1; BPFB 1; CA 17-20R; 73-76; CANR 8, 34, 61; CMW 4; DLB 226; EWL 3; MSW; MTCW 1; RGAL 4
Caine, Hall 1853-1931 .... TCLC 97
See also RHW
Caine, Mark
See Raphael, Frederic (Michael)
Calasso, Roberto 1941- .... CLC 81
See also CA 143; CANR 89
Calderon de la Barca, Pedro 1600-1681
.... DC 3; HLCS 1; LC 23
See also EW 2; RGWL 2, 3; TWA
Caldwell, Erskine (Preston) 1903-1987
.. CLC 1, 8, 14, 50, 60; SSC 19; TCLC 117
See also AITN 1; AMW; BPFB 1; CA 1-4R; 121; CAAS 1; CANR 2, 33; DA3; DAM NOV; DLB 9, 86; EWL 3; MTCW 1, 2; RGAL 4; RGSF 2; TUS
Caldwell, (Janet Miriam) Taylor (Holland)
1900-1985 .... CLC 2, 28, 39
See also BPFB 1; CA 5-8R; 116; CANR 5; DA3; DAM NOV, POP; DLBD 17; RHW
Calhoun, John Caldwell 1782-1850
.... NCLC 15
See also DLB 3, 248
Calisher, Hortense 1911- .... CLC 2, 4, 8, 38, 134; SSC 15
See also CA 1-4R; CANR 1, 22, 117; CN 7; DA3; DAM NOV; DLB 2, 218; INT CANR-22; MTCW 1, 2; RGAL 4; RGSF 2

Callaghan, Morley Edward 1903-1990
.... **CLC 3, 14, 41, 65**
See also CA 9-12R; 132; CANR 33, 73; DAC; DAM MST; DLB 68; EWL 3; MTCW 1, 2; RGEL 2; RGSF 2

Callimachus c. 305B.C.-c. 240B.C.
.... **CMLC 18**
See also AW 1; DLB 176; RGWL 2, 3

Calvin, Jean
See Calvin, John
See also GFL Beginnings to 1789

Calvin, John 1509-1564 .... **LC 37**
See Calvin, Jean

Calvino, Italo 1923-1985 .. **CLC 5, 8, 11, 22, 33, 39, 73; SSC 3, 48**
See also CA 85-88; 116; CANR 23, 61; DAM NOV; DLB 196; EW 13; EWL 3; MTCW 1, 2; RGSF 2; RGWL 2, 3; SFW 4; SSFS 12

Camara Laye
See Laye, Camara
See also EWL 3

Camden, William 1551-1623 .... **LC 77**
See also DLB 172

Cameron, Carey 1952- .... **CLC 59**
See also CA 135

Cameron, Peter 1959- .... **CLC 44**
See also AMWS 12; CA 125; CANR 50, 117; DLB 234; GLL 2

Camoens, Luis Vaz de 1524(?)-1580
See Camoes, Luis de
See also EW 2

Camoes, Luis de 1524(?)-1580 .... **HLCS 1; LC 62; PC 31**
See Camoens, Luis Vaz de
See also RGWL 2, 3

Campana, Dino 1885-1932 .... **TCLC 20**
See also CA 117; DLB 114; EWL 3

Campanella, Tommaso 1568-1639 ... **LC 32**
See also RGWL 2, 3

Campbell, John W(ood, Jr.) 1910-1971
.... **CLC 32**
See also CA 21-22; 29-32R; CANR 34; CAP 2; DLB 8; MTCW 1; SCFW; SFW 4

Campbell, Joseph 1904-1987 .... **CLC 69**
See also AAYA 3; BEST 89:2; CA 1-4R; 124; CANR 3, 28, 61, 107; DA3; MTCW 1, 2

Campbell, Maria 1940- .... **CLC 85; NNAL**
See also CA 102; CANR 54; CCA 1; DAC

Campbell, Paul N. 1923-
See hooks, bell
See also CA 21-24R

Campbell, (John) Ramsey 1946- ... **CLC 42; SSC 19**
See also CA 57-60; CANR 7, 102; DLB 261; HGG; INT CANR-7; SUFW 1, 2

Campbell, (Ignatius) Roy (Dunnachie) 1901-1957 .... **TCLC 5**
See also AFW; CA 104; 155; DLB 20, 225; EWL 3; MTCW 2; RGEL 2

Campbell, Thomas 1777-1844 .... **NCLC 19**
See also DLB 93, 144; RGEL 2

Campbell, Wilfred .... **TCLC 9**
See Campbell, William

Campbell, William 1858(?)-1918
See Campbell, Wilfred
See also CA 106; DLB 92

Campion, Jane 1954- .... **CLC 95**
See also AAYA 33; CA 138; CANR 37

Campion, Thomas 1567-1620 .... **LC 78**
See also CDBLB Before 1660; DAM POET; DLB 58, 172; RGEL 2

Camus, Albert 1913-1960 ..... **CLC 1, 2, 4, 9, 11, 14, 32, 63, 69, 124; DC 2; SSC 9; WLC**
See also AAYA 36; AFW; BPFB 1; CA 89-92; DA; DA3; DAB; DAC; DAM DRAM, MST, NOV; DLB 72; EW 13; EWL 3; EXPN; EXPS; GFL 1789 to the Present; LMFS 2; MTCW 1, 2; NFS 6, 16; RGSF 2; RGWL 2, 3; SSFS 4; TWA

Canby, Vincent 1924-2000 .... **CLC 13**
See also CA 81-84; 191

Cancale
See Desnos, Robert

Canetti, Elias 1905-1994 ...... **CLC 3, 14, 25, 75, 86**
See also CA 21-24R; 146; CANR 23, 61, 79; CDWLB 2; CWW 2; DA3; DLB 85, 124; EW 12; EWL 3; MTCW 1, 2; RGWL 2, 3; TWA

Canfield, Dorothea F.
See Fisher, Dorothy (Frances) Canfield

Canfield, Dorothea Frances
See Fisher, Dorothy (Frances) Canfield

Canfield, Dorothy
See Fisher, Dorothy (Frances) Canfield

Canin, Ethan 1960- .... **CLC 55**
See also CA 131; 135

Cankar, Ivan 1876-1918 .... **TCLC 105**
See also CDWLB 4; DLB 147; EWL 3

Cannon, Curt
See Hunter, Evan

Cao, Lan 1961- .... **CLC 109**
See also CA 165

Cape, Judith
See Page, P(atricia) K(athleen)
See also CCA 1

Capek, Karel 1890-1938 .... **DC 1; SSC 36; TCLC 6, 37; WLC**
See also CA 104; 140; CDWLB 4; DA; DA3; DAB; DAC; DAM DRAM, MST, NOV; DFS 7, 11; DLB 215; EW 10; EWL 3; MTCW 1; RGSF 2; RGWL 2, 3; SCFW 2; SFW 4

Capote, Truman 1924-1984 ..... **CLC 1, 3, 8, 13, 19, 34, 38, 58; SSC 2, 47; WLC**
See also AMWS 3; BPFB 1; CA 5-8R; 113; CANR 18, 62; CDALB 1941-1968; CPW; DA; DA3; DAB; DAC; DAM MST, NOV, POP; DLB 2, 185, 227; DLBY 1980, 1984; EWL 3; EXPS; GLL 1; LAIT 3; MTCW 1, 2; NCFS 2; RGAL 4; RGSF 2; SATA 91; SSFS 2; TUS

Capra, Frank 1897-1991 .... **CLC 16**
See also CA 61-64; 135

Caputo, Philip 1941- .... **CLC 32**
See also CA 73-76; CANR 40; YAW

Caragiale, Ion Luca 1852-1912 .... **TCLC 76**
See also CA 157

Card, Orson Scott 1951- ...... **CLC 44, 47, 50**
See also AAYA 11, 42; BPFB 1; BYA 5, 8; CA 102; CANR 27, 47, 73, 102, 106; CPW; DA3; DAM POP; FANT; INT CANR-27; MTCW 1, 2; NFS 5; SATA 83, 127; SCFW 2; SFW 4; SUFW 2; YAW

Cardenal, Ernesto 1925- .... **CLC 31, 161; HLC 1; PC 22**
See also CA 49-52; CANR 2, 32, 66; CWW 2; DAM MULT, POET; EWL 3; HW 1, 2; LAWS 1; MTCW 1, 2; RGWL 2, 3

Cardozo, Benjamin N(athan) 1870-1938
.... **TCLC 65**
See also CA 117; 164

Carducci, Giosue (Alessandro Giuseppe) 1835-1907 .... **PC 46; TCLC 32**
See also CA 163; EW 7; RGWL 2, 3

Carew, Thomas 1595(?)-1640 .... **LC 13; PC 29**
See also BRW 2; DLB 126; PAB; RGEL 2

Carey, Ernestine Gilbreth 1908- ...... **CLC 17**
See also CA 5-8R; CANR 71; SATA 2

Carey, Peter 1943- .... **CLC 40, 55, 96**
See also CA 123; 127; CANR 53, 76, 117; CN 7; EWL 3; INT CA-127; MTCW 1, 2; RGSF 2; SATA 94

Carleton, William 1794-1869 .... **NCLC 3**
See also DLB 159; RGEL 2; RGSF 2

Carlisle, Henry (Coffin) 1926- ...... **CLC 33**
See also CA 13-16R; CANR 15, 85

Carlsen, Chris
See Holdstock, Robert P.

Carlson, Ron(ald F.) 1947- .... **CLC 54**
See also CA 105; CAAE 189; CANR 27; DLB 244

Carlyle, Thomas 1795-1881 .... **NCLC 22, 70**
See also BRW 4; CDBLB 1789-1832; DA; DAB; DAC; DAM MST; DLB 55, 144, 254; RGEL 2; TEA

Carman, (William) Bliss 1861-1929 . **PC 34; TCLC 7**
See also CA 104; 152; DAC; DLB 92; RGEL 2

Carnegie, Dale 1888-1955 .... **TCLC 53**

Carossa, Hans 1878-1956 .... **TCLC 48**
See also CA 170; DLB 66; EWL 3

Carpenter, Don(ald Richard) 1931-1995
.... **CLC 41**
See also CA 45-48; 149; CANR 1, 71

Carpenter, Edward 1844-1929 ...... **TCLC 88**
See also CA 163; GLL 1

Carpenter, John (Howard) 1948- .. **CLC 161**
See also AAYA 2; CA 134; SATA 58

Carpenter, Johnny
See Carpenter, John (Howard)

Carpentier (y Valmont), Alejo 1904-1980
.... **CLC 8, 11, 38, 110; HLC 1; SSC 35**
See also CA 65-68; 97-100; CANR 11, 70; CDWLB 3; DAM MULT; DLB 113; EWL 3; HW 1, 2; LAW; LMFS 2; RGSF 2; RGWL 2, 3; WLIT 1

Carr, Caleb 1955(?)- .... **CLC 86**
See also CA 147; CANR 73; DA3

Carr, Emily 1871-1945 .... **TCLC 32**
See also CA 159; DLB 68; FW; GLL 2

Carr, John Dickson 1906-1977 .... **CLC 3**
See Fairbairn, Roger
See also CA 49-52; 69-72; CANR 3, 33, 60; CMW 4; MSW; MTCW 1, 2

Carr, Philippa
See Hibbert, Eleanor Alice Burford

Carr, Virginia Spencer 1929- .... **CLC 34**
See also CA 61-64; DLB 111

Carrere, Emmanuel 1957- .... **CLC 89**
See also CA 200

Carrier, Roch 1937- .... **CLC 13, 78**
See also CA 130; CANR 61; CCA 1; DAC; DAM MST; DLB 53; SATA 105

Carroll, James Dennis
See Carroll, Jim

Carroll, James P. 1943(?)- .... **CLC 38**
See also CA 81-84; CANR 73; MTCW 1

Carroll, Jim 1951- .... **CLC 35, 143**
See Carroll, James Dennis
See also AAYA 17; CA 45-48; CANR 42, 115

Carroll, Lewis ... **NCLC 2, 53; PC 18; WLC**
See Dodgson, Charles L(utwidge)
See also AAYA 39; BRW 5; BYA 5, 13; CD-BLB 1832-1890; CLR 2, 18; DLB 18, 163, 178; DLBY 1998; EXPN; EXPP; FANT; JRDA; LAIT 1; NFS 7; PFS 11; RGEL 2; SUFW 1; TEA; WCH

Carroll, Paul Vincent 1900-1968 ...... **CLC 10**
See also CA 9-12R; 25-28R; DLB 10; EWL 3; RGEL 2

Carruth, Hayden 1921- .... **CLC 4, 7, 10, 18, 84; PC 10**
See also CA 9-12R; CANR 4, 38, 59, 110; CP 7; DLB 5, 165; INT CANR-4; MTCW 1, 2; SATA 47

Carson, Rachel
See Carson, Rachel Louise
See also AAYA 49; DLB 275

Carson, Rachel Louise 1907-1964 ... **CLC 71**
See Carson, Rachel
See also AMWS 9; ANW; CA 77-80; CANR 35; DA3; DAM POP; FW; LAIT 4; MTCW 1, 2; NCFS 1; SATA 23

Carter, Angela (Olive) 1940-1992 .... **CLC 5, 41, 76; SSC 13**
See also BRWS 3; CA 53-56; 136; CANR 12, 36, 61, 106; DA3; DAB; DLB 14, 207, 261; EXPS; FANT; FW; MTCW 1, 2; RGSF 2; SATA 66; SATA-Obit 70; SFW 4; SSFS 4, 12; SUFW 2; WLIT 4

Carter, Nick
See Smith, Martin Cruz

Carver, Raymond 1938-1988 .... **CLC 22, 36, 53, 55, 126; SSC 8, 51**
See also AAYA 44; AMWS 3; BPFB 1; CA 33-36R; 126; CANR 17, 34, 61, 103; CPW; DA3; DAM NOV; DLB 130; DLBY 1984, 1988; EWL 3; MTCW 1, 2; PFS 17; RGAL 4; RGSF 2; SSFS 3, 6, 12, 13; TCWW 2; TUS

Cary, Elizabeth, Lady Falkland 1585-1639
.... **LC 30**

Cary, (Arthur) Joyce (Lunel) 1888-1957
.... **TCLC 1, 29**
See also BRW 7; CA 104; 164; CDBLB 1914-1945; DLB 15, 100; EWL 3; MTCW 2; RGEL 2; TEA

Casanova de Seingalt, Giovanni Jacopo 1725-1798 .... **LC 13**

Casares, Adolfo Bioy
See Bioy Casares, Adolfo
See also RGSF 2

Casas, Bartolome de las 1474-1566
See Las Casas, Bartolome de
See also WLIT 1

Casely-Hayford, J(oseph) E(phraim) 1866-1903 .... **BLC 1; TCLC 24**
See also BW 2; CA 123; 152; DAM MULT

Casey, John (Dudley) 1939- .... **CLC 59**
See also BEST 90:2; CA 69-72; CANR 23, 100

Casey, Michael 1947- .... **CLC 2**
See also CA 65-68; CANR 109; DLB 5

Casey, Patrick
See Thurman, Wallace (Henry)

Casey, Warren (Peter) 1935-1988 ... **CLC 12**
See also CA 101; 127; INT 101

Casona, Alejandro .... **CLC 49**
See Alvarez, Alejandro Rodriguez
See also EWL 3

Cassavetes, John 1929-1989 .... **CLC 20**
See also CA 85-88; 127; CANR 82

Cassian, Nina 1924- .... **PC 17**
See also CWP; CWW 2

Cassill, R(onald) V(erlin) 1919-2002
.... **CLC 4, 23**
See also CA 9-12R; 208; CAAS 1; CANR 7, 45; CN 7; DLB 6, 218; DLBY 2002

Cassiodorus, Flavius Magnus c. 490(?)-c. 583(?) .... **CMLC 43**

Cassirer, Ernst 1874-1945 .... **TCLC 61**
See also CA 157

Cassity, (Allen) Turner 1929- .... **CLC 6, 42**
See also CA 17-20R; CAAS 8; CANR 11; CSW; DLB 105

Castaneda, Carlos (Cesar Aranha) 1931(?)-1998 .... **CLC 12, 119**
See also CA 25-28R; CANR 32, 66, 105; DNFS 1; HW 1; MTCW 1

Castedo, Elena 1937- .... **CLC 65**
See also CA 132

Castedo-Ellerman, Elena
See Castedo, Elena

Castellanos, Rosario 1925-1974 ..... **CLC 66; HLC 1; SSC 39**
See also CA 131; 53-56; CANR 58; CDWLB 3; DAM MULT; DLB 113; EWL 3; FW; HW 1; LAW; MTCW 1; RGSF 2; RGWL 2, 3

Castelvetro, Lodovico 1505-1571 .... **LC 12**

Castiglione, Baldassare 1478-1529 ..... **LC 12**
See Castiglione, Baldesar
See also LMFS 1; RGWL 2, 3

Castiglione, Baldesar
See Castiglione, Baldassare
See also EW 2

Castillo, Ana (Hernandez Del) 1953-
.... **CLC 151**
See also AAYA 42; CA 131; CANR 51, 86; CWP; DLB 122, 227; DNFS 2; FW; HW 1

Castle, Robert
See Hamilton, Edmond

Castro (Ruz), Fidel 1926(?)- .... **HLC 1**
See also CA 110; 129; CANR 81; DAM MULT; HW 2

Castro, Guillen de 1569-1631 .... **LC 19**

Castro, Rosalia de 1837-1885 . **NCLC 3, 78; PC 41**
See also DAM MULT

Cather, Willa (Sibert) 1873-1947 .... **SSC 2, 50; TCLC 1, 11, 31, 99, 132; WLC**
See also AAYA 24; AMW; AMWC 1; AMWR 1; BPFB 1; CA 104; 128; CDALB 1865-1917; DA; DA3; DAB; DAC; DAM MST, NOV; DLB 9, 54, 78, 256; DLBD 1; EWL 3; EXPN; EXPS; LAIT 3; MAWW; MTCW 1, 2; NFS 2; RGAL 4; RGSF 2; RHW; SATA 30; SSFS 2, 7, 16; TCWW 2; TUS

Catherine II
See Catherine the Great
See also DLB 150

Catherine the Great 1729-1796 .... **LC 69**
See Catherine II

Cato, Marcus Porcius 234B.C.-149B.C.
.... **CMLC 21**
See Cato the Elder

Cato, Marcus Porcius, the Elder
See Cato, Marcus Porcius

Cato the Elder
See Cato, Marcus Porcius
See also DLB 211

Catton, (Charles) Bruce 1899-1978
.... **CLC 35**
See also AITN 1; CA 5-8R; 81-84; CANR 7, 74; DLB 17; SATA 2; SATA-Obit 24

Catullus c. 84B.C.-54B.C. .... **CMLC 18**
See also AW 2; CDWLB 1; DLB 211; RGWL 2, 3

Cauldwell, Frank
See King, Francis (Henry)

Caunitz, William J. 1933-1996 .... **CLC 34**
See also BEST 89:3; CA 125; 130; 152; CANR 73; INT 130

Causley, Charles (Stanley) 1917- .... **CLC 7**
See also CA 9-12R; CANR 5, 35, 94; CLR 30; CWRI 5; DLB 27; MTCW 1; SATA 3, 66

Caute, (John) David 1936- .... **CLC 29**
See also CA 1-4R; CAAS 4; CANR 1, 33, 64; CBD; CD 5; CN 7; DAM NOV; DLB 14, 231

Cavafy, C(onstantine) P(eter) .... **PC 36; TCLC 2, 7**
See Kavafis, Konstantinos Petrou
See also CA 148; DA3; DAM POET; EW 8; EWL 3; MTCW 1; RGWL 2, 3; WP

Cavalcanti, Guido c. 1250-c. 1300
.... **CMLC 54**

Cavallo, Evelyn
See Spark, Muriel (Sarah)

Cavanna, Betty .... **CLC 12**
See Harrison, Elizabeth (Allen) Cavanna
See also JRDA; MAICYA 1; SAAS 4; SATA 1, 30

Cavendish, Margaret Lucas 1623-1673
.... **LC 30**
See also DLB 131, 252; RGEL 2

Caxton, William 1421(?)-1491(?) .... **LC 17**
See also DLB 170

Cayer, D. M.
See Duffy, Maureen

Cayrol, Jean 1911- .... **CLC 11**
See also CA 89-92; DLB 83; EWL 3

Cela, Camilo Jose 1916-2002 ..... **CLC 4, 13, 59, 122; HLC 1**
See also BEST 90:2; CA 21-24R; 206; CAAS 10; CANR 21, 32, 76; DAM MULT; DLBY 1989; EW 13; EWL 3; HW 1; MTCW 1, 2; RGSF 2; RGWL 2, 3

Celan, Paul .... **CLC 10, 19, 53, 82; PC 10**
See Antschel, Paul
See also CDWLB 2; DLB 69; EWL 3; RGWL 2, 3

Celine, Louis-Ferdinand .. **CLC 1, 3, 4, 7, 9, 15, 47, 124**
See Destouches, Louis-Ferdinand
See also DLB 72; EW 11; EWL 3; GFL 1789 to the Present; RGWL 2, 3

Cellini, Benvenuto 1500-1571 .... **LC 7**

Cendrars, Blaise .... **CLC 18, 106**
See Sauser-Hall, Frederic
See also DLB 258; EWL 3; GFL 1789 to the Present; RGWL 2, 3; WP

Centlivre, Susanna 1669(?)-1723 .... **LC 65**
See also DLB 84; RGEL 2

Cernuda (y Bidon), Luis 1902-1963
.... **CLC 54**
See also CA 131; 89-92; DAM POET; DLB 134; EWL 3; GLL 1; HW 1; RGWL 2, 3

Cervantes, Lorna Dee 1954- ... **HLCS 1; PC 35**
See also CA 131; CANR 80; CWP; DLB 82; EXPP; HW 1

Cervantes (Saavedra), Miguel de 1547-1616
.... **HLCS; LC 6, 23; SSC 12; WLC**
See also BYA 1, 14; DA; DAB; DAC; DAM MST, NOV; EW 2; LAIT 1; LMFS 1; NFS 8; RGSF 2; RGWL 2, 3; TWA

Cesaire, Aime (Fernand) 1913- .... **BLC 1; CLC 19, 32, 112; PC 25**
See also BW 2, 3; CA 65-68; CANR 24, 43, 81; DA3; DAM MULT, POET; EWL 3; GFL 1789 to the Present; MTCW 1, 2; WP

Chabon, Michael 1963- .. **CLC 55, 149; SSC 59**
See also AAYA 45; AMWS 11; CA 139; CANR 57, 96; DLB 278

Chabrol, Claude 1930- .... **CLC 16**
See also CA 110

Chairil Anwar
See Anwar, Chairil
See also EWL 3

Challans, Mary 1905-1983
See Renault, Mary
See also CA 81-84; 111; CANR 74; DA3; MTCW 2; SATA 23; SATA-Obit 36; TEA

Challis, George
See Faust, Frederick (Schiller)
See also TCWW 2

Chambers, Aidan 1934- .... **CLC 35**
See also AAYA 27; CA 25-28R; CANR 12, 31, 58, 116; JRDA; MAICYA 1, 2; SAAS 12; SATA 1, 69, 108; WYA; YAW

Chambers, James 1948-
See Cliff, Jimmy
See also CA 124

Chambers, Jessie
See Lawrence, D(avid) H(erbert Richards)
See also GLL 1

Chambers, Robert W(illiam) 1865-1933 .... **TCLC 41**
See also CA 165; DLB 202; HGG; SATA 107; SUFW 1

Chambers, (David) Whittaker 1901-1961 .... **TCLC 129**
See also CA 89-92

Chamisso, Adelbert von 1781-1838 .... **NCLC 82**
See also DLB 90; RGWL 2, 3; SUFW 1

Chance, James T.
See Carpenter, John (Howard)

Chance, John T.
See Carpenter, John (Howard)

Chandler, Raymond (Thornton) 1888-1959 .... **SSC 23; TCLC 1, 7**
See also AAYA 25; AMWS 4; BPFB 1; CA 104; 129; CANR 60, 107; CDALB 1929-1941; CMW 4; DA3; DLB 226, 253; DLBD 6; EWL 3; MSW; MTCW 1, 2; NFS 17; RGAL 4; TUS

Chang, Diana 1934- .... **AAL**
See also CWP; EXPP

Chang, Eileen 1921-1995 .... **AAL; SSC 28**
See Chang Ai-Ling
See also CA 166; CWW 2

Chang, Jung 1952- .... **CLC 71**
See also CA 142

Chang Ai-Ling
See Chang, Eileen
See also EWL 3

Channing, William Ellery 1780-1842 .... **NCLC 17**
See also DLB 1, 59, 235; RGAL 4

Chao, Patricia 1955- .... **CLC 119**
See also CA 163

Chaplin, Charles Spencer 1889-1977 .... **CLC 16**
See Chaplin, Charlie
See also CA 81-84; 73-76

Chaplin, Charlie
See Chaplin, Charles Spencer
See also DLB 44

Chapman, George 1559(?)-1634 .... **DC 19; LC 22**
See also BRW 1; DAM DRAM; DLB 62, 121; LMFS 1; RGEL 2

Chapman, Graham 1941-1989 .... **CLC 21**
See Monty Python
See also CA 116; 129; CANR 35, 95

Chapman, John Jay 1862-1933 .... **TCLC 7**
See also CA 104; 191

Chapman, Lee
See Bradley, Marion Zimmer
See also GLL 1

Chapman, Walker
See Silverberg, Robert

Chappell, Fred (Davis) 1936- .... **CLC 40, 78, 162**
See also CA 5-8R; CAAE 198; CAAS 4; CANR 8, 33, 67, 110; CN 7; CP 7; CSW; DLB 6, 105; HGG

Char, Rene(-Emile) 1907-1988 .... **CLC 9, 11, 14, 55**
See also CA 13-16R; 124; CANR 32; DAM POET; DLB 258; EWL 3; GFL 1789 to the Present; MTCW 1, 2; RGWL 2, 3

Charby, Jay
See Ellison, Harlan (Jay)

Chardin, Pierre Teilhard de
See Teilhard de Chardin, (Marie Joseph) Pierre

Chariton fl. 1st cent. (?)- .... **CMLC 49**

Charlemagne 742-814 .... **CMLC 37**

Charles I 1600-1649 .... **LC 13**

Charriere, Isabelle de 1740-1805 .... **NCLC 66**

Chartier, Emile-Auguste
See Alain

Charyn, Jerome 1937- .... **CLC 5, 8, 18**
See also CA 5-8R; CAAS 1; CANR 7, 61, 101; CMW 4; CN 7; DLBY 1983; MTCW 1

Chase, Adam
See Marlowe, Stephen

Chase, Mary (Coyle) 1907-1981 .... **DC 1**
See also CA 77-80; 105; CAD; CWD; DFS 11; DLB 228; SATA 17; SATA-Obit 29

Chase, Mary Ellen 1887-1973 .... **CLC 2; TCLC 124**
See also CA 13-16; 41-44R; CAP 1; SATA 10

Chase, Nicholas
See Hyde, Anthony
See also CCA 1

Chateaubriand, Francois Rene de 1768-1848 .... **NCLC 3**
See also DLB 119; EW 5; GFL 1789 to the Present; RGWL 2, 3; TWA

Chatterje, Sarat Chandra 1876-1936(?)
See Chatterji, Saratchandra
See also CA 109

Chatterji, Bankim Chandra 1838-1894 .... **NCLC 19**

Chatterji, Saratchandra .... **TCLC 13**
See Chatterje, Sarat Chandra
See also CA 186; EWL 3

Chatterton, Thomas 1752-1770 .... **LC 3, 54**
See also DAM POET; DLB 109; RGEL 2

Chatwin, (Charles) Bruce 1940-1989 .... **CLC 28, 57, 59**
See also AAYA 4; BEST 90:1; BRWS 4; CA 85-88; 127; CPW; DAM POP; DLB 194, 204; EWL 3

Chaucer, Daniel
See Ford, Ford Madox
See also RHW

Chaucer, Geoffrey 1340(?)-1400 .... **LC 17, 56; PC 19; WLCS**
See also BRW 1; BRWC 1; BRWR 2; CD-BLB Before 1660; DA; DA3; DAB; DAC; DAM MST, POET; DLB 146; LAIT 1; PAB; PFS 14; RGEL 2; TEA; WLIT 3; WP

Chavez, Denise (Elia) 1948- .... **HLC 1**
See also CA 131; CANR 56, 81; DAM MULT; DLB 122; FW; HW 1, 2; MTCW 2

Chaviaras, Strates 1935-
See Haviaras, Stratis
See also CA 105

Chayefsky, Paddy .... **CLC 23**
See Chayefsky, Sidney
See also CAD; DLB 7, 44; DLBY 1981; RGAL 4

Chayefsky, Sidney 1923-1981
See Chayefsky, Paddy
See also CA 9-12R; 104; CANR 18; DAM DRAM

Chedid, Andree 1920- .... **CLC 47**
See also CA 145; CANR 95; EWL 3

Cheever, John 1912-1982 .... **CLC 3, 7, 8, 11, 15, 25, 64; SSC 1, 38, 57; WLC**
See also AMWS 1; BPFB 1; CA 5-8R; 106; CABS 1; CANR 5, 27, 76; CDALB 1941-1968; CPW; DA; DA3; DAB; DAC; DAM MST, NOV, POP; DLB 2, 102, 227; DLBY 1980, 1982; EWL 3; EXPS; INT CANR-5; MTCW 1, 2; RGAL 4; RGSF 2; SSFS 2, 14; TUS

Cheever, Susan 1943- .... **CLC 18, 48**
See also CA 103; CANR 27, 51, 92; DLBY 1982; INT CANR-27

Chekhonte, Antosha
See Chekhov, Anton (Pavlovich)

Chekhov, Anton (Pavlovich) 1860-1904 .... **DC 9; SSC 2, 28, 41, 51; TCLC 3, 10, 31, 55, 96; WLC**
See also BYA 14; CA 104; 124; DA; DA3; DAB; DAC; DAM DRAM, MST; DFS 5, 10, 12; DLB 277; EW 7; EWL 3; EXPS; LAIT 3; RGSF 2; RGWL 2, 3; SATA 90; SSFS 5, 13, 14; TWA

Cheney, Lynne V. 1941- .... **CLC 70**
See also CA 89-92; CANR 58, 117

Chernyshevsky, Nikolai Gavrilovich
See Chernyshevsky, Nikolay Gavrilovich
See also DLB 238

Chernyshevsky, Nikolay Gavrilovich 1828-1889 .... **NCLC 1**
See Chernyshevsky, Nikolai Gavrilovich

Cherry, Carolyn Janice 1942-
See Cherryh, C. J.
See also CA 65-68; CANR 10

Cherryh, C. J. .... **CLC 35**
See Cherry, Carolyn Janice
See also AAYA 24; BPFB 1; DLBY 1980; FANT; SATA 93; SCFW 2; SFW 4; YAW

Chesnutt, Charles W(addell) 1858-1932 .... **BLC 1; SSC 7, 54; TCLC 5, 39**
See also AFAW 1, 2; BW 1, 3; CA 106; 125; CANR 76; DAM MULT; DLB 12, 50, 78; EWL 3; MTCW 1, 2; RGAL 4; RGSF 2; SSFS 11

Chester, Alfred 1929(?)-1971 .... **CLC 49**
See also CA 196; 33-36R; DLB 130

Chesterton, G(ilbert) K(eith) 1874-1936 .... **PC 28; SSC 1, 46; TCLC 1, 6, 64**
See also BRW 6; CA 104; 132; CANR 73; CDBLB 1914-1945; CMW 4; DAM NOV, POET; DLB 10, 19, 34, 70, 98, 149, 178; EWL 3; FANT; MSW; MTCW 1, 2; RGEL 2; RGSF 2; SATA 27; SUFW 1

Chiang, Pin-chin 1904-1986
See Ding Ling
See also CA 118

Chief Joseph 1840-1904 .... **NNAL**
See also CA 152; DA3; DAM MULT

Chief Seattle 1786(?)-1866 .... **NNAL**
See also DA3; DAM MULT

Ch'ien, Chung-shu 1910-1998 .... **CLC 22**
See also CA 130; CANR 73; MTCW 1, 2

Chikamatsu Monzaemon 1653-1724 .... **LC 66**
See also RGWL 2, 3

Child, L. Maria
See Child, Lydia Maria

Child, Lydia Maria 1802-1880 .... **NCLC 6, 73**
See also DLB 1, 74, 243; RGAL 4; SATA 67

Child, Mrs.
See Child, Lydia Maria

Child, Philip 1898-1978 .... **CLC 19, 68**
See also CA 13-14; CAP 1; DLB 68; RHW; SATA 47

Childers, (Robert) Erskine 1870-1922 .... **TCLC 65**
See also CA 113; 153; DLB 70

Childress, Alice 1920-1994 .... **BLC 1; CLC 12, 15, 86, 96; DC 4; TCLC 116**
See also AAYA 8; BW 2, 3; BYA 2; CA 45-48; CAD; CANR 3, 27, 50, 74; CLR 14; CWD; DA3; DAM DRAM, MULT, NOV; DFS 2, 8, 14; DLB 7, 38, 249; JRDA; LAIT 5; MAICYA 1, 2; MAICYAS 1; MTCW 1, 2; RGAL 4; SATA 7, 48, 81; TUS; WYA; YAW

Chin, Frank (Chew, Jr.) 1940- ..... **CLC 135; DC 7**
See also CA 33-36R; CANR 71; CD 5; DAM MULT; DLB 206; LAIT 5; RGAL 4

Chin, Marilyn (Mei Ling) 1955- .... **PC 40**
See also CA 129; CANR 70, 113; CWP

Chislett, (Margaret) Anne 1943- ..... **CLC 34**
See also CA 151

Chitty, Thomas Willes 1926- .... **CLC 11**
See Hinde, Thomas
See also CA 5-8R; CN 7

Chivers, Thomas Holley 1809-1858
.... **NCLC 49**
See also DLB 3, 248; RGAL 4

Choi, Susan .... **CLC 119**

Chomette, Rene Lucien 1898-1981
See Clair, Rene
See also CA 103

Chomsky, (Avram) Noam 1928- ... **CLC 132**
See also CA 17-20R; CANR 28, 62, 110; DA3; DLB 246; MTCW 1, 2

Chona, Maria 1845(?)-1936 .... **NNAL**
See also CA 144

Chopin, Kate ..... **SSC 8; TCLC 127; WLCS**
See Chopin, Katherine
See also AAYA 33; AMWR 2; AMWS 1; CDALB 1865-1917; DA; DAB; DLB 12, 78; EXPN; EXPS; FW; LAIT 3; MAWW; NFS 3; RGAL 4; RGSF 2; SSFS 17; TUS

Chopin, Katherine 1851-1904
See Chopin, Kate
See also CA 104; 122; DA3; DAC; DAM MST, NOV

Chretien de Troyes c. 12th cent. -
.... **CMLC 10**
See also DLB 208; EW 1; RGWL 2, 3; TWA

Christie
See Ichikawa, Kon

Christie, Agatha (Mary Clarissa) 1890-1976
.... **CLC 1, 6, 8, 12, 39, 48, 110**
See also AAYA 9; AITN 1, 2; BPFB 1; BRWS 2; CA 17-20R; 61-64; CANR 10, 37, 108; CBD; CDBLB 1914-1945; CMW 4; CPW; CWD; DA3; DAB; DAC; DAM NOV; DFS 2; DLB 13, 77, 245; MSW; MTCW 1, 2; NFS 8; RGEL 2; RHW; SATA 36; TEA; YAW

Christie, Philippa .... **CLC 21**
See Pearce, Philippa
See also BYA 5; CANR 109; CLR 9; DLB 161; MAICYA 1; SATA 1, 67, 129

Christine de Pizan 1365(?)-1431(?) ...... **LC 9**
See also DLB 208; RGWL 2, 3

Chuang Tzu c. 369B.C.-c. 286B.C.
.... **CMLC 57**

Chubb, Elmer
See Masters, Edgar Lee

Chulkov, Mikhail Dmitrievich 1743-1792
.... **LC 2**
See also DLB 150

Churchill, Caryl 1938- ..... **CLC 31, 55, 157; DC 5**
See also BRWS 4; CA 102; CANR 22, 46, 108; CBD; CWD; DFS 12, 16; DLB 13; EWL 3; FW; MTCW 1; RGEL 2

Churchill, Charles 1731-1764 .... **LC 3**
See also DLB 109; RGEL 2

Churchill, Sir Winston (Leonard Spencer) 1874-1965 .... **TCLC 113**
See also BRW 6; CA 97-100; CDBLB 1890-1914; DA3; DLB 100; DLBD 16; LAIT 4; MTCW 1, 2

Chute, Carolyn 1947- .... **CLC 39**
See also CA 123

Ciardi, John (Anthony) 1916-1986
.... **CLC 10, 40, 44, 129**
See also CA 5-8R; 118; CAAS 2; CANR 5, 33; CLR 19; CWRI 5; DAM POET; DLB 5; DLBY 1986; INT CANR-5; MAICYA 1, 2; MTCW 1, 2; RGAL 4; SAAS 26; SATA 1, 65; SATA-Obit 46

Cibber, Colley 1671-1757 .... **LC 66**
See also DLB 84; RGEL 2

Cicero, Marcus Tullius 106B.C.-43B.C.
.... **CMLC 3**
See also AW 1; CDWLB 1; DLB 211; RGWL 2, 3

Cimino, Michael 1943- .... **CLC 16**
See also CA 105

Cioran, E(mil) M. 1911-1995 .... **CLC 64**
See also CA 25-28R; 149; CANR 91; DLB 220; EWL 3

Cisneros, Sandra 1954- . **CLC 69, 118; HLC 1; SSC 32**
See also AAYA 9; AMWS 7; CA 131; CANR 64; CWP; DA3; DAM MULT; DLB 122, 152; EWL 3; EXPN; FW; HW 1, 2; LAIT 5; MAICYA 2; MTCW 2; NFS 2; RGAL 4; RGSF 2; SSFS 3, 13; WLIT 1; YAW

Cixous, Helene 1937- .... **CLC 92**
See also CA 126; CANR 55; CWW 2; DLB 83, 242; EWL 3; FW; GLL 2; MTCW 1, 2; TWA

Clair, Rene .... **CLC 20**
See Chomette, Rene Lucien

Clampitt, Amy 1920-1994 ... **CLC 32; PC 19**
See also AMWS 9; CA 110; 146; CANR 29, 79; DLB 105

Clancy, Thomas L., Jr. 1947-
See Clancy, Tom
See also CA 125; 131; CANR 62, 105; DA3; INT CA-131; MTCW 1, 2

Clancy, Tom .... **CLC 45, 112**
See Clancy, Thomas L., Jr.
See also AAYA 9; BEST 89:1, 90:1; BPFB 1; BYA 10, 11; CMW 4; CPW; DAM NOV, POP; DLB 227

Clare, John 1793-1864 . **NCLC 9, 86; PC 23**
See also DAB; DAM POET; DLB 55, 96; RGEL 2

Clarin
See Alas (y Urena), Leopoldo (Enrique Garcia)

Clark, Al C.
See Goines, Donald

Clark, (Robert) Brian 1932- .... **CLC 29**
See also CA 41-44R; CANR 67; CBD; CD 5

Clark, Curt
See Westlake, Donald E(dwin)

Clark, Eleanor 1913-1996 .... **CLC 5, 19**
See also CA 9-12R; 151; CANR 41; CN 7; DLB 6

Clark, J. P.
See Clark Bekederemo, J(ohnson) P(epper)
See also CDWLB 3; DLB 117

Clark, John Pepper
See Clark Bekederemo, J(ohnson) P(epper)
See also AFW; CD 5; CP 7; RGEL 2

Clark, M. R.
See Clark, Mavis Thorpe

Clark, Mavis Thorpe 1909-1999 ..... **CLC 12**
See also CA 57-60; CANR 8, 37, 107; CLR 30; CWRI 5; MAICYA 1, 2; SAAS 5; SATA 8, 74

Clark, Walter Van Tilburg 1909-1971
.... **CLC 28**
See also CA 9-12R; 33-36R; CANR 63, 113; DLB 9, 206; LAIT 2; RGAL 4; SATA 8

Clark Bekederemo, J(ohnson) P(epper) 1935- .... **BLC 1; CLC 38; DC 5**
See Clark, J. P.; Clark, John Pepper
See also BW 1; CA 65-68; CANR 16, 72; DAM DRAM, MULT; DFS 13; EWL 3; MTCW 1

Clarke, Arthur C(harles) 1917- ... **CLC 1, 4, 13, 18, 35, 136; SSC 3**
See also AAYA 4, 33; BPFB 1; BYA 13; CA 1-4R; CANR 2, 28, 55, 74; CN 7; CPW; DA3; DAM POP; DLB 261; JRDA; LAIT 5; MAICYA 1, 2; MTCW 1, 2; SATA 13, 70, 115; SCFW; SFW 4; SSFS 4; YAW

Clarke, Austin 1896-1974 .... **CLC 6, 9**
See also CA 29-32; 49-52; CAP 2; DAM POET; DLB 10, 20; EWL 3; RGEL 2

Clarke, Austin C(hesterfield) 1934- . **BLC 1; CLC 8, 53; SSC 45**
See also BW 1; CA 25-28R; CAAS 16; CANR 14, 32, 68; CN 7; DAC; DAM MULT; DLB 53, 125; DNFS 2; RGSF 2

Clarke, Gillian 1937- .... **CLC 61**
See also CA 106; CP 7; CWP; DLB 40

Clarke, Marcus (Andrew Hislop) 1846-1881
.... **NCLC 19**
See also DLB 230; RGEL 2; RGSF 2

Clarke, Shirley 1925-1997 .... **CLC 16**
See also CA 189

Clash, The
See Headon, (Nicky) Topper; Jones, Mick; Simonon, Paul; Strummer, Joe

Claudel, Paul (Louis Charles Marie) 1868-1955 .... **TCLC 2, 10**
See also CA 104; 165; DLB 192, 258; EW 8; EWL 3; GFL 1789 to the Present; RGWL 2, 3; TWA

Claudian 370(?)-404(?) .... **CMLC 46**
See also RGWL 2, 3

Claudius, Matthias 1740-1815 .... **NCLC 75**
See also DLB 97

Clavell, James (duMaresq) 1925-1994
.... **CLC 6, 25, 87**
See also BPFB 1; CA 25-28R; 146; CANR 26, 48; CPW; DA3; DAM NOV, POP; MTCW 1, 2; NFS 10; RHW

Clayman, Gregory .... **CLC 65**

Cleaver, (Leroy) Eldridge 1935-1998
.... **BLC 1; CLC 30, 119**
See also BW 1, 3; CA 21-24R; 167; CANR 16, 75; DA3; DAM MULT; MTCW 2; YAW

Cleese, John (Marwood) 1939- .... **CLC 21**
See Monty Python
See also CA 112; 116; CANR 35; MTCW 1

Cleishbotham, Jebediah
See Scott, Sir Walter

Cleland, John 1710-1789 .... **LC 2, 48**
See also DLB 39; RGEL 2

Clemens, Samuel Langhorne 1835-1910
See Twain, Mark
See also CA 104; 135; CDALB 1865-1917; DA; DA3; DAB; DAC; DAM MST, NOV; DLB 12, 23, 64, 74, 186, 189; JRDA; LMFS 1; MAICYA 1, 2; NCFS 4; SATA 100; SSFS 16; YABC 2

Clement of Alexandria 150(?)-215(?)
.... **CMLC 41**

Cleophil
See Congreve, William

Clerihew, E.
See Bentley, E(dmund) C(lerihew)

Clerk, N. W.
See Lewis, C(live) S(taples)

Cliff, Jimmy .... **CLC 21**
See Chambers, James
See also CA 193

Cliff, Michelle 1946- .... **BLCS; CLC 120**
See also BW 2; CA 116; CANR 39, 72; CDWLB 3; DLB 157; FW; GLL 2

Clifford, Lady Anne 1590-1676 .... **LC 76**
See also DLB 151

Clifton, (Thelma) Lucille 1936- .... **BLC 1; CLC 19, 66, 162; PC 17**
See also AFAW 2; BW 2, 3; CA 49-52; CANR 2, 24, 42, 76, 97; CLR 5; CP 7; CSW; CWP; CWRI 5; DA3; DAM MULT, POET; DLB 5, 41; EXPP; MAICYA 1, 2; MTCW 1, 2; PFS 1, 14; SATA 20, 69, 128; WP

Clinton, Dirk
See Silverberg, Robert

Clough, Arthur Hugh 1819-1861 . **NCLC 27**
See also BRW 5; DLB 32; RGEL 2

Clutha, Janet Paterson Frame 1924-
See Frame, Janet
See also CA 1-4R; CANR 2, 36, 76; MTCW 1, 2; SATA 119

Clyne, Terence
See Blatty, William Peter

Cobalt, Martin
See Mayne, William (James Carter)

Cobb, Irvin S(hrewsbury) 1876-1944
.... **TCLC 77**
See also CA 175; DLB 11, 25, 86

Cobbett, William 1763-1835 .... **NCLC 49**
See also DLB 43, 107, 158; RGEL 2

Coburn, D(onald) L(ee) 1938- .... **CLC 10**
See also CA 89-92

Cocteau, Jean (Maurice Eugene Clement) 1889-1963 ..... **CLC 1, 8, 15, 16, 43; DC 17; TCLC 119; WLC**
See also CA 25-28; CANR 40; CAP 2; DA; DA3; DAB; DAC; DAM DRAM, MST, NOV; DLB 65, 258; EW 10; EWL 3; GFL 1789 to the Present; MTCW 1, 2; RGWL 2, 3; TWA

Codrescu, Andrei 1946- .... **CLC 46, 121**
See also CA 33-36R; CAAS 19; CANR 13, 34, 53, 76; DA3; DAM POET; MTCW 2

Coe, Max
See Bourne, Randolph S(illiman)

Coe, Tucker
See Westlake, Donald E(dwin)

Coen, Ethan 1958- .... **CLC 108**
See also CA 126; CANR 85

Coen, Joel 1955- .... **CLC 108**
See also CA 126

The Coen Brothers
See Coen, Ethan; Coen, Joel

Coetzee, J(ohn) M(ichael) 1940- .... **CLC 23, 33, 66, 117, 161, 162**
See also AAYA 37; AFW; BRWS 6; CA 77-80; CANR 41, 54, 74, 114; CN 7; DA3; DAM NOV; DLB 225; EWL 3; LMFS 2; MTCW 1, 2; WLIT 2

Coffey, Brian
See Koontz, Dean R(ay)

Coffin, Robert P(eter) Tristram 1892-1955
.... **TCLC 95**
See also CA 123; 169; DLB 45

Cohan, George M(ichael) 1878-1942
.... **TCLC 60**
See also CA 157; DLB 249; RGAL 4

Cohen, Arthur A(llen) 1928-1986 .... **CLC 7, 31**
See also CA 1-4R; 120; CANR 1, 17, 42; DLB 28

Cohen, Leonard (Norman) 1934- .... **CLC 3, 38**
See also CA 21-24R; CANR 14, 69; CN 7; CP 7; DAC; DAM MST; DLB 53; EWL 3; MTCW 1

Cohen, Matt(hew) 1942-1999 .... **CLC 19**
See also CA 61-64; 187; CAAS 18; CANR 40; CN 7; DAC; DLB 53

Cohen-Solal, Annie 19(?)- .... **CLC 50**

Colegate, Isabel 1931- .... **CLC 36**
See also CA 17-20R; CANR 8, 22, 74; CN 7; DLB 14, 231; INT CANR-22; MTCW 1

Coleman, Emmett
See Reed, Ishmael

Coleridge, Hartley 1796-1849 .... **NCLC 90**
See also DLB 96

Coleridge, M. E.
See Coleridge, Mary E(lizabeth)

Coleridge, Mary E(lizabeth) 1861-1907
.... **TCLC 73**
See also CA 116; 166; DLB 19, 98

Coleridge, Samuel Taylor 1772-1834
.... **NCLC 9, 54, 99, 111; PC 11, 39; WLC**
See also BRW 4; BRWR 2; BYA 4; CDBLB 1789-1832; DA; DA3; DAB; DAC; DAM MST, POET; DLB 93, 107; EXPP; LMFS 1; PAB; PFS 4, 5; RGEL 2; TEA; WLIT 3; WP

Coleridge, Sara 1802-1852 .... **NCLC 31**
See also DLB 199

Coles, Don 1928- .... **CLC 46**
See also CA 115; CANR 38; CP 7

Coles, Robert (Martin) 1929- .... **CLC 108**
See also CA 45-48; CANR 3, 32, 66, 70; INT CANR-32; SATA 23

Colette, (Sidonie-Gabrielle) 1873-1954
.... **SSC 10; TCLC 1, 5, 16**
See also CA 104; 131; DA3; DAM NOV; DLB 65; EW 9; EWL 3; GFL 1789 to the Present; MTCW 1, 2; RGWL 2, 3; TWA

Collett, (Jacobine) Camilla (Wergeland) 1813-1895 .... **NCLC 22**

Collier, Christopher 1930- .... **CLC 30**
See also AAYA 13; BYA 2; CA 33-36R; CANR 13, 33, 102; JRDA; MAICYA 1, 2; SATA 16, 70; WYA; YAW 1

Collier, James Lincoln 1928- .... **CLC 30**
See also AAYA 13; BYA 2; CA 9-12R; CANR 4, 33, 60, 102; CLR 3; DAM POP; JRDA; MAICYA 1, 2; SAAS 21; SATA 8, 70; WYA; YAW 1

Collier, Jeremy 1650-1726 .... **LC 6**

Collier, John 1901-1980 .... **SSC 19; TCLC 127**
See also CA 65-68; 97-100; CANR 10; DLB 77, 255; FANT; SUFW 1

Collier, Mary 1690-1762 .... **LC 86**
See also DLB 95

Collingwood, R(obin) G(eorge) 1889(?)-1943
.... **TCLC 67**
See also CA 117; 155; DLB 262

Collins, Hunt
See Hunter, Evan

Collins, Linda 1931- .... **CLC 44**
See also CA 125

Collins, Tom
See Furphy, Joseph
See also RGEL 2

Collins, (William) Wilkie 1824-1889
.... **NCLC 1, 18, 93**
See also BRWS 6; CDBLB 1832-1890; CMW 4; DLB 18, 70, 159; MSW; RGEL 2; RGSF 2; SUFW 1; WLIT 4

Collins, William 1721-1759 .... **LC 4, 40**
See also BRW 3; DAM POET; DLB 109; RGEL 2

Collodi, Carlo .... **NCLC 54**
See Lorenzini, Carlo
See also CLR 5; WCH

Colman, George
See Glassco, John

Colonna, Vittoria 1492-1547 .... **LC 71**
See also RGWL 2, 3

Colt, Winchester Remington
See Hubbard, L(afayette) Ron(ald)

Colter, Cyrus J. 1910-2002 .... **CLC 58**
See also BW 1; CA 65-68; 205; CANR 10, 66; CN 7; DLB 33

Colton, James
See Hansen, Joseph
See also GLL 1

Colum, Padraic 1881-1972 .... **CLC 28**
See also BYA 4; CA 73-76; 33-36R; CANR 35; CLR 36; CWRI 5; DLB 19; MAICYA 1, 2; MTCW 1; RGEL 2; SATA 15; WCH

Colvin, James
See Moorcock, Michael (John)

Colwin, Laurie (E.) 1944-1992 ... **CLC 5, 13, 23, 84**
See also CA 89-92; 139; CANR 20, 46; DLB 218; DLBY 1980; MTCW 1

Comfort, Alex(ander) 1920-2000 .... **CLC 7**
See also CA 1-4R; 190; CANR 1, 45; CP 7; DAM POP; MTCW 1

Comfort, Montgomery
See Campbell, (John) Ramsey

Compton-Burnett, I(vy) 1892(?)-1969
.... **CLC 1, 3, 10, 15, 34**
See also BRW 7; CA 1-4R; 25-28R; CANR 4; DAM NOV; DLB 36; EWL 3; MTCW 1; RGEL 2

Comstock, Anthony 1844-1915 ..... **TCLC 13**
See also CA 110; 169

Comte, Auguste 1798-1857 .... **NCLC 54**

Conan Doyle, Arthur
See Doyle, Sir Arthur Conan
See also BPFB 1; BYA 4, 5, 11

Conde (Abellan), Carmen 1901-1996
.... **HLCS 1**
See also CA 177; DLB 108; EWL 3; HW 2

Conde, Maryse 1937- .... **BLCS; CLC 52, 92**
See also BW 2, 3; CA 110; CAAE 190; CANR 30, 53, 76; CWW 2; DAM MULT; EWL 3; MTCW 1

Condillac, Etienne Bonnot de 1714-1780
.... **LC 26**

Condon, Richard (Thomas) 1915-1996
.... **CLC 4, 6, 8, 10, 45, 100**
See also BEST 90:3; BPFB 1; CA 1-4R; 151; CAAS 1; CANR 2, 23; CMW 4; CN 7; DAM NOV; INT CANR-23; MTCW 1, 2

Confucius 551B.C.-479B.C. .... **CMLC 19; WLCS**
See also DA; DA3; DAB; DAC; DAM MST

Congreve, William 1670-1729 .. **DC 2; LC 5, 21; WLC**
See also BRW 2; CDBLB 1660-1789; DA; DAB; DAC; DAM DRAM, MST, POET; DFS 15; DLB 39, 84; RGEL 2; WLIT 3

Conley, Robert J(ackson) 1940- .... **NNAL**
See also CA 41-44R; CANR 15, 34, 45, 96; DAM MULT

Connell, Evan S(helby), Jr. 1924- .... **CLC 4, 6, 45**
See also AAYA 7; CA 1-4R; CAAS 2; CANR 2, 39, 76, 97; CN 7; DAM NOV; DLB 2; DLBY 1981; MTCW 1, 2

Connelly, Marc(us Cook) 1890-1980
.... **CLC 7**
See also CA 85-88; 102; CANR 30; DFS 12; DLB 7; DLBY 1980; RGAL 4; SATA-Obit 25

Connor, Ralph .... **TCLC 31**
See Gordon, Charles William
See also DLB 92; TCWW 2

Conrad, Joseph 1857-1924 .... **SSC 9; TCLC 1, 6, 13, 25, 43, 57; WLC**
See also AAYA 26; BPFB 1; BRW 6; BRWC 1; BRWR 2; BYA 2; CA 104; 131; CANR 60; CDBLB 1890-1914; DA; DA3;

DAB; DAC; DAM MST, NOV; DLB 10, 34, 98, 156; EWL 3; EXPN; EXPS; LAIT 2; LMFS 1; MTCW 1, 2; NFS 2, 16; RGEL 2; RGSF 2; SATA 27; SSFS 1, 12; TEA; WLIT 4

Conrad, Robert Arnold
See Hart, Moss

Conroy, (Donald) Pat(rick) 1945- .. **CLC 30, 74**
See also AAYA 8; AITN 1; BPFB 1; CA 85-88; CANR 24, 53; CPW; CSW; DA3; DAM NOV, POP; DLB 6; LAIT 5; MTCW 1, 2

Constant (de Rebecque), (Henri) Benjamin 1767-1830 .... **NCLC 6**
See also DLB 119; EW 4; GFL 1789 to the Present

Conway, Jill K(er) 1934- .... **CLC 152**
See also CA 130; CANR 94

Conybeare, Charles Augustus
See Eliot, T(homas) S(tearns)

Cook, Michael 1933-1994 .... **CLC 58**
See also CA 93-96; CANR 68; DLB 53

Cook, Robin 1940- .... **CLC 14**
See also AAYA 32; BEST 90:2; BPFB 1; CA 108; 111; CANR 41, 90, 109; CPW; DA3; DAM POP; HGG; INT CA-111

Cook, Roy
See Silverberg, Robert

Cooke, Elizabeth 1948- .... **CLC 55**
See also CA 129

Cooke, John Esten 1830-1886 .... **NCLC 5**
See also DLB 3, 248; RGAL 4

Cooke, John Estes
See Baum, L(yman) Frank

Cooke, M. E.
See Creasey, John

Cooke, Margaret
See Creasey, John

Cooke, Rose Terry 1827-1892 ..... **NCLC 110**
See also DLB 12, 74

Cook-Lynn, Elizabeth 1930- .... **CLC 93; NNAL**
See also CA 133; DAM MULT; DLB 175

Cooney, Ray .... **CLC 62**
See also CBD

Cooper, Douglas 1960- .... **CLC 86**

Cooper, Henry St. John
See Creasey, John

Cooper, J(oan) California (?)- .... **CLC 56**
See also AAYA 12; BW 1; CA 125; CANR 55; DAM MULT; DLB 212

Cooper, James Fenimore 1789-1851
.... **NCLC 1, 27, 54**
See also AAYA 22; AMW; BPFB 1; CDALB 1640-1865; DA3; DLB 3, 183, 250, 254; LAIT 1; NFS 9; RGAL 4; SATA 19; TUS; WCH

Coover, Robert (Lowell) 1932- ..... **CLC 3, 7, 15, 32, 46, 87, 161; SSC 15**
See also AMWS 5; BPFB 1; CA 45-48; CANR 3, 37, 58, 115; CN 7; DAM NOV; DLB 2, 227; DLBY 1981; EWL 3; MTCW 1, 2; RGAL 4; RGSF 2

Copeland, Stewart (Armstrong) 1952-
.... **CLC 26**

Copernicus, Nicolaus 1473-1543 .... **LC 45**

Coppard, A(lfred) E(dgar) 1878-1957
.... **SSC 21; TCLC 5**
See also BRWS 8; CA 114; 167; DLB 162; EWL 3; HGG; RGEL 2; RGSF 2; SUFW 1; YABC 1

Coppee, Francois 1842-1908 .... **TCLC 25**
See also CA 170; DLB 217

Coppola, Francis Ford 1939- .. **CLC 16, 126**
See also AAYA 39; CA 77-80; CANR 40, 78; DLB 44

Copway, George 1818-1869 .... **NNAL**
See also DAM MULT; DLB 175, 183

Corbiere, Tristan 1845-1875 .... **NCLC 43**
See also DLB 217; GFL 1789 to the Present

Corcoran, Barbara (Asenath) 1911-
.... **CLC 17**
See also AAYA 14; CA 21-24R; CAAE 191; CAAS 2; CANR 11, 28, 48; CLR 50; DLB 52; JRDA; MAICYA 2; MAICYAS 1; RHW; SAAS 20; SATA 3, 77, 125

Cordelier, Maurice
See Giraudoux, Jean(-Hippolyte)

Corelli, Marie .... **TCLC 51**
See Mackay, Mary
See also DLB 34, 156; RGEL 2; SUFW 1

Corman, Cid .... **CLC 9**
See Corman, Sidney
See also CAAS 2; DLB 5, 193

Corman, Sidney 1924-
See Corman, Cid
See also CA 85-88; CANR 44; CP 7; DAM POET

Cormier, Robert (Edmund) 1925-2000
.... **CLC 12, 30**
See also AAYA 3, 19; BYA 1, 2, 6, 8, 9; CA 1-4R; CANR 5, 23, 76, 93; CDALB 1968-1988; CLR 12, 55; DA; DAB; DAC; DAM MST, NOV; DLB 52; EXPN; INT CANR-23; JRDA; LAIT 5; MAICYA 1, 2; MTCW 1, 2; NFS 2; RHW; SATA 10, 45, 83; SATA-Obit 122; WYA; YAW

Corn, Alfred (DeWitt III) 1943- ...... **CLC 33**
See also CA 179; CAAE 179; CAAS 25; CANR 44; CP 7; CSW; DLB 120, 282; DLBY 1980

Corneille, Pierre 1606-1684 .... **LC 28**
See also DAB; DAM MST; DLB 268; EW 3; GFL Beginnings to 1789; RGWL 2, 3; TWA

Cornwell, David (John Moore) 1931-
.... **CLC 9, 15**
See le Carre, John
See also CA 5-8R; CANR 13, 33, 59, 107; DA3; DAM POP; MTCW 1, 2

Cornwell, Patricia (Daniels) 1956-
.... **CLC 155**
See also AAYA 16; BPFB 1; CA 134; CANR 53; CMW 4; CPW; CSW; DAM POP; MSW; MTCW 1

Corso, (Nunzio) Gregory 1930-2001
.... **CLC 1, 11; PC 33**
See also AMWS 12; BG 2; CA 5-8R; 193; CANR 41, 76; CP 7; DA3; DLB 5, 16, 237; LMFS 2; MTCW 1, 2; WP

Cortazar, Julio 1914-1984 .. **CLC 2, 3, 5, 10, 13, 15, 33, 34, 92; HLC 1; SSC 7**
See also BPFB 1; CA 21-24R; CANR 12, 32, 81; CDWLB 3; DA3; DAM MULT, NOV; DLB 113; EWL 3; EXPS; HW 1, 2; LAW; MTCW 1, 2; RGSF 2; RGWL 2, 3; SSFS 3; TWA; WLIT 1

Cortes, Hernan 1485-1547 .... **LC 31**

Corvinus, Jakob
See Raabe, Wilhelm (Karl)

Corvo, Baron
See Rolfe, Frederick (William Serafino Austin Lewis Mary)
See also GLL 1; RGEL 2

Corwin, Cecil
See Kornbluth, C(yril) M.

Cosic, Dobrica 1921- .... **CLC 14**
See also CA 122; 138; CDWLB 4; CWW 2; DLB 181; EWL 3

Costain, Thomas B(ertram) 1885-1965
.... **CLC 30**
See also BYA 3; CA 5-8R; 25-28R; DLB 9; RHW

Costantini, Humberto 1924(?)-1987
.... **CLC 49**
See also CA 131; 122; EWL 3; HW 1

Costello, Elvis 1954- .... **CLC 21**
See also CA 204

Costenoble, Philostene
See Ghelderode, Michel de

Cotes, Cecil V.
See Duncan, Sara Jeannette

Cotter, Joseph Seamon Sr. 1861-1949
.... **BLC 1; TCLC 28**
See also BW 1; CA 124; DAM MULT; DLB 50

Couch, Arthur Thomas Quiller
See Quiller-Couch, Sir Arthur (Thomas)

Coulton, James
See Hansen, Joseph

Couperus, Louis (Marie Anne) 1863-1923
.... **TCLC 15**
See also CA 115; EWL 3; RGWL 2, 3

Coupland, Douglas 1961- .... **CLC 85, 133**
See also AAYA 34; CA 142; CANR 57, 90; CCA 1; CPW; DAC; DAM POP

Court, Wesli
See Turco, Lewis (Putnam)

Courtenay, Bryce 1933- .... **CLC 59**
See also CA 138; CPW

Courtney, Robert
See Ellison, Harlan (Jay)

Cousteau, Jacques-Yves 1910-1997 . **CLC 30**
See also CA 65-68; 159; CANR 15, 67; MTCW 1; SATA 38, 98

Coventry, Francis 1725-1754 .... **LC 46**

Coverdale, Miles c. 1487-1569 .... **LC 77**
See also DLB 167

Cowan, Peter (Walkinshaw) 1914- .. **SSC 28**
See also CA 21-24R; CANR 9, 25, 50, 83; CN 7; DLB 260; RGSF 2

Coward, Noel (Peirce) 1899-1973 .... **CLC 1, 9, 29, 51**
See also AITN 1; BRWS 2; CA 17-18; 41-44R; CANR 35; CAP 2; CBDLB 1914-1945; DA3; DAM DRAM; DFS 3, 6; DLB 10, 245; EWL 3; IDFW 3, 4; MTCW 1, 2; RGEL 2; TEA

Cowley, Abraham 1618-1667 .... **LC 43**
See also BRW 2; DLB 131, 151; PAB; RGEL 2

Cowley, Malcolm 1898-1989 .... **CLC 39**
See also AMWS 2; CA 5-8R; 128; CANR 3, 55; DLB 4, 48; DLBY 1981, 1989; EWL 3; MTCW 1, 2

Cowper, William 1731-1800 ..... **NCLC 8, 94; PC 40**
See also BRW 3; DA3; DAM POET; DLB 104, 109; RGEL 2

Cox, William Trevor 1928-
See Trevor, William
See also CA 9-12R; CANR 4, 37, 55, 76, 102; DAM NOV; INT CANR-37; MTCW 1, 2; TEA

Coyne, P. J.
See Masters, Hilary

Cozzens, James Gould 1903-1978 .... **CLC 1, 4, 11, 92**
See also AMW; BPFB 1; CA 9-12R; 81-84; CANR 19; CDALB 1941-1968; DLB 9; DLBD 2; DLBY 1984, 1997; EWL 3; MTCW 1, 2; RGAL 4

Crabbe, George 1754-1832 ... **NCLC 26, 121**
See also BRW 3; DLB 93; RGEL 2

Crace, Jim 1946- .... **CLC 157; SSC 61**
See also CA 128; 135; CANR 55, 70; CN 7; DLB 231; INT CA-135

Craddock, Charles Egbert
See Murfree, Mary Noailles

Craig, A. A.
See Anderson, Poul (William)

Craik, Mrs.
See Craik, Dinah Maria (Mulock)
See also RGEL 2

Craik, Dinah Maria (Mulock) 1826-1887
.... NCLC 38
See Craik, Mrs.; Mulock, Dinah Maria
See also DLB 35, 163; MAICYA 1, 2; SATA 34

Cram, Ralph Adams 1863-1942 .. TCLC 45
See also CA 160

Cranch, Christopher Pearse 1813-1892
.... NCLC 115
See also DLB 1, 42, 243

Crane, (Harold) Hart 1899-1932 .... PC 3;
TCLC 2, 5, 80; WLC
See also AMW; AMWR 2; CA 104; 127; CDALB 1917-1929; DA; DA3; DAB; DAC; DAM MST, POET; DLB 4, 48; EWL 3; MTCW 1, 2; RGAL 4; TUS

Crane, R(onald) S(almon) 1886-1967
.... CLC 27
See also CA 85-88; DLB 63

Crane, Stephen (Townley) 1871-1900
...... SSC 7, 56; TCLC 11, 17, 32; WLC
See also AAYA 21; AMW; AMWC 1; BPFB 1; BYA 3; CA 109; 140; CANR 84; CDALB 1865-1917; DA; DA3; DAB; DAC; DAM MST, NOV, POET; DLB 12, 54, 78; EXPN; EXPS; LAIT 2; LMFS 2; NFS 4; PFS 9; RGAL 4; RGSF 2; SSFS 4; TUS; WYA; YABC 2

Cranshaw, Stanley
See Fisher, Dorothy (Frances) Canfield

Crase, Douglas 1944- .... CLC 58
See also CA 106

Crashaw, Richard 1612(?)-1649 .... LC 24
See also BRW 2; DLB 126; PAB; RGEL 2

Cratinus c. 519B.C.-c. 422B.C. .... CMLC 54
See also LMFS 1

Craven, Margaret 1901-1980 .... CLC 17
See also BYA 2; CA 103; CCA 1; DAC; LAIT 5

Crawford, F(rancis) Marion 1854-1909
.... TCLC 10
See also CA 107; 168; DLB 71; HGG; RGAL 4; SUFW 1

Crawford, Isabella Valancy 1850-1887
.... NCLC 12
See also DLB 92; RGEL 2

Crayon, Geoffrey
See Irving, Washington

Creasey, John 1908-1973 .... CLC 11
See Marric, J. J.
See also CA 5-8R; 41-44R; CANR 8, 59; CMW 4; DLB 77; MTCW 1

Crebillon, Claude Prosper Jolyot de (fils) 1707-1777 .... LC 1, 28
See also GFL Beginnings to 1789

Credo
See Creasey, John

Credo, Alvaro J. de
See Prado (Calvo), Pedro

Creeley, Robert (White) 1926- . CLC 1, 2, 4, 8, 11, 15, 36, 78
See also AMWS 4; CA 1-4R; CAAS 10; CANR 23, 43, 89; CP 7; DA3; DAM POET; DLB 5, 16, 169; DLBD 17; EWL 3; MTCW 1, 2; RGAL 4; WP

Crevecoeur, Hector St. John de
See Crevecoeur, Michel Guillaume Jean de
See also ANW

Crevecoeur, Michel Guillaume Jean de 1735-1813 .... NCLC 105
See Crevecoeur, Hector St. John de
See also AMWS 1; DLB 37

Crevel, Rene 1900-1935 .... TCLC 112
See also GLL 2

Crews, Harry (Eugene) 1935- .... CLC 6, 23, 49
See also AITN 1; AMWS 11; BPFB 1; CA 25-28R; CANR 20, 57; CN 7; CSW; DA3; DLB 6, 143, 185; MTCW 1, 2; RGAL 4

Crichton, (John) Michael 1942- ... CLC 2, 6, 54, 90
See also AAYA 10, 49; AITN 2; BPFB 1; CA 25-28R; CANR 13, 40, 54, 76; CMW 4; CN 7; CPW; DA3; DAM NOV, POP; DLBY 1981; INT CANR-13; JRDA; MTCW 1, 2; SATA 9, 88; SFW 4; YAW

Crispin, Edmund .... CLC 22
See Montgomery, (Robert) Bruce
See also DLB 87; MSW

Cristofer, Michael 1945(?)- .... CLC 28
See also CA 110; 152; CAD; CD 5; DAM DRAM; DFS 15; DLB 7

Criton
See Alain

Croce, Benedetto 1866-1952 .... TCLC 37
See also CA 120; 155; EW 8; EWL 3

Crockett, David 1786-1836 .... NCLC 8
See also DLB 3, 11, 183, 248

Crockett, Davy
See Crockett, David

Crofts, Freeman Wills 1879-1957 . TCLC 55
See also CA 115; 195; CMW 4; DLB 77; MSW

Croker, John Wilson 1780-1857 ... NCLC 10
See also DLB 110

Crommelynck, Fernand 1885-1970
.... CLC 75
See also CA 189; 89-92; EWL 3

Cromwell, Oliver 1599-1658 .... LC 43

Cronenberg, David 1943- .... CLC 143
See also CA 138; CCA 1

Cronin, A(rchibald) J(oseph) 1896-1981
.... CLC 32
See also BPFB 1; CA 1-4R; 102; CANR 5; DLB 191; SATA 47; SATA-Obit 25

Cross, Amanda
See Heilbrun, Carolyn G(old)
See also BPFB 1; CMW; CPW; MSW

Crothers, Rachel 1878-1958 .... TCLC 19
See also CA 113; 194; CAD; CWD; DLB 7, 266; RGAL 4

Croves, Hal
See Traven, B.

Crow Dog, Mary (Ellen) (?)- .... CLC 93
See Brave Bird, Mary
See also CA 154

Crowfield, Christopher
See Stowe, Harriet (Elizabeth) Beecher

Crowley, Aleister .... TCLC 7
See Crowley, Edward Alexander
See also GLL 1

Crowley, Edward Alexander 1875-1947
See Crowley, Aleister
See also CA 104; HGG

Crowley, John 1942- .... CLC 57
See also BPFB 1; CA 61-64; CANR 43, 98; DLBY 1982; SATA 65; SFW 4; SUFW 2

Crud
See Crumb, R(obert)

Crumarums
See Crumb, R(obert)

Crumb, R(obert) 1943- .... CLC 17
See also CA 106; CANR 107

Crumbum
See Crumb, R(obert)

Crumski
See Crumb, R(obert)

Crum the Bum
See Crumb, R(obert)

Crunk
See Crumb, R(obert)

Crustt
See Crumb, R(obert)

Crutchfield, Les
See Trumbo, Dalton

Cruz, Victor Hernandez 1949- .. HLC 1; PC 37
See also BW 2; CA 65-68; CAAS 17; CANR 14, 32, 74; CP 7; DAM MULT, POET; DLB 41; DNFS 1; EXPP; HW 1, 2; MTCW 1; PFS 16; WP

Cryer, Gretchen (Kiger) 1935- .... CLC 21
See also CA 114; 123

Csath, Geza 1887-1919 .... TCLC 13
See also CA 111

Cudlip, David R(ockwell) 1933- ...... CLC 34
See also CA 177

Cullen, Countee 1903-1946 ... BLC 1; HR 2; PC 20; TCLC 4, 37; WLCS
See also AFAW 2; AMWS 4; BW 1; CA 108; 124; CDALB 1917-1929; DA; DA3; DAC; DAM MST, MULT, POET; DLB 4, 48, 51; EWL 3; EXPP; LMFS 2; MTCW 1, 2; PFS 3; RGAL 4; SATA 18; WP

Culleton, Beatrice 1949- .... NNAL
See also CA 120; CANR 83; DAC

Cum, R.
See Crumb, R(obert)

Cummings, Bruce F(rederick) 1889-1919
See Barbellion, W. N. P.
See also CA 123

Cummings, E(dward) E(stlin) 1894-1962
...... CLC 1, 3, 8, 12, 15, 68; PC 5; WLC
See also AAYA 41; AMW; CA 73-76; CANR 31; CDALB 1929-1941; DA; DA3; DAB; DAC; DAM MST, POET; DLB 4, 48 EWL 3; EXPP; MTCW 1, 2; PAB; PFS 1, 3, 12, 13; RGAL 4; TUS; WP

Cunha, Euclides (Rodrigues Pimenta) da 1866-1909 .... TCLC 24
See also CA 123; LAW; WLIT 1

Cunningham, E. V.
See Fast, Howard (Melvin)

Cunningham, J(ames) V(incent) 1911-1985
.... CLC 3, 31
See also CA 1-4R; 115; CANR 1, 72; DLB 5

Cunningham, Julia (Woolfolk) 1916-
.... CLC 12
See also CA 9-12R; CANR 4, 19, 36; CWRI 5; JRDA; MAICYA 1, 2; SAAS 2; SATA 1, 26, 132

Cunningham, Michael 1952- .... CLC 34
See also CA 136; CANR 96; GLL 2

Cunninghame Graham, R. B.
See Cunninghame Graham, Robert (Gallnigad) Bontine

Cunninghame Graham, Robert (Gallnigad) Bontine 1852-1936 .... TCLC 19
See Graham, R(obert) B(ontine) Cunninghame
See also CA 119; 184

Currie, Ellen 19(?)- .... CLC 44

Curtin, Philip
See Lowndes, Marie Adelaide (Belloc)

Curtin, Phillip
See Lowndes, Marie Adelaide (Belloc)

Curtis, Price
See Ellison, Harlan (Jay)

Cusanus, Nicolaus 1401-1464 .... LC 80
See Nicholas of Cusa

Cutrate, Joe
See Spiegelman, Art

Cynewulf c. 770- .... CMLC 23
See also DLB 146; RGEL 2

Cyrano de Bergerac, Savinien de 1619-1655
.... LC 65
See also DLB 268; GFL Beginnings to 1789; RGWL 2, 3

Cyril of Alexandria c. 375-c. 430
.... CMLC 59

Czaczkes, Shmuel Yosef Halevi
See Agnon, S(hmuel) Y(osef Halevi)

Dabrowska, Maria (Szumska) 1889-1965 .... **CLC 15**
See also CA 106; CDWLB 4; DLB 215; EWL 3
Dabydeen, David 1955- .... **CLC 34**
See also BW 1; CA 125; CANR 56, 92; CN 7; CP 7
Dacey, Philip 1939- .... **CLC 51**
See also CA 37-40R; CAAS 17; CANR 14, 32, 64; CP 7; DLB 105
Dagerman, Stig (Halvard) 1923-1954 .... **TCLC 17**
See also CA 117; 155; DLB 259; EWL 3
D'Aguiar, Fred 1960- .... **CLC 145**
See also CA 148; CANR 83, 101; CP 7; DLB 157; EWL 3
Dahl, Roald 1916-1990 .... **CLC 1, 6, 18, 79**
See also AAYA 15; BPFB 1; BRWS 4; BYA 5; CA 1-4R; 133; CANR 6, 32, 37, 62; CLR 1, 7, 41; CPW; DA3; DAB; DAC; DAM MST, NOV, POP; DLB 139, 255; HGG; JRDA; MAICYA 1, 2; MTCW 1, 2; RGSF 2; SATA 1, 26, 73; SATA-Obit 65; SSFS 4; TEA; YAW
Dahlberg, Edward 1900-1977 . **CLC 1, 7, 14**
See also CA 9-12R; 69-72; CANR 31, 62; DLB 48; MTCW 1; RGAL 4
Daitch, Susan 1954- .... **CLC 103**
See also CA 161
Dale, Colin .... **TCLC 18**
See Lawrence, T(homas) E(dward)
Dale, George E.
See Asimov, Isaac
Dalton, Roque 1935-1975(?) .... **HLCS 1; PC 36**
See also CA 176; HW 2
Daly, Elizabeth 1878-1967 .... **CLC 52**
See also CA 23-24; 25-28R; CANR 60; CAP 2; CMW 4
Daly, Mary 1928- .... **CLC 173**
See also CA 25-28R; CANR 30, 62; FW; GLL 1; MTCW 1
Daly, Maureen 1921- .... **CLC 17**
See also AAYA 5; BYA 6; CANR 37, 83, 108; JRDA; MAICYA 1, 2; SAAS 1; SATA 2, 129; WYA; YAW
Damas, Leon-Gontran 1912-1978 ... **CLC 84**
See also BW 1; CA 125; 73-76; EWL 3
Dana, Richard Henry Sr. 1787-1879 .... **NCLC 53**
Daniel, Samuel 1562(?)-1619 .... **LC 24**
See also DLB 62; RGEL 2
Daniels, Brett
See Adler, Renata
Dannay, Frederic 1905-1982 .... **CLC 11**
See Queen, Ellery
See also CA 1-4R; 107; CANR 1, 39; CMW 4; DAM POP; DLB 137; MTCW 1
D'Annunzio, Gabriele 1863-1938 .. **TCLC 6, 40**
See also CA 104; 155; EW 8; EWL 3; RGWL 2, 3; TWA
Danois, N. le
See Gourmont, Remy(-Marie-Charles) de
Dante 1265-1321 .. **CMLC 3, 18, 39; PC 21; WLCS**
See also DA; DA3; DAB; DAC; DAM MST, POET; EFS 1; EW 1; LAIT 1; RGWL 2, 3; TWA; WP
d'Antibes, Germain
See Simenon, Georges (Jacques Christian)
Danticat, Edwidge 1969- .... **CLC 94, 139**
See also AAYA 29; CA 152; CAAE 192; CANR 73; DNFS 1; EXPS; MTCW 1; SSFS 1; YAW
Danvers, Dennis 1947- .... **CLC 70**
Danziger, Paula 1944- .... **CLC 21**
See also AAYA 4, 36; BYA 6, 7, 14; CA 112; 115; CANR 37; CLR 20; JRDA; MAICYA 1, 2; SATA 36, 63, 102; SATA-Brief 30; WYA; YAW
Da Ponte, Lorenzo 1749-1838 ...... **NCLC 50**
Dario, Ruben 1867-1916 ..... **HLC 1; PC 15; TCLC 4**
See also CA 131; CANR 81; DAM MULT; EWL 3; HW 1, 2; LAW; MTCW 1, 2; RGWL 2, 3
Darley, George 1795-1846 .... **NCLC 2**
See also DLB 96; RGEL 2
Darrow, Clarence (Seward) 1857-1938 .... **TCLC 81**
See also CA 164
Darwin, Charles 1809-1882 .... **NCLC 57**
See also BRWS 7; DLB 57, 166; RGEL 2; TEA; WLIT 4
Darwin, Erasmus 1731-1802 .... **NCLC 106**
See also DLB 93; RGEL 2
Daryush, Elizabeth 1887-1977 .... **CLC 6, 19**
See also CA 49-52; CANR 3, 81; DLB 20
Das, Kamala 1934- .... **PC 43**
See also CA 101; CANR 27, 59; CP 7; CWP; FW
Dasgupta, Surendranath 1887-1952 .... **TCLC 81**
See also CA 157
Dashwood, Edmee Elizabeth Monica de la Pasture 1890-1943
See Delafield, E. M.
See also CA 119; 154
da Silva, Antonio Jose 1705-1739 .... **NCLC 114**
See Silva, Jose Asuncion
Daudet, (Louis Marie) Alphonse 1840-1897 .... **NCLC 1**
See also DLB 123; GFL 1789 to the Present; RGSF 2
Daumal, Rene 1908-1944 .... **TCLC 14**
See also CA 114; EWL 3
Davenant, William 1606-1668 .... **LC 13**
See also DLB 58, 126; RGEL 2
Davenport, Guy (Mattison, Jr.) 1927- .... **CLC 6, 14, 38; SSC 16**
See also CA 33-36R; CANR 23, 73; CN 7; CSW; DLB 130
David, Robert
See Nezval, Vitezslav
Davidson, Avram (James) 1923-1993
See Queen, Ellery
See also CA 101; 171; CANR 26; DLB 8; FANT; SFW 4; SUFW 1, 2
Davidson, Donald (Grady) 1893-1968 .... **CLC 2, 13, 19**
See also CA 5-8R; 25-28R; CANR 4, 84; DLB 45
Davidson, Hugh
See Hamilton, Edmond
Davidson, John 1857-1909 .... **TCLC 24**
See also CA 118; DLB 19; RGEL 2
Davidson, Sara 1943- .... **CLC 9**
See also CA 81-84; CANR 44, 68; DLB 185
Davie, Donald (Alfred) 1922-1995 ... **CLC 5, 8, 10, 31; PC 29**
See also BRWS 6; CA 1-4R; 149; CAAS 3; CANR 1, 44; CP 7; DLB 27; MTCW 1; RGEL 2
Davie, Elspeth 1919-1995 .... **SSC 52**
See also CA 120; 126; 150; DLB 139
Davies, Ray(mond Douglas) 1944- .. **CLC 21**
See also CA 116; 146; CANR 92
Davies, Rhys 1901-1978 .... **CLC 23**
See also CA 9-12R; 81-84; CANR 4; DLB 139, 191
Davies, (William) Robertson 1913-1995 .... **CLC 2, 7, 13, 25, 42, 75, 91; WLC**
See Marchbanks, Samuel
See also BEST 89:2; BPFB 1; CA 33-36R; 150; CANR 17, 42, 103; CN 7; CPW; DA; DA3; DAB; DAC; DAM MST, NOV, POP; DLB 68; EWL 3; HGG; INT CANR-17; MTCW 1, 2; RGEL 2; TWA
Davies, Sir John 1569-1626 .... **LC 85**
See also DLB 172
Davies, Walter C.
See Kornbluth, C(yril) M.
Davies, William Henry 1871-1940 .. **TCLC 5**
See also CA 104; 179; DLB 19, 174; EWL 3; RGEL 2
Da Vinci, Leonardo 1452-1519 ... **LC 12, 57, 60**
See also AAYA 40
Davis, Angela (Yvonne) 1944- .... **CLC 77**
See also BW 2, 3; CA 57-60; CANR 10, 81; CSW; DA3; DAM MULT; FW
Davis, B. Lynch
See Bioy Casares, Adolfo; Borges, Jorge Luis
Davis, Frank Marshall 1905-1987 ..... **BLC 1**
See also BW 2, 3; CA 125; 123; CANR 42, 80; DAM MULT; DLB 51
Davis, Gordon
See Hunt, E(verette) Howard, (Jr.)
Davis, H(arold) L(enoir) 1896-1960 .... **CLC 49**
See also ANW; CA 178; 89-92; DLB 9, 206; SATA 114
Davis, Rebecca (Blaine) Harding 1831-1910 .... **SSC 38; TCLC 6**
See also CA 104; 179; DLB 74, 239; FW; NFS 14; RGAL 4; TUS
Davis, Richard Harding 1864-1916 .... **TCLC 24**
See also CA 114; 179; DLB 12, 23, 78, 79, 189; DLBD 13; RGAL 4
Davison, Frank Dalby 1893-1970 ... **CLC 15**
See also CA 116; DLB 260
Davison, Lawrence H.
See Lawrence, D(avid) H(erbert Richards)
Davison, Peter (Hubert) 1928- .... **CLC 28**
See also CA 9-12R; CAAS 4; CANR 3, 43, 84; CP 7; DLB 5
Davys, Mary 1674-1732 .... **LC 1, 46**
See also DLB 39
Dawson, (Guy) Fielding (Lewis) 1930-2002 .... **CLC 6**
See also CA 85-88; 202; CANR 108; DLB 130; DLBY 2002
Dawson, Peter
See Faust, Frederick (Schiller)
See also TCWW 2, 2
Day, Clarence (Shepard, Jr.) 1874-1935 .... **TCLC 25**
See also CA 108; 199; DLB 11
Day, John 1574(?)-1640(?) .... **LC 70**
See also DLB 62, 170; RGEL 2
Day, Thomas 1748-1789 .... **LC 1**
See also DLB 39; YABC 1
Day Lewis, C(ecil) 1904-1972 .... **CLC 1, 6, 10; PC 11**
See Blake, Nicholas
See also BRWS 3; CA 13-16; 33-36R; CANR 34; CAP 1; CWRI 5; DAM POET; DLB 15, 20; EWL 3; MTCW 1, 2; RGEL 2
Dazai Osamu .... **SSC 41; TCLC 11**
See Tsushima, Shuji
See also CA 164; DLB 182; EWL 3; MJW; RGSF 2; RGWL 2, 3; TWA
de Andrade, Carlos Drummond
See Drummond de Andrade, Carlos
de Andrade, Mario 1892-1945
See Andrade, Mario de
See also CA 178; HW 2
Deane, Norman
See Creasey, John
Deane, Seamus (Francis) 1940- ..... **CLC 122**
See also CA 118; CANR 42

de Beauvoir, Simone (Lucie Ernestine Marie Bertrand)
See Beauvoir, Simone (Lucie Ernestine Marie Bertrand) de
de Beer, P.
See Bosman, Herman Charles
de Brissac, Malcolm
See Dickinson, Peter (Malcolm)
de Campos, Alvaro
See Pessoa, Fernando (Antonio Nogueira)
de Chardin, Pierre Teilhard
See Teilhard de Chardin, (Marie Joseph) Pierre
Dee, John 1527-1608 .... **LC 20**
See also DLB 136, 213
Deer, Sandra 1940- .... **CLC 45**
See also CA 186
De Ferrari, Gabriella 1941- .... **CLC 65**
See also CA 146
de Filippo, Eduardo 1900-1984 .. **TCLC 127**
See also CA 132; 114; EWL 3; MTCW 1; RGWL 2, 3
Defoe, Daniel 1660(?)-1731 . **LC 1, 42; WLC**
See also AAYA 27; BRW 3; BRWR 1; BYA 4; CDBLB 1660-1789; CLR 61; DA; DA3; DAB; DAC; DAM MST, NOV; DLB 39, 95, 101; JRDA; LAIT 1; LMFS 1; MAICYA 1, 2; NFS 9, 13; RGEL 2; SATA 22; TEA; WCH; WLIT 3
de Gourmont, Remy(-Marie-Charles)
See Gourmont, Remy(-Marie-Charles) de
de Hartog, Jan 1914- .... **CLC 19**
See also CA 1-4R; CANR 1; DFS 12
de Hostos, E. M.
See Hostos (y Bonilla), Eugenio Maria de
de Hostos, Eugenio M.
See Hostos (y Bonilla), Eugenio Maria de
Deighton, Len .... **CLC 4, 7, 22, 46**
See Deighton, Leonard Cyril
See also AAYA 6; BEST 89:2; BPFB 1; CDBLB 1960 to Present; CMW 4; CN 7; CPW; DLB 87
Deighton, Leonard Cyril 1929-
See Deighton, Len
See also CA 9-12R; CANR 19, 33, 68; DA3; DAM NOV, POP; MTCW 1, 2
Dekker, Thomas 1572(?)-1632 ... **DC 12; LC 22**
See also CDBLB Before 1660; DAM DRAM; DLB 62, 172; LMFS 1; RGEL 2
de Laclos, Pierre Ambroise Franois
See Laclos, Pierre Ambroise Francois
Delafield, E. M. .... **TCLC 61**
See Dashwood, Edmee Elizabeth Monica de la Pasture
See also DLB 34; RHW
de la Mare, Walter (John) 1873-1956
.... **SSC 14; TCLC 4, 53; WLC**
See also CA 163; CDBLB 1914-1945; CLR 23; CWRI 5; DA3; DAB; DAC; DAM MST, POET; DLB 19, 153, 162, 255; EWL 3; EXPP; HGG; MAICYA 1, 2; MTCW 1; RGEL 2; RGSF 2; SATA 16; SUFW 1; TEA; WCH
de Lamartine, Alphonse (Marie Louis Prat)
See Lamartine, Alphonse (Marie Louis Prat) de
Delaney, Franey
See O'Hara, John (Henry)
Delaney, Shelagh 1939- .... **CLC 29**
See also CA 17-20R; CANR 30, 67; CBD; CD 5; CDBLB 1960 to Present; CWD; DAM DRAM; DFS 7; DLB 13; MTCW 1
Delany, Martin Robison 1812-1885
.... **NCLC 93**
See also DLB 50; RGAL 4

Delany, Mary (Granville Pendarves) 1700-1788 .... **LC 12**
Delany, Samuel R(ay), Jr. 1942- ...... **BLC 1; CLC 8, 14, 38, 141**
See also AAYA 24; AFAW 2; BPFB 1; BW 2, 3; CA 81-84; CANR 27, 43, 115, 116; CN 7; DAM MULT; DLB 8, 33; FANT; MTCW 1, 2; RGAL 4; SATA 92; SCFW; SFW 4; SUFW 2
De la Ramee, Marie Louise (Ouida) 1839-1908
See Ouida
See also CA 204; SATA 20
de la Roche, Mazo 1879-1961 .... **CLC 14**
See also CA 85-88; CANR 30; DLB 68; RGEL 2; RHW; SATA 64
De La Salle, Innocent
See Hartmann, Sadakichi
de Laureamont, Comte
See Lautreamont
Delbanco, Nicholas (Franklin) 1942-
.... **CLC 6, 13, 167**
See also CA 17-20R; CAAE 189; CAAS 2; CANR 29, 55, 116; DLB 6, 234
del Castillo, Michel 1933- .... **CLC 38**
See also CA 109; CANR 77
Deledda, Grazia (Cosima) 1875(?)-1936
.... **TCLC 23**
See also CA 123; 205; DLB 264; EWL 3; RGWL 2, 3
Deleuze, Gilles 1925-1995 .... **TCLC 116**
Delgado, Abelardo (Lalo) B(arrientos) 1930-
.... **HLC 1**
See also CA 131; CAAS 15; CANR 90; DAM MST, MULT; DLB 82; HW 1, 2
Delibes, Miguel .... **CLC 8, 18**
See Delibes Setien, Miguel
See also EWL 3
Delibes Setien, Miguel 1920-
See Delibes, Miguel
See also CA 45-48; CANR 1, 32; HW 1; MTCW 1
DeLillo, Don 1936- .... **CLC 8, 10, 13, 27, 39, 54, 76, 143**
See also AMWS 6; BEST 89:1; BPFB 1; CA 81-84; CANR 21, 76, 92; CN 7; CPW; DA3; DAM NOV, POP; DLB 6, 173; EWL 3; MTCW 1, 2; RGAL 4; TUS
de Lisser, H. G.
See De Lisser, H(erbert) G(eorge)
See also DLB 117
De Lisser, H(erbert) G(eorge) 1878-1944
.... **TCLC 12**
See de Lisser, H. G.
See also BW 2; CA 109; 152
Deloire, Pierre
See Peguy, Charles (Pierre)
Deloney, Thomas 1543(?)-1600 .... **LC 41**
See also DLB 167; RGEL 2
Deloria, Ella (Cara) 1889-1971(?) .... **NNAL**
See also CA 152; DAM MULT; DLB 175
Deloria, Vine (Victor), Jr. 1933- ...... **CLC 21, 122; NNAL**
See also CA 53-56; CANR 5, 20, 48, 98; DAM MULT; DLB 175; MTCW 1; SATA 21
del Valle-Inclan, Ramon (Maria)
See Valle-Inclan, Ramon (Maria) del
Del Vecchio, John M(ichael) 1947- . **CLC 29**
See also CA 110; DLBD 9
de Man, Paul (Adolph Michel) 1919-1983
.... **CLC 55**
See also CA 128; 111; CANR 61; DLB 67; MTCW 1, 2
DeMarinis, Rick 1934- .... **CLC 54**
See also CA 57-60, 184; CAAE 184; CAAS 24; CANR 9, 25, 50; DLB 218

de Maupassant, (Henri Rene Albert) Guy
See Maupassant, (Henri Rene Albert) Guy de
Dembry, R. Emmet
See Murfree, Mary Noailles
Demby, William 1922- .... **BLC 1; CLC 53**
See also BW 1, 3; CA 81-84; CANR 81; DAM MULT; DLB 33
de Menton, Francisco
See Chin, Frank (Chew, Jr.)
Demetrius of Phalerum c. 307B.C.-
.... **CMLC 34**
Demijohn, Thom
See Disch, Thomas M(ichael)
De Mille, James 1833-1880 .... **NCLC 123**
See also DLB 99, 251
Deming, Richard 1915-1983
See Queen, Ellery
See also CA 9-12R; CANR 3, 94; SATA 24
Democritus c. 460B.C.-c. 370B.C.
.... **CMLC 47**
de Montaigne, Michel (Eyquem)
See Montaigne, Michel (Eyquem) de
de Montherlant, Henry (Milon)
See Montherlant, Henry (Milon) de
Demosthenes 384B.C.-322B.C. ...... **CMLC 13**
See also AW 1; DLB 176; RGWL 2, 3
de Musset, (Louis Charles) Alfred
See Musset, (Louis Charles) Alfred de
de Natale, Francine
See Malzberg, Barry N(athaniel)
de Navarre, Marguerite 1492-1549 ... **LC 61**
See Marguerite d'Angouleme; Marguerite de Navarre
Denby, Edwin (Orr) 1903-1983 .... **CLC 48**
See also CA 138; 110
de Nerval, Gerard
See Nerval, Gerard de
Denham, John 1615-1669 .... **LC 73**
See also DLB 58, 126; RGEL 2
Denis, Julio
See Cortazar, Julio
Denmark, Harrison
See Zelazny, Roger (Joseph)
Dennis, John 1658-1734 .... **LC 11**
See also DLB 101; RGEL 2
Dennis, Nigel (Forbes) 1912-1989 ..... **CLC 8**
See also CA 25-28R; 129; DLB 13, 15, 233; EWL 3; MTCW 1
Dent, Lester 1904(?)-1959 .... **TCLC 72**
See also CA 112; 161; CMW 4; SFW 4
De Palma, Brian (Russell) 1940- ..... **CLC 20**
See also CA 109
De Quincey, Thomas 1785-1859 .... **NCLC 4, 87**
See also BRW 4; CDBLB 1789-1832; DLB 110, 144; RGEL 2
Deren, Eleanora 1908(?)-1961
See Deren, Maya
See also CA 192; 111
Deren, Maya .... **CLC 16, 102**
See Deren, Eleanora
Derleth, August (William) 1909-1971
.... **CLC 31**
See also BPFB 1; BYA 9, 10; CA 1-4R; 29-32R; CANR 4; CMW 4; DLB 9; DLBD 17; HGG; SATA 5; SUFW 1
Der Nister 1884-1950 .... **TCLC 56**
See Nister, Der
de Routisie, Albert
See Aragon, Louis
Derrida, Jacques 1930- .... **CLC 24, 87**
See also CA 124; 127; CANR 76, 98; DLB 242; EWL 3; LMFS 2; MTCW 1; TWA
Derry Down Derry
See Lear, Edward
Dersonnes, Jacques
See Simenon, Georges (Jacques Christian)

Desai, Anita 1937- .... **CLC 19, 37, 97**
See also BRWS 5; CA 81-84; CANR 33, 53, 95; CN 7; CWRI 5; DA3; DAB; DAM NOV; DLB 271; DNFS 2; EWL 3; FW; MTCW 1, 2; SATA 63, 126

Desai, Kiran 1971- .... **CLC 119**
See also CA 171

de Saint-Luc, Jean
See Glassco, John

de Saint Roman, Arnaud
See Aragon, Louis

Desbordes-Valmore, Marceline 1786-1859
.... **NCLC 97**
See also DLB 217

Descartes, Rene 1596-1650 .... **LC 20, 35**
See also DLB 268; EW 3; GFL Beginnings to 1789

De Sica, Vittorio 1901(?)-1974 .... **CLC 20**
See also CA 117

Desnos, Robert 1900-1945 .... **TCLC 22**
See also CA 121; 151; CANR 107; DLB 258; EWL 3; LMFS 2

Destouches, Louis-Ferdinand 1894-1961
.... **CLC 9, 15**
See Celine, Louis-Ferdinand
See also CA 85-88; CANR 28; MTCW 1

de Tolignac, Gaston
See Griffith, D(avid Lewelyn) W(ark)

Deutsch, Babette 1895-1982 .... **CLC 18**
See also BYA 3; CA 1-4R; 108; CANR 4, 79; DLB 45; SATA 1; SATA-Obit 33

Devenant, William 1606-1649 .... **LC 13**

Devkota, Laxmiprasad 1909-1959
.... **TCLC 23**
See also CA 123

De Voto, Bernard (Augustine) 1897-1955
.... **TCLC 29**
See also CA 113; 160; DLB 9, 256

De Vries, Peter 1910-1993 .... **CLC 1, 2, 3, 7, 10, 28, 46**
See also CA 17-20R; 142; CANR 41; DAM NOV; DLB 6; DLBY 1982; MTCW 1, 2

Dewey, John 1859-1952 .... **TCLC 95**
See also CA 114; 170; DLB 246, 270; RGAL 4

Dexter, John
See Bradley, Marion Zimmer
See also GLL 1

Dexter, Martin
See Faust, Frederick (Schiller)
See also TCWW 2

Dexter, Pete 1943- .... **CLC 34, 55**
See also BEST 89:2; CA 127; 131; CPW; DAM POP; INT 131; MTCW 1

Diamano, Silmang
See Senghor, Leopold Sedar

Diamond, Neil 1941- .... **CLC 30**
See also CA 108

Diaz del Castillo, Bernal 1496-1584
.... **HLCS 1; LC 31**
See also LAW

di Bassetto, Corno
See Shaw, George Bernard

Dick, Philip K(indred) 1928-1982 .. **CLC 10, 30, 72; SSC 57**
See also AAYA 24; BPFB 1; BYA 11; CA 49-52; 106; CANR 2, 16; CPW; DA3; DAM NOV, POP; DLB 8; MTCW 1, 2; NFS 5; SCFW; SFW 4

Dickens, Charles (John Huffam) 1812-1870
.... **NCLC 3, 8, 18, 26, 37, 50, 86, 105, 113; SSC 17, 49; WLC**
See also AAYA 23; BRW 5; BRWC 1; BYA 1, 2, 3, 13, 14; CDBLB 1832-1890; CMW 4; DA; DA3; DAB; DAC; DAM MST, NOV; DLB 21, 55, 70, 159, 166; EXPN; HGG; JRDA; LAIT 1, 2; LMFS 1; MAI- CYA 1, 2; NFS 4, 5, 10, 14; RGEL 2; RGSF 2; SATA 15; SUFW 1; TEA; WCH; WLIT 4; WYA

Dickey, James (Lafayette) 1923-1997
. **CLC 1, 2, 4, 7, 10, 15, 47, 109; PC 40**
See also AITN 1, 2; AMWS 4; BPFB 1; CA 9-12R; 156; CABS 2; CANR 10, 48, 61, 105; CDALB 1968-1988; CP 7; CPW; CSW; DA3; DAM NOV, POET, POP; DLB 5, 193; DLBD 7; DLBY 1982, 1993, 1996, 1997, 1998; EWL 3; INT CANR-10; MTCW 1, 2; NFS 9; PFS 6, 11; RGAL 4; TUS

Dickey, William 1928-1994 .... **CLC 3, 28**
See also CA 9-12R; 145; CANR 24, 79; DLB 5

Dickinson, Charles 1951- .... **CLC 49**
See also CA 128

Dickinson, Emily (Elizabeth) 1830-1886
.... **NCLC 21, 77; PC 1; WLC**
See also AAYA 22; AMW; AMWR 1; CDALB 1865-1917; DA; DA3; DAB; DAC; DAM MST, POET; DLB 1, 243; EXPP; MAWW; PAB; PFS 1, 2, 3, 4, 5, 6, 8, 10, 11, 13, 16; RGAL 4; SATA 29; TUS; WP; WYA

Dickinson, Mrs. Herbert Ward
See Phelps, Elizabeth Stuart

Dickinson, Peter (Malcolm) 1927- . **CLC 12, 35**
See also AAYA 9, 49; BYA 5; CA 41-44R; CANR 31, 58, 88; CLR 29; CMW 4; DLB 87, 161, 276; JRDA; MAICYA 1, 2; SATA 5, 62, 95; SFW 4; WYA; YAW

Dickson, Carr
See Carr, John Dickson

Dickson, Carter
See Carr, John Dickson

Diderot, Denis 1713-1784 .... **LC 26**
See also EW 4; GFL Beginnings to 1789; LMFS 1; RGWL 2, 3

Didion, Joan 1934- .... **CLC 1, 3, 8, 14, 32, 129**
See also AITN 1; AMWS 4; CA 5-8R; CANR 14, 52, 76; CDALB 1968-1988; CN 7; DA3; DAM NOV; DLB 2, 173, 185; DLBY 1981, 1986; EWL 3; MAWW; MTCW 1, 2; NFS 3; RGAL 4; TCWW 2; TUS

Dietrich, Robert
See Hunt, E(verette) Howard, (Jr.)

Difusa, Pati
See Almodovar, Pedro

Dillard, Annie 1945- .... **CLC 9, 60, 115**
See also AAYA 6, 43; AMWS 6; ANW; CA 49-52; CANR 3, 43, 62, 90; DA3; DAM NOV; DLB 275, 278; DLBY 1980; LAIT 4, 5; MTCW 1, 2; NCFS 1; RGAL 4; SATA 10; TUS

Dillard, R(ichard) H(enry) W(ilde) 1937-
.... **CLC 5**
See also CA 21-24R; CAAS 7; CANR 10; CP 7; CSW; DLB 5, 244

Dillon, Eilis 1920-1994 .... **CLC 17**
See also CA 9-12R, 182; 147; CAAE 182; CAAS 3; CANR 4, 38, 78; CLR 26; MAI-CYA 1, 2; MAICYAS 1; SATA 2, 74; SATA-Essay 105; SATA-Obit 83; YAW

Dimont, Penelope
See Mortimer, Penelope (Ruth)

Dinesen, Isak .... **CLC 10, 29, 95; SSC 7**
See Blixen, Karen (Christentze Dinesen)
See also EW 10; EWL 3; EXPS; FW; HGG; LAIT 3; MTCW 1; NCFS 2; NFS 9; RGSF 2; RGWL 2, 3; SSFS 3, 6, 13; WLIT 2

Ding Ling .... **CLC 68**
See Chiang, Pin-chin
See also RGWL 3

Diphusa, Patty
See Almodovar, Pedro

Disch, Thomas M(ichael) 1940- .. **CLC 7, 36**
See Disch, Tom
See also AAYA 17; BPFB 1; CA 21-24R; CAAS 4; CANR 17, 36, 54, 89; CLR 18; CP 7; DA3; DLB 8; HGG; MAICYA 1, 2; MTCW 1, 2; SAAS 15; SATA 92; SCFW 4; SFW 4; SUFW 2

Disch, Tom
See Disch, Thomas M(ichael)
See also DLB 282

d'Isly, Georges
See Simenon, Georges (Jacques Christian)

Disraeli, Benjamin 1804-1881 . **NCLC 2, 39, 79**
See also BRW 4; DLB 21, 55; RGEL 2

Ditcum, Steve
See Crumb, R(obert)

Dixon, Paige
See Corcoran, Barbara (Asenath)

Dixon, Stephen 1936- .... **CLC 52; SSC 16**
See also AMWS 12; CA 89-92; CANR 17, 40, 54, 91; CN 7; DLB 130

Doak, Annie
See Dillard, Annie

Dobell, Sydney Thompson 1824-1874
.... **NCLC 43**
See also DLB 32; RGEL 2

Doblin, Alfred .... **TCLC 13**
See Doeblin, Alfred
See also CDWLB 2; EWL 3; RGWL 2, 3

Dobroliubov, Nikolai Aleksandrovich
See Dobrolyubov, Nikolai Alexandrovich
See also DLB 277

Dobrolyubov, Nikolai Alexandrovich
1836-1861 .... **NCLC 5**
See Dobroliubov, Nikolai Aleksandrovich

Dobson, Austin 1840-1921 .... **TCLC 79**
See also DLB 35, 144

Dobyns, Stephen 1941- .... **CLC 37**
See also CA 45-48; CANR 2, 18, 99; CMW 4; CP 7

Doctorow, E(dgar) L(aurence) 1931-
.... **CLC 6, 11, 15, 18, 37, 44, 65, 113**
See also AAYA 22; AITN 2; AMWS 4; BEST 89:3; BPFB 1; CA 45-48; CANR 2, 33, 51, 76, 97; CDALB 1968-1988; CN 7; CPW; DA3; DAM NOV, POP; DLB 2, 28, 173; DLBY 1980; EWL 3; LAIT 3; MTCW 1, 2; NFS 6; RGAL 4; RHW; TUS

Dodgson, Charles L(utwidge) 1832-1898
See Carroll, Lewis
See also CLR 2; DA; DA3; DAB; DAC; DAM MST, NOV, POET; MAICYA 1, 2; SATA 100; YABC 2

Dodson, Owen (Vincent) 1914-1983
.... **BLC 1; CLC 79**
See also BW 1; CA 65-68; 110; CANR 24; DAM MULT; DLB 76

Doeblin, Alfred 1878-1957 .... **TCLC 13**
See Doblin, Alfred
See also CA 110; 141; DLB 66

Doerr, Harriet 1910- .... **CLC 34**
See also CA 117; 122; CANR 47; INT 122

Domecq, H(onorio Bustos)
See Bioy Casares, Adolfo

Domecq, H(onorio) Bustos
See Bioy Casares, Adolfo; Borges, Jorge Luis

Domini, Rey
See Lorde, Audre (Geraldine)
See also GLL 1

Dominique
See Proust, (Valentin-Louis-George-Eugene-)Marcel

Don, A
See Stephen, Sir Leslie

Donaldson, Stephen R(eeder) 1947- .... CLC 46, 138
See also AAYA 36; BPFB 1; CA 89-92; CANR 13, 55, 99; CPW; DAM POP; FANT; INT CANR-13; SATA 121; SFW 4; SUFW 1, 2

Donleavy, J(ames) P(atrick) 1926- ... CLC 1, 4, 6, 10, 45
See also AITN 2; BPFB 1; CA 9-12R; CANR 24, 49, 62, 80; CBD; CD 5; CN 7; DLB 6, 173; INT CANR-24; MTCW 1, 2; RGAL 4

Donnadieu, Marguerite
See Duras, Marguerite
See also CWW 2

Donne, John 1572-1631 .... LC 10, 24; PC 1, 43; WLC
See also BRW 1; BRWC 1; BRWR 2; CDBLB Before 1660; DA; DAB; DAC; DAM MST, POET; DLB 121, 151; EXPP; PAB; PFS 2, 11; RGEL 2; TEA WLIT 3; WP

Donnell, David 1939(?)- .... CLC 34
See also CA 197

Donoghue, P. S.
See Hunt, E(verette) Howard, (Jr.)

Donoso (Yanez), Jose 1924-1996 .. CLC 4, 8, 11, 32, 99; HLC 1; SSC 34; TCLC 133
See also CA 81-84; 155; CANR 32, 73; CDWLB 3; DAM MULT; DLB 113 EWL 3; HW 1, 2; LAW; LAWS 1; MTCW 1, 2; RGSF 2; WLIT 1

Donovan, John 1928-1992 .... CLC 35
See also AAYA 20; CA 97-100; 137; CLR 3; MAICYA 1, 2; SATA 72; SATA-Brief 29; YAW

Don Roberto
See Cunninghame Graham, Robert (Gallnigad) Bontine

Doolittle, Hilda 1886-1961 ...... CLC 3, 8, 14, 31, 34, 73; PC 5; WLC
See H. D.
See also AMWS 1; CA 97-100; CANR 35; DA; DAC; DAM MST, POET; DLB 4, 45; EWL 3; FW; GLL 1; LMFS 2; MAWW; MTCW 1, 2; PFS 6; RGAL 4

Doppo, Kunikida .... TCLC 99
See Kunikida Doppo

Dorfman, Ariel 1942- .. CLC 48, 77; HLC 1
See also CA 124; 130; CANR 67, 70; CWW 2; DAM MULT; DFS 4; EWL 3; HW 1, 2; INT CA-130; WLIT 1

Dorn, Edward (Merton) 1929-1999 .... CLC 10, 18
See also CA 93-96; 187; CANR 42, 79; CP 7; DLB 5; INT 93-96; WP

Dor-Ner, Zvi .... CLC 70

Dorris, Michael (Anthony) 1945-1997 .... CLC 109; NNAL
See also AAYA 20; BEST 90:1; BYA 12; CA 102; 157; CANR 19, 46, 75; CLR 58; DA3; DAM MULT, NOV; DLE 175; LAIT 5; MTCW 2; NFS 3; RGAL 4; SATA 75; SATA-Obit 94; TCWW 2 YAW

Dorris, Michael A.
See Dorris, Michael (Anthony)

Dorsan, Luc
See Simenon, Georges (Jacques Christian)

Dorsange, Jean
See Simenon, Georges (Jacques Christian)

Dos Passos, John (Roderigo) 1896-1970 .. CLC 1, 4, 8, 11, 15, 25, 34, 82; WLC
See also AMW; BPFB 1; CA 1-4R; 29-32R; CANR 3; CDALB 1929-1941; DA; DA3; DAB; DAC; DAM MST, NOV; DLB 4, 9; DLBD 1, 15, 274; DLBY 1996; EWL 3; MTCW 1, 2; NFS 14; RGAL 4; TUS

Dossage, Jean
See Simenon, Georges (Jacques Christian)

Dostoevsky, Fedor Mikhailovich 1821-1881 ...... NCLC 2, 7, 21, 33, 43, 119; SSC 2, 33, 44; WLC
See Dostoevsky, Fyodor
See also AAYA 40; DA; DA3; DAB; DAC; DAM MST, NOV; EW 7; EXPN; NFS 3, 8; RGSF 2; RGWL 2, 3; SSFS 8; TWA

Dostoevsky, Fyodor
See Dostoevsky, Fedor Mikhailovich
See also DLB 238; LMFS 1, 2

Doughty, Charles M(ontagu) 1843-1926 .... TCLC 27
See also CA 115; 178; DLB 19, 57, 174

Douglas, Ellen .... CLC 73
See Haxton, Josephine Ayres; Williamson, Ellen Douglas
See also CN 7; CSW

Douglas, Gavin 1475(?)-1522 .... LC 20
See also DLB 132; RGEL 2

Douglas, George
See Brown, George Douglas
See also RGEL 2

Douglas, Keith (Castellain) 1920-1944 .... TCLC 40
See also BRW 7; CA 160; DLB 27; EWL 3; PAB; RGEL 2

Douglas, Leonard
See Bradbury, Ray (Douglas)

Douglas, Michael
See Crichton, (John) Michael

Douglas, (George) Norman 1868-1952 .... TCLC 68
See also BRW 6; CA 119; 157; DLB 34, 195; RGEL 2

Douglas, William
See Brown, George Douglas

Douglass, Frederick 1817(?)-1895 .... BLC 1; NCLC 7, 55; WLC
See also AAYA 48; AFAW 1, 2; AMWC 1; AMWS 3; CDALB 1640-1865; DA; DA3; DAC; DAM MST, MULT; DLB 1, 43, 50, 79, 243; FW; LAIT 2; NCFS 2; RGAL 4; SATA 29

Dourado, (Waldomiro Freitas) Autran 1926- .... CLC 23, 60
See also CA 25-28R; 179; CANR 34, 81; DLB 145; HW 2

Dourado, Waldomiro Autran
See Dourado, (Waldomiro Freitas) Autran
See also CA 179

Dove, Rita (Frances) 1952- ...... BLCS; CLC 50, 81; PC 6
See also AAYA 46; AMWS 4; BW 2; CA 109; CAAS 19; CANR 27, 42, 68, 76, 97; CDALBS; CP 7; CSW; CWP; DA3; DAM MULT, POET; DLB 120; EWL 3; EXPP; MTCW 1; PFS 1, 15; RGAL 4

Doveglion
See Villa, Jose Garcia

Dowell, Coleman 1925-1985 .... CLC 60
See also CA 25-28R; 117; CANR 10; DLB 130; GLL 2

Dowson, Ernest (Christopher) 1867-1900 .... TCLC 4
See also CA 105; 150; DLB 19, 135; RGEL 2

Doyle, A. Conan
See Doyle, Sir Arthur Conan

Doyle, Sir Arthur Conan 1859-1930 .... SSC 12; TCLC 7; WLC
See Conan Doyle, Arthur
See also AAYA 14; BRWS 2; CA 104; 122; CDBLB 1890-1914; CMW 4; DA; DA3; DAB; DAC; DAM MST, NOV; DLB 18, 70, 156, 178; EXPS; HCG; LAIT 2; MSW; MTCW 1, 2; RGEL 2; RGSF 2; RHW; SATA 24; SCFW 2; SFW 4; SSFS 2; TEA; WCH; WLIT 4; WYA; YAW

Doyle, Conan
See Doyle, Sir Arthur Conan

Doyle, John
See Graves, Robert (von Ranke)

Doyle, Roddy 1958(?)- .... CLC 81
See also AAYA 14; BRWS 5; CA 143; CANR 73; CN 7; DA3; DLB 194

Doyle, Sir A. Conan
See Doyle, Sir Arthur Conan

Dr. A
See Asimov, Isaac; Silverstein, Alvin; Silverstein, Virginia B(arbara Opshelor)

Drabble, Margaret 1939- ...... CLC 2, 3, 5, 8, 10, 22, 53, 129
See also BRWS 4; CA 13-16R; CANR 18, 35, 63, 112; CDBLB 1960 to Present; CN 7; CPW; DA3; DAB; DAC; DAM MST, NOV, POP; DLB 14, 155, 231; EWL 3; FW; MTCW 1, 2; RGEL 2; SATA 48; TEA

Drakulic, Slavenka 1949- .... CLC 173
See also CA 144; CANR 92

Drakulic-Ilic, Slavenka
See Drakulic, Slavenka

Drapier, M. B.
See Swift, Jonathan

Drayham, James
See Mencken, H(enry) L(ouis)

Drayton, Michael 1563-1631 .... LC 8
See also DAM POET; DLB 121; RGEL 2

Dreadstone, Carl
See Campbell, (John) Ramsey

Dreiser, Theodore (Herman Albert) 1871-1945 .. SSC 30; TCLC 10, 18, 35, 83; WLC
See also AMW; AMWR 2; CA 106; 132; CDALB 1865-1917; DA; DA3; DAC; DAM MST NOV; DLB 9, 12, 102, 137; DLBD 2; EWL 3; LAIT 2; LMFS 2; MTCW 1, 2; NFS 17; RGAL 4; TUS

Drexler, Rosalyn 1926- .... CLC 2, 6
See also CA 81-84; CAD; CANR 68; CD 5; CWD

Dreyer, Carl Theodor 1889-1968 .... CLC 16
See also CA 116

Drieu la Rochelle, Pierre(-Eugene) 1893-1945 .... TCLC 21
See also CA 117; DLB 72; EWL 3; GFL 1789 to the Present

Drinkwater, John 1882-1937 .... TCLC 57
See also CA 109; 149; DLB 10, 19, 149; RGEL 2

Drop Shot
See Cable, George Washington

Droste-Hulshoff, Annette Freiin von 1797-1848 .... NCLC 3
See also CDWLB 2; DLB 133; RGSF 2; RGWL 2, 3

Drummond, Walter
See Silverberg, Robert

Drummond, William Henry 1854-1907 .... TCLC 25
See also CA 160; DLB 92

Drummond de Andrade, Carlos 1902-1987 .... CLC 18
See Andrade, Carlos Drummond de
See also CA 132; 123; LAW

Drummond of Hawthornden, William 1585-1649 .... LC 83
See also DLB 121, 213; RGEL 2

Drury, Allen (Stuart) 1918-1998 ...... CLC 37
See also CA 57-60; 170; CANR 18, 52; CN 7; INT CANR-18

Dryden, John 1631-1700 .... DC 3; LC 3, 21; PC 25; WLC
See also BRW 2; CDBLB 1660-1789; DA; DAB; DAC; DAM DRAM, MST, POET; DLB 80, 101, 131; EXPP; IDTP; LMFS 1; RGEL 2; TEA; WLIT 3

Duberman, Martin (Bauml) 1930- ... **CLC 8**
See also CA 1-4R; CAD; CANR 2, 63; CD 5

Dubie, Norman (Evans) 1945- .... **CLC 36**
See also CA 69-72; CANR 12, 115; CP 7; DLB 120; PFS 12

Du Bois, W(illiam) E(dward) B(urghardt) 1868-1963 ...... **BLC 1; CLC 1, 2, 13, 64, 96; HR 2; WLC**
See also AAYA 40; AFAW 1, 2; AMWC 1; AMWS 2; BW 1, 3; CA 85-88; CANR 34, 82; CDALB 1865-1917; DA; DA3; DAC; DAM MST, MULT, NOV; DLB 47, 50, 91, 246; EWL 3; EXPP; LAIT 2; LMFS 2; MTCW 1, 2; NCFS 1; PFS 13; RGAL 4; SATA 42

Dubus, Andre 1936-1999 .... **CLC 13, 36, 97; SSC 15**
See also AMWS 7; CA 21-24R; 177; CANR 17; CN 7; CSW; DLB 130; INT CANR-17; RGAL 4; SSFS 10

Duca Minimo
See D'Annunzio, Gabriele

Ducharme, Rejean 1941- .... **CLC 74**
See also CA 165; DLB 60

Duchen, Claire .... **CLC 65**

Duclos, Charles Pinot- 1704-1772 .... **LC 1**
See also GFL Beginnings to 1789

Dudek, Louis 1918- .... **CLC 11, 19**
See also CA 45-48; CAAS 14; CANR 1; CP 7; DLB 88

Duerrenmatt, Friedrich 1921-1990 .. **CLC 1, 4, 8, 11, 15, 43, 102**
See Durrenmatt, Friedrich
See also CA 17-20R; CANR 33; CMW 4; DAM DRAM; DLB 69, 124; MTCW 1, 2

Duffy, Bruce 1953(?)- .... **CLC 50**
See also CA 172

Duffy, Maureen 1933- .... **CLC 37**
See also CA 25-28R; CANR 33, 68; CBD; CN 7; CP 7; CWD; CWP; DFS 15; DLB 14; FW; MTCW 1

Du Fu
See Tu Fu
See also RGWL 2, 3

Dugan, Alan 1923- .... **CLC 2, 6**
See also CA 81-84; CP 7; DLB 5; PFS 10

du Gard, Roger Martin
See Martin du Gard, Roger

Duhamel, Georges 1884-1966 .... **CLC 8**
See also CA 81-84; 25-28R; CANR 35; DLB 65; EWL 3; GFL 1789 to the Present; MTCW 1

Dujardin, Edouard (Emile Louis) 1861-1949 .... **TCLC 13**
See also CA 109; DLB 123

Duke, Raoul
See Thompson, Hunter S(tockton)

Dulles, John Foster 1888-1959 ...... **TCLC 72**
See also CA 115; 149

Dumas, Alexandre (pere) 1802-1870 .... **NCLC 11, 71; WLC**
See also AAYA 22; BYA 3; DA; DA3; DAB; DAC; DAM MST, NOV; DLB 119, 192; EW 6; GFL 1789 to the Present; LAIT 1; NFS 14; RGWL 2, 3; SATA 18; TWA; WCH

Dumas, Alexandre (fils) 1824-1895 ..... **DC 1; NCLC 9**
See also DLB 192; GFL 1789 to the Present; RGWL 2, 3

Dumas, Claudine
See Malzberg, Barry N(athaniel)

Dumas, Henry L. 1934-1968 .... **CLC 6, 62**
See also BW 1; CA 85-88; DLB 41; RGAL 4

du Maurier, Daphne 1907-1989 . **CLC 6, 11, 59; SSC 18**
See also AAYA 37; BPFB 1; BRWS 3; CA 5-8R; 128; CANR 6, 55; CMW 4; CPW; DA3; DAB; DAC; DAM MST, POP; DLB 191; HGG; LAIT 3; MSW; MTCW 1, 2; NFS 12; RGEL 2; RGSF 2; RHW; SATA 27; SATA-Obit 60; SSFS 14, 16; TEA

Du Maurier, George 1834-1896 .... **NCLC 86**
See also DLB 153, 178; RGEL 2

Dunbar, Paul Laurence 1872-1906 .. **BLC 1; PC 5; SSC 8; TCLC 2, 12; WLC**
See also AFAW 1, 2; AMWS 2; BW 1, 3; CA 104; 124; CDALB 1865-1917; DA; DA3; DAC; DAM MST, MULT, POET; DLB 50, 54, 78; EXPP; RGAL 4; SATA 34

Dunbar, William 1460(?)-1520(?) .... **LC 20**
See also BRWS 8; DLB 132, 146; RGEL 2

Dunbar-Nelson, Alice .... **HR 2**
See Nelson, Alice Ruth Moore Dunbar

Duncan, Dora Angela
See Duncan, Isadora

Duncan, Isadora 1877(?)-1927 ...... **TCLC 68**
See also CA 118; 149

Duncan, Lois 1934- .... **CLC 26**
See also AAYA 4, 34; BYA 6, 8; CA 1-4R; CANR 2, 23, 36, 111; CLR 29; JRDA; MAICYA 1, 2; MAICYAS 1; SAAS 2; SATA 1, 36, 75, 133; WYA; YAW

Duncan, Robert (Edward) 1919-1988 .... **CLC 1, 2, 4, 7, 15, 41, 55; PC 2**
See also BG 2; CA 9-12R; 124; CANR 28, 62; DAM POET; DLB 5, 16, 193; EWL 3; MTCW 1, 2; PFS 13; RGAL 4; WP

Duncan, Sara Jeannette 1861-1922 .... **TCLC 60**
See also CA 157; DLB 92

Dunlap, William 1766-1839 .... **NCLC 2**
See also DLB 30, 37, 59; RGAL 4

Dunn, Douglas (Eaglesham) 1942- .. **CLC 6, 40**
See also CA 45-48; CANR 2, 33; CP 7; DLB 40; MTCW 1

Dunn, Katherine (Karen) 1945- .... **CLC 71**
See also CA 33-36R; CANR 72; HGG; MTCW 1

Dunn, Stephen (Elliott) 1939- .... **CLC 36**
See also AMWS 11; CA 33-36R; CANR 12, 48, 53, 105; CP 7; DLB 105

Dunne, Finley Peter 1867-1936 .... **TCLC 28**
See also CA 108; 178; DLB 11, 23; RGAL 4

Dunne, John Gregory 1932- .... **CLC 28**
See also CA 25-28R; CANR 14, 50; CN 7; DLBY 1980

Dunsany, Lord .... **TCLC 2, 59**
See Dunsany, Edward John Moreton Drax Plunkett
See also DLB 77, 153, 156, 255; FANT; IDTP; RGEL 2; SFW 4; SUFW 1

Dunsany, Edward John Moreton Drax Plunkett 1878-1957
See Dunsany, Lord
See also CA 104; 148; DLB 10; MTCW 1

Duns Scotus, John 1266(?)-1308 . **CMLC 59**
See also DLB 115

du Perry, Jean
See Simenon, Georges (Jacques Christian)

Durang, Christopher (Ferdinand) 1949- .... **CLC 27, 38**
See also CA 105; CAD; CANR 50, 76; CD 5; MTCW 1

Duras, Marguerite 1914-1996 .... **CLC 3, 6, 11, 20, 34, 40, 68, 100; SSC 40**
See Donnadieu, Marguerite
See also BPFB 1; CA 25-28R; 151; CANR 50; CWW 2; DLB 83; EWL 3; GFL 1789 to the Present; IDFW 4; MTCW 1, 2; RGWL 2, 3; TWA

Durban, (Rosa) Pam 1947- .... **CLC 39**
See also CA 123; CANR 98; CSW

Durcan, Paul 1944- .... **CLC 43, 70**
See also CA 134; CP 7; DAM POET; EWL 3

Durkheim, Emile 1858-1917 .... **TCLC 55**

Durrell, Lawrence (George) 1912-1990 .... **CLC 1, 4, 6, 8, 13, 27, 41**
See also BPFB 1; BRWS 1; CA 9-12R; 132; CANR 40, 77; CDBLB 1945-1960; DAM NOV; DLB 15, 27, 204; DLBY 1990; EWL 3; MTCW 1, 2; RGEL 2; SFW 4; TEA

Durrenmatt, Friedrich
See Duerrenmatt, Friedrich
See also CDWLB 2; EW 13; EWL 3; RGWL 2, 3

Dutt, Michael Madhusudan 1824-1873 .... **NCLC 118**

Dutt, Toru 1856-1877 .... **NCLC 29**
See also DLB 240

Dwight, Timothy 1752-1817 .... **NCLC 13**
See also DLB 37; RGAL 4

Dworkin, Andrea 1946- .... **CLC 43, 123**
See also CA 77-80; CAAS 21; CANR 16, 39, 76, 96; FW; GLL 1; INT CANR-16; MTCW 1, 2

Dwyer, Deanna
See Koontz, Dean R(ay)

Dwyer, K. R.
See Koontz, Dean R(ay)

Dybek, Stuart 1942- .... **CLC 114; SSC 55**
See also CA 97-100; CANR 39; DLB 130

Dye, Richard
See De Voto, Bernard (Augustine)

Dyer, Geoff 1958- .... **CLC 149**
See also CA 125; CANR 88

Dylan, Bob 1941- ... **CLC 3, 4, 6, 12, 77; PC 37**
See also CA 41-44R; CANR 108; CP 7; DLB 16

Dyson, John 1943- .... **CLC 70**
See also CA 144

Dzyubin, Eduard Georgievich 1895-1934
See Bagritsky, Eduard
See also CA 170

E. V. L.
See Lucas, E(dward) V(errall)

Eagleton, Terence (Francis) 1943- . **CLC 63, 132**
See also CA 57-60; CANR 7, 23, 68, 115; DLB 242; LMFS 2; MTCW 1, 2

Eagleton, Terry
See Eagleton, Terence (Francis)

Early, Jack
See Scoppettone, Sandra
See also GLL 1

East, Michael
See West, Morris L(anglo)

Eastaway, Edward
See Thomas, (Philip) Edward

Eastlake, William (Derry) 1917-1997 .... **CLC 8**
See also CA 5-8R; 158; CAAS 1; CANR 5, 63; CN 7; DLB 6, 206; INT CANR-5; TCWW 2

Eastman, Charles A(lexander) 1858-1939 .... **NNAL; TCLC 55**
See also CA 179; CANR 91; DAM MULT; DLB 175; YABC 1

Eaton, Edith Maude 1865-1914 .... **AAL**
See Far, Sui Sin
See also CA 154; DLB 221; FW

Eaton, Winnifred 1875-1954 .... **AAL**
See also DLB 221; RGAL 4

Eberhart, Richard (Ghormley) 1904- .... CLC **3, 11, 19, 56**
See also AMW; CA 1-4R; CANR 2; CDALB 1941-1968; CP 7; DAM POET; DLB 48; MTCW 1; RGAL 4

Eberstadt, Fernanda 1960- .... CLC **39**
See also CA 136; CANR 69

Echegaray (y Eizaguirre), Jose (Maria Waldo) 1832-1916 ... HLCS **1**; TCLC **4**
See also CA 104; CANR 32; EWL 3; HW 1; MTCW 1

Echeverría, (Jose) Esteban (Antonino) 1805-1851 .... NCLC **18**
See also LAW

Echo
See Proust, (Valentin-Louis-George-Eugene-)Marcel

Eckert, Allan W. 1931- .... CLC **17**
See also AAYA 18; BYA 2; CA 13-16R; CANR 14, 45; INT CANR-14; MAICYA 2; MAICYAS 1; SAAS 21; SATA 29, 91; SATA-Brief 27

Eckhart, Meister 1260(?)-1327(?) .. CMLC **9**
See also DLB 115; LMFS 1

Eckmar, F. R.
See de Hartog, Jan

Eco, Umberto 1932- .... CLC **28, 60, 142**
See also BEST 90:1; BPFB 1; CA 77-80; CANR 12, 33, 55, 110; CPW; CWW 2; DA3; DAM NOV, POP; DLB 196, 242; EWL 3; MSW; MTCW 1, 2; RGWL 3

Eddison, E(ric) R(ucker) 1882-1945 .... TCLC **15**
See also CA 109; 156; DLB 255; FANT; SFW 4; SUFW 1

Eddy, Mary (Ann Morse) Baker 1821-1910 .... TCLC **71**
See also CA 113; 174

Edel, (Joseph) Leon 1907-1997 . CLC **29, 34**
See also CA 1-4R; 161; CANR 1, 22, 112; DLB 103; INT CANR-22

Eden, Emily 1797-1869 .... NCLC **10**

Edgar, David 1948- .... CLC **42**
See also CA 57-60; CANR 12, 61, 112; CBD; CD 5; DAM DRAM; DFS 15; DLB 13, 233; MTCW 1

Edgerton, Clyde (Carlyle) 1944- ..... CLC **39**
See also AAYA 17; CA 118; 134; CANR 64; CSW; DLB 278; INT 134; YAW

Edgeworth, Maria 1768-1849 ... NCLC **1, 51**
See also BRWS 3; DLB 116, 159, 163; FW; RGEL 2; SATA 21; TEA; WLIT 3

Edmonds, Paul
See Kuttner, Henry

Edmonds, Walter D(umaux) 1903-1998 .... CLC **35**
See also BYA 2; CA 5-8R; CANR 2; CWRI 5; DLB 9; LAIT 1; MAICYA 1, 2; RHW; SAAS 4; SATA 1, 27; SATA-Obit 99

Edmondson, Wallace
See Ellison, Harlan (Jay)

Edson, Russell 1935- .... CLC **13**
See also CA 33-36R; CANR 115; DLB 244; WP

Edwards, Bronwen Elizabeth
See Rose, Wendy

Edwards, G(erald) B(asil) 1899-1976 .... CLC **25**
See also CA 201; 110

Edwards, Gus 1939- .... CLC **43**
See also CA 108; INT 108

Edwards, Jonathan 1703-1758 .... LC **7, 54**
See also AMW; DA; DAC; DAM MST; DLB 24, 270; RGAL 4; TUS

Edwards, Sarah Pierpont 1710-1758 . LC **87**
See also DLB 200

Efron, Marina Ivanovna Tsvetaeva
See Tsvetaeva (Efron), Marina (Ivanovna)

Egoyan, Atom 1960- .... CLC **151**
See also CA 157

Ehle, John (Marsden, Jr.) 1925- ..... CLC **27**
See also CA 9-12R; CSW

Ehrenbourg, Ilya (Grigoryevich)
See Ehrenburg, Ilya (Grigoryevich)

Ehrenburg, Ilya (Grigoryevich) 1891-1967 .... CLC **18, 34, 62**
See Erenburg, Il'ia Grigor'evich
See also CA 102; 25-28R; EWL 3

Ehrenburg, Ilyo (Grigoryevich)
See Ehrenburg, Ilya (Grigoryevich)

Ehrenreich, Barbara 1941- .... CLC **110**
See also BEST 90:4; CA 73-76; CANR 16, 37, 62, 117; DLB 246; FW; MTCW 1, 2

Eich, Gunter
See Eich, Gunter
See also RGWL 2, 3

Eich, Gunter 1907-1972 .... CLC **15**
See Eich, Gunter
See also CA 111; 93-96; DLB 69, 124; EWL 3

Eichendorff, Joseph 1788-1857 .... NCLC **8**
See also DLB 90; RGWL 2, 3

Eigner, Larry .... CLC **9**
See Eigner, Laurence (Joe)
See also CAAS 23; DLB 5; WP

Eigner, Laurence (Joel) 1927-1996
See Eigner, Larry
See also CA 9-12R; 151; CANR 6, 84; CP 7; DLB 193

Einhard c. 770-840 .... CMLC **50**
See also DLB 148

Einstein, Albert 1879-1955 .... TCLC **65**
See also CA 121; 133; MTCW 1, 2

Eiseley, Loren
See Eiseley, Loren Corey
See also DLB 275

Eiseley, Loren Corey 1907-1977 .... CLC **7**
See Eiseley, Loren
See also AAYA 5; ANW; CA 1-4R; 73-76; CANR 6; DLBD 17

Eisenstadt, Jill 1963- .... CLC **50**
See also CA 140

Eisenstein, Sergei (Mikhailovich) 1898-1948 .... TCLC **57**
See also CA 114; 149

Eisner, Simon
See Kornbluth, C(yril) M.

Ekeloef, (Bengt) Gunnar 1907-1968 .... CLC **27**; PC **23**
See Ekelof, (Bengt) Gunnar
See also CA 123; 25-28R; DAM POET

Ekelof, (Bengt) Gunnar 1907-1968
See Ekeloef, (Bengt) Gunnar
See also DLB 259; EW 12; EWL 3

Ekelund, Vilhelm 1880-1949 .... TCLC **75**
See also CA 189; EWL 3

Ekwensi, C. O. D.
See Ekwensi, Cyprian (Odiatu Duaka)

Ekwensi, Cyprian (Odiatu Duaka) 1921- .... BLC **1**; CLC **4**
See also AFW; BW 2, 3; CA 29-32R; CANR 18, 42, 74; CDWLB 3; CN 7; CWRI 5; DAM MULT; DLB 117; EWL 3; MTCW 1, 2; RGEL 2; SATA 66; WLIT 2

Elaine .... TCLC **18**
See Leverson, Ada Esther

El Crummo
See Crumb, R(obert)

Elder, Lonne III 1931-1996 ... BLC **1**; DC **8**
See also BW 1, 3; CA 81-84; 152; CAD; CANR 25; DAM MULT; DLB 7, 38, 44

Eleanor of Aquitaine 1122-1204 .. CMLC **39**

Elia
See Lamb, Charles

Eliade, Mircea 1907-1986 .... CLC **19**
See also CA 65-68; 119; CANR 30, 62; CDWLB 4; DLB 220; EWL 3; MTCW 1; RGWL 3; SFW 4

Eliot, A. D.
See Jewett, (Theodora) Sarah Orne

Eliot, Alice
See Jewett, (Theodora) Sarah Orne

Eliot, Dan
See Silverberg, Robert

Eliot, George 1819-1880 .... NCLC **4, 13, 23, 41, 49, 89, 118**; PC **20**; WLC
See also BRW 5; BRWC 1; BRWR 2; CDBLB 1832-1890; CN 7; CPW; DA; DA3; DAB; DAC; DAM MST, NOV; DLB 21, 35, 55; LMFS 1; NFS 17; RGEL 2; RGSF 2; SSFS 8; TEA; WLIT 3

Eliot, John 1604-1690 .... LC **5**
See also DLB 24

Eliot, T(homas) S(tearns) 1888-1965 .... CLC **1, 2, 3, 6, 9, 10, 13, 15, 24, 34, 41, 55, 57, 113**; PC **5, 31**; WLC
See also AAYA 28; AMW; AMWC 1; AMWR 1; BRW 7; BRWR 2; CA 5-8R; 25-28R; CANR 41; CDALB 1929-1941; DA; DA3; DAB; DAC; DAM DRAM, MST, POET; DFS 4, 13; DLB 7, 10, 45, 63, 245; DLBY 1988; EWL 3; EXPP; LAIT 3; LMFS 2; MTCW 1, 2; PAB; PFS 1, 7; RGAL 4; RGEL 2; TUS; WLIT 4; WP

Elizabeth 1866-1941 .... TCLC **41**

Elkin, Stanley L(awrence) 1930-1995 .... CLC **4, 6, 9, 14, 27, 51, 91**; SSC **12**
See also AMWS 6; BPFB 1; CA 9-12R; 148; CANR 8, 46; CN 7; CPW; DAM NOV, POP; DLB 2, 28, 218, 278; DLBY 1980; EWL 3; INT CANR-8; MTCW 1, 2; RGAL 4

Elledge, Scott .... CLC **34**

Elliot, Don
See Silverberg, Robert

Elliott, Don
See Silverberg, Robert

Elliott, George P(aul) 1918-1980 .... CLC **2**
See also CA 1-4R; 97-100; CANR 2; DLB 244

Elliott, Janice 1931-1995 .... CLC **47**
See also CA 13-16R; CANR 8, 29, 84; CN 7; DLB 14; SATA 119

Elliott, Sumner Locke 1917-1991 ... CLC **38**
See also CA 5-8R; 134; CANR 2, 21

Elliott, William
See Bradbury, Ray (Douglas)

Ellis, A. E. .... CLC **7**

Ellis, Alice Thomas .... CLC **40**
See Haycraft, Anna (Margaret)
See also DLB 194; MTCW 1

Ellis, Bret Easton 1964- ..... CLC **39, 71, 117**
See also AAYA 2, 43; CA 118; 123; CANR 51, 74; CN 7; CPW; DA3; DAM POP; HGG; INT CA-123; MTCW 1; NFS 11

Ellis, (Henry) Havelock 1859-1939 .... TCLC **14**
See also CA 109; 169; DLB 190

Ellis, Landon
See Ellison, Harlan (Jay)

Ellis, Trey 1962- .... CLC **55**
See also CA 146; CANR 92

Ellison, Harlan (Jay) 1934- .. CLC **1, 13, 42, 139**; SSC **14**
See also AAYA 29; BPFB 1; BYA 14; CA 5-8R; CANR 5, 46, 115; CPW; DAM POP; DLB 8; HGG; INT CANR-5; MTCW 1, 2; SCFW 2; SFW 4; SSFS 13, 14, 15; SUFW 1, 2

Ellison, Ralph (Waldo) 1914-1994 ... BLC 1; CLC **1, 3, 11, 54, 86, 114**; SSC **26**; WLC
See also AAYA 19; AFAW 1, 2; AMWR 2; AMWS 2; BPFB 1; BW 1, 3; BYA 2; CA 9-12R; 145; CANR 24, 53; CDALB 1941-1968; CSW; DA; DA3; DAB; DAC; DAM MST, MULT, NOV; DLB 2, 76, 227; DLBY 1994; EWL 3; EXPN; EXPS; LAIT 4; MTCW 1, 2; NCFS 3; NFS 2; RGAL 4; RGSF 2; SSFS 1, 11; YAW

Ellmann, Lucy (Elizabeth) 1956- .... CLC **61**
See also CA 128

Ellmann, Richard (David) 1918-1987
.... CLC **50**
See also BEST 89:2; CA 1-4R; 122; CANR 2, 28, 61; DLB 103; DLBY 1987; MTCW 1, 2

Elman, Richard (Martin) 1934-1997
.... CLC **19**
See also CA 17-20R; 163; CAAS 3; CANR 47

Elron
See Hubbard, L(afayette) Ron(ald)

Eluard, Paul .... PC **38**; TCLC **7, 41**
See Grindel, Eugene
See also EWL 3; GFL 1789 to the Present; RGWL 2, 3

Elyot, Thomas 1490(?)-1546 .... LC **11**
See also DLB 136; RGEL 2

Elytis, Odysseus 1911-1996 ...... CLC **15, 49, 100**; PC **21**
See Alepoudelis, Odysseus
See also CA 102; 151; CANR 94; CWW 2; DAM POET; EW 13; EWL 3; MTCW 1, 2; RGWL 2, 3

Emecheta, (Florence Onye) Buchi 1944-
.... BLC **2**; CLC **14, 48, 128**
See also AFW; BW 2, 3; CA 81-84; CANR 27, 81; CDWLB 3; CN 7; CWRI 5; DA3; DAM MULT; DLB 117; EWL 3; FW; MTCW 1, 2; NFS 12, 14; SATA 66; WLIT 2

Emerson, Mary Moody 1774-1863
.... NCLC **66**

Emerson, Ralph Waldo 1803-1882
.... NCLC **1, 38, 98**; PC **18**; WLC
See also AMW; ANW; CDALB 1640-1865; DA; DA3; DAB; DAC; DAM MST, POET; DLB 1, 59, 73, 183, 223, 270; EXPP; LAIT 2; LMFS 1; NCFS 3; PFS 4, 17; RGAL 4; TUS; WP

Eminescu, Mihail 1850-1889 .... NCLC **33**

Empedocles 5th cent. B.C.- .... CMLC **50**
See also DLB 176

Empson, William 1906-1984 .. CLC **3, 8, 19, 33, 34**
See also BRWS 2; CA 17-20R; 112; CANR 31, 61; DLB 20; EWL 3; MTCW 1, 2; RGEL 2

Enchi, Fumiko (Ueda) 1905-1986 ... CLC **31**
See Enchi Fumiko
See also CA 129; 121; FW; MJW

Enchi Fumiko
See Enchi, Fumiko (Ueda)
See also DLB 182; EWL 3

Ende, Michael (Andreas Helmuth) 1929-1995 .... CLC **31**
See also BYA 5; CA 118; 124; 149; CANR 36, 110; CLR 14; DLB 75; MAICYA 1, 2; MAICYAS 1; SATA 61, 130; SATA-Brief 42; SATA-Obit 86

Endo, Shusaku 1923-1996 .... CLC **7, 14, 19, 54, 99**; SSC **48**
See Endo Shusaku
See also CA 29-32R; 153; CANR 21, 54; DA3; DAM NOV; MTCW 1, 2; RGSF 2; RGWL 2, 3

Endo Shusaku
See Endo, Shusaku
See also DLB 182; EWL 3

Engel, Marian 1933-1985 .... CLC **36**
See also CA 25-28R; CANR 12; DLB 53; FW; INT CANR-12

Engelhardt, Frederick
See Hubbard, L(afayette) Ron(ald)

Engels, Friedrich 1820-1895 . NCLC **85, 114**
See also DLB 129

Enright, D(ennis) J(oseph) 1920- . CLC **4, 8, 31**
See also CA 1-4R; CANR 1, 42, 83; CP 7; DLB 27; EWL 3; SATA 25

Enzensberger, Hans Magnus 1929-
.... CLC **43**; PC **28**
See also CA 116; 119; CANR 103; EWL 3

Ephron, Nora 1941- .... CLC **17, 31**
See also AAYA 35; AITN 2; CA 65-68; CANR 12, 39, 83

Epicurus 341B.C.-270B.C. .... CMLC **21**
See also DLB 176

Epsilon
See Betjeman, John

Epstein, Daniel Mark 1948- .... CLC **7**
See also CA 49-52; CANR 2, 53, 90

Epstein, Jacob 1956- .... CLC **19**
See also CA 114

Epstein, Jean 1897-1953 .... TCLC **92**

Epstein, Joseph 1937- .... CLC **39**
See also CA 112; 119; CANR 50, 65, 117

Epstein, Leslie 1938- .... CLC **27**
See also AMWS 12; CA 73-76; CAAS 12; CANR 23, 69

Equiano, Olaudah 1745(?)-1797 .... BLC **2**; LC **16**
See also AFAW 1, 2; CDWLB 3; DAM MULT; DLB 37, 50; WLIT 2

Erasmus, Desiderius 1469(?)-1536 ..... LC **16**
See also DLB 136; EW 2; LMFS 1; RGWL 2, 3; TWA

Erdman, Paul E(mil) 1932- .... CLC **25**
See also AITN 1; CA 61-64; CANR 13, 43, 84

Erdrich, Louise 1954- .... CLC **39, 54, 120**; NNAL
See also AAYA 10, 47; AMWS 4; BEST 89:1; BPFB 1; CA 114; CANR 41, 62; CDALBS; CN 7; CP 7; CPW; CWP; DA3; DAM MULT, NOV, POP; DLB 152, 175, 206; EWL 3; EXPP; LAIT 5; MTCW 1; NFS 5; PFS 14; RGAL 4; SATA 94; SSFS 14; TCWW 2

Erenburg, Ilya (Grigoryevich)
See Ehrenburg, Ilya (Grigoryevich)

Erickson, Stephen Michael 1950-
See Erickson, Steve
See also CA 129; SFW 4

Erickson, Steve .... CLC **64**
See Erickson, Stephen Michael
See also CANR 60, 68; SUFW 2

Ericson, Walter
See Fast, Howard (Melvin)

Eriksson, Buntel
See Bergman, (Ernst) Ingmar

Ernaux, Annie 1940- .... CLC **88**
See also CA 147; CANR 93; NCFS 3

Erskine, John 1879-1951 .... TCLC **84**
See also CA 112; 159; DLB 9, 102; FANT

Eschenbach, Wolfram von
See Wolfram von Eschenbach
See also RGWL 3

Eseki, Bruno
See Mphahlele, Ezekiel

Esenin, Sergei (Alexandrovich) 1895-1925
.... TCLC **4**
See also CA 104; RGWL 2, 3

Eshleman, Clayton 1935- .... CLC **7**
See also CA 33-36R; CAAS 6; CANR 93; CP 7; DLB 5

Espriella, Don Manuel Alvarez
See Southey, Robert

Espriu, Salvador 1913-1985 .... CLC **9**
See also CA 154; 115; DLB 134; EWL 3

Espronceda, Jose de 1808-1842 .... NCLC **39**

Esquivel, Laura 1951(?)- .. CLC **141**; HLCS **1**
See also AAYA 29; CA 143; CANR 68, 113; DA3; DNFS 2; LAIT 3; LMFS 2; MTCW 1; NFS 5; WLIT 1

Esse, James
See Stephens, James

Esterbrook, Tom
See Hubbard, L(afayette) Ron(ald)

Estleman, Loren D. 1952- .... CLC **48**
See also AAYA 27; CA 85-88; CANR 27, 74; CMW 4; CPW; DA3; DAM NOV, POP; DLB 226; INT CANR-27; MTCW 1, 2

Etherege, Sir George 1636-1692 .... LC **78**
See also BRW 2; DAM DRAM; DLB 80; PAB; RGEL 2

Euclid 306B.C.-283B.C. .... CMLC **25**

Eugenides, Jeffrey 1960(?)- .... CLC **81**
See also CA 144

Euripides c. 484B.C.-406B.C. .... CMLC **23, 51**; DC **4**; WLCS
See also AW 1; CDWLB 1; DA; DA3; DAB; DAC; DAM DRAM, MST; DFS 1, 4, 6; DLB 176; LAIT 1; LMFS 1; RGWL 2, 3

Evan, Evin
See Faust, Frederick (Schiller)

Evans, Caradoc 1878-1945 .. SSC **43**; TCLC **85**
See also DLB 162

Evans, Evan
See Faust, Frederick (Schiller)
See also TCWW 2

Evans, Marian
See Eliot, George

Evans, Mary Ann
See Eliot, George

Evarts, Esther
See Benson, Sally

Everett, Percival
See Everett, Percival L.
See also CSW

Everett, Percival L. 1956- .... CLC **57**
See Everett, Percival
See also BW 2; CA 129; CANR 94

Everson, R(onald) G(ilmour) 1903-1992
.... CLC **27**
See also CA 17-20R; DLB 88

Everson, William (Oliver) 1912-1994
.... CLC **1, 5, 14**
See also BG 2; CA 9-12R; 145; CANR 20; DLB 5, 16, 212; MTCW 1

Evtushenko, Evgenii Aleksandrovich
See Yevtushenko, Yevgeny (Alexandrovich)
See also RGWL 2, 3

Ewart, Gavin (Buchanan) 1916-1995
.... CLC **13, 46**
See also BRWS 7; CA 89-92; 150; CANR 17, 46; CP 7; DLB 40; MTCW 1

Ewers, Hanns Heinz 1871-1943 .... TCLC **12**
See also CA 109; 149

Ewing, Frederick R.
See Sturgeon, Theodore (Hamilton)

Exley, Frederick (Earl) 1929-1992 ... CLC **6, 11**
See also AITN 2; BPFB 1; CA 81-84; 138; CANR 117; DLB 143; DLBY 1981

Eynhardt, Guillermo
See Quiroga, Horacio (Sylvestre)

Ezekiel, Nissim 1924- .... CLC 61
See also CA 61-64; CP 7; EWL 3

Ezekiel, Tish O'Dowd 1943- .... CLC 34
See also CA 129

Fadeev, Aleksandr Aleksandrovich
See Bulgya, Alexander Alexandrovich
See also DLB 272

Fadeev, Alexandr Alexandrovich
See Bulgya, Alexander Alexandrovich
See also EWL 3

Fadeyev, A.
See Bulgya, Alexander Alexandrovich

Fadeyev, Alexander .... TCLC 53
See Bulgya, Alexander Alexandrovich

Fagen, Donald 1948- .... CLC 26

Fainzilberg, Ilya Arnoldovich 1897-1937
See Ilf, Ilya
See also CA 120; 165

Fair, Ronald L. 1932- .... CLC 18
See also BW 1; CA 69-72; CANR 25; DLB 33

Fairbairn, Roger
See Carr, John Dickson

Fairbairns, Zoe (Ann) 1948- .... CLC 32
See also CA 103; CANR 21, 85; CN 7

Fairfield, Flora
See Alcott, Louisa May

Fairman, Paul W. 1916-1977
See Queen, Ellery
See also CA 114; SFW 4

Falco, Gian
See Papini, Giovanni

Falconer, James
See Kirkup, James

Falconer, Kenneth
See Kornbluth, C(yril) M.

Falkland, Samuel
See Heijermans, Herman

Fallaci, Oriana 1930- .... CLC 11, 110
See also CA 77-80; CANR 15, 58; FW; MTCW 1

Faludi, Susan 1959- .... CLC 140
See also CA 138; FW; MTCW 1; NCFS 3

Faludy, George 1913- .... CLC 42
See also CA 21-24R

Faludy, Gyoergy
See Faludy, George

Fanon, Frantz 1925-1961 ... BLC 2; CLC 74
See also BW 1; CA 116; 89-92; DAM MULT; LMFS 2; WLIT 2

Fanshawe, Ann 1625-1680 .... LC 11

Fante, John (Thomas) 1911-1983 .... CLC 60
See also AMWS 11; CA 69-72; 109; CANR 23, 104; DLB 130; DLBY 1983

Farah, Nuruddin 1945- ...... BLC 2; CLC 53, 137
See also AFW; BW 2, 3; CA 106; CANR 81; CDWLB 3; CN 7; DAM MULT; DLB 125; EWL 3; WLIT 2

Fargue, Leon-Paul 1876(?)-1947 ... TCLC 11
See also CA 109; CANR 107; DLB 258; EWL 3

Farigoule, Louis
See Romains, Jules

Farina, Richard 1936(?)-1966 .... CLC 9
See also CA 81-84; 25-28R

Farley, Walter (Lorimer) 1915-1989
.... CLC 17
See also BYA 14; CA 17-20R; CANR 8, 29, 84; DLB 22; JRDA; MAICYA 1, 2; SATA 2, 43, 132; YAW

Farmer, Philip Jose 1918- .... CLC 1, 19
See also AAYA 28; BPFB 1; CA 1-4R; CANR 4, 35, 111; DLB 8; MTCW 1; SATA 93; SCFW 4; SFW 4

Farquhar, George 1677-1707 .... LC 21
See also BRW 2; DAM DRAM; DLB 84; RGEL 2

Farrell, J(ames) G(ordon) 1935-1979
.... CLC 6
See also CA 73-76; 89-92; CANR 36; DLB 14, 271; MTCW 1; RGEL 2; RHW; WLIT 4

Farrell, James T(homas) 1904-1979
.... CLC 1, 4, 8, 11, 66; SSC 28
See also AMW; BPFB 1; CA 5-8R; 89-92; CANR 9, 61; DLB 4, 9, 86; DLBD 2; EWL 3; MTCW 1, 2; RGAL 4

Farrell, Warren (Thomas) 1943- ..... CLC 70
See also CA 146

Farren, Richard J.
See Betjeman, John

Farren, Richard M.
See Betjeman, John

Fassbinder, Rainer Werner 1946-1982
.... CLC 20
See also CA 93-96; 106; CANR 31

Fast, Howard (Melvin) 1914-2003 . CLC 23, 131
See also AAYA 16; BPFB 1; CA 1-4R, 181; CAAE 181; CAAS 18; CANR 1, 33, 54, 75, 98; CMW 4; CN 7; CPW; DAM NOV; DLB 9; INT CANR-33; MTCW 1; RHW; SATA 7; SATA-Essay 107; TCWW 2; YAW

Faulcon, Robert
See Holdstock, Robert P.

Faulkner, William (Cuthbert) 1897-1962
..... CLC 1, 3, 6, 8, 9, 11, 14, 18, 28, 52, 68; SSC 1, 35, 42; WLC
See also AAYA 7; AMW; AMWR 1; BPFB 1; BYA 5; CA 81-84; CANR 33; CDALB 1929-1941; DA; DA3; DAB; DAC; DAM MST, NOV; DLB 9, 11, 44, 102; DLBD 2; DLBY 1986, 1997; EWL 3; EXPN; EXPS; LAIT 2; LMFS 2; MTCW 1, 2; NFS 4, 8, 13; RGAL 4; RGSF 2; SSFS 2, 5, 6, 12; TUS

Fauset, Jessie Redmon 1882(?)-1961
.... BLC 2; CLC 19, 54; HR 2
See also AFAW 2; BW 1; CA 109; CANR 83; DAM MULT; DLB 51; FW; LMFS 2; MAWW

Faust, Frederick (Schiller) 1892-1944(?)
.... TCLC 49
See Austin, Frank; Brand, Max; Challis, George; Dawson, Peter; Dexter, Martin; Evans, Evan; Frederick, John; Frost, Frederick; Manning, David; Silver, Nicholas
See also CA 108; 152; DAM POP; DLB 256; TUS

Faust, Irvin 1924- .... CLC 8
See also CA 33-36R; CANR 28, 67; CN 7; DLB 2, 28, 218, 278; DLBY 1980

Faustino, Domingo 1811-1888 .... NCLC 123

Fawkes, Guy
See Benchley, Robert (Charles)

Fearing, Kenneth (Flexner) 1902-1961
.... CLC 51
See also CA 93-96; CANR 59; CMW 4; DLB 9; RGAL 4

Fecamps, Elise
See Creasey, John

Federman, Raymond 1928- .... CLC 6, 47
See also CA 17-20R; CAAE 208; CAAS 8; CANR 10, 43, 83, 108; CN 7; DLBY 1980

Federspiel, J(uerg) F. 1931- .... CLC 42
See also CA 146

Feiffer, Jules (Ralph) 1929- ..... CLC 2, 8, 64
See also AAYA 3; CA 17-20R; CAD; CANR 30, 59; CD 5; DAM DRAM; DLB 7, 44; INT CANR-30; MTCW 1; SATA 8, 61, 111

Feige, Hermann Albert Otto Maximilian
See Traven, B.

Feinberg, David B. 1956-1994 .... CLC 59
See also CA 135; 147

Feinstein, Elaine 1930- .... CLC 36
See also CA 69-72; CAAS 1; CANR 31, 68; CN 7; CP 7; CWP; DLB 14, 40; MTCW 1

Feke, Gilbert David .... CLC 65

Feldman, Irving (Mordecai) 1928- ... CLC 7
See also CA 1-4R; CANR 1; CP 7; DLB 169

Felix-Tchicaya, Gerald
See Tchicaya, Gerald Felix

Fellini, Federico 1920-1993 .... CLC 16, 85
See also CA 65-68; 143; CANR 33

Felsen, Henry Gregor 1916-1995 .... CLC 17
See also CA 1-4R; 180; CANR 1; SAAS 2; SATA 1

Felski, Rita .... CLC 65

Fenno, Jack
See Calisher, Hortense

Fenollosa, Ernest (Francisco) 1853-1908
.... TCLC 91

Fenton, James Martin 1949- .... CLC 32
See also CA 102; CANR 108; CP 7; DLB 40; PFS 11

Ferber, Edna 1887-1968 .... CLC 18, 93
See also AITN 1; CA 5-8R; 25-28R; CANR 68, 105; DLB 9, 28, 86, 266; MTCW 1, 2; RGAL 4; RHW; SATA 7; TCWW 2

Ferdowsi, Abu'l Qasem 940-1020
.... CMLC 43
See also RGWL 2, 3

Ferguson, Helen
See Kavan, Anna

Ferguson, Niall 1964- .... CLC 134
See also CA 190

Ferguson, Samuel 1310-1886 .... NCLC 33
See also DLB 32; RGEL 2

Fergusson, Robert 1750-1774 .... LC 29
See also DLB 109; RGEL 2

Ferling, Lawrence
See Ferlinghetti, Lawrence (Monsanto)

Ferlinghetti, Lawrence (Monsanto) 1919(?)-
.... CLC 2, 6, 10, 27, 111; PC 1
See also CA 5-8R; CANR 3, 41, 73; CDALB 1941-1968; CP 7; DA3; DAM POET; DLB 5, 16; MTCW 1, 2; RGAL 4; WP

Fern, Fanny
See Parton, Sara Payson Willis

Fernandez, Vicente Garcia Huidobro
See Huidobro Fernandez, Vicente Garcia

Fernandez-Armesto, Felipe .... CLC 70

Fernandez de Lizardi, Jose Joaquin
See Lizardi, Jose Joaquin Fernandez de

Ferre, Rosario 1938- .... CLC 139; HLCS 1; SSC 36
See also CA 131; CANR 55, 81; CWW 2; DLB 145; EWL 3; HW 1, 2; LAWS 1; MTCW 1; WLIT 1

Ferrer, Gabriel (Francisco Victor) Miro
See Miro (Ferrer), Gabriel (Francisco Victor)

Ferrier, Susan (Edmonstone) 1782-1854
.... NCLC 8
See also DLB 116; RGEL 2

Ferrigno, Robert 1948(?)- .... CLC 65
See also CA 140

Ferron, Jacques 1921-1985 .... CLC 94
See also CA 117; 129; CCA 1; DAC; DLB 60; EWL 3

Feuchtwanger, Lion 1884-1958 .... TCLC 3
See also CA 104; 187; DLB 66; EWL 3

Feuillet, Octave 1821-1890 .... NCLC 45
See also DLB 192

Feydeau, Georges (Leon Jules Marie) 1862-1921 .... TCLC 22
See also CA 113; 152; CANR 84; DAM DRAM; DLB 192; EWL 3; GFL 1789 to the Present; RGWL 2, 3

Fichte, Johann Gottlieb 1762-1814
.... **NCLC 62**
See also DLB 90

Ficino, Marsilio 1433-1499 .... **LC 12**
See also LMFS 1

Fiedeler, Hans
See Doeblin, Alfred

Fiedler, Leslie A(aron) 1917-2003 .... **CLC 4, 13, 24**
See also CA 9-12R; CANR 7, 63; CN 7; DLB 28, 67; EWL 3; MTCW 1, 2; RGAL 4; TUS

Field, Andrew 1938- .... **CLC 44**
See also CA 97-100; CANR 25

Field, Eugene 1850-1895 .... **NCLC 3**
See also DLB 23, 42, 140; DLBD 13; MAICYA 1, 2; RGAL 4; SATA 16

Field, Gans T.
See Wellman, Manly Wade

Field, Michael 1915-1971 .... **TCLC 43**
See also CA 29-32R

Field, Peter
See Hobson, Laura Z(ametkin)
See also TCWW 2

Fielding, Helen 1959(?)- .... **CLC 146**
See also CA 172; DLB 231

Fielding, Henry 1707-1754 ..... **LC 1, 46, 85; WLC**
See also BRW 3; BRWR 1; CDBLB 1660-1789; DA; DA3; DAB; DAC; DAM DRAM, MST, NOV; DLB 39, 84, 101; RGEL 2; TEA; WLIT 3

Fielding, Sarah 1710-1768 .... **LC 1, 44**
See also DLB 39; RGEL 2; TEA

Fields, W. C. 1880-1946 .... **TCLC 80**
See also DLB 44

Fierstein, Harvey (Forbes) 1954- .... **CLC 33**
See also CA 123; 129; CAD; CD 5; CPW; DA3; DAM DRAM, POP; DFS 6; DLB 266; GLL

Figes, Eva 1932- .... **CLC 31**
See also CA 53-56; CANR 4, 44, 83; CN 7; DLB 14, 271; FW

Filippo, Eduardo de
See de Filippo, Eduardo

Finch, Anne 1661-1720 .... **LC 3; PC 21**
See also DLB 95

Finch, Robert (Duer Claydon) 1900-1995
.... **CLC 18**
See also CA 57-60; CANR 9, 24, 49; CP 7; DLB 88

Findley, Timothy (Irving Frederick) 1930-2002 .... **CLC 27, 102**
See also CA 25-28R; 206; CANR 12, 42, 69, 109; CCA 1; CN 7; DAC; DAM MST; DLB 53; FANT; RHW

Fink, William
See Mencken, H(enry) L(ouis)

Firbank, Louis 1942-
See Reed, Lou
See also CA 117

Firbank, (Arthur Annesley) Ronald 1886-1926 .... **TCLC 1**
See also BRWS 2; CA 104; 177; DLB 36; EWL 3; RGEL 2

Fish, Stanley
See Fish, Stanley Eugene

Fish, Stanley E.
See Fish, Stanley Eugene

Fish, Stanley Eugene 1938- .... **CLC 142**
See also CA 112; 132; CANR 90; DLB 67

Fisher, Dorothy (Frances) Canfield 1879-1958 .... **TCLC 87**
See also CA 114; 136; CANR 80; CLR 71,; CWRI 5; DLB 9, 102; MAICYA 1, 2; YABC 1

Fisher, M(ary) F(rances) K(ennedy) 1908-1992 .... **CLC 76, 87**
See also CA 77-80; 138; CANR 44; MTCW 1

Fisher, Roy 1930- .... **CLC 25**
See also CA 81-84; CAAS 10; CANR 16; CP 7; DLB 40

Fisher, Rudolph 1897-1934 ... **BLC 2; HR 2; SSC 25; TCLC 11**
See also BW 1, 3; CA 107; 124; CANR 80; DAM MULT; DLB 51, 102

Fisher, Vardis (Alvero) 1895-1968 .... **CLC 7**
See also CA 5-8R; 25-28R; CANR 68; DLB 9, 206; RGAL 4; TCWW 2

Fiske, Tarleton
See Bloch, Robert (Albert)

Fitch, Clarke
See Sinclair, Upton (Beall)

Fitch, John IV
See Cormier, Robert (Edmund)

Fitzgerald, Captain Hugh
See Baum, L(yman) Frank

FitzGerald, Edward 1809-1883 ...... **NCLC 9**
See also BRW 4; DLB 32; RGEL 2

Fitzgerald, F(rancis) Scott (Key) 1896-1940
.... **SSC 6, 31; TCLC 1, 6, 14, 28, 55; WLC**
See also AAYA 24; AITN 1; AMW; AMWR 1; BPFB 1; CA 110; 123; CDALB 1917-1929; DA; DA3; DAB; DAC; DAM MST, NOV; DLB 4, 9, 86, 219; DLBD 1, 15, 16, 273; DLBY 1981, 1996; EWL 3; EXPN; EXPS; LAIT 3; MTCW 1, 2; NFS 2; RGAL 4; RGSF 2; SSFS 4, 15; TUS

Fitzgerald, Penelope 1916-2000 ...... **CLC 19, 51, 61, 143**
See also BRWS 5; CA 85-88; 190; CAAS 10; CANR 56, 86; CN 7; DLB 14, 194; EWL 3; MTCW 2

Fitzgerald, Robert (Stuart) 1910-1985
.... **CLC 39**
See also CA 1-4R; 114; CANR 1; DLBY 1980

FitzGerald, Robert D(avid) 1902-1987
.... **CLC 19**
See also CA 17-20R; DLB 260; RGEL 2

Fitzgerald, Zelda (Sayre) 1900-1948
.... **TCLC 52**
See also AMWS 9; CA 117; 126; DLBY 1984

Flanagan, Thomas (James Bonner) 1923-2002 .... **CLC 25, 52**
See also CA 108; 206; CANR 55; CN 7; DLBY 1980; INT 108; MTCW 1; RHW

Flaubert, Gustave 1821-1880 .. **NCLC 2, 10, 19, 62, 66; SSC 11, 60; WLC**
See also DA; DA3; DAB; DAC; DAM MST, NOV; DLB 119; EW 7; EXPS; GFL 1789 to the Present; LAIT 2; LMFS 1; NFS 14; RGSF 2; RGWL 2, 3; SSFS 6; TWA

Flavius Josephus
See Josephus, Flavius

Flecker, Herman Elroy
See Flecker, (Herman) James Elroy

Flecker, (Herman) James Elroy 1884-1915
.... **TCLC 43**
See also CA 109; 150; DLB 10, 19; RGEL 2

Fleming, Ian (Lancaster) 1908-1964
.... **CLC 3, 30**
See also AAYA 26; BPFB 1; CA 5-8R; CANR 59; CDBLB 1945-1960; CMW 4; CPW; DA3; DAM POP; DLB 87, 201; MSW; MTCW 1, 2; RGEL 2; SATA 9; TEA; YAW

Fleming, Thomas (James) 1927- ..... **CLC 37**
See also CA 5-8R; CANR 10, 102; INT CANR-10; SATA 8

Fletcher, John 1579-1625 .... **DC 6; LC 33**
See also BRW 2; CDBLB Before 1660; DLB 58; RGEL 2; TEA

Fletcher, John Gould 1886-1950 .. **TCLC 35**
See also CA 107; 167; DLB 4, 45; LMFS 2; RGAL 4

Fleur, Paul
See Pohl, Frederik

Flooglebuckle, Al
See Spiegelman, Art

Flora, Fletcher 1914-1969
See Queen, Ellery
See also CA 1-4R; CANR 3, 85

Flying Officer X
See Bates, H(erbert) E(rnest)

Fo, Dario 1926- .... **CLC 32, 109; DC 10**
See also CA 116; 128; CANR 68, 114; CWW 2; DA3; DAM DRAM; DLBY 1997; EWL 3; MTCW 1, 2

Fogarty, Jonathan Titulescu Esq.
See Farrell, James T(homas)

Follett, Ken(neth Martin) 1949- ...... **CLC 18**
See also AAYA 6; BEST 89:4; BPFB 1; CA 81-84; CANR 13, 33, 54, 102; CMW 4; CPW; DA3; DAM NOV, POP; DLB 87; DLBY 1981; INT CANR-33; MTCW 1

Fontane, Theodor 1819-1898 .... **NCLC 26**
See also CDWLB 2; DLB 129; EW 6; RGWL 2, 3; TWA

Fontenot, Chester .... **CLC 65**

Fonvizin, Denis Ivanovich 1744(?)-1792
.... **LC 81**
See also DLB 150; RGWL 2, 3

Foote, Horton 1916- .... **CLC 51, 91**
See also CA 73-76; CAD; CANR 34, 51, 110; CP 5; CSW; DA3; DAM DRAM; DLB 26, 266; EWL 3; INT CANR-34

Foote, Mary Hallock 1847-1938 . **TCLC 108**
See also DLB 186, 188, 202, 221

Foote, Shelby 1916- .... **CLC 75**
See also AAYA 40; CA 5-8R; CANR 3, 45, 74; CN 7; CPW; CSW; DA3; DAM NOV, POP; DLB 2, 17; MTCW 2; RHW

Forbes, Cosmo
See Lewton, Val

Forbes, Esther 1891-1967 .... **CLC 12**
See also AAYA 17; BYA 2; CA 13-14; 25-28R; CAP 1; CLR 27; DLB 22; JRDA; MAICYA 1, 2; RHW; SATA 2, 100; YAW

Forche, Carolyn (Louise) 1950- ..... **CLC 25, 83, 86; PC 10**
See also CA 109; 117; CANR 50, 74; CP 7; CWP; DA3; DAM POET; DLB 5, 193; INT CA-117; MTCW 1; RGAL 4

Ford, Elbur
See Hibbert, Eleanor Alice Burford

Ford, Ford Madox 1873-1939 . **TCLC 1, 15, 39, 57**
See Chaucer, Daniel
See also BRW 6; CA 104; 132; CANR 74; CDBLB 1914-1945; DA3; DAM NOV; DLB 34, 98, 162; EWL 3; MTCW 1, 2; RGEL 2; TEA

Ford, Henry 1863-1947 .... **TCLC 73**
See also CA 115; 148

Ford, Jack
See Ford, John

Ford, John 1586-1639 .... **DC 8; LC 68**
See also BRW 2; CDBLB Before 1660; DA3; DAM DRAM; DFS 7; DLB 58; IDTP; RGEL 2

Ford, John 1895-1973 .... **CLC 16**
See also CA 187; 45-48

Ford, Richard 1944- .... **CLC 46, 99**
See also AMWS 5; CA 69-72; CANR 11, 47, 86; CN 7; CSW; DLB 227; EWL 3; MTCW 1; RGAL 4; RGSF 2

Ford, Webster
See Masters, Edgar Lee

Foreman, Richard 1937- .... **CLC 50**
See also CA 65-68; CAD; CANR 32, 63; CD 5

Forester, C(ecil) S(cott) 1899-1966 . **CLC 35**
See also CA 73-76; 25-28R; CANR 83; DLB 191; RGEL 2; RHW; SATA 13

Forez
See Mauriac, Francois (Charles)

Forman, James
See Forman, James D(ouglas)

Forman, James D(ouglas) 1932- ..... **CLC 21**
See also AAYA 17; CA 9-12R; CANR 4, 19, 42; JRDA; MAICYA 1, 2; SATA 8, 70; YAW

Forman, Milos 1932- .... **CLC 164**
See also CA 109

Fornes, Maria Irene 1930- .... **CLC 39, 61; DC 10; HLCS 1**
See also CA 25-28R; CAD; CANR 28, 81; CD 5; CWD; DLB 7; HW 1, 2; INT CANR-28; MTCW 1; RGAL 4

Forrest, Leon (Richard) 1937-1997
.... **BLCS; CLC 4**
See also AFAW 2; BW 2; CA 89-92; 162; CAAS 7; CANR 25, 52, 87; CN 7; DLB 33

Forster, E(dward) M(organ) 1879-1970
..... **CLC 1, 2, 3, 4, 9, 10, 13, 15, 22, 45, 77; SSC 27; TCLC 125; WLC**
See also AAYA 2, 37; BRW 6; BRWR 2; CA 13-14; 25-28R; CANR 45; CAP 1; CDBLB 1914-1945; DA; DA3; DAB; DAC; DAM MST, NOV; DLB 34, 98, 162, 178, 195; DLBD 10; EWL 3; EXPN; LAIT 3; LMFS 1; MTCW 1, 2; NCFS 1; NFS 3, 10, 11; RGEL 2; RGSF 2; SATA 57; SUFW 1; TEA; WLIT 4

Forster, John 1812-1876 .... **NCLC 11**
See also DLB 144, 184

Forster, Margaret 1938- .... **CLC 149**
See also CA 133; CANR 62, 115; CN 7; DLB 155, 271

Forsyth, Frederick 1938- .... **CLC 2, 5, 36**
See also BEST 89:4; CA 85-88; CANR 38, 62, 115; CMW 4; CN 7; CPW; DAM NOV, POP; DLB 87; MTCW 1, 2

Forten, Charlotte L. 1837-1914 .... **BLC 2; TCLC 16**
See Grimke, Charlotte L(ottie) Forten
See also DLB 50, 239

Fortinbras
See Grieg, (Johan) Nordahl (Brun)

Foscolo, Ugo 1778-1827 .... **NCLC 8, 97**
See also EW 5

Fosse, Bob .... **CLC 20**
See Fosse, Robert Louis

Fosse, Robert Louis 1927-1987
See Fosse, Bob
See also CA 110; 123

Foster, Hannah Webster 1758-1840
.... **NCLC 99**
See also DLB 37, 200; RGAL 4

Foster, Stephen Collins 1826-1864
.... **NCLC 26**
See also RGAL 4

Foucault, Michel 1926-1984 ..... **CLC 31, 34, 69**
See also CA 105; 113; CANR 34; DLB 242; EW 13; EWL 3; GFL 1789 to the Present; GLL 1; LMFS 2; MTCW 1, 2; TWA

Fouque, Friedrich (Heinrich Karl) de la Motte 1777-1843 .... **NCLC 2**
See also DLB 90; RGWL 2, 3; SUFW 1

Fourier, Charles 1772-1837 .... **NCLC 51**

Fournier, Henri-Alban 1886-1914
See Alain-Fournier
See also CA 104; 179

Fournier, Pierre 1916- .... **CLC 11**
See Gascar, Pierre
See also CA 89-92; CANR 16, 40

Fowles, John (Robert) 1926- .... **CLC 1, 2, 3, 4, 6, 9, 10, 15, 33, 87; SSC 33**
See also BPFB 1; BRWS 1; CA 5-8R; CANR 25, 71, 103; CDBLB 1960 to Present; CN 7; DA3; DAB; DAC; DAM MST; DLB 14, 139, 207; EWL 3; HGG; MTCW 1, 2; RGEL 2; RHW; SATA 22; TEA; WLIT 4

Fox, Paula 1923- .... **CLC 2, 8, 121**
See also AAYA 3, 37; BYA 3, 8; CA 73-76; CANR 20, 36, 62, 105; CLR 1, 44; DLB 52; JRDA; MAICYA 1, 2; MTCW 1; NFS 12; SATA 17, 60, 120; WYA; YAW

Fox, William Price (Jr.) 1926- .... **CLC 22**
See also CA 17-20R; CAAS 19; CANR 11; CSW; DLB 2; DLBY 1981

Foxe, John 1517(?)-1587 .... **LC 14**
See also DLB 132

Frame, Janet .. **CLC 2, 3, 6, 22, 66, 96; SSC 29**
See Clutha, Janet Paterson Frame
See also CN 7; CWP; EWL 3; RGEL 2; RGSF 2; TWA

France, Anatole .... **TCLC 9**
See Thibault, Jacques Anatole Francois
See also DLB 123; EWL 3; GFL 1789 to the Present; MTCW 1; RGWL 2, 3; SUFW 1

Francis, Claude .... **CLC 50**
See also CA 192

Francis, Dick 1920- .... **CLC 2, 22, 42, 102**
See also AAYA 5, 21; BEST 89:3; BPFB 1; CA 5-8R; CANR 9, 42, 68, 100; CDBLB 1960 to Present; CMW 4; CN 7; DA3; DAM POP; DLB 87; INT CANR-9; MSW; MTCW 1, 2

Francis, Robert (Churchill) 1901-1987
.... **CLC 15; PC 34**
See also AMWS 9; CA 1-4R; 123; CANR 1; EXPP; PFS 12

Francis, Lord Jeffrey
See Jeffrey, Francis
See also DLB 107

Frank, Anne(lies Marie) 1929-1945
.... **TCLC 17; WLC**
See also AAYA 12; BYA 1; CA 113; 133; CANR 68; DA; DA3; DAB; DAC; DAM MST; LAIT 4; MAICYA 2; MAICYAS 1; MTCW 1, 2; NCFS 2; SATA 87; SATA-Brief 42; WYA; YAW

Frank, Bruno 1887-1945 .... **TCLC 81**
See also CA 189; DLB 118; EWL 3

Frank, Elizabeth 1945- .... **CLC 39**
See also CA 121; 126; CANR 78; INT 126

Frankl, Viktor E(mil) 1905-1997 .... **CLC 93**
See also CA 65-68; 161

Franklin, Benjamin
See Hasek, Jaroslav (Matej Frantisek)

Franklin, Benjamin 1706-1790 .... **LC 25; WLCS**
See also AMW; CDALB 1640-1865; DA; DA3; DAB; DAC; DAM MST; DLB 24, 43, 73, 183; LAIT 1; RGAL 4; TUS

Franklin, (Stella Maria Sarah) Miles (Lampe) 1879-1954 .... **TCLC 7**
See also CA 104; 164; DLB 230; FW; MTCW 2; RGEL 2; TWA

Fraser, (Lady) Antonia (Pakenham) 1932-
.... **CLC 32, 107**
See also CA 85-88; CANR 44, 65; CMW; DLB 276; MTCW 1, 2; SATA-Brief 32

Fraser, George MacDonald 1925- ..... **CLC 7**
See also AAYA 48; CA 45-48, 180; CAAE 180; CANR 2, 48, 74; MTCW 1; RHW

Fraser, Sylvia 1935- .... **CLC 64**
See also CA 45-48; CANR 1, 16, 60; CCA 1

Frayn, Michael 1933- .... **CLC 3, 7, 31, 47**
See also BRWS 7; CA 5-8R; CANR 30, 69, 114; CBD; CD 5; CN 7; DAM DRAM, NOV; DLB 13, 14, 194, 245; FANT; MTCW 1, 2; SFW 4

Fraze, Candida (Merrill) 1945- .... **CLC 50**
See also CA 126

Frazer, Andrew
See Marlowe, Stephen

Frazer, J(ames) G(eorge) 1854-1941
.... **TCLC 32**
See also BRWS 3; CA 118

Frazer, Robert Caine
See Creasey, John

Frazer, Sir James George
See Frazer, J(ames) G(eorge)

Frazier, Charles 1950- .... **CLC 109**
See also AAYA 34; CA 161; CSW

Frazier, Ian 1951- .... **CLC 46**
See also CA 130; CANR 54, 93

Frederic, Harold 1856-1898 .... **NCLC 10**
See also AMW; DLB 12, 23; DLBD 13; RGAL 4

Frederick, John
See Faust, Frederick (Schiller)
See also TCWW 2

Frederick the Great 1712-1786 .... **LC 14**

Fredro, Aleksander 1793-1876 .... **NCLC 8**

Freeling, Nicolas 1927- .... **CLC 38**
See also CA 49-52; CAAS 12; CANR 1, 17, 50, 84; CMW 4; CN 7; DLB 87

Freeman, Douglas Southall 1886-1953
.... **TCLC 11**
See also CA 109; 195; DLB 17; DLBD 17

Freeman, Judith 1946- .... **CLC 55**
See also CA 148; DLB 256

Freeman, Mary E(leanor) Wilkins 1852-1930
.... **SSC 1, 47; TCLC 9**
See also CA 106; 177; DLB 12, 78, 221; EXPS; FW; HGG; MAWW; RGAL 4; RGSF 2; SSFS 4, 8; SUFW 1; TUS

Freeman, R(ichard) Austin 1862-1943
.... **TCLC 21**
See also CA 113; CANR 84; CMW 4; DLB 70

French, Albert 1943- .... **CLC 86**
See also BW 3; CA 167

French, Antonia
See Kureishi, Hanif

French, Marilyn 1929- .... **CLC 10, 18, 60**
See also BPFB 1; CA 69-72; CANR 3, 31; CN 7; CPW; DAM DRAM, NOV, POP; FW; INT CANR-31; MTCW 1, 2

French, Paul
See Asimov, Isaac

Freneau, Philip Morin 1752-1832 . **NCLC 1, 111**
See also AMWS 2; DLB 37, 43; RGAL 4

Freud, Sigmund 1856-1939 .... **TCLC 52**
See also CA 115; 133; CANR 69; EW 8; EWL 3; MTCW 1, 2; NCFS 3; TWA

Freytag, Gustav 1816-1895 .... **NCLC 109**
See also DLB 129

Friedan, Betty (Naomi) 1921- .... **CLC 74**
See also CA 65-68; CANR 18, 45, 74; DLB 246; FW; MTCW 1, 2

Friedlander, Saul 1932- .... **CLC 90**
See also CA 117; 130; CANR 72

Friedman, B(ernard) H(arper) 1926-
.... **CLC 7**
See also CA 1-4R; CANR 3, 48

Friedman, Bruce Jay 1930- .... **CLC 3, 5, 56**
See also CA 9-12R; CAD; CANR 25, 52, 101; CD 5; CN 7; DLB 2, 28, 244; INT CANR-25

Friel, Brian 1929- .. **CLC 5, 42, 59, 115; DC 8**
See also BRWS 5; CA 21-24R; CANR 33, 69; CBD; CD 5; DFS 11; DLB 13; EWL 3; MTCW 1; RGEL 2; TEA

Friis-Baastad, Babbis Ellinor 1921-1970
.... **CLC 12**
See also CA 17-20R; 134; SATA 7

Frisch, Max (Rudolf) 1911-1991 .. **CLC 3, 9, 14, 18, 32, 44; TCLC 121**
See also CA 85-88; 134; CANR 32, 74; CDWLB 2; DAM DRAM, NOV; DLB 69, 124; EW 13; EWL 3; MTCW 1, 2; RGWL 2, 3

Fromentin, Eugene (Samuel Auguste) 1820-1876 .... **NCLC 10, 125**
See also DLB 123; GFL 1789 to the Present

Frost, Frederick
See Faust, Frederick (Schiller)
See also TCWW 2

Frost, Robert (Lee) 1874-1963 . **CLC 1, 3, 4, 9, 10, 13, 15, 26, 34, 44; PC 1, 39; WLC**
See also AAYA 21; AMW; AMWR 1; CA 89-92; CANR 33; CDALB 1917-1929; CLR 67; DA; DA3; DAB; DAC; DAM MST, POET; DLB 54; DLBD 7; EWL 3; EXPP; MTCW 1, 2; PAB; PFS 1, 2, 3, 4, 5, 6, 7, 10, 13; RGAL 4; SATA 14; TUS; WP; WYA

Froude, James Anthony 1818-1894
.... **NCLC 43**
See also DLB 18, 57, 144

Froy, Herald
See Waterhouse, Keith (Spencer)

Fry, Christopher 1907- .... **CLC 2, 10, 14**
See also BRWS 3; CA 17-20R; CAAS 23; CANR 9, 30, 74; CBD; CD 5; CP 7; DAM DRAM; DLB 13; EWL 3; MTCW 1, 2; RGEL 2; SATA 66; TEA

Frye, (Herman) Northrop 1912-1991
.... **CLC 24, 70**
See also CA 5-8R; 133; CANR 8, 37; DLB 67, 68, 246; EWL 3; MTCW 1, 2; RGAL 4; TWA

Fuchs, Daniel 1909-1993 .... **CLC 8, 22**
See also CA 81-84; 142; CAAS 5; CANR 40; DLB 9, 26, 28; DLBY 1993

Fuchs, Daniel 1934- .... **CLC 34**
See also CA 37-40R; CANR 14, 48

Fuentes, Carlos 1928- .... **CLC 3, 8, 10, 13, 22, 41, 60, 113; HLC 1; SSC 24; WLC**
See also AAYA 4, 45; AITN 2; BPFB 1; CA 69-72; CANR 10, 32, 68, 104; CDWLB 3; CWW 2; DA; DA3; DAB; DAC; DAM MST, MULT, NOV; DLB 113; DNFS 2; EWL 3; HW 1, 2; LAIT 3; LAW; LAWS 1; LMFS 2; MTCW 1, 2; NFS 8; RGSF 2; RGWL 2, 3; TWA; WLIT 1

Fuentes, Gregorio Lopez y
See Lopez y Fuentes, Gregorio

Fuertes, Gloria 1918-1998 .... **PC 27**
See also CA 178, 180; DLB 108; HW 2; SATA 115

Fugard, (Harold) Athol 1932- ...... **CLC 5, 9, 14, 25, 40, 80; DC 3**
See also AAYA 17; AFW; CA 85-88; CANR 32, 54; CD 5; DAM DRAM; DFS 3, 6, 10; DLB 225; DNFS 1, 2; EWL 3; MTCW 1; RGEL 2; WLIT 2

Fugard, Sheila 1932- .... **CLC 48**
See also CA 125

Fukuyama, Francis 1952- .... **CLC 131**
See also CA 140; CANR 72

Fuller, Charles (H., Jr.) 1939- .... **BLC 2; CLC 25; DC 1**
See also BW 2; CA 108; 112; CAD; CANR 87; CD 5; DAM DRAM, MULT; DFS 8; DLB 38, 266; EWL 3; INT CA-112; MTCW 1

Fuller, Henry Blake 1857-1929 ... **TCLC 103**
See also CA 108; 177; DLB 12; RGAL 4

Fuller, John (Leopold) 1937- .... **CLC 62**
See also CA 21-24R; CANR 9, 44; CP 7; DLB 40

Fuller, Margaret
See Ossoli, Sarah Margaret (Fuller)
See also AMWS 2; DLB 183, 223, 239

Fuller, Roy (Broadbent) 1912-1991 . **CLC 4, 28**
See also BRWS 7; CA 5-8R; 135; CAAS 10; CANR 53, 83; CWRI 5; DLB 15, 20; EWL 3; RGEL 2; SATA 87

Fuller, Sarah Margaret
See Ossoli, Sarah Margaret (Fuller)

Fuller, Sarah Margaret
See Ossoli, Sarah Margaret (Fuller)
See also DLB 1, 59, 73

Fulton, Alice 1952- .... **CLC 52**
See also CA 116; CANR 57, 88; CP 7; CWP; DLB 193

Furphy, Joseph 1843-1912 .... **TCLC 25**
See Collins, Tom
See also CA 163; DLB 230; EWL 3; RGEL 2

Fuson, Robert H(enderson) 1927- .. **CLC 70**
See also CA 89-92; CANR 103

Fussell, Paul 1924- .... **CLC 74**
See also BEST 90:1; CA 17-20R; CANR 8, 21, 35, 69; INT CANR-21; MTCW 1, 2

Futabatei, Shimei 1864-1909 .... **TCLC 44**
See Futabatei Shimei
See also CA 162; MJW

Futabatei Shimei
See Futabatei, Shimei
See also DLB 180; EWL 3

Futrelle, Jacques 1875-1912 .... **TCLC 19**
See also CA 113; 155; CMW 4

Gaboriau, Emile 1835-1873 .... **NCLC 14**
See also CMW 4; MSW

Gadda, Carlo Emilio 1893-1973 .... **CLC 11**
See also CA 89-92; DLB 177; EWL 3

Gaddis, William 1922-1998 .. **CLC 1, 3, 6, 8, 10, 19, 43, 86**
See also AMWS 4; BPFB 1; CA 17-20R; 172; CANR 21, 48; CN 7; DLB 2, 278; EWL 3; MTCW 1, 2; RGAL 4

Gaelique, Moruen le
See Jacob, (Cyprien-)Max

Gage, Walter
See Inge, William (Motter)

Gaines, Ernest J(ames) 1933- . **BLC 2; CLC 3, 11, 18, 86**
See also AAYA 18; AFAW 1, 2; AITN 1; BPFB 1; BW 2, 3; BYA 6; CA 9-12R; CANR 6, 24, 42, 75; CDALB 1968-1988; CLR 62; CN 7; CSW; DA3; DAM MULT; DLB 2, 33, 152; DLBY 1980; EWL 3; EXPN; LAIT 5; MTCW 1, 2; NFS 5, 7, 16; RGAL 4; RGSF 2; RHW; SATA 86; SSFS 5; YAW

Gaitskill, Mary 1954- .... **CLC 69**
See also CA 128; CANR 61; DLB 244

Galdos, Benito Perez
See Perez Galdos, Benito
See also EW 7

Gale, Zona 1874-1938 .... **TCLC 7**
See also CA 105; 153; CANR 84; DAM DRAM; DFS 17; DLB 9, 78, 228; RGAL 4

Galeano, Eduardo (Hughes) 1940-
.... **CLC 72; HLCS 1**
See also CA 29-32R; CANR 13, 32, 100; HW 1

Galiano, Juan Valera y Alcala
See Valera y Alcala-Galiano, Juan

Galilei, Galileo 1564-1642 .... **LC 45**

Gallagher, Tess 1943- .... **CLC 18, 63; PC 9**
See also CA 106; CP 7; CWP; DAM POET; DLB 120, 212, 244; PFS 16

Gallant, Mavis 1922- .... **CLC 7, 18, 38, 172; SSC 5**
See also CA 69-72; CANR 29, 69, 117; CCA 1; CN 7; DAC; DAM MST; DLB 53; EWL 3; MTCW 1, 2; RGEL 2; RGSF 2

Gallant, Roy A(rthur) 1924- .... **CLC 17**
See also CA 5-8R; CANR 4, 29, 54, 117; CLR 30; MAICYA 1; SATA 4, 68, 110

Gallico, Paul (William) 1897-1976 .... **CLC 2**
See also AITN 1; CA 5-8R; 69-72; CANR 23; DLB 9, 171; FANT; MAICYA 1, 2; SATA 13

Gallo, Max Louis 1932- .... **CLC 95**
See also CA 85-88

Gallois, Lucien
See Desnos, Robert

Gallup, Ralph
See Whitemore, Hugh (John)

Galsworthy, John 1867-1933 .... **SSC 22; TCLC 1, 45; WLC**
See also BRW 6; CA 104; 141; CANR 75; CDBLB 1890-1914; DA; DA3; DAB; DAC; DAM DRAM, MST, NOV; DLB 10, 34, 98, 162; DLBD 16; EWL 3; MTCW 1; RGEL 2; SSFS 3; TEA

Galt, John 1779-1839 .... **NCLC 1, 110**
See also DLB 99, 116, 159; RGEL 2; RGSF 2

Galvin, James 1951- .... **CLC 38**
See also CA 108; CANR 26

Gamboa, Federico 1864-1939 .... **TCLC 36**
See also CA 167; HW 2; LAW

Gandhi, M. K.
See Gandhi, Mohandas Karamchand

Gandhi, Mahatma
See Gandhi, Mohandas Karamchand

Gandhi, Mohandas Karamchand 1869-1948
.... **TCLC 59**
See also CA 121; 132; DA3; DAM MULT; MTCW 1, 2

Gann, Ernest Kellogg 1910-1991 .... **CLC 23**
See also AITN 1; BPFB 2; CA 1-4R; 136; CANR 1, 83; RHW

Gao Xingjian 1940- .... **CLC 167**
See Xingjian, Gao

Garber, Eric 1943(?)-
See Holleran, Andrew
See also CANR 89

Garcia, Cristina 1958- .... **CLC 76**
See also AMWS 11; CA 141; CANR 73; DNFS 1; EWL 3; HW 2

Garcia Lorca, Federico 1898-1936 ...... **DC 2; HLC 2; PC 3; TCLC 1, 7, 49; WLC**
See Lorca, Federico Garcia
See also AAYA 46; CA 104; 131; CANR 81; DA; DA3; DAB; DAC; DAM DRAM, MST, MULT, POET; DFS 10; DLB 108; EWL 3; HW 1, 2; MTCW 1, 2; TWA

Garcia Marquez, Gabriel (Jose) 1928-
.... **CLC 2, 3, 8, 10, 15, 27, 47, 55, 68, 170; HLC 1; SSC 8; WLC**
See also AAYA 3, 33; BEST 89:1, 90:4; BPFB 2; BYA 12; CA 33-36R; CANR 10, 28, 50, 75, 82; CDWLB 3; CPW; DA; DA3; DAB; DAC; DAM MST, MULT, NOV, POP; DLB 113; DNFS 1, 2; EWL 3; EXPN; EXPS; HW 1, 2; LAIT 2; LAW; LAWS 1; LMFS 2; MTCW 1, 2; NCFS 3; NFS 1, 5, 10; RGSF 2; RGWL 2, 3; SSFS 1, 6, 16; TWA; WLIT 1

Garcilaso de la Vega, El Inca 1503-1536
.... **HLCS 1**
See also LAW

Gard, Janice
See Latham, Jean Lee
Gard, Roger Martin du
See Martin du Gard, Roger
Gardam, Jane (Mary) 1928- .... **CLC 43**
See also CA 49-52; CANR 2, 18, 33, 54, 106; CLR 12; DLB 14, 161, 231; MAICYA 1, 2; MTCW 1; SAAS 9; SATA 39, 76, 130; SATA-Brief 28; YAW
Gardner, Herb(ert) 1934- .... **CLC 44**
See also CA 149; CAD; CD 5
Gardner, John (Champlin), Jr. 1933-1982
.. **CLC 2, 3, 5, 7, 8, 10, 18, 28, 34; SSC 7**
See also AAYA 45; AITN 1; AMWS 6; BPFB 2; CA 65-68; 107; CANR 33, 73; CDALBS; CPW; DA3; DAM NOV, POP; DLB 2; DLBY 1982; EWL 3; FANT; MTCW 1; NFS 3; RGAL 4; RGSF 2; SATA 40; SATA-Obit 31; SSFS 8
Gardner, John (Edmund) 1926- ...... **CLC 30**
See also CA 103; CANR 15, 69; CMW 4; CPW; DAM POP; MTCW 1
Gardner, Miriam
See Bradley, Marion Zimmer
See also GLL 1
Gardner, Noel
See Kuttner, Henry
Gardons, S. S.
See Snodgrass, W(illiam) D(e Witt)
Garfield, Leon 1921-1996 .... **CLC 12**
See also AAYA 8; BYA 1, 3; CA 17-20R; 152; CANR 38, 41, 78; CLR 21; DLB 161; JRDA; MAICYA 1, 2; MAICYAS 1; SATA 1, 32, 76; SATA-Obit 90; TEA; WYA; YAW
Garland, (Hannibal) Hamlin 1860-1940
.... **SSC 18; TCLC 3**
See also CA 104; DLB 12, 71, 78, 186; RGAL 4; RGSF 2; TCWW 2
Garneau, (Hector de) Saint-Denys 1912-1943
.... **TCLC 13**
See also CA 111; DLB 88
Garner, Alan 1934- .... **CLC 17**
See also AAYA 18; BYA 3, 5; CA 73-76, 178; CAAE 178; CANR 15, 64; CLR 20; CPW; DAB; DAM POP; DLB 161, 261; FANT; MAICYA 1, 2; MTCW 1, 2; SATA 18, 69; SATA-Essay 108; SUFW 1, 2; YAW
Garner, Hugh 1913-1979 .... **CLC 13**
See Warwick, Jarvis
See also CA 69-72; CANR 31; CCA 1; DLB 68
Garnett, David 1892-1981 .... **CLC 3**
See also CA 5-8R; 103; CANR 17, 79; DLB 34; FANT; MTCW 2; RGEL 2; SFW 4; SUFW 1
Garos, Stephanie
See Katz, Steve
Garrett, George (Palmer) 1929- .... **CLC 3, 11, 51; SSC 30**
See also AMWS 7; BPFB 2; CA 1-4R; CAAE 202; CAAS 5; CANR 1, 42, 67, 109; CN 7; CP 7; CSW; DLB 2, 5, 130, 152; DLBY 1983
Garrick, David 1717-1779 .... **LC 15**
See also DAM DRAM; DLB 84, 213; RGEL 2
Garrigue, Jean 1914-1972 .... **CLC 2, 8**
See also CA 5-8R; 37-40R; CANR 20
Garrison, Frederick
See Sinclair, Upton (Beall)
Garro, Elena 1920(?)-1998 .... **HLCS 1**
See also CA 131; 169; CWW 2; DLB 145; EWL 3; HW 1; LAWS 1; WLIT 1
Garth, Will
See Hamilton, Edmond; Kuttner, Henry
Garvey, Marcus (Moziah, Jr.) 1887-1940
.... **BLC 2; HR 2; TCLC 41**
See also BW 1; CA 120; 124; CANR 79; DAM MULT
Gary, Romain .... **CLC 25**
See Kacew, Romain
See also DLB 83
Gascar, Pierre .... **CLC 11**
See Fournier, Pierre
See also EWL 3
Gascoyne, David (Emery) 1916-2001
.... **CLC 45**
See also CA 65-68; 200; CANR 10, 28, 54; CP 7; DLB 20; MTCW 1; RGEL 2
Gaskell, Elizabeth Cleghorn 1810-1865
.... **NCLC 5, 70, 97; SSC 25**
See also BRW 5; CDBLB 1832-1890; DAB; DAM MST; DLB 21, 144, 159; RGEL 2; RGSF 2; TEA
Gass, William H(oward) 1924- .... **CLC 1, 2, 8, 11, 15, 39, 132; SSC 12**
See also AMWS 6; CA 17-20R; CANR 30, 71, 100; CN 7; DLB 2, 227; EWL 3; MTCW 1, 2; RGAL 4
Gassendi, Pierre 1592-1655 .... **LC 54**
See also GFL Beginnings to 1789
Gasset, Jose Ortega y
See Ortega y Gasset, Jose
Gates, Henry Louis, Jr. 1950- . **BLCS; CLC 65**
See also BW 2, 3; CA 109; CANR 25, 53, 75; CSW; DA3; DAM MULT; DLB 67; EWL 3; MTCW 1; RGAL 4
Gautier, Theophile 1811-1872 . **NCLC 1, 59; PC 18; SSC 20**
See also DAM POET; DLB 119; EW 6; GFL 1789 to the Present; RGWL 2, 3; SUFW; TWA
Gawsworth, John
See Bates, H(erbert) E(rnest)
Gay, John 1685-1732 .... **LC 49**
See also BRW 3; DAM DRAM; DLB 84, 95; RGEL 2; WLIT 3
Gay, Oliver
See Gogarty, Oliver St. John
Gay, Peter (Jack) 1923- .... **CLC 158**
See also CA 13-16R; CANR 18, 41, 77; INT CANR-18
Gaye, Marvin (Pentz, Jr.) 1939-1984
.... **CLC 26**
See also CA 195; 112
Gebler, Carlo (Ernest) 1954- .... **CLC 39**
See also CA 119; 133; CANR 96; DLB 271
Gee, Maggie (Mary) 1948- .... **CLC 57**
See also CA 130; CN 7; DLB 207
Gee, Maurice (Gough) 1931- .... **CLC 29**
See also AAYA 42; CA 97-100; CANR 67; CLR 56; CN 7; CWRI 5; EWL 3; MAICYA 2; RGSF 2; SATA 46, 101
Geiogamah, Hanay 1945- .... **NNAL**
See also CA 153; DAM MULT; DLB 175
Gelbart, Larry (Simon) 1928- ... **CLC 21, 61**
See Gelbart, Larry
See also CA 73-76; CANR 45, 94
Gelbart, Larry 1928-
See Gelbart, Larry (Simon)
See also CAD; CD 5
Gelber, Jack 1932- .... **CLC 1, 6, 14, 79**
See also CA 1-4R; CAD; CANR 2; DLB 7, 228
Gellhorn, Martha (Ellis) 1908-1998
.... **CLC 14, 60**
See also CA 77-80; 164; CANR 44; CN 7; DLBY 1982, 1998
Genet, Jean 1910-1986 . **CLC 1, 2, 5, 10, 14, 44, 46; TCLC 128**
See also CA 13-16R; CANR 18; DA3; DAM DRAM; DFS 10; DLB 72; DLBY 1986; EW 13; EWL 3; GFL 1789 to the Present; GLL 1; LMFS 2; MTCW 1, 2; RGWL 2, 3; TWA
Gent, Peter 1942- .... **CLC 29**
See also AITN 1; CA 89-92; DLBY 1982
Gentile, Giovanni 1875-1944 .... **TCLC 96**
See also CA 119
Gentlewoman in New England, A
See Bradstreet, Anne
Gentlewoman in Those Parts, A
See Bradstreet, Anne
Geoffrey of Monmouth c. 1100-1155
.... **CMLC 44**
See also DLB 146; TEA
George, Jean
See George, Jean Craighead
George, Jean Craighead 1919- .... **CLC 35**
See also AAYA 8; BYA 2, 4; CA 5-8R; CANR 25; CLR 1; 80; DLB 52; JRDA; MAICYA 1, 2; SATA 2, 68, 124; WYA; YAW
George, Stefan (Anton) 1868-1933
.... **TCLC 2, 14**
See also CA 104; 193; EW 8; EWL 3
Georges, Georges Martin
See Simenon, Georges (Jacques Christian)
Gerhardi, William Alexander
See Gerhardie, William Alexander
Gerhardie, William Alexander 1895-1977
.... **CLC 5**
See also CA 25-28R; 73-76; CANR 18; DLB 36; RGEL 2
Gerson, Jean 1363-1429 .... **LC 77**
See also DLB 208
Gersonides 1288-1344 .... **CMLC 49**
See also DLB 115
Gerstler, Amy 1956- .... **CLC 70**
See also CA 146; CANR 99
Gertler, T. .... **CLC 34**
See also CA 116; 121
Gertsen, Aleksandr Ivanovich
See Herzen, Aleksandr Ivanovich
Ghalib .... **NCLC 39, 78**
See Ghalib, Asadullah Khan
Ghalib, Asadullah Khan 1797-1869
See Ghalib
See also DAM POET; RGWL 2, 3
Ghelderode, Michel de 1898-1962 ... **CLC 6, 11; DC 15**
See also CA 85-88; CANR 40, 77; DAM DRAM; EW 11; EWL 3; TWA
Ghiselin, Brewster 1903-2001 .... **CLC 23**
See also CA 13-16R; CAAS 10; CANR 13; CP 7
Ghose, Aurabinda 1872-1950 .... **TCLC 63**
See Ghose, Aurobindo
See also CA 163
Ghose, Aurobindo
See Ghose, Aurabinda
See also EWL 3
Ghose, Zulfikar 1935- .... **CLC 42**
See also CA 65-68; CANR 67; CN 7; CP 7; EWL 3
Ghosh, Amitav 1956- .... **CLC 44, 153**
See also CA 147; CANR 80; CN 7
Giacosa, Giuseppe 1847-1906 .... **TCLC 7**
See also CA 104
Gibb, Lee
See Waterhouse, Keith (Spencer)
Gibbon, Lewis Grassic .... **TCLC 4**
See Mitchell, James Leslie
See also RGEL 2
Gibbons, Kaye 1960- .... **CLC 50, 88, 145**
See also AAYA 34; AMWS 10; CA 151; CANR 75; CSW; DA3; DAM POP; MTCW 1; NFS 3; RGAL 4; SATA 117

Gibran, Kahlil 1883-1931 ... **PC 9; TCLC 1, 9**
See also CA 104; 150; DA3; DAM POET, POP; EWL 3; MTCW 2

Gibran, Khalil
See Gibran, Kahlil

Gibson, William 1914- .... **CLC 23**
See also CA 9-12R; CAD 2; CANR 9, 42, 75; CD 5; DA; DAB; DAC; DAM DRAM, MST; DFS 2; DLB 7; LAIT 2; MTCW 2; SATA 66; YAW

Gibson, William (Ford) 1948- . **CLC 39, 63; SSC 52**
See also AAYA 12; BPFB 2; CA 126; 133; CANR 52, 90, 106; CN 7; CPW; DA3; DAM POP; DLB 251; MTCW 2; SCFW 2; SFW 4

Gide, Andre (Paul Guillaume) 1869-1951 .... **SSC 13; TCLC 5, 12, 36; WLC**
See also CA 104; 124; DA; DA3; DAB; DAC; DAM MST, NOV; DLB 65; EW 8; EWL 3; GFL 1789 to the Present; MTCW 1, 2; RGSF 2; RGWL 2, 3; TWA

Gifford, Barry (Colby) 1946- .... **CLC 34**
See also CA 65-68; CANR 9, 30, 40, 90

Gilbert, Frank
See De Voto, Bernard (Augustine)

Gilbert, W(illiam) S(chwenck) 1836-1911 .... **TCLC 3**
See also CA 104; 173; DAM DRAM, POET; RGEL 2; SATA 36

Gilbreth, Frank B(unker), Jr. 1911-2001 .... **CLC 17**
See also CA 9-12R; SATA 2

Gilchrist, Ellen (Louise) 1935- . **CLC 34, 48, 143; SSC 14**
See also BPFB 2; CA 113; 116; CANR 41, 61, 104; CN 7; CPW; CSW; DAM POP; DLB 130; EWL 3; EXPS; MTCW 1, 2; RGAL 4; RGSF 2; SSFS 9

Giles, Molly 1942- .... **CLC 39**
See also CA 126; CANR 98

Gill, Eric 1882-1940 .... **TCLC 85**
See Gill, (Arthur) Eric (Rowton Peter Joseph)

Gill, (Arthur) Eric (Rowton Peter Joseph) 1882-1940
See Gill, Eric
See also CA 120; DLB 98

Gill, Patrick
See Creasey, John

Gillette, Douglas .... **CLC 70**

Gilliam, Terry (Vance) 1940- .. **CLC 21, 141**
See Monty Python
See also AAYA 19; CA 108; 113; CANR 35; INT 113

Gillian, Jerry
See Gilliam, Terry (Vance)

Gilliatt, Penelope (Ann Douglass) 1932-1993 .... **CLC 2, 10, 13, 53**
See also AITN 2; CA 13-16R; 141; CANR 49; DLB 14

Gilman, Charlotte (Anna) Perkins (Stetson) 1860-1935 .... **SSC 13; TCLC 9, 37, 117**
See also AMWS 11; BYA 11; CA 106; 150; DLB 221; EXPS; FW; HGG; LAIT 2; MAWW; MTCW 1; RGAL 4; RGSF 2; SFW 4; SSFS 1

Gilmour, David 1946- .... **CLC 35**

Gilpin, William 1724-1804 .... **NCLC 30**

Gilray, J. D.
See Mencken, H(enry) L(ouis)

Gilroy, Frank D(aniel) 1925- .... **CLC 2**
See also CA 81-84; CAD; CANR 32, 64, 86; CD 5; DFS 17; DLB 7

Gilstrap, John 1957(?)- .... **CLC 99**
See also CA 160; CANR 101

Ginsberg, Allen 1926-1997 ... **CLC 1, 2, 3, 4, 6, 13, 36, 69, 109; PC 4, 47; TCLC 120; WLC**
See also AAYA 33; AITN 1; AMWC 1; AMWS 2; BG 2; CA 1-4R; 157; CANR 2, 41, 63, 95; CDALB 1941-1968; CP 7; DA; DA3; DAB; DAC; DAM MST, POET; DLB 5, 16, 169, 237; EWL 3; GLL 1; LMFS 2; MTCW 1, 2; PAB; PFS 5; RGAL 4; TUS; WP

Ginzburg, Eugenia .... **CLC 59**

Ginzburg, Natalia 1916-1991 ..... **CLC 5, 11, 54, 70**
See also CA 85-88; 135; CANR 33; DFS 14; DLB 177; EW 13; EWL 3; MTCW 1, 2; RGWL 2, 3

Giono, Jean 1895-1970 ... **CLC 4, 11; TCLC 124**
See also CA 45-48; 29-32R; CANR 2, 35; DLB 72; EWL 3; GFL 1789 to the Present; MTCW 1; RGWL 2, 3

Giovanni, Nikki 1943- ..... **BLC 2; CLC 2, 4, 19, 64, 117; PC 19; WLCS**
See also AAYA 22; AITN 1; BW 2, 3; CA 29-32R; CAAS 2; CANR 18, 41, 60, 91; CDALBS; CLR 6, 73; CP 7; CSW; CWP; CWRI 5; DA; DA3; DAB; DAC; DAM MST, MULT, POET; DLB 5, 41; EWL 3; EXPP; INT CANR-18; MAICYA 1, 2; MTCW 1, 2; PFS 17; RGAL 4; SATA 24, 107; TUS; YAW

Giovene, Andrea 1904-1998 .... **CLC 7**
See also CA 85-88

Gippius, Zinaida (Nikolayevna) 1869-1945
See Hippius, Zinaida
See also CA 106

Giraudoux, Jean(-Hippolyte) 1882-1944 .... **TCLC 2, 7**
See also CA 104; 196; DAM DRAM; DLB 65; EW 9; EWL 3; GFL 1789 to the Present; RGWL 2, 3; TWA

Gironella, Jose Maria 1917-1991 .... **CLC 11**
See also CA 101; EWL 3; RGWL 2, 3

Gissing, George (Robert) 1857-1903 .... **SSC 37; TCLC 3, 24, 47**
See also BRW 5; CA 105; 167; DLB 18, 135, 184; RGEL 2; TEA

Giurlani, Aldo
See Palazzeschi, Aldo

Gladkov, Fedor Vasil'evich
See Gladkov, Fyodor (Vasilyevich)
See also DLB 272

Gladkov, Fyodor (Vasilyevich) 1883-1958 .... **TCLC 27**
See Gladkov, Fedor Vasil'evich
See also CA 170; EWL 3

Glancy, Diane 1941- .... **NNAL**
See also CA 136; CAAS 24; CANR 87; DLB 175

Glanville, Brian (Lester) 1931- .... **CLC 6**
See also CA 5-8R; CAAS 9; CANR 3, 70; CN 7; DLB 15, 139; SATA 42

Glasgow, Ellen (Anderson Gholson) 1873-1945 .... **SSC 34; TCLC 2, 7**
See also AMW; CA 104; 164; DLB 9, 12; MAWW; MTCW 2; RGAL 4; RHW; SSFS 9; TUS

Glaspell, Susan 1882(?)-1948 ... **DC 10; SSC 41; TCLC 55**
See also AMWS 3; CA 110; 154; DFS 8; DLB 7, 9, 78, 228; MAWW; RGAL 4; SSFS 3; TCWW 2; TUS; YABC 2

Glassco, John 1909-1981 .... **CLC 9**
See also CA 13-16R; 102; CANR 15; DLB 68

Glasscock, Amnesia
See Steinbeck, John (Ernst)

Glasser, Ronald J. 1940(?)- .... **CLC 37**
See also CA 209

Glassman, Joyce
See Johnson, Joyce

Gleick, James (W.) 1954- .... **CLC 147**
See also CA 131; 137; CANR 97; INT CA-137

Glendinning, Victoria 1937- .... **CLC 50**
See also CA 120; 127; CANR 59, 89; DLB 155

Glissant, Edouard (Mathieu) 1928- .... **CLC 10, 68**
See also CA 153; CANR 111; CWW 2; DAM MULT; EWL 3; RGWL 3

Gloag, Julian 1930- .... **CLC 40**
See also AITN 1; CA 65-68; CANR 10, 70; CN 7

Glowacki, Aleksander
See Prus, Boleslaw

Gluck, Louise (Elisabeth) 1943- .... **CLC 7, 22, 44, 81, 160; PC 16**
See also AMWS 5; CA 33-36R; CANR 40, 69, 108; CP 7; CWP; DA3; DAM POET; DLB 5; MTCW 2; PFS 5, 15; RGAL 4

Glyn, Elinor 1864-1943 .... **TCLC 72**
See also DLB 153; RHW

Gobineau, Joseph-Arthur 1816-1882 .... **NCLC 17**
See also DLB 123; GFL 1789 to the Present

Godard, Jean-Luc 1930- .... **CLC 20**
See also CA 93-96

Godden, (Margaret) Rumer 1907-1998 .... **CLC 53**
See also AAYA 6; BPFB 2; BYA 2, 5; CA 5-8R; 172; CANR 4, 27, 36, 55, 80; CLR 20; CN 7; CWRI 5; DLB 161; MAICYA 1, 2; RHW; SAAS 12; SATA 3, 36; SATA-Obit 109; TEA

Godoy Alcayaga, Lucila 1899-1957 . **HLC 2; PC 32; TCLC 2**
See Mistral, Gabriela
See also BW 2; CA 104; 131; CANR 81; DAM MULT; DNFS; HW 1, 2; MTCW 1, 2

Godwin, Gail (Kathleen) 1937- .... **CLC 5, 8, 22, 31, 69, 125**
See also BPFB 2; CA 29-32R; CANR 15, 43, 69; CN 7; CPW; CSW; DA3; DAM POP; DLB 6, 234; INT CANR-15; MTCW 1, 2

Godwin, William 1756-1836 .... **NCLC 14**
See also CDBLB 1789-1832; CMW 4; DLB 39, 104, 142, 158, 163, 262; HGG; RGEL 2

Goebbels, Josef
See Goebbels, (Paul) Joseph

Goebbels, (Paul) Joseph 1897-1945 .... **TCLC 68**
See also CA 115; 148

Goebbels, Joseph Paul
See Goebbels, (Paul) Joseph

Goethe, Johann Wolfgang von 1749-1832 ...... **DC 20; NCLC 4, 22, 34, 90; PC 5; SSC 38; WLC**
See also CDWLB 2; DA; DA3; DAB; DAC; DAM DRAM, MST, POET; DLB 94; EW 5; LMFS 1; RGWL 2, 3; TWA

Gogarty, Oliver St. John 1878-1957 .... **TCLC 15**
See also CA 109; 150; DLB 15, 19; RGEL 2

Gogol, Nikolai (Vasilyevich) 1809-1852 .... **DC 1; NCLC 5, 15, 31; SSC 4, 29, 52; WLC**
See also DA; DAB; DAC; DAM DRAM, MST; DFS 12; DLB 198; EW 6; EXPS; RGSF 2; RGWL 2, 3; SSFS 7; TWA

Goines, Donald 1937(?)-1974 .. **BLC 2; CLC 80**
See also AITN 1; BW 1, 3; CA 124; 114; CANR 82; CMW 4; DA3; DAM MULT, POP; DLB 33

Gold, Herbert 1924- .... CLC **4, 7, 14, 42, 152**
See also CA 9-12R; CANR 17, 45; CN 7; DLB 2; DLBY 1981

Goldbarth, Albert 1948- .... CLC **5, 38**
See also AMWS 12; CA 53-56; CANR 6, 40; CP 7; DLB 120

Goldberg, Anatol 1910-1982 .... CLC **34**
See also CA 131; 117

Goldemberg, Isaac 1945- .... CLC **52**
See also CA 69-72; CAAS 12; CANR 11, 32; EWL 3; HW 1; WLIT 1

Golding, William (Gerald) 1911-1993
.... CLC **1, 2, 3, 8, 10, 17, 27, 58, 81;** WLC
See also AAYA 5, 44; BPFB 2; BRWR 1; BRWS 1; BYA 2; CA 5-8R; 141; CANR 13, 33, 54; CDBLB 1945-1960; DA; DA3; DAB; DAC; DAM MST, NOV; DLB 15, 100, 255; EWL 3; EXPN; HGG; LAIT 4; MTCW 1, 2; NFS 2; RGEL 2; RHW; SFW 4; TEA; WLIT 4; YAW

Goldman, Emma 1869-1940 .... TCLC **13**
See also CA 110; 150; DLB 221; FW; RGAL 4; TUS

Goldman, Francisco 1954- .... CLC **76**
See also CA 162

Goldman, William (W.) 1931- ..... CLC **1, 48**
See also BPFB 2; CA 9-12R; CANR 29, 69, 106; CN 7; DLB 44; FANT; IDFW 3, 4

Goldmann, Lucien 1913-1970 .... CLC **24**
See also CA 25-28; CAP 2

Goldoni, Carlo 1707-1793 .... LC **4**
See also DAM DRAM; EW 4; RGWL 2, 3

Goldsberry, Steven 1949- .... CLC **34**
See also CA 131

Goldsmith, Oliver 1730-1774 ... DC **8;** LC **2, 48;** WLC
See also BRW 3; CDBLB 1660-1789; DA; DAB; DAC; DAM DRAM, MST, NOV, POET; DFS 1; DLB 39, 89, 104, 109, 142; IDTP; RGEL 2; SATA 26; TEA; WLIT 3

Goldsmith, Peter
See Priestley, J(ohn) B(oynton)

Gombrowicz, Witold 1904-1969 ... CLC **4, 7, 11, 49**
See also CA 19-20; 25-28R; CANR 105; CAP 2; CDWLB 4; DAM DRAM; DLB 215; EW 12; EWL 3; RGWL 2, 3; TWA

Gomez de Avellaneda, Gertrudis 1814-1873
.... NCLC **111**
See also LAW

Gomez de la Serna, Ramon 1888-1963
.... CLC **9**
See also CA 153; 116; CANR 79; EWL 3; HW 1, 2

Goncharov, Ivan Alexandrovich 1812-1891
.... NCLC **1, 63**
See also DLB 238; EW 6; RGWL 2, 3

Goncourt, Edmond (Louis Antoine Huot) de 1822-1896 .... NCLC **7**
See also DLB 123; EW 7; GFL 1789 to the Present; RGWL 2, 3

Goncourt, Jules (Alfred Huot) de 1830-1870
.... NCLC **7**
See also DLB 123; EW 7; GFL 1789 to the Present; RGWL 2, 3

Gongora (y Argote), Luis de 1561-1627
.... LC **72**
See also RGWL 2, 3

Gontier, Fernande 19(?)- .... CLC **50**

Gonzalez Martinez, Enrique 1871-1952
.... TCLC **72**
See also CA 166; CANR 81; EWL 3; HW 1, 2

Goodison, Lorna 1947- .... PC **36**
See also CA 142; CANR 88; CP 7; CWP; DLB 157; EWL 3

Goodman, Paul 1911-1972 .... CLC **1, 2, 4, 7**
See also CA 19-20; 37-40R; CAD; CANR 34; CAP 2; DLB 130, 246; MTCW 1; RGAL 4

Gordimer, Nadine 1923- .... CLC **3, 5, 7, 10, 18, 33, 51, 70, 123, 160, 161;** SSC **17;** WLCS
See also AAYA 39; AFW; BRWS 2; CA 5-8R; CANR 3, 28, 56, 88; CN 7; DA; DA3; DAB; DAC; DAM MST, NOV; DLB 225; EWL 3; EXPS; INT CANR-28; MTCW 1, 2; NFS 4; RGEL 2; RGSF 2; SSFS 2, 14; TWA; WLIT 2; YAW

Gordon, Adam Lindsay 1833-1870
.... NCLC **21**
See also DLB 230

Gordon, Caroline 1895-1981 ...... CLC **6, 13, 29, 83;** SSC **15**
See also AMW; CA 11-12; 103; CANR 36; CAP 1; DLB 4, 9, 102; DLBD 17; DLBY 1981; EWL 3; MTCW 1, 2; RGAL 4; RGSF 2

Gordon, Charles William 1860-1937
See Connor, Ralph
See also CA 109

Gordon, Mary (Catherine) 1949- .. CLC **13, 22, 128;** SSC **59**
See also AMWS 4; BPFB 2; CA 102; CANR 44, 92; CN 7; DLB 6; DLBY 1981; FW; INT CA-102; MTCW 1

Gordon, N. J.
See Bosman, Herman Charles

Gordon, Sol 1923- .... CLC **26**
See also CA 53-56; CANR 4; SATA 11

Gordone, Charles 1925-1995 .... CLC **1, 4;** DC **8**
See also BW 1, 3; CA 93-96; 180; 150; CAAE 180; CAD; CANR 55; DAM DRAM; DLB 7; INT 93-96; MTCW 1

Gore, Catherine 1800-1861 .... NCLC **65**
See also DLB 116; RGEL 2

Gorenko, Anna Andreevna
See Akhmatova, Anna

Gorky, Maxim .... SSC **28;** TCLC **8;** WLC
See Peshkov, Alexei Maximovich
See also DAB; DFS 9; EW 8; EWL 3; MTCW 2; TWA

Goryan, Sirak
See Saroyan, William

Gosse, Edmund (William) 1849-1928
.... TCLC **28**
See also CA 117; DLB 57, 144, 184; RGEL 2

Gotlieb, Phyllis Fay (Bloom) 1926-
.... CLC **18**
See also CA 13-16R; CANR 7; DLB 88, 251; SFW 4

Gottesman, S. D.
See Kornbluth, C(yril) M.; Pohl, Frederik

Gottfried von Strassburg fl. c. 1170-1215
.... CMLC **10**
See also CDWLB 2; DLB 138; EW 1; RGWL 2, 3

Gotthelf, Jeremias 1797-1854 ..... NCLC **117**
See also DLB 133; RGWL 2, 3

Gottschalk, Laura Riding
See Jackson, Laura (Riding)

Gould, Lois 1932(?)-2002 .... CLC **4, 10**
See also CA 77-80; 208; CANR 29; MTCW 1

Gould, Stephen Jay 1941-2002 .... CLC **163**
See also AAYA 26; BEST 90:2; CA 77-80; 205; CANR 10, 27, 56, 75; CPW; INT CANR-27; MTCW 1, 2

Gourmont, Remy(-Marie-Charles) de 1858-1915 .... TCLC **17**
See also CA 109; 150; GFL 1789 to the Present; MTCW 2

Govier, Katherine 1948- .... CLC **51**
See also CA 101; CANR 18, 40; CCA 1

Gower, John c. 1330-1408 .... LC **76**
See also BRW 1; DLB 146; RGEL 2

Goyen, (Charles) William 1915-1983
.... CLC **5, 8, 14, 40**
See also AITN 2; CA 5-8R; 110; CANR 6, 71; DLB 2, 218; DLBY 1983; EWL 3; INT CANR-6

Goytisolo, Juan 1931- .. CLC **5, 10, 23, 133;** HLC **1**
See also CA 85-88; CANR 32, 61; CWW 2; DAM MULT; EWL 3; GLL 2; HW 1, 2; MTCW 1, 2

Gozzano, Guido 1883-1916 .... PC **10**
See also CA 154; DLB 114; EWL 3

Gozzi, (Conte) Carlo 1720-1806 ... NCLC **23**

Grabbe, Christian Dietrich 1801-1836
.... NCLC **2**
See also DLB 133; RGWL 2, 3

Grace, Patricia Frances 1937- .... CLC **56**
See also CA 176; CN 7; EWL 3; RGSF 2

Gracian y Morales, Baltasar 1601-1658
.... LC **15**

Gracq, Julien .... CLC **11, 48**
See Poirier, Louis
See also CWW 2; DLB 83; GFL 1789 to the Present

Grade, Chaim 1910-1982 .... CLC **10**
See also CA 93-96; 107; EWL 3

Graduate of Oxford, A
See Ruskin, John

Grafton, Garth
See Duncan, Sara Jeannette

Grafton, Sue 1940- .... CLC **163**
See also AAYA 11, 49; BEST 90:3; CA 108; CANR 31, 55, 111; CMW 4; CPW; CSW; DA3; DAM POP; DLB 226; FW; MSW

Graham, John
See Phillips, David Graham

Graham, Jorie 1951- .... CLC **48, 118**
See also CA 111; CANR 63; CP 7; CWP; DLB 120; EWL 3; PFS 10, 17

Graham, R(obert) B(ontine) Cunninghame
See Cunninghame Graham, Robert (Gallnigad) Bontine
See also DLB 98, 135, 174; RGEL 2; RGSF 2

Graham, Robert
See Haldeman, Joe (William)

Graham, Tom
See Lewis, (Harry) Sinclair

Graham, W(illiam) S(idney) 1918-1986
.... CLC **29**
See also BRWS 7; CA 73-76; 118; DLB 20; RGEL 2

Graham, Winston (Mawdsley) 1910-
.... CLC **23**
See also CA 49-52; CANR 2, 22, 45, 66; CMW 4; CN 7; DLB 77; RHW

Grahame, Kenneth 1859-1932 .... TCLC **64**
See also BYA 5; CA 108; 136; CANR 80; CLR 5; CWRI 5; DA3; DAB; DLB 34, 141, 178; FANT; MAICYA 1, 2; MTCW 2; RGEL 2; SATA 100; TEA; WCH; YABC 1

Granger, Darius John
See Marlowe, Stephen

Granin, Daniil .... CLC **59**

Granovsky, Timofei Nikolaevich 1813-1855
.... NCLC **75**
See also DLB 198

Grant, Skeeter
See Spiegelman, Art

Granville-Barker, Harley 1877-1946
.... TCLC **2**
See Barker, Harley Granville
See also CA 104; 204; DAM DRAM; RGEL 2

Granzotto, Gianni
See Granzotto, Giovanni Battista
Granzotto, Giovanni Battista 1914-1985 .... **CLC 70**
See also CA 166
Grass, Guenter (Wilhelm) 1927- . **CLC 1, 2, 4, 6, 11, 15, 22, 32, 49, 88; WLC**
See also BPFB 2; CA 13-16R; CANR 20, 75, 93; CDWLB 2; DA; DA3; DAB; DAC; DAM MST, NOV; DLB 75, 124; EW 13; EWL 3; MTCW 1, 2; RGWL 2, 3; TWA
Gratton, Thomas
See Hulme, T(homas) E(rnest)
Grau, Shirley Ann 1929- ...... **CLC 4, 9, 146; SSC 15**
See also CA 89-92; CANR 22, 69; CN 7; CSW; DLB 2, 218; INT CA-89-92, CANR-22; MTCW 1
Gravel, Fern
See Hall, James Norman
Graver, Elizabeth 1964- .... **CLC 70**
See also CA 135; CANR 71
Graves, Richard Perceval 1895-1985 .... **CLC 44**
See also CA 65-68; CANR 9, 26, 51
Graves, Robert (von Ranke) 1895-1985 .... **CLC 1, 2, 6, 11, 39, 44, 45; PC 6**
See also BPFB 2; BRW 7; BYA 4; CA 5-8R; 117; CANR 5, 36; CDBLB 1914-1945; DA3; DAB; DAC; DAM MST, POET; DLB 20, 100, 191; DLBD 18; DLBY 1985; EWL 3; MTCW 1, 2; NCFS 2; RGEL 2; RHW; SATA 45; TEA
Graves, Valerie
See Bradley, Marion Zimmer
Gray, Alasdair (James) 1934- .... **CLC 41**
See also CA 126; CANR 47, 69, 106; CN 7; DLB 194, 261; HGG; INT CA-126; MTCW 1, 2; RGSF 2; SUFW 2
Gray, Amlin 1946- .... **CLC 29**
See also CA 138
Gray, Francine du Plessix 1930- .... **CLC 22, 153**
See also BEST 90:3; CA 61-64; CAAS 2; CANR 11, 33, 75, 81; DAM NOV; INT CANR-11; MTCW 1, 2
Gray, John (Henry) 1866-1934 ..... **TCLC 19**
See also CA 119; 162; RGEL 2
Gray, Simon (James Holliday) 1936- .... **CLC 9, 14, 36**
See also AITN 1; CA 21-24R; CAAS 3; CANR 32, 69; CD 5; DLB 13; EWL 3; MTCW 1; RGEL 2
Gray, Spalding 1941- .... **CLC 49, 112; DC 7**
See also CA 128; CAD; CANR 74; CD 5; CPW; DAM POP; MTCW 2
Gray, Thomas 1716-1771 ... **LC 4, 40; PC 2; WLC**
See also BRW 3; CDBLB 1660-1789; DA; DA3; DAB; DAC; DAM MST; DLB 109; EXPP; PAB; PFS 9; RGEL 2; TEA; WP
Grayson, David
See Baker, Ray Stannard
Grayson, Richard (A.) 1951- .... **CLC 38**
See also CA 85-88; CANR 14, 31, 57; DLB 234
Greeley, Andrew M(oran) 1928- ..... **CLC 28**
See also BPFB 2; CA 5-8R; CAAS 7; CANR 7, 43, 69, 104; CMW 4; CPW; DA3; DAM POP; MTCW 1, 2
Green, Anna Katharine 1846-1935 .... **TCLC 63**
See also CA 112; 159; CMW 4; DLB 202, 221; MSW
Green, Brian
See Card, Orson Scott
Green, Hannah
See Greenberg, Joanne (Goldenberg)

Green, Hannah 1927(?)-1996 .... **CLC 3**
See also CA 73-76; CANR 59, 93; NFS 10
Green, Henry .... **CLC 2, 13, 97**
See Yorke, Henry Vincent
See also BRWS 2; CA 175; DLB 15; EWL 3; RGEL 2
Green, Julian (Hartridge) 1900-1998
See Green, Julien
See also CA 21-24R; 169; CANR 33, 87; DLB 4, 72; MTCW 1
Green, Julien .... **CLC 3, 11, 77**
See Green, Julian (Hartridge)
See also EWL 3; GFL 1789 to the Present; MTCW 2
Green, Paul (Eliot) 1894-1981 .... **CLC 25**
See also AITN 1; CA 5-8R; 103; CANR 3; DAM DRAM; DLB 7, 9, 249; DLBY 1981; RGAL 4
Greenaway, Peter 1942- .... **CLC 159**
See also CA 127
Greenberg, Ivan 1908-1973
See Rahv, Philip
See also CA 85-88
Greenberg, Joanne (Goldenberg) 1932- .... **CLC 7, 30**
See also AAYA 12; CA 5-8R; CANR 14, 32, 69; CN 7; SATA 25; YAW
Greenberg, Richard 1959(?)- .... **CLC 57**
See also CA 138; CAD; CD 5
Greenblatt, Stephen J(ay) 1943- ..... **CLC 70**
See also CA 49-52; CANR 115
Greene, Bette 1934- .... **CLC 30**
See also AAYA 7; BYA 3; CA 53-56; CANR 4; CLR 2; CWRI 5; JRDA; LAIT 4; MAICYA 1, 2; NFS 10; SAAS 16; SATA 8, 102; WYA; YAW
Greene, Gael .... **CLC 8**
See also CA 13-16R; CANR 10
Greene, Graham (Henry) 1904-1991
... **CLC 1, 3, 6, 9, 14, 18, 27, 37, 70, 72, 125; SSC 29; WLC**
See also AITN 2; BPFB 2; BRWR 2; BRWS 1; BYA 3; CA 13-16R; 133; CANR 35, 61; CBD; CDBLB 1945-1960; CMW 4; DA; DA3; DAB; DAC; DAM MST, NOV; DLB 13, 15, 77, 100, 162, 201, 204; DLBY 1991; EWL 3; MSW; MTCW 1, 2; NFS 16; RGEL 2; SATA 20; SSFS 14; TEA; WLIT 4
Greene, Robert 1558-1592 .... **LC 41**
See also BRWS 8; DLB 62, 167; IDTP; RGEL 2; TEA
Greer, Germaine 1939- .... **CLC 131**
See also AITN 1; CA 81-84; CANR 33, 70, 115; FW; MTCW 1, 2
Greer, Richard
See Silverberg, Robert
Gregor, Arthur 1923- .... **CLC 9**
See also CA 25-28R; CAAS 10; CANR 11; CP 7; SATA 36
Gregor, Lee
See Pohl, Frederik
Gregory, Lady Isabella Augusta (Persse) 1852-1932 .... **TCLC 1**
See also BRW 6; CA 104; 184; DLB 10; IDTP; RGEL 2
Gregory, J. Dennis
See Williams, John A(lfred)
Grekova, I. .... **CLC 59**
Grendon, Stephen
See Derleth, August (William)
Grenville, Kate 1950- .... **CLC 61**
See also CA 118; CANR 53, 93
Grenville, Pelham
See Wodehouse, P(elham) G(renville)

Greve, Felix Paul (Berthold Friedrich) 1879-1948
See Grove, Frederick Philip
See also CA 104; 141, 175; CANR 79; DAC; DAM MST
Greville, Fulke 1554-1628 .... **LC 79**
See also DLB 62, 172; RGEL 2
Grey, Zane 1872-1939 .... **TCLC 6**
See also BPFB 2; CA 104; 132; DA3; DAM POP; DLB 9, 212; MTCW 1, 2; RGAL 4; TCWW 2; TUS
Grieg, (Johan) Nordahl (Brun) 1902-1943 .... **TCLC 10**
See also CA 107; 189; EWL 3
Grieve, C(hristopher) M(urray) 1892-1978 .... **CLC 11, 19**
See MacDiarmid, Hugh; Pteleon
See also CA 5-8R; 85-88; CANR 33, 107; DAM POET; MTCW 1; RGEL 2
Griffin, Gerald 1803-1840 .... **NCLC 7**
See also DLB 159; RGEL 2
Griffin, John Howard 1920-1980 .... **CLC 68**
See also AITN 1; CA 1-4R; 101; CANR 2
Griffin, Peter 1942- .... **CLC 39**
See also CA 136
Griffith, D(avid) Lewelyn) W(ark) 1875(?)-1948 .... **TCLC 68**
See also CA 119; 150; CANR 80
Griffith, Lawrence
See Griffith, D(avid) Lewelyn) W(ark)
Griffiths, Trevor 1935- .... **CLC 13, 52**
See also CA 97-100; CANR 45; CBD; CD 5; DLB 13, 245
Griggs, Sutton (Elbert) 1872-1930 .... **TCLC 77**
See also CA 123; 186; DLB 50
Grigson, Geoffrey (Edward Harvey) 1905-1985 .... **CLC 7, 39**
See also CA 25-28R; 118; CANR 20, 33; DLB 27; MTCW 1, 2
Grile, Dod
See Bierce, Ambrose (Gwinett)
Grillparzer, Franz 1791-1872 .... **DC 14; NCLC 1, 102; SSC 37**
See also CDWLB 2; DLB 133; EW 5; RGWL 2, 3; TWA
Grimble, Reverend Charles James
See Eliot, T(homas) S(tearns)
Grimke, Angelina (Emily) Weld 1880-1958 .... **HR 2**
See Weld, Angelina (Emily) Grimke
See also BW 1; CA 124; DAM POET; DLB 50, 54
Grimke, Charlotte L(ottie) Forten 1837(?)-1914
See Forten, Charlotte L.
See also BW 1; CA 117; 124; DAM MULT, POET
Grimm, Jacob Ludwig Karl 1785-1863 .... **NCLC 3, 77; SSC 36**
See also DLB 90; MAICYA 1, 2; RGSF 2; RGWL 2, 3; SATA 22; WCH
Grimm, Wilhelm Karl 1786-1859 . **NCLC 3, 77; SSC 36**
See also CDWLB 2; DLB 90; MAICYA 1, 2; RGSF 2; RGWL 2, 3; SATA 22; WCH
Grimmelshausen, Hans Jakob Christoffel von
See Grimmelshausen, Johann Jakob Christoffel von
See also RGWL 2, 3
Grimmelshausen, Johann Jakob Christoffel von 1621-1676 .... **LC 6**
See Grimmelshausen, Hans Jakob Christoffel von
See also CDWLB 2; DLB 168
Grindel, Eugene 1895-1952
See Eluard, Paul
See also CA 104; 193; LMFS 2

Grisham, John 1955- .... CLC 84
See also AAYA 14, 47; BPFB 2; CA 138; CANR 47, 69, 114; CMW 4; CN 7; CPW; CSW; DA3; DAM POP; MSW; MTCW 2

Grossman, David 1954- .... CLC 67
See also CA 138; CANR 114; CWW 2; EWL 3

Grossman, Vasilii Semenovich
See Grossman, Vasily (Semenovich)
See also DLB 272

Grossman, Vasily (Semenovich) 1905-1964 .... CLC 41
See Grossman, Vasilii Semenovich
See also CA 124; 130; MTCW 1

Grove, Frederick Philip .... TCLC 4
See Greve, Felix Paul (Berthold Friedrich)
See also DLB 92; RGEL 2

Grubb
See Crumb, R(obert)

Grumbach, Doris (Isaac) 1918- ...... CLC 13, 22, 64
See also CA 5-8R; CAAS 2; CANR 9, 42, 70; CN 7; INT CANR-9; MTCW 2

Grundtvig, Nicolai Frederik Severin 1783-1872 .... NCLC 1

Grunge
See Crumb, R(obert)

Grunwald, Lisa 1959- .... CLC 44
See also CA 120

Gryphius, Andreas 1616-1664 .... LC 89
See also CDWLB 2; DLB 164; RGWL 2, 3

Guare, John 1938- ... CLC 8, 14, 29, 67; DC 20
See also CA 73-76; CAD; CANR 21, 69; CD 5; DAM DRAM; DFS 8, 13; DLB 7, 249; EWL 3; MTCW 1, 2; RGAL 4

Gubar, Susan (David) 1944- .... CLC 145
See also CA 108; CANR 45, 70; FW; MTCW 1; RGAL 4

Gudjonsson, Halldor Kiljan 1902-1998
See Laxness, Halldor
See also CA 103; 164; CWW 2

Guenter, Erich
See Eich, Gunter

Guest, Barbara 1920- .... CLC 34
See also BG 2; CA 25-28R; CANR 11, 44, 84; CP 7; CWP; DLB 5, 193

Guest, Edgar A(lbert) 1881-1959 . TCLC 95
See also CA 112; 168

Guest, Judith (Ann) 1936- .... CLC 8, 30
See also AAYA 7; CA 77-80; CANR 15, 75; DA3; DAM NOV, POP; EXPN; INT CANR-15; LAIT 5; MTCW 1, 2; NFS 1

Guevara, Che .... CLC 87; HLC 1
See Guevara (Serna), Ernesto

Guevara (Serna), Ernesto 1928-1967 .... CLC 87; HLC 1
See Guevara, Che
See also CA 127; 111; CANR 56; DAM MULT; HW 1

Guicciardini, Francesco 1483-1540 ... LC 49

Guild, Nicholas M. 1944- .... CLC 33
See also CA 93-96

Guillemin, Jacques
See Sartre, Jean-Paul

Guillen, Jorge 1893-1984 .... CLC 11; HLCS 1; PC 35
See also CA 89-92; 112; DAM MULT, POET; DLB 108; EWL 3; HW 1; RGWL 2, 3

Guillen, Nicolas (Cristobal) 1902-1989 .... BLC 2; CLC 48, 79; HLC 1; PC 23
See also BW 2; CA 116; 125; 129; CANR 84; DAM MST, MULT, POET; EWL 3; HW 1; LAW; RGWL 2, 3; WP

Guillen y Alvarez, Jorge
See Guillen, Jorge

Guillevic, (Eugene) 1907-1997 .... CLC 33
See also CA 93-96; CWW 2

Guillois
See Desnos, Robert

Guillois, Valentin
See Desnos, Robert

Guimaraes Rosa, Joao 1908-1967 .. HLCS 2
See also CA 175; LAW; RGSF 2; RGWL 2, 3

Guiney, Louise Imogen 1861-1920 .... TCLC 41
See also CA 160; DLB 54; RGAL 4

Guinizelli, Guido c. 1230-1276 .... CMLC 49

Guiraldes, Ricardo (Guillermo) 1886-1927 .... TCLC 39
See also CA 131; EWL 3; HW 1; LAW; MTCW 1

Gumilev, Nikolai (Stepanovich) 1886-1921 .... TCLC 60
See Gumilyov, Nikolay Stepanovich
See also CA 165

Gumilyov, Nikolay Stepanovich
See Gumilev, Nikolai (Stepanovich)
See also EWL 3

Gunesekera, Romesh 1954- .... CLC 91
See also CA 159; CN 7; DLB 267

Gunn, Bill .... CLC 5
See Gunn, William Harrison
See also DLB 38

Gunn, Thom(son William) 1929- . CLC 3, 6, 18, 32, 81; PC 26
See also BRWS 4; CA 17-20R; CANR 9, 33, 116; CDBLB 1960 to Present; CP 7; DAM POET; DLB 27; INT CANR-33; MTCW 1; PFS 9; RGEL 2

Gunn, William Harrison 1934(?)-1989
See Gunn, Bill
See also AITN 1; BW 1, 3; CA 13-16R; 128; CANR 12, 25, 76

Gunn Allen, Paula
See Allen, Paula Gunn

Gunnars, Kristjana 1948- .... CLC 69
See also CA 113; CCA 1; CP 7; CWP; DLB 60

Gunter, Erich
See Eich, Gunter

Gurdjieff, G(eorgei) I(vanovich) 1877(?)-1949 .... TCLC 71
See also CA 157

Gurganus, Allan 1947- .... CLC 70
See also BEST 90:1; CA 135; CANR 114; CN 7; CPW; CSW; DAM POP; GLL 1

Gurney, A. R.
See Gurney, A(lbert) R(amsdell), Jr.
See also DLB 266

Gurney, A(lbert) R(amsdell), Jr. 1930- .... CLC 32, 50, 54
See Gurney, A. R.
See also AMWS 5; CA 77-80; CAD; CANR 32, 64; CD 5; DAM DRAM; EWL 3

Gurney, Ivor (Bertie) 1890-1937 .. TCLC 33
See also BRW 6; CA 167; DLBY 2002; PAB; RGEL 2

Gurney, Peter
See Gurney, A(lbert) R(amsdell), Jr.

Guro, Elena 1877-1913 .... TCLC 56

Gustafson, James M(oody) 1925- .... CLC 100
See also CA 25-28R; CANR 37

Gustafson, Ralph (Barker) 1909-1995 .... CLC 36
See also CA 21-24R; CANR 8, 45, 84; CP 7; DLB 88; RGEL 2

Gut, Gom
See Simenon, Georges (Jacques Christian)

Guterson, David 1956- .... CLC 91
See also CA 132; CANR 73; MTCW 2; NFS 13

Guthrie, A(lfred) B(ertram), Jr. 1901-1991 .... CLC 23
See also CA 57-60; 134; CANR 24; DLB 6, 212; SATA 62; SATA-Obit 67

Guthrie, Isobel
See Grieve, C(hristopher) M(urray)

Guthrie, Woodrow Wilson 1912-1967
See Guthrie, Woody
See also CA 113; 93-96

Guthrie, Woody .... CLC 35
See Guthrie, Woodrow Wilson
See also LAIT 3

Gutierrez Najera, Manuel 1859-1895 .... HLCS 2
See also LAW

Guy, Rosa (Cuthbert) 1925- .... CLC 26
See also AAYA 4, 37; BW 2; CA 17-20R; CANR 14, 34, 83; CLR 13; DLB 33; DNFS 1; JRDA; MAICYA 1, 2; SATA 14, 62, 122; YAW

Gwendolyn
See Bennett, (Enoch) Arnold

H. D. .... CLC 3, 8, 14, 31, 34, 73; PC 5
See Doolittle, Hilda

H. de V.
See Buchan, John

Haavikko, Paavo Juhani 1931- . CLC 18, 34
See also CA 106; EWL 3

Habbema, Koos
See Heijermans, Herman

Habermas, Juergen 1929- .... CLC 104
See also CA 109; CANR 85; DLB 242

Habermas, Jurgen
See Habermas, Juergen

Hacker, Marilyn 1942- ...... CLC 5, 9, 23, 72, 91; PC 47
See also CA 77-80; CANR 68; CP 7; CWP; DAM POET; DLB 120, 282; FW; GLL 2

Hadrian 76-138 .... CMLC 52

Haeckel, Ernst Heinrich (Philipp August) 1834-1919 .... TCLC 83
See also CA 157

Hafiz c. 1326-1389(?) .... CMLC 34
See also RGWL 2, 3

Haggard, H(enry) Rider 1856-1925 .... TCLC 11
See also BRWS 3; BYA 4, 5; CA 108; 148; CANR 112; DLB 70, 156, 174, 178; FANT; LMFS 1; MTCW 2; RGEL 2; RHW; SATA 16; SCFW; SFW 4; SUFW 1; WLIT 4

Hagiosy, L.
See Larbaud, Valery (Nicolas)

Hagiwara, Sakutaro 1886-1942 .... PC 18; TCLC 60
See Hagiwara Sakutaro
See also CA 154; RGWL 3

Hagiwara Sakutaro
See Hagiwara, Sakutaro
See also EWL 3

Haig, Fenil
See Ford, Ford Madox

Haig-Brown, Roderick (Langmere) 1908-1976 .... CLC 21
See also CA 5-8R; 69-72; CANR 4, 38, 83; CLR 31; CWRI 5; DLB 88; MAICYA 1, 2; SATA 12

Haight, Rip
See Carpenter, John (Howard)

Hailey, Arthur 1920- .... CLC 5
See also AITN 2; BEST 90:3; BPFB 2; CA 1-4R; CANR 2, 36, 75; CCA 1; CN 7; CPW; DAM NOV, POP; DLB 88; DLBY 1982; MTCW 1, 2

Hailey, Elizabeth Forsythe 1938- .... CLC 40
See also CA 93-96; CAAE 188; CAAS 1; CANR 15, 48; INT CANR-15

Haines, John (Meade) 1924- .... CLC 58
See also AMWS 12; CA 17-20R; CANR 13, 34; CSW; DLB 5, 212

Hakluyt, Richard 1552-1616 .... LC 31
See also DLB 136; RGEL 2

Haldeman, Joe (William) 1943- ...... **CLC 61**
See Graham, Robert
See also AAYA 38; CA 53-56, 179; CAAE 179; CAAS 25; CANR 6, 70, 72; DLB 8; INT CANR-6; SCFW 2; SFW 4

Hale, Janet Campbell 1947- .... **NNAL**
See also CA 49-52; CANR 45, 75; DAM MULT; DLB 175; MTCW 2

Hale, Sarah Josepha (Buell) 1788-1879
.... **NCLC 75**
See also DLB 1, 42, 73, 243

Halevy, Elie 1870-1937 .... **TCLC 104**

Haley, Alex(ander Murray Palmer) 1921-1992 .... **BLC 2; CLC 8, 12, 76**
See also AAYA 26; BPFB 2; BW 2, 3; CA 77-80; 136; CANR 61; CDALBS; CPW; CSW; DA; DA3; DAB; DAC; DAM MST, MULT, POP; DLB 38; LAIT 5; MTCW 1, 2; NFS 9

Haliburton, Thomas Chandler 1796-1865
.... **NCLC 15**
See also DLB 11, 99; RGEL 2; RGSF 2

Hall, Donald (Andrew, Jr.) 1928- .... **CLC 1, 13, 37, 59, 151**
See also CA 5-8R; CAAS 7; CANR 2, 44, 64, 106; CP 7; DAM POET; DLB 5; MTCW 1; RGAL 4; SATA 23, 97

Hall, Frederic Sauser
See Sauser-Hall, Frederic

Hall, James
See Kuttner, Henry

Hall, James Norman 1887-1951 ... **TCLC 23**
See also CA 123; 173; LAIT 1; RHW 1; SATA 21

Hall, (Marguerite) Radclyffe 1880-1943
.... **TCLC 12**
See also BRWS 6; CA 110; 150; CANR 83; DLB 191; MTCW 2; RGEL 2; RHW

Hall, Rodney 1935- .... **CLC 51**
See also CA 109; CANR 69; CN 7; CP 7

Hallam, Arthur Henry 1811-1833
.... **NCLC 110**
See also DLB 32

Halleck, Fitz-Greene 1790-1867 ... **NCLC 47**
See also DLB 3, 250; RGAL 4

Halliday, Michael
See Creasey, John

Halpern, Daniel 1945- .... **CLC 14**
See also CA 33-36R; CANR 93; CP 7

Hamburger, Michael (Peter Leopold) 1924-
.... **CLC 5, 14**
See also CA 5-8R; CAAE 196; CAAS 4; CANR 2, 47; CP 7; DLB 27

Hamill, Pete 1935- .... **CLC 10**
See also CA 25-28R; CANR 18, 71

Hamilton, Alexander 1755(?)-1804
.... **NCLC 49**
See also DLB 37

Hamilton, Clive
See Lewis, C(live) S(taples)

Hamilton, Edmond 1904-1977 .... **CLC 1**
See also CA 1-4R; CANR 3, 84; DLB 8; SATA 118; SFW 4

Hamilton, Eugene (Jacob) Lee
See Lee-Hamilton, Eugene (Jacob)

Hamilton, Franklin
See Silverberg, Robert

Hamilton, Gail
See Corcoran, Barbara (Asenath)

Hamilton, Mollie
See Kaye, M(ary) M(argaret)

Hamilton, (Anthony Walter) Patrick 1904-1962 .... **CLC 51**
See also CA 176; 113; DLB 10, 191

Hamilton, Virginia (Esther) 1936-2002
.... **CLC 26**
See also AAYA 2, 21; BW 2, 3; BYA 1, 2, 8; CA 25-28R; 206; CANR 20, 37, 73; CLR 1, 11, 40; DAM MULT; DLB 33, 52; DLBY 01; INT CANR-20; JRDA; LAIT 5; MAICYA 1, 2; MAICYAS 1; MTCW 1, 2; SATA 4, 56, 79, 123; SATA-Obit 132; WYA; YAW

Hammett, (Samuel) Dashiell 1894-1961
.... **CLC 3, 5, 10, 19, 47; SSC 17**
See also AITN 1; AMWS 4; BPFB 2; CA 81-84; CANR 42; CDALB 1929-1941; CMW 4; DA3; DLB 226; DLBD 6; DLBY 1996; EWL 3; LAIT 3; MSW; MTCW 1, 2; RGAL 4; RGSF 2; TUS

Hammon, Jupiter 1720(?)-1800(?) ... **BLC 2; NCLC 5; PC 16**
See also DAM MULT, POET; DLB 31, 50

Hammond, Keith
See Kuttner, Henry

Hamner, Earl (Henry), Jr. 1923- .... **CLC 12**
See also AITN 2; CA 73-76; DLB 6

Hampton, Christopher (James) 1946-
.... **CLC 4**
See also CA 25-28R; CD 5; DLB 13; MTCW 1

Hamsun, Knut .... **TCLC 2, 14, 49**
See Pedersen, Knut
See also EW 8; EWL 3; RGWL 2, 3

Handke, Peter 1942- .. **CLC 5, 8, 10, 15, 38, 134; DC 17**
See also CA 77-80; CANR 33, 75, 104; CWW 2; DAM DRAM, NOV; DLB 85, 124; EWL 3; MTCW 1, 2; TWA

Handy, W(illiam) C(hristopher) 1873-1958
.... **TCLC 97**
See also BW 3; CA 121; 167

Hanley, James 1901-1985 .... **CLC 3, 5, 8, 13**
See also CA 73-76; 117; CANR 36; CBD; DLB 191; EWL 3; MTCW 1; RGEL 2

Hannah, Barry 1942- .... **CLC 23, 38, 90**
See also BPFB 2; CA 108; 110; CANR 43, 68, 113; CN 7; CSW; DLB 6, 234; INT CA-110; MTCW 1; RGSF 2

Hannon, Ezra
See Hunter, Evan

Hansberry, Lorraine (Vivian) 1930-1965
.... **BLC 2; CLC 17, 62; DC 2**
See also AAYA 25; AFAW 1, 2; AMWS 4; BW 1, 3; CA 109; 25-28R; CABS 3; CAD; CANR 58; CDALB 1941-1968; CWD; DA; DA3; DAB; DAC; DAM DRAM, MST, MULT; DFS 2; DLB 7, 38; EWL 3; FW; LAIT 4; MTCW 1, 2; RGAL 4; TUS

Hansen, Joseph 1923- .... **CLC 38**
See Brock, Rose; Colton, James
See also BPFB 2; CA 29-32R; CAAS 17; CANR 16, 44, 66; CMW 4; DLB 226; GLL 1; INT CANR-16

Hansen, Martin A(lfred) 1909-1955
.... **TCLC 32**
See also CA 167; DLB 214; EWL 3

Hansen and Philipson eds. .... **CLC 65**

Hanson, Kenneth O(stlin) 1922- ..... **CLC 13**
See also CA 53-56; CANR 7

Hardwick, Elizabeth (Bruce) 1916-
.... **CLC 13**
See also AMWS 3; CA 5-8R; CANR 3, 32, 70, 100; CN 7; CSW; DA3; DAM NOV; DLB 6; MAWW; MTCW 1, 2

Hardy, Thomas 1840-1928 ...... **PC 8; SSC 2, 60; TCLC 4, 10, 18, 32, 48, 53, 72; WLC**
See also BRW 6; BRWC 1; BRWR 1; CA 104; 123; CDBLB 1890-1914; DA; DA3; DAB; DAC; DAM MST, NOV, POET; DLB 18, 19, 135; EWL 3; EXPN; EXPP; LAIT 2; MTCW 1, 2; NFS 3, 11, 15; PFS 3, 4; RGEL 2; RGSF 2; TEA; WLIT 4

Hare, David 1947- .... **CLC 29, 58, 136**
See also BRWS 4; CA 97-100; CANR 39, 91; CBD; CD 5; DFS 4, 7, 16; DLB 13; MTCW 1; TEA

Harewood, John
See Van Druten, John (William)

Harford, Henry
See Hudson, W(illiam) H(enry)

Hargrave, Leonie
See Disch, Thomas M(ichael)

Harjo, Joy 1951- .... **CLC 83; NNAL; PC 27**
See also AMWS 12; CA 114; CANR 35, 67, 91; CP 7; CWP; DAM MULT; DLB 120, 175; EWL 3; MTCW 2; PFS 15; RGAL 4

Harlan, Louis R(udolph) 1922- .... **CLC 34**
See also CA 21-24R; CANR 25, 55, 80

Harling, Robert 1951(?)- .... **CLC 53**
See also CA 147

Harmon, William (Ruth) 1938- .... **CLC 38**
See also CA 33-36R; CANR 14, 32, 35; SATA 65

Harper, F. E. W.
See Harper, Frances Ellen Watkins

Harper, Frances E. W.
See Harper, Frances Ellen Watkins

Harper, Frances E. Watkins
See Harper, Frances Ellen Watkins

Harper, Frances Ellen
See Harper, Frances Ellen Watkins

Harper, Frances Ellen Watkins 1825-1911
.... **BLC 2; PC 21; TCLC 14**
See also AFAW 1, 2; BW 1, 3; CA 111; 125; CANR 79; DAM MULT, POET; DLB 50, 221; MAWW; RGAL 4

Harper, Michael S(teven) 1938- .. **CLC 7, 22**
See also AFAW 2; BW 1; CA 33-36R; CANR 24, 108; CP 7; DLB 41; RGAL 4

Harper, Mrs. F. E. W.
See Harper, Frances Ellen Watkins

Harpur, Charles 1813-1868 .... **NCLC 114**
See also DLB 230; RGEL 2

Harris, Christie 1907-
See Harris, Christie (Lucy) Irwin

Harris, Christie (Lucy) Irwin 1907-2002
.... **CLC 12**
See also CA 5-8R; CANR 6, 83; CLR 47; DLB 88; JRDA; MAICYA 1, 2; SAAS 10; SATA 6, 74; SATA-Essay 116

Harris, Frank 1856-1931 .... **TCLC 24**
See also CA 109; 150; CANR 80; DLB 156, 197; RGEL 2

Harris, George Washington 1814-1869
.... **NCLC 23**
See also DLB 3, 11, 248; RGAL 4

Harris, Joel Chandler 1848-1908 ... **SSC 19; TCLC 2**
See also CA 104; 137; CANR 80; CLR 49; DLB 11, 23, 42, 78, 91; LAIT 2; MAICYA 1, 2; RGSF 2; SATA 100; WCH; YABC 1

Harris, John (Wyndham Parkes Lucas) Beynon 1903-1969
See Wyndham, John
See also CA 102; 89-92; CANR 84; SATA 118; SFW 4

Harris, MacDonald .... **CLC 9**
See Heiney, Donald (William)

Harris, Mark 1922- .... **CLC 19**
See also CA 5-8R; CAAS 3; CANR 2, 55, 83; CN 7; DLB 2; DLBY 1980

Harris, Norman .... **CLC 65**

Harris, (Theodore) Wilson 1921- ... **CLC 25, 159**
See also BRWS 5; BW 2, 3; CA 65-68; CAAS 16; CANR 11, 27, 69, 114; CDWLB 3; CN 7; CP 7; DLB 117; EWL 3; MTCW 1; RGEL 2

Harrison, Barbara Grizzuti 1934-2002
.... **CLC 144**
See also CA 77-80; 205; CANR 15, 48; INT CANR-15

Harrison, Elizabeth (Allen) Cavanna
1909-2001
See Cavanna, Betty
See also CA 9-12R; 200; CANR 6, 27, 85, 104; MAICYA 2; YAW

Harrison, Harry (Max) 1925- .... **CLC 42**
See also CA 1-4R; CANR 5, 21, 84; DLB 8; SATA 4; SCFW 2; SFW 4

Harrison, James (Thomas) 1937- .... **CLC 6, 14, 33, 66, 143; SSC 19**
See Harrison, Jim
See also CA 13-16R; CANR 8, 51, 79; CN 7; CP 7; DLBY 1982; INT CANR-8

Harrison, Jim
See Harrison, James (Thomas)
See also AMWS 8; RGAL 4; TCWW 2; TUS

Harrison, Kathryn 1961- .... **CLC 70, 151**
See also CA 144; CANR 68

Harrison, Tony 1937- .... **CLC 43, 129**
See also BRWS 5; CA 65-68; CANR 44, 98; CBD; CD 5; CP 7; DLB 40, 245; MTCW 1; RGEL 2

Harriss, Will(ard Irvin) 1922- .... **CLC 34**
See also CA 111

Hart, Ellis
See Ellison, Harlan (Jay)

Hart, Josephine 1942(?)- .... **CLC 70**
See also CA 138; CANR 70; CPW; DAM POP

Hart, Moss 1904-1961 .... **CLC 66**
See also CA 109; 89-92; CANR 84; DAM DRAM; DFS 1; DLB 7, 266; RGAL 4

Harte, (Francis) Bret(t) 1836(?)-1902
.... **SSC 8, 59; TCLC 1, 25; WLC**
See also AMWS 2; CA 104; 140; CANR 80; CDALB 1865-1917; DA; DA3; DAB; DAC; DAM MST; DLB 12, 64, 74, 79, 186; EXPS; LAIT 2; RGAL 4; RGSF 2; SATA 26; SSFS 3; TUS

Hartley, L(eslie) P(oles) 1895-1972 .. **CLC 2, 22**
See also BRWS 7; CA 45-48; 37-40R; CANR 33; DLB 15, 139; EWL 3; HGG; MTCW 1, 2; RGEL 2; RGSF 2; SUFW 1

Hartman, Geoffrey H. 1929- .... **CLC 27**
See also CA 117; 125; CANR 79; DLB 67

Hartmann, Sadakichi 1869-1944 .. **TCLC 73**
See also CA 157; DLB 54

Hartmann von Aue c. 1170-c. 1210
.... **CMLC 15**
See also CDWLB 2; DLB 138; RGWL 2, 3

Hartog, Jan de
See de Hartog, Jan

Haruf, Kent 1943- .... **CLC 34**
See also AAYA 44; CA 149; CANR 91

Harvey, Gabriel 1550(?)-1631 .... **LC 88**
See also DLB 167, 213

Harwood, Ronald 1934- .... **CLC 32**
See also CA 1-4R; CANR 4, 55; CBD; CD 5; DAM DRAM, MST; DLB 13

Hasegawa Tatsunosuke
See Futabatei, Shimei

Hasek, Jaroslav (Matej Frantisek)
1883-1923 .... **TCLC 4**
See also CA 104; 129; CDWLB 4; DLB 215; EW 9; EWL 3; MTCW 1, 2; RGSF 2; RGWL 2, 3

Hass, Robert 1941- . **CLC 18, 39, 99; PC 16**
See also AMWS 6; CA 111; CANR 30, 50, 71; CP 7; DLB 105, 206; EWL 3; RGAL 4; SATA 94

Hastings, Hudson
See Kuttner, Henry

Hastings, Selina .... **CLC 44**

Hathorne, John 1641-1717 .... **LC 38**

Hatteras, Amelia
See Mencken, H(enry) L(ouis)

Hatteras, Owen .... **TCLC 18**
See Mencken, H(enry) L(ouis); Nathan, George Jean

Hauptmann, Gerhart (Johann Robert)
1862-1946 .... **SSC 37; TCLC 4**
See also CA 104; 153; CDWLB 2; DAM DRAM; DLB 66, 118; EW 8; EWL 3; RGSF 2; RGWL 2, 3; TWA

Havel, Vaclav 1936- .... **CLC 25, 58, 65, 123; DC 6**
See also CA 104; CANR 36, 63; CDWLB 4; CWW 2; DA3; DAM DRAM; DFS 10; DLB 232; EWL 3; LMFS 2; MTCW 1, 2; RGWL 3

Haviaras, Stratis .... **CLC 33**
See Chaviaras, Strates

Hawes, Stephen 1475(?)-1529(?) .... **LC 17**
See also DLB 132; RGEL 2

Hawkes, John (Clendennin Burne, Jr.)
1925-1998 . **CLC 1, 2, 3, 4, 7, 9, 14, 15, 27, 49**
See also BPFB 2; CA 1-4R; 167; CANR 2, 47, 64; CN 7; DLB 2, 7, 227; DLBY 1980, 1998; EWL 3; MTCW 1, 2; RGAL 4

Hawking, S. W.
See Hawking, Stephen W(illiam)

Hawking, Stephen W(illiam) 1942-
.... **CLC 63, 105**
See also AAYA 13; BEST 89:1; CA 126; 129; CANR 48, 115; CPW; DA3; MTCW 2

Hawkins, Anthony Hope
See Hope, Anthony

Hawthorne, Julian 1846-1934 .... **TCLC 25**
See also CA 165; HGG

Hawthorne, Nathaniel 1804-1864 .. **NCLC 2, 10, 17, 23, 39, 79, 95; SSC 3, 29, 39; WLC**
See also AAYA 18; AMW; AMWC 1; AMWR 1; BPFB 2; BYA 3; CDALB 1640-1865; DA; DA3; DAB; DAC; DAM MST, NOV; DLB 1, 74, 183, 223, 269; EXPN; EXPS; HGG; LAIT 1; NFS 1; RGAL 4; RGSF 2; SSFS 1, 7, 11, 15; SUFW 1; TUS; WCH; YABC 2

Haxton, Josephine Ayres 1921-
See Douglas, Ellen
See also CA 115; CANR 41, 83

Hayaseca y Eizaguirre, Jorge
See Echegaray (y Eizaguirre), Jose (Maria Waldo)

Hayashi, Fumiko 1904-1951 .... **TCLC 27**
See Hayashi Fumiko
See also CA 161

Hayashi Fumiko
See Hayashi, Fumiko
See also DLB 180; EWL 3

Haycraft, Anna (Margaret) 1932-
See Ellis, Alice Thomas
See also CA 122; CANR 85, 90; MTCW 2

Hayden, Robert E(arl) 1913-1980 ... **BLC 2; CLC 5, 9, 14, 37; PC 6**
See also AFAW 1, 2; AMWS 2; BW 1, 3; CA 69-72; 97-100; CABS 2; CANR 24, 75, 82; CDALB 1941-1968; DA; DAC; DAM MST, MULT, POET; DLB 5, 76; EWL 3; EXPP; MTCW 1, 2; PFS 1; RGAL 4; SATA 19; SATA-Obit 26; WP

Hayek, F(riedrich) A(ugust von) 1899-1992
.... **TCLC 109**
See also CA 93-96; 137; CANR 20; MTCW 1, 2

Hayford, J(oseph) E(phraim) Casely
See Casely-Hayford, J(oseph) E(phraim)

Hayman, Ronald 1932- .... **CLC 44**
See also CA 25-28R; CANR 18, 50, 88; CD 5; DLB 155

Hayne, Paul Hamilton 1830-1886
.... **NCLC 94**
See also DLB 3, 64, 79, 248; RGAL 4

Hays, Mary 1760-1843 .... **NCLC 114**
See also DLB 142, 158; RGEL 2

Haywood, Eliza (Fowler) 1693(?)-1756
.... **LC 1, 44**
See also DLB 39; RGEL 2

Hazlitt, William 1778-1830 ..... **NCLC 29, 82**
See also BRW 4; DLB 110, 158; RGEL 2; TEA

Hazzard, Shirley 1931- .... **CLC 18**
See also CA 9-12R; CANR 4, 70; CN 7; DLBY 1982; MTCW 1

Head, Bessie 1937-1986 ..... **BLC 2; CLC 25, 67; SSC 52**
See also AFW; BW 2, 3; CA 29-32R; 119; CANR 25, 82; CDWLB 3; DA3; DAM MULT; DLB 117, 225; EWL 3; EXPS; FW; MTCW 1, 2; RGSF 2; SSFS 5, 13; WLIT 2

Headon, (Nicky) Topper 1956(?)- ... **CLC 30**

Heaney, Seamus (Justin) 1939- ..... **CLC 5, 7, 14, 25, 37, 74, 91, 171; PC 18; WLCS**
See also ERWR 1; BRWS 2; CA 85-88; CANR 25, 48, 75, 91; CDBLB 1960 to Present; CP 7; DA3; DAB; DAM POET; DLB 40; DLBY 1995; EWL 3; EXPP; MTCW 1, 2; PAB; PFS 2, 5, 8, 17; RGEL 2; TEA; WLIT 4

Hearn, (Patricio) Lafcadio (Tessima Carlos)
1850-1904 .... **TCLC 9**
See also CA 105; 166; DLB 12, 78, 189; HGG; RGAL 4

Hearne, Vicki 1946-2001 .... **CLC 56**
See also CA 139; 201

Hearon, Shelby 1931- .... **CLC 63**
See also AITN 2; AMWS 8; CA 25-28R; CANR 18, 48, 103; CSW

Heat-Moon, William Least .... **CLC 29**
See Trogdon, William (Lewis)
See also AAYA 9

Hebbel, Friedrich 1813-1863 .... **NCLC 43**
See also CDWLB 2; DAM DRAM; DLB 129; EW 6 RGWL 2, 3

Hebert, Anne 1916-2000 .... **CLC 4, 13, 29**
See also CA 85-88; 187; CANR 69; CCA 1; CWP; CWW 2; DA3; DAC; DAM MST, POET; DLB 68; EWL 3; GFL 1789 to the Present; MTCW 1, 2

Hecht, Anthony (Evan) 1923- .... **CLC 8, 13, 19**
See also AMWS 10; CA 9-12R; CANR 6, 108; CP 7; DAM POET; DLB 5, 169; EWL 3; PFS 6; WP

Hecht, Ben 1894-1964 .... **CLC 8; TCLC 101**
See also CA 85-88; DFS 9; DLB 7, 9, 25, 26, 28, 86; FANT; IDFW 3, 4; RGAL 4

Hedayat, Sadeq 1903-1951 .... **TCLC 21**
See also CA 120; EWL 3; RGSF 2

Hegel, Georg Wilhelm Friedrich 1770-1831
.... **NCLC 46**
See also DLB 90; TWA

Heidegger, Martin 1889-1976 .... **CLC 24**
See also CA 81-84; 65-68; CANR 34; MTCW 1, 2

Heidenstam, (Carl Gustaf) Verner von
1859-1940 .... **TCLC 5**
See also CA 104

Heifner, Jack 1946- .... **CLC 11**
See also CA 105; CANR 47

Heijermans, Herman 1864-1924 ... **TCLC 24**
See also CA 123; EWL 3

Heilbrun, Carolyn G(old) 1926- .... **CLC 25, 173**
See Cross, Amanda
See also CA 45-48; CANR 1, 28, 58, 94; FW

Hein, Christoph 1944- .... **CLC 154**
   See also CA 158; CANR 108; CDWLB 2; CWW 2; DLB 124
Heine, Heinrich 1797-1856 ...... **NCLC 4, 54; PC 25**
   See also CDWLB 2; DLB 90; EW 5; RGWL 2, 3; TWA
Heinemann, Larry (Curtiss) 1944- . **CLC 50**
   See also CA 110; CAAS 21; CANR 31, 81; DLBD 9; INT CANR-31
Heiney, Donald (William) 1921-1993
   See Harris, MacDonald
   See also CA 1-4R; 142; CANR 3, 58; FANT
Heinlein, Robert A(nson) 1907-1988
   .... **CLC 1, 3, 8, 14, 26, 55; SSC 55**
   See also AAYA 17; BPFB 2; BYA 4, 13; CA 1-4R; 125; CANR 1, 20, 53; CLR 75; CPW; DA3; DAM POP; DLB 8; EXPS; JRDA; LAIT 5; LMFS 2; MAICYA 1, 2; MTCW 1, 2; RGAL 4; SATA 9, 69; SATA-Obit 56; SCFW; SFW 4; SSFS 7; YAW
Helforth, John
   See Doolittle, Hilda
Heliodorus fl. 3rd cent. - .... **CMLC 52**
Hellenhofferu, Vojtech Kapristian z
   See Hasek, Jaroslav (Matej Frantisek)
Heller, Joseph 1923-1999 ..... **CLC 1, 3, 5, 8, 11, 36, 63; TCLC 131; WLC**
   See also AAYA 24; AITN 1; AMWS 4; BPFB 2; BYA 1; CA 5-8R; 187; CABS 1; CANR 8, 42, 66; CN 7; CPW; DA; DA3; DAB; DAC; DAM MST, NOV, POP; DLB 2, 28, 227; DLBY 1980, 2002; EWL 3; EXPN; INT CANR-8; LAIT 4; MTCW 1, 2; NFS 1; RGAL 4; TUS; YAW
Hellman, Lillian (Florence) 1906-1984
   . **CLC 2, 4, 8, 14, 18, 34, 44, 52; DC 1; TCLC 119**
   See also AAYA 47; AITN 1, 2; AMWS 1; CA 13-16R; 112; CAD; CANR 33; CWD; DA3; DAM DRAM; DFS 1, 3, 14; DLB 7, 228; DLBY 1984; EWL 3; FW; LAIT 3; MAWW; MTCW 1, 2; RGAL 4; TUS
Helprin, Mark 1947- .... **CLC 7, 10, 22, 32**
   See also CA 81-84; CANR 47, 64; CDALBS; CPW; DA3; DAM NOV, POP; DLBY 1985; FANT; MTCW 1, 2; SUFW 2
Helvetius, Claude-Adrien 1715-1771 . **LC 26**
Helyar, Jane Penelope Josephine 1933-
   See Poole, Josephine
   See also CA 21-24R; CANR 10, 26; CWRI 5; SATA 82; SATA-Essay 138
Hemans, Felicia 1793-1835 ...... **NCLC 29, 71**
   See also DLB 96; RGEL 2
Hemingway, Ernest (Miller) 1899-1961
   ... **CLC 1, 3, 6, 8, 10, 13, 19, 30, 34, 39, 41, 44, 50, 61, 80; SSC 1, 25, 36, 40; TCLC 115; WLC**
   See also AAYA 19; AMW; AMWC 1; AMWR 1; BPFB 2; BYA 2, 3, 13; CA 77-80; CANR 34; CDALB 1917-1929; DA; DA3; DAB; DAC; DAM MST, NOV, DLB 4, 9, 102, 210; DLBD 1, 15, 16; DLBY 1981, 1987, 1996, 1998; EWL 3; EXPN; EXPS; LAIT 3, 4; MTCW 1, 2; NFS 1, 5, 6, 14; RGAL 4; RGSF 2; SSFS 17; TUS; WYA
Hempel, Amy 1951- .... **CLC 39**
   See also CA 118; 137; CANR 70; DA3; DLB 218; EXPS; MTCW 2; SSFS 2
Henderson, F. C.
   See Mencken, H(enry) L(ouis)
Henderson, Sylvia
   See Ashton-Warner, Sylvia (Constance)
Henderson, Zenna (Chlarson) 1917-1983
   .... **SSC 29**
   See also CA 1-4R; 133; CANR 1, 84; DLB 8; SATA 5; SFW 4

Henkin, Joshua .... **CLC 119**
   See also CA 161
Henley, Beth .... **CLC 23; DC 6, 14**
   See Henley, Elizabeth Becker
   See also CABS 3; CAD; CD 5; CSW; CWD; DFS 2; DLBY 1986; FW
Henley, Elizabeth Becker 1952-
   See Henley, Beth
   See also CA 107; CANR 32, 73; DA3; DAM DRAM, MST; MTCW 1, 2
Henley, William Ernest 1849-1903 . **TCLC 8**
   See also CA 105; DLB 19; RGEL 2
Hennissart, Martha
   See Lathen, Emma
   See also CA 85-88; CANR 64
Henry VIII 1491-1547 .... **LC 10**
   See also DLB 132
Henry, O. ..... **SSC 5, 49; TCLC 1, 19; WLC**
   See Porter, William Sydney
   See also AAYA 41; AMWS 2; EXPS; RGAL 4; RGSF 2; SSFS 2
Henry, Patrick 1736-1799 .... **LC 25**
   See also LAIT 1
Henryson, Robert 1430(?)-1506(?) ...... **LC 20**
   See also BRWS 7; DLB 146; RGEL 2
Henschke, Alfred
   See Klabund
Henson, Lance 1944- .... **NNAL**
   See also CA 146; DLB 175
Hentoff, Nat(han Irving) 1925- .... **CLC 26**
   See also AAYA 4, 42; BYA 6; CA 1-4R; CAAS 6; CANR 5, 25, 77, 114; CLR 52; INT CANR-25; JRDA; MAICYA 1, 2; SATA 42, 69, 133; SATA-Brief 27; WYA; YAW
Heppenstall, (John) Rayner 1911-1981
   .... **CLC 10**
   See also CA 1-4R; 103; CANR 29; EWL 3
Heraclitus c. 540B.C.-c. 450B.C. . **CMLC 22**
   See also DLB 176
Herbert, Frank (Patrick) 1920-1986
   .... **CLC 12, 23, 35, 44, 85**
   See also AAYA 21; BPFB 2; BYA 4, 14; CA 53-56; 118; CANR 5, 43; CDALBS; CPW; DAM POP; DLB 8; INT CANR-5; LAIT 5; MTCW 1, 2; NFS 17; SATA 9, 37; SATA-Obit 47; SCFW 2; SFW 4; YAW
Herbert, George 1593-1633 ...... **LC 24; PC 4**
   See also BRW 2; BRWR 2; CDBLB Before 1660; DAB; DAM POET; DLB 126; EXPP; RGEL 2; TEA; WP
Herbert, Zbigniew 1924-1998 ..... **CLC 9, 43**
   See also CA 89-92; 169; CANR 36, 74; CDWLB 4; CWW 2; DAM POET; DLB 232; EWL 3; MTCW 1
Herbst, Josephine (Frey) 1897-1969
   .... **CLC 34**
   See also CA 5-8R; 25-28R; DLB 9
Herder, Johann Gottfried von 1744-1803
   .... **NCLC 8**
   See also DLB 97; EW 4; TWA
Heredia, Jose Maria 1803-1839 ...... **HLCS 2**
   See also LAW
Hergesheimer, Joseph 1880-1954 .. **TCLC 11**
   See also CA 109; 194; DLB 102, 9; RGAL 4
Herlihy, James Leo 1927-1993 .... **CLC 6**
   See also CA 1-4R; 143; CAD; CANR 2
Herman, William
   See Bierce, Ambrose (Gwinett)
Hermogenes fl. c. 175- .... **CMLC 6**
Hernandez, Jose 1834-1886 .... **NCLC 17**
   See also LAW; RGWL 2, 3; WLIT 1
Herodotus c. 484B.C.-c. 420B.C. . **CMLC 17**
   See also AW 1; CDWLB 1; DLB 176; RGWL 2, 3; TWA

Herrick, Robert 1591-1674 ..... **LC 13; PC 9**
   See also BRW 2; DA; DAB; DAC; DAM MST, POP; DLB 126; EXPP; PFS 13; RGAL 4; RGEL 2; TEA; WP
Herring, Guilles
   See Somerville, Edith Oenone
Herriot, James 1916-1995 .... **CLC 12**
   See Wight, James Alfred
   See also AAYA 1; BPFB 2; CA 148; CANR 40; CLR 80; CPW; DAM POP; LAIT 3; MAICYA 2; MAICYAS 1; MTCW 2; SATA 86, 135; TEA; YAW
Herris, Violet
   See Hunt, Violet
Herrmann, Dorothy 1941- .... **CLC 44**
   See also CA 107
Herrmann, Taffy
   See Herrmann, Dorothy
Hersey, John (Richard) 1914-1993 .. **CLC 1, 2, 7, 9, 40, 81, 97**
   See also AAYA 29; BPFB 2; CA 17-20R; 140; CANR 33; CDALBS; CPW; DAM POP; DLB 6, 185, 278; MTCW 1, 2; SATA 25; SATA-Obit 76; TUS
Herzen, Aleksandr Ivanovich 1812-1870
   .... **NCLC 10, 61**
   See Herzen, Alexander
Herzen, Alexander
   See Herzen, Aleksandr Ivanovich
   See also DLB 277
Herzl, Theodor 1860-1904 .... **TCLC 36**
   See also CA 168
Herzog, Werner 1942- .... **CLC 16**
   See also CA 89-92
Hesiod c. 8th cent. B.C.- .... **CMLC 5**
   See also AW 1; DLB 176; RGWL 2, 3
Hesse, Hermann 1877-1962 . **CLC 1, 2, 3, 6, 11, 17, 25, 69; SSC 9, 49; WLC**
   See also AAYA 43; BPFB 2; CA 17-18; CAP 2; CDWLB 2; DA; DA3; DAB; DAC; DAM MST, NOV; DLB 66; EW 9; EWL 3; EXPN; LAIT 1; MTCW 1, 2; NFS 6, 15; RGWL 2, 3; SATA 50; TWA
Hewes, Cady
   See De Voto, Bernard (Augustine)
Heyen, William 1940- .... **CLC 13, 18**
   See also CA 33-36R; CAAS 9; CANR 98; CP 7; DLB 5
Heyerdahl, Thor 1914-2002 .... **CLC 26**
   See also CA 5-8R; 207; CANR 5, 22, 66, 73; LAIT 4; MTCW 1, 2; SATA 2, 52
Heym, Georg (Theodor Franz Arthur) 1887-1912 .... **TCLC 9**
   See also CA 106; 181
Heym, Stefan 1913-2001 .... **CLC 41**
   See also CA 9-12R; 203; CANR 4; CWW 2; DLB 69; EWL 3
Heyse, Paul (Johann Ludwig von) 1830-1914
   .... **TCLC 8**
   See also CA 104; DLB 129
Heyward, (Edwin) DuBose 1885-1940
   .... **HR 2; TCLC 59**
   See also CA 108; 157; DLB 7, 9, 45, 249; SATA 21
Heywood, John 1497(?)-1580(?) .... **LC 65**
   See also DLB 136; RGEL 2
Hibbert, Eleanor Alice Burford 1906-1993
   .... **CLC 7**
   See Holt, Victoria
   See also BEST 90:4; CA 17-20R; 140; CANR 9, 28, 59; CMW 4; CPW; DAM POP; MTCW 2; RHW; SATA 2; SATA-Obit 74
Hichens, Robert (Smythe) 1864-1950
   .... **TCLC 64**
   See also CA 162; DLB 153; HGG; RHW; SUFW

Higgins, George V(incent) 1939-1999 .... CLC 4, 7, 10, 18
See also BPFB 2; CA 77-80; 186; CAAS 5; CANR 17, 51, 89, 96; CMW 4; CN 7; DLB 2; DLBY 1981, 1998; INT CANR-17; MSW; MTCW 1

Higginson, Thomas Wentworth 1823-1911 .... TCLC 36
See also CA 162; DLB 1, 64, 243

Higgonet, Margaret ed. .... CLC 65

Highet, Helen
See MacInnes, Helen (Clark)

Highsmith, (Mary) Patricia 1921-1995 .... CLC 2, 4, 14, 42, 102
See Morgan, Claire
See also AAYA 48; BRWS 5; CA 1-4R; 147; CANR 1, 20, 48, 62, 108; CMW 4; CPW; DA3; DAM NOV, POP; MSW; MTCW 1, 2

Highwater, Jamake (Mamake) 1942(?)-2001 .... CLC 12
See also AAYA 7; BPFB 2; BYA 4; CA 65-68; 199; CAAS 7; CANR 10, 34, 84; CLR 17; CWRI 5; DLB 52; DLBY 1985; JRDA; MAICYA 1, 2; SATA 32, 69; SATA-Brief 30

Highway, Tomson 1951- ..... CLC 92; NNAL
See also CA 151; CANR 75; CCA 1; CD 5; DAC; DAM MULT; DFS 2; MTCW 2

Hijuelos, Oscar 1951- .... CLC 65; HLC 1
See also AAYA 25; AMWS 8; BEST 90:1; CA 123; CANR 50, 75; CPW; DA3; DAM MULT, POP; DLB 145; HW 1, 2; MTCW 2; NFS 17; RGAL 4; WLIT 1

Hikmet, Nazim 1902(?)-1963 .... CLC 40
See also CA 141; 93-96; EWL 3

Hildegard von Bingen 1098-1179 .... CMLC 20
See also DLB 148

Hildesheimer, Wolfgang 1916-1991 . CLC 49
See also CA 101; 135; DLB 69, 124; EWL 3

Hill, Geoffrey (William) 1932- ..... CLC 5, 8, 18, 45
See also BRWS 5; CA 81-84; CANR 21, 89; CDBLB 1960 to Present; CP 7; DAM POET; DLB 40; EWL 3; MTCW 1; RGEL 2

Hill, George Roy 1921- .... CLC 26
See also CA 110; 122

Hill, John
See Koontz, Dean R(ay)

Hill, Susan (Elizabeth) 1942- ..... CLC 4, 113
See also CA 33-36R; CANR 29, 69; CN 7; DAB; DAM MST, NOV; DLB 14, 139; HGG; MTCW 1; RHW

Hillard, Asa G. III .... CLC 70

Hillerman, Tony 1925- .... CLC 62, 170
See also AAYA 40; BEST 89:1; BPFB 2; CA 29-32R; CANR 21, 42, 65, 97; CMW 4; CPW; DA3; DAM POP; DLB 206; MSW; RGAL 4; SATA 6; TCWW 2; YAW

Hillesum, Etty 1914-1943 .... TCLC 49
See also CA 137

Hilliard, Noel (Harvey) 1929-1996 . CLC 15
See also CA 9-12R; CANR 7, 69; CN 7

Hillis, Rick 1956- .... CLC 66
See also CA 134

Hilton, James 1900-1954 .... TCLC 21
See also CA 108; 169; DLB 34, 77; FANT; SATA 34

Hilton, Walter (?)-1396 .... CMLC 58
See also DLB 146; RGEL 2

Himes, Chester (Bomar) 1909-1984 .... BLC 2; CLC 2, 4, 7, 18, 58, 108
See also AFAW 2; BPFB 2; BW 2; CA 25-28R; 114; CANR 22, 89; CMW 4; DAM MULT; DLB 2, 76, 143, 226; EWL 3; MSW; MTCW 1, 2; RGAL 4

Hinde, Thomas .... CLC 6, 11
See Chitty, Thomas Willes
See also EWL 3

Hine, (William) Daryl 1936- .... CLC 15
See also CA 1-4R; CAAS 15; CANR 1, 20; CP 7; DLB 60

Hinkson, Katharine Tynan
See Tynan, Katharine

Hinojosa(-Smith), Rolando (R.) 1929- .... HLC 1
See Hinojosa-Smith, Rolando
See also CA 131; CAAS 16; CANR 62; DAM MULT; DLB 82; HW 1, 2; MTCW 2; RGAL 4

Hinton, S(usan) E(loise) 1950- .... CLC 30, 111
See also AAYA 2, 33; BPFB 2; BYA 2, 3; CA 81-84; CANR 32, 62, 92; CDALBS; CLR 3, 23; CPW; DA; DA3; DAB; DAC; DAM MST, NOV; JRDA; LAIT 5; MAICYA 1, 2; MTCW 1, 2; NFS 5, 9, 15, 16; SATA 19, 58, 115; WYA; YAW

Hippius, Zinaida .... TCLC 9
See Gippius, Zinaida (Nikolayevna)
See also EWL 3

Hiraoka, Kimitake 1925-1970
See Mishima, Yukio
See also CA 97-100; 29-32R; DA3; DAM DRAM; GLL 1; MTCW 1, 2

Hirsch, E(ric) D(onald), Jr. 1928- ... CLC 79
See also CA 25-28R; CANR 27, 51; DLB 67; INT CANR-27; MTCW 1

Hirsch, Edward 1950- .... CLC 31, 50
See also CA 104; CANR 20, 42, 102; CP 7; DLB 120

Hitchcock, Alfred (Joseph) 1899-1980 .... CLC 16
See also AAYA 22; CA 159; 97-100; SATA 27; SATA-Obit 24

Hitchens, Christopher (Eric) 1949- .... CLC 157
See also CA 152; CANR 89

Hitler, Adolf 1889-1945 .... TCLC 53
See also CA 117; 147

Hoagland, Edward 1932- .... CLC 28
See also ANW; CA 1-4R; CANR 2, 31, 57, 107; CN 7; DLB 6; SATA 51; TCWW 2

Hoban, Russell (Conwell) 1925- . CLC 7, 25
See also BPFB 2; CA 5-8R; CANR 23, 37, 66, 114; CLR 3, 69; CN 7; CWRI 5; DAM NOV; DLB 52; FANT; MAICYA 1, 2; MTCW 1, 2; SATA 1, 40, 78, 136; SFW 4; SUFW 2

Hobbes, Thomas 1588-1679 .... LC 36
See also DLB 151, 252; RGEL 2

Hobbs, Perry
See Blackmur, R(ichard) P(almer)

Hobson, Laura Z(ametkin) 1900-1986 .... CLC 7, 25
See Field, Peter
See also BPFB 2; CA 17-20R; 118; CANR 55; DLB 28; SATA 52

Hoccleve, Thomas c. 1368-c. 1437 ..... LC 75
See also DLB 146; RGEL 2

Hoch, Edward D(entinger) 1930-
See Queen, Ellery
See also CA 29-32R; CANR 11, 27, 51, 97; CMW 4; SFW 4

Hochhuth, Rolf 1931- .... CLC 4, 11, 18
See also CA 5-8R; CANR 33, 75; CWW 2; DAM DRAM; DLB 124; EWL 3; MTCW 1, 2

Hochman, Sandra 1936- .... CLC 3, 8
See also CA 5-8R; DLB 5

Hochwaelder, Fritz 1911-1986 .... CLC 36
See Hochwalder, Fritz
See also CA 29-32R; 120; CANR 42; DAM DRAM; MTCW 1; RGWL 3

Hochwalder, Fritz
See Hochwaelder, Fritz
See also EWL 3; RGWL 2

Hocking, Mary (Eunice) 1921- .... CLC 13
See also CA 101; CANR 18, 40

Hodgins, Jack 1938- .... CLC 23
See also CA 93-96; CN 7; DLB 60

Hodgson, William Hope 1877(?)-1918 .... TCLC 13
See also CA 111; 164; CMW 4; DLB 70, 153, 156, 178; HGG; MTCW 2; SFW 4; SUFW 1

Hoeg, Peter 1957- .... CLC 95, 156
See also CA 151; CANR 75; CMW 4; DA3; DLB 214; EWL 3; MTCW 2; NFS 17; RGWL 3

Hoffman, Alice 1952- .... CLC 51
See also AAYA 37; AMWS 10; CA 77-80; CANR 34, 66, 100; CN 7; CPW; DAM NOV; MTCW 1, 2

Hoffman, Daniel (Gerard) 1923- ...... CLC 6, 13, 23
See also CA 1-4R; CANR 4; CP 7; DLB 5

Hoffman, Stanley 1944- .... CLC 5
See also CA 77-80

Hoffman, William 1925- .... CLC 141
See also CA 21-24R; CANR 9, 103; CSW; DLB 234

Hoffman, William M(oses) 1939- .... CLC 40
See Hoffman, William M.
See also CA 57-60; CANR 11, 71

Hoffmann, E(rnst) T(heodor) A(madeus) 1776-1822 .... NCLC 2; SSC 13
See also CDWLB 2; DLB 90; EW 5; RGSF 2; RGWL 2, 3; SATA 27; SUFW 1; WCH

Hofmann, Gert 1931- .... CLC 54
See also CA 128; EWL 3

Hofmannsthal, Hugo von 1874-1929 . DC 4; TCLC 11
See also CA 106 153; CDWLB 2; DAM DRAM; DFS 17; DLB 81, 118; EW 9; EWL 3; RGWL 2, 3

Hogan, Linda 1947- ..... CLC 73; NNAL; PC 35
See also AMWS 4; ANW; BYA 12; CA 120; CANR 45, 73; CWP; DAM MULT; DLB 175; SATA 132; TCWW 2

Hogarth, Charles
See Creasey, John

Hogarth, Emmett
See Polonsky, Abraham (Lincoln)

Hogg, James 1770-1835 .... NCLC 4, 109
See also DLB 93, 116, 159; HGG; RGEL 2; SUFW 1

Holbach, Paul Henri Thiry Baron 1723-1789 .... LC 14

Holberg, Ludvig 1684-1754 .... LC 6
See also RGWL 2, 3

Holcroft, Thomas 1745-1809 .... NCLC 85
See also DLB 39, 89, 158; RGEL 2

Holden, Ursula 1921- .... CLC 18
See also CA 101; CAAS 8; CANR 22

Holderlin, (Johann Christian) Friedrich 1770-1843 .... NCLC 16; PC 4
See also CDWLB 2; DLB 90; EW 5; RGWL 2, 3

Holdstock, Robert
See Holdstock, Robert P.

Holdstock, Robert P. 1948- .... CLC 39
See also CA 131; CANR 81; DLB 261; FANT; HGG SFW 4; SUFW 2

Holinshed, Raphael fl. 1580- .... LC 69
See also DLB 167; RGEL 2

Holland, Isabelle (Christian) 1920-2002 .... CLC 21
See also AAYA 11; CA 21-24R; 181; 205; CAAS 181; CANR 10, 25, 47; CLR 57;

CWRI 5; JRDA; LAIT 4; MAICYA 1, 2; SATA 8, 70; SATA-Essay 103; SATA-Obit 132; WYA

Holland, Marcus
See Caldwell, (Janet Miriam) Taylor (Holland)

Hollander, John 1929- .... CLC 2, 5, 8, 14
See also CA 1-4R; CANR 1, 52; CP 7; DLB 5; SATA 13

Hollander, Paul
See Silverberg, Robert

Holleran, Andrew 1943(?)- .... CLC 38
See Garber, Eric
See also CA 144; GLL 1

Holley, Marietta 1836(?)-1926 ...... TCLC 99
See also CA 118; DLB 11

Hollinghurst, Alan 1954- .... CLC 55, 91
See also CA 114; CN 7; DLB 207; GLL 1

Hollis, Jim
See Summers, Hollis (Spurgeon, Jr.)

Holly, Buddy 1936-1959 .... TCLC 65

Holmes, Gordon
See Shiel, M(atthew) P(hipps)

Holmes, John
See Souster, (Holmes) Raymond

Holmes, John Clellon 1926-1988 ..... CLC 56
See also BG 2; CA 9-12R; 125; CANR 4; DLB 16, 237

Holmes, Oliver Wendell, Jr. 1841-1935
.... TCLC 77
See also CA 114; 186

Holmes, Oliver Wendell 1809-1894
.... NCLC 14, 81
See also AMWS 1; CDALB 1640-1865; DLB 1, 189, 235; EXPP; RGAL 4; SATA 34

Holmes, Raymond
See Souster, (Holmes) Raymond

Holt, Victoria
See Hibbert, Eleanor Alice Burford
See also BPFB 2

Holub, Miroslav 1923-1998 .... CLC 4
See also CA 21-24R; 169; CANR 10; CDWLB 4; CWW 2; DLB 232; EWL 3; RGWL 3

Holz, Detlev
See Benjamin, Walter

Homer c. 8th cent. B.C.- ..... CMLC 1, 16; PC 23; WLCS
See also AW 1; CDWLB 1; DA; DA3; DAB; DAC; DAM MST, POET; DLB 176; EFS 1; LAIT 1; LMFS 1; RGWL 2, 3; TWA; WP

Hongo, Garrett Kaoru 1951- .... PC 23
See also CA 133; CAAS 22; CP 7; DLB 120; EWL 3; EXPP; RGAL 4

Honig, Edwin 1919- .... CLC 33
See also CA 5-8R; CAAS 8; CANR 4, 45; CP 7; DLB 5

Hood, Hugh (John Blagdon) 1928-
.... CLC 15, 28; SSC 42
See also CA 49-52; CAAS 17; CANR 1, 33, 87; CN 7; DLB 53; RGSF 2

Hood, Thomas 1799-1845 .... NCLC 16
See also BRW 4; DLB 96; RGEL 2

Hooker, (Peter) Jeremy 1941- .... CLC 43
See also CA 77-80; CANR 22; CP 7; DLB 40

hooks, bell .... CLC 94
See Watkins, Gloria Jean
See also DLB 246

Hope, A(lec) D(erwent) 1907-2000 ... CLC 3, 51
See also BRWS 7; CA 21-24R; 188; CANR 33, 74; EWL 3; MTCW 1, 2; PFS 8; RGEL 2

Hope, Anthony 1863-1933 .... TCLC 83
See also CA 157; DLB 153, 156; RGEL 2; RHW

Hope, Brian
See Creasey, John

Hope, Christopher (David Tully) 1944-
.... CLC 52
See also AFW; CA 106; CANR 47, 101; CN 7; DLB 225; SATA 62

Hopkins, Gerard Manley 1844-1889
.... NCLC 17; PC 15; WLC
See also BRW 5; BRWR 2; CDBLB 1890-1914; DA; DA3; DAB; DAC; DAM MST, POET; DLB 35, 57; EXPP; PAB; RGEL 2; TEA; WP

Hopkins, John (Richard) 1931-1998 . CLC 4
See also CA 85-88; 169; CBD; CD 5

Hopkins, Pauline Elizabeth 1859-1930
.... BLC 2; TCLC 28
See also AFAW 2; BW 2, 3; CA 141; CANR 82; DAM MULT; DLB 50

Hopkinson, Francis 1737-1791 .... LC 25
See also DLB 31; RGAL 4

Hopley-Woolrich, Cornell George 1903-1968
See Woolrich, Cornell
See also CA 13-14; CANR 58; CAP 1; CMW 4; DLB 226; MTCW 2

Horace 65B.C.-8B.C. .... CMLC 39; PC 46
See also AW 2; CDWLB 1; DLB 211; RGWL 2, 3

Horatio
See Proust, (Valentin-Louis-George-Eugene-)Marcel

Horgan, Paul (George Vincent O'Shaughnessy) 1903-1995 . CLC 9, 53
See also BPFB 2; CA 13-16R; 147; CANR 9, 35; DAM NOV; DLB 102, 212; DLBY 1985; INT CANR-9; MTCW 1, 2; SATA 13; SATA-Obit 84; TCWW 2

Horkheimer, Max 1895-1973 ...... TCLC 132
See also CA 41-44R

Horn, Peter
See Kuttner, Henry

Horne, Frank (Smith) 1899-1974 .... HR 2
See also BW 1; CA 125; 53-56; DLB 51; WP

Hornem, Horace Esq.
See Byron, George Gordon (Noel)

Horney, Karen (Clementine Theodore Danielsen) 1885-1952 .... TCLC 71
See also CA 114; 165; DLB 246; FW

Hornung, E(rnest) W(illiam) 1866-1921
.... TCLC 59
See also CA 108; 160; CMW 4; DLB 70

Horovitz, Israel (Arthur) 1939- .... CLC 56
See also CA 33-36R; CAD; CANR 46, 59; CD 5; DAM DRAM; DLB 7

Horton, George Moses 1797(?)-1883(?)
.... NCLC 87
See also DLB 50

Horvath, odon von 1901-1938
See von Horvath, Odon
See also EWL 3

Horvath, Oedoen von -1938
See von Horvath, Odon

Horwitz, Julius 1920-1986 .... CLC 14
See also CA 9-12R; 119; CANR 12

Hospital, Janette Turner 1942- ...... CLC 42, 145
See also CA 108; CANR 48; CN 7; DLBY 2002; RGSF 2

Hostos, E. M. de
See Hostos (y Bonilla), Eugenio Maria de

Hostos, Eugenio M. de
See Hostos (y Bonilla), Eugenio Maria de

Hostos, Eugenio Maria
See Hostos (y Bonilla), Eugenio Maria de

Hostos (y Bonilla), Eugenio Maria de 1839-1903 .... TCLC 24
See also CA 123; 131; HW 1

Houdini
See Lovecraft, H(oward) P(hillips)

Hougan, Carolyn 1943- .... CLC 34
See also CA 139

Household, Geoffrey (Edward West) 1900-1988 .... CLC 11
See also CA 77-80; 126; CANR 58; CMW 4; DLB 87; SATA 14; SATA-Obit 59

Housman, A(lfred) E(dward) 1859-1936
.... PC 2, 43; TCLC 1, 10; WLCS
See also BRW 6; CA 104; 125; DA; DA3; DAB; DAC; DAM MST, POET; DLB 19; EWL 3; EXPP; MTCW 1, 2; PAB; PFS 4, 7; RGEL 2; TEA; WP

Housman, Laurence 1865-1959 ...... TCLC 7
See also CA 106; 155; DLB 10; FANT; RGEL 2; SATA 25

Houston, Jeanne (Toyo) Wakatsuki 1934-
.... AAL
See also AAYA 49; CA 103; CAAS 16; CANR 29; LAIT 4; SATA 78

Howard, Elizabeth Jane 1923- .... CLC 7, 29
See also CA 5-8R; CANR 8, 62; CN 7

Howard, Maureen 1930- ...... CLC 5, 14, 46, 151
See also CA 53-56; CANR 31, 75; CN 7; DLBY 1983; INT CANR-31; MTCW 1, 2

Howard, Richard 1929- .... CLC 7, 10, 47
See also AITN 1; CA 85-88; CANR 25, 80; CP 7; DLB 5; INT CANR-25

Howard, Robert E(rvin) 1906-1936
.... TCLC 8
See also BPFB 2; BYA 5; CA 105; 157; FANT; SUFW 1

Howard, Warren F.
See Pohl, Frederik

Howe, Fanny (Quincy) 1940- .... CLC 47
See also CA 117; CAAE 187; CAAS 27; CANR 70, 116; CP 7; CWP; SATA-Brief 52

Howe, Irving 1920-1993 .... CLC 85
See also AMWS 6; CA 9-12R; 141; CANR 21, 50; DLB 67; EWL 3; MTCW 1, 2

Howe, Julia Ward 1819-1910 .... TCLC 21
See also CA 117; 191; DLB 1, 189, 235; FW

Howe, Susan 1937- .... CLC 72, 152
See also AMWS 4; CA 160; CP 7; CWP; DLB 120; FW; RGAL 4

Howe, Tina 1937- .... CLC 48
See also CA 109; CAD; CD 5; CWD

Howell, James 1594(?)-1666 .... LC 13
See also DLB 151

Howells, W. D.
See Howells, William Dean

Howells, William D.
See Howells, William Dean

Howells, William Dean 1837-1920 .. SSC 36; TCLC 7, 17, 41
See also AMW; CA 104; 134; CDALB 1865-1917; DLB 12, 64, 74, 79, 189; LMFS 1; MTCW 2; RGAL 4; TUS

Howes, Barbara 1914-1996 .... CLC 15
See also CA 9-12R; 151; CAAS 3; CANR 53; CP 7; SATA 5

Hrabal, Bohumil 1914-1997 ...... CLC 13, 67
See also CA 106; 156; CAAS 12; CANR 57; CWW 2; DLB 232; EWL 3; RGSF 2

Hrotsvit of Gandersheim c. 935-c. 1000
.... CMLC 29
See also DLB 148

Hsi, Chu 1130-1200 .... CMLC 42

Hsun, Lu
See Lu Hsun

Hubbard, L(afayette) Ron(ald) 1911-1986
.... CLC 43
See also CA 77-80; 118; CANR 52; CPW; DA3; DAM POP; FANT; MTCW 2; SFW 4

Huch, Ricarda (Octavia) 1864-1947
.... TCLC 13
See also CA 111; 189; DLB 66; EWL 3

Huddle, David 1942- .... CLC 49
See also CA 57-60; CAAS 20; CANR 89; DLB 130

Hudson, Jeffrey
See Crichton, (John) Michael

Hudson, W(illiam) H(enry) 1841-1922
.... TCLC 29
See also CA 115; 190; DLB 98, 153, 174; RGEL 2; SATA 35

Hueffer, Ford Madox
See Ford, Ford Madox

Hughart, Barry 1934- .... CLC 39
See also CA 137; FANT; SFW 4; SUFW 2

Hughes, Colin
See Creasey, John

Hughes, David (John) 1930- .... CLC 48
See also CA 116; 129; CN 7; DLB 14

Hughes, Edward James
See Hughes, Ted
See also DA3; DAM MST, POET

Hughes, (James Mercer) Langston
1902-1967 .... BLC 2; CLC 1, 5, 10, 15, 35, 44, 108; DC 3; HR 2; PC 1; SSC 6; WLC
See also AAYA 12; AFAW 1, 2; AMWR 1; AMWS 1; BW 1, 3; CA 1-4R; 25-28R; CANR 1, 34, 82; CDALB 1929-1941; CLR 17; DA; DA3; DAB; DAC; DAM DRAM, MST, MULT, POET; DLB 4, 7, 48, 51, 86, 228; EWL 3; EXPP; EXPS; JRDA; LAIT 3; LMFS 2; MAICYA 1, 2; MTCW 1, 2; PAB; PFS 1, 3, 6, 10, 15; RGAL 4; RGSF 2; SATA 4, 33; SSFS 4, 7; TUS; WCH; WP; YAW

Hughes, Richard (Arthur Warren)
1900-1976 .... CLC 1, 11
See also CA 5-8R; 65-68; CANR 4; DAM NOV; DLB 15, 161; EWL 3; MTCW 1; RGEL 2; SATA 8; SATA-Obit 25

Hughes, Ted 1930-1998 ...... CLC 2, 4, 9, 14, 37, 119; PC 7
See Hughes, Edward James
See also BRWR 2; BRWS 1; CA 1-4R; 171; CANR 1, 33, 66, 108; CLR 3; CP 7; DAB; DAC; DLB 40, 161; EWL 3; EXPP; MAICYA 1, 2; MTCW 1, 2; PAB; PFS 4; RGEL 2; SATA 49; SATA-Brief 27; SATA-Obit 107; TEA; YAW

Hugo, Richard
See Huch, Ricarda (Octavia)

Hugo, Richard F(ranklin) 1923-1982
.... CLC 6, 18, 32
See also AMWS 6; CA 49-52; 108; CANR 3; DAM POET; DLB 5, 206; EWL 3; PFS 17; RGAL 4

Hugo, Victor (Marie) 1802-1885 ... NCLC 3, 10, 21; PC 17; WLC
See also AAYA 28; DA; DA3; DAB; DAC; DAM DRAM, MST, NOV, POET; DLB 119, 192, 217; EFS 2; EW 7; EXPN; GFL 1789 to the Present; LAIT 1, 2; NFS 5; RGWL 2, 3; SATA 47; TWA

Huidobro, Vicente
See Huidobro Fernandez, Vicente Garcia
See also EWL 3; LAW

Huidobro Fernandez, Vicente Garcia
1893-1948 .... TCLC 31
See Huidobro, Vicente
See also CA 131; HW 1

Hulme, Keri 1947- .... CLC 39, 130
See also CA 125; CANR 69; CN 7; CP 7; CWP; EWL 3; FW; INT 125

Hulme, T(homas) E(rnest) 1883-1917
.... TCLC 21
See also BRWS 6; CA 117; 203; DLB 19

Hume, David 1711-1776 .... LC 7, 56
See also BRWS 3; DLB 104, 252; LMFS 1; TEA

Humphrey, William 1924-1997 .... CLC 45
See also AMWS 9; CA 77-80; 160; CANR 68; CN 7; CSW; DLB 6, 212, 234, 278; TCWW 2

Humphreys, Emyr Owen 1919- ...... CLC 47
See also CA 5-8R; CANR 3, 24; CN 7; DLB 15

Humphreys, Josephine 1945- .... CLC 34, 57
See also CA 121; 127; CANR 97; CSW; INT 127

Huneker, James Gibbons 1860-1921
.... TCLC 65
See also CA 193; DLB 71; RGAL 4

Hungerford, Hesba Fay
See Brinsmead, H(esba) F(ay)

Hungerford, Pixie
See Brinsmead, H(esba) F(ay)

Hunt, E(verette) Howard, (Jr.) 1918-
.... CLC 3
See also AITN 1; CA 45-48; CANR 2, 47, 103; CMW 4

Hunt, Francesca
See Holland, Isabelle (Christian)

Hunt, Howard
See Hunt, E(verette) Howard, (Jr.)

Hunt, Kyle
See Creasey, John

Hunt, (James Henry) Leigh 1784-1859
.... NCLC 1, 70
See also DAM POET; DLB 96, 110, 144; RGEL 2; TEA

Hunt, Marsha 1946- .... CLC 70
See also BW 2, 3; CA 143; CANR 79

Hunt, Violet 1866(?)-1942 .... TCLC 53
See also CA 184; DLB 162, 197

Hunter, E. Waldo
See Sturgeon, Theodore (Hamilton)

Hunter, Evan 1926- .... CLC 11, 31
See McBain, Ed
See also AAYA 39; BPFB 2; CA 5-8R; CANR 5, 38, 62, 97; CMW 4; CN 7; CPW; DAM POP; DLBY 1982; INT CANR-5; MSW; MTCW 1; SATA 25; SFW 4

Hunter, Kristin 1931-
See Lattany, Kristin (Elaine Eggleston) Hunter

Hunter, Mary
See Austin, Mary (Hunter)

Hunter, Mollie 1922- .... CLC 21
See McIlwraith, Maureen Mollie Hunter
See also AAYA 13; BYA 6; CANR 37, 78; CLR 25; DLB 161; JRDA; MAICYA 1, 2; SAAS 7; SATA 54, 106, 139; WYA; YAW

Hunter, Robert (?)-1734 .... LC 7

Hurston, Zora Neale 1891-1960 .... BLC 2; CLC 7, 30, 61; DC 12; HR 2; SSC 4; TCLC 121, 131; WLCS
See also AAYA 15; AFAW 1, 2; AMWS 6; BW 1, 3; BYA 12; CA 85-88; CANR 61; CDALBS; DA; DA3; DAC; DAM MST, MULT, NOV; DFS 6; DLB 51, 86; EWL 3; EXPN; EXPS; FW; LAIT 3; LMFS 2; MAWW; MTCW 1, 2; NFS 3; RGAL 4; RGSF 2; SSFS 1, 6, 11; TUS; YAW

Husserl, E. G.
See Husserl, Edmund (Gustav Albrecht)

Husserl, Edmund (Gustav Albrecht)
1859-1938 .... TCLC 100
See also CA 116; 133

Huston, John (Marcellus) 1906-1987
.... CLC 20
See also CA 73-76; 123; CANR 34; DLB 26

Hustvedt, Siri 1955- .... CLC 76
See also CA 137

Hutten, Ulrich von 1488-1523 .... LC 16
See also DLB 179

Huxley, Aldous (Leonard) 1894-1963
.. CLC 1, 3, 4, 5, 8, 11, 18, 35, 79; SSC 39; WLC
See also AAYA 11; BPFB 2; BRW 7; CA 85-88; CANR 44, 99; CDBLB 1914-1945; DA; DA3; DAB; DAC; DAM MST, NOV; DLB 36, 100, 162, 195, 255; EWL 3; EXPN; LAIT 5; LMFS 2; MTCW 1, 2; NFS 6; RGEL 2; SATA 63; SCFW 2; SFW 4; TEA; YAW

Huxley, T(homas) H(enry) 1825-1895
.... NCLC 67
See also DLB 57; TEA

Huysmans, Joris-Karl 1848-1907 .. TCLC 7, 69
See also CA 104; 165; DLB 123; EW 7; GFL 1789 to the Present; LMFS 2; RGWL 2, 3

Hwang, David Henry 1957- . CLC 55; DC 4
See also CA 127; 132; CAD; CANR 76; CD 5; DA3; DAM DRAM; DFS 11; DLB 212, 228; INT CA-132; MTCW 2; RGAL 4

Hyde, Anthony 1946- .... CLC 42
See Chase, Nicholas
See also CA 136; CCA 1

Hyde, Margaret O(ldroyd) 1917- ..... CLC 21
See also CA 1-4R; CANR 1, 36; CLR 23; JRDA; MAICYA 1, 2; SAAS 8; SATA 1, 42, 76, 139

Hynes, James 1956(?)- .... CLC 65
See also CA 164 CANR 105

Hypatia c. 370-415 .... CMLC 35

Ian, Janis 1951- .... CLC 21
See also CA 105; 187

Ibanez, Vicente Blasco
See Blasco Ibanez, Vicente

Ibarbourou, Juana de 1895-1979 ... HLCS 2
See also HW 1; LAW

Ibarguengoitia, Jorge 1928-1983 .... CLC 37
See also CA 124; 113; EWL 3; HW 1

Ibn Battuta, Abu Abdalla 1304-1368(?)
.... CMLC 57
See also WLIT 2

Ibsen, Henrik (Johan) 1828-1906 .... DC 2; TCLC 2, 8, 16, 37, 52; WLC
See also AAYA 46; CA 104; 141; DA; DA3; DAB; DAC; DAM DRAM, MST; DFS 1, 6, 8, 10, 11, 15, 16; EW 7; LAIT 2; RGWL 2, 3

Ibuse, Masuji 1898-1993 .... CLC 22
See Ibuse Masuji
See also CA 127; 141; MJW; RGWL 3

Ibuse Masuji
See Ibuse, Masuji
See also DLB 180; EWL 3

Ichikawa, Kon 1915- .... CLC 20
See also CA 121

Ichiyo, Higuchi 1872-1896 .... NCLC 49
See also MJW

Idle, Eric 1943-2000 .... CLC 21
See Monty Python
See also CA 116; CANR 35, 91

Ignatow, David 1914-1997 ...... CLC 4, 7, 14, 40; PC 34
See also CA 9-12R 162; CAAS 3; CANR 31, 57, 96; CP 7; DLB 5; EWL 3

Ignotus
See Strachey, (Giles) Lytton

Ihimaera, Witi 1944- .... CLC 46
See also CA 77-80; CN 7; RGSF 2

Ilf, Ilya .... TCLC 21
See Fainzilberg, Ilya Arnoldovich
See also EWL 3

Illyes, Gyula 1902-1983 .... **PC 16**
See also CA 114; 109; CDWLB 4; DLB 215; EWL 3; RGWL 2, 3
Immermann, Karl (Lebrecht) 1796-1840
.... **NCLC 4, 49**
See also DLB 133
Ince, Thomas H. 1882-1924 .... **TCLC 89**
See also IDFW 3, 4
Inchbald, Elizabeth 1753-1821 ...... **NCLC 62**
See also DLB 39, 89; RGEL 2
Inclan, Ramon (Maria) del Valle
See Valle-Inclan, Ramon (Maria) del
Infante, G(uillermo) Cabrera
See Cabrera Infante, G(uillermo)
Ingalls, Rachel (Holmes) 1940- .... **CLC 42**
See also CA 123; 127
Ingamells, Reginald Charles
See Ingamells, Rex
Ingamells, Rex 1913-1955 .... **TCLC 35**
See also CA 167; DLB 260
Inge, William (Motter) 1913-1973 ... **CLC 1, 8, 19**
See also CA 9-12R; CDALB 1941-1968; DA3; DAM DRAM; DFS 1, 5, 8; DLB 7, 249; EWL 3; MTCW 1, 2; RGAL 4; TUS
Ingelow, Jean 1820-1897 .... **NCLC 39, 107**
See also DLB 35, 163; FANT; SATA 33
Ingram, Willis J.
See Harris, Mark
Innaurato, Albert (F.) 1948(?)- . **CLC 21, 60**
See also CA 115; 122; CAD; CANR 78; CD 5; INT CA-122
Innes, Michael
See Stewart, J(ohn) I(nnes) M(ackintosh)
See also DLB 276; MSW
Innis, Harold Adams 1894-1952 ... **TCLC 77**
See also CA 181; DLB 88
Insluis, Alanus de
See Alain de Lille
Iola
See Wells-Barnett, Ida B(ell)
Ionesco, Eugene 1912-1994 .. **CLC 1, 4, 6, 9, 11, 15, 41, 86; DC 12; WLC**
See also CA 9-12R; 144; CANR 55; CWW 2; DA; DA3; DAB; DAC; DAM DRAM, MST; DFS 4, 9; EW 13; EWL 3; GFL 1789 to the Present; LMFS 2; MTCW 1, 2; RGWL 2, 3; SATA 7; SATA-Obit 79; TWA
Iqbal, Muhammad 1877-1938 .... **TCLC 28**
See also EWL 3
Ireland, Patrick
See O'Doherty, Brian
Irenaeus St. 130- .... **CMLC 42**
Irigaray, Luce 1930- .... **CLC 164**
See also CA 154; FW
Iron, Ralph
See Schreiner, Olive (Emilie Albertina)
Irving, John (Winslow) 1942- .. **CLC 13, 23, 38, 112**
See also AAYA 8; AMWS 6; BEST 89:3; BPFB 2; CA 25-28R; CANR 28, 73, 112; CN 7; CPW; DA3; DAM NOV, POP; DLB 6, 278; DLBY 1982; EWL 3; MTCW 1, 2; NFS 12, 14; RGAL 4; TUS
Irving, Washington 1783-1859 .... **NCLC 2, 19, 95; SSC 2, 37; WLC**
See also AMW; CDALB 1640-1865; DA; DA3; DAB; DAC; DAM MST; DLB 3, 11, 30, 59, 73, 74, 183, 186, 250, 254; EXPS; LAIT 1; RGAL 4; RGSF 2; SSFS 1, 8, 16; SUFW 1; TUS; WCH; YABC 2
Irwin, P. K.
See Page, P(atricia) K(athleen)
Isaacs, Jorge Ricardo 1837-1895 . **NCLC 70**
See also LAW

Isaacs, Susan 1943- .... **CLC 32**
See also BEST 89:1; BPFB 2; CA 89-92; CANR 20, 41, 65, 112; CPW; DA3; DAM POP; INT CANR-20; MTCW 1, 2
Isherwood, Christopher (William Bradshaw) 1904-1986 ... **CLC 1, 9, 11, 14, 44; SSC 56**
See also BRW 7; CA 13-16R; 117; CANR 35, 97; DA3; DAM DRAM, NOV; DLB 15, 195; DLBY 1986; EWL 3; IDTP; MTCW 1, 2; RGAL 4; RGEL 2; TUS; WLIT 4
Ishiguro, Kazuo 1954- . **CLC 27, 56, 59, 110**
See also BEST 90:2; BPFB 2; BRWS 4; CA 120; CANR 49, 95; CN 7; DA3; DAM NOV; DLB 194; EWL 3; MTCW 1, 2; NFS 13; WLIT 4
Ishikawa, Hakuhin
See Ishikawa, Takuboku
Ishikawa, Takuboku 1886(?)-1912 .... **PC 10; TCLC 15**
See Ishikawa Takuboku
See also CA 113; 153; DAM POET
Iskander, Fazil (Abdulovich) 1929-
.... **CLC 47**
See also CA 102; EWL 3
Isler, Alan (David) 1934- .... **CLC 91**
See also CA 156; CANR 105
Ivan IV 1530-1584 .... **LC 17**
Ivanov, Vyacheslav Ivanovich 1866-1949
.... **TCLC 33**
See also CA 122; EWL 3
Ivask, Ivar Vidrik 1927-1992 .... **CLC 14**
See also CA 37-40R; 139; CANR 24
Ives, Morgan
See Bradley, Marion Zimmer
See also GLL 1
Izumi Shikibu c. 973-c. 1034 .... **CMLC 33**
J .... **CLC 24, 83; TCLC 135**
See also CA 130; 97-100; CANR 66; EW 13; EWL 3; GFL 1789 to the Present; MTCW 1, 2; TWA
J. R. S.
See Gogarty, Oliver St. John
Jabran, Kahlil
See Gibran, Kahlil
Jabran, Khalil
See Gibran, Kahlil
Jackson, Daniel
See Wingrove, David (John)
Jackson, Helen Hunt 1830-1885 ... **NCLC 90**
See also DLB 42, 47, 186, 189; RGAL 4
Jackson, Jesse 1908-1983 .... **CLC 12**
See also BW 1; CA 25-28R; 109; CANR 27; CLR 28; CWRI 5; MAICYA 1, 2; SATA 2, 29; SATA-Obit 48
Jackson, Laura (Riding) 1901-1991 ... **PC 44**
See Riding, Laura
See also CA 65-68; 135; CANR 28, 89; DLB 48
Jackson, Sam
See Trumbo, Dalton
Jackson, Sara
See Wingrove, David (John)
Jackson, Shirley 1919-1965 .... **CLC 11, 60, 87; SSC 9, 39; WLC**
See also AAYA 9; AMWS 9; BPFB 2; CA 1-4R; 25-28R; CANR 4, 52; CDALB 1941-1968; DA; DA3; DAC; DAM MST; DLB 6, 234; EXPS; HGG; LAIT 4; MTCW 2; RGAL 4; RGSF 2; SATA 2; SSFS 1; SUFW 1, 2
Jacob, (Cyprien-)Max 1876-1944 ... **TCLC 6**
See also CA 104; 193; DLB 258; EWL 3; GFL 1789 to the Present; GLL 2; RGWL 2, 3

Jacobs, Harriet A(nn) 1813(?)-1897
.... **NCLC 67**
See also AFAW 1, 2; DLB 239; FW; LAIT 2; RGAL 4
Jacobs, Jim 1942- .... **CLC 12**
See also CA 97-100; INT 97-100
Jacobs, W(illiam) W(ymark) 1863-1943
.... **TCLC 22**
See also CA 121; 167; DLB 135; EXPS; HGG; RGEL 2; RGSF 2; SSFS 2; SUFW 1
Jacobsen, Jens Peter 1847-1885 ... **NCLC 34**
Jacobsen, Josephine 1908- .... **CLC 48, 102**
See also CA 33-36R; CAAS 18; CANR 23, 48; CCA 1; CP 7; DLB 244
Jacobson, Dan 1929- .... **CLC 4, 14**
See also AFW; CA 1-4R; CANR 2, 25, 66; CN 7; DLB 14, 207, 225; EWL 3; MTCW 1; RGSF 2
Jacqueline
See Carpentier (y Valmont), Alejo
Jagger, Mick 1944- .... **CLC 17**
Jahiz, al- c. 780-c. 869 .... **CMLC 25**
Jakes, John (William) 1932- .... **CLC 29**
See also AAYA 32; BEST 89:4; BPFB 2; CA 57-60; CANR 10, 43, 66, 111; CPW; CSW; DA3; DAM NOV, POP; DLB 278; DLBY 1983; FANT; INT CANR-10; MTCW 1, 2; RHW; SATA 62; SFW 4; TCWW 2
James I 1394-1437 .... **LC 20**
See also RGEL 2
James, Andrew
See Kirkup, James
James, C(yril) L(ionel) R(obert) 1901-1989
.... **BLCS; CLC 33**
See also BW 2; CA 117; 125; 128; CANR 62; DLB 125; MTCW 1
James, Daniel (Lewis) 1911-1988
See Santiago, Danny
See also CA 174; 125
James, Dynely
See Mayne, William (James Carter)
James, Henry Sr. 1811-1882 .... **NCLC 53**
James, Henry 1843-1916 .... **SSC 8, 32, 47; TCLC 2, 11, 24, 40, 47, 64; WLC**
See also AMW; AMWC 1; AMWR 1; BPFB 2; BRW 6; CA 104; 132; CDALB 1865-1917; DA; DA3; DAB; DAC; DAM MST, NOV; DLB 12, 71, 74, 189; DLBD 13; EWL 3; EXPS; HGG; LAIT 2; MTCW 1, 2; NFS 12, 16; RGAL 4; RGEL 2; RGSF 2; SSFS 9; SUFW 1; TUS
James, M. R.
See James, Montague (Rhodes)
See also DLB 156, 201
James, Montague (Rhodes) 1862-1936
.... **SSC 16; TCLC 6**
See James, M. R.
See also CA 104; 203; HGG; RGEL 2; RGSF 2; SUFW 1
James, P. D. .... **CLC 18, 46, 122**
See White, Phyllis Dorothy James
See also BEST 90:2; BPFB 2; BRWS 4; CDBLB 1960 to Present; DLB 87, 276; DLBD 17; MSW
James, Philip
See Moorcock, Michael (John)
James, Samuel
See Stephens, James
James, Seumas
See Stephens, James
James, Stephen
See Stephens, James
James, William 1842-1910 .... **TCLC 15, 32**
See also AMW; CA 109; 193; DLB 270; RGAL 4
Jameson, Anna 1794-1860 .... **NCLC 43**
See also DLB 99, 166

Jameson, Fredric (R.) 1934- .... **CLC 142**
See also CA 196; DLB 67; LMFS 2

Jami, Nur al-Din 'Abd al-Rahman
1414-1492 .... **LC 9**

Jammes, Francis 1868-1938 .... **TCLC 75**
See also CA 198; EWL 3; GFL 1789 to the Present

Jandl, Ernst 1925-2000 .... **CLC 34**
See also CA 200; EWL 3

Janowitz, Tama 1957- .... **CLC 43, 145**
See also CA 106; CANR 52, 89; CN 7; CPW; DAM POP

Japrisot, Sebastien 1931- .... **CLC 90**
See Rossi, Jean Baptiste
See also CMW 4

Jarrell, Randall 1914-1965 .. **CLC 1, 2, 6, 9, 13, 49; PC 41**
See also AMW; BYA 5; CA 5-8R; 25-28R; CABS 2; CANR 6, 34; CDALB 1941-1968; CLR 6; CWRI 5; DA3; DAM POET; DLB 48, 52; EWL 3; EXPP; MAICYA 1, 2; MTCW 1, 2; PAB; PFS 2; RGAL 4; SATA 7

Jarry, Alfred 1873-1907 .. **SSC 20; TCLC 2, 14**
See also CA 104; 153; DA3; DAM DRAM; DFS 8; DLB 192, 258; EW 9; EWL 3; GFL 1789 to the Present; RGWL 2, 3; TWA

Jarvis, E. K.
See Ellison, Harlan (Jay)

Jawien, Andrzej
See John Paul II, Pope

Jaynes, Roderick
See Coen, Ethan

Jeake, Samuel, Jr.
See Aiken, Conrad (Potter)

Jean Paul 1763-1825 .... **NCLC 7**

Jefferies, (John) Richard 1848-1887
.... **NCLC 47**
See also DLB 98, 141; RGEL 2; SATA 16; SFW 4

Jeffers, (John) Robinson 1887-1962
...... **CLC 2, 3, 11, 15, 54; PC 17; WLC**
See also AMWS 2; CA 85-88; CANR 35; CDALB 1917-1929; DA; DAC; DAM MST, POET; DLB 45, 212; EWL 3; MTCW 1, 2; PAB; PFS 3, 4; RGAL 4

Jefferson, Janet
See Mencken, H(enry) L(ouis)

Jefferson, Thomas 1743-1826 .... **NCLC 11, 103**
See also ANW; CDALB 1640-1865; DA3; DLB 31, 183; LAIT 1; RGAL 4

Jeffrey, Francis 1773-1850 .... **NCLC 33**
See Francis, Lord Jeffrey

Jelakowitch, Ivan
See Heijermans, Herman

Jelinek, Elfriede 1946- .... **CLC 169**
See also CA 154; DLB 85; FW

Jellicoe, (Patricia) Ann 1927- .... **CLC 27**
See also CA 85-88; CBD; CD 5; CWD; CWRI 5; DLB 13, 233; FW

Jemyma
See Holley, Marietta

Jen, Gish .... **CLC 70**
See Jen, Lillian

Jen, Lillian 1956(?)-
See Jen, Gish
See also CA 135; CANR 89

Jenkins, (John) Robin 1912- .... **CLC 52**
See also CA 1-4R; CANR 1; CN 7; DLB 14, 271

Jennings, Elizabeth (Joan) 1926-2001
.... **CLC 5, 14, 131**
See also BRWS 5; CA 61-64; 200; CAAS 5; CANR 8, 39, 66; CP 7; CWP; DLB 27; EWL 3; MTCW 1; SATA 66

Jennings, Waylon 1937- .... **CLC 21**

Jensen, Johannes V(ilhelm) 1873-1950
.... **TCLC 41**
See also CA 170; DLB 214; EWL 3; RGWL 3

Jensen, Laura (Linnea) 1948- .... **CLC 37**
See also CA 103

Jerome, Saint 345-420 .... **CMLC 30**
See also RGWL 3

Jerome, Jerome K(lapka) 1859-1927
.... **TCLC 23**
See also CA 119; 177; DLB 10, 34, 135; RGEL 2

Jerrold, Douglas William 1803-1857
.... **NCLC 2**
See also DLB 158, 159; RGEL 2

Jewett, (Theodora) Sarah Orne 1849-1909
.... **SSC 6, 44; TCLC 1, 22**
See also AMW; AMWR 2; CA 108; 127; CANR 71; DLB 12, 74, 221; EXPS; FW; MAWW; NFS 15; RGAL 4; RGSF 2; SATA 15; SSFS 4

Jewsbury, Geraldine (Endsor) 1812-1880
.... **NCLC 22**
See also DLB 21

Jhabvala, Ruth Prawer 1927- ...... **CLC 4, 8, 29, 94, 138**
See also BRWS 5; CA 1-4R; CANR 2, 29, 51, 74, 91; CN 7; DAB; DAM NOV; DLB 139, 194; EWL 3; IDFW 3, 4; INT CANR-29; MTCW 1, 2; RGSF 2; RGWL 2; RHW; TEA

Jibran, Kahlil
See Gibran, Kahlil

Jibran, Khalil
See Gibran, Kahlil

Jiles, Paulette 1943- .... **CLC 13, 58**
See also CA 101; CANR 70; CWP

Jimenez (Mantecon), Juan Ramon
1881-1958 .... **HLC 1; PC 7; TCLC 4**
See also CA 104; 131; CANR 74; DAM MULT, POET; DLB 134; EW 9; EWL 3; HW 1; MTCW 1, 2; RGWL 2, 3

Jimenez, Ramon
See Jimenez (Mantecon), Juan Ramon

Jimenez Mantecon, Juan
See Jimenez (Mantecon), Juan Ramon

Jin, Ha .... **CLC 109**
See Jin, Xuefei
See also CA 152; DLB 244; SSFS 17

Jin, Xuefei 1956-
See Jin, Ha
See also CANR 91

Joel, Billy .... **CLC 26**
See Joel, William Martin

Joel, William Martin 1949-
See Joel, Billy
See also CA 108

John, Saint 107th cent. -100 .... **CMLC 27**

John of the Cross, St. 1542-1591 .... **LC 18**
See also RGWL 2, 3

John Paul II, Pope 1920- .... **CLC 128**
See also CA 106; 133

Johnson, B(ryan) S(tanley William)
1933-1973 .... **CLC 6, 9**
See also CA 9-12R; 53-56; CANR 9; DLB 14, 40; EWL 3; RGEL 2

Johnson, Benjamin F., of Boone
See Riley, James Whitcomb

Johnson, Charles (Richard) 1948- ... **BLC 2; CLC 7, 51, 65, 163**
See also AFAW 2; AMWS 6; BW 2, 3; CA 116; CAAS 18; CANR 42, 66, 82; CN 7; DAM MULT; DLB 33, 278; MTCW 2; RGAL 4; SSFS 16

Johnson, Charles S(purgeon) 1893-1956
.... **HR 3**
See also BW 1, 3; CA 125; CANR 82; DLB 51, 91

Johnson, Denis 1949- ..... **CLC 52, 160; SSC 56**
See also CA 117; 121; CANR 71, 99; CN 7; DLB 120

Johnson, Diane 1934- .... **CLC 5, 13, 48**
See also BPFB 2; CA 41-44R; CANR 17, 40, 62, 95; CN 7; DLBY 1980; INT CANR-17; MTCW 1

Johnson, E. Pauline 1861-1913 .... **NNAL**
See also CA 150; DAC; DAM MULT; DLB 92, 175

Johnson, Eyvind (Olof Verner) 1900-1976
.... **CLC 14**
See also CA 73-76; 69-72; CANR 34, 101; DLB 259; EW 12; EWL 3

Johnson, Fenton 1883-1958 .... **BLC 2**
See also BW 1; CA 118; 124; DAM MULT; DLB 45, 50

Johnson, Georgia Douglas (Camp)
1880-1966 .... **HR 3**
See also BW 1; CA 125; DLB 51, 249; WP

Johnson, Helene 1907-1995 .... **HR 3**
See also CA 181; DLB 51; WP

Johnson, J. R.
See James, C(yril) L(ionel) R(obert)

Johnson, James Weldon 1871-1938 . **BLC 2; HR 3; PC 24; TCLC 3, 19**
See also AFAW 1, 2; BW 1, 3; CA 104; 125; CANR 82; CDALB 1917-1929; CLR 32; DA3; DAM MULT, POET; DLB 51; EWL 3; EXPP; LMFS 2; MTCW 1, 2; PFS 1; RGAL 4; SATA 31; TUS

Johnson, Joyce 1935- .... **CLC 58**
See also BG 3; CA 125; 129; CANR 102

Johnson, Judith (Emlyn) 1936- .. **CLC 7, 15**
See Sherwin, Judith Johnson
See also CA 25-28R; 153; CANR 34

Johnson, Lionel (Pigot) 1867-1902
.... **TCLC 19**
See also CA 117; DLB 19; RGEL 2

Johnson, Marguerite Annie
See Angelou, Maya

Johnson, Mel
See Malzberg, Barry N(athaniel)

Johnson, Pamela Hansford 1912-1981
.... **CLC 1, 7, 27**
See also CA 1-4R; 134; CANR 2, 28; DLB 15; MTCW 1, 2; RGEL 2

Johnson, Paul (Bede) 1928- .... **CLC 147**
See also BEST 89:4; CA 17-20R; CANR 34, 62, 100

Johnson, Robert .... **CLC 70**

Johnson, Robert 1911(?)-1938 .... **TCLC 69**
See also BW 3; CA 174

Johnson, Samuel 1709-1784 .... **LC 15, 52; WLC**
See also BRW 3; BRWR 1; CDBLB 1660-1789; DA; DAB; DAC; DAM MST; DLB 39, 95, 104, 142, 213; LMFS 1; RGEL 2; TEA

Johnson, Uwe 1934-1984 . **CLC 5, 10, 15, 40**
See also CA 1-4R; 112; CANR 1, 39; CD-WLB 2; DLB 75; EWL 3; MTCW 1, 2; RGWL 2, 3

Johnston, Basil H. 1929- .... **NNAL**
See also CA 69-72; CANR 11, 28, 66; DAC; DAM MULT; DLB 60

Johnston, George (Benson) 1913- ... **CLC 51**
See also CA 1-4R; CANR 5, 20; CP 7; DLB 88

Johnston, Jennifer (Prudence) 1930-
.... **CLC 7, 150**
See also CA 85-88; CANR 92; CN 7; DLB 14

Joinville, Jean de 1224(?)-1317 ..... **CMLC 38**

Jolley, (Monica) Elizabeth 1923- ... **CLC 46; SSC 19**
See also CA 127; CAAS 13; CANR 59; CN 7; EWL 3; RGSF 2

Jones, Arthur Llewellyn 1863-1947
See Machen, Arthur
See also CA 104; 179; HGG

Jones, D(ouglas) G(ordon) 1929- .... **CLC 10**
See also CA 29-32R; CANR 13, 90; CP 7; DLB 53

Jones, David (Michael) 1895-1974 ... **CLC 2, 4, 7, 13, 42**
See also BRW 6; BRWS 7; CA 9-12R; 53-56; CANR 28; CDBLB 1945-1960; DLB 20, 100; EWL 3; MTCW 1; PAB; RGEL 2

Jones, David Robert 1947-
See Bowie, David
See also CA 103; CANR 104

Jones, Diana Wynne 1934- .... **CLC 26**
See also AAYA 12; BYA 6, 7, 9, 11, 13; CA 49-52; CANR 4, 26, 56; CLR 23; DLB 161; FANT; JRDA; MAICYA 1, 2; SAAS 7; SATA 9, 70, 108; SFW 4; SUFW 2; YAW

Jones, Edward P. 1950- .... **CLC 76**
See also BW 2, 3; CA 142; CANR 79; CSW

Jones, Gayl 1949- ..... **BLC 2; CLC 6, 9, 131**
See also AFAW 1, 2; BW 2, 3; CA 77-80; CANR 27, 66; CN 7; CSW; DA3; DAM MULT; DLB 33, 278; MTCW 1, 2; RGAL 4

Jones, James 1921-1977 .... **CLC 1, 3, 10, 39**
See also AITN 1, 2; AMWS 11; BPFB 2; CA 1-4R; 69-72; CANR 6; DLB 2, 143; DLBD 17; DLBY 1998; EWL 3; MTCW 1; RGAL 4

Jones, John J.
See Lovecraft, H(oward) P(hillips)

Jones, LeRoi .... **CLC 1, 2, 3, 5, 10, 14**
See Baraka, Amiri
See also MTCW 2

Jones, Louis B. 1953- .... **CLC 65**
See also CA 141; CANR 73

Jones, Madison (Percy, Jr.) 1925- ..... **CLC 4**
See also CA 13-16R; CAAS 11; CANR 7, 54, 83; CN 7; CSW; DLB 152

Jones, Mervyn 1922- .... **CLC 10, 52**
See also CA 45-48; CAAS 5; CANR 1, 91; CN 7; MTCW 1

Jones, Mick 1956(?)- .... **CLC 30**

Jones, Nettie (Pearl) 1941- .... **CLC 34**
See also BW 2; CA 137; CAAS 20; CANR 88

Jones, Peter 1802-1856 .... **NNAL**

Jones, Preston 1936-1979 .... **CLC 10**
See also CA 73-76; 89-92; DLB 7

Jones, Robert F(rancis) 1934- .... **CLC 7**
See also CA 49-52; CANR 2, 61

Jones, Rod 1953- .... **CLC 50**
See also CA 128

Jones, Terence Graham Parry 1942-
.... **CLC 21**
See Jones, Terry; Monty Python
See also CA 112; 116; CANR 35, 93; INT 116; SATA 127

Jones, Terry
See Jones, Terence Graham Parry
See also SATA 67; SATA-Brief 51

Jones, Thom (Douglas) 1945(?)- .... **CLC 81; SSC 56**
See also CA 157; CANR 88; DLB 244

Jong, Erica 1942- .... **CLC 4, 6, 8, 18, 83**
See also AITN 1; AMWS 5; BEST 90:2; BPFB 2; CA 73-76; CANR 26, 52, 75; CN 7; CP 7; CPW; DA3; DAM NOV, POP; DLB 2, 5, 28, 152; FW; INT CANR-26; MTCW 1, 2

Jonson, Ben(jamin) 1572(?)-1637 .... **DC 4; LC 6, 33; PC 17; WLC**
See also BRW 1; BRWC 1; BRWR 1; CDBLB Before 1660; DA; DAB; DAC; DAM DRAM, MST, POET; DFS 4, 10; DLB 62, 121; LMFS 1; RGEL 2; TEA; WLIT 3

Jordan, June (Meyer) 1936-2002
.... **BLCS; CLC 5, 11, 23, 114; PC 38**
See also AAYA 2; AFAW 1, 2; BW 2, 3; CA 33-36R; 206; CANR 25, 70, 114; CLR 10; CP 7; CWP; DAM MULT, POET; DLB 38; GLL 2; LAIT 5; MAICYA 1, 2; MTCW 1; SATA 4, 136; YAW

Jordan, Neil (Patrick) 1950- .... **CLC 110**
See also CA 124; 130; CANR 54; CN 7; GLL 2; INT 130

Jordan, Pat(rick M.) 1941- .... **CLC 37**
See also CA 33-36R

Jorgensen, Ivar
See Ellison, Harlan (Jay)

Jorgenson, Ivar
See Silverberg, Robert

Joseph, George Ghevarughese .... **CLC 70**

Josephson, Mary
See O'Doherty, Brian

Josephus, Flavius c. 37-100 .... **CMLC 13**
See also AW 2; DLB 176

Josiah Allen's Wife
See Holley, Marietta

Josipovici, Gabriel (David) 1940- .... **CLC 6, 43, 153**
See also CA 37-40R; CAAS 8; CANR 47, 84; CN 7; DLB 14

Joubert, Joseph 1754-1824 .... **NCLC 9**

Jouve, Pierre Jean 1887-1976 .... **CLC 47**
See also CA 65-68; DLB 258; EWL 3

Jovine, Francesco 1902-1950 .... **TCLC 79**
See also DLB 264; EWL 3

Joyce, James (Augustine Aloysius) 1882-1941 ... **DC 16; PC 22; SSC 3, 26, 44; TCLC 3, 8, 16, 35, 52; WLC**
See also AAYA 42; BRW 7; BRWC 1; BRWR 1; BYA 11, 13; CA 104; 126; CDBLB 1914-1945; DA; DA3; DAB; DAC; DAM MST, NOV, POET; DLB 10, 19, 36, 162, 247; EWL 3; EXPN; EXPS; LAIT 3; LMFS 1, 2; MTCW 1; NFS 7; RGSF 2; SSFS 1; TEA; WLIT 4

Jozsef, Attila 1905-1937 .... **TCLC 22**
See also CA 116; CDWLB 4; DLB 215; EWL 3

Juana Ines de la Cruz, Sor 1651(?)-1695
.... **HLCS 1; LC 5; PC 24**
See also FW; LAW; RGWL 2, 3; WLIT 1

Juana Inez de La Cruz, Sor
See Juana Ines de la Cruz, Sor

Judd, Cyril
See Kornbluth, C(yril) M.; Pohl, Frederik

Juenger, Ernst 1895-1998 .... **CLC 125**
See Junger, Ernst
See also CA 101; 167; CANR 21, 47, 106; DLB 56

Julian of Norwich 1342(?)-1416(?) ..... **LC 6, 52**
See also DLB 146; LMFS 1

Julius Caesar 100B.C.-44B.C.
See Caesar, Julius
See also CDWLB 1; DLB 211

Junger, Ernst
See Juenger, Ernst
See also CDWLB 2; EWL 3; RGWL 2, 3

Junger, Sebastian 1962- .... **CLC 109**
See also AAYA 28; CA 165

Juniper, Alex
See Hospital, Janette Turner

Junius
See Luxemburg, Rosa

Just, Ward (Swift) 1935- .... **CLC 4, 27**
See also CA 25-28R; CANR 32, 87; CN 7; INT CANR-32

Justice, Donald (Rodney) 1925- . **CLC 6, 19, 102**
See also AMWS 7; CA 5-8R; CANR 26, 54, 74; CP 7; CSW; DAM POET; DLBY 1983; EWL 3; INT CANR-26; MTCW 2; PFS 14

Juvenal c. 60-c. 130 .... **CMLC 8**
See also AW 2; CDWLB 1; DLB 211; RGWL 2, 3

Juvenis
See Bourne, Randolph S(illiman)

K., Alice
See Knapp, Caroline

Kabakov, Sasha .... **CLC 59**

Kacew, Romain 1914-1980
See Gary, Romain
See also CA 108; 102

Kadare, Ismail 1936- .... **CLC 52**
See also CA 161; EWL 3; RGWL 3

Kadohata, Cynthia .... **CLC 59, 122**
See also CA 140

Kafka, Franz 1883-1924 . **SSC 5, 29, 35, 60; TCLC 2, 6, 13, 29, 47, 53, 112; WLC**
See also AAYA 31; BPFB 2; CA 105; 126; CDWLB 2; DA; DA3; DAB; DAC; DAM MST, NOV; DLB 81; EW 9; EWL 3; EXPS; LMFS 2; MTCW 1, 2; NFS 7; RGSF 2; RGWL 2, 3; SFW 4; SSFS 3, 7, 12; TWA

Kahanovitsch, Pinkhes
See Der Nister

Kahn, Roger 1927- .... **CLC 30**
See also CA 25-28R; CANR 44, 69; DLB 171; SATA 37

Kain, Saul
See Sassoon, Siegfried (Lorraine)

Kaiser, Georg 1878-1945 .... **TCLC 9**
See also CA 106; 190; CDWLB 2; DLB 124; EWL 3; LMFS 2; RGWL 2, 3

Kaledin, Sergei .... **CLC 59**

Kaletski, Alexander 1946- .... **CLC 39**
See also CA 118; 143

Kalidasa fl. c. 400-455 .... **CMLC 9; PC 22**
See also RGWL 2, 3

Kallman, Chester (Simon) 1921-1975
.... **CLC 2**
See also CA 45-48; 53-56; CANR 3

Kaminsky, Melvin 1926-
See Brooks, Mel
See also CA 65-68; CANR 16

Kaminsky, Stuart M(elvin) 1934- ... **CLC 59**
See also CA 73-76; CANR 29, 53, 89; CMW 4

Kandinsky, Wassily 1866-1944 ..... **TCLC 92**
See also CA 118; 155

Kane, Francis
See Robbins, Harold

Kane, Henry 1918-
See Queen, Ellery
See also CA 156; CMW 4

Kane, Paul
See Simon, Paul (Frederick)

Kanin, Garson 1912-1999 .... **CLC 22**
See also AITN 1; CA 5-8R; 177; CAD; CANR 7, 78; DLB 7; IDFW 3, 4

Kaniuk, Yoram 1930- .... **CLC 19**
See also CA 134

Kant, Immanuel 1724-1804 .... **NCLC 27, 67**
See also DLB 94

Kantor, MacKinlay 1904-1977 .... **CLC 7**
See also CA 61-64; 73-76; CANR 60, 63; DLB 9, 102; MTCW 2; RHW; TCWW 2

Kanze Motokiyo
See Zeami

Kaplan, David Michael 1946- .... **CLC 50**
See also CA 187

Kaplan, James 1951- .... **CLC 59**
See also CA 135

Karadzic, Vuk Stefanovic 1787-1864
.... **NCLC 115**
See also CDWLB 4; DLB 147

Karageorge, Michael
See Anderson, Poul (William)

Karamzin, Nikolai Mikhailovich 1766-1826
.... **NCLC 3**
See also DLB 150; RGSF 2

Karapanou, Margarita 1946- .... **CLC 13**
See also CA 101

Karinthy, Frigyes 1887-1938 .... **TCLC 47**
See also CA 170; DLB 215; EWL 3

Karl, Frederick R(obert) 1927- .... **CLC 34**
See also CA 5-8R; CANR 3, 44

Kastel, Warren
See Silverberg, Robert

Kataev, Evgeny Petrovich 1903-1942
See Petrov, Evgeny
See also CA 120

Kataphusin
See Ruskin, John

Katz, Steve 1935- .... **CLC 47**
See also CA 25-28R; CAAS 14, 64; CANR 12; CN 7; DLBY 1983

Kauffman, Janet 1945- .... **CLC 42**
See also CA 117; CANR 43, 84; DLB 218; DLBY 1986

Kaufman, Bob (Garnell) 1925-1986
.... **CLC 49**
See also BG 3; BW 1; CA 41-44R; 118; CANR 22; DLB 16, 41

Kaufman, George S. 1889-1961 ..... **CLC 38; DC 17**
See also CA 108; 93-96; DAM DRAM; DFS 1, 10; DLB 7; INT CA-108; MTCW 2; RGAL 4; TUS

Kaufman, Sue .... **CLC 3, 8**
See Barondess, Sue K(aufman)

Kavafis, Konstantinos Petrou 1863-1933
See Cavafy, C(onstantine) P(eter)
See also CA 104

Kavan, Anna 1901-1968 .... **CLC 5, 13, 82**
See also BRWS 7; CA 5-8R; CANR 6, 57; DLB 255; MTCW 1; RGEL 2; SFW 4

Kavanagh, Dan
See Barnes, Julian (Patrick)

Kavanagh, Julie 1952- .... **CLC 119**
See also CA 163

Kavanagh, Patrick (Joseph) 1904-1967
.... **CLC 22; PC 33**
See also BRWS 7; CA 123; 25-28R; DLB 15, 20; EWL 3; MTCW 1; RGEL 2

Kawabata, Yasunari 1899-1972 ... **CLC 2, 5, 9, 18, 107; SSC 17**
See Kawabata Yasunari
See also CA 93-96; 33-36R; CANR 88; DAM MULT; MJW; MTCW 2; RGSF 2; RGWL 2, 3

Kawabata Yasunari
See Kawabata, Yasunari
See also DLB 180; EWL 3

Kaye, M(ary) M(argaret) 1909- ...... **CLC 28**
See also CA 89-92; CANR 24, 60, 102; MTCW 1, 2; RHW; SATA 62

Kaye, Mollie
See Kaye, M(ary) M(argaret)

Kaye-Smith, Sheila 1887-1956 ...... **TCLC 20**
See also CA 118; 203; DLB 36

Kaymor, Patrice Maguilene
See Senghor, Leopold Sedar

Kazakov, Yuri Pavlovich 1927-1982
.... **SSC 43**
See Kazakov, Yury
See also CA 5-8R; CANR 36; MTCW 1; RGSF 2

Kazakov, Yury
See Kazakov, Yuri Pavlovich
See also EWL 3

Kazan, Elia 1909- .... **CLC 6, 16, 63**
See also CA 21-24R; CANR 32, 78

Kazantzakis, Nikos 1883(?)-1957 .. **TCLC 2, 5, 33**
See also BPFB 2; CA 105; 132; DA3; EW 9; EWL 3; MTCW 1, 2 RGWL 2, 3

Kazin, Alfred 1915-1998 ... **CLC 34, 38, 119**
See also AMWS 8; CA 1-4R; CAAS 7; CANR 1, 45, 79; DLB 67; EWL 3

Keane, Mary Nesta (Skrine) 1904-1996
See Keane, Molly
See also CA 108; 114; 151; CN 7; RHW

Keane, Molly .... **CLC 31**
See Keane, Mary Nesta (Skrine)
See also INT 114

Keates, Jonathan 1946(?)- .... **CLC 34**
See also CA 163

Keaton, Buster 1895-1966 .... **CLC 20**
See also CA 194

Keats, John 1795-1821 .... **NCLC 8, 73, 121; PC 1; WLC**
See also BRW 4; BRWR 2; CDBLB 1789-1832; DA; DA3; DAB; DAC; DAM MST, POET; DLB 96, 110; EXPP; LMFS 1; PAB; PFS 1, 2, 3, 9, 16; RGEL 2; TEA; WLIT 3; WP

Keble, John 1792-1866 .... **NCLC 87**
See also DLB 32, 55; RGEL 2

Keene, Donald 1922- .... **CLC 34**
See also CA 1-4R; CANR 5

Keillor, Garrison .... **CLC 40, 115**
See Keillor, Gary (Edward)
See also AAYA 2; BEST 89:3; BPFB 2; DLBY 1987; EWL 3; SATA 58; TUS

Keillor, Gary (Edward) 1942-
See Keillor, Garrison
See also CA 111; 117; CANR 36, 59; CPW; DA3; DAM POP; MTCW 1, 2

Keith, Carlos
See Lewton, Val

Keith, Michael
See Hubbard, L(afayette) Ron(ald)

Keller, Gottfried 1819-1890 .. **NCLC 2; SSC 26**
See also CDWLB 2; DLB 129; EW; RGSF 2; RGWL 2, 3

Keller, Nora Okja 1965- .... **CLC 109**
See also CA 187

Kellerman, Jonathan 1949- .... **CLC 44**
See also AAYA 35; BEST 90:1; CA 106; CANR 29, 51; CMW 4; CPW; DA3; DAM POP; INT CANR-29

Kelley, William Melvin 1937- .... **CLC 22**
See also BW 1; CA 77-80; CANR 27, 83; CN 7; DLB 33; EWL 3

Kellogg, Marjorie 1922- .... **CLC 2**
See also CA 81-84

Kellow, Kathleen
See Hibbert, Eleanor Alice Burford

Kelly, M(ilton) T(errence) 1947- ...... **CLC 55**
See also CA 97-100; CAAS 22; CANR 19, 43, 84; CN 7

Kelly, Robert 1935- .... **SSC 50**
See also CA 17-20R; CAAS 19; CANR 47; CP 7; DLB 5, 130, 165

Kelman, James 1946- .... **CLC 58, 86**
See also BRWS 5; CA 148; CANR 85; CN 7; DLB 194; RGSF 2; WLIT 4

Kemal, Yashar 1923- .... **CLC 14, 29**
See also CA 89-92; CANR 44; CWW 2

Kemble, Fanny 1809-1893 .... **NCLC 18**
See also DLB 32

Kemelman, Harry 1908-1996 .... **CLC 2**
See also AITN 1; BPFB 2; CA 9-12R; 155; CANR 6, 71; CMW 4; DLB 28

Kempe, Margery 1373(?)-1440(?) .. **LC 6, 56**
See also DLB 146; RGEL 2

Kempis, Thomas a 1380-1471 .... **LC 11**

Kendall, Henry 1839-1882 .... **NCLC 12**
See also DLB 230

Keneally, Thomas (Michael) 1935- .. **CLC 5, 8, 10, 14, 19, 27, 43, 117**
See also BRWS 4; CA 85-88; CANR 10, 50, 74; CN 7; CPW; DA3; DAM NOV; EWL 3; MTCW 1, 2; NFS 17; RGEL 2; RHW

Kennedy, Adrienne (Lita) 1931- ...... **BLC 2; CLC 66; DC 5**
See also AFAW 2; BW 2, 3; CA 103; CAAS 20; CABS 3; CANR 26, 53, 82; CD 5; DAM MULT; DFS 9; DLB 38; FW

Kennedy, John Pendleton 1795-1870
.... **NCLC 2**
See also DLB 3, 248, 254; RGAL 4

Kennedy, Joseph Charles 1929-
See Kennedy, X. J.
See also CA 1-4R; CAAE 201; CANR 4, 30, 40; CP 7; CWRI 5; MAICYA 2; MAICYAS 1; SATA 14, 86; SATA-Essay 130

Kennedy, William 1928- .. **CLC 6, 28, 34, 53**
See also AAYA 1; AMWS 7; BPFB 2; CA 85-88; CANR 14, 31, 76; CN 7; DA3; DAM NOV; DLB 143; DLBY 1985; EWL 3; INT CANR-31; MTCW 1, 2; SATA 57

Kennedy, X. J. .... **CLC 8, 42**
See Kennedy, Joseph Charles
See also CAAS 9; CLR 27; DLB 5; SAAS 22

Kenny, Maurice (Francis) 1929- .... **CLC 87; NNAL**
See also CA 144; CAAS 22; DAM MULT; DLB 175

Kent, Kelvin
See Kuttner, Henry

Kenton, Maxwell
See Southern, Terry

Kenyon, Robert O.
See Kuttner, Henry

Kepler, Johannes 1571-1630 .... **LC 45**

Ker, Jill
See Conway, Jill K(er)

Kerkow, H. C.
See Lewton, Val

Kerouac, Jack 1922-1969 ..... **CLC 1, 2, 3, 5, 14, 29, 61; TCLC 117; WLC**
See Kerouac, Jean-Louis Lebris de
See also AAYA 25; AMWC 1; AMWS 3; BG 3; BPFB 2; CDALB 1941-1968; CPW; DLB 2, 16, 237; DLBD 3; DLBY 1995; EWL 3; GLL 1; LMFS 2; MTCW 2; NFS 8; RGAL 4; TUS; WP

Kerouac, Jean-Louis Lebris de 1922-1969
See Kerouac, Jack
See also AITN 1; CA 5-8R; 25-28R; CANR 26, 54, 95; DA; DA3; DAB; DAC; DAM MST, NOV, POET, POP; MTCW 1, 2

Kerr, Jean 1923- .... **CLC 22**
See also CA 5-8R; CANR 7; INT CANR-7

Kerr, M. E. .... **CLC 12, 35**
See Meaker, Marijane (Agnes)
See also AAYA 2, 23; BYA 1, 7, 8; CLR 29; SAAS 1; WYA

Kerr, Robert .... **CLC 55**

Kerrigan, (Thomas) Anthony 1918-
.... **CLC 4, 6**
See also CA 49-52; CAAS 11; CANR 4

Kerry, Lois
See Duncan, Lois

Kesey, Ken (Elton) 1935-2001 . **CLC 1, 3, 6, 11, 46, 64; WLC**
See also AAYA 25; BG 3; BPFB 2; CA 1-4R; 204; CANR 22, 38, 66; CDALB 1968-1988; CN 7; CPW; DA; DA3; DAB; DAC; DAM MST, NOV, POP; DLB 2, 16, 206; EWL 3; EXPN; LAIT 4; MTCW

1, 2; NFS 2; RGAL 4; SATA 66; SATA-Obit 131; TUS; YAW

Kesselring, Joseph (Otto) 1902-1967
.... **CLC 45**
See also CA 150; DAM DRAM, MST

Kessler, Jascha (Frederick) 1929- ..... **CLC 4**
See also CA 17-20R; CANR 8, 48, 111

Kettelkamp, Larry (Dale) 1933- ..... **CLC 12**
See also CA 29-32R; CANR 16; SAAS 3; SATA 2

Key, Ellen (Karolina Sofia) 1849-1926
.... **TCLC 65**
See also DLB 259

Keyber, Conny
See Fielding, Henry

Keyes, Daniel 1927- .... **CLC 80**
See also AAYA 23; BYA 11; CA 17-20R, 181; CAAE 181; CANR 10, 26, 54, 74; DA; DA3; DAC; DAM MST, NOV; EXPN; LAIT 4; MTCW 2; NFS 2; SATA 37; SFW 4

Keynes, John Maynard 1883-1946
.... **TCLC 64**
See also CA 114; 162, 163; DLBD 10; MTCW 2

Khanshendel, Chiron
See Rose, Wendy

Khayyam, Omar 1048-1131 . **CMLC 11; PC 8**
See Omar Khayyam
See also DA3; DAM POET

Kherdian, David 1931- .... **CLC 6, 9**
See also AAYA 42; CA 21-24R; CAAE 192; CAAS 2; CANR 39, 78; CLR 24; JRDA; LAIT 5; MAICYA 1, 2; SATA 16, 74; SATA-Essay 125

Khlebnikov, Velimir .... **TCLC 20**
See Khlebnikov, Viktor Vladimirovich
See also EW 10; EWL 3; RGWL 2, 3

Khlebnikov, Viktor Vladimirovich 1885-1922
See Khlebnikov, Velimir
See also CA 117

Khodasevich, Vladislav (Felitsianovich) 1886-1939 .... **TCLC 15**
See also CA 115; EWL 3

Kielland, Alexander Lange 1849-1906
.... **TCLC 5**
See also CA 104

Kiely, Benedict 1919- .. **CLC 23, 43; SSC 58**
See also CA 1-4R; CANR 2, 84; CN 7; DLB 15

Kienzle, William X(avier) 1928-2001
.... **CLC 25**
See also CA 93-96; 203; CAAS 1; CANR 9, 31, 59, 111; CMW 4; DA3; DAM POP; INT CANR-31; MSW; MTCW 1, 2

Kierkegaard, Soren 1813-1855 .... **NCLC 34, 78, 125**
See also EW 6; LMFS 2; RGWL 3; TWA

Kieslowski, Krzysztof 1941-1996 .. **CLC 120**
See also CA 147; 151

Killens, John Oliver 1916-1987 .... **CLC 10**
See also BW 2; CA 77-80; 123; CAAS 2; CANR 26; DLB 33; EWL 3

Killigrew, Anne 1660-1685 .... **LC 4, 73**
See also DLB 131

Killigrew, Thomas 1612-1683 .... **LC 57**
See also DLB 58; RGEL 2

Kim
See Simenon, Georges (Jacques Christian)

Kincaid, Jamaica 1949- .... **BLC 2; CLC 43, 68, 137**
See also AAYA 13; AFAW 2; AMWS 7; BRWS 7; BW 2, 3; CA 125; CANR 47, 59, 95; CDALBS; CDWLB 3; CLR 63; CN 7; DA3; DAM MULT, NOV; DLB 157, 227; DNFS 1; EWL 3; EXPS; FW; LMFS 2; MTCW 2; NCFS 1; NFS 3; SSFS 5, 7; TUS; YAW

King, Francis (Henry) 1923- ...... **CLC 8, 53, 145**
See also CA 1-4R; CANR 1, 33, 86; CN 7; DAM NOV; DLB 15, 139; MTCW 1

King, Kennedy
See Brown, George Douglas

King, Martin Luther, Jr. 1929-1968
.... **BLC 2; CLC 83; WLCS**
See also BW 2, 3; CA 25-28; CANR 27, 44; CAP 2; DA; DA3; DAB; DAC; DAM MST, MULT; LAIT 5; MTCW 1, 2; SATA 14

King, Stephen (Edwin) 1947- ... **CLC 12, 26, 37, 61, 113; SSC 17, 55**
See also AAYA 1, 17; AMWS 5; BEST 90:1; BPFB 2; CA 61-64; CANR 1, 30, 52, 76; CPW; DA3; DAM NOV, POP; DLB 143; DLBY 1980; HGG; JRDA; LAIT 5; MTCW 1, 2; RGAL 4; SATA 9, 55; SUFW 1, 2; WYAS 1; YAW

King, Steve
See King, Stephen (Edwin)

King, Thomas 1943- ... **CLC 89, 171; NNAL**
See also CA 144; CANR 95; CCA 1; CN 7; DAC; DAM MULT; DLB 175; SATA 96

Kingman, Lee .... **CLC 17**
See Natti, (Mary) Lee
See also CWRI 5; SAAS 3; SATA 1, 67

Kingsley, Charles 1819-1875 .... **NCLC 35**
See also CLR 77; DLB 21, 32, 163, 178, 190; FANT; MAICYA 2; MAICYAS 1; RGEL 2; WCH; YABC 2

Kingsley, Henry 1830-1876 .... **NCLC 107**
See also DLB 21, 230; RGEL 2

Kingsley, Sidney 1906-1995 .... **CLC 44**
See also CA 85-88; 147; CAD; DFS 14; DLB 7; RGAL 4

Kingsolver, Barbara 1955- .... **CLC 55, 81, 130**
See also AAYA 15; AMWS 7; CA 129; 134; CANR 60, 96; CDALBS; CPW; CSW; DA3; DAM POP; DLB 206; INT CA-134; LAIT 5; MTCW 2; NFS 5, 10, 12; RGAL 4

Kingston, Maxine (Ting Ting) Hong 1940-
...... **AAL; CLC 12, 19, 58, 121; WLCS**
See also AAYA 8; AMWS 5; BPFB 2; CA 69-72; CANR 13, 38, 74, 87; CDALBS; CN 7; DA3; DAM MULT, NOV; DLB 173, 212; DLBY 1980; EWL 3; FW; INT CANR-13; LAIT 5; MAWW; MTCW 1, 2; NFS 6; RGAL 4; SATA 53; SSFS 3

Kinnell, Galway 1927- ... **CLC 1, 2, 3, 5, 13, 29, 129; PC 26**
See also AMWS 3; CA 9-12R; CANR 10, 34, 66, 116; CP 7; DLB 5; DLBY 1987; EWL 3; INT CANR-34; MTCW 1, 2; PAB; PFS 9; RGAL 4; WP

Kinsella, Thomas 1928- .... **CLC 4, 19, 138**
See also BRWS 5; CA 17-20R; CANR 15; CP 7; DLB 27; EWL 3; MTCW 1, 2; RGEL 2; TEA

Kinsella, W(illiam) P(atrick) 1935-
.... **CLC 27, 43, 166**
See also AAYA 7; BPFB 2; CA 97-100; CAAS 7; CANR 21, 35, 66, 75; CN 7; CPW; DAC; DAM NOV, POP; FANT; INT CANR-21; LAIT 5; MTCW 1, 2; NFS 15; RGSF 2

Kinsey, Alfred C(harles) 1894-1956
.... **TCLC 91**
See also CA 115; 170; MTCW 2

Kipling, (Joseph) Rudyard 1865-1936
... **PC 3; SSC 5, 54; TCLC 8, 17; WLC**
See also AAYA 32; BRW 6; BRWC 1; BYA 4; CA 105; 120; CANR 33; CDBLB 1890-1914; CLR 39, 65; CWRI 5; DA; DA3; DAB; DAC; DAM MST, POET; DLB 19, 34, 141, 156; EWL 3; EXPS; FANT; LAIT 3; LMFS 1; MAICYA 1, 2;

MTCW 1, 2; RGEL 2; RGSF 2; SATA 100; SFW 4; SSFS 8; SUFW 1; TEA; WCH; WLIT 4; YABC 2

Kirk, Russell (Amos) 1918-1994 . **TCLC 119**
See also AITN 1; CA 1-4R; 145; CAAS 9; CANR 1, 20, 60; HGG; INT CANR-20; MTCW 1, 2

Kirkland, Caroline M. 1801-1864
.... **NCLC 85**
See also DLB 3, 73, 74, 250, 254; DLBD 13

Kirkup, James 1918- .... **CLC 1**
See also CA 1-4R; CAAS 4; CANR 2; CP 7; DLB 27; SATA 12

Kirkwood, James 1930(?)-1989 .... **CLC 9**
See also AITN 2; CA 1-4R; 128; CANR 6, 40; GLL 2

Kirshner, Sidney
See Kingsley, Sidney

Kis, Danilo 1935-1989 .... **CLC 57**
See also CA 109; 118; 129; CANR 61; CD-WLB 4; DLB 181; EWL 3; MTCW 1; RGSF 2; RGWL 2, 3

Kissinger, Henry A(lfred) 1923- .... **CLC 137**
See also CA 1-4R; CANR 2, 33, 66, 109; MTCW 1

Kivi, Aleksis 1834-1872 .... **NCLC 30**

Kizer, Carolyn (Ashley) 1925- . **CLC 15, 39, 80**
See also CA 65-68; CAAS 5; CANR 24, 70; CP 7; CWP; DAM POET; DLB 5, 169; EWL 3; MTCW 2

Klabund 1890-1928 .... **TCLC 44**
See also CA 162; DLB 66

Klappert, Peter 1942- .... **CLC 57**
See also CA 33-36R; CSW; DLB 5

Klein, A(braham) M(oses) 1909-1972
.... **CLC 19**
See also CA 101; 37-40R; DAB; DAC; DAM MST; DLB 68; EWL 3; RGEL 2

Klein, Joe
See Klein, Joseph

Klein, Joseph 1946- .... **CLC 154**
See also CA 85-88; CANR 55

Klein, Norma 1938-1989 .... **CLC 30**
See also AAYA 2, 35; BPFB 2; BYA 6, 7, 8; CA 41-44R; 128; CANR 15, 37; CLR 2, 19; INT CANR-15; JRDA; MAICYA 1, 2; SAAS 1; SATA 7, 57; WYA; YAW

Klein, T(heodore) E(ibon) D(onald) 1947-
.... **CLC 34**
See also CA 119; CANR 44, 75; HGG

Kleist, Heinrich von 1777-1811 ..... **NCLC 2, 37; SSC 22**
See also CDWLB 2; DAM DRAM; DLB 90; EW 5; RGSF 2; RGWL 2, 3

Klima, Ivan 1931- .... **CLC 56, 172**
See also CA 25-28R; CANR 17, 50, 91; CDWLB 4; CWW 2; DAM NOV; DLB 232; EWL 3; RGWL 3

Klimentev, Andrei Platonovich
See Klimentov, Andrei Platonovich

Klimentov, Andrei Platonovich 1899-1951
.... **SSC 42; TCLC 14**
See Platonov, Andrei Platonovich; Platonov, Andrey Platonovich
See also CA 108

Klinger, Friedrich Maximilian von 1752-1831 .... **NCLC 1**
See also DLB 94

Klingsor the Magician
See Hartmann, Sadakichi

Klopstock, Friedrich Gottlieb 1724-1803
.... **NCLC 11**
See also DLB 97; EW 4; RGWL 2, 3

Kluge, Alexander 1932- .... **SSC 61**
See also CA 81-84; DLB 75

Knapp, Caroline 1959-2002 .... **CLC 99**
See also CA 154; 207

Knebel, Fletcher 1911-1993 .... **CLC 14**
See also AITN 1; CA 1-4R; 140; CAAS 3; CANR 1, 36; SATA 36; SATA-Obit 75

Knickerbocker, Diedrich
See Irving, Washington

Knight, Etheridge 1931-1991 .. **BLC 2; CLC 40; PC 14**
See also BW 1, 3; CA 21-24R; 133; CANR 23, 82; DAM POET; DLB 41; MTCW 2; RGAL 4

Knight, Sarah Kemble 1666-1727 .... **LC 7**
See also DLB 24, 200

Knister, Raymond 1899-1932 .... **TCLC 56**
See also CA 186; DLB 68; RGEL 2

Knowles, John 1926-2001 . **CLC 1, 4, 10, 26**
See also AAYA 10; AMWS 12; BPFB 2; BYA 3; CA 17-20R; 203; CANR 40, 74, 76; CDALB 1968-1988; CN 7; DA; DAC; DAM MST, NOV; DLB 6; EXPN; MTCW 1, 2; NFS 2; RGAL 4; SATA 8, 89; SATA-Obit 134; YAW

Knox, Calvin M.
See Silverberg, Robert

Knox, John c. 1505-1572 .... **LC 37**
See also DLB 132

Knye, Cassandra
See Disch, Thomas M(ichael)

Koch, C(hristopher) J(ohn) 1932- .. **CLC 42**
See also CA 127; CANR 84; CN 7

Koch, Christopher
See Koch, C(hristopher) J(ohn)

Koch, Kenneth (Jay) 1925-2002 .. **CLC 5, 8, 44**
See also CA 1-4R; 207; CAD; CANR 6, 36, 57, 97; CD 5; CP 7; DAM POET; DLB 5; INT CANR-36; MTCW 2; SATA 65; WP

Kochanowski, Jan 1530-1584 .... **LC 10**
See also RGWL 2, 3

Kock, Charles Paul de 1794-1871
.... **NCLC 16**

Koda Rohan
See Koda Shigeyuki

Koda Rohan
See Koda Shigeyuki
See also DLB 180

Koda Shigeyuki 1867-1947 .... **TCLC 22**
See Koda Rohan
See also CA 121; 183

Koestler, Arthur 1905-1983 . **CLC 1, 3, 6, 8, 15, 33**
See also BRWS 1; CA 1-4R; 109; CANR 1, 33; CDBLB 1945-1960; DLBY 1983; EWL 3; MTCW 1, 2; RGEL 2

Kogawa, Joy Nozomi 1935- ..... **CLC 78, 129**
See also AAYA 47; CA 101; CANR 19, 62; CN 7; CWP; DAC; DAM MST, MULT; FW; MTCW 2; NFS 3; SATA 99

Kohout, Pavel 1928- .... **CLC 13**
See also CA 45-48; CANR 3

Koizumi, Yakumo
See Hearn, (Patricio) Lafcadio (Tessima Carlos)

Kolmar, Gertrud 1894-1943 .... **TCLC 40**
See also CA 167; EWL 3

Komunyakaa, Yusef 1947- . **BLCS; CLC 86, 94**
See also AFAW 2; CA 147; CANR 83; CP 7; CSW; DLB 120; EWL 3; PFS 5; RGAL 4

Konrad, George
See Konrad, Gyorgy
See also CWW 2

Konrad, Gyorgy 1933- .... **CLC 4, 10, 73**
See Konrad, George
See also CA 85-88; CANR 97; CDWLB 4; CWW 2; DLB 232; EWL 3

Konwicki, Tadeusz 1926- ..... **CLC 8, 28, 54, 117**
See also CA 101; CAAS 9; CANR 39, 59; CWW 2; DLB 232; EWL 3; IDFW 3; MTCW 1

Koontz, Dean R(ay) 1945- .... **CLC 78**
See also AAYA 9, 31; BEST 89:3, 90:2; CA 108; CANR 19, 36, 52, 95; CMW 4; CPW; DA3; DAM NOV, POP; HGG; MTCW 1; SATA 92; SFW 4; SUFW 2; YAW

Kopernik, Mikolaj
See Copernicus, Nicolaus

Kopit, Arthur (Lee) 1937- .... **CLC 1, 18, 33**
See also AITN 1; CA 81-84; CABS 3; CD 5; DAM DRAM; DFS 7, 14; DLB 7; MTCW 1; RGAL 4

Kopitar, Jernej (Bartholomaus) 1780-1844
.... **NCLC 117**

Kops, Bernard 1926- .... **CLC 4**
See also CA 5-8R; CANR 84; CBD; CN 7; CP 7; DLB 13

Kornbluth, C(yril) M. 1923-1958 ... **TCLC 8**
See also CA 105; 160; DLB 8; SFW 4

Korolenko, V. G.
See Korolenko, Vladimir Galaktionovich

Korolenko, Vladimir
See Korolenko, Vladimir Galaktionovich

Korolenko, Vladimir G.
See Korolenko, Vladimir Galaktionovich

Korolenko, Vladimir Galaktionovich 1853-1921 .... **TCLC 22**
See also CA 121; DLB 277

Korzybski, Alfred (Habdank Skarbek) 1879-1950 .... **TCLC 61**
See also CA 123; 160

Kosinski, Jerzy (Nikodem) 1933-1991
.... **CLC 1, 2, 3, 6, 10, 15, 53, 70**
See also AMWS 7; BPFB 2; CA 17-20R; 134; CANR 9, 46; DA3; DAM NOV; DLB 2; DLBY 1982; EWL 3; HGG; MTCW 1, 2; NFS 12; RGAL 4; TUS

Kostelanetz, Richard (Cory) 1940- . **CLC 28**
See also CA 13-16R; CAAS 8; CANR 38, 77; CN 7; CP 7

Kostrowitzki, Wilhelm Apollinaris de 1880-1918
See Apollinaire, Guillaume
See also CA 104

Kotlowitz, Robert 1924- .... **CLC 4**
See also CA 33-36R; CANR 36

Kotzebue, August (Friedrich Ferdinand) von 1761-1819 .... **NCLC 25**
See also DLB 94

Kotzwinkle, William 1938- ..... **CLC 5, 14, 35**
See also BPFB 2; CA 45-48; CANR 3, 44, 84; CLR 6; DLB 173; FANT; MAICYA 1, 2; SATA 24, 70; SFW 4; SUFW 2; YAW

Kowna, Stancy
See Szymborska, Wislawa

Kozol, Jonathan 1936- .... **CLC 17**
See also AAYA 46; CA 61-64; CANR 16, 45, 96

Kozoll, Michael 1940(?)- .... **CLC 35**

Kramer, Kathryn 19(?)- .... **CLC 34**

Kramer, Larry 1935- .... **CLC 42; DC 8**
See also CA 124; 126; CANR 60; DAM POP; DLB 249; GLL 1

Krasicki, Ignacy 1735-1801 .... **NCLC 8**

Krasinski, Zygmunt 1812-1859 .... **NCLC 4**
See also RGWL 2, 3

Kraus, Karl 1874-1936 .... **TCLC 5**
See also CA 104; DLB 118; EWL 3

Kreve (Mickevicius), Vincas 1882-1954
.... **TCLC 27**
See also CA 170; DLB 220; EWL 3

Kristeva, Julia 1941- .... **CLC 77, 140**
See also CA 154; CANR 99; DLB 242; EWL 3; FW; LMFS 2

Kristofferson, Kris 1936- .... **CLC 26**
See also CA 104

Krizanc, John 1956- .... **CLC 57**
See also CA 187

Krleza, Miroslav 1893-1981 ...... **CLC 8, 114**
See also CA 97-100; 105; CANR 50; CDWLB 4; DLB 147; EW 11; RGWL 2, 3

Kroetsch, Robert 1927- . **CLC 5, 23, 57, 132**
See also CA 17-20R; CANR 8, 38; CCA 1; CN 7; CP 7; DAC; DAM POET; DLB 53; MTCW 1

Kroetz, Franz
See Kroetz, Franz Xaver

Kroetz, Franz Xaver 1946- .... **CLC 41**
See also CA 130; EWL 3

Kroker, Arthur (W.) 1945- .... **CLC 77**
See also CA 161

Kropotkin, Peter (Alekseevich) 1842-1921
.... **TCLC 36**
See Kropotkin, Petr Alekseevich
See also CA 119

Kropotkin, Petr Alekseevich
See Kropotkin, Peter (Alekseevich)
See also DLB 277

Krotkov, Yuri 1917-1981 .... **CLC 19**
See also CA 102

Krumb
See Crumb, R(obert)

Krumgold, Joseph (Quincy) 1908-1980
.... **CLC 12**
See also BYA 1, 2; CA 9-12R; 101; CANR 7; MAICYA 1, 2; SATA 1, 48; SATA-Obit 23; YAW

Krumwitz
See Crumb, R(obert)

Krutch, Joseph Wood 1893-1970 .... **CLC 24**
See also ANW; CA 1-4R; 25-28R; CANR 4; DLB 63, 206, 275

Krutzch, Gus
See Eliot, T(homas) S(tearns)

Krylov, Ivan Andreevich 1768(?)-1844
.... **NCLC 1**
See also DLB 150

Kubin, Alfred (Leopold Isidor) 1877-1959
.... **TCLC 23**
See also CA 112; 149; CANR 104; DLB 81

Kubrick, Stanley 1928-1999 .... **CLC 16; TCLC 112**
See also AAYA 30; CA 81-84; 177; CANR 33; DLB 26

Kueng, Hans 1928-
See Kung, Hans
See also CA 53-56; CANR 66; MTCW 1, 2

Kumin, Maxine (Winokur) 1925- .... **CLC 5, 13, 28, 164; PC 15**
See also AITN 2; AMWS 4; ANW; CA 1-4R; CAAS 8; CANR 1, 21, 69, 115; CP 7; CWP; DA3; DAM POET; DLB 5; EWL 3; EXPP; MTCW 1, 2; PAB; SATA 12

Kundera, Milan 1929- ..... **CLC 4, 9, 19, 32, 68, 115, 135; SSC 24**
See also AAYA 2; BPFB 2; CA 85-88; CANR 19, 52, 74; CDWLB 4; CWW 2; DA3; DAM NOV; DLB 232; EW 13; EWL 3; MTCW 1, 2; RGSF; RGWL 3; SSFS 10

Kunene, Mazisi (Raymond) 1930- ... **CLC 85**
See also BW 1, 3; CA 125; CANR 81; CP 7; DLB 117

Kung, Hans .... **CLC 130**
See Kueng, Hans

Kunikida Doppo 1859(?)-1908
See Doppo, Kunikida
See also DLB 180; EWL 3

Kunitz, Stanley (Jasspon) 1905- ...... **CLC 6, 11, 14, 148; PC 19**
See also AMWS 3; CA 41-44R; CANR 26, 57, 98; CP 7; DA3; DLB 48; INT CANR-26; MTCW 1, 2; PFS 11; RGAL 4

Kunze, Reiner 1933- .... **CLC 10**
See also CA 93-96; CWW 2; DLB 75; EWL 3

Kuprin, Aleksander Ivanovich 1870-1938
.... **TCLC 5**
See Kuprin, Alexandr Ivanovich
See also CA 104; 182

Kuprin, Alexandr Ivanovich
See Kuprin, Aleksander Ivanovich
See also EWL 3

Kureishi, Hanif 1954(?)- .... **CLC 64, 135**
See also CA 139; CANR 113; CBD; CD 5; CN 7; DLB 194, 245; GLL 2; IDFW 4; WLIT 4

Kurosawa, Akira 1910-1998 .... **CLC 16, 119**
See also AAYA 11; CA 101; 170; CANR 46; DAM MULT

Kushner, Tony 1957(?)- .... **CLC 81; DC 10**
See also AMWS 9; CA 144; CAD; CANR 74; CD 5; DA3; DAM DRAM; DFS 5; DLB 228; EWL 3; GLL 1; LAIT 5; MTCW 2; RGAL 4

Kuttner, Henry 1915-1958 .... **TCLC 10**
See also CA 107; 157; DLB 8; FANT; SCFW 2; SFW 4

Kutty, Madhavi
See Das, Kamala

Kuzma, Greg 1944- .... **CLC 7**
See also CA 33-36R; CANR 70

Kuzmin, Mikhail 1872(?)-1936 ..... **TCLC 40**
See also CA 170; EWL 3

Kyd, Thomas 1558-1594 .... **DC 3; LC 22**
See also BRW 1; DAM DRAM; DLB 62; IDTP; LMFS 1; RGEL 2; TEA; WLIT 3

Kyprianos, Iossif
See Samarakis, Antonis

L. S.
See Stephen, Sir Leslie

Labrunie, Gerard
See Nerval, Gerard de

La Bruyere, Jean de 1645-1696 .... **LC 17**
See also DLB 268; EW 3; GFL Beginnings to 1789

Lacan, Jacques (Marie Emile) 1901-1981
.... **CLC 75**
See also CA 121; 104; EWL 3; TWA

Laclos, Pierre Ambroise Francois 1741-1803
.... **NCLC 4, 87**
See also EW 4; GFL Beginnings to 1789; RGWL 2, 3

Lacolere, Francois
See Aragon, Louis

La Colere, Francois
See Aragon, Louis

La Deshabilleuse
See Simenon, Georges (Jacques Christian)

Lady Gregory
See Gregory, Lady Isabella Augusta (Persse)

Lady of Quality, A
See Bagnold, Enid

La Fayette, Marie-(Madelaine Pioche de la Vergne) 1634-1693 .... **LC 2**
See Lafayette, Marie-Madeleine
See also GFL Beginnings to 1789; RGWL 2, 3

Lafayette, Marie-Madeleine
See La Fayette, Marie-(Madelaine Pioche de la Vergne)
See also DLB 268

Lafayette, Rene
See Hubbard, L(afayette) Ron(ald)

La Flesche, Francis 1857(?)-1932 ..... **NNAL**
See also CA 144; CANR 83; DLB 175

La Fontaine, Jean de 1621-1695 .... **LC 50**
See also DLB 268; EW 3; GFL Beginnings to 1789; MAICYA 1, 2; RGWL 2, 3; SATA 18

Laforgue, Jules 1860-1887 ...... **NCLC 5, 53; PC 14; SSC 20**
See also DLB 217; EW 7; GFL 1789 to the Present; RGWL 2, 3

Layamon
See Layamon
See also DLB 146

Lagerkvist, Paer (Fabian) 1891-1974
.... **CLC 7, 10, 13, 54**
See Lagerkvist, Par
See also CA 85-88; 49-52; DA3; DAM DRAM, NOV; MTCW 1, 2; TWA

Lagerkvist, Par .... **SSC 12**
See Lagerkvist, Paer (Fabian)
See also DLB 259; EW 10; EWL 3; MTCW 2; RGSF 2; RGWL 2, 3

Lagerloef, Selma (Ottiliana Lovisa)
1858-1940 .... **TCLC 4, 36**
See Lagerlof, Selma (Ottiliana Lovisa)
See also CA 108; MTCW 2; SATA 15

Lagerlof, Selma (Ottiliana Lovisa)
See Lagerloef, Selma (Ottiliana Lovisa)
See also CLR 7; SATA 15

La Guma, (Justin) Alex(ander) 1925-1985
.... **BLCS; CLC 19**
See also AFW; BW 1, 3; CA 49-52; 118; CANR 25, 81; CDWLB 3; DAM NOV; DLB 117, 225; EWL 3; MTCW 1, 2; WLIT 2

Laidlaw, A. K.
See Grieve, C(hristopher) M(urray)

Lainez, Manuel Mujica
See Mujica Lainez, Manuel
See also HW 1

Laing, R(onald) D(avid) 1927-1989
.... **CLC 95**
See also CA 107; 129; CANR 34; MTCW 1

Lamartine, Alphonse (Marie Louis Prat) de
1790-1869 .... **NCLC 11; PC 16**
See also DAM POET; DLB 217; GFL 1789 to the Present; RGWL 2, 3

Lamb, Charles 1775-1834 .... **NCLC 10, 113; WLC**
See also BRW 4; CDBLB 1789-1832; DA; DAB; DAC; DAM MST; DLB 93, 107, 163; RGEL 2; SATA 17; TEA

Lamb, Lady Caroline 1785-1828 . **NCLC 38**
See also DLB 116

Lamb, Mary Ann 1764-1847 ...... **NCLC 125**
See also DLB 163; SATA 17

Lame Deer 1903(?)-1976 .... **NNAL**
See also CA 69-72

Lamming, George (William) 1927- . **BLC 2; CLC 2, 4, 66, 144**
See also BW 2, 3; CA 85-88; CANR 26, 76; CDWLB 3; CN 7; DAM MULT; DLB 125; EWL 3; MTCW 1, 2; NFS 15; RGEL 2

L'Amour, Louis (Dearborn) 1908-1988
.... **CLC 25, 55**
See Burns, Tex; Mayo, Jim
See also AAYA 16; AITN 2; BEST 89:2; BPFB 2; CA 1-4R; 125; CANR 3, 25, 40; CPW; DA3; DAM NOV, POP; DLB 206; DLBY 1980; MTCW 1, 2; RGAL 4

Lampedusa, Giuseppe (Tomasi) di
.... **TCLC 13**
See Tomasi di Lampedusa, Giuseppe
See also CA 164; EW 11; MTCW 2; RGWL 2, 3

Lampman, Archibald 1861-1899 .. **NCLC 25**
See also DLB 92; RGEL 2; TWA

Lancaster, Bruce 1896-1963 .... **CLC 36**
See also CA 9-10; CANR 70; CAP 1; SATA 9

Lanchester, John 1962- .... **CLC 99**
See also CA 194; DLB 267

Landau, Mark Alexandrovich
See Aldanov, Mark (Alexandrovich)

Landau-Aldanov, Mark Alexandrovich
See Aldanov, Mark (Alexandrovich)

Landis, Jerry
See Simon, Paul (Frederick)

Landis, John 1950- .... **CLC 26**
See also CA 112; 122

Landolfi, Tommaso 1908-1979 .. **CLC 11, 49**
See also CA 127; 117; DLB 177; EWL 3

Landon, Letitia Elizabeth 1802-1838
.... **NCLC 15**
See also DLB 96

Landor, Walter Savage 1775-1864
.... **NCLC 14**
See also BRW 4; DLB 93, 107; RGEL 2

Landwirth, Heinz 1927-
See Lind, Jakov
See also CA 9-12R; CANR 7

Lane, Patrick 1939- .... **CLC 25**
See also CA 97-100; CANR 54; CP 7; DAM POET; DLB 53; INT 97-100

Lang, Andrew 1844-1912 .... **TCLC 16**
See also CA 114; 137; CANR 85; DLB 98, 141, 184; FANT; MAICYA 1, 2; RGEL 2; SATA 16; WCH

Lang, Fritz 1890-1976 .... **CLC 20, 103**
See also CA 77-80; 69-72; CANR 30

Lange, John
See Crichton, (John) Michael

Langer, Elinor 1939- .... **CLC 34**
See also CA 121

Langland, William 1332(?)-1400(?) ... **LC 19**
See also BRW 1; DA; DAB; DAC; DAM MST, POET; DLB 146; RGEL 2; TEA; WLIT 3

Langstaff, Launcelot
See Irving, Washington

Lanier, Sidney 1842-1881 .... **NCLC 6, 118**
See also AMWS 1; DAM POET; DLB 64; DLBD 13; EXPP; MAICYA 1; PFS 14; RGAL 4; SATA 18

Lanyer, Aemilia 1569-1645 .... **LC 10, 30, 83**
See also DLB 121

Lao-Tzu
See Lao Tzu

Lao Tzu c. 6th cent. B.C.-3rd cent. B.C.
.... **CMLC 7**

Lapine, James (Elliot) 1949- .... **CLC 39**
See also CA 123; 130; CANR 54; INT 130

Larbaud, Valery (Nicolas) 1881-1957
.... **TCLC 9**
See also CA 106; 152; EWL 3; GFL 1789 to the Present

Lardner, Ring
See Lardner, Ring(gold) W(ilmer)
See also BPFB 2; CDALB 1917-1929; DLB 11, 25, 86, 171; DLBD 16; RGAL 4; RGSF 2

Lardner, Ring W., Jr.
See Lardner, Ring(gold) W(ilmer)

Lardner, Ring(gold) W(ilmer) 1885-1933
.... **SSC 32; TCLC 2, 14**
See Lardner, Ring
See also AMW; CA 104; 131; MTCW 1, 2; TUS

Laredo, Betty
See Codrescu, Andrei

Larkin, Maia
See Wojciechowska, Maia (Teresa)

Larkin, Philip (Arthur) 1922-1985 .. **CLC 3, 5, 8, 9, 13, 18, 33, 39, 64; PC 21**
See also BRWS 1; CA 5-8R; 117; CANR 24, 62; CDBLB 1960 to Present; DA3; DAB; DAM MST, POET; DLB 27; EWL 3; MTCW 1, 2; PFS 3, 4, 12; RGEL 2

La Roche, Sophie von 1730-1807 .... NCLC 121
  See also DLB 94
Larra (y Sanchez de Castro), Mariano Jose de 1809-1837 .... NCLC 17
Larsen, Eric 1941- .... CLC 55
  See also CA 132
Larsen, Nella 1893(?)-1963 ..... BLC 2; CLC 37; HR 3
  See also AFAW 1, 2; BW 1; CA 125; CANR 83; DAM MULT; DLB 51; FW; LMFS 2
Larson, Charles R(aymond) 1938- . CLC 31
  See also CA 53-56; CANR 4
Larson, Jonathan 1961-1996 .... CLC 99
  See also AAYA 28; CA 156
Las Casas, Bartolome de 1474-1566
  .... HLCS; LC 31
  See Casas, Bartolome de las
  See also LAW
Lasch, Christopher 1932-1994 ...... CLC 102
  See also CA 73-76; 144; CANR 25; DLB 246; MTCW 1, 2
Lasker-Schueler, Else 1869-1945 .. TCLC 57
  See Lasker-Schuler, Else
  See also CA 183; DLB 66, 124
Lasker-Schuler, Else
  See Lasker-Schueler, Else
  See also EWL 3
Laski, Harold J(oseph) 1893-1950
  .... TCLC 79
  See also CA 188
Latham, Jean Lee 1902-1995 .... CLC 12
  See also AITN 1; BYA 1; CA 5-8R; CANR 7, 84; CLR 50; MAICYA 1, 2; SATA 2, 68; YAW
Latham, Mavis
  See Clark, Mavis Thorpe
Lathen, Emma .... CLC 2
  See Hennissart, Martha; Latsis, Mary J(ane)
  See also BPFB 2; CMW 4
Lathrop, Francis
  See Leiber, Fritz (Reuter, Jr.)
Latsis, Mary J(ane) 1927(?)-1997
  See Lathen, Emma
  See also CA 85-88; 162; CMW 4
Lattany, Kristin
  See Lattany, Kristin (Elaine Eggleston) Hunter
Lattany, Kristin (Elaine Eggleston) Hunter 1931- .... CLC 35
  See also AITN 1; BW 1; BYA 3; CA 13-16R; CANR 13, 108; CLR 3; CN 7; DLB 33; INT CANR-13; MAICYA 1, 2; SAAS 10; SATA 12, 132; YAW
Lattimore, Richmond (Alexander) 1906-1984
  .... CLC 3
  See also CA 1-4R; 112; CANR 1
Laughlin, James 1914-1997 .... CLC 49
  See also CA 21-24R; 162; CAAS 22; CANR 9, 47; DLB 48; DLBY 1996, 1997
Laurence, (Jean) Margaret (Wemyss) 1926-1987 ... CLC 3, 6, 13, 50, 62; SSC 7
  See also BYA 13; CA 5-8R; 121; CANR 33; DAC; DAM MST; DLB 53; EWL 3; FW; MTCW 1, 2; NFS 11; RGEL 2; RGSF 2; SATA-Obit 50; TCWW 2
Laurent, Antoine 1952- .... CLC 50
Lauscher, Hermann
  See Hesse, Hermann
Lautreamont 1846-1870 . NCLC 12; SSC 14
  See Lautreamont, Isidore Lucien Ducasse
  See also GFL 1789 to the Present; RGWL 2, 3
Lautreamont, Isidore Lucien Ducasse
  See Lautreamont
  See also DLB 217
Laverty, Donald
  See Blish, James (Benjamin)

Lavin, Mary 1912-1996 .... CLC 4, 18, 99; SSC 4
  See also CA 9-12R; 151; CANR 33; CN 7; DLB 15; FW; MTCW 1; RGEL 2; RGSF 2
Lavond, Paul Dennis
  See Kornbluth, C(yril) M; Pohl, Frederik
Lawler, Raymond Evenor 1922- ...... CLC 58
  See also CA 103; CD 5; RGEL 2
Lawrence, D(avid) H(erbert Richards) 1885-1930 .. SSC 4, 19; TCLC 2, 9, 16, 33, 48, 61, 93; WLC
  See Chambers, Jessie
  See also BPFB 2; BRW 7; BRWR 2; CA 104; 121; CDBLB 1914-1945; DA; DA3; DAB; DAC; DAM MST, NOV, POET; DLB 10, 19, 36, 98, 162, 195; EWL 3; EXPP; EXPS; LAIT 2, 3; MTCW 1, 2; PFS 6; RGEL 2; RGSF 2; SSFS 2, 6; TEA; WLIT 4; WP
Lawrence, T(homas) E(dward) 1888-1935
  .... TCLC 18
  See Dale, Colin
  See also BRWS 2; CA 115; 167; DLB 195
Lawrence of Arabia
  See Lawrence, T(homas) E(dward)
Lawson, Henry (Archibald Hertzberg) 1867-1922 .... SSC 18; TCLC 27
  See also CA 120; 181; DLB 230; RGEL 2; RGSF 2
Lawton, Dennis
  See Faust, Frederick (Schiller)
Laxness, Halldor .... CLC 25
  See Gudjonsson, Halldor Kiljan
  See also EW 12; EWL 3; RGWL 2, 3
Layamon fl. c. 1200- .... CMLC 10
  See Layamon
  See also RGEL 2
Laye, Camara 1928-1980 .... BLC 2; CLC 4, 38
  See Camara Laye
  See also AFW; BW 1; CA 85-88; 97-100; CANR 25; DAM MULT; MTCW 1, 2; WLIT 2
Layton, Irving (Peter) 1912- .... CLC 2, 15, 164
  See also CA 1-4R; CANR 2, 33, 43, 66; CP 7; DAC; DAM MST, POET; DLB 88; EWL 3; MTCW 1, 2; PFS 12; RGEL 2
Lazarus, Emma 1849-1887 ..... NCLC 8, 109
Lazarus, Felix
  See Cable, George Washington
Lazarus, Henry
  See Slavitt, David R(ytman)
Lea, Joan
  See Neufeld, John (Arthur)
Leacock, Stephen (Butler) 1869-1944
  .... SSC 39; TCLC 2
  See also CA 104; 141; CANR 80; DAC; DAM MST; DLB 92; EWL 3; MTCW 2; RGEL 2; RGSF 2
Lead, Jane Ward 1623-1704 .... LC 72
  See also DLB 131
Leapor, Mary 1722-1746 .... LC 80
  See also DLB 109
Lear, Edward 1812-1888 .... NCLC 3
  See also AAYA 48; BRW 5; CLR 1, 75; DLB 32, 163, 166; MAICYA 1, 2; RGEL 2; SATA 18, 100; WCH; WP
Lear, Norman (Milton) 1922- .... CLC 12
  See also CA 73-76
Leautaud, Paul 1872-1956 .... TCLC 83
  See also CA 203; DLB 65; GFL 1789 to the Present
Leavis, F(rank) R(aymond) 1895-1978
  .... CLC 24
  See also BRW 7; CA 21-24R; 77-80; CANR 44; DLB 242; EWL 3; MTCW 1, 2; RGEL 2

Leavitt, David 1961- .... CLC 34
  See also CA 116; 122; CANR 50, 62, 101; CPW; DA3; DAM POP; DLB 130; GLL 1; INT 122; MTCW 2
Leblanc, Maurice (Marie Emile) 1864-1941
  .... TCLC 49
  See also CA 110; CMW 4
Lebowitz, Fran(ces Ann) 1951(?)- .. CLC 11, 36
  See also CA 81-84; CANR 14, 60, 70; INT CANR-14; MTCW 1
Lebrecht, Peter
  See Tieck, (Johann) Ludwig
le Carre, John .... CLC 3, 5, 9, 15, 28
  See Cornwell, David (John Moore)
  See also AAYA 42; BEST 89:4; BPFB 2; BRWS 2; CDBLB 1960 to Present; CMW 4; CN 7; CPW; DLB 87; EWL 3; MSW; MTCW 2; RGEL 2; TEA
Le Clezio, J(ean) M(arie) G(ustave) 1940-
  .... CLC 31, 155
  See also CA 116; 128; DLB 83; EWL 3; GFL 1789 to the Present; RGSF 2
Leconte de Lisle, Charles-Marie-Rene 1818-1894 .... NCLC 29
  See also DLB 217; EW 6; GFL 1789 to the Present
Le Coq, Monsieur
  See Simenon, Georges (Jacques Christian)
Leduc, Violette 1907-1972 .... CLC 22
  See also CA 13-14; 33-36R; CANR 69; CAP 1; EWL 3; GFL 1789 to the Present; GLL 1
Ledwidge, Francis 1887(?)-1917 ... TCLC 23
  See also CA 123; 203; DLB 20
Lee, Andrea 1953- .... BLC 2; CLC 36
  See also BW 1, 3; CA 125; CANR 82; DAM MULT
Lee, Andrew
  See Auchincloss, Louis (Stanton)
Lee, Chang-rae 1965- .... CLC 91
  See also CA 148; CANR 89
Lee, Don L. .... CLC 2
  See Madhubuti, Haki R.
Lee, George W(ashington) 1894-1976
  .... BLC 2; CLC 52
  See also BW 1; CA 125; CANR 83; DAM MULT; DLB 51
Lee, (Nelle) Harper 1926- .... CLC 12, 60; WLC
  See also AAYA 13; AMWS 8; BPFB 2; BYA 3; CA 13-16R; CANR 51; CDALB 1941-1968; CSW; DA; DA3; DAB; DAC; DAM MST, NOV; DLB 6; EXPN; LAIT 3; MTCW 1, 2; NFS 2; SATA 11; WYA; YAW
Lee, Helen Elaine 1959(?)- .... CLC 86
  See also CA 148
Lee, John .... CLC 70
Lee, Julian
  See Latham, Jean Lee
Lee, Larry
  See Lee, Lawrence
Lee, Laurie 1914-1997 .... CLC 90
  See also CA 77-80; 158; CANR 33, 73; CP 7; CPW; DAB; DAM POP; DLB 27; MTCW 1; RGEL 2
Lee, Lawrence 1941-1990 .... CLC 34
  See also CA 131; CANR 43
Lee, Li-Young 1957- .... CLC 164; PC 24
  See also CA 153; CP 7; DLB 165; LMFS 2; PFS 11, 15, 17
Lee, Manfred B(ennington) 1905-1971
  .... CLC 11
  See Queen, Ellery
  See also CA 1-4R; 29-32R; CANR 2; CMW 4; DLB 137

Lee, Shelton Jackson 1957(?)- . BLCS; CLC 105
See Lee, Spike
See also BW 2, 3; CA 125; CANR 42; DAM MULT

Lee, Spike
See Lee, Shelton Jackson
See also AAYA 4, 29

Lee, Stan 1922- .... CLC 17
See also AAYA 5, 49; CA 108; 111; INT 111

Lee, Tanith 1947- .... CLC 46
See also AAYA 15; CA 37-40R; CANR 53, 102; DLB 261; FANT; SATA 8, 88, 134; SFW 4; SUFW 1, 2; YAW

Lee, Vernon .... SSC 33; TCLC 5
See Paget, Violet
See also DLB 57, 153, 156, 174, 178; GLL 1; SUFW 1

Lee, William
See Burroughs, William S(eward)
See also GLL 1

Lee, Willy
See Burroughs, William S(eward)
See also GLL 1

Lee-Hamilton, Eugene (Jacob) 1845-1907
.... TCLC 22
See also CA 117

Leet, Judith 1935- .... CLC 11
See also CA 187

Le Fanu, Joseph Sheridan 1814-1873
.... NCLC 9, 58; SSC 14
See also CMW 4; DA3; DAM POP; DLB 21, 70, 159, 178; HGG; RGEL 2; RGSF 2; SUFW 1

Leffland, Ella 1931- .... CLC 19
See also CA 29-32R; CANR 35, 78, 82; DLBY 1984; INT CANR-35; SATA 65

Leger, Alexis
See Leger, (Marie-Rene Auguste) Alexis Saint-Leger

Leger, (Marie-Rene Auguste) Alexis Saint-Leger 1887-1975 . CLC 4, 11, 46; PC 23
See Perse, Saint-John; Saint-John Perse
See also CA 13-16R; 61-64; CANR 43; DAM POET; MTCW 1

Leger, Saintleger
See Leger, (Marie-Rene Auguste) Alexis Saint-Leger

Le Guin, Ursula K(roeber) 1929- .... CLC 8, 13, 22, 45, 71, 136; SSC 12
See also AAYA 9, 27; AITN 1; BPFB 2; BYA 5, 8, 11, 14; CA 21-24R; CANR 9, 32, 52, 74; CDALB 1968-1988; CLR 3, 28; CN 7; CPW; DA3; DAB; DAC; DAM MST, POP; DLB 8, 52, 256, 275; EXPS; FANT; FW; INT CANR-32; JRDA; LAIT 5; MAICYA 1, 2; MTCW 1, 2; NFS 6, 9; SATA 4, 52, 99; SCFW; SFW 4; SSFS 2; SUFW 1, 2; WYA; YAW

Lehmann, Rosamond (Nina) 1901-1990
.... CLC 5
See also CA 77-80; 131; CANR 8, 73; DLB 15; MTCW 2; RGEL 2; RHW

Leiber, Fritz (Reuter, Jr.) 1910-1992
.... CLC 25
See also BPFB 2; CA 45-48; 139; CANR 2, 40, 86; DLB 8; FANT; HGG; MTCW 1, 2; SATA 45; SATA-Obit 73; SCFW 2; SFW 4; SUFW 1, 2

Leibniz, Gottfried Wilhelm von 1646-1716
.... LC 35
See also DLB 168

Leimbach, Martha 1963-
See Leimbach, Marti
See also CA 130

Leimbach, Marti .... CLC 65
See Leimbach, Martha

Leino, Eino .... TCLC 24
See Lonnbohm, Armas Eino Leopold
See also EWL 3

Leiris, Michel (Julien) 1901-1990 ... CLC 61
See also CA 119; 128; 132; EWL 3; GFL 1789 to the Present

Leithauser, Brad 1953- .... CLC 27
See also CA 107; CANR 27, 81; CP 7; DLB 120, 282

Lelchuk, Alan 1938- .... CLC 5
See also CA 45-48; CAAS 20; CANR 1, 70; CN 7

Lem, Stanislaw 1921- .... CLC 8, 15, 40, 149
See also CA 105; CAAS 1; CANR 32; CWW 2; MTCW 1; SCFW 2; SFW 4

Lemann, Nancy 1956- .... CLC 39
See also CA 118; 136

Lemonnier, (Antoine Louis) Camille 1844-1913 .... TCLC 22
See also CA 121

Lenau, Nikolaus 1802-1850 .... NCLC 16

L'Engle, Madeleine (Camp Franklin) 1918-
.... CLC 12
See also AAYA 28; AITN 2; BPFB 2; BYA 2, 4, 5, 7; CA 1-4R; CANR 3, 21, 39, 66, 107; CLR 1, 14, 57; CPW; CWRI 5; DA3; DAM POP; DLB 52; JRDA; MAICYA 1, 2; MTCW 1, 2; SAAS 15; SATA 1, 27, 75, 128; SFW 4; WYA; YAW

Lengyel, Jozsef 1896-1975 .... CLC 7
See also CA 85-88; 57-60; CANR 71; RGSF 2

Lenin 1870-1924
See Lenin, V. I.
See also CA 121; 168

Lenin, V. I. .... TCLC 67
See Lenin

Lennon, John (Ono) 1940-1980 ...... CLC 12, 35
See also CA 102; SATA 114

Lennox, Charlotte Ramsay 1729(?)-1804
.... NCLC 23
See also DLB 39; RGEL 2

Lentricchia, Frank, (Jr.) 1940- .... CLC 34
See also CA 25-28R; CANR 19, 106; DLB 246

Lenz, Gunter .... CLC 65

Lenz, Siegfried 1926- .... CLC 27; SSC 33
See also CA 89-92; CANR 80; CWW 2; DLB 75; EWL 3; RGSF 2; RGWL 2, 3

Leon, David
See Jacob, (Cyprien-)Max

Leonard, Elmore (John, Jr.) 1925-
.... CLC 28, 34, 71, 120
See also AAYA 22; AITN 1; BEST 89:1, 90:4; BPFB 2; CA 81-84; CANR 12, 28, 53, 76, 96; CMW 4; CN 7; CPW; DA3; DAM POP; DLB 173, 226; INT CANR-28; MSW; MTCW 1, 2; RGAL 4; TCWW 2

Leonard, Hugh .... CLC 19
See Byrne, John Keyes
See also CBD; CD 5; DFS 13; DLB 13

Leonov, Leonid (Maximovich) 1899-1994
.... CLC 92
See Leonov, Leonid Maksimovich
See also CA 129; CANR 74, 76; DAM NOV; EWL 3; MTCW 1, 2

Leonov, Leonid Maksimovich
See Leonov, Leonid (Maximovich)
See also DLB 272

Leopardi, (Conte) Giacomo 1798-1837
.... NCLC 22; PC 37
See also EW 5; RGWL 2, 3; WP

Le Reveler
See Artaud, Antonin (Marie Joseph)

Lerman, Eleanor 1952- .... CLC 9
See also CA 85-88; CANR 69

Lerman, Rhoda 1936- .... CLC 56
See also CA 49-52; CANR 70

Lermontov, Mikhail
See Lermontov, Mikhail Yuryevich

Lermontov, Mikhail Iur'evich
See Lermontov, Mikhail Yuryevich
See also DLB 205

Lermontov, Mikhail Yuryevich 1814-1841
.... NCLC 5, 47; PC 18
See Lermontov, Mikhail Iur'evich
See also EW 6; RGWL 2, 3; TWA

Leroux, Gaston 1868-1927 .... TCLC 25
See also CA 108; 136; CANR 69; CMW 4; SATA 65

Lesage, Alain-Rene 1668-1747 .... LC 2, 28
See also EW 3; GFL Beginnings to 1789; RGWL 2, 3

Leskov, N(ikolai) S(emenovich) 1831-1895
See Leskov, Nikolai (Semyonovich)

Leskov, Nikolai (Semyonovich) 1831-1895
.... NCLC 25; SSC 34
See Leskov, Nikolai Semenovich

Leskov, Nikolai Semenovich
See Leskov, Nikolai (Semyonovich)
See also DLB 238

Lesser, Milton
See Marlowe, Stephen

Lessing, Doris (May) 1919- . CLC 1, 2, 3, 6, 10, 15, 22, 40, 94, 170; SSC 6, 61; WLCS
See also AFW; BRWS 1; CA 9-12R; CAAS 14; CANR 33, 54, 76; CD 5; CDBLB 1960 to Present; CN 7; DA; DA3; DAB; DAC; DAM MST, NOV; DLB 15, 139; DLBY 1985; EWL 3; EXPS; FW; LAIT 4; MTCW 1, 2; RGEL 2; RGSF 2; SFW 4; SSFS 1, 12; TEA; WLIT 2, 4

Lessing, Gotthold Ephraim 1729-1781
.... LC 8
See also CDWLB 2; DLB 97; EW 4; RGWL 2, 3

Lester, Richard 1932- .... CLC 20

Levenson, Jay .... CLC 70

Lever, Charles (James) 1806-1872
.... NCLC 23
See also DLB 21; RGEL 2

Leverson, Ada Esther 1862(?)-1933(?)
.... TCLC 18
See Elaine
See also CA 117; 202; DLB 153; RGEL 2

Levertov, Denise 1923-1997 . CLC 1, 2, 3, 5, 8, 15, 28, 66; PC 11
See also AMWS 3; CA 1-4R; 178; 163; CAAE 178; CAAS 19; CANR 3, 29, 50, 108; CDALBS; CP 7; CWP; DAM POET; DLB 5, 165; EWL 3; EXPP; FW; INT CANR-29; MTCW 1, 2; PAB; PFS 7, 16; RGAL 4; TUS; WP

Levi, Carlo 1902-1975 .... TCLC 125
See also CA 65-68; 53-56; CANR 10; EWL 3; RGWL 2, 3

Levi, Jonathan .... CLC 76
See also CA 197

Levi, Peter (Chad Tigar) 1931-2000
.... CLC 41
See also CA 5-8R; 187; CANR 34, 80; CP 7; DLB 40

Levi, Primo 1919-1987 ...... CLC 37, 50; SSC 12; TCLC 109
See also CA 13-16R; 122; CANR 12, 33, 61, 70; DLB 177; EWL 3; MTCW 1, 2; RGWL 2, 3

Levin, Ira 1929- .... CLC 3, 6
See also CA 21-24R; CANR 17, 44, 74; CMW 4; CN 7; CPW; DA3; DAM POP; HGG; MTCW 1, 2; SATA 66; SFW 4

Levin, Meyer 1905-1981 .... **CLC 7**
See also AITN 1; CA 9-12R; 104; CANR 15; DAM POP; DLB 9, 28; DLBY 1981; SATA 21; SATA-Obit 27

Levine, Norman 1924- .... **CLC 54**
See also CA 73-76; CAAS 23; CANR 14, 70; DLB 88

Levine, Philip 1928- . **CLC 2, 4, 5, 9, 14, 33, 118; PC 22**
See also AMWS 5; CA 9-12R; CANR 9, 37, 52, 116; CP 7; DAM POET; DLB 5; EWL 3; PFS 8

Levinson, Deirdre 1931- .... **CLC 49**
See also CA 73-76; CANR 70

Levi-Strauss, Claude 1908- .... **CLC 38**
See also CA 1-4R; CANR 6, 32, 57; DLB 242; EWL 3; GFL 1789 to the Present; MTCW 1, 2; TWA

Levitin, Sonia (Wolff) 1934- .... **CLC 17**
See also AAYA 13, 48; CA 29-32R; CANR 14, 32, 79; CLR 53; JRDA; MAICYA 1, 2; SAAS 2; SATA 4, 68, 119; SATA-Essay 131; YAW

Levon, O. U.
See Kesey, Ken (Elton)

Levy, Amy 1861-1889 .... **NCLC 59**
See also DLB 156, 240

Lewes, George Henry 1817-1878 . **NCLC 25**
See also DLB 55, 144

Lewis, Alun 1915-1944 ..... **SSC 40; TCLC 3**
See also BRW 7; CA 104; 188; DLB 20, 162; PAB; RGEL 2

Lewis, C. Day
See Day Lewis, C(ecil)

Lewis, C(live) S(taples) 1898-1963 ... **CLC 1, 3, 6, 14, 27, 124; WLC**
See also AAYA 3, 39; BPFB 2; BRWS 3; CA 81-84; CANR 33, 71; CDBLB 1945-1960; CLR 3, 27; CWRI 5; DA; DA3; DAB; DAC; DAM MST, NOV, POP; DLB 15, 100, 160, 255; EWL 3; FANT; JRDA; LMFS 2; MAICYA 1, 2; MTCW 1, 2; RGEL 2; SATA 13, 100; SCFW; SFW 4; SUFW 1; TEA; WCH; WYA; YAW

Lewis, Cecil Day
See Day Lewis, C(ecil)

Lewis, Janet 1899-1998 .... **CLC 41**
See Winters, Janet Lewis
See also CA 9-12R; 172; CANR 29, 63; CAP 1; CN 7; DLBY 1987; RHW; TCWW 2

Lewis, Matthew Gregory 1775-1818
.... **NCLC 11, 62**
See also DLB 39, 158, 178; HGG; LMFS 1; RGEL 2; SUFW

Lewis, (Harry) Sinclair 1885-1951
.... **TCLC 4, 13, 23, 39; WLC**
See also AMW; AMWC 1; BPFB 2; CA 104; 133; CDALB 1917-1929; DA; DA3; DAB; DAC; DAM MST, NOV; DLB 9, 102; DLBD 1; EWL 3; LAIT 3; MTCW 1, 2; NFS 15; RGAL 4; TUS

Lewis, (Percy) Wyndham 1884(?)-1957
.... **SSC 34; TCLC 2, 9, 104**
See also BRW 7; CA 104; 157; DLB 15; EWL 3; FANT; MTCW 2; RGEL 2

Lewisohn, Ludwig 1883-1955 .... **TCLC 19**
See also CA 107; 203; DLB 4, 9, 28, 102

Lewton, Val 1904-1951 .... **TCLC 76**
See also CA 199; IDFW 3, 4

Leyner, Mark 1956- .... **CLC 92**
See also CA 110; CANR 28, 53; DA3; MTCW 2

Lezama Lima, Jose 1910-1976 ... **CLC 4, 10, 101; HLCS 2**
See also CA 77-80; CANR 71; DAM MULT; DLB 113; EWL 3; HW 1, 2; LAW; RGWL 2, 3

L'Heureux, John (Clarke) 1934- .... **CLC 52**
See also CA 13-16R; CANR 23, 45, 88; DLB 244

Liddell, C. H.
See Kuttner, Henry

Lie, Jonas (Lauritz Idemil) 1833-1908(?)
.... **TCLC 5**
See also CA 115

Lieber, Joel 1937-1971 .... **CLC 6**
See also CA 73-76; 29-32R

Lieber, Stanley Martin
See Lee, Stan

Lieberman, Laurence (James) 1935-
.... **CLC 4, 36**
See also CA 17-20R; CANR 8, 36, 89; CP 7

Lieh Tzu fl. 7th cent. B.C.-5th cent. B.C.
.... **CMLC 27**

Lieksman, Anders
See Haavikko, Paavo Juhani

Li Fei-kan 1904-
See Pa Chin
See also CA 105; TWA

Lifton, Robert Jay 1926- .... **CLC 67**
See also CA 17-20R; CANR 27, 78; INT CANR-27; SATA 66

Lightfoot, Gordon 1938- .... **CLC 26**
See also CA 109

Lightman, Alan P(aige) 1948- .... **CLC 81**
See also CA 141; CANR 63, 105

Ligotti, Thomas (Robert) 1953- ..... **CLC 44; SSC 16**
See also CA 123; CANR 49; HGG; SUFW 2

Li Ho 791-817 .... **PC 13**

Liliencron, (Friedrich Adolf Axel) Detlev von 1844-1909 .... **TCLC 18**
See also CA 117

Lille, Alain de
See Alain de Lille

Lilly, William 1602-1681 .... **LC 27**

Lima, Jose Lezama
See Lezama Lima, Jose

Lima Barreto, Afonso Henrique de 1881-1922 .... **TCLC 23**
See also CA 117; 181; LAW

Lima Barreto, Afonso Henriques de
See Lima Barreto, Afonso Henrique de

Limonov, Edward 1944- .... **CLC 67**
See also CA 137

Lin, Frank
See Atherton, Gertrude (Franklin Horn)

Lincoln, Abraham 1809-1865 .... **NCLC 18**
See also LAIT 2

Lind, Jakov .... **CLC 1, 2, 4, 27, 82**
See Landwirth, Heinz
See also CAAS 4; EWL 3

Lindbergh, Anne (Spencer) Morrow 1906-2001 .... **CLC 82**
See also BPFB 2; CA 17-20R; 193; CANR 16, 73; DAM NOV; MTCW 1, 2; SATA 33; SATA-Obit 125; TUS

Lindsay, David 1878(?)-1945 .... **TCLC 15**
See also CA 113; 187; DLB 255; FANT; SFW 4; SUFW 1

Lindsay, (Nicholas) Vachel 1879-1931
.... **PC 23; TCLC 17; WLC**
See also AMWS 1; CA 114; 135; CANR 79; CDALB 1865-1917; DA; DA3; DAC; DAM MST, POET; DLB 54; EWL 3; EXPP; RGAL 4; SATA 40; WP

Linke-Poot
See Doeblin, Alfred

Linney, Romulus 1930- .... **CLC 51**
See also CA 1-4R; CAD; CANR 40, 44, 79; CD 5; CSW; RGAL 4

Linton, Eliza Lynn 1822-1898 ...... **NCLC 41**
See also DLB 18

Li Po 701-763 .... **CMLC 2; PC 29**
See also WP

Lipsius, Justus 1547-1606 .... **LC 16**

Lipsyte, Robert (Michael) 1938- .... **CLC 21**
See also AAYA 7, 45; CA 17-20R; CANR 8, 57; CLR 23, 76; DA; DAC; DAM MST, NOV; JRDA; LAIT 5; MAICYA 1, 2; SATA 5, 68, 113; WYA; YAW

Lish, Gordon (Jay) 1934- . **CLC 45; SSC 18**
See also CA 113; 117; CANR 79; DLB 130; INT 117

Lispector, Clarice 1925(?)-1977 ..... **CLC 43; HLCS 2; SSC 34**
See also CA 139; 116; CANR 71; CDWLB 3; DLB 113; DNFS 1; EWL 3; FW; HW 2; LAW; RGSF 2; RGWL 2, 3; WLIT 1

Littell, Robert 1935(?)- .... **CLC 42**
See also CA 109; 112; CANR 64, 115; CMW 4

Little, Malcolm 1925-1965
See Malcolm X
See also BW 1, 3; CA 125; 111; CANR 82; DA; DA3; DAB; DAC; DAM MST, MULT; MTCW 1, 2; NCFS 3

Littlewit, Humphrey Gent.
See Lovecraft, H(oward) P(hillips)

Litwos
See Sienkiewicz, Henryk (Adam Alexander Pius)

Liu, E. 1857-1909 .... **TCLC 15**
See also CA 115; 190

Lively, Penelope (Margaret) 1933-
.... **CLC 32, 50**
See also BPFB 2; CA 41-44R; CANR 29, 67, 79; CLR 7; CN 7; CWRI 5; DAM NOV; DLB 14, 161, 207; FANT; JRDA; MAICYA 1, 2; MTCW 1, 2; SATA 7, 60, 101; TEA

Livesay, Dorothy (Kathleen) 1909-1996
.... **CLC 4, 15, 79**
See also AITN 2; CA 25-28R; CAAS 8; CANR 36, 67; DAC; DAM MST, POET; DLB 68; FW; MTCW 1; RGEL 2; TWA

Livy c. 59B.C.-c. 12 .... **CMLC 11**
See also AW 2; CDWLB 1; DLB 211; RGWL 2, 3

Lizardi, Jose Joaquin Fernandez de 1776-1827 .... **NCLC 30**
See also LAW

Llewellyn, Richard
See Llewellyn Lloyd, Richard Dafydd Vivian
See also DLB 15

Llewellyn Lloyd, Richard Dafydd Vivian 1906-1983 .... **CLC 7, 80**
See Llewellyn, Richard
See also CA 53-56; 111; CANR 7, 71; SATA 11; SATA-Obit 37

Llosa, (Jorge) Mario (Pedro) Vargas
See Vargas Llosa, (Jorge) Mario (Pedro)
See also RGWL 3

Llosa, Mario Vargas
See Vargas Llosa, (Jorge) Mario (Pedro)

Lloyd, Manda
See Mander, (Mary) Jane

Lloyd Webber, Andrew 1948-
See Webber, Andrew Lloyd
See also AAYA 1, 38; CA 116; 149; DAM DRAM; SATA 56

Llull, Ramon c. 1235-c. 1316 .... **CMLC 12**

Lobb, Ebenezer
See Upward, Allen

Locke, Alain (Le Roy) 1886-1954
.... **BLCS; HR 3; TCLC 43**
See also BW 1, 3; CA 106; 124; CANR 79; DLB 51; LMFS 2; RGAL 4

Locke, John 1632-1704 .... **LC 7, 35**
See also DLB 31, 101, 213, 252; RGEL 2; WLIT 3

Locke-Elliott, Sumner
See Elliott, Sumner Locke
Lockhart, John Gibson 1794-1854 . **NCLC 6**
See also DLB 110, 116, 144
Lockridge, Ross (Franklin), Jr. 1914-1948
.... **TCLC 111**
See also CA 108; 145; CANR 79; DLB 143; DLBY 1980; RGAL 4; RHW
Lockwood, Robert
See Johnson, Robert
Lodge, David (John) 1935- ...... **CLC 36, 141**
See also BEST 90:1; BRWS 4; CA 17-20R; CANR 19, 53, 92; CN 7; CPW; DAM POP; DLB 14, 194; EWL 3; INT CANR-19; MTCW 1, 2
Lodge, Thomas 1558-1625 .... **LC 41**
See also DLB 172; RGEL 2
Loewinsohn, Ron(ald William) 1937-
.... **CLC 52**
See also CA 25-28R; CANR 71
Logan, Jake
See Smith, Martin Cruz
Logan, John (Burton) 1923-1987 ...... **CLC 5**
See also CA 77-80; 124; CANR 45; DLB 5
Lo Kuan-chung 1330(?)-1400(?) .... **LC 12**
Lombard, Nap
See Johnson, Pamela Hansford
Lomotey (editor), Kofi .... **CLC 70**
London, Jack 1876-1916 . **SSC 4, 49; TCLC 9, 15, 39; WLC**
See London, John Griffith
See also AAYA 13; AITN 2; AMW; BPFB 2; BYA 4, 13; CDALB 1865-1917; DLB 8, 12, 78, 212; EWL 3; EXPS; LAIT 3; NFS 8; RGAL 4; RGSF 2; SATA 18; SFW 4; SSFS 7; TCWW 2; TUS; WYA; YAW
London, John Griffith 1876-1916
See London, Jack
See also CA 110; 119; CANR 73; DA; DA3; DAB; DAC; DAM MST, NOV; JRDA; MAICYA 1, 2; MTCW 1, 2
Long, Emmett
See Leonard, Elmore (John, Jr.)
Longbaugh, Harry
See Goldman, William (W.)
Longfellow, Henry Wadsworth 1807-1882
. **NCLC 2, 45, 101, 103; PC 30; WLCS**
See also AMW; AMWR 2; CDALB 1640-1865; DA; DA3; DAB; DAC; DAM MST, POET; DLB 1, 59, 235; EXPP; PAB; PFS 2, 7, 17; RGAL 4; SATA 19; TUS; WP
Longinus c. 1st cent. - .... **CMLC 27**
See also AW 2; DLB 176
Longley, Michael 1939- .... **CLC 29**
See also BRWS 8; CA 102; CP 7; DLB 40
Longus fl. c. 2nd cent. - .... **CMLC 7**
Longway, A. Hugh
See Lang, Andrew
Lonnbohm, Armas Eino Leopold 1878-1926
See Leino, Eino
See also CA 123
Lonnrot, Elias 1802-1884 .... **NCLC 53**
See also EFS 1
Lonsdale, Roger ed. .... **CLC 65**
Lopate, Phillip 1943- .... **CLC 29**
See also CA 97-100; CANR 88; DLBY 1980; INT 97-100
Lopez, Barry (Holstun) 1945- .... **CLC 70**
See also AAYA 9; ANW; CA 65-68; CANR 7, 23, 47, 68, 92; DLB 256, 275; INT CANR-7, -23; MTCW 1; RGAL 4; SATA 67
Lopez Portillo (y Pacheco), Jose 1920-
.... **CLC 46**
See also CA 129; HW 1
Lopez y Fuentes, Gregorio 1897(?)-1966
.... **CLC 32**
See also CA 131; EWL 3; HW 1

Lorca, Federico Garcia
See Garcia Lorca, Federico
See also DFS 4; EW 11; RGWL 2, 3; WP
Lord, Audre
See Lorde, Audre (Geraldine)
See also EWL 3
Lord, Bette Bao 1938- .... **AAL; CLC 23**
See also BEST 90:3; BPFB 2; CA 107; CANR 41, 79; INT CA-107; SATA 58
Lord Auch
See Bataille, Georges
Lord Brooke
See Greville, Fulke
Lord Byron
See Byron, George Gordon (Noel)
Lorde, Audre (Geraldine) 1934-1992
.... **BLC 2; CLC 18, 71; PC 12**
See Domini, Rey; Lord, Audre
See also AFAW 1, 2; BW 1, 3; CA 25-28R; 142; CANR 16, 26, 46, 82; DA3; DAM MULT, POET; DLB 41; FW; MTCW 1, 2; PFS 16; RGAL 4
Lord Houghton
See Milnes, Richard Monckton
Lord Jeffrey
See Jeffrey, Francis
Loreaux, Nichol .... **CLC 65**
Lorenzini, Carlo 1826-1890
See Collodi, Carlo
See also MAICYA 1, 2; SATA 29, 100
Lorenzo, Heberto Padilla
See Padilla (Lorenzo), Heberto
Loris
See Hofmannsthal, Hugo von
Loti, Pierre .... **TCLC 11**
See Viaud, (Louis Marie) Julien
See also DLB 123; GFL 1789 to the Present
Lou, Henri
See Andreas-Salome, Lou
Louie, David Wong 1954- .... **CLC 70**
See also CA 139
Louis, Adrian C. .... **NNAL**
Louis, Father M.
See Merton, Thomas (James)
Lovecraft, H(oward) P(hillips) 1890-1937
.... **SSC 3, 52; TCLC 4, 22**
See also AAYA 14; BPFB 2; CA 104; 133; CANR 106; DA3; DAM POP; HGG; MTCW 1, 2; RGAL 4; SCFW; SFW 4; SUFW
Lovelace, Earl 1935- .... **CLC 51**
See also BW 2; CA 77-80; CANR 41, 72, 114; CD 5; CDWLB 3; CN 7; DLB 125; EWL 3; MTCW 1
Lovelace, Richard 1618-1657 .... **LC 24**
See also BRW 2; DLB 131; EXPP; PAB; RGEL 2
Lowe, Pardee 1904- .... **AAL**
Lowell, Amy 1874-1925 .. **PC 13; TCLC 1, 8**
See also AMW; CA 104; 151; DAM POET; DLB 54, 140; EWL 3; EXPP; LMFS 2; MAWW; MTCW 2; RGAL 4; TUS
Lowell, James Russell 1819-1891 .. **NCLC 2, 90**
See also AMWS 1; CDALB 1640-1865; DLB 1, 11, 64, 79, 189, 235; RGAL 4
Lowell, Robert (Traill Spence, Jr.) 1917-1977 ... **CLC 1, 2, 3, 4, 5, 8, 9, 11, 15, 37, 124; PC 3; WLC**
See also AMW; AMWR 2; CA 9-12R; 73-76; CABS 2; CANR 26, 60; CDALBS; DA; DA3; DAB; DAC; DAM MST, NOV; DLB 5, 169; EWL 3; MTCW 1, 2; PAB; PFS 6, 7; RGAL 4; WP
Lowenthal, Michael (Francis) 1969-
.... **CLC 119**
See also CA 150; CANR 115

Lowndes, Marie Adelaide (Belloc) 1868-1947
.... **TCLC 12**
See also CA 107; CMW 4; DLB 70; RHW
Lowry, (Clarence) Malcolm 1909-1957
.... **SSC 31; TCLC 6, 40**
See also BPFB 2; BRWS 3; CA 105; 131; CANR 62, 105; CDBLB 1945-1960; DLB 15; EWL 3; MTCW 1, 2; RGEL 2
Lowry, Mina Gertrude 1882-1966
See Loy, Mina
See also CA 113
Loxsmith, John
See Brunner, John (Kilian Houston)
Loy, Mina .... **CLC 28; PC 16**
See Lowry, Mina Gertrude
See also DAM POET; DLB 4, 54
Loyson-Bridet
See Schwob, Marcel (Mayer Andre)
Lucan 39-65 .... **CMLC 33**
See also AW 2; DLB 211; EFS 2; RGWL 2, 3
Lucas, Craig 1951- .... **CLC 64**
See also CA 137; CAD; CANR 71, 109; CD 5; GLL 2
Lucas, E(dward) V(errall) 1868-1938
.... **TCLC 73**
See also CA 176; DLB 98, 149, 153; SATA 20
Lucas, George 1944- .... **CLC 16**
See also AAYA 1, 23; CA 77-80; CANR 30; SATA 56
Lucas, Hans
See Godard, Jean-Luc
Lucas, Victoria
See Plath, Sylvia
Lucian c. 125-c. 180 .... **CMLC 32**
See also AW 2; DLB 176; RGWL 2, 3
Lucretius c. 94B.C.-c. 49B.C. .... **CMLC 48**
See also AW 2; CDWLB 1; DLB 211; EFS 2; RGWL 2, 3
Ludlam, Charles 1943-1987 ...... **CLC 46, 50**
See also CA 85-88; 122; CAD; CANR 72, 86; DLB 266
Ludlum, Robert 1927-2001 .... **CLC 22, 43**
See also AAYA 10; BEST 89:1, 90:3; BPFB 2; CA 33-36R; 195; CANR 25, 41, 68, 105; CMW 4; CPW; DA3; DAM NOV, POP; DLBY 1982; MSW; MTCW 1, 2
Ludwig, Ken .... **CLC 60**
See also CA 195; CAD
Ludwig, Otto 1813-1865 .... **NCLC 4**
See also DLB 129
Lugones, Leopoldo 1874-1938 .... **HLCS 2; TCLC 15**
See also CA 116; 131; CANR 104; EWL 3; HW 1; LAW
Lu Hsun .... **SSC 20; TCLC 3**
See Shu-Jen, Chou
See also EWL 3
Lukacs, George .... **CLC 24**
See Lukacs, Gyorgy (Szegeny von)
Lukacs, Gyorgy (Szegeny von) 1885-1971
See Lukacs, George
See also CA 101; 29-32R; CANR 62; CD-WLB 4; DLB 215, 242; EW 10; EWL 3; MTCW 2
Luke, Peter (Ambrose Cyprian) 1919-1995
.... **CLC 38**
See also CA 81-84; 147; CANR 72; CBD; CD 5; DLB 13
Lunar, Dennis
See Mungo, Raymond
Lurie, Alison 1926- .... **CLC 4, 5, 18, 39**
See also BPFB 2; CA 1-4R; CANR 2, 17, 50, 88; CN 7; DLB 2; MTCW 1; SATA 46, 112

Lustig, Arnost 1926- .... **CLC 56**
See also AAYA 3; CA 69-72; CANR 47, 102; CWW 2; DLB 232; EWL 3; SATA 56

Luther, Martin 1483-1546 .... **LC 9, 37**
See also CDWLB 2; DLB 179; EW 2; RGWL 2, 3

Luxemburg, Rosa 1870(?)-1919 .... **TCLC 63**
See also CA 118

Luzi, Mario 1914- .... **CLC 13**
See also CA 61-64; CANR 9, 70; CWW 2; DLB 128; EWL 3

L'vov, Arkady .... **CLC 59**

Lydgate, John c. 1370-1450(?) .... **LC 81**
See also BRW 1; DLB 146; RGEL 2

Lyly, John 1554(?)-1606 .... **DC 7; LC 41**
See also BRW 1; DAM DRAM; DLB 62, 167; RGEL 2

L'Ymagier
See Gourmont, Remy(-Marie-Charles) de

Lynch, B. Suarez
See Borges, Jorge Luis

Lynch, David (Keith) 1946- ..... **CLC 66, 162**
See also CA 124; 129; CANR 111

Lynch, James
See Andreyev, Leonid (Nikolaevich)

Lyndsay, Sir David 1485-1555 .... **LC 20**
See also RGEL 2

Lynn, Kenneth S(chuyler) 1923-2001
.... **CLC 50**
See also CA 1-4R; 196; CANR 3, 27, 65

Lynx
See West, Rebecca

Lyons, Marcus
See Blish, James (Benjamin)

Lyotard, Jean-Francois 1924-1998
.... **TCLC 103**
See also DLB 242; EWL 3

Lyre, Pinchbeck
See Sassoon, Siegfried (Lorraine)

Lytle, Andrew (Nelson) 1902-1995 .. **CLC 22**
See also CA 9-12R; 150; CANR 70; CN 7; CSW; DLB 6; DLBY 1995; RGAL 4; RHW

Lyttelton, George 1709-1773 .... **LC 10**
See also RGEL 2

Lytton of Knebworth, Baron
See Bulwer-Lytton, Edward (George Earle Lytton)

Maas, Peter 1929-2001 .... **CLC 29**
See also CA 93-96; 201; INT CA-93-96; MTCW 2

Macaulay, Catherine 1731-1791 .... **LC 64**
See also DLB 104

Macaulay, (Emilie) Rose 1881(?)-1958
.... **TCLC 7, 44**
See also CA 104; DLB 36; EWL 3; RGEL 2; RHW

Macaulay, Thomas Babington 1800-1859
.... **NCLC 42**
See also BRW 4; CDBLB 1832-1890; DLB 32, 55; RGEL 2

MacBeth, George (Mann) 1932-1992
.... **CLC 2, 5, 9**
See also CA 25-28R; 136; CANR 61, 66; DLB 40; MTCW 1; PFS 8; SATA 4; SATA-Obit 70

MacCaig, Norman (Alexander) 1910-1996
.... **CLC 36**
See also BRWS 6; CA 9-12R; CANR 3, 34; CP 7; DAB; DAM POET; DLB 27; EWL 3; RGEL 2

MacCarthy, Sir (Charles Otto) Desmond 1877-1952 .... **TCLC 36**
See also CA 167

MacDiarmid, Hugh .... **CLC 2, 4, 11, 19, 63; PC 9**
See Grieve, C(hristopher) M(urray)
See also CDBLB 1945-1960; DLB 20; EWL 3; RGEL 2

MacDonald, Anson
See Heinlein, Robert A(nson)

Macdonald, Cynthia 1928- .... **CLC 13, 19**
See also CA 49-52; CANR 4, 44; DLB 105

MacDonald, George 1824-1905 ..... **TCLC 9, 113**
See also BYA 5; CA 106; 137; CANR 80; CLR 67; DLB 18, 163, 178; FANT; MAICYA 1, 2; RGEL 2; SATA 33, 100; SFW 4; SUFW; WCH

Macdonald, John
See Millar, Kenneth

MacDonald, John D(ann) 1916-1986
.... **CLC 3, 27, 44**
See also BPFB 2; CA 1-4R; 121; CANR 1, 19, 60; CMW 4; CPW; DAM NOV, POP; DLB 8; DLBY 1986; MSW; MTCW 1, 2; SFW 4

Macdonald, John Ross
See Millar, Kenneth

Macdonald, Ross ..... **CLC 1, 2, 3, 14, 34, 41**
See Millar, Kenneth
See also AMWS 4; BPFB 2; DLBD 6; MSW; RGAL 4

MacDougal, John
See Blish, James (Benjamin)

MacDougal, John
See Blish, James (Benjamin)

MacDowell, John
See Parks, Tim(othy Harold)

MacEwen, Gwendolyn (Margaret) 1941-1987 .... **CLC 13, 55**
See also CA 9-12R; 124; CANR 7, 22; DLB 53, 251; SATA 50; SATA-Obit 55

Macha, Karel Hynek 1810-1846 .. **NCLC 46**

Machado (y Ruiz), Antonio 1875-1939
.... **TCLC 3**
See also CA 104; 174; DLB 108; EW 9; EWL 3; HW 2; RGWL 2, 3

Machado de Assis, Joaquim Maria 1839-1908 ... **BLC 2; HLCS 2; SSC 24; TCLC 10**
See also CA 107; 153; CANR 91; LAW; RGSF 2; RGWL 2, 3; TWA; WLIT 1

Machen, Arthur .... **SSC 20; TCLC 4**
See Jones, Arthur Llewellyn
See also CA 179; DLB 156, 178; RGEL 2; SUFW 1

Machiavelli, Niccolo 1469-1527 . **DC 16; LC 8, 36; WLCS**
See also CA; DAB; DAC; DAM MST; EW 2; LAIT 1; LMFS 1; NFS 9; RGWL 2, 3; TWA

MacInnes, Colin 1914-1976 .... **CLC 4, 23**
See also CA 69-72; 65-68; CANR 21; DLB 14; MTCW 1, 2; RGEL 2; RHW

MacInnes, Helen (Clark) 1907-1985
.... **CLC 27, 39**
See also BPFB 2; CA 1-4R; 117; CANR 1, 28, 58; CMW 4; CPW; DAM POP; DLB 87; MSW; MTCW 1, 2; SATA 22; SATA-Obit 44

Mackay, Mary 1855-1924
See Corelli, Marie
See also CA 118; 177; FANT; RHW

Mackenzie, Compton (Edward Montague) 1883-1972 .... **CLC 18; TCLC 116**
See also CA 21-22; 37-40R; CAP 2; DLB 34, 100; RGEL 2

Mackenzie, Henry 1745-1831 .... **NCLC 41**
See also DLB 39; RGEL 2

Mackintosh, Elizabeth 1896(?)-1952
See Tey, Josephine
See also CA 110; CMW 4

MacLaren, James
See Grieve, C(hristopher) M(urray)

Mac Laverty, Bernard 1942- .... **CLC 31**
See also CA 116; 118; CANR 43, 88; CN 7; DLB 267; INT CA-118; RGSF 2

MacLean, Alistair (Stuart) 1922(?)-1987
.... **CLC 3, 13, 50, 63**
See also CA 57-60; 121; CANR 28, 61; CMW 4; CPW; DAM POP; DLB 276; MTCW 1; SATA 23; SATA-Obit 50; TCWW 2

Maclean, Norman (Fitzroy) 1902-1990
.... **CLC 78; SSC 13**
See also CA 102; 132; CANR 49; CPW; DAM POP; DLB 206; TCWW 2

MacLeish, Archibald 1892-1982 .. **CLC 3, 8, 14, 68; PC 47**
See also AMW; CA 9-12R; 106; CAD; CANR 33, 63; CDALBS; DAM POET; DFS 4, 7, 45; DLBY 1982; EWL 3; EXPP; MTCW 1, 2; PAB; PFS 5; RGAL 4; TUS

MacLennan, (John) Hugh 1907-1990
.... **CLC 2, 14, 92**
See also CA 5-8R; 142; CANR 33; DAC; DAM MST; DLB 68; EWL 3; MTCW 1, 2; RGEL 2; TWA

MacLeod, Alistair 1936- .... **CLC 56, 165**
See also CA 123; CCA 1; DAC; DAM MST; DLB 60; MTCW 2; RGSF 2

Macleod, Fiona
See Sharp, William
See also RGEL 2; SUFW

MacNeice, (Frederick) Louis 1907-1963
.... **CLC 1, 4, 10, 53**
See also BRW 7; CA 85-88; CANR 61; DAB; DAM POET; DLB 10, 20; EWL 3; MTCW 1, 2; RGEL 2

MacNeill, Dand
See Fraser, George MacDonald

Macpherson, James 1736-1796 .... **LC 29**
See Ossian
See also BRWS 8; DLB 109; RGEL 2

Macpherson, (Jean) Jay 1931- .... **CLC 14**
See also CA 5-8R; CANR 90; CP 7; CWP; DLB 53

Macrobius fl. 430- .... **CMLC 48**

MacShane, Frank 1927-1999 .... **CLC 39**
See also CA 9-12R; 186; CANR 3, 33; DLB 111

Macumber, Mari
See Sandoz, Mari(e Susette)

Madach, Imre 1823-1854 .... **NCLC 19**

Madden, (Jerry) David 1933- ...... **CLC 5, 15**
See also CA 1-4R; CAAS 3; CANR 4, 45; CN 7; CSW; DLB 6; MTCW 1

Maddern, Al(an)
See Ellison, Harlan (Jay)

Madhubuti, Haki R. 1942- . **BLC 2; CLC 6, 73; PC 5**
See Lee, Don L.
See also BW 2, 3; CA 73-76; CANR 24, 51, 73; CP 7; CSW; DAM MULT, POET; DLB 5, 41; DLBD 8; EWL 3; MTCW 2; RGAL 4

Maepenn, Hugh
See Kuttner, Henry

Maepenn, K. H.
See Kuttner, Henry

Maeterlinck, Maurice 1862-1949 ... **TCLC 3**
See also CA 104; 136; CANR 80; DAM DRAM; DLB 192; EW 8; EWL 3; GFL 1789 to the Present; LMFS 2; RGWL 2, 3; SATA 66; TWA

Maginn, William 1794-1842 .... **NCLC 8**
See also DLB 110, 159

Mahapatra, Jayanta 1928- .... **CLC 33**
See also CA 73-76; CAAS 9; CANR 15, 33, 66, 87; CP 7; DAM MULT

Mahfouz, Naguib (Abdel Aziz Al-Sabilgi)
1911(?)- .... CLC 153
See Mahfuz, Najib (Abdel Aziz al-Sabilgi)
See also AAYA 49; BEST 89:2; CA 128;
CANR 55, 101; CWW 2; DA3; DAM
NOV; MTCW 1, 2; RGWL 2, 3; SSFS 9

Mahfuz, Najib (Abdel Aziz al-Sabilgi)
.... CLC 52, 55
See Mahfouz, Naguib (Abdel Aziz Al-Sabilgi)
See also AFW; DLBY 1988; EWL 3; RGSF 2; WLIT 2

Mahon, Derek 1941- .... CLC 27
See also BRWS 6; CA 113; 128; CANR 88; CP 7; DLB 40; EWL 3

Maiakovskii, Vladimir
See Mayakovski, Vladimir (Vladimirovich)
See also IDTP; RGWL 2, 3

Mailer, Norman 1923- . CLC 1, 2, 3, 4, 5, 8, 11, 14, 28, 39, 74, 111
See also AAYA 31; AITN 2; AMW; AMWR 2; BPFB 2; CA 9-12R; CABS 1; CANR 28, 74, 77; CDALB 1968-1988; CN 7; CPW; DA; DA3; DAB; DAC; DAM MST, NOV, POP; DLB 2, 16, 28, 185, 278; DLBD 3; DLBY 1980, 1983; EWL 3; MTCW 1, 2; NFS 10; RGAL 4; TUS

Maillet, Antonine 1929- .... CLC 54, 118
See also CA 115; 120; CANR 46, 74, 77; CCA 1; CWW 2; DAC; DLB 60; INT 120; MTCW 2

Mais, Roger 1905-1955 .... TCLC 8
See also BW 1, 3; CA 105; 124; CANR 82; CDWLB 3; DLB 125; EWL 3; MTCW 1; RGEL 2

Maistre, Joseph 1753-1821 .... NCLC 37
See also GFL 1789 to the Present

Maitland, Frederic William 1850-1906
.... TCLC 65

Maitland, Sara (Louise) 1950- .... CLC 49
See also CA 69-72; CANR 13, 59; DLB 271; FW

Major, Clarence 1936- .. BLC 2; CLC 3, 19, 48
See also AFAW 2; BW 2, 3; CA 21-24R; CAAS 6; CANR 13, 25, 53, 82; CN 7; CP 7; CSW; DAM MULT; DLB 33; EWL 3; MSW

Major, Kevin (Gerald) 1949- .... CLC 26
See also AAYA 16; CA 97-100; CANR 21, 38, 112; CLR 11; DAC; DLB 60; INT CANR-21; JRDA; MAICYA 1, 2; MAICYAS 1; SATA 32, 82, 134; WYA; YAW

Maki, James
See Ozu, Yasujiro

Malabaila, Damiano
See Levi, Primo

Malamud, Bernard 1914-1986 . CLC 1, 2, 3, 5, 8, 9, 11, 18, 27, 44, 78, 85; SSC 15; TCLC 129; WLC
See also AAYA 16; AMWS 1; BPFB 2; CA 5-8R; 118; CABS 1; CANR 28, 62, 114; CDALB 1941-1968; CPW; DA; DA3; DAB; DAC; DAM MST, NOV, POP; DLB 2, 28, 152; DLBY 1980, 1986; EWL 3; EXPS; LAIT 4; MTCW 1, 2; NFS 4, 9; RGAL 4; RGSF 2; SSFS 8, 13, 16; TUS

Malan, Herman
See Bosman, Herman Charles; Bosman, Herman Charles

Malaparte, Curzio 1898-1957 .... TCLC 52
See also DLB 264

Malcolm, Dan
See Silverberg, Robert

Malcolm X .... BLC 2; CLC 82, 117; WLCS
See Little, Malcolm
See also LAIT 5

Malherbe, Francois de 1555-1628 .... LC 5
See also GFL Beginnings to 1789

Mallarme, Stephane 1842-1898 ..... NCLC 4, 41; PC 4
See also DAM POET; DLB 217; EW 7; GFL 1789 to the Present; LMFS 2; RGWL 2, 3; TWA

Mallet-Joris, Francoise 1930- .... CLC 11
See also CA 65-68; CANR 17; DLB 83; EWL 3; GFL 1789 to the Present

Malley, Ern
See McAuley, James Phillip

Mallon, Thomas 1951- .... CLC 172
See also CA 110; CANR 29, 57, 92

Mallowan, Agatha Christie
See Christie, Agatha (Mary Clarissa)

Maloff, Saul 1922- .... CLC 5
See also CA 33-36R

Malone, Louis
See MacNeice, (Frederick) Louis

Malone, Michael (Christopher) 1942-
.... CLC 43
See also CA 77-80; CANR 14, 32, 57, 114

Malory, Sir Thomas 1410(?)-1471(?)
.... LC 11, 88; WLCS
See also BRW 1; BRWR 2; CDBLB Before 1660; DA; DAB; DAC; DAM MST; DLB 146; EFS 2; RGEL 2; SATA 59; SATA-Brief 33; TEA; WLIT 3

Malouf, (George Joseph) David 1934-
.... CLC 28, 86
See also CA 124; CANR 50, 76; CN 7; CP 7; EWL 3; MTCW 2

Malraux, (Georges-)Andre 1901-1976
.... CLC 1, 4, 9, 13, 15, 57
See also BPFB 2; CA 21-22; 69-72; CANR 34, 58; CAP 2; DA3; DAM NOV; DLB 72; EW 12; EWL 3; GFL 1789 to the Present; MTCW 1, 2; RGWL 2, 3; TWA

Malzberg, Barry N(athaniel) 1939- .. CLC 7
See also CA 61-64; CAAS 4; CANR 16; CMW 4; DLB 8; SFW 4

Mamet, David (Alan) 1947- . CLC 9, 15, 34, 46, 91, 166; DC 4
See also AAYA 3; CA 81-84; CABS 3; CANR 15, 41, 67, 72; CD 5; DA3; DAM DRAM; DFS 15; DLB 7; EWL 3; IDFW 4; MTCW 1, 2; RGAL 4

Mamoulian, Rouben (Zachary) 1897-1987
.... CLC 16
See also CA 25-28R; 124; CANR 85

Mandelshtam, Osip
See Mandelstam, Osip (Emilievich)
See also EW 10; EWL 3; RGWL 2, 3

Mandelstam, Osip (Emilievich)
1891(?)-1943(?) .... PC 14; TCLC 2, 6
See Mandelshtam, Osip
See also CA 104; 150; MTCW 2; TWA

Mander, (Mary) Jane 1877-1949 .. TCLC 31
See also CA 162; RGEL 2

Mandeville, Bernard 1670-1733 .... LC 82
See also DLB 101

Mandeville, Sir John fl. 1350- ..... CMLC 19
See also DLB 146

Mandiargues, Andre Pieyre de .... CLC 41
See Pieyre de Mandiargues, Andre
See also DLB 83

Mandrake, Ethel Belle
See Thurman, Wallace (Henry)

Mangan, James Clarence 1803-1849
.... NCLC 27
See also RGEL 2

Maniere, J.-E.
See Giraudoux, Jean(-Hippolyte)

Mankiewicz, Herman (Jacob) 1897-1953
.... TCLC 85
See also CA 120; 169; DLB 26; IDFW 3, 4

Manley, (Mary) Delariviere 1672(?)-1724
.... LC 1, 42
See also DLB 39, 80; RGEL 2

Mann, Abel
See Creasey, John

Mann, Emily 1952- .... DC 7
See also CA 130; CAD; CANR 55; CD 5; CWD; DLB 266

Mann, (Luiz) Heinrich 1871-1950 .. TCLC 9
See also CA 106; 164; 181; DLB 66, 118; EW 8; EWL 3; RGWL 2, 3

Mann, (Paul) Thomas 1875-1955 ...... SSC 5; TCLC 2, 8, 14, 21, 35, 44, 60; WLC
See also BPFB 2; CA 104; 128; CDWLB 2; DA; DA3; DAB; DAC; DAM MST, NOV; DLB 66; EW 9; EWL 3; GLL 1; LMFS 1; MTCW 1, 2; NFS 17; RGSF 2; RGWL 2, 3; SSFS 4, 9; TWA

Mannheim, Karl 1893-1947 .... TCLC 65
See also CA 204

Manning, David
See Faust, Frederick (Schiller)
See also TCWW 2

Manning, Frederic 1887(?)-1935 .. TCLC 25
See also CA 124; DLB 260

Manning, Olivia 1915-1980 .... CLC 5, 19
See also CA 5-8R; 101; CANR 29; EWL 3; FW; MTCW 1; RGEL 2

Mano, D. Keith 1942- .... CLC 2, 10
See also CA 25-28R; CAAS 6; CANR 26, 57; DLB 6

Mansfield, Katherine . SSC 9, 23, 38; TCLC 2, 8, 39; WLC
See Beauchamp, Kathleen Mansfield
See also BPFB 2; BRW 7; DAB; DLB 162; EWL 3; EXPS; FW; GLL 1; RGEL 2; RGSF 2; SSFS 2, 8, 10, 11

Manso, Peter 1940- .... CLC 39
See also CA 29-32R; CANR 44

Mantecon, Juan Jimenez
See Jimenez (Mantecon), Juan Ramon

Mantel, Hilary (Mary) 1952- .... CLC 144
See also CA 125; CANR 54, 101; CN 7; DLB 271; RHW

Manton, Peter
See Creasey, John

Man Without a Spleen, A
See Chekhov, Anton (Pavlovich)

Manzoni, Alessandro 1785-1873 .. NCLC 29, 98
See also EW 5; RGWL 2, 3; TWA

Map, Walter 1140-1209 .... CMLC 32

Mapu, Abraham (ben Jekutiel) 1808-1867
.... NCLC 18

Mara, Sally
See Queneau, Raymond

Maracle, Lee 1950- .... NNAL
See also CA 149

Marat, Jean Paul 1743-1793 .... LC 10

Marcel, Gabriel Honore 1889-1973
.... CLC 15
See also CA 102; 45-48; EWL 3; MTCW 1, 2

March, William 1893-1954 .... TCLC 96

Marchbanks, Samuel
See Davies, (William) Robertson
See also CCA 1

Marchi, Giacomo
See Bassani, Giorgio

Marcus Aurelius
See Aurelius, Marcus
See also AW 2

Marguerite
See de Navarre, Marguerite

Marguerite d'Angouleme
See de Navarre, Marguerite
See also GFL Beginnings to 1789

Marguerite de Navarre
See de Navarre, Marguerite
See also RGWL 2, 3

Margulies, Donald 1954- .... CLC 76
See also CA 200; DFS 13; DLB 228
Marie de France c. 12th cent. - .... CMLC 8; PC 22
See also DLB 208; FW; RGWL 2, 3
Marie de l'Incarnation 1599-1672 ..... LC 10
Marier, Captain Victor
See Griffith, D(avid Lewelyn) W(ark)
Mariner, Scott
See Pohl, Frederik
Marinetti, Filippo Tommaso 1876-1944
.... TCLC 10
See also CA 107; DLB 114, 264; EW 9; EWL 3
Marivaux, Pierre Carlet de Chamblain de 1688-1763 .... DC 7; LC 4
See also GFL Beginnings to 1789; RGWL 2, 3; TWA
Markandaya, Kamala .... CLC 8, 38
See Taylor, Kamala (Purnaiya)
See also BYA 13; CN 7; EWL 3
Markfield, Wallace 1926-2002 .... CLC 8
See also CA 69-72; 208; CAAS 3; CN 7; DLB 2, 28; DLBY 2002
Markham, Edwin 1852-1940 .... TCLC 47
See also CA 160; DLB 54, 186; RGAL 4
Markham, Robert
See Amis, Kingsley (William)
Markoosie .... NNAL
See Markoosie, Patsauq
See also CLR 23; DAM MULT
Marks, J
See Highwater, Jamake (Mamake)
Marks, J.
See Highwater, Jamake (Mamake)
Marks-Highwater, J
See Highwater, Jamake (Mamake)
Marks-Highwater, J.
See Highwater, Jamake (Mamake)
Markson, David M(errill) 1927- ..... CLC 67
See also CA 49-52; CANR 1, 91; CN 7
Marlatt, Daphne (Buckle) 1942- ... CLC 168
See also CA 25-28R; CANR 17, 39; CN 7; CP 7; CWP; DLB 60; FW
Marley, Bob .... CLC 17
See Marley, Robert Nesta
Marley, Robert Nesta 1945-1981
See Marley, Bob
See also CA 107; 103
Marlowe, Christopher 1564-1593 .... DC 1; LC 22, 47; WLC
See also BRW 1; BRWR 1; CDBLB Before 1660; DA; DA3; DAB; DAC; DAM DRAM, MST; DFS 1, 5, 13; DLB 62; EXPP; LMFS 1; RGEL 2; TEA; WLIT 3
Marlowe, Stephen 1928- .... CLC 70
See Queen, Ellery
See also CA 13-16R; CANR 6, 55; CMW 4; SFW 4
Marmion, Shakerley 1603-1639 .... LC 89
See also DLB 58; RGEL 2
Marmontel, Jean-Francois 1723-1799 . LC 2
Maron, Monika 1941- .... CLC 165
See also CA 201
Marquand, John P(hillips) 1893-1960
.... CLC 2, 10
See also AMW; BPFB 2; CA 85-88; CANR 73; CMW 4; DLB 9, 102; EWL 3; MTCW 2; RGAL 4
Marques, Rene 1919-1979 . CLC 96; HLC 2
See also CA 97-100; 85-88; CANR 78; DAM MULT; DLB 113; EWL 3; HW 1, 2; LAW; RGSF 2
Marquez, Gabriel (Jose) Garcia
See Garcia Marquez, Gabriel (Jose)
Marquis, Don(ald Robert Perry) 1878-1937
.... TCLC 7
See also CA 104; 166; DLB 11, 25; RGAL 4

Marquis de Sade
See Sade, Donatien Alphonse Francois
Marric, J. J.
See Creasey, John
See also MSW
Marryat, Frederick 1792-1848 .... NCLC 3
See also DLB 21, 163; RGEL 2; WCH
Marsden, James
See Creasey, John
Marsh, Edward 1872-1953 .... TCLC 99
Marsh, (Edith) Ngaio 1899-1982 ...... CLC 7, 53
See also CA 9-12R; CANR 6, 58; CMW 4; CPW; DAM POP; DLB 77; MSW; MTCW 1, 2; RGEL 2; TEA
Marshall, Garry 1934- .... CLC 17
See also AAYA 3; CA 111; SATA 60
Marshall, Paule 1929- .... BLC 3; CLC 27, 72; SSC 3
See also AFAW 1, 2; AMWS 11; BPFB 2; BW 2, 3; CA 77-80; CANR 25, 73; CN 7; DA3; DAM MULT; DLB 33, 157, 227; EWL 3; MTCW 1, 2; RGAL 4; SSFS 15
Marshallik
See Zangwill, Israel
Marsten, Richard
See Hunter, Evan
Marston, John 1576-1634 .... LC 33
See also BRW 2; DAM DRAM; DLB 58, 172; RGEL 2
Martha, Henry
See Harris, Mark
Marti (y Perez), Jose (Julian) 1853-1895
.... HLC 2; NCLC 63
See also DAM MULT; HW 2; LAW; RGWL 2, 3; WLIT 1
Martial c. 40-c. 104 .... CMLC 35; PC 10
See also AW 2; CDWLB 1; DLB 211; RGWL 2, 3
Martin, Ken
See Hubbard, L(afayette) Ron(ald)
Martin, Richard
See Creasey, John
Martin, Steve 1945- .... CLC 30
See also CA 97-100; CANR 30, 100; MTCW 1
Martin, Valerie 1948- .... CLC 89
See also BEST 90:2; CA 85-88; CANR 49, 89
Martin, Violet Florence 1862-1915 . SSC 56; TCLC 51
Martin, Webber
See Silverberg, Robert
Martindale, Patrick Victor
See White, Patrick (Victor Martindale)
Martin du Gard, Roger 1881-1958
.... TCLC 24
See also CA 118; CANR 94; DLB 65; EWL 3; GFL 1789 to the Present; RGWL 2, 3
Martineau, Harriet 1802-1876 ..... NCLC 26
See also DLB 21, 55, 159, 163, 166, 190; FW; RGEL 2; YABC 2
Martines, Julia
See O'Faolain, Julia
Martinez, Enrique Gonzalez
See Gonzalez Martinez, Enrique
Martinez, Jacinto Benavente y
See Benavente (y Martinez), Jacinto
Martinez de la Rosa, Francisco de Paula 1787-1862 .... NCLC 102
See also TWA
Martinez Ruiz, Jose 1873-1967
See Azorin; Ruiz, Jose Martinez
See also CA 93-96; HW 1
Martinez Sierra, Gregorio 1881-1947
.... TCLC 6
See also CA 115; EWL 3

Martinez Sierra, Maria (de la O'LeJarraga) 1874-1974 .... TCLC 6
See also CA 115; EWL 3
Martinsen, Martin
See Follett, Ken(neth Martin)
Martinson, Harry (Edmund) 1904-1978
.... CLC 14
See also CA 77-80; CANR 34; DLB 259; EWL 3
Martyn, Edward 1859-1923 .... TCLC 131
See also CA 179; DLB 10; RGEL 2
Marut, Ret
See Traven, B.
Marut, Robert
See Traven, B.
Marvell, Andrew 1621-1678 ... LC 4, 43; PC 10; WLC
See also BRW 2; BRWR 2; CDBLB 1660-1789; DA; DAB; DAC; DAM MST, POET; DLB 131 EXPP; PFS 5; RGEL 2; TEA; WP
Marx, Karl (Heinrich) 1818-1883
.... NCLC 17, 114
See also DLB 129; TWA
Masaoka, Shiki -1902 .... TCLC 18
See Masaoka, Tsunenori
See also RGWL 3
Masaoka, Tsunenori 1867-1902
See Masaoka, Shiki
See also CA 117; 191; TWA
Masefield, John (Edward) 1878-1967
.... CLC 11, 47
See also CA 19-20; 25-28R; CANR 33; CAP 2; CDBLB 1890-1914; DAM POET; DLB 10, 19, 153, 160; EWL 3; EXPP; FANT; MTCW 1, 2; PFS 5; RGEL 2; SATA 19
Maso, Carole 19(?)- .... CLC 44
See also CA 170; GLL 2; RGAL 4
Mason, Bobbie Ann 1940- .. CLC 28, 43, 82, 154; SSC 4
See also AAYA 5, 42; AMWS 8; BPFB 2; CA 53-56; CANR 11, 31, 58, 83; CDALBS; CN 7; CSW; DA3; DLB 173; DLBY 1987; EWL 3; EXPS; INT CANR-31; MTCW 1, 2; NFS 4; RGAL 4; RGSF 2; SSFS 3,8; YAW
Mason, Ernst
See Pohl, Frederik
Mason, Hunni B.
See Sternheim, (William Adolf) Carl
Mason, Lee W.
See Malzberg, Barry N(athaniel)
Mason, Nick 1945- ...... CLC 35
Mason, Tally
See Derleth, August (William)
Mass, Anna .... CLC 59
Mass, William
See Gibson, William
Massinger, Philip 1583-1640 .... LC 70
See also DLB 58; RGEL 2
Master Lao
See Lao Tzu
Masters, Edgar Lee 1868-1950 ..... PC 1, 36; TCLC 2, 25; WLCS
See also AMWS 1; CA 104; 133; CDALB 1865-1917; DA; DAC; DAM MST, POET; DLB 54; EWL 3; EXPP; MTCW 1, 2; RGAL 4; TUS; WP
Masters, Hilary 1928- .... CLC 48
See also CA 25-28R; CANR 13, 47, 97; CN 7; DLB 244
Mastrosimone, William 19(?)- .... CLC 36
See also CA 186; CAD; CD 5
Mathe, Albert
See Camus, Albert
Mather, Cotton 1663-1728 .... LC 38
See also AMWS 2; CDALB 1640-1865; DLB 24, 30, 140; RGAL 4; TUS

Mather, Increase 1639-1723 .... **LC 38**
See also DLB 24

Matheson, Richard (Burton) 1926- .... **CLC 37**
See also AAYA 31; CA 97-100; CANR 88, 99; DLB 8, 44; HGG; INT 97-100; SCFW 2; SFW 4; SUFW 2

Mathews, Harry 1930- .... **CLC 6, 52**
See also CA 21-24R; CAAS 6; CANR 18, 40, 98; CN 7

Mathews, John Joseph 1894-1979 . **CLC 84; NNAL**
See also CA 19-20; 142; CANR 45; CAP 2; DAM MULT; DLB 175

Mathias, Roland (Glyn) 1915- .... **CLC 45**
See also CA 97-100; CANR 19, 41; CP 7; DLB 27

Matsuo Basho 1644-1694 .... **LC 62; PC 3**
See Basho, Matsuo
See also DAM POET; PFS 2, 7

Mattheson, Rodney
See Creasey, John

Matthews, (James) Brander 1852-1929 .... **TCLC 95**
See also DLB 71, 78; DLBD 13

Matthews, Greg 1949- .... **CLC 45**
See also CA 135

Matthews, William (Procter III) 1942-1997 .... **CLC 40**
See also AMWS 9; CA 29-32R; 162; CAAS 18; CANR 12, 57; CP 7; DLB 5

Matthias, John (Edward) 1941- .... **CLC 9**
See also CA 33-36R; CANR 56; CP 7

Matthiessen, F(rancis) O(tto) 1902-1950 .... **TCLC 100**
See also CA 185; DLB 63

Matthiessen, Peter 1927- .. **CLC 5, 7, 11, 32, 64**
See also AAYA 6, 40; AMWS 5; ANW; BEST 90:4; BPFB 2; CA 9-12R; CANR 21, 50, 73, 100; CN 7; DA3; DAM NOV; DLB 6, 173, 275; MTCW 1, 2; SATA 27

Maturin, Charles Robert 1780(?)-1824 .... **NCLC 6**
See also BRWS 8; DLB 178; HGG; LMFS 1; RGEL 2; SUFW

Matute (Ausejo), Ana Maria 1925- . **CLC 11**
See also CA 89-92; EWL 3; MTCW 1; RGSF 2

Maugham, W. S.
See Maugham, W(illiam) Somerset

Maugham, W(illiam) Somerset 1874-1965 .... **CLC 1, 11, 15, 67, 93; SSC 8; WLC**
See also BPFB 2; BRW 6; CA 5-8R; 25-28R; CANR 40; CDBLB 1914-1945; CMW 4; DA; DA3; DAB; DAC; DAM DRAM, MST, NOV; DLB 10, 36, 77, 100, 162, 195; EWL 3; LAIT 3; MTCW 1, 2; RGEL 2; RGSF 2; SATA 54; SSFS 17

Maugham, William Somerset
See Maugham, W(illiam) Somerset

Maupassant, (Henri Rene Albert) Guy de 1850-1893 ...... **NCLC 1, 42, 83; SSC 1; WLC**
See also BYA 14; DA; DA3; DAB; DAC; DAM MST; DLB 123; EXPS; GFL 1789 to the Present; LAIT 2; LMFS 1; RGSF 2; RGWL 2, 3; SSFS 4; SUFW; TWA

Maupin, Armistead (Jones, Jr.) 1944- .... **CLC 95**
See also CA 125; 130; CANR 58, 101; CPW; DA3; DAM POP; DLB 278; GLL 1; INT 130; MTCW 2

Maurhut, Richard
See Traven, B.

Mauriac, Claude 1914-1996 .... **CLC 9**
See also CA 89-92; 152; CWW 2; DLB 83; EWL 3; GFL 1789 to the Present

Mauriac, Francois (Charles) 1885-1970 .... **CLC 4, 9, 56; SSC 24**
See also CA 25-28; CAP 2; DLB 65; EW 10; EWL 3; GFL 1789 to the Present; MTCW 1, 2; RGWL 2, 3; TWA

Mavor, Osborne Henry 1888-1951
See Bridie, James
See also CA 104

Maxwell, William (Keepers, Jr.) 1908-2000 .... **CLC 19**
See also AMWS 8; CA 93-96; 189; CANR 54, 95; CN 7; DLB 218, 278; DLBY 1980; INT CA-93-96; SATA-Obit 128

May, Elaine 1932- .... **CLC 16**
See also CA 124; 142; CAD; CWD; DLB 44

Mayakovski, Vladimir (Vladimirovich) 1893-1930 .... **TCLC 4, 18**
See Maiakovskii, Vladimir; Mayakovsky, Vladimir
See also CA 104; 158; EWL 3; MTCW 2; SFW 4; TWA

Mayakovsky, Vladimir
See Mayakovski, Vladimir (Vladimirovich)
See also EW 11; WP

Mayhew, Henry 1812-1887 .... **NCLC 31**
See also DLB 18, 55, 190

Mayle, Peter 1939(?)- .... **CLC 89**
See also CA 139; CANR 64, 109

Maynard, Joyce 1953- .... **CLC 23**
See also CA 111; 129; CANR 64

Mayne, William (James Carter) 1928- .... **CLC 12**
See also AAYA 20; CA 9-12R; CANR 37, 80, 100; CLR 25; FANT; JRDA; MAI-CYA 1, 2; MAICYAS 1; SAAS 11; SATA 6, 68, 122; SUFW 2; YAW

Mayo, Jim
See L'Amour, Louis (Dearborn)
See also TCWW 2

Maysles, Albert 1926- .... **CLC 16**
See also CA 29-32R

Maysles, David 1932-1987 .... **CLC 16**
See also CA 191

Mazer, Norma Fox 1931- .... **CLC 26**
See also AAYA 5, 36; BYA 1, 8; CA 69-72; CANR 12, 32, 66; CLR 23; JRDA; MAI-CYA 1, 2; SAAS 1; SATA 24, 67, 105; WYA; YAW

Mazzini, Guiseppe 1805-1872 .... **NCLC 34**

McAlmon, Robert (Menzies) 1895-1956 .... **TCLC 97**
See also CA 107; 168; DLB 4, 45; DLBD 15; GLL 1

McAuley, James Phillip 1917-1976 . **CLC 45**
See also CA 97-100; DLB 260; RGEL 2

McBain, Ed
See Hunter, Evan
See also MSW

McBrien, William (Augustine) 1930- .... **CLC 44**
See also CA 107; CANR 90

McCabe, Patrick 1955- .... **CLC 133**
See also CA 130; CANR 50, 90; CN 7; DLB 194

McCaffrey, Anne (Inez) 1926- .... **CLC 17**
See also AAYA 6, 34; AITN; BEST 89:2; BPFB 2; BYA 5; CA 25-28R; CANR 15, 35, 55, 96; CLR 49; CPW; DA3; DAM NOV, POP; DLB 8; JRDA; MAICYA 1, 2; MTCW 1, 2; SAAS 11; SATA 8, 70, 116; SFW 4; SUFW 2; WYA; YAW

McCall, Nathan 1955(?)- .... **CLC 86**
See also BW 3; CA 146; CANR 88

McCann, Arthur
See Campbell, John W(ood, Jr.)

McCann, Edson
See Pohl, Frederik

McCarthy, Charles, Jr. 1933-
See McCarthy, Cormac
See also CANR 42, 69, 101; CN 7; CPW; CSW; DA3; DAM POP; MTCW 2

McCarthy, Cormac .... **CLC 4, 57, 59, 101**
See McCarthy, Charles, Jr.
See also AAYA 41; AMWS 8; BPFB 2; CA 13-16R; CANR 10; DLB 6, 143, 256; EWL 3; TCWW 2

McCarthy, Mary (Therese) 1912-1989 ..... **CLC 1, 3, 5, 14, 24, 39, 59; SSC 24**
See also AMW; BPFB 2; CA 5-8R; 129; CANR 16, 50, 64; DA3; DLB 2; DLBY 1981; EWL 3; FW; INT CANR-16; MAWW; MTCW 1, 2; RGAL 4; TUS

McCartney, (James) Paul 1942- ..... **CLC 12, 35**
See also CA 146; CANR 111

McCauley, Stephen (D.) 1955- .... **CLC 50**
See also CA 141

McClaren, Peter .... **CLC 70**

McClure, Michael (Thomas) 1932- .. **CLC 6, 10**
See also BG 3; CA 21-24R; CAD; CANR 17, 46, 77; CD 5; CP 7; DLB 16; WP

McCorkle, Jill (Collins) 1958- .... **CLC 51**
See also CA 121; CANR 113; CSW; DLB 234; DLBY 1987

McCourt, Frank 1930- .... **CLC 109**
See also AMWS 12; CA 157; CANR 97; NCFS 1

McCourt, James 1941- .... **CLC 5**
See also CA 57-60; CANR 98

McCourt, Malachy 1931- .... **CLC 119**
See also SATA 126

McCoy, Horace (Stanley) 1897-1955 .... **TCLC 28**
See also CA 108; 155; CMW 4; DLB 9

McCrae, John 1872-1918 .... **TCLC 12**
See also CA 109; DLB 92; PFS 5

McCreigh, James
See Pohl, Frederik

McCullers, (Lula) Carson (Smith) 1917-1967 .. **CLC 1, 4, 10, 12, 48, 100; SSC 9, 24; WLC**
See also AAYA 21; AMW; BPFB 2; CA 5-8R; 25-28R; CABS 1, 3; CANR 18; CDALB 1941-1968; DA; DA3; DAB; DAC; DAM MST, NOV; DFS 5; DLB 2, 7, 173, 228; EWL 3; EXPS; FW; GLL 1; LAIT 3, 4; MAWW; MTCW 1, 2; NFS 6, 13; RGAL 4; RGSF 2; SATA 27; SSFS 5; TUS; YAW

McCulloch, John Tyler
See Burroughs, Edgar Rice

McCullough, Colleen 1938(?)- .... **CLC 27, 107**
See also AAYA 36; BPFB 2; CA 81-84; CANR 17, 46, 67, 98; CPW; DA3; DAM NOV, POP; MTCW 1, 2; RHW

McCunn, Ruthanne Lum 1946- .... **AAL**
See also CA 119; CANR 43, 96; LAIT 2; SATA 63

McDermott, Alice 1953- .... **CLC 90**
See also CA 109; CANR 40, 90

McElroy, Joseph 1930- .... **CLC 5, 47**
See also CA 17-20R; CN 7

McEwan, Ian (Russell) 1948- ... **CLC 13, 66, 169**
See also BEST 90:4; BRWS 4; CA 61-64; CANR 14, 41, 69, 87; CN 7; DAM NOV; DLB 14, 194; HGG; MTCW 1, 2; RGSF 2; SUFW 2; TEA

McFadden, David 1940- .... **CLC 48**
See also CA 104; CP 7; DLB 60; INT 104

McFarland, Dennis 1950- .... **CLC 65**
See also CA 165; CANR 110

McGahern, John 1934- .. CLC **5, 9, 48, 156;** SSC **17**
See also CA 17-20R; CANR 29, 68, 113; CN 7; DLB 14, 231; MTCW 1

McGinley, Patrick (Anthony) 1937- .... CLC **41**
See also CA 120; 127; CANR 56; INT 127

McGinley, Phyllis 1905-1978 .... CLC **14**
See also CA 9-12R; 77-80; CANR 19; CWRI 5; DLB 11, 48; PFS 9, 13; SATA 2, 44; SATA-Obit 24

McGinniss, Joe 1942- .... CLC **32**
See also AITN 2; BEST 89:2; CA 25-28R; CANR 26, 70; CPW; DLB 135; INT CANR-26

McGivern, Maureen Daly
See Daly, Maureen

McGrath, Patrick 1950- .... CLC **55**
See also CA 136; CANR 65; CN 7; DLB 231; HGG; SUFW 2

McGrath, Thomas (Matthew) 1916-1990
.... CLC **28, 59**
See also AMWS 10; CA 9-12R; 132; CANR 6, 33, 95; DAM POET; MTCW 1; SATA 41; SATA-Obit 66

McGuane, Thomas (Francis III) 1939-
.... CLC **3, 7, 18, 45, 127**
See also AITN 2; BPFB 2; CA 49-52; CANR 5, 24, 49, 94; CN 7; DLB 2, 212; DLBY 1980; EWL 3; INT CANR-24; MTCW 1; TCWW 2

McGuckian, Medbh 1950- .. CLC **48;** PC **27**
See also BRWS 5; CA 143; CP 7; CWP; DAM POET; DLB 40

McHale, Tom 1942(?)-1982 .... CLC **3, 5**
See also AITN 1; CA 77-80; 106

McIlvanney, William 1936- .... CLC **42**
See also CA 25-28R; CANR 61; CMW 4; DLB 14, 207

McIlwraith, Maureen Mollie Hunter
See Hunter, Mollie
See also SATA 2

McInerney, Jay 1955- .... CLC **34, 112**
See also AAYA 18; BPFB 2; CA 116; 123; CANR 45, 68, 116; CN 7; CPW; DA3; DAM POP; INT 123; MTCW 2

McIntyre, Vonda N(eel) 1948- .... CLC **18**
See also CA 81-84; CANR 17, 34, 69; MTCW 1; SFW 4; YAW

McKay, Claude .... BLC **3;** HR **3;** PC **2;** TCLC **7, 41;** WLC
See McKay, Festus Claudius
See also AFAW 1, 2; AMWS 10; DAB; DLB 4, 45, 51, 117; EWL 3; EXPP; GLL 2; LAIT 3; LMFS 2; PAB; PFS 4; RGAL 4; WP

McKay, Festus Claudius 1889-1948
See McKay, Claude
See also BW 1, 3; CA 104; 124; CANR 73; DA; DAC; DAM MST, MULT, NOV, POET; MTCW 1, 2; TUS

McKuen, Rod 1933- .... CLC **1, 3**
See also AITN 1; CA 41-44R; CANR 40

McLoughlin, R. B.
See Mencken, H(enry) L(ouis)

McLuhan, (Herbert) Marshall 1911-1980
.... CLC **37, 83**
See also CA 9-12R; 102; CANR 12, 34, 61; DLB 88; INT CANR-12; MTCW 1, 2

McManus, Declan Patrick Aloysius
See Costello, Elvis

McMillan, Terry (L.) 1951- ...... BLCS; CLC **50, 61, 112**
See also AAYA 21; BPFB 2; BW 2, 3; CA 140; CANR 60, 104; CPW; DA3; DAM MULT, NOV, POP; MTCW 2; RGAL 4; YAW

McMurtry, Larry (Jeff) 1936- . CLC **2, 3, 7, 11, 27, 44, 127**
See also AAYA 15; AITN 2; AMWS 5; BEST 89:2; BPFB 2; CA 5-8R; CANR 19, 43, 64, 103; CDALB 1968-1988; CN 7; CPW; CSW; DA3; DAM NOV, POP; DLB 2, 143, 256; DLBY 1980, 1987; EWL 3; MTCW 1, 2; RGAL 4; TCWW 2

McNally, T. M. 1961- .... CLC **82**

McNally, Terrence 1939- ... CLC **4, 7, 41, 91**
See also CA 45-48; CAD; CANR 2, 56, 116; CD 5; DA3; DAM DRAM; DFS 16; DLB 7, 249; EWL 3; GLL 1; MTCW 2

McNamer, Deirdre 1950- .... CLC **70**

McNeal, Tom .... CLC **119**

McNeile, Herman Cyril 1888-1937
See Sapper
See also CA 184; CMW 4; DLB 77

McNickle, (William) D'Arcy 1904-1977
.... CLC **89;** NNAL
See also CA 9-12R; 85-88; CANR 5, 45; DAM MULT; DLB 175, 212; RGAL 4; SATA-Obit 22

McPhee, John (Angus) 1931- .... CLC **36**
See also AMWS 3; ANW; BEST 90:1; CA 65-68; CANR 20, 46, 64, 69; CPW; DLB 185, 275; MTCW 1, 2; TUS

McPherson, James Alan 1943-
.... BLCS; CLC **19, 77**
See also BW 1, 3; CA 25-28R; CAAS 17; CANR 24, 74; CN 7; CSW; DLB 38, 244; EWL 3; MTCW 1, 2; RGAL 4; RGSF 2

McPherson, William (Alexander) 1933-
.... CLC **34**
See also CA 69-72; CANR 28; INT CANR-28

McTaggart, J. McT. Ellis
See McTaggart, John McTaggart Ellis

McTaggart, John McTaggart Ellis 1866-1925
.... TCLC **105**
See also CA 120; DLB 262

Mead, George Herbert 1863-1931
.... TCLC **89**
See also DLB 270

Mead, Margaret 1901-1978 .... CLC **37**
See also AITN 1; CA 1-4R; 81-84; CANR 4; DA3; FW; MTCW 1, 2; SATA-Obit 20

Meaker, Marijane (Agnes) 1927-
See Kerr, M. E.
See also CA 107; CANR 37, 63; INT 107; JRDA; MAICYA 1, 2; MAICYAS 1; MTCW 1; SATA 20, 61, 99; SATA-Essay 111; YAW

Medoff, Mark (Howard) 1940- ... CLC **6, 23**
See also AITN 1; CA 53-56; CAD; CANR 5; CD 5; DAM DRAM; DFS 4; DLB 7; INT CANR-5

Medvedev, P. N.
See Bakhtin, Mikhail Mikhailovich

Meged, Aharon
See Megged, Aharon

Meged, Aron
See Megged, Aharon

Megged, Aharon 1920- .... CLC **9**
See also CA 49-52; CAAS 13; CANR 1; EWL 3

Mehta, Ved (Parkash) 1934- .... CLC **37**
See also CA 1-4R; CANR 2, 23, 69; MTCW 1

Melanter
See Blackmore, R(ichard) D(oddridge)

Meleager c. 140B.C.-c. 70B.C. ..... CMLC **53**

Melies, Georges 1861-1938 .... TCLC **81**

Melikow, Loris
See Hofmannsthal, Hugo von

Melmoth, Sebastian
See Wilde, Oscar (Fingal O'Flahertie Wills)

Melo Neto, Joao Cabral de
See Cabral de Melo Neto, Joao
See also EWL 3

Meltzer, Milton 1915- .... CLC **26**
See also AAYA 8, 45; BYA 2, 6; CA 13-16R; CANR 38, 92, 107; CLR 13; DLB 61; JRDA; MAICYA 1, 2; SAAS 1; SATA 1, 50, 80, 128; SATA-Essay 124; WYA; YAW

Melville, Herman 1819-1891 ... NCLC **3, 12, 29, 45, 49, 91, 93, 123;** SSC **1, 17, 46;** WLC
See also AAYA 25; AMW; AMWR 1; CDALB 1640-1865; DA; DA3; DAB; DAC; DAM MST, NOV; DLB 3, 74, 250, 254; EXPN; EXPS; LAIT 1, 2; NFS 7, 9; RGAL 4; RGSF 2; SATA 59; SSFS 3; TUS

Members, Mark
See Powell, Anthony (Dymoke)

Membreno, Alejandro .... CLC **59**

Menander c. 342B.C.-c. 293B.C. .. CMLC **9, 51;** DC **3**
See also AW 1; CDWLB 1; DAM DRAM; DLB 176; LMFS 1; RGWL 2, 3

Menchu, Rigoberta 1959- . CLC **160;** HLCS **2**
See also CA 175; DNFS 1; WLIT 1

Mencken, H(enry) L(ouis) 1880-1956
.... TCLC **13**
See also AMW; CA 105; 125; CDALB 1917-1929; DLB 11, 29, 63, 137, 222; EWL 3; MTCW 1, 2; NCFS 4; RGAL 4; TUS

Mendelsohn, Jane 1965- .... CLC **99**
See also CA 154; CANR 94

Menton, Francisco de
See Chin, Frank (Chew, Jr.)

Mercer, David 1928-1980 .... CLC **5**
See also CA 9-12R; 102; CANR 23; CBD; DAM DRAM; DLB 13; MTCW 1; RGEL 2

Merchant, Paul
See Ellison, Harlan (Jay)

Meredith, George 1828-1909 .. TCLC **17, 43**
See also CA 117; 153; CANR 80; CDBLB 1832-1890; DAM POET; DLB 18, 35, 57, 159; RGEL 2; TEA

Meredith, William (Morris) 1919- ... CLC **4, 13, 22, 55;** PC **28**
See also CA 9-12R; CAAS 14; CANR 6, 40; CP 7; DAM POET; DLB 5

Merezhkovsky, Dmitry Sergeevich
See Merezhkovsky, Dmitry Sergeyevich
See also EWL 3

Merezhkovsky, Dmitry Sergeyevich 1865-1941 .... TCLC **29**
See Merezhkovsky, Dmitry Sergeyevich
See also CA 169

Merimee, Prosper 1803-1870 .. NCLC **6, 65;** SSC **7**
See also DLB 119, 192; EW 6; EXPS; GFL 1789 to the Present; RGSF 2; RGWL 2, 3; SSFS 8; SUFW

Merkin, Daphne 1954- .... CLC **44**
See also CA 123

Merlin, Arthur
See Blish, James (Benjamin)

Mernissi, Fatima 1940- .... CLC **171**
See also CA 152; FW

Merrill, James (Ingram) 1926-1995
... CLC **2, 3, 6, 8, 13, 18, 34, 91;** PC **28**
See also AMWS 3; CA 13-16R; 147; CANR 10, 49, 63, 108; DA3; DAM POET; DLB 5, 165; DLBY 1985; EWL 3; INT CANR-10; MTCW 1, 2; PAB; RGAL 4

Merriman, Alex
See Silverberg, Robert

Merriman, Brian 1747-1805 .... **NCLC 70**
Merritt, E. B.
See Waddington, Miriam
Merton, Thomas (James) 1915-1968
.... **CLC 1, 3, 11, 34, 83; PC 10**
See also AMWS 8; CA 5-8R; 25-28R; CANR 22, 53, 111; DA3; DLB 48; DLBY 1981; MTCW 1, 2
Merwin, W(illiam) S(tanley) 1927- .. **CLC 1, 2, 3, 5, 8, 13, 18, 45, 88; PC 45**
See also AMWS 3; CA 13-16R; CANR 15, 51, 112; CP 7; DA3; DAM POET; DLB 5, 169; EWL 3; INT CANR-15; MTCW 1, 2; PAB; PFS 5, 15; RGAL 4
Metcalf, John 1938- .... **CLC 37; SSC 43**
See also CA 113; CN 7; DLB 60; RGSF 2; TWA
Metcalf, Suzanne
See Baum, L(yman) Frank
Mew, Charlotte (Mary) 1870-1928 . **TCLC 8**
See also CA 105; 189; DLB 19, 135; RGEL 2
Mewshaw, Michael 1943- .... **CLC 9**
See also CA 53-56; CANR 7, 47; DLBY 1980
Meyer, Conrad Ferdinand 1825-1898
.... **NCLC 81**
See also DLB 129; EW; RGWL 2, 3
Meyer, Gustav 1868-1932
See Meyrink, Gustav
See also CA 117; 190
Meyer, June
See Jordan, June (Meyer)
Meyer, Lynn
See Slavitt, David R(ytman)
Meyers, Jeffrey 1939- .... **CLC 39**
See also CA 73-76; CAAE 186; CANR 54, 102; DLB 111
Meynell, Alice (Christina Gertrude Thompson) 1847-1922 .... **TCLC 6**
See also CA 104; 177; DLB 19, 98; RGEL 2
Meyrink, Gustav .... **TCLC 21**
See Meyer, Gustav
See also DLB 81; EWL 3
Michaels, Leonard 1933- ... **CLC 6, 25; SSC 16**
See also CA 61-64; CANR 21, 62; CN 7; DLB 130; MTCW 1
Michaux, Henri 1899-1984 .... **CLC 8, 19**
See also CA 85-88; 114; DLB 258; EWL 3; GFL 1789 to the Present; RGWL 2, 3
Micheaux, Oscar (Devereaux) 1884-1951
.... **TCLC 76**
See also BW 3; CA 174; DLB 50; TCWW 2
Michelangelo 1475-1564 .... **LC 12**
See also AAYA 43
Michelet, Jules 1798-1874 .... **NCLC 31**
See also EW 5; GFL 1789 to the Present
Michels, Robert 1876-1936 .... **TCLC 88**
Michener, James A(lbert) 1907(?)-1997
.... **CLC 1, 5, 11, 29, 60, 109**
See also AAYA 27; AITN 1; BEST 90:1; BPFB 2; CA 5-8R; 161; CANR 21, 45, 68; CN 7; CPW; DA3; DAM NOV, POP; DLB 6; MTCW 1, 2; RHW
Mickiewicz, Adam 1798-1855 .... **NCLC 3, 101; PC 38**
See also EW 5; RGWL 2, 3
Middleton, (John) Christopher
See Middleton, (John) Christopher
Middleton, (John) Christopher 1926-
.... **CLC 13**
See also CA 13-16R; CANR 29, 54, 117; CP 7; DLB 40
Middleton, Richard (Barham) 1882-1911
.... **TCLC 56**
See also CA 187; DLB 156; HGG

Middleton, Stanley 1919- .... **CLC 7, 38**
See also CA 25-28R; CAAS 23; CANR 21, 46, 81; CN 7; DLB 14
Middleton, Thomas 1580-1627 .... **DC 5; LC 33**
See also BRW 2; DAM DRAM, MST; DLB 58; RGEL 2
Migueis, Jose Rodrigues 1901- .... **CLC 10**
Mikszath, Kalman 1847-1910 .... **TCLC 31**
See also CA 170
Miles, Jack .... **CLC 100**
See also CA 200
Miles, John Russiano
See Miles, Jack
Miles, Josephine (Louise) 1911-1985
.... **CLC 1, 2, 14, 34, 39**
See also CA 1-4R; 116; CANR 2, 55; DAM POET; DLB 48
Militant
See Sandburg, Carl (August)
Mill, Harriet (Hardy) Taylor 1807-1858
.... **NCLC 102**
See also FW
Mill, John Stuart 1806-1873 ... **NCLC 11, 58**
See also CDBLB 1832-1890; DLB 55, 190, 262; FW 1; RGEL 2; TEA
Millar, Kenneth 1915-1983 .... **CLC 14**
See Macdonald, Ross
See also CA 9-12R; 110; CANR 16, 63, 107; CMW 4; CPW; DA3; DAM POP; DLB 2, 226; DLBD 6; DLBY 1983; MTCW 1, 2
Millay, E. Vincent
See Millay, Edna St. Vincent
Millay, Edna St. Vincent 1892-1950 ... **PC 6; TCLC 4, 49; WLCS**
See Boyd, Nancy
See also AMW; CA 104; 130; CDALB 1917-1929; DA; DA3; DAB; DAC; DAM MST, POET; DLB 45, 249; EWL 3; EXPP; MAWW; MTCW 1, 2; PAB; PFS 3, 17; RGAL 4; TUS; WP
Miller, Arthur 1915- ... **CLC 1, 2, 6, 10, 15, 26, 47, 78; DC 1; WLC**
See also AAYA 15; AITN 1; AMW; AMWC 1; CA 1-4R; CABS 3; CAD; CANR 2, 30, 54, 76; CD 5; CDALB 1941-1968; DA; DA3; DAB; DAC; DAM DRAM, MST; DFS 1, 3; DLB 7, 266; EWL 3; LAIT 1, 4; MTCW 1, 2; RGAL 4; TUS; WYAS 1
Miller, Henry (Valentine) 1891-1980
.... **CLC 1, 2, 4, 9, 14, 43, 84; WLC**
See also AMW; BPFB 2; CA 9-12R; 97-100; CANR 33, 64; CDALB 1929-1941; DA; DA3; DAB; DAC; DAM MST, NOV; DLB 4, 9; DLBY 1980; EWL 3; MTCW 1, 2; RGAL 4; TUS
Miller, Jason 1939(?)-2001 .... **CLC 2**
See also AITN 1; CA 73-76; 197; CAD; DFS 12; DLB 7
Miller, Sue 1943- .... **CLC 44**
See also AMWS 12; BEST 90:3; CA 139; CANR 59, 91; DA3; DAM POP; DLB 143
Miller, Walter M(ichael, Jr.) 1923-1996
.... **CLC 4, 30**
See also BPFB 2; CA 85-88; CANR 108; DLB 8; SCFW; SFW 4
Millett, Kate 1934- .... **CLC 67**
See also AITN 1; CA 73-76; CANR 32, 53, 76, 110; DA3; DLB 246; FW; GLL 1; MTCW 1, 2
Millhauser, Steven (Lewis) 1943- ... **CLC 21, 54, 109; SSC 57**
See also CA 110; 111; CANR 63, 114; CN 7; DA3; DLB 2; FANT; INT CA-111; MTCW 2
Millin, Sarah Gertrude 1889-1968 . **CLC 49**
See also CA 102; 93-96; DLB 225; EWL 3

Milne, A(lan) A(lexander) 1882-1956
.... **TCLC 6, 88**
See also BRWS 5; CA 104; 133; CLR 1, 26; CMW 4; CWRI 5; DA3; DAB; DAC; DAM MST; DLB 10, 77, 100, 160; FANT; MAICYA 1, 2; MTCW 1, 2; RGEL 2; SATA 100; WCH; YABC 1
Milner, Ron(ald) 1938- .... **BLC 3; CLC 56**
See also AITN 1; BW 1; CA 73-76; CAD; CANR 24, 81; CD 5; DAM MULT; DLB 38; MTCW 1
Milnes, Richard Monckton 1809-1885
.... **NCLC 61**
See also DLB 32, 184
Milosz, Czeslaw 1911- .... **CLC 5, 11, 22, 31, 56, 82; PC 8; WLCS**
See also CA 81-84; CANR 23, 51, 91; CD-WLB 4; CWW 2; DA3; DAM MST, POET; DLB 215; EW 13; EWL 3; MTCW 1, 2; PFS 16; RGWL 2, 3
Milton, John 1608-1674 .... **LC 9, 43; PC 19, 29; WLC**
See also BRW 2; BRWR 2; CDBLB 1660-1789; DA; DA3; DAB; DAC; DAM MST, POET; DLB 131, 151; EFS 1; EXPP; LAIT 1; PAB; PFS 3, 17; RGEL 2; TEA; WLIT 3; WP
Min, Anchee 1957- .... **CLC 86**
See also CA 146; CANR 94
Minehaha, Cornelius
See Wedekind, (Benjamin) Frank(lin)
Miner, Valerie 1947- .... **CLC 40**
See also CA 97-100; CANR 59; FW; GLL 2
Minimo, Duca
See D'Annunzio, Gabriele
Minot, Susan 1956- .... **CLC 44, 159**
See also AMWS 6; CA 134; CN 7
Minus, Ed 1938- .... **CLC 39**
See also CA 185
Miranda, Javier
See Bioy Casares, Adolfo
See also CWW 2
Mirbeau, Octave 1848-1917 .... **TCLC 55**
See also DLB 123, 192; GFL 1789 to the Present
Mirikitani, Janice 1942- .... **AAL**
See also RGAL 4
Miro (Ferrer), Gabriel (Francisco Victor) 1879-1930 .... **TCLC 5**
See also CA 104; 185; EWL 3
Misharin, Alexandr .... **CLC 59**
Mishima, Yukio ... **CLC 2, 4, 6, 9, 27; DC 1; SSC 4**
See Hiraoka, Kimitake
See also BPFB 2; GLL 1; MJW; MTCW 2; RGSF 2; RGWL 2, 3; SSFS 5, 12
Mistral, Frederic 1830-1914 .... **TCLC 51**
See also CA 122; GFL 1789 to the Present
Mistral, Gabriela
See Godoy Alcayaga, Lucila
See also DNFS 1; EWL 3; LAW; RGWL 2, 3; WP
Mistry, Rohinton 1952- .... **CLC 71**
See also CA 141; CANR 86, 114; CCA 1; CN 7; DAC; SSFS 6
Mitchell, Clyde
See Ellison, Harlan (Jay)
Mitchell, Emerson Blackhorse Barney 1945-
.... **NNAL**
See also CA 45-48
Mitchell, James Leslie 1901-1935
See Gibbon, Lewis Grassic
See also CA 104; 188; DLB 15
Mitchell, Joni 1943- .... **CLC 12**
See also CA 112; CCA 1

Mitchell, Joseph (Quincy) 1908-1996 .... **CLC 98**
See also CA 77-80; 152; CANR 69; CN 7; CSW; DLB 185; DLBY 1996

Mitchell, Margaret (Munnerlyn) 1900-1949 .... **TCLC 11**
See also AAYA 23; BPFB 2; BYA 1; CA 109; 125; CANR 55, 94; CDALBS; DA3; DAM NOV, POP; DLB 9; LAIT 2; MTCW 1, 2; NFS 9; RGAL 4; RHW; TUS; WYAS 1; YAW

Mitchell, Peggy
See Mitchell, Margaret (Munnerlyn)

Mitchell, S(ilas) Weir 1829-1914 .. **TCLC 36**
See also CA 165; DLB 202; RGAL 4

Mitchell, W(illiam) O(rmond) 1914-1998 .... **CLC 25**
See also CA 77-80; 165; CANR 15, 43; CN 7; DAC; DAM MST; DLB 88

Mitchell, William 1879-1936 .... **TCLC 81**

Mitford, Mary Russell 1787-1855 .. **NCLC 4**
See also DLB 110, 116; RGEL 2

Mitford, Nancy 1904-1973 .... **CLC 44**
See also CA 9-12R; DLB 191; RGEL 2

Miyamoto, (Chujo) Yuriko 1899-1951 .... **TCLC 37**
See Miyamoto Yuriko
See also CA 170, 174

Miyamoto Yuriko
See Miyamoto, (Chujo) Yuriko
See also DLB 180

Miyazawa, Kenji 1896-1933 .... **TCLC 76**
See Miyazawa Kenji
See also CA 157; RGWL 3

Miyazawa Kenji
See Miyazawa, Kenji
See also EWL 3

Mizoguchi, Kenji 1898-1956 .... **TCLC 72**
See also CA 167

Mo, Timothy (Peter) 1950(?)- . **CLC 46, 134**
See also CA 117; CN 7; DLB 194; MTCW 1; WLIT 4

Modarressi, Taghi (M.) 1931-1997 . **CLC 44**
See also CA 121; 134; INT 134

Modiano, Patrick (Jean) 1945- ...... **CLC 18**
See also CA 85-88; CANR 17, 40, 115; CWW 2; DLB 83; EWL 3

Mofolo, Thomas (Mokopu) 1875(?)-1948 .... **BLC 3; TCLC 22**
See also AFW; CA 121; 153; CANR 83; DAM MULT; DLB 225; EWL 3 MTCW 2; WLIT 2

Mohr, Nicholasa 1938- .... **CLC 12; HLC 2**
See also AAYA 8, 46; CA 49-52; CANR 1, 32, 64; CLR 22; DAM MULT; DLB 145; HW 1, 2; JRDA; LAIT 5; MAICYA 2; MAICYAS 1; RGAL 4; SAAS 8; SATA 8, 97; SATA-Essay 113; WYA; YAW

Moi, Toril 1953- .... **CLC 172**
See also CA 154; CANR 102; FW

Mojtabai, A(nn) G(race) 1938- .... **CLC 5, 9, 15, 29**
See also CA 85-88; CANR 88

Moliere 1622-1673 .... **DC 13; LC 10, 28, 64; WLC**
See also DA; DA3; DAB; DAC DAM DRAM, MST; DFS 13; DLB 268; EW 3; GFL Beginnings to 1789; RGWL 2, 3; TWA

Molin, Charles
See Mayne, William (James Carter)

Molnar, Ferenc 1878-1952 .... **TCLC 20**
See also CA 109; 153; CANR 83; CDWLB 4; DAM DRAM; DLB 215; EWL 3; RGWL 2, 3

Momaday, N(avarre) Scott 1934- .... **CLC 2, 19, 85, 95, 160; NNAL; PC 25; WLCS**
See also AAYA 11; AMWS 4; ANW; BPFB 2; CA 25-28R; CANR 14, 34, 68;
CDALBS; CN 7; CPW; DA; DA3; DAB; DAC; DAM MST, MULT, NOV, POP; DLB 143, 175, 256; EWL 3; EXPP; INT CANR-14; LAIT 4; MTCW 1, 2; NFS 10; PFS 2, 11; RGAL 4; SATA 48; SATA-Brief 30; WP; YAW

Monette, Paul 1945-1995 .... **CLC 82**
See also AMWS 10; CA 139; 147; CN 7; GLL 1

Monroe, Harriet 1860-1936 .... **TCLC 12**
See also CA 109; 204; DLB 54, 91

Monroe, Lyle
See Heinlein, Robert A(nson)

Montagu, Elizabeth 1720-1800 ...... **NCLC 7, 117**
See also FW

Montagu, Mary (Pierrepont) Wortley 1689-1762 .... **LC 9, 57; PC 16**
See also DLB 95, 101; RGEL 2

Montagu, W. H.
See Coleridge, Samuel Taylor

Montague, John (Patrick) 1929- .... **CLC 13, 46**
See also CA 9-12R; CANR 9, 69; CP 7; DLB 40; EWL 3; MTCW 1; PFS 12; RGEL 2

Montaigne, Michel (Eyquem) de 1533-1592 .... **LC 8; WLC**
See also DA; DAB; DAC; DAM MST; EW 2; GFL Beginnings to 1789; LMFS 1; RGWL 2, 3; TWA

Montale, Eugenio 1896-1981 . **CLC 7, 9, 18; PC 13**
See also CA 17-20R; 104; CANR 30; DLB 114; EW 11; EWL 3; MTCW 1; RGWL 2, 3; TWA

Montesquieu, Charles-Louis de Secondat 1689-1755 .... **LC 7, 69**
See also EW 3; GFL Beginnings to 1789; TWA

Montessori, Maria 1870-1952 ..... **TCLC 103**
See also CA 115; 147

Montgomery, (Robert) Bruce 1921(?)-1978
See Crispin, Edmund
See also CA 179; 104; CMW 4

Montgomery, L(ucy) M(aud) 1874-1942 .... **TCLC 51**
See also AAYA 12; BYA 1; CA 108; 137; CLR 8; DA; DA3; DAC; DAM MST; DLB 92; DLBD 14; JRDA; MAICYA 1, 2; MTCW 2; RGEL 2; SATA 100; TWA; WCH; WYA; YABC 1

Montgomery, Marion H., Jr. 1925- .. **CLC 7**
See also AITN 1; CA 1-4R; CANR 3, 48; CSW; DLB 6

Montgomery, Max
See Davenport, Guy (Mattison, Jr.)

Montherlant, Henry (Milon) de 1896-1972 .... **CLC 8, 19**
See also CA 85-88; 37-40R; DAM DRAM; DLB 72; EW 11; EWL 3; GFL 1789 to the Present; MTCW 1

Monty Python
See Chapman, Graham; Cleese, John (Marwood); Gilliam, Terry (Vance); Idle, Eric; Jones, Terence Graham Parry; Palin, Michael (Edward)
See also AAYA 7

Moodie, Susanna (Strickland) 1803-1885 .... **NCLC 14, 113**
See also DLB 99

Moody, Hiram (F. III) 1961-
See Moody, Rick
See also CA 138; CANR 64, 112

Moody, Minerva
See Alcott, Louisa May

Moody, Rick .... **CLC 147**
See Moody, Hiram (F. III)

Moody, William Vaughn 1869-1910 .... **TCLC 105**
See also CA 110; 178; DLB 7, 54; RGAL 4

Mooney, Edward 1951-
See Mooney, Ted
See also CA 130

Mooney, Ted .... **CLC 25**
See Mooney, Edward

Moorcock, Michael (John) 1939- ..... **CLC 5, 27, 58**
See Bradbury, Edward P.
See also AAYA 26; CA 45-48; CAAS 5; CANR 2, 17, 38, 64; CN 7; DLB 14, 231, 261; FANT; MTCW 1, 2; SATA 93; SCFW 2; SFW 4; SUFW 1, 2

Moore, Brian 1921-1999 .. **CLC 1, 3, 5, 7, 8, 19, 32, 90**
See Bryan Michael
See also CA 1-4R; 174; CANR 1, 25, 42, 63; CCA 1; CN 7; DAB; DAC; DAM MST; DLB 251; EWL 3; FANT; MTCW 1, 2; RGEL 2

Moore, Edward
See Muir, Edwin
See also RGEL 2

Moore, G. E. 1873-1958 .... **TCLC 89**
See also DLB 262

Moore, George Augustus 1852-1933 .... **SSC 19; TCLC 7**
See also BRW 6; CA 104; 177; DLB 10, 18, 57, 135; EWL 3; RGEL 2; RGSF 2

Moore, Lorrie .... **CLC 39, 45, 68**
See Moore, Marie Lorena
See also AMWS 10; DLB 234

Moore, Marianne (Craig) 1887-1972 .... **CLC 1, 2, 4, 8, 10, 13, 19, 47; PC 4; WLCS**
See also AMW; CA 1-4R; 33-36R; CANR 3, 61; CDALB 1929-1941; DA; DA3; DAB; DAC; DAM MST, POET; DLB 45; DLBD 7; EWL 3; EXPP; MAWW; MTCW 1, 2; PAB; PFS 14, 17; RGAL 4; SATA 20; TUS; WP

Moore, Marie Lorena 1957- .... **CLC 165**
See Moore, Lorrie
See also CA 116; CANR 39, 83; CN 7; DLB 234

Moore, Thomas 1779-1852 ..... **NCLC 6, 110**
See also DLB 96, 144; RGEL 2

Moorhouse, Frank 1938- .... **SSC 40**
See also CA 118; CANR 92; CN 7; RGSF 2

Mora, Pat(ricia) 1942- .... **HLC 2**
See also CA 129; CANR 57, 81, 112; CLR 58; DAM MULT; DLB 209; HW 1, 2; MAICYA 2 SATA 92, 134

Moraga, Cherrie 1952- .... **CLC 126**
See also CA 131; CANR 66; DAM MULT; DLB 82, 249; FW; GLL 1; HW 1, 2

Morand, Paul 1888-1976 .. **CLC 41; SSC 22**
See also CA 184; 69-72; DLB 65; EWL 3

Morante, Elsa 1918-1985 .... **CLC 8, 47**
See also CA 85-88 117; CANR 35; DLB 177; EWL 3; MTCW 1, 2; RGWL 2, 3

Moravia, Alberto .... **CLC 2, 7, 11, 27, 46; SSC 26**
See Pincherle, Alberto
See also DLB 177; EW 12; EWL 3; MTCW 2; RGSF 2; RGWL 2, 3

More, Hannah 1745-1833 .... **NCLC 27**
See also DLB 107, 109, 116, 158; RGEL 2

More, Henry 1614-1687 .... **LC 9**
See also DLB 126, 252

More, Sir Thomas 1478(?)-1535 .. **LC 10, 32**
See also BRWC 1; BRWS 7; DLB 136; LMFS 1; RGEL 2; TEA

Moreas, Jean .... **TCLC 18**
See Papadiamantopoulos, Johannes
See also GFL 1789 to the Present

Moreton, Andrew Esq.
See Defoe, Daniel
Morgan, Berry 1919-2002 .... **CLC 6**
See also CA 49-52; 208; DLB 6
Morgan, Claire
See Highsmith, (Mary) Patricia
See also GLL 1
Morgan, Edwin (George) 1920- ...... **CLC 31**
See also CA 5-8R; CANR 3, 43, 90; CP 7; DLB 27
Morgan, (George) Frederick 1922-
.... **CLC 23**
See also CA 17-20R; CANR 21; CP 7
Morgan, Harriet
See Mencken, H(enry) L(ouis)
Morgan, Jane
See Cooper, James Fenimore
Morgan, Janet 1945- .... **CLC 39**
See also CA 65-68
Morgan, Lady 1776(?)-1859 .... **NCLC 29**
See also DLB 116, 158; RGEL 2
Morgan, Robin (Evonne) 1941- .... **CLC 2**
See also CA 69-72; CANR 29, 68; FW; GLL 2; MTCW 1; SATA 80
Morgan, Scott
See Kuttner, Henry
Morgan, Seth 1949(?)-1990 .... **CLC 65**
See also CA 185; 132
Morgenstern, Christian (Otto Josef Wolfgang) 1871-1914 .... **TCLC 8**
See also CA 105; 191; EWL 3
Morgenstern, S.
See Goldman, William (W.)
Mori, Rintaro
See Mori Ogai
See also CA 110
Moricz, Zsigmond 1879-1942 .... **TCLC 33**
See also CA 165; DLB 215; EWL 3
Morike, Eduard (Friedrich) 1804-1875
.... **NCLC 10**
See also DLB 133; RGWL 2, 3
Mori Ogai 1862-1922 .... **TCLC 14**
See Ogai
See also CA 164; DLB 180; EWL 3; RGWL 3; TWA
Moritz, Karl Philipp 1756-1793 .... **LC 2**
See also DLB 94
Morland, Peter Henry
See Faust, Frederick (Schiller)
Morley, Christopher (Darlington) 1890-1957
.... **TCLC 87**
See also CA 112; DLB 9; RGAL 4
Morren, Theophil
See Hofmannsthal, Hugo von
Morris, Bill 1952- .... **CLC 76**
Morris, Julian
See West, Morris L(anglo)
Morris, Steveland Judkins 1950(?)-
See Wonder, Stevie
See also CA 111
Morris, William 1834-1896 .... **NCLC 4**
See also BRW 5; CDBLB 1832-1890; DLB 18, 35, 57, 156, 178, 184; FANT; RGEL 2; SFW 4; SUFW
Morris, Wright 1910-1998 . **CLC 1, 3, 7, 18, 37; TCLC 107**
See also AMW; CA 9-12R; 167; CANR 21, 81; CN 7; DLB 2, 206, 218; DLBY 1981; EWL 3; MTCW 1, 2; RGAL 4; TCWW 2
Morrison, Arthur 1863-1945 .... **SSC 40; TCLC 72**
See also CA 120; 157; CMW 4; DLB 70, 135, 197; RGEL 2
Morrison, James Douglas 1943-1971
See Morrison, Jim
See also CA 73-76; CANR 40
Morrison, Jim .... **CLC 17**
See Morrison, James Douglas

Morrison, Toni 1931- .... **BLC 3; CLC 4, 10, 22, 55, 81, 87, 173**
See also AAYA 1, 22; AFAW 1, 2; AMWC 1; AMWS 3; BPFB 2; BW 2, 3; CA 29-32R; CANR 27, 42, 67, 113; CDALB 1968-1988; CN 7; CPW; DA; DA3; DAB; DAC; DAM MST, MULT, NOV, POP; DLB 6, 33, 143; DLBY 1981; EWL 3; EXPN; FW; LAIT 2, 4; LMFS 2; MAWW; MTCW 1, 2; NFS 1, 6, 8, 14; RGAL 4; RHW; SATA 57; SSFS 5; TUS; YAW
Morrison, Van 1945- .... **CLC 21**
See also CA 116; 168
Morrissy, Mary 1957- .... **CLC 99**
See also CA 205; DLB 267
Mortimer, John (Clifford) 1923- .... **CLC 28, 43**
See also CA 13-16R; CANR 21, 69, 109; CD 5; CDBLB 1960 to Present; CMW 4; CN 7; CPW; DA3; DAM DRAM, POP; DLB 13, 245, 271; INT CANR-21; MSW; MTCW 1, 2; RGEL 2
Mortimer, Penelope (Ruth) 1918-1999
.... **CLC 5**
See also CA 57-60; 187; CANR 45, 88; CN 7
Mortimer, Sir John
See Mortimer, John (Clifford)
Morton, Anthony
See Creasey, John
Morton, Thomas 1579(?)-1647(?) .... **LC 72**
See also DLB 24; RGEL 2
Mosca, Gaetano 1858-1941 .... **TCLC 75**
Moses, Daniel David 1952- .... **NNAL**
See also CA 186
Mosher, Howard Frank 1943- .... **CLC 62**
See also CA 139; CANR 65, 115
Mosley, Nicholas 1923- .... **CLC 43, 70**
See also CA 69-72; CANR 41, 60, 108; CN 7; DLB 14, 207
Mosley, Walter 1952- .... **BLCS; CLC 97**
See also AAYA 17; BPFB 2; BW 2; CA 142; CANR 57, 92; CMW 4; CPW; DA3; DAM MULT, POP; MSW; MTCW 2
Moss, Howard 1922-1987 ..... **CLC 7, 14, 45, 50**
See also CA 1-4R; 123; CANR 1, 44; DAM POET; DLB 5
Mossgiel, Rab
See Burns, Robert
Motion, Andrew (Peter) 1952- .... **CLC 47**
See also BRWS 7; CA 146; CANR 90; CP 7; DLB 40
Motley, Willard (Francis) 1909-1965
.... **CLC 18**
See also BW 1; CA 117; 106; CANR 88; DLB 76, 143
Motoori, Noringa 1730-1801 .... **NCLC 45**
Mott, Michael (Charles Alston) 1930-
.... **CLC 15, 34**
See also CA 5-8R; CAAS 7; CANR 7, 29
Mountain Wolf Woman 1884-1960
.... **CLC 92; NNAL**
See also CA 144; CANR 90
Moure, Erin 1955- .... **CLC 88**
See also CA 113; CP 7; CWP; DLB 60
Mourning Dove 1885(?)-1936 .... **NNAL**
See also CA 144; CANR 90; DAM MULT; DLB 175, 221
Mowat, Farley (McGill) 1921- .... **CLC 26**
See also AAYA 1; BYA 2; CA 1-4R; CANR 4, 24, 42, 68, 108; CLR 20; CPW; DAC; DAM MST; DLB 68; INT CANR-24; JRDA; MAICYA 1, 2; MTCW 1, 2; SATA 3, 55; YAW
Mowatt, Anna Cora 1819-1870 .... **NCLC 74**
See also RGAL 4
Moyers, Bill 1934- .... **CLC 74**
See also AITN 2; CA 61-64; CANR 31, 52

Mphahlele, Es'kia
See Mphahlele, Ezekiel
See also AFW; CDWLB 3; DLB 125, 225; RGSF 2; SSFS 11
Mphahlele, Ezekiel 1919- .. **BLC 3; CLC 25, 133**
See Mphahlele, Es'kia
See also BW 2, 3; CA 81-84; CANR 26, 76; CN 7; DA3; DAM MULT; EWL 3; MTCW 2; SATA 119
Mqhayi, S(amuel) E(dward) K(rune Loliwe) 1875-1945 .... **BLC 3; TCLC 25**
See also CA 153; CANR 87; DAM MULT
Mrozek, Slawomir 1930- .... **CLC 3, 13**
See also CA 13-16R; CAAS 10; CANR 29; CDWLB 4; CWW 2; DLB 232; EWL 3; MTCW 1
Mrs. Belloc-Lowndes
See Lowndes, Marie Adelaide (Belloc)
M'Taggart, John M'Taggart Ellis
See McTaggart, John McTaggart Ellis
Mtwa, Percy (?)- .... **CLC 47**
Mueller, Lisel 1924- .... **CLC 13, 51; PC 33**
See also CA 93-96; CP 7; DLB 105; PFS 9, 13
Muggeridge, Malcolm (Thomas) 1903-1990
.... **TCLC 120**
See also AITN 1; CA 101; CANR 33, 63; MTCW 1, 2
Muhammad 570-632 .... **WLCS**
See also DA; DAB; DAC; DAM MST
Muir, Edwin 1887-1959 .... **TCLC 2, 87**
See Moore, Edward
See also BRWS 6; CA 104; 193; DLB 20, 100, 191; EWL 3; RGEL 2
Muir, John 1838-1914 .... **TCLC 28**
See also AMWS 9; ANW; CA 165; DLB 186, 275
Mujica Lainez, Manuel 1910-1984 . **CLC 31**
See Lainez, Manuel Mujica
See also CA 81-84; 112; CANR 32; EWL 3; HW 1
Mukherjee, Bharati 1940- ... **AAL; CLC 53, 115; SSC 38**
See also AAYA 46; BEST 89:2; CA 107; CANR 45, 72; CN 7; DAM NOV; DLB 60, 218; DNFS 1, 2; EWL 3; FW; MTCW 1, 2; RGAL 4; RGSF 2; SSFS 7; TUS
Muldoon, Paul 1951- .... **CLC 32, 72, 166**
See also BRWS 4; CA 113; 129; CANR 52, 91; CP 7; DAM POET; DLB 40; INT 129; PFS 7
Mulisch, Harry 1927- .... **CLC 42**
See also CA 9-12R; CANR 6, 26, 56, 110; EWL 3
Mull, Martin 1943- .... **CLC 17**
See also CA 105
Muller, Wilhelm .... **NCLC 73**
Mulock, Dinah Maria
See Craik, Dinah Maria (Mulock)
See also RGEL 2
Munday, Anthony 1560-1633 .... **LC 87**
See also DLB 62, 172; RGEL 2
Munford, Robert 1737(?)-1783 .... **LC 5**
See also DLB 31
Mungo, Raymond 1946- .... **CLC 72**
See also CA 49-52; CANR 2
Munro, Alice 1931- .. **CLC 6, 10, 19, 50, 95; SSC 3; WLCS**
See also AITN 2; BPFB 2; CA 33-36R; CANR 33, 53, 75, 114; CCA 1; CN 7; DA3; DAC; DAM MST, NOV; DLB 53; EWL 3; MTCW 1, 2; RGEL 2; RGSF 2; SATA 29; SSFS 5, 13
Munro, H(ector) H(ugh) 1870-1916 .. **WLC**
See Saki
See also CA 104; 130; CANR 104; CDBLB 1890-1914; DA; DA3; DAB; DAC; DAM

MST, NOV; DLB 34, 162; EXPS; MTCW 1, 2; RGEL 2; SSFS 15

Murakami, Haruki 1949- .... CLC 150
See Murakami Haruki
See also CA 165; CANR 102; MJW; RGWL 3; SFW 4

Murakami Haruki
See Murakami, Haruki
See also DLB 182; EWL 3

Murasaki, Lady
See Murasaki Shikibu

Murasaki Shikibu 978(?)-1026(?) .. CMLC 1
See also EFS 2; RGWL 2, 3

Murdoch, (Jean) Iris 1919-1999 .. CLC 1, 2, 3, 4, 6, 8, 11, 15, 22, 31, 51
See also BRWS 1; CA 13-16R; 179; CANR 8, 43, 68, 103; CDBLB 1960 to Present; CN 7; CWD; DA3; DAB; DAC; DAM MST, NOV; DLB 14, 194, 233; EWL 3; INT CANR-8; MTCW 1, 2; RGEL 2; TEA; WLIT 4

Murfree, Mary Noailles 1850-1922
.... SSC 22; TCLC 135
See also CA 122; 176; DLB 12, 74; RGAL 4

Murnau, Friedrich Wilhelm
See Plumpe, Friedrich Wilhelm

Murphy, Richard 1927- .... CLC 41
See also BRWS 5; CA 29-32R; CP 7; DLB 40; EWL 3

Murphy, Sylvia 1937- .... CLC 34
See also CA 121

Murphy, Thomas (Bernard) 1935- . CLC 51
See also CA 101

Murray, Albert L. 1916- .... CLC 73
See also BW 2; CA 49-52; CANR 26, 52, 78; CSW; DLB 38

Murray, James Augustus Henry 1837-1915
.... TCLC 117

Murray, Judith Sargent 1751-1820
.... NCLC 63
See also DLB 37, 200

Murray, Les(lie Allan) 1938- .... CLC 40
See also BRWS 7; CA 21-24R; CANR 11, 27, 56, 103; CP 7; DAM POET; DLBY 2001; EWL 3; RGEL 2

Murry, J. Middleton
See Murry, John Middleton

Murry, John Middleton 1889-1957
.... TCLC 16
See also CA 118; DLB 149

Musgrave, Susan 1951- .... CLC 13, 54
See also CA 69-72; CANR 45, 84; CCA 1; CP 7; CWP

Musil, Robert (Edler von) 1880-1942
.... SSC 18; TCLC 12, 68
See also CA 109; CANR 55, 84; CDWLB 2; DLB 81, 124; EW 9; EWL 3; MTCW 2; RGSF 2; RGWL 2, 3

Muske, Carol .... CLC 90
See Muske-Dukes, Carol (Anne)

Muske-Dukes, Carol (Anne) 1945-
See Muske, Carol
See also CA 65-68; CAAE 203; CANR 32, 70; CWP

Musset, (Louis Charles) Alfred de 1810-1857
.... NCLC 7
See also DLB 192, 217; EW 6; GFL 1789 to the Present; RGWL 2, 3; TWA

Mussolini, Benito (Amilcare Andrea) 1883-1945 .... TCLC 96
See also CA 116

My Brother's Brother
See Chekhov, Anton (Pavlovich)

Myers, L(eopold) H(amilton) 1881-1944
.... TCLC 59
See also CA 157; DLB 15; EWL 3; RGEL 2

Myers, Walter Dean 1937- ...... BLC 3; CLC 35
See also AAYA 4, 23; BW 2; BYA 6, 8, 11; CA 33-36R; CANR 20, 42, 67, 108; CLR 4, 16, 35; DAM MULT, NOV; DLB 33; INT CANR-20; JRDA; LAIT 5; MAICYA 1, 2; MAICYAS 1; MTCW 2; SAAS 2; SATA 41, 71, 109; SATA-Brief 27; WYA; YAW

Myers, Walter M.
See Myers, Walter Dean

Myles, Symon
See Follett, Ken(neth Martin)

Nabokov, Vladimir (Vladimirovich) 1899-1977 ..... CLC 1, 2, 3, 6, 8, 11, 15, 23, 44, 46, 64; SSC 11; TCLC 108; WLC
See also AAYA 45; AMW; AMWC 1; AMWR 1; BPFB 2; CA 5-8R; 69-72; CANR 20, 102; CDALB 1941-1968; DA; DA3; DAB; DAC; DAM MST, NOV; DLB 2, 244, 278; DLBD 3; DLBY 1980, 1991; EWL 3; EXPS; MTCW 1, 2; NCFS 4; NFS 9; RGAL 4; RGSF 2; SSFS 6, 15; TUS

Naevius c. 265B.C.-201B.C. .... CMLC 37
See also DLB 211

Nagai, Kafu .... TCLC 51
See Nagai, Sokichi
See also DLB 180

Nagai, Sokichi 1879-1959
See Nagai, Kafu
See also CA 117

Nagy, Laszlo 1925-1978 .... CLC 7
See also CA 129; 112

Naidu, Sarojini 1879-1949 .... TCLC 80
See also EWL 3; RGEL 2

Naipaul, Shiva(dhar Srinivasa) 1945-1985
.... CLC 32, 39
See also CA 110; 112; 116; CANR 33; DA3; DAM NOV; DLB 157; DLBY 1985; EWL 3; MTCW 1, 2

Naipaul, V(idiadhar) S(urajprasad) 1932-
... CLC 4, 7, 9, 13, 18, 37, 105; SSC 38
See also BPFB 2; BRWS 1; CA 1-4R; CANR 1, 33, 51, 91; CDBLB 1960 to Present; CDWLB 3; CN 7; DA3; DAB; DAC; DAM MST, NOV; DLB 125, 204, 207; DLBY 1985, 2001; EWL 3; MTCW 1, 2; RGEL 2; RGSF 2; TWA; WLIT 4

Nakos, Lilika 1899(?)- .... CLC 29

Narayan, R(asipuram) K(rishnaswami) 1906-2001 ..... CLC 7, 28, 47, 121; SSC 25
See also BPFB 2; CA 81-84; 196; CANR 33, 61, 112; CN 7; DA3; DAM NOV; DNFS 1; EWL 3; MTCW 1, 2; RGEL 2; RGSF 2; SATA 62; SSFS 5

Nash, (Frediric) Ogden 1902-1971
.... CLC 23; PC 21; TCLC 109
See also CA 13-14; 29-32R; CANR 34, 61; CAP 1; DAM POET; DLB 11; MAICYA 1, 2; MTCW 1, 2; RGAL 4; SATA 2, 46; WP

Nashe, Thomas 1567-1601(?) .... LC 41, 59
See also DLB 167; RGEL 2

Nathan, Daniel
See Dannay, Frederic

Nathan, George Jean 1882-1958 .. TCLC 18
See Hatteras, Owen
See also CA 114; 169; DLB 137

Natsume, Kinnosuke
See Natsume, Soseki

Natsume, Soseki 1867-1916 ..... TCLC 2, 10
See Natsume Soseki; Soseki
See also CA 104; 195; RGWL 2, 3; TWA

Natsume Soseki
See Natsume, Soseki
See also DLB 180; EWL 3

Natti, (Mary) Lee 1919-
See Kingman, Lee
See also CA 5-3R; CANR 2

Navarre, Marguerite de
See de Navarre, Marguerite

Naylor, Gloria 1950- ... BLC 3; CLC 28, 52, 156; WLCS
See also AAYA 6, 39; AFAW 1, 2; AMWS 8; BW 2, 3; CA 107; CANR 27, 51, 74; CN 7; CPW; DA; DA3; DAC; DAM MST, MULT, NOV, POP; DLB 173; EWL 3; FW; MTCW 1, 2; NFS 4, 7; RGAL 4; TUS

Neff, Debra .... CLC 59

Neihardt, John Gneisenau 1881-1973
.... CLC 32
See also CA 13-14; CANR 65; CAP 1; DLB 9, 54, 256; LAIT 2

Nekrasov, Nikolai Alekseevich 1821-1878
.... NCLC 11

Nelligan, Emile 1879-1941 .... TCLC 14
See also CA 114; 204; DLB 92; EWL 3

Nelson, Willie 1933- .... CLC 17
See also CA 107; CANR 114

Nemerov, Howard (Stanley) 1920-1991
..... CLC 2, 6, 9, 36; PC 24; TCLC 124
See also AMW; CA 1-4R; 134; CABS 2; CANR 1, 27, 53; DAM POET; DLB 5, 6; DLBY 1983; EWL 3; INT CANR-27; MTCW 1, 2; PFS 10, 14; RGAL 4

Neruda, Pablo 1904-1973 ..... CLC 1, 2, 5, 7, 9, 28, 62; HLC 2; PC 4; WLC
See also CA 19-20; 45-48; CAP 2; DA; DA3; DAB; DAC; DAM MST, MULT, POET; DNFS 2; EWL 3; HW 1; LAW; MTCW 1, 2; PFS 11; RGWL 2, 3; TWA; WLIT 1; WP

Nerval, Gerard de 1808-1855 . NCLC 1, 67; PC 13; SSC 18
See also DLB 217; EW 6; GFL 1789 to the Present; RGSF 2; RGWL 2, 3

Nervo, (Jose) Amado (Ruiz de) 1870-1919
.... HLCS 2; TCLC 11
See also CA 109; 131; EWL 3; HW 1; LAW

Nesbit, Malcolm
See Chester, Alfred

Nessi, Pio Baroja y
See Baroja (y Nessi), Pio

Nestroy, Johann 1801-1862 .... NCLC 42
See also DLB 133; RGWL 2, 3

Netterville, Luke
See O'Grady, Standish (James)

Neufeld, John (Arthur) 1938- .... CLC 17
See also AAYA 11; CA 25-28R; CANR 11, 37, 56; CLR 52; MAICYA 1, 2; SAAS 3; SATA 6, 81; SATA-Essay 131; YAW

Neumann, Alfred 1895-1952 .... TCLC 100
See also CA 183; DLB 56

Neumann, Ferenc
See Molnar, Ferenc

Neville, Emily Cheney 1919- .... CLC 12
See also BYA 2; CA 5-8R; CANR 3, 37, 85; JRDA; MAICYA 1, 2; SAAS 2; SATA 1; YAW

Newbound, Bernard Slade 1930-
See Slade, Bernard
See also CA 81-84; CANR 49; CD 5; DAM DRAM

Newby, P(ercy) H(oward) 1918-1997
.... CLC 2, 13
See also CA 5-8R; 161; CANR 32, 67; CN 7; DAM NOV; DLB 15; MTCW 1; RGEL 2

Newcastle
See Cavendish, Margaret Lucas

Newlove, Donald 1928- .... CLC 6
See also CA 29-32R; CANR 25

Newlove, John (Herbert) 1938- .... **CLC 14**
See also CA 21-24R; CANR 9, 25; CP 7
Newman, Charles 1938- .... **CLC 2, 8**
See also CA 21-24R; CANR 84; CN 7
Newman, Edwin (Harold) 1919- ..... **CLC 14**
See also AITN 1; CA 69-72; CANR 5
Newman, John Henry 1801-1890
.... **NCLC 38, 99**
See also BRWS 7; DLB 18, 32, 55; RGEL 2
Newton, (Sir) Isaac 1642-1727 ..... **LC 35, 53**
See also DLB 252
Newton, Suzanne 1936- .... **CLC 35**
See also BYA 7; CA 41-44R; CANR 14; JRDA; SATA 5, 77
New York Dept. of Ed. .... **CLC 70**
Nexo, Martin Andersen 1869-1954
.... **TCLC 43**
See also CA 202; DLB 214; EWL 3
Nezval, Vitezslav 1900-1958 .... **TCLC 44**
See also CA 123; CDWLB 4; DLB 215; EWL 3
Ng, Fae Myenne 1957(?)- .... **CLC 81**
See also CA 146
Ngema, Mbongeni 1955- .... **CLC 57**
See also BW 2; CA 143; CANR 84; CD 5
Ngugi, James T(hiong'o) .... **CLC 3, 7, 13**
See Ngugi wa Thiong'o
Ngugi wa Thiong'o
See Ngugi wa Thiong'o
See also DLB 125; EWL 3
Ngugi wa Thiong'o 1938- .. **BLC 3; CLC 36**
See Ngugi, James T(hiong'o); Ngugi wa Thiong'o
See also AFW; BRWS 8; BW 2; CA 81-84; CANR 27, 58; CDWLB 3; DAM MULT, NOV; DNFS 2; MTCW 1, 2; RGEL 2
Niatum, Duane 1938- .... **NNAL**
See also CA 41-44R; CANR 21, 45, 83; DLB 175
Nichol, B(arrie) P(hillip) 1944-1988
.... **CLC 18**
See also CA 53-56; DLB 53; SATA 66
Nicholas of Cusa 1401-1464 .... **LC 80**
See also DLB 115
Nichols, John (Treadwell) 1940- ..... **CLC 38**
See also CA 9-12R; CAAE 190; CAAS 2; CANR 6, 70; DLBY 1982; TCWW 2
Nichols, Leigh
See Koontz, Dean R(ay)
Nichols, Peter (Richard) 1927- .. **CLC 5, 36, 65**
See also CA 104; CANR 33, 86; CBD; CD 5; DLB 13, 245; MTCW 1
Nicholson, Linda ed. .... **CLC 65**
Ni Chuilleanain, Eilean 1942- .... **PC 34**
See also CA 126; CANR 53, 83; CP 7; CWP; DLB 40
Nicolas, F. R. E.
See Freeling, Nicolas
Niedecker, Lorine 1903-1970 ... **CLC 10, 42; PC 42**
See also CA 25-28; CAP 2; DAM POET; DLB 48
Nietzsche, Friedrich (Wilhelm) 1844-1900
.... **TCLC 10, 18, 55**
See also CA 107; 121; CDWLB 2; DLB 129; EW 7; RGWL 2, 3; TWA
Nievo, Ippolito 1831-1861 .... **NCLC 22**
Nightingale, Anne Redmon 1943-
See Redmon, Anne
See also CA 103
Nightingale, Florence 1820-1910 .. **TCLC 85**
See also CA 188; DLB 166
Nijo Yoshimoto 1320-1388 .... **CMLC 49**
See also DLB 203
Nik. T. O.
See Annensky, Innokenty (Fyodorovich)

Nin, Anais 1903-1977 .... **CLC 1, 4, 8, 11, 14, 60, 127; SSC 10**
See also AITN 2; AMWS 10; BPFB 2; CA 13-16R; 69-72; CANR 22, 53; DAM NOV, POP; DLB 2, 4, 152; EWL 3; GLL 2; MAWW; MTCW 1, 2; RGAL 4; RGSF 2
Nisbet, Robert A(lexander) 1913-1996
.... **TCLC 117**
See also CA 25-28R; 153; CANR 17; INT CANR-17
Nishida, Kitaro 1870-1945 .... **TCLC 83**
Nishiwaki, Junzaburo
See Nishiwaki, Junzaburo
See also CA 194
Nishiwaki, Junzaburo 1894-1982 .... **PC 15**
See Nishiwaki, Junzaburo; Nishiwaki Junzaburo
See also CA 194; 107; MJW; RGWL 3
Nishiwaki Junzaburo
See Nishiwaki, Junzaburo
See also EWL 3
Nissenson, Hugh 1933- .... **CLC 4, 9**
See also CA 17-20R; CANR 27, 108; CN 7; DLB 28
Nister, Der
See Der Nister
See also EWL 3
Niven, Larry .... **CLC 8**
See Niven, Laurence Van Cott
See also AAYA 27; BPFB 2; BYA 10; CAAE 207; DLB 8; SCFW 2
Niven, Laurence Van Cott 1938-
See Niven, Larry
See also CA 21-24R; CAAE 207; CAAS 12; CANR 14, 44, 66, 113; CPW; DAM POP; MTCW 1, 2; SATA 95; SFW 4
Nixon, Agnes Eckhardt 1927- .... **CLC 21**
See also CA 110
Nizan, Paul 1905-1940 .... **TCLC 40**
See also CA 161; DLB 72; EWL 3; GFL 1789 to the Present
Nkosi, Lewis 1936- .... **BLC 3; CLC 45**
See also BW 1, 3; CA 65-68; CANR 27, 81; CBD; CD 5; DAM MULT; DLB 157, 225
Nodier, (Jean) Charles (Emmanuel) 1780-1844 .... **NCLC 19**
See also DLB 119; GFL 1789 to the Present
Noguchi, Yone 1875-1947 .... **TCLC 80**
Nolan, Christopher 1965- .... **CLC 58**
See also CA 111; CANR 88
Noon, Jeff 1957- .... **CLC 91**
See also CA 148; CANR 83; DLB 267; SFW 4
Norden, Charles
See Durrell, Lawrence (George)
Nordhoff, Charles (Bernard) 1887-1947
.... **TCLC 23**
See also CA 108; DLB 9; LAIT 1; RHW 1; SATA 23
Norfolk, Lawrence 1963- .... **CLC 76**
See also CA 144; CANR 85; CN 7; DLB 267
Norman, Marsha 1947- .... **CLC 28; DC 8**
See also CA 105; CABS 3; CAD; CANR 41; CD 5; CSW; CWD; DAM DRAM; DFS 2; DLB 266; DLBY 1984; FW
Normyx
See Douglas, (George) Norman
Norris, (Benjamin) Frank(lin, Jr.) 1870-1902
.... **SSC 28; TCLC 24**
See also AMW; BPFB 2; CA 110; 160; CDALB 1865-1917; DLB 12, 71, 186; LMFS 2; NFS 12; RGAL 4; TCWW 2; TUS
Norris, Leslie 1921- .... **CLC 14**
See also CA 11-12; CANR 14, 117; CAP 1; CP 7; DLB 27, 256

North, Andrew
See Norton, Andre
North, Anthony
See Koontz, Dean R(ay)
North, Captain George
See Stevenson, Robert Louis (Balfour)
North, Captain George
See Stevenson, Robert Louis (Balfour)
North, Milou
See Erdrich, Louise
Northrup, B. A.
See Hubbard, L(afayette) Ron(ald)
North Staffs
See Hulme, T(homas) E(rnest)
Northup, Solomon 1808-1863 ..... **NCLC 105**
Norton, Alice Mary
See Norton, Andre
See also MAICYA 1; SATA 1, 43
Norton, Andre 1912- .... **CLC 12**
See Norton, Alice Mary
See also AAYA 14; BPFB 2; BYA 4, 10, 12; CA 1-4R; CANR 68; CLR 50; DLB 8, 52; JRDA; MAICYA 2; MTCW 1; SATA 91; SUFW 1, 2; YAW
Norton, Caroline 1808-1877 .... **NCLC 47**
See also DLB 21, 159, 199
Norway, Nevil Shute 1899-1960
See Shute, Nevil
See also CA 102; 93-96; CANR 85; MTCW 2
Norwid, Cyprian Kamil 1821-1883
.... **NCLC 17**
See also RGWL 3
Nosille, Nabrah
See Ellison, Harlan (Jay)
Nossack, Hans Erich 1901-1978 .... **CLC 6**
See also CA 93-96; 85-88; DLB 69; EWL 3
Nostradamus 1503-1566 .... **LC 27**
Nosu, Chuji
See Ozu, Yasujiro
Notenburg, Eleanora (Genrikhovna) von
See Guro, Elena
Nova, Craig 1945- .... **CLC 7, 31**
See also CA 45-48; CANR 2, 53
Novak, Joseph
See Kosinski, Jerzy (Nikodem)
Novalis 1772-1801 .... **NCLC 13**
See also CDWLB 2; DLB 90; EW 5; RGWL 2, 3
Novick, Peter 1934- .... **CLC 164**
See also CA 188
Novis, Emile
See Weil, Simone (Adolphine)
Nowlan, Alden (Albert) 1933-1983 . **CLC 15**
See also CA 9-12R; CANR 5; DAC; DAM MST; DLB 53; PFS 12
Noyes, Alfred 1880-1958 .... **PC 27; TCLC 7**
See also CA 104; 188; DLB 20; EXPP; FANT; PFS 4; RGEL 2
Nugent, Richard Bruce 1906(?)-1987 . **HR 3**
See also BW 1; CA 125; DLB 51; GLL 2
Nunn, Kem .... **CLC 34**
See also CA 159
Nwapa, Flora (Nwanzuruaha) 1931-1993
.... **BLCS; CLC 133**
See also BW 2; CA 143; CANR 83; CDWLB 3; CWRI 5; DLB 125; EWL 3; WLIT 2
Nye, Robert 1939- .... **CLC 13, 42**
See also CA 33-36R; CANR 29, 67, 107; CN 7; CP 7; CWRI 5; DAM NOV; DLB 14, 271; FANT; HGG; MTCW 1; RHW; SATA 6
Nyro, Laura 1947-1997 .... **CLC 17**
See also CA 194

Oates, Joyce Carol 1938- . CLC 1, 2, 3, 6, 9, 11, 15, 19, 33, 52, 108, 134; SSC 6; WLC
See also AAYA 15; AITN 1; AMWS 2; BEST 89:2; BPFB 2; BYA 11; CA 5-8R; CANR 25, 45, 74, 113, 113; CDALB 1968-1988; CN 7; CP 7; CPW; CWP; DA; DA3; DAB; DAC; DAM MST, NOV, POP; DLB 2, 5, 130; DLBY 1981; EWL 3; EXPS; FW; HGG; INT CANR-25; LAIT 4; MAWW; MTCW 1, 2; NFS 8; RGAL 4; RGSF 2; SSFS 17; SUFW 2; TUS

O'Brian, E. G.
See Clarke, Arthur C(harles)

O'Brian, Patrick 1914-2000 .... CLC 152
See also CA 144; 187; CANR 74; CPW; MTCW 2; RHW

O'Brien, Darcy 1939-1998 .... CLC 11
See also CA 21-24R; 167; CANR 8, 59

O'Brien, Edna 1936- .... CLC 3, 5, 8, 13, 36, 65, 116; SSC 10
See also BRWS 5; CA 1-4R; CANR 6, 41, 65, 102; CDBLB 1960 to Present; CN 7; DA3; DAM NOV; DLB 14, 231; EWL 3; FW; MTCW 1, 2; RGSF 2; WLIT 4

O'Brien, Fitz-James 1828-1862 ...... NCLC 21
See also DLB 74; RGAL 4; SUFW

O'Brien, Flann .... CLC 1, 4, 5, 7, 10, 47
See O Nuallain, Brian
See also BRWS 2; DLB 231; EWL 3; RGEL 2

O'Brien, Richard 1942- .... CLC 17
See also CA 124

O'Brien, (William) Tim(othy) 1946-
.... CLC 7, 19, 40, 103
See also AAYA 16; AMWS 5; CA 85-88; CANR 40, 58; CDALBS; CN 7; CPW; DA3; DAM POP; DLB 152; DLBD 9; DLBY 1980; MTCW 2; RGAL 4; SSFS 5, 15

Obstfelder, Sigbjoern 1866-1900 .. TCLC 23
See also CA 123

O'Casey, Sean 1880-1964 ... CLC 1, 5, 9, 11, 15, 88; DC 12; WLCS
See also BRW 7; CA 89-92; CANR 62; CBD; CDBLB 1914-1945; DA3; DAB; DAC; DAM DRAM, MST; DLB 10; EWL 3; MTCW 1, 2; RGEL 2; TEA; WLIT 4

O'Cathasaigh, Sean
See O'Casey, Sean

Occom, Samson 1723-1792 ... LC 60; NNAL
See also DLB 175

Ochs, Phil(ip David) 1940-1976 .... CLC 17
See also CA 185; 65-68

O'Connor, Edwin (Greene) 1918-1968
.... CLC 14
See also CA 93-96; 25-28R

O'Connor, (Mary) Flannery 1925-1964
.... CLC 1, 2, 3, 6, 10, 13, 15, 21, 66, 104; SSC 1, 23, 61; TCLC 132; WLC
See also AAYA 7; AMW; AMWR 2; BPFB 3; CA 1-4R; CANR 3, 41; CDALB 1941-1968; DA; DA3; DAB; DAC; DAM MST, NOV; DLB 2, 152; DLBD 12; DLBY 1980; EWL 3; EXPS; LAIT 5; MAWW; MTCW 1, 2; NFS 3; RGAL 4; RGSF 2; SSFS 2, 7, 10; TUS

O'Connor, Frank .... CLC 23; SSC 5
See O'Donovan, Michael Francis
See also DLB 162; EWL 3; RGSF 2; SSFS 5

O'Dell, Scott 1898-1989 .... CLC 30
See also AAYA 3, 44; BPFB 3; BYA 1, 2, 3, 5; CA 61-64; 129; CANR 12, 30, 112; CLR 1, 16; DLB 52; JRDA; MAICYA 1, 2; SATA 12, 60, 134; WYA; YAW

Odets, Clifford 1906-1963 .... CLC 2, 28, 98; DC 6
See also AMWS 2; CA 85-88; CAD; CANR 62; DAM DRAM; DFS 17; DLB 7, 26; EWL 3; MTCW 1, 2; RGAL 4; TUS

O'Doherty, Brian 1928- .... CLC 76
See also CA 105; CANR 108

O'Donnell, K. M.
See Malzberg, Barry N(athaniel)

O'Donnell, Lawrence
See Kuttner, Henry

O'Donovan, Michael Francis 1903-1966
.... CLC 14
See O'Connor, Frank
See also CA 93-96; CANR 84

Oe, Kenzaburo 1935- . CLC 10, 36, 86; SSC 20
See Oe Kenzaburo
See also CA 97-100; CANR 36, 50, 74; CWW 2; DA3; DAM NOV; DLB 182; DLBY 1994; EWL 3; MJW; MTCW 1, 2; RGSF 2; RGWL 2, 3

Oe Kenzaburo
See Oe, Kenzaburo
See also EWL 3

O'Faolain, Julia 1932- ... CLC 6, 19, 47, 108
See also CA 81-84; CAAS 2; CANR 12, 61; CN 7; DLB 14, 231; FW; MTCW 1; RHW

O'Faolain, Sean 1900-1991 .... CLC 1, 7, 14, 32, 70; SSC 13
See also CA 61-64; 134; CANR 12, 66; DLB 15, 162; MTCW 1, 2; RGEL 2; RGSF 2

O'Flaherty, Liam 1896-1984 ...... CLC 5, 34; SSC 6
See also CA 101; 113; CANR 35; DLB 36, 162; DLBY 1984; MTCW 1, 2; RGEL 2; RGSF 2; SSFS 5

Ogai
See Mori Ogai
See also MJW

Ogilvy, Gavin
See Barrie, J(ames) M(atthew)

O'Grady, Standish (James) 1846-1928
.... TCLC 5
See also CA 104; 157

O'Grady, Timothy 1951- .... CLC 59
See also CA 138

O'Hara, Frank 1926-1966 ...... CLC 2, 5, 13, 78; PC 45
See also CA 9-12R; 25-28R; CANR 33; DA3; DAM POET; DLB 5, 16, 193; EWL 3; MTCW 1, 2; PFS 8; 12; RGAL 4; WP

O'Hara, John (Henry) 1905-1970 .... CLC 1, 2, 3, 6, 11, 42; SSC 15
See also AMW; BPFB 3; CA 5-8R; 25-28R; CANR 31, 60; CDALB 1929-1941; DAM NOV; DLB 9, 86; DLBD 2; EWL 3; MTCW 1, 2; NFS 11; RGAL 4; RGSF 2

O Hehir, Diana 1922- .... CLC 41
See also CA 93-96

Ohiyesa
See Eastman, Charles A(lexander)

Okada, John 1923-1971 .... AAL
See also BYA 14

Okigbo, Christopher (Ifenayichukwu) 1932-1967 .. BLC 3; CLC 25, 84; PC 7
See also AFW; BW 1, 3; CA 77-80; CANR 74; CDWLB 3; DAM MULT, POET; DLB 125; EWL 3; MTCW 1, 2; RGEL 2

Okri, Ben 1959- .... CLC 87
See also AFW; BRWS 5; BW 2, 3; CA 130; 138; CANR 65; CN 7; DLB 157, 231; EWL 3; INT CA-138; MTCW 2; RGSF 2; WLIT 2

Olds, Sharon 1942- . CLC 32, 39, 85; PC 22
See also AMWS 10; CA 101; CANR 18, 41, 66, 98; CP 7; CPW; CWP; DAM POET; DLB 120; MTCW 2; PFS 17

Oldstyle, Jonathan
See Irving, Washington

Olesha, Iurii
See Olesha, Yuri (Karlovich)
See also EGWL 2

Olesha, Iurii Karlovich
See Olesha, Yuri (Karlovich)
See also DLB 272

Olesha, Yuri (Karlovich) 1899-1960 . CLC 8
See Olesha, Iurii; Olesha, Iurii Karlovich; Olesha, Yury Karlovich
See also CA 85-88; EW 11; RGWL 3

Olesha, Yury Karlovich
See Olesha, Yuri (Karlovich)
See also EWL 3

Oliphant, Mrs.
See Oliphant, Margaret (Oliphant Wilson)
See also SUFW

Oliphant, Laurence 1829(?)-1888 . NCLC 47
See also DLB 18, 166

Oliphant, Margaret (Oliphant Wilson) 1828-1897 ...... NCLC 11, 61; SSC 25
See Oliphant, Mrs.
See also DLB 18, 159, 190; HGG; RGEL 2; RGSF 2

Oliver, Mary 1935- .... CLC 19, 34, 98
See also AMWS 7; CA 21-24R; CANR 9, 43, 84, 92; CP 7; CWP; DLB 5, 193; EWL 3; PFS 15

Olivier, Laurence (Kerr) 1907-1989
.... CLC 20
See also CA 111; 150; 129

Olsen, Tillie 1912- . CLC 4, 13, 114; SSC 11
See also BYA 11; CA 1-4R; CANR 1, 43, 74; CDALBS; CN 7; DA; DA3; DAB; DAC; DAM MST; DLB 28, 206; DLBY 1980; EWL 3; EXPS; FW; MTCW 1, 2; RGAL 4; RGSF 2; SSFS 1; TUS

Olson, Charles (John) 1910-1970 ..... CLC 1, 2, 5, 6, 9, 11, 29; PC 19
See also AMWS 2; CA 13-16; 25-28R; CABS 2; CANR 35, 61; CAP 1; DAM POET; DLB 5, 16, 193; EWL 3; MTCW 1, 2; RGAL 4; WP

Olson, Toby 1937- .... CLC 28
See also CA 65-68; CANR 9, 31, 84; CP 7

Olyesha, Yuri
See Olesha, Yuri (Karlovich)

Olympiodorus of Thebes c. 375-c. 430
.... CMLC 59

Omar Khayyam
See Khayyam, Omar
See also RGWL 2, 3

Ondaatje, (Philip) Michael 1943- .. CLC 14, 29, 51, 76; PC 28
See also CA 77-80; CANR 42, 74, 109; CN 7; CP 7; DA3; DAB; DAC; DAM MST; DLB 60; EWL 3; LMFS 2; MTCW 2; PFS 8; TWA

Oneal, Elizabeth 1934-
See Oneal, Zibby
See also CA 106; CANR 28, 84; MAICYA 1, 2; SATA 30, 82; YAW

Oneal, Zibby .... CLC 30
See Oneal, Elizabeth
See also AAYA 5, 41; BYA 13; CLR 13; JRDA; WYA

O'Neill, Eugene (Gladstone) 1888-1953
.... DC 20; TCLC 1, 6, 27, 49; WLC
See also AITN 1; AMW; AMWC 1; CA 110; 132; CAD; CDALB 1929-1941; DA; DA3; DAB; DAC; DAM DRAM, MST; DFS 2, 4, 5, 6, 9, 11, 12, 16; DLB 7; EWL 3; LAIT 3; LMFS 2; MTCW 1, 2; RGAL 4; TUS

Onetti, Juan Carlos 1909-1994 .. **CLC 7, 10; HLCS 2; SSC 23; TCLC 131**
See also CA 85-88; 145; CANR 32, 63; CDWLB 3; DAM MULT, NOV; DLB 113; EWL 3; HW 1, 2; LAW; MTCW 1, 2; RGSF 2

O Nuallain, Brian 1911-1966
See O'Brien, Flann
See also CA 21-22; 25-28R; CAP 2; DLB 231; FANT; TEA

Ophuls, Max 1902-1957 .... **TCLC 79**
See also CA 113

Opie, Amelia 1769-1853 .... **NCLC 65**
See also DLB 116, 159; RGEL 2

Oppen, George 1908-1984 ... **CLC 7, 13, 34; PC 35; TCLC 107**
See also CA 13-16R; 113; CANR 8, 82; DLB 5, 165

Oppenheim, E(dward) Phillips 1866-1946
.... **TCLC 45**
See also CA 111; 202; CMW 4; DLB 70

Opuls, Max
See Ophuls, Max

Origen c. 185-c. 254 .... **CMLC 19**

Orlovitz, Gil 1918-1973 .... **CLC 22**
See also CA 77-80; 45-48; DLB 2, 5

Orris
See Ingelow, Jean

Ortega y Gasset, Jose 1883-1955 ..... **HLC 2; TCLC 9**
See also CA 106; 130; DAM MULT; EW 9; EWL 3; HW 1, 2; MTCW 1, 2

Ortese, Anna Maria 1914-1998 .... **CLC 89**
See also DLB 177; EWL 3

Ortiz, Simon J(oseph) 1941- .... **CLC 45; NNAL; PC 17**
See also AMWS 4; CA 134; CANR 69; CP 7; DAM MULT, POET; DLB 120, 175, 256; EXPP; PFS 4, 16; RGAL 4

Orton, Joe .... **CLC 4, 13, 43; DC 3**
See Orton, John Kingsley
See also BRWS 5; CBD; CDBLB 1960 to Present; DFS 3, 6; DLB 13; GLL 1; MTCW 2; RGEL; TEA; WLIT 4

Orton, John Kingsley 1933-1967
See Orton, Joe
See also CA 85-88; CANR 35, 66; DAM DRAM; MTCW 1, 2

Orwell, George . **TCLC 2, 6, 15, 31, 51, 128, 129; WLC**
See Blair, Eric (Arthur)
See also BPFB 3; BRW 7; BYA 5; CDBLB 1945-1960; CLR 68; DAB; DLB 15, 98, 195, 255; EWL 3; EXPN; LAIT 4, 5; NFS 3, 7; RGEL 2; SCFW 2; SFW 4; SSFS 4; TEA; WLIT 4; YAW

Osborne, David
See Silverberg, Robert

Osborne, George
See Silverberg, Robert

Osborne, John (James) 1929-1994 ... **CLC 1, 2, 5, 11, 45; WLC**
See also BRWS 1; CA 13-16R; 147; CANR 21, 56; CDBLB 1945-1960; DA; DAB; DAC; DAM DRAM, MST; DFS 4; DLB 13; EWL 3; MTCW 1, 2; RGEL 2

Osborne, Lawrence 1958- .... **CLC 50**
See also CA 189

Osbourne, Lloyd 1868-1947 .... **TCLC 93**

Oshima, Nagisa 1932- .... **CLC 20**
See also CA 116; 121; CANR 78

Oskison, John Milton 1874-1947
.... **NNAL; TCLC 35**
See also CA 144; CANR 84; DAM MULT; DLB 175

Ossian c. 3rd cent. - .... **CMLC 28**
See Macpherson, James

Ossoli, Sarah Margaret (Fuller) 1810-1850
.... **NCLC 5, 50**
See Fuller, Margaret; Fuller, Sarah Margaret
See also CDALB 1640-1865; FW; LMFS 1; SATA 25

Ostriker, Alicia (Suskin) 1937- ...... **CLC 132**
See also CA 25-28R; CAAS 24; CANR 10, 30, 62, 99; CWP; DLB 120; EXPP

Ostrovsky, Aleksandr Nikolaevich
See Ostrovsky, Alexander
See also DLB 277

Ostrovsky, Alexander 1823-1886 . **NCLC 30, 57**
See Ostrovsky, Aleksandr Nikolaevich

Otero, Blas de 1916-1979 .... **CLC 11**
See also CA 89-92; DLB 134; EWL 3

Otto, Rudolf 1869-1937 .... **TCLC 85**

Otto, Whitney 1955- .... **CLC 70**
See also CA 140

Ouida .... **TCLC 43**
See De la Ramee, Marie Louise (Ouida)
See also DLB 18, 156; RGEL 2

Ouologuem, Yambo 1940- .... **CLC 146**
See also CA 111; 176

Ousmane, Sembene 1923- .. **BLC 3; CLC 66**
See Sembene, Ousmane
See also BW 1, 3; CA 117; 125; CANR 81; CWW 2; MTCW 1

Ovid 43B.C.-17 .... **CMLC 7; PC 2**
See also AW 2; CDWLB 1; DA3; DAM POET; DLB 211; RGWL 2, 3; WP

Owen, Hugh
See Faust, Frederick (Schiller)

Owen, Wilfred (Edward Salter) 1893-1918
.... **PC 19; TCLC 5, 27; WLC**
See also BRW 6; CA 104; 141; CDBLB 1914-1945; DA; DAB; DAC; DAM MST, POET; DLB 20; EWL 3; EXPP; MTCW 2; PFS 10; RGEL 2; WLIT 4

Owens, Louis (Dean) 1948-2002 .... **NNAL**
See also CA 137; 179; 207; CAAE 179; CAAS 24; CANR 71

Owens, Rochelle 1936- .... **CLC 8**
See also CA 17-20R; CAAS 2; CAD; CANR 39; CD 5; CP 7; CWD; CWP

Oz, Amos 1939- ...... **CLC 5, 8, 11, 27, 33, 54**
See also CA 53-56; CANR 27, 47, 65, 113; CWW 2; DAM NOV; EWL 3; MTCW 1, 2; RGSF 2; RGWL 3

Ozick, Cynthia 1928- .... **CLC 3, 7, 28, 62, 155; SSC 15, 60**
See also AMWS 5; BEST 90:1; CA 17-20R; CANR 23, 58, 116; CN 7; CPW; DA3; DAM NOV, POP; DLB 28, 152; DLBY 1982; EWL 3; EXPS; INT CANR-23; MTCW 1, 2; RGAL 4; RGSF 2; SSFS 3, 12

Ozu, Yasujiro 1903-1963 .... **CLC 16**
See also CA 112

Pabst, G. W. 1885-1967 .... **TCLC 127**

Pacheco, C.
See Pessoa, Fernando (Antonio Nogueira)

Pacheco, Jose Emilio 1939- .... **HLC 2**
See also CA 111; 131; CANR 65; DAM MULT; EWL 3; HW 1, 2; RGSF 2

Pa Chin .... **CLC 18**
See Li Fei-kan
See also EWL 3

Pack, Robert 1929- .... **CLC 13**
See also CA 1-4R; CANR 3, 44, 82; CP 7; DLB 5; SATA 118

Padgett, Lewis
See Kuttner, Henry

Padilla (Lorenzo), Heberto 1932-2000
.... **CLC 38**
See also AITN 1; CA 123; 131; 189; EWL 3; HW 1

Page, James Patrick 1944-
See Page, Jimmy
See also CA 204

Page, Jimmy 1944- .... **CLC 12**
See Page, James Patrick

Page, Louise 1955- .... **CLC 40**
See also CA 140; CANR 76; CBD; CD 5; CWD; DLB 233

Page, P(atricia) K(athleen) 1916- .... **CLC 7, 18; PC 12**
See Cape, Judith
See also CA 53-56; CANR 4, 22, 65; CP 7; DAC; DAM MST; DLB 68; MTCW 1; RGEL 2

Page, Stanton
See Fuller, Henry Blake

Page, Stanton
See Fuller, Henry Blake

Page, Thomas Nelson 1853-1922 ...... **SSC 23**
See also CA 118; 177; DLB 12, 78; DLBD 13; RGAL 4

Pagels, Elaine Hiesey 1943- .... **CLC 104**
See also CA 45-48; CANR 2, 24, 51; FW; NCFS 4

Paget, Violet 1856-1935
See Lee, Vernon
See also CA 104; 166; GLL 1; HGG

Paget-Lowe, Henry
See Lovecraft, H(oward) P(hillips)

Paglia, Camille (Anna) 1947- .... **CLC 68**
See also CA 140; CANR 72; CPW; FW; GLL 2; MTCW 2

Paige, Richard
See Koontz, Dean R(ay)

Paine, Thomas 1737-1809 .... **NCLC 62**
See also AMWS 1; CDALB 1640-1865; DLB 31, 43, 73, 158; LAIT 1; RGAL 4; RGEL 2; TUS

Pakenham, Antonia
See Fraser, (Lady) Antonia (Pakenham)

Palamas, Costis
See Palamas, Kostes

Palamas, Kostes 1859-1943 .... **TCLC 5**
See Palamas, Kostis
See also CA 105; 190; RGWL 2, 3

Palamas, Kostis
See Palamas, Kostes
See also EWL 3

Palazzeschi, Aldo 1885-1974 .... **CLC 11**
See also CA 89-92; 53-56; DLB 114, 264; EWL 3

Pales Matos, Luis 1898-1959 .... **HLCS 2**
See Pales Matos, Luis
See also HW 1; LAW

Paley, Grace 1922- . **CLC 4, 6, 37, 140; SSC 8**
See also AMWS 6; CA 25-28R; CANR 13, 46, 74; CN 7; CPW; DA3; DAM POP; DLB 28, 218; EWL 3; EXPS; FW; INT CANR-13; MAWW; MTCW 1, 2; RGAL 4; RGSF 2; SSFS 3

Palin, Michael (Edward) 1943- .... **CLC 21**
See Monty Python
See also CA 107; CANR 35, 109; SATA 67

Palliser, Charles 1947- .... **CLC 65**
See also CA 136; CANR 76; CN 7

Palma, Ricardo 1833-1919 .... **TCLC 29**
See also CA 168; LAW

Pancake, Breece Dexter 1952-1979
See Pancake, Breece D'J
See also CA 123; 109

Pancake, Breece D'J .... **CLC 29; SSC 61**
See Pancake, Breece Dexter
See also DLB 130

Panchenko, Nikolai .... **CLC 59**

Pankhurst, Emmeline (Goulden) 1858-1928
.... **TCLC 100**
See also CA 116; FW

Panko, Rudy
See Gogol, Nikolai (Vasilyevich)
Papadiamantis, Alexandros 1851-1911
.... **TCLC 29**
See also CA 168; EWL 3
Papadiamantopoulos, Johannes 1856-1910
See Moreas, Jean
See also CA 117
Papini, Giovanni 1881-1956 .... **TCLC 22**
See also CA 121; 180; DLB 264
Paracelsus 1493-1541 .... **LC 14**
See also DLB 179
Parasol, Peter
See Stevens, Wallace
Pardo Bazan, Emilia 1851-1921 ..... **SSC 30**
See also EWL 3; FW; RGSF 2; RGWL 2, 3
Pareto, Vilfredo 1848-1923 .... **TCLC 69**
See also CA 175
Paretsky, Sara 1947- .... **CLC 135**
See also AAYA 30; BEST 90:3; CA 125; 129; CANR 59, 95; CMW 4; CPW; DA3; DAM POP; INT CA-129; MSW; RGAL 4
Parfenie, Maria
See Codrescu, Andrei
Parini, Jay (Lee) 1948- .... **CLC 54, 133**
See also CA 97-100; CAAS 16; CANR 32, 87
Park, Jordan
See Kornbluth, C(yril) M.; Pohl, Frederik
Park, Robert E(zra) 1864-1944 .... **TCLC 73**
See also CA 122; 165
Parker, Bert
See Ellison, Harlan (Jay)
Parker, Dorothy (Rothschild) 1893-1967
.... **CLC 15, 68; PC 28; SSC 2**
See also AMWS 9; CA 19-20; 25-28R; CAP 2; DA3; DAM POET; DLB 11, 45, 86; EXPP; FW; MAWW; MTCW 1, 2; RGAL 4; RGSF 2; TUS
Parker, Robert B(rown) 1932- .... **CLC 27**
See also AAYA 28; BEST 89:4; BPFB 3; CA 49-52; CANR 1, 26, 52, 89; CMW 4; CPW; DAM NOV, POP; INT CANR-26; MSW; MTCW 1
Parkin, Frank 1940- .... **CLC 43**
See also CA 147
Parkman, Francis, Jr. 1823-1893 . **NCLC 12**
See also AMWS 2; DLB 1, 30, 183, 186, 235; RGAL 4
Parks, Gordon (Alexander Buchanan) 1912-
.... **BLC 3; CLC 1, 16**
See also AAYA 36; AITN 2; BW 2, 3; CA 41-44R; CANR 26, 66; DA3; DAM MULT; DLB 33; MTCW 2; SATA 8, 108
Parks, Tim(othy Harold) 1954- ..... **CLC 147**
See also CA 126; 131; CANR 77; DLB 231; INT CA-131
Parmenides c. 515B.C.-c. 450B.C.
.... **CMLC 22**
See also DLB 176
Parnell, Thomas 1679-1718 .... **LC 3**
See also DLB 95; RGEL 2
Parr, Catherine c. 1513(?)-1548 .... **LC 86**
See also DLB 136
Parra, Nicanor 1914- . **CLC 2, 102; HLC 2; PC 39**
See also CA 85-88; CANR 32; CWW 2; DAM MULT; EWL 3; HW 1; LAW; MTCW 1
Parra Sanojo, Ana Teresa de la 1890-1936
.... **HLCS 2**
See de la Parra, (Ana) Teresa (Sonojo)
See also LAW
Parrish, Mary Frances
See Fisher, M(ary) F(rances) K(ennedy)
Parshchikov, Aleksei .... **CLC 59**
Parson, Professor
See Coleridge, Samuel Taylor

Parson Lot
See Kingsley, Charles
Parton, Sara Payson Willis 1811-1872
.... **NCLC 86**
See also DLB 43, 74, 239
Partridge, Anthony
See Oppenheim, E(dward) Phillips
Pascal, Blaise 1623-1662 .... **LC 35**
See also DLB 268; EW 3; GFL Beginnings to 1789; RGWL 2, 3; TWA
Pascoli, Giovanni 1855-1912 .... **TCLC 45**
See also CA 170; EW 7; EWL 3
Pasolini, Pier Paolo 1922-1975 . **CLC 20, 37, 106; PC 17**
See also CA 93-96; 61-64; CANR 63; DLB 128, 177; EWL 3; MTCW 1; RGWL 2, 3
Pasquini
See Silone, Ignazio
Pastan, Linda (Olenik) 1932- .... **CLC 27**
See also CA 61-64; CANR 18, 40, 61, 113; CP 7; CSW; CWP; DAM POET; DLB 5; PFS 8
Pasternak, Boris (Leonidovich) 1890-1960
.... **CLC 7, 10, 18, 63; PC 6; SSC 31; WLC**
See also BPFB 3; CA 127; 116; DA; DA3; DAB; DAC; DAM MST, NOV, POET; EW 10; MTCW 1, 2; RGSF 2; RGWL 2, 3; TWA; WP
Patchen, Kenneth 1911-1972 .. **CLC 1, 2, 18**
See also BG 3; CA 1-4R; 33-36R; CANR 3, 35; DAM POET; DLB 16, 48; EWL 3; MTCW 1; RGAL 4
Pater, Walter (Horatio) 1839-1894
.... **NCLC 7, 90**
See also BRW 5; CDBLB 1832-1890; DLB 57, 156; RGEL 2; TEA
Paterson, A(ndrew) B(arton) 1864-1941
.... **TCLC 32**
See also CA 155; DLB 230; RGEL 2; SATA 97
Paterson, Banjo
See Paterson, A(ndrew) B(arton)
Paterson, Katherine (Womeldorf) 1932-
.... **CLC 12, 30**
See also AAYA 1, 31; BYA 1, 2, 7; CA 21-24R; CANR 28, 59, 111; CLR 7, 50; CWRI 5; DLB 52; JRDA; LAIT 4; MAICYA 1, 2; MAICYAS 1; MTCW 1; SATA 13, 53, 92, 133; WYA; YAW
Patmore, Coventry Kersey Dighton 1823-1896 .... **NCLC 9**
See also DLB 35, 98; RGEL 2; TEA
Paton, Alan (Stewart) 1903-1988 ...... **CLC 4, 10, 25, 55, 106; WLC**
See also AAYA 26; AFW; BPFB 3; BRWS 2; BYA 1; CA 13-16; 125; CANR 22; CAP 1; DA; DA3; DAB; DAC; DAM MST, NOV; DLB 225; DLBD 17; EWL 3; EXPN; LAIT 4; MTCW 1, 2; NFS 3, 12; RGEL 2; SATA 11; SATA-Obit 56; TWA; WLIT 2
Paton Walsh, Gillian 1937- .... **CLC 35**
See Paton Walsh, Jill; Walsh, Jill Paton
See also AAYA 11; CANR 38, 83; CLR 2, 65; DLB 161; JRDA; MAICYA 1, 2; SAAS 3; SATA 4, 72, 109; YAW
Paton Walsh, Jill
See Paton Walsh, Gillian
See also AAYA 47; BYA 1, 8
Patterson, (Horace) Orlando (Lloyd) 1940-
.... **BLCS**
See also BW 1; CA 65-68; CANR 27, 84; CN 7
Patton, George S(mith), Jr. 1885-1945
.... **TCLC 79**
See also CA 189
Paulding, James Kirke 1778-1860 . **NCLC 2**
See also DLB 3, 59, 74, 250; RGAL 4

Paulin, Thomas Neilson 1949-
See Paulin, Tom
See also CA 123; 128; CANR 98; CP 7
Paulin, Tom .... **CLC 37**
See Paulin, Thomas Neilson
See also DLB 40
Pausanias c. 1st cent. - .... **CMLC 36**
Paustovsky, Konstantin (Georgievich) 1892-1968 .... **CLC 40**
See also CA 93-96; 25-28R; DLB 272; EWL 3
Pavese, Cesare 1903-1950 ... **PC 13; SSC 19; TCLC 3**
See also CA 104; 169; DLB 128, 177; EW 12; EWL 3; RGSF 2; RGWL 2, 3; TWA
Pavic, Milorad 1929- .... **CLC 60**
See also CA 136; CDWLB 4; CWW 2; DLB 181; EWL 3; RGWL 3
Pavlov, Ivan Petrovich 1849-1936
.... **TCLC 91**
See also CA 118; 180
Payne, Alan
See Jakes, John (William)
Paz, Gil
See Lugones, Leopoldo
Paz, Octavio 1914-1998 ...... **CLC 3, 4, 6, 10, 19, 51, 65, 119; HLC 2; PC 1; WLC**
See also CA 73-76; 165; CANR 32, 65, 104; CWW 2; DA; DA3; DAB; DAC; DAM MST, MULT, POET; DLBY 1990, 1998; DNFS 1; EWL 3; HW 1, 2; LAW; LAWS 1; MTCW 1, 2; RGWL 2, 3; SSFS 13; TWA; WLIT 1
p'Bitek, Okot 1931-1982 .... **BLC 3; CLC 96**
See also AFW; BW 2, 3; CA 124; 107; CANR 82; DAM MULT; DLB 125; EWL 3; MTCW 1, 2; RGEL 2; WLIT 2
Peacock, Molly 1947- .... **CLC 60**
See also CA 103; CAAS 21; CANR 52, 84; CP 7; CWP; DLB 120, 282
Peacock, Thomas Love 1785-1866
.... **NCLC 22**
See also BRW 4; DLB 96, 116; RGEL 2; RGSF 2
Peake, Mervyn 1911-1968 .... **CLC 7, 54**
See also CA 5-8R; 25-28R; CANR 3; DLB 15, 160, 255; FANT; MTCW 1; RGEL 2; SATA 23; SFW 4
Pearce, Philippa
See Christie, Philippa
See also CA 5-8R; CANR 4, 109; CWRI 5; FANT; MAICYA 2
Pearl, Eric
See Elman, Richard (Martin)
Pearson, T(homas) R(eid) 1956- ...... **CLC 39**
See also CA 120; 130; CANR 97; CSW; INT 130
Peck, Dale 1967- .... **CLC 81**
See also CA 146; CANR 72; GLL 2
Peck, John (Frederick) 1941- .... **CLC 3**
See also CA 49-52; CANR 3, 100; CP 7
Peck, Richard (Wayne) 1934- .... **CLC 21**
See also AAYA 1, 24; BYA 1, 6, 8, 11; CA 85-88; CANR 19, 38; CLR 15; INT CANR-19; JRDA; MAICYA 1, 2; SAAS 2; SATA 18, 55, 97; SATA-Essay 110; WYA; YAW
Peck, Robert Newton 1928- .... **CLC 17**
See also AAYA 3, 43; BYA 1, 6; CA 81-84, 182; CAAE 182; CANR 31, 63; CLR 45; DA; DAC; DAM MST; JRDA; LAIT 3; MAICYA 1, 2; SAAS 1; SATA 21, 62, 111; SATA-Essay 108; WYA; YAW
Peckinpah, (David) Sam(uel) 1925-1984
.... **CLC 20**
See also CA 109; 114; CANR 82

Pedersen, Knut 1859-1952
　See Hamsun, Knut
　See also CA 104; 119; CANR 63; MTCW 1, 2
Peeslake, Gaffer
　See Durrell, Lawrence (George)
Peguy, Charles (Pierre) 1873-1914 .... **TCLC 10**
　See also CA 107; 193; DLB 258; EWL 3; GFL 1789 to the Present
Peirce, Charles Sanders 1839-1914 .... **TCLC 81**
　See also CA 194; DLB 270
Pellicer, Carlos 1900(?)-1977 .... **HLCS 2**
　See also CA 153; 69-72; EWL 3; HW 1
Pena, Ramon del Valle y
　See Valle-Inclan, Ramon (Maria) del
Pendennis, Arthur Esquir
　See Thackeray, William Makepeace
Penn, William 1644-1718 .... **LC 25**
　See also DLB 24
PEPECE
　See Prado (Calvo), Pedro
Pepys, Samuel 1633-1703 . **LC 11, 58; WLC**
　See also BRW 2; CDBLB 1660-1789; DA; DA3; DAB; DAC; DAM MST; DLB 101, 213; NCFS 4; RGEL 2; TEA; WLIT 3
Percy, Thomas 1729-1811 .... **NCLC 95**
　See also DLB 104
Percy, Walker 1916-1990 ..... **CLC 2, 3, 6, 8, 14, 18, 47, 65**
　See also AMWS 3; BPFB 3; CA 1-4R; 131; CANR 1, 23, 64; CPW; CSW; DA3; DAM NOV, POP; DLB 2; DLBY 1980, 1990; EWL 3; MTCW 1, 2; RGAL 4; TUS
Percy, William Alexander 1885-1942 .... **TCLC 84**
　See also CA 163; MTCW 2
Perec, Georges 1936-1982 .... **CLC 56, 116**
　See also CA 141; DLB 83; EWL 3; GFL 1789 to the Present; RGWL 3
Pereda (y Sanchez de Porrua), Jose Maria de 1833-1906 .... **TCLC 16**
　See also CA 117
Pereda y Porrua, Jose Maria de
　See Pereda (y Sanchez de Porrua), Jose Maria de
Peregoy, George Weems
　See Mencken, H(enry) L(ouis)
Perelman, S(idney) J(oseph) 1904-1979
　..... **CLC 3, 5, 9, 15, 23, 44, 49; SSC 32**
　See also AITN 1, 2; BPFB 3; CA 73-76; 89-92; CANR 18; DAM DRAM; DLB 11, 44; MTCW 1, 2; RGAL 4
Peret, Benjamin 1899-1959 ... **PC 33; TCLC 20**
　See also CA 117; 186; GFL 1789 to the Present
Peretz, Isaac Leib 1851(?)-1915
　See Peretz, Isaac Loeb
　See also CA 201
Peretz, Isaac Loeb 1851(?)-1915 ..... **SSC 26; TCLC 16**
　See Peretz, Isaac Leib
　See also CA 109
Peretz, Yitzkhok Leibush
　See Peretz, Isaac Loeb
Perez Galdos, Benito 1843-1920 .... **HLCS 2; TCLC 27**
　See Galdos, Benito Perez
　See also CA 125; 153; EWL 3; HW 1; RGWL 2, 3
Peri Rossi, Cristina 1941- .... **CLC 156; HLCS 2**
　See also CA 131; CANR 59, 81; DLB 145; EWL 3; HW 1, 2
Perlata
　See Peret, Benjamin

Perloff, Marjorie G(abrielle) 1931- .... **CLC 137**
　See also CA 57-60; CANR 7, 22, 49, 104
Perrault, Charles 1628-1703 .. **DC 12; LC 2, 56**
　See also BYA 4; CLR 79; DLB 268; GFL Beginnings to 1789; MAICYA 1, 2; RGWL 2, 3; SATA 25; WCH
Perry, Anne 1938- .... **CLC 126**
　See also CA 101; CANR 22, 50, 84; CMW 4; CN 7; CPW; DLB 276
Perry, Brighton
　See Sherwood, Robert E(mmet)
Perse, St.-John
　See Leger, (Marie-Rene Auguste) Alexis Saint-Leger
Perse, Saint-John
　See Leger, (Marie-Rene Auguste) Alexis Saint-Leger
　See also DLB 258; RGWL 3
Perutz, Leo(pold) 1882-1957 .... **TCLC 60**
　See also CA 147; DLB 81
Peseenz, Tulio F.
　See Lopez y Fuentes, Gregorio
Pesetsky, Bette 1932- .... **CLC 28**
　See also CA 133; DLB 130
Peshkov, Alexei Maximovich 1868-1936
　See Gorky, Maxim
　See also CA 105; 141; CANR 83; DA; DAC; DAM DRAM, MST, NOV; MTCW 2
Pessoa, Fernando (Antonio Nogueira) 1898-1935 ... **HLC 2; PC 20; TCLC 27**
　See also CA 125; 183; DAM MULT; EW 10; EWL 3; RGWL 2, 3; WP
Peterkin, Julia Mood 1880-1961 ..... **CLC 31**
　See also CA 102; DLB 9
Peters, Joan K(aren) 1945- .... **CLC 39**
　See also CA 158; CANR 109
Peters, Robert L(ouis) 1924- .... **CLC 7**
　See also CA 13-16R; CAAS 8; CP 7; DLB 105
Petofi, Sandor 1823-1849 .... **NCLC 21**
　See also RGWL 2, 3
Petrakis, Harry Mark 1923- .... **CLC 3**
　See also CA 9-12R; CANR 4, 30, 85; CN 7
Petrarch 1304-1374 .... **CMLC 20; PC 8**
　See also DA3; DAM POET; EW 2; LMFS 1; RGWL 2, 3
Petronius c. 20-66 .... **CMLC 34**
　See also AW 2; CDWLB 1; DLB 211; RGWL 2, 3
Petrov, Evgeny .... **TCLC 21**
　See Kataev, Evgeny Petrovich
Petry, Ann (Lane) 1908-1997 . **CLC 1, 7, 18; TCLC 112**
　See also AFAW 1, 2; BPFB 3; BW 1, 3; BYA 2; CA 5-8R; 157; CAAS 6; CANR 4, 46; CLR 12; CN 7; DLB 76; EWL 3; JRDA; LAIT 1; MAICYA 1, 2; MAIC-YAS 1; MTCW 1; RGAL 4; SATA 5; SATA-Obit 94; TUS
Petursson, Hallgrimur 1614-1674 .... **LC 8**
Peychinovich
　See Vazov, Ivan (Minchov)
Phaedrus c. 15B.C.-c. 50 .... **CMLC 25**
　See also DLB 211
Phelps (Ward), Elizabeth Stuart
　See Phelps, Elizabeth Stuart
　See also FW
Phelps, Elizabeth Stuart 1844-1911 .... **TCLC 113**
　See Phelps (Ward), Elizabeth Stuart
　See also DLB 74
Philips, Katherine 1632-1664 ..... **LC 30; PC 40**
　See also DLB 131; RGEL 2
Philipson, Morris H. 1926- .... **CLC 53**
　See also CA 1-4R; CANR 4

Phillips, Caryl 1958- .... **BLCS; CLC 96**
　See also BRWS 5; BW 2; CA 141; CANR 63, 104; CBD; CD 5; CN 7; DA3; DAM MULT; DLB 157; EWL 3; MTCW 2; WLIT 4
Phillips, David Graham 1867-1911 .... **TCLC 44**
　See also CA 108; 176; DLB 9, 12; RGAL 4
Phillips, Jack
　See Sandburg, Carl (August)
Phillips, Jayne Anne 1952- .... **CLC 15, 33, 139; SSC 16**
　See also BPFB 3; CA 101; CANR 24, 50, 96; CN 7; CSW; DLBY 1980; INT CANR-24; MTCW 1, 2; RGAL 4; RGSF 2; SSFS 4
Phillips, Richard
　See Dick, Philip K(indred)
Phillips, Robert (Schaeffer) 1938- ... **CLC 28**
　See also CA 17-20R; CAAS 13; CANR 8; DLB 105
Phillips, Ward
　See Lovecraft, H(oward) P(hillips)
Piccolo, Lucio 1901-1969 .... **CLC 13**
　See also CA 97-100; DLB 114; EWL 3
Pickthall, Marjorie L(owry) C(hristie) 1883-1922 .... **TCLC 21**
　See also CA 107; DLB 92
Pico della Mirandola, Giovanni 1463-1494 .... **LC 15**
　See also LMFS 1
Piercy, Marge 1936- ... **CLC 3, 6, 14, 18, 27, 62, 128; PC 29**
　See also BPFB 3; CA 21-24R; CAAE 187; CAAS 1; CANR 13, 43, 66, 111; CN 7; CP 7; CWP; DLB 120, 227; EXPP; FW; MTCW 1, 2; PFS 9; SFW 4
Piers, Robert
　See Anthony, Piers
Pieyre de Mandiargues, Andre 1909-1991
　See Mandiargues, Andre Pieyre de
　See also CA 103; 136; CANR 22, 82; EWL 3; GFL 1789 to the Present
Pilnyak, Boris 1894-1938 ..... **SSC 48; TCLC 23**
　See Vogau, Boris Andreyevich
　See also EWL 3
Pinchback, Eugene
　See Toomer, Jean
Pincherle, Alberto 1907-1990 .... **CLC 11, 18**
　See Moravia, Alberto
　See also CA 25-28R; 132; CANR 33, 63; DAM NOV; MTCW 1
Pinckney, Darryl 1953- .... **CLC 76**
　See also BW 2, 3; CA 143; CANR 79
Pindar 518(?)B.C.-438(?)B.C. ..... **CMLC 12; PC 19**
　See also AW 1; CDWLB 1; DLB 176; RGWL 2
Pineda, Cecile 1942- .... **CLC 39**
　See also CA 118; DLB 209
Pinero, Arthur Wing 1855-1934 ... **TCLC 32**
　See also CA 110; 153; DAM DRAM; DLB 10; RGEL 2
Pinero, Miguel (Antonio Gomez) 1946-1988 .... **CLC 4, 55**
　See also CA 61-64; 125; CAD; CANR 29, 90; DLB 266; HW 1
Pinget, Robert 1919-1997 .... **CLC 7, 13, 37**
　See also CA 85-88; 160; CWW 2; DLB 83; EWL 3; GFL 1789 to the Present
Pink Floyd
　See Barrett, (Roger) Syd; Gilmour, David; Mason, Nick; Waters, Roger; Wright, Rick
Pinkney, Edward 1802-1828 .... **NCLC 31**
　See also DLB 248
Pinkwater, Daniel
　See Pinkwater, Daniel Manus

Pinkwater, Daniel Manus 1941- ...... **CLC 35**
See also AAYA 1, 46; BYA 9; CA 29-32R; CANR 12, 38, 89; CLR 4; CSW; FANT; JRDA; MAICYA 1, 2; SAAS 3; SATA 8, 46, 76, 114; SFW 4; YAW

Pinkwater, Manus
See Pinkwater, Daniel Manus

Pinsky, Robert 1940- ...... **CLC 9, 19, 38, 94, 121; PC 27**
See also AMWS 6; CA 29-32R; CAAS 4 CANR 58, 97; CP 7; DA3; DAM POET; DLBY 1982, 1998; MTCW 2; RGAL 4

Pinta, Harold
See Pinter, Harold

Pinter, Harold 1930- . **CLC 1, 3, 6, 9, 11, 15, 27, 58, 73; DC 15; WLC**
See also BRWR 1; BRWS 1; CA 5-8R; CANR 33, 65, 112; CBD; CD 5; CDBLB 1960 to Present; DA; DA3; DAB; DAC; DAM DRAM, MST; DFS 3, 5, 7, 14; DLB 13; EWL 3; IDFW 3, 4; LMFS 2; MTCW 1, 2; RGEL 2; TEA

Piozzi, Hester Lynch (Thrale) 1741-1821
...... **NCLC 57**
See also DLB 104, 142

Pirandello, Luigi 1867-1936 . **DC 5; SSC 22; TCLC 4, 29; WLC**
See also CA 104; 153; CANR 103; DA; DA3; DAB; DAC; DAM DRAM, MST; DFS 4, 9; DLB 264; EW 8; EWL 3; MTCW 2; RGSF 2; RGWL 2, 3

Pirsig, Robert M(aynard) 1928- .. **CLC 4, 6, 73**
See also CA 53-56; CANR 42, 74; CPW 1; DA3; DAM POP; MTCW 1, 2; SATA 39

Pisarev, Dmitrii Ivanovich
See Pisarev, Dmitry Ivanovich
See also DLB 277

Pisarev, Dmitry Ivanovich 1840-1868
...... **NCLC 25**
See Pisarev, Dmitrii Ivanovich

Pix, Mary (Griffith) 1666-1709 .... **LC 8**
See also DLB 80

Pixerecourt, (Rene Charles) Guilbert de 1773-1844 ...... **NCLC 39**
See also DLB 192; GFL 1789 to the Present

Plaatje, Sol(omon) T(shekisho) 1878-1932
...... **BLCS; TCLC 73**
See also BW 2, 3; CA 141; CANR 79; DLB 125, 225

Plaidy, Jean
See Hibbert, Eleanor Alice Burford

Planche, James Robinson 1796-1880
...... **NCLC 42**
See also RGEL 2

Plant, Robert 1948- ...... **CLC 12**

Plante, David (Robert) 1940- ...... **CLC 7, 23, 38**
See also CA 37-40R; CANR 12, 36, 58, 82; CN 7; DAM NOV; DLBY 1983; INT CANR-12; MTCW 1

Plath, Sylvia 1932-1963 .... **CLC 1, 2, 3, 5, 9, 11, 14, 17, 50, 51, 62, 111; PC 1, 37; WLC**
See also AAYA 13; AMWR 2; AMWS 1; BPFB 3; CA 19-20; CANR 34, 101; CAP 2; CDALB 1941-1968; DA; DA3; DAB; DAC; DAM MST, POET; DLB 5, 6, 152; EWL 3; EXPN; EXPP; FW; LAIT 4; MAWW; MTCW 1, 2; NFS 1; PAB; PFS 1, 15; RGAL 4; SATA 96; TUS; WP; YAW

Plato c. 428B.C.-347B.C. .. **CMLC 8; WLCS**
See also AW 1; CDWLB 1; DA; DA3; DAB; DAC; DAM MST; DLB 176; LAIT 1; RGWL 2, 3

Platonov, Andrei
See Klimentov, Andrei Platonovich

Platonov, Andrei Platonovich
See Klimentov, Andrei Platonovich
See also DLB 272

Platonov, Andrey Platonovich
See Klimentov, Andrei Platonovich
See also EWL 3

Platt, Kin 1911- ...... **CLC 26**
See also AAYA 11; CA 17-20R; CANR 11; JRDA; SAAS 17; SATA 21, 86; WYA

Plautus c. 254B.C.-c. 184B.C. ..... **CMLC 24; DC 6**
See also AW 1; CDWLB 1; DLB 211; RGWL 2, 3

Plick et Plock
See Simenon, Georges (Jacques Christian)

Plieksans, Janis
See Rainis, Janis

Plimpton, George (Ames) 1927- ...... **CLC 36**
See also AITN 1; CA 21-24R; CANR 32, 70, 103; DLB 185, 241; MTCW 1, 2; SATA 10

Pliny the Elder c. 23-79 ...... **CMLC 23**
See also DLB 211

Plomer, William Charles Franklin 1903-1973
...... **CLC 4, 8**
See also AFW; CA 21-22; CANR 34; CAP 2; DLB 20, 162, 191, 225; EWL 3; MTCW 1; RGEL 2; RGSF 2; SATA 24

Plotinus 204-270 ...... **CMLC 46**
See also CDWLB 1; DLB 176

Plowman, Piers
See Kavanagh, Patrick (Joseph)

Plum, J.
See Wodehouse, P(elham) G(renville)

Plumly, Stanley (Ross) 1939- ...... **CLC 33**
See also CA 108; 110; CANR 97; CP 7; DLB 5, 193; INT 110

Plumpe, Friedrich Wilhelm 1888-1931
...... **TCLC 53**
See also CA 112

Po Chu-i 772-846 ...... **CMLC 24**

Poe, Edgar Allan 1809-1849 .... **NCLC 1, 16, 55, 78, 94, 97, 117; PC 1; SSC 1, 22, 34, 35, 54; WLC**
See also AAYA 14; AMW; AMWC 1; AMWR 2; BPFB 3; BYA 5, 11; CDALB 1640-1865; CMW 4; DA; DA3; DAB; DAC; DAM MST, POET; DLB 3, 59, 73, 74, 248, 254; EXPP; EXPS; HGG; LAIT 2; LMFS 1; MSW; PAB; PFS 1, 3, 9; RGAL 4; RGSF 2; SATA 23; SCFW 2; SFW 4; SSFS 2, 4, 7, 8, 16; SUFW; TUS; WP; WYA

Poet of Titchfield Street, The
See Pound, Ezra (Weston Loomis)

Pohl, Frederik 1919- ...... **CLC 18; SSC 25**
See also AAYA 24; CA 61-64; CAAE 188; CAAS 1; CANR 11, 37, 81; CN 7; DLB 8; INT CANR-11; MTCW 1; SATA 24; SCFW 2; SFW 4

Poirier, Louis 1910-
See Gracq, Julien
See also CA 122; 126; CWW 2

Poitier, Sidney 1927- ...... **CLC 26**
See also BW 1; CA 117; CANR 94

Pokagon, Simon 1830-1899 ...... **NNAL**
See also DAM MULT

Polanski, Roman 1933- ...... **CLC 16**
See also CA 77-80

Poliakoff, Stephen 1952- ...... **CLC 38**
See also CA 106; CANR 116; CBD; CD 5; DLB 13

Police, The
See Copeland, Stewart (Armstrong); Summers, Andrew James; Sumner, Gordon Matthew

Polidori, John William 1795-1821
...... **NCLC 51**
See also DLB 116; HGG

Pollitt, Katha 1949- ...... **CLC 28, 122**
See also CA 120; 122; CANR 66, 108; MTCW 1, 2

Pollock, (Mary) Sharon 1936- ...... **CLC 50**
See also CA 141; CD 5; CWD; DAC; DAM DRAM, MST; DFS 3; DLB 60; FW

Pollock, Sharon 1936- ...... **DC 20**

Polo, Marco 1254-1324 ...... **CMLC 15**

Polonsky, Abraham (Lincoln) 1910-1999
...... **CLC 92**
See also CA 104; 187; DLB 26; INT 104

Polybius c. 200B.C.-c. 118B.C. ...... **CMLC 17**
See also AW 1; DLB 176; RGWL 2, 3

Pomerance, Bernard 1940- ...... **CLC 13**
See also CA 101; CAD; CANR 49; CD 5; DAM DRAM; DFS 9; LAIT 2

Ponge, Francis 1899-1988 ...... **CLC 6, 18**
See also CA 85-88; 126; CANR 40, 86; DAM POET; DLBY 2002; EWL 3; GFL 1789 to the Present; RGWL 2, 3

Poniatowska, Elena 1933- ... **CLC 140; HLC 2**
See also CA 101; CANR 32, 66, 107; CDWLB 3; DAM MULT; DLB 113; EWL 3; HW 1, 2; LAWS 1; WLIT 1

Pontoppidan, Henrik 1857-1943 ... **TCLC 29**
See also CA 170

Poole, Josephine ...... **CLC 17**
See Helyar, Jane Penelope Josephine
See also SAAS 2; SATA 5

Popa, Vasko 1922-1991 ...... **CLC 19**
See also CA 112; 148; CDWLB 4; DLB 181; EWL 3; RGWL 2, 3

Pope, Alexander 1688-1744 ...... **LC 3, 58, 60, 64; PC 26; WLC**
See also BRW 3; BRWC 1; BRWR 1; CDBLB 1660-1789; DA; DA3; DAB; DAC; DAM MST, POET; DLB 95, 101, 213; EXPP; PAB; PFS 12; RGEL 2; WLIT 3; WP

Popov, Yevgeny ...... **CLC 59**

Poquelin, Jean-Baptiste
See Moliere

Porter, Connie (Rose) 1959(?)- ...... **CLC 70**
See also BW 2, 3; CA 142; CANR 90, 109; SATA 81, 129

Porter, Gene(va Grace) Stratton .. **TCLC 21**
See Stratton-Porter, Gene(va Grace)
See also BPFB 3; CA 112; CWRI 5; RHW

Porter, Katherine Anne 1890-1980 .. **CLC 1, 3, 7, 10, 13, 15, 27, 101; SSC 4, 31, 43**
See also AAYA 42; AITN 2; AMW; BPFB 3; CA 1-4R; 101; CANR 1, 65; CDALBS; DA; DA3; DAB; DAC; DAM MST, NOV; DLB 4, 9, 102; DLBD 12; DLBY 1980; EWL 3; EXPS; LAIT 3; MAWW; MTCW 1, 2; NFS 14; RGAL 4; RGSF 2; SATA 39; SATA-Obit 23; SSFS 1, 8, 11, 16; TUS

Porter, Peter (Neville Frederick) 1929-
...... **CLC 5, 13, 33**
See also CA 85-88; CP 7; DLB 40

Porter, William Sydney 1862-1910
See Henry, O.
See also CA 104; 131; CDALB 1865-1917; DA; DA3; DAB; DAC; DAM MST; DLB 12, 78, 79; MTCW 1, 2; TUS; YABC 2

Portillo (y Pacheco), Jose Lopez
See Lopez Portillo (y Pacheco), Jose

Portillo Trambley, Estela 1927-1998
...... **HLC 2**
See Trambley, Estela Portillo
See also CANR 32; DAM MULT; DLB 209; HW 1

Posey, Alexander (Lawrence) 1873-1908
...... **NNAL**
See also CA 144; CANR 80; DAM MULT; DLB 175

Posse, Abel .... CLC 70
Post, Melville Davisson 1869-1930
.... TCLC 39
See also CA 110; 202; CMW 4
Potok, Chaim 1929-2002 .. CLC 2, 7, 14, 26, 112
See also AAYA 15; AITN 1, 2; BPFB 3; BYA 1; CA 17-20R; 208; CANR 19, 35, 64, 98; CN 7; DA3; DAM NOV; DLB 28, 152; EXPN; INT CANR-19; LAIT 4; MTCW 1, 2; NFS 4; SATA 33, 106; SATA-Obit 134; TUS; YAW
Potok, Herbert Harold -2002
See Potok, Chaim
Potok, Herman Harold
See Potok, Chaim
Potter, Dennis (Christopher George) 1935-1994 .... CLC 58, 86, 123
See also CA 107; 145; CANR 33, 61; CBD; DLB 233; MTCW 1
Pound, Ezra (Weston Loomis) 1885-1972
.... CLC 1, 2, 3, 4, 5, 7, 10, 13, 18, 34, 48, 50, 112; PC 4; WLC
See also AAYA 47; AMW; AMWR 1; CA 5-8R; 37-40R; CANR 40; CDALB 1917-1929; DA; DA3; DAB; DAC; DAM MST, POET; DLB 4, 45, 63; DLBD 15; EFS 2; EWL 3; EXPP; LMFS 2; MTCW 1, 2; PAB; PFS 2, 8, 16; RGAL 4; TUS; WP
Povod, Reinaldo 1959-1994 .... CLC 44
See also CA 136; 146; CANR 83
Powell, Adam Clayton, Jr.
.... BLC 3; CLC 89
See also BW 1, 3; CA 102; 33-36R; CANR 86; DAM MULT
Powell, Anthony (Dymoke) 1905-2000
.... CLC 1, 3, 7, 9, 10, 31
See also BRW 7; CA 1-4R; 189; CANR 1, 32, 62, 107; CDBLB 1945-1960; CN 7; DLB 15; EWL 3; MTCW 1, 2; RGEL 2; TEA
Powell, Dawn 1896(?)-1965 .... CLC 66
See also CA 5-8R; DLBY 1997
Powell, Padgett 1952- .... CLC 34
See also CA 126; CANR 63, 101; CSW; DLB 234; DLBY 01
Powell, (Oval) Talmage 1920-2000
See Queen, Ellery
See also CA 5-8R; CANR 2, 80
Power, Susan 1961- .... CLC 91
See also BYA 14; CA 160; NFS 11
Powers, J(ames) F(arl) 1917-1999 ... CLC 1, 4, 8, 57; SSC 4
See also CA 1-4R; 181; CANR 2, 61; CN 7; DLB 130; MTCW 1; RGAL 4; RGSF 2
Powers, John J(ames) 1945-
See Powers, John R.
See also CA 69-72
Powers, John R. .... CLC 66
See Powers, John J(ames)
Powers, Richard (S.) 1957- .... CLC 93
See also AMWS 9; BPFB 3; CA 148; CANR 80; CN 7
Pownall, David 1938- .... CLC 10
See also CA 89-92, 180; CAAS 18; CANR 49, 101; CBD; CD 5; CN 7; DLB 14
Powys, John Cowper 1872-1963 .. CLC 7, 9, 15, 46, 125
See also CA 85-88; CANR 106; DLB 15, 255; EWL 3; FANT; MTCW 1, 2; RGEL 2; SUFW
Powys, T(heodore) F(rancis) 1875-1953
.... TCLC 9
See also BRWS 8; CA 106; 189; DLB 36, 162; EWL 3; FANT; RGEL 2; SUFW
Prado (Calvo), Pedro 1886-1952 .. TCLC 75
See also CA 131; HW 1; LAW

Prager, Emily 1952- .... CLC 56
See also CA 204
Pratolini, Vasco 1913-1991 .... TCLC 124
See also DLB 177; EWL 3; RGWL 2, 3
Pratt, E(dwin) J(ohn) 1883(?)-1964
.... CLC 19
See also CA 141; 93-96; CANR 77; DAC; DAM POET; DLB 92; EWL 3; RGEL 2; TWA
Premchand .... TCLC 21
See Srivastava, Dhanpat Rai
See also EWL 3
Preussler, Otfried 1923- .... CLC 17
See also CA 77-80; SATA 24
Prevert, Jacques (Henri Marie) 1900-1977
.... CLC 15
See also CA 77-80; 69-72; CANR 29, 61; DLB 258; EWL 3; GFL 1789 to the Present; IDFW 3, 4; MTCW 1; RGWL 2, 3; SATA-Obit 30
Prevost, (Antoine Francois) 1697-1763
.... LC 1
See also EW 4; GFL Beginnings to 1789; RGWL 2, 3
Price, (Edward) Reynolds 1933- .. CLC 3, 6, 13, 43, 50, 63; SSC 22
See also AMWS 6; CA 1-4R; CANR 1, 37, 57, 87; CN 7; CSW; DAM NOV; DLB 2, 218, 278; EWL 3; INT CANR-37
Price, Richard 1949- .... CLC 6, 12
See also CA 49-52; CANR 3; DLBY 1981
Prichard, Katharine Susannah 1883-1969
.... CLC 46
See also CA 11-12; CANR 33; CAP 1; DLB 260; MTCW 1; RGEL 2; RGSF 2; SATA 66
Priestley, J(ohn) B(oynton) 1894-1984
.... CLC 2, 5, 9, 34
See also BRW 7; CA 9-12R; 113; CANR 33; CDBLB 1914-1945; DA3; DAM DRAM, NOV; DLB 10, 34, 77, 100, 139; DLBY 1984; EWL 3; MTCW 1, 2; RGEL 2; SFW 4
Prince 1958(?)- .... CLC 35
Prince, F(rank) T(empleton) 1912- . CLC 22
See also CA 101; CANR 43, 79; CP 7; DLB 20
Prince Kropotkin
See Kropotkin, Peter (Alekseevich)
Prior, Matthew 1664-1721 .... LC 4
See also DLB 95; RGEL 2
Prishvin, Mikhail 1873-1954 .... TCLC 75
See Prishvin, Mikhail Mikhailovich
Prishvin, Mikhail Mikhailovich
See Prishvin, Mikhail
See also DLB 272; EWL 3
Pritchard, William H(arrison) 1932-
.... CLC 34
See also CA 65-68; CANR 23, 95; DLB 111
Pritchett, V(ictor) S(awdon) 1900-1997
.... CLC 5, 13, 15, 41; SSC 14
See also BPFB 3; BRWS 3; CA 61-64; 157; CANR 31, 63; CN 7; DA3; DAM NOV; DLB 15, 139; EWL 3; MTCW 1, 2; RGEL 2; RGSF 2; TEA
Private 19022
See Manning, Frederic
Probst, Mark 1925- .... CLC 59
See also CA 130
Prokosch, Frederic 1908-1989 ..... CLC 4, 48
See also CA 73-76; 128; CANR 82; DLB 48; MTCW 2
Propertius, Sextus c. 50B.C.-c. 16B.C.
.... CMLC 32
See also AW 2; CDWLB 1; DLB 211; RGWL 2, 3
Prophet, The
See Dreiser, Theodore (Herman Albert)

Prose, Francine 1947- .... CLC 45
See also CA 109; 112; CANR 46, 95; DLB 234; SATA 101
Proudhon
See Cunha, Euclides (Rodrigues Pimenta) da
Proulx, Annie
See Proulx, E(dna) Annie
Proulx, E(dna) Annie 1935- .... CLC 81, 158
See also AMWS 7; BPFB 3; CA 145; CANR 65, 110; CN 7; CPW 1; DA3; DAM POP; MTCW 2
Proust, (Valentin-Louis-George-Eugene-)Marcel 1871-1922 .... TCLC 7, 13, 33; WLC
See also BPFB 3; CA 104; 120; CANR 110; DA; DA3; DAB; DAC; DAM MST, NOV; DLB 65; EW 8; EWL 3; GFL 1789 to the Present; MTCW 1, 2; RGWL 2, 3; TWA
Prowler, Harley
See Masters, Edgar Lee
Prus, Boleslaw 1845-1912 .... TCLC 48
See also RGWL 2, 3
Pryor, Richard (Franklin Lenox Thomas) 1940- .... CLC 26
See also CA 122; 152
Przybyszewski, Stanislaw 1868-1927
.... TCLC 36
See also CA 160; DLB 66; EWL 3
Pteleon
See Grieve, C(hristopher) M(urray)
See also DAM POET
Puckett, Lute
See Masters, Edgar Lee
Puig, Manuel 1932-1990 ... CLC 3, 5, 10, 28, 65, 133; HLC 2
See also BPFB 3; CA 45-48; CANR 2, 32, 63; CDWLB 3; DA3; DAM MULT; DLB 113; DNFS 1; EWL 3; GLL 1; HW 1, 2; LAW; MTCW 1, 2; RGWL 2, 3; TWA; WLIT 1
Pulitzer, Joseph 1847-1911 .... TCLC 76
See also CA 114; DLB 23
Purchas, Samuel 1577(?)-1626 .... LC 70
See also DLB 151
Purdy, A(lfred) W(ellington) 1918-2000
.... CLC 3, 6, 14, 50
See also CA 81-84; 189; CAAS 17; CANR 42, 66; CP 7; DAC; DAM MST, POET; DLB 88; PFS 5; RGEL 2
Purdy, James (Amos) 1923- ... CLC 2, 4, 10, 28, 52
See also AMWS 7; CA 33-36R; CAAS 1; CANR 19, 51; CN 7; DLB 2, 218; EWL 3; INT CANR-19; MTCW 1; RGAL 4
Pure, Simon
See Swinnerton, Frank Arthur
Pushkin, Aleksandr Sergeevich
See Pushkin, Alexander (Sergeyevich)
See also DLB 205
Pushkin, Alexander (Sergeyevich) 1799-1837
... NCLC 3, 27, 83; PC 10; SSC 27, 55; WLC
See Pushkin, Aleksandr Sergeevich
See also DA; DA3; DAB; DAC; DAM DRAM, MST, POET; EW 5; EXPS; RGSF 2; RGWL 2, 3; SATA 61; SSFS 9; TWA
P'u Sung-ling 1640-1715 ...... LC 49; SSC 31
Putnam, Arthur Lee
See Alger, Horatio, Jr.
Puzo, Mario 1920-1999 .... CLC 1, 2, 6, 36, 107
See also BPFB 3; CA 65-68; 185; CANR 4, 42, 65, 99; CN 7; CPW; DA3; DAM NOV, POP; DLB 6; MTCW 1, 2; NFS 16; RGAL 4
Pygge, Edward
See Barnes, Julian (Patrick)

Pyle, Ernest Taylor 1900-1945
See Pyle, Ernie
See also CA 115; 160

Pyle, Ernie .... TCLC 75
See Pyle, Ernest Taylor
See also DLB 29; MTCW 2

Pyle, Howard 1853-1911 .... TCLC 81
See also BYA 2, 4; CA 109; 137; CLR 22; DLB 42, 188; DLBD 13; LAIT 1; MAICYA 1, 2; SATA 16, 100; WCH; YAW

Pym, Barbara (Mary Crampton) 1913-1980
.... CLC 13, 19, 37, 111
See also BPFB 3; BRWS 2; CA 13-14; 97-100; CANR 13, 34; CAP 1; DLB 14, 207; DLBY 1987; EWL 3; MTCW 1, 2; RGEL 2; TEA

Pynchon, Thomas (Ruggles, Jr.) 1937-
.... CLC 2, 3, 6, 9, 11, 18, 33, 62, 72, 123; SSC 14; WLC
See also AMWS 2; BEST 90:2; BPFB 3; CA 17-20R; CANR 22, 46, 73; CN 7; CPW 1; DA; DA3; DAB; DAC; DAM MST, NOV, POP; DLB 2, 173; EWL 3; MTCW 1, 2; RGAL 4; SFW 4; TUS

Pythagoras c. 582B.C.-c. 507B.C.
.... CMLC 22
See also DLB 176

Q
See Quiller-Couch, Sir Arthur (Thomas)

Qian, Chongzhu
See Ch'ien, Chung-shu

Qian Zhongshu
See Ch'ien, Chung-shu

Qroll
See Dagerman, Stig (Halvard)

Quarrington, Paul (Lewis) 1953- .... CLC 65
See also CA 129; CANR 62, 95

Quasimodo, Salvatore 1901-1968 .. CLC 10; PC 47
See also CA 13-16; 25-28R; CAP 1; DLB 114; EW 12; EWL 3; MTCW 1; RGWL 2, 3

Quatermass, Martin
See Carpenter, John (Howard)

Quay, Stephen 1947- .... CLC 95
See also CA 189

Quay, Timothy 1947- .... CLC 95
See also CA 189

Queen, Ellery .... CLC 3, 11
See Dannay, Frederic; Davidson, Avram (James); Deming, Richard; Fairman, Paul W.; Flora, Fletcher; Hoch, Edward D(entinger); Kane, Henry; Lee, Manfred B(ennington); Marlowe, Stephen; Powell, (Oval) Talmage; Sheldon, Walter J(ames); Sturgeon, Theodore (Hamilton); Tracy, Don(ald Fiske); Vance, John Holbrook
See also BPFB 3; CMW 4; MSW; RGAL 4

Queen, Ellery, Jr.
See Dannay, Frederic; Lee, Manfred B(ennington)

Queneau, Raymond 1903-1976 .... CLC 2, 5, 10, 42
See also CA 77-80; 69-72; CANR 32; DLB 72, 258; EW 12; EWL 3; GFL 1789 to the Present; MTCW 1, 2; RGWL 2, 3

Quevedo, Francisco de 1580-1645 ..... LC 23

Quiller-Couch, Sir Arthur (Thomas) 1863-1944 .... TCLC 53
See also CA 118; 166; DLB 135, 153, 190; HGG; RGEL 2; SUFW 1

Quin, Ann (Marie) 1936-1973 .... CLC 6
See also CA 9-12R; 45-48; DLB 14, 231

Quincey, Thomas de
See De Quincey, Thomas

Quinn, Martin
See Smith, Martin Cruz

Quinn, Peter 1947- .... CLC 91
See also CA 197

Quinn, Simon
See Smith, Martin Cruz

Quintana, Leroy V. 1944- ..... HLC 2; PC 36
See also CA 131; CANR 65; DAM MULT; DLB 82; HW 1, 2

Quiroga, Horacio (Sylvestre) 1878-1937
.... HLC 2; TCLC 20
See also CA 117; 131; DAM MULT; EWL 3; HW 1; LAW; MTCW 1; RGSF 2; WLIT 1

Quoirez, Francoise 1935- .... CLC 9
See Sagan, Francoise
See also CA 49-52; CANR 6, 39, 73; CWW 2; MTCW 1, 2; TWA

Raabe, Wilhelm (Karl) 1831-1910
.... TCLC 45
See also CA 167; DLB 129

Rabe, David (William) 1940- . CLC 4, 8, 33; DC 16
See also CA 85-88; CABS 3; CAD; CANR 59; CD 5; DAM DRAM; DFS 3, 8, 13; DLB 7, 228; EWL 3

Rabelais, Francois 1494-1553 .... LC 5, 60; WLC
See also DA; DAB; DAC; DAM MST; EW 2; GFL Beginnings to 1789; LMFS 1; RGWL 2, 3; TWA

Rabinovitch, Sholem 1859-1916
See Aleichem, Sholom
See also CA 104

Rabinyan, Dorit 1972- .... CLC 119
See also CA 170

Rachilde
See Vallette, Marguerite Eymery; Vallette, Marguerite Eymery
See also EWL 3

Racine, Jean 1639-1699 .... LC 28
See also DA3; DAB; DAM MST; DLB 268; EW 3; GFL Beginnings to 1789; LMFS 1; RGWL 2, 3; TWA

Radcliffe, Ann (Ward) 1764-1823 . NCLC 6, 55, 106
See also DLB 39, 178; HGG; LMFS 1; RGEL 2; SUFW; WLIT 3

Radclyffe-Hall, Marguerite
See Hall, (Marguerite) Radclyffe

Radiguet, Raymond 1903-1923 ..... TCLC 29
See also CA 162; DLB 65; EWL 3; GFL 1789 to the Present; RGWL 2, 3

Radnoti, Miklos 1909-1944 .... TCLC 16
See also CA 118; CDWLB 4; DLB 215; EWL 3; RGWL 2, 3

Rado, James 1939- .... CLC 17
See also CA 105

Radvanyi, Netty 1900-1983
See Seghers, Anna
See also CA 85-88; 110; CANR 82

Rae, Ben
See Griffiths, Trevor

Raeburn, John (Hay) 1941- .... CLC 34
See also CA 57-60

Ragni, Gerome 1942-1991 .... CLC 17
See also CA 105; 134

Rahv, Philip .... CLC 24
See Greenberg, Ivan
See also DLB 137

Raimund, Ferdinand Jakob 1790-1836
.... NCLC 69
See also DLB 90

Raine, Craig (Anthony) 1944- .... CLC 32, 103
See also CA 108; CANR 29, 51, 103; CP 7; DLB 40; PFS 7

Raine, Kathleen (Jessie) 1908- .... CLC 7, 45
See also CA 85-88; CANR 46, 109; CP 7; DLB 20; EWL 3; MTCW 1; RGEL 2

Rainis, Janis 1865-1929 .... TCLC 29
See also CA 170; CDWLB 4; DLB 220; EWL 3

Rakosi, Carl .... CLC 47
See Rawley, Callman
See also CAAS 5; CP 7; DLB 193

Ralegh, Sir Walter
See Raleigh, Sir Walter
See also ERW 1; RGEL 2; WP

Raleigh, Richard
See Lovecraft, H(oward) P(hillips)

Raleigh, Sir Walter 1554(?)-1618 ...... LC 31, 39; PC 31
See Ralegh, Sir Walter
See also CDBLB Before 1660; DLB 172; EXPP; PFS 14; TEA

Rallentando, H. P.
See Sayers, Dorothy L(eigh)

Ramal, Walter
See de la Mare, Walter (John)

Ramana Maharshi 1879-1950 .... TCLC 84

Ramoacn y Cajal, Santiago 1852-1934
.... TCLC 93

Ramon, Juan
See Jimenez (Mantecon), Juan Ramon

Ramos, Graciliano 1892-1953 .... TCLC 32
See also CA 167; EWL 3; HW 2; LAW; WLIT 1

Rampersad, Arnold 1941- .... CLC 44
See also BW 2, 3; CA 127; 133; CANR 81; DLB 111; INT 133

Rampling, Anne
See Rice, Anne
See also GLL 2

Ramsay, Allan 1686(?)-1758 .... LC 29
See also DLB 95; RGEL 2

Ramsay, Jay
See Campbell, (John) Ramsey

Ramuz, Charles-Ferdinand 1878-1947
.... TCLC 33
See also CA 165; EWL 3

Rand, Ayn 1905-1982 ..... CLC 3, 30, 44, 79; WLC
See also AAYA 10; AMWS 4; BPFB 3; BYA 12; CA 13-16R; 105; CANR 27, 73; CDALBS; CPW; DA; DA3; DAC; DAM MST, NOV, POP; DLB 227, 279; MTCW 1, 2; NFS 10, 16; RGAL 4; SFW 4; TUS; YAW

Randall, Dudley (Felker) 1914-2000
.... BLC 3; CLC 1, 135
See also BW 1, 3; CA 25-28R; 189; CANR 23, 82; DAM MULT; DLB 41; PFS 5

Randall, Robert
See Silverberg, Robert

Ranger, Ken
See Creasey, John

Rank, Otto 1884-1939 .... TCLC 115

Ransom, John Crowe 1888-1974 . CLC 2, 4, 5, 11, 24
See also AMW; CA 5-8R; 49-52; CANR 6, 34; CDALBS; DA3; DAM POET; DLB 45, 63; EWL 3; EXPP; MTCW 1, 2; RGAL 4; TUS

Rao, Raja 1909- .... CLC 25, 56
See also CA 73-76; CANR 51; CN 7; DAM NOV; EWL 3; MTCW 1, 2; RGEL 2; RGSF 2

Raphael, Frederic (Michael) 1931- .. CLC 2, 14
See also CA 1-4R; CANR 1, 86; CN 7; DLB 14

Ratcliffe, James P.
See Mencken, H(enry) L(ouis)

Rathbone, Julian 1935- .... CLC 41
See also CA 101; CANR 34, 73

Rattigan, Terence (Mervyn) 1911-1977
.... CLC 7; DC 18
See also BRWS 7; CA 85-88; 73-76; CBD; CDBLB 1945-1960 DAM DRAM; DFS 8; DLB 13; IDFW 3, 4; MTCW 1, 2; RGEL 2

Ratushinskaya, Irina 1954- .... **CLC 54**
See also CA 129; CANR 68; CWW 2
Raven, Simon (Arthur Noel) 1927-2001
.... **CLC 14**
See also CA 81-84; 197; CANR 86; CN 7;
DLB 271
Ravenna, Michael
See Welty, Eudora (Alice)
Rawley, Callman 1903-
See Rakosi, Carl
See also CA 21-24R; CANR 12, 32, 91
Rawlings, Marjorie Kinnan 1896-1953
.... **TCLC 4**
See also AAYA 20; AMWS 10; ANW;
BPFB 3; BYA 3; CA 104; 137; CANR 74;
CLR 63; DLB 9, 22, 102; DLBD 17;
JRDA; MAICYA 1, 2; MTCW 2; RGAL
4; SATA 100; WCH; YABC 1; YAW
Ray, Satyajit 1921-1992 .... **CLC 16, 76**
See also CA 114; 137; DAM MULT
Read, Herbert Edward 1893-1968 .... **CLC 4**
See also BRW 6; CA 85-88; 25-28R; DLB
20, 149; EWL 3; PAB; RGEL 2
Read, Piers Paul 1941- .... **CLC 4, 10, 25**
See also CA 21-24R; CANR 38, 86; CN 7;
DLB 14; SATA 21
Reade, Charles 1814-1884 .... **NCLC 2, 74**
See also DLB 21; RGEL 2
Reade, Hamish
See Gray, Simon (James Holliday)
Reading, Peter 1946- .... **CLC 47**
See also BRWS 8; CA 103; CANR 46, 96;
CP 7; DLB 40
Reaney, James 1926- .... **CLC 13**
See also CA 41-44R; CAAS 15; CANR 42;
CD 5; CP 7; DAC; DAM MST; DLB 68;
RGEL 2; SATA 43
Rebreanu, Liviu 1885-1944 .... **TCLC 28**
See also CA 165; DLB 220; EWL 3
Rechy, John (Francisco) 1934- ..... **CLC 1, 7, 14, 18, 107; HLC 2**
See also CA 5-8R; CAAE 195; CAAS 4;
CANR 6, 32, 64; CN 7; DAM MULT;
DLB 122, 278; DLBY 1982; HW 1, 2;
INT CANR-6; RGAL 4
Redcam, Tom 1870-1933 .... **TCLC 25**
Reddin, Keith .... **CLC 67**
See also CAD
Redgrove, Peter (William) 1932- ..... **CLC 6, 41**
See also BRWS 6; CA 1-4R; CANR 3, 39,
77; CP 7; DLB 40
Redmon, Anne .... **CLC 22**
See Nightingale, Anne Redmon
See also DLBY 1986
Reed, Eliot
See Ambler, Eric
Reed, Ishmael 1938- ... **BLC 3; CLC 2, 3, 5, 6, 13, 32, 60**
See also AFAW 1, 2; AMWS 10; BPFB 3;
BW 2, 3; CA 21-24R; CANR 25, 48, 74;
CN 7; CP 7; CSW; DA3; DAM MULT;
DLB 2, 5, 33, 169, 227; DLBD 8; EWL
3; LMFS 2; MSW; MTCW 1, 2; PFS 6;
RGAL 4; TCWW 2
Reed, John (Silas) 1887-1920 .... **TCLC 9**
See also CA 106; 195; TUS
Reed, Lou .... **CLC 21**
See Firbank, Louis
Reese, Lizette Woodworth 1856-1935
.... **PC 29**
See also CA 180; DLB 54
Reeve, Clara 1729-1807 .... **NCLC 19**
See also DLB 39; RGEL 2
Reich, Wilhelm 1897-1957 .... **TCLC 57**
See also CA 199
Reid, Christopher (John) 1949- ...... **CLC 33**
See also CA 140; CANR 89; CP 7; DLB
40; EWL 3

Reid, Desmond
See Moorcock, Michael (John)
Reid Banks, Lynne 1929-
See Banks, Lynne Reid
See also AAYA 49; CA 1-4R; CANR 6, 22,
38, 87; CLR 24; CN 7; JRDA; MAICYA
1, 2; SATA 22, 75, 111; YAW
Reilly, William K.
See Creasey, John
Reiner, Max
See Caldwell, (Janet Miriam) Taylor
(Holland)
Reis, Ricardo
See Pessoa, Fernando (Antonio Nogueira)
Reizenstein, Elmer Leopold
See Rice, Elmer (Leopold)
See also EWL 3
Remarque, Erich Maria 1898-1970
.... **CLC 21**
See also AAYA 27; BPFB 3; CA 77-80; 29-
32R; CDWLB 2; DA; DA3; DAB; DAC;
DAM MST, NOV; DLB 56; EWL 3;
EXPN; LAIT 3; MTCW 1, 2; NFS 4;
RGWL 2, 3
Remington, Frederic 1861-1909 ... **TCLC 89**
See also CA 108; 169; DLB 12, 186, 188;
SATA 41
Remizov, A.
See Remizov, Aleksei (Mikhailovich)
Remizov, A. M.
See Remizov, Aleksei (Mikhailovich)
Remizov, Aleksei (Mikhailovich) 1877-1957
.... **TCLC 27**
See Remizov, Alexey Mikhaylovich
See also CA 125; 133
Remizov, Alexey Mikhaylovich
See Remizov, Aleksei (Mikhailovich)
See also EWL 3
Renan, Joseph Ernest 1823-1892 . **NCLC 26**
See also GFL 1789 to the Present
Renard, Jules(-Pierre) 1864-1910 . **TCLC 17**
See also CA 117; 202; GFL 1789 to the
Present
Renault, Mary .... **CLC 3, 11, 17**
See Challans, Mary
See also BPFB 3; BYA 2; DLBY 1983;
EWL 3; GLL 1; LAIT 1; MTCW 2; RGEL
2; RHW
Rendell, Ruth (Barbara) 1930- . **CLC 28, 48**
See Vine, Barbara
See also BPFB 3; CA 109; CANR 32, 52,
74; CN 7; CPW; DAM POP; DLB 87,
276; INT CANR-32; MSW; MTCW 1, 2
Renoir, Jean 1894-1979 .... **CLC 20**
See also CA 129; 85-88
Resnais, Alain 1922- .... **CLC 16**
Revard, Carter (Curtis) 1931- .... **NNAL**
See also CA 144; CANR 81; PFS 5
Reverdy, Pierre 1889-1960 .... **CLC 53**
See also CA 97-100; 89-92; DLB 258; EWL
3; GFL 1789 to the Present
Rexroth, Kenneth 1905-1982 ... **CLC 1, 2, 6, 11, 22, 49, 112; PC 20**
See also BG 3; CA 5-8R; 107; CANR 14,
34, 63; CDALB 1941-1968; DAM POET;
DLB 16, 48, 165, 212; DLBY 1982; EWL
3; INT CANR-14; MTCW 1, 2; RGAL 4
Reyes, Alfonso 1889-1959 .. **HLCS 2; TCLC 33**
See also CA 131; EWL 3; HW 1; LAW
Reyes y Basoalto, Ricardo Eliecer Neftali
See Neruda, Pablo
Reymont, Wladyslaw (Stanislaw)
1868(?)-1925 .... **TCLC 5**
See also CA 104; EWL 3
Reynolds, Jonathan 1942- .... **CLC 6, 38**
See also CA 65-68; CANR 28
Reynolds, Joshua 1723-1792 .... **LC 15**
See also DLB 104

Reynolds, Michael S(hane) 1937-2000
.... **CLC 44**
See also CA 65-68; 189; CANR 9, 89, 97
Reznikoff, Charles 1894-1976 .... **CLC 9**
See also CA 33-36; 61-64; CAP 2; DLB 28,
45; WP
Rezzori (d'Arezzo), Gregor von 1914-1998
.... **CLC 25**
See also CA 122; 136; 167
Rhine, Richard
See Silverstein, Alvin; Silverstein, Virginia
B(arbara Opshelor)
Rhodes, Eugene Manlove 1869-1934
.... **TCLC 53**
See also CA 198; DLB 256
R'hoone, Lord
See Balzac, Honore de
Rhys, Jean 1894(?)-1979 .... **CLC 2, 4, 6, 14, 19, 51, 124; SSC 21**
See also BRWS 2; CA 25-28R; 85-88;
CANR 35, 62; CDBLB 1945-1960; CD-
WLB 3; DA3; DAM NOV; DLB 36, 117,
162; DNFS 2; EWL 3; MTCW 1, 2;
RGEL 2; RGSF 2; RHW; TEA
Ribeiro, Darcy 1922-1997 .... **CLC 34**
See also CA 33-36R; 156; EWL 3
Ribeiro, Joao Ubaldo (Osorio Pimentel)
1941- .... **CLC 10, 67**
See also CA 81-84; EWL 3
Ribman, Ronald (Burt) 1932- .... **CLC 7**
See also CA 21-24R; CAD; CANR 46, 80;
CD 5
Ricci, Nino 1959- .... **CLC 70**
See also CA 137; CCA 1
Rice, Anne 1941- .... **CLC 41, 128**
See Rampling, Anne
See also AAYA 9; AMWS 7; BEST 89:2;
BPFB 3; CA 65-68; CANR 12, 36, 53,
74, 100; CN 7; CPW; CSW; DA3; DAM
POP; GLL 2; HGG; MTCW 2; SUFW 2;
YAW
Rice, Elmer (Leopold) 1892-1967 .... **CLC 7, 49**
See Reizenstein, Elmer Leopold
See also CA 21-22; 25-28R; CAP 2; DAM
DRAM; DFS 12; DLB 4, 7; MTCW 1, 2;
RGAL 4
Rice, Tim(othy Miles Bindon) 1944-
.... **CLC 21**
See also CA 103; CANR 46; DFS 7
Rich, Adrienne (Cecile) 1929- .. **CLC 3, 6, 7, 11, 18, 36, 73, 76, 125; PC 5**
See also AMWR 2; AMWS 1; CA 9-12R;
CANR 20, 53, 74; CDALBS; CP 7; CSW;
CWP; DA3; DAM POET; DLB 5, 67;
EWL 3; EXPP; FW; MAWW; MTCW 1,
2; PAB; PFS 15; RGAL 4; WP
Rich, Barbara
See Graves, Robert (von Ranke)
Rich, Robert
See Trumbo, Dalton
Richard, Keith .... **CLC 17**
See Richards, Keith
Richards, David Adams 1950- .... **CLC 59**
See also CA 93-96; CANR 60, 110; DAC;
DLB 53
Richards, I(vor) A(rmstrong) 1893-1979
.... **CLC 14, 24**
See also BRWS 2; CA 41-44R; 89-92;
CANR 34, 74; DLB 27; EWL 3; MTCW
2; RGEL 2
Richards, Keith 1943-
See Richard, Keith
See also CA 107; CANR 77
Richardson, Anne
See Roiphe, Anne (Richardson)

Richardson, Dorothy Miller 1873-1957 .... **TCLC 3**
See also CA 104; 192; DLB 36; EWL 3; FW; RGEL 2

Richardson (Robertson), Ethel Florence Lindesay 1870-1946
See Richardson, Henry Handel
See also CA 105; 190; DLB 230; RHW

Richardson, Henry Handel .... **TCLC 4**
See Richardson (Robertson), Ethel Florence Lindesay
See also DLB 197; EWL 3; RGEL 2; RGSF 2

Richardson, John 1796-1852 .... **NCLC 55**
See also CCA 1; DAC; DLB 99

Richardson, Samuel 1689-1761 .... **LC 1, 44; WLC**
See also BRW 3; CDBLB 1660-1789; DA; DAB; DAC; DAM MST, NOV; DLB 39; RGEL 2; TEA; WLIT 3

Richardson, Willis 1889-1977 .... **HR 3**
See also BW 1; CA 124; DLB 51; SATA 60

Richler, Mordecai 1931-2001 ... **CLC 3, 5, 9, 13, 18, 46, 70**
See also AITN 1; CA 65-68; 201; CANR 31, 62, 111; CCA 1; CLR 17; CWRI 5; DAC; DAM MST, NOV; DLB 53; EWL 3; MAICYA 1, 2; MTCW 1, 2; RGEL 2; SATA 44, 98; SATA-Brief 27; TWA

Richter, Conrad (Michael) 1890-1968 .... **CLC 30**
See also AAYA 21; BYA 2; CA 5-8R; 25-28R; CANR 23; DLB 9, 212; LAIT 1; MTCW 1, 2; RGAL 4; SATA 3; TCWW 2; TUS; YAW

Ricostranza, Tom
See Ellis, Trey

Riddell, Charlotte 1832-1906 .... **TCLC 40**
See Riddell, Mrs. J. H.
See also CA 165; DLB 156

Riddell, Mrs. J. H.
See Riddell, Charlotte
See also HGG; SUFW

Ridge, John Rollin 1827-1867 ..... **NCLC 82; NNAL**
See also CA 144; DAM MULT; DLB 175

Ridgeway, Jason
See Marlowe, Stephen

Ridgway, Keith 1965- .... **CLC 119**
See also CA 172

Riding, Laura .... **CLC 3, 7**
See Jackson, Laura (Riding)
See also RGAL 4

Riefenstahl, Berta Helene Amalia 1902-
See Riefenstahl, Leni
See also CA 108

Riefenstahl, Leni .... **CLC 16**
See Riefenstahl, Berta Helene Amalia

Riffe, Ernest
See Bergman, (Ernst) Ingmar

Riggs, (Rolla) Lynn 1899-1954
.... **NNAL; TCLC 56**
See also CA 144; DAM MULT; DLB 175

Riis, Jacob A(ugust) 1849-1914 .... **TCLC 80**
See also CA 113; 168; DLB 23

Riley, James Whitcomb 1849-1916
.... **TCLC 51**
See also CA 118; 137; DAM POET; MAICYA 1, 2; RGAL 4; SATA 17

Riley, Tex
See Creasey, John

Rilke, Rainer Maria 1875-1926 .... **PC 2; TCLC 1, 6, 19**
See also CA 104; 132; CANR 62, 99; CDWLB 2; DA3; DAM POET; DLB 81; EW 9; EWL 3; MTCW 1, 2; RGWL 2, 3; TWA; WP

Rimbaud, (Jean Nicolas) Arthur 1854-1891
.... **NCLC 4, 35, 82; PC 3; WLC**
See also DA; DA3; DAB; DAC; DAM MST, POET; DLB 217; EW 7; GFL 1789 to the Present; LMFS 2; RGWL 2, 3; TWA; WP

Rinehart, Mary Roberts 1876-1958
.... **TCLC 52**
See also BPFB 3; CA 108; 166; RGAL 4; RHW

Ringmaster, The
See Mencken, H(enry) L(ouis)

Ringwood, Gwen(dolyn Margaret) Pharis 1910-1984 .... **CLC 48**
See also CA 148; 112; DLB 88

Rio, Michel 1945(?)- .... **CLC 43**
See also CA 201

Ritsos, Giannes
See Ritsos, Yannis

Ritsos, Yannis 1909-1990 .... **CLC 6, 13, 31**
See also CA 77-80; 133; CANR 39, 61; EW 12; EWL 3; MTCW 1; RGWL 2, 3

Ritter, Erika 1948(?)- .... **CLC 52**
See also CD 5; CWD

Rivera, Jose Eustasio 1889-1928 .. **TCLC 35**
See also CA 162; EWL 3; HW 1, 2; LAW

Rivera, Tomas 1935-1984 .... **HLCS 2**
See also CA 49-52; CANR 32; DLB 82; HW 1; RGAL 4; SSFS 15; TCWW 2; WLIT 1

Rivers, Conrad Kent 1933-1968 .... **CLC 1**
See also BW 1; CA 85-88; DLB 41

Rivers, Elfrida
See Bradley, Marion Zimmer
See also GLL 1

Riverside, John
See Heinlein, Robert A(nson)

Rizal, Jose 1861-1896 .... **NCLC 27**

Roa Bastos, Augusto (Antonio) 1917-
.... **CLC 45; HLC 2**
See also CA 131; DAM MULT; DLB 113; EWL 3; HW 1; LAW; RGSF 2; WLIT 1

Robbe-Grillet, Alain 1922- ... **CLC 1, 2, 4, 6, 8, 10, 14, 43, 128**
See also BPFB 3; CA 9-12R; CANR 33, 65, 115; DLB 83; EW 13; EWL 3; GFL 1789 to the Present; IDFW 3, 4; MTCW 1, 2; RGWL 2, 3; SSFS 15

Robbins, Harold 1916-1997 .... **CLC 5**
See also BPFB 3; CA 73-76; 162; CANR 26, 54, 112; DA3; DAM NOV; MTCW 1, 2

Robbins, Thomas Eugene 1936-
See Robbins, Tom
See also CA 81-84; CANR 29, 59, 95; CN 7; CPW; CSW; DA3; DAM NOV, POP; MTCW 1, 2

Robbins, Tom .... **CLC 9, 32, 64**
See Robbins, Thomas Eugene
See also AAYA 32; AMWS 10; BEST 90:3; BPFB 3; DLBY 1980; MTCW 2

Robbins, Trina 1938- .... **CLC 21**
See also CA 128

Roberts, Charles G(eorge) D(ouglas) 1860-1943 .... **TCLC 8**
See also CA 105; 188; CLR 33; CWRI 5; DLB 92; RGEL 2; RGSF 2; SATA 88; SATA-Brief 29

Roberts, Elizabeth Madox 1886-1941
.... **TCLC 68**
See also CA 111; 166; CWRI 5; DLB 9, 54, 102; RGAL 4; RHW; SATA 33; SATA-Brief 27; WCH

Roberts, Kate 1891-1985 .... **CLC 15**
See also CA 107; 116

Roberts, Keith (John Kingston) 1935-2000
.... **CLC 14**
See also CA 25-28R; CANR 46; DLB 261; SFW 4

Roberts, Kenneth (Lewis) 1885-1957
.... **TCLC 23**
See also CA 109; 199; DLB 9; RGAL 4; RHW

Roberts, Michele (Brigitte) 1949- ... **CLC 48**
See also CA 115; CANR 58; CN 7; DLB 231; FW

Robertson, Ellis
See Ellison, Harlan (Jay); Silverberg, Robert

Robertson, Thomas William 1829-1871
.... **NCLC 35**
See Robertson, Tom
See also DAM DRAM

Robertson, Tom
See Robertson, Thomas William
See also RGEL 2

Robeson, Kenneth
See Dent, Lester

Robinson, Edwin Arlington 1869-1935
.... **PC 1, 35; TCLC 5, 101**
See also AMW; CA 104; 133; CDALB 1865-1917; DA; DAC; DAM MST, POET; DLB 54; EWL 3; EXPP; MTCW 1, 2; PAB; PFS 4; RGAL 4; WP

Robinson, Henry Crabb 1775-1867
.... **NCLC 15**
See also DLB 107

Robinson, Jill 1936- .... **CLC 10**
See also CA 102; INT 102

Robinson, Kim Stanley 1952- .... **CLC 34**
See also AAYA 26; CA 126; CANR 113; CN 7; SATA 109; SCFW 2; SFW 4

Robinson, Lloyd
See Silverberg, Robert

Robinson, Marilynne 1944- .... **CLC 25**
See also CA 116; CANR 80; CN 7; DLB 206

Robinson, Smokey .... **CLC 21**
See Robinson, William, Jr.

Robinson, William, Jr. 1940-
See Robinson, Smokey
See also CA 116

Robison, Mary 1949- .... **CLC 42, 98**
See also CA 113; 116; CANR 87; CN 7; DLB 130; INT 116; RGSF 2

Rochester
See Wilmot, John
See also RGEL 2

Rod, Edouard 1857-1910 .... **TCLC 52**

Roddenberry, Eugene Wesley 1921-1991
See Roddenberry, Gene
See also CA 110; 135; CANR 37; SATA 45; SATA-Obit 69

Roddenberry, Gene .... **CLC 17**
See Roddenberry, Eugene Wesley
See also AAYA 5; SATA-Obit 69

Rodgers, Mary 1931- .... **CLC 12**
See also BYA 5; CA 49-52; CANR 8, 55, 90; CLR 20; CWRI 5; INT CANR-8; JRDA; MAICYA 1, 2; SATA 8, 130

Rodgers, W(illiam) R(obert) 1909-1969
.... **CLC 7**
See also CA 85-88; DLB 20; RGEL 2

Rodman, Eric
See Silverberg, Robert

Rodman, Howard 1920(?)-1985 .... **CLC 65**
See also CA 118

Rodman, Maia
See Wojciechowska, Maia (Teresa)

Rodo, Jose Enrique 1871(?)-1917 ... **HLCS 2**
See also CA 178; EWL 3; HW 2; LAW

Rodolph, Utto
See Ouologuem, Yambo

Rodriguez, Claudio 1934-1999 .... **CLC 10**
See also CA 188; DLB 134

Rodriguez, Richard 1944- .. **CLC 155; HLC 2**
See also CA 110; CANR 66, 116; DAM MULT; DLB 82, 256; HW 1, 2; LAIT 5; NCFS 3; WLIT 1

Roelvaag, O(le) E(dvart) 1876-1931
See Rolvaag, O(le) E(dvart)
See also CA 117; 171

Roethke, Theodore (Huebner) 1908-1963
.... **CLC 1, 3, 8, 11, 19, 46, 101; PC 15**
See also AMW; CA 81-84; CABS 2; CDALB 1941-1968; DA3; DAM POET; DLB 5, 206; EWL 3; EXPP; MTCW 1, 2; PAB; PFS 3; RGAL 4; WP

Rogers, Carl R(ansom) 1902-1987
.... **TCLC 125**
See also CA 1-4R; 121; CANR 1, 18; MTCW 1

Rogers, Samuel 1763-1855 .... **NCLC 69**
See also DLB 93; RGEL 2

Rogers, Thomas Hunton 1927- .... **CLC 57**
See also CA 89-92; INT 89-92

Rogers, Will(iam Penn Adair) 1879-1935
.... **NNAL; TCLC 8, 71**
See also CA 105; 144; DA3; DAM MULT; DLB 11; MTCW 2

Rogin, Gilbert 1929- .... **CLC 18**
See also CA 65-68; CANR 15

Rohan, Koda
See Koda Shigeyuki

Rohlfs, Anna Katharine Green
See Green, Anna Katharine

Rohmer, Eric .... **CLC 16**
See Scherer, Jean-Marie Maurice

Rohmer, Sax .... **TCLC 28**
See Ward, Arthur Henry Sarsfield
See also DLB 70; MSW; SUFW

Roiphe, Anne (Richardson) 1935- .... **CLC 3, 9**
See also CA 89-92; CANR 45, 73; DLBY 1980; INT 89-92

Rojas, Fernando de 1475-1541 ...... **HLCS 1; LC 23**
See also RGWL 2, 3

Rojas, Gonzalo 1917- .... **HLCS 2**
See also CA 178; HW 2; LAWS 1

Rolfe, Frederick (William Serafino Austin Lewis Mary) 1860-1913 .... **TCLC 12**
See Corvo, Baron
See also CA 107; DLB 34, 156; RGEL 2

Rolland, Romain 1866-1944 .... **TCLC 23**
See also CA 118; 197; DLB 65; EWL 3; GFL 1789 to the Present; RGWL 2, 3

Rolle, Richard c. 1300-c. 1349 ...... **CMLC 21**
See also DLB 146; LMFS 1; RGEL 2

Rolvaag, O(le) E(dvart) .... **TCLC 17**
See Roelvaag, O(le) E(dvart)
See also DLB 9, 212; NFS 5; RGAL 4

Romain Arnaud, Saint
See Aragon, Louis

Romains, Jules 1885-1972 .... **CLC 7**
See also CA 85-88; CANR 34; DLB 65; EWL 3; GFL 1789 to the Present; MTCW 1

Romero, Jose Ruben 1890-1952 ... **TCLC 14**
See also CA 114; 131; EWL 3; HW 1; LAW

Ronsard, Pierre de 1524-1585 ...... **LC 6, 54; PC 11**
See also EW 2; GFL Beginnings to 1789; RGWL 2, 3; TWA

Rooke, Leon 1934- .... **CLC 25, 34**
See also CA 25-28R; CANR 23, 53; CCA 1; CPW; DAM POP

Roosevelt, Franklin Delano 1882-1945
.... **TCLC 93**
See also CA 116; 173; LAIT 3

Roosevelt, Theodore 1858-1919 .... **TCLC 69**
See also CA 115; 170; DLB 47, 186, 275

Roper, William 1498-1578 .... **LC 10**

Roquelaure, A. N.
See Rice, Anne

Rosa, Joao Guimaraes 1908-1967 . **CLC 23; HLCS 1**
See also CA 89-92; DLB 113; EWL 3; WLIT 1

Rose, Wendy 1948- ..... **CLC 85; NNAL; PC 13**
See also CA 53-56; CANR 5, 51; CWP; DAM MULT; DLB 175; PFS 13; RGAL 4; SATA 12

Rosen, R. D.
See Rosen, Richard (Dean)

Rosen, Richard (Dean) 1949- .... **CLC 39**
See also CA 77-80; CANR 62; CMW 4; INT CANR-30

Rosenberg, Isaac 1890-1918 .... **TCLC 12**
See also BRW 6; CA 107; 188; DLB 20, 216; EWL 3; PAB; RGEL 2

Rosenblatt, Joe .... **CLC 15**
See Rosenblatt, Joseph

Rosenblatt, Joseph 1933-
See Rosenblatt, Joe
See also CA 89-92; CP 7; INT 89-92

Rosenfeld, Samuel
See Tzara, Tristan

Rosenstock, Sami
See Tzara, Tristan

Rosenstock, Samuel
See Tzara, Tristan

Rosenthal, M(acha) L(ouis) 1917-1996
.... **CLC 28**
See also CA 1-4R; 152; CAAS 6; CANR 4, 51; CP 7; DLB 5; SATA 59

Ross, Barnaby
See Dannay, Frederic

Ross, Bernard L.
See Follett, Ken(neth Martin)

Ross, J. H.
See Lawrence, T(homas) E(dward)

Ross, John Hume
See Lawrence, T(homas) E(dward)

Ross, Martin 1862-1915
See Martin, Violet Florence
See also DLB 135; GLL 2; RGEL 2; RGSF 2

Ross, (James) Sinclair 1908-1996 .. **CLC 13; SSC 24**
See also CA 73-76; CANR 81; CN 7; DAC; DAM MST; DLB 88; RGEL 2; RGSF 2; TCWW 2

Rossetti, Christina (Georgina) 1830-1894
.... **NCLC 2, 50, 66; PC 7; WLC**
See also BRW 5; BYA 4; DA; DAB; DAC; DAM MST, POET; DLB 35, 163, 240; EXPP; MAICYA 1, 2; PFS 10, 14; RGEL 2; SATA 20; TEA; WCH

Rossetti, Dante Gabriel 1828-1882
.... **NCLC 4, 77; PC 44; WLC**
See also BRW 5; CDBLB 1832-1890; DA; DAB; DAC; DAM MST, POET; DLB 35; EXPP; RGEL 2; TEA

Rossi, Cristina Peri
See Peri Rossi, Cristina

Rossi, Jean Baptiste 1931-
See Japrisot, Sebastien
See also CA 201

Rossner, Judith (Perelman) 1935- .... **CLC 6, 9, 29**
See also AITN 2; BEST 90:3; BPFB 3; CA 17-20R; CANR 18, 51, 73; CN 7; DLB 6; INT CANR-18; MTCW 1, 2

Rostand, Edmond (Eugene Alexis) 1868-1918 .... **DC 10; TCLC 6, 37**
See also CA 104; 126; DA; DA3; DAB; DAC; DAM DRAM, MST; DFS 1; DLB 192; LAIT 1; MTCW 1; RGWL 2, 3; TWA

Roth, Henry 1906-1995 ... **CLC 2, 6, 11, 104**
See also AMWS 9; CA 11-12; 149; CANR 38, 63; CAP 1; CN 7; DA3; DLB 28; EWL 3; MTCW 1, 2; RGAL 4

Roth, (Moses) Joseph 1894-1939 ... **TCLC 33**
See also CA 160; DLB 85; EWL 3; RGWL 2, 3

Roth, Philip (Milton) 1933- . **CLC 1, 2, 3, 4, 6, 9, 15, 22, 31, 47, 66, 86, 119; SSC 26; WLC**
See also AMWR 2; AMWS 3; BEST 90:3; BPFB 3; CA 1-4R; CANR 1, 22, 36, 55, 89; CDALB 1968-1988; CN 7; CPW 1; DA; DA3; DAB; DAC; DAM MST, NOV, POP; DLB 2, 28, 173; DLBY 1982; EWL 3; MTCW 1, 2; RGAL 4; RGSF 2; SSFS 12; TUS

Rothenberg, Jerome 1931- .... **CLC 6, 57**
See also CA 45-48; CANR 1, 106; CP 7; DLB 5, 193

Rotter, Pat ed. .... **CLC 65**

Roumain, Jacques (Jean Baptiste) 1907-1944
.... **BLC 3; TCLC 19**
See also BW 1; CA 117; 125; DAM MULT; EWL 3

Rourke, Constance Mayfield 1885-1941
.... **TCLC 12**
See also CA 107; 200; YABC 1

Rousseau, Jean-Baptiste 1671-1741 ..... **LC 9**

Rousseau, Jean-Jacques 1712-1778 .. **LC 14, 36; WLC**
See also DA; DA3; DAB; DAC; DAM MST; EW 4; GFL Beginnings to 1789; LMFS 1; RGWL 2, 3; TWA

Roussel, Raymond 1877-1933 .... **TCLC 20**
See also CA 117; 201; EWL 3; GFL 1789 to the Present

Rovit, Earl (Herbert) 1927- .... **CLC 7**
See also CA 5-8R; CANR 12

Rowe, Elizabeth Singer 1674-1737 .... **LC 44**
See also DLB 39, 95

Rowe, Nicholas 1674-1718 .... **LC 8**
See also DLB 84; RGEL 2

Rowlandson, Mary 1637(?)-1678 .... **LC 66**
See also DLB 24, 200; RGAL 4

Rowley, Ames Dorrance
See Lovecraft, H(oward) P(hillips)

Rowling, J(oanne) K(athleen) 1965-
.... **CLC 137**
See also AAYA 34; BYA 13, 14; CA 173; CLR 66, 80; MAICYA 2; SATA 109; SUFW 2

Rowson, Susanna Haswell 1762(?)-1824
.... **NCLC 5, 69**
See also DLB 37, 200; RGAL 4

Roy, Arundhati 1960(?)- .... **CLC 109**
See also CA 163; CANR 90; DLBY 1997; EWL 3

Roy, Gabrielle 1909-1983 .... **CLC 10, 14**
See also CA 53-56; 110; CANR 5, 61; CCA 1; DAB; DAC; DAM MST; DLB 68; EWL 3; MTCW 1; RGWL 2, 3; SATA 104

Royko, Mike 1932-1997 .... **CLC 109**
See also CA 89-92; 157; CANR 26, 111; CPW

Rozanov, Vasily Vasilyevich
See Rozanov, Vassili
See also EWL 3

Rozanov, Vassili 1856-1919 .... **TCLC 104**
See Rozanov, Vasily Vasilyevich

Rozewicz, Tadeusz 1921- ..... **CLC 9, 23, 139**
See also CA 108; CANR 36, 66; CWW 2; DA3; DAM POET; DLB 232; EWL 3; MTCW 1, 2; RGWL 3

Ruark, Gibbons 1941- .... **CLC 3**
See also CA 33-36R; CAAS 23; CANR 14, 31, 57; DLB 120

Rubens, Bernice (Ruth) 1923- . **CLC 19, 31**
See also CA 25-28R; CANR 33, 65; CN 7; DLB 14, 207; MTCW 1

Rubin, Harold
See Robbins, Harold

Rudkin, (James) David 1936- .... **CLC 14**
See also CA 89-92; CBD; CD 5; DLB 13

Rudnik, Raphael 1933- .... **CLC 7**
See also CA 29-32R

Ruffian, M.
See Hasek, Jaroslav (Matej Frantisek)

Ruiz, Jose Martinez .... **CLC 11**
See Martinez Ruiz, Jose

Rukeyser, Muriel 1913-1980 ...... **CLC 6, 10, 15, 27; PC 12**
See also AMWS 6; CA 5-8R; 93-96; CANR 26, 60; DA3; DAM POET; DLB 48; EWL 3; FW; GLL 2; MTCW 1, 2; PFS 10; RGAL 4; SATA-Obit 22

Rule, Jane (Vance) 1931- .... **CLC 27**
See also CA 25-28R; CAAS 18; CANR 12, 87; CN 7; DLB 60; FW

Rulfo, Juan 1918-1986 . **CLC 8, 80; HLC 2; SSC 25**
See also CA 85-88; 118; CANR 26; CD-WLB 3; DAM MULT; DLB 113; EWL 3; HW 1, 2; LAW; MTCW 1, 2; RGSF 2; RGWL 2, 3; WLIT 1

Rumi, Jalal al-Din 1207-1273 ..... **CMLC 20; PC 45**
See also RGWL 2, 3; WP

Runeberg, Johan 1804-1877 ...... **NCLC 41**

Runyon, (Alfred) Damon 1884(?)-1946
.... **TCLC 10**
See also CA 107; 165; DLB 11, 86, 171; MTCW 2; RGAL 4

Rush, Norman 1933- .... **CLC 44**
See also CA 121; 126; INT 126

Rushdie, (Ahmed) Salman 1947- ... **CLC 23, 31, 55, 100; WLCS**
See also BEST 89:3; BPFB 3; BRWS 4; CA 108; 111; CANR 33, 56, 108; CN 7; CPW 1; DA3; DAB; DAC; DAM MST, NOV, POP; DLB 194; EWL 3; FANT; INT CA-111; LMFS 2; MTCW 1, 2; RGEL 2; RGSF 2; TEA; WLIT 4

Rushforth, Peter (Scott) 1945- .... **CLC 19**
See also CA 101

Ruskin, John 1819-1900 .... **TCLC 63**
See also BRW 5; BYA 5; CA 114; 129; CDBLB 1832-1890; DLB 55, 163, 190; RGEL 2; SATA 24; TEA; WCH

Russ, Joanna 1937- .... **CLC 15**
See also BPFB 3; BRWS 4; CA 5-8R; CANR 11, 31, 65; CN 7; DLB 8; FW; GLL 1; MTCW 1; SCFW 2; SFW 4

Russ, Richard Patrick
See O'Brian, Patrick

Russell, George William 1867-1935
See A.E.; Baker, Jean H.
See also BRWS 8; CA 104; 153; CDBLB 1890-1914; DAM POET; EWL 3; RGEL 2

Russell, Jeffrey Burton 1934- .... **CLC 70**
See also CA 25-28R; CANR 11, 28, 52

Russell, (Henry) Ken(neth Alfred) 1927-
.... **CLC 16**
See also CA 105

Russell, William Martin 1947-
See Russell, Willy
See also CA 164; CANR 107

Russell, Willy .... **CLC 60**
See Russell, William Martin
See CBD; CD 5; DLB 233

Rutherford, Mark .... **TCLC 25**
See White, William Hale
See also DLB 18; RGEL 2

Ruyslinck, Ward .... **CLC 14**
See Belser, Reimond Karel Maria de

Ryan, Cornelius (John) 1920-1974 ... **CLC 7**
See also CA 69-72; 53-56; CANR 38

Ryan, Michael 1946- .... **CLC 65**
See also CA 49-52; CANR 109; DLBY 1982

Ryan, Tim
See Dent, Lester

Rybakov, Anatoli (Naumovich) 1911-1998
.... **CLC 23, 53**
See also CA 126; 135; 172; SATA 79; SATA-Obit 108

Ryder, Jonathan
See Ludlum, Robert

Ryga, George 1932-1987 .... **CLC 14**
See also CA 101; 124; CANR 43, 90; CCA 1; DAC; DAM MST; DLB 60

S. H.
See Hartmann, Sadakichi

S. S.
See Sassoon, Siegfried (Lorraine)

Saba, Umberto 1883-1957 .... **TCLC 33**
See also CA 144; CANR 79; DLB 114; EWL 3; RGWL 2, 3

Sabatini, Rafael 1875-1950 .... **TCLC 47**
See also BPFB 3; CA 162; RHW

Sabato, Ernesto (R.) 1911- .... **CLC 10, 23; HLC 2**
See also CA 97-100; CANR 32, 65; CD-WLB 3; DAM MULT; DLB 145; EWL 3; HW 1, 2; LAW; MTCW 1, 2

Sa-Carniero, Mario de 1890-1916
.... **TCLC 83**
See also EWL 3

Sacastru, Martin
See Bioy Casares, Adolfo
See also CWW 2

Sacher-Masoch, Leopold von 1836(?)-1895
.... **NCLC 31**

Sachs, Marilyn (Stickle) 1927- .... **CLC 35**
See also AAYA 2; BYA 6; CA 17-20R; CANR 13, 47; CLR 2; JRDA; MAICYA 1, 2; SAAS 2; SATA 3, 68; SATA-Essay 110; WYA; YAW

Sachs, Nelly 1891-1970 .... **CLC 14, 98**
See also CA 17-18; 25-28R; CANR 87; CAP 2; EWL 3; MTCW 2; RGWL 2, 3

Sackler, Howard (Oliver) 1929-1982
.... **CLC 14**
See also CA 61-64; 108; CAD; CANR 30; DFS 15; DLB 7

Sacks, Oliver (Wolf) 1933- .... **CLC 67**
See also CA 53-56; CANR 28, 50, 76; CPW; DA3; INT CANR-28; MTCW 1, 2

Sadakichi
See Hartmann, Sadakichi

Sade, Donatien Alphonse Francois
1740-1814 .... **NCLC 3, 47**
See also EW 4; GFL Beginnings to 1789; RGWL 2, 3

Sade, Marquis de
See Sade, Donatien Alphonse Francois

Sadoff, Ira 1945- .... **CLC 9**
See also CA 53-56; CANR 5, 21, 109; DLB 120

Saetone
See Camus, Albert

Safire, William 1929- .... **CLC 10**
See also CA 17-20R; CANR 31, 54, 91

Sagan, Carl (Edward) 1934-1996 .. **CLC 30, 112**
See also AAYA 2; CA 25-28R; 155; CANR 11, 36, 74; CPW; DA3; MTCW 1, 2; SATA 58; SATA-Obit 94

Sagan, Francoise .... **CLC 3, 6, 9, 17, 36**
See Quoirez, Francoise
See also CWW 2; DLB 83; EWL 3; GFL 1789 to the Present; MTCW 2

Sahgal, Nayantara (Pandit) 1927- .. **CLC 41**
See also CA 9-12R; CANR 11, 88; CN 7

Said, Edward W. 1935- .... **CLC 123**
See also CA 21-24R; CANR 45, 74, 107; DLB 67; MTCW 2

Saint, H(arry) F. 1941- .... **CLC 50**
See also CA 127

St. Aubin de Teran, Lisa 1953-
See Teran, Lisa St. Aubin de
See also CA 118; 126; CN 7; INT 126

Saint Birgitta of Sweden c. 1303-1373
.... **CMLC 24**

Sainte-Beuve, Charles Augustin 1804-1869
.... **NCLC 5**
See also DLB 217; EW 6; GFL 1789 to the Present

Saint-Exupery, Antoine (Jean Baptiste Marie Roger) de 1900-1944 .. **TCLC 2, 56; WLC**
See also BPFB 3; BYA 3; CA 108; 132; CLR 10; DA3; DAM NOV; DLB 72; EW 12; EWL 3; GFL 1789 to the Present; LAIT 3; MAICYA 1, 2; MTCW 1, 2; RGWL 2, 3; SATA 20; TWA

St. John, David
See Hunt, E(verette) Howard, (Jr.)

St. John, J. Hector
See Crevecoeur, Michel Guillaume Jean de

Saint-John Perse
See Leger, (Marie-Rene Auguste) Alexis Saint-Leger
See also EW 10; EWL 3; GFL 1789 to the Present; RGWL 2

Saintsbury, George (Edward Bateman)
1845-1933 .... **TCLC 31**
See also CA 160; DLB 57, 149

Sait Faik .... **TCLC 23**
See Abasiyanik, Sait Faik

Saki .... **SSC 12; TCLC 3**
See Munro, H(ector) H(ugh)
See also BRWS 6; LAIT 2; MTCW 2; RGEL 2; SSFS 1; SUFW

Sala, George Augustus 1828-1895
.... **NCLC 46**

Saladin 1138-1193 .... **CMLC 38**

Salama, Hannu 1936- .... **CLC 18**
See also EWL 3

Salamanca, J(ack) R(ichard) 1922- . **CLC 4, 15**
See also CA 25-28R; CAAE 193

Salas, Floyd Francis 1931- .... **HLC 2**
See also CA 119; CAAS 27; CANR 44, 75, 93; DAM MULT; DLB 82; HW 1, 2; MTCW 2

Sale, J. Kirkpatrick
See Sale, Kirkpatrick

Sale, Kirkpatrick 1937- .... **CLC 68**
See also CA 13-16R; CANR 10

Salinas, Luis Omar 1937- . **CLC 90; HLC 2**
See also CA 131; CANR 81; DAM MULT; DLB 82; HW 1, 2

Salinas (y Serrano), Pedro 1891(?)-1951
.... **TCLC 17**
See also CA 117; DLB 134; EWL 3

Salinger, J(erome) D(avid) 1919- . **CLC 1, 3, 8, 12, 55, 56, 138; SSC 2, 28; WLC**
See also AAYA 2, 36; AMW; AMWC 1; BPFB 3; CA 5-8R; CANR 39; CDALB 1941-1968; CLR 18; CN 7; CPW 1; DA; DA3; DAB; DAC; DAM MST, NOV, POP; DLB 2, 102, 173; EWL 3; EXPN; LAIT 4; MAICYA 1, 2; MTCW 1, 2; NFS 1; RGAL 4; RGSF 2; SATA 67; SSFS 17; TUS; WYA; YAW

Salisbury, John
See Caute, (John) David

Salter, James 1925- . **CLC 7, 52, 59; SSC 58**
See also AMWS 9; CA 73-76; CANR 107; DLB 130

Saltus, Edgar (Everton) 1855-1921
.... **TCLC 8**
See also CA 105; DLB 202; RGAL 4

Saltykov, Mikhail Evgrafovich 1826-1889
.... **NCLC 16**
See also DLB 238:

Saltykov-Shchedrin, N.
See Saltykov, Mikhail Evgrafovich

Samarakis, Andonis
See Samarakis, Antonis
See also EWL 3

Samarakis, Antonis 1919- .... **CLC 5**
See also CA 25-28R; CAAS 16; CANR 36

Sanchez, Florencio 1875-1910 .... **TCLC 37**
See also CA 153; EWL 3; HW 1; LAW

Sanchez, Luis Rafael 1936- .... **CLC 23**
See also CA 128; DLB 145; EWL 3; HW 1; WLIT 1

Sanchez, Sonia 1934- .. **BLC 3; CLC 5, 116; PC 9**
See also BW 2, 3; CA 33-36R; CANR 24, 49, 74, 115; CLR 18; CP 7; CSW; CWP; DA3; DAM MULT; DLB 41; DLBD 8; EWL 3; MAICYA 1, 2; MTCW 1, 2; SATA 22, 136; WP

Sancho, Ignatius 1729-1780 .... **LC 84**

Sand, George 1804-1876 ... **NCLC 2, 42, 57; WLC**
See also DA; DA3; DAB; DAC; DAM MST, NOV; DLB 119, 192; EW 6; FW; GFL 1789 to the Present; RGWL 2, 3; TWA

Sandburg, Carl (August) 1878-1967
.. **CLC 1, 4, 10, 15, 35; PC 2, 41; WLC**
See also AAYA 24; AMW; BYA 1, 3; CA 5-8R; 25-28R; CANR 35; CDALB 1865-1917; CLR 67; DA; DA3; DAB; DAC; DAM MST, POET; DLB 17, 54; EWL 3; EXPP; LAIT 2; MAICYA 1, 2; MTCW 1, 2; PAB; PFS 3, 6, 12; RGAL 4; SATA 8; TUS; WCH; WP; WYA

Sandburg, Charles
See Sandburg, Carl (August)

Sandburg, Charles A.
See Sandburg, Carl (August)

Sanders, (James) Ed(ward) 1939- ... **CLC 53**
See Sanders, Edward
See also BG 3; CA 13-16R; CAAS 21; CANR 13, 44, 78; CP 7; DAM POET; DLB 16, 244

Sanders, Edward
See Sanders, (James) Ed(ward)
See also DLB 244

Sanders, Lawrence 1920-1998 .... **CLC 41**
See also BEST 89:4; BPFB 3; CA 81-84; 165; CANR 33, 62; CMW 4; CPW; DA3; DAM POP; MTCW 1

Sanders, Noah
See Blount, Roy (Alton), Jr.

Sanders, Winston P.
See Anderson, Poul (William)

Sandoz, Mari(e Susette) 1900-1966
.... **CLC 28**
See also CA 1-4R; 25-28R; CANR 17, 64; DLB 9, 212; LAIT 2; MTCW 1, 2; SATA 5; TCWW 2

Sandys, George 1578-1644 .... **LC 80**
See also DLB 24, 121

Saner, Reg(inald Anthony) 1931- ...... **CLC 9**
See also CA 65-68; CP 7

Sankara 788-820 .... **CMLC 32**

Sannazaro, Jacopo 1456(?)-1530 .... **LC 8**
See also RGWL 2, 3

Sansom, William 1912-1976 .... **CLC 2, 6; SSC 21**
See also CA 5-8R; 65-68; CANR 42; DAM NOV; DLB 139; EWL 3; MTCW 1; RGEL 2; RGSF 2

Santayana, George 1863-1952 ...... **TCLC 40**
See also AMW; CA 115; 194; DLB 54, 71, 246, 270; DLBD 13; EWL 3; RGAL 4; TUS

Santiago, Danny .... **CLC 33**
See James, Daniel (Lewis)
See also DLB 122

Santmyer, Helen Hooven 1895-1986
.... **CLC 33; TCLC 133**
See also CA 1-4R; 118; CANR 15, 33; DLBY 1984; MTCW 1; RHW

Santoka, Taneda 1882-1940 .... **TCLC 72**

Santos, Bienvenido N(uqui) 1911-1996
.... **AAL; CLC 22**
See also CA 101; 151; CANR 19, 46; DAM MULT; EWL; RGAL 4

Sapir, Edward 1884-1939 .... **TCLC 108**
See also DLB 92

Sapper .... **TCLC 44**
See McNeile, Herman Cyril

Sapphire
See Sapphire, Brenda

Sapphire, Brenda 1950- .... **CLC 99**

Sappho fl. 6th cent. B.C.- ...... **CMLC 3; PC 5**
See also CDWLB 1; DA3; DAM POET; DLB 176; RGWL 2, 3; WP

Saramago, Jose 1922- .... **CLC 119; HLCS 1**
See also CA 153; CANR 96; EWL 3

Sarduy, Severo 1937-1993 .... **CLC 6, 97; HLCS 2**
See also CA 89-92; 142; CANR 58, 81; CWW 2; DLB 113; EWL 3; HW 1, 2; LAW

Sargeson, Frank 1903-1982 .... **CLC 31**
See also CA 25-28R; 106; CANR 38, 79; EWL 3; GLL 2; RGEL 2; RGSF 2

Sarmiento, Domingo Faustino 1811-1888
.... **HLCS 2**
See also LAW; WLIT 1

Sarmiento, Felix Ruben Garcia
See Dario, Ruben

Saro-Wiwa, Ken(ule Beeson) 1941-1995
.... **CLC 114**
See also BW 2; CA 142; 150; CANR 60; DLB 157

Saroyan, William 1908-1981 .. **CLC 1, 8, 10, 29, 34, 56; SSC 21; WLC**
See also CA 5-8R; 103; CAD; CANR 30; CDALBS; DA; DA3; DAB; DAC; DAM DRAM, MST, NOV; DFS 17; DLB 7, 9, 86; DLBY 1981; EWL 3; LAIT 4; MTCW 1, 2; RGAL 4; RGSF 2; SATA 23; SATA-Obit 24; SSFS 14; TUS

Sarraute, Nathalie 1900-1999 .. **CLC 1, 2, 4, 8, 10, 31, 80**
See also BPFB 3; CA 9-12R; 187; CANR 23, 66; CWW 2; DLB 83; EW 12; EWL 3; GFL 1789 to the Present; MTCW 1, 2; RGWL 2, 3

Sarton, (Eleanor) May 1912-1995 .... **CLC 4, 14, 49, 91; PC 39; TCLC 120**
See also AMWS 8; CA 1-4R; 149; CANR 1, 34, 55, 116; CN 7; CP 7; DAM POET; DLB 48; DLBY 1981; EWL 3; FW; INT CANR-34; MTCW 1, 2; RGAL 4; SATA 36; SATA-Obit 86; TUS

Sartre, Jean-Paul 1905-1980 .... **CLC 1, 4, 7, 9, 13, 18, 24, 44, 50, 52; DC 3; SSC 32; WLC**
See also CA 9-12R; 97-100; CANR 21; DA; DA3; DAB; DAC; DAM DRAM, MST, NOV; DFS 5; DLB 72; EW 12; EWL 3; GFL 1789 to the Present; LMFS 2; MTCW 1, 2; RGSF 2; RGWL 2, 3; SSFS 9; TWA

Sassoon, Siegfried (Lorraine) 1886-1967
.... **CLC 36, 130; PC 12**
See also BRW 6; CA 104; 25-28R; CANR 36; DAB; DAM MST, NOV, POET; DLB 20, 191; DLBD 18; EWL 3; MTCW 1, 2; PAB; RGEL 2; TEA

Satterfield, Charles
See Pohl, Frederik

Satyremont
See Peret, Benjamin

Saul, John (W. III) 1942- .... **CLC 46**
See also AAYA 10; BEST 90:4; CA 81-84; CANR 16, 40, 81; CPW; DAM NOV, POP; HGG; SATA 98

Saunders, Caleb
See Heinlein, Robert A(nson)

Saura (Atares), Carlos 1932-1998 ... **CLC 20**
See also CA 114; 131; CANR 79; HW 1

Sauser, Frederic Louis
See Sauser-Hall, Frederic

Sauser-Hall, Frederic 1887-1961 ..... **CLC 18**
See Cendrars, Blaise
See also CA 102; 93-96; CANR 36, 62; MTCW 1

Saussure, Ferdinand de 1857-1913
.... **TCLC 49**
See also DLB 242

Savage, Catharine
See Brosman, Catharine Savage

Savage, Thomas 1915- .... **CLC 40**
See also CA 126; 132; CAAS 15; CN 7; INT 132; TCWW 2

Savan, Glenn (?)- .... **CLC 50**

Sax, Robert
See Johnson, Robert

Saxo Grammaticus c. 1150-c. 1222
.... **CMLC 58**

Saxton, Robert
See Johnson, Robert

Sayers, Dorothy L(eigh) 1893-1957
.... **TCLC 2, 15**
See also BPFB 3; BRWS 3; CA 104; 119; CANR 60; CDBLB 1914-1945; CMW 4; DAM POP; DLB 10, 36, 77, 100; MSW; MTCW 1, 2; RGEL 2; SSFS 12; TEA

Sayers, Valerie 1952- .... **CLC 50, 122**
See also CA 134; CANR 61; CSW

Sayles, John (Thomas) 1950- ...... **CLC 7, 10, 14**
See also CA 57-60; CANR 41, 84; DLB 44

Scammell, Michael 1935- .... **CLC 34**
See also CA 156

Scannell, Vernon 1922- .... **CLC 49**
See also CA 5-8R; CANR 8, 24, 57; CP 7; CWRI 5; DLB 27; SATA 59

Scarlett, Susan
See Streatfeild, (Mary) Noel

Scarron 1847-1910
See Mikszath, Kalman

Schaeffer, Susan Fromberg 1941- ..... **CLC 6, 11, 22**
See also CA 49-52; CANR 18, 65; CN 7; DLB 28; MTCW 1, 2; SATA 22

Schama, Simon (Michael) 1945- ... **CLC 150**
See also BEST 89:4; CA 105; CANR 39, 91

Schary, Jill
See Robinson, Jill

Schell, Jonathan 1943- .... **CLC 35**
See also CA 73-76; CANR 12, 117

Schelling, Friedrich Wilhelm Joseph von
1775-1854 .... **NCLC 30**
See also DLB 90

Scherer, Jean-Marie Maurice 1920-
See Rohmer, Eric
See also CA 110

Schevill, James (Erwin) 1920- .... **CLC 7**
See also CA 5-8R; CAAS 12; CAD; CD 5

Schiller, Friedrich von 1759-1805 .... **DC 12; NCLC 39, 69**
See also CDWLB 2; DAM DRAM; DLB 94; EW 5; RGWL 2, 3; TWA

Schisgal, Murray (Joseph) 1926- ...... **CLC 6**
See also CA 21-24R; CAD; CANR 48, 86; CD 5

Schlee, Ann 1934- .... **CLC 35**
See also CA 101; CANR 29, 88; SATA 44; SATA-Brief 36

Schlegel, August Wilhelm von 1767-1845
.... **NCLC 15**
See also DLB 94; RGWL 2, 3

Schlegel, Friedrich 1772-1829 ...... **NCLC 45**
See also DLB 90; EW 5; RGWL 2, 3; TWA

Schlegel, Johann Elias (von) 1719(?)-1749
.... **LC 5**

Schleiermacher, Friedrich 1768-1834
.... **NCLC 107**
See also DLB 90

Schlesinger, Arthur M(eier), Jr. 1917-
.... **CLC 84**
See also AITN 1; CA 1-4R; CANR 1, 28, 58, 105; DLB 17; INT CANR-28; MTCW 1, 2; SATA 61

Schmidt, Arno (Otto) 1914-1979 ..... **CLC 56**
See also CA 128; 109; DLB 69; EWL 3

Schmitz, Aron Hector 1861-1928
See Svevo, Italo
See also CA 104; 122; MTCW 1

Schnackenberg, Gjertrud (Cecelia) 1953-
.... **CLC 40; PC 45**
See also CA 116; CANR 100; CP 7; CWP; DLB 120, 282; PFS 13

Schneider, Leonard Alfred 1925-1966
See Bruce, Lenny
See also CA 89-92

Schnitzler, Arthur 1862-1931 ... **DC 17; SSC 15, 61; TCLC 4**
See also CA 104; CDWLB 2; DLB 81, 118; EW 8; EWL 3; RGSF 2; RGWL 2, 3

Schoenberg, Arnold Franz Walter 1874-1951
.... **TCLC 75**
See also CA 109; 188

Schonberg, Arnold
See Schoenberg, Arnold Franz Walter

Schopenhauer, Arthur 1788-1860 . **NCLC 51**
See also DLB 90; EW 5

Schor, Sandra (M.) 1932(?)-1990 .... **CLC 65**
See also CA 132

Schorer, Mark 1908-1977 .... **CLC 9**
See also CA 5-8R; 73-76; CANR 7; DLB 103

Schrader, Paul (Joseph) 1946- .... **CLC 26**
See also CA 37-40R; CANR 41; DLB 44

Schreber, Daniel 1842-1911 .... **TCLC 123**

Schreiner, Olive (Emilie Albertina)
1855-1920 .... **TCLC 9**
See also AFW; BRWS 2; CA 105; 154; DLB 18, 156, 190, 225; EWL 3; FW; RGEL 2; TWA; WLIT 2

Schulberg, Budd (Wilson) 1914- ...... **CLC 7, 48**
See also BPFB 3; CA 25-28R; CANR 19, 87; CN 7; DLB 6, 26, 28; DLBY 1981, 2001

Schulman, Arnold
See Trumbo, Dalton

Schulz, Bruno 1892-1942 ..... **SSC 13; TCLC 5, 51**
See also CA 115; 123; CANR 86; CDWLB 4; DLB 215; EWL 3; MTCW 2; RGSF 2; RGWL 2, 3

Schulz, Charles M(onroe) 1922-2000
.... **CLC 12**
See also AAYA 39; CA 9-12R; 187; CANR 6; INT CANR-6; SATA 10; SATA-Obit 118

Schumacher, E(rnst) F(riedrich) 1911-1977
.... **CLC 80**
See also CA 81-84; 73-76; CANR 34, 85

Schuyler, George Samuel 1895-1977 ... **HR 3**
See also BW 2; CA 81-84; 73-76; CANR 42; DLB 29, 51

Schuyler, James Marcus 1923-1991 . **CLC 5, 23**
See also CA 101; 134; DAM POET; DLB 5, 169; EWL 3; INT 101; WP

Schwartz, Delmore (David) 1913-1966
.... **CLC 2, 4, 10, 45, 87; PC 8**
See also AMWS 2; CA 17-18; 25-28R; CANR 35; CAP 2; DLB 28, 48; EWL 3; MTCW 1, 2; PAB; RGAL 4; TUS

Schwartz, Ernst
See Ozu, Yasujiro

Schwartz, John Burnham 1965- ..... **CLC 59**
See also CA 132; CANR 116

Schwartz, Lynne Sharon 1939- .... **CLC 31**
See also CA 103; CANR 44, 89; DLB 218; MTCW 2

Schwartz, Muriel A.
See Eliot, T(homas) S(tearns)

Schwarz-Bart, Andre 1928- .... **CLC 2, 4**
See also CA 89-92; CANR 109

Schwarz-Bart, Simone 1938- ... **BLCS; CLC 7**
See also BW 2; CA 97-100; CANR 117; EWL 3

Schwerner, Armand 1927-1999 .... **PC 42**
See also CA 9-12R; 179; CANR 50, 85; CP 7; DLB 165

Schwitters, Kurt (Hermann Edward Karl Julius) 1887-1948 .... **TCLC 95**
See also CA 158

Schwob, Marcel (Mayer Andre) 1867-1905
.... **TCLC 20**
See also CA 117; 168; DLB 123; GFL 1789 to the Present

Sciascia, Leonardo 1921-1989 . **CLC 8, 9, 41**
See also CA 85-88; 130; CANR 35; DLB 177; EWL 3; MTCW 1; RGWL 2, 3

Scoppettone, Sandra 1936- .... **CLC 26**
See Early, Jack
See also AAYA 11; BYA 8; CA 5-8R; CANR 41, 73; GLL 1; MAICYA 2; MAICYAS 1; SATA 9, 92; WYA; YAW

Scorsese, Martin 1942- .... **CLC 20, 89**
See also AAYA 38; CA 110; 114; CANR 46, 85

Scotland, Jay
See Jakes, John (William)

Scott, Duncan Campbell 1862-1947
.... **TCLC 6**
See also CA 104; 153; DAC; DLB 92; RGEL 2

Scott, Evelyn 1893-1963 .... **CLC 43**
See also CA 104; 112; CANR 64; DLB 9, 48; RHW

Scott, F(rancis) R(eginald) 1899-1985
.... **CLC 22**
See also CA 101; 114; CANR 87; DLB 88; INT CA-101; RGEL 2

Scott, Frank
See Scott, F(rancis) R(eginald)

Scott, Joan .... **CLC 65**

Scott, Joanna 1960- .... **CLC 50**
See also CA 126; CANR 53, 92

Scott, Paul (Mark) 1920-1978 ..... **CLC 9, 60**
See also BRWS 1; CA 81-84; 77-80; CANR 33; DLB 14, 207; EWL 3; MTCW 1; RGEL 2; RHW

Scott, Sarah 1723-1795 .... **LC 44**
See also DLB 39

Scott, Sir Walter 1771-1832 ... **NCLC 15, 69, 110; PC 13; SSC 32; WLC**
See also AAYA 22; BRW 4; BYA 2; CD-BLB 1789-1832; DA; DAB; DAC; DAM MST, NOV, POET; DLB 93, 107, 116, 144, 159; HGG; LAIT 1; RGEL 2; RGSF 2; SSFS 10; SUFW 1; TEA; WLIT 3; YABC 2

Scribe, (Augustin) Eugene 1791-1861
.... **DC 5; NCLC 16**
See also DAM DRAM; DLB 192; GFL 1789 to the Present; RGWL 2, 3

Scrum, R.
See Crumb, R(obert)

Scudery, Georges de 1601-1667 .... **LC 75**
See also GFL Beginnings to 1789

Scudery, Madeleine de 1607-1701 . **LC 2, 58**
See also DLB 268; GFL Beginnings to 1789

Scum
See Crumb, R(obert)

Scumbag, Little Bobby
See Crumb, R(obert)

Seabrook, John
See Hubbard, L(afayette) Ron(ald)

Sealy, I(rwin) Allan 1951- .... **CLC 55**
See also CA 136; CN 7

Search, Alexander
See Pessoa, Fernando (Antonio Nogueira)

Sebastian, Lee
See Silverberg, Robert

Sebastian Owl
See Thompson, Hunter S(tockton)

Sebestyen, Igen
See Sebestyen, Ouida

Sebestyen, Ouida 1924- .... **CLC 30**
See also AAYA 8; BYA 7; CA 107; CANR 40, 114; CLR 17; JRDA; MAICYA 1, 2; SAAS 10; SATA 39; WYA; YAW

Secundus, H. Scriblerus
See Fielding, Henry

Sedges, John
See Buck, Pearl S(ydenstricker)

Sedgwick, Catharine Maria 1789-1867
.... **NCLC 19, 98**
See also DLB 1, 74, 183, 239, 243, 254; RGAL 4

Seelye, John (Douglas) 1931- .... **CLC 7**
See also CA 97-100; CANR 70; INT 97-100; TCWW 2

Seferiades, Giorgos Stylianou 1900-1971
See Seferis, George
See also CA 5-8R; 33-36R; CANR 5, 36; MTCW 1

Seferis, George .... **CLC 5, 11**
See Seferiades, Giorgos Stylianou
See also EW 12; EWL 3; RGWL 2, 3

Segal, Erich (Wolf) 1937- .... **CLC 3, 10**
See also BEST 89:1; BPFB 3; CA 25-28R; CANR 20, 36, 65, 113; CPW; DAM POP; DLBY 1986; INT CANR-20; MTCW 1

Seger, Bob 1945- .... **CLC 35**

Seghers, Anna .... **CLC 7**
See Radvanyi, Netty
See also CDWLB 2; DLB 69; EWL 3

Seidel, Frederick (Lewis) 1936- ...... **CLC 18**
See also CA 13-16R; CANR 8, 99; CP 7; DLBY 1984

Seifert, Jaroslav 1901-1986 ...... **CLC 34, 44, 93; PC 47**
See also CA 127; CDWLB 4; DLB 215; EWL 3; MTCW 1, 2

Sei Shonagon c. 966-1017(?) .... **CMLC 6**

Sejour, Victor 1817-1874 .... **DC 10**
See also DLB 50

Sejour Marcou et Ferrand, Juan Victor
See Sejour, Victor

Selby, Hubert, Jr. 1928- .... **CLC 1, 2, 4, 8; SSC 20**
See also CA 13-16R; CANR 33, 85; CN 7; DLB 2, 227

Selzer, Richard 1928- .... **CLC 74**
See also CA 65-68; CANR 14, 106

Sembene, Ousmane
See Ousmane, Sembene
See also AFW; CWW 2; EWL 3; WLIT 2

Senancour, Etienne Pivert de 1770-1846
.... NCLC 16
See also DLB 119; GFL 1789 to the Present

Sender, Ramon (Jose) 1902-1982 ..... CLC 8;
HLC 2
See also CA 5-8R; 105; CANR 8; DAM MULT; EWL 3; HW 1; MTCW 1; RGWL 2, 3

Seneca, Lucius Annaeus c. 4B.C.-c. 65
.... CMLC 6; DC 5
See also AW 2; CDWLB 1; DAM DRAM; DLB 211; RGWL 2, 3; TWA

Senghor, Leopold Sedar 1906-2001 . **BLC 3;**
CLC 54, 130; PC 25
See also AFW; BW 2; CA 116; 125; 203; CANR 47, 74; DAM MULT; POET; DNFS 2; EWL 3; GFL 1789 to the Present; MTCW 1, 2; TWA

Senna, Danzy 1970- .... CLC 119
See also CA 169

Serling, (Edward) Rod(man) 1924-1975
.... CLC 30
See also AAYA 14; AITN 1; CA 162; 57-60; DLB 26; SFW 4

Serna, Ramon Gomez de la
See Gomez de la Serna, Ramon

Serpieres
See Guillevic, (Eugene)

Service, Robert
See Service, Robert W(illiam)
See also BYA 4; DAB; DLB 92

Service, Robert W(illiam) 1874(?)-1958
.... TCLC 15; WLC
See Service, Robert
See also CA 115; 140; CANR 84; DA; DAC; DAM MST, POET; PFS 10; RGEL 2; SATA 20

Seth, Vikram 1952- .... CLC 43, 90
See also CA 121; 127; CANR 50, 74; CN 7; CP 7; DA3; DAM MULT; DLB 120, 271, 282; EWL 3; INT 127; MTCW 2

Seton, Cynthia Propper 1926-1982 . CLC 27
See also CA 5-8R; 108; CANR 7

Seton, Ernest (Evan) Thompson 1860-1946
.... TCLC 31
See also ANW; BYA; CA 109; 204; CLR 59; DLB 92; DLBD 13; JRDA; SATA 18

Seton-Thompson, Ernest
See Seton, Ernest (Evan) Thompson

Settle, Mary Lee 1918- .... CLC 19, 61
See also BPFB 3; CA 89-92; CAAS 1; CANR 44, 87; CN 7; CSW; DLB 6; INT 89-92

Seuphor, Michel
See Arp, Jean

Sevigne, Marie (de Rabutin-Chantal)
1626-1696 .... LC 11
See Sevigne, Marie de Rabutin Chantal
See also GFL Beginnings to 1789; TWA

Sevigne, Marie de Rabutin Chantal
See Sevigne, Marie (de Rabutin-Chantal)
See also DLB 268

Sewall, Samuel 1652-1730 .... LC 38
See also DLB 24; RGAL 4

Sexton, Anne (Harvey) 1928-1974 ... CLC 2,
4, 6, 8, 10, 15, 53, 123; PC 2; WLC
See also AMWS 2; CA 1-4R; 53-56; CABS 2; CANR 3, 36; CDALB 1941-1968; DA; DA3; DAB; DAC; DAM MST, POET; DLB 5, 169; EWL 3; EXPP; FW; MAWW; MTCW 1, 2; PAB; PFS 4, 14; RGAL 4; SATA 10; TUS

Shaara, Jeff 1952- .... CLC 119
See also CA 163; CANR 109

Shaara, Michael (Joseph, Jr.) 1929-1988
.... CLC 15
See also AITN 1; BPFB 3; CA 102; 125; CANR 52, 85; DAM POP; DLBY 1983

Shackleton, C. C.
See Aldiss, Brian W(ilson)

Shacochis, Bob .... CLC 39
See Shacochis, Robert G.

Shacochis, Robert G. 1951-
See Shacochis, Bob
See also CA 119; 124; CANR 100; INT 124

Shaffer, Anthony (Joshua) 1926-2001
.... CLC 19
See also CA 110; 116; 200; CBD; CD 5; DAM DRAM; DFS 13; DLB 13

Shaffer, Peter (Levin) 1926- . CLC 5, 14, 18, 37, 60; DC 7
See also BRWS 1; CA 25-28R; CANR 25, 47, 74; CBD; CD 5; CDBLB 1960 to Present; DA3; DAB; DAM DRAM, MST; DFS 5, 13; DLB 13, 233; EWL 3; MTCW 1, 2; RGEL 2; TEA

Shakespeare, William 1564-1616 .... WLC
See also AAYA 35; BRW 1; CDBLB Before 1660; DA; DA3; DAB; DAC; DAM DRAM, MST, POET; DLB 62, 172, 263; EXPP; LAIT 1; LMFS 1; PAB; PFS 1, 2, 3, 4, 5, 8, 9; RGEL 2; TEA; WLIT 3; WP; WS; WYA

Shakey, Bernard
See Young, Neil

Shalamov, Varlam (Tikhonovich)
1907(?)-1982 .... CLC 18
See also CA 129; 105; RGSF 2

Shamlu, Ahmad 1925-2000 .... CLC 10
See also CWW 2

Shammas, Anton 1951- .... CLC 55
See also CA 199

Shandling, Arline
See Berriault, Gina

Shange, Ntozake 1948- . **BLC 3; CLC 8, 25, 38, 74, 126; DC 3**
See also AAYA 9; AFAW 1, 2; BW 2; CA 85-88; CABS 3; CAD; CANR 27, 48, 74; CD 5; CP 7; CWD; CWP; DA3; DAM DRAM, MULT; DFS 2, 11; DLB 38, 249; FW; LAIT 4; MTCW 1, 2; NFS 11; RGAL 4; YAW

Shanley, John Patrick 1950- .... CLC 75
See also CA 128; 133; CAD; CANR 83; CD 5

Shapcott, Thomas W(illiam) 1935- . CLC 38
See also CA 69-72; CANR 49, 83, 103; CP 7

Shapiro, Jane 1942- .... CLC 76
See also CA 196

Shapiro, Karl (Jay) 1913-2000 ..... CLC 4, 8, 15, 53; PC 25
See also AMWS 2; CA 1-4R; 188; CAAS 6; CANR 1, 36, 66; CP 7; DLB 48; EWL 3; EXPP; MTCW 1, 2; PFS 3; RGAL 4

Sharp, William 1855-1905 .... TCLC 39
See Macleod, Fiona
See also CA 160; DLB 156; RGEL 2

Sharpe, Thomas Ridley 1928-
See Sharpe, Tom
See also CA 114; 122; CANR 85; INT CA-122

Sharpe, Tom .... CLC 36
See Sharpe, Thomas Ridley
See also CN 7; DLB 14, 231

Shatrov, Mikhail .... CLC 59

Shaw, Bernard
See Shaw, George Bernard
See also DLB 190

Shaw, G. Bernard
See Shaw, George Bernard

Shaw, George Bernard 1856-1950
.... TCLC 3, 9, 21, 45; WLC
See Shaw, Bernard
See also BRW 6; BRWC 1; BRWR 2; CA 104; 128; CDBLB 1914-1945; DA; DA3; DAB; DAC; DAM DRAM, MST; DFS 1, 3, 6, 11; DLB 10, 57; EWL 3; LAIT 3; MTCW 1, 2; RGEL 2; TEA; WLIT 4

Shaw, Henry Wheeler 1818-1885 . NCLC 15
See also DLB 11; RGAL 4

Shaw, Irwin 1913-1984 .... CLC 7, 23, 34
See also AITN 1; BPFB 3; CA 13-16R; 112; CANR 21; CDALB 1941-1968; CPW; DAM DRAM, POP; DLB 6, 102; DLBY 1984; MTCW 1, 21

Shaw, Robert 1927-1978 .... CLC 5
See also AITN 1; CA 1-4R; 81-84; CANR 4; DLB 13, 14

Shaw, T. E.
See Lawrence, T(homas) E(dward)

Shawn, Wallace 1943- .... CLC 41
See also CA 112; CAD; CD 5; DLB 266

Shchedrin, N.
See Saltykov, Mikhail Evgrafovich

Shea, Lisa 1953- .... CLC 86
See also CA 147

Sheed, Wilfrid (John Joseph) 1930-
.... CLC 2, 4, 10, 53
See also CA 65-68; CANR 30, 66; CN 7; DLB 6; MTCW 1, 2

Sheehy, Gail 1937- .... CLC 171
See also CA 49-52; CANR 1, 33, 55, 92; CPW; MTCW 1

Sheldon, Alice Hastings Bradley
1915(?)-1987
See Tiptree, James, Jr.
See also CA 108; 122; CANR 34; INT 108; MTCW 1

Sheldon, John
See Bloch, Robert (Albert)

Sheldon, Walter J(ames) 1917-1996
See Queen, Ellery
See also AITN 1; CA 25-28R; CANR 10

Shelley, Mary Wollstonecraft (Godwin)
1797-1851 .... NCLC 14, 59, 103; WLC
See also AAYA 20; BPFB 3; BRW 3; BRWS 3; BYA 5; CDBLB 1789-1832; DA; DA3; DAB; DAC; DAM MST, NOV; DLB 110, 116, 159, 178; EXPN; HGG; LAIT 1; LMFS 1, 2; NFS 1; RGEL 2; SATA 29; SCFW; SFW 4; TEA; WLIT 3

Shelley, Percy Bysshe 1792-1822 . **NCLC 18, 93; PC 14; WLC**
See also BRW 4; BRWR 1; CDBLB 1789-1832; DA; DA3; DAB; DAC; DAM MST, POET; DLB 96, 110, 158; EXPP; LMFS 1; PAB; PFS 2; RGEL 2; TEA; WLIT 3; WP

Shepard, Jim 1956- .... CLC 36
See also CA 137; CANR 59, 104; SATA 90

Shepard, Lucius 1947- .... CLC 34
See also CA 128; 141; CANR 81; HGG; SCFW 2; SFW 4; SUFW 2

Shepard, Sam 1943- ... **CLC 4, 6, 17, 34, 41, 44, 169; DC 5**
See also AAYA 1; AMWS 3; CA 69-72; CABS 3; CAD; CANR 22; CD 5; DA3; DAM DRAM; DFS 3, 6, 7, 14; DLB 7, 212; EWL 3; IDFW 3, 4; MTCW 1, 2; RGAL 4

Shepherd, Michael
See Ludlum, Robert

Sherburne, Zoa (Lillian Morin) 1912-1995
.... CLC 30
See also AAYA 13; CA 1-4R; 176; CANR 3, 37; MAICYA 1, 2; SAAS 18; SATA 3; YAW

Sheridan, Frances 1724-1766 .... LC 7
See also DLB 39, 84

Sheridan, Richard Brinsley 1751-1816
.... **DC 1; NCLC 5, 91; WLC**
See also BRW 3; CDBLB 1660-1789; DA; DAB; DAC; DAM DRAM, MST; DFS 15; DLB 89; WLIT 3

Sherman, Jonathan Marc .... **CLC 55**

Sherman, Martin 1941(?)- .... **CLC 19**
See also CA 116; 123; CAD; CANR 86; CD 5; DLB 228; GLL 1; IDTP

Sherwin, Judith Johnson
See Johnson, Judith (Emlyn)
See also CANR 85; CP 7; CWP

Sherwood, Frances 1940- .... **CLC 81**
See also CA 146

Sherwood, Robert E(mmet) 1896-1955
.... **TCLC 3**
See also CA 104; 153; CANR 86; DAM DRAM; DFS 17; DLB 7, 26, 249; IDFW 3, 4; RGAL 4

Shestov, Lev 1866-1938 .... **TCLC 56**

Shevchenko, Taras 1814-1861 .... **NCLC 54**

Shiel, M(atthew) P(hipps) 1865-1947
.... **TCLC 8**
See Holmes, Gordon
See also CA 106; 160; DLB 153; HGG; MTCW 2; SFW 4; SUFW

Shields, Carol 1935- .... **CLC 91, 113**
See also AMWS 7; CA 81-84; CANR 51, 74, 98; CCA 1; CN 7; CPW; DA3; DAC; MTCW 2

Shields, David 1956- .... **CLC 97**
See also CA 124; CANR 48, 99, 112

Shiga, Naoya 1883-1971 .... **CLC 33; SSC 23**
See Shiga Naoya
See also CA 101; 33-36R; MJW; RGWL 3

Shiga Naoya
See Shiga, Naoya
See also DLB 180; EWL 3; RGWL 3

Shilts, Randy 1951-1994 .... **CLC 85**
See also AAYA 19; CA 115; 127; 144; CANR 45; DA3; GLL 1; INT 127; MTCW 2

Shimazaki, Haruki 1872-1943
See Shimazaki Toson
See also CA 105; 134; CANR 84; RGWL 3

Shimazaki Toson .... **TCLC 5**
See Shimazaki, Haruki
See also DLB 180; EWL 3

Sholokhov, Mikhail (Aleksandrovich)
1905-1984 .... **CLC 7, 15**
See also CA 101; 112; DLB 272; EWL 3; MTCW 1, 2; RGWL 2, 3; SATA-Obit 36

Shone, Patric
See Hanley, James

Showalter, Elaine 1941- .... **CLC 169**
See also CA 57-60; CANR 58, 106; DLB 67; FW; GLL 2

Shreve, Susan Richards 1939- .... **CLC 23**
See also CA 49-52; CAAS 5; CANR 5, 38, 69, 100; MAICYA 1, 2; SATA 46, 95; SATA-Brief 41

Shue, Larry 1946-1985 .... **CLC 52**
See also CA 145; 117; DAM DRAM; DFS 7

Shu-Jen, Chou 1881-1936
See Lu Hsun
See also CA 104

Shulman, Alix Kates 1932- .... **CLC 2, 10**
See also CA 29-32R; CANR 43; FW; SATA 7

Shusaku, Endo
See Endo, Shusaku

Shuster, Joe 1914-1992 .... **CLC 21**

Shute, Nevil .... **CLC 30**
See Norway, Nevil Shute
See also BPFB 3; DLB 255; NFS 9; RHW; SFW 4

Shuttle, Penelope (Diane) 1947- .... **CLC 7**
See also CA 93-96; CANR 39, 84, 92, 108; CP 7; CWP; DLB 14, 40

Sidhwa, Bapsy (N.) 1938- .... **CLC 168**
See also CA 108; CANR 25, 57; CN 7; FW

Sidney, Mary 1561-1621 .... **LC 19, 39**
See Sidney Herbert, Mary

Sidney, Sir Philip 1554-1586 .... **LC 19, 39; PC 32**
See also BRW 1; BRWR 2; CDBLB Before 1660; DA; DA3; DAB; DAC; DAM MST, POET; DLB 167; EXPP; PAB; RGEL 2; TEA; WP

Sidney Herbert, Mary
See Sidney, Mary
See also DLB 167

Siegel, Jerome 1914-1996 .... **CLC 21**
See also CA 116; 169; 151

Siegel, Jerry
See Siegel, Jerome

Sienkiewicz, Henryk (Adam Alexander Pius)
1846-1916 .... **TCLC 3**
See also CA 104; 134; CANR 84; EWL 3; RGSF 2; RGWL 2, 3

Sierra, Gregorio Martinez
See Martinez Sierra, Gregorio

Sierra, Maria (de la O'LeJarraga) Martinez
See Martinez Sierra, Maria (de la O'LeJarraga)

Sigal, Clancy 1926- .... **CLC 7**
See also CA 1-4R; CANR 85; CN 7

Sigourney, Lydia H.
See Sigourney, Lydia Howard (Huntley)
See also DLB 73, 183

Sigourney, Lydia Howard (Huntley)
1791-1865 .... **NCLC 21, 87**
See Sigourney, Lydia H.; Sigourney, Lydia Huntley
See also DLB 1

Sigourney, Lydia Huntley
See Sigourney, Lydia Howard (Huntley)
See also DLB 42, 239, 243

Siguenza y Gongora, Carlos de 1645-1700
.... **HLCS 2; LC 8**
See also LAW

Sigurjonsson, Johann 1880-1919 .. **TCLC 27**
See also CA 170; EWL 3

Sikelianos, Angelos 1884-1951 .... **PC 29; TCLC 39**
See also EWL 3; RGWL 2, 3

Silkin, Jon 1930-1997 .... **CLC 2, 6, 43**
See also CA 5-8R; CAAS 5; CANR 89; CP 7; DLB 27

Silko, Leslie (Marmon) 1948- .. **CLC 23, 74, 114; NNAL; SSC 37; WLCS**
See also AAYA 14; AMWS 4; ANW; BYA 12; CA 115; 122; CANR 45, 65; CN 7; CP 7; CPW 1; CWP; DA; DA3; DAC; DAM MST, MULT, POP; DLB 143, 175, 256, 275; EWL 3; EXPP; EXPS; LAIT 4; MTCW 2; NFS 4; PFS 9, 16; RGAL 4; RGSF 2; SSFS 4, 8, 10, 11

Sillanpaa, Frans Eemil 1888-1964 .. **CLC 19**
See also CA 129; 93-96; EWL 3; MTCW 1

Sillitoe, Alan 1928- . **CLC 1, 3, 6, 10, 19, 57, 148**
See also AITN 1; BRWS 5; CA 9-12R; CAAE 191; CAAS 2; CANR 8, 26, 55; CDBLB 1960 to Present; CN 7; DLB 14, 139; EWL 3; MTCW 1, 2; RGEL 2; RGSF 2; SATA 61

Silone, Ignazio 1900-1978 .... **CLC 4**
See also CA 25-28; 81-84; CANR 34; CAP 2; DLB 264; EW 12; EWL 3; MTCW 1; RGSF 2; RGWL 2, 3

Silone, Ignazione
See Silone, Ignazio

Silva, Jose Asuncion
See da Silva, Antonio Jose
See also LAW

Silver, Joan Micklin 1935- .... **CLC 20**
See also CA 114; 121; INT 121

Silver, Nicholas
See Faust, Frederick (Schiller)
See also TCWW 2

Silverberg, Robert 1935- .... **CLC 7, 140**
See also AAYA 24; BPFB 3; BYA 7, 9; CA 1-4R, 186; CAAE 186; CAAS 3; CANR 1, 20, 36, 85; CLR 59; CN 7; CPW; DAM POP; DLB 8; INT CANR-20; MAICYA 1, 2; MTCW 1, 2; SATA 13, 91; SATA-Essay 104; SCFW 2; SFW 4; SUFW 2

Silverstein, Alvin 1933- .... **CLC 17**
See also CA 49-52; CANR 2; CLR 25; JRDA; MAICYA 1, 2; SATA 8, 69, 124

Silverstein, Virginia B(arbara Opshelor)
1937- .... **CLC 17**
See also CA 49-52; CANR 2; CLR 25; JRDA; MAICYA 1, 2; SATA 8, 69, 124

Sim, Georges
See Simenon, Georges (Jacques Christian)

Simak, Clifford D(onald) 1904-1988
.... **CLC 1, 55**
See also CA 1-4R; 125; CANR 1, 35; DLB 8; MTCW 1; SATA-Obit 56; SFW 4

Simenon, Georges (Jacques Christian)
1903-1989 .... **CLC 1, 2, 3, 8, 18, 47**
See also BPFB 3; CA 85-88; 129; CANR 35; CMW 4; DA3; DAM POP; DLB 72; DLBY 1989; EW 12; EWL 3; GFL 1789 to the Present; MSW; MTCW 1, 2; RGWL 2, 3

Simic, Charles 1938- .. **CLC 6, 9, 22, 49, 68, 130**
See also AMWS 8; CA 29-32R; CAAS 4; CANR 12, 33, 52, 61, 96; CP 7; DA3; DAM POET; DLB 105; MTCW 2; PFS 7; RGAL 4; WP

Simmel, Georg 1858-1918 .... **TCLC 64**
See also CA 157

Simmons, Charles (Paul) 1924- .... **CLC 57**
See also CA 89-92; INT 89-92

Simmons, Dan 1948- .... **CLC 44**
See also AAYA 16; CA 138; CANR 53, 81; CPW; DAM POP; HGG; SUFW 2

Simmons, James (Stewart Alexander) 1933-
.... **CLC 43**
See also CA 105; CAAS 21; CP 7; DLB 40

Simms, William Gilmore 1806-1870
.... **NCLC 3**
See also DLB 3, 30, 59, 73, 248, 254; RGAL 4

Simon, Carly 1945- .... **CLC 26**
See also CA 105

Simon, Claude (Henri Eugene) 1913-1984
.... **CLC 4, 9, 15, 39**
See also CA 89-92; CANR 33, 117; DAM NOV; DLB 83; EW 13; EWL 3; GFL 1789 to the Present; MTCW 1

Simon, Myles
See Follett, Kenneth Martin)

Simon, (Marvin) Neil 1927- . **CLC 6, 11, 31, 39, 70; DC 14**
See also AAYA 32; AITN 1; AMWS 4; CA 21-24R; CANR 26, 54, 87; CD 5; DA3; DAM DRAM; DFS 2, 6, 12; DLB 7, 266; LAIT 4; MTCW 1, 2; RGAL 4; TUS

Simon, Paul (Frederick) 1941(?)- ... **CLC 17**
See also CA 116; 153

Simonon, Paul 1956(?)- .... **CLC 30**

Simonson, Rick ed. .... **CLC 70**

Simpson, Harriette
See Arnow, Harriette (Louisa) Simpson

Simpson, Louis (Aston Marantz) 1923-
.... CLC **4, 7, 9, 32, 149**
See also AMWS 9; CA 1-4R; CAAS 4;
CANR 1, 61; CP 7; DAM POET; DLB 5;
MTCW 1, 2; PFS 7, 11, 14; RGAL 4

Simpson, Mona (Elizabeth) 1957- .. CLC **44, 146**
See also CA 122; 135; CANR 68, 103; CN 7; EWL 3

Simpson, N(orman) F(rederick) 1919-
.... CLC **29**
See also CA 13-16R; CBD; DLB 13; RGEL 2

Sinclair, Andrew (Annandale) 1935-
.... CLC **2, 14**
See also CA 9-12R; CAAS 5; CANR 14, 38, 91; CN 7; DLB 14; FANT; MTCW 1

Sinclair, Emil
See Hesse, Hermann

Sinclair, Iain 1943- .... CLC **76**
See also CA 132; CANR 81; CP 7; HGG

Sinclair, Iain MacGregor
See Sinclair, Iain

Sinclair, Irene
See Griffith, D(avid Lewelyn) W(ark)

Sinclair, Mary Amelia St. Clair 1865(?)-1946
See Sinclair, May
See also CA 104; HGG; RHW

Sinclair, May .... TCLC **3, 11**
See Sinclair, Mary Amelia St. Clair
See also CA 166; DLB 36, 135; EWL 3; RGEL 2; SUFW

Sinclair, Roy
See Griffith, D(avid Lewelyn) W(ark)

Sinclair, Upton (Beall) 1878-1968 .... CLC **1, 11, 15, 63**; WLC
See also AMWS 5; BPFB 3; BYA 2; CA 5-8R; 25-28R; CANR 7; CDALB 1929-1941; DA; DA3; DAB; DAC; DAM MST, NOV; DLB 9; EWL 3; INT CANR-7; LAIT 3; MTCW 1, 2; NFS 6; RGAL 4; SATA 9; TUS; YAW

Singe, (Edmund) J(ohn) M(illington) 1871-1909 .... WLC

Singer, Isaac
See Singer, Isaac Bashevis

Singer, Isaac Bashevis 1904-1991 ..... CLC **1, 3, 6, 9, 11, 15, 23, 38, 69, 111**; SSC **3, 53**; WLC
See also AAYA 32; AITN 1, 2; AMW; AMWR 2; BPFB 3; BYA 1, 4; CA 1-4R; 134; CANR 1, 39, 106; CDALB 1941-1968; CLR 1; CWRI 5; DA; DA3; DAB; DAC; DAM MST, NOV; DLB 6, 28, 52, 278; DLBY 1991; EWL 3; EXPS; HGG; JRDA; LAIT 3; MAICYA 1, 2; MTCW 1, 2; RGAL 4; RGSF 2; SATA 3, 27; SATA-Obit 68; SSFS 2, 12, 16; TUS; TWA

Singer, Israel Joshua 1893-1944 ... TCLC **33**
See also CA 169; EWL 3

Singh, Khushwant 1915- .... CLC **11**
See also CA 9-12R; CAAS 9; CANR 6, 84; CN 7; EWL 3; RGEL 2

Singleton, Ann
See Benedict, Ruth (Fulton)

Singleton, John 1968(?)- .... CLC **156**
See also BW 2, 3; CA 138; CANR 67, 82; DAM MULT

Sinjohn, John
See Galsworthy, John

Sinyavsky, Andrei (Donatevich) 1925-1997
.... CLC **8**
See Sinyavsky, Andrey Donatovich; Tertz, Abram
See also CA 85-88; 159

Sirin, V.
See Nabokov, Vladimir (Vladimirovich)

Sissman, L(ouis) E(dward) 1928-1976
.... CLC **9, 18**
See also CA 21-24R; 65-68; CANR 13; DLB 5

Sisson, C(harles) H(ubert) 1914- ...... CLC **8**
See also CA 1-4R; CAAS 3; CANR 3, 48, 84; CP 7; DLB 27

Sitting Bull 1831(?)-1890 .... NNAL
See also DA3; DAM MULT

Sitwell, Dame Edith 1887-1964 .... CLC **2, 9, 67**; PC **3**
See also BRW 7; CA 9-12R; CANR 35; CDBLB 1945-1960; DAM POET; DLB 20; EWL 3; MTCW 1, 2; RGEL 2; TEA

Siwaarmill, H. P.
See Sharp, William

Sjoewall, Maj 1935- .... CLC **7**
See Sjowall, Maj
See also CA 65-68; CANR 73

Sjowall, Maj
See Sjoewall, Maj
See also BPFB 3; CMW 4; MSW

Skelton, John 1460(?)-1529 ... LC **71**; PC **25**
See also BRW 1; DLB 136; RGEL 2

Skelton, Robin 1925-1997 .... CLC **13**
See Zuk, Georges
See also AITN 2; CA 5-8R; 160; CAAS 5; CANR 28, 89; CCA 1; CP 7; DLB 27, 53

Skolimowski, Jerzy 1938- .... CLC **20**
See also CA 128

Skram, Amalie (Bertha) 1847-1905
.... TCLC **25**
See also CA 165

Skvorecky, Josef (Vaclav) 1924- ..... CLC **15, 39, 69, 152**
See also CA 61-64; CAAS 1; CANR 10, 34, 63, 108; CDWLB 4; DA3; DAC; DAM NOV; DLB 232; EWL 3; MTCW 1, 2

Slade, Bernard .... CLC **11, 46**
See Newbound, Bernard Slade
See also CAAS 9; CCA 1; DLB 53

Slaughter, Carolyn 1946- .... CLC **56**
See also CA 85-88; CANR 85; CN 7

Slaughter, Frank G(ill) 1908-2001 .. CLC **29**
See also AITN 2; CA 5-8R; 197; CANR 5, 85; INT CANR-5; RHW

Slavitt, David R(ytman) 1935- .... CLC **5, 14**
See also CA 21-24R; CAAS 3; CANR 41, 83; CP 7; DLB 5, 6

Slesinger, Tess 1905-1945 .... TCLC **10**
See also CA 107; 199; DLB 102

Slessor, Kenneth 1901-1971 .... CLC **14**
See also CA 102; 89-92; DLB 260; RGEL 2

Slowacki, Juliusz 1809-1849 .... NCLC **15**
See also RGWL 3

Smart, Christopher 1722-1771 ..... LC **3**; PC **13**
See also DAM POET; DLB 109; RGEL 2

Smart, Elizabeth 1913-1986 .... CLC **54**
See also CA 81-84; 118; DLB 88

Smiley, Jane (Graves) 1949- ..... CLC **53, 76, 144**
See also AMWS 6; BPFB 3; CA 104; CANR 30, 50, 74, 96; CN 7; CPW 1; DA3; DAM POP; DLB 227, 234; EWL 3; INT CANR-30

Smith, A(rthur) J(ames) M(arshall) 1902-1980 .... CLC **15**
See also CA 1-4R; 102; CANR 4; DAC; DLB 88; RGEL 2

Smith, Adam 1723(?)-1790 .... LC **36**
See also DLB 104, 252; RGEL 2

Smith, Alexander 1829-1867 .... NCLC **59**
See also DLB 32, 55

Smith, Anna Deavere 1950- .... CLC **86**
See also CA 133; CANR 103; CD 5; DFS 2

Smith, Betty (Wehner) 1904-1972 ... CLC **19**
See also BPFB 3; BYA 3; CA 5-8R; 33-36R; DLBY 1982; LAIT 3; RGAL 4; SATA 6

Smith, Charlotte (Turner) 1749-1806
.... NCLC **23, 115**
See also DLB 39, 109; RGEL 2; TEA

Smith, Clark Ashton 1893-1961 .... CLC **43**
See also CA 143; CANR 81; FANT; HGG; MTCW 2; SCFW 2; SFW 4; SUFW

Smith, Dave .... CLC **22, 42**
See Smith, David (Jeddie)
See also CAAS 7; DLB 5

Smith, David (Jeddie) 1942-
See Smith, Dave
See also CA 49-52; CANR 1, 59; CP 7; CSW; DAM POET

Smith, Florence Margaret 1902-1971
See Smith, Stevie
See also CA 17-18; 29-32R; CANR 35; CAP 2; DAM POET; MTCW 1, 2; TEA

Smith, Iain Crichton 1928-1998 .... CLC **64**
See also CA 21-24R; 171; CN 7; CP 7; DLB 40, 139; RGSF 2

Smith, John 1580(?)-1631 .... LC **9**
See also DLB 24, 30; TUS

Smith, Johnston
See Crane, Stephen (Townley)

Smith, Joseph, Jr. 1805-1844 .... NCLC **53**

Smith, Lee 1944- .... CLC **25, 73**
See also CA 114; 119; CANR 46; CSW; DLB 143; DLBY 1983; EWL 3; INT CA-119; RGAL 4

Smith, Martin
See Smith, Martin Cruz

Smith, Martin Cruz 1942- . CLC **25**; NNAL
See also BEST 89:4; BPFB 3; CA 85-88; CANR 6, 23, 43, 65; CMW 4; CPW; DAM MULT, POP; HGG; INT CANR-23; MTCW 2; RGAL 4

Smith, Patti 1946- .... CLC **12**
See also CA 93-96; CANR 63

Smith, Pauline (Urmson) 1882-1959
.... TCLC **25**
See also DLB 225; EWL 3

Smith, Rosamond
See Oates, Joyce Carol

Smith, Sheila Kaye
See Kaye-Smith, Sheila

Smith, Stevie .... CLC **3, 8, 25, 44**; PC **12**
See Smith, Florence Margaret
See also BRWS 2; DLB 20; EWL 3; MTCW 2; PAB; PFS 3; RGEL 2

Smith, Wilbur (Addison) 1933- .... CLC **33**
See also CA 13-16R; CANR 7, 46, 66; CPW; MTCW 1, 2

Smith, William Jay 1918- .... CLC **6**
See also CA 5-8R; CANR 44, 106; CP 7; CSW; CWRI 5; DLB 5; MAICYA 1, 2; SAAS 22; SATA 2, 68

Smith, Woodrow Wilson
See Kuttner, Henry

Smith, Zadie 1976- .... CLC **158**
See also CA 193

Smolenskin, Peretz 1842-1885 .... NCLC **30**

Smollett, Tobias (George) 1721-1771 .. LC **2, 46**
See also BRW 3; CDBLB 1660-1789; DLB 39, 104; RGEL 2; TEA

Snodgrass, W(illiam) D(e Witt) 1926-
.... CLC **2, 6, 10, 18, 68**
See also AMWS 6; CA 1-4R; CANR 6, 36, 65, 85; CP 7; DAM POET; DLB 5; MTCW 1, 2; RGAL 4

Snorri Sturluson 1179-1241 .... CMLC **56**
See also RGWL 2, 3

Snow, C(harles) P(ercy) 1905-1980 .. **CLC 1, 4, 6, 9, 13, 19**
See also BRW 7; CA 5-8R; 101; CANR 28; CDBLB 1945-1960; DAM NOV; DLB 15, 77; DLBD 17; EWL 3; MTCW 1, 2; RGEL 2; TEA

Snow, Frances Compton
See Adams, Henry (Brooks)

Snyder, Gary (Sherman) 1930- .... **CLC 1, 2, 5, 9, 32, 120; PC 21**
See also AMWS 8; ANW; BG 3; CA 17-20R; CANR 30, 60; CP 7; DA3; DAM POET; DLB 5, 16, 165, 212, 237, 275; EWL 3; MTCW 2; PFS 9; RGAL 4; WP

Snyder, Zilpha Keatley 1927- .... **CLC 17**
See also AAYA 15; BYA 1; CA 9-12R; CANR 38; CLR 31; JRDA; MAICYA 1, 2; SAAS 1, 28, 75, 110; SATA-Essay 112; YAW

Soares, Bernardo
See Pessoa, Fernando (Antonio Nogueira)

Sobh, A.
See Shamlu, Ahmad

Sobol, Joshua 1939- .... **CLC 60**
See Sobol, Yehoshua
See also CA 200; CWW 2

Sobol, Yehoshua 1939-
See Sobol, Joshua
See also CWW 2

Socrates 470B.C.-399B.C. .... **CMLC 27**

Soderberg, Hjalmar 1869-1941 .... **TCLC 39**
See also DLB 259; EWL 3; RGSF 2

Soderbergh, Steven 1963- .... **CLC 154**
See also AAYA 43

Sodergran, Edith (Irene) 1892-1923
See Soedergran, Edith (Irene)
See also CA 202; DLB 259; EW 11; EWL 3; RGWL 2, 3

Soedergran, Edith (Irene) 1892-1923
.... **TCLC 31**
See Sodergran, Edith (Irene)

Softly, Edgar
See Lovecraft, H(oward) P(hillips)

Softly, Edward
See Lovecraft, H(oward) P(hillips)

Sokolov, Alexander V(sevolodovich) 1943-
See Sokolov, Sasha
See also CA 73-76

Sokolov, Raymond 1941- .... **CLC 7**
See also CA 85-88

Sokolov, Sasha .... **CLC 59**
See Sokolov, Alexander V(sevolodovich)
See also CWW 2; EWL 3; RGWL 2, 3

Sokolov, Sasha .... **CLC 59**

Solo, Jay
See Ellison, Harlan (Jay)

Sologub, Fyodor .... **TCLC 9**
See Teternikov, Fyodor Kuzmich
See also EWL 3

Solomons, Ikey Esquir
See Thackeray, William Makepeace

Solomos, Dionysios 1798-1857 ...... **NCLC 15**

Solwoska, Mara
See French, Marilyn

Solzhenitsyn, Aleksandr I(sayevich) 1918-
..... **CLC 1, 2, 4, 7, 9, 10, 18, 26, 34, 78, 134; SSC 32; WLC**
See Solzhenitsyn, Aleksandr Isaevich
See also AAYA 49; AITN 1; BPFB 3; CA 69-72; CANR 40, 65, 116; DA; DA3; DAB; DAC; DAM MST, NOV; EW 13; EXPS; LAIT 4; MTCW 1, 2; NFS 6; RGSF 2; RGWL 2, 3; SSFS 9; TWA

Somers, Jane
See Lessing, Doris (May)

Somerville, Edith Oenone 1858-1949
.... **SSC 56; TCLC 51**
See also CA 196; DLB 135; RGEL 2; RGSF 2

Somerville & Ross
See Martin, Violet Florence; Somerville, Edith Oenone

Sommer, Scott 1951- .... **CLC 25**
See also CA 106

Sondheim, Stephen (Joshua) 1930-
.... **CLC 30, 39, 147**
See also AAYA 11; CA 103; CANR 47, 67; DAM DRAM; LAIT 4

Sone, Monica 1919- .... **AAL**

Song, Cathy 1955- .... **AAL; PC 21**
See also CA 154; CWP; DLB 169; EXPP; FW; PFS 5

Sontag, Susan 1933- ... **CLC 1, 2, 10, 13, 31, 105**
See also AMWS 3; CA 17-20R; CANR 25, 51, 74, 97; CN 7; CPW; DA3; DAM POP; DLB 2, 67; EWL 3; MAWW; MTCW 1, 2; RGAL 4; RHW; SSFS 10

Sophocles 496(?)B.C.-406(?)B.C. ... **CMLC 2, 47, 51; DC 1; WLCS**
See also AW 1; CDWLB 1; DA; DA3; DAB; DAC; DAM DRAM, MST; DFS 1, 4, 8; DLB 176; LAIT 1; LMFS 1; RGWL 2, 3; TWA

Sordello 1189-1269 .... **CMLC 15**

Sorel, Georges 1847-1922 .... **TCLC 91**
See also CA 118; 188

Sorel, Julia
See Drexler, Rosalyn

Sorokin, Vladimir .... **CLC 59**

Sorrentino, Gilbert 1929- . **CLC 3, 7, 14, 22, 40**
See also CA 77-80; CANR 14, 33, 115; CN 7; CP 7; DLB 5, 173; DLBY 1980; INT CANR-14

Soseki
See Natsume, Soseki
See also MJW

Soto, Gary 1952- .. **CLC 32, 80; HLC 2; PC 28**
See also AAYA 10, 37; BYA 11; CA 119; 125; CANR 50, 74, 107; CLR 38; CP 7; DAM MULT; DLB 82; EWL 3; EXPP; HW 1, 2; INT CA-125; JRDA; MAICYA 2; MAICYAS 1; MTCW 2; PFS 7; RGAL 4; SATA 80, 120; WYA; YAW

Soupault, Philippe 1897-1990 .... **CLC 68**
See also CA 116; 147; 131; EWL 3; GFL 1789 to the Present; LMFS 2

Souster, (Holmes) Raymond 1921- .. **CLC 5, 14**
See also CA 13-16R; CAAS 14; CANR 13, 29, 53; CP 7; DA3; DAC; DAM POET; DLB 88; RGEL 2; SATA 63

Southern, Terry 1924(?)-1995 .... **CLC 7**
See also AMWS 11; BPFB 3; CA 1-4R; 150; CANR 1, 55, 107; CN 7; DLB 2; IDFW 3, 4

Southey, Robert 1774-1843 .... **NCLC 8, 97**
See also BRW 4; DLB 93, 107, 142; RGEL 2; SATA 54

Southworth, Emma Dorothy Eliza Nevitte 1819-1899 .... **NCLC 26**
See also DLB 239

Souza, Ernest
See Scott, Evelyn

Soyinka, Wole 1934- . **BLC 3; CLC 3, 5, 14, 36, 44; DC 2; WLC**
See also AFW; BW 2, 3; CA 13-16R; CANR 27, 39, 82; CD 5; CDWLB 3; CN 7; CP 7; DA; DA3; DAB; DAC; DAM DRAM, MST, MULT; DFS 10; DLB 125; EWL 3; MTCW 1, 2; RGEL 2; TWA; WLIT 2

Spackman, W(illiam) M(ode) 1905-1990
.... **CLC 46**
See also CA 81-84; 132

Spacks, Barry (Bernard) 1931- .... **CLC 14**
See also CA 154; CANR 33, 109; CP 7; DLB 105

Spanidou, Irini 1946- .... **CLC 44**
See also CA 185

Spark, Muriel (Sarah) 1918- ... **CLC 2, 3, 5, 8, 13, 18, 40, 94; SSC 10**
See also BRWS 1; CA 5-8R; CANR 12, 36, 76, 89; CDBLB 1945-1960; CN 7; CP 7; DA3; DAB; DAC; DAM MST, NOV; DLB 15, 139; EWL 3; FW; INT CANR-12; LAIT 4; MTCW 1, 2; RGEL 2; TEA; WLIT 4; YAW

Spaulding, Douglas
See Bradbury, Ray (Douglas)

Spaulding, Leonard
See Bradbury, Ray (Douglas)

Spelman, Elizabeth .... **CLC 65**

Spence, J. A. D.
See Eliot, T(homas) S(tearns)

Spencer, Anne 1882-1975 .... **HR 3**
See also BW 2; CA 161; DLB 51, 54

Spencer, Elizabeth 1921- .. **CLC 22; SSC 57**
See also CA 13-16R; CANR 32, 65, 87; CN 7; CSW; DLB 6, 218; EWL 3; MTCW 1; RGAL 4; SATA 14

Spencer, Leonard G.
See Silverberg, Robert

Spencer, Scott 1945- .... **CLC 30**
See also CA 113; CANR 51; DLBY 1986

Spender, Stephen (Harold) 1909-1995
.... **CLC 1, 2, 5, 10, 41, 91**
See also BRWS 2; CA 9-12R; 149; CANR 31, 54; CDBLB 1945-1960; CP 7; DA3; DAM POET; DLB 20; EWL 3; MTCW 1, 2; PAB; RGEL 2; TEA

Spengler, Oswald (Arnold Gottfried) 1880-1936 .... **TCLC 25**
See also CA 118; 189

Spenser, Edmund 1552(?)-1599 .... **LC 5, 39; PC 8, 42; WLC**
See also BRW 1; CDBLB Before 1660; DA; DA3; DAB; DAC; DAM MST, POET; DLB 167; EFS 2; EXPP; PAB; RGEL 2; TEA; WLIT 3; WP

Spicer, Jack 1925-1965 .... **CLC 8, 18, 72**
See also BG 3; CA 85-88; DAM POET; DLB 5, 16, 193; GLL 1; WP

Spiegelman, Art 1948- .... **CLC 76**
See also AAYA 10, 46; CA 125; CANR 41, 55, 74; MTCW 2; SATA 109; YAW

Spielberg, Peter 1929- .... **CLC 6**
See also CA 5-8R; CANR 4, 48; DLBY 1981

Spielberg, Steven 1947- .... **CLC 20**
See also AAYA 8, 24; CA 77-80; CANR 32; SATA 32

Spillane, Frank Morrison 1918-
See Spillane, Mickey
See also CA 25-28R; CANR 28, 63; DA3; MTCW 1, 2; SATA 66

Spillane, Mickey .... **CLC 3, 13**
See Spillane, Frank Morrison
See also BPFB 3; CMW 4; DLB 226; MSW; MTCW 2

Spinoza, Benedictus de 1632-1677 .... **LC 9, 58**

Spinrad, Norman (Richard) 1940- .. **CLC 46**
See also BPFB 3; CA 37-40R; CAAS 19; CANR 20, 91; DLB 8; INT CANR-20; SFW 4

Spitteler, Carl (Friedrich Georg) 1845-1924
.... **TCLC 12**
See also CA 109; DLB 129; EWL 3

Spivack, Kathleen (Romola Drucker) 1938-
.... **CLC 6**
See also CA 49-52

Spoto, Donald 1941- .... **CLC 39**
See also CA 65-68; CANR 11, 57, 93**

Springsteen, Bruce (F.) 1949- .... **CLC 17**
See also CA 111

Spurling, Hilary 1940- .... **CLC 34**
See also CA 104; CANR 25, 52, 94

Spyker, John Howland
See Elman, Richard (Martin)

Squires, (James) Radcliffe 1917-1993
.... **CLC 51**
See also CA 1-4R; 140; CANR 6, 21

Srivastava, Dhanpat Rai 1880(?)-1936
See Premchand
See also CA 118; 197

Stacy, Donald
See Pohl, Frederik

Stael
See Stael-Holstein, Anne Louise Germaine Necker
See also EW 5; RGWL 2, 3

Stael, Germaine de
See Stael-Holstein, Anne Louise Germaine Necker
See also DLB 119, 192; FW; GFL 1789 to the Present; TWA

Stael-Holstein, Anne Louise Germaine Necker 1766-1817 .... **NCLC 3, 91**
See Stael; Stael, Germaine de

Stafford, Jean 1915-1979 . **CLC 4, 7, 19, 68; SSC 26**
See also CA 1-4R; 85-88; CANR 3, 65; DLB 2, 173; MTCW 1, 2; RGAL 4; RGSF 2; SATA-Obit 22; TCWW 2; TUS

Stafford, William (Edgar) 1914-1993
.... **CLC 4, 7, 29**
See also AMWS 11; CA 5-8R; 142; CAAS 3; CANR 5, 22; DAM POET; DLB 5, 206; EXPP; INT CANR-22; PFS 2, 8, 16; RGAL 4; WP

Stagnelius, Eric Johan 1793-1823
.... **NCLC 61**

Staines, Trevor
See Brunner, John (Kilian Houston)

Stairs, Gordon
See Austin, Mary (Hunter)
See also TCWW 2

Stalin, Joseph 1879-1953 .... **TCLC 92**

Stampa, Gaspara c. 1524-1554 .... **PC 43**
See also RGWL 2, 3

Stampflinger, K. A.
See Benjamin, Walter

Stancykowna
See Szymborska, Wislawa

Standing Bear, Luther 1868(?)-1939(?)
.... **NNAL**
See also CA 113; 144; DAM MULT

Stannard, Martin 1947- .... **CLC 44**
See also CA 142; DLB 155

Stanton, Elizabeth Cady 1815-1902
.... **TCLC 73**
See also CA 171; DLB 79; FW

Stanton, Maura 1946- .... **CLC 9**
See also CA 89-92; CANR 15; DLB 120

Stanton, Schuyler
See Baum, L(yman) Frank

Stapledon, (William) Olaf 1886-1950
.... **TCLC 22**
See also CA 111; 162; DLB 15, 255; SFW 4

Starbuck, George (Edwin) 1931-1996
.... **CLC 53**
See also CA 21-24R; 153; CANR 23; DAM POET

Stark, Richard
See Westlake, Donald E(dwin)

Staunton, Schuyler
See Baum, L(yman) Frank

Stead, Christina (Ellen) 1902-1983 .. **CLC 2, 5, 8, 32, 80**
See also BRWS 4; CA 13-16R; 109; CANR 33, 40; DLB 260; EWL 3; FW; MTCW 1, 2; RGEL 2; RGSF 2

Stead, William Thomas 1849-1912
.... **TCLC 48**
See also CA 167

Stebnitsky, M.
See Leskov, Nikolai (Semyonovich)

Steele, Sir Richard 1672-1729 .... **LC 18**
See also BRW 3; CDBLB 1660-1789; DLB 84, 101; RGEL 2; WLIT 3

Steele, Timothy (Reid) 1948- .... **CLC 45**
See also CA 93-96; CANR 16, 50, 92; CP 7; DLB 120, 282

Steffens, (Joseph) Lincoln 1866-1936
.... **TCLC 20**
See also CA 117; 198

Stegner, Wallace (Earle) 1909-1993 . **CLC 9, 49, 81; SSC 27**
See also AITN 1; AMWS 4; ANW; BEST 90:3; BPFB 3; CA 1-4R; 141; CAAS 9; CANR 1, 21, 46; DAM NOV; DLB 9, 206, 275; DLBY 1993; EWL 3; MTCW 1, 2; RGAL 4; TCWW 2; TUS

Stein, Gertrude 1874-1946 ...... **DC 19; PC 18; SSC 42; TCLC 1, 6, 28, 48; WLC**
See also AMW; CA 104; 132; CANR 108; CDALB 1917-1929; DA; DA3; DAB; DAC; DAM MST, NOV, POET; DLB 4, 54, 86, 228; DLBD 15; EWL 3; EXPS; GLL 1; MAWW; MTCW 1, 2; NCFS 4; RGAL 4; RGSF 2; SSFS 5; TUS; WP

Steinbeck, John (Ernst) 1902-1968 .. **CLC 1, 5, 9, 13, 21, 34, 45, 75, 124; SSC 11, 37; TCLC 135; WLC**
See also AAYA 12; AMW; BPFB 3; BYA 2, 3, 13; CA 1-4R; 25-28R; CANR 1, 35; CDALB 1929-1941; DA; DA3; DAB; DAC; DAM DRAM, MST, NOV; DLB 7, 9, 212, 275; DLBD 2; EWL 3; EXPS; LAIT 3; MTCW 1, 2; NFS 17; RGAL 4; RGSF 2; RHW; SATA 9; SSFS 3, 6; TCWW 2; TUS; WYA; YAW

Steinem, Gloria 1934- .... **CLC 63**
See also CA 53-56; CANR 28, 51; DLB 246; FW; MTCW 1, 2

Steiner, George 1929- .... **CLC 24**
See also CA 73-76; CANR 31, 67, 108; DAM NOV; DLB 67; EWL 3; MTCW 1, 2; SATA 62

Steiner, K. Leslie
See Delany, Samuel R(ay), Jr.

Steiner, Rudolf 1861-1925 .... **TCLC 13**
See also CA 107

Stendhal 1783-1842 . **NCLC 23, 46; SSC 27; WLC**
See also DA; DA3; DAB; DAC; DAM MST, NOV; DLB 119; EW 5; GFL 1789 to the Present; RGWL 2, 3; TWA

Stephen, Adeline Virginia
See Woolf, (Adeline) Virginia

Stephen, Sir Leslie 1832-1904 .... **TCLC 23**
See also BRW 5; CA 123; DLB 57, 144, 190

Stephen, Sir Leslie
See Stephen, Sir Leslie

Stephen, Virginia
See Woolf, (Adeline) Virginia

Stephens, James 1882(?)-1950 .... **SSC 50; TCLC 4**
See also CA 104; 192; DLB 19, 153, 162; EWL 3; FANT; RGEL 2; SUFW

Stephens, Reed
See Donaldson, Stephen R(eeder)

Steptoe, Lydia
See Barnes, Djuna
See also GLL 1

Sterchi, Beat 1949- .... **CLC 65**
See also CA 203

Sterling, Brett
See Bradbury, Ray (Douglas); Hamilton, Edmond

Sterling, Bruce 1954- .... **CLC 72**
See also CA 119; CANR 44; SCFW 2; SFW 4

Sterling, George 1869-1926 .... **TCLC 20**
See also CA 117; 165; DLB 54

Stern, Gerald 1925- .... **CLC 40, 100**
See also AMWS 9; CA 81-84; CANR 28, 94; CP 7; DLB 105; RGAL 4

Stern, Richard (Gustave) 1928- .. **CLC 4, 39**
See also CA 1-4R; CANR 1, 25, 52; CN 7; DLB 218; DLBY 1987; INT CANR-25

Sternberg, Josef von 1894-1969 ...... **CLC 20**
See also CA 81-84

Sterne, Laurence 1713-1768 .... **LC 2, 48; WLC**
See also BRW 3; BRWC 1; CDBLB 1660-1789; DA; DAB; DAC; DAM MST, NOV; DLB 39; RGEL 2; TEA

Sternheim, (William Adolf) Carl 1878-1942
.... **TCLC 8**
See also CA 105; 193; DLB 56, 118; EWL 3; RGWL 2, 3

Stevens, Mark 1951- .... **CLC 34**
See also CA 122

Stevens, Wallace 1879-1955 .... **PC 6; TCLC 3, 12, 45; WLC**
See also AMW; AMWR 1; CA 104; 124; CDALB 1929-1941; DA; DA3; DAB; DAC; DAM MST, POET; DLB 54; EWL 3; EXPP; MTCW 1, 2; PAB; PFS 13, 16; RGAL 4; TUS; WP

Stevenson, Anne (Katharine) 1933- . **CLC 7, 33**
See also BRWS 6; CA 17-20R; CAAS 9; CANR 9, 33; CP 7; CWP; DLB 40; MTCW 1; RHW

Stevenson, Robert Louis (Balfour) 1850-1894 .... **NCLC 5, 14, 63; SSC 11, 51; WLC**
See also AAYA 24; BPFB 3; BRW 5; BRWC 1; BRWR 1; BYA 1, 2, 4, 13; CDBLB 1890-1914; CLR 10, 11; DA; DA3; DAB; DAC; DAM MST, NOV; DLB 18, 57, 141, 156, 174; DLBD 13; HGG; JRDA; LAIT 1, 3; MAICYA 1, 2; NFS 11; RGEL 2; RGSF 2; SATA 100; SUFW; TEA; WCH; WLIT 4; WYA; YABC 2; YAW

Stewart, J(ohn) I(nnes) M(ackintosh) 1906-1994 .... **CLC 7, 14, 32**
See Innes, Michael
See also CA 85-88; 147; CAAS 3; CANR 47; CMW 4; MTCW 1, 2

Stewart, Mary (Florence Elinor) 1916-
.... **CLC 7, 35, 117**
See also AAYA 29; BPFB 3; CA 1-4R; CANR 1, 59; CMW 4; CPW; DAB; FANT; RHW; SATA 12; YAW

Stewart, Mary Rainbow
See Stewart, Mary (Florence Elinor)

Stifle, June
See Campbell, Maria

Stifter, Adalbert 1805-1868 . **NCLC 41; SSC 28**
See also CDWLB 2; DLB 133; RGSF 2; RGWL 2, 3

Still, James 1906-2001 .... **CLC 49**
See also CA 65-68; 195; CAAS 17; CANR 10, 26; CSW; DLB 9; DLBY 01; SATA 29; SATA-Obit 127

Sting 1951-
See Sumner, Gordon Matthew
See also CA 167

Stirling, Arthur
See Sinclair, Upton (Beall)

Stitt, Milan 1941- .... **CLC 29**
See also CA 69-72

Stockton, Francis Richard 1834-1902
See Stockton, Frank R.
See also CA 108; 137; MAICYA 1, 2; SATA 44; SFW 4

Stockton, Frank R. .... **TCLC 47**
See Stockton, Francis Richard
See also BYA 4, 13; DLB 42, 74; DLBD 13; EXPS; SATA-Brief 32; SSFS 3; SUFW; WCH

Stoddard, Charles
See Kuttner, Henry

Stoker, Abraham 1847-1912
See Stoker, Bram
See also CA 105; 150; DA; DA3; DAC; DAM MST, NOV; HGG; SATA 29

Stoker, Bram .... **TCLC 8; WLC**
See Stoker, Abraham
See also AAYA 23; BPFB 3; BRWS 3; BYA 5; CDBLB 1890-1914; DAB; DLB 36, 70, 178; RGEL 2; SUFW; TEA; WLIT 4

Stolz, Mary (Slattery) 1920- .... **CLC 12**
See also AAYA 8; AITN 1; CA 5-8R; CANR 13, 41, 112; JRDA; MAICYA 1, 2; SAAS 3; SATA 10, 71, 133; YAW

Stone, Irving 1903-1989 .... **CLC 7**
See also AITN 1; BPFB 3; CA 1-4R; 129; CAAS 3; CANR 1, 23; CPW; DA3; DAM POP; INT CANR-23; MTCW 1, 2; RHW; SATA 3; SATA-Obit 64

Stone, Oliver (William) 1946- .... **CLC 73**
See also AAYA 15; CA 110; CANR 55

Stone, Robert (Anthony) 1937- .. **CLC 5, 23, 42**
See also AMWS 5; BPFB 3; CA 85-88; CANR 23, 66, 95; CN 7; DLB 152; EWL 3; INT CANR-23; MTCW 1

Stone, Zachary
See Follett, Ken(neth Martin)

Stoppard, Tom 1937- . **CLC 1, 3, 4, 5, 8, 15, 29, 34, 63, 91; DC 6; WLC**
See also BRWC 1; BRWR 2; BRWS 1; CA 81-84; CANR 39, 67; CBD; CD 5; CDBLB 1960 to Present; DA; DA3; DAB; DAC; DAM DRAM, MST; DFS 2, 5, 8, 11, 13, 16; DLB 13, 233; DLBY 1985; EWL 3; MTCW 1, 2; RGEL 2; TEA; WLIT 4

Storey, David (Malcolm) 1933- .... **CLC 2, 4, 5, 8**
See also BRWS 1; CA 81-84; CANR 36; CBD; CD 5; CN 7; DAM DRAM; DLB 13, 14, 207, 245; EWL 3; MTCW 1; RGEL 2

Storm, Hyemeyohsts 1935- .. **CLC 3; NNAL**
See also CA 81-84; CANR 45; DAM MULT

Storm, (Hans) Theodor (Woldsen) 1817-1888
.... **NCLC 1; SSC 27**
See also CDWLB 2; DLB 129; EW; RGSF 2; RGWL 2, 3

Storni, Alfonsina 1892-1938 ...... **HLC 2; PC 33; TCLC 5**
See also CA 104; 131; DAM MULT; HW 1; LAW

Stoughton, William 1631-1701 .... **LC 38**
See also DLB 24

Stout, Rex (Todhunter) 1886-1975 .... **CLC 3**
See also AITN 2; BPFB 3; CA 61-64; CANR 71; CMW 4; MSW; RGAL 4

Stow, (Julian) Randolph 1935- . **CLC 23, 48**
See also CA 13-16R; CANR 33; CN 7; DLB 260; MTCW 1; RGEL 2

Stowe, Harriet (Elizabeth) Beecher 1811-1896 .... **NCLC 3, 50; WLC**
See also AMWS 1; CDALB 1865-1917; DA; DA3; DAB; DAC; DAM MST, NOV; DLB 1, 12, 42, 74, 189, 239, 243; EXPN; JRDA; LAIT 2; MAICYA 1, 2; NFS 6; RGAL 4; TUS; YABC 1

Strabo c. 64B.C.-c. 25 .... **CMLC 37**
See also DLB 176

Strachey, (Giles) Lytton 1880-1932
.... **TCLC 12**
See also BRWS 2; CA 110; 178; DLB 149; DLBD 10; EWL 3; MTCW 2; NCFS 4

Strand, Mark 1934- .... **CLC 6, 18, 41, 71**
See also AMWS 4; CA 21-24R; CANR 40, 65, 100; CP 7; DAM POET; DLB 5; EWL 3; PAB; PFS 9; RGAL 4; SATA 41

Stratton-Porter, Gene(va Grace) 1863-1924
See Porter, Gene(va Grace) Stratton
See also ANW; CA 137; CLR 87; DLB 221; DLBD 14; MAICYA 1, 2; SATA 15

Straub, Peter (Francis) 1943- . **CLC 28, 107**
See also BEST 89:1; BPFB 3; CA 85-88; CANR 28, 65, 109; CPW; DAM POP; DLBY 1984; HGG; MTCW 1, 2; SUFW 2

Strauss, Botho 1944- .... **CLC 22**
See also CA 157; CWW 2; DLB 124

Streatfeild, (Mary) Noel 1897(?)-1986
.... **CLC 21**
See also CA 81-84; 120; CANR 31; CLR 17, 83; CWRI 5; DLB 160; MAICYA 1, 2; SATA 20; SATA-Obit 48

Stribling, T(homas) S(igismund) 1881-1965
.... **CLC 23**
See also CA 189; 107; CMW 4; DLB 9; RGAL 4

Strindberg, (Johan) August 1849-1912
.... **DC 18; TCLC 1, 8, 21, 47; WLC**
See also CA 104; 135; DA; DA3; DAB; DAC; DAM DRAM, MST; DFS 4, 9; DLB 259; EW 7; EWL 3; IDTP; LMFS 2; MTCW 2; RGWL 2, 3; TWA

Stringer, Arthur 1874-1950 .... **TCLC 37**
See also CA 161; DLB 92

Stringer, David
See Roberts, Keith (John Kingston)

Stroheim, Erich von 1885-1957 .... **TCLC 71**

Strugatskii, Arkadii (Natanovich) 1925-1991
.... **CLC 27**
See also CA 106; 135; SFW 4

Strugatskii, Boris (Natanovich) 1933-
.... **CLC 27**
See also CA 106; SFW 4

Strummer, Joe 1953(?)- .... **CLC 30**

Strunk, William, Jr. 1869-1946 .... **TCLC 92**
See also CA 118; 164

Stryk, Lucien 1924- .... **PC 27**
See also CA 13-16R; CANR 10, 28, 55, 110; CP 7

Stuart, Don A.
See Campbell, John W(ood, Jr.)

Stuart, Ian
See MacLean, Alistair (Stuart)

Stuart, Jesse (Hilton) 1906-1984 .. **CLC 1, 8, 11, 14, 34; SSC 31**
See also CA 5-8R; 112; CANR 31; DLB 9, 48, 102; DLBY 1984; SATA 2; SATA-Obit 36

Stubblefield, Sally
See Trumbo, Dalton

Sturgeon, Theodore (Hamilton) 1918-1985
.... **CLC 22, 39**
See Queen, Ellery
See also BPFB 3; BYA 9, 10; CA 81-84; 116; CANR 32, 103; DLB 8; DLBY 1985; HGG; MTCW 1, 2; SCFW; SFW 4; SUFW

Sturges, Preston 1898-1959 .... **TCLC 48**
See also CA 114; 149; DLB 26

Styron, William 1925- .. **CLC 1, 3, 5, 11, 15, 60; SSC 25**
See also AMW; BEST 90:4; BPFB 3; CA 5-8R; CANR 6, 33, 74; CDALB 1968-1988; CN 7; CPW; CSW; DA3; DAM NOV, POP; DLB 2, 143; DLBY 1980; EWL 3; INT CANR-6; LAIT 2; MTCW 1, 2; NCFS 1; RGAL 4; RHW; TUS

Su, Chien 1884-1918
See Su Man-shu
See also CA 123

Suarez Lynch, B.
See Bioy Casares, Adolfo; Borges, Jorge Luis

Suassuna, Ariano Vilar 1927- .... **HLCS 1**
See also CA 178; HW 2; LAW

Suckert, Kurt Erich
See Malaparte, Curzio

Suckling, Sir John 1609-1642 ..... **LC 75; PC 30**
See also BRW 2; DAM POET; DLB 58, 126; EXPP; PAB; RGEL 2

Suckow, Ruth 1892-1960 .... **SSC 18**
See also CA 193; 113; DLB 9, 102; RGAL 4; TCWW 2

Sudermann, Hermann 1857-1928
.... **TCLC 15**
See also CA 107; 201; DLB 118

Sue, Eugene 1804-1857 .... **NCLC 1**
See also DLB 119

Sueskind, Patrick 1949- .... **CLC 44**
See Suskind, Patrick

Sukenick, Ronald 1932- ...... **CLC 3, 4, 6, 48**
See also CA 25-28R; CAAE 209; CAAS 8; CANR 32, 89; CN 7; DLB 173; DLBY 1981

Suknaski, Andrew 1942- .... **CLC 19**
See also CA 101; CP 7; DLB 53

Sullivan, Vernon
See Vian, Boris

Sully Prudhomme, Rene-Francois-Armand 1839-1907 .... **TCLC 31**
See also GFL 1789 to the Present

Su Man-shu .... **TCLC 24**
See Su, Chien
See also EWL 3

Summerforest, Ivy B.
See Kirkup, James

Summers, Andrew James 1942- ...... **CLC 26**

Summers, Andy
See Summers, Andrew James

Summers, Hollis (Spurgeon, Jr.) 1916-
.... **CLC 10**
See also CA 5-8R; CANR 3; DLB 6

Summers, (Alphonsus Joseph-Mary Augustus) Montague 1880-1948
.... **TCLC 16**
See also CA 118; 163

Sumner, Gordon Matthew .... **CLC 26**
See Police, The; Sting

Sun Tzu c. 400B.C.-c. 320B.C. .... **CMLC 56**

Surtees, Robert Smith 1805-1864
.... **NCLC 14**
See also DLB 21; RGEL 2

Susann, Jacqueline 1921-1974 .... **CLC 3**
See also AITN 1; BPFB 3; CA 65-68; 53-56; MTCW 1, 2

Su Shi
See Su Shih
See also RGWL 2, 3

Su Shih 1036-1101 .... **CMLC 15**
See Su Shi

Suskind, Patrick
See Sueskind, Patrick
See also BPFB 3; CA 145; CWW 2

Sutcliff, Rosemary 1920-1992 .... **CLC 26**
See also AAYA 10; BYA 1, 4; CA 5-8R; 139; CANR 37; CLR 1, 37; CPW; DAB; DAC; DAM MST, POP; JRDA; MAICYA 1, 2; MAICYAS 1; RHW; SATA 6, 44, 78; SATA-Obit 73; WYA; YAW

Sutro, Alfred 1863-1933 .... **TCLC 6**
See also CA 105; 185; DLB 10; RGEL 2

Sutton, Henry
See Slavitt, David R(ytman)

Suzuki, D. T.
See Suzuki, Daisetz Teitaro

Suzuki, Daisetz T.
See Suzuki, Daisetz Teitaro

Suzuki, Daisetz Teitaro 1870-1966
.... TCLC 109
See also CA 121; 111; MTCW 1, 2

Suzuki, Teitaro
See Suzuki, Daisetz Teitaro

Svevo, Italo .... SSC 25; TCLC 2, 35
See Schmitz, Aron Hector
See also DLB 264; EW 8; EWL 3; RGWL 2, 3

Swados, Elizabeth (A.) 1951- .... CLC 12
See also CA 97-100; CANR 49; INT 97-100

Swados, Harvey 1920-1972 .... CLC 5
See also CA 5-8R; 37-40R; CANR 6; DLB 2

Swan, Gladys 1934- .... CLC 69
See also CA 101; CANR 17, 39

Swanson, Logan
See Matheson, Richard (Burton)

Swarthout, Glendon (Fred) 1918-1992
.... CLC 35
See also CA 1-4R; 139; CANR 1, 47; LAIT 5; SATA 26; TCWW 2; YAW

Sweet, Sarah C.
See Jewett, (Theodora) Sarah Orne

Swenson, May 1919-1989 ..... CLC 4, 14, 61, 106; PC 14
See also AMWS 4; CA 5-8R; 130; CANR 36, 61; DA; DAB; DAC; DAM MST, POET; DLB 5; EXPP; GLL 2; MTCW 1, 2; PFS 16; SATA 15; WP

Swift, Augustus
See Lovecraft, H(oward) P(hillips)

Swift, Graham (Colin) 1949- .... CLC 41, 88
See also BRWS 5; CA 117; 122; CANR 46, 71; CN 7; DLB 194; MTCW 2; RGSF 2

Swift, Jonathan 1667-1745 ..... LC 1, 42; PC 9; WLC
See also AAYA 41; BRW 3; BRWC 1; BRWR 1; BYA 5, 14; CDBLB 1660-1789; CLR 53; DA; DA3; DAB; DAC; DAM MST, NOV, POET; DLB 39, 95, 101; EXPN; LAIT 1; NFS 6; RGEL 2; SATA 19; TEA; WCH; WLIT 3

Swinburne, Algernon Charles 1837-1909
.... PC 24; TCLC 8, 36; WLC
See also BRW 5; CA 105; 140; CDBLB 1832-1890; DA; DA3; DAB; DAC; DAM MST, POET; DLB 35, 57; PAB; RGEL 2; TEA

Swinfen, Ann .... CLC 34
See also CA 202

Swinnerton, Frank Arthur 1884-1982
.... CLC 31
See also CA 108; DLB 34

Swithen, John
See King, Stephen (Edwin)

Sylvia
See Ashton-Warner, Sylvia (Constance)

Symmes, Robert Edward
See Duncan, Robert (Edward)

Symonds, John Addington 1840-1893
.... NCLC 34
See also DLB 57, 144

Symons, Arthur 1865-1945 .... TCLC 11
See also CA 107; 189; DLB 19, 57, 149; RGEL 2

Symons, Julian (Gustave) 1912-1994
.... CLC 2, 14, 32
See also CA 49-52; 147; CAAS 3; CANR 3, 33, 59; CMW 4; DLB 87, 155; DLBY 1992; MSW; MTCW 1

Synge, (Edmund) J(ohn) M(illington)
1871-1909 .... DC 2; TCLC 6, 37
See also BRW 6; BRWR 1; CA 104; 141; CDBLB 1890-1914; DAM DRAM; DLB 10, 19; EWL 3; RGEL 2; TEA; WLIT 4

Syruc, J.
See Milosz, Czeslaw

Szirtes, George 1948- .... CLC 46
See also CA 109; CANR 27, 61, 117; CP 7

Szymborska, Wislawa 1923- .... CLC 99; PC 44
See also CA 154; CANR 91; CDWLB 4; CWP; CWW 2; DA3; DLB 232; DLBY 1996; EWL 3; MTCW 2; PFS 15; RGWL 2, 3

T. O., Nik
See Annensky, Innokenty (Fyodorovich)

Tabori, George 1914- .... CLC 19
See also CA 49-52; CANR 4, 69; CBD; CD 5; DLB 245

Tacitus c. 55-c. 117 .... CMLC 56
See also AW 2; CDWLB 1; DLB 211; RGWL 2, 3

Tagore, Rabindranath 1861-1941 .... PC 8; SSC 48; TCLC 3, 53
See also CA 104; 120; DA3; DAM DRAM, POET; EWL 3; MTCW 1, 2; RGEL 2; RGSF 2; RGWL 2, 3; TWA

Taine, Hippolyte Adolphe 1828-1893
.... NCLC 15
See also EW 7; GFL 1789 to the Present

Talayesva, Don C. 1890-(?) .... NNAL

Talese, Gay 1932- .... CLC 37
See also AITN 1; CA 1-4R; CANR 9, 58; DLB 185; INT CANR-9; MTCW 1, 2

Tallent, Elizabeth (Ann) 1954- .... CLC 45
See also CA 117; CANR 72; DLB 130

Tallmountain, Mary 1918-1997 .... NNAL
See also CA 146; 161; DLB 193

Tally, Ted 1952- .... CLC 42
See also CA 120; 124; CAD; CD 5; INT 124

Talvik, Heiti 1904-1947 .... TCLC 87
See also EWL 3

Tamayo y Baus, Manuel 1829-1898
.... NCLC 1

Tammsaare, A(nton) H(ansen) 1878-1940
.... TCLC 27
See also CA 164; CDWLB 4; DLB 220; EWL 3

Tam'si, Tchicaya U
See Tchicaya, Gerald Felix

Tan, Amy (Ruth) 1952- .... AAL; CLC 59, 120, 151
See also AAYA 9, 48; AMWS 10; BEST 89:3; BPFB 3; CA 136; CANR 54, 105; CDALBS; CN 7; CPW 1; DA3; DAM MULT, NOV, POP; DLB 173; EXPN; FW; LAIT 3, 5; MTCW 2; NFS 1, 13, 16; RGAL 4; SATA 75; SSFS 9; YAW

Tandem, Felix
See Spitteler, Carl (Friedrich Georg)

Tanizaki, Jun'ichiro 1886-1965 .. CLC 8, 14, 28; SSC 21
See Tanizaki Jun'ichiro
See also CA 93-96; 25-28R; MJW; MTCW 2; RGSF 2; RGWL 2

Tanizaki Jun'ichiro
See Tanizaki, Jun'ichiro
See also DLB 180; EWL 3

Tanner, William
See Amis, Kingsley (William)

Tao Lao
See Storni, Alfonsina

Tapahonso, Luci 1953- .... NNAL
See also CA 145; CANR 72; DLB 175

Tarantino, Quentin (Jerome) 1963-
.... CLC 125
See also CA 171

Tarassoff, Lev
See Troyat, Henri

Tarbell, Ida M(inerva) 1857-1944
.... TCLC 40
See also CA 122; 181; DLB 47

Tarkington, (Newton) Booth 1869-1946
.... TCLC 9
See also BPFB 3; BYA 3; CA 110; 143; CWRI 5; DLB 9, 102; MTCW 2; RGAL 4; SATA 17

Tarkovskii, Andrei Arsen'evich
See Tarkovsky, Andrei (Arsenyevich)

Tarkovsky, Andrei (Arsenyevich) 1932-1986
.... CLC 75
See also CA 127

Tartt, Donna 1964(?)- .... CLC 76
See also CA 142

Tasso, Torquato 1544-1595 .... LC 5
See also EFS 2; EW 2; RGWL 2, 3

Tate, (John Orley) Allen 1899-1979 . CLC 2, 4, 6, 9, 11, 14, 24
See also AMW; CA 5-8R; 85-88; CANR 32, 108; DLB 4, 45, 63; DLBD 17; EWL 3; MTCW 1, 2; RGAL 4; RHW

Tate, Ellalice
See Hibbert, Eleanor Alice Burford

Tate, James (Vincent) 1943- .... CLC 2, 6, 25
See also CA 21-24R; CANR 29, 57, 114; CP 7; DLB 5, 169; EWL 3; PFS 10, 15; RGAL 4; WP

Tauler, Johannes c. 1300-1361 ..... CMLC 37
See also DLB 179; LMFS 1

Tavel, Ronald 1940- .... CLC 6
See also CA 21-24R; CAD; CANR 33; CD 5

Taviani, Paolo 1931- .... CLC 70
See also CA 153

Taylor, Bayard 1825-1878 .... NCLC 89
See also DLB 3, 189, 250, 254; RGAL 4

Taylor, C(ecil) P(hilip) 1929-1981 .... CLC 27
See also CA 25-28R; 105; CANR 47; CBD

Taylor, Edward 1642(?)-1729 .... LC 11
See also AMW; DA; DAB; DAC; DAM MST, POET; DLB 24; EXPP; RGAL 4; TUS

Taylor, Eleanor Ross 1920- .... CLC 5
See also CA 81-84; CANR 70

Taylor, Elizabeth 1932-1975 .... CLC 2, 4, 29
See also CA 13-16R; CANR 9, 70; DLB 139; MTCW 1, 2; RGEL 2; SATA 13

Taylor, Frederick Winslow 1856-1915
.... TCLC 76
See also CA 188

Taylor, Henry (Splawn) 1942- .... CLC 44
See also CA 33-36R; CAAS 7; CANR 31; CP 7; DLB 5; PFS 10

Taylor, Kamala (Purnaiya) 1924-
See Markandaya, Kamala
See also CA 77-80; NFS 13

Taylor, Mildred D(elois) 1943- .... CLC 21
See also AAYA 10, 47; BW 1; BYA 3, 8; CA 85-88; CANR 25, 115; CLR 9, 59; CSW; DLB 52; JRDA; LAIT 3; MAICYA 1, 2; SAAS 5; SATA 135; WYA; YAW

Taylor, Peter (Hillsman) 1917-1994 . CLC 1, 4, 18, 37, 44, 50, 71; SSC 10
See also AMWS 5; BPFB 3; CA 13-16R; 147; CANR 9, 50; CSW; DLB 218, 278; DLBY 1981, 1994; EWL 3; EXPS; INT CANR-9; MTCW 1, 2; RGSF 2; SSFS 9; TUS

Taylor, Robert Lewis 1912-1998 ..... CLC 14
See also CA 1-4R; 170; CANR 3, 64; SATA 10

Tchekhov, Anton
See Chekhov, Anton (Pavlovich)

Tchicaya, Gerald Felix 1931-1988
.... CLC 101
See Tchicaya U Tam'si
See also CA 129; 125; CANR 81

Tchicaya U Tam'si
See Tchicaya, Gerald Felix
See also EWL 3

Teasdale, Sara 1884-1933 ... PC 31; TCLC 4
See also CA 104; 163; DLB 45; GLL 1; PFS 14; RGAL 4; SATA 32; TUS

Tecumseh 1768-1813 .... NNAL
See also DAM MULT

Tegner, Esaias 1782-1846 .... NCLC 2

Teilhard de Chardin, (Marie Joseph) Pierre 1881-1955 .... TCLC 9
See also CA 105; GFL 1789 to the Present

Temple, Ann
See Mortimer, Penelope (Ruth)

Tennant, Emma (Christina) 1937- . CLC 13, 52
See also CA 65-68; CAAS 9; CANR 10, 38, 59, 88; CN 7; DLB 14; EWL 3; SFW 4

Tenneshaw, S. M.
See Silverberg, Robert

Tenney, Tabitha Gilman 1762-1837
.... NCLC 122
See also DLB 37, 200

Tennyson, Alfred 1809-1892 .. NCLC 30, 65, 115; PC 6; WLC
See also BRW 4; CDBLB 1832-1890; DA; DA3; DAB; DAC; DAM MST, POET; DLB 32; EXPP; PAB; PFS 1, 2, 4, 11, 15; RGEL 2; TEA; WLIT 4; WP

Teran, Lisa St. Aubin de .... CLC 36
See St. Aubin de Teran, Lisa

Terence c. 184B.C.-c. 159B.C. .... CMLC 14; DC 7
See also AW 1; CDWLB 1; DLB 211; RGWL 2, 3; TWA

Teresa de Jesus, St. 1515-1582 .... LC 18

Terkel, Louis 1912-
See Terkel, Studs
See also CA 57-60; CANR 18, 45, 67; DA3; MTCW 1, 2

Terkel, Studs .... CLC 38
See Terkel, Louis
See also AAYA 32; AITN 1; MTCW 2; TUS

Terry, C. V.
See Slaughter, Frank G(ill)

Terry, Megan 1932- .... CLC 19; DC 13
See also CA 77-80; CABS 3; CAD; CANR 43; CD 5; CWD; DLB 7, 249; GLL 2

Tertullian c. 155-c. 245 .... CMLC 29

Tertz, Abram
See Sinyavsky, Andrei (Donatevich)
See also CWW 2; RGSF 2

Tesich, Steve 1943(?)-1996 .... CLC 40, 69
See also CA 105; 152; CAD; DLBY 1983

Tesla, Nikola 1856-1943 .... TCLC 88

Teternikov, Fyodor Kuzmich 1863-1927
See Sologub, Fyodor
See also CA 104

Tevis, Walter 1928-1984 .... CLC 42
See also CA 113; SFW 4

Tey, Josephine .... TCLC 14
See Mackintosh, Elizabeth
See also DLB 77; MSW

Thackeray, William Makepeace 1811-1863
.... NCLC 5, 14, 22, 43; WLC
See also BRW 5; CDBLB 1832-1890; DA; DA3; DAB; DAC; DAM MST, NOV; DLB 21, 55, 159, 163; NFS 13; RGEL 2; SATA 23; TEA; WLIT 3

Thakura, Ravindranatha
See Tagore, Rabindranath

Thames, C. H.
See Marlowe, Stephen

Tharoor, Shashi 1956- .... CLC 70
See also CA 141; CANR 91; CN 7

Thelwell, Michael Miles 1939- .... CLC 22
See also BW 2; CA 101

Theobald, Lewis, Jr.
See Lovecraft, H(oward) P(hillips)

Theocritus c. 310B.C.- .... CMLC 45
See also AW 1; DLB 176; RGWL 2, 3

Theodorescu, Ion N. 1880-1967
See Arghezi, Tudor
See also CA 116

Theriault, Yves 1915-1983 .... CLC 79
See also CA 102; CCA 1; DAC; DAM MST; DLB 88; EWL 3

Theroux, Alexander (Louis) 1939- ... CLC 2, 25
See also CA 85-88; CANR 20, 63; CN 7

Theroux, Paul (Edward) 1941- .... CLC 5, 8, 11, 15, 28, 46
See also AAYA 28; AMWS 8; BEST 89:4; BPFB 3; CA 33-36R; CANR 20, 45, 74; CDALBS; CN 7; CPW 1; DA3; DAM POP; DLB 2, 218; EWL 3; HGG; MTCW 1, 2; RGAL 4; SATA 44, 109; TUS

Thesen, Sharon 1946- .... CLC 56
See also CA 163; CP 7; CWP

Thespis fl. 6th cent. B.C.- .... CMLC 51
See also LMFS 1

Thevenin, Denis
See Duhamel, Georges

Thibault, Jacques Anatole Francois 1844-1924
See France, Anatole
See also CA 106; 127; DA3; DAM NOV; MTCW 1, 2; TWA

Thiele, Colin (Milton) 1920- .... CLC 17
See also CA 29-32R; CANR 12, 28, 53, 105; CLR 27; MAICYA 1, 2; SAAS 2; SATA 14, 72, 125; YAW

Thistlethwaite, Bel
See Wetherald, Agnes Ethelwyn

Thomas, Audrey (Callahan) 1935- .. CLC 7, 13, 37, 107; SSC 20
See also AITN 2; CA 21-24R; CAAS 19; CANR 36, 58; CN 7; DLB 60; MTCW 1; RGSF 2

Thomas, Augustus 1857-1934 .... TCLC 97

Thomas, D(onald) M(ichael) 1935-
.... CLC 13, 22, 31, 132
See also BPFB 3; BRWS 4; CA 61-64; CAAS 11; CANR 17, 45, 75; CDBLB 1960 to Present; CN 7; CP 7; DA3; DLB 40, 207; HGG; INT CANR-17; MTCW 1, 2; SFW 4

Thomas, Dylan (Marlais) 1914-1953 .. PC 2; SSC 3, 44; TCLC 1, 8, 45, 105; WLC
See also AAYA 45; BRWS 1; CA 104; 120; CANR 65; CDBLB 1945-1960; DA; DA3; DAB; DAC; DAM DRAM, MST, POET; DLB 13, 20, 139; EWL 3; EXPP; LAIT 3; MTCW 1, 2; PAB; PFS 1, 3, 8; RGEL 2; RGSF 2; SATA 60; TEA; WLIT 4; WP

Thomas, (Philip) Edward 1878-1917
.... TCLC 10
See also BRW 6; BRWS 3; CA 106; 153; DAM POET; DLB 19, 98, 156, 216; PAB; RGEL 2

Thomas, Joyce Carol 1938- .... CLC 35
See also AAYA 12; BW 2, 3; CA 113; 116; CANR 48, CA 17, 39; CLR 19; DLB 33; INT CA-116; JRDA; MAICYA 1, 2; MTCW 1, 2; SAAS 7; SATA 40, 78, 123, 137; WYA; YAW

Thomas, Lewis 1913-1993 .... CLC 35
See also ANW; CA 85-88; 143; CANR 38, 60; DLB 275; MTCW 1, 2

Thomas, M. Carey 1857-1935 .... TCLC 89
See also FW

Thomas, Paul
See Mann, (Paul) Thomas

Thomas, Piri 1928- .... CLC 17; HLCS 2
See also CA 73-76; HW 1

Thomas, R(onald) S(tuart) 1913-2000
.... CLC 6, 13, 48
See also CA 89-92; 189; CAAS 4; CANR 30; CDBLB 1960 to Present; CP 7; DAB; DAM POET; DLB 27; EWL 3; MTCW 1; RGEL 2

Thomas, Ross (Elmore) 1926-1995 . CLC 39
See also CA 33-36R; 150; CANR 22, 63; CMW 4

Thompson, Francis (Joseph) 1859-1907
.... TCLC 4
See also BRW 5; CA 104; 189; CDBLB 1890-1914; DLB 19; RGEL 2; TEA

Thompson, Francis Clegg
See Mencken, H(enry) L(ouis)

Thompson, Hunter S(tockton) 1937(?)-
.... CLC 9, 17, 40, 104
See also AAYA 45; BEST 89:1; BPFB 3; CA 17-20R; CANR 23, 46, 74, 77, 111; CPW; CSW; DA3; DAM POP; DLB 185; MTCW 1, 2; TUS

Thompson, James Myers
See Thompson, Jim (Myers)

Thompson, Jim (Myers) 1906-1977(?)
.... CLC 69
See also BPFB 3; CA 140; CMW 4; CPW; DLB 226; MSW

Thompson, Judith .... CLC 39
See also CWD

Thomson, James 1700-1748 ... LC 16, 29, 40
See also BRWS 3; DAM POET; DLB 95; RGEL 2

Thomson, James 1834-1882 .... NCLC 18
See also DAM POET; DLB 35; RGEL 2

Thoreau, Henry David 1817-1862
.... NCLC 7, 21, 61; PC 30; WLC
See also AAYA 42; AMW; ANW; BYA 3; CDALB 1640-1865; DA; DA3; DAB; DAC; DAM MST; DLB 1, 183, 223, 270; LAIT 2; LMFS 1; NCFS 3; RGAL 4; TUS

Thorndike, E. L.
See Thorndike, Edward L(ee)

Thorndike, Edward L(ee) 1874-1949
.... TCLC 107
See also CA 121

Thornton, Hall
See Silverberg, Robert

Thubron, Colin (Gerald Dryden) 1939-
.... CLC 163
See also CA 25-28R; CANR 12, 29, 59, 95; CN 7; DLB 204, 231

Thucydides c. 455B.C.-c. 395B.C.
.... CMLC 17
See also AW 1; DLB 176; RGWL 2, 3

Thumboo, Edwin Nadason 1933- .... PC 30
See also CA 94

Thurber, James (Grover) 1894-1961
.... CLC 5, 11, 25, 125; SSC 1, 47
See also AMWS 1; BPFB 3; BYA 5; CA 73-76; CANR 17, 39; CDALB 1929-1941; CWRI 5; DA; DA3; DAB; DAC; DAM DRAM, MST, NOV; DLB 4, 11, 22, 102; EXPS; FANT; LAIT 3; MAICYA 1, 2; MTCW 1, 2; RGAL 4; RGSF 2; SATA 13; SSFS 1, 10; SUFW 2; TUS

Thurman, Wallace (Henry) 1902-1934
.... BLC 3; HR 3; TCLC 6
See also BW 1, 3; CA 104; 124; CANR 81; DAM MULT; DLB 51

Tibullus c. 54B.C.-c. 18B.C. .... CMLC 36
See also AW 2; DLB 211; RGWL 2, 3

Ticheburn, Cheviot
See Ainsworth, William Harrison

Tieck, (Johann) Ludwig 1773-1853
.... **NCLC 5, 46; SSC 31**
See also CDWLB 2; DLB 90; EW 5; IDTP; RGSF 2; RGWL 2, 3; SUFW

Tiger, Derry
See Ellison, Harlan (Jay)

Tilghman, Christopher 1948(?)- ...... **CLC 65**
See also CA 159; CSW; DLB 244

Tillich, Paul (Johannes) 1886-1965
.... **CLC 131**
See also CA 5-8R; 25-28R; CANR 33; MTCW 1, 2

Tillinghast, Richard (Williford) 1940-
.... **CLC 29**
See also CA 29-32R; CAAS 23; CANR 26, 51, 96; CP 7; CSW

Timrod, Henry 1828-1867 .... **NCLC 25**
See also DLB 3, 248; RGAL 4

Tindall, Gillian (Elizabeth) 1938- ...... **CLC 7**
See also CA 21-24R; CANR 11, 65, 107; CN 7

Tiptree, James, Jr. .... **CLC 48, 50**
See Sheldon, Alice Hastings Bradley
See also DLB 8; SCFW 2; SFW 4

Tirone Smith, Mary-Ann 1944- ...... **CLC 39**
See also CA 118; 136; CANR 113

Tirso de Molina 1580(?)-1648 .... **DC 13; HLCS 2; LC 73**
See also RGWL 2, 3

Titmarsh, Michael Angelo
See Thackeray, William Makepeace

Tocqueville, Alexis (Charles Henri Maurice Clerel Comte) de 1805-1859 . **NCLC 7, 63**
See also EW 6; GFL 1789 to the Present; TWA

Toffler, Alvin 1928- .... **CLC 168**
See also CA 13-16R; CANR 15, 46, 67; CPW; DAM POP; MTCW 1, 2

Toibin, Colm
See Toibin, Colm
See also DLB 271

Toibin, Colm 1955- .... **CLC 162**
See Toibin, Colm
See also CA 142; CANR 81

Tolkien, J(ohn) R(onald) R(euel) 1892-1973
.... **CLC 1, 2, 3, 8, 12, 38; WLC**
See also AAYA 10; AITN 1; BPFB 3; BRWS 2; CA 17-18; 45-48; CANR 36; CAP 2; CDBLB 1914-1945; CLR 56; CPW 1; CWRI 5; DA; DA3; DAB; DAC; DAM MST, NOV, POP; DLB 15, 160, 255; EFS 2; FANT; JRDA; LAIT 1; LMFS 2; MAICYA 1, 2; MTCW 1, 2; NFS 8; RGEL 2; SATA 2, 32, 100; SATA-Obit 24; SFW 4; SUFW; TEA; WCH; WYA; YAW

Toller, Ernst 1893-1939 .... **TCLC 10**
See also CA 107; 186; DLB 124; RGWL 2, 3

Tolson, M. B.
See Tolson, Melvin B(eaunorus)

Tolson, Melvin B(eaunorus) 1898(?)-1966
.... **BLC 3; CLC 36, 105**
See also AFAW 1, 2; BW 1, 3; CA 124; 89-92; CANR 80; DAM MULT, POET; DLB 48, 76; RGAL 4

Tolstoi, Aleksei Nikolaevich
See Tolstoy, Alexey Nikolaevich

Tolstoi, Lev
See Tolstoy, Leo (Nikolaevich)
See also RGSF 2; RGWL 2, 3

Tolstoy, Aleksei Nikolaevich
See Tolstoy, Alexey Nikolaevich
See also DLB 272

Tolstoy, Alexey Nikolaevich 1882-1945
.... **TCLC 18**
See Tolstoy, Aleksei Nikolaevich
See also CA 107; 158; SFW 4

Tolstoy, Leo (Nikolaevich) 1828-1910
...... **SSC 9, 30, 45, 54; TCLC 4, 11, 17, 28, 44, 79; WLC**
See Tolstoi, Lev
See also CA 104; 123; DA; DA3; DAB; DAC; DAM MST, NOV; DLB 238; EFS 2; EW 7; EXPS; IDTP; LAIT 2; LMFS 1; NFS 10; SATA 26; SSFS 5; TWA

Tolstoy, Count Leo
See Tolstoy, Leo (Nikolaevich)

Tomalin, Claire 1933- .... **CLC 166**
See also CA 89-92; CANR 52, 88; DLB 155

Tomasi di Lampedusa, Giuseppe 1896-1957
See Lampedusa, Giuseppe (Tomasi) di
See also CA 111; DLB 177

Tomlin, Lily .... **CLC 17**
See Tomlin, Mary Jean

Tomlin, Mary Jean 1939(?)-
See Tomlin, Lily
See also CA 117

Tomline, F. Latour
See Gilbert, W(illiam) S(chwenck)

Tomlinson, (Alfred) Charles 1927- .. **CLC 2, 4, 6, 13, 45; PC 17**
See also CA 5-8R; CANR 33; CP 7; DAM POET; DLB 40

Tomlinson, H(enry) M(ajor) 1873-1958
.... **TCLC 71**
See also CA 118; 161; DLB 36, 100, 195

Tonson, Jacob fl. 1655(?)-1736 .... **LC 86**
See also DLB 170

Toole, John Kennedy 1937-1969 .... **CLC 19, 64**
See also BPFB 3; CA 104; DLBY 1981; MTCW 2

Toomer, Eugene
See Toomer, Jean

Toomer, Eugene Pinchback
See Toomer, Jean

Toomer, Jean 1894-1967 . **BLC 3; CLC 1, 4, 13, 22; HR 3; PC 7; SSC 1, 45; WLCS**
See also AFAW 1, 2; AMWS 3, 9; BW 1; CA 85-88; CDALB 1917-1929; DA3; DAM MULT; DLB 45, 51; EXPP; EXPS; LMFS 2; MTCW 1, 2; NFS 11; RGAL 4; RGSF 2; SSFS 5

Toomer, Nathan Jean
See Toomer, Jean

Toomer, Nathan Pinchback
See Toomer, Jean

Torley, Luke
See Blish, James (Benjamin)

Tornimparte, Alessandra
See Ginzburg, Natalia

Torre, Raoul della
See Mencken, H(enry) L(ouis)

Torrence, Ridgely 1874-1950 .... **TCLC 97**
See also DLB 54, 249

Torrey, E(dwin) Fuller 1937- .... **CLC 34**
See also CA 119; CANR 71

Torsvan, Ben Traven
See Traven, B.

Torsvan, Benno Traven
See Traven, B.

Torsvan, Berick Traven
See Traven, B.

Torsvan, Berwick Traven
See Traven, B.

Torsvan, Bruno Traven
See Traven, B.

Torsvan, Traven
See Traven, B.

Tourneur, Cyril 1575(?)-1626 .... **LC 66**
See also BRW 2; DAM DRAM; DLB 58; RGEL 2

Tournier, Michel (Edouard) 1924- ... **CLC 6, 23, 36, 95**
See also CA 49-52; CANR 3, 36, 74; DLB 83; GFL 1789 to the Present; MTCW 1, 2; SATA 23

Tournimparte, Alessandra
See Ginzburg, Natalia

Towers, Ivar
See Kornbluth, C(yril) M.

Towne, Robert (Burton) 1936(?)- .... **CLC 87**
See also CA 108; DLB 44; IDFW 3, 4

Townsend, Sue .... **CLC 61**
See Townsend, Susan Lilian
See also AAYA 28; CA 119; 127; CANR 65, 107; CBD; CD 5; CPW; CWD; DAB; DAC; DAM MST; DLB 271; INT 127; SATA 55, 93; SATA-Brief 48; YAW

Townsend, Susan Lilian 1946-
See Townsend, Sue

Townshend, Pete
See Townshend, Peter (Dennis Blandford)

Townshend, Peter (Dennis Blandford) 1945-
.... **CLC 17, 42**
See also CA 107

Tozzi, Federigo 1883-1920 .... **TCLC 31**
See also CA 160; CANR 110; DLB 264

Tracy, Don(ald Fiske) 1905-1970(?)
See Queen, Ellery
See also CA 1-4R; 176; CANR 2

Trafford, F. G.
See Riddell, Charlotte

Traill, Catharine Parr 1802-1899
.... **NCLC 31**
See also DLB 99

Trakl, Georg 1887-1914 ...... **PC 20; TCLC 5**
See also CA 104; 165; EW 10; LMFS 2; MTCW 2; RGWL 2, 3

Tranquilli, Secondino
See Silone, Ignazio

Transtroemer, Tomas Gosta
See Transtromer, Tomas (Goesta)

Transtromer, Tomas
See Transtromer, Tomas (Goesta)

Transtromer, Tomas (Goesta) 1931-
.... **CLC 52, 65**
See also CA 117; 129; CAAS 17; CANR 115; DAM POET; DLB 257

Transtromer, Tomas Gosta
See Transtromer, Tomas (Goesta)

Traven, B. 1882(?)-1969 .... **CLC 8, 11**
See also CA 19-20; 25-28R; CAP 2; DLB 9, 56; MTCW 1; RGAL 4

Trediakovsky, Vasilii Kirillovich 1703-1769
.... **LC 68**
See also DLB 150

Treitel, Jonathan 1959- .... **CLC 70**
See also DLB 267

Trelawny, Edward John 1792-1881
.... **NCLC 85**
See also DLB 110, 116, 144

Tremain, Rose 1943- .... **CLC 42**
See also CA 97-100; CANR 44, 95; CN 7; DLB 14, 271; RGSF 2; RHW

Tremblay, Michel 1942- .... **CLC 29, 102**
See also CA 116; 128; CCA 1; CWW 2; DAC; DAM MST; DLB 60; GLL 1; MTCW 1, 2

Trevanian .... **CLC 29**
See Whitaker, Rod(ney)

Trevor, Glen
See Hilton, James

Trevor, William .. **CLC 7, 9, 14, 25, 71, 116; SSC 21, 58**
See Cox, William Trevor
See also BRWS 4; CBD; CD 5; CN 7; DLB 14, 139; MTCW 2; RGEL 2; RGSF 2; SSFS 10

Trifonov, Iurii (Valentinovich)
See Trifonov, Yuri (Valentinovich)
See also RGWL 2, 3

Trifonov, Yuri (Valentinovich) 1925-1981
.... CLC 45
See Trifonov, Iurii (Valentinovich)
See also CA 126; 103; MTCW 1

Trilling, Diana (Rubin) 1905-1996
.... CLC 129
See also CA 5-8R; 154; CANR 10, 46; INT CANR-10; MTCW 1, 2

Trilling, Lionel 1905-1975 ..... CLC 9, 11, 24
See also AMWS 3; CA 9-12R; 61-64; CANR 10, 105; DLB 28, 63; INT CANR-10; MTCW 1, 2; RGAL 4; TUS

Trimball, W. H.
See Mencken, H(enry) L(ouis)

Tristan
See Gomez de la Serna, Ramon

Tristram
See Housman, A(lfred) E(dward)

Trogdon, William (Lewis) 1939-
See Heat-Moon, William Least
See also CA 115; 119; CANR 47, 89; CPW; INT CA-119

Trollope, Anthony 1815-1882 .. NCLC 6, 33, **101; SSC 28; WLC**
See also BRW 5; CDBLB 1832-1890; DA; DA3; DAB; DAC; DAM MST, NOV; DLB 21, 57, 159; RGEL 2; RGSF 2; SATA 22

Trollope, Frances 1779-1863 .... NCLC 30
See also DLB 21, 166

Trotsky, Leon 1879-1940 .... TCLC 22
See also CA 118; 167

Trotter (Cockburn), Catharine 1679-1749
.... LC 8
See also DLB 84, 252

Trotter, Wilfred 1872-1939 .... TCLC 97

Trout, Kilgore
See Farmer, Philip Jose

Trow, George W. S. 1943- .... CLC 52
See also CA 126; CANR 91

Troyat, Henri 1911- .... CLC 23
See also CA 45-48; CANR 2, 33, 67, 117; GFL 1789 to the Present; MTCW 1

Trudeau, G(arretson) B(eekman) 1948-
See Trudeau, Garry B.
See also CA 81-84; CANR 31; SATA 35

Trudeau, Garry B. .... CLC 12
See Trudeau, G(arretson) B(eekman)
See also AAYA 10; AITN 2

Truffaut, Francois 1932-1984 .. CLC 20, 101
See also CA 81-84; 113; CANR 34

Trumbo, Dalton 1905-1976 .... CLC 19
See also CA 21-24R; 69-72; CANR 10; DLB 26; IDFW 3, 4; YAW

Trumbull, John 1750-1831 .... NCLC 30
See also DLB 31; RGAL 4

Trundlett, Helen B.
See Eliot, T(homas) S(tearns)

Truth, Sojourner 1797(?)-1883 ..... NCLC 94
See also DLB 239; FW; LAIT 2

Tryon, Thomas 1926-1991 .... CLC 3, 11
See also AITN 1; BPFB 3; CA 29-32R; 135; CANR 32, 77; CPW; DA3; DAM POP; HGG; MTCW 1

Tryon, Tom
See Tryon, Thomas

Ts'ao Hsueh-ch'in 1715(?)-1763 .... LC 1

Tsushima, Shuji 1909-1948
See Dazai Osamu
See also CA 107

Tsvetaeva (Efron), Marina (Ivanovna) 1892-1941 .... PC 14; TCLC 7, 35
See also CA 104; 128; CANR 73; EW 11; MTCW 1, 2; RGWL 2, 3

Tuck, Lily 1938- .... CLC 70
See also CA 139; CANR 90

Tu Fu 712-770 .... PC 9
See Du Fu
See also DAM MULT; TWA; WP

Tunis, John R(oberts) 1889-1975 .... CLC 12
See also BYA 1; CA 61-64; CANR 62; DLB 22, 171; JRDA; MAICYA 1, 2; SATA 37; SATA-Brief 30; YAW

Tuohy, Frank .... CLC 37
See Tuohy, John Francis
See also DLB 14, 139

Tuohy, John Francis 1925-
See Tuohy, Frank
See also CA 5-8R; 178; CANR 3, 47; CN 7

Turco, Lewis (Putnam) 1934- .... CLC 11, 63
See also CA 13-16R; CAAS 22; CANR 24, 51; CP 7; DLBY 1984

Turgenev, Ivan (Sergeevich) 1818-1883
.. DC 7; NCLC 21, 37, 122; SSC 7, 57; **WLC**
See also DA; DAB; DAC; DAM MST, NOV; DFS 6; DLB 238; EW 6; NFS 16; RGSF 2; RGWL 2, 3; TWA

Turgot, Anne-Robert-Jacques 1727-1781
.... LC 26

Turner, Frederick 1943- .... CLC 48
See also CA 73-76; CAAS 10; CANR 12, 30, 56; DLB 40, 282

Turton, James
See Crace, Jim

Tutu, Desmond M(pilo) 1931- .... BLC 3; **CLC 80**
See also BW 1, 3; CA 125; CANR 67, 81; DAM MULT

Tutuola, Amos 1920-1997 ... BLC 3; CLC 5, **14, 29**
See also AFW; BW 2, 3; CA 9-12R; 159; CANR 27, 66; CDWLB 3; CN 7; DA3; DAM MULT; DLB 125; DNFS 1, 2; MTCW 1, 2; RGEL 2; WLIT 2

Twain, Mark .. SSC 34; TCLC 6, 12, 19, 36, **48, 59; WLC**
See Clemens, Samuel Langhorne
See also AAYA 20; AMW; AMWC 1; BPFB 3; BYA 2, 3, 11, 14; CLR 58, 60, 66; DLB 11; EXPN; EXPS; FANT; LAIT 2; NFS 1, 6; RGAL 4; RGSF 2; SFW 4; SSFS 1, 7; SUFW; TUS; WCH; WYA; YAW

Tyler, Anne 1941- ...... CLC 7, 11, 18, 28, 44, **59, 103**
See also AAYA 18; AMWS 4; BEST 89:1; BPFB 3; BYA 12; CA 9-12R; CANR 11, 33, 53, 109; CDALBS; CN 7; CPW; CSW; DAM NOV, POP; DLB 6, 143; DLBY 1982; EXPN; MAWW; MTCW 1, 2; NFS 2, 7, 10; RGAL 4; SATA 7, 90; SSFS 17; TUS; YAW

Tyler, Royall 1757-1826 .... NCLC 3
See also DLB 37; RGAL 4

Tynan, Katharine 1861-1931 .... TCLC 3
See also CA 104; 167; DLB 153, 240; FW

Tyutchev, Fyodor 1803-1873 .... NCLC 34

Tzara, Tristan 1896-1963 .... CLC 47; PC 27
See also CA 153; 89-92; DAM POET; MTCW 2

Uchida, Yoshiko 1921-1992 .... AAL
See also AAYA 16; BYA 2, 3; CA 13-16R; 139; CANR 6, 22, 47, 61; CDALBS; CLR 6, 56; CWRI 5; JRDA; MAICYA 1, 2; MTCW 1, 2; SAAS 1; SATA 1, 53; SATA-Obit 72

Udall, Nicholas 1504-1556 .... LC 84
See also DLB 62; RGEL 2

Uhry, Alfred 1936- .... CLC 55
See also CA 127; 133; CAD; CANR 112; CD 5; CSW; DA3; DAM DRAM, POP; DFS 15; INT CA-133

Ulf, Haerved
See Strindberg, (Johan) August

Ulf, Harved
See Strindberg, (Johan) August

Ulibarri, Sabine R(eyes) 1919- .... CLC 83; **HLCS 2**
See also CA 131; CANR 81; DAM MULT; DLB 82; HW 1, 2; RGSF 2

Unamuno (y Jugo), Miguel de 1864-1936
.... HLC 2; SSC 11; TCLC 2, 9
See also CA 104; 131; CANR 81; DAM MULT, NOV; DLB 108; EW 8; HW 1, 2; MTCW 1, 2; RGSF 2; RGWL 2, 3; TWA

Undercliffe, Errol
See Campbell, (John) Ramsey

Underwood, Miles
See Glassco, John

Undset, Sigrid 1882-1949 .... TCLC 3; WLC
See also CA 104; 129; DA; DA3; DAB; DAC; DAM MST, NOV; EW 9; FW; MTCW 1, 2; RGWL 2, 3

Ungaretti, Giuseppe 1888-1970 .. CLC 7, 11, **15**
See also CA 19-20; 25-28R; CAP 2; DLB 114; EW 10; RGWL 2, 3

Unger, Douglas 1952- .... CLC 34
See also CA 130; CANR 94

Unsworth, Barry (Forster) 1930- ... CLC 76, **127**
See also BRWS 7; CA 25-28R; CANR 30, 54; CN 7; DLB 194

Updike, John (Hoyer) 1932- .... CLC 1, 2, 3, **5, 7, 9, 13, 15, 23, 34, 43, 70, 139; SSC 13, 27; WLC**
See also AAYA 36; AMW; AMWC 1; AMWR 1; BPFB 3; BYA 12; CA 1-4R; CABS 1; CANR 4, 33, 51, 94; CDALB 1968-1988; CN 7; CP 7; CPW 1; DA; DA3; DAB; DAC; DAM MST, NOV, POET, POP; DLB 2, 5, 143, 218, 227; DLBD 3; DLBY 1980, 1982, 1997; EXPP; HGG; MTCW 1, 2; NFS 12; RGAL 4; RGSF 2; SSFS 3; TUS

Upshaw, Margaret Mitchell
See Mitchell, Margaret (Munnerlyn)

Upton, Mark
See Sanders, Lawrence

Upward, Allen 1863-1926 .... TCLC 85
See also CA 117; 187; DLB 36

Urdang, Constance (Henriette) 1922-1996
.... CLC 47
See also CA 21-24R; CANR 9, 24; CP 7; CWP

Uriel, Henry
See Faust, Frederick (Schiller)

Uris, Leon (Marcus) 1924- .... CLC 7, 32
See also AITN 1, 2; BEST 89:2; BPFB 3; CA 1-4R; CANR 1, 40, 65; CN 7; CPW 1; DA3; DAM NOV, POP; MTCW 1, 2; SATA 49

Urista, Alberto H. 1947- ..... HLCS 1; PC 34
See Alurista
See also CA 45-48; 182; CANR 2, 32; HW 1

Urmuz
See Codrescu, Andrei

Urquhart, Guy
See McAlmon, Robert (Menzies)

Urquhart, Jane 1949- .... CLC 90
See also CA 113; CANR 32, 68, 116; CCA 1; DAC

Usigli, Rodolfo 1905-1979 .... HLCS 1
See also CA 131; HW 1; LAW

Ustinov, Peter (Alexander) 1921- ...... CLC 1
See also AITN 1; CA 13-16R; CANR 25, 51; CBD; CD 5; DLB 13; MTCW 2

U Tam'si, Gerald Felix Tchicaya
See Tchicaya, Gerald Felix

U Tam'si, Tchicaya
See Tchicaya, Gerald Felix

Vachss, Andrew (Henry) 1942- ..... **CLC 106**
See also CA 118; CANR 44, 95; CMW 4
Vachss, Andrew H.
See Vachss, Andrew (Henry)
Vaculik, Ludvik 1926- .... **CLC 7**
See also CA 53-56; CANR 72; CWW 2; DLB 232
Vaihinger, Hans 1852-1933 .... **TCLC 71**
See also CA 116; 166
Valdez, Luis (Miguel) 1940- .... **CLC 84; DC 10; HLC 2**
See also CA 101; CAD; CANR 32, 81; CD 5; DAM MULT; DFS 5; DLB 122; HW 1; LAIT 4
Valenzuela, Luisa 1938- .... **CLC 31, 104; HLCS 2; SSC 14**
See also CA 101; CANR 32, 65; CDWLB 3; CWW 2; DAM MULT; DLB 113; FW; HW 1, 2; LAW; RGSF 2; RGWL 3
Valera y Alcala-Galiano, Juan 1824-1905
.... **TCLC 10**
See also CA 106
Valery, (Ambroise) Paul (Toussaint Jules)
1871-1945 .... **PC 9; TCLC 4, 15**
See also CA 104; 122; DA3; DAM POET; DLB 258; EW 8; GFL 1789 to the Present; MTCW 1, 2; RGWL 2, 3; TWA
Valle-Inclan, Ramon (Maria) del 1866-1936
.... **HLC 2; TCLC 5**
See also CA 106; 153; CANR 80; DAM MULT; DLB 134; EW 8; HW 2; RGSF 2; RGWL 2, 3
Vallejo, Antonio Buero
See Buero Vallejo, Antonio
Vallejo, Cesar (Abraham) 1892-1938
.... **HLC 2; TCLC 3, 56**
See also CA 105; 153; DAM MULT; HW 1; LAW; RGWL 2, 3
Valles, Jules 1832-1885 .... **NCLC 71**
See also DLB 123; GFL 1789 to the Present
Vallette, Marguerite Eymery 1860-1953
.... **TCLC 67**
See Rachilde
See also CA 182; DLB 123, 192
Valle Y Pena, Ramon del
See Valle-Inclan, Ramon (Maria) del
Van Ash, Cay 1918- .... **CLC 34**
Vanbrugh, Sir John 1664-1726 .... **LC 21**
See also BRW 2; DAM DRAM; DLB 80; IDTP; RGEL 2
Van Campen, Karl
See Campbell, John W(ood, Jr.)
Vance, Gerald
See Silverberg, Robert
Vance, Jack .... **CLC 35**
See Vance, John Holbrook
See also DLB 8; FANT; SCFW 2; SFW 4; SUFW 1, 2
Vance, John Holbrook 1916-
See Queen, Ellery; Vance, Jack
See also CA 29-32R; CANR 17, 65; CMW 4; MTCW 1
Van Den Bogarde, Derek Jules Gaspard Ulric Niven 1921-1999 .... **CLC 14**
See Bogarde, Dirk
See also CA 77-80; 179
Vandenburgh, Jane .... **CLC 59**
See also CA 168
Vanderhaeghe, Guy 1951- .... **CLC 41**
See also BPFB 3; CA 113; CANR 72
van der Post, Laurens (Jan) 1906-1996
.... **CLC 5**
See also AFW; CA 5-8R; 155; CANR 35; CN 7; DLB 204; RGEL 2
van de Wetering, Janwillem 1931- . **CLC 47**
See also CA 49-52; CANR 4, 62, 90; CMW 4

Van Dine, S. S. .... **TCLC 23**
See Wright, Willard Huntington
See also MSW
Van Doren, Carl (Clinton) 1885-1950
.... **TCLC 18**
See also CA 111; 168
Van Doren, Mark 1894-1972 .... **CLC 6, 10**
See also CA 1-4R; 37-40R; CANR 3; DLB 45; MTCW 1, 2; RGAL 4
Van Druten, John (William) 1901-1957
.... **TCLC 2**
See also CA 104; 161; DLB 10; RGAL 4
Van Duyn, Mona (Jane) 1921- ..... **CLC 3, 7, 63, 116**
See also CA 9-12R; CANR 7, 38, 60, 116; CP 7; CWP; DAM POET; DLB 5
Van Dyne, Edith
See Baum, L(yman) Frank
van Itallie, Jean-Claude 1936- .... **CLC 3**
See also CA 45-48; CAAS 2; CAD; CANR 1, 48; CD 5; DLB 7
Van Loot, Cornelius Obenchain
See Roberts, Kenneth (Lewis)
van Ostaijen, Paul 1896-1928 .... **TCLC 33**
See also CA 163
Van Peebles, Melvin 1932- .... **CLC 2, 20**
See also BW 2, 3; CA 85-88; CANR 27, 67, 82; DAM MULT
van Schendel, Arthur(-Francois-Emile)
1874-1946 .... **TCLC 56**
Vansittart, Peter 1920- .... **CLC 42**
See also CA 1-4R; CANR 3, 49, 90; CN 7; RHW
Van Vechten, Carl 1880-1964 . **CLC 33; HR 3**
See also AMWS 2; CA 183; 89-92; DLB 4, 9, 51; RGAL 4
van Vogt, A(lfred) E(lton) 1912-2000
.... **CLC 1**
See also BPFB 3; BYA 13, 14; CA 21-24R; 190; CANR 28; DLB 8, 251; SATA 14; SATA-Obit 124; SCFW; SFW 4
Vara, Madeleine
See Jackson, Laura (Riding)
Varda, Agnes 1928- .... **CLC 16**
See also CA 116; 122
Vargas Llosa, (Jorge) Mario (Pedro) 1939-
... **CLC 3, 6, 9, 10, 15, 31, 42, 85; HLC 2**
See Llosa, (Jorge) Mario (Pedro) Vargas
See also BPFB 3; CA 73-76; CANR 18, 32, 42, 67, 116; CDWLB 3; DA; DA3; DAB; DAC; DAM MST, MULT, NOV; DLB 145; DNFS 2; HW 1, 2; LAIT 5; LAW; LAWS 1; MTCW 1, 2; RGWL 2; SSFS 14; TWA; WLIT 1
Vasiliu, George
See Bacovia, George
Vasiliu, Gheorghe
See Bacovia, George
See also CA 123; 189
Vassa, Gustavus
See Equiano, Olaudah
Vassilikos, Vassilis 1933- .... **CLC 4, 8**
See also CA 81-84; CANR 75
Vaughan, Henry 1621-1695 .... **LC 27**
See also BRW 2; DLB 131; PAB; RGEL 2
Vaughn, Stephanie .... **CLC 62**
Vazov, Ivan (Minchov) 1850-1921
.... **TCLC 25**
See also CA 121; 167; CDWLB 4; DLB 147
Veblen, Thorstein B(unde) 1857-1929
.... **TCLC 31**
See also AMWS 1; CA 115; 165; DLB 246
Vega, Lope de 1562-1635 ... **HLCS 2; LC 23**
See also EW 2; RGWL 2, 3

Vendler, Helen (Hennessy) 1933- .. **CLC 138**
See also CA 41-44R; CANR 25, 72; MTCW 1, 2
Venison, Alfred
See Pound, Ezra (Weston Loomis)
Verdi, Marie de
See Mencken, H(enry) L(ouis)
Verdu, Matilde
See Cela, Camilo Jose
Verga, Giovanni (Carmelo) 1840-1922
.... **SSC 21; TCLC 3**
See also CA 104; 123; CANR 101; EW 7; RGSF 2; RGWL 2, 3
Vergil 70B.C.-19B.C. .. **CMLC 9, 40; PC 12; WLCS**
See Virgil
See also AW 2; DA; DA3; DAB; DAC; DAM MST, POET; EFS 1; LMFS 1
Verhaeren, Emile (Adolphe Gustave)
1855-1916 .... **TCLC 12**
See also CA 109; GFL 1789 to the Present
Verlaine, Paul (Marie) 1844-1896 . **NCLC 2, 51; PC 2, 32**
See also DAM POET; DLB 217; EW 7; GFL 1789 to the Present; LMFS 2; RGWL 2, 3; TWA
Verne, Jules (Gabriel) 1828-1905 .. **TCLC 6, 52**
See also AAYA 16; BYA 4; CA 110; 131; CLR 88; DA3; DLB 123; GFL 1789 to the Present; JRDA; LAIT 2; LMFS 2; MAICYA 1, 2; RGWL 2, 3; SATA 21; SCFW; SFW 4; TWA; WCH
Verus, Marcus Annius
See Aurelius, Marcus
Very, Jones 1813-1880 .... **NCLC 9**
See also DLB 1, 243; RGAL 4
Vesaas, Tarjei 1897-1970 .... **CLC 48**
See also CA 190; 29-32R; EW 11; RGWL 3
Vialis, Gaston
See Simenon, Georges (Jacques Christian)
Vian, Boris 1920-1959 .... **TCLC 9**
See also CA 106; 164; CANR 111; DLB 72; GFL 1789 to the Present; MTCW 2; RGWL 2, 3
Viaud, (Louis Marie) Julien 1850-1923
See Loti, Pierre
See also CA 107
Vicar, Henry
See Felsen, Henry Gregor
Vicker, Angus
See Felsen, Henry Gregor
Vidal, Gore 1925- ...... **CLC 2, 4, 6, 8, 10, 22, 33, 72, 142**
See Box, Edgar
See also AITN 1; AMWS 4; BEST 90:2; BPFB 3; CA 5-8R; CAD; CANR 13, 45, 65, 100; CD 5; CDALBS; CN 7; CPW; DA3; DAM NOV, POP; DFS 2; DLB 6, 152; INT CANR-13; MTCW 1, 2; RGAL 4; RHW; TUS
Viereck, Peter (Robert Edwin) 1916-
.... **CLC 4; PC 27**
See also CA 1-4R; CANR 1, 47; CP 7; DLB 5; PFS 9, 14
Vigny, Alfred (Victor) de 1797-1863
.... **NCLC 7, 102; PC 26**
See also DAM POET; DLB 119, 192, 217; EW 5; GFL 1789 to the Present; RGWL 2, 3
Vilakazi, Benedict Wallet 1906-1947
.... **TCLC 37**
See also CA 168
Villa, Jose Garcia 1914-1997 ... **AAL; PC 22**
See also CA 25-28R; CANR 12; EXPP
Villarreal, Jose Antonio 1924- .... **HLC 2**
See also CA 133; CANR 93; DAM MULT; DLB 82; HW 1; LAIT 4; RGAL 4

Villaurrutia, Xavier 1903-1950 ..... **TCLC 80**
See also CA 192; HW 1; LAW

Villaverde, Cirilo 1812-1894 .... **NCLC 121**
See also LAW

Villehardouin, Geoffroi de 1150(?)-1218(?)
.... **CMLC 38**

Villiers de l'Isle Adam, Jean Marie Mathias Philippe Auguste 1838-1889 . **NCLC 3; SSC 14**
See also DLB 123, 192; GFL 1789 to the Present; RGSF 2

Villon, François 1431-1463(?) ..... **LC 62; PC 13**
See also DLB 208; EW 2; RGWL 2, 3; TWA

Vine, Barbara .... **CLC 50**
See Rendell, Ruth (Barbara)
See also BEST 90:4

Vinge, Joan (Carol) D(ennison) 1948-
.... **CLC 30; SSC 24**
See also AAYA 32; BPFB 3; CA 93-96; CANR 72; SATA 36, 113; SFW 4; YAW

Viola, Herman J(oseph) 1938- .... **CLC 70**
See also CA 61-64; CANR 8, 23, 48, 91; SATA 126

Violis, G.
See Simenon, Georges (Jacques Christian)

Viramontes, Helena Maria 1954- ... **HLCS 2**
See also CA 159; DLB 122; HW 2

Virgil
See Vergil
See also CDWLB 1; DLB 211; LAIT 1; RGWL 2, 3; WP

Visconti, Luchino 1906-1976 .... **CLC 16**
See also CA 81-84; 65-68; CANR 39

Vittorini, Elio 1908-1966 .... **CLC 6, 9, 14**
See also CA 133; 25-28R; DLB 264; EW 12; RGWL 2, 3

Vivekananda, Swami 1863-1902 ... **TCLC 88**

Vizenor, Gerald Robert 1934- .... **CLC 103; NNAL**
See also CA 13-16R; CAAE 205; CAAS 22; CANR 5, 21, 44, 67; DAM MULT; DLB 175, 227; MTCW 2; TCWW 2

Vizinczey, Stephen 1933- .... **CLC 40**
See also CA 128; CCA 1; INT 128

Vliet, R(ussell) G(ordon) 1929-1984
.... **CLC 22**
See also CA 37-40R; 112; CANR 18

Vogau, Boris Andreyevich 1894-1937(?)
See Pilnyak, Boris
See also CA 123

Vogel, Paula A(nne) 1951- .. **CLC 76; DC 19**
See also CA 108; CAD; CD 5; CWD; DFS 14; RGAL 4

Voigt, Cynthia 1942- .... **CLC 30**
See also AAYA 3, 30; BYA 1, 3, 6, 7, 8; CA 106; CANR 18, 37, 40, 94; CLR 13, 48; INT CANR-18; JRDA; LAIT 5; MAICYA 1, 2; MAICYAS 1; SATA 48, 79, 116; SATA-Brief 33; WYA; YAW

Voigt, Ellen Bryant 1943- .... **CLC 54**
See also CA 69-72; CANR 11, 29, 55, 115; CP 7; CSW; CWP; DLB 120

Voinovich, Vladimir (Nikolaevich) 1932-
.... **CLC 10, 49, 147**
See also CA 81-84; CAAS 12; CANR 33, 67; MTCW 1

Vollmann, William T. 1959- .... **CLC 89**
See also CA 134; CANR 67, 116; CPW; DA3; DAM NOV, POP; MTCW 2

Voloshinov, V. N.
See Bakhtin, Mikhail Mikhailovich

Voltaire 1694-1778 .... **LC 14, 79; SSC 12; WLC**
See also BYA 13; DA; DA3; DAB; DAC; DAM DRAM, MST; EW 4; GFL Beginnings to 1789; LMFS 1; NFS 7; RGWL 2, 3; TWA

von Aschendrof, Baron Ignatz
See Ford, Ford Madox

von Chamisso, Adelbert
See Chamisso, Adelbert von

von Daeniken, Erich 1935- .... **CLC 30**
See also AITN 1; CA 37-40R; CANR 17, 44

von Daniken, Erich
See von Daeniken, Erich

von Hartmann, Eduard 1842-1906
.... **TCLC 96**

von Hayek, Friedrich August
See Hayek, F(riedrich) A(ugust von)

von Heidenstam, (Carl Gustaf) Verner
See Heidenstam, (Carl Gustaf) Verner von

von Heyse, Paul (Johann Ludwig)
See Heyse, Paul (Johann Ludwig von)

von Hofmannsthal, Hugo
See Hofmannsthal, Hugo von

von Horvath, Odon
See von Horvath, Odon

von Horvath, Odon
See von Horvath, Odon

von Horvath, Odon 1901-1938 ..... **TCLC 45**
See von Horvath, Oedoen
See also CA 118; 194; DLB 85, 124; RGWL 2, 3

von Horvath, Oedoen
See von Horvath, Odon
See also CA 184

von Kleist, Heinrich
See Kleist, Heinrich von

von Liliencron, (Friedrich Adolf Axel) Detlev
See Liliencron, (Friedrich Adolf Axel) Detlev von

Vonnegut, Kurt, Jr. 1922- .... **CLC 1, 2, 3, 4, 5, 8, 12, 22, 40, 60, 111; SSC 8; WLC**
See also AAYA 6, 44; AITN 1; AMWS 2; BEST 90:4; BPFB 3; BYA 3, 14; CA 1-4R; CANR 1, 25, 49, 75, 92; CDALB 1968-1988; CN 7; CPW 1; DA; DA3; DAB; DAC; DAM MST, NOV, POP; DLB 2, 8, 152; DLBD 3; DLBY 1980; EXPN; EXPS; LAIT 4; LMFS 2; MTCW 1, 2; NFS 3; RGAL 4; SCFW; SFW 4; SSFS 5; TUS; YAW

Von Rachen, Kurt
See Hubbard, L(afayette) Ron(ald)

von Rezzori (d'Arezzo), Gregor
See Rezzori (d'Arezzo), Gregor von

von Sternberg, Josef
See Sternberg, Josef von

Vorster, Gordon 1924- .... **CLC 34**
See also CA 133

Vosce, Trudie
See Ozick, Cynthia

Voznesensky, Andrei (Andreievich) 1933-
.... **CLC 1, 15, 57**
See also CA 89-92; CANR 37; CWW 2; DAM POET; MTCW 1

Wace, Robert c. 1100-c. 1175 ...... **CMLC 55**
See also DLB 146

Waddington, Miriam 1917- .... **CLC 28**
See also CA 21-24R; CANR 12, 30; CCA 1; CP 7; DLB 68

Wagman, Fredrica 1937- .... **CLC 7**
See also CA 97-100; INT 97-100

Wagner, Linda W.
See Wagner-Martin, Linda (C.)

Wagner, Linda Welshimer
See Wagner-Martin, Linda (C.)

Wagner, Richard 1813-1883 .. **NCLC 9, 119**
See also DLB 129; EW 6

Wagner-Martin, Linda (C.) 1936- .. **CLC 50**
See also CA 159

Wagoner, David (Russell) 1926- .. **CLC 3, 5, 15; PC 33**
See also AMWS 9; CA 1-4R; CAAS 3; CANR 2, 71; CN 7; CP 7; DLB 5, 256; SATA 14; TCWW 2

Wah, Fred(erick James) 1939- .... **CLC 44**
See also CA 107; 141; CP 7; DLB 60

Wahloo, Per 1926-1975 .... **CLC 7**
See also BPFB 3; CA 61-64; CANR 73; CMW 4; MSW

Wahloo, Peter
See Wahloo, Per

Wain, John (Barrington) 1925-1994
.... **CLC 2, 11, 15, 46**
See also CA 5-8R; 145; CAAS 4; CANR 23, 54; CDBLB 1960 to Present; DLB 15, 27, 139, 155; MTCW 1, 2

Wajda, Andrzej 1926- .... **CLC 16**
See also CA 102

Wakefield, Dan 1932- .... **CLC 7**
See also CA 21-24R; CAAS 7; CN 7

Wakefield, Herbert Russell 1888-1965
.... **TCLC 120**
See also CA 5-8R; CANR 77; HGG; SUFW

Wakoski, Diane 1937- .... **CLC 2, 4, 7, 9, 11, 40; PC 15**
See also CA 13-16R; CAAS 1; CANR 9, 60, 106; CP 7; CWP; DAM POET; DLB 5; INT CANR-9; MTCW 2

Wakoski-Sherbell, Diane
See Wakoski, Diane

Walcott, Derek (Alton) 1930- . **BLC 3; CLC 2, 4, 9, 14, 25, 42, 67, 76, 160; DC 7; PC 46**
See also BW 2; CA 89-92; CANR 26, 47, 75, 80; CBD; CD 5; CDWLB 3; CP 7; DA3; DAB; DAC; DAM MST, MULT, POET; DLB 117; DLBY 1981; DNFS 1; EFS 1; LMFS 2; MTCW 1, 2; PFS 6; RGEL 2; TWA

Waldman, Anne (Lesley) 1945- .... **CLC 7**
See also BG 3; CA 37-40R; CAAS 17; CANR 34, 69, 116; CP 7; CWP; DLB 16

Waldo, E. Hunter
See Sturgeon, Theodore (Hamilton)

Waldo, Edward Hamilton
See Sturgeon, Theodore (Hamilton)

Walker, Alice (Malsenior) 1944- ...... **BLC 3; CLC 5, 6, 9, 19, 27, 46, 58, 103, 167; PC 30; SSC 5; WLCS**
See also AAYA 3, 33; AFAW 1, 2; AMWS 3; BEST 89:4; BFFB 3; BW 2, 3; CA 37-40R; CANR 9, 27, 49, 66, 82; CDALB 1968-1988; CN 7; CPW; CSW; DA; DA3; DAB; DAC; DAM MST, MULT, NOV, POET, POP; DLB 6, 33, 143; EXPN; EXPS; FW; INT CANR-27; LAIT 3; MAWW; MTCW 1, 2; NFS 5; RGAL 4; RGSF 2; SATA 31; SSFS 2, 11; TUS; YAW

Walker, David Harry 1911-1992 ..... **CLC 14**
See also CA 1-4R; 137; CANR 1; CWRI 5; SATA 8; SATA-Obit 71

Walker, Edward Joseph 1934-
See Walker, Ted
See also CA 21-24R; CANR 12, 28, 53; CP 7

Walker, George F. 1947- .... **CLC 44, 61**
See also CA 103; CANR 21, 43, 59; CD 5; DAB; DAC; DAM MST; DLB 60

Walker, Joseph A. 1935- .... **CLC 19**
See also BW 1, 3; CA 89-92; CAD; CANR 26; CD 5; DAM DRAM, MST; DFS 12; DLB 38

Walker, Margaret (Abigail) 1915-1998
..... **BLC; CLC 1, 6; PC 20; TCLC 129**
See also AFAW 1, 2; BW 2, 3; CA 73-76; 172; CANR 26, 54, 76; CN 7; CP 7; CSW; DAM MULT; DLB 76, 152; EXPP; FW; MTCW 1, 2; RGAL 4; RHW

Walker, Ted .... **CLC 13**
See Walker, Edward Joseph
See also DLB 40

Wallace, David Foster 1962- ... **CLC 50, 114**
See also AMWS 10; CA 132; CANR 59; DA3; MTCW 2

Wallace, Dexter
See Masters, Edgar Lee

Wallace, (Richard Horatio) Edgar 1875-1932
.... **TCLC 57**
See also CA 115; CMW 4; DLB 70; MSW; RGEL 2

Wallace, Irving 1916-1990 .... **CLC 7, 13**
See also AITN 1; BPFB 3; CA 1-4R; 132; CAAS 1; CANR 1, 27; CPW; DAM NOV, POP; INT CANR-27; MTCW 1, 2

Wallant, Edward Lewis 1926-1962 .. **CLC 5, 10**
See also CA 1-4R; CANR 22; DLB 2, 28, 143; MTCW 1, 2; RGAL 4

Wallas, Graham 1858-1932 .... **TCLC 91**

Waller, Edmund 1606-1687 .... **LC 86**
See also BRW 2; DAM POET; DLB 126; PAB; RGEL 2

Walley, Byron
See Card, Orson Scott

Walpole, Horace 1717-1797 .... **LC 2, 49**
See also BRW 3; DLB 39, 104, 213; HGG; LMFS 1; RGEL 2; SUFW 1; TEA

Walpole, Hugh (Seymour) 1884-1941
.... **TCLC 5**
See also CA 104; 165; DLB 34; HGG; MTCW 2; RGEL 2; RHW

Walrond, Eric (Derwent) 1898-1966 ... **HR 3**
See also BW 1; CA 125; DLB 51

Walser, Martin 1927- .... **CLC 27**
See also CA 57-60; CANR 8, 46; CWW 2; DLB 75, 124

Walser, Robert 1878-1956 ... **SSC 20; TCLC 18**
See also CA 118; 165; CANR 100; DLB 66

Walsh, Gillian Paton
See Paton Walsh, Gillian

Walsh, Jill Paton .... **CLC 35**
See Paton Walsh, Gillian
See also CLR 2, 65; WYA

Walter, Villiam Christian
See Andersen, Hans Christian

Walters, Anna L(ee) 1946- .... **NNAL**
See also CA 73-76

Walther von der Vogelweide c. 1170-1228
.... **CMLC 56**

Walton, Izaak 1593-1683 .... **LC 72**
See also BRW 2; CDBLB Before 1660; DLB 151, 213; RGEL 2

Wambaugh, Joseph (Aloysius), Jr. 1937-
.... **CLC 3, 18**
See also AITN 1; BEST 89:3; BPFB 3; CA 33-36R; CANR 42, 65, 115; CMW 4; CPW 1; DA3; DAM NOV, POP; DLB 6; DLBY 1983; MSW; MTCW 1, 2

Wang Wei 699(?)-761(?) .... **PC 18**
See also TWA

Ward, Arthur Henry Sarsfield 1883-1959
See Rohmer, Sax
See also CA 108; 173; CMW 4; HGG

Ward, Douglas Turner 1930- .... **CLC 19**
See also BW 1; CA 81-84; CAD; CANR 27; CD 5; DLB 7, 38

Ward, E. D.
See Lucas, E(dward) V(errall)

Ward, Mrs. Humphry 1851-1920
See Ward, Mary Augusta
See also RGEL 2

Ward, Mary Augusta 1851-1920 .. **TCLC 55**
See Ward, Mrs. Humphry
See also DLB 18

Ward, Peter
See Faust, Frederick (Schiller)

Warhol, Andy 1928(?)-1987 .... **CLC 20**
See also AAYA 12; BEST 89:4; CA 89-92; 121; CANR 34

Warner, Francis (Robert le Plastrier) 1937-
.... **CLC 14**
See also CA 53-56; CANR 11

Warner, Marina 1946- .... **CLC 59**
See also CA 65-68; CANR 21, 55; CN 7; DLB 194

Warner, Rex (Ernest) 1905-1986 .... **CLC 45**
See also CA 89-92; 119; DLB 15; RGEL 2; RHW

Warner, Susan (Bogert) 1819-1885
.... **NCLC 31**
See also DLB 3, 42, 239, 250, 254

Warner, Sylvia (Constance) Ashton
See Ashton-Warner, Sylvia (Constance)

Warner, Sylvia Townsend 1893-1978
.... **CLC 7, 19; SSC 23; TCLC 131**
See also BRWS 7; CA 61-64; 77-80; CANR 16, 60, 104; DLB 34, 139; FANT; FW; MTCW 1, 2; RGEL 2; RGSF 2; RHW

Warren, Mercy Otis 1728-1814 .... **NCLC 13**
See also DLB 31, 200; RGAL 4; TUS

Warren, Robert Penn 1905-1989 . **CLC 1, 4, 6, 8, 10, 13, 18, 39, 53, 59; PC 37; SSC 4, 58; WLC**
See also AITN 1; AMW; BPFB 3; BYA 1; CA 13-16R; 129; CANR 10, 47; CDALB 1968-1988; DA; DA3; DAB; DAC; DAM MST, NOV, POET; DLB 2, 48, 152; DLBY 1980, 1989; INT CANR-10; MTCW 1, 2; NFS 13; RGAL 4; RGSF 2; RHW; SATA 46; SATA-Obit 63; SSFS 8; TUS

Warrigal, Jack
See Furphy, Joseph

Warshofsky, Isaac
See Singer, Isaac Bashevis

Warton, Joseph 1722-1800 .... **NCLC 118**
See also DLB 104, 109; RGEL 2

Warton, Thomas 1728-1790 .... **LC 15, 82**
See also DAM POET; DLB 104, 109; RGEL 2

Waruk, Kona
See Harris, (Theodore) Wilson

Warung, Price .... **TCLC 45**
See Astley, William
See also DLB 230; RGEL 2

Warwick, Jarvis
See Garner, Hugh
See also CCA 1

Washington, Alex
See Harris, Mark

Washington, Booker T(aliaferro) 1856-1915
.... **BLC 3; TCLC 10**
See also BW 1; CA 114; 125; DA3; DAM MULT; LAIT 2; RGAL 4; SATA 28

Washington, George 1732-1799 .... **LC 25**
See also DLB 31

Wassermann, (Karl) Jakob 1873-1934
.... **TCLC 6**
See also CA 104; 163; DLB 66

Wasserstein, Wendy 1950- . **CLC 32, 59, 90; DC 4**
See also CA 121; 129; CABS 3; CAD; CANR 53, 75; CD 5; CWD; DA3; DAM DRAM; DFS 17; DLB 228; FW; INT CA-129; MTCW 2; SATA 94

Waterhouse, Keith (Spencer) 1929-
.... **CLC 47**
See also CA 5-8R; CANR 38, 67, 109; CBD; CN 7; DLB 13, 15; MTCW 1, 2

Waters, Frank (Joseph) 1902-1995 . **CLC 88**
See also CA 5-8R; 149; CAAS 13; CANR 3, 18, 63; DLB 212; DLBY 1986; RGAL 4; TCWW 2

Waters, Mary C. .... **CLC 70**

Waters, Roger 1944- .... **CLC 35**

Watkins, Frances Ellen
See Harper, Frances Ellen Watkins

Watkins, Gerrold
See Malzberg, Barry N(athaniel)

Watkins, Gloria Jean 1952(?)-
See hooks, bell
See also BW 2; CA 143; CANR 87; MTCW 2; SATA 115

Watkins, Paul 1964- .... **CLC 55**
See also CA 132; CANR 62, 98

Watkins, Vernon Phillips 1906-1967
.... **CLC 43**
See also CA 9-10; 25-28R; CAP 1; DLB 20; RGEL 2

Watson, Irving S.
See Mencken, H(enry) L(ouis)

Watson, John H.
See Farmer, Philip Jose

Watson, Richard F.
See Silverberg, Robert

Waugh, Auberon (Alexander) 1939-2001
.... **CLC 7**
See also CA 45-48; 192; CANR 6, 22, 92; DLB 14, 194

Waugh, Evelyn (Arthur St. John) 1903-1966
.. **CLC 1, 3, 8, 13, 19, 27, 44, 107; SSC 41; WLC**
See also BPFB 3; BRW 7; CA 85-88; 25-28R; CANR 22; CDBLB 1914-1945; DA; DA3; DAB; DAC; DAM MST, NOV, POP; DLB 15, 162, 195; MTCW 1, 2; NFS 17; RGEL 2; RGSF 2; TEA; WLIT 4

Waugh, Harriet 1944- .... **CLC 6**
See also CA 85-88; CANR 22

Ways, C. R.
See Blount, Roy (Alton), Jr.

Waystaff, Simon
See Swift, Jonathan

Webb, Beatrice (Martha Potter) 1858-1943
.... **TCLC 22**
See also CA 117; 162; DLB 190; FW

Webb, Charles (Richard) 1939- .... **CLC 7**
See also CA 25-28R; CANR 114

Webb, James H(enry), Jr. 1946- ..... **CLC 22**
See also CA 81-84

Webb, Mary Gladys (Meredith) 1881-1927
.... **TCLC 24**
See also CA 182; 123; DLB 34; FW

Webb, Mrs. Sidney
See Webb, Beatrice (Martha Potter)

Webb, Phyllis 1927- .... **CLC 18**
See also CA 104; CANR 23; CCA 1; CP 7; CWP; DLB 53

Webb, Sidney (James) 1859-1947 . **TCLC 22**
See also CA 117; 163; DLB 190

Webber, Andrew Lloyd .... **CLC 21**
See Lloyd Webber, Andrew
See also DFS 7

Weber, Lenora Mattingly 1895-1971
.... **CLC 12**
See also CA 19-20; 29-32R; CAP 1; SATA 2; SATA-Obit 26

Weber, Max 1864-1920 .... **TCLC 69**
See also CA 109; 189

Webster, John 1580(?)-1634(?) ..... **DC 2; LC 33, 84; WLC**
See also BRW 2; CDBLB Before 1660; DA; DAB; DAC; DAM DRAM, MST, DFS 17; DLB 58; IDTP; RGEL 2; WLIT 3

Webster, Noah 1758-1843 .... **NCLC 30**
See also DLB 1, 37, 42, 43, 73, 243

Wedekind, (Benjamin) Frank(lin) 1864-1918
.... **TCLC 7**
See also CA 104; 153; CDWLB 2; DAM DRAM; DLB 118; EW 8; LMFS 2; RGWL 2, 3

Wehr, Demaris .... **CLC 65**
Weidman, Jerome 1913-1998 .... **CLC 7**
See also AITN 2; CA 1-4R; 171; CAD; CANR 1; DLB 28
Weil, Simone (Adolphine) 1909-1943
.... **TCLC 23**
See also CA 117; 159; EW 12; FW; GFL 1789 to the Present; MTCW 2
Weininger, Otto 1880-1903 .... **TCLC 84**
Weinstein, Nathan
See West, Nathanael
Weinstein, Nathan von Wallenstein
See West, Nathanael
Weir, Peter (Lindsay) 1944- .... **CLC 20**
See also CA 113; 123
Weiss, Peter (Ulrich) 1916-1982 .... **CLC 3, 15, 51**
See also CA 45-48; 106; CANR 3; DAM DRAM; DFS 3; DLB 69, 124; EGWL 2, 3
Weiss, Theodore (Russell) 1916- .. **CLC 3, 8, 14**
See also CA 9-12R; CAAE 189; CAAS 2; CANR 46, 94; CP 7; DLB 5
Welch, (Maurice) Denton 1915-1948
.... **TCLC 22**
See also BRWS 8; CA 121; 148; RGEL 2
Welch, James 1940- . **CLC 6, 14, 52; NNAL**
See also CA 85-88; CANR 42, 66, 107; CN 7; CP 7; CPW; DAM MULT, POP; DLB 175, 256; RGAL 4; TCWW 2
Weldon, Fay 1931- ...... **CLC 6, 9, 11, 19, 36, 59, 122**
See also BRWS 4; CA 21-24R; CANR 16, 46, 63, 97; CDBLB 1960 to Present; CN 7; CPW; DAM POP; DLB 14, 194; FW; HGG; INT CANR-16; MTCW 1, 2; RGEL 2; RGSF 2
Wellek, Rene 1903-1995 .... **CLC 28**
See also CA 5-8R; 150; CAAS 7; CANR 8; DLB 63; INT CANR-8
Weller, Michael 1942- .... **CLC 10, 53**
See also CA 85-88; CAD; CD 5
Weller, Paul 1958- .... **CLC 26**
Wellershoff, Dieter 1925- .... **CLC 46**
See also CA 89-92; CANR 16, 37
Welles, (George) Orson 1915-1985
.... **CLC 20, 80**
See also AAYA 40; CA 93-96; 117
Wellman, John McDowell 1945-
See Wellman, Mac
See also CA 166; CD 5
Wellman, Mac .... **CLC 65**
See Wellman, John McDowell; Wellman, John McDowell
See also CAD; RGAL 4
Wellman, Manly Wade 1903-1986 .. **CLC 49**
See also CA 1-4R; 118; CANR 6, 16, 44; FANT; SATA 6; SATA-Obit 47; SFW 4; SUFW
Wells, Carolyn 1869(?)-1942 .... **TCLC 35**
See also CA 113; 185; CMW 4; DLB 11
Wells, H(erbert) G(eorge) 1866-1946
...... **SSC 6; TCLC 6, 12, 19, 133; WLC**
See also AAYA 18; BPFB 3; BRW 6 CA 110; 121; CDBLB 1914-1945; CLR 64; DA; DA3; DAB; DAC; DAM MST, NOV; DLB 34, 70, 156, 178; EXPS; HGG; LAIT 3; LMFS 2; MTCW 1, 2; NFS 17; RGEL 2; RGSF 2; SATA 20; SCFW 4; SSFS 3; SUFW; TEA; WCH; WLIT 4; YAW
Wells, Rosemary 1943- .... **CLC 12**
See also AAYA 13; BYA 7, 8; CA 85-88; CANR 48; CLR 16, 69; CWRI 5; MAICYA 1, 2; SAAS 1; SATA 18, 69, 114; YAW

Wells-Barnett, Ida B(ell) 1862-1931
.... **TCLC 125**
See also CA 182; DLB 23, 221
Welsh, Irvine 1958- .... **CLC 144**
See also CA 173; DLB 271
Welty, Eudora (Alice) 1909-2001 . **CLC 1, 2, 5, 14, 22, 33, 105; SSC 1, 27, 51; WLC**
See also AAYA 48; AMW; AMWR 1; BPFB 3; CA 9-12R; 199; CABS 1; CANR 32, 65; CDALB 1941-1968; CN 7; CSW; DA; DA3; DAB; DAC; DAM MST, NOV; DLB 2, 102, 143; DLBD 12; DLBY 1987, 2001; EXPS; HGG; LAIT 3; MAWW; MTCW 1, 2; NFS 13, 15; RGAL 4; RGSF 2; RHW; SSFS 2, 10; TUS
Wen I-to 1899-1946 .... **TCLC 28**
Wentworth, Robert
See Hamilton, Edmond
Werfel, Franz (Viktor) 1890-1945 .. **TCLC 8**
See also CA 104; 161; DLB 81, 124; RGWL 2, 3
Wergeland, Henrik Arnold 1808-1845
.... **NCLC 5**
Wersba, Barbara 1932- .... **CLC 30**
See also AAYA 2, 30; BYA 6, 12, 13; CA 29-32R, 182; CAAE 182 CANR 16, 38; CLR 3, 78; DLB 52; JRDA; MAICYA 1, 2; SAAS 2; SATA 1, 58; SATA-Essay 103; WYA; YAW
Wertmueller, Lina 1928- .... **CLC 16**
See also CA 97-100; CANR 39, 78
Wescott, Glenway 1901-1987 . **CLC 13; SSC 35**
See also CA 13-16R; 121; CANR 23, 70; DLB 4, 9, 102; RGAL 4
Wesker, Arnold 1932- .... **CLC 3, 5, 42**
See also CA 1-4R; CAAS 7; CANR 1, 33; CBD; CD 5; CDBLB 1960 to Present; DAB; DAM DRAM; DLB 13; MTCW 1; RGEL 2; TEA
Wesley, John 1703-1791 .... **LC 88**
See also DLB 104
Wesley, Richard (Errol) 1945- .... **CLC 7**
See also BW 1; CA 57-60; CAD; CANR 27; CD 5; DLB 38
Wessel, Johan Herman 1742-1785 .... **LC 7**
West, Anthony (Panther) 1914-1987
.... **CLC 50**
See also CA 45-48; 124; CANR 3, 19; DLB 15
West, C. P.
See Wodehouse, P(elham) G(renville)
West, Cornel (Ronald) 1953- .. **BLCS; CLC 134**
See also CA 144; CANR 91; DLB 246
West, Delno C(loyde), Jr. 1936- ...... **CLC 70**
See also CA 57-60
West, Dorothy 1907-1998 .... **HR 3; TCLC 108**
See also BW 2; CA 143; 169; DLB 76
West, (Mary) Jessamyn 1902-1984 .. **CLC 7, 17**
See also CA 9-12R; 112; CANR 27; DLB 6; DLBY 1984; MTCW 1, 2; RGAL 4; RHW; SATA-Obit 37; TCWW 2; TUS; YAW
West, Morris L(anglo) 1916-1999 .... **CLC 6, 33**
See also BPFB 3; CA 5-8R; 187; CANR 24, 49, 64; CN 7; CPW; MTCW 1, 2
West, Nathanael 1903-1940 . **SSC 16; TCLC 1, 14, 44**
See also AMW; AMWR 2; BPFB 3; CA 104; 125; CDALB 1929-1941; DA3; DLB 4, 9, 28; MTCW 1, 2; NFS 16; RGAL 4; TUS
West, Owen
See Koontz, Dean R(ay)

West, Paul 1930- .... **CLC 7, 14, 96**
See also CA 13-16R; CAAS 7; CANR 22, 53, 76, 89; CN 7; DLB 14; INT CANR-22; MTCW 2
West, Rebecca 1892-1983 .. **CLC 7, 9, 31, 50**
See also BPFB 3; BRWS 3; CA 5-8R; 109; CANR 19; DLB 36; DLBY 1983; FW; MTCW 1, 2; NCFS 4; RGEL 2; TEA
Westall, Robert (Atkinson) 1929-1993
.... **CLC 17**
See also AAYA 12; BYA 2, 6, 7, 8, 9; CA 69-72; 141; CANR 18, 68; CLR 13; FANT; JRDA; MAICYA 1, 2; MAICYAS 1; SAAS 2; SATA 23, 69; SATA-Obit 75; WYA; YAW
Westermarck, Edward 1862-1939
.... **TCLC 87**
Westlake, Donald E(dwin) 1933- ...... **CLC 7, 33**
See also BPFB 3; CA 17-20R; CAAS 13; CANR 16, 44, 65, 94; CMW 4; CPW; DAM POP; INT CANR-16; MSW; MTCW 2
Westmacott, Mary
See Christie, Agatha (Mary Clarissa)
Weston, Allen
See Norton, Andre
Wetcheek, J. L.
See Feuchtwanger, Lion
Wetering, Janwillem van de
See van de Wetering, Janwillem
Wetherald, Agnes Ethelwyn 1857-1940
.... **TCLC 81**
See also CA 202; DLB 99
Wetherell, Elizabeth
See Warner, Susan (Bogert)
Whale, James 1889-1957 .... **TCLC 63**
Whalen, Philip (Glenn) 1923-2002 .. **CLC 6, 29**
See also BG 3; CA 9-12R; 209; CANR 5, 39; CP 7; DLB 16; WP
Wharton, Edith (Newbold Jones) 1862-1937
. **SSC 6; TCLC 3, 9, 27, 53, 129; WLC**
See also AAYA 25; AMW; AMWR 1; BPFB 3; CA 104; 132; CDALB 1865-1917; DA; DA3; DAB; DAC; DAM MST, NOV; DLB 4, 9, 12, 78, 189; DLBD 13; EXPS; HGG; LAIT 2, 3; MAWW; MTCW 1, 2; NFS 5, 11, 15; RGAL 4; RGSF 2; RHW; SSFS 6, 7; SUFW; TUS
Wharton, James
See Mencken, H(enry) L(ouis)
Wharton, William (a pseudonym) . **CLC 18, 37**
See also CA 93-96; DLBY 1980; INT 93-96
Wheatley (Peters), Phillis 1753(?)-1784
.... **BLC 3; LC 3, 50; PC 3; WLC**
See also AFAW 1, 2; CDALB 1640-1865; DA; DA3; DAC; DAM MST, MULT, POET; DLB 31, 50; EXPP; PFS 13; RGAL 4
Wheelock, John Hall 1886-1978 ..... **CLC 14**
See also CA 13-16R; 77-80; CANR 14; DLB 45
White, Babington
See Braddon, Mary Elizabeth
White, E(lwyn) B(rooks) 1899-1985
.... **CLC 10, 34, 39**
See also AITN 2; AMWS 1; CA 13-16R; 116; CANR 16, 37; CDALBS; CLR 1, 21; CPW; DA3; DAM POP; DLB 11, 22; FANT; MAICYA 1, 2; MTCW 1, 2; RGAL 4; SATA 2, 29, 100; SATA-Obit 44; TUS
White, Edmund (Valentine III) 1940-
.... **CLC 27, 110**
See also AAYA 7; CA 45-48; CANR 3, 19, 36, 62, 107; CN 7; DA3; DAM POP; DLB 227; MTCW 1, 2

White, Hayden V. 1928- .... **CLC 148**
See also CA 128; DLB 246

White, Patrick (Victor Martindale)
1912-1990 ..... **CLC 3, 4, 5, 7, 9, 18, 65, 69; SSC 39**
See also BRWS 1; CA 81-84; 132; CANR 43; DLB 260; MTCW 1; RGEL 2; RGSF 2; RHW; TWA

White, Phyllis Dorothy James 1920-
See James, P. D.
See also CA 21-24R; CANR 17, 43, 65, 112; CMW 4; CN 7; CPW; DA3; DAM POP; MTCW 1, 2; TEA

White, T(erence) H(anbury) 1906-1964
.... **CLC 30**
See also AAYA 22; BPFB 3; BYA 4, 5; CA 73-76; CANR 37; DLB 160; FANT; JRDA; LAIT 1; MAICYA 1, 2; RGEL 2; SATA 12; SUFW 1; YAW

White, Terence de Vere 1912-1994 . **CLC 49**
See also CA 49-52; 145; CANR 3

White, Walter
See White, Walter F(rancis)

White, Walter F(rancis) 1893-1955 . **BLC 3; HR 3; TCLC 15**
See also BW 1; CA 115; 124; DAM MULT; DLB 51

White, William Hale 1831-1913
See Rutherford, Mark
See also CA 121; 189

Whitehead, Alfred North 1861-1947
.... **TCLC 97**
See also CA 117; 165; DLB 100, 262

Whitehead, E(dward) A(nthony) 1933-
.... **CLC 5**
See also CA 65-68; CANR 58; CBD; CD 5

Whitehead, Ted
See Whitehead, E(dward) A(nthony)

Whiteman, Roberta J. Hill 1947- ..... **NNAL**
See also CA 146

Whitemore, Hugh (John) 1936- ...... **CLC 37**
See also CA 132; CANR 77; CBD; CD 5; INT CA-132

Whitman, Sarah Helen (Power) 1803-1878
.... **NCLC 19**
See also DLB 1, 243

Whitman, Walt(er) 1819-1892 . **NCLC 4, 31, 81; PC 3; WLC**
See also AAYA 42; AMW; AMWR 1; CDALB 1640-1865; DA; DA3; DAB; DAC; DAM MST, POET; DLB 3, 64, 224, 250; EXPP; LAIT 2; LMFS 1; PAB; PFS 2, 3, 13; RGAL 4; SATA 20; TUS; WP; WYAS 1

Whitney, Phyllis A(yame) 1903- ...... **CLC 42**
See also AAYA 36; AITN 2; BEST 90:3; CA 1-4R; CANR 3, 25, 38, 60; CLR 59; CMW 4; CPW; DA3; DAM POP; JRDA; MAICYA 1, 2; MTCW 2; RHW; SATA 1, 30; YAW

Whittemore, (Edward) Reed (Jr.) 1919-
.... **CLC 4**
See also CA 9-12R; CAAS 8; CANR 4; CP 7; DLB 5

Whittier, John Greenleaf 1807-1892
.... **NCLC 8, 59**
See also AMWS 1; DLB 1, 243; RGAL 4

Whittlebot, Hernia
See Coward, Noel (Peirce)

Wicker, Thomas Grey 1926-
See Wicker, Tom
See also CA 65-68; CANR 21, 46

Wicker, Tom .... **CLC 7**
See Wicker, Thomas Grey

Wideman, John Edgar 1941- .. **BLC 3; CLC 5, 34, 36, 67, 122**
See also AFAW 1, 2; AMWS 10; BPFB 4; BW 2, 3; CA 85-88; CANR 14, 42, 67, 109; CN 7; DAM MULT; DLB 33, 143; MTCW 2; RGAL 4; RGSF 2; SSFS 6, 12

Wiebe, Rudy (Henry) 1934- . **CLC 6, 11, 14, 138**
See also CA 37-40R; CANR 42, 67; CN 7; DAC; DAM MST; DLB 60; RHW

Wieland, Christoph Martin 1733-1813
.... **NCLC 17**
See also DLB 97; EW 4; LMFS 1; RGWL 2, 3

Wiene, Robert 1881-1938 .... **TCLC 56**

Wieners, John 1934- .... **CLC 7**
See also BG 3; CA 13-16R; CP 7; DLB 16; WP

Wiesel, Elie(zer) 1928- ...... **CLC 3, 5, 11, 37, 165; WLCS**
See also AAYA 7; AITN 1; CA 5-8R; CAAS 4; CANR 8, 40, 65; CDALBS; DA; DA3; DAB; DAC; DAM MST, NOV; DLB 83; DLBY 1987; INT CANR-8; LAIT 4; MTCW 1, 2; NCFS 4; NFS 4; RGWL 3; SATA 56; YAW

Wiggins, Marianne 1947- .... **CLC 57**
See also BEST 89:3; CA 130; CANR 60

Wiggs, Susan .... **CLC 70**
See also CA 201

Wight, James Alfred 1916-1995
See Herriot, James
See also CA 77-80; SATA 55; SATA-Brief 44

Wilbur, Richard (Purdy) 1921- ... **CLC 3, 6, 9, 14, 53, 110**
See also AMWS 3; CA 1-4R; CABS 2; CANR 2, 29, 76, 93; CDALBS; CP 7; DA; DAB; DAC; DAM MST, POET; DLB 5, 169; EXPP; INT CANR-29; MTCW 1, 2; PAB; PFS 11, 12, 16; RGAL 4; SATA 9, 108; WP

Wild, Peter 1940- .... **CLC 14**
See also CA 37-40R; CP 7; DLB 5

Wilde, Oscar (Fingal O'Flahertie Wills)
1854(?)-1900 ... **DC 17; SSC 11; TCLC 1, 8, 23, 41; WLC**
See also AAYA 49; BRW 5; BRWC 1; BRWR 2; CA 104; 119; CANR 112; CDBLB 1890-1914; DA; DA3; DAB; DAC; DAM DRAM, MST, NOV; DFS 4, 8, 9; DLB 10, 19, 34, 57, 141, 156, 190; EXPS; FANT; RGEL 2; RGSF 2; SATA 24; SSFS 7; SUFW; TEA; WCH; WLIT 4

Wilder, Billy .... **CLC 20**
See Wilder, Samuel
See also DLB 26

Wilder, Samuel 1906-2002
See Wilder, Billy
See also CA 89-92; 205

Wilder, Stephen
See Marlowe, Stephen

Wilder, Thornton (Niven) 1897-1975
.... **CLC 1, 5, 6, 10, 15, 35, 82; DC 1; WLC**
See also AAYA 29; AITN 2; AMW; CA 13-16R; 61-64; CAD; CANR 40; CDALBS; DA; DA3; DAB; DAC; DAM DRAM, MST, NOV; DFS 1, 4, 16; DLB 4, 7, 9, 228; DLBY 1997; LAIT 3; MTCW 1, 2; RGAL 4; RHW; WYAS 1

Wilding, Michael 1942- ...... **CLC 73; SSC 50**
See also CA 104; CANR 24, 49, 106; CN 7; RGSF 2

Wiley, Richard 1944- .... **CLC 44**
See also CA 121; 129; CANR 71

Wilhelm, Kate .... **CLC 7**
See Wilhelm, Katie (Gertrude)
See also AAYA 20; CAAS 5; DLB 8; INT CANR-17; SCFW 2

Wilhelm, Katie (Gertrude) 1928-
See Wilhelm, Kate
See also CA 37-40R; CANR 17, 36, 60, 94; MTCW 1; SFW 4

Wilkins, Mary
See Freeman, Mary E(leanor) Wilkins

Willard, Nancy 1936- .... **CLC 7, 37**
See also BYA 5; CA 89-92; CANR 10, 39, 68, 107; CLR 5; CWP; CWRI 5; DLB 5, 52; FANT; MAICYA 1, 2; MTCW 1; SATA 37, 71, 127; SATA-Brief 30; SUFW 2

William of Malmesbury c. 1090B.C.-c. 1140B.C. .... **CMLC 57**

William of Ockham 1290-1349 .... **CMLC 32**

Williams, Ben Ames 1889-1953 .... **TCLC 89**
See also CA 183; DLB 102

Williams, C(harles) K(enneth) 1936-
.... **CLC 33, 56, 148**
See also CA 37-40R; CAAS 26; CANR 57, 106; CP 7; DAM POET; DLB 5

Williams, Charles
See Collier, James Lincoln

Williams, Charles (Walter Stansby)
1886-1945 .... **TCLC 1, 11**
See also CA 104; 163; DLB 100, 153, 255; FANT; RGEL 2; SUFW 1

Williams, Ella Gwendolen Rees
See Rhys, Jean

Williams, (George) Emlyn 1905-1987
.... **CLC 15**
See also CA 104; 123; CANR 36; DAM DRAM; DLB 10, 77; MTCW 1

Williams, Hank 1923-1953 .... **TCLC 81**
See Williams, Hiram King

Williams, Hiram Hank
See Williams, Hank

Williams, Hiram King
See Williams, Hank
See also CA 188

Williams, Hugo 1942- .... **CLC 42**
See also CA 17-20R; CANR 45; CP 7; DLB 40

Williams, J. Walker
See Wodehouse, P(elham) G(renville)

Williams, John A(lfred) 1925- .... **BLC 3; CLC 5, 13**
See also AFAW 2; BW 2, 3; CA 53-56; CAAS 3; CANR 6, 26, 51; CN 7; CSW; DAM MULT; DLB 2, 33; INT CANR-6; RGAL 4; SFW 4

Williams, Jonathan (Chamberlain) 1929-
.... **CLC 13**
See also CA 9-12R; CAAS 12; CANR 8, 108; CP 7; DLB 5

Williams, Joy 1944- .... **CLC 31**
See also CA 41-44R; CANR 22, 48, 97

Williams, Norman 1952- .... **CLC 39**
See also CA 118

Williams, Sherley Anne 1944-1999 .. **BLC 3; CLC 89**
See also AFAW 2; BW 2, 3; CA 73-76; 185; CANR 25, 82; DAM MULT, POET; DLB 41; INT CANR-25; SATA 78; SATA-Obit 116

Williams, Shirley
See Williams, Sherley Anne

Williams, Tennessee 1911-1983 .... **CLC 1, 2, 5, 7, 8, 11, 15, 19, 30, 39, 45, 71, 111; DC 4; WLC**
See also AAYA 31; AITN 1, 2; AMW; AMWC 1; CA 5-8R; 108; CABS 3; CAD; CANR 31; CDALB 1941-1968; DA; DA3; DAB; DAC; DAM DRAM, MST; DFS 17; DLB 7; DLBD 4; DLBY 1983; GLL 1; LAIT 4; MTCW 1, 2; RGAL 4; TUS

Williams, Thomas (Alonzo) 1926-1990
.... **CLC 14**
See also CA 1-4R; 132; CANR 2

Williams, William C.
See Williams, William Carlos

Williams, William Carlos 1883-1963
.... **CLC 1, 2, 5, 9, 13, 22, 42, 67; PC 7; SSC 31**
See also AAYA 46; AMW; AMWR 1; CA 89-92; CANR 34; CDALB 1917-1929; DA; DA3; DAB; DAC; DAM MST, POET; DLB 4, 16, 54, 86; EXPP; MTCW 1, 2; NCFS 4; PAB; PFS 1, 6, 11; RGAL 4; RGSF 2; TUS; WP

Williamson, David (Keith) 1942- .... **CLC 56**
See also CA 103; CANR 41; CD 5

Williamson, Ellen Douglas 1905-1984
See Douglas, Ellen
See also CA 17-20R; 114; CANR 39

Williamson, Jack .... **CLC 29**
See Williamson, John Stewart
See also CAAS 8; DLB 8; SCFW 2

Williamson, John Stewart 1908-
See Williamson, Jack
See also CA 17-20R; CANR 23, 70; SFW 4

Willie, Frederick
See Lovecraft, H(oward) P(hillips)

Willingham, Calder (Baynard, Jr.) 1922-1995 .... **CLC 5, 51**
See also CA 5-8R; 147; CANR 3; CSW; DLB 2, 44; IDFW 3, 4; MTCW 1

Willis, Charles
See Clarke, Arthur C(harles)

Willy
See Colette, (Sidonie-Gabrielle)

Willy, Colette
See Colette, (Sidonie-Gabrielle)
See also GLL 1

Wilmot, John 1647-1680 .... **LC 75**
See Rochester
See also BRW 2; DLB 131; PAB

Wilson, A(ndrew) N(orman) 1950- . **CLC 33**
See also BRWS 6; CA 112; 122; CN 7; DLB 14, 155, 194; MTCW 2

Wilson, Angus (Frank Johnstone) 1913-1991
.... **CLC 2, 3, 5, 25, 34; SSC 21**
See also BRWS 1; CA 5-8R; 134; CANR 21; DLB 15, 139, 155; MTCW 1, 2; RGEL 2; RGSF 2

Wilson, August 1945- .. **BLC 3; CLC 39, 50, 63, 118; DC 2; WLCS**
See also AAYA 16; AFAW 2; AMWS 8; BW 2, 3; CA 115; 122; CAD; CANR 42, 54, 76; CD 5; DA; DA3; DAB; DAC; DAM DRAM, MST, MULT; DFS 17; DLB 228; LAIT 4; MTCW 1, 2; RGAL 4

Wilson, Brian 1942- .... **CLC 12**

Wilson, Colin 1931- .... **CLC 3, 14**
See also CA 1-4R; CAAS 5; CANR 1, 22, 33, 77; CMW 4; CN 7; DLB 14, 194; HGG; MTCW 1; SFW 4

Wilson, Dirk
See Pohl, Frederick

Wilson, Edmund 1895-1972 . **CLC 1, 2, 3, 8, 24**
See also AMW; CA 1-4R; 37-40R; CANR 1, 46, 110; DLB 63; MTCW 1, 2; RGAL 4; TUS

Wilson, Ethel Davis (Bryant) 1888(?)-1980
.... **CLC 13**
See also CA 102; DAC; DAM POET; DLB 68; MTCW 1; RGEL 2

Wilson, Harriet
See Wilson, Harriet E. Adams
See also DLB 239

Wilson, Harriet E.
See Wilson, Harriet E. Adams
See also DLB 243

Wilson, Harriet E. Adams 1827(?)-1863(?)
.... **BLC 3; NCLC 78**
See Wilson, Harriet; Wilson, Harriet E.
See also DAM MULT; DLB 50

Wilson, John 1785-1854 .... **NCLC 5**

Wilson, John (Anthony) Burgess 1917-1993
See Burgess, Anthony
See also CA 1-4R; 143; CANR 2, 46; DA3; DAC; DAM NOV; MTCW 1, 2; NFS 15; TEA

Wilson, Lanford 1937- .. **CLC 7, 14, 36; DC 19**
See also CA 17-20R; CABS 3; CAD; CANR 45, 96; CD 5; DAM DRAM; DFS 4, 9, 12, 16; DLB 7; TUS

Wilson, Robert M. 1944- .... **CLC 7, 9**
See also CA 49-52; CAD; CANR 2, 41; CD 5; MTCW 1

Wilson, Robert McLiam 1964- .... **CLC 59**
See also CA 132; DLB 267

Wilson, Sloan 1920- .... **CLC 32**
See also CA 1-4R; CANR 1, 44; CN 7

Wilson, Snoo 1948- .... **CLC 33**
See also CA 69-72; CBD; CD 5

Wilson, William S(mith) 1932- .... **CLC 49**
See also CA 81-84

Wilson, (Thomas) Woodrow 1856-1924
.... **TCLC 79**
See also CA 166; DLB 47

Wilson and Warnke eds. .... **CLC 65**

Winchilsea, Anne (Kingsmill) Finch 1661-1720
See Finch, Anne
See also RGEL 2

Windham, Basil
See Wodehouse, P(elham) G(renville)

Wingrove, David (John) 1954- .... **CLC 68**
See also CA 133; SFW 4

Winnemucca, Sarah 1844-1891 ... **NCLC 79; NNAL**
See also DAM MULT; DLB 175; RGAL 4

Winstanley, Gerrard 1609-1676 .... **LC 52**

Wintergreen, Jane
See Duncan, Sara Jeannette

Winters, Janet Lewis .... **CLC 41**
See Lewis, Janet
See also DLBY 1987

Winters, (Arthur) Yvor 1900-1968 .. **CLC 4, 8, 32**
See also AMWS 2; CA 11-12; 25-28R; CAP 1; DLB 48; MTCW 1; RGAL 4

Winterson, Jeanette 1959- .... **CLC 64, 158**
See also BRWS 4; CA 136; CANR 58, 116; CN 7; CPW; DA3; DAM POP; DLB 207, 261; FANT; FW; GLL 1; MTCW 2; RHW

Winthrop, John 1588-1649 .... **LC 31**
See also DLB 24, 30

Wirth, Louis 1897-1952 .... **TCLC 92**
See also CA 159

Wiseman, Frederick 1930- .... **CLC 20**
See also CA 159

Wister, Owen 1860-1938 .... **TCLC 21**
See also BPFB 3; CA 108; 162; DLB 9, 78, 186; RGAL 4; SATA 62; TCWW 2

Witkacy
See Witkiewicz, Stanislaw Ignacy

Witkiewicz, Stanislaw Ignacy 1885-1939
.... **TCLC 8**
See also CA 105; 162; CDWLB 4; DLB 215; EW 10; RGWL 2, 3; SFW 4

Wittgenstein, Ludwig (Josef Johann) 1889-1951 .... **TCLC 59**
See also CA 113; 164; DLB 262; MTCW 2

Wittig, Monique 1935(?)- .... **CLC 22**
See also CA 116; 135; CWW 2; DLB 83; FW; GLL 1

Wittlin, Jozef 1896-1976 .... **CLC 25**
See also CA 49-52; 65-68; CANR 3

Wodehouse, P(elham) G(renville) 1881-1975
.... **CLC 1, 2, 5, 10, 22; SSC 2; TCLC 108**
See also AITN 2; BRWS 3; CA 45-48; 57-60; CANR 3, 33; CDBLB 1914-1945; CPW 1; DA3; DAB; DAC; DAM NOV; DLB 34, 162; MTCW 1, 2; RGEL 2; RGSF 2; SATA 22; SSFS 10

Woiwode, L.
See Woiwode, Larry (Alfred)

Woiwode, Larry (Alfred) 1941- .. **CLC 6, 10**
See also CA 73-76; CANR 16, 94; CN 7; DLB 6; INT CANR-16

Wojciechowska, Maia (Teresa) 1927-2002
.... **CLC 26**
See also AAYA 8, 46; BYA; CA 9-12R; 183; 209; CAAE 183; CANR 4, 41; CLR 1; JRDA; MAICYA 1, 2; SAAS 1; SATA 1, 28, 83; SATA-Essay 104; SATA-Obit 134; YAW

Wojtyla, Karol
See John Paul II, Pope

Wolf, Christa 1929- ...... **CLC 14, 29, 58, 150**
See also CA 85-88; CANR 45; CDWLB 2; CWW 2; DLB 75; FW; MTCW 1; RGWL 2, 3; SSFS 14

Wolf, Naomi 1962- .... **CLC 157**
See also CA 141; CANR 110; FW

Wolfe, Gene (Rodman) 1931- .... **CLC 25**
See also AAYA 35; CA 57-60; CAAS 9; CANR 6, 32, 60; CPW; DAM POP; DLB 8; FANT; MTCW 2; SATA 118; SCFW 2; SFW 4; SUFW 2

Wolfe, George C. 1954- .... **BLCS; CLC 49**
See also CA 149; CAD; CD 5

Wolfe, Thomas (Clayton) 1900-1938
.... **SSC 33; TCLC 4, 13, 29, 61; WLC**
See also AMW; BPFB 3; CA 104; 132; CANR 102; CDALB 1929-1941; DA; DA3; DAB; DAC; DAM MST, NOV; DLB 9, 102, 229; DLBD 2, 16; DLBY 1985, 1997; MTCW 1, 2; RGAL 4; TUS

Wolfe, Thomas Kennerly, Jr. 1930-
.... **CLC 147**
See Wolfe, Tom
See also CA 13-16R; CANR 9, 33, 70, 104; DA3; DAM POP; DLB 185; INT CANR-9; MTCW 1, 2; TUS

Wolfe, Tom .... **CLC 1, 2, 9, 15, 35, 51**
See Wolfe, Thomas Kennerly, Jr.
See also AAYA 8; AITN 2; AMWS 3; BEST 89:1; BPFB 3; CN 7; CPW; CSW; DLB 152; LAIT 5; RGAL 4

Wolff, Geoffrey (Ansell) 1937- .... **CLC 41**
See also CA 29-32R; CANR 29, 43, 78

Wolff, Sonia
See Levitin, Sonia (Wolff)

Wolff, Tobias (Jonathan Ansell) 1945-
.... **CLC 39, 64, 172**
See also AAYA 16; AMWS 7; BEST 90:2; BYA 12; CA 114; 117; CAAS 22; CANR 54, 76, 96; CN 7; CSW; DA3; DLB 130; INT CA-117; MTCW 2; RGAL 4; RGSF 2; SSFS 4, 11

Wolfram von Eschenbach c. 1170-c. 1220
.... **CMLC 5**
See Eschenbach, Wolfram von
See also CDWLB 2; DLB 138; EW 1; RGWL 2

Wolitzer, Hilma 1930- .... **CLC 17**
See also CA 65-68; CANR 18, 40; INT CANR-18; SATA 31; YAW

Wollstonecraft, Mary 1759-1797 ... **LC 5, 50**
See also BRWS 3; CDBLB 1789-1832; DLB 39, 104, 153, 252; FW; LAIT 1; RGEL 2; TEA; WLIT 3

Wonder, Stevie .... **CLC 12**
See Morris, Steveland Judkins

Wong, Jade Snow 1922- .... **CLC 17**
See also CA 109; CANR 91; SATA 112

Woodberry, George Edward 1855-1930
.... **TCLC 73**
See also CA 165; DLB 71, 103

Woodcott, Keith
See Brunner, John (Kilian Houston)

Woodruff, Robert W.
See Mencken, H(enry) L(ouis)

Woolf, (Adeline) Virginia 1882-1941
...... SSC 7; TCLC 1, 5, 20, 43, 56, 101, 123, 128; WLC
See also AAYA 44; BPFB 3; BRW 7; BRWR 1; CA 104; 130; CANR 64; CDBLB 1914-1945; DA; DA3; DAB; DAC; DAM MST, NOV; DLB 36, 100, 162; DLBD 10; EXPS; FW; LAIT 3; LMFS 2; MTCW 1, 2; NCFS 2; NFS 8, 12; RGEL 2; RGSF 2; SSFS 4, 12; TEA; WLIT 4

Woollcott, Alexander (Humphreys) 1887-1943 .... TCLC 5
See also CA 105; 161; DLB 29

Woolrich, Cornell .... CLC 77
See Hopley-Woolrich, Cornell George
See also MSW

Woolson, Constance Fenimore 1840-1894
.... NCLC 82
See also DLB 12, 74, 189, 221; RGAL 4

Wordsworth, Dorothy 1771-1855 . NCLC 25
See also DLB 107

Wordsworth, William 1770-1850
.... NCLC 12, 38, 111; PC 4; WLC
See also BRW 4; BRWC 1; CDBLB 1789-1832; DA; DA3; DAB; DAC; DAM MST, POET; DLB 93, 107; EXPP; LMFS 1; PAB; PFS 2; RGEL 2; TEA; WLIT 3; WP

Wotton, Sir Henry 1568-1639 .... LC 68
See also DLB 121; RGEL 2

Wouk, Herman 1915- .... CLC 1, 9, 38
See also BPFB 2, 3; CA 5-8R; CANR 6, 33, 67; CDALBS; CN 7; CPW; DA3; DAM NOV, POP; DLBY 1982; INT CANR-6; LAIT 4; MTCW 1, 2; NFS 7; TUS

Wright, Charles (Penzel, Jr.) 1935- . CLC 6, 13, 28, 119, 146
See also AMWS 5; CA 29-32R; CAAS 7; CANR 23, 36, 62, 88; CP 7; DLB 165; DLBY 1982; MTCW 1, 2; PFS 10

Wright, Charles Stevenson 1932- .... BLC 3; CLC 49
See also BW 1; CA 9-12R; CANR 26; CN 7; DAM MULT, POET; DLB 33

Wright, Frances 1795-1852 .... NCLC 74
See also DLB 73

Wright, Frank Lloyd 1867-1959 .. TCLC 95
See also AAYA 33; CA 174

Wright, Jack R.
See Harris, Mark

Wright, James (Arlington) 1927-1980
.... CLC 3, 5, 10, 28; PC 36
See also AITN 2; AMWS 3; CA 49-52; 97-100; CANR 4, 34, 64; CDALBS; DAM POET; DLB 5, 169; EXPP; MTCW 1, 2; PFS 7, 8; RGAL 4; TUS; WP

Wright, Judith (Arundell) 1915-2000
.... CLC 11, 53; PC 14
See also CA 13-16R; 188; CANR 31, 76, 93; CP 7; CWP; DLB 260; MTCW 1, 2; PFS 8; RGEL 2; SATA 14; SATA-Obit 121

Wright, L(aurali) R. 1939- .... CLC 44
See also CA 138; CMW 4

Wright, Richard (Nathaniel) 1908-1960
. BLC 3; CLC 1, 3, 4, 9, 14, 21, 48, 74; SSC 2; WLC
See also AAYA 5, 42; AFAW 1, 2; AMW; BPFB 3; BW 1; BYA 2; CA 108; CANR 64; CDALB 1929-1941; DA; DA3; DAB; DAC; DAM MST, MULT, NOV; DLB 76, 102; DLBD 2; EXPN; LAIT 3, 4; MTCW 1, 2; NCFS 1; NFS 1, 7; RGAL 4; RGSF 2; SSFS 3, 9, 15; TUS; YAW

Wright, Richard B(ruce) 1937- .... CLC 6
See also CA 85-88; DLB 53

Wright, Rick 1945- .... CLC 35

Wright, Rowland
See Wells, Carolyn

Wright, Stephen 1946- .... CLC 33

Wright, Willard Huntington 1888-1939
See Van Dine, S. S.
See also CA 115; 189; CMW 4; DLBD 16

Wright, William 1930- .... CLC 44
See also CA 53-56; CANR 7, 23

Wroth, Lady Mary 1587-1653(?) ...... LC 30; PC 38
See also DLB 121

Wu Ch'eng-en 1500(?)-1582(?) .... LC 7

Wu Ching-tzu 1701-1754 .... LC 2

Wulfstan c. 10th cent. -1023 .... CMLC 59

Wurlitzer, Rudolph 1938(?)- ... CLC 2, 4, 15
See also CA 85-88; CN 7; DLB 173

Wyatt, Sir Thomas c. 1503-1542 ...... LC 70; PC 27
See also BRW 1; DLB 132; EXPP; RGEL 2; TEA

Wycherley, William 1640-1716 ...... LC 8, 21
See also BRW 2; CDBLB 1660-1789; DAM DRAM; DLB 80; RGEL 2

Wylie, Elinor (Morton Hoyt) 1885-1928
.... PC 23; TCLC 8
See also AMWS 1; CA 105; 162; DLB 9, 45; EXPP; RGAL 4

Wylie, Philip (Gordon) 1902-1971 .. CLC 43
See also CA 21-22; 33-36R; CAP 2; DLB 9; SFW 4

Wyndham, John .... CLC 19
See Harris, John (Wyndham Parkes Lucas) Beynon
See also DLB 255; SCFW 2

Wyss, Johann David Von 1743-1818
.... NCLC 10
See also JRDA; MAICYA 1, 2; SATA 29; SATA-Brief 27

Xenophon c. 430B.C.-c. 354B.C. ... CMLC 17
See also AW 1; DLB 176; RGWL 2, 3

Xingjian, Gao 1940-
See Gao Xingjian
See also CA 193; RGWL 3

Yakumo Koizumi
See Hearn, (Patricio) Lafcadio (Tessima Carlos)

Yamada, Mitsuye (May) 1923- .... PC 44
See also CA 77-80

Yamamoto, Hisaye 1921- .... AAL; SSC 34
See also DAM MULT; LAIT 4; SSFS 14

Yamauchi, Wakako 1924- .... AAL

Yanez, Jose Donoso
See Donoso (Yanez), Jose

Yanovsky, Basile S.
See Yanovsky, V(assily) S(emenovich)

Yanovsky, V(assily) S(emenovich) 1906-1989
.... CLC 2, 18
See also CA 97-100; 129

Yates, Richard 1926-1992 .... CLC 7, 8, 23
See also AMWS 11; CA 5-8R; 139; CANR 10, 43; DLB 2, 234; DLBY 1981, 1992; INT CANR-10

Yeats, W. B.
See Yeats, William Butler

Yeats, William Butler 1865-1939 .... PC 20; TCLC 1, 11, 18, 31, 93, 116; WLC
See also AAYA 48; BRW 6; BRWR 1; CA 104; 127; CANR 45; CDBLB 1890-1914; DA; DA3; DAB; DAC; DAM DRAM, MST, POET; DLB 10, 19, 98, 156; EXPP; MTCW 1, 2; NCFS 3; PAB; PFS 1, 2, 5, 7, 13, 15; RGEL 2; TEA; WLIT 4; WP

Yehoshua, A(braham) B. 1936- . CLC 13, 31
See also CA 33-36R; CANR 43, 90; RGSF 2; RGWL 3

Yellow Bird
See Ridge, John Rollin

Yep, Laurence Michael 1948- .... CLC 35
See also AAYA 5, 31; BYA 7; CA 49-52; CANR 1, 46, 92; CLR 3, 17, 54; DLB 52; FANT; JRDA; MAICYA 1, 2; MAICYAS 1; SATA 7, 69, 123; WYA; YAW

Yerby, Frank G(arvin) 1916-1991 ... BLC 3; CLC 1, 7, 22
See also BPFB 3; BW 1, 3; CA 9-12R; 136; CANR 16, 52; DAM MULT; DLB 76; INT CANR-16; MTCW 1; RGAL 4; RHW

Yesenin, Sergei Alexandrovich
See Esenin, Sergei (Alexandrovich)

Yevtushenko, Yevgeny (Alexandrovich) 1933-
.... CLC 1, 3, 13, 26, 51, 126; PC 40
See Evtushenko, Evgenii Aleksandrovich
See also CA 81-84; CANR 33, 54; CWW 2; DAM POET; MTCW 1

Yezierska, Anzia 1885(?)-1970 .... CLC 46
See also CA 126; 89-92; DLB 28, 221; FW; MTCW 1; RGAL 4; SSFS 15

Yglesias, Helen 1915- .... CLC 7, 22
See also CA 37-40R; CAAS 20; CANR 15, 65, 95; CN 7; INT CANR-15; MTCW 1

Yokomitsu, Riichi 1898-1947 .... TCLC 47
See also CA 170

Yonge, Charlotte (Mary) 1823-1901
.... TCLC 48
See also CA 109; 163; DLB 18, 163; RGEL 2; SATA 17; WCH

York, Jeremy
See Creasey, John

York, Simon
See Heinlein, Robert A(nson)

Yorke, Henry Vincent 1905-1974 .... CLC 13
See Green, Henry
See also CA 85-88; 49-52

Yosano Akiko 1878-1942 .. PC 11; TCLC 59
See also CA 161; RGWL 3

Yoshimoto, Banana .... CLC 84
See Yoshimoto, Mahoko
See also NFS 7

Yoshimoto, Mahoko 1964-
See Yoshimoto, Banana
See also CA 144; CANR 98; SSFS 16

Young, Al(bert James) 1939- .. BLC 3; CLC 19
See also BW 2, 3; CA 29-32R; CANR 26, 65, 109; CN 7; CP 7; DAM MULT; DLB 33

Young, Andrew (John) 1885-1971 ..... CLC 5
See also CA 5-8R; CANR 7, 29; RGEL 2

Young, Collier
See Bloch, Robert (Albert)

Young, Edward 1683-1765 .... LC 3, 40
See also DLB 95; RGEL 2

Young, Marguerite (Vivian) 1909-1995
.... CLC 82
See also CA 13-16; 150; CAP 1; CN 7

Young, Neil 1945- .... CLC 17
See also CA 110; CCA 1

Young Bear, Ray A. 1950- . CLC 94; NNAL
See also CA 146; DAM MULT; DLB 175

Yourcenar, Marguerite 1903-1987 . CLC 19, 38, 50, 87
See also BPFB 3; CA 69-72; CANR 23, 60, 93; DAM NOV; DLB 72; DLBY 1988; EW 12; GFL 1789 to the Present; GLL 1; MTCW 1, 2; RGWL 2, 3

Yuan, Chu 340(?)B.C.-278(?)B.C.
.... CMLC 36

Yurick, Sol 1925- .... CLC 6
See also CA 13-16R; CANR 25; CN 7

Zabolotsky, Nikolai Alekseevich 1903-1958
.... TCLC 52
See also CA 116; 164

Zagajewski, Adam 1945- .... PC 27
See also CA 186; DLB 232

Zalygin, Sergei -2000 .... **CLC 59**
Zamiatin, Evgenii
 See Zamyatin, Evgeny Ivanovich
 See also RGSF 2; RGWL 2, 3
Zamiatin, Evgenii Ivanovich
 See Zamyatin, Evgeny Ivanovich
 See also DLB 272
Zamiatin, Yevgenii
 See Zamyatin, Evgeny Ivanovich
Zamora, Bernice (B. Ortiz) 1938- . **CLC 89; HLC 2**
 See also CA 151; CANR 80; DAM MULT; DLB 82; HW 1, 2
Zamyatin, Evgeny Ivanovich 1884-1937
 .... **TCLC 8, 37**
 See Zamiatin, Evgenii; Zamiatin, Evgenii Ivanovich
 See also CA 105; 166; EW 10; SFW 4
Zangwill, Israel 1864-1926 .. **SSC 44; TCLC 16**
 See also CA 109; 167; CMW 4; DLB 10, 135, 197; RGEL 2
Zappa, Francis Vincent, Jr. 1940-1993
 See Zappa, Frank
 See also CA 108; 143; CANR 57
Zappa, Frank .... **CLC 17**
 See Zappa, Francis Vincent, Jr.
Zaturenska, Marya 1902-1982 .... **CLC 6, 11**
 See also CA 13-16R; 105; CANR 22
Zeami 1363-1443 .... **DC 7; LC 86**
 See also DLB 203; RGWL 2, 3

Zelazny, Roger (Joseph) 1937-1995
 .... **CLC 21**
 See also AAYA 7; BPFB 3; CA 21-24R; 148; CANR 26, 60; CN 7; DLB 8; FANT; MTCW 1, 2; SATA 57; SATA-Brief 39; SCFW; SFW 4; SUFW 1, 2
Zhdanov, Andrei Alexandrovich 1896-1948
 .... **TCLC 18**
 See also CA 117; 167
Zhukovsky, Vasilii Andreevich
 See Zhukovsky, Vasily (Andreevich)
 See also DLB 205
Zhukovsky, Vasily (Andreevich) 1783-1852
 .... **NCLC 35**
 See Zhukovsky, Vasilii Andreevich
Ziegenhagen, Eric .... **CLC 55**
Zimmer, Jill Schary
 See Robinson, Jill
Zimmerman, Robert
 See Dylan, Bob
Zindel, Paul 1936-2003 .... **CLC 6, 26; DC 5**
 See also AAYA 2, 37; BYA 2, 3, 8, 11, 14; CA 73-76; CAD; CANR 31, 65, 108; CD 5; CDALBS; CLR 3, 45, 85; DA; DA3; DAB; DAC; DAM DRAM, MST, NOV; DFS 12; DLB 7, 52; JRDA; LAIT 5; MAICYA 1, 2; MTCW 1, 2; NFS 14; SATA 16, 58, 102; WYA; YAW
Zinov'Ev, A. A.
 See Zinoviev, Alexander (Aleksandrovich)
Zinoviev, Alexander (Aleksandrovich) 1922-
 .... **CLC 19**
 See also CA 116; 133; CAAS 10

Zoilus
 See Lovecraft, H(oward) P(hillips)
Zola, Emile (Edouard Charles Antoine) 1840-1902 .... **TCLC 1, 6, 21, 41; WLC**
 See also CA 104; 138; DA; DA3; DAB; DAC; DAM MST, NOV; DLB 123; EW 7; GFL 1789 to the Present; IDTP; LMFS 1, 2; RGWL 2; TWA
Zoline, Pamela 1941- .... **CLC 62**
 See also CA 161; SFW 4
Zoroaster 628(?)B.C.-551(?)B.C. .. **CMLC 40**
Zorrilla y Moral, Jose 1817-1893 .. **NCLC 6**
Zoshchenko, Mikhail (Mikhailovich) 1895-1958 .... **SSC 15; TCLC 15**
 See also CA 115; 160; RGSF 2; RGWL 3
Zuckmayer, Carl 1896-1977 .... **CLC 18**
 See also CA 69-72; DLB 56, 124; RGWL 2, 3
Zuk, Georges
 See Skelton, Robin
 See also CCA 1
Zukofsky, Louis 1904-1978 .. **CLC 1, 2, 4, 7, 11, 18; PC 11**
 See also AMWS 3; CA 9-12R; 77-80; CANR 39; DAM POET; DLB 5, 165; MTCW 1; RGAL 4
Zweig, Paul 1935-1984 .... **CLC 34, 42**
 See also CA 85-88; 113
Zweig, Stefan 1881-1942 .... **TCLC 17**
 See also CA 112; 170; DLB 81, 118
Zwingli, Huldreich 1484-1531 .... **LC 37**
 See also DLB 179

Literary Criticism Series Cumulative Topic Index

This index lists all topic entries in Gale's *Classical and Medieval Literature Criticism* (CMLC), *Contemporary Literary Criticism* (CLC), *Drama Criticism* (DC), *Literature Criticism from 1400 to 1800* (LC), *Nineteenth-Century Literature Criticism* (NCLC), *Short Story Criticism* (SSC), and *Twentieth-Century Literary Criticism* (TCLC). The index also lists topic entries in the Gale Critical Companion Collection, which includes the following publications: *The Beat Generation* (BG), and *Harlem Renaissance* (HR).

Aborigine in Nineteenth-Century Australian Literature, The NCLC 120: 1-88
  overviews, 2-27
  representations of the Aborigine in Australian literature, 27-58
  Aboriginal myth, literature, and oral tradition, 58-88

Aesopic Fable, The LC 51: 1-100
  the British Aesopic Fable, 1-54
  the Aesopic tradition in non-English-speaking cultures, 55-66
  political uses of the Aesopic fable, 67-88
  the evolution of the Aesopic fable, 89-99

African-American Folklore and Literature TCLC 126: 1-67
  African-American folk tradition, 1-16
  representative writers, 16-34
  hallmark works, 35-48
  the study of African-American literature and folklore, 48-64

Age of Johnson LC 15: 1-87
  Johnson's London, 3-15
  aesthetics of neoclassicism, 15-36
  "age of prose and reason," 36-45
  clubmen and bluestockings, 45-56
  printing technology, 56-62
  periodicals: "a map of busy life," 62-74
  transition, 74-86

Age of Spenser LC 39: 1-70
  overviews and general studies, 2-21
  literary style, 22-34
  poets and the crown, 34-70

AIDS in Literature CLC 81: 365-416

Alcohol and Literature TCLC 70: 1-58
  overview, 2-8
  fiction, 8-48
  poetry and drama, 48-58

American Abolitionism NCLC 44: 1-73
  overviews and general studies, 2-26
  abolitionist ideals, 26-46
  the literature of abolitionism, 46-72

American Autobiography TCLC 86: 1-115
  overviews and general studies, 3-36
  American authors and autobiography, 36-82
  African-American autobiography, 82-114

American Black Humor Fiction TCLC 54: 1-85
  characteristics of black humor, 2-13
  origins and development, 13-38
  black humor distinguished from related literary trends, 38-60
  black humor and society, 60-75
  black humor reconsidered, 75-83

American Civil War in Literature NCLC 32: 1-109
  overviews and general studies, 2-20
  regional perspectives, 20-54
  fiction popular during the war, 54-79
  the historical novel, 79-108

American Frontier in Literature NCLC 28: 1-103
  definitions, 2-12
  development, 12-17
  nonfiction writing about the frontier, 17-30
  frontier fiction, 30-45
  frontier protagonists, 45-66
  portrayals of Native Americans, 66-86
  feminist readings, 86-98
  twentieth-century reaction against frontier literature, 98-100

American Humor Writing NCLC 52: 1-59
  overviews and general studies, 2-12
  the Old Southwest, 12-42
  broader impacts, 42-5
  women humorists, 45-58

American Novel of Manners TCLC 130: 1-42
  history of the Novel of Manners in America, 4-10
  representative writers, 10-18
  relevancy of the Novel of Manners, 18-24
  hallmark works in the Novel of Manners, 24-36
  Novel of Manners and other media, 36-40

American Mercury, The TCLC 74: 1-80

American Popular Song, Golden Age of TCLC 42: 1-49
  background and major figures, 2-34
  the lyrics of popular songs, 34-47

American Proletarian Literature TCLC 54: 86-175
  overviews and general studies, 87-95
  American proletarian literature and the American Communist Party, 95-111
  ideology and literary merit, 111-17
  novels, 117-36

  Gastonia, 136-48
  drama, 148-54
  journalism, 154-9
  proletarian literature in the United States, 159-74

American Realism NCLC 120: 89-246
  overviews, 91-112
  background and sources, 112-72
  social issues, 172-223
  women and realism, 223-45

American Romanticism NCLC 44: 74-138
  overviews and general studies, 74-84
  sociopolitical influences, 84-104
  Romanticism and the American frontier, 104-15
  thematic concerns, 115-37

American Western Literature TCLC 46: 1-100
  definition and development of American Western literature, 2-7
  characteristics of the Western novel, 8-23
  Westerns as history and fiction, 23-34
  critical reception of American Western literature, 34-41
  the Western hero, 41-73
  women in Western fiction, 73-91
  later Western fiction, 91-9

American Writers in Paris TCLC 98: 1-156
  overviews and general studies, 2-155

Anarchism NCLC 84: 1-97
  overviews and general studies, 2-23
  the French anarchist tradition, 23-56
  Anglo-American anarchism, 56-68
  anarchism: incidents and issues, 68-97

Animals in Literature TCLC 106: 1-120
  overviews and general studies, 2-8
  animals in American literature, 8-45
  animals in Canadian literature, 45-57
  animals in European literature, 57-100
  animals in Latin American literature, 100-06
  animals in women's literature, 106-20

Antebellum South, Literature of the NCLC 112:1-188
  overviews, 4-55
  culture of the Old South, 55-68
  antebellum fiction: pastoral and heroic romance, 58-120

469

role of women: a subdued rebellion, 120-59
slavery and the slave narrative, 159-85

The Apocalyptic Movement TCLC 106: 121-69

Aristotle CMLC 31:1-397
philosophy, 3-100
poetics, 101-219
rhetoric, 220-301
science, 302-397

Art and Literature TCLC 54: 176-248
overviews and general studies, 176-93
definitions, 193-219
influence of visual arts on literature, 219-31
spatial form in literature, 231-47

Arthurian Literature CMLC 10: 1-127
historical context and literary beginnings, 2-27
development of the legend through Malory, 27-64
development of the legend from Malory to the Victorian Age, 65-81
themes and motifs, 81-95
principal characters, 95-125

Arthurian Revival NCLC 36: 1-77
overviews and general studies, 2-12
Tennyson and his influence, 12-43
other leading figures, 43-73
the Arthurian legend in the visual arts, 73-6

Australian Cultural Identity in Nineteenth-Century Literature NCLC 124: 1-164
overviews and general studies, 4-22
poetry, 22-67
fiction, 67-135
role of women writers, 135-64

Australian Literature TCLC 50: 1-94
origins and development, 2-21
characteristics of Australian literature, 21-33
historical and critical perspectives, 33-41
poetry, 41-58
fiction, 58-76
drama, 76-82
Aboriginal literature, 82-91

Beat Generation, The BG 1:1-562
the Beat Generation: an overview, 1-137
primary sources, 3-32
overviews and general studies, 32-47
Beat Generation as a social phenomenon, 47-65
drugs, inspiration, and the Beat Generation, 65-92
religion and the Beat Generation, 92-124
women of the Beat Generation, 124-36
Beat "scene": East and West, 139-259
primary sources, 141-77
Beat scene in the East, 177-218
Beat scene in the West, 218-59
Beat Generation publishing: periodicals, small presses, and censorship, 261-349
primary sources, 263-74
overview, 274-88
Beat periodicals: "little magazines," 288-311
Beat publishing: small presses, 311-24
Beat battles with censorship, 324-49
performing arts and the Beat Generation, 351-417
primary sources, 353-58
Beats and film, 358-81
Beats and music, 381-415
visual arts and the Beat Generation, 419-91
primary sources, 421-24
critical commentary, 424-90

Beat Generation, Literature of the TCLC 42: 50-102
overviews and general studies, 51-9
the Beat generation as a social phenomenon, 59-62

development, 62-5
Beat literature, 66-96
influence, 97-100

The Bell Curve Controversy CLC 91: 281-330

Bildungsroman **in Nineteenth-Century Literature** NCLC 20: 92-168
surveys, 93-113
in Germany, 113-40
in England, 140-56
female *Bildungsroman*, 156-67

Bloomsbury Group TCLC 34: 1-73
history and major figures, 2-13
definitions, 13-7
influences, 17-27
thought, 27-40
prose, 40-52
and literary criticism, 52-4
political ideals, 54-61
response to, 61-71

The Blues in Literature TCLC 82: 1-71

Bly, Robert, *Iron John: A Book about Men and Men's Work* CLC 70: 414-62

The Book of J CLC 65: 289-311

Brazilian Literature TCLC 134: 1-126
overviews and general studies, 3-33
Brazilian poetry, 33-48
contemporary Brazilian writing, 48-76
culture, politics, and race in Brazilian writing, 76-100
modernism and postmodernism in Brazil, 100-25

British Ephemeral Literature LC 59: 1-70
overviews and general studies, 1-9
broadside ballads, 10-40
chapbooks, jestbooks, pamphlets, and newspapers, 40-69

Buddhism and Literature TCLC 70: 59-164
eastern literature, 60-113
western literature, 113-63

The *Bulletin* **and the Rise of Australian Literary Nationalism** NCLC 116: 1-121
overviews, 3-32
legend of the nineties, 32-55
Bulletin style, 55-71
Australian literary nationalism, 71-98
myth of the bush, 98-120

Businessman in American Literature TCLC 26: 1-48
portrayal of the businessman, 1-32
themes and techniques in business fiction, 32-47

The Calendar LC 55: 1-92
overviews and general studies, 2-19
measuring time, 19-28
calendars and culture, 28-60
calendar reform, 60-92

Captivity Narratives LC 82: 71-172
overviews, 72-107
captivity narratives and Puritanism, 108-34
captivity narratives and Native Americans, 134-49
influence on American literature, 149-72

Catholicism in Nineteenth-Century American Literature NCLC 64: 1-58
overviews, 3-14
polemical literature, 14-46
Catholicism in literature, 47-57

Celtic Mythology CMLC 26: 1-111
overviews and general studies, 2-22
Celtic myth as literature and history, 22-48
Celtic religion: Druids and divinities, 48-80
Fionn MacCuhaill and the Fenian cycle, 80-111

Celtic Twilight See Irish Literary Renaissance

Chartist Movement and Literature, The NCLC 60: 1-84
overview: nineteenth-century working-class fiction, 2-19
Chartist fiction and poetry, 19-73
the Chartist press, 73-84

Child Labor in Nineteenth-Century Literature NCLC 108: 1-133
overviews, 3-10
climbing boys and chimney sweeps, 10-16
the international traffic in children, 16-45
critics and reformers, 45-82
fictional representations of child laborers, 83-132

Children's Literature, Nineteenth-Century NCLC 52: 60-135
overviews and general studies, 61-72
moral tales, 72-89
fairy tales and fantasy, 90-119
making men/making women, 119-34

Christianity in Twentieth-Century Literature TCLC 110: 1-79
overviews and general studies, 2-31
Christianity in twentieth-century fiction, 31-78

The City and Literature TCLC 90: 1-124
overviews and general studies, 2-9
the city in American literature, 9-86
the city in European literature, 86-124

Civic Critics, Russian NCLC 20: 402-46
principal figures and background, 402-9
and Russian Nihilism, 410-6
aesthetic and critical views, 416-45

The Cockney School NCLC 68: 1-64
overview, 2-7
Blackwood's Magazine and the contemporary critical response, 7-24
the political and social import of the Cockneys and their critics, 24-63

Colonial America: The Intellectual Background LC 25: 1-98
overviews and general studies, 2-17
philosophy and politics, 17-31
early religious influences in Colonial America, 31-60
consequences of the Revolution, 60-78
religious influences in post-revolutionary America, 78-87
colonial literary genres, 87-97

Colonialism in Victorian English Literature NCLC 56: 1-77
overviews and general studies, 2-34
colonialism and gender, 34-51
monsters and the occult, 51-76

Columbus, Christopher, Books on the Quincentennial of His Arrival in the New World CLC 70: 329-60

Comic Books TCLC 66: 1-139
historical and critical perspectives, 2-48
superheroes, 48-67
underground comix, 67-88
comic books and society, 88-122
adult comics and graphic novels, 122-36

Commedia dell'Arte LC 83: 1-147
overviews, 2-7
origins and development, 7-23
characters and actors, 23-45
performance, 45-62
texts and authors, 62-100
influence in Europe, 100-46

Connecticut Wits NCLC 48: 1-95
overviews and general studies, 2-40
major works, 40-76
intellectual context, 76-95

Contemporary Gay and Lesbian Literature
CLC 171: 1-130
　　overviews and general studies, 2-43
　　contemporary gay literature, 44-95
　　lesbianism in contemporary literature, 95-129

Contemporary Southern Literature CLC 167: 1-132
　　criticism, 2-131

Crime in Literature TCLC 54: 249-307
　　evolution of the criminal figure in literature, 250-61
　　crime and society, 261-77
　　literary perspectives on crime and punishment, 277-88
　　writings by criminals, 288-306

Crime-Mystery-Detective Stories SSC 59:89-226
　　overviews and general studies, 90-140
　　origins and early masters of the crime-mystery-detective story, 140-73
　　hard-boiled crime-mystery-detective fiction, 173-209
　　diversity in the crime-mystery-detective story, 210-25

The Crusades CMLC 38: 1-144
　　history of the Crusades, 3-60
　　literature of the Crusades, 60-116
　　the Crusades and the people: attitudes and influences, 116-44

Cyberpunk TCLC 106: 170-366
　　overviews and general studies, 171-88
　　feminism and cyberpunk, 188-230
　　history and cyberpunk, 230-70
　　sexuality and cyberpunk, 270-98
　　social issues and cyberpunk, 299-366

Cyberpunk Short Fiction SSC 60: 44-108
　　overviews and general studies, 46-78
　　major writers of cyberpunk fiction, 78-81
　　sexuality and cyberpunk fiction, 81-97
　　additional pieces, 97-108

Czechoslovakian Literature of the Twentieth Century TCLC 42:103-96
　　through World War II, 104-35
　　de-Stalinization, the Prague Spring, and contemporary literature, 135-72
　　Slovak literature, 172-85
　　Czech science fiction, 185-93

Dadaism TCLC 46: 101-71
　　background and major figures, 102-16
　　definitions, 116-26
　　manifestos and commentary by Dadaists, 126-40
　　theater and film, 140-58
　　nature and characteristics of Dadaist writing, 158-70

Darwinism and Literature NCLC 32: 110-206
　　background, 110-31
　　direct responses to Darwin, 131-71
　　collateral effects of Darwinism, 171-205

Death in American Literature NCLC 92: 1-170
　　overviews and general studies, 2-32
　　death in the works of Emily Dickinson, 32-72
　　death in the works of Herman Melville, 72-101
　　death in the works of Edgar Allan Poe, 101-43
　　death in the works of Walt Whitman, 143-70

Death in Nineteenth-Century British Literature NCLC 68: 65-142
　　overviews and general studies, 66-92
　　responses to death, 92-102
　　feminist perspectives, 103-17
　　striving for immortality, 117-41

Death in Literature TCLC 78:1-183
　　fiction, 2-115
　　poetry, 115-46
　　drama, 146-81

de Man, Paul, Wartime Journalism of CLC 55: 382-424

Detective Fiction, Nineteenth-Century NCLC 36: 78-148
　　origins of the genre, 79-100
　　history of nineteenth-century detective fiction, 101-33
　　significance of nineteenth-century detective fiction, 133-46

Detective Fiction, Twentieth-Century TCLC 38: 1-96
　　genesis and history of the detective story, 3-22
　　defining detective fiction, 22-32
　　evolution and varieties, 32-77
　　the appeal of detective fiction, 77-90

Detective Story See **Crime-Mystery-Detective Stories**

Dime Novels NCLC 84: 98-168
　　overviews and general studies, 99-123
　　popular characters, 123-39
　　major figures and influences, 139-52
　　socio-political concerns, 152-167

Disease and Literature TCLC 66: 140-283
　　overviews and general studies, 141-65
　　disease in nineteenth-century literature, 165-81
　　tuberculosis and literature, 181-94
　　women and disease in literature, 194-221
　　plague literature, 221-53
　　AIDS in literature, 253-82

El Dorado, The Legend of See **Legend of El Dorado, The**

The Double in Nineteenth-Century Literature NCLC 40: 1-95
　　genesis and development of the theme, 2-15
　　the double and Romanticism, 16-27
　　sociological views, 27-52
　　psychological interpretations, 52-87
　　philosophical considerations, 87-95

Dramatic Realism NCLC 44: 139-202
　　overviews and general studies, 140-50
　　origins and definitions, 150-66
　　impact and influence, 166-93
　　realist drama and tragedy, 193-201

Drugs and Literature TCLC 78: 184-282
　　overviews and general studies, 185-201
　　pre-twentieth-century literature, 201-42
　　twentieth-century literature, 242-82

Dystopias in Contemporary Literature CLC 168: 1-91
　　overviews and general studies, 2-52
　　dystopian views in Margaret Atwood's *The Handmaid's Tale* (1985), 52-71
　　feminist readings of dystopias, 71-90

Eastern Mythology CMLC 26: 112-92
　　heroes and kings, 113-51
　　cross-cultural perspective, 151-69
　　relations to history and society, 169-92

Eighteenth-Century British Periodicals LC 63: 1-123
　　rise of periodicals, 2-31
　　impact and influence of periodicals, 31-64
　　periodicals and society, 64-122

Eighteenth-Century Travel Narratives LC 77: 252-355
　　overviews and general studies, 254-79
　　eighteenth-century European travel narratives, 279-334
　　non-European eighteenth-century travel narratives, 334-55

Electronic "Books": Hypertext and Hyperfiction CLC 86: 367-404
　　books vs. CD-ROMs, 367-76
　　hypertext and hyperfiction, 376-95
　　implications for publishing, libraries, and the public, 395-403

Eliot, T. S., Centenary of Birth CLC 55: 345-75

Elizabethan Drama LC 22: 140-240
　　origins and influences, 142-67
　　characteristics and conventions, 167-83
　　theatrical production, 184-200
　　histories, 200-12
　　comedy, 213-20
　　tragedy, 220-30

Elizabethan Prose Fiction LC 41: 1-70
　　overviews and general studies, 1-15
　　origins and influences, 15-43
　　style and structure, 43-69

Enclosure of the English Common NCLC 88: 1-57
　　overviews and general studies, 1-12
　　early reaction to enclosure, 12-23
　　nineteenth-century reaction to enclosure, 23-56

The Encyclopedists LC 26: 172-253
　　overviews and general studies, 173-210
　　intellectual background, 210-32
　　views on esthetics, 232-41
　　views on women, 241-52

English Caroline Literature LC 13: 221-307
　　background, 222-41
　　evolution and varieties, 241-62
　　the Cavalier mode, 262-75
　　court and society, 275-91
　　politics and religion, 291-306

English Decadent Literature of the 1890s NCLC 28: 104-200
　　fin de siècle: the Decadent period, 105-19
　　definitions, 120-37
　　major figures: "the tragic generation," 137-50
　　French literature and English literary Decadence, 150-7
　　themes, 157-61
　　poetry, 161-82
　　periodicals, 182-96

English Essay, Rise of the LC 18: 238-308
　　definitions and origins, 236-54
　　influence on the essay, 254-69
　　historical background, 269-78
　　the essay in the seventeenth century, 279-93
　　the essay in the eighteenth century, 293-307

English Mystery Cycle Dramas LC 34: 1-88
　　overviews and general studies, 1-27
　　the nature of dramatic performances, 27-42
　　the medieval worldview and the mystery cycles, 43-67
　　the doctrine of repentance and the mystery cycles, 67-76
　　the fall from grace in the mystery cycles, 76-88

The English Realist Novel, 1740-1771 LC 51: 102-98
　　overviews and general studies, 103-22
　　from Romanticism to Realism, 123-58
　　women and the novel, 159-175
　　the novel and other literary forms, 176-197

English Revolution, Literature of the LC 43: 1-58
　　overviews and general studies, 2-24
　　pamphlets of the English Revolution, 24-38
　　political sermons of the English Revolution, 38-48
　　poetry of the English Revolution, 48-57

CUMULATIVE TOPIC INDEX

English Romantic Hellenism NCLC 68: 143-250
- overviews and general studies, 144-69
- historical development of English Romantic Hellenism, 169-91
- influence of Greek mythology on the Romantics, 191-229
- influence of Greek literature, art, and culture on the Romantics, 229-50

English Romantic Poetry NCLC 28: 201-327
- overviews and reputation, 202-37
- major subjects and themes, 237-67
- forms of Romantic poetry, 267-78
- politics, society, and Romantic poetry, 278-99
- philosophy, religion, and Romantic poetry, 299-324

The Epistolary Novel LC 59: 71-170
- overviews and general studies, 72-96
- women and the Epistolary novel, 96-138
- principal figures: Britain, 138-53
- principal figures: France, 153-69

Espionage Literature TCLC 50: 95-159
- overviews and general studies, 96-113
- espionage fiction/formula fiction, 113-26
- spies in fact and fiction, 126-38
- the female spy, 138-44
- social and psychological perspectives, 144-58

European Debates on the Conquest of the Americas LC 67: 1-129
- overviews and general studies, 3-56
- major Spanish figures, 56-98
- English perceptions of Native Americans, 98-129

European Romanticism NCLC 36: 149-284
- definitions, 149-77
- origins of the movement, 177-82
- Romantic theory, 182-200
- themes and techniques, 200-23
- Romanticism in Germany, 223-39
- Romanticism in France, 240-61
- Romanticism in Italy, 261-4
- Romanticism in Spain, 264-8
- impact and legacy, 268-82

Exile in Literature TCLC 122: 1-129
- overviews and general studies, 2-33
- exile in fiction, 33-92
- German literature in exile, 92-129

Existentialism and Literature TCLC 42: 197-268
- overviews and definitions, 198-209
- history and influences, 209-19
- Existentialism critiqued and defended, 220-35
- philosophical and religious perspectives, 235-41
- Existentialist fiction and drama, 241-67

Familiar Essay NCLC 48: 96-211
- definitions and origins, 97-130
- overview of the genre, 130-43
- elements of form and style, 143-59
- elements of content, 159-73
- the Cockneys: Hazlitt, Lamb, and Hunt, 173-91
- status of the genre, 191-210

The Faust Legend LC 47: 1-117

Fear in Literature TCLC 74: 81-258
- overviews and general studies, 81
- pre-twentieth-century literature, 123
- twentieth-century literature, 182

Feminism in the 1990s: Commentary on Works by Naomi Wolf, Susan Faludi, and Camille Paglia CLC 76: 377-415

Feminist Criticism in 1990 CLC 65: 312-60

Fifteenth-Century English Literature LC 17: 248-334
- background, 249-72
- poetry, 272-315
- drama, 315-23
- prose, 323-33

Film and Literature TCLC 38: 97-226
- overviews and general studies, 97-119
- film and theater, 119-34
- film and the novel, 134-45
- the art of the screenplay, 145-66
- genre literature/genre film, 167-79
- the writer and the film industry, 179-90
- authors on film adaptations of their works, 190-200
- fiction into film: comparative essays, 200-23

Finance and Money as Represented in Nineteenth-Century Literature NCLC 76: 1-69
- historical perspectives, 2-20
- the image of money, 20-37
- the dangers of money, 37-50
- women and money, 50-69

Folklore and Literature TCLC 86: 116-293
- overviews and general studies, 118-144
- Native American literature, 144-67
- African-American literature, 167-238
- folklore and the American West, 238-57
- modern and postmodern literature, 257-91

Food in Literature TCLC 114: 1-133
- food and children's literature, 2-14
- food as a literary device, 14-32
- rituals involving food, 33-45
- food and social and ethnic identity, 45-90
- women's relationship with food, 91-132

Food in Nineteenth-Century Literature NCLC 108: 134-288
- overviews, 136-74
- food and social class, 174-85
- food and gender, 185-219
- food and love, 219-31
- food and sex, 231-48
- eating disorders, 248-70
- vegetarians, carnivores, and cannibals, 270-87

French Drama in the Age of Louis XIV LC 28: 94-185
- overview, 95-127
- tragedy, 127-46
- comedy, 146-66
- tragicomedy, 166-84

French Enlightenment LC 14: 81-145
- the question of definition, 82-9
- le siècle des lumières, 89-94
- women and the salons, 94-105
- censorship, 105-15
- the philosophy of reason, 115-31
- influence and legacy, 131-44

French New Novel TCLC 98: 158-234
- overviews and general studies, 158-92
- influences, 192-213
- themes, 213-33

French Realism NCLC 52: 136-216
- origins and definitions, 137-70
- issues and influence, 170-98
- realism and representation, 198-215

French Revolution and English Literature NCLC 40: 96-195
- history and theory, 96-123
- romantic poetry, 123-50
- the novel, 150-81
- drama, 181-92
- children's literature, 192-5

Futurism, Italian TCLC 42: 269-354
- principles and formative influences, 271-9
- manifestos, 279-88

- literature, 288-303
- theater, 303-19
- art, 320-30
- music, 330-6
- architecture, 336-9
- and politics, 339-46
- reputation and significance, 346-51

Gaelic Revival See Irish Literary Renaissance

Gates, Henry Louis, Jr., and African-American Literary Criticism CLC 65: 361-405

Gay and Lesbian Literature CLC 76: 416-39

Gay and Lesbian Literature See also Contemporary Gay and Lesbian Literature

German Exile Literature TCLC 30: 1-58
- the writer and the Nazi state, 1-10
- definition of, 10-4
- life in exile, 14-32
- surveys, 32-50
- Austrian literature in exile, 50-2
- German publishing in the United States, 52-7

German Expressionism TCLC 34: 74-160
- history and major figures, 76-85
- aesthetic theories, 85-109
- drama, 109-26
- poetry, 126-38
- film, 138-42
- painting, 142-7
- music, 147-53
- and politics, 153-8

The Ghost Story SSC 58: 1-142
- overviews and general studies, 1-21
- the ghost story in American literature, 21-49
- the ghost story in Asian literature, 49-53
- the ghost story in European and English literature, 54-89
- major figures, 89-141

The Gilded Age NCLC 84: 169-271
- popular themes, 170-90
- Realism, 190-208
- Aestheticism, 208-26
- socio-political concerns, 226-70

Glasnost **and Contemporary Soviet Literature** CLC 59: 355-97

Gothic Novel NCLC 28: 328-402
- development and major works, 328-34
- definitions, 334-50
- themes and techniques, 350-78
- in America, 378-85
- in Scotland, 385-91
- influence and legacy, 391-400

The Governess in Nineteenth-Century Literature NCLC 104: 1-131
- overviews and general studies, 3-28
- social roles and economic conditions, 28-86
- fictional governesses, 86-131

Graphic Narratives CLC 86: 405-32
- history and overviews, 406-21
- the "Classics Illustrated" series, 421-2
- reviews of recent works, 422-32

Graveyard Poets LC 67: 131-212
- origins and development, 131-52
- major figures, 152-75
- major works, 175-212

Greek Historiography CMLC 17: 1-49

Greek Mythology CMLC 26: 193-320
- overviews and general studies, 194-209
- origins and development of Greek mythology, 209-29
- cosmogonies and divinities in Greek mythology, 229-54

heroes and heroines in Greek mythology, 254-80
women in Greek mythology, 280-320

Greek Theater CMLC 51: 1-58
criticism, 2-58

Hard-Boiled Fiction TCLC 118: 1-109
overviews and general studies, 2-39
major authors, 39-76
women and hard-boiled fiction, 76-109

The Harlem Renaissance HR 1: 1-563
overviews and general studies of the Harlem Renaissance, 1-137
primary sources, 3-12
overviews, 12-38
background and sources of the Harlem Renaissance, 38-56
the New Negro aesthetic, 56-91
patrons, promoters, and the New York Public Library, 91-121
women of the Harlem Renaissance, 121-37
social, economic, and political factors that influenced the Harlem Renaissance, 139-240
primary sources, 141-53
overviews, 153-87
social and economic factors, 187-213
Black intellectual and political thought, 213-40
publishing and periodicals during the Harlem Renaissance, 243-339
primary sources, 246-52
overviews, 252-68
African American writers and mainstream publishers, 268-91
anthologies: *The New Negro* and others, 291-309
African American periodicals and the Harlem Renaissance, 309-39
performing arts during the Harlem Renaissance, 341-465
primary sources, 343-48
overviews, 348-64
drama of the Harlem Renaissance, 364-92
influence of music on Harlem Renaissance writing, 437-65
visual arts during the Harlem Renaissance, 467-563
primary sources, 470-71
overviews, 471-517
painters, 517-36
sculptors, 536-58
photographers, 558-63

Harlem Renaissance TCLC 26: 49-125
principal issues and figures, 50-67
the literature and its audience, 67-74
theme and technique in poetry, fiction, and drama, 74-115
and American society, 115-21
achievement and influence, 121-2

Havel, Václav, Playwright and President CLC 65: 406-63

Historical Fiction, Nineteenth-Century NCLC 48: 212-307
definitions and characteristics, 213-36
Victorian historical fiction, 236-65
American historical fiction, 265-88
realism in historical fiction, 288-306

Hollywood and Literature TCLC 118: 110-251
overviews and general studies, 111-20
adaptations, 120-65
socio-historical and cultural impact, 165-206
theater and hollywood, 206-51

Holocaust and the Atomic Bomb: Fifty Years Later CLC 91: 331-82
the Holocaust remembered, 333-52

Anne Frank revisited, 352-62
the atomic bomb and American memory, 362-81

Holocaust Denial Literature TCLC 58: 1-110
overviews and general studies, 1-30
Robert Faurisson and Noam Chomsky, 30-52
Holocaust denial literature in America, 52-71
library access to Holocaust denial literature, 72-5
the authenticity of Anne Frank's diary, 76-90
David Irving and the "normalization" of Hitler, 90-109

Holocaust, Literature of the TCLC 42: 355-450
historical overview, 357-61
critical overview, 361-70
diaries and memoirs, 370-95
novels and short stories, 395-425
poetry, 425-41
drama, 441-8

Homosexuality in Nineteenth-Century Literature NCLC 56: 78-182
defining homosexuality, 80-111
Greek love, 111-44
trial and danger, 144-81

Humors Comedy LC 85: 194-324
overviews, 195-251
major figures: Ben Jonson, 251-93
major figures: William Shakespeare, 293-324

Hungarian Literature of the Twentieth Century TCLC 26: 126-88
surveys of, 126-47
Nyugat and early twentieth-century literature, 147-56
mid-century literature, 156-68
and politics, 168-78
since the 1956 revolt, 178-87

Hysteria in Nineteenth-Century Literature NCLC 64: 59-184
the history of hysteria, 60-75
the gender of hysteria, 75-103
hysteria and women's narratives, 103-57
hysteria in nineteenth-century poetry, 157-83

Image of the Noble Savage in Literature LC 79: 136-252
overviews and development, 136-76
the Noble Savage in the New World, 176-221
Rousseau and the French Enlightenment's view of the noble savage, 221-51

Imagism TCLC 74: 259-454
history and development, 260
major figures, 288
sources and influences, 352
Imagism and other movements, 397
influence and legacy, 431

Immigrants in Nineteenth-Century Literature, Representation of NCLC 112: 188-298
overview, 189-99
immigrants in America, 199-223
immigrants and labor, 223-60
immigrants in England, 260-97

Incest in Nineteenth-Century American Literature NCLC 76: 70-141
overview, 71-88
the concern for social order, 88-117
authority and authorship, 117-40

Incest in Victorian Literature NCLC 92: 172-318
overviews and general studies, 173-85
novels, 185-276

plays, 276-84
poetry, 284-318

Indian Literature in English TCLC 54: 308-406
overview, 309-13
origins and major figures, 313-25
the Indo-English novel, 325-55
Indo-English poetry, 355-67
Indo-English drama, 367-72
critical perspectives on Indo-English literature, 372-80
modern Indo-English literature, 380-9
Indo-English authors on their work, 389-404

The Industrial Revolution in Literature NCLC 56: 183-273
historical and cultural perspectives, 184-201
contemporary reactions to the machine, 201-21
themes and symbols in literature, 221-73

The Irish Famine as Represented in Nineteenth-Century Literature NCLC 64: 185-261
overviews and general studies, 187-98
historical background, 198-212
famine novels, 212-34
famine poetry, 234-44
famine letters and eye-witness accounts, 245-61

Irish Literary Renaissance TCLC 46: 172-287
overview, 173-83
development and major figures, 184-202
influence of Irish folklore and mythology, 202-22
Irish poetry, 222-34
Irish drama and the Abbey Theatre, 234-56
Irish fiction, 256-86

Irish Nationalism and Literature NCLC 44: 203-73
the Celtic element in literature, 203-19
anti-Irish sentiment and the Celtic response, 219-34
literary ideals in Ireland, 234-45
literary expressions, 245-73

Irish Novel, The NCLC 80: 1-130
overviews and general studies, 3-9
principal figures, 9-22
peasant and middle class Irish novelists, 22-76
aristocratic Irish and Anglo-Irish novelists, 76-129

Israeli Literature TCLC 94: 1-137
overviews and general studies, 2-18
Israeli fiction, 18-33
Israeli poetry, 33-62
Israeli drama, 62-91
women and Israeli literature, 91-112
Arab characters in Israeli literature, 112-36

Italian Futurism See Futurism, Italian

Italian Humanism LC 12: 205-77
origins and early development, 206-18
revival of classical letters, 218-23
humanism and other philosophies, 224-39
humanism and humanists, 239-46
the plastic arts, 246-57
achievement and significance, 258-76

Italian Romanticism NCLC 60: 85-145
origins and overviews, 86-101
Italian Romantic theory, 101-25
the language of Romanticism, 125-45

Jacobean Drama LC 33: 1-37
the Jacobean worldview: an era of transition, 2-14
the moral vision of Jacobean drama, 14-22

Jacobean tragedy, 22-3
the Jacobean masque, 23-36

Jazz and Literature TCLC 102: 3-124

Jewish-American Fiction TCLC 62: 1-181
overviews and general studies, 2-24
major figures, 24-48
Jewish writers and American life, 48-78
Jewish characters in American fiction, 78-108
themes in Jewish-American fiction, 108-43
Jewish-American women writers, 143-59
the Holocaust and Jewish-American fiction, 159-81

Jews in Literature TCLC 118: 252-417
overviews and general studies, 253-97
representing the Jew in literature, 297-351
the Holocaust in literature, 351-416

Journals of Lewis and Clark, The NCLC 100: 1-88
overviews and general studies, 4-30
journal-keeping methods, 30-46
Fort Mandan, 46-51
the Clark journal, 51-65
the journals as literary texts, 65-87

Kabuki LC 73: 118-232
overviews and general studies, 120-40
the development of Kabuki, 140-65
major works, 165-95
Kabuki and society, 195-231

Kit-Kat Club, The LC 71: 66-112
overviews and general studies, 67-88
major figures, 88-107
attacks on the Kit-Kat Club, 107-12

Knickerbocker Group, The NCLC 56: 274-341
overviews and general studies, 276-314
Knickerbocker periodicals, 314-26
writers and artists, 326-40

Lake Poets, The NCLC 52: 217-304
characteristics of the Lake Poets and their works, 218-27
literary influences and collaborations, 227-66
defining and developing Romantic ideals, 266-84
embracing Conservatism, 284-303

Language Poets TCLC 126: 66-172
overviews and general studies, 67-122
selected major figures in language poetry, 122-72

Larkin, Philip, Controversy CLC 81: 417-64

Latin American Literature, Twentieth-Century TCLC 58: 111-98
historical and critical perspectives, 112-36
the novel, 136-45
the short story, 145-9
drama, 149-60
poetry, 160-7
the writer and society, 167-86
Native Americans in Latin American literature, 186-97

Law and Literature TCLC 126: 173-347
overviews and general studies, 174-253
fiction critiquing the law, 253-88
literary responses to the law, 289-346

Legend of El Dorado, The LC 74: 248-350
overviews, 249-308
major explorations for El Dorado, 308-50

The Levellers LC 51: 200-312
overviews and general studies, 201-29
principal figures, 230-86
religion, political philosophy, and pamphleteering, 287-311

Literary Prizes TCLC 122: 130-203
overviews and general studies, 131-34
the Nobel Prize in Literature, 135-83
the Pulitzer Prize, 183-203

Literature and Millenial Lists CLC 119: 431-67
The Modern Library list, 433
The Waterstone list, 438-439

Literature of the American Cowboy NCLC 96: 1-60
overview, 3-20
cowboy fiction, 20-36
cowboy poetry and songs, 36-59

Literature of the California Gold Rush NCLC 92: 320-85
overviews and general studies, 322-24
early California Gold Rush fiction, 324-44
Gold Rush folklore and legend, 344-51
the rise of Western local color, 351-60
social relations and social change, 360-385

Living Theatre, The DC 16: 154-214

Madness in Nineteenth-Century Literature NCLC 76: 142-284
overview, 143-54
autobiography, 154-68
poetry, 168-215
fiction, 215-83

Madness in Twentieth-Century Literature TCLC 50: 160-225
overviews and general studies, 161-71
madness and the creative process, 171-86
suicide, 186-91
madness in American literature, 191-207
madness in German literature, 207-13
madness and feminist artists, 213-24

Magic Realism TCLC 110: 80-327
overviews and general studies, 81-94
magic realism in African literature, 95-110
magic realism in American literature, 110-32
magic realism in Canadian literature, 132-46
magic realism in European literature, 146-66
magic realism in Asian literature, 166-79
magic realism in Latin-American literature, 179-223
magic realism in Israeli literature and the novels of Salman Rushdie, 223-38
magic realism in literature written by women, 239-326

Marxist Criticism TCLC 134: 127-57
overviews and general studies, 128-67
Marxist interpretations, 167-209
cultural and literary Marxist theory, 209-49
Marxism and feminist critical theory, 250-56

The Masque LC 63: 124-265
development of the masque, 125-62
sources and structure, 162-220
race and gender in the masque, 221-64

Medical Writing LC 55: 93-195
colonial America, 94-110
enlightenment, 110-24
medieval writing, 124-40
sexuality, 140-83
vernacular, 185-95

Memoirs of Trauma CLC 109: 419-466
overview, 420
criticism, 429

Metafiction TCLC 130: 43-228
overviews and general studies, 44-85
Spanish metafiction, 85-117
studies of metafictional authors and works, 118-228

Metaphysical Poets LC 24: 356-439
early definitions, 358-67
surveys and overviews, 367-92
cultural and social influences, 392-406
stylistic and thematic variations, 407-38

Missionaries in the Nineteenth-Century, Literature of NCLC 112: 299-392
history and development, 300-16
uses of ethnography, 316-31
sociopolitical concerns, 331-82
David Livingstone, 382-91

Modern Essay, The TCLC 58: 199-273
overview, 200-7
the essay in the early twentieth century, 207-19
characteristics of the modern essay, 219-32
modern essayists, 232-45
the essay as a literary genre, 245-73

Modern French Literature TCLC 122: 205-359
overviews and general studies, 207-43
French theater, 243-77
gender issues and French women writers, 277-315
ideology and politics, 315-24
modern French poetry, 324-41
resistance literature, 341-58

Modern Irish Literature TCLC 102: 125-321
overview, 129-44
dramas, 144-70
fiction, 170-247
poetry, 247-321

Modern Japanese Literature TCLC 66: 284-389
poetry, 285-305
drama, 305-29
fiction, 329-61
western influences, 361-87

Modernism TCLC 70: 165-275
definitions, 166-184
Modernism and earlier influences, 184-200
stylistic and thematic traits, 200-229
poetry and drama, 229-242
redefining Modernism, 242-275

Muckraking Movement in American Journalism TCLC 34: 161-242
development, principles, and major figures, 162-70
publications, 170-9
social and political ideas, 179-86
targets, 186-208
fiction, 208-19
decline, 219-29
impact and accomplishments, 229-40

Multiculturalism in Literature and Education CLC 70: 361-413

Music and Modern Literature TCLC 62: 182-329
overviews and general studies, 182-211
musical form/literary form, 211-32
music in literature, 232-50
the influence of music on literature, 250-73
literature and popular music, 273-303
jazz and poetry, 303-28

Mystery Story See Crime-Mystery-Detective Stories

Native American Literature CLC 76: 440-76

Natural School, Russian NCLC 24: 205-40
history and characteristics, 205-25
contemporary criticism, 225-40

Naturalism NCLC 36: 285-382
definitions and theories, 286-305
critical debates on Naturalism, 305-16
Naturalism in theater, 316-32
European Naturalism, 332-61
American Naturalism, 361-72
the legacy of Naturalism, 372-81

Negritude TCLC 50: 226-361
origins and evolution, 227-56

definitions, 256-91
Negritude in literature, 291-343
Negritude reconsidered, 343-58
New Criticism TCLC 34: 243-318
development and ideas, 244-70
debate and defense, 270-99
influence and legacy, 299-315
New South, Literature of the NCLC 116: 122-240
overviews, 124-66
the novel in the New South, 166-209
myth of the Old South in the New, 209-39
The New World in Renaissance Literature LC 31: 1-51
overview, 1-18
utopia vs. terror, 18-31
explorers and Native Americans, 31-51
New York Intellectuals and *Partisan Review* TCLC 30: 117-98
development and major figures, 118-28
influence of Judaism, 128-39
Partisan Review, 139-57
literary philosophy and practice, 157-75
political philosophy, 175-87
achievement and significance, 187-97
The New Yorker TCLC 58: 274-357
overviews and general studies, 274-95
major figures, 295-304
New Yorker style, 304-33
fiction, journalism, and humor at *The New Yorker*, 333-48
the new *New Yorker*, 348-56
Newgate Novel NCLC 24: 166-204
development of Newgate literature, 166-73
Newgate Calendar, 173-7
Newgate fiction, 177-95
Newgate drama, 195-204
New Zealand Literature TCLC 134: 258-368
overviews and general studies, 260-300
Maori literature, 300-22
New Zealand drama, 322-32
New Zealand fiction, 332-51
New Zealand poetry, 351-67
Nigerian Literature of the Twentieth Century TCLC 30: 199-265
surveys of, 199-227
English language and African life, 227-45
politics and the Nigerian writer, 245-54
Nigerian writers and society, 255-62
Nihilism and Literature TCLC 110: 328-93
overviews and general studies, 328-44
European and Russian nihilism, 344-73
nihilism in the works of Albert Camus, Franz Kafka, and John Barth, 373-92
Nineteenth-Century Captivity Narratives NCLC 80:131-218
overview, 132-37
the political significance of captivity narratives, 137-67
images of gender, 167-96
moral instruction, 197-217
Nineteenth-Century Euro-American Literary Representations of Native Americans NCLC 104: 132-264
overviews and general studies, 134-53
Native American history, 153-72
the Indians of the Northeast, 172-93
the Indians of the Southeast, 193-212
the Indians of the West, 212-27
Indian-hater fiction, 227-43
the Indian as exhibit, 243-63
Nineteenth-Century Native American Autobiography NCLC 64: 262-389
overview, 263-8
problems of authorship, 268-81
the evolution of Native American autobiography, 281-304

political issues, 304-15
gender and autobiography, 316-62
autobiographical works during the turn of the century, 362-88
Norse Mythology CMLC 26: 321-85
history and mythological tradition, 322-44
Eddic poetry, 344-74
Norse mythology and other traditions, 374-85
Northern Humanism LC 16: 281-356
background, 282-305
precursor of the Reformation, 305-14
the Brethren of the Common Life, the Devotio Moderna, and education, 314-40
the impact of printing, 340-56
Novel of Manners, The NCLC 56: 342-96
social and political order, 343-53
domestic order, 353-73
depictions of gender, 373-83
the American novel of manners, 383-95
Novels of the Ming and Early Ch'ing Dynasties LC 76: 213-356
overviews and historical development, 214-45
major works—overview, 245-85
genre studies, 285-325
cultural and social themes, 325-55
Nuclear Literature: Writings and Criticism in the Nuclear Age TCLC 46: 288-390
overviews and general studies, 290-301
fiction, 301-35
poetry, 335-8
nuclear war in Russo-Japanese literature, 338-55
nuclear war and women writers, 355-67
the nuclear referent and literary criticism, 367-88
Occultism in Modern Literature TCLC 50: 362-406
influence of occultism on literature, 363-72
occultism, literature, and society, 372-87
fiction, 387-96
drama, 396-405
Opium and the Nineteenth-Century Literary Imagination NCLC 20:250-301
original sources, 250-62
historical background, 262-71
and literary society, 271-9
and literary creativity, 279-300
Orientalism NCLC 96: 149-364
overviews and general studies, 150-98
Orientalism and imperialism, 198-229
Orientalism and gender, 229-59
Orientalism and the nineteenth-century novel, 259-321
Orientalism in nineteenth-century poetry, 321-63
The Oxford Movement NCLC 72: 1-197
overviews and general studies, 2-24
background, 24-59
and education, 59-69
religious responses, 69-128
literary aspects, 128-178
political implications, 178-196
The Parnassian Movement NCLC 72: 198-241
overviews and general studies, 199-231
and epic form, 231-38
and positivism, 238-41
Pastoral Literature of the English Renaissance LC 59: 171-282
overviews and general studies, 172-214
principal figures of the Elizabethan period, 214-33
principal figures of the later Renaissance, 233-50
pastoral drama, 250-81

Periodicals, Nineteenth-Century British NCLC 24: 100-65
overviews and general studies, 100-30
in the Romantic Age, 130-41
in the Victorian era, 142-54
and the reviewer, 154-64
Picaresque Literature of the Sixteenth and Seventeenth Centuries LC 78: 223-355
context and development, 224-71
genre, 271-98
the picaro, 299-326
the picara 326-53
Plath, Sylvia, and the Nature of Biography CLC 86: 433-62
the nature of biography, 433-52
reviews of *The Silent Woman*, 452-61
Political Theory from the 15th to the 18th Century LC 36: 1-55
overview, 1-26
natural law, 26-42
empiricism, 42-55
Polish Romanticism NCLC 52: 305-71
overviews and general studies, 306-26
major figures, 326-40
Polish Romantic drama, 340-62
influences, 362-71
Politics and Literature TCLC 94: 138-61
overviews and general studies, 139-96
Europe, 196-226
Latin America, 226-48
Africa and the Caribbean, 248-60
Popular Literature TCLC 70: 279-382
overviews and general studies, 280-324
"formula" fiction 324-336
readers of popular literature, 336-351
evolution of popular literature, 351-382
The Portrayal of Jews in Nineteenth-Century English Literature NCLC 72: 242-368
overviews and general studies, 244-77
Anglo-Jewish novels, 277-303
depictions by non-Jewish writers, 303-44
Hebraism versus Hellenism, 344-67
The Portrayal of Mormonism NCLC 96: 61-148
overview, 63-72
early Mormon literature, 72-100
Mormon periodicals and journals, 100-10
women writers, 110-22
Mormonism and nineteenth-century literature, 122-42
Mormon poetry, 142-47
Postcolonialism TCLC 114: 134-239
overviews and general studies, 135-153
African postcolonial writing, 153-72
Asian/Pacific literature, 172-78
postcolonial literary theory, 178-213
postcolonial women's writing, 213-38
Postmodernism TCLC 90:125-307
overview, 125-166
criticism, 166-224
fiction, 224-282
poetry, 282-300
drama, 300-307
Pre-Raphaelite Movement NCLC 20: 302-401
overview, 302-4
genesis, 304-12
Germ and *Oxford and Cambridge Magazine*, 312-20
Robert Buchanan and the "Fleshly School of Poetry," 320-31
satires and parodies, 331-4
surveys, 334-51
aesthetics, 351-75
sister arts of poetry and painting, 375-94
influence, 394-9
Pre-romanticism LC 40: 1-56
overviews and general studies, 2-14

defining the period, 14-23
new directions in poetry and prose, 23-45
the focus on the self, 45-56

Pre-Socratic Philosophy CMLC 22: 1-56
overviews and general studies, 3-24
the Ionians and the Pythagoreans, 25-35
Heraclitus, the Eleatics, and the Atomists, 36-47
the Sophists, 47-55

Prison in Nineteenth-Century Literature, The NCLC 116: 241-357
overview, 242-60
romantic prison, 260-78
domestic prison, 278-316
America as prison, 316-24
physical prisons and prison authors, 324-56

Protestant Hagiography and Martyrology LC 84: 106-217
overview, 106-37
John Foxe's *Book of Martyrs*, 137-97
martyrology and the feminine perspective, 198-216

Protestant Reformation, Literature of the LC 37: 1-83
overviews and general studies, 1-49
humanism and scholasticism, 49-69
the reformation and literature, 69-82

Psychoanalysis and Literature TCLC 38: 227-338
overviews and general studies, 227-46
Freud on literature, 246-51
psychoanalytic views of the literary process, 251-61
psychoanalytic theories of response to literature, 261-88
psychoanalysis and literary criticism, 288-312
psychoanalysis as literature/literature as psychoanalysis, 313-34

The Quarrel between the Ancients and the Moderns LC 63: 266-381
overviews and general studies, 267-301
Renaissance origins, 301-32
Quarrel between the Ancients and the Moderns in France, 332-58
Battle of the Books in England, 358-80

Rap Music CLC 76: 477-50

Renaissance Natural Philosophy LC 27: 201-87
cosmology, 201-28
astrology, 228-54
magic, 254-86

Representations of the Devil in Nineteenth-Century Literature NCLC 100: 89-223
overviews and general studies, 90-115
the Devil in American fiction, 116-43
English Romanticism: the satanic school, 143-89
Luciferian discourse in European literature, 189-222

Restoration Drama LC 21: 184-275
general overviews and general studies, 185-230
Jeremy Collier stage controversy, 230-9
other critical interpretations, 240-75

Revenge Tragedy LC 71: 113-242
overviews and general studies, 113-51
Elizabethan attitudes toward revenge, 151-88
the morality of revenge, 188-216
reminders and remembrance, 217-41

Revising the Literary Canon CLC 81: 465-509

Revising the Literary Canon TCLC 114: 240-84
overviews and general studies, 241-85
canon change in American literature, 285-339
gender and the literary canon, 339-59
minority and third-world literature and the canon, 359-84

Revolutionary Astronomers LC 51: 314-65
overviews and general studies, 316-25
principal figures, 325-51
Revolutionary astronomical models, 352-64

Robin Hood, Legend of LC 19: 205-58
origins and development of the Robin Hood legend, 206-20
representations of Robin Hood, 220-44
Robin Hood as hero, 244-56

Rushdie, Salman, *Satanic Verses* Controversy CLC 55: 214-63; 59:404-56

Russian Nihilism NCLC 28: 403-47
definitions and overviews, 404-17
women and Nihilism, 417-27
literature as reform: the Civic Critics, 427-33
Nihilism and the Russian novel: Turgenev and Dostoevsky, 433-47

Russian Thaw TCLC 26: 189-247
literary history of the period, 190-206
theoretical debate of socialist realism, 206-11
Novy Mir, 211-7
Literary Moscow, 217-24
Pasternak, *Zhivago*, and the Nobel prize, 224-7
poetry of liberation, 228-31
Brodsky trial and the end of the Thaw, 231-6
achievement and influence, 236-46

Salem Witch Trials LC 38: 1-145
overviews and general studies, 2-30
historical background, 30-65
judicial background, 65-78
the search for causes, 78-115
the role of women in the trials, 115-44

Salinger, J. D., Controversy Surrounding *In Search of J. D. Salinger* CLC 55: 325-44

Sanitation Reform, Nineteenth-Century NCLC 124: 165-257
overviews and general studies, 166
primary texts, 186-89
social context, 189-221
public health in literature, 221-56

Science and Modern Literature TCLC 90: 308-419
overviews and general studies, 295-333
fiction, 333-95
poetry, 395-405
drama, 405-19

Science in Nineteenth-Century Literature NCLC 100: 224-366
overviews and general studies, 225-65
major figures, 265-336
sociopolitical concerns, 336-65

Science Fiction, Nineteenth-Century NCLC 24: 241-306
background, 242-50
definitions of the genre, 251-56
representative works and writers, 256-75
themes and conventions, 276-305

Scottish Chaucerians LC 20: 363-412

Scottish Poetry, Eighteenth-Century LC 29: 95-167
overviews and general studies, 96-114
the Scottish Augustans, 114-28
the Scots Vernacular Revival, 132-63
Scottish poetry after Burns, 163-66

Sea in Literature, The TCLC 82: 72-191
drama, 73-9
poetry, 79-119
fiction, 119-91

Sea in Nineteenth-Century English and American Literature, The NCLC 104: 265-362
overviews and general studies, 267-306
major figures in American sea fiction—Cooper and Melville, 306-29
American sea poetry and short stories, 329-45
English sea literature, 345-61

Sensation Novel, The NCLC 80: 219-330
overviews and general studies, 221-46
principal figures, 246-62
nineteenth-century reaction, 262-91
feminist criticism, 291-329

Sentimental Novel, The NCLC 60: 146-245
overviews and general studies, 147-58
the politics of domestic fiction, 158-79
a literature of resistance and repression, 179-212
the reception of sentimental fiction, 213-44

Sex and Literature TCLC 82: 192-434
overviews and general studies, 193-216
drama, 216-63
poetry, 263-87
fiction, 287-431

Sherlock Holmes Centenary TCLC 26: 248-310
Doyle's life and the composition of the Holmes stories, 248-59
life and character of Holmes, 259-78
method, 278-79
Holmes and the Victorian world, 279-92
Sherlockian scholarship, 292-301
Doyle and the development of the detective story, 301-07
Holmes's continuing popularity, 307-09

The Silver Fork Novel NCLC 88: 58-140
criticism, 59-139

Slave Narratives, American NCLC 20: 1-91
background, 2-9
overviews and general studies, 9-24
contemporary responses, 24-7
language, theme, and technique, 27-70
historical authenticity, 70-5
antecedents, 75-83
role in development of Black American literature, 83-8

The Slave Trade in British and American Literature LC 59: 283-369
overviews and general studies, 284-91
depictions by white writers, 291-331
depictions by former slaves, 331-67

Social Conduct Literature LC 55: 196-298
overviews and general studies, 196-223
prescriptive ideology in other literary forms, 223-38
role of the press, 238-63
impact of conduct literature, 263-87
conduct literature and the perception of women, 287-96
women writing for women, 296-98

Social Protest Literature Outside England, Nineteenth-Century NCLC 124: 258-350
overviews and general studies, 259-72
oppression revealed, 272-306
literature to incite or prevent reform, 306-50

Socialism NCLC 88: 141-237
origins, 142-54

French socialism, 154-83
Anglo-American socialism, 183-205
Socialist-Feminism, 205-36

Southern Literature See **Contemporary Southern Literature**

Southern Literature of the Reconstruction NCLC 108: 289-369
overview, 290-91
reconstruction literature: the consequences of war, 291-321
old south to new: continuities in southern culture, 321-68

Spanish Civil War Literature TCLC 26: 311-85
topics in, 312-33
British and American literature, 333-59
French literature, 359-62
Spanish literature, 362-73
German literature, 373-75
political idealism and war literature, 375-83

Spanish Golden Age Literature LC 23: 262-332
overviews and general studies, 253-81
verse drama, 281-304
prose fiction, 304-19
lyric poetry, 319-31

Spasmodic School of Poetry NCLC 24: 307-52
history and major figures, 307-21
the Spasmodics on poetry, 321-7
Firmilian and critical disfavor, 327-39
theme and technique, 339-47
influence, 347-51

Sports in Literature TCLC 86: 294-445
overviews and general studies, 295-324
major writers and works, 324-402
sports, literature, and social issues, 402-45

Steinbeck, John, Fiftieth Anniversary of *The Grapes of Wrath* CLC 59: 311-54

Sturm und Drang NCLC 40: 196-275
definitions, 197-238
poetry and poetics, 238-58
drama, 258-75

Supernatural Fiction in the Nineteenth Century NCLC 32: 207-87
major figures and influences, 208-35
the Victorian ghost story, 236-54
the influence of science and occultism, 254-66
supernatural fiction and society, 266-86

Supernatural Fiction, Modern TCLC 30: 59-116
evolution and varieties, 60-74
"decline" of the ghost story, 74-86
as a literary genre, 86-92
technique, 92-101
nature and appeal, 101-15

Surrealism TCLC 30: 334-406
history and formative influences, 335-43
manifestos, 343-54
philosophic, aesthetic, and political principles, 354-75
poetry, 375-81
novel, 381-6
drama, 386-92
film, 392-8
painting and sculpture, 398-403
achievement, 403-5

Symbolism, Russian TCLC 30: 266-333
doctrines and major figures, 267-92
theories, 293-8
and French Symbolism, 298-310
themes in poetry, 310-4
theater, 314-20
and the fine arts, 320-32

Symbolist Movement, French NCLC 20: 169-249
background and characteristics, 170-86
principles, 186-91
attacked and defended, 191-7
influences and predecessors, 197-211
and Decadence, 211-6
theater, 216-26
prose, 226-33
decline and influence, 233-47

Television and Literature TCLC 78: 283-426
television and literacy, 283-98
reading vs. watching, 298-341
adaptations, 341-62
literary genres and television, 362-90
television genres and literature, 390-410
children's literature/children's television, 410-25

Theater of the Absurd TCLC 38: 339-415
"The Theater of the Absurd," 340-7
major plays and playwrights, 347-58
and the concept of the absurd, 358-86
theatrical techniques, 386-94
predecessors of, 394-402
influence of, 402-13

Tin Pan Alley See **American Popular Song, Golden Age of**

Tobacco Culture LC 55: 299-366
social and economic attitudes toward tobacco, 299-344
tobacco trade between the old world and the new world, 344-55
tobacco smuggling in Great Britain, 355-66

Transcendentalism, American NCLC 24: 1-99
overviews and general studies, 3-23
contemporary documents, 23-41
theological aspects of, 42-52
and social issues, 52-74
literature of, 74-96

Travel Writing in the Nineteenth Century NCLC 44: 274-392
the European grand tour, 275-303
the Orient, 303-47
North America, 347-91

Travel Writing in the Twentieth Century TCLC 30: 407-56
conventions and traditions, 407-27
and fiction writing, 427-43
comparative essays on travel writers, 443-54

Tristan and Isolde Legend CMLC 42: 311-404

True-Crime Literature CLC 99: 333-433
history and analysis, 334-407
reviews of true-crime publications, 407-23
writing instruction, 424-29
author profiles, 429-33

***Ulysses* and the Process of Textual Reconstruction** TCLC 26: 386-416
evaluations of the new *Ulysses*, 386-94
editorial principles and procedures, 394-401
theoretical issues, 401-16

Utilitarianism NCLC 84: 272-340
J. S. Mill's Utilitarianism: liberty, equality, justice, 273-313
Jeremy Bentham's Utilitarianism: the science of happiness, 313-39

Utopianism NCLC 88: 238-346
overviews: Utopian literature, 239-59
Utopianism in American literature, 259-99
Utopianism in British literature, 299-311
Utopianism and Feminism, 311-45

Utopian Literature, Nineteenth-Century NCLC 24: 353-473
definitions, 354-74
overviews and general studies, 374-88
theory, 388-408
communities, 409-26
fiction, 426-53
women and fiction, 454-71

Utopian Literature, Renaissance LC 32: 1-63
overviews and general studies, 2-25
classical background, 25-33
utopia and the social contract, 33-9
origins in mythology, 39-48
utopia and the Renaissance country house, 48-52
influence of millenarianism, 52-62

Vampire in Literature TCLC 46: 391-454
origins and evolution, 392-412
social and psychological perspectives, 413-44
vampire fiction and science fiction, 445-53

Vernacular Bibles LC 67: 214-388
overviews and general studies, 215-59
the English Bible, 259-355
the German Bible, 355-88

Victorian Autobiography NCLC 40: 277-363
development and major characteristics, 278-88
themes and techniques, 289-313
the autobiographical tendency in Victorian prose and poetry, 313-47
Victorian women's autobiographies, 347-62

Victorian Fantasy Literature NCLC 60: 246-384
overviews and general studies, 247-91
major figures, 292-366
women in Victorian fantasy literature, 366-83

Victorian Hellenism NCLC 68: 251-376
overviews and general studies, 252-78
the meanings of Hellenism, 278-335
the literary influence, 335-75

Victorian Illustrated Fiction NCLC 120: 247-356
overviews and development, 128-76
technical and material aspects of book illustration, 276-84
Charles Dickens and his illustrators, 284-320
William Makepeace Thackeray, 320-31
George Eliot and Frederic Leighton, 331-51
Lewis Carroll and John Tenniel, 351-56

Victorian Novel NCLC 32: 288-454
development and major characteristics, 290-310
themes and techniques, 310-58
social criticism in the Victorian novel, 359-97
urban and rural life in the Victorian novel, 397-406
women in the Victorian novel, 406-25
Mudie's Circulating Library, 425-34
the late-Victorian novel, 434-51

Vietnamese Literature TCLC 102: 322-386

Vietnam War in Literature and Film CLC 91: 383-437
overview, 384-8
prose, 388-412
film and drama, 412-24
poetry, 424-35

Violence in Literature TCLC 98: 235-358
overviews and general studies, 236-74
violence in the works of modern authors, 274-358

CUMULATIVE TOPIC INDEX

Vorticism TCLC 62: 330-426
    Wyndham Lewis and Vorticism, 330-8
    characteristics and principles of Vorticism, 338-65
    Lewis and Pound, 365-82
    Vorticist writing, 382-416
    Vorticist painting, 416-26

Well-Made Play, The NCLC 80: 331-370
    overviews and general studies, 332-45
    Scribe's style, 345-56
    the influence of the well-made play, 356-69

Women's Autobiography, Nineteenth Century NCLC 76: 285-368
    overviews and general studies, 287-300
    autobiographies concerned with religious and political issues, 300-15
    autobiographies by women of color, 315-38
    autobiographies by women pioneers, 338-51
    autobiographies by women of letters, 351-68

Women's Diaries, Nineteenth-Century NCLC 48: 308-54
    overview, 308-13
    diary as history, 314-25
    sociology of diaries, 325-34
    diaries as psychological scholarship, 334-43
    diary as autobiography, 343-8
    diary as literature, 348-53

Women in Modern Literature TCLC 94: 262-425
    overviews and general studies, 263-86
    American literature, 286-304
    other national literatures, 304-33
    fiction, 333-94
    poetry, 394-407
    drama, 407-24

Women Writers, Seventeenth-Century LC 30: 2-58
    overview, 2-15
    women and education, 15-9
    women and autobiography, 19-31
    women's diaries, 31-9
    early feminists, 39-58

World War I Literature TCLC 34: 392-486
    overview, 393-403
    English, 403-27
    German, 427-50
    American, 450-66
    French, 466-74
    and modern history, 474-82

Yellow Journalism NCLC 36: 383-456
    overviews and general studies, 384-96
    major figures, 396-413

Yiddish Literature TCLC 130: 229-364
    overviews and general studies, 230-54
    major authors, 254-305
    Yiddish literature in America, 305-34
    Yiddish and Judaism, 334-64

Young Playwrights Festival
    1988 CLC 55: 376-81
    1989 CLC 59: 398-403
    1990 CLC 65: 444-8

CLC Cumulative Nationality Index

ALBANIAN

Kadare, Ismail **52**

ALGERIAN

Althusser, Louis **106**
Camus, Albert **1, 2, 4, 9, 11, 14, 32, 63, 69, 124**
Cixous, Hélène **92**
Cohen-Solal, Annie **50**

AMERICAN

Abbey, Edward **36, 59**
Abbott, Lee K(ittredge) **48**
Abish, Walter **22**
Abrams, M(eyer) H(oward) **24**
Acker, Kathy **45, 111**
Adams, Alice (Boyd) **6, 13, 46**
Addams, Charles (Samuel) **30**
Adler, C(arole) S(chwerdtfeger) **35**
Adler, Renata **8, 31**
Ai **4, 14, 69**
Aiken, Conrad (Potter) **1, 3, 5, 10, 52**
Albee, Edward (Franklin III) **1, 2, 3, 5, 9, 11, 13, 25, 53, 86, 113**
Alexander, Lloyd (Chudley) **35**
Alexie, Sherman (Joseph Jr.) **96, 154**
Algren, Nelson **4, 10, 33**
Allen, Edward **59**
Allen, Paula Gunn **84**
Allen, Woody **16, 52**
Allison, Dorothy E. **78, 153**
Alta **19**
Alter, Robert B(ernard) **34**
Alther, Lisa **7, 41**
Altman, Robert **16, 116**
Alvarez, Julia **93**
Ambrose, Stephen E(dward) **145**
Ammons, A(rchie) R(andolph) **2, 3, 5, 8, 9, 25, 57, 108**
L'Amour, Louis (Dearborn) **25, 55**
Anaya, Rudolfo A(lfonso) **23, 148**
Anderson, Jon (Victor) **9**
Anderson, Poul (William) **15**
Anderson, Robert (Woodruff) **23**
Angell, Roger **26**
Angelou, Maya **12, 35, 64, 77, 155**
Anthony, Piers **35**
Apple, Max (Isaac) **9, 33**
Appleman, Philip (Dean) **51**
Archer, Jules **12**
Arendt, Hannah **66, 98**
Arnow, Harriette (Louisa) Simpson **2, 7, 18**
Arrick, Fran **30**
Arzner, Dorothy **98**
Ashbery, John (Lawrence) **2, 3, 4, 6, 9, 13, 15, 25, 41, 77, 125**
Asimov, Isaac **1, 3, 9, 19, 26, 76, 92**
Attaway, William (Alexander) **92**
Auchincloss, Louis (Stanton) **4, 6, 9, 18, 45**
Auden, W(ystan) H(ugh) **1, 2, 3, 4, 6, 9, 11, 14, 43, 123**
Auel, Jean M(arie) **31, 107**

Auster, Paul **47, 131**
Bach, Richard (David) **14**
Badanes, Jerome **59**
Baker, Elliott **8**
Baker, Nicholson **61, 165**
Baker, Russell (Wayne) **31**
Bakshi, Ralph **26**
Baldwin, James (Arthur) **1, 2, 3, 4, 5, 8, 13, 15, 17, 42, 50, 67, 90, 127**
Bambara, Toni Cade **19, 88**
Banks, Russell **37, 72**
Baraka, Amiri **1, 2, 3, 5, 10, 14, 33, 115**
Barber, Benjamin R. **141**
Barbera, Jack (Vincent) **44**
Barnard, Mary (Ethel) **48**
Barnes, Djuna **3, 4, 8, 11, 29, 127**
Barondess, Sue K(aufman) **8**
Barrett, Andrea **150**
Barrett, William (Christopher) **27**
Barth, John (Simmons) **1, 2, 3, 5, 7, 9, 10, 14, 27, 51, 89**
Barthelme, Donald **1, 2, 3, 5, 6, 8, 13, 23, 46, 59, 115**
Barthelme, Frederick **36, 117**
Barzun, Jacques (Martin) **51, 145**
Bass, Rick **79, 143**
Baumbach, Jonathan **6, 23**
Bausch, Richard (Carl) **51**
Baxter, Charles (Morley) **45, 78**
Beagle, Peter S(oyer) **7, 104**
Beattie, Ann **8, 13, 18, 40, 63, 146**
Becker, Walter **26**
Beecher, John **6**
Begiebing, Robert J(ohn) **70**
Behrman, S(amuel) N(athaniel) **40**
Belitt, Ben **22**
Bell, Madison Smartt **41, 102**
Bell, Marvin (Hartley) **8, 31**
Bellow, Saul **1, 2, 3, 6, 8, 10, 13, 15, 25, 33, 34, 63, 79**
Benary-Isbert, Margot **12**
Benchley, Peter (Bradford) **4, 8**
Benedikt, Michael **4, 14**
Benford, Gregory (Albert) **52**
Bennett, Jay **35**
Benson, Jackson J. **34**
Benson, Sally **17**
Bentley, Eric (Russell) **24**
Berendt, John (Lawrence) **86**
Berger, Melvin H. **12**
Berger, Thomas (Louis) **3, 5, 8, 11, 18, 38**
Bergstein, Eleanor **4**
Bernard, April **59**
Bernstein, Charles **142,**
Berriault, Gina **54, 109**
Berrigan, Daniel **4**
Berry, Chuck **17**
Berry, Wendell (Erdman) **4, 6, 8, 27, 46**
Berryman, John **1, 2, 3, 4, 6, 8, 10, 13, 25, 62**
Bessie, Alvah **23**
Bettelheim, Bruno **79**
Betts, Doris (Waugh) **3, 6, 28**

Bidart, Frank **33**
Birkerts, Sven **116**
Bishop, Elizabeth **1, 4, 9, 13, 15, 32**
Bishop, John **10**
Blackburn, Paul **9, 43**
Blackmur, R(ichard) P(almer) **2, 24**
Blaise, Clark **29**
Blatty, William Peter **2**
Blessing, Lee **54**
Blish, James (Benjamin) **14**
Bloch, Robert (Albert) **33**
Bloom, Harold **24, 103**
Blount, Roy (Alton) Jr. **38**
Blume, Judy (Sussman) **12, 30**
Bly, Robert (Elwood) **1, 2, 5, 10, 15, 38, 128**
Bochco, Steven **35**
Bogan, Louise **4, 39, 46, 93**
Bogosian, Eric **45, 141**
Bograd, Larry **35**
Bonham, Frank **12**
Bontemps, Arna(ud Wendell) **1, 18**
Booth, Philip **23**
Booth, Wayne C(layson) **24**
Bottoms, David **53**
Bourjaily, Vance (Nye) **8, 62**
Bova, Ben(jamin William) **45**
Bowers, Edgar **9**
Bowles, Jane (Sydney) **3, 68**
Bowles, Paul (Frederick) **1, 2, 19, 53**
Boyle, Kay **1, 5, 19, 58, 121**
Boyle, T(homas) Coraghessan **36, 55, 90**
Bradbury, Ray (Douglas) **1, 3, 10, 15, 42, 98**
Bradley, David (Henry) Jr. **23, 118**
Bradley, John Ed(mund Jr.) **55**
Bradley, Marion Zimmer **30**
Bradshaw, John **70**
Brady, Joan **86**
Brammer, William **31**
Brancato, Robin F(idler) **35**
Brand, Millen **7**
Branden, Barbara **44**
Branley, Franklyn M(ansfield) **21**
Brautigan, Richard (Gary) **1, 3, 5, 9, 12, 34, 42**
Braverman, Kate **67**
Brennan, Maeve **5**
Bridgers, Sue Ellen **26**
Brin, David **34**
Brodkey, Harold (Roy) **56**
Brodsky, Joseph **4, 6, 13, 36, 100**
Brodsky, Michael (Mark) **19**
Bromell, Henry **5**
Broner, E(sther) M(asserman) **19**
Bronk, William (M.) **10**
Brooks, Cleanth **24, 86, 110**
Brooks, Gwendolyn (Elizabeth) **1, 2, 4, 5, 15, 49, 125**
Brooks, Mel **12**
Brooks, Peter **34**
Brooks, Van Wyck **29**
Brosman, Catharine Savage **9**
Broughton, T(homas) Alan **19**
Broumas, Olga **10, 73**

CUMULATIVE NATIONALITY INDEX

Brown, Claude **30**
Brown, Dee (Alexander) **18, 47**
Brown, Rita Mae **18, 43, 79**
Brown, Rosellen **32, 170**
Brown, Sterling Allen **1, 23, 59**
Brown, (William) Larry **73**
Brownmiller, Susan **159**
Browne, (Clyde) Jackson **21**
Browning, Tod **16**
Bruccoli, Matthew J(oseph) **34**
Bruce, Lenny **21**
Bryan, C(ourtlandt) D(ixon) B(arnes) **29**
Buchwald, Art(hur) **33**
Buck, Pearl S(ydenstricker) **7, 11, 18, 127**
Buckley, Christopher **165**
Buckley, William F(rank) Jr. **7, 18, 37**
Buechner, (Carl) Frederick **2, 4, 6, 9**
Bukowski, Charles **2, 5, 9, 41, 82, 108**
Bullins, Ed **1, 5, 7**
Burke, Kenneth (Duva) **2, 24**
Burnshaw, Stanley **3, 13, 44**
Burr, Anne **6**
Burroughs, William S(eward) **1, 2, 5, 15, 22, 42, 75, 109**
Busch, Frederick **7, 10, 18, 47, 166**
Bush, Ronald **34**
Butler, Octavia E(stelle) **38, 121**
Butler, Robert Olen (Jr.) **81, 162**
Byars, Betsy (Cromer) **35**
Byrne, David **26**
Cage, John (Milton Jr.) **41**
Cain, James M(allahan) **3, 11, 28**
Caldwell, Erskine (Preston) **1, 8, 14, 50, 60**
Caldwell, (Janet Miriam) Taylor (Holland) **2, 28, 39**
Calisher, Hortense **2, 4, 8, 38, 134**
Cameron, Carey **59**
Cameron, Peter **44**
Campbell, John W(ood Jr.) **32**
Campbell, Joseph **69**
Campion, Jane **95**
Canby, Vincent **13**
Canin, Ethan **55**
Capote, Truman **1, 3, 8, 13, 19, 34, 38, 58**
Capra, Frank **16**
Caputo, Philip **32**
Card, Orson Scott **44, 47, 50**
Carey, Ernestine Gilbreth **17**
Carlisle, Henry (Coffin) **33**
Carlson, Ron(ald F.) **54**
Carpenter, Don(ald Richard) **41**
Carpenter, John **161**
Carr, Caleb **86**
Carr, John Dickson **3**
Carr, Virginia Spencer **34**
Carroll, James P. **38**
Carroll, Jim **35, 143**
Carruth, Hayden **4, 7, 10, 18, 84**
Carson, Rachel Louise **71**
Carver, Raymond **22, 36, 53, 55, 126**
Casey, John (Dudley) **59**
Casey, Michael **2**
Casey, Warren (Peter) **12**
Cassavetes, John **20**
Cassill, R(onald) V(erlin) **4, 23**
Cassity, (Allen) Turner **6, 42**
Castaneda, Carlos (Cesar Aranha) **12, 119**
Castedo, Elena **65**
Castillo, Ana (Hernandez Del) **151**
Catton, (Charles) Bruce **35**
Caunitz, William J. **34**
Chabon, Michael **55, 149**
Chappell, Fred (Davis) **40, 78, 162**
Charyn, Jerome **5, 8, 18**
Chase, Mary Ellen **2**
Chayefsky, Paddy **23**
Cheever, John **3, 7, 8, 11, 15, 25, 64**
Cheever, Susan **18, 48**
Cheney, Lynne V. **70**
Chester, Alfred **49**
Childress, Alice **12, 15, 86, 96**
Chin, Frank (Chew Jr.) **135**

Choi, Susan **119**
Chomsky, (Avram) Noam **132**
Chute, Carolyn **39**
Ciardi, John (Anthony) **10, 40, 44, 129**
Cimino, Michael **16**
Cisneros, Sandra **69, 118**
Clampitt, Amy **32**
Clancy, Tom **45, 112**
Clark, Eleanor **5, 19**
Clark, Walter Van Tilburg **28**
Clarke, Shirley **16**
Clavell, James (duMaresq) **6, 25, 87**
Cleaver, (Leroy) Eldridge **30, 119**
Clifton, (Thelma) Lucille **19, 66, 162**
Coburn, D(onald) L(ee) **10**
Codrescu, Andrei **46, 121**
Coen, Ethan **108**
Coen, Joel **108**
Cohen, Arthur A(llen) **7, 31**
Coles, Robert (Martin) **108**
Collier, Christopher **30**
Collier, James Lincoln **30**
Collins, Linda **44**
Colter, Cyrus **58**
Colum, Padraic **28**
Colwin, Laurie (E.) **5, 13, 23, 84**
Condon, Richard (Thomas) **4, 6, 8, 10, 45, 100**
Connell, Evan S(helby) Jr. **4, 6, 45**
Connelly, Marc(us Cook) **7**
Conroy, (Donald) Pat(rick) **30, 74**
Cook, Robin **14**
Cooke, Elizabeth **55**
Cook-Lynn, Elizabeth **93**
Cooper, J(oan) California **56**
Coover, Robert (Lowell) **3, 7, 15, 32, 46, 87, 161**
Coppola, Francis Ford **16, 126**
Corcoran, Barbara (Asenath) **17**
Corman, Cid **9**
Cormier, Robert (Edmund) **12, 30**
Corn, Alfred (DeWitt III) **33**
Cornwell, Patricia (Daniels) **155**
Corso, (Nunzio) Gregory **1, 11**
Costain, Thomas B(ertram) **30**
Cowley, Malcolm **39**
Cozzens, James Gould **1, 4, 11, 92**
Crane, R(onald) S(almon) **27**
Crase, Douglas **58**
Creeley, Robert (White) **1, 2, 4, 8, 11, 15, 36, 78**
Crews, Harry (Eugene) **6, 23, 49**
Crichton, (John) Michael **2, 6, 54, 90**
Cristofer, Michael **28**
Cronenberg, David **143**
Crow Dog, Mary (Ellen) **93**
Crowley, John **57**
Crumb, R(obert) **17**
Cryer, Gretchen (Kiger) **21**
Cudlip, David R(ockwell) **34**
Cummings, E(dward) E(stlin) **1, 3, 8, 12, 15, 68**
Cunningham, J(ames) V(incent) **3, 31**
Cunningham, Julia (Woolfolk) **12**
Cunningham, Michael **34**
Currie, Ellen **44**
Dacey, Philip **51**
Dahlberg, Edward **1, 7, 14**
Daitch, Susan **103**
Daly, Elizabeth **52**
Daly, Mary **173**
Daly, Maureen **17**
Dannay, Frederic **11**
Danvers, Dennis **70**
Danziger, Paula **21**
Davenport, Guy (Mattison Jr.) **6, 14, 38**
Davidson, Donald (Grady) **2, 13, 19**
Davidson, Sara **9**
Davis, Angela (Yvonne) **77**
Davis, H(arold) L(enoir) **49**
Davison, Peter (Hubert) **28**
Dawson, Fielding **6**

Deer, Sandra **45**
Delany, Samuel R(ay) Jr. **8, 14, 38, 141**
Delbanco, Nicholas (Franklin) **6, 13, 167**
DeLillo, Don **8, 10, 13, 27, 39, 54, 76, 143**
Deloria, Vine (Victor) Jr. **21, 122**
Del Vecchio, John M(ichael) **29**
de Man, Paul (Adolph Michel) **55**
DeMarinis, Rick **54**
Demby, William **53**
Denby, Edwin (Orr) **48**
De Palma, Brian (Russell) **20**
Deren, Maya **16, 102**
Derleth, August (William) **31**
Deutsch, Babette **18**
De Vries, Peter **1, 2, 3, 7, 10, 28, 46**
Dexter, Pete **34, 55**
Diamond, Neil **30**
Dick, Philip K(indred) **10, 30, 72**
Dickey, James (Lafayette) **1, 2, 4, 7, 10, 15, 47, 109**
Dickey, William **3, 28**
Dickinson, Charles **49**
Didion, Joan **1, 3, 8, 14, 32, 129**
Dillard, Annie **9, 60, 115**
Dillard, R(ichard) H(enry) W(ilde) **5**
Disch, Thomas M(ichael) **7, 36**
Dixon, Stephen **52**
Dobyns, Stephen **37**
Doctorow, E(dgar) L(aurence) **6, 11, 15, 18, 37, 44, 65, 113**
Dodson, Owen (Vincent) **79**
Doerr, Harriet **34**
Donaldson, Stephen R(eeder) **46, 138**
Donleavy, J(ames) P(atrick) **1, 4, 6, 10, 45**
Donovan, John **35**
Dorn, Edward (Merton) **10, 18**
Dorris, Michael (Anthony) **109**
Dos Passos, John (Roderigo) **1, 4, 8, 11, 15, 25, 34, 82**
Douglas, Ellen **73**
Dove, Rita (Frances) **50, 81**
Dowell, Coleman **60**
Drexler, Rosalyn **2, 6**
Drury, Allen (Stuart) **37**
Duberman, Martin (Bauml) **8**
Dubie, Norman (Evans) **36**
Du Bois, W(illiam) E(dward) B(urghardt) **1, 2, 13, 64, 96**
Dubus, André **13, 36, 97**
Duffy, Bruce **50**
Dugan, Alan **2, 6**
Dumas, Henry L. **6, 62**
Duncan, Lois **26**
Duncan, Robert (Edward) **1, 2, 4, 7, 15, 41, 55**
Dunn, Katherine (Karen) **71**
Dunn, Stephen (Elliott) **36**
Dunne, John Gregory **28**
Durang, Christopher (Ferdinand) **27, 38**
Durban, (Rosa) Pam **39**
Dworkin, Andrea **43, 123**
Dwyer, Thomas A. **114**
Dybek, Stuart **114**
Dylan, Bob **3, 4, 6, 12, 77**
Eastlake, William (Derry) **8**
Eberhart, Richard (Ghormley) **3, 11, 19, 56**
Eberstadt, Fernanda **39**
Eckert, Allan W. **17**
Edel, (Joseph) Leon **29, 34**
Edgerton, Clyde (Carlyle) **39**
Edmonds, Walter D(umaux) **35**
Edson, Russell **13**
Edwards, Gus **43**
Ehle, John (Marsden Jr.) **27**
Ehrenreich, Barbara **110**
Eigner, Larry **9**
Eiseley, Loren Corey **7**
Eisenstadt, Jill **50**
Eliade, Mircea **19**
Eliot, T(homas) S(tearns) **1, 2, 3, 6, 9, 10, 13, 15, 24, 34, 41, 55, 57, 113**

Elkin, Stanley L(awrence) **4, 6, 9, 14, 27, 51, 91**
Elledge, Scott **34**
Elliott, George P(aul) **2**
Ellis, Bret Easton **39, 71, 117**
Ellison, Harlan (Jay) **1, 13, 42, 139**
Ellison, Ralph (Waldo) **1, 3, 11, 54, 86, 114**
Ellmann, Lucy (Elizabeth) **61**
Ellmann, Richard (David) **50**
Elman, Richard (Martin) **19**
L'Engle, Madeleine (Camp Franklin) **12**
Ephron, Nora **17, 31**
Epstein, Daniel Mark **7**
Epstein, Jacob **19**
Epstein, Joseph **39**
Epstein, Leslie **27**
Erdman, Paul E(mil) **25**
Erdrich, Louise **39, 54, 120**
Erickson, Steve **64**
Eshleman, Clayton **7**
Estleman, Loren D. **48**
Eugenides, Jeffrey **81**
Everett, Percival L. **57**
Everson, William (Oliver) **1, 5, 14**
Exley, Frederick (Earl) **6, 11**
Ezekiel, Tish O'Dowd **34**
Fagen, Donald **26**
Fair, Ronald L. **18**
Faludi, Susan **140**
Fante, John (Thomas) **60**
Farina, Richard **9**
Farley, Walter (Lorimer) **17**
Farmer, Philip José **1, 19**
Farrell, James T(homas) **1, 4, 8, 11, 66**
Fast, Howard (Melvin) **23, 131**
Faulkner, William (Cuthbert) **1, 3, 6, 8, 9, 11, 14, 18, 28, 52, 68**
Fauset, Jessie Redmon **19, 54**
Faust, Irvin **8**
Fearing, Kenneth (Flexner) **51**
Federman, Raymond **6, 47**
Feiffer, Jules (Ralph) **2, 8, 64**
Feinberg, David B. **59**
Feldman, Irving (Mordecai) **7**
Felsen, Henry Gregor **17**
Ferber, Edna **18, 93**
Ferlinghetti, Lawrence (Monsanto) **2, 6, 10, 27, 111**
Ferrigno, Robert **65**
Fiedler, Leslie A(aron) **4, 13, 24**
Field, Andrew **44**
Fierstein, Harvey (Forbes) **33**
Fish, Stanley Eugene **142**
Fisher, M(ary) F(rances) K(ennedy) **76, 87**
Fisher, Vardis (Alvero) **7**
Fitzgerald, Robert (Stuart) **39**
Flanagan, Thomas (James Bonner) **25, 52**
Fleming, Thomas (James) **37**
Foote, Horton **51, 91**
Foote, Shelby **75**
Forbes, Esther **12**
Forché, Carolyn (Louise) **25, 83, 86**
Ford, John **16**
Ford, Richard **46, 99**
Foreman, Richard **50**
Forman, James Douglas **21**
Fornés, María Irene **39, 61**
Forrest, Leon (Richard) **4**
Fosse, Bob **20**
Fox, Paula **2, 8, 121**
Fox, William Price (Jr.) **22**
Francis, Robert (Churchill) **15**
Frank, Elizabeth **39**
Fraze, Candida (Merrill) **50**
Frazier, Ian **46**
Freeman, Judith **55**
French, Albert **86**
French, Marilyn **10, 18, 60**
Friedan, Betty (Naomi) **74**
Friedman, B(ernard) H(arper) **7**
Friedman, Bruce Jay **3, 5, 56**

Frost, Robert (Lee) **1, 3, 4, 9, 10, 13, 15, 26, 34, 44**
Frye, (Herman) Northrop **24, 70**
Fuchs, Daniel **34**
Fuchs, Daniel **8, 22**
Fukuyama, Francis **131**
Fuller, Charles (H. Jr.) **25**
Fulton, Alice **52**
Fuson, Robert H(enderson) **70**
Fussell, Paul **74**
Gaddis, William **1, 3, 6, 8, 10, 19, 43, 86**
Gaines, Ernest J(ames) **3, 11, 18, 86**
Gaitskill, Mary **69**
Gallagher, Tess **18, 63**
Gallant, Roy A(rthur) **17**
Gallico, Paul (William) **2**
Galvin, James **38**
Gann, Ernest Kellogg **23**
Garcia, Cristina **76**
Gardner, Herb(ert) **44**
Gardner, John (Champlin) Jr. **2, 3, 5, 7, 8, 10, 18, 28, 34**
Garrett, George (Palmer) **3, 11, 51**
Garrigue, Jean **2, 8**
Gass, William H(oward) **1, 2, 8, 11, 15, 39, 132**
Gates, Henry Louis Jr. **65**
Gay, Peter (Jack) **158**
Gaye, Marvin (Pentz Jr.) **26**
Gelbart, Larry (Simon) **21, 61**
Gelber, Jack **1, 6, 14, 79**
Gellhorn, Martha (Ellis) **14, 60**
Gent, Peter **29**
George, Jean Craighead **35**
Gertler, T. **134**
Ghiselin, Brewster **23**
Gibbons, Kaye **50, 88, 145**
Gibson, William **23**
Gibson, William (Ford) **39, 63**
Gifford, Barry (Colby) **34**
Gilbreth, Frank B(unker) Jr. **17**
Gilchrist, Ellen (Louise) **34, 48, 143**
Giles, Molly **39**
Gilliam, Terry (Vance) **21, 141**
Gilroy, Frank D(aniel) **2**
Gilstrap, John **99**
Ginsberg, Allen **1, 2, 3, 4, 6, 13, 36, 69, 109**
Giovanni, Nikki **2, 4, 19, 64, 117**
Glasser, Ronald J. **37**
Gleick, James (W.) **147**
Glück, Louise (Elisabeth) **7, 22, 44, 81, 160**
Godwin, Gail (Kathleen) **5, 8, 22, 31, 69, 125**
Goines, Donald **80**
Gold, Herbert **4, 7, 14, 42, 152**
Goldbarth, Albert **5, 38**
Goldman, Francisco **76**
Goldman, William (W.) **1, 48**
Goldsberry, Steven **34**
Goodman, Paul **1, 2, 4, 7**
Gordon, Caroline **6, 13, 29, 83**
Gordon, Mary (Catherine) **13, 22, 128**
Gordon, Sol **26**
Gordone, Charles **1, 4**
Gould, Lois **4, 10**
Gould, Stephen Jay **163**
Goyen, (Charles) William **5, 8, 14, 40**
Grafton, Sue **163**
Graham, Jorie **48, 118**
Grau, Shirley Ann **4, 9, 146**
Graver, Elizabeth **70**
Gray, Amlin **29**
Gray, Francine du Plessix **22, 153**
Gray, Spalding **49, 112**
Grayson, Richard (A.) **38**
Greeley, Andrew M(oran) **28**
Green, Hannah **3**
Green, Julien **3, 11, 77**
Green, Paul (Eliot) **25**
Greenberg, Joanne (Goldenberg) **7, 30**
Greenberg, Richard **57**
Greenblatt, Stephen J(ay) **70**

Greene, Bette **30**
Greene, Gael **8**
Gregor, Arthur **9**
Griffin, John Howard **68**
Griffin, Peter **39**
Grisham, John **84**
Grumbach, Doris (Isaac) **13, 22, 64**
Grunwald, Lisa **44**
Guare, John **8, 14, 29, 67**
Gubar, Susan (David) **145**
Guest, Barbara **34**
Guest, Judith (Ann) **8, 30**
Guild, Nicholas M. **33**
Gunn, Bill **5**
Gurganus, Allan **70**
Gurney, A(lbert) R(amsdell) Jr. **32, 50, 54**
Gustafson, James M(oody) **100**
Guterson, David **91**
Guthrie, A(lfred) B(ertram) Jr. **23**
Guy, Rosa (Cuthbert) **26**
Hacker, Marilyn **5, 9, 23, 72, 91**
Hailey, Elizabeth Forsythe **40**
Haines, John (Meade) **58**
Haldeman, Joe (William) **61**
Haley, Alex(ander Murray Palmer) **8, 12, 76**
Hall, Donald (Andrew Jr.) **1, 13, 37, 59, 151**
Halpern, Daniel **14**
Hamill, Pete **10**
Hamilton, Edmond **1**
Hamilton, Virginia (Esther) **26**
Hammett, (Samuel) Dashiell **3, 5, 10, 19, 47**
Hamner, Earl (Henry) Jr. **12**
Hannah, Barry **23, 38, 90**
Hansberry, Lorraine (Vivian) **17, 62**
Hansen, Joseph **38**
Hanson, Kenneth O(stlin) **13**
Hardwick, Elizabeth (Bruce) **13**
Harjo, Joy **83**
Harlan, Louis R(udolph) **34**
Harling, Robert **53**
Harmon, William (Ruth) **38**
Harper, Michael S(teven) **7, 22**
Harris, MacDonald **9**
Harris, Mark **19**
Harrison, Barbara Grizzuti **144**
Harrison, Harry (Max) **42**
Harrison, James (Thomas) **6, 14, 33, 66, 143**
Harrison, Kathryn **70, 151**
Harriss, Will(ard Irvin) **34**
Hart, Moss **66**
Hartman, Geoffrey H. **27**
Haruf, Kent **34**
Hass, Robert **18, 39, 99**
Haviaras, Stratis **33**
Hawkes, John (Clendennin Burne Jr.) **1, 2, 3, 4, 7, 9, 14, 15, 27, 49**
Hayden, Robert E(arl) **5, 9, 14, 37**
Hayman, Ronald **44**
H. D. **3, 8, 14, 31, 34, 73**
Hearne, Vicki **56**
Hearon, Shelby **63**
Hecht, Anthony (Evan) **8, 13, 19**
Hecht, Ben **8**
Heifner, Jack **11**
Heilbrun, Carolyn G(old) **25, 173**
Heinemann, Larry (Curtiss) **50**
Heinlein, Robert A(nson) **1, 3, 8, 14, 26, 55**
Heller, Joseph **1, 3, 5, 8, 11, 36, 63**
Hellman, Lillian (Florence) **2, 4, 8, 14, 18, 34, 44, 52**
Helprin, Mark **7, 10, 22, 32**
Hemingway, Ernest (Miller) **1, 3, 6, 8, 10, 13, 19, 30, 34, 39, 41, 44, 50, 61, 80**
Hempel, Amy **39**
Henley, Beth **23**
Hentoff, Nat(han Irving) **26**
Herbert, Frank (Patrick) **12, 23, 35, 44, 85**
Herbst, Josephine (Frey) **34**
Herlihy, James Leo **6**
Herrmann, Dorothy **44**
Hersey, John (Richard) **1, 2, 7, 9, 40, 81, 97**
L'Heureux, John (Clarke) **52**

Heyen, William **13, 18**
Higgins, George V(incent) **4, 7, 10, 18**
Highsmith, (Mary) Patricia **2, 4, 14, 42, 102**
Highwater, Jamake (Mamake) **12**
Hijuelos, Oscar **65**
Hill, George Roy **26**
Hillerman, Tony **62, 170**
Himes, Chester (Bomar) **2, 4, 7, 18, 58, 108**
Hinton, S(usan) E(loise) **30, 111**
Hirsch, Edward **31, 50**
Hirsch, E(ric) D(onald) Jr. **79**
Hoagland, Edward **28**
Hoban, Russell (Conwell) **7, 25**
Hobson, Laura Z(ametkin) **7, 25**
Hochman, Sandra **3, 8**
Hoffman, Alice **51**
Hoffman, Daniel (Gerard) **6, 13, 23**
Hoffman, Stanley **5**
Hoffman, William **141**
Hoffman, William M(oses) **40**
Hogan, Linda **73**
Holland, Isabelle **21**
Hollander, John **2, 5, 8, 14**
Holleran, Andrew **38**
Holmes, John Clellon **56**
Honig, Edwin **33**
Horgan, Paul (George Vincent O'Shaughnessy) **9, 53**
Horovitz, Israel (Arthur) **56**
Horwitz, Julius **14**
Hougan, Carolyn **34**
Howard, Maureen **5, 14, 46, 151**
Howard, Richard **7, 10, 47**
Howe, Fanny (Quincy) **47**
Howe, Irving **85**
Howe, Susan **72, 152**
Howe, Tina **48**
Howes, Barbara **15**
Hubbard, L(afayette) Ron(ald) **43**
Huddle, David **49**
Hughart, Barry **39**
Hughes, (James) Langston **1, 5, 10, 15, 35, 44, 108**
Hugo, Richard F(ranklin) **6, 18, 32**
Humphrey, William **45**
Humphreys, Josephine **34, 57**
Hunt, E(verette) Howard (Jr.) **3**
Hunt, Marsha **70**
Hunter, Evan **11, 31**
Hunter, Kristin (Eggleston) **35**
Hurston, Zora Neale **7, 30, 61**
Huston, John (Marcellus) **20**
Hustvedt, Siri **76**
Huxley, Aldous (Leonard) **1, 3, 4, 5, 8, 11, 18, 35, 79**
Hwang, David Henry **55**
Hyde, Margaret O(ldroyd) **21**
Hynes, James **65**
Ian, Janis **21**
Ignatow, David **4, 7, 14, 40**
Ingalls, Rachel (Holmes) **42**
Inge, William (Motter) **1, 8, 19**
Innaurato, Albert (F.) **21, 60**
Irving, John (Winslow) **13, 23, 38, 112**
Isaacs, Susan **32**
Isler, Alan (David) **91**
Ivask, Ivar Vidrik **14**
Jackson, Jesse **12**
Jackson, Shirley **11, 60, 87**
Jacobs, Jim **12**
Jacobsen, Josephine **48, 102**
Jakes, John (William) **29**
Jameson, Fredric (R.) **142**
Janowitz, Tama **43, 145**
Jarrell, Randall **1, 2, 6, 9, 13, 49**
Jeffers, (John) Robinson **2, 3, 11, 15, 54**
Jen, Gish **70**
Jennings, Waylon **21**
Jensen, Laura (Linnea) **37**
Jin, Xuefei **109**
Joel, Billy **26**
Johnson, Charles (Richard) **7, 51, 65, 163**

Johnson, Denis **52, 160**
Johnson, Diane **5, 13, 48**
Johnson, Joyce **58**
Johnson, Judith (Emlyn) **7, 15**
Jones, Edward P. **76**
Jones, Gayl **6, 9, 131**
Jones, James **1, 3, 10, 39**
Jones, LeRoi **1, 2, 3, 5, 10, 14**
Jones, Louis B. **65**
Jones, Madison (Percy Jr.) **4**
Jones, Nettie (Pearl) **34**
Jones, Preston **10**
Jones, Robert F(rancis) **7**
Jones, Thom (Douglas) **81**
Jong, Erica **4, 6, 8, 18, 83**
Jordan, June **5, 11, 23, 114**
Jordan, Pat(rick M.) **37**
Just, Ward (Swift) **4, 27**
Justice, Donald (Rodney) **6, 19, 102**
Kadohata, Cynthia **59, 122**
Kahn, Roger **30**
Kaletski, Alexander **39**
Kallman, Chester (Simon) **2**
Kaminsky, Stuart M(elvin) **59**
Kanin, Garson **22**
Kantor, MacKinlay **7**
Kaplan, David Michael **50**
Kaplan, James **59**
Karl, Frederick R(obert) **34**
Katz, Steve **47**
Kauffman, Janet **42**
Kaufman, Bob (Garnell) **49**
Kaufman, George S. **38**
Kaufman, Sue **3, 8**
Kazan, Elia **6, 16, 63**
Kazin, Alfred **34, 38, 119**
Keaton, Buster **20**
Keene, Donald **34**
Keillor, Garrison **40, 115**
Kellerman, Jonathan **44**
Kelley, William Melvin **22**
Kellogg, Marjorie **2**
Kemelman, Harry **2**
Kennedy, Adrienne (Lita) **66**
Kennedy, William **6, 28, 34, 53**
Kennedy, X. J. **8, 42**
Kenny, Maurice (Francis) **87**
Kerouac, Jack **1, 2, 3, 5, 14, 29, 61**
Kerr, Jean **22**
Kerr, M. E. **12, 35**
Kerr, Robert **55**
Kerrigan, (Thomas) Anthony **4, 6**
Kesey, Ken (Elton) **1, 3, 6, 11, 46, 64**
Kesselring, Joseph (Otto) **45**
Kessler, Jascha (Frederick) **4**
Kettelkamp, Larry (Dale) **12**
Keyes, Daniel **80**
Kherdian, David **6, 9**
Kienzle, William X(avier) **25**
Killens, John Oliver **10**
Kincaid, Jamaica **43, 68, 137**
King, Martin Luther Jr. **83**
King, Stephen (Edwin) **12, 26, 37, 61, 113**
King, Thomas **89, 171**
Kingman, Lee **17**
Kingsley, Sidney **44**
Kingsolver, Barbara **55, 81, 130**
Kingston, Maxine (Ting Ting) Hong **12, 19, 58, 121**
Kinnell, Galway **1, 2, 3, 5, 13, 29, 129**
Kirkwood, James **9**
Kissinger, Henry A(lfred) **137**
Kizer, Carolyn (Ashley) **15, 39, 80**
Klappert, Peter **57**
Klein, Joe **154**
Klein, Norma **30**
Klein, T(heodore) E(ibon) D(onald) **34**
Knapp, Caroline **99**
Knebel, Fletcher **14**
Knight, Etheridge **40**
Knowles, John **1, 4, 10, 26**
Koch, Kenneth **5, 8, 44**

Komunyakaa, Yusef **86, 94**
Koontz, Dean R(ay) **78**
Kopit, Arthur (Lee) **1, 18, 33**
Kosinski, Jerzy (Nikodem) **1, 2, 3, 6, 10, 15, 53, 70**
Kostelanetz, Richard (Cory) **28**
Kotlowitz, Robert **4**
Kotzwinkle, William **5, 14, 35**
Kozol, Jonathan **17**
Kozoll, Michael **35**
Kramer, Kathryn **34**
Kramer, Larry **42**
Kristofferson, Kris **26**
Krumgold, Joseph (Quincy) **12**
Krutch, Joseph Wood **24**
Kubrick, Stanley **16**
Kumin, Maxine (Winokur) **5, 13, 28, 164**
Kunitz, Stanley (Jasspon) **6, 11, 14, 148**
Kushner, Tony **81**
Kuzma, Greg **7**
Lancaster, Bruce **36**
Landis, John **26**
Langer, Elinor **34**
Lapine, James (Elliot) **39**
Larsen, Eric **55**
Larsen, Nella **37**
Larson, Charles R(aymond) **31**
Lasch, Christopher **102**
Latham, Jean Lee **12**
Lattimore, Richmond (Alexander) **3**
Laughlin, James **49**
Lear, Norman (Milton) **12**
Leavitt, David **34**
Lebowitz, Fran(ces Ann) **11, 36**
Lee, Andrea **36**
Lee, Chang-rae **91**
Lee, Don L. **2**
Lee, George W(ashington) **52**
Lee, Helen Elaine **86**
Lee, Lawrence **34**
Lee, Manfred B(ennington) **11**
Lee, (Nelle) Harper **12, 60**
Lee, Shelton Jackson **105**
Lee, Stan **17**
Leet, Judith **11**
Leffland, Ella **19**
Le Guin, Ursula K(roeber) **8, 13, 22, 45, 71, 136**
Leiber, Fritz (Reuter Jr.) **25**
Leimbach, Marti **65**
Leithauser, Brad **27**
Lelchuk, Alan **5**
Lemann, Nancy **39**
Lentricchia, Frank (Jr.) **34**
Leonard, Elmore (John Jr.) **28, 34, 71, 120**
Lerman, Eleanor **9**
Lerman, Rhoda **56**
Lester, Richard **20**
Levertov, Denise **1, 2, 3, 5, 8, 15, 28, 66**
Levi, Jonathan **76**
Levin, Ira **3, 6**
Levin, Meyer **7**
Levine, Philip **2, 4, 5, 9, 14, 33, 118**
Levinson, Deirdre **49**
Levitin, Sonia (Wolff) **17**
Lewis, Janet **41**
Leyner, Mark **92**
Lieber, Joel **6**
Lieberman, Laurence (James) **4, 36**
Lifton, Robert Jay **67**
Lightman, Alan P(aige) **81**
Ligotti, Thomas (Robert) **44**
Lindbergh, Anne (Spencer) Morrow **82**
Linney, Romulus **51**
Lipsyte, Robert (Michael) **21**
Lish, Gordon (Jay) **45**
Littell, Robert **42**
Loewinsohn, Ron(ald William) **52**
Logan, John (Burton) **5**
Lopate, Phillip **29**
Lopez, Barry (Holstun) **70**
Lord, Bette Bao **23**

Lorde, Audre (Geraldine) **18, 71**
Louie, David Wong **70**
Lowell, Robert (Traill Spence Jr.) **1, 2, 3, 4, 5, 8, 9, 11, 15, 37, 124**
Loy, Mina **28**
Lucas, Craig **64**
Lucas, George **16**
Ludlam, Charles **46, 50**
Ludlum, Robert **22, 43**
Ludwig, Ken **60**
Lurie, Alison **4, 5, 18, 39**
Lynch, David (K.) **66, 162**
Lynn, Kenneth S(chuyler) **50**
Lytle, Andrew (Nelson) **22**
Maas, Peter **29**
Macdonald, Cynthia **13, 19**
MacDonald, John D(ann) **3, 27, 44**
MacInnes, Helen (Clark) **27, 39**
Maclean, Norman (Fitzroy) **78**
MacLeish, Archibald **3, 8, 14, 68**
MacShane, Frank **39**
Madden, (Jerry) David **5, 15**
Madhubuti, Haki R. **6, 73**
Mailer, Norman **1, 2, 3, 4, 5, 8, 11, 14, 28, 39, 74, 111**
Major, Clarence **3, 19, 48**
Malamud, Bernard **1, 2, 3, 5, 8, 9, 11, 18, 27, 44, 78, 85**
Malcolm X **82, 117**
Mallon, Thomas **172**
Maloff, Saul **5**
Malone, Michael (Christopher) **43**
Malzberg, Barry N(athaniel) **7**
Mamet, David (Alan) **9, 15, 34, 46, 91, 166**
Mamoulian, Rouben (Zachary) **16**
Mano, D. Keith **2, 10**
Manso, Peter **39**
Margulies, Donald **76**
Markfield, Wallace **8**
Markson, David M(errill) **67**
Marlowe, Stephen **70**
Marquand, John P(hillips) **2, 10**
Marqués, René **96**
Marshall, Garry **17**
Marshall, Paule **27, 72**
Martin, Steve **30**
Martin, Valerie **89**
Maso, Carole **44**
Mason, Bobbie Ann **28, 43, 82, 154**
Masters, Hilary **48**
Mastrosimone, William **36**
Matheson, Richard (Burton) **37**
Mathews, Harry **6, 52**
Mathews, John Joseph **84**
Matthews, William (Procter III) **40**
Matthias, John (Edward) **9**
Matthiessen, Peter **5, 7, 11, 32, 64**
Maupin, Armistead (Jones Jr.) **95**
Maxwell, William (Keepers Jr.) **19**
May, Elaine **16**
Maynard, Joyce **23**
Maysles, Albert **16**
Maysles, David **16**
Mazer, Norma Fox **26**
McBrien, William (Augustine) **44**
McCaffrey, Anne (Inez) **17**
McCall, Nathan **86**
McCarthy, Mary (Therese) **1, 3, 5, 14, 24, 39, 59**
McCauley, Stephen (D.) **50**
McClure, Michael (Thomas) **6, 10**
McCorkle, Jill (Collins) **51**
McCourt, James **5**
McCourt, Malachy **119**
McCullers, (Lula) Carson (Smith) **1, 4, 10, 12, 48, 100**
McDermott, Alice **90**
McElroy, Joseph **5, 47**
McFarland, Dennis **65**
McGinley, Phyllis **14**
McGinniss, Joe **32**
McGrath, Thomas (Matthew) **28, 59**

McGuane, Thomas (Francis III) **3, 7, 18, 45, 127**
McHale, Tom **3, 5**
McInerney, Jay **34, 112**
McIntyre, Vonda N(eel) **18**
McKuen, Rod **1, 3**
McMillan, Terry (L.) **50, 61, 112**
McMurtry, Larry (Jeff) **2, 3, 7, 11, 27, 44, 127**
McNally, Terrence **4, 7, 41, 91**
McNally, T. M. **82**
McNamer, Deirdre **70**
McNeal, Tom **119**
McNickle, (William) D'Arcy **89**
McPhee, John (Angus) **36**
McPherson, James Alan **19, 77**
McPherson, William (Alexander) **34**
Mead, Margaret **37**
Medoff, Mark (Howard) **6, 23**
Mehta, Ved (Parkash) **37**
Meltzer, Milton **26**
Mendelsohn, Jane **99**
Meredith, William (Morris) **4, 13, 22, 55**
Merkin, Daphne **44**
Merrill, James (Ingram) **2, 3, 6, 8, 13, 18, 34, 91**
Merton, Thomas **1, 3, 11, 34, 83**
Merwin, W(illiam) S(tanley) **1, 2, 3, 5, 8, 13, 18, 45, 88**
Mewshaw, Michael **9**
Meyers, Jeffrey **39**
Michaels, Leonard **6, 25**
Michener, James A(lbert) **1, 5, 11, 29, 60, 109**
Miles, Jack **100**
Miles, Josephine (Louise) **1, 2, 14, 34, 39**
Millar, Kenneth **14**
Miller, Arthur **1, 2, 6, 10, 15, 26, 47, 78**
Miller, Henry (Valentine) **1, 2, 4, 9, 14, 43, 84**
Miller, Jason **2**
Miller, Sue **44**
Miller, Walter M(ichael Jr.) **4, 30**
Millett, Kate **67**
Millhauser, Steven (Lewis) **21, 54, 109**
Milner, Ron(ald) **56**
Miner, Valerie **40**
Minot, Susan **44, 159**
Minus, Ed **39**
Mitchell, Joseph (Quincy) **98**
Modarressi, Taghi (M.) **44**
Mohr, Nicholasa **12**
Mojtabai, A(nn) G(race) **5, 9, 15, 29**
Momaday, N(avarre) Scott **2, 19, 85, 95, 160**
Monette, Paul **82**
Montague, John (Patrick) **13, 46**
Montgomery, Marion H. Jr. **7**
Moody, Rick **147**
Mooney, Ted **25**
Moore, Lorrie **39, 45, 68, 165**
Moore, Marianne (Craig) **1, 2, 4, 8, 10, 13, 19, 47**
Moraga, Cherrie **126**
Morgan, Berry **6**
Morgan, (George) Frederick **23**
Morgan, Robin (Evonne) **2**
Morgan, Seth **65**
Morris, Bill **76**
Morris, Wright **1, 3, 7, 18, 37**
Morrison, Jim **17**
Morrison, Toni **4, 10, 22, 55, 81, 87, 173**
Mosher, Howard Frank **62**
Mosley, Walter **97**
Moss, Howard **7, 14, 45, 50**
Motley, Willard (Francis) **18**
Mountain Wolf Woman **92**
Moyers, Bill **74**
Mueller, Lisel **13, 51**
Mull, Martin **17**
Mungo, Raymond **72**
Murphy, Sylvia **34**
Murray, Albert L. **73**

Muske, Carol **90**
Myers, Walter Dean **35**
Nabokov, Vladimir (Vladimirovich) **1, 2, 3, 6, 8, 11, 15, 23, 44, 46, 64**
Nash, (Frediric) Ogden **23**
Naylor, Gloria **28, 52, 156**
Neihardt, John Gneisenau **32**
Nelson, Willie **17**
Nemerov, Howard (Stanley) **2, 6, 9, 36**
Neufeld, John (Arthur) **17**
Neville, Emily Cheney **12**
Newlove, Donald **6**
Newman, Charles **2, 8**
Newman, Edwin (Harold) **14**
Newton, Suzanne **35**
Nichols, John (Treadwell) **38**
Niedecker, Lorine **10, 42**
Nin, Anaïs **1, 4, 8, 11, 14, 60, 127**
Nissenson, Hugh **4, 9**
Nixon, Agnes Eckhardt **21**
Norman, Marsha **28**
Norton, Andre **12**
Nova, Craig **7, 31**
Nunn, Kem **34**
Nyro, Laura **17**
Oates, Joyce Carol **1, 2, 3, 6, 9, 11, 15, 19, 33, 52, 108, 134**
O'Brien, Darcy **11**
O'Brien, (William) Tim(othy) **7, 19, 40, 103**
Ochs, Phil(ip David) **17**
O'Connor, Edwin (Greene) **14**
O'Connor, (Mary) Flannery **1, 2, 3, 6, 10, 13, 15, 21, 66, 104**
O'Dell, Scott **30**
Odets, Clifford **2, 28, 98**
O'Donovan, Michael John **14**
O'Grady, Timothy **59**
O'Hara, Frank **2, 5, 13, 78**
O'Hara, John (Henry) **1, 2, 3, 6, 11, 42**
O Hehir, Diana **41**
Olds, Sharon **32, 39, 85**
Oliver, Mary **19, 34, 98**
Olsen, Tillie **4, 13, 114**
Olson, Charles (John) **1, 2, 5, 6, 9, 11, 29**
Olson, Toby **28**
Oppen, George **7, 13, 34**
Orlovitz, Gil **22**
Ortiz, Simon J(oseph) **45**
Ostriker, Alicia (Suskin) **132**
Otto, Whitney **70**
Owens, Rochelle **8**
Ozick, Cynthia **3, 7, 28, 62, 155**
Pack, Robert **13**
Pagels, Elaine Hiesey **104**
Paglia, Camille (Anna) **68**
Paley, Grace **4, 6, 37, 140**
Palliser, Charles **65**
Pancake, Breece D'J **29**
Paretsky, Sara **135**
Parini, Jay (Lee) **54, 133**
Parker, Dorothy (Rothschild) **15, 68**
Parker, Robert B(rown) **27**
Parks, Gordon (Alexander Buchanan) **1, 16**
Pastan, Linda (Olenik) **27**
Patchen, Kenneth **1, 2, 18**
Paterson, Katherine (Womeldorf) **12, 30**
Peacock, Molly **60**
Pearson, T(homas) R(eid) **39**
Peck, John (Frederick) **3**
Peck, Richard (Wayne) **21**
Peck, Robert Newton **17**
Peckinpah, (David) Sam(uel) **20**
Percy, Walker **2, 3, 6, 8, 14, 18, 47, 65**
Perelman, S(idney) J(oseph) **3, 5, 9, 15, 23, 44, 49**
Perloff, Marjorie G(abrielle) **137**
Pesetsky, Bette **28**
Peterkin, Julia Mood **31**
Peters, Joan K(aren) **39**
Peters, Robert L(ouis) **7**
Petrakis, Harry Mark **3**
Petry, Ann (Lane) **1, 7, 18**

CUMULATIVE NATIONALITY INDEX

Philipson, Morris H. **53**
Phillips, Jayne Anne **15, 33, 139**
Phillips, Robert (Schaeffer) **28**
Piercy, Marge **3, 6, 14, 18, 27, 62, 128**
Pinckney, Darryl **76**
Pineda, Cecile **39**
Pinkwater, Daniel Manus **35**
Pinsky, Robert **9, 19, 38, 94, 121**
Pirsig, Robert M(aynard) **4, 6, 73**
Plante, David (Robert) **7, 23, 38**
Plath, Sylvia **1, 2, 3, 5, 9, 11, 14, 17, 50, 51, 62, 111**
Platt, Kin **26**
Plimpton, George (Ames) **36**
Plumly, Stanley (Ross) **33**
Pohl, Frederick **18**
Poitier, Sidney **26**
Pollitt, Katha **28, 122**
Polonsky, Abraham (Lincoln) **92**
Pomerance, Bernard **13**
Porter, Connie (Rose) **70**
Porter, Katherine Anne **1, 3, 7, 10, 13, 15, 27, 101**
Potok, Chaim **2, 7, 14, 26, 112**
Pound, Ezra (Weston Loomis) **1, 2, 3, 4, 5, 7, 10, 13, 18, 34, 48, 50, 112**
Povod, Reinaldo **44**
Powell, Adam Clayton Jr. **89**
Powell, Dawn **66**
Powell, Padgett **34**
Power, Susan **91**
Powers, J(ames) F(arl) **1, 4, 8, 57**
Powers, John R. **66**
Powers, Richard (S.) **93**
Prager, Emily **56**
Price, (Edward) Reynolds **3, 6, 13, 43, 50, 63**
Price, Richard **6, 12**
Prince **35**
Pritchard, William H(arrison) **34**
Probst, Mark **59**
Prokosch, Frederic **4, 48**
Prose, Francine **45**
Proulx, E(dna) Annie **81, 158**
Pryor, Richard (Franklin Lenox Thomas) **26**
Purdy, James (Amos) **2, 4, 10, 28, 52**
Puzo, Mario **1, 2, 6, 36, 107**
Pynchon, Thomas (Ruggles Jr.) **2, 3, 6, 9, 11, 18, 33, 62, 72, 123**
Quay, Stephen **95**
Quay, Timothy **95**
Queen, Ellery **3, 11**
Quinn, Peter **91**
Rabe, David (William) **4, 8, 33**
Rado, James **17**
Raeburn, John (Hay) **34**
Ragni, Gerome **17**
Rahv, Philip **24**
Rakosi, Carl **47**
Rampersad, Arnold **44**
Rand, Ayn **3, 30, 44, 79**
Randall, Dudley (Felker) **1, 135**
Ransom, John Crowe **2, 4, 5, 11, 24**
Raphael, Frederic (Michael) **2, 14**
Rechy, John (Francisco) **1, 7, 14, 18, 107**
Reddin, Keith **67**
Redmon, Anne **22**
Reed, Ishmael **2, 3, 5, 6, 13, 32, 60**
Reed, Lou **21**
Remarque, Erich Maria **21**
Rexroth, Kenneth **1, 2, 6, 11, 22, 49, 112**
Reynolds, Jonathan **6, 38**
Reynolds, Michael S(hane) **44**
Reznikoff, Charles **9**
Ribman, Ronald (Burt) **7**
Rice, Anne **41, 128**
Rice, Elmer (Leopold) **7, 49**
Rich, Adrienne (Cecile) **3, 6, 7, 11, 18, 36, 73, 76, 125**
Richter, Conrad (Michael) **30**
Riding, Laura **3, 7**
Ringwood, Gwen(dolyn Margaret) Pharis **48**

Rivers, Conrad Kent **1**
Robbins, Harold **5**
Robbins, Trina **21**
Robinson, Jill **10**
Robinson, Kim Stanley **34**
Robinson, Marilynne **25**
Robinson, Smokey **21**
Robison, Mary **42, 98**
Roddenberry, Gene **17**
Rodgers, Mary **12**
Rodman, Howard **65**
Rodriguez, Richard **155**
Roethke, Theodore (Huebner) **1, 3, 8, 11, 19, 46, 101**
Rogers, Thomas Hunton **57**
Rogin, Gilbert **18**
Roiphe, Anne (Richardson) **3, 9**
Rooke, Leon **25, 34**
Rose, Wendy **85**
Rosen, Richard (Dean) **39**
Rosenthal, M(acha) L(ouis) **28**
Rossner, Judith (Perelman) **6, 9, 29**
Roth, Henry **2, 6, 11, 104**
Roth, Philip (Milton) **1, 2, 3, 4, 6, 9, 15, 22, 31, 47, 66, 86, 119**
Rothenberg, Jerome **6, 57**
Rovit, Earl (Herbert) **7**
Royko, Mike **109**
Ruark, Gibbons **3**
Rudnik, Raphael **7**
Rukeyser, Muriel **6, 10, 15, 27**
Rule, Jane (Vance) **27**
Rush, Norman **44**
Russ, Joanna **15**
Russell, Jeffrey Burton **70**
Ryan, Cornelius (John) **7**
Ryan, Michael **65**
Sachs, Marilyn (Stickle) **35**
Sackler, Howard (Oliver) **14**
Sadoff, Ira **9**
Safire, William **10**
Sagan, Carl (Edward) **30, 112**
Said, Edward W. **123**
Saint, H(arry) F. **50**
Salamanca, J(ack) R(ichard) **4, 15**
Sale, Kirkpatrick **68**
Salinas, Luis Omar **90**
Salinger, J(erome) D(avid) **1, 3, 8, 12, 55, 56, 138**
Salter, James **7, 52, 59**
Sanchez, Sonia **5, 116**
Sandburg, Carl (August) **1, 4, 10, 15, 35**
Sanders, (James) Ed(ward) **53**
Sanders, Lawrence **41**
Sandoz, Mari(e Susette) **28**
Saner, Reg(inald Anthony) **9**
Santiago, Danny **33**
Santmyer, Helen Hooven **33**
Santos, Bienvenido N(uqui) **22**
Sapphire, Brenda **99**
Saroyan, William **1, 8, 10, 29, 34, 56**
Sarton, (Eleanor) May **4, 14, 49, 91**
Saul, John (W. III) **46**
Savage, Thomas **40**
Savan, Glenn **50**
Sayers, Valerie **50, 122**
Sayles, John (Thomas) **7, 10, 14**
Schaeffer, Susan Fromberg **6, 11, 22**
Schell, Jonathan **35**
Schevill, James (Erwin) **7**
Schisgal, Murray (Joseph) **6**
Schlesinger, Arthur M(eier) Jr. **84**
Schnackenberg, Gjertrud (Cecelia) **40**
Schor, Sandra (M.) **65**
Schorer, Mark **9**
Schrader, Paul (Joseph) **26**
Schulberg, Budd (Wilson) **7, 48**
Schulz, Charles M(onroe) **12**
Schuyler, James Marcus **5, 23**
Schwartz, Delmore (David) **2, 4, 10, 45, 87**
Schwartz, John Burnham **59**
Schwartz, Lynne Sharon **31**

Scoppettone, Sandra **26**
Scorsese, Martin **20, 89**
Scott, Evelyn **43**
Scott, Joanna **50**
Sebestyen, Ouida **30**
Seelye, John (Douglas) **7**
Segal, Erich (Wolf) **3, 10**
Seger, Bob **35**
Seidel, Frederick (Lewis) **18**
Selby, Hubert Jr. **1, 2, 4, 8**
Selzer, Richard **74**
Serling, (Edward) Rod(man) **30**
Seton, Cynthia Propper **27**
Settle, Mary Lee **19, 61**
Sexton, Anne (Harvey) **2, 4, 6, 8, 10, 15, 53, 123**
Shaara, Michael (Joseph Jr.) **15**
Shacochis, Bob **39**
Shange, Ntozake **8, 25, 38, 74, 126**
Shanley, John Patrick **75**
Shapiro, Jane **76**
Shapiro, Karl (Jay) **4, 8, 15, 53**
Shaw, Irwin **7, 23, 34**
Shawn, Wallace **41**
Shea, Lisa **86**
Sheed, Wilfrid (John Joseph) **2, 4, 10, 53**
Sheehy, Gail **171**
Shepard, Jim **36**
Shepard, Lucius **34**
Shepard, Sam **4, 6, 17, 34, 41, 44, 169**
Sherburne, Zoa (Lillian Morin) **30**
Sherman, Jonathan Marc **55**
Sherman, Martin **19**
Shields, Carol **91, 113**
Shields, David **97**
Shilts, Randy **85**
Showalter, Elaine **169**
Shreve, Susan Richards **23**
Shue, Larry **52**
Shulman, Alix Kates **2, 10**
Shuster, Joe **21**
Sidhwa, Bapsi **168**
Siegel, Jerome **21**
Sigal, Clancy **7**
Silko, Leslie (Marmon) **23, 74, 114**
Silver, Joan Micklin **20**
Silverberg, Robert **7, 140**
Silverstein, Alvin **17**
Silverstein, Virginia B(arbara Opshelor) **17**
Simak, Clifford D(onald) **1, 55**
Simic, Charles **6, 9, 22, 49, 68, 130**
Simmons, Charles (Paul) **57**
Simmons, Dan **44**
Simon, Carly **26**
Simon, (Marvin) Neil **6, 11, 31, 39, 70**
Simon, Paul (Frederick) **17**
Simpson, Louis (Aston Marantz) **4, 7, 9, 32, 149**
Simpson, Mona (Elizabeth) **44, 146**
Sinclair, Upton (Beall) **1, 11, 15, 63**
Singer, Isaac Bashevis **1, 3, 6, 9, 11, 15, 23, 38, 69, 111**
Singleton, John **156**
Sissman, L(ouis) E(dward) **9, 18**
Slaughter, Frank G(ill) **29**
Slavitt, David R(ytman) **5, 14**
Smiley, Jane (Graves) **53, 76, 144**
Smith, Anna Deavere **86**
Smith, Betty (Wehner) **19**
Smith, Clark Ashton **43**
Smith, Dave **22, 42**
Smith, Lee **25, 73**
Smith, Martin Cruz **25**
Smith, Mary-Ann Tirone **39**
Smith, Patti **12**
Smith, William Jay **6**
Snodgrass, W(illiam) D(e Witt) **2, 6, 10, 18, 68**
Snyder, Gary (Sherman) **1, 2, 5, 9, 32, 120**
Snyder, Zilpha Keatley **17**
Soderbergh, Steven **154**
Sokolov, Raymond **7**

Sommer, Scott 25
Sondheim, Stephen (Joshua) 30, 39, 147
Sontag, Susan 1, 2, 10, 13, 31, 105
Sorrentino, Gilbert 3, 7, 14, 22, 40
Soto, Gary 32, 80
Southern, Terry 7
Spackman, W(illiam) M(ode) 46
Spacks, Barry (Bernard) 14
Spanidou, Irini 44
Spencer, Elizabeth 22
Spencer, Scott 30
Spicer, Jack 8, 18, 72
Spiegelman, Art 76
Spielberg, Peter 6
Spielberg, Steven 20
Spinrad, Norman (Richard) 46
Spivack, Kathleen (Romola Drucker) 6
Spoto, Donald 39
Springsteen, Bruce (F.) 17
Squires, (James) Radcliffe 51
Stafford, Jean 4, 7, 19, 68
Stafford, William (Edgar) 4, 7, 29
Stanton, Maura 9
Starbuck, George (Edwin) 53
Steele, Timothy (Reid) 45
Stegner, Wallace (Earle) 9, 49, 81
Steinbeck, John (Ernst) 1, 5, 9, 13, 21, 34, 45, 75, 124
Steinem, Gloria 63
Steiner, George 24
Sterling, Bruce 72
Stern, Gerald 40, 100
Stern, Richard (Gustave) 4, 39
Sternberg, Josef von 20
Stevens, Mark 34
Stevenson, Anne (Katharine) 7, 33
Still, James 49
Stitt, Milan 29
Stolz, Mary (Slattery) 12
Stone, Irving 7
Stone, Oliver (William) 73
Stone, Robert (Anthony) 5, 23, 42
Storm, Hyemeyohsts 3
Stout, Rex (Todhunter) 3
Strand, Mark 6, 18, 41, 71
Straub, Peter (Francis) 28, 107
Stribling, T(homas) S(igismund) 23
Stuart, Jesse (Hilton) 1, 8, 11, 14, 34
Sturgeon, Theodore (Hamilton) 22, 39
Styron, William 1, 3, 5, 11, 15, 60
Sukenick, Ronald 3, 4, 6, 48
Summers, Hollis (Spurgeon Jr.) 10
Susann, Jacqueline 3
Swados, Elizabeth (A.) 12
Swados, Harvey 5
Swan, Gladys 69
Swarthout, Glendon (Fred) 35
Swenson, May 4, 14, 61, 106
Talese, Gay 37
Tallent, Elizabeth (Ann) 45
Tally, Ted 42
Tan, Amy (Ruth) 59, 120, 151
Tartt, Donna 76
Tate, James (Vincent) 2, 6, 25
Tate, (John Orley) Allen 2, 4, 6, 9, 11, 14, 24
Tavel, Ronald 6
Taylor, Eleanor Ross 5
Taylor, Henry (Splawn) 44
Taylor, Mildred D(elois) 21
Taylor, Peter (Hillsman) 1, 4, 18, 37, 44, 50, 71
Taylor, Robert Lewis 14
Terkel, Studs 38
Terry, Megan 19
Tesich, Steve 40, 69
Tevis, Walter 42
Theroux, Alexander (Louis) 2, 25
Theroux, Paul (Edward) 5, 8, 11, 15, 28, 46, 159
Thomas, Audrey (Callahan) 7, 13, 37, 107
Thomas, Joyce Carol 35
Thomas, Lewis 35

Thomas, Piri 17
Thomas, Ross (Elmore) 39
Thompson, Hunter S(tockton) 9, 17, 40, 104
Thompson, Jim (Myers) 69
Thurber, James (Grover) 5, 11, 25, 125
Tilghman, Christopher 65
Tillich, Paul (Johannes) 131
Tillinghast, Richard (Williford) 29
Toffler, Alvin
Tolson, Melvin B(eaunorus) 36, 105
Tomlin, Lily 17
Toole, John Kennedy 19, 64
Toomer, Jean 1, 4, 13, 22
Torrey, E(dwin) Fuller 34
Towne, Robert (Burton) 87
Traven, B. 8, 11
Trevanian 29
Trilling, Diana (Rubin) 129
Trilling, Lionel 9, 11, 24
Trow, George W. S. 52
Trudeau, Garry B. 12
Trumbo, Dalton 19
Tryon, Thomas 3, 11
Tuck, Lily 70
Tunis, John R(oberts) 12
Turco, Lewis (Putnam) 11, 63
Turner, Frederick 48
Tyler, Anne 7, 11, 18, 28, 44, 59, 103
Uhry, Alfred 55
Ulibarrí, Sabine R(eyes) 83
Unger, Douglas 34
Updike, John (Hoyer) 1, 2, 3, 5, 7, 9, 13, 15, 23, 34, 43, 70, 139
Urdang, Constance (Henriette) 47
Uris, Leon (Marcus) 7, 32
Vachss, Andrew (Henry) 106
Valdez, Luis (Miguel) 84
Van Ash, Cay 34
Vandenburgh, Jane 59
Van Doren, Mark 6, 10
Van Duyn, Mona (Jane) 3, 7, 63, 116
Van Peebles, Melvin 2, 20
Van Vechten, Carl 33
Vaughn, Stephanie 62
Vendler, Helen (Hennessy) 138
Vidal, Gore 2, 4, 6, 8, 10, 22, 33, 72, 142
Viereck, Peter (Robert Edwin) 4
Vinge, Joan (Carol) D(ennison) 30
Viola, Herman J(oseph) 70
Vizenor, Gerald Robert 103
Vliet, R(ussell) G(ordon) 22
Vogel, Paula A(nne) 76
Voigt, Cynthia 30
Voigt, Ellen Bryant 54
Vollmann, William T. 89
Vonnegut, Kurt Jr. 1, 2, 3, 4, 5, 8, 12, 22, 40, 60, 111
Wagman, Fredrica 7
Wagner-Martin, Linda (C.) 50
Wagoner, David (Russell) 3, 5, 15
Wakefield, Dan 7
Wakoski, Diane 2, 4, 7, 9, 11, 40
Waldman, Anne (Lesley) 7
Walker, Alice (Malsenior) 5, 6, 9, 19, 27, 46, 58, 103, 167
Walker, Joseph A. 19
Walker, Margaret (Abigail) 1, 6
Wallace, David Foster 50, 114
Wallace, Irving 7, 13
Wallant, Edward Lewis 5, 10
Wambaugh, Joseph (Aloysius Jr.) 3, 18
Ward, Douglas Turner 19
Warhol, Andy 20
Warren, Robert Penn 1, 4, 6, 8, 10, 13, 18, 39, 53, 59
Wasserstein, Wendy 32, 59, 90
Waters, Frank (Joseph) 88
Watkins, Paul 55
Webb, Charles (Richard) 7
Webb, James H(enry) Jr. 22
Weber, Lenora Mattingly 12
Weidman, Jerome 7

Weiss, Theodore (Russell) 3, 8, 14
Welch, James 6, 14, 52
Wellek, Rene 28
Weller, Michael 10, 53
Welles, (George) Orson 20, 80
Wellman, Mac 65
Wellman, Manly Wade 49
Wells, Rosemary 12
Welty, Eudora 1, 2, 5, 14, 22, 33, 105
Wersba, Barbara 30
Wescott, Glenway 13
Wesley, Richard (Errol) 7
West, Cornel (Ronald) 134
West, Delno C(loyde) Jr. 70
West, (Mary) Jessamyn 7, 17
West, Paul 7, 14, 96
Westlake, Donald E(dwin) 7, 33
Whalen, Philip 6, 29
Wharton, William (a pseudonym) 18, 37
Wheelock, John Hall 14
White, Edmund (Valentine III) 27, 110
White, E(lwyn) B(rooks) 10, 34, 39
White, Hayden V. 148
Whitney, Phyllis A(yame) 42
Whittemore, (Edward) Reed (Jr.) 4
Wicker, Tom 7
Wideman, John Edgar 5, 34, 36, 67, 122
Wieners, John 7
Wiesel, Elie(zer) 3, 5, 11, 37, 165
Wiggins, Marianne 57
Wilbur, Richard (Purdy) 3, 6, 9, 14, 53, 110
Wild, Peter 14
Wilder, Billy 20
Wilder, Thornton (Niven) 1, 5, 6, 10, 15, 35, 82
Wiley, Richard 44
Willard, Nancy 7, 37
Williams, C(harles) K(enneth) 33, 56, 148
Williams, John A(lfred) 5, 13
Williams, Jonathan (Chamberlain) 13
Williams, Joy 31
Williams, Norman 39
Williams, Sherley Anne 89
Williams, Tennessee 1, 2, 5, 7, 8, 11, 15, 19, 30, 39, 45, 71, 111
Williams, Thomas (Alonzo) 14
Williams, William Carlos 1, 2, 5, 9, 13, 22, 42, 67
Willingham, Calder (Baynard Jr.) 5, 51
Wilson, August 39, 50, 63, 118
Wilson, Brian 12
Wilson, Edmund 1, 2, 3, 8, 24
Wilson, Lanford 7, 14, 36
Wilson, Robert M. 7, 9
Wilson, Sloan 32
Wilson, William S(mith) 49
Winters, (Arthur) Yvor 4, 8, 32
Winters, Janet Lewis 41
Wiseman, Frederick 20
Wodehouse, P(elham) G(renville) 1, 2, 5, 10, 22
Woiwode, Larry (Alfred) 6, 10
Wojciechowska, Maia (Teresa) 26
Wolf, Naomi 157
Wolfe, Gene (Rodman) 25
Wolfe, George C. 49
Wolfe, Thomas Kennerly Jr. 147
Wolff, Geoffrey (Ansell) 41
Wolff, Tobias (Jonathan Ansell) 39, 64, 172
Wolitzer, Hilma 17
Wonder, Stevie 12
Wong, Jade Snow 17
Woolrich, Cornell 77
Wouk, Herman 1, 9, 38
Wright, Charles (Penzel Jr.) 6, 13, 28, 119, 146
Wright, Charles Stevenson 49
Wright, James (Arlington) 3, 5, 10, 28
Wright, Richard (Nathaniel) 1, 3, 4, 9, 14, 21, 48, 74
Wright, Stephen 33
Wright, William 44

Wurlitzer, Rudolph **2, 4, 15**
Wylie, Philip (Gordon) **43**
Yates, Richard **7, 8, 23**
Yep, Laurence Michael **35**
Yerby, Frank G(arvin) **1, 7, 22**
Yglesias, Helen **7, 22**
Young, Al(bert James) **19**
Young, Marguerite (Vivian) **82**
Young Bear, Ray A. **94**
Yurick, Sol **6**
Zamora, Bernice (B. Ortiz) **89**
Zappa, Frank **17**
Zaturenska, Marya **6, 11**
Zelazny, Roger (Joseph) **21**
Ziegenhagen, Eric **55**
Zindel, Paul **6, 26**
Zoline, Pamela **62**
Zukofsky, Louis **1, 2, 4, 7, 11, 18**
Zweig, Paul **34, 42**

ANGOLAN

Wellman, Manly Wade **49**

ANTIGUAN

Edwards, Gus **43**
Kincaid, Jamaica **43, 68, 137**

ARGENTINIAN

Bioy Casares, Adolfo **4, 8, 13, 88**
Borges, Jorge Luis **1, 2, 3, 4, 6, 8, 9, 10, 13, 19, 44, 48, 83**
Cortázar, Julio **2, 3, 5, 10, 13, 15, 33, 34, 92**
Costantini, Humberto **49**
Dorfman, Ariel **48, 77**
Guevara, Che **87**
Guevara (Serna), Ernesto **87**
Mujica Lainez, Manuel **31**
Puig, Manuel **3, 5, 10, 28, 65, 133**
Sabato, Ernesto (R.) **10, 23**
Valenzuela, Luisa **31, 104**

ARMENIAN

Mamoulian, Rouben (Zachary) **16**

AUSTRALIAN

Anderson, Jessica (Margaret) Queale **37**
Astley, Thea (Beatrice May) **41**
Brinsmead, H(esba) F(ay) **21**
Buckley, Vincent (Thomas) **57**
Buzo, Alexander (John) **61**
Carey, Peter **40, 55, 96**
Clark, Mavis Thorpe **12**
Clavell, James (duMaresq) **6, 25, 87**
Conway, Jill K(er) **152**
Courtenay, Bryce **59**
Davison, Frank Dalby **15**
Elliott, Sumner Locke **38**
FitzGerald, Robert D(avid) **19**
Greer, Germaine **131**
Grenville, Kate **61**
Hall, Rodney **51**
Hazzard, Shirley **18**
Hope, A(lec) D(erwent) **3, 51**
Hospital, Janette Turner **42, 145**
Jolley, (Monica) Elizabeth **46**
Jones, Rod **50**
Keneally, Thomas (Michael) **5, 8, 10, 14, 19, 27, 43, 117**
Koch, C(hristopher) J(ohn) **42**
Lawler, Raymond Evenor **58**
Malouf, (George Joseph) David **28, 86**
Matthews, Greg **45**
McAuley, James Phillip **45**
McCullough, Colleen **27, 107**
Murray, Les(lie Allan) **40**
Porter, Peter (Neville Frederick) **5, 13, 33**
Prichard, Katharine Susannah **46**
Shapcott, Thomas W(illiam) **38**
Slessor, Kenneth **14**
Stead, Christina (Ellen) **2, 5, 8, 32, 80**
Stow, (Julian) Randolph **23, 48**
Thiele, Colin (Milton) **17**
Weir, Peter (Lindsay) **20**
West, Morris L(anglo) **6, 33**
White, Patrick (Victor Martindale) **3, 4, 5, 7, 9, 18, 65, 69**
Wilding, Michael **73**
Williamson, David (Keith) **56**
Wright, Judith (Arundell) **11, 53**

AUSTRIAN

Adamson, Joy(-Friederike Victoria) **17**
Bachmann, Ingeborg **69**
Bernhard, Thomas **3, 32, 61**
Bettelheim, Bruno **79**
Frankl, Viktor E(mil) **93**
Gregor, Arthur **9**
Handke, Peter **5, 8, 10, 15, 38, 134**
Hochwaelder, Fritz **36**
Jelinek, Elfriede **169**
Jandl, Ernst **34**
Lang, Fritz **20, 103**
Lind, Jakov **1, 2, 4, 27, 82**
Perloff, Marjorie G(abrielle) **137**
Sternberg, Josef von **20**
Wellek, Rene **28**
Wilder, Billy **20**

BARBADIAN

Brathwaite, Edward (Kamau) **11**
Clarke, Austin C(hesterfield) **8, 53**
Kennedy, Adrienne (Lita) **66**
Lamming, George (William) **2, 4, 66, 144**

BELGIAN

Crommelynck, Fernand **75**
Ghelderode, Michel de **6, 11**
Lévi-Strauss, Claude **38**
Mallet-Joris, Françoise **11**
Michaux, Henri **8, 19**
Sarton, (Eleanor) May **4, 14, 49, 91**
Simenon, Georges (Jacques Christian) **1, 2, 3, 8, 18, 47**
van Itallie, Jean-Claude **3**
Yourcenar, Marguerite **19, 38, 50, 87**

BOTSWANAN

Head, Bessie **25, 67**

BRAZILIAN

Amado, Jorge **13, 40, 106**
Boff, Leonardo (Genezio Darci) **70**
Cabral de Melo Neto, João **76**
Castaneda, Carlos (Cesar Aranha) **12, 119**
Dourado, (Waldomiro Freitas) Autran **23, 60**
Drummond de Andrade, Carlos **18**
Lispector, Clarice **43**
Ribeiro, Darcy **34**
Ribeiro, Joao Ubaldo (Osorio Pimentel) **10, 67**
Rosa, João Guimarães **23**

BULGARIAN

Belcheva, Elisaveta Lyubomirova **10**
Canetti, Elias **3, 14, 25, 75, 86**
Kristeva, Julia **77, 140**

CAMEROONIAN

Beti, Mongo **27**

CANADIAN

Acorn, Milton **15**
Aquin, Hubert **15**
Atwood, Margaret (Eleanor) **2, 3, 4, 8, 13, 15, 25, 44, 84, 135**
Avison, Margaret **2, 4, 97**
Barfoot, Joan **18**
Bellow, Saul **1, 2, 3, 6, 8, 10, 13, 15, 25, 33, 34, 63, 79**
Berton, Pierre (Francis Demarigny) **104**
Birney, (Alfred) Earle **1, 4, 6, 11**
Bissett, Bill **18**
Blais, Marie-Claire **2, 4, 6, 13, 22**
Blaise, Clark **29**
Bowering, George **15, 47**
Bowering, Marilyn R(uthe) **32**
Brossard, Nicole **115, 169**
Buckler, Ernest **13**
Buell, John (Edward) **10**
Callaghan, Morley Edward **3, 14, 41, 65**
Campbell, Maria **85**
Carrier, Roch **13, 78**
Child, Philip **19, 68**
Chislett, (Margaret) Anne **34**
Clarke, Austin C(hesterfield) **8, 53**
Cohen, Leonard (Norman) **3, 38**
Cohen, Matt(hew) **19**
Coles, Don **46**
Cook, Michael **58**
Cooper, Douglas **86**
Coupland, Douglas **85, 133**
Craven, Margaret **17**
Cronenberg, David **143**
Davies, (William) Robertson **2, 7, 13, 25, 42, 75, 91**
de la Roche, Mazo **14**
Donnell, David **34**
Ducharme, Rejean **74**
Dudek, Louis **11, 19**
Egoyan, Atom **151**
Engel, Marian **36**
Everson, R(onald) G(ilmour) **27**
Faludy, George **42**
Ferron, Jacques **94**
Finch, Robert (Duer Claydon) **18**
Findley, Timothy **27, 102**
Fraser, Sylvia **64**
Frye, (Herman) Northrop **24, 70**
Gallant, Mavis **7, 18, 38, 172**
Garner, Hugh **13**
Gibson, William (Ford) **39, 63**
Gilmour, David **35**
Glassco, John **9**
Gotlieb, Phyllis Fay (Bloom) **18**
Govier, Katherine **51**
Gunnars, Kristjana **69**
Gustafson, Ralph (Barker) **36**
Haig-Brown, Roderick (Langmere) **21**
Hailey, Arthur **5**
Harris, Christie (Lucy) Irwin **12**
Hébert, Anne **4, 13, 29**
Highway, Tomson **92**
Hillis, Rick **66**
Hine, (William) Daryl **15**
Hodgins, Jack **23**
Hood, Hugh (John Blagdon) **15, 28**
Hyde, Anthony **42**
Jacobsen, Josephine **48, 102**
Jiles, Paulette **13, 58**
Johnston, George (Benson) **51**
Jones, D(ouglas) G(ordon) **10**
Kelly, M(ilton) T(errence) **55**
King, Thomas **89**
Kinsella, W(illiam) P(atrick) **27, 43, 166**
Klein, A(braham) M(oses) **19**
Kogawa, Joy Nozomi **78, 129**
Krizanc, John **57**
Kroetsch, Robert **5, 23, 57, 132**
Kroker, Arthur (W.) **77**
Lane, Patrick **25**
Laurence, (Jean) Margaret (Wemyss) **3, 6, 13, 50, 62**
Layton, Irving (Peter) **2, 15, 164**
Levine, Norman **54**
Lightfoot, Gordon **26**
Livesay, Dorothy (Kathleen) **4, 15, 79**
MacEwen, Gwendolyn (Margaret) **13, 55**
MacLennan, (John) Hugh **2, 14, 92**
MacLeod, Alistair **56, 165**
Macpherson, (Jean) Jay **14**
Maillet, Antonine **54, 118**

Major, Kevin (Gerald) **26**
Marlatt, Daphne **168**
McFadden, David **48**
McLuhan, (Herbert) Marshall **37, 83**
Metcalf, John **37**
Mistry, Rohinton **71**
Mitchell, Joni **12**
Mitchell, W(illiam) O(rmond) **25**
Moore, Brian **1, 3, 5, 7, 8, 19, 32, 90**
Morgan, Janet **39**
Moure, Erin **88**
Mowat, Farley (McGill) **26**
Mukherjee, Bharati **53, 115**
Munro, Alice **6, 10, 19, 50, 95**
Musgrave, Susan **13, 54**
Newlove, John (Herbert) **14**
Nichol, B(arrie) P(hillip) **18**
Nowlan, Alden (Albert) **15**
Ondaatje, (Philip) Michael **14, 29, 51, 76**
Page, P(atricia) K(athleen) **7, 18**
Pollock, (Mary) Sharon **50**
Pratt, E(dwin) J(ohn) **19**
Purdy, A(lfred) W(ellington) **3, 6, 14, 50**
Quarrington, Paul (Lewis) **65**
Reaney, James **13**
Ricci, Nino **70**
Richards, David Adams **59**
Richler, Mordecai **3, 5, 9, 13, 18, 46, 70**
Ringwood, Gwen(dolyn Margaret) Pharis **48**
Ritter, Erika **52**
Rooke, Leon **25, 34**
Rosenblatt, Joe **15**
Ross, (James) Sinclair **13**
Roy, Gabrielle **10, 14**
Rule, Jane (Vance) **27**
Ryga, George **14**
Scott, F(rancis) R(eginald) **22**
Shields, Carol **91, 113**
Skelton, Robin **13**
Škvorecký, Josef (Vaclav) **15, 39, 69, 152**
Slade, Bernard **11, 46**
Smart, Elizabeth **54**
Smith, A(rthur) J(ames) M(arshall) **15**
Souster, (Holmes) Raymond **5, 14**
Suknaski, Andrew **19**
Theriault, Yves **79**
Thesen, Sharon **56**
Thomas, Audrey (Callahan) **7, 13, 37, 107**
Thompson, Judith **39**
Tremblay, Michel **29, 102**
Urquhart, Jane **90**
Vanderhaeghe, Guy **41**
van Vogt, A(lfred) E(lton) **1**
Vizinczey, Stephen **40**
Waddington, Miriam **28**
Wah, Fred(erick James) **44**
Walker, David Harry **14**
Walker, George F. **44, 61**
Webb, Phyllis **18**
Wiebe, Rudy (Henry) **6, 11, 14, 138**
Wilson, Ethel Davis (Bryant) **13**
Wright, L(aurali) R. **44**
Wright, Richard B(ruce) **6**
Young, Neil **17**

CHILEAN

Alegria, Fernando **57**
Allende, Isabel **39, 57, 97, 170**
Donoso (Yañez), José **4, 8, 11, 32, 99**
Dorfman, Ariel **48, 77**
Neruda, Pablo **1, 2, 5, 7, 9, 28, 62**
Parra, Nicanor **2, 102**

CHINESE

Chang, Jung **71**
Ch'ien, Chung-shu **22**
Ding Ling **68**
Lord, Bette Bao **23**
Mo, Timothy (Peter) **46, 134**
Pa Chin **18**

Peake, Mervyn **7, 54**
Wong, Jade Snow **17**

COLOMBIAN

García Márquez, Gabriel (Jose) **2, 3, 8, 10, 15, 27, 47, 55, 68, 170**

CONGOLESE

Tchicaya, Gerald Felix **101**

CROATION

Drakulic, Slavenka **173**

CUBAN

Arenas, Reinaldo **41**
Cabrera Infante, G(uillermo) **5, 25, 45, 120**
Calvino, Italo **5, 8, 11, 22, 33, 39, 73**
Carpentier (y Valmont), Alejo **8, 11, 38, 110**
Fornés, María Irene **39, 61**
Garcia, Cristina **76**
Guevara, Che **87**
Guillén, Nicolás (Cristobal) **48, 79**
Lezama Lima, José **4, 10, 101**
Padilla (Lorenzo), Heberto **38**
Sarduy, Severo **6, 97**

CZECH

Forman, Milos **164**
Friedlander, Saul **90**
Havel, Václav **25, 58, 65, 123**
Holub, Miroslav **4**
Hrabal, Bohumil **13, 67**
Klima, Ivan **56, 172**
Kohout, Pavel **13**
Kundera, Milan **4, 9, 19, 32, 68, 115, 135**
Lustig, Arnost **56**
Seifert, Jaroslav **34, 44, 93**
Škvorecký, Josef (Vaclav) **15, 39, 69, 152**
Vaculik, Ludvik **7**

DANISH

Abell, Kjeld **15**
Bodker, Cecil **21**
Dreyer, Carl Theodor **16**
Hoeg, Peter **95, 156**

DOMINICAN REPUBLICAN

Alvarez, Julia **93**

DUTCH

Bernhard, Thomas **3, 32, 61**
Buruma, Ian **163**
de Hartog, Jan **19**
Mulisch, Harry **42**
Ruyslinck, Ward **14**
van de Wetering, Janwillem **47**

EGYPTIAN

Chedid, Andree **47**
Mahfouz, Naguīb (Abdel Azīz Al-Sabilgi) **153**

ENGLISH

Ackroyd, Peter **34, 52, 140**
Adams, Douglas (Noel) **27, 60**
Adams, Richard (George) **4, 5, 18**
Adcock, Fleur **41**
Aickman, Robert (Fordyce) **57**
Aiken, Joan (Delano) **35**
Aldington, Richard **49**
Aldiss, Brian W(ilson) **5, 14, 40**
Allingham, Margery (Louise) **19**
Almedingen, E. M. **12**
Alvarez, A(lfred) **5, 13**
Ambler, Eric **4, 6, 9**
Amis, Kingsley (William) **1, 2, 3, 5, 8, 13, 40, 44, 129**
Amis, Martin (Louis) **4, 9, 38, 62, 101**

Anderson, Lindsay (Gordon) **20**
Anthony, Piers **35**
Archer, Jeffrey (Howard) **28**
Arden, John **6, 13, 15**
Armatrading, Joan **17**
Arthur, Ruth M(abel) **12**
Arundel, Honor (Morfydd) **17**
Atkinson, Kate **99**
Auden, W(ystan) H(ugh) **1, 2, 3, 4, 6, 9, 11, 14, 43, 123**
Ayckbourn, Alan **5, 8, 18, 33, 74**
Ayrton, Michael **7**
Bagnold, Enid **25**
Bailey, Paul **45**
Bainbridge, Beryl (Margaret) **4, 5, 8, 10, 14, 18, 22, 62, 130**
Ballard, J(ames) G(raham) **3, 6, 14, 36, 137**
Banks, Lynne Reid **23**
Barker, Clive **52**
Barker, George Granville **8, 48**
Barker, Howard **37**
Barker, Pat(ricia) **32, 94, 146**
Barnes, Julian (Patrick) **42, 141**
Barnes, Peter **5, 56**
Barrett, (Roger) Syd **35**
Bates, H(erbert) E(rnest) **46**
Beer, Patricia **58**
Bennett, Alan **45, 77**
Berger, John (Peter) **2, 19**
Berkoff, Steven **56**
Bermant, Chaim (Icyk) **40**
Betjeman, John **2, 6, 10, 34, 43**
Billington, (Lady) Rachel (Mary) **43**
Binyon, T(imothy) J(ohn) **34**
Blunden, Edmund (Charles) **2, 56**
Bolt, Robert (Oxton) **14**
Bond, Edward **4, 6, 13, 23**
Booth, Martin **13**
Bowen, Elizabeth (Dorothea Cole) **1, 3, 6, 11, 15, 22, 118**
Bowie, David **17**
Boyd, William **28, 53, 70**
Bradbury, Malcolm (Stanley) **32, 61**
Bragg, Melvyn **10**
Braine, John (Gerard) **1, 3, 41**
Brenton, Howard **31**
Brittain, Vera (Mary) **23**
Brooke-Rose, Christine **40**
Brookner, Anita **32, 34, 51, 136**
Brophy, Brigid (Antonia) **6, 11, 29, 105**
Brunner, John (Kilian Houston) **8, 10**
Bunting, Basil **10, 39, 47**
Burgess, Anthony **1, 2, 4, 5, 8, 10, 13, 15, 22, 40, 62, 81, 94**
Byatt, A(ntonia) S(usan Drabble) **19, 65, 136**
Caldwell, (Janet Miriam) Taylor (Holland) **2, 28, 39**
Campbell, (John) Ramsey **42**
Carter, Angela (Olive) **5, 41, 76**
Causley, Charles (Stanley) **7**
Caute, (John) David **29**
Chambers, Aidan **35**
Chaplin, Charles Spencer **16**
Chapman, Graham **21**
Chatwin, (Charles) Bruce **28, 57, 59**
Chitty, Thomas Willes **11**
Christie, Agatha (Mary Clarissa) **1, 6, 8, 12, 39, 48, 110**
Churchill, Caryl **31, 55, 157**
Clark, (Robert) Brian **29**
Clarke, Arthur C(harles) **1, 4, 13, 18, 35, 136**
Cleese, John (Marwood) **21**
Colegate, Isabel **36**
Comfort, Alex(ander) **7**
Compton-Burnett, I(vy) **1, 3, 10, 15, 34**
Cooney, Ray **62**
Copeland, Stewart (Armstrong) **26**
Cornwell, David (John Moore) **9, 15**
Costello, Elvis **21**
Coward, Noël (Peirce) **1, 9, 29, 51**
Crace, Jim **157**
Creasey, John **11**

Crispin, Edmund 22
Dabydeen, David 34
D'Aguiar, Fred 145
Dahl, Roald 1, 6, 18, 79
Daryush, Elizabeth 6, 19
Davie, Donald (Alfred) 5, 8, 10, 31
Davies, Rhys 23
Day Lewis, C(ecil) 1, 6, 10
Deighton, Len 4, 7, 22, 46
Delaney, Shelagh 29
Dennis, Nigel (Forbes) 8
Dickinson, Peter (Malcolm) 12, 35
Drabble, Margaret 2, 3, 5, 8, 10, 22, 53, 129
Duffy, Maureen 37
du Maurier, Daphne 6, 11, 59
Durrell, Lawrence (George) 1, 4, 6, 8, 13, 27, 41
Dyer, Geoff 149
Eagleton, Terence (Francis) 63, 132
Edgar, David 42
Edwards, G(erald) B(asil) 25
Eliot, T(homas) S(tearns) 1, 2, 3, 6, 9, 10, 13, 15, 24, 34, 41, 55, 57, 113
Elliott, Janice 47
Ellis, A. E. 7
Ellis, Alice Thomas 40
Empson, William 3, 8, 19, 33, 34
Enright, D(ennis) J(oseph) 4, 8, 31
Ewart, Gavin (Buchanan) 13, 46
Fairbairns, Zoe (Ann) 32
Farrell, J(ames) G(ordon) 6
Feinstein, Elaine 36
Fenton, James Martin 32
Ferguson, Niall 134
Fielding, Helen 146
Figes, Eva 31
Fisher, Roy 25
Fitzgerald, Penelope 19, 51, 61, 143
Fleming, Ian (Lancaster) 3, 30
Follett, Ken(neth Martin) 18
Forester, C(ecil) S(cott) 35
Forster, E(dward) M(organ) 1, 2, 3, 4, 9, 10, 13, 15, 22, 45, 77
Forster, Margaret 149
Forsyth, Frederick 2, 5, 36
Fowles, John (Robert) 1, 2, 3, 4, 6, 9, 10, 15, 33, 87
Francis, Dick 2, 22, 42, 102
Fraser, George MacDonald 7
Frayn, Michael 3, 7, 31, 47
Freeling, Nicolas 38
Fry, Christopher 2, 10, 14
Fugard, Sheila 48
Fuller, John (Leopold) 62
Fuller, Roy (Broadbent) 4, 28
Gardam, Jane (Mary) 43
Gardner, John (Edmund) 30
Garfield, Leon 12
Garner, Alan 17
Garnett, David 3
Gascoyne, David (Emery) 45
Gee, Maggie (Mary) 57
Gerhardie, William Alexander 5
Gilliatt, Penelope (Ann Douglass) 2, 10, 13, 53
Glanville, Brian (Lester) 6
Glendinning, Victoria 50
Gloag, Julian 40
Godden, (Margaret) Rumer 53
Golding, William (Gerald) 1, 2, 3, 8, 10, 17, 27, 58, 81
Graham, Winston (Mawdsley) 23
Graves, Richard Perceval 44
Graves, Robert (von Ranke) 1, 2, 6, 11, 39, 44, 45
Gray, Simon (James Holliday) 9, 14, 36
Green, Henry 2, 13, 97
Greenaway, Peter 159
Greene, Graham (Henry) 1, 3, 6, 9, 14, 18, 27, 37, 70, 72, 125
Griffiths, Trevor 13, 52
Grigson, Geoffrey (Edward Harvey) 7, 39

Gunn, Thom(son William) 3, 6, 18, 32, 81
Haig-Brown, Roderick (Langmere) 21
Hailey, Arthur 5
Hall, Rodney 51
Hamburger, Michael (Peter Leopold) 5, 14
Hamilton, (Anthony Walter) Patrick 51
Hampton, Christopher (James) 4
Hare, David 29, 58, 136
Harris, (Theodore) Wilson 25, 159
Harrison, Tony 43, 129
Hartley, L(eslie) P(oles) 2, 22
Harwood, Ronald 32
Hastings, Selina 44
Hawking, Stephen W(illiam) 63, 105
Headon, (Nicky) Topper 30
Heppenstall, (John) Rayner 10
Hibbert, Eleanor Alice Burford 7
Hill, Geoffrey (William) 5, 8, 18, 45
Hill, Susan (Elizabeth) 4, 113
Hinde, Thomas 6, 11
Hitchcock, Alfred (Joseph) 16
Hitchens, Christopher 157
Hocking, Mary (Eunice) 13
Holden, Ursula 18
Holdstock, Robert P. 39
Hollinghurst, Alan 55, 91
Hooker, (Peter) Jeremy 43
Hopkins, John (Richard) 4
Household, Geoffrey (Edward West) 11
Howard, Elizabeth Jane 7, 29
Hughes, David (John) 48
Hughes, Richard (Arthur Warren) 1, 11
Hughes, Ted 2, 4, 9, 14, 37, 119
Huxley, Aldous (Leonard) 1, 3, 4, 5, 8, 11, 18, 35, 79
Idle, Eric 21
Ingalls, Rachel (Holmes) 42
Isherwood, Christopher (William Bradshaw) 1, 9, 11, 14, 44
Ishiguro, Kazuo 27, 56, 59, 110
Jacobson, Dan 4, 14
Jagger, Mick 17
James, C(yril) L(ionel) R(obert) 33
James, P. D. 18, 46, 122
Jellicoe, (Patricia) Ann 27
Jennings, Elizabeth (Joan) 5, 14, 131
Jhabvala, Ruth Prawer 4, 8, 29, 94, 138
Johnson, B(ryan) S(tanley William) 6, 9
Johnson, Pamela Hansford 1, 7, 27
Johnson, Paul (Bede) 147
Jolley, (Monica) Elizabeth 46
Jones, David (Michael) 2, 4, 7, 13, 42
Jones, Diana Wynne 26
Jones, Mervyn 10, 52
Jones, Mick 30
Josipovici, Gabriel (David) 6, 43, 153
Kavan, Anna 5, 13, 82
Kaye, M(ary) M(argaret) 28
Keates, Jonathan 34
King, Francis (Henry) 8, 53, 145
Kirkup, James 1
Koestler, Arthur 1, 3, 6, 8, 15, 33
Kops, Bernard 4
Kureishi, Hanif 64, 135
Lanchester, John 99
Larkin, Philip (Arthur) 3, 5, 8, 9, 13, 18, 33, 39, 64
Leavis, F(rank) R(aymond) 24
Lee, Laurie 90
Lee, Tanith 46
Lehmann, Rosamond (Nina) 5
Lennon, John (Ono) 12, 35
Lessing, Doris (May) 1, 2, 3, 6, 10, 15, 22, 40, 94, 170
Levertov, Denise 1, 2, 3, 5, 8, 15, 28, 66
Levi, Peter (Chad Tigar) 41
Lewis, C(live) S(taples) 1, 3, 6, 14, 27, 124
Lively, Penelope (Margaret) 32, 50
Lodge, David (John) 36, 141
Loy, Mina 28
Luke, Peter (Ambrose Cyprian) 38
MacInnes, Colin 4, 23

Mackenzie, Compton (Edward Montague) 18
Macpherson, (Jean) Jay 14
Maitland, Sara (Louise) 49
Manning, Olivia 5, 19
Mantel, Hilary (Mary) 144
Masefield, John (Edward) 11, 47
Mason, Nick 35
Maugham, W(illiam) Somerset 1, 11, 15, 67, 93
Mayle, Peter 89
Mayne, William (James Carter) 12
McEwan, Ian (Russell) 13, 66, 169
McGrath, Patrick 55
Mercer, David 5
Middleton, Christopher 13
Middleton, Stanley 7, 38
Mitford, Nancy 44
Mo, Timothy (Peter) 46, 134
Moorcock, Michael (John) 5, 27, 58
Mortimer, John (Clifford) 28, 43
Mortimer, Penelope (Ruth) 5
Mosley, Nicholas 43, 70
Motion, Andrew (Peter) 47
Mott, Michael (Charles Alston) 15, 34
Murdoch, (Jean) Iris 1, 2, 3, 4, 6, 8, 11, 15, 22, 31, 51
Naipaul, V(idiadhar) S(urajprasad) 4, 7, 9, 13, 18, 37, 105
Newby, P(ercy) H(oward) 2, 13
Nichols, Peter (Richard) 5, 36, 65
Noon, Jeff 91
Norfolk, Lawrence 76
Nye, Robert 13, 42
O'Brien, Richard 17
O'Faolain, Julia 6, 19, 47, 108
Olivier, Laurence (Kerr) 20
Orton, Joe 4, 13, 43
Osborne, John (James) 1, 2, 5, 11, 45
Osborne, Lawrence 50
Page, Jimmy 12
Page, Louise 40
Page, P(atricia) K(athleen) 7, 18
Palin, Michael (Edward) 21
Parkin, Frank 43
Parks, Tim(othy Harold) 147
Paton Walsh, Gillian 35
Paulin, Tom 37
Peake, Mervyn 7, 54
Perry, Anne 126
Phillips, Caryl 96
Pinter, Harold 1, 3, 6, 9, 11, 15, 27, 58, 73
Plant, Robert 12
Poliakoff, Stephen 38
Potter, Dennis (Christopher George) 58, 86, 123
Powell, Anthony (Dymoke) 1, 3, 7, 9, 10, 31
Pownall, David 10
Powys, John Cowper 7, 9, 15, 46, 125
Priestley, J(ohn) B(oynton) 2, 5, 9, 34
Prince, F(rank) T(empleton) 22
Pritchett, V(ictor) S(awdon) 5, 13, 15, 41
Pym, Barbara (Mary Crampton) 13, 19, 37, 111
Quin, Ann (Marie) 6
Raine, Craig (Anthony) 32, 103
Raine, Kathleen (Jessie) 7, 45
Rathbone, Julian 41
Rattigan, Terence (Mervyn) 7
Raven, Simon (Arthur Noel) 14
Read, Herbert Edward 4
Read, Piers Paul 4, 10, 25
Reading, Peter 47
Redgrove, Peter (William) 6, 41
Reid, Christopher (John) 33
Rendell, Ruth (Barbara) 28, 48
Rhys, Jean 2, 4, 6, 14, 19, 51, 124
Rice, Tim(othy Miles Bindon) 21
Richard, Keith 17
Richards, I(vor) A(rmstrong) 14, 24
Roberts, Keith (John Kingston) 14
Roberts, Michele (Brigitte) 48
Rowling, J(oanne) K(athleen) 137

Rudkin, (James) David **14**
Rushdie, (Ahmed) Salman **23, 31, 55, 100**
Rushforth, Peter (Scott) **19**
Russell, (Henry) Ken(neth Alfred) **16**
Russell, William Martin **60**
Sacks, Oliver (Wolf) **67**
Sansom, William **2, 6**
Sassoon, Siegfried (Lorraine) **36, 130**
Scammell, Michael **34**
Scannell, Vernon **49**
Schama, Simon (Michael) **150**
Schlee, Ann **35**
Schumacher, E(rnst) F(riedrich) **80**
Scott, Paul (Mark) **9, 60**
Shaffer, Anthony (Joshua) **19**
Shaffer, Peter (Levin) **5, 14, 18, 37, 60**
Sharpe, Tom **36**
Shaw, Robert **5**
Sheed, Wilfrid (John Joseph) **2, 4, 10, 53**
Shute, Nevil **30**
Shuttle, Penelope (Diane) **7**
Silkin, Jon **2, 6, 43**
Sillitoe, Alan **1, 3, 6, 10, 19, 57, 148**
Simonon, Paul **30**
Simpson, N(orman) F(rederick) **29**
Sinclair, Andrew (Annandale) **2, 14**
Sinclair, Iain **76**
Sisson, C(harles) H(ubert) **8**
Sitwell, Edith **2, 9, 67**
Slaughter, Carolyn **56**
Smith, Stevie **3, 8, 25, 44**
Smith, Zadie **158**
Snow, C(harles) P(ercy) **1, 4, 6, 9, 13, 19**
Spender, Stephen (Harold) **1, 2, 5, 10, 41, 91**
Spurling, Hilary **34**
Stannard, Martin **44**
Stewart, J(ohn) I(nnes) M(ackintosh) **7, 14, 32**
Stewart, Mary (Florence Elinor) **7, 35, 117**
Stoppard, Tom **1, 3, 4, 5, 8, 15, 29, 34, 63, 91**
Storey, David (Malcolm) **2, 4, 5, 8**
Streatfeild, (Mary) Noel **21**
Strummer, Joe **30**
Summers, Andrew James **26**
Sumner, Gordon Matthew **26**
Sutcliff, Rosemary **26**
Swift, Graham (Colin) **41, 88**
Swinfen, Ann **34**
Swinnerton, Frank Arthur **31**
Symons, Julian (Gustave) **2, 14, 32**
Szirtes, George **46**
Taylor, Elizabeth **2, 4, 29**
Tennant, Emma (Christina) **13, 52**
Teran, Lisa St. Aubin de **36**
Thomas, D(onald) M(ichael) **13, 22, 31, 132**
Thubron, Colin (Gerald Dryden) **163**
Tindall, Gillian (Elizabeth) **7**
Tolkien, J(ohn) R(onald) R(euel) **1, 2, 3, 8, 12, 38**
Tomalin, Claire **166**
Tomlinson, (Alfred) Charles **2, 4, 6, 13, 45**
Townshend, Peter (Dennis Blandford) **17, 42**
Treitel, Jonathan **70**
Tremain, Rose **42**
Tuohy, Frank **37**
Turner, Frederick **48**
Unsworth, Barry (Forster) **76, 127**
Ustinov, Peter (Alexander) **1**
Van Den Bogarde, Derek Jules Gaspard Ulric Niven
Vansittart, Peter **42**
Wain, John (Barrington) **2, 11, 15, 46**
Walker, Ted **13**
Walsh, Jill Paton **35**
Warner, Francis (Robert le Plastrier) **14**
Warner, Marina **59**
Warner, Rex (Ernest) **45**
Warner, Sylvia Townsend **7, 19**
Waterhouse, Keith (Spencer) **47**
Waters, Roger **35**
Waugh, Auberon (Alexander) **7**
Waugh, Evelyn (Arthur St. John) **1, 3, 8, 13, 19, 27, 44, 107**
Waugh, Harriet **6**
Webber, Andrew Lloyd **21**
Weldon, Fay **6, 9, 11, 19, 36, 59, 122**
Weller, Paul **26**
Wesker, Arnold **3, 5, 42**
West, Anthony (Panther) **50**
West, Paul **7, 14, 96**
West, Rebecca **7, 9, 31, 50**
Westall, Robert (Atkinson) **17**
White, Patrick (Victor Martindale) **3, 4, 5, 7, 9, 18, 65, 69**
White, T(erence) H(anbury) **30**
Whitehead, E(dward) A(nthony) **5**
Whitemore, Hugh (John) **37**
Wilding, Michael **73**
Williams, Hugo **42**
Wilson, A(ndrew) N(orman) **33**
Wilson, Angus (Frank Johnstone) **2, 3, 5, 25, 34**
Wilson, Colin **3, 14**
Wilson, Snoo **33**
Wingrove, David (John) **68**
Winterson, Jeanette **64, 158**
Wodehouse, P(elham) G(renville) **1, 2, 5, 10, 22**
Wright, Rick **35**
Yorke, Henry Vincent **13**
Young, Andrew (John) **5**

ESTONIAN

Ivask, Ivar Vidrik **14**

FIJI ISLANDER

Prichard, Katharine Susannah **46**

FILIPINO

Santos, Bienvenido N(uqui) **22**

FINNISH

Haavikko, Paavo Juhani **18, 34**
Salama, Hannu **18**
Sillanpaa, Frans Eemil **19**

FRENCH

Adamov, Arthur **4, 25**
Anouilh, Jean (Marie Lucien Pierre) **1, 3, 8, 13, 40, 50**
Aragon, Louis **3, 22**
Arp, Jean **5**
Audiberti, Jacques **38**
Aymé, Marcel (Andre) **11**
Barthes, Roland (Gérard) **24, 83**
Barzun, Jacques (Martin) **51, 145**
Bataille, Georges **29**
Baudrillard, Jean **60**
Beauvoir, Simone (Lucie Ernestine Marie Bertrand) de **1, 2, 4, 8, 14, 31, 44, 50, 71, 124**
Beckett, Samuel (Barclay) **1, 2, 3, 4, 6, 9, 10, 11, 14, 18, 29, 57, 59, 83**
Blanchot, Maurice **135**
Bonnefoy, Yves **9, 15, 58**
Bresson, Robert **16**
Breton, André **2, 9, 15, 54**
Butor, Michel (Marie François) **1, 3, 8, 11, 15, 161**
Camus, Albert **1, 2, 4, 9, 11, 14, 32, 63, 69, 124**
Carrere, Emmanuel **89**
Cayrol, Jean **11**
Chabrol, Claude **16**
Char, René(-émile) **9, 11, 14, 55**
Chedid, Andree **47**
Cixous, Hélène **92**
Clair, Rene **20**
Cocteau, Jean (Maurice Eugène Clément) **1, 8, 15, 16, 43**
Cousteau, Jacques-Yves **30**
del Castillo, Michel **38**
Derrida, Jacques **24, 87**
Destouches, Louis-Ferdinand **9, 15**
Duhamel, Georges **8**
Duras, Marguerite **3, 6, 11, 20, 34, 40, 68, 100**
Ernaux, Annie **88**
Federman, Raymond **6, 47**
Foucault, Michel **31, 34, 69**
Fournier, Pierre **11**
Francis, Claude **50**
Gallo, Max Louis **95**
Gao Xingjian **167**
Gary, Romain **25**
Gascar, Pierre **11**
Genet, Jean **1, 2, 5, 10, 14, 44, 46**
Giono, Jean **4, 11**
Godard, Jean-Luc **20**
Goldmann, Lucien **24**
Gontier, Fernande **50**
Gray, Francine du Plessix **22, 153**
Green, Julien **3, 11, 77**
Guillevic, (Eugene) **33**
Ionesco, Eugène **1, 4, 6, 9, 11, 15, 41, 86**
Irigarary, Luce **164**
Japrisot, Sébastien **90**
Josipovici, Gabriel (David) **6, 43, 153**
Jouve, Pierre Jean **47**
Kristeva, Julia **77, 140**
Lacan, Jacques (Marie Emile) **75**
Laurent, Antoine **50**
Le Clézio, J(ean) M(arie) G(ustave) **31, 155**
Leduc, Violette **22**
Leger, (Marie-Rene Auguste) Alexis Saint-Leger **4, 11, 46**
Leiris, Michel (Julien) **61**
Lévi-Strauss, Claude **38**
Mallet-Joris, Françoise **11**
Malraux, (Georges-)André **1, 4, 9, 13, 15, 57**
Mandiargues, Andre Pieyre de **41**
Marcel, Gabriel Honore **15**
Mauriac, Claude **9**
Mauriac, François (Charles) **4, 9, 56**
Merton, Thomas **1, 3, 11, 34, 83**
Modiano, Patrick (Jean) **18**
Montherlant, Henry (Milon) de **8, 19**
Morand, Paul **41**
Nin, Anaïs **1, 4, 8, 11, 14, 60, 127**
Perec, Georges **56, 116**
Pinget, Robert **7, 13, 37**
Ponge, Francis **6, 18**
Poniatowska, Elena **140**
Prévert, Jacques (Henri Marie) **15**
Queneau, Raymond **2, 5, 10, 42**
Quoirez, Francoise **9**
Renoir, Jean **20**
Resnais, Alain **16**
Reverdy, Pierre **53**
Rio, Michel **43**
Robbe-Grillet, Alain **1, 2, 4, 6, 8, 10, 14, 43, 128**
Rohmer, Eric **16**
Romains, Jules **7**
Sachs, Nelly **14, 98**
Sarraute, Nathalie **1, 2, 4, 8, 10, 31, 80**
Sartre, Jean-Paul **1, 4, 7, 9, 13, 18, 24, 44, 50, 52**
Sauser-Hall, Frederic **18**
Schwarz-Bart, André **2, 4**
Schwarz-Bart, Simone **7**
Simenon, Georges (Jacques Christian) **1, 2, 3, 8, 18, 47**
Simon, Claude **4, 9, 15, 39**
Soupault, Philippe **68**
Steiner, George **24**
Tournier, Michel (édouard) **6, 23, 36, 95**
Troyat, Henri **23**
Truffaut, Francois **20, 101**
Tuck, Lily **70**
Tzara, Tristan **47**
Varda, Agnes **16**

Wittig, Monique **22**
Yourcenar, Marguerite **19, 38, 50, 87**

FRENCH GUINEAN

Damas, Leon-Gontran **84**

GERMAN

Amichai, Yehuda **9, 22, 57, 116**
Arendt, Hannah **66, 98**
Arp, Jean **5**
Becker, Jurek **7, 19**
Benary-Isbert, Margot **12**
Bienek, Horst **7, 11**
Boell, Heinrich (Theodor) **2, 3, 6, 9, 11, 15, 27, 32, 72**
Buchheim, Lothar-Guenther **6**
Bukowski, Charles **2, 5, 9, 41, 82, 108**
Eich, Guenter **15**
Ende, Michael (Andreas Helmuth) **31**
Enzensberger, Hans Magnus **43**
Fassbinder, Rainer Werner **20**
Figes, Eva **31**
Grass, Guenter (Wilhelm) **1, 2, 4, 6, 11, 15, 22, 32, 49, 88**
Habermas, Juergen **104**
Hamburger, Michael (Peter Leopold) **5, 14**
Handke, Peter **5, 8, 10, 15, 38, 134**
Heidegger, Martin **24**
Hein, Christoph **154**
Herzog, Werner **16**
Hesse, Hermann **1, 2, 3, 6, 11, 17, 25, 69**
Heym, Stefan **41**
Hildesheimer, Wolfgang **49**
Hochhuth, Rolf **4, 11, 18**
Hofmann, Gert **54**
Jhabvala, Ruth Prawer **4, 8, 29, 94, 138**
Johnson, Uwe **5, 10, 15, 40**
Juenger, Ernst **125**
Kissinger, Henry A(lfred) **137**
Kroetz, Franz Xaver **41**
Kunze, Reiner **10**
Lenz, Siegfried **27**
Levitin, Sonia (Wolff) **17**
Maron, Monika **165**
Mueller, Lisel **13, 51**
Nossack, Hans Erich **6**
Preussler, Otfried **17**
Remarque, Erich Maria **21**
Riefenstahl, Leni **16**
Sachs, Nelly **14, 98**
Schmidt, Arno (Otto) **56**
Schumacher, E(rnst) F(riedrich) **80**
Seghers, Anna **7**
Strauss, Botho **22**
Sueskind, Patrick **44**
Tillich, Paul (Johannes) **131**
Walser, Martin **27**
Weiss, Peter (Ulrich) **3, 15, 51**
Wellershoff, Dieter **46**
Wolf, Christa **14, 29, 58, 150**
Zuckmayer, Carl **18**

GHANIAN

Armah, Ayi Kwei **5, 33, 136**

GREEK

Broumas, Olga **10, 73**
Elytis, Odysseus **15, 49, 100**
Haviaras, Stratis **33**
Karapanou, Margarita **13**
Nakos, Lilika **29**
Ritsos, Yannis **6, 13, 31**
Samarakis, Antonis **5**
Seferis, George **5, 11**
Spanidou, Irini **44**
Vassilikos, Vassilis **4, 8**

GUADELOUPEAN

Condé, Maryse **52, 92**
Schwarz-Bart, Simone **7**

GUATEMALAN

Asturias, Miguel Ángel **3, 8, 13**

GUINEAN

Laye, Camara **4, 38**

GUYANESE

Dabydeen, David **34**
Harris, (Theodore) Wilson **25**

HAITIAN

Danticat, Edwidge **94, 139**

HUNGARIAN

Faludy, George **42**
Koestler, Arthur **1, 3, 6, 8, 15, 33**
Konrád, György **4, 10, 73**
Lengyel, József **7**
Lukacs, George **24**
Nagy, Laszlo **7**
Szirtes, George **46**
Tabori, George **19**
Vizinczey, Stephen **40**

ICELANDIC

Gunnars, Kristjana **69**

INDIAN

Alexander, Meena **121**
Ali, Ahmed **69**
Anand, Mulk Raj **23, 93**
Desai, Anita **19, 37, 97**
Ezekiel, Nissim **61**
Ghosh, Amitav **44, 153**
Mahapatra, Jayanta **33**
Mehta, Ved (Parkash) **37**
Mistry, Rohinton **71**
Mukherjee, Bharati **53, 115**
Narayan, R(asipuram) K(rishnaswami) **7, 28, 47, 121**
Rao, Raja **25, 56**
Ray, Satyajit **16, 76**
Rushdie, (Ahmed) Salman **23, 31, 55, 100**
Sahgal, Nayantara (Pandit) **41**
Sealy, I(rwin) Allan **55**
Seth, Vikram **43, 90**
Singh, Khushwant **11**
Tharoor, Shashi **70**
White, T(erence) H(anbury) **30**

INDONESIAN

Lee, Li-Young **164**

IRANIAN

Modarressi, Taghi (M.) **44**
Shamlu, Ahmad **10**

IRISH

Banville, John **46, 118**
Beckett, Samuel (Barclay) **1, 2, 3, 4, 6, 9, 10, 11, 14, 18, 29, 57, 59, 83**
Behan, Brendan **1, 8, 11, 15, 79**
Binchy, Maeve **153**
Blackwood, Caroline **6, 9, 100**
Boland, Eavan (Aisling) **40, 67, 113**
Bowen, Elizabeth (Dorothea Cole) **1, 3, 6, 11, 15, 22, 118**
Boyle, Patrick **19**
Brennan, Maeve **5**
Brown, Christy **63**
Carroll, Paul Vincent **10**
Clarke, Austin **6, 9**
Colum, Padraic **28**
Day Lewis, C(ecil) **1, 6, 10**
Dillon, Eilis **17**
Donleavy, J(ames) P(atrick) **1, 4, 6, 10, 45**
Doyle, Roddy **81**
Durcan, Paul **43, 70**
Friel, Brian **5, 42, 59, 115**
Gébler, Carlo (Ernest) **39**
Hanley, James **3, 5, 8, 13**
Hart, Josephine **70**
Heaney, Seamus (Justin) **5, 7, 14, 25, 37, 74, 91, 171**
Johnston, Jennifer (Prudence) **7, 150**
Jordan, Neil (Patrick) **110**
Kavanagh, Patrick (Joseph) **22**
Keane, Molly **31**
Kiely, Benedict **23, 43**
Kinsella, Thomas **4, 19, 138**
Lavin, Mary **4, 18, 99**
Leonard, Hugh **19**
Longley, Michael **29**
Mac Laverty, Bernard **31**
MacNeice, (Frederick) Louis **1, 4, 10, 53**
Mahon, Derek **27**
McCabe, Patrick **133**
McGahern, John **5, 9, 48, 156**
McGinley, Patrick (Anthony) **41**
McGuckian, Medbh **48**
Montague, John (Patrick) **13, 46**
Moore, Brian **1, 3, 5, 7, 8, 19, 32, 90**
Morrison, Van **21**
Morrissy, Mary **99**
Muldoon, Paul **32, 72, 166**
Murphy, Richard **41**
Murphy, Thomas (Bernard) **51**
Nolan, Christopher **58**
O'Brian, Patrick **152**
O'Brien, Edna **3, 5, 8, 13, 36, 65, 116**
O'Casey, Sean **1, 5, 9, 11, 15, 88**
O'Doherty, Brian **76**
O'Faolain, Julia **6, 19, 47, 108**
O'Faolain, Sean **1, 7, 14, 32, 70**
O'Flaherty, Liam **5, 34**
Paulin, Tom **37**
Rodgers, W(illiam) R(obert) **7**
Simmons, James (Stewart Alexander) **43**
Toibin, Colm **162**
Trevor, William **7, 9, 14, 25, 71, 116**
White, Terence de Vere **49**
Wilson, Robert McLiam **59**

ISRAELI

Agnon, S(hmuel) Y(osef Halevi) **4, 8, 14**
Amichai, Yehuda **9, 22, 57, 116**
Appelfeld, Aharon **23, 47**
Bakshi, Ralph **26**
Friedlander, Saul **90**
Grossman, David **67**
Kaniuk, Yoram **19**
Levin, Meyer **7**
Megged, Aharon **9**
Oz, Amos **5, 8, 11, 27, 33, 54**
Shammas, Anton **55**
Sobol, Joshua **60**
Yehoshua, A(braham) B. **13, 31**

ITALIAN

Antonioni, Michelangelo **20, 144**
Bacchelli, Riccardo **19**
Bassani, Giorgio **9**
Bertolucci, Bernardo **16, 157**
Bufalino, Gesualdo **74**
Buzzati, Dino **36**
Calasso, Roberto **81**
Calvino, Italo **5, 8, 11, 22, 33, 39, 73**
De Sica, Vittorio **20**
Eco, Umberto **28, 60, 142**
Fallaci, Oriana **11, 110**
Fellini, Federico **16, 85**
Fo, Dario **32, 109**
Gadda, Carlo Emilio **11**
Ginzburg, Natalia **5, 11, 54, 70**
Giovene, Andrea **7**
Landolfi, Tommaso **11, 49**
Levi, Primo **37, 50**
Luzi, Mario **13**
Montale, Eugenio **7, 9, 18**

Morante, Elsa **8, 47**
Moravia, Alberto **2, 7, 11, 27, 46**
Ortese, Anna Maria **89**
Palazzeschi, Aldo **11**
Pasolini, Pier Paolo **20, 37, 106**
Piccolo, Lucio **13**
Pincherle, Alberto **11, 18**
Quasimodo, Salvatore **10**
Ricci, Nino **70**
Sciascia, Leonardo **8, 9, 41**
Silone, Ignazio **4**
Ungaretti, Giuseppe **7, 11, 15**
Visconti, Luchino **16**
Vittorini, Elio **6, 9, 14**
Wertmueller, Lina **16**

JAMAICAN

Bennett, Louise (Simone) **28**
Cliff, Jimmy **21**
Cliff, Michelle **120**
Marley, Bob **17**
Thelwell, Michael Miles **22**

JAPANESE

Abe, Kōbō **8, 22, 53, 81**
Enchi, Fumiko (Ueda) **31**
Endō, Shūsaku **7, 14, 19, 54, 99**
Ibuse, Masuji **22**
Ichikawa, Kon **20**
Ishiguro, Kazuo **27, 56, 59, 110**
Kawabata, Yasunari **2, 5, 9, 18, 107**
Kurosawa, Akira **16, 119**
Murakami, Haruki
Oe, Kenzaburo **10, 36, 86**
Oshima, Nagisa **20**
Ozu, Yasujiro **16**
Shiga, Naoya **33**
Tanizaki, Jun'ichirō **8, 14, 28**
Whitney, Phyllis A(yame) **42**
Yoshimoto, Banana **84**

KENYAN

Ngugi, James T(hiong'o) **3, 7, 13**
Ngũgĩ wa Thiong'o **36**

MALIAN

Ouologuem, Yambo **146**

MARTINICAN

Césaire, Aimé (Fernand) **19, 32, 112**
Fanon, Frantz **74**
Glissant, Edouard **10, 68**

MEXICAN

Arreola, Juan José **147**
Castellanos, Rosario **66**
Esquivel, Laura **141**
Fuentes, Carlos **3, 8, 10, 13, 22, 41, 60, 113**
Ibarguengoitia, Jorge **37**
Lopez Portillo (y Pacheco), Jose **46**
Lopez y Fuentes, Gregorio **32**
Paz, Octavio **3, 4, 6, 10, 19, 51, 65, 119**
Poniatowska, Elena **140**
Rulfo, Juan **8, 80**

MOROCCAN

Arrabal, Fernando **2, 9, 18, 58**
Mernissi, Fatima **171**

NEW ZEALANDER

Adcock, Fleur **41**
Ashton-Warner, Sylvia (Constance) **19**
Baxter, James K(eir) **14**
Campion, Jane **95**
Gee, Maurice (Gough) **29**
Grace, Patricia Frances **56**
Hilliard, Noel (Harvey) **15**
Hulme, Keri **39, 130**
Ihimaera, Witi **46**

Marsh, (Edith) Ngaio **7, 53**
Sargeson, Frank **31**

NICARAGUAN

Alegria, Claribel **75**
Cardenal, Ernesto **31, 161**

NIGERIAN

Achebe, (Albert) Chinua(lumogu) **1, 3, 5, 7, 11, 26, 51, 75, 127, 152**
Clark Bekedermo, J(ohnson) P(epper) **38**
Ekwensi, Cyprian (Odiatu Duaka) **4**
Emecheta, (Florence Onye) Buchi **14, 48, 128**
Nwapa, Flora **133**
Okigbo, Christopher (Ifenayichukwu) **25, 84**
Okri, Ben **87**
Saro-Wiwa, Ken(ule Beeson) **114**
Soyinka, Wole **3, 5, 14, 36, 44**
Tutuola, Amos **5, 14, 29**

NORTHERN IRISH

Deane, Seamus (Francis) **122**
Simmons, James (Stewart Alexander) **43**
Wilson, Robert McLiam **59**

NORWEGIAN

Friis-Baastad, Babbis Ellinor **12**
Heyerdahl, Thor **26**
Moi, Toril **172**
Vesaas, Tarjei **48**

PAKISTANI

Ali, Ahmed **69**
Ali, Tariq **173**
Ghose, Zulfikar **42**

PARAGUAYAN

Roa Bastos, Augusto (Antonio) **45**

PERUVIAN

Allende, Isabel **39, 57, 97**
Arguedas, José María **10, 18**
Goldemberg, Isaac **52**
Vargas Llosa, (Jorge) Mario (Pedro) **3, 6, 9, 10, 15, 31, 42, 85**

POLISH

Agnon, S(hmuel) Y(osef Halevi) **4, 8, 14**
Becker, Jurek **7, 19**
Bermant, Chaim (Icyk) **40**
Bienek, Horst **7, 11**
Brandys, Kazimierz **62**
Dabrowska, Maria (Szumska) **15**
Gombrowicz, Witold **4, 7, 11, 49**
Herbert, Zbigniew **9, 43**
John Paul II, Pope **128**
Kieslowski, Krzysztof **120**
Konwicki, Tadeusz **8, 28, 54, 117**
Kosinski, Jerzy (Nikodem) **1, 2, 3, 6, 10, 15, 53, 70**
Lem, Stanislaw **8, 15, 40, 149**
Milosz, Czeslaw **5, 11, 22, 31, 56, 82**
Mrozek, Slawomir **3, 13**
Polanski, Roman **16**
Rozewicz, Tadeusz **9, 23, 139**
Singer, Isaac Bashevis **1, 3, 6, 9, 11, 15, 23, 38, 69, 111**
Skolimowski, Jerzy **20**
Szymborska, Wislawa **99**
Wajda, Andrzej **16**
Wittlin, Jozef **25**
Wojciechowska, Maia (Teresa) **26**

PORTUGUESE

Migueis, Jose Rodrigues **10**
Saramago, José **119**

PUERTO RICAN

Ferré, Rosario **139**
Marqués, René **96**
Piñero, Miguel (Antonio Gomez) **4, 55**
Sánchez, Luis Rafael **23**

ROMANIAN

Celan, Paul **10, 19, 53, 82**
Cioran, E(mil) M. **64**
Codrescu, Andrei **46, 121**
Ionesco, Eugène **1, 4, 6, 9, 11, 15, 41, 86**
Rezzori (d'Arezzo), Gregor von **25**
Tzara, Tristan **47**
Wiesel, Elie(zer) **3, 5, 11, 37**

RUSSIAN

Aitmatov, Chingiz (Torekulovich) **71**
Akhmadulina, Bella Akhatovna **53**
Akhmatova, Anna **11, 25, 64, 126**
Aksyonov, Vassily (Pavlovich) **22, 37, 101**
Aleshkovsky, Yuz **44**
Almedingen, E. M. **12**
Asimov, Isaac **1, 3, 9, 19, 26, 76, 92**
Bakhtin, Mikhail M(khailovich) **83**
Bitov, Andrei (Georgievich) **57**
Brodsky, Joseph **4, 6, 13, 36, 100**
Deren, Maya **16, 102**
Ehrenburg, Ilya (Grigoryevich) **18, 34, 62**
Eliade, Mircea **19**
Gary, Romain **25**
Goldberg, Anatol **34**
Grade, Chaim **10**
Grossman, Vasily (Semenovich) **41**
Iskander, Fazil **47**
Kabakov, Sasha **59**
Kaletski, Alexander **39**
Krotkov, Yuri **19**
Leonov, Leonid (Maximovich) **92**
Limonov, Edward **67**
Nabokov, Vladimir (Vladimirovich) **1, 2, 3, 6, 8, 11, 15, 23, 44, 46, 64**
Olesha, Yuri (Karlovich) **8**
Pasternak, Boris (Leonidovich) **7, 10, 18, 63**
Paustovsky, Konstantin (Georgievich) **40**
Rahv, Philip **24**
Rand, Ayn **3, 30, 44, 79**
Ratushinskaya, Irina **54**
Rybakov, Anatoli (Naumovich) **23, 53**
Sarraute, Nathalie **1, 2, 4, 8, 10, 31, 80**
Shalamov, Varlam (Tikhonovich) **18**
Shatrov, Mikhail **59**
Sholokhov, Mikhail (Aleksandrovich) **7, 15**
Sinyavsky, Andrei (Donatevich) **8**
Solzhenitsyn, Aleksandr I(sayevich) **1, 2, 4, 7, 9, 10, 18, 26, 34, 78, 134**
Strugatskii, Arkadii (Natanovich) **27**
Strugatskii, Boris (Natanovich) **27**
Tarkovsky, Andrei (Arsenyevich) **75**
Trifonov, Yuri (Valentinovich) **45**
Troyat, Henri **23**
Voinovich, Vladimir (Nikolaevich) **10, 49, 147**
Voznesensky, Andrei (Andreievich) **1, 15, 57**
Yanovsky, V(assily) S(emenovich) **2, 18**
Yevtushenko, Yevgeny (Alexandrovich) **1, 3, 13, 26, 51, 126**
Yezierska, Anzia **46**
Zaturenska, Marya **6, 11**
Zinoviev, Alexander (Aleksandrovich) **19**

SALVADORAN

Alegria, Claribel **75**
Argueta, Manlio **31**

SCOTTISH

Banks, Iain M(enzies) **34**
Brown, George Mackay **5, 48, 100**
Cronin, A(rchibald) J(oseph) **32**
Dunn, Douglas (Eaglesham) **6, 40**
Graham, W(illiam) S(idney) **29**

Gray, Alasdair (James) **41**
Grieve, C(hristopher) M(urray) **11, 19**
Hunter, Mollie **21**
Jenkins, (John) Robin **52**
Kelman, James **58, 86**
Laing, R(onald) D(avid) **95**
MacBeth, George (Mann) **2, 5, 9**
MacCaig, Norman (Alexander) **36**
MacInnes, Helen (Clark) **27, 39**
MacLean, Alistair (Stuart) **3, 13, 50, 63**
McIlvanney, William **42**
Morgan, Edwin (George) **31**
Smith, Iain Crichton **64**
Spark, Muriel (Sarah) **2, 3, 5, 8, 13, 18, 40, 94**
Taylor, C(ecil) P(hilip) **27**
Walker, David Harry **14**
Welsh, Irvine **144**
Young, Andrew (John) **5**

SENEGALESE

Ousmane, Sembene **66**
Senghor, Léopold Sédar **54, 130**

SOMALIAN

Farah, Nuruddin **53, 137**

SOUTH AFRICAN

Abrahams, Peter (Henry) **4**
Breytenbach, Breyten **23, 37, 126**
Brink, André (Philippus) **18, 36, 106**
Brutus, Dennis **43**
Coetzee, J(ohn) M(ichael) **23, 33, 66, 117, 161, 162**
Courtenay, Bryce **59**
Fugard, (Harold) Athol **5, 9, 14, 25, 40, 80**
Fugard, Sheila **48**
Gordimer, Nadine **3, 5, 7, 10, 18, 33, 51, 70, 123, 160, 161**
Harwood, Ronald **32**
Head, Bessie **25, 67**
Hope, Christopher (David Tully) **52**
Kunene, Mazisi (Raymond) **85**
La Guma, (Justin) Alex(ander) **19**
Millin, Sarah Gertrude **49**
Mphahlele, Ezekiel **25, 133**
Mtwa, Percy **47**
Ngema, Mbongeni **57**
Nkosi, Lewis **45**
Paton, Alan (Stewart) **4, 10, 25, 55, 106**
Plomer, William Charles Franklin **4, 8**
Prince, F(rank) T(empleton) **22**
Smith, Wilbur (Addison) **33**
Tolkien, J(ohn) R(onald) R(euel) **1, 2, 3, 8, 12, 38**
Tutu, Desmond M(pilo) **80**

van der Post, Laurens (Jan) **5**
Vorster, Gordon **34**

SPANISH

Alberti, Rafael **7**
Alfau, Felipe **66**
Almodovar, Pedro **114**
Alonso, Damaso **14**
Arrabal, Fernando **2, 9, 18, 58**
Benet, Juan **28**
Buero Vallejo, Antonio **15, 46, 139**
Bunuel, Luis **16, 80**
Casona, Alejandro **49**
Castedo, Elena **65**
Cela, Camilo José **4, 13, 59, 122**
Cernuda (y Bidón), Luis **54**
del Castillo, Michel **38**
Delibes, Miguel **8, 18**
Espriu, Salvador **9**
Gironella, José María **11**
Gomez de la Serna, Ramon **9**
Goytisolo, Juan **5, 10, 23, 133**
Guillén, Jorge **11**
Matute (Ausejo), Ana María **11**
Otero, Blas de **11**
Rodriguez, Claudio **10**
Ruiz, Jose Martinez **11**
Saura (Atares), Carlos **20**
Sender, Ramón (José) **8**

SRI LANKAN

Gunesekera, Romesh **91**

ST. LUCIAN

Walcott, Derek (Alton) **2, 4, 9, 14, 25, 42, 67, 76, 160**

SWEDISH

Beckman, Gunnel **26**
Bergman, (Ernst) Ingmar **16, 72**
Ekeloef, (Bengt) Gunnar **27**
Johnson, Eyvind (Olof Verner) **14**
Lagerkvist, Paer (Fabian) **7, 10, 13, 54**
Martinson, Harry (Edmund) **14**
Sjoewall, Maj **7**
Spiegelman, Art **76**
Transtroemer, Tomas (Goesta) **52, 65**
Wahlöö, Per **7**
Weiss, Peter (Ulrich) **3, 15, 51**

SWISS

Canetti, Elias **3, 14, 25, 75, 86**
Duerrenmatt, Friedrich **1, 4, 8, 11, 15, 43, 102**
Frisch, Max (Rudolf) **3, 9, 14, 18, 32, 44**
Hesse, Hermann **1, 2, 3, 6, 11, 17, 25, 69**
King, Francis (Henry) **8, 53, 145**

Kung, Hans **130**
Pinget, Robert **7, 13, 37**
Sauser-Hall, Frederic **18**
Sterchi, Beat **65**
von Daeniken, Erich **30**

TRINIDADIAN

Guy, Rosa (Cuthbert) **26**
James, C(yril) L(ionel) R(obert) **33**
Lovelace, Earl **51**
Naipaul, Shiva(dhar Srinivasa) **32, 39**
Naipaul, V(idiadhar) S(urajprasad) **4, 7, 9, 13, 18, 37, 105**
Rampersad, Arnold **44**

TURKISH

Hikmet, Nazim **40**
Kemal, Yashar **14, 29**
Seferis, George **5, 11**

UGANDAN

p'Bitek, Okot **96**

URUGUAYAN

Galeano, Eduardo (Hughes) **72**
Onetti, Juan Carlos **7, 10**
Peri Rossi, Cristina **156**

WELSH

Abse, Dannie **7, 29**
Arundel, Honor (Morfydd) **17**
Clarke, Gillian **61**
Dahl, Roald **1, 6, 18, 79**
Davies, Rhys **23**
Francis, Dick **2, 22, 42, 102**
Hughes, Richard (Arthur Warren) **1, 11**
Humphreys, Emyr Owen **47**
Jones, David (Michael) **2, 4, 7, 13, 42**
Jones, Terence Graham Parry **21**
Levinson, Deirdre **49**
Llewellyn Lloyd, Richard Dafydd Vivian **7, 80**
Mathias, Roland (Glyn) **45**
Norris, Leslie **14**
Roberts, Kate **15**
Rubens, Bernice (Ruth) **19, 31**
Thomas, R(onald) S(tuart) **6, 13, 48**
Watkins, Vernon Phillips **43**
Williams, (George) Emlyn **15**

YUGOSLAVIAN

Andrić, Ivo **8**
Cosic, Dobrica **14**
Kĭ, Danilo **57**
Krlĕa, Miroslav **8, 114**
Pavic, Milorad **60**
Popa, Vasko **19**
Simic, Charles **6, 9, 22, 49, 68, 130**
Tesich, Steve **40, 69**

CLC-173 Title Index

"An Actress Who Lost Her Homeland" (Drakulic) **173**:183
As If I Am Not There: A Novel about the Balkans (Drakulic)
See *A Novel about the Balkans*
Balkan Express: Fragments from the Other Side of War (Drakulic)
See *Sterben in Kroatian: Vom Krieg mitten in Europa*
Beloved (Morrison) **173**:327
Beyond God the Father: Toward a Philosophy of Women's Liberation (Daly) **173**:55, 57-61, 66, 69, 73, 78-79, 81, 93-95, 98, 100-101, 104, 116-17, 122, 130, 132, 135-39, 149, 151-53, 155, 160, 162
"A Bitter Capuccino" (Drakulic) **173**:201
The Bluest Eye (Morrison) **173**:271-369
The Book of Saladin (Ali) **173**:33-34, 39-42
"Bosnia, or What Europe Means to Us" (Drakulic) **173**:206
Café Europa: Life After Communism (Drakulic) **173**:203, 205-7, 212-13
"Café Europa" (Drakulic) **173**:206
Can Pakistan Survive? (Ali) **173**:3-5, 23
"The Character of Hamlet's Mother" (Heilbrun) **173**:235
The Church and the Second Sex (Daly) **173**:58, 79, 81, 94, 105-6, 110, 115-16, 132, 134-35, 148-51, 159
The Clash of Fundamentalism: Crusades, Jihad, and Modernity (Ali) **173**:42, 45, 47, 49-52
Collateral Damage (Ali) **173**:35-36
Death in a Tenured Position (Heilbrun) **173**:226, 236, 253-54, 256-58
The Education of a Woman: The Life of Gloria Steinem (Heilbrun) **173**:237, 239, 241-42, 245-47, 249
"Ein Brief an meine Tochter" (Drakulic) **173**:201
"Embracing the Paradox" (Heilbrun) **173**:251
"The Evolution of the Female Memoir" (Heilbrun) **173**:251
"Exemplary Women" (Heilbrun) **173**:235
"The Family Lost and Found" (Heilbrun) **173**:249
Fear of Mirrors (Ali) **173**:31-32, 34, 42
"Feminism and the Profession of Literature" (Heilbrun) **173**:235
The Gender Division of Welfare; The Impact of the British and German Welfare States (Daly) **173**:164
Gyn/Ecology: The Metaethics of Radical Feminism (Daly) **173**:61-62, 66, 68, 70, 73, 77-79, 81, 93-108, 110, 116-17, 122, 125-26, 136-40, 148-49, 151-53, 155, 161
Hamlet's Mother and Other Women (Heilbrun) **173**:235
"High-heeled Shoes" (Drakulic) **173**:184-85
Hologrami straha (Drakulic) **173**:169-70, 207, 210
Holograms of Fear (Drakulic)
See *Hologrami straha*
Honest Doubt (Heilbrun) **173**:264
How We Survived Communism and Even Laughed (Drakulic) **173**:169-71, 173, 175, 179, 182, 201-2, 205, 207, 210
"If I Had a Son" (Drakulic) **173**:174
An Imperfect Spy (Heilbrun) **173**:236
In the Last Analysis (Heilbrun) **173**:225
An Indian Dynasty: the Story of the Nehru-Gandhi Family (Ali) **173**:6-8, 23
"Introduction: First-Person Singular" (Drakulic) **173**:214
Iranian Nights (Ali) **173**:13, 22, 24-25, 27, 36
The Last Gift of Time: Life beyond Sixty (Heilbrun) **173**:248-50, 267
"A Letter to My Daughter" (Drakulic) **173**:182
"Literature and Women" (Heilbrun) **173**:235
"Living with Men" (Heilbrun) **173**:249, 251
"Love Story" (Drakulic) **173**:205
Marble Skin (Drakulic)
See *Mramorna kosa*
Moscow Gold (Ali) **173**:17-18, 24-28, 35
Mramorna koza (Drakulic) **173**:182-83, 207, 210
"My Father's Guilt" (Drakulic) **173**:203
"My Father's Pistol" (Drakulic) **173**:201
1968: Marching in the Streets (Ali) **173**:30
1968 and After (Ali) **173**:12
No Word from Winifred (Heilbrun) **173**:225-26
A Novel about the Balkans (Drakulic) **173**:208, 210-11
"On Not Wearing Dresses" (Heilbrun) **173**:250
Outercourse: The Bedazzling Voyage: Containing Recollections from My Logbook of a Radical Feminist Philosopher (Daly) **173**:77-80, 94, 116-18, 149
"Overcome by Nationhood" (Drakulic) **173**:177, 195
"The Pillbox Effect" (Drakulic) **173**:206
Poetic Justice (Heilbrun) **173**:268
"Post-Christian Introduction" (Daly) **173**:135
Pure Lust: Elemental Feminist Philosophy (Daly) **173**:62-66, 73-74, 77-79, 81, 94-96, 98, 100-109, 116-17, 122, 124, 130, 136-37, 149, 151, 153-54, 162
The Puzzled Heart (Heilbrun) **173**:264
Quintessence . . . Realizing the Archaic Future: A Radical Elemental Feminist Manifesto (Daly) **173**:112, 116-23, 127-29, 159, 161-63
Redemption (Ali) **173**:18-21, 42
Reinventing Womanhood (Heilbrun) **173**:248
The Representation of Women in Fiction (Heilbrun) **173**:224
Revolution from Above (Ali) **173**:13-16, 19, 23-24
"Rootedness: The Ancestor as Foundation" (Morrison) **173**:290
Shadows of the Pomegranate Tree (Ali) **173**:20-22, 40-42
"The Small House" (Heilbrun) **173**:249
Snogging Ken (Ali) **173**:35-36
Song of Solomon (Morrison) **173**:342, 355
The Stalinist Legacy (Ali) **173**:18
Sterben in Kroatian: Vom Krieg mitten in Europa (Drakulic) **173**:173-75, 177, 179, 182-84, 194, 201-2, 205, 207, 210, 212
The Stone Woman (Ali) **173**:37-42
Street Fighting Years: An Autobiography of the Sixties (Ali) **173**:12, 23
Sula (Morrison) **173**:318-19, 342, 358
Sweet Death, Kind Death (Heilbrun) **173**:225-26
Tar Baby (Morrison) **173**:327, 355
The Taste of a Man (Drakulic) **173**:204-7, 210
"Three Little Hens" (Drakulic) **173**:185
"To Have or Have Not" (Drakulic) **173**:206
Toward a Recognition of Androgyny (Heilbrun) **173**:265
"Trashing" (Heilbrun) **173**:244
Ugly Rumours (Ali) **173**:32, 35
"A Unique Person" (Heilbrun) **173**:249-50
"An Unmet Friend" (Heilbrun) **173**:249
Websters' First New Intergalactic Wickedary of the English Language (Daly) **173**:66-74, 78-79, 81, 94-95, 97-108, 116-18, 120, 122, 126-27, 149, 152, 154
"What Ivan Said" (Drakulic) **173**:198
"What Was Penelope Unweaving?" (Heilbrun) **173**:235
When Men Were the Only Models We Had: My Teachers Barzun, Fadiman, Trilling (Heilbrun) **173**:265-67
Women's Lives (Heilbrun) **173**:251-52
Writing a Woman's Life (Heilbrun) **173**:226-31, 234-35, 237, 239, 245, 249, 265

ISBN 0-7876-6746-3

90000